C000176615

# HERETICS AND BELIEVERS

# HERETICS
## AND
# BELIEVERS
## A HISTORY OF
## THE ENGLISH REFORMATION

PETER MARSHALL

YALE UNIVERSITY PRESS
NEW HAVEN AND LONDON

Published with assistance from the foundation established in memory of
Oliver Baty Cunningham of the Class for 1917, Yale College.

For information about this and other Yale University Press publications, please contact:
U.S. Office:   sales.press@yale.edu   yalebooks.com
Europe Office:   sales@yaleup.co.uk   yalebooks.co.uk

Typeset in Minion Pro by IDSUK (DataConnection) Ltd
Printed in Great Britain by TJ International Ltd, Padstow, Cornwall

Library of Congress Cataloging-in-Publication Data

Names: Marshall, Peter, 1964 October 26- author.
Title: Heretics and believers : a history of the English Reformation / Peter
    Marshall.
Description: New Haven : Yale University Press, 2017. | Includes
    bibliographical references and index.
Identifiers: LCCN 2016055372 | ISBN 9780300170627 (hardback)
Subjects: LCSH: Reformation—England. | England—Religious life and customs.
    | England—Church history—16th century. | BISAC: RELIGION / Christian
    Church / History. | HISTORY / Modern / 16th Century. | HISTORY / Europe /
    Great Britain. | RELIGION / Christianity / Anglican.
Classification: LCC BR377 .M34 2017 | DDC 274.2/06—dc23
LC record available at https://lccn.loc.gov/2016055372

A catalogue record for this book is available from the British Library.

10 9 8 7 6 5 4 3 2 1

*For Ali, again*

# CONTENTS

## IV   UNATTAINABLE PRIZES

# PLATES

# PREFACE

THIS BOOK INVITES readers to take a new look at one of the best-known and most widely discussed epochs of English history: the Reformation of the sixteenth century. It does so by retelling the story of what happened to English people, of all sorts and conditions, in the course of a long and traumatic national quarrel about the correct ways to worship God. As far as possible, my book proceeds in chronological sequence, and without much if any direct reference to the numerous academic debates and controversies in which the study of the Reformation abounds. (Should readers wish to consult them, the endnotes reveal the extent of my debts to other scholars in the field.) But threaded through my narrative is a series of fresh arguments about what sort of process the English Reformation was, and about why it mattered then and continues to matter now. It may be helpful at the outset to state what some of these arguments are.

In the first place, it is an unapologetic assumption of what follows that the conflicts of the Reformation were indeed principally about religion; that questions of faith were not merely a convenient covering for more fundamental or 'real' concerns about political power, social domination or economic assets. That said, it would be absurd to assert that the Reformation was 'just' about religion, for to do so would be to imply that religion was a disconnected phenomenon, separable from the other spheres of value and meaning in which sixteenth-century people lived their lives.

On the contrary, 'religion' was woven inextricably into the fabric of virtually all the other artificial abstractions from the messy interplay of collective human existence: society, politics, culture, gender, art, literature, economy. That religious symbolism or argument sometimes patently served what we might regard as political or economic ends should be regarded as demonstrating the depth of religion's importance, rather than exposing its precarious shallowness.

It is for these reasons that the refashioning, the 'Reformation', of religion was a matter of such significance, for it inevitably had profound effects across the entire spectrum of organized social activity and lived human experience. At the same time, one of the key contentions of this book is that over the course of the Reformation, and as a result of the pressures it produced on people, the meaning of 'religion' itself began fundamentally and permanently to change. This was not so much because one variant of Christian faith (Catholicism) was largely replaced by another (Protestantism), as because ways and habits of 'doing' religion themselves underwent transformative, irreversible changes in a crucible of political calculation and of individual initiative and response.

Almost the most unhelpful thing that can be said about the English Reformation is that it was an 'Act of State', simply imposed upon the nation by its successive governments. In one sense, this traditional assessment has merits. The lasting changes of the period would not have taken the forms that they did without sustained assertions of state power, assertions that gave a legal and coercive basis to far-reaching changes in doctrine, worship and governance in the English Church. Without the precise circumstances of Henry VIII's marriage and divorce, events would have taken a very different turn, and – as in most other parts of Europe – the overall direction and broad outcomes of religious change were at each stage usually the ones the regime of the day wanted to see.

And yet, I will argue, virtually from the start, the imposition of the Reformation was the pyrrhic victory of the English state. It was achieved at the cost of eroding the government's power to command, and of empowering ordinary English people to think and reflect – and sometimes to refuse and resist. Not the least among the ironies of the process was that, in raising the monarch to an unprecedentedly elevated official status – supreme head, under Christ, of the Church within England – the Reformation fatally undermined the monarchy's majesty and mystique among significant numbers of its subjects.

The one objective that, whatever their complexion, all Tudor governments shared was that there should be national 'uniformity' in matters of religious belief and practice. Edwin Sandys, Protestant bishop of London, spoke for the political assumptions of the age when he declared to Members of Parliament assembled in Westminster Abbey in 1571 that 'this liberty, that men may openly profess diversity of religion, must needs be dangerous to the commonwealth . . . Let conformity and unity in religion be provided for; and it shall be a wall of defence unto this realm.'[1]

As I demonstrate in the first part of this book, absolute uniformity in these matters had never, in fact, existed. Nonetheless, a broad and flexible consensus around most core matters of faith obtained in the late medieval period. It blew apart in the sixteenth century, and was never subsequently repaired. Increasingly, pluralism and division, rather than underlying unity, were the defining characteristics of English religious life: a development that in itself helped to transform the very nature of religion, and the role it occupied within society.

This development took place, I will argue, not just despite, but to a considerable extent because of, government strategies and policies. Some shared assumptions of faith were already breaking down in the 1520s, but Henry VIII opened a Pandora's box of plurality, licensing 'evangelical' reformers to make their frequently persuasive but invariably divisive case in front of the English public. At the same time, the King's fitful and erratic attempts to rein in the reformers and promote his own idiosyncratic versions of traditional Christianity fuelled intense rivalries within the Church, emboldening idealists of varying kinds to pursue and promote their own agendas for change.

In these circumstances, even the mechanisms for imposing uniformity often had the effect of advertising alternative possibilities. A turn to the propaganda potential of the printing press – the core and consistent strategy of political regimes across the century – made appeals to, and to a considerable extent called into being, the volatile phenomenon of public 'opinion'. Yet all attempts to persuade through force of argument implicitly concede the possibility of failure; they recognize the existence of different ways of looking at the world. Even direct efforts to control and constrain the consciences of subjects, through – for example – an insistence on the swearing of solemn oaths or the making of formal public declarations of assent, could in practice serve to galvanize resistance, and provide rallying calls for opposition.

The most coercive of all government policies in the sixteenth century – the putting to death of dissidents – was only ever partially successful as an instrument of enforced uniformity. The fate of heretics and traitors was an object lesson in the consequences of nonconformity. But the meaning of those deaths could never be entirely controlled by the oppressors, and events seen by some as legitimate judicial punishments were inevitably interpreted by others as divinely sanctioned martyrdoms. Martyrs were by definition unusual and exceptional Christians, but their symbolic importance for the creation and strengthening of new religious identities is difficult to overstate. The English Reformation was, as we shall see, unusually and bloodily prolific in its creation of martyrs, through successive decades, and across the entire spectrum of religious belief.

There were many other places in Europe where official religion changed, and changed more than once, over the course of the sixteenth century. But among the major west European powers England was unique in its sequence of dramatic swings of official policy, taking place over the course of a relatively short span of years. It is often suggested that the main effect of these oscillations was to bewilder and confuse people, or at least to encourage in them an attitude of quiet, wait-and-see conformity, and of widespread indifference – except among a noisy minority – to the obscure obsessions of their governors and betters.

It will be a central argument of this book that the opposite of this is very likely to be true; that a constantly changing diet of religious proclamations, injunctions, articles, catechisms, liturgies, homilies, iconoclastic spectacles and rearrangements of church interiors had the cumulative effect, to a hitherto unprecedented degree, of informing and educating English people about contested religious and doctrinal issues. No doubt there were some who let it all wash over them. But there is a great deal of evidence, from all levels of society, for people thinking very seriously about questions of faith and salvation, and being prepared to discuss them with others: in their homes, on the road, after church services and sermons, in alehouses, marketplaces and shops.

There is also good reason for scepticism about another often-repeated judgement on the unfolding of the English Reformation: that the overwhelming popular response to it was one of acquiescence, compliance and obedience, and that a surprising absence of protest and resistance is one of its abiding mysteries. This is often accompanied by assertions that the progress of reformation in England was, by and large, an orderly and peaceful affair.

It is true that England avoided – in the sixteenth century at least – any outbreak of full-scale religious civil war, such as that which afflicted France from the 1560s onwards. Yet the Reformation's progress in England was at nearly every stage lubricated by copious effusions of blood, and – as we shall see – in every decade between the 1530s and the 1570s, some of that blood was spilled in skirmishes and battles between armed forces in the field. Resistance to reformation – in any of its variant guises – only looks 'limited' if we actually expect riot and rebellion to be the default response of political subordinates to the reception of unpopular orders: a profoundly unrealistic scenario in any of the strongly hierarchical societies of sixteenth-century Europe.

As it was, each of a succession of political crises and breakdowns of order in England, several of which had potential for developing into larger conflagrations, had a discernibly religious complexion, if not a fundamentally religious character. In the sixteenth century, England's wars of religion remained – largely – metaphorical ones. But this was never something that could be taken for granted, and it needs to be explained by detailed attention to the interplay of events, rather than by vague appeals to overarching social structures, or any putative national disposition towards moderation and compromise.

The instinct of obedience was hard-wired into late medieval and sixteenth-century English people, but the Reformation stretched and strained that instinct to breaking point and beyond. It was an inherited assumption of the age that all political authority was ordained by God, yet the unavoidable fact of religious division in itself demonstrated that not all expressions of that authority were approved of by God. A growing and alarming realization on the part of many subjects that their monarch was acting contrary to God's will – as revealed in scripture, or by the inherited traditions of the Christian faith – impelled a few determined souls to develop justifications for non-obedience, for resistance, and even for the overthrow and replacement of an ungodly ruler. More common, however, was a widespread and novel experience of disconnect, of uncomfortable consciousness that the version of Christian truth approved and promoted by the highest authorities in the land was not one the individual could necessarily recognize or share.

The implications of this were multiple and profound. In England, from the reign of Henry VIII onwards, parallel processes were underway of what is sometimes called 'confessionalization'.[2] This refers to the growing perception on the part of individuals that they were possessed of a distinctive identity of faith, shared with other committed adherents, at home and often abroad. These processes took place alongside, but not necessarily in tandem with, official programmes of religious renewal and reform. Sometimes, as with evangelicals in the reigns of Henry and Edward VI, the patterns of identity-formation sought to outrun the pace of officially sanctioned change. Other paths of confessionalization diverged dramatically from approved routes. This, other than in the reign of Mary I, was the case of Catholics – many of whom, as we shall see, can begin meaningfully to be called Roman Catholics only as a result of choices imposed upon them in the maelstrom of Reformation politics. A still more dramatic path of divergence was taken by the various radical, experimentalist Christians derisively labelled by contemporaries as 'anabaptists': men and women whose conscientious views were consistently rejected, and whose persons were periodically persecuted, by state-sanctioned authority. In the reign of Elizabeth I, explored in the final part of the book, a key theme is the growth spurt, from earlier embryonic development, of a godly, 'Puritan' identity, whose bearers perceived a duty to take over the primary responsibility for reformation from a delinquent and ineffective state.

Growing divisions within and between communities in themselves underlined and accelerated the process of fragmentation: the awareness of being a Catholic by virtue of not being a Protestant (and vice versa) lent new and sharper edges to the social importance of belief – whether or not this trend was always accompanied by greater intellectual understanding of the actual content of disputed doctrines.

Another of the themes of this book is the way in which language itself became increasingly critical to the dynamics of disunity. The devising of insulting labels and names for opponents was a blatant polemical strategy, but its effect, not always foreseen, was often to shore up identity and solidarity – both of the name-callers and of the people being named. Repeated, forlorn pleas from the authorities for English men and women not to asperse each other with the titles of 'papist', 'heretic' or 'Puritan' are a backhanded tribute to the effectiveness of hostile labelling in policing the boundaries of religious differentiation. In the sixteenth century, competing forms of Christian faith were on their way to becoming, in the literal meaning of the word, denominations.

Just as significant was a puzzling and paradoxical fact: the pluralization of English religion took place in a context of consistent official intolerance of any form of dissent. There was, more or less, only ever one approved pattern of religious worship and practice at any one time in England in the sixteenth century, with threats of significant legal penalties for anyone refusing outwardly to take part. Since relatively few people, even among the seriously devout, had either the stomach for martyrdom or the stamina for exile, one result was the growth of a pervasive culture of dissembling and concealment, against which clerical leaders on all sides indignantly railed, but which they could do little to prevent.

Outward conformity is sometimes regarded as an unheroically banal pattern of behaviour. In fact, it could represent a complex and sophisticated adaptation of conscience to conditions. It also served to compartmentalize religion, and the questions of authenticity and duty that went with it, in new and creative ways. When, for example, Elizabethan Catholics declared a loyal willingness to obey the Queen in all 'civil' matters, they were drawing a distinction between things that scarcely existed as separate spheres before, and which would have made little sense to their medieval forebears. Here was the germ of a familiar modern idea: religion as a purely private matter, divorced from the necessary terms of participation in wider public life.

The tendency was reinforced by the messy realities of life in religiously mixed communities. The divisions of England provoked real hatreds of the 'other', in abstract and sometimes in viscerally embodied forms. As a result of the Reformation, English society became an uneasy aggregate of true and false Christians, of 'heretics' and 'believers' – people who knew they were in the right by their ability to point out those who were in the wrong. But neighbours of different faiths remained neighbours still, and much of the time they had to find ways of making do and muddling along – like the inn-keeper in later Elizabethan Norfolk who scolded customers for letting an argument about the mass and religious images get out of hand: 'he must be for all companies, and all men's money'.[3]

Before the Reformation, 'religion' meant primarily an attitude of devoted living in the service of God, one that encompassed public duty and private piety in ways difficult to prise apart. Something of that aura continued to adhere to the concept throughout the period covered by this book, and indeed beyond it. But 'religion' emerged from the convulsions of the sixteenth century in a state of fragmented, almost schizophrenic reinvention. On the one hand, it now represented the sectarian ideology of self-selecting membership groups – the 'true religion', the 'Catholic religion' – arming those groups with a new confidence to resist what might once have seemed the incontestable demands of legitimate authority. On the other, it had the potential to manifest itself as a matter of inner conscience, private and protected, a subjective abstraction – 'my religion', or even just 'religion'. Emphasis on the former implied an impulse to seek total Reformation, total victory; on the latter, a willingness to consider the suspension of outward hostilities in the pursuit of social peace. In failing to resolve which of these imperatives would prevail, the Reformation proved to be a highly creative, as well as profoundly destabilizing, force for societal change.

The structure of this book – as well as seeking to provide the framework for telling an engaging and compelling story – aims to map a series of broad stages in the unfolding of these transformations. The four chapters comprising Part I, 'Reformations before Reformation', collectively portray late medieval English religion as the basis of a principled and intelligible world-view, but also as remarkably dynamic and diverse; they attempt to explain why English society around the turn of the sixteenth century was often convinced of the necessity for 'reformation', but unable to find agreed strategies for implementing it.

The intention in these thematic chapters, viewing the period c. 1480–1525 from a variety of angles, is not to offer systematic analysis of the 'causes' of the English Reformation – I have no wish to assert the inevitability of developments that in reality were often unpredictable and usually avoidable. But neither is the aim here to portray an innocent and untroubled 'pre-Reformation' world. The Reformation, it is vital to recognize, was neither a detached and unheralded post-medieval arrival, nor simply a reaction against the religious culture of the Middle Ages. It was itself a flowering of late medieval developments, seeded and germinated in the political, cultural and religious soil of the decades around 1500. My account of patterns in devotional life, of the aspirations and deficiencies of the institutional Church, of the relationship between that Church and secular authority, and of the temptations of religious dissidence, is designed to make later developments seem, if not predictable, then at least explicable.

Part II, 'Separations', shifts the tempo of the book into a forward-flowing, if not always rigidly strict, chronological narrative of events. It describes the emergence of the bitter divisions within English Christianity following from two, seemingly unconnected, developments of the 1520s: the reverberations from Martin Luther's protest against papal authority, and the frustrated desire of Henry VIII to secure an annulment of his marriage to Catherine of Aragon. The early and remarkable convergence between these processes, I argue, explains much about the dynamic character, and the instability and incoherence, of the so-called 'Henrician Reformation'.

The fitful emergence, after the fluidity and confusion of the early Reformation years, of more confident and enduring patterns of religious identity and solidarity is the predominant theme of Part III, 'New Christianities'. These identities were already emerging in the later years of Henry VIII, and continued to solidify through the short but eventful reigns of Edward VI and Mary I, when rival visions of Reformation, political and religious, convulsed the conscience of the nation, and impacted heavily on communities throughout the realm.

My final section, Part IV, 'Unattainable Prizes', coincides with the reign of Elizabeth I. It is a mixed story of triumphs and defeat. These chapters describe how Protestantism established a powerful political hegemony in England, and began to put down roots in the localities; and how Catholicism, only recently the establishment faith, surmounted threats to its very survival in order to reinvent itself as a vibrant vehicle of dissident expression. At the same time, they chart several parallel odysseys of disillusionment; I explain why it was that none of the idealistic programmes of Reformation proclaimed in the later sixteenth century – not even Elizabeth I's own – were ultimately able to triumph.

The account in this book comes to a close in the years around 1590, near the beginning of Elizabeth's last decade. There is no obvious point at which the English Reformation 'ends', and no one alive at the time thought officially to declare one. Some historians will probably think my Reformation (if not my book itself) is a little on the short side. They will point out that the consequences of England's momentous break with Catholic Christendom were still working themselves out, in politics, religion and the experiences of daily life, far beyond 1600. While this is perfectly true, it is also the case that a number of crucial questions had been settled, or shown themselves incapable of being settled, before the sixteenth century drew to a close. A broad-based Protestantism was established as the majority faith of the nation. But thickets of Roman Catholicism, and other, still more exotic, plants, were ineradicably rooted across the religious landscape of England. A plurality of religious attitudes and identities, in bristling array, had assumed their recognizable forms; and, by the early 1590s, the purest proponents of Protestant Reformation had staked their claim, and shot their bolt.

Readers will notice there are a lot of names in this book. Some – like Henry VIII, Thomas More, Hugh Latimer or Elizabeth I – appear repeatedly; others, less well known, on only one or two occasions. I hope this will bolster a key argument of the unfolding story: that 'the Reformation' was not a mysterious, faceless force, obtruding upon individuals and their communities from somewhere beyond their reckoning. Rather, it was a transformative historical moment enacted by the calculations and decisions, sometimes heroic and sometimes shameful, of innumerable men and women, both great and small, at the centres of high policy-making, and in myriad localities where ordinary people lived.

It was not all about making choices. Compulsion and coercion feature prominently in the narrative that follows, and for many people, much of the time, the sensible choice was to keep their heads down and do as they were told. Nonetheless, over the course of the sixteenth century, and for the first time in securely documented history, everyone in England became acutely aware that the most important questions of human existence were capable of demanding divergent – indeed, mutually incompatible – answers. That fundamentally new dynamic had a momentous impact, on existing patterns of collective allegiance and on conceptions of individual identity: it redefined people's relationships to both 'vertical' structures of authority and 'horizontal' bonds of community. In a world of plural possibility, even quiet adherence to the status quo was now an act of meaningful affirmation. The English Reformation, and with it the future course of the nation's history, was made by a great multitude of heretics and believers.

# PART I

## Reformations before Reformation

# I

# THE IMITATION OF CHRIST

## Before the Rood

THE CARVINGS DEPICT a near-naked man being slowly tortured to death. He has been nailed through the hands and feet to a pair of crossed wooden staves, raised to stand upright in the ground. In his last agonies, he looks outward towards the viewer, or up towards the sky. Sometimes, he has died already, and the eyes are cast down. Blood drips from a freshly opened wound in his right side.

No one in England, in the years around the start of the sixteenth century, could fail to recognize this image. The crucifix – from the Latin, meaning 'fixed to a cross' – was to be found in the streets, in private homes, or worn about the person, often at the end of a set of prayer beads known as a rosary. Most commonly, it was seen in churches, themselves often constructed in the shape of a cross, with north and south transepts perpendicular to the main structure. All places of worship, from the grandest city cathedrals to the humble chapels of the remote countryside, displayed a large crucifix, commanding the sight-lines within the building. It rested on a beam, running the upper length of the archway separating the main body of the church, known as the nave, from the east-end chancel, where the sacred mysteries were performed.

This crucifix was referred to as the rood, from an Old English word for cross. A small gallery, the rood loft, was often attached to the beam: it was accessible by stairs, and allowed lit candles to be placed in front of the rood as a gesture of piety and devotion. Under this structure, an ornately carved screen, solid in its bottom half, marked the boundary between nave and chancel.

The death portrayed on the rood was no random act of cruelty and violence. It was an event foreseen by God from before the creation of the world; an event that transformed the relationship between God and the world of living beings he created. According to ancient Hebrew scripture, the first humans,

Adam and Eve, defied their Maker and were expelled from the place of paradise he had prepared for them. Their disobedience, theologians believed, constituted an 'original sin', a permanent stain on the character of humanity. It demanded some extraordinary act of cleansing and restitution before relations between God and humankind could be restored and it became possible for people to be 'saved', for their immortal souls to live eternally with God as he intended.

The 'Atonement', the making right of the primordial wrong, was too great a task for humans alone to undertake. God himself decided to assume human flesh, to become 'incarnated', the miraculous offspring of a virgin birth, in the person of Jesus of Nazareth. This man, who lived in Jewish Palestine in the early years of the Roman Empire, was called by his followers the Christ, the anointed one. Jesus, at once true God and true man, taught a code of loving ethical behaviour that challenged the severity of the old Jewish ceremonial law. But the ultimate purpose of his life was his suffering and death, his 'passion', at the hands of the Roman authorities in Jerusalem.

Jesus' act of willing self-sacrifice restored the broken relationship between humanity and God; salvation was possible once more. The gruesome instrument of Roman torture, the cross, became a sign of hope; the day on which Christ suffered became 'Good' Friday. A symbolic triumph over death was also a literal one: three days after dying on the cross, Christ rose bodily to life on Easter Sunday. Forty days later, he ascended to his Father in heaven. One day he would return, to judge the world and destroy it, and preside over the creation of a new heaven and a new earth. All people who ever lived would then be resurrected in the body, as Christ had been – some to live with him in glory, others to suffer unspeakable torments in hell, a place of despair, ruled by the fallen angel, Satan. This judgement, or Doom, was often in front of people's eyes, portrayed in vibrant painting on a plastered surface or wooden board filling the top of the chancel arch: a backdrop to, and forward projection from, the carved figure of the rood.

There was a lot for people to think about when they looked up in church to behold the rood. It spoke of an amazing act of love and generosity performed on their behalf, provoking feelings of gratitude, but perhaps also of unworthiness and guilt. It commemorated an event from the distant past, but reminded people of a present reality, while pointing them towards a literally earth-shattering future. It encapsulated an idea grounded in the incarnation itself: that the powers of the sacred could be localized in physical space, and in material form. Most of all, it represented an invitation and a challenge. Christ's work of stunning self-sacrifice opened the doorway to heaven, but it did not guarantee entry there. It summoned people to seize the opportunities offered them: to avoid sin and better themselves spiritually, to become more Christ-like, and strive to follow his teachings in their lives. Only in so doing could the healing work of the atonement be made a reality for them as individual Christians; only thus could they be saved.

The enormous convulsion in English social, political and cultural life that came to be known as 'the Reformation' was a long collective argument about what was truly involved in the imitation of Christ; about what people needed to do, or avoid doing, in order to achieve salvation. It does not have any single starting point, and too much talk about 'origins' or 'roots' risks either making it seem inevitable, or reducing its complex and fecund beginnings to a single thread of traceable development.

Christianity was in existence for a millennium and a half before the events described in this book took place. It had endured and survived many previous trials. Attempts to reform Christianity, and by Christians to reform themselves, were as old as the Jesus movement itself. The urge to pursue 'Reformation' was a congenital condition of the serious Christian life, and – given the fallible nature of humanity – a perhaps incurable one, but it had led over the centuries to many changes. Christians towards the end of what is conventionally called the Middle Ages often prided themselves on the antiquity of their faith, but theirs in fact was a system of belief and practice undergoing continual evolutionary alteration. There was no static 'pre-Reformation Catholicism', into which the Reformation suddenly inserted itself.

'The Reformation', indeed, is itself an abstraction – a later attempt to make sense out of a pattern of events whose unfolding mostly seemed fitful and strange to the people living through them. Those events were unpredictable, and not infrequently implausible; but they are not unfathomable. The dramatic changes of the Reformation, which transformed in countless ways the lives of the English people, arose out of the ideals and assumptions of a culture that was intensely serious about an obligation to follow the teachings of Christ, not from one neglectful of it. The changes took the precise forms they did for a variety of social, political and religious reasons this book will do its best to describe and explain. There is no simple explanation for why in the sixteenth century growing numbers of English Christians came to believe that true discipleship of Jesus meant demanding that the sacred figure of the rood be pulled down from its lofty perch, broken into pieces and burned to ashes.

### To Be a Christian

Imitation of Christ began with becoming a Christian. That was the easy part. It happened within days of being born, when a baby was baptized in the stone font usually found, in symbolic placement, near the entrance of the church. The ceremony involved a ritual cleansing with water, and the bestowal of a name, while an officiating priest invoked on the child the power of 'the Father, the Son and the Holy Spirit', the three 'persons' of a single Trinitarian God.

Baptism could be an elaborate affair. A few days after his birth on 28 June 1491, Henry, second son of King Henry VII and his wife Elizabeth, was baptized in the church of the Observant Franciscan friars at Greenwich, on a specially constructed platform hung with richly embroidered cloths and canopies. The font was made of silver, and the priest was a leading clergyman of the realm, Bishop Richard Fox of Winchester. Yet, spiritually, the little prince did not get anything more out of it than a child of the lowliest of his father's subjects. In a rite that was part exorcism, the curse of original sin was erased from the infant's soul; he or she was literally 'christened'. Mothers remained at home for six weeks after the birth of a child, and fathers generally stayed away from the ceremony. But the godparents, who made statements of faith on the baby's behalf, would be huddled around the font. A contemporary describes them nervously asking the priest, 'How say you . . . is this child christened enough? Hath it his full Christendom?'[1]

There was always an element of anxiety in an age when so many infants failed to survive their first days and weeks. Babies dying unbaptized were not Christians, could not be saved. Logically, this implied the eternal torments of hell. But, long before 1500, the idea gained near-universal acceptance that their souls went not to hell but to a neighbouring 'limbo' (from the Latin for fringe or boundary) – a place without vision of God but equally without pain. Another limbo housed 'good pagans' who lived and died before the incarnation of Christ. In an emergency, not just a priest, but anyone – even a female midwife – could validly baptize a child. All this suggests how, over time, the rigid rules of the Church might soften, in response to theological reflection, or the demands of simple humanity; there was flexibility in the system, and a dose of perplexing untidiness.

Baptism illuminates some other core assumptions of Christianity, as it was lived and taught across western Europe in the later Middle Ages. The faith was inclusive, and all-embracing. With the exception of a small number of Jews and a still smaller number of Muslims, no one 'chose' to be a Christian. Membership of the Church, and formal profession of Christian faith, was simply coterminous with human community. This makes it profoundly unhelpful to speak, as historians still tend to do, about 'religion and society', as it is impossible to identify where the one stopped and the other began.

Perhaps it is even unhelpful to speak about 'religion' at all, in the modern sense of a contained sphere of thought and activity, separable from other aspects of experience. Early sixteenth-century people did use the word 'religion', but they nearly always meant by it the specialized ritual practices undertaken in monasteries (see Chapter 2). When it came to ordinary 'lay' folk, people might praise their faith, piety or devotion – words signifying an intensified presence of universally valued ideals and beliefs that underpinned all social and political order. There were certainly people, perhaps significant numbers of people, who were 'irreligious', in the sense of not taking seriously enough the moral demands of their Christian faith. Baptism removed 'original sin', but it did not remove the propensity to sinful behaviour that was the common lot and legacy of humankind. Others did not believe precisely what they were supposed to believe, and became stigmatized as 'heretics' (see Chapter 4). But it is unlikely that late medieval England contained 'atheists' in anything akin to our modern understanding of the term. God's presence was ubiquitous, and if winning his favour was not always at the forefront of people's minds, his judgement on them was the inescapable backdrop to their lives.

Baptism also illustrates the means through which God's presence was sought and experienced. It was a sacrament, one of seven such rituals, which, by the late Middle Ages, the Church had designated with this title. The others were confirmation, marriage, ordination, anointing of the sick (extreme unction), penance (confession) and the eucharist. Sacraments were symbols and more than symbols. They actually effected what they signified: the washing away of sins, in the case of baptism. In the technical jargon of the Church, a sacrament comprised 'matter' and 'form'. The matter was some raw material or point of departure – water, oil for anointing, bread and wine for the eucharist, sorrow for sins, mutual consent, and subsequent consummation, in marriage. The form was a recital of prescribed words. Together they guaranteed God's life-giving favour to the recipient; they produced the presence of 'grace'.

Late medieval religion (we can now allow ourselves, with appropriate wariness, to use the word) was profoundly 'sacramental'. That is, it accepted the idea that material things could be made holy, and that the sacred could be captured in ritual, gesture and spatial experience. Other objects, rites and blessings, of second-tier status, were designated 'sacramentals' – they were not assured vehicles of grace, but could convey it if approached in an appropriate spirit of piety. These included church bells; holy water used for the blessing of houses and crops; candles taken home on the feast of the Purification of the Blessed Virgin Mary (Candlemas), which were believed to offer protection during thunderstorms; ashes daubed on the foreheads of believers at the start of the penitential season of Lent; palm leaves distributed in church at the end of Lent to recreate the entry of Christ into Jerusalem.[2] In domestic, and sometimes frankly quasi-magical, uses of such objects, the distinctions between Church and society, official and unofficial religion, became blurred still further.

Of the formal sacraments, some, like baptism, were performed only once. Confirmation, as the name implied, supplied a sealing and strengthening of the commitments of baptism. It seems a frequently neglected ritual; perhaps because it could only be performed by a bishop, and bishops had other things to do than tour the parishes offering it. Marriage was another sacrament of the life-cycle; it could be repeated, though not while a first partner lived. Ordination as a priest was firmly once and for all; an alternative to marriage, and, of course, confined to men. The anointing of the sick was also, theoretically, repeatable, should a recipient regain health. But popular belief viewed it as part of the ritual of the deathbed, a final sentence from which there was no coming back.

The two remaining sacraments were also performed on the deathbed, part of a triad of 'last rites'. But they differed from the others in representing regular, cyclical sources for renewal of grace. Penance regulated the flow of sinfulness in the world. It offered God's forgiveness in return for penitence and confession of sins to a priest, acting as God's representative. Theologians argued over whether for the sacrament to take effect people needed to feel genuine sorrow for sins ('contrition') or just a desire to want to feel sorry ('attrition'). The latter interpretation placed more weight on the sacramental power of the priest. But it is unlikely the distinction mattered greatly to most ordinary layfolk, struggling to remember their misdeeds and get over the embarrassment of admitting them to a pastor who was also a neighbour.

The existence of elaborate manuals for confessors, with endless categorizations of sin, and lists of intrusive questions, has led some historians to conclude the transaction was traumatic and spiritually oppressive, inducing in laypeople an obsession with sinfulness and deep anxieties about the likelihood of salvation. It is possible that some were affected in this way: the process was certainly designed to induce feelings of guilt (though also to assuage them).

Yet it seems unlikely that most Christians lived in a semi-permanent state of confession-induced dread. The requirement to confess was no more than an annual one. The duty was nearly always fulfilled in the run-up to Easter, usually in Holy Week (the week preceding Easter Sunday), when the sheer volume of people waiting to make their confessions to hard-pressed priests rendered a detailed grilling improbable. In the bustling Yorkshire town of Doncaster, it was reported, later in Henry VIII's reign, that the vicar and seven other priests 'can scarce hear the confessions of the said parishioners from the beginning of Lent unto Palm Sunday'.

Still, we know that some, and perhaps most, early Tudor people took the obligation seriously, using mnemonic systems recommended in the confessors' manuals. At Faversham in Kent, a man declared an intention to go to his 'ghostly father' (a common name for the priest-confessor) and 'show to him I have sinned in the Seven Deadly Sins and have broken the Ten Commandments, and misspent my Five Wits [senses]'. In Lent 1536, a Londoner likewise 'rehearsed the Seven Deadly Sins particularly, and then the misspending of his Five Wits'. 'Have you not,' the priest wanted to know, 'sinned in not doing the Five Works of Mercy?' The man confessed he had: 'I cry God mercy.'[3]

Confession was performed before Easter, because it was a prerequisite for full participation in the most important sacrament of all. The eucharist, a Greek word meaning 'thanksgiving', was a re-enactment of the Last Supper that Jesus, just before his arrest, shared with his closest followers. According to accounts in three of the four gospels, Jesus took bread, broke it and gave it to his disciples, saying 'this is my body, do this in memory of me'. He did the same with a cup of wine, 'this is my blood of the covenant, which is poured out for many' (Matt. 26:26–8; Mark 14:22–4; Luke 22:19–20).

These seemingly clear instructions, from the mouth of God himself, obliged Christians to make this observance a centrepiece of their ritual. By the later Middle Ages it had long since assumed an elaborate ceremonial form, with a priest robed in long vestments – a residue of the formal wear of the late Roman Empire – playing the part of Jesus. The ceremony, like all services, or liturgies, of the medieval Church, was recited in Latin – another hangover from the world of late antiquity, when Latin had been the language of government, the army and of many ordinary people. In England, the ritual was performed, with minor local variations, according to the 'use' of various dioceses, principally Salisbury (Sarum). It was known as the mass, from the mysterious closing words of the ancient liturgy, *Ite, missa est*: 'Go, it is sent'.

What was being sent, by whom and to whom, was a good question, for the mass was a conduit of communication between worlds. On the one hand, it was an offering made by the Church to God, a sacrifice like the blood sacrifices of the Old Testament. For that reason it was performed at a stone altar, situated at the far east end of the church, behind the rood screen. In a system of sacred topography, east – the direction of Jerusalem, where Christ would return – always signified holiness. The sacrifice, theologians decided, was the same as that offered by Jesus himself. Bread for the mass took the form of flat, unleavened wheaten discs, known as hosts, from the Latin *ostia*, victim. Every mass, in every church in Christendom, re-enacted and re-constituted Christ's death on the cross, making this daily event a 'work' of extraordinary power.

At the mass God became truly, physically present among his people. When Christ took bread and declared 'this is my body', he meant what he said. At the high point of the mass, the priest repeated those words, 'Hoc est enim corpus meum', and the host in his hands miraculously turned into the actual body of Jesus. Theologians long pondered how, contrary to all evidence of human senses, this could be so. The predominant theory rested on a philosophical distinction (inherited from Aristotle) between the 'substance' and 'accidents' of an entity; between its true inner nature and its external attributes of colour, shape, smell, taste. The consecration, or 'sacring', of bread and wine during the mass was a 'transubstantiation', by which their original substance was obliterated and replaced with the body and blood of Christ.

This was, literally, something to see. Immediately after pronouncing the words of consecration, the priest raised the host above his head. Up to this point, laypeople in the nave, unable to follow in detail the low Latin chanting of the priest at his altar beyond the rood screen, concentrated on their own private prayers. A Venetian diplomat, visiting England in about 1500, commented approvingly on the piety of the people: 'they all attend mass every day . . . the women carrying long rosaries in their hands, and any who can read taking the Office of Our Lady with them'. But at the elevation, beads and books were laid aside. A sacring bell, rung by the assisting altar server, alerted people to look, and to adore. The main church bells might be tolled, so that people out in the fields or on the roads would know to stop, and make gestures of respect. For those present, it was a moment of direct visual contact with the most sacred of imaginable things. William Hampden, a Buckinghamshire parishioner, wanted to appropriate for himself the moment in perpetuity: his will of 1521 specified his body should be buried 'within the chancel of Hartwell, before the midst of the high altar, so that the priest may stand upon my feet in the sacring of the mass'.

The consecrated host was – quite appropriately – worshipped, for it was God in material form. Surplus hosts were reserved in a special container, a pyx, suspended above the altar, a focal point of reverence for anyone entering church. The benefits of seeing the host might be more than spiritual: no one would go blind that day, travellers would reach their destination unharmed, expectant mothers give birth in safety. This was not 'official' teaching, but was affirmed in numerous respectable sources.[4] Here again, the modern instinct might be to recoil at a blurring of the line between religion and magic. But this is to take an anachronistic approach to a world suffused with a sense of God's power and presence.

To a considerable extent, seeing substituted for another aspect of Christ's mandate of memory: to eat and drink. Communion for laypeople was required, but no more than annually; taking communion more regularly was a sign of uncommon devotion. It generally took place at Easter, and people made their confession in preparation for it; to consume the body of Christ unworthily was a truly perilous act.

Layfolk received 'in one kind' only. Centuries earlier, clerical fears that people might carelessly spill the consecrated wine restricted their consumption to the bread. Laypeople were not – they could be reassured – short-changed. The complete Christ, body and blood, was present under each of the forms. Most were probably content, though the issue's potential to pick at a lurking sense of grievance was suggested by events in distant Bohemia. Here, in the early fifteenth century, a remarkably successful movement of rebellion, inspired by the dissident priest Jan Hus, made demands for 'the chalice' for the laity.

Communion was a spiritual experience, but also a social one. It designated full membership of the local community, and people commonly referred to 'taking their rights'. Reception was by turn of social precedence, something that also dictated where people sat or stood in the church: 'religion' reflected the social and political order, and helped construct it. On Corpus Christi, the special summer feast that celebrated the miracle of the eucharist, in London,

Bristol, Coventry, York and elsewhere, the consecrated host was carried in procession through the streets. Townspeople processed by order of rank, with mayor, aldermen and other luminaries marching in their full dignity behind the canopy at the front.

Corpus Christi processions underlined disparities of status between people in urban communities, but were also intended to express an essential unity. Since no one 'out of charity' with neighbours was supposed to be allowed to receive communion, this ritual too restored – in theory – harmony within the community. Peace was a declared purpose of every mass, whether there was lay communion or not. After the great prayer of consecration, worshippers exchanged the 'kiss of peace'. By the later Middle Ages this had assumed more decorous form: an engraved wooden or silver plate, a *pax* or *paxbrede*, was passed around for people to kiss in turn.

Such rituals contained a potential for bringing to the surface the social tensions they were intended to dissolve. In 1496, Joanna Dyaca, of the London parish of All Hallows, Staining, cast the pax in fury to the ground because another woman was allowed to kiss it before her. John Browne, of the Essex parish of Theydon-Garnon, went further in 1522, and smashed the pax over the head of the parish clerk, in his anger at being placed lower than he assessed himself in the order of local importance.[5]

Such histrionic incidents – for which the perpetrators were reported by outraged neighbours – underline rather than undermine the role of ritual and shared faith in articulating a sense of common identity. Another ritual of the mass contributed. Households took turns to bake and present a 'holy loaf' to the church: a not insignificant quasi-liturgical role for local women. This was blessed, broken and distributed at the end of mass, sometimes in pieces of varying size reflecting the status of the recipient. People generally understood how this was supposed to work, and there was genuine anger at Hartford, Huntingdonshire, in 1518, where John Kareles habitually took such large pieces of holy bread that his neighbours were left without. His wife was said to be a stirrer of discord, who went running to the vicar with tales about other parishioners.[6] 'Community' in the early sixteenth century was not a state of cosy togetherness. Hell has always been other people. But in struggles to contain and arbitrate the inevitable discords of proximate living, the rituals and symbols of a shared religious culture came invariably to the fore.

The communities where English people lived were extremely diverse. A key requirement of being Christian was to be a member of a parish. The parish was a geographical unit of ecclesiastical administration, about 9,000 of them in the country as a whole. Clusters of parishes formed deaneries, grouped into archdeaconries, which were themselves subdivisions of dioceses, each presided over by a bishop. This bald summary creates a false impression of neatness and order. The parish system came into existence in a haphazard way over the earlier part of the Middle Ages, as landowners endowed churches on their estates. Parishes were thick on the ground over much of southern and midland England, where they were often coterminous with the manor, the basic unit of lordship and agricultural organization. In the north, they were more thinly spread, especially in the moorland regions of counties like Yorkshire, Lancashire or Northumberland. Here, people often worshipped in small dependent chapelries, and had little day-to-day contact with a parish church some dozen or more miles away. In parts of the north, the parish network overlapped with remnants of the old Anglo-Saxon minster system, with large churches staffed by teams of resident priests. There were impressive minsters at Beverley, Ripon, Southwell and other places.

Parishes were most densely clustered in towns, especially long-standing regional centres like Norwich, with about 12,000 inhabitants in the early sixteenth century, and Bristol, Coventry, Exeter and York, with something under 10,000 each. In contrast to France, the German territories of the Holy Roman Empire, or the commercial powerhouses of Italy and the Netherlands, England possessed only one city worthy of the name. London's population was approaching 50,000 in 1500, and rising rapidly. It had a whopping 107 parish churches within its ancient walls, and another ten in the expanding suburbs. But most English parishioners were rural, not urban; agricultural labourers, not craftsmen or merchants. At the start of the sixteenth century, only about 3 per cent of an English and Welsh population of around two and a half million lived in towns of 5,000 or more inhabitants.[7]

Membership of a parish meant attending services in its church, confessing and communicating at Easter, paying tithes to its presiding priest, and submitting ultimately to burial in its church or churchyard. Presence at mass, matins and evensong, monitored fitfully by the church courts (see Chapter 3), was required not only on Sundays, but on around forty to fifty special feasts or holy days each year – 'holidays' when cessation from all manual labour was expected.

Laypeople's awareness of time passing was profoundly influenced by the cyclical patterns of the Church's liturgical calendar.[8] This was in two halves. The first traced and commemorated the life of Jesus, starting in the season of Advent preceding celebration of Christ's nativity at the midwinter festival of Christmas. It culminated in ceremonies marking Christ's death and resurrection – then, as now, a movable feast, with Easter (the first Sunday after the first full moon after the vernal equinox) falling between late March and late April.

Forty days after Easter, the feast of the Ascension celebrated Christ's return to heaven, and ten days after that, Pentecost (Whitsunday) recalled the coming of the Holy Spirit to the disciples as they gathered in an upper room in Jerusalem. This was reckoned the real birth-date of the Catholic (Greek: *katholikos*, universal) Church to which everyone still belonged. The second half of the year, spanning high summer and autumn, was punctuated by numerous feast days honouring the saints: John the Baptist on 24 June; Mary Magdalene on 22 July; the Assumption (bodily ascent into heaven) of the Virgin Mary on 15 August; St Michael and All Angels on 29 September; a remembrance of All Saints on 1 November.

Lent, the period of forty days (recalling time Christ spent in the wilderness) preceding Easter, was a season of solemn fasting, which required abstinence not just from meat, but from dairy products and eggs – items making a welcome reappearance on Easter Sunday. Consumption of meat was also forbidden on all Fridays, in commemoration of Christ's passion, and on vigils of various other important feasts throughout the year. Marriages were not celebrated in Advent or Lent, and some rigorist confessors suggested to female penitents that Lent was an inappropriate time for them to sleep with their husbands. The liturgical calendar was no high-minded abstraction, but an ordering of daily experience that touched the lives of the laity in numerous domestic and intimate ways.

For the most part, though, it worked with rather than against the grain of everyday life. Rituals were interwoven with the rhythms of the agricultural year. After the extended festivities of Christmas were over the serious business began of ploughing fields ready for planting, though this too had celebratory aspects. On 'Plough Monday', immediately following Epiphany, ploughs were festively dragged through village streets. They were often blessed in church, where special plough lights were maintained before the rood or holy sacrament. The sprouting of crops coincided with the feast of the Ascension, and in the preceding week, parishioners would go around the fields with their priests asking God's blessing and protection for the new shoots. These Rogation processions (Latin: *rogare*, to beseech) also supplied an occasion to 'beat the bounds' of the parish; to remind everyone of its geographical extent by walking around the boundaries – a striking instance of the community defining itself through collective ritual action. Harvests were brought in before the feast of St Michael (Michaelmas), a date when rents were due to be paid, and university and law terms began.

Arguably, Catholicism was a better 'fit' for the traditional agricultural communities of late medieval England than for its developing urban centres. Townspeople seem to have leapt on the feast of Corpus Christi (observed in England from 1318) as an opportunity, otherwise barely afforded them by the liturgical calendar, to parade their faith and distinctive social priorities. But the argument should not be pressed too far. All parishes celebrated the same major feasts, as well as the special day of whichever saint was the named patron of their local church.

In any case, the minimal expectations of Catholic Christianity were universal ones. Detailed doctrinal understanding was not high on the list of requirements, though it was generally expected that parishioners would at least learn by heart the *paternoster* (Our Father), *Ave Maria* (Hail Mary) and *Credo* or Creed – the statement of affirmation of core Christian beliefs beginning *Credo in unum Deum* (I believe in one God). True to its incarnational instincts, late medieval Catholicism exhibited a comprehensively 'embodied belief', a set of understandings expressed primarily in symbolic gesture and ritual activity.[9] The interwovenness of faith and action was the beating heart of a vigorous cultural system. But it was also, potentially, a point of weakness. What if someone were to demand the justification for ceremonies and observances? Many would have struggled to say more than that they did as their forebears had always done. Not everyone would prove satisfied with such an explanation.

### The Living and the Dead

On Sunday 9 September 1515, the parishioners of Louth, a small market town on the boundary between the high wolds and low-lying marshlands of Lincolnshire, gathered in front of their parish church of St James. The occasion was the setting of a weathercock, recently purchased at York, on top of the church's newly completed spire:

> There being William Ayleby, parish priest, with many of his brethren priests, there present, hallowing the said weathercock and the stone that it stands upon, and so conveyed upon the said broach [spire]. And then all the priests sung *Te Deum Laudamus* (We praise thee, O God) with organs, and the churchwardens garred ring [caused to be rung] all the bells, and caused all the people there to have bread and ale. And all to the loving of God, Our Lady and All Saints.

The spire – the tallest of any parish church in England – took fifteen years to construct, and cost the parish the enormous sum of £305 7s. 5d. Various parishioners – Thomas Bradley, Agnes English and others – proudly wanted it put on record that they 'saw the first stone set upon the steeple, and also the last stone set upon the broach'.[10]

Parish churches were more than functional houses of worship. At Louth, and elsewhere, they were communal resources and objects of considerable local pride. Lay parishioners were required by law to keep the church – or at least their part of it, the nave – in good repair, an obligation overseen by part-time officials known as churchwardens. These were chosen by the rest of the parishioners, usually in pairs, on a rotating basis. Accounts kept by churchwardens – of which there are over 200 surviving sets for the period before the Reformation – show that, as at Louth, expenditure frequently went beyond necessary repairs and extended to ambitious schemes of construction and beautification.

Churchwardens were also responsible for ensuring parishes possessed everything necessary for performance of the liturgy, inside and outside the church: chalices and plates for the mass, altar coverings, candles, bells, crosses and processional banners, a variety of service books, vestments in the appropriate liturgical colours – green for ordinary Sundays, purple for Advent and Lent, white for important feasts, red for commemoration of martyrs, black for requiem.

Raising money for these purposes itself nurtured community and lay participation. In some places, particularly London and major urban centres, parishes could rely on rental income from church properties. Small town and rural parishes typically depended on a wider range of fund-generating activities. The commonest was the church ale, which combined marking an appropriate Christian festival with feasting in the churchyard or parish-owned church house, and sale of parish-brewed ale to locals and visitors. At Yatton in Somerset, the thrice-yearly ale paid in the fifteenth century for a complete rebuilding of the nave, and replacement of the wooden rood screen with an elaborately carved stone one.

Another form of fund-raising was the staging of plays and revels, sometimes featuring Robin Hood – an appropriate figure for collection of contributions. Such parish productions were less sophisticated affairs than the (often loosely) biblically based miracle and mystery plays performed in the streets of towns like Chester, Coventry, Wakefield and York under the auspices of local craft guilds. But like them, they helped disseminate Christian knowledge in entertaining form. The small town of Wymondham in Norfolk had an annual play honouring St Thomas Becket; New Romney in Kent staged a regular Whitsuntide passion play; a 'play of St Swithin' was acted in the church at Braintree in Essex in 1523.[11]

Parish churches varied in standards of repair, and in lavishness of equipment for worship. But minimum requirements were usually, and sometimes impressively, exceeded. A 1529 inventory from the parish of Long Melford, in the wealthy wool-producing region of south Suffolk, reveals an embarrassment of liturgical riches. The wardens recorded their possession, among many other items, of fifteen chasubles (the coloured upper garment worn by a priest at mass) and seventeen copes (a cape-like vestment used for processions and various liturgical occasions); thirteen chalices, nineteen silver and brass candlesticks, three gilded paxes, three gilded vessels for burning incense, two silver chrismatories (for oil) – and a relic, encased in silver, of the pillar to which Christ had been bound. Parish churches like this were, literally, treasure houses, and their painstakingly acquired riches fostered understandably proprietorial feelings among leading layfolk. The parishioners of Luddenham in Kent were angered in 1511 by the carelessness of their rector, who 'dealeth not fairly with the vestments when he putteth them on'. In 1518, the churchwardens of Louth recorded expenses for escorting to trial at Lincoln a priest – perhaps one of those participating in the celebrations of 1515 – who robbed the contents of the parish chest.[12]

To a great extent, the accumulation of objects in parish churches was the result not of procurement but of benefaction. In wills written at, or near to, the point of death, laypeople in their tens of thousands made gifts of money and valuable things to the parishes where they lived and worshipped. The acquired items, whether a lavish bequest of stained-glass windows or rood screen, or relatively more modest gifts of vestments, chalice or service book, were frequently personalized with the name or coat of arms of the donor. The intention was to prompt priest and people to call to mind the generous benefactors.[13] This desire to be remembered was more than a natural human impulse; it was interwoven with the process of salvation itself.

To remember the dead meant to pray for them, as the dead were in need of the prayers of the living. Near the heart of late medieval religion, and therefore near the heart of late medieval culture, lay a compelling and unsettling landscape of the imagination: the place known as purgatory, an alternative to hell and the prelude to heaven.

Purgatory was a doctrine that 'evolved', achieving its more or less settled form by the late twelfth century. It was, perhaps, the preeminent case of the Church's responsiveness to pastoral and practical necessities. Most dying humans were too fallible to deserve immediate entry to heaven – an honour traditionally reserved for ascetic saints and heroic martyrs. Yet it was hard to believe that a loving God, who wanted to redeem humanity, would wish the great mass of the morally mediocre to suffer for eternity in hell. Purgatory supplied a logically satisfying method of admitting such people to heaven. The atonement removed the collective barrier to salvation; baptism washed away the individual impediment of original sin, and God's absolution, delivered via the priest in the sacrament of penance, forgave any further disqualifying ('mortal') sins it was human habit to commit.

But legally minded medieval theologians drew a distinction between the guilt attached to a sin, and a penalty or 'satisfaction' still due to God for it when the guilt was removed. Penances imposed by priests in confession made a start with this, but most people would end their lives with a great deal of 'satisfaction' still due. Purgatory was where the debt would finally be paid.

The existence of purgatory was formally defined by church councils in 1274 and 1439, but official formulations were remarkably vague about what sort of place it was, and what departed souls could expect to experience there. The vacuum was filled by preachers and authors of devotional books who described a place of intense fiery torment; a place, indeed, hardly distinguishable from hell, and often imagined as situated next to it under the earth.

'Time' in the next life was a mysterious, almost metaphorical concept. But most Christians, clergy as well as layfolk, expected tariffs due in the 'prison' of purgatory to be measurable in tens, hundreds or thousands of years. To anyone facing the prospect of death, it was imperative to consider how that sentence might be reduced. This entailed considerable degrees of diversity and choice. Men and women hoping to reduce time in purgatory were supplicants for mercy, but they were also active consumers, contemplating a range of competing offers of assistance.

One expedient was purchase of an indulgence. These seemed to offer a great deal, in both senses of the phrase. Indulgences were certificates remitting part or all of the satisfaction due for sins, expressed in terms of 'days' and 'years'. They were a logical, even ingenious, conclusion from an attractive premise. All Christians, living and dead, on earth, in purgatory and in heaven, formed part of a single Church – what the Apostles' Creed called the 'communion of saints'. Some members of the communion passed into heaven with a superabundance of 'merit', more satisfaction than they personally needed. This was pre-eminently true of Christ himself, but also of great saints and martyrs down the ages. Their surplus of satisfaction was available for redistribution to less holy members of the communion of saints, from a 'Treasury of Merit' administered by the Church. Only the Pope could offer a plenary indulgence, removing all punishment due for sins – a claim grounded in Christ's pledge to St Peter and his successors (Matt. 16:19): 'I will give to you the keys of the kingdom of heaven, and whatever you shall bind on earth shall be bound in heaven, and whatever you shall loose on earth shall be loosed in heaven.' Other authorities, including bishops, were delegated to remit lesser amounts.

Technically, it was not possible to purchase satisfaction. An indulgence was a reward for performance of some specified good work, or for supporting a worthwhile cause, such as the rebuilding of a church, through making financial contribution. Indulgences were invariably issued for some explicit purpose. Nor were the spiritual benefits automatic, but depended on confession and absolution, and a correct devotional attitude on the part of purchasers.

Nonetheless, 'pardons' were everywhere in late fifteenth- and early sixteenth-century England, with many churches and other bodies securing grants to help fund favoured projects. Indulgences were repeatedly offered, for example, for supporting the pious work of repairing the bridge across the River Torridge at Bideford in North Devon. In such cases, the primary motivation of purchasers may have been to assist the cause in question. Yet a widespread and genuine interest in the spiritual benefits is suggested by the frequency with which offers of indulgence appeared in the prayer books for the laity known as primers or Books of Hours, and were displayed on title pages as an inducement to purchase. Many of these were in return for saying specified prayers in front of a picture of Christ surrounded by the instruments of his passion. Promised returns were implausibly large, and entirely bogus, in that they rested on no episcopal or papal grant: 26,000 years or more of remission for successive repetitions of the prayers.[14]

Similarly questionable guarantees sometimes appeared on memorials. A 'pardon brass' of 1506, commemorating Roger and Elizabeth Legh in the church of St Michael, Macclesfield, offered 26,000 years and twenty-six days of remission in purgatory to anyone saying for their souls five *paternosters*, five *aves* and a Creed – the prayers everyone was expected to know. Tombs and brasses were routinely emblazoned with the imprecations 'ora pro anima . . .' or 'pray for the soul of . . .' A principal purpose of funerary monuments was to serve as tinderboxes of memory, and spark in by-passers the burning impulse of intercession.

It was an opportunity largely confined to those with sufficient wealth and status to be buried inside churches – churchmen, landed gentry, merchants, the occasional yeoman farmer. The mass of the people were interred in parish churchyards without permanent grave-markers. Tombs, particularly for the gentry, were indicators of rank, and emblems of a family's enduring social importance. Yet significant numbers of monuments employed a symbolism of humility and vulnerability. Brasses depicting the body in its burial shroud became common in the last quarter of the fifteenth century, and some brasses and sculpted figural tombs represented the deceased's corpse as a skeletal, worm-eaten cadaver – shock tactics, calculated to arouse the pity of spectators, and move them to prayer, as well as remind them of their own impending mortality.

In ways less readily quantified, but paradoxically more dependable than indulgences, the prayers of the living benefited the dead. The prayers of the poor were considered especially beneficial, an inversion of the normal rules of social influence. The London merchant John Hosier was unusually ambitious in hoping 4,800 paupers would attend his burial in 1518, each to receive a penny. But bequests of alms in money or food to the poor at funerals were commonplace. Wills didn't always explicitly state this was in return for prayers, but the contract was invariably understood. To a modern, utilitarian mind-set, the exchange seems mildly shocking: medieval 'charity' was not altruistic, but nakedly self-interested. Once more, we need to move beyond anachronistic ways of thinking. Each element in the transaction – the relief of the poor, the act of prayer, the remission of purgatorial penalties – was intrinsically pleasing to God. The reciprocal flow of benefits was the communion of saints in action.[15]

The quest for remembrance and prayer was a motivation behind a near-ubiquitous feature of the contemporary scene: the proliferation of guilds and fraternities, voluntary lay associations dedicated to a saint or devotion. Like much in late medieval religion, the diversity of these institutions almost overwhelms their common features. Urban guilds – most notably, the grand 'livery companies' of London – were often principally trade associations, regulating the activities of butchers, tanners, coopers or brewers. In some boroughs, like Coventry or Stratford-upon-Avon, guild membership was intimately tied up with governance structures of the town. A few large urban guilds operated on a national scale: Corpus Christi at York, for example, or the guild of Our Lady at Boston in Lincolnshire, which by the end of the fifteenth century was employing ten chaplains and a choir.

The majority of guilds were, literally, parochial, focusing activities on an annual feast, the maintenance of lights before a statue of their saintly patron, and assistance with parish fund-raising activities. Many parishes had more than one such guild, their existence sometimes known to us only through fleeting mention in a will. There were nineteen guilds in the Norfolk port town of Great Yarmouth, and over 150 in London, in the century before the Reformation.[16]

Parish guilds illustrate the voluntarist impulse in late medieval religion, though doubtless there were sometimes social pressures to join. It is a mistake to see them as symptoms of dissatisfaction with the parish structure, still less with the orthodox teachings of the wider Church. But they show laypeople's readiness to assume degrees of responsibility for their own salvation. Postmortem benefits of membership loomed large in people's minds. Guilds organized your funeral, and guaranteed for it an imposing turn-out of brethren, sometimes clad in distinctive fraternity costume. Most importantly, they arranged masses for the soul of the deceased.

Of all the means of intercession, the mass was most powerful. Because it constituted an application in space and time of Christ's redemptive death on the cross, the mass came to be seen as a quantifiable unit of spiritual power: two masses were better than one, and a thousand were a thousand times better. Masses themselves were not technically for sale, but priests deserved and expected compensation for their labour. For laypeople, the challenge, within their means, was to maximize the merits of the mass for their soul.

A requiem mass, along with the vespers and matins of the dead known as *placebo* and *dirige*, was integral to the burial ritual. One popular supplement was the 'obit', an exact recreation of funeral rites, down to the placing of a hearse in the parish church, to take place each year on the anniversary of death. Its ostentatious, performative character was designed to jog memories, prompting participants and onlookers to recollect and pray. Obits were particularly popular in towns, and more than half of those founded in fifteenth-century Bristol were intended to continue 'as long as the world standeth'.[17]

An alternative, and sometimes an addition, was to establish an institution known as a chantry. At their most lavish, these were housed in purpose-built chantry chapels, though most commonly chantry priests conducted their business at subsidiary altars within the parish church. The most serious, or wealthiest, testators left endowments of land or property for a 'perpetual' chantry, where a priest and his successors would 'sing' for the soul of the founder, and other named beneficiaries, until the world came to an end and purgatory itself was no more. Others left sums for a priest to celebrate masses for a specified period, very often a year.

Some masses might represent better value than others. Trentals were special sets of thirty masses, to be celebrated in the month following death, claimed by their advocates to be uniquely powerful in easing the passage of the soul. There were distinct variants. The Trental of St Gregory, the formula for which was supposedly revealed to the saint by the soul of his suffering mother, was popular in all parts of England in the early sixteenth century. Laypeople showed interest in various other themed 'votive' masses: of the Trinity, of the Name of Jesus, of the Five Wounds, or in the set of so-called 'golden masses', said to produce souls 'flying out of purgatory as thick as sparks of fire'.

The glorious untidiness of the system of intercession was its strength and its weakness. Attempts to use data from wills to suggest belief in purgatory was already waning from the late fifteenth century are unconvincing. The percentage of testators endowing masses varied from region to region, but everywhere an acceptance of the need for some form of intercession was the obvious norm. A discernible shift from establishment of permanent chantries to more temporary ones is related to the phenomenon of 'mortmain' legislation, which from the end of the fourteenth century made it increasingly difficult and expensive to alienate lands permanently into the 'dead hand' of the Church.

Voices of direct criticism were few and muted, though the author of *Dives and Pauper*, a fifteenth-century commentary on the Ten Commandments, printed in the early 1530s, disapproved of showy devotions claiming to be better than ordinary masses of requiem; he thought the Gregory Trental was the cause of 'much hypocrisy and much folly'.

Nor do contemporaries seem to have anticipated a view of modern critics: that an economy of salvation based on post-mortem intercession lent itself to the 'purchase of paradise', and was intrinsically biased against the poor. Perhaps this was due to widespread acceptance of the notion that the greater pride and sinfulness of the rich weighted the scales against them, and they needed all the help they could get. Chantries were certainly the preserve of the rich, but any bequest to the parish, however modest, led to entry of the donor's name onto the parish 'bede roll' – a list of benefactors read at least annually in full, and in shortened form at the weekly mass, with exhortations to remember and pray.

In theory, no one was entirely and finally forgotten: the feast of All Souls, immediately following All Saints on 2 November, was the occasion of praying for an otherwise nameless army of the dead. It was also, close to the onset of winter, a moment of slippage between worlds, when it was popularly believed the dead might return to make demands on the living. The widespread custom of ringing church bells on the night of Halloween (All Hallows' Eve) was partly a form of intercession for the dead, partly a means of protection against them.[18]

Purgatory was 'the defining doctrine of late medieval Catholicism', a religion which has even been called 'a cult of the living in the service of the dead'.[19] It was an undeniably dismal prospect: some self-proclaimed authorities talked of devils, skewers, brandings, in addition to purgation by fire – all inflicted over the course of what would seem like centuries and millennia. The suspicion persists that behind the intense devotional activity of late medieval laity lurked a pervasive, unhealthy fear of punishment in store.

Elizabeth, widow of the knight Sir John Bicknell, of South Perrot in Dorset, left precise, anxious instructions in her will of June 1504. After she received the sacrament of extreme unction, and 'immediately as by man earthly it may be perceived that my soul should be from my body separate', four 'discreet priests' were to begin singing Trentals of St Gregory. Or at least 'as soon as the law of Holy Church ordaineth, after the appearing of the daylight' – even in extremis, the rules should be observed. Priests were not supposed to say more than one mass daily, so at other times the chaplains were to recite psalms for her soul, 'one of them to be occupied night and day' in the month following her death.

Elizabeth Bicknell clearly aimed to take heaven by storm, and there are other examples of testators demanding large sequences of masses to start as soon as the breath passed from their bodies.[20] But such twitchy wills stand out by virtue of their rarity. We cannot finally know the state of mind with which most people approached death, but the general impression is of people sensibly making provision to navigate their way through an inescapable destiny. The most unsettling preaching on the horrors of purgatory was in any case designed to warn people what they could expect if they did *not* behave better in this life, or arrange suffrages for the next; one writer justified his concern with the punishments of purgatory on the grounds that 'few it dread'.[21]

For the health of the purgatorial system as a whole, perhaps a greater dormant danger than the terror of the dying was the complacency, and occasional resentment, of the survivors. The demand to be remembered was, potentially, insatiable, absorbing a significant percentage both of individual legacies and of communal resources. The neglectfulness of heirs and executors was a contemporary cliché not entirely without foundation in fact. The Norfolk gentleman John Paston conspicuously failed to establish the chantry asked for by his father, while the sluggishness of John's own son in making a start on the elaborate tomb he requested was a cause of local scandal through the 1470s.

After decades passed and revenues started to decline, chantries and obits, even those intended to continue while the world endured, were often quietly abandoned, amalgamated, or confiscated by descendants of the original founder. The obligation of memory weighed heavily on people's time as well as purse strings. In 1497, the London Goldsmiths decided that the twenty-five obits they were required to attend each year were 'to the great unease and trouble of the wardens and of all the livery'. The number was cut to fourteen – and in an attempt to encourage flagging attendances, drink was to be provided at all of them. Even after such rationalizations, 368 obits were taking place in London through to the later part of Henry VIII's reign.[22]

Late medieval Catholicism was not oppressively monolithic. If anything, it was alarmingly unregulated. A religious system that advocated the limitless performance of 'good works' as a necessary response to Christ's offer of salvation encouraged an exponential growth of pious lay initiatives, a dazzling array of devotional choices, and some occasional shameless hucksterism – all illustrated in vibrant colour by the practices of purgatory.

It was certainly not a structure collapsing inevitably under the weight of its own contradictions. Under the umbrella of a broad sacramental orthodoxy, Catholicism managed to contain its divergent energies in generally harmonious tension. But the pursuit of varying objectives, and a lack of consensus about what the real priorities should be, were fissures in the fabric of faith – holes for the rain to find, should the weather ever change. The dynamism of late medieval religion, accelerating not decelerating in the early Tudor decades, encompassed an extraordinary devotional agility, alongside an unexpected, almost imperceptible, but nonetheless real spiritual fragility.

### Print, Piety and Pilgrimage

In 1476, after half a lifetime of overseas residence in the service of trade, the merchant William Caxton returned to settle permanently in England. He brought with him a device already widely used in Germany and Italy. It allowed type – small metal blocks in carved forms of letters – to be arranged on a frame, inked, and have their impression conveyed onto pressured sheets of paper. The printing press was a relatively simple technology, and the most revolutionary discovery of the age. It allowed texts, which previously needed to be copied laboriously by hand, to be duplicated quickly, in multiple and standardized copies. It met, and helped fuel, a commercial demand for reading matter, and it slowly began to transform the possibilities for religious practice.

The earliest datable piece of printing to emerge from Caxton's press was very topical: a 1476 bull of Pope Sixtus IV, which for the first time formally extended the benefits of indulgences to souls already in purgatory. The first proper book Caxton printed was Chaucer's *Canterbury Tales*, a work containing sly satire of an unscrupulous pardoner, hawking indulgences with a comic selection of fake relics. It is unlikely Caxton saw any irony or contradiction: printers produced what they perceived the market wanted, and in around 1500 Caxton's assistant and successor, the naturalized Englishman Wynkyn de Worde, moved the operation from the governmental centre of Westminster to the commercial hub of the city of London, where other printers were already open for business.[23]

Printing both reflected and invigorated lay piety. Almost half the output of de Worde and other early printers comprised religious works of various kinds. The topics mirrored the characteristic breadth and variety of late medieval pious interests: sermons, saints' lives (hagiographies), treatises on making a good death, accounts – condensed from scripture – of the life of Jesus, garish visions of purgatory, sombre expositions of the penitential psalms. Among the most popular items were primers or Books of Hours, adapted versions of the cycle of monastic prayer 'offices', with additional material (such as indulgences) thrown in. Up to the early 1530s, at least 500 separate editions of Books of Hours were produced for the English market, representing tens of thousands of copies in circulation.

The advent of printing, and an associated slow but steady rise in literacy rates, did not create any fundamental divide between 'elite' and 'popular' religion, with the wealthy or literate inclined to look cerebrally down their noses on the sensual and ritual devotions of the masses. Books of Hours and other printed texts often contained devotional images, to be prayed in front of like statues in church. A widely shared frame of religious reference is also suggested by the contents of 'common-place books' – compilations of instructive and improving passages – kept in the late fifteenth and early sixteenth centuries by some gentry and wealthy merchants, as well as the odd parish churchwarden. These draw on a wide yet common repertoire. There are pious prayers, and dutiful expositions of commandments and sacraments, but also some decidedly unofficial and folkloric elements: charms against the toothache, verse instructions on divination using dice.[24] Nonetheless, it would be perverse to maintain that literacy and access to printed books did not open up any new possibilities for religious practice and reflective meditation on the part of the laity.

Exact boundaries between literacy and illiteracy are difficult to establish. Calculations based on the ability of witnesses in legal settings to write their names tend to produce minimal estimates: at the start of the sixteenth century, a 90 per cent illiteracy rate among men, and 99 per cent among women. Yet writing is a harder task than reading, and children might be taught one skill but not the other.

Both skills were certainly more heavily concentrated in towns than in the countryside. In the early sixteenth century, perhaps a third to a half of male Londoners were able to read. The Venetian visitor who saw literate laypeople taking the Office of Our Lady along to mass observed them 'with some companion reciting it in the church verse by verse, in a low voice, after the manner of churchmen'.

But the dominant mode of lay literacy was not, in fact, that of churchmen. The word *literatus*, in the earlier Middle Ages, usually meant a 'clerk' (*clericus*, clergyman), and signalled proficiency in Latin. The religious output of the English presses, however, was overwhelmingly vernacular; more technically complex Latin service books tended to be printed on the continent and imported. Books of Hours were Latin texts, but they were increasingly accoutred with translations and paraphrases of the key prayers. There was an unmistakable lay appetite for devotional material in English.[25] This did not – necessarily – represent any immediate threat to the teaching or authority of the Church, even when the appetite extended to the bible itself in vernacular translation (see Chapter 4). The materials in demand were almost invariably orthodox in character, intended to foster deeper understanding of the mysteries, and by-ways, of the faith. But their popularity provides further testimony that growing numbers of laymen and women were active participants in the production and consumption of religious culture, not passive receptacles of clerical instruction.

Sometimes, lay religious activism required the great and good to sit up and take notice. In November 1515, a twelve-year-old girl, Anne, daughter of an Essex gentleman, Sir Roger Wentworth, began to suffer violent and disturbing convulsions, seemingly possessed by the devil. The fits lasted until 25 March 1516, Feast of the Annunciation, when Christ's coming was revealed to the Virgin Mary by the Angel Gabriel. Anne had on that day a radiant vision of Mary, 'in the picture and stature of the image of Our Lady of Grace in Ipswich'. This was a famous statue, housed in a chapel to which Anne demanded to be taken on pilgrimage. There, over several days, and before a crowd of more than a thousand, she was miraculously cured, while reportedly showing prophetic knowledge of 'many things said and done at the same time in other places'. Witnesses included the abbot of Bury St Edmunds, so overcome with emotion that he promised to make a pilgrimage there every year on foot, and the nobleman Robert, Lord Curzon, who wrote up an excitable account of the affair.

Speculations as to the 'real' cause of Anne's condition, or her motivation, are not particularly helpful. There were clearly tensions within the family, and her symptoms recurred when her parents initially reneged on a promise to return to the shrine after eleven days. The second visit was yet more spectacular than the first: a crowd of 4,000 gathered to see Anne, and hear her deliver a two-hour sermon, in the course of which she reproached her parents for having 'put me again to these great pains'.

Anne's celebrity was short-lived. Despite her father's objections, she turned to the life of a Franciscan nun, and fourteen years later was reported to be living in a convent 'well and graciously'. At the time of her cure, the Ipswich chapel's custodian, Dr John Bailey, preached in the town hailing the greatest miracle since the conversion of England. He perhaps had a vested interest in thinking so, but the affair renewed national interest in the shrine. The following year, Queen Catherine paid a visit there, as did the most important man in England after the King: Thomas, Cardinal Wolsey.[26]

The affair of the Maid of Ipswich, unusual though it was, reveals a society prepared to believe in the intrusion of the miraculous, even – or perhaps especially – when its conduit was a twelve-year-old girl. Anne's temporary inversion of the usual hierarchies of age, gender, family and status could be accepted because her messages reinforced orthodox teaching. The crowds she commanded, spanning all social classes, affirmed the importance to them of the saints, and particularly of Christ's mother, the Blessed Virgin Mary.

Anne's vision was of a specific, materialized face of the Virgin, 'Our Lady of Ipswich'. There were other renowned statues that earthed the transcendent Queen of Heaven to a particular piece of English soil. Our Lady of Walsingham in Norfolk was perhaps the most famous. Others included Our Lady of Doncaster in Yorkshire; of Caversham in Berkshire; Our Lady of Willesden, just to the north-west of London; Our Lady of Worcester; Our Lady of the Tower, set in the city walls of Coventry. Such hubs of devotion suggest ways in which late medieval religion was at once instinctively universal and intensely local.

Pilgrimage in general illuminates this theme. Spiritual journeys to holy places might be expeditions to the exotic and unknown. The holiest of all places was Jerusalem, and a handful of English travellers undertook this risky trek. The courtier Sir Richard Guildford set off for Jerusalem in April 1506, and died there in September. An account of the journey by his chaplain, printed in London in 1511, allowed English readers to experience vicariously the glamorous sights and ceremonies of the Church of the Holy Sepulchre, its custodianship uneasily shared between 'divers sects of Christian men' – a phenomenon as yet unknown in the Catholic Latin west.

A decade later, a Warwickshire squire, Sir Robert Throckmorton, made the same journey, and likewise failed to return. The will he made on the eve of his departure in May 1518 testified to a strong belief in the power of intercession. Throckmorton established a chantry, and requested masses from the Benedictine monks of Evesham and Augustinian canons of Studley, the Franciscan and Dominican friars at Oxford and Cambridge, as well as the prayers of paupers in the almshouse he had founded at Worcester. The suspicions of some historians, that gentry were not emotionally invested in their local parish church, are dispelled in Throckmorton's careful prescriptions for St Peter's, Coughton, the place he wanted to be buried. The east window in the chancel was to be glazed 'at my cost and charge' with scenes of Doomsday. Other new windows were to depict the seven sacraments, and seven works of mercy. In detailed instructions for the gilding, painting and placing of new statues in the church, Throckmorton brought the universal symbols of Christian cosmology to the parochial gaze of rural Warwickshire: images of the Trinity; the Annunciation of Gabriel to Mary; the Archangels Michael and Raphael.[27]

Ardent or adventurous souls also journeyed to the shrine of St James at Compostela in Galicia, or to Rome, in greater numbers than they did to Muslim-occupied Jerusalem. Canterbury attracted pilgrims from across

England, as did Walsingham. The presence of relics, a physical remnant of the once-living saint, was the usual allurement. Canterbury, perhaps the only English shrine of truly international significance, possessed the remains of its martyred archbishop, Thomas Becket; Walsingham, a remarkable relic of the milk of the Virgin Mary. Yet the principal draw of the chapel of Our Lady at Walsingham was its statue of an enthroned and crowned Virgin holding the Christ-child on her lap; by the later Middle Ages, an image too could serve as principal physical site of a saint's sacred power, the role once confined to their relics.

Some shrines were embodiments of regional identity, such as the corpse of St Cuthbert, apostle to the Anglo-Saxon north, in Durham Cathedral. Here, veneration extended beyond the body itself to an important 'contact relic': a banner, supposedly incorporating the *corporal*, or white linen cloth, used by the saint in his celebrations of the mass. On several occasions in the Middle Ages, the banner was carried into victorious battle against the Scots. The shrine at Hereford Cathedral of St Thomas Cantilupe, a holy thirteenth-century bishop, was a similar rallying symbol for the Welsh border country, though its popularity had passed its peak by the early sixteenth century. Saints, like stocks and shares, rose and fell with fashions, and with shrewd or lax management of the assets and public promotion of the shrine.

Much pilgrim traffic was in fact remarkably local, involving distances comparable to travel for buying and selling at the nearest market town, and saints as internationally obscure as St Urith of Chittelhampton (Devon) or St Walstan of Bawburgh (Norfolk). A poem in celebration of Walstan, a putative Saxon prince, written around the turn of the sixteenth century, recorded eleven healing miracles performed at his shrine: four of the fortunate pilgrims came from Bawburgh itself, and another three lived within a half day's walk.[28]

The saints were a mixed crew, and performed a variety of roles. As holy people who once inhabited the earth, they were peerless exemplars of Christian living, and as current denizens at the court of heaven, they were in the definitive position to lobby for the interests of devotees. People prayed to saints, including the Virgin Mary, so that they could intercede with Christ on their behalf. In practice, it seems likely that most people thought of saints as possessing and exercising sacred power in their own right. The recorded favours resulting from visits to shrines were overwhelmingly miracles of healing, and it may be that people sometimes took to local saints relatively minor ailments they did not wish to bother St Peter or the Virgin about. Particular specialisms were well known: St Erasmus for bowel complaints, St Apollonia for the toothache, St Margaret of Antioch for help with childbirth.[29]

Did the cult of saints eclipse the figure of Jesus? It is sometimes suggested that the focus on Christ was blurred in late medieval Christianity, that the real significance of his passion was somehow lost or obscured amidst a blizzard of saints' legends and questionable 'superstitious' devotions.

Yet the subordinate place of saints in a celestial hierarchy was well under-stood by people like the Hull merchant John Dalton, whose will of 1487 bequeathed his soul to 'Our Lord Jesus Christ, when it shall depart from my body, and to Our Lady St Mary, St Michael, St John Baptist, St John the Evangelist, St Katherine, and St Barbara and all the holy company and saints of heaven'. By far the most popular 'cult' at the start of the sixteenth century, in England as in all other parts of Europe, was the cult of Jesus himself – a cult whose intensity was in fervent advance over the course of the fifteenth century.

At an official and liturgical level, it was encouraged by the institution of new feast days. Papally approved celebrations of the Transfiguration and the Holy Name of Jesus were absorbed into service books and liturgical practice in England in the 1480s and '90s, and many parishes quickly established Jesus altars, or gilds dedicated to the Holy Name. The great feast of Corpus Christi was also, of course, a supremely 'Christocentric' one. Devotions to the Five Wounds and the Lamentation (for Jesus) of the Virgin Mary did not quite make it to the status of fully fledged feasts, but were authorized as special votive cele-brations for inclusion in missals (mass books).

The 'image of pity', an affecting picture of Christ's dead upper body, surrounded by instruments of his passion, was widely reproduced in Books of Hours, and also in churches on painted walls, bench-ends, funeral brasses, panels and pyxes. It was closely associated with the image of 'Our Lady of Pity', or pietà: a depiction of a grieving mother cradling the lifeless Jesus in her arms, and a much favoured subject for paintings and statues in churches.[30]

It betrays misunderstanding of the late medieval mind-set to see the cult of the Virgin as a rival focus of devotion, diverting attention from her divine son. In fact, it was itself part of the 'Christocentric' impulse, as it was based around Mary's role in the life of Jesus, and particularly in the passion narrative. Even devotional themes without clear scriptural provenance – such as carvings of Mary's coronation as Queen of Heaven – placed her in close, and subordinate, proximity to Christ. The phrase, 'Jesus mercy, Lady help' came naturally to prayerful lips. The most prominent statue of the Virgin in every English church was one that placed her at the foot of the cross, alongside St John, the disciple Jesus loved, atop the parish rood beam.

The growing popularity of Marian shrines like Walsingham and Ipswich was matched by that of sites associated with the person of Christ. Pilgrims travelling to the Cistercian monastery of Hailes in Gloucestershire could view and venerate a vial containing a portion of the Holy Blood of Jesus. An unsym-pathetic commentator in the early 1530s observed 'how they come by flocks out of the west country . . . And they believe verily that it is the very blood that was in Christ's body, shed upon the mount of Calvary for our salvation'.

A localized manifestation of the Virgin, in her statues at Walsingham, Willesden, Worcester and elsewhere, was paralleled in the devotion shown to individual wonder-working roods, some of which were credited with containing actual pieces of the True Cross. Pilgrims trooped to the Rood of Bromholm in Norfolk, the Rood of Dovercourt in Essex, the Rood of Bermondsey in Surrey, the 'Rood of Grace' at Boxley Abbey in Kent, a great cross at the north door of St Paul's Cathedral in London. There were further miraculous roods at Brecon and Llangynwyd in Wales, and just across the English border at Chester.[31]

The devotions to Jesus, just like late medieval popular devotions as a whole, were not moribund, but florid; not sterile, but fertile; not modestly monotone, but confidently cacophonous. For some, it was all too much. Among the plural pieties, sacred materiality and sensuous ritual of late medieval Catholicism, various individuals longed for clarity, simplicity and spiritual purity. Those longings might take rebellious, heretical forms (see Chapter 4), but they need not do. Fifteenth- and early sixteenth-century will-makers, across different regions of England, who asked for burial 'without any pomp', were in every likelihood entirely orthodox. So too were the testators in parts of Kent who in the first decades of the sixteenth century requested in disproportionate numbers masses of the Holy Name of Jesus, while conspicuously neglecting other traditional forms of intercession.

Within the ranks of the clergy, there had always been a chorus of austere, moralistic voices, warning against 'superstition' in popular piety and a lack of true devotion in the practice of pilgrimage. Such voices were particularly audible around the turn of the fifteenth century, and some of the works produced by restrained and self-consciously reformist Lancastrian Catholics, such as *Dives and Pauper*, were printed for a new audience in the age of Caxton and his successors. A common refrain was that while images had an instructive value for the unlearned – they were 'laymen's books' – it was necessary to be on vigilant guard lest people start offering them the kind of worship and devotion that was the due of God alone.[32]

How, then, amidst the noise and clutter, to live the kind of life God wanted, to practise the imitation of Christ? One book claimed to know the answer. The *Imitatio Christi* was composed in Latin at the beginning of the fifteenth century, probably by a Dutch monk called Thomas Kempis. Offering guidance for a close spiritual relationship with Jesus, and a disciplined interior life of prayer and self-knowledge, it was received with enthusiasm in pious circles across Europe. In England, the *Imitatio* circulated in manuscript translation in the fifteenth century, but became better known after Henry VII's mother, Lady Margaret Beaufort, commissioned a new translation by William Atkinson, fellow of Jesus College, Cambridge, which appeared in 1503.

The *Imitatio* had little time for lavish saints' cults, images and pilgrimage, and Atkinson played down and even omitted some passages where Kempis was sharply critical of popular religion and monastic life – such as a tart observation that 'they that go much on pilgrimage be seldom thereby made perfect and holy'. The censored passages were restored in a second vernacular edition of 1531. Its translator – in keeping with the *Imitatio*'s themes of humility and self-abnegation – was uncredited, but seems very likely to have been a priest called Richard Whitford. In all, ten printed editions of the two sixteenth-century translations appeared up to 1535.[33]

Whitford was no radical, dissident or rebel; rather, he was a serious-minded, orthodox member of the Catholic clerical establishment. But his admiration for the stripped-down message of the *Imitatio Christi* underlines the long-standing concerns in some church circles about a loss of vision and clarity in the presentation of the essential Christian message – anxieties shared by some literate lay readers. Around the turn of the sixteenth century, such concerns were being repackaged in eye-catchingly new ways. The eye-catcher-in-chief was a personal friend of Whitford, and a marvel to Europe as a whole.

### Humanists and Barbarians

In early 1512, a group of student-pilgrims made their way from Cambridge to the shrine at Walsingham. They were accompanied by an older mentor, a foreigner resident in England since 1509, and well acquainted with the English and their ways. Erasmus of Rotterdam was a name to conjure with in the first years of the sixteenth century, and its bearer was disinclined to let people forget it: international man of letters, friend of scholars, prelates, kings and popes, runaway monk and lightning-rod of controversy, a self-appointed scourge of ignorance, obscurantism, superstition and abuse of power. Erasmus took up residence in Cambridge in 1511, and in May 1512 wrote to his friend Andrea Ammonio to say 'I am going to pay a visit to our Lady of Walsingham', adding 'I will there hang up a votive offering of a Greek poem.'[34] The composition began by praising the Virgin in conventional terms, but where other worshippers brought gifts of silver and gold, requesting health or other blessings, Erasmus offered nothing but the verses themselves, and asked in return for the greatest of rewards, 'a heart that honours God, and is free from all blemishes'. Here, in a scallop shell, was Erasmus's religious philosophy, the 'philosophy of Christ', as he liked to call it. In place of the fearful, servile and self-interested devotion of the masses, he offered a true piety of the heart, sincere and secure in its love of God.

Years later, Erasmus composed a semi-fictionalized description of the Walsingham visit as one of his set of moralizing tales known as *The Colloquies*. Its title, 'A Pilgrimage for Religion's Sake', is ironic, for the intention of the piece is to satirize the greed and corruption of the Augustinian monks administering the shrine, and the superstitious credulity of pilgrims frequenting it. The work contained an account of a second visit, to the shrine of Thomas Becket at Canterbury, where the emphasis again is on the sumptuous wealth generated by the pilgrim trade, and the superstitious veneration of spiritually doubtful relics.[35]

Erasmus's companion on the journey to Canterbury was reportedly even more revolted than he was by the mendacity and superstition of the shrine and relic business. The colloquy calls him 'Gratian Pullus': a scholar's joke, for *pullus* is both a classical term of endearment, and a Latin word meaning young animal or colt. John Colet (1467–1519) was a renowned preacher, the dean of St Paul's Cathedral, and an educational reformer, who founded St Paul's School and personally planned its curriculum. Colet was a leading light in England of the movement known to historians as humanism, though the term itself is anachronistic, and the word 'movement' gives too great an impression of clarity and organization to what was in fact a mishmash of attitudes and values.

Humanism is inextricably linked with another made-up category of historians, 'the Renaissance' – the enthusiastic rediscovery of classical learning that began in Italy in the late fourteenth century. Nineteenth-century writers like the Swiss scholar Jacob Burckhardt associated the Renaissance with the rise of 'individualism', with a kind of neo-pagan celebration of the joys of life, and a relative dethroning of God and elevation of humanity. Even if this holds true for Italy (and it is questionable), Erasmus, Colet and those associated with them in England are best described as *Christian* humanists, eager to apply the insights of Greek and Latin learning, and the critical analysis of texts, to the renewal and reform of the Church. They were not voices crying in the wilderness, but influential opinion-makers, with friends in the highest of places.

Like other early exponents of humanism in England, such as William Grocyn, Thomas Linacre and William Lyly, Colet caught the bug in Italy, where he travelled and studied between 1492 and 1495. He was particularly drawn to the writings of the Florentine Marsilio Ficino (1433–99), a leading exponent of the mystical philosophy of neo-platonism. In Plato's teaching, the 'Demiurge' (God) created the world as an image of an eternal archetype, planting the idea of that ultimate reality in the human mind or soul. Neo-platonism concerned itself with how the soul could 'ascend' to embrace the divine ideal lying beyond and behind the perishable things of the material world. For Colet, this meant an unceasing effort to imitate Jesus Christ, whose whole life 'was nothing other than an ascent from this place into heaven'.[36] Colet was, quite literally, a perfectionist, considering it the duty of Christians, especially priests, to nurture and radiate an intensely purified holiness.

Conformity to the pattern of Christ through perfection of conduct was the theme of an influential sequence of lectures on the epistles of St Paul that Colet delivered in Oxford in 1496–7. Great claims have been made for these sermons, though they in fact neither revolutionized medieval patterns of scriptural interpretation, nor anticipated the theology of Martin Luther. Nonetheless,

Colet saw little role for rites and ceremonies in the process of becoming Christ-like. He emphasized the centrality of scripture as a source of divine grace, and neglected scholarly authorities in order to engage directly with the character and letters of St Paul. Close scrutiny of the written text was characteristic of the humanist approach, as was the impetus to return *ad fontes*: to the purest, most original sources of the faith.

Colet was obsessively concerned with the failures of the clergy to assume their rightful role in the divine plan, yet there is little indication he trusted the laity to take matters into their own hands. That approach was more character-istic of Erasmus. His hugely popular *Enchiridion Militis Christiani* (1503) exudes an emphasis on simple Christ-centred piety, unencumbered by complex ritual or ceremonial demands, and nurtured by close engagement with the text of the New Testament. It was a work intended to be owned and read by laypeople.

The title translates as handbook of a Christian knight (or soldier), though *Enchiridion* can also mean 'dagger'. When the occasion demanded, Erasmus was not averse to sticking the knife in. During his first stay in England, he worked on a book called *Antibarbari* – against the barbarians. What Erasmus meant by 'barbarians' were people hostile to the *studia humanitatis* (the 'humanities'), which in the sixteenth century meant the classically inspired study of rhetoric, grammar, poetry, history and moral philosophy, in addition to, or in place of, a focus on formal theology. Such barbarians were to be found everywhere. Erasmus came across them in the Augustinian monastery at Steyn in the Netherlands, which he entered as a young man in 1487, and from which he departed a few years later, never to return. Throughout his life, Erasmus retained a distaste for the cloistered religious existence, and an almost paranoid conviction that the religious, particularly the friars, were out to get him.

The worst barbarians were high guardians of learning itself: the university teachers of the theology 'schools'. Medieval academic divinity – scholasticism – was a highly sophisticated and diverse system of didactic and exploratory investigation, combining characteristics of the disciplines we today would call theology and philosophy. Contrary to later myth-making, scholastics never debated the question of how many angels could dance on the head of a pin. But they did apply logic and dialectical reasoning to the elucidation of Christian revelation, and to a host of existential and metaphysical problems.

To Erasmus's way of thinking, scholastics were men who derived their philo-sophical method from Aristotle, and who mangled the simple truths of the Gospel in a bear-pit of abstract speculations. 'In saying that you dislike this modern school of divines, who spend their lives on mere subtleties and quib-bling of sophistry, you are quite of the same way of thinking as myself,' Erasmus wrote to Colet in the autumn of 1499.[37] It is revealing that Erasmus described the centuries-old traditions of scholastic learning as 'modern'. In an age suspicious of novelty, the humanists did not consider their approach 'new learning', but rather the restoration of an earlier purity and probity.[38]

The primordial sin of the scholastics, so humanists believed, was their separation of theology from piety. This led, on the one hand, to the pure stream of gospel teaching becoming polluted by human logic and disputatiousness; on the other, to the religion actually practised by the majority descending into empty ceremonies and external rituals, a pointless imitation of styles of devotion found in religious houses. Erasmus was a man of his age in characterizing such worthless externalism as 'Jewish'. Sound textual and linguistic scholarship, re-establishing the authentic meanings of ancient Christian writings – including the scriptures themselves – was one weapon against the barbarians; another was ridicule and satire.

In England, Erasmus soon found a kindred spirit, a brilliant young London lawyer, rising in city and royal service. Erasmus was introduced to Thomas More in 1499 by his pupil and patron, William Blount, Lord Mountjoy, a friend of the More family. Although Erasmus was More's senior by a decade, they were to become lifelong friends. During a stay at More's house in 1505, the two men found serious amusement in translating from Greek into Latin the satirical dialogues of Lucian of Samosata, a second-century writer whose works were rediscovered by fifteenth-century humanists. A biting commentator on the popular religion of his day, Lucian's satires were, Erasmus reflected, 'most serviceable for the detection and refutation of the impostures of certain persons who even today cheat the populace, either by conjuring up miracles, or with a pretence of holiness'.[39]

Thomas was Erasmus's muse for a more famous satirical work of 1511, the *Moriae Encomium* (Praise of Folly), which punned affectionately on his friend's surname. Speaking ironically through the figure of Folly, Erasmus castigated the pointless speculations of 'Thomists, Albertists, Ockhamists and Scotists' – disciples of the thirteenth- and fourteenth-century theologians Thomas Aquinas, Albertus Magnus, William of Ockham and Duns Scotus. Among questions they were said to have formally debated are: 'is it a possible proposition that God the father could hate his son? Could God have taken on the form of a woman, a devil, a donkey, a gourd or a flintstone? Shall we be permitted to eat and drink after the Resurrection?'

The metaphysical subtleties applied by school doctors to the sacraments, and to the technicalities of grace, penance and transubstantiation, would surely have baffled the apostles. Scorn was poured too on the numerous orders of friars and monks, who 'aren't interested in being like Christ but in being unlike each other', as well as on the 'silliness' of excessive popular devotion to the saints and their images, 'encouraged by priests who are not unaware of the profit to be made thereby'.[40] That all these critiques were, to varying degrees, unfair did not make them any less effective.

In 1516 More published his own counterpart to the *Praise of Folly* – a description of the recently discovered island of *Utopia* (Greek: 'no place') from the mouth of the traveller Raphael Hythlodaeus ('speaker of nonsense'). This too was a piquant satire of the society, politics and customs of early sixteenth-century Europe, though a more subtle and ambiguous one than that of Erasmus, who seems not to have known quite what to make of it. Despite posterity's appropriation of the word, Utopia itself is not a perfect society, and modern critics have been perplexed by the layers of irony More wove into the approbation of practices he himself surely disapproved of: rigid control of freedom of movement, euthanasia, religious toleration.

*Utopia* contains a few jibes at the condition of the Church. There is a playful sideswipe at 'inventions of our modern logicians'; a laconic observation that the priests of the Utopians are 'of great holiness, and therefore very few'; an ironic explanation of why, while the Utopians avoid making treaties, Europeans always uphold them because of the respect and reverence everyone feels for the popes, who themselves 'never promise anything that they do not scrupulously perform'.[41]

Yet *Utopia* lacks the programmatic reform agenda found in *Praise of Folly* and other of Erasmus's works. More was perfectly capable of exasperation with knuckle-headed friars, such as the Franciscan he encountered in Coventry preaching that anyone saying the Psalter of the Blessed Virgin every day could not be damned.[42] But he never shared Erasmus's instinctive disdain for the vowed religious life as a whole. As a young man More resided for some months with the London Carthusians, possibly testing a vocation to the cloister. Even at the knot of its closest personal threads, humanism was never a tapestry of a single tint.

If his 'philosophy of Christ' was to become a widely lived reality, Erasmus believed it could only be on the basis of renewed engagement with the original source text of Christian faith, the New Testament. The idea that medieval religious culture ignored or marginalized the bible is profoundly misguided; on the contrary, vast intellectual and pastoral efforts were devoted to its interpretation.[43] For Erasmus, however, the issue was not so much attention to scripture *per se*, as the quality of the bible on offer. The standard Latin version used by the Church was the Vulgate (Latin, *vulgatus*: popular or common) translation made by St Jerome in the fourth century. For some time, its merits had been under the critical lens of humanist scholarship. The Roman humanist Lorenzo Valla (1407–57) set himself the task of comparing the Greek against the Latin Vulgate and found hundreds of minor errors. Erasmus came across Valla's *Adnotationes* (Annotations) in a monastic library near Louvain, and published them in 1505.[44]

He later decided to prepare a new Latin translation, or at least a corrected version of the Vulgate, and publish it alongside a version of the Greek original. This was an endeavour with a remarkably English pedigree. Having acquired sufficient knowledge of the Greek language, Erasmus began the project during his visit to England in 1505–6, using Greek and Latin manu-scripts lent to him by Colet from the library of St Paul's. The bulk of the work on the Greek edition was undertaken during an extended Cambridge stay in 1511–14. In February 1512, Erasmus claimed to have been 'almost entirely transformed into an Englishman'.[45]

Erasmus's *Novum Instrumentum* was published at Basel in February 1516: a parallel Greek and Latin text of the New Testament, with 450 pages of appended notes. It was an instant sensation. Everything about it was controversial, starting with the title. *Instrumentum* means in classical Latin a tool, piece of equipment or furniture, and Erasmus thus seemed to be making a bold claim about the significance of his endeavour (it became the *Novum Testamentum* again in a second edition of 1519). His prefatory *Paraclesis* – exhortation or admonition – was a clarion call for the philosophy of Christ. His was 'a new and wonderful philosophy', requiring only a pious and open mind, and a pure and simple faith; it rendered redundant 'those huge commentaries of the inter-preters at odds with one another'.

Looking beyond his present labours, Erasmus issued a call for Holy Scripture to be available in vernacular languages – even those of the 'Scots and Irish', no doubt the most obscure and barbarous European peoples to which Erasmus's Anglophile mind could run. The gospels and epistles should be read by 'even the lowliest women'. Would that 'the farmer sing some portion of them at the plough, the weaver hum some parts of them to the movement of his shuttle, the traveller lighten the weariness of the journey with stories of this kind!' Indeed, anyone who encouraged others to charity, simplicity of life, forgiveness of wrongs, and to welcome the embrace of death should be consid-ered a theologian, even if they were a common labourer or weaver. And if preachers were to teach this philosophy, then Christendom would not be disturbed by almost continuous war, men would not drive themselves frantic in pursuit of riches, and every subject under the sun would cease to resound with 'noisy disputation'. It was a powerful and provocative manifesto: return to the life-giving sources of the Christian message; back to basics.[46]

Taking a leaf out of Valla's book, Erasmus believed the task of establishing correct meaning from the original biblical languages belonged to scholarly philologists, not theologians. Some of Erasmus's translation choices were none-theless heavy with theological implication, which his notes were not chary of pointing out. *Metanoiete* – John the Baptist's imperative command in expecta-tion of the kingdom of God (Matt. 3:2) – was rendered by the Vulgate as *poeni-tentiam agite* (do penance). Erasmus proposed as a better Latin translation *resipiscite* (repent) or *ad mentem redite* (turn to yourself). The text was taken by the 'common herd' of theologians as a proof-text for confession and sacramental penance, but Erasmus argued the Greek term had nothing to do with 'the prescribed penalties by which one atones for sins'.

Similarly, his notes marvelled that Christ's words to Peter ('thou art Peter, and upon this rock I will build my Church'; Matt. 16:18) had been 'twisted' by theologians, 'making it refer to the Roman Pontiff' rather than to Peter's faith, or to all Christians, or to Christ himself.[47] Most controversial, however, was Erasmus's decision, in the second edition of 1519, to translate the resounding opening to St John's Gospel – 'In the beginning was the Word, and the Word was with God, and the Word was God' – using *sermo* rather than *verbum* for the Greek *logos*. *Sermo* carried added connotations of communication, dialogue or conversation, which Erasmus considered more fitting than the one-dimensional 'word' of *verbum*. This was typical of humanist educational ideals, and notions of spiritual improvement through colloquy and discussion: Christ was the 'argument' of God!

The 'barbarians' did not take this lying down. After publication of the *Annotations*, Erasmus was told of a Dominican friar complaining tearfully to his congregation that all his efforts to defend the faith were for nothing: 'what is left for us, except to throw our books into the fire, now that men have arisen who write new books to put right the *Paternoster* and the *Magnificat*? [prayer of Mary; Luke 1: 46–55]'[48] A more notable critic, going on the offensive even before the *Novum Instrumentum* was published, was Martin van Dorp of the Theology Faculty at Louvain, a body notable for lack of enthusiasm about Erasmus. Dorp feared attacking the Vulgate would undermine the teachings of the Church: how could God have allowed it to continue in error for more than a thousand years? And what of the authority of theological texts and decrees of councils based on the established translation? More rallied to Erasmus's defence in an emollient *Letter to Dorp* (1515), but was soon warning him that other critics in England, including the Provincial of the Franciscans, Henry Standish, were conspiring to find and attack errors in the *Novum Instrumentum*, fuelling Erasmus's paranoia about the malevolent hostility of friars.[49]

Reports reached Erasmus of one Cambridge college where the fellows had sworn by solemn resolution that no copy of his New Testament be allowed into the precincts, whether 'by horse, boat, wagon or porter'. Such men, he scoffed, hadn't read the book: 'they have merely heard over their cups or in little gatherings in the marketplace that a new book has come out which tries to peck the crow's eyes out and give the theologians a taste of their own medicine'.[50] There was little enthusiasm for Erasmus either at Merton College, Oxford, where the intellectual tone had been set by almost a quarter century under the wardenship of Richard Fitzjames, an earnest and irascible West Countryman. In 1506 Fitzjames was appointed bishop of London, and though details are hazy, he was sufficiently perturbed by the reformist critiques of Erasmus's friend Colet to threaten in 1513 to bring heresy charges against him. Erasmus thought the bishop 'an insuperably superstitious Scotist'.[51]

Not all of Erasmus's critics, in England or elsewhere, were ignorant backwoodsmen, or unreconstructed scholastic theologians. Dorp had respectable humanist credentials, and Erasmus sparred over details of the translation with the leading French humanist, Jacques Lefèvre d'Étaples. Even Fitzjames had a volume of Cicero in his generally old-fashioned library.[52] Embarrassingly for both Erasmus and Thomas More, the most vocal English critic was a mutual friend, Edward Lee, who actually assisted Erasmus with his work on the New Testament, but took umbrage when his suggestions were ignored, and published in pique a heavily critical set of *Annotations on the Annotations of the New Testament*. Despite More's attempts at mediation, the feud festered nastily for years. Robert Ridley, fellow of King's Hall, Cambridge, and a humanist scholar who avidly read Erasmus's works, was also less than completely bowled over. His marginal comments reveal a deep concern about the corrosive effect of Erasmus's freewheeling scholarship on traditional piety. An observation that 'Erasmus is always blind about the monastic life and the monastery' was not wide of the mark.[53]

Erasmus and his English allies were scarcely a small, heroic insurgency withstanding a massive establishment backlash. In the main, it was the critics of the *Novum Instrumentum* who felt threatened and beleaguered. If humanist scholarship was the thin end of a dangerous wedge, most guardians of orthodoxy seem not to have realized it. Erasmus himself boasted in a letter of July 1514 that 'there isn't a bishop in England but rejoices to be greeted by me', adding that the archbishop of Canterbury, William Warham, was 'so devoted to me that he could be no more loving if he were my father or my brother'. What was more, the King himself 'still speaks often of me, with as much admiration and devotion as anyone else'.

### Colleges, Trojans and Greeks

In 1516, Cambridge acquaintances rushed to congratulate Erasmus on the appearance of the New Testament. John Watson, fellow of Peterhouse, told him his notes had 'placed mightily in your debt every student of Our Lord'. Henry Bullock, a close friend and future vice-chancellor of the university, waxed lyrical: 'great gods, how clever it is, how clearly reasoned, and to all men of sound judgement how pleasing and how indispensable!' The current chancellor, Bishop John Fisher, wrote in more measured but still enthusiastic tones: 'in the translation of the New Testament, made by you for the common profit of all, no man of sense could find offence'.

The printing of the *Novum Testamentum* in 1519 was publicly endorsed by no lower an authority than Pope Leo X, to whom Erasmus tactfully dedicated the first edition in 1516. Erasmus could wave a pile of supportive letters from a clutch of leading prelates and secular rulers, including Francis I of France and Henry VIII. In a letter of 1519, he reported with satisfaction how Henry intervened to 'put to silence' certain 'rascals' attacking the study of Greek at Oxford.[54]

This episode, recounted at greater length in a letter of Thomas More to the university authorities in March 1518, involved a self-styled group of 'Trojans', who set themselves to oppose all forms of 'polite learning', and specifically the introduction of the teaching of Greek.[55] Some academics will always oppose changes to the curriculum. But, at both Oxford and Cambridge, Christian humanism was in the ascendant in the early years of the sixteenth century, and was, for now, at the service of a profoundly Catholic vision of Christian reformation.

Oxford and Cambridge were ecclesiastical institutions, providing for the education of clergymen to serve the needs of Church and state. The handful of colleges in both places were endowed institutions comprising groups of scholars attached to the 'higher' faculties of Theology, Medicine and Law. Those studying in the Faculty of Arts – whom we today would call undergraduates – were more loosely affiliated, and usually housed in halls or private lodgings. The various religious houses in the university towns, particularly those of Franciscan and Dominican friars, were historically of great significance, especially in the Faculty of Theology, though by the later fifteenth century the friars did not enjoy the academic prestige they once did. Other religious communities sent members to study at the universities; the Benedictines maintained houses of study at both Oxford and Cambridge in the fifteenth and sixteenth centuries.[56]

A loosening grip of the religious orders was accompanied by an intensification of the collegiate system. Six new colleges were founded between 1495 and 1525: at Cambridge, Jesus (1496), Christ's (1506) and St John's (1511); at Oxford, Brasenose (1512), Corpus Christi (1517) and Cardinal (1525). In each case, a wealthy founder endowed the institution in the hope of advancing the cause of learning, and of helping their own soul through the prayers of beneficiaries.

New foundations represented an opportunity to reshape priorities. This was particularly evident in the activities of one of the early sixteenth century's most remarkable double acts: that of Lady Margaret Beaufort and her chaplain and confessor, Bishop John Fisher. Lady Margaret lived through more 'history' than anyone should reasonably be expected to. Born in 1443 during the last act of the Hundred Years War, her royal ancestry – she was a great-granddaughter, by the illegitimate line, of John of Gaunt, Duke of Lancaster – made her a dynastic and marital asset during more than three decades of Wars of the Roses. Married four times, her only child (by Edmund Tudor, Earl of Richmond) emerged victorious at Bosworth in 1485, and she survived to see her grandson ascend the throne in 1509.

A woman of the pronounced piety characteristic of a number of fifteenth-century aristocratic ladies, Lady Margaret was deeply impressed by the devout and learned John Fisher, a young Cambridge don of Yorkshire extraction, whom she met when he was visiting the court on university business in 1495–6. Margaret wanted to do good, and Fisher was the man to show her how, steering her benefactions away from the conventional chantry foundations she had begun to make, and towards support of education on a lavish scale. At Fisher's prompting, in 1497 Lady Margaret endowed professorships in divinity at Oxford and Cambridge; the first Cambridge Lady Margaret Professor was Fisher himself. Margaret's largesse to the struggling mid-fifteenth-century Cambridge foundation of God's House transformed it into the impressive Christ's College. Legacies in her will produced, under Fisher's close supervision, the still more imposing St John's. She stepped in earlier to secure the legal and financial status of Jesus College, founded by the devout and learned bishop of Ely, John Alcock. Jesus was established on the site of the moribund Benedictine nunnery of St Radegund. St John's too was a phoenix from the ashes of an earlier foundation: the Hospital of St John run by a skeleton staff of Augustinian canons. 'Top-up' funding in the early 1520s came through the dissolution of small and ill-disciplined nunneries at Higham in Kent and Broomhill in Berkshire.

The suppressions were indicative of new priorities in the world of institutionalized religion. Changes of emphasis were still more apparent in Oxford in 1525, when Cardinal Wolsey planted his lavish new foundation of Cardinal College on top of the Augustinian priory of St Frideswide, the endowment secured by the suppression of no fewer than a further twenty-one small religious houses from across the Midlands and the south-east.[57]

Another changing priority was a greater emphasis on preaching. In 1504 Henry VII granted his mother the right to establish a university preachership at Cambridge: holders of the post were to give six sermons a year, including one at the high-profile London pulpit of St Paul's Cross, or another city church. Shortly prior to this, Thomas Cabold, fellow of Gonville, secured a notable grant of favour from the notorious Borgia pope, Alexander VI. Twelve preachers, and two from Cabold's own college, were licensed to go annually from Cambridge to preach in any diocese in the country. Over the next eighteen years some 175 such licences were granted, to a roll-call of the university's great and good. Fisher's foundation statutes for St John's laid down that a quarter of the fellows were to preach regularly to the people in English, giving them 'the fruit of their studies'.[58]

Notwithstanding rear-guard action by the Oxford 'Trojans', the wooden horse of Greek language teaching, and with it a more open spirit of critical enquiry, was brought firmly within the walls of both Cambridge and Oxford by the middle of the second decade of the sixteenth century, along with admiration for the more polished neoclassical Latin that was the international humanist idiom. In 1516, Fisher, already in his late forties, led his juniors by example in beginning to learn the Greek language.

The following year, Fisher's friend Richard Fox, bishop of Winchester, sought to atone for a lifetime of government service away from the pastoral needs of his diocese by founding Corpus Christi College, Oxford. Originally intended as a base for the Benedictines of the cathedral priory in Winchester, Fox was persuaded by his friend Bishop Hugh Oldham of Exeter not to lavish his money on 'a company of bussing [chattering] monks'. Instead, Corpus was to be a showcase of Christian humanist scholarship. Fox's statutes provided for lecturers in Greek and Latin, to speak publicly on the Old and New Testaments in a cycle of alternate years. Their interpretations should imitate 'holy and ancient doctors' – Jerome, Augustine, Ambrose, Origen, Chrysostom – in preference to those 'in time and therefore doctrine much more recent', such as the Franciscan Nicolas of Lyra, and the Dominican Hugo of Vienne. The term used, *posterior*, had implications of 'inferior' as well as 'later'.[59]

This was a slap in the face to the friars, and music to Erasmian ears. The Greek lectureship briefly galvanized the Oxford Trojans, with a preacher at St Mary's Church castigating the advocates of Greek learning as heretics.[60] But the big guns of Church and state were massed on the side of Agamemnon. On the recommendation of Henry VIII himself, Cambridge appointed Richard Croke as Lecturer in Greek in 1517. He came hotfoot from Germany, where he had introduced study of the language at Leipzig, and declined a job offer at the dull provincial university of Wittenberg – somewhere about to become a much more interesting location. Erasmus enthused in December 1517 that 'Cambridge is a changed place. The university there has no use for this hairsplitting [old-fashioned scholastic theology], which is more conducive to wrangling than religion.'[61]

Yet it is unlikely that Erasmus's sense of a sharp fork in the road – the dead end of scholasticism or the shining path of the *studia humanitatis* – was widely shared by English intellectuals. The wills and library lists of university scholars from these years, like that of Fisher's mentor, William Melton, fellow of Michaelhouse, reveal humanist and scholastic works frequently sitting together on the shelves – Aquinas and Duns Scotus alongside Valla, Erasmus and More's *Utopia*. Only in later and very different times would 'Dunce' become a synonym for ignoramus.

Humphrey Walkenden of Queens' College, a friend of Erasmus, lectured on Scotus's *Sentences* in 1519–20. Fisher's revised statutes for St John's specified a regular Hebrew lecture, but allowed the master and senior fellows to substitute one in (good) Latin on Scotus if that seemed more useful to the students. Wolsey's statutes for Cardinal College prescribed daily public lectures on Roman and Greek rhetoric or poetry, and students were to study the works of Plautus and Terence. But scholastic philosophy and logic remained at the heart of the curriculum, and a new professor of theology was to spend half his time expounding scripture; half exploring the 'subtle questions' of Duns Scotus.

In an address of 1519, Richard Croke, the Cambridge Greek specialist, extolled the study of classical literature, painting it as preferable to the traditional university curriculum. But at the same time he praised Scotus and Aquinas, urging that attention to classical writers should supplement not supplant traditional theological authorities. This seems to have been the instinct of Robert Joseph, an Oxford-educated humanist monk of Evesham Abbey, who wrote a few years later to chide a correspondent for calling the teaching of the Scotists 'dirty puddles'. Joseph condemned those 'who spend their whole life weaving syllogisms out of Scotist subtleties', but he was reluctant to throw the baby out with the puddle water. 'I would treat Scotus and the Scotists so as to take ideas from them, but take a pure Latinity from more cultivated works.'[62]

Scholastic message, humanist packaging. For some, enthusiasm for Latin and Greek letters was little more than a fashionable pose, a semblance of style over substance. But for significant numbers of leading clergymen – Colet, Fisher and other English admirers of Erasmus like the new (1522) bishop of London, Cuthbert Tunstall – the renewal of learning was a token of great moral earnestness, a mainspring of a longed-for revitalization of faith through profound meditation on the life and passion of Jesus.

Late medieval Catholicism was defined by tradition but not enshrined in timelessness. Powerful currents of renewal and regeneration were in motion in early Tudor England, the tidal stirrings of an English Catholic Reformation eager to wash away unsightly encrustations from the abiding rock of the Church. Among pious, literate and attentive laypeople, expectations of a purer practice of the faith were undoubtedly being heightened. But as things looked from episcopal palaces, and from the cloisters and quadrangles of Cambridge and Oxford, this was to be a reformation of the institution undertaken and led by the institutionalized themselves. The clergy, greater and less, must rise to the challenge of their calling, inspire the laity to greater clarity of Christian vision, and reinvigorate the life of the Church. The extent to which they would prove eager for, or equal to, the task was to be of profound significance for the very different directions reform would in the end take.

# 2

## LIGHTS OF THE WORLD

### Like People, Like Priest

'YOU ARE THE salt of the earth . . . You are the light of the world . . . Your light must shine so brightly before men that they can see your good works.' Jesus' words were addressed to his disciples, but they had special meaning for those who saw themselves as the apostles' direct descendants: the priests and bishops leading Christ's Church upon earth.

Priests were men set apart. At ordination, they were anointed with oil by a bishop, vested in the priestly robes of stole and chasuble, and presented with bread and a chalice. New priests took on a sacramental 'character', becoming walking icons of Christ. They alone were empowered to re-enact at mass Jesus' role at the Last Supper: 'This is my body . . . this is my blood.'

The clergy looked different. Priests shaved the upper crown of the head, a 'tonsure' leaving a circlet of hair calling to mind Christ's crown of thorns. Clerical cheeks were clean-shaven, in an age when beards were becoming fashionable again among those – like the young Henry VIII – important enough to have their portraits painted. Beards were signs of masculinity and virility, but priests were supposed to shun the familiar company of women. Virginity, so the clergy taught, pleased God more than marriage. Even the humblest priest qualified for the Latin honorific *Dominus* (lord), rendered into English as 'Sir'. Most 'Sir Johns' and 'Sir Roberts' in the early sixteenth century were parish priests, not chivalric knights. The honour came with heavy responsibility. Nearly everyone would have agreed with Thomas Crabbe, a parishioner of Axminster in Devon, that 'every man must needs have a priest at his coming into the world, and a priest at his departing'.

In one sense, priests did not need to be good. Theologians taught that sacraments worked *ex opere operato*, not *ex opere operantis* – that is, by virtue of the ritual itself, not the personal merits of the celebrant. The mass of an immoral priest was as valid as that of a living saint.

Nonetheless, the biblical author of the Book of Hosea surely had it right: 'like people, like priest'. The spiritual and moral well-being of society depended on the clergy. 'Reformation of holy Church', insisted one author, required the 'reformation of curates and good heads of holy Church'. It was evident to Bishop Fisher that 'all fear of God, also the contempt of God cometh and is grounded of the clergy . . . if the clergy live desolately in manner, as they should give no account of their life past and done before, will not the lay people do the same?'

The responsibility sat heavily on the shoulders of reform-minded clerics. In 1510, Archbishop William Warham presided over a meeting of the Convocation of Canterbury – a gathering, sitting alongside the secular Parliament, of bishops, abbots and other clergy. Convocations (there was a separate one for the northern province of York) often restricted themselves to financial matters, but this one passed constitutions on clerical reform, regulation of chaplains, clerical dress and simony – the crime of buying or selling spiritual office.[1] Around the same time, Fisher's mentor, William Melton, preached a hard-hitting sermon to new ordinands in the diocese of York. Melton was no anti-clerical: he believed priests were 'celsior angelis' (higher than angels). But he feared the ideal was undermined by multitudes of 'ill-educated' and 'stupid' clergy, getting drunk in taverns and wasting time on secular pursuits. Good humanist that he was, Melton saw solutions in Latin learning, and study of the scriptures. And he begged unworthy candidates to refrain from coming forward, anticipating the dictum of Thomas More's *Utopia* – fewer yet holier priests. Utopian indeed, for York was a diocese churning out record priestly numbers in the first years of the sixteenth century.

Foremost among the counsellors of perfection was the man who approved Melton's sermon for publication, Dean Colet of London. In his Oxford lectures on St Paul, Colet spoke excoriatingly of churchmen 'profoundly ignorant of the teaching of the Gospels', and obsessed with pursuit of wealth under self-serving slogans: 'the rights of the Church, the heritage of Christ, the property of the priesthood'. Priests, he bemoaned, now hardly differed at all from laymen 'except by our tonsured hair and crown'.

Colet revisited the theme in February 1512, preaching at Warham's invita-tion at the opening of Convocation.[2] It was an eye-opening address, designed – quite possibly with Warham's approval – to knock the complacency out of his distinguished audience, and inspire them to 'reformation of the Church's estate'. Only when the clergy, 'the light of the world', put their own house in order could there be 'reformation of the lay's part'. Four evils blighted the Church: devilish pride, carnal concupiscence, secular business and worldly covetousness (espe-cially grasping after tithes and promotions). New legislation was not needed, merely enforcement of existing laws, and careful screening of candidates: the 'broad gate of holy orders' was itself 'the well of evils'. Priests were the essential instruments of reformation, and also the principal obstacles to it.

Colet's diatribe was once regarded as a reliable description of the woeful condition of the institutional Church. More recent assessments have concluded his prognosis and prescriptions were at best impossibly idealistic, and at worst downright unfair. They have noted too the apparent hypocrisy of Colet's own position as a non-resident 'pluralist': his glittering scholarly career was funded by revenues from a rich Suffolk rectory, and canonries at York and Salisbury.[3]

It was all very well for reformers to demand fewer and better priests, but the Church needed large numbers of them, a result of lay demand for services. In addition to staffing the 9,000 or so parishes, and numerous dependent chapelries, priests were needed as chaplains for fraternities, and to sing endless numbers of intercessory masses. The result was a wave of ordinations around the turn of the sixteenth century: not including monks and friars, an average of 187 priests were ordained annually at York between 1501 and 1527; 126 per annum for the diocese of Lincoln in 1514–21. The total number of clergy in England may have been about 40,000 in the parishes, with another 10,000 or so in the religious orders. Everyone knew some priests, for they were to be found in all places and all walks of life.

Priesthood required no formal training. Significant numbers attended one or other of the universities, but those with degrees, or any experience of higher education, remained a small minority of the body as a whole. Graduates were well represented in the upper echelons, in diocesan administration, and among the rectors and vicars appointed to the wealthiest parishes or 'benefices'. Clergy in London were the best educated, and, in light of relatively high literacy rates among their parishioners, perhaps needed to be: between 1479 and 1529 some 60 per cent of priests appointed to benefices in the capital were graduates. The proportion among the beneficed clergy was much lower elsewhere: a figure of around one in six presented to parishes in Norwich diocese in 1503–28 was probably typical. It was everywhere minimal among the unbeneficed – curates and parish priests performing much of the actual work in the parishes.[4] These acquired what learning they had at one of the grammar schools springing up across England from the later fifteenth century, or received some instruction from their local curate and picked up tricks of the trade serving as altar boys in the parish church.

Humanists scoffed at the priestly proletariat. Thomas More's whip-smart daughter, Margaret Roper, in the preface to her translation of a treatise by Erasmus, defended the teaching of classical languages to women against accusations it would lead to over-familiarity with priests. 'Nowadays a man could not devise a better way to keep his wife safe from them, than if he should teach her the Latin and Greek tongue.' In 1517, the priest and diplomat Richard Pace, about to succeed Colet as dean of St Paul's, lifted an anecdote from a letter of

Erasmus and fathered it on 'a certain boorish English priest'. This character possessed a badly printed missal, and thus in the mass always said the nonsense word *mumpsimus* rather than *sumpsimus* ('we have taken up'). When corrected, the priest swore he would not give up his old mumpsimus for some newfangled sumpsimus.

Apocryphal tales of this sort did the rounds in sophisticated circles. John Mason, English ambassador in Spain, a former protégé of Thomas More, recalled in the early 1530s the story of an English priest so scrupulously pious that he would not suffer the name of Satan to appear anywhere in his mass book. Striking it out and substituting the name of God had predictably comic results: *abrenuncio Deo et omnibus operibus eius* – I renounce God and all his works.[5]

It seems unlikely that many priests were functionally illiterate in Latin. Their job involved daily recital of Latin services, in a Church using the language for countless legal and administrative purposes. And even if they were, it provoked few objections from the laity. Of more than 1,000 parishes in the vast diocese of Lincoln, 'visited' (inspected) by Bishop William Atwater and his deputies between 1514 and 1521, only two registered complaints that their curate was 'ignorant'.

Parish clergy come rather well out of the early sixteenth-century visitation material. Complaints about pastoral performance surfaced in a mere forty-one (4 per cent) of the Lincoln parishes overseen by Atwater, and other dioceses for which we have records – Canterbury, Chichester, Norwich, Winchester – produce only isolated cases of priestly neglect and nastiness.

Pluralism was certainly widespread: revenues from parishes and cathedral canonries eased the ascent of well-connected clerics making their way up the administrative ladder in Church or state. A consequence was non-residence: 14 per cent of rectors and vicars were absent from the Kent parishes visited by Archbishop Warham in 1511, and about a quarter of the incumbents in Lincoln diocese in 1518 did not reside.[6] If parishes were properly served by deputies, it was not necessarily a pastoral disaster. Nonetheless, reforming bishops were keen to crack down on unlicensed pluralism, particularly where incumbents abandoned unglamorous rural livings for the bright lights of the capital. In February 1521, an official sent by John Worthial, diocesan chancellor of the disciplinarian Bishop Robert Sherburne of Chichester, tracked down a priest 'fussing and croaking in London' and forced him to return and reside.[7]

Colet was right about relentless pursuit of tithes; few issues were as likely to get lay backs up. Tithing was in theory straightforward: an obligation based on biblical precedent to support the clergy with an annual offering of 10 per cent of all profits and produce. In practice, it could be immensely complicated. What was a tenth of three calves, or a dozen eggs? Tricky enough in the agricultural contexts for which they were designed, tithe arrangements in urban areas, particularly London, could be fraught and difficult, as priests struggled to keep track of shifting rents and wages.

It is easy enough to rack up examples of conflict – legal, verbal and sometimes physical – between clergy and parishioners, and a handful of parishes were convulsed by intractable disputes. Yet tithing in the main worked, regulated at the local level by custom and compromise, and commutation of hard-to-tithe items into fixed money payments. Church court records reveal remarkably few parishes producing tithe suits in any given year: ten on average from the 1,148 parishes in the diocese of Norwich in the early 1520s; two from 339 Winchester parishes in 1527; four from 650 Lichfield parishes in 1530. No doubt people rarely paid more than they ought, and often paid less than they owed. But the principle was seldom directly questioned. In the first three decades of the sixteenth century, well over half the laypeople making wills gestured towards virtue by setting aside small sums for 'tithes forgotten.'[8]

The moral character of priests – so close to the heart of reformers like Colet – eludes statistical certainty. The extent to which young men pursued ordination with a genuine sense of spiritual vocation was rarely commented on in individual cases. Without doubt, the most challenging obligation was to live celibate and chaste. Early medieval parish clergy were routinely married, and serious attempts to enforce clerical celibacy were first undertaken in the late eleventh and twelfth centuries as part of the reform movement initiated by the energetic Pope Gregory VII. This had mixed results: de facto clerical marriage was never eradicated in medieval Wales and Ireland, and in parts of Switzerland clerical 'concubinage' was effectively institutionalized, the bishops making tidy sums from fining their clergy, and legitimizing their children.

In England, for whatever reason, Gregorian ideals took firmer root. Bishop Fox's boast that he never tolerated 'manifest fornication' is borne out by visitation evidence: Winchester produced only eleven allegations from 230 parishes inspected in 1527–8. There were five complaints from 478 Suffolk parishes in 1499, and nine from 260 Kentish ones in 1511. Bishop Atwater's officials in Lincoln diocese were scrupulous in requiring the churchwardens to tell them whether priests had any 'suspect woman' (*mulier suspecte*) in the parsonage. By a generous interpretation, that might mean any female under forty who was not a close blood relation, including domestic servants. In any case, the figures are low: a minimum of twenty-five and maximum of 102 priests from 1,006 parishes were suspected to be up to no good.[9]

These findings suggest that, on average, well over 90 per cent of clergy were routinely maintaining chaste lives. Later Protestants (and some modern psychologists) would be frankly unbelieving that such an 'unnatural' state of affairs could have pertained. It may well be that the incidence of sexual activity was higher than the visitation evidence implies – if laypeople turned a strategically blind eye to the situation of priests living quietly with their housekeepers who were in other ways good pastors. Yet, in contrast to modern western society, the prestige of virginity was high, and strong cultural pressures operated in its favour.

An evidential audit of the late medieval clergy is likely to conclude that laypeople were broadly content, and priests were doing a good job. But optimistic generalizations about overall popular 'satisfaction' with the clergy risk skating too quickly over the aspirations and frustrations of key constituencies, and over some persistent and uneasy questions pertaining to clerical roles and rank.

### Princes and Paupers

The priesthood's collective claim to present an icon of Christ to the people was mocked by disparities of wealth, status and power. At the apex were the bishops, ecclesiastical lords holding significant landed estates. By European standards, dioceses were large: there were only seventeen for the whole of England; a further four for Wales. They were also exceptionally wealthy: twelve of the forty richest bishoprics in Europe were said to have been English. The diocese of Lincoln was worth £3,300 a year to its holder; that of Ely, £2,134. Combined tenure of York and Durham supplied Thomas Wolsey with about £5,000 a year in the 1520s, which he supplemented with the abbacy of St Albans, fees as Lord Chancellor and a lavish pension from the King of France. Wolsey, the worldliest of early Tudor bishops, enjoyed an income on a par with the greatest secular nobles. By contrast, the least worldly, John Fisher, occupied the smallest and poorest English diocese: Rochester brought him a measly £300 a year.[10]

A handful of parishes were worth more than £100 a year, and tended to go to well-connected, often absentee, careerists. Most parish livings were valued at under £15, vicarages (where the right to collect most of the tithes belonged to a local monastery) usually considerably less than rectories. The majority of the beneficed clergy enjoyed an income roughly on a par with comfortably off yeoman farmers, the class from which many of them originated. The prevalence, in the wills of rectors and vicars, of livestock, agricultural implements, and loads of wheat, barley and hay, shows that many felt the need to supplement the income from tithes, and did not devote all their energies to the performance of sacred duties.

Curates, and the assistants usually called 'parish priests', drew salaries ranging from £4 to £6 per annum – little more than an unskilled agricultural labourer. Chantry priests did a little better, but not much. Unbeneficed clergy of all kinds needed to supplement their salaries, engaging in secular occupations, picking up fees for occasional masses, or signing up for extra parish duties at Easter and Christmas.[11]

There was no formal career structure, no reasonable expectation that a curate would ever secure promotion to a parish living, let alone one of the higher dignities. Yet unlike other social and political entities, the Church did not operate under rules of hereditary succession, and it permitted a degree of social mobility found in no other walk of life. Only two early Tudor bishops were children of noblemen: the idle and disreputable James Stanley, bishop of Ely (1506–1515), was the sixth son of the Earl of Derby, while the learned and serious Edmund Audley of Salisbury (1502–1524) was a second son of Lord Audley. The others came of mixed gentry, merchant and yeoman backgrounds. Wolsey, as his enemies never tired of whispering, was a 'butcher's cur', the son of an Ipswich tradesman.[12]

In the importance it afforded to patronage and clientage, the Church embraced rather than resisted the values of the secular world. Advancement depended on whom you knew, and on what they might do for you in return for what they imagined you could do for them. The power to nominate priests to vacant parish livings did not, in the main, belong to bishops. This right, called an 'advowson' (from the Latin *advocatio*, I summon or call), originally pertained to lords of manors establishing parishes on their lands. By the later Middle Ages it had become a piece of property, to be inherited, sold or rented out by the turn.

Much patronage was in the hands of religious houses. This was the result of a medieval pattern whereby decaying parishes became 'appropriated' to an outside body, usually a monastery, which as corporate rector appointed a permanent deputy, or 'vicar'. In the East Riding of Yorkshire, monasteries presented to just over 50 per cent of the 165 parishes, collegiate churches to 8.5 per cent, and assorted other ecclesiastics to 18.2 per cent. Various lay patrons had 17.6 per cent of advowsons, though fewer than 2 per cent were in the hands of the crown. A mere four belonged to the archbishop of York. In Essex, by contrast, 37.4 per cent of advowson numbers were in the hands of laymen, with 8.4 per cent for the bishop and 4.6 per cent for the King. But just about everywhere, religious houses were the largest category of patron, and a significant proportion was in lay hands.[13]

The figures underestimate the reach of royal patronage, for a petitioning letter from the King was not lightly ignored. Bishops could reject a candidate as unsuitable, though they had little control over the appointments process as a whole. Nobles promoted their chaplains; crown and churchmen put forward servants and officials. Gentry families looked after their own: Colet was presented to the Suffolk rectory of Dennington by his cousin, Sir William Knevet, and to that of Thurning in Northamptonshire by his father, Sir Henry Colet. From the 1440s to the 1550s, the Longley family of Cheshire ensured one of that name was rector of Prestwich. Bishops, even reforming ones, acknowledged the claims of blood. John Longland of Lincoln paved the glittering career path of his nephew, the diplomat Richard Pate, while Warham showered preferment on a namesake who might have been an illegitimate son rather than a nephew. Even the saintly John Fisher appointed his nephew Henry White to a Suffolk living in 1514.[14]

Where a clergyman's relatives, or agents acting on his behalf, purchased a 'right of next presentation', the result was perilously close to simony. Henry VII's councillor, Edmund Dudley, castigated simony and pluralism in a reforming treatise, *The Tree of Commonwealth*, composed in the Tower at the start of Henry VIII's reign. Yet Dudley himself was involved in such transactions on behalf of clients, relatives and royal servants.[15] It was a system in which everyone could see the potential for abuse, but from which even would-be reformers could seldom easily extricate themselves.

Further down the social scale, the stakes were lower, but opportunities for patronage over the clergy were considerable. Middle-ranking laity appointed priests to serve as fraternity chaplains, and engaged them to sing intercessory masses. In many parishes, the wages of the curate or parish priest were paid, not by the rector, but by churchwardens, who hired in extra clerical manpower at Easter. Laypeople owed deference to the 'lights of the world', but often exercised considerable practical authority over them. At times, the lowly social status of priests bred a familiarity perilously close to contempt. References to priests known locally as 'Little Sir John' or 'Black Sir John' hardly suggest a sense of awe in the face of the charisma conferred by ordination.[16]

## Dumb Dogs and Pulpit Men

Priests were technicians of salvation, distributors of sacramental grace. But they were also supposed to be instructors in knowledge and virtue. The 1281 decree of archbishop of Canterbury John Pecham, *De Informacione Simplicium* (On the instruction of the unlearned), better known by its frank opening words *Ignorantia Sacerdotum* (the ignorance of priests), ordered that clergy with cure of souls should preach in English four times a year, on the Creed, the Ten Commandments, Christ's precept to love God and neighbour, the seven works of mercy, seven deadly sins and seven sacraments. Conscientious bishops like Fox of Winchester and Nicholas West of Ely still enforced its provisions in the 1520s. It inspired the composition of helpful sermon compilations: the *Quattuor Sermones*, the *Festial* of John Mirk, the *Exonoratorium Curatorum*. Along with the *Sermones Discipuli* of the German Dominican friar Johannes Herolt, these were the books most frequently found in the wills of early sixteenth-century English clergy.

There was a difference between trotting out a pre-packaged homily from one of these volumes, or from the ever-popular collection of saints' lives, *The Golden Legend*, and composing an inspirational sermon of one's own. Most priests were not up to the latter task. The specialists in set-piece, outdoor sermons were the friars, who delivered them at market or churchyard crosses.

Cathedrals were important too. Even if the bishop was not himself a habitual preacher, cathedral clergy made the diocesan mother church a centre of God's Word, and went on tours of surrounding parishes.[17]

Even if only a minority did it regularly, the notion that every priest was, potentially, a preacher of God's Word was a familiar one, with not the slightest whiff of heresy about it. Later Protestants had a tag for those who could or would not preach, a category into which they thrust almost the whole of the medieval priesthood: 'dumb dogs'. It was no new coinage. In William Langland's prophetic *Piers Plowman*, abbots, priors, priests and curates are reminded of a duty 'to teach and preach to all mankind'. Its neglect has layfolk calling them 'dumb hounds' – an echo of Isaiah 56:10: 'here are none but blind watchmen; here are dumb dogs that cannot bark'. These were not the eccentric views of a visionary outsider: the standard compilation of canon law for the late medieval English Church, William Lyndwood's *Provinciale*, admonished rectors and vicars to fulfil their obligation to preach, lest they justly be accounted dumb dogs.

How much laypeople wanted to be barked at is another matter. There were just four complaints of neglect of preaching from Lincoln parishes in 1517–31 – reflecting either an extraordinary level of diligence by the clergy, or, more likely, a lack of concern on the part of rural laity. Quarterly sermons were mandated, but there was no legal requirement for Sunday homilies. Nonetheless, the growing number of both pulpits and pews in fifteenth- and early sixteenth-century parish churches points to their emergence as a more regular and expected feature of weekly worship.[18]

Complaints by preachers that audiences were slothful about coming to sermons, and inattentive when they got there, are to be found in nearly every surviving medieval sermon collection. There was a formulaic, self-regarding aspect to this – the faithful preacher serves as a prophet without honour. Yet the churchwardens of Bishophill near York admitted in 1481 that 'when the Word of God is declared in the said church, and the said parishioners have warning to come hear it, the most part of them cometh not at all'.

Whether or not *most* people got excited about sermons, some layfolk certainly did. Enthusiasm for preaching was rife among the merchant classes of London and the major provincial towns. In the early fifteenth century, Margery Kempe, visionary and pious troublemaker, declared that, if she had the money, she would give a gold coin 'to have every day a sermon'. She reported 'much multitude of people' assembling for the preaching of a monk at York, and 'much people gathered to hear the sermon' of a holy friar at King's Lynn in Norfolk. On this occasion, the preacher 'spoke much of Our Lord's passion', and Margery, as was her habit, wept tears of pure devotion.[19]

Townsfolk's zeal for preaching showed no sign of waning over the ensuing decades, particularly in London, where the famous outdoor pulpit on the north side of St Paul's Cathedral attracted big crowds. Preaching there in 1497, Bishop Alcock observed with pride how 'many a noble sermon is said in this place in the year'. In 1508, a saintly Franciscan Observant, Friar Donald, expounded there the letters of St Paul, as Colet did in Oxford.

London preaching made a strong impression, but did not always produce peace and charity. In 1517, a xenophobic sermon at St Mary Spital triggered 'Evil May Day', when resident aliens were set upon in the streets by rioting apprentices. The lead plotter, John Lincoln, recruited an Augustinian canon, Dr Bell, to preach on the Tuesday of Easter Week on the Psalm *Coelum coeli Domino: terram autem dedit filiis hominum* ('The heaven of heaven is the Lord's: but the earth he has given to the children of men'). Bell drew the lesson that 'this land was given to Englishmen, and as birds would defend their nest, so ought Englishmen to cherish and defend themselves'.[20]

The public, persuasive character of sermons accounts for their regular appearance in the wills of urban worthies. Bertram Dawson, wealthy alderman of York, left 3s. 4d. in 1515 to 'the doctor that shall show the Word of God at my eight day' (i.e. the conclusion of an extended week of funeral celebrations). The London merchant tailor, and former sheriff, James Wilford, left money in 1526 for a learned Franciscan to preach every Good Friday in perpetuity 'a sermon of the passion of Our Lord' at his parish church of St Bartholomew the Less. Another sheriff, John Thurston, made the substantial bequest of £40 in 1520 to support two scholars 'studying holy divinity' at Oxford and Cambridge, so that 'the faith of Christ may be increased'. His widow, Dame Elizabeth, augmented the provision in her will, with further exhibitions to scholars, priests and students, 'being pulpit men'.

Such bequests were hardly proto-Protestant. These sermons were one element of a package of commemoration and intercession for the donor's soul. The same approach, on a more lavish scale, was taken by Henry VII, whose elaborate schema for regular preaching on Sundays and feast days at Westminster Abbey, established in 1504, was part and parcel of a sumptuous chantry. Chantry foundations with specific provisions for preaching were never the norm, but they proliferated from the later fifteenth century, and it is likely there was at least one in every decent-sized provincial town. Sermons of all sorts, at Paul's Cross and elsewhere, conventionally started with the bidding of the bedes, which called to remembrance the needs of living and dead. Pulpits were engines of intercessory prayer, as much as they were beacons of edification – a fact graphically illustrated by the 1529 will of the Devon merchant John Lane, which contained bequests to no fewer than one hundred churches 'to pray for me in their pulpits'.[21]

Yet it is significant that Elizabeth Thurston described her favoured priests as 'pulpit men'. A feeling was growing, among both laypeople and clergy, that an ability to expound the Word of God was the highest and purest manifestation of the priestly calling. John Fisher, himself a maestro of the preacher's art, strongly encouraged Erasmus in his project of compiling a handbook on the techniques of preaching, *Ecclesiastae sive de ratione concionandi*. Finally published in 1535, Erasmus's treatise put forward an evangelical, charismatic vision of the sermon, in which the Holy Spirit flowed through the words of the eloquent preacher to fill the hearts of his auditors. All priests, not just a cadre of specialists, were called to exercise this ministry.

Like many medieval theologians, Fisher saw Word and Sacrament as complementary, not competing, channels of grace. The *Imitation of Christ*, in William Atkinson's translation, thanked God equally for the gift of the eucharist 'to the refreshing of my soul and body', and for putting 'before my faith the light of thy holy word'.

Yet sometimes people were willing explicitly to juxtapose these twin priestly vocations. *Dives and Pauper*, printed three times between 1493 and 1536, articulated a high doctrine of the importance of preaching. God's Word was 'life and salvation of man's soul', and persons trying to hinder preaching were nothing less than 'manslayers ghostly'. In a choice between hearing a sermon and attending a mass, one should forgo the latter, for 'it is more profitable to hear God's Word in preaching than to hear any mass'.[22]

*Dives and Pauper* was a text on the uncomfortable edges of orthodoxy. But its take on the respective merits of mass and sermon was neither eccentric nor unique. The great revivalist preacher of fifteenth-century Italy, Bernardino of Siena, told audiences that if it came to it 'you should let the mass go, rather than the sermon. . . . There is less peril for your soul in not hearing mass than in not hearing the sermon.' The message was repeated by the most impeccably orthodox of early Tudor Englishmen (actually, most probably a Welshman by birth), the Bridgettine monk Richard Whitford. His advice to heads of households was to ensure that everyone under their authority was present 'if there be a sermon any time of the day', and to 'let them ever keep the preachings rather than the mass, if (by case) they may not hear both'.[23]

There was no inherent incompatibility between priests' sacramental roles and their duty to edify and instruct. But the clergy were obliged to carry a mixed bundle of expectations, and their mission was complicated by what could often seem a mismatch between exalted ideals and a frequently shabby reality. Laypeople's utter dependence on priests for securing salvation, and their awareness – heightened by the jeremiads of clerical reformers – that priests were typically frail and fallible human beings was a source of tension that could be creative and constructive, but could also fuel recrimination and resentment. The future Protestant insistence on the clergyman's identity as a preacher grew out of, as much as it reacted against, the evolving attitudes of the late Middle Ages. Long before the Reformation, spirited conversations were underway about what priests were really for, and whether their privileges were really justified.

## The State of the Regulars

Questions of purpose and identity dogged the steps of the 'regular' clergy: the monks and friars, as well as nuns, living in community under authority of a religious superior, and the discipline of a rule (*regula*), as opposed to the 'secular' clergy out in the world (*seculum*). To contemporaries, they were simply 'the religious'. Their lives of communal prayer – an *Opus Dei* (work of God) structured by vows of poverty, chastity and obedience – were to be conspicuous casualties of the Reformation. Yet many of the first generation of Reformation rebels, including Luther himself, were members of religious orders. The capacity of late medieval Catholicism to mould and nurture its own critics is nowhere on clearer display.

There were perhaps 10,000 persons 'in religion' at the start of the sixteenth century, in around 900 separate establishments. Recruitment to individual houses went up and down, but the aggregate numbers were not on any path of long-term decline, and may in fact have been higher than ever.[24] The only safe generalization about the religious orders is that they were extraordinarily diverse, even within broad bands of distinction between contemplative monks and nuns, 'enclosed' (in theory) within their cloisters, and the friars, usually based in towns, and pursuing more active vocations of preaching and hearing confessions. The friars or 'mendicants' (*mendicare*, to beg) lived off the alms and offerings of the laity, in contrast to the landed estates of 'possessioner' orders. About a quarter of the religious were 'canons regular', communities of priests observing the rule of St Augustine. The Austin canons were thought of as monks, but resembled friars in their engagement with the world.

The backbone of the monastic establishment were the Benedictines or Black Monks. In a situation virtually unique to England, they supplied personnel for nine priories that were also cathedral churches, including Canterbury, Durham and Winchester. The other cathedrals, except for Augustinian Carlisle, had a secular dean and chapter. Many of the wealthiest and most prestigious houses, such as Westminster and St Albans, were Benedictine.

The Cistercians or White Monks, prided themselves on greater austerity and simplicity of life, and situated their houses away from centres of habitation, at Rievaulx and Fountains in North Yorkshire, or Tintern in the secluded Wye Valley along the Welsh border. Stricter still were the Carthusians, with a slim total of nine 'Charterhouses'. There was one house of Bridgettines, an order founded by St Bridget of Sweden: Syon Abbey at Isleworth in Middlesex. Syon's location, and its distinctive character as a double-house of monks and nuns, lent it visibility and prestige. Most nuns followed the Benedictine rule, though some were Cistercian or Augustinian. Their vocation provided a rare opportunity, in a deeply patriarchal society, to pursue lives of status and dignity independent of immediate male oversight.

Friars might be – depending on the colour of their habits – White, Black or Grey: Carmelite, Dominican or Franciscan. The Franciscans were split between the main branch, and a reformed group of 'Observant' Franciscans, pledged to a stricter observance of the rule of St Francis. Between 1482 and 1507, six Observant houses were established in England, largely through royal patronage; there were nearly ten times that number of 'Conventual' friaries. There were also Augustinian friars (Luther's order), as well as smaller numbers of Friars of the Holy Cross ('Crutched Friars'), and Trinitarian Friars who specialized in redeeming Christian captives held by Muslims. Rounding out the roster was the single English affiliation to a crusading order. The Knights Hospitaller of St John of Jerusalem had their priory at Clerkenwell, just north of London, while their properties were administered from widely scattered dependent houses known as commanderies.[25]

In later years, reformers would contemptuously dismiss the religious orders as a rabble of contending 'sects', obsessed with their own rites, ceremonies and privileges. There were, undoubtedly, rivalries and tensions. Conventual Franciscans, three of whose houses were transferred to the Observants by royal command in 1499, nursed an understandable grievance. Yet the most serious turf wars were not among the various religious orders, but between the secular clergy and the mendicants. The friars' pastoral activities, as preachers and confessors, had the potential, so parish clergy feared, to draw their congregations away. Much of the sometimes vitriolic 'anti-fraternal' satire of the Middle Ages originated in circles sympathetic to the secular clergy.[26]

The sheer diversity of religious life complicates assessments of its overall health. Visitations can be enjoyably mined for eye-catching scandal. At Littlemore (Oxfordshire) in 1517, the prioress had borne a child to the nuns' chaplain, and ordered the sisters to remain quiet about it. The wealthy Benedictine abbey of Ramsey in Cambridgeshire was in a sad state that same year. Numbers were down, and formation of the junior monks was shamefully neglected. The seniors swore and gambled, under the oversight of a drunken, bad-tempered prior. Matters were scarcely better at Walsingham Priory in 1514, about the time Erasmus visited the shrine. The canons were said to spend their nights drinking and singing in the household of the seneschal's (lay steward's) wife.

Revelations of criminal or sexual misbehaviour were always, however, relatively few, and disproportionately affected smaller houses, where patterns of orderly life and discipline were harder to maintain. More pervasive were reports suggesting a wearied attrition of religious fervour and community feeling. Bishops uncovered numerous cases of absenteeism, services at irregular times, monks gossiping after compline, financial mismanagement, or abbots and priors leading disengaged, leisured lives in comfortable abbatial chambers. Bishop Alcock took it for granted that as a fish dies outside water, 'so a man or woman of religion being without their cloister is dead in their souls'.[27] Yet almost everywhere there was neglect of 'enclosure', and much toing and froing between religious community and lay society. If English monasticism was 'corrupt', it was the corruption of comfort, convention and compromise, rather than of depravity, decadence and dissipation. There is not much evidence there had ever been a monastic 'golden age' when such problems did not exist.

'Worldliness' might in any case more charitably be interpreted as a pragmatic readjustment to the expectations of a changing world. Monasteries hired professional singers to enhance their liturgy, and professional scribes to spruce up their manuscripts. Libraries, in the larger houses at least, were well stocked and expanding, and several monasteries, particularly cathedral priories, established schools for instruction of local children.

English monasticism was not irretrievably stuck in the past. Hardly any early printing presses were found outside London. But the few that were belonged to the Benedictines: in the 1520s and '30s books were produced on presses at Abingdon, Tavistock, St Augustine's Canterbury and St Albans. The early sixteenth century was a heyday of monastic building: new chantries at Tewkesbury, Peterborough and St Albans; new towers at Shap, Furness, Bolton, Canterbury and – an exquisite survival – at Fountains; rebuilt cloisters at Hailes and Lacock; extensive refurbishments at Westminster, Chester, Sherborne, Winchcombe, Evesham and Glastonbury; a brand new abbey church, never completed, at Bath.[28]

### Bishops, Legate and Reform

Whatever judgement historians might make, many contemporaries believed the reform of religious orders to be an urgently pressing task. There were several strands to this. One was the attitude of Erasmus – unsympathetic towards monasticism as a whole, and still, in the later 1520s, complaining to English correspondents about the malevolence towards him of monks and friars. There are echoes in a manuscript treatise of the early 1530s, a fictional *Dialogue between Pole and Lupset*. It was written by Erasmus's admirer, Thomas Starkey, secretary to the aristocratic scholar Reginald Pole, and a friend of the humanist churchman Thomas Lupset. Starkey did not advocate abolishing monasteries, but he considered them full of 'ill occupied' persons, and in need of 'good reformation'. It would be better if only mature men and not youths were admitted, so there might be 'fewer in number religious men, but better in life'. Overall, monasteries played a very marginal role in Starkey's conception of the well-ordered Christian commonwealth, and nunneries didn't enter his consciousness at all.

This was not the attitude of reform-minded bishops, who took very seriously their responsibility to elevate standards of monastic life. Longland of

Lincoln generally left parish visitations to his deputies, but visited many of the 111 religious houses in his diocese personally. In extreme cases, Longland removed superiors – such as the abbess of Elstow in Bedfordshire, who ignored orders to enforce communal dining, and allowed the sisters to wear unseemly low-cut dresses.[29]

The willingness of bishops – Alcock of Ely, Fox of Winchester, Fisher of Rochester – to suppress religious houses in order to endow university colleges did not reflect a low opinion of religious life. In 1497, Alcock published a sermon preached at the consecration of some nuns. He explained the matrimonial symbolism of their profession, and promised that if they continued faithfully as spouses of Christ, their jointure (marriage settlement) would 'exceed all rewards that can be thought'. In 1517, Fox translated the Benedictine rule into English for the benefit of nuns of his diocese. Fisher routinely took in person the professions of new monks, hermits and nuns. His 1522 suppression of the Benedictine nunnery of Higham marked the expiry of efforts, stretching over a decade, to reform the behaviour of its inmates. Fisher reconfirmed his concern for the spiritual formation of nuns at the very end of his life, when, incarcerated in the Tower, he composed two devotional treatises for his half-sister, Elizabeth White, a Dominican nun of Dartford.[30]

Cardinal Wolsey's suppressions of religious houses in the cause of education were on a scale larger than any other bishop's. In his last months in office, in 1528–9, he secured papal bulls allowing further suppressions to add to the endowments of Eton and Cambridge. He was also empowered to dissolve and amalgamate houses with fewer than twelve inmates, and to establish an undetermined number of new dioceses using monastic churches and wealth – measures that, had they not been overtaken by events, would have left the map of monastic England substantially redrawn.

Wolsey was less than scrupulous about only dissolving houses shown to be incapable of reform. The Benedictine priory of Daventry, suppressed in 1525, came quite well out of a recent visitation, and there is no evidence of very much amiss with the Augustinian community of St Frideswide's, Oxford, the kernel of the new foundation for Cardinal College. Wolsey's absentee abbotship of wealthy St Albans was also a flagrant contradiction of his expressed concern for reform.[31]

Wolsey's credentials as monastic reformer are not entirely negligible. In 1519, he issued detailed constitutions for the Austin canons, a back-to-basics manifesto whose provisions included a ban on polyphonic music – 'wanton melodies' that 'flatter the ear' – in favour of good, old-fashioned monastic plainchant. Heads of Augustinian, Benedictine and Cistercian houses were summoned to a meeting in November that year to discuss matters 'concerning their reformation', and for the Benedictines a new set of statutes was issued. The text does not survive, but it was demanding enough to provoke a letter of protest, arguing that 'if everything in the reformation of the order should tend to excessive austerity and rigour, we should not have the monks (at least not a decent and sufficient number) to inhabit so many and so great monasteries'. It was simply unreasonable to expect everyone to emulate the ascetic rigour of Carthusians, Bridgettines and Franciscan Observants.

This *cri de coeur* is often regarded as a patent self-indictment of mainstream monasticism, though one might choose to see it as recognition of the variegated character of religious life, and a sensible warning against letting the best become enemy of the good. Nonetheless, a rhetoric of monastic reformation was in the ascendant at the start of Henry VIII's second decade. The Benedictines of Westminster must have squirmed in the choir stalls in January 1519, when Wolsey visited their abbey, and Longland preached from Genesis 18:21: 'I will go down and see whether they have deserved the ill report that has reached me.'[32]

Monastic reform was not just a moral question, but a jurisdictional and political one. It was an obstacle to disciplinary oversight that so many houses could claim immunity from episcopal visitation. The 'exempt' orders included all the friars, the Premonstratensian canons, Cistercians, Carthusians and almost three dozen 'Cluniac' priories, under the supervision of the reformed Benedictine Abbey of Cluny in Burgundy. In addition, some of the most prestigious Benedictine abbeys – Glastonbury, St Albans, Evesham, Malmesbury – claimed exempt status on the basis of treasured papal privileges. Freedom from episcopal oversight need not mean moral anarchy. Exempt orders were responsible for organizing their own inspection regimes, and surviving evidence proves this could be done conscientiously and effectively.[33] Bishops, however, resented infringement of their jurisdictional powers. Wolsey, flush with royal favour, was in a unique position to do something about it.

In 1518, with Henry VIII's backing, Wolsey secured from Leo X appointment as legate *a latere* in England – a representative sent 'from the side' of the Holy Father. The formal basis for the request was a need to reform the religious orders. The legateship, made permanent in 1524, conferred the right to issue new constitutions and depose unworthy heads. Wolsey interfered repeatedly in monastic elections, and removed at least eight unsuitable superiors. Legateship also empowered Wolsey to visit exempt houses, and though he exercised the right only sporadically, bishops could turn to him for help. Longland, for example, appealed to Wolsey in 1528 to get rid of the philandering Dominican prior of King's Langley, Hertfordshire.[34]

The one exemplary demonstration of legatine power against an exempt order underlines the contradictory character of 'reform' in the early Tudor Church. The targets were, of all people, the Observant Franciscans of Greenwich – by virtually unanimous consent the most devout and disciplined of the friars. The house at Greenwich was closely associated with the court: a foundation of

Edward IV, it lay adjacent to the royal palace. It was where Prince Henry was baptized in 1491, and where he married Catherine of Aragon in 1509. Their daughter Mary was in turn baptized in the chapel at Greenwich in 1516.

For the Observants, episcopal oversight did not seem like a prescription for spiritual health. On the contrary, after their controversial split from the main branch of the order in the early fifteenth century, Observants repeatedly resisted bishops' attempts to suppress their distinctive identity. Their best guarantee of survival was the direct endorsement of the papacy, and they jealously guarded their independence from jurisdictions short of Rome itself.

Their loyalty was only tepidly rewarded. Clement VII begged Wolsey not to stir up trouble by visiting the order, but nonetheless issued a bull in August 1524, specifically empowering him to override the Observants' exemptions. The visitation took place in January 1525, prompting a mass walkout by nineteen of the brethren. They were brought to heel by excommunication, and incarceration in the porter's lodge at Wolsey's London residence. The visitation did nothing to enhance spiritual standards, and succeeded only in stirring factionalism and ill will among the community. That was to erupt again in the following decade, when the order faced a much greater crisis of identity and obedience.[35]

## Observance and Imitation

The sorry episode at Greenwich points to a noticeable deficiency of religious life in the generation before the break with Rome: the failure of English monasticism to manifest much internally generated revival, or participate wholeheartedly in reform movements sweeping other parts of the western Church. Religious orders across Europe in the fifteenth century were gripped by the spirit of 'Observance' – reform as return to an imagined past.

Observantism was most influential among the Franciscans. By the start of the sixteenth century, Observant houses matched Conventual ones in most provinces of the order, and in some places achieved dominance. In Ireland, two-thirds of Franciscan houses became Observant, and in Spain observance was imposed on all Franciscans by the ascetic friar, royal minister, and Cardinal Archbishop of Toledo, Francisco Jiménez de Cisneros (1436–1517) – a much more plausible symbol of ecclesiastical reform than his English counterpart, Wolsey. In 1517, Leo X took the step of declaring Observant Franciscans to be the true heirs of St Francis, henceforth to elect the minister general of the order. The Conventuals were reconstituted as a separate and subordinate branch.[36]

Of these convulsions, there was little sign in England. The Franciscan Observants were established late, on a limited scale, and as a result of direct royal patronage. Perhaps there was no gaping crisis of Franciscan vision demanding redress. It is hard to imagine an English equivalent to the situation confronting Cisneros in Andalusia, where, rather than give up their concubines, 400 friars fled to North Africa and converted to Islam. But neither was there much urgency about internal regeneration. The English friars were learned enough, in a traditional kind of way, and produced solid and seemingly popular sermons. But their ranks produced no superstar revivalist preacher, no English equivalent of Bernardino of Siena, John of Capistrano, Vincent Ferrer or Girolamo Savonarola.

Across Europe, the Observant movement also deeply influenced the Dominicans, Carmelites and Augustinian friars. In the early sixteenth century, the Observant Augustinians produced a great reforming prior general, Giles of Viterbo, who in 1512 delivered a prophetic plea for Church reform at the opening of the Fifth Lateran Council.[37] Yet none of the English friaries, with the limited exception of the Franciscans, attached themselves to the Observant movement at all. English Benedictines were equally immune to the bug of strict observance spreading through the provinces of the order in the fifteenth century, and associated particularly with the houses of Subiaco in central Italy and Melk in Lower Austria.[38] In an era of incessant talk about 'reformation' in the English Church, the religious orders were conspicuously backward at coming forward.

Reasons for the retardation of Observant renewal in English religious life are not immediately obvious. Ironically, it may in part be a backhanded tribute to the fact that standards were not so shockingly low as to demand urgent remedial action. The untypical (in European terms) power of the English bishops, who had little desire to see the proliferation of assertively independent-minded reform movements within their dioceses, may also have been a factor. Yet a culture of contentment and complacency, and a relative deficit of charismatic leadership, left the religious houses, the wealthiest and most institutionally exposed sector of the English Church, ill-prepared to play much more than a passive, onlooking role, when the world they had known began, suddenly, to shift on its axes.

Monks were primarily concerned with the worship of God, and with salvation of their own souls. Yet a compelling argument in favour of religious life was its ability to inspire wider society to higher levels of spirituality. Reform currents among the Augustinian canons in the later Middle Ages – which again failed to make headway across the Channel – impacted strongly on the lives of the laity. From the late fourteenth century, the Observant house at Windesheim near Deventer in the Netherlands was epicentre of a reform movement spanning Augustinian priories in the Low Countries, Rhineland, Saxony and Switzerland. From this nexus emerged the most influential book of late medieval spiritual direction. Thomas Kempis, sub-prior of Mount St Agnes, near Zwolle in the Dutch province of Overijssel, is likeliest candidate for authorship of the *Imitatio Christi* (see pp. 28–9).

Both the *Imitatio* and the wider Windesheim congregation were linked to the *Devotio Moderna* (modern devotion), a movement of spiritual renewal embracing both clergy and laity and producing 'brethren of the common life' – groups of laypeople living lives of prayer and chastity in community without formal vows. These were similar to earlier groups of beguines (female) and beghards (male) in Germany and the Low Countries, which, despite arousing suspicions of heresy, survived with official support into the Reformation period and beyond. There is some sparse and scattered evidence for informal communities of pious laywomen in England in the fourteenth and fifteenth centuries, but these seem to have been neither widespread nor of long duration. England also missed out on establishment of 'tertiary' groupings of the mendicant orders, found in France, Germany and Italy. Tertiaries constituted a lay third branch, after the friars and the nuns, committed to regular recitation of the divine office, and extensive charitable work.

English people were not, then, much inspired to imitate the pattern of the cloister in specific forms of organization, preferring the more relaxed model of parish fraternities. But they were not entirely indifferent to the values of religious life. The Book of Hours or primer was after all based on monastic forms of prayer. There is also evidence in some elite circles of a shared reading culture, with books passing between nuns and aristocratic and gentry women.[39]

A monastic-style spirituality was successfully 'marketed' for the laity by the one off-shoot of reformed Augustinianism to establish a toe-hold in England: the Bridgettine house of Syon. In addition to overseeing the spiritual health of the community's nuns, the brothers had pastoral responsibility for pious laymen and women visiting or staying within the precincts. The Bridgettines also assigned themselves a more ambitious spiritual responsibility. Through preaching and the medium of print, they aimed to reach out to a constituency of pious lay questers. A miscellany of prayers and exhortations in English, published by the Syon brother Thomas Betson in 1500, was designed to be 'meedful [meritorious] to religious people as to the laypeople'. Bridgettines were advocates of what the fourteenth-century mystic Walter Hilton dubbed the mixed or 'medled' life, a balanced vocation of meditative contemplation and external, charitable action. It was promoted between 1494 and 1533 in four successive editions of Hilton's vernacular *Scala perfectionis* (ladder of perfection), and in an extracted text of 1530.[40]

In the same tradition stood Richard Whitford's *Werke for Housholders*, a book that went through a remarkable seven editions between 1530 and 1537. Whitford prescribed a 'customable course of good and profitable exercise' for responsible heads of lay households, with demanding, but not absurdly unmanageable, expectations. The day should begin with elaborate makings of the sign of the cross, and end with a detailed mental inspection of 'work, word or thought'. A practical-minded man, who spent years in the world as a secular priest, Whitford recognized that where people roomed together, and such shows of piety were performed, 'some would laugh us to scorn and mock us'.

Thoughtful expositions of religious life, framed with attentive lay audiences in view, were also produced by Whitford's fellow-Bridgettine, William Bonde, in his *Pylgrimage of Perfection* (1526) and *Directory of Conscience* (1527). A third Syon monk, John Fewterer, offered lay readers his *Myrrour or Glasse of Christes Passion* (1534), a deeply Christocentric reflection on the mixed life. Fewterer, as Confessor General of the Abbey, and in partnership with a redoubtable abbess, Agnes Jordan, spearheaded a concerted, commercially savvy campaign of vernacular publication. The period of their joint headship witnessed publication of eleven of fourteen English printed books emanating from Syon.[41]

The wills of wealthy Londoners expressed admiration for the Bridgettines. Other beneficiaries were the Observants of Greenwich and Richmond, and the Charterhouses of London and Sheen. Carthusians are the exception to the rule of cyclical stagnation and reform characterizing the religious orders. There were no Carthusians 'of the observance'. As a later pope was to put it, *numquam reformata quia numquam deformata* (never reformed because never deformed).

Like Syon, the London Charterhouse was a powerhouse of lay spiritual direction. The young Thomas More lodged with (or close to) the Carthusians, 'religiously living there without vow about four years'. Carthusians were often 'late vocations', either laymen of status looking to withdraw from the cares of the world, or priests and monks seeking more authentic forms of religious expression. With limited places, and plenty of applicants to fill them, the order could afford to be picky. In 1522, Lord Clifford wrote to Prior John Wilson of Mount Grace in Yorkshire, soliciting a place there for his chaplain; Wilson courteously but firmly explained that the house could accept no novices without evidence of a long-standing vocation to the Carthusian life. A cell was potentially free, but there were already four applicants for it.[42]

The Carthusians were relatively little affected by the humanist enthusiasms of the first years of the sixteenth century, remaining closer to a native tradition of mystical contemplation found in works like *The Cloud of Unknowing*. John Batmanson, a brother of the London Charterhouse, was egged on by Edward Lee to attack Erasmus's New Testament, and earned a put-down from Thomas More, admiration for the Carthusians notwithstanding, as 'an unlearned, obscure little monk'.

They lacked the panache and polish of the Syon brethren, but Carthusians were also concerned with making spiritual literature available to the laity. *The Pomander of Prayer*, a work going rapidly through four editions in 1528–32, was written by a 'devout father of the Charterhouse of Sheen'. The author explained how he chose to write in English so that he might instruct 'the unlearned that lack knowledge of holy scripture'. There was no flurry of new

Carthusian books to match the Bridgettine output, but an older vernacular work, Nicholas Love's *Myrrour of the Blessed Lyfe of Jesu Criste*, remained popular with lay readers.

Carthusians were the monks you knew were going to heaven. Even Erasmus was capable of writing respectfully about their vocation. English laypeople voted, not so much with their feet, as with their corpses, requesting burial in Carthusian houses in considerable numbers. If this was not possible, they requested the prayers and suffrages of the order.[43] Like the Bridgettines and Franciscan Observants, these exemplars of the monastic ideal combined sanctification of their own lives with a mission of spiritual service to the wider Church. Perhaps this raised the reputation of the monastic body as a whole in the eyes of the laity; more likely it simply showed up the shortcomings of the others.

### The Cloister and the World

There is little clear evidence of admiration or rejection of monasticism as a whole because people did not experience it as a whole. They interacted with individual houses, and individual religious, in a wide variety of settings. Monasteries were major landowners, usually leasing rather than farming their estates. They were notable local employers, engaging gentlemen as bailiffs and stewards at the top end, and recruiting domestic servants in significant numbers at the other. The Benedictine nuns of St Michael's, Stamford, in Northamptonshire employed a valet, cook, gardener, carter, porter, brewster, shepherd, oxherd and swineherd, along with a host of other, unspecified servants. On the payroll at the great Benedictine house of Westminster were nearly a hundred servants to care for the community of fifty brethren, a figure not including personal attendants paid for out of monks' private funds.[44]

The number of laypeople reliant on religious houses rises when we include those in possession of a corrody – an annuity, or an allowance of food, drink and accommodation, given in return for gifts of land or a cash down payment. There were fewer of these by the 1530s than in earlier centuries: perhaps a national average of one corrodian per ten religious. Yet in Devon the ratio was just under 1:3, and it could determine the ambience of individual houses. Eight corrodians lived alongside eight nuns at Thetford Priory, Norfolk in 1532.[45]

Such schemes were not motivated by altruism: like modern medical insurers, monasteries stood to gain if laypeople died shortly after claiming on the policy. Yet they were a needed and valued social service. Just as valued was the tradition of monastic hospitality to travellers, though this was open to exploitation from social elites, happy to be entertained comfortably while on the road with their retinues. An Augustinian chronicler at Butley Priory in

Suffolk recorded with evident pride multiple visits to his house between 1526 and 1534 by the Duke of Norfolk, and the Duke and Duchess of Suffolk, though these must have been a very significant drain on priory finances.

Less easy to subvert was the obligation to give alms to paupers. After a long stretch of historical scepticism, modern research is inclined to think its scale was significant, and that it provided an important safety net for local indigents: nationally, about 7 per cent of monastic revenue was disbursed annually to the poor, along with informal distribution of foodstuffs at abbey gates.[46]

Most communities were rooted in a locality. Recruitment drew heavily on the vicinity and the hinterland, a pattern traceable by the Benedictine habit of adopting birthplace as a new surname 'in religion'. A succession of remarkable superiors – William Selling, Richard Kidderminster, Hugh Faringdon, John Feckenham – were professed at houses less than a day's ride from the villages giving them their name. Nunneries too recruited from the locality, and predominantly from middling social backgrounds: they were not 'dumping grounds' for unmarriable aristocratic daughters. A few houses – Syon, most notably – were socially exclusive, but most relied for recruits on the merchant classes and the lower 'parish gentry'.[47]

Unsurprisingly, the religious remained in contact with their local kinsfolk; a perennial visitation complaint was of monks giving to family members the excess food earmarked for distribution to the poor. Ties of kindred and affinity, and the significance for economic and social activity, meant laypeople often valued the presence of local houses. In July 1525, a delegation of sixteen inhabitants from Tonbridge in Kent appeared in front of Archbishop Warham to denounce Wolsey's recent suppression of the Augustinian priory. There was still more vigorous protest that summer at Bayham in Sussex, where a former canon of the Premonstratensian abbey orchestrated a riot of 100 persons to restore religious life.[48]

Bequests in wills supply a rough-and-ready index of the standing of the religious orders. These were much less common than to parish churches, and do not appear to have been subject to strong social convention. Yet this in itself speaks for the authenticity of the bequests that were made. In the 1520s, a substantial minority of testators remembered one or more monastic houses. In the dioceses of Exeter, London, York and Durham, some 17–18 per cent did so, as did 15 per cent in the diocese of Salisbury and 11 per cent in Lincolnshire, though the figure was markedly, and somewhat inexplicably, lower in Suffolk (3 per cent).

The friars did better. In Yorkshire and County Durham, 28 per cent of wills made bequests to them in the 1520s, as did nearly a quarter in Devon and Cornwall and in Lincolnshire. In urban settings, the friars' natural habitat, proportions were noticeably higher: 43 per cent in London in 1523–5; 47 per cent in Norwich in 1490–1517; 33 per cent in York in 1501–36, and 38 per cent in

Salisbury over the same period. Especially among the gentry, who had more choice and flexibility in such matters, requests to be buried in friary churches were common.[49]

Nearly all religious houses offered a special form of association through issuing letters of confraternity, assigning the recipient a fraternal status and a promised share of spiritual benefits. These could be a form of favour-seeking with the great and good: in 1502 Durham Cathedral Priory issued letters of confraternity to Lady Margaret Beaufort, and also to her advisor, Henry VII's tough councillor and enforcer, Sir Reginald Bray, who probably had need of them. Such grants formed part of a nexus of good relations between the prominent gentry of a county and its leading religious institutions – the Warwickshire and Worcestershire landowner Sir Robert Throckmorton was admitted in 1491, along with his wife and infant son, to confraternity with Evesham Abbey. Other grants of confraternity were proactively sought, or sold for cash – an illustration of how material, spiritual and social bonds between religious houses and lay society were inextricably intertwined.[50]

The ties that bind sometimes chafe. Laypeople periodically quarrelled with abbeys over tithes and tenancies. Competition to control local resources could turn nasty. In 1527, 300 rioters in Devon destroyed a weir on the River Tamar, maintained by the Benedictines of Tavistock Abbey. Several English towns were monastic boroughs, where inhabitants were subject to the jurisdiction of an abbot's court and paid tolls on markets and mills. Assertions of independence and self-governance by townspeople caused tensions, and occasional violence, in a number of these places in the thirteenth and fourteenth centuries. Most such disputes had run their course by the later fifteenth century. But some were stubbornly persistent. The townsmen of Bury St Edmunds in Suffolk pursued a series of unsuccessful lawsuits against the abbey into the 1480s and '90s, while those at Reading kept up legal pressure until a settlement was finally reached in 1507.[51]

Negative stereotypes of monks and friars circulated widely in late medieval England – a lively and evergreen cultural phenomenon, seemingly consumed for pleasure and recreation as much as articulated in righteous anger. Multiple editions of the *Canterbury Tales* were printed around the turn of the sixteenth century (1478, 1484, 1492, 1498, 1526). Perennially popular were ballads of Robin Hood, which pitted a bold and pious outlaw, the name of the Virgin ever on his lips, against corpulent, uncharitable and grasping Benedictines.[52]

Lively Chauceresque satire of hypocritical friars and pardoners was revived at the start of the 1530s in the knockabout interludes of the musician and playwright John Heywood. But an existing taste for it is revealed by English translations of the German humanist Sebastian Brandt's popular 1494 verse satire, *The Ship of Fools*. One (via the French) was made by Wynkyn de Worde's assistant Henry Watson in 1509. Another, also in 1509, was produced by Alexander

Barclay, an erudite priest of the collegiate church of Ottery St Mary in Devon. Along with other ranks of society, the religious orders come in for a sharp lashing: 'O holy Benet, Francis and Augustine, see how your children despiseth your doctrine!'[53] There was more in the same vein in the rhymester-priest John Skelton's 1522 verse, *Colyn Cloute* – a poetic blunderbuss of playfully satirical invective, aimed indiscriminately at clergy failing to meet the exalted standards Skelton knew he himself fell short of: delinquent bishops, ignorant parish priests, worldly monks, gluttonous hypocrite friars, determined to grasp for every passing penny. 'All is fish that cometh to the net.'

Around the turn of the 1530s, *Colyn Cloute*, along with *Speke Parrot*, another Skelton poem strongly critical of the clergy, was copied into the commonplace book of the London mercer John Collins. Other anonymous verses in his compilation attributed 'The Ruin of a Realm' to rule of 'spiritual men', and beseeched Christ to 'amend our priests and make them good'. In affluent urban circles, priestly shortcomings were, literally, proverbial. The expression 'as tender as a parson's leman [i.e. concubine]' appeared in an early sixteenth-century collection of aphorisms. Another proverb is preserved for us by Thomas More: 'if a woman be fair then she is young, and if a priest be good then he is old'. More himself professed exasperation that, if a good priest preached, 'a short tale shall serve us ... but let a lewd friar be taken with a wench, we will jest and rail upon the whole order all the year after!'[54]

Is all this evidence of widespread 'anticlericalism'? There was no swelling tide of seething resentment, poised to sweep all vestiges of the old order away. It is clear that most anticlerical talk, even of the jokey variety, was the expression, not the negation, of a genuine Catholic piety – an echo of disappointed expectation. Alongside the anticlerical verses, John Collins inscribed miracle stories and prayers for souls in purgatory into his manuscript volume, carefully heading each page 'Jesus'. There were similar juxtapositions in other early sixteenth-century commonplace books.

Authors of overtly anticlerical writings were generally not disenfranchised rebels, but religious insiders, with strong connections to the institutional Church. Heywood was a pious, orthodox Catholic of Erasmian stamp, a relative and protégé of Thomas More. Like More, he was a married layman. But his brother was an Augustinian friar (and two sons were in later decades to become Jesuit priests). Skelton and Barclay were well-connected scholar-priests with links to the court. Despite – or perhaps because of – the critiques of religious orders in his *Ship of Fools* translation, Barclay went on to become, successively, a Benedictine monk and an Observant Franciscan. Watson's translation even claimed to have been undertaken at 'the enticement and exhortation of the excellent Princess Margaret, Countess of Richmond and Derby'. Whether the pious Lady Margaret Beaufort really sponsored the exercise is dubious, but readers were not expected to find anything incongruous in the claim.[55]

Yet if anticlerical feelings were typically orthodox and idealistic, that did not make them innocuous or inert. Impatience with the shortcomings of the clergy was a sentiment energized by the zeal of its own self-evident rightness. It was a product of the centrality of sacramental priesthood to the spiritual objectives of society, and of the entrenched position of clergymen across swathes of social, economic and cultural life. Hopes for salvation in the next world, and for the triumph of virtue in this, required good priests. But the religious needs of society also demanded there must be many priests. England was not Utopia, where the priests were very good and very few. Anticlericalism was the unavoidable by-product of a widespread craving for reform, and its significance for eventual Reformation should not be underestimated.

The church authorities were hopeful the circle could be squared. Archbishops and bishops would gradually bring about 'reformation of the Church's estate' by vigilant and ever more comprehensive regimes of inspection, by acquiring greater control over patterns of clerical appointments, by exercising to the full the disciplinary powers of the church courts – in other words, by asserting and enhancing the political and jurisdictional authority of bishops within the realm. Lay society, from the palace to the parish, had things to say about that.

## 3

## HEAD AND MEMBERS

### The Body of Christ

IN NOVEMBER 1515, a messenger disembarked at Dover with a precious object in a bag. The bearer was the Protonotary Apostolic of the papal court, and the encased object was the red, tasselled and broad-brimmed hat of a Roman cardinal. It was sent by Pope Leo X to adorn the head of Thomas Wolsey, archbishop of York, and trusted favourite of the young King of England, Henry VIII. Within days, the envoy was met by assorted lay and ecclesiastical dignitaries at Blackheath, and escorted across old London Bridge into the city. At the door of Westminster Abbey, the hat was received by Abbot Islip and eight other abbots in full regalia, and laid reverently on the high altar. Three days later, Wolsey was installed as cardinal in the abbey, amidst such splendour that an eyewitness declared he had never seen the like 'unless it had been at the coronation of a mighty prince or king'.[1]

A hat for a head, a head for a body. Society's resemblance to a human body was the commonest of medieval metaphors. The idea had strong mystical and sacral underpinnings, for St Paul taught that the Church was the body of Christ. The analogy appealed to people wishing to live in a state that was hierarchical but not tyrannical – the head governs but does not vex the other body parts.

If the Church was a body, then clearly, as Bishop Alcock declared in 1497, 'in every realm of Christianity, the head thereof is Christ'.[2] For practical purposes, it needed a head attached to its members in more concrete and visible ways. The bishops of Rome – known as popes, from the Latin *papa*, father – exercised this role for the Church in the west. They based their claim on Christ's commission to St Peter to 'feed my sheep' (John 21:17), and on his pledge that Peter was the rock on which 'I will build my Church' (Matt. 16:18–19). For centuries before 1500, popes were accustomed to refer to themselves as 'vicars of St Peter', and also as 'vicars of Christ'.

Yet the precise scope and character of their authority had long been a matter of contention. It was placed in the spotlight by the scandal of the Great Schism. From 1378, rival lines of popes, one based in Rome, the other in Avignon in southern France, hurled anathemas at each other and competed for the allegiance of European powers. The eventual remedy was a little used but venerable instrument of discipline and reform, a General Council of the Church. A council meeting at Constance in southern Germany between 1414 and 1418 achieved what an earlier council at Pisa failed to enforce: the deposition of all rival claimants and the election of a universally recognized new pope. Furthermore, Constance set itself the task of reforming the Church 'in head and members', and in the process asserted that the authority of a General Council came directly from Christ, and all, even popes, were bound to obey it.[3]

The conciliar movement of the early fifteenth century was an emergency response to crisis circumstances. Despite the hopes of its proponents, it failed to transform itself into a new model of church government. Subsequent popes refused to recognize conciliar claims, and spent much of the century clawing back their authority. But the slogan of reform in 'head and members' remained in the memory of those who cared about the health of the Church, and kept alive the question of whether the papacy was the key agent of reform, or its first and necessary object.

In the meantime, the real winners from this crisis of authority were those other heads of the body politic, the secular rulers of European states. Their interests did not always coincide with those of a supra-national Church, and they had reason to begrudge the idea that its local manifestation constituted a separate 'body' within the realm, with its own rights and privileges. To earlier generations of tidy-minded national and constitutional historians, it was self-evident that the Reformation grew out of this problem of too many bodies inhabiting the same skin, and of rival heads seeking to direct them. The decisive showdown between 'Church' and 'State' was only a matter of time.

That idea now seems naïve, underestimating the extent to which contemporaries could cope with complexity and compromise. But more recent assessments of the Reformation in England, emphasizing a general cultural and doctrinal satisfaction with the late medieval Church, have paid too little attention to tensions and rivalries surrounding its legal and constitutional position.[4] These did not make a reformation inevitable. Yet they are an important part of the explanation for why a largely dutiful and devout Catholic nation proved in the end unable to meet an unexpected doctrinal challenge with a powerfully united front. They also tell a story of opportunities missed, of preventative action not taken. Disagreements about who should have primary responsibility for reform of Church and society, and about the forms it should take, acted to inhibit a thoroughgoing reformation that stayed within the bounds of Catholic orthodoxy. Wolsey's red hat – supplied by the Pope, but ordered by the King – could have been the instrument and symbol of just such a reformation. Its failure was conspicuous, and left a legacy of disappointment and frustration.

In July 1511, the papacy produced a powerful statement of intent regarding the process of reform. Julius II published a bull summoning a universal council of the Church to assemble the following year in Rome, at the palace of the Lateran. In England, the King commissioned an impressive team to represent the nation there. John Fisher, bishop of Rochester, Thomas Docwra, prior of the Knights Hospitaller, and Richard Kidderminster, abbot of Winchcombe, were to attend, along with the diplomat Sir Robert Wingfield, and the Italian Silvestro Gigli, absentee bishop of Worcester, who helped keep an eye on English interests at the Roman curia (court). Fisher, characteristically, invited Erasmus to accompany him to the council, though, for reasons not entirely clear, it seems most of the English delegation did not make it to Rome, and it may have been Gigli alone who travelled to the council.[5]

The prospect of a reforming council struck a chord with those longing for a clergy-led renewal of the Church in England: in the same week that Fisher and his colleagues were commissioned to go to Rome, Colet delivered his rousing reformist manifesto to the Convocation of Canterbury.[6]

Yet the Fifth Lateran Council proved a false dawn. There were some moderate achievements – a doctrinal decree on the immortality of the soul, greater restrictions on the exemption of regulars from episcopal oversight, and a renewed assertion of the dignity of clerical office. But the council did not effect any fundamental reforms. Its very existence was in fact fundamentally political and reactive. Julius II was locked in conflict with Louis XII of France, over territory and influence in northern Italy. In 1511, to put pressure on the Pope, Louis summoned a group of rebellious cardinals to attend a council at Pisa; the principal purpose of the Lateran Council was to anathematize its Pisan rival.

Julius saw off the French-sponsored, half-hearted revival of conciliarism, but in the process he did little to enhance the dignity of the papal office. That dignity was already severely compromised by the shameless nepotism, opulent lifestyle and relaxed morality of what we have come to know as the 'Renaissance papacy' – an institution of whose excesses Julius's predecessor, the Borgia pope Alexander VI, was the most scandalous but scarcely the sole exemplar. A few years earlier, sensitive observers looked on open-mouthed as Julius, clad in full plate armour, led armies to victory over the bothersome rulers of Perugia and Bologna.[7] The episode underlines how the papacy was locked into the politics of the Italian peninsula, especially after the French invasion of 1494, and the extent to which its priorities had become those of a local territorial prince, rather than a universal Christian pastor.

There were sound reasons for popes to be masters of their own independent territorial state. A papacy under the thumb of either of the two great powers with a hand in the Italian pie – the French or the Spanish – was everyone else's worst nightmare. But a loss of moral authority was the price for playing the part of Italian princeling.

Shortly after Julius II's death, a text called the *Julius Exclusus e Coelis* ('Julius Excluded from Heaven') circulated in manuscript; it was printed in 1518. In this merciless satire, Julius tries to bluster his way past St Peter at the heavenly gates, threatening to return with an army when entry is refused. It is usually attributed to Erasmus (who always denied writing it), though just possibly its author may have been the English humanist Richard Pace.

On Good Friday 1513, as Henry VIII prepared to lead an army into France, John Colet preached a sermon at court. He extolled the virtues of peace, and urged Catholics 'to imitate Christ their king, rather than characters like Alexander and Julius'.[8] He referred here to the ancient warrior rulers of Macedonia and Rome, but a coincidence with the regnal names of two preceding popes was scarcely accidental. Catholic reformers were sceptical, and sometimes cynical, about the wise judgement of the head.

### Popes and People

What ordinary English people thought about popes and the papacy is an elusive but not impenetrable question. We should not expect to find what could not have existed: a late medieval equivalent to the modern Catholic personality cult of the papacy, sustained by the possibilities of air travel, photography and instant mass communications. The Pope was, in every sense, a distant figure. But distance need not imply dislike or indifference.

Everyone knew the Pope was head of the Church. The prayers of intercession, or bidding of the bedes, taking place during mass every Sunday, began with the priest calling on people in English to pray for 'our holy father the Pope of Rome with all his true cardinals'. Awareness of the Pope's position of primacy was reinforced by commentaries on the Ten Commandments, which ranked him first in the requirement to honour your (spiritual) father and mother, and by passing references to 'our holy father, the Pope' in a broad range of printed works. A papal presence in the cultural landscape of English people was further enshrined by images in churches of popes who happened also to be saints – in particular, the figure of St Gregory, one of the four Latin doctors adorning large numbers of rood screens. Images of the Mass of Pope Gregory, during which the pontiff experienced a vision of Christ at the altar, proliferated in devotional books.[9]

More than any other artefact, printed indulgences – of which vast quantities were proclaimed, produced and purchased in England – promoted popular consciousness of papal authority, and its significance for the life of the Church.[10] Emblazoned with the papal arms, indulgences were neatly packaged distillations of the spiritual authority of the Holy Father, and of his ability to offer remission from the penalties of sin. They depended for efficacy, not on vague invocations of papal authority, but on specific grants from named occupants of the chair of St Peter. Popes took their share of the proceeds, but as most indulgences were issued in response to requests from the English individuals and institutions to whose advantage they accrued, they can scarcely be considered merely a money-making scam on the part of the Holy See.

In light of later events, it is remarkable how few rumblings of anti-papal satire or complaint are to be heard in England around the turn of the sixteenth century. Conceivably, the absence of overt hostility is a marker of the relatively low importance of the Pope. For other than enticing them to purchase indulgences, what practical impact on the lives of English laypeople did the authority of the papacy have? Perhaps a few hundred men and women – including merchants with good business reasons for being in Italy – journeyed to Rome each year and took advantage of the indulgences on offer for visiting Roman churches. Some lodged gratefully at the hospice for English pilgrims. No fewer than 489 visitors stayed in the hospice between November 1504 and May 1507, and an impressive 750 English pilgrims were welcomed there, receiving alms, if not accommodation, during the papal jubilee year of 1500.[11]

Rome was not always where the heart was. Luther, still an ardent friar, travelled there on the business of his order in 1510–11, and was famously turned off by the louche character of the papal court. A few years earlier, Colet and More's friend Cuthbert Tunstall attended a papal audience in the city. He was appalled by the haughty demeanour of Julius II, who caused a chamberlain to lift the hem of his robe so that 'a nobleman of great age' might prostrate himself before the pontiff and kiss his shoe. But this was a recollection from 1539, when there was only one politic way to speak about popes in England.[12]

The vast majority of English people never came physically close to the person of the Pope. We cannot know, when they were invited to pray for their Holy Father, how many did so with fervent sincerity, how many carelessly or perfunctorily. Yet Rome was far from an absolute irrelevance. The curia, in the words of the Norfolk gentleman Sir John Paston, was 'the well of grace', and a 'salve sufficient for such a sore'.

The sore in question was Paston's betrothal to Anne Hault, now to be broken off, an action that, for satisfaction of the lady's conscience, required a dispensation from the Pope's tribunal. Rome was Christendom's supreme licensing agency, the ultimate source of legal resolution for a host of practical, personal and professional problems.[13] The Pope was universally recognized to possess power to dispense from the prescriptions of the canon law, and the archives of the two main curial offices, the chancery and penitentiary, record the concerns and successes of a steady stream of supplicants: the number of English and Welsh petitioners to the apostolic penitentiary was certainly much greater than the 4,085 recorded in an incomplete set of registers between 1411 and 1503.

Many requests were of a technical and ecclesiastical variety: clergymen sought dispensations to hold benefices in plurality, be ordained to the priesthood despite the canonical bar on illegitimate birth or physical deformity, or receive promotions before the required canonical age. Complex tithe disputes were sometimes referred to Rome for resolution, though in these and other cases authority to rule on the matter was often referred back to judges-delegate in England, and after 1518 were increasingly remitted to Wolsey as papal legate.

Laypeople petitioned the papacy for an equally wide range of permissions and dispensations. These included requests to be released from vows – perhaps rashly made in time of sickness – to go on pilgrimage to the Holy Land, or to live a life of perpetual chastity, a pledge sometimes made by bereaved wives in the emotionally intense first days of widowhood.

Most commonly, it was the business of marriage that impelled laypeople to seek guidance and grace from Rome. Medieval canon law closely regulated pools of potential marriage partners, setting out the just causes why a man and woman might not be joined in holy wedlock. The principal barriers were those of consanguinity (relationship in blood), affinity (a form of kinship created by marriage or sexual relations, preventing union with an 'in-law' or step-relation), and spiritual kinship (the relationship created between godparents and godchildren, and their respective families). The prohibitions were extensive. Consanguinity and affinity applied to the fourth degree; that is, a man and woman might not legally marry if they had a great-great-grandparent in common, or if one of them had previously married, or slept with, a sibling or a first, second or third cousin of the other.[14]

Applied rigidly, the rules severely constricted choice in marriage, for the small worlds of English villages, and for the socially small world of the gentry and aristocracy. But other than in cases of close consanguinity, the Church was generally prepared to dispense from its own rules. Prohibitions so extensive, and frankly difficult to demonstrate or even know about, must often have been quietly ignored. But considerable numbers of laypeople did seek and secure dispensations, in some cases retrospectively, to validate a marriage contracted in ignorance of consanguinal or affinal relationship.

In such ways, the formal legal structures of the Church interacted with the intimate transactions of daily life. The Pope's ability, even at a remove or two, to wave a restorative hand over the messy realities of lived experience subtly reinforced popular awareness of the overarching character of papal authority. In 1490, for example, John Speke and Isabel Beaumond were granted a dispensation to marry, despite the unfortunate circumstance that John had earlier committed fornication with an illegitimate daughter of Isabel's maternal grandfather.[15] Of rather greater interest, at the time and subsequently, was the dispensation granted by Julius II in 1502 to allow Henry, Prince of Wales, to marry Catherine of Aragon, widow of his elder brother, Arthur.

## Crown and Tiara

One layman in particular – the King – had a pronounced interest in the power of the Pope, and in how it might strengthen, sanctify or subvert the sinews of his own authority. Popes and kings had many mutual and compatible interests, and where their interests clashed, there were strong motives and mechanisms for working things out. Periodic quarrels between the King and the Pope, like rain on a Scottish holiday, were things simply to be expected, and they would always pass. Or so it seemed.

The Tudors came to the English throne in 1485 with a strong papal wind at their back. Richard III was unpopular in Rome – a result of his bloody usurpation, and of his outrageous attempt to bastardize the sons of Edward IV with wild assertions about the invalidity of their parents' marriage. Richard also failed to seek a dispensation for his own marriage to Anne Neville, a consanguinal cousin, as well as an affinal sister-in-law. Pointedly, after his victory at Bosworth, Henry VII requested and received a dispensation for his marriage to Edward IV's daughter, Elizabeth of York, to whom he was related in the fourth degree of consanguinity. Crucially, and unusually, Pope Innocent VIII followed this with a bull confirming the legitimacy of any children from the marriage, and of the Act of Parliament that declared Henry's title.

Henry VII valued papal support. In 1487 he successfully requested the Pope to excommunicate Irish bishops who supported the pretender Lambert Simnel. He also reported with satisfaction that after his victory over the rebels at the battle of Stoke, a criminal named John Swit, seeking sanctuary at Westminster, tried spreading a false report of Henry's supposed defeat: 'And what then for the censures of the Church or the powers of the Pontiff? Don't you see that the interdicts have no force, since you have before your eyes the very men who hurl them at you put to flight?' But Swit was instantly struck down dead for his lying and blasphemous words, his body becoming blacker than soot and emitting an unbearable stench.[16]

There was a strong scent of co-operation around Anglo-papal relations in Henry VII's first years. Henry had the 1486 papal bull of dispensation printed as a broadsheet in English translation, with further editions in 1494, 1495 and 1497.[17] Successive popes indulged the English usurper-king, bestowing on him the traditional honours of presentation with a papal cap and sword of maintenance, and an ornamental Golden Rose, as well as graciously dispensing him to eat cheese and eggs during the Lenten fast. The papacy also responded benignly, if cautiously, to Henry's desire to see the last of the direct Lancastrian line, Henry VI, canonized as a saint – excessive sanctity being the only plausible excuse for the disastrous levels of incompetence Henry demonstrated in the exercise of his kingship.

Of more immediate concern were the concessions Henry wrung out of Pope Innocent in 1489 regarding privileges of sanctuary, the long-standing claims of particular churches to provide protection from prosecution to those seeking refuge within their precincts. Henry did not object to sanctuary in principle, but would not tolerate immunity for rebels. He had already hauled out of sanctuary the Yorkist fugitives Humphrey and Thomas Stafford, the judges ruling, controversially but decisively, that rights of sanctuary did not apply to traitors. The Pope agreed that malefactors who left sanctuary could not claim it a second time, and that guards could be posted around sanctuaries to prevent nefarious comings and goings.[18]

For his part, Henry was prepared to invest effort in cultivating good relations with Rome, no fewer than ten English ambassadors arriving to receive an audience with Innocent VIII in 1489. In 1492, Henry established the office of cardinal-protector, a permanent representative of English interests at the curia, and an innovation soon emulated by other European monarchs. The first of the English cardinal-protectors, a reform-minded Sienese prelate, Francesco Piccolomini, was in 1503 elected to the papacy as Pius III, though his death within a month makes it impossible to judge the extent to which his elevation would have paid policy dividends. Henry also bestowed the bishopric of Worcester on the papal officials Giovanni Gigli (1497–8) and his cousin Silvestro (1499–1521). The bishoprics of Hereford (1502) and Bath and Wells (1504) were given to another reliably pro-English papal bureaucrat, Adriano Castellesi. In 1496, in a further nod to the diplomatic importance of Rome, the English hospice there became 'The King's Hospice', Henry assuming the right to appoint its warden from the autonomous confraternity that previously performed the task.[19]

Henry VII's policies could scarcely be described as slavishly enthralled to the Pope. He was dilatory and evasive, for example, in support for the persistent preoccupation of successive popes, a crusade against the Ottoman Turks. Yet, as a pious Christian king, Henry liked to be seen on the side of Christ's vicar; never more so than when the latter was at odds with the English monarchy's old rival, the King of France. In 1496, Henry signed up to membership of the Holy League, an alliance of the Emperor, the King of Aragon, the Venetian Republic, Milan and – supplying the holiness – Pope Alexander VI: a coalition designed to constrain French ambitions in Italy.[20] That Henry himself had no such territorial ambitions undoubtedly made diplomatic relations between England and the papacy less fraught than those between popes and other west European monarchs often were.

There were few signs of any of this changing when, in 1509, following Henry VII's death, the reins of power passed to his seventeen-year-old son. The younger Henry, epitome of a cultivated Renaissance prince, lauded by the humanists Erasmus and More, was if anything still more outwardly pro-papal than his father. English diplomatic ties with Rome were strengthened with the appointment of Christopher Bainbridge, archbishop of York, as permanent ambassador in September 1509. When Bainbridge was elevated to the Sacred

College in March 1511, he became the first English cardinal resident in Rome in more than a hundred years. His principal brief was to foment intrigues against the French.

Papalism and Francophobia were the coffee and cream of early Henrician foreign policy. Henry VIII's adherence to a reconstituted Holy League was celebrated with bonfires and processions in Rome in 1511, and a supportive letter from Henry was read at the second session of the Fifth Lateran Council in May 1512. By then, in emulation of the monarchical heroes of the Hundred Years War, Henry had formally declared war on France. He cited as *casus belli* the 'great sin of the King of France' in seeking to 'lacerate the seamless garment of Christ'. Specially commissioned ballads called upon true Englishmen to help their King 'against the Frenchmen in the field to fight / In the quarrel of the Church and in the right'.[21]

Julius II was eager to embolden the ardent young English sovereign. In the summer of 1511 he sent him a hundred Parmesan cheeses. A probably more motivational gift was the promise, in a secret brief dated 20 March 1512, to strip the Kingdom of France from Louis XII.[22] The Pope was reportedly willing to come to Paris to place the crown on Henry's head. Alas, there was a condition: Henry had actually to defeat Louis before the ruling could take effect. The campaign Henry led in northern France in the summer of 1513 was long on pageantry and bombast, short on practical results.

Still, Henry had continuing hopes of honours beyond the conventional golden rose and papal cap and sword. It was a sore point that his rival of France was *Rex Christianissimus* (the most Christian King), while Ferdinand and Isabella and their successors of Castile and Aragon had been dubbed *Reyes Católicos* (Catholic monarchs) by Alexander VI in 1496, a reward for their role in ruthlessly Christianizing their once multi-faith kingdoms.

Silvestro Gigli worked hard to secure a comparable title for his English master. 'Protector' was considered, but rejected as properly pertaining to the Emperor; likewise 'Defender', a style Julius II had already bestowed on the Swiss. Other ideas were to dub Henry 'Orthodox King', or the 'King Apostolic', on the intriguing grounds that a petitionary prayer for all *apostolicae fidei cultoribus* (guardians of the apostolic faith) occurred in the canon of the mass. But the Pope did not like these suggestions. By January 1516, Gigli had secured a bull for recognition of Henry as *Sanctae Romanae Ecclesiae Defensor* (defender of the Holy Roman Church). But nothing happened on this score, Wolsey suspecting the Pope of having been intimidated into inaction by the French.[23] In the event, Henry was obliged to wait until 1521 to receive his coveted title of *Fidei Defensor* (Defender of the Faith), in recognition of literary efforts against the upstart friar, Martin Luther.

Ironically, the sole gain from Henry's holy little war against the French, the captured Flemish fortress-town of Tournai, precipitated a minor but revealing spat with the papacy. When the French bishop-elect, Louis Guillard, refused to recognize Henry's claim to sovereignty over the territory, Leo X appointed Wolsey administrator of the see, and the rising star of Henry's government strongly pressed his claims to be recognized as bishop. But after the new French King, Francis I, triumphed over Swiss and papal forces at the battle of Marignano in September 1515, Leo was obliged to come to terms with him. Under the December Concordat of Bologna, Leo conceded considerable royal authority over the French Church, and in a secret ruling of August 1516 granted the diocese of Tournai back to Guillard, allowing him to seek military assistance from the French King to re-establish his authority.

When all this emerged, Henry was furious. In a letter to Gigli he fulminated against the Pope for seeking to 'take from us the superiority, regal pre-eminence, jurisdiction and authority that we have in the region and dominion of Tournai'. Henry was dismayed by the ingratitude towards someone who had done so much for the Church, and he hinted darkly about dangers to the Pope if he were to carry on granting bulls 'against the sovereignty of princes'. A more measured, but still angry, letter of protest was despatched to Leo himself.

Much has been made of this affair, though in fact it did not articulate any radical new doctrine of sovereignty, or prefigure claims Henry was to make in 1533–4.[24] The King's grievance was that Leo was acting beyond the scope of his powers in granting 'temporalities' (estates and income) of a bishopric in Henry's territory to someone who was in effect a disobedient subject. The row slowly blew over. Leo protested feebly he had not realized Guillard would refuse to swear allegiance to Henry, and more or less admitted he had been pressured into reversing policy by Francis I. Tournai was returned to the French by the 1518 Treaty of London, and Wolsey accepted a pension of £1,200 a year as compensation for the loss of a diocese he had never properly controlled.[25]

Nonetheless, the episode is revealing about the limits of co-operation between crown and papacy. Both parties derived ideological capital from an amicable and reciprocal relationship of honour and respect. Henry was the pious and dutiful son; Julius, Leo and their successors the benevolent fathers in God. Only a couple of years after the return of Tournai, Henry was lauding the papacy in extravagant terms in his *Defence of the Seven Sacraments* against Luther. Thomas More helped sort out a draft of the text, and, as he later recalled, advised Henry to tone down his high papalism in case it embarrass him in any future political or diplomatic quarrels. But the King apparently retorted that 'we are so much bounden unto the See of Rome that we cannot do too much honour unto it.' Intriguingly, he added this was because 'we have received from that See our crown imperial'.

The remark is typically opaque. Perhaps Henry was acknowledging a debt of gratitude owed for papal support of his father's accession. But his emphasis on an *imperial* crown sounds like he was claiming a relationship of equality and autonomy. The Arthurian legends verified (or rather, invented) as history by medieval chroniclers like Geoffrey of Monmouth, and popularized by Thomas Malory's *Morte D'Arthur*, reported a defining episode. Lucius, Emperor of Rome, demanded tribute from the British King. Arthur acknowledged that the status of empire had devolved on his realm through kings of Britain, such as Constantine, who were also rulers of the Empire. But for that very reason, there was now no requirement for tribute or fealty to Rome. Henry's elder brother, Prince Arthur, never lived to be king, but Arthurianism was in the Tudor life-blood. It was probably in 1516, on the occasion of a royal visit to Winchester, that the Round Table there, believed to be Arthur's own, was repainted, its figure of Arthur given an imperial crown and the features of the young Henry VIII.[26]

Despite all the talk of piety and fatherhood, the King of England and the Pope of Rome made use of each other for political ends. The papacy hoped western pressure would weaken the French hold in northern Italy, while Henry sought a blanket of sanctification to cast over his atavistic ambitions to sit as a crowned king in Paris. Henry's petulance in 1516–17, no less than his gracious-ness in 1521, suggests the contingent and quasi-contractual character of his attachment to the Holy See. To put it more simply, it reveals how Henry VIII was capable of reacting when he didn't get his own way.

### Tax and Benefice

In most practical matters the King did get his own way. His ability to tax the English Church was a case in point. Churchmen were, by papal insistence, exempt from royal taxes imposed on the laity. But English rulers had long since learned the habit of levying parallel demands through Parliament, and through Convocations of the clergy, whenever they needed to raise revenue for defence or other pressing causes. In fact, royal taxation of the clergy increasingly aban-doned the convention of making demands in wartime only, and turned into a regular part of crown income, averaging £7,600 per annum in the fifteenth century, and £9,000 a year (a slight real-terms decrease due to inflation) between 1485 and 1534. Voices of complaint were sometimes raised, but Convocation invariably granted the request and appointed local collectors, generally heads of monastic houses, to implement it.[27]

On top of formal demands for taxation and forced loans, the crown could exact considerable sums (perhaps £3,500 a year) in its guise as feudal overlord of ecclesiastical estates: fees for restitution of temporalities, and – still more profitably – income from the temporalities themselves during vacancy of an episcopal see or major religious house. In addition, there were fees for confir-mation of privileges, and for retention of plural benefices, as well as fines to secure indemnity from a range of offences, real or cooked up.

The Church was emphatically not exempt from Henry VII's notorious 'fiscalism' – his determination, through agents like Edmund Dudley, to scour the crannies and crevices of the law to maximize his income. Between 1504 and 1508, Dudley managed to squeeze over £38,000 from English churchmen, in cash and bonds. For some, it was all too much. Robert Freeman, prior of the Gilbertine house of Shouldham in Norfolk, complained over dinner in 1505 about how the King 'polleth us'. Ominously, he added that, rather than put up with such exactions, he would welcome the return of 'yon gentleman beyond the sea' – the Yorkist claimant, Edmund de la Pole. Other clergy, including the King's almoner, Christopher Urswick, owned copies of a work by an Italian monk, printed in London in 1505, which denounced encroachment on the goods of the Church.

Such grumbling availed little, and there was scant support for it in Rome, which depended on the co-operation of the English crown to levy its own taxation in England. Religious houses with papal privileges paid a small regular charge for them, and payments known as annates were due from clergymen on first appointment to their benefices. In addition, laypeople were liable to contribute to the annual levy sent to Rome, known colloquially as Peter's Pence. All of these charges between them amounted to an average of £4,816 a year in the early sixteenth century, barely two-fifths of what the crown was taking annually from the Church in England.[28]

More significant even than taxation, the papacy had sold the pass over appointment of clergy to English benefices. Papal rights to override the wishes of the patron had long been challenged by the crown, and popes de facto conceded restrictions that were spelled out in the 1351 Statute of Provisors. The most important benefices – the bishoprics – remained in theory a matter of papal provision. Newly appointed bishops were required to take an oath of obedience to the Pope, and, in principle, to attend personally in Rome. In practice, these obligations were regularly fudged to the King's advantage. Weakened by the Great Schism, and anxious for political support against conciliarists and rival Italian powers, successive popes simply provided to English bishoprics whomever the King nominated. The pattern was so taken for granted that the crown regularly bestowed the temporalities of the see on its nominees before formal ratification by the papacy. The requirement to visit Rome became a formality, performed by proxies.

In important and obvious public respects the English and Welsh bishops were servants of two masters. They were bound to the Pope by oath, and, according to many reputable theologians, were directly dependent on the papacy for spiritual authority: the Pope delegated power and jurisdiction to bishops, just as St Peter had to the other apostles. But bishops were also feudal subjects of the King, doing homage for the temporalities of their sees. It was standard practice for episcopal oaths of obedience to the King to renounce clauses in the papal bull of provision to the bishopric that could be regarded as prejudicial to the rights of the crown.[29]

The power to nominate bishops, and exercise patronage at a variety of levels in the Church, mattered to Henry VII and Henry VIII for a variety of reasons, good and not so good. As major landowners, bishops were figures of real social and political power, and as 'lords spiritual' they sat in the Upper House of Parliament along with a comparable number of mitred abbots. The crown could do little to change or influence inheritance patterns among the aristocracy. But it could at least try to ensure their ecclesiastical equivalents were politically reliable and more than minimally competent, a combination particularly desirable for the troubled border regions of the north. The Wars of the Roses were an object lesson in the dangers of 'bastard feudal' power exercised by 'overmighty subjects'. Bishops did not found dynasties, and their followings were often dependably linked to the crown's own webs of patronage and favour.

Those nominated to bishoprics had usually already proved loyal and effective in royal service. Their appointment ensured that the coffers of the Church, rather than the crown, were an immediate source of incentive and reward for high-flying administrators. It was no accident that high offices of state had long tended to be bestowed on churchmen. Lord Keepership of the Privy Seal was held between 1485 and 1523 by Peter Courtenay, bishop of Exeter, Richard Fox, bishop of Winchester, and Thomas Ruthall, bishop of Durham; the Lord Chancellorship over the same period resided in the hands of Thomas Rotherham, archbishop of York, John Alcock, bishop of Worcester, three successive archbishops of Canterbury (John Morton, Henry Deane and William Warham), and Thomas Wolsey, archbishop of York.[30]

It was, in a sense, blatant exploitation. But the Church benefited too from having capable administrators. It is questionable whether a papacy granted free rein in the matter, and subject to the pleading of a plethora of suitors, would have managed to select candidates of comparable talent and dedication.

In the main, the early Tudor bishops deserve the positive reputation they have accrued with modern historians. They were virtually without exception graduates, mostly in law rather than theology. Hardly any of them showed blatant disregard for their priestly obligation to celibacy. James Stanley, the anomalously aristocratic bishop of Ely, and Thomas Wolsey are the exceptions here. Also out of character were the couple of sees held by the almost permanently absentee Italians, and the tenure of York by the curial Cardinal Bainbridge, who was literally never there.

Other bishops were non-resident for considerable periods, but most made an effort to return when they could. As archbishop of Canterbury (1504–32), William Warham resided only a third of the year there; yet others like Richard Nykke of Norwich (1501–35), Hugh Oldham of Exeter (1505–19) and Nicholas West of Ely (1515–33) all managed to spend around three-quarters of their time in their dioceses. Even absentees generally felt a strong sense of obligation to ensure the diocese was competently managed, working through assistant or suffragan bishops for spiritual tasks like ordinations and confirmations, and through commissaries and diocesan chancellors for administrative ones.[31]

The pastoral aspects of episcopal office, and the plethora of legal, administrative, political and diplomatic responsibilities it also involved, nonetheless sometimes chafed. William Smith, bishop of Lincoln, petitioned Henry VII in vain to be allowed to give up his duties as a member of Prince Arthur's Council governing the Marches of Wales, in order to see to the needs of his diocese: its neglected state 'runneth in my mind both day and night'. Richard Fox, bishop successively of Exeter, Bath and Wells, Durham and Winchester, tirelessly served Henry VII and Henry VIII as Lord Privy Seal for nearly thirty years. His sometime chaplain, the humanist monk Richard Whitford, remarked to Thomas More that the bishop was one that 'to serve the King's turn, will not stick to agree to his own father's death'.

But by 1516, Fox had had enough. He resigned his offices, writing to Wolsey that to continue 'to serve worldly' would mean 'the damnation of my soul'. He now intended to devote himself to the running of his diocese 'whereby I may do some satisfaction for twenty-eight years negligence'. John Fisher, though never a major office-holder of state, still felt the pressures acutely. In a speech to a synod of bishops summoned by Wolsey in 1519, Fisher complained of an unrelenting burden of secular business on the clergy:

> For sundry times when I have settled and fully bent myself to the care of my flock committed unto me, to visit my diocese, to govern my church and to answer the enemies of Christ, straightways hath come a messenger for one cause or other sent from higher authority by whom I have been called to other business . . .[32]

## Cardinal Legate

Fisher's speech, and Fox's resignation letter, contained barely hidden barbs. Their target was the unparalleled accumulation of spiritual and secular authority resting in the hands of Thomas Wolsey. One of the most written-about figures of early Tudor history, Wolsey remains in many respects an enigma. Some see him as a serious reformer, others as the epitome of moral and ecclesiastical corruption. There is disagreement too over whether he was widely hated, or whether most of the secular and ecclesiastical establishment managed to work with him effectively and amiably, only turning pack-like against him after his fall from royal favour in 1529. Most of all, historians ask whether his ascendancy over the Church was a warning cloud of a coming storm, or a period of constructive stability, knocked off the rails by unforeseeable events.[33]

There had been powerful cardinal-ministers before: Henry Beaufort in Henry VI's reign, Thomas Bourchier in Edward IV's, John Morton under Henry VII. Nor did Wolsey's lowly social origins make him exceptional – the Church always provided for the talented and ambitious a meritocratic entry scheme to the corridors of power. What made Wolsey unusual, and unusually powerful, was his delegated papal authority, his legateship.

It was as resident legate that Wolsey could override the exemptions of privileged religious orders, convoke an impromptu reform synod of bishops of Canterbury province (1519), or summon a Convocation of the clergy of York in 1518 to codify canon law and issue decrees against clerical absenteeism and (somewhat hypocritically) the keeping of mistresses. It was as legate that Wolsey received petitions and issued dispensations in cases reserved to the judgement of the Holy See. And as legate that he could cut across the demarcated structures of the English Church, imposing his authority without respect of difference on the provinces of York (of which he happened also to be archbishop), and of Canterbury, the 'primatial' see, of whose possession only the stubborn longevity of Archbishop William Warham (c. 1450–1532) managed to deprive him.

By 1522, Wolsey had set up his own legatine court, staffed it with aggressively efficient church lawyers, and claimed precedence in testamentary cases. Warham was not alone among the bishops in feeling resentful, and tensions were only partially resolved when in 1524 Wolsey agreed to a series of compositions with the bishops, which in effect allowed them to purchase back the ordinary episcopal authority his legateship had taken away from them.

The bishops, like the secular nobles, were capable of courteous co-operation with the cardinal-minister in the course of carrying out their duties. In truth, they had little choice, for Wolsey was first and last the King's man, and his actions, even when they seemed arrogant or self-aggrandizing, nearly always had behind them the warm, scented breeze of royal favour. It was as a result of Henry's petitioning that Leo X created Wolsey a cardinal in 1515, and in 1518 appointed him legate. The stated reasons were, of course, laudable ones: in January 1520, Henry complained to Leo that the time-limit imposed on Wolsey's legateship was making it difficult for him to 'to proceed with greater vigour in the reformation of the clergy'.[34] In 1524, a second cultured Medici pope, Leo's cousin Clement VII, was reluctantly persuaded to extend Wolsey's legatine powers indefinitely.

Henry VIII was neither perverse nor unique in this scarcely concealed sleight of hand. Prior to his dramatic falling-out with the warrior-pope, Louis XII of France persuaded Julius II to provide, and then extend, sweeping legatine powers for Georges, Cardinal d'Amboise. Around the same time, Emperor Maximilian I negotiated hard to try to secure a permanent legateship a latere for his minister, Cardinal Matthias Lang.[35]

In all these cases, popes were colluding in an erosion of their ability to control the day-to-day running of national churches. There was nothing in this pointing inexorably towards heresy, schism or separation. On the contrary, here was a pattern for local centralization and streamlining of church institutions, under remote papal auspices and immediate royal stewardship, to bring about the meaningful structural changes reformers had long prayed for, but which were always prevented by the power of vested and sectional interests. The perfect medicinal partnership of a pious Catholic ruler and an energetic reforming prelate, blessed from a distance by the therapeutic authority of the Pope, could shake off the lethargy afflicting the body of Christ, and provide inoculation against more radical, doctrinal solutions to that body's ills. Something of the sort did happen in Spain, a country whose lack of enthusiasm for Lutheran reforms was in part a legacy of the immense spiritual and political authority wielded by the gaunt Franciscan reformer, Cardinal Cisneros, and the trust reposed in him by the 'Catholic monarchs' Isabella and Ferdinand.[36]

In England, this potential for systematic local reform in head and members never came to fruition. Wolsey's reform initiatives were fitful and erratic, more often concerned with scoring points against rivals and subordinates, and with justifying retention of his legateship, than with change and renewal for its own sake. His incursions into the authority of fellow prelates encouraged an unhealthy preoccupation on their part with the defence of sectional rights and privileges. And in a culture that looked for clergymen, even bishops, to be exemplars of holiness, Wolsey's worldliness underlined a failure of inspirational leadership for which the Church would pay a heavy price.

Henry, meanwhile, was a pious enough Catholic ruler, but his priorities were elsewhere, principally in the resolve, inherited from his father, to secure dynastic and political authority at home, and in a determination, departing from his father's concerns, to cut an imposing figure on the European stage. Henry was eager for churchmen to assist him in realizing these objectives; when they asserted and pursued priorities of their own, his patience with them waned.

## Common Law and Canon Law

In 1515, the year of Wolsey's elevation to the Sacred College, rival understandings of what was meant by 'reform' came into open conflict. Churchmen threw out accusations of heresy at laymen and at each other; lawyers fulminated against abuses committed in the name of ecclesiastical jurisdiction. In the end, the King forced his new cardinal to seek mercy on his knees for the infractions of the Church, and sententiously declared that 'Kings of England in time past have never had any superior but God alone'.[37]

The origins of the 1515 crisis lie in the existence of parallel systems of justice and jurisdiction. For centuries, royal courts had applied and adjudicated the

body of legal authority known as 'common law', the mass of acknowledged precedent and established procedure that provided a necessary complement to the
relatively few matters explicitly defined by parliamentary statute. The common
law was administered in the central courts of King's Bench, Common Pleas, and
the Exchequer, meeting at Westminster Hall, and it radiated to the localities
through assize courts presided over in the shires by itinerant royal justices, and
through regular quarter sessions and petty sessions convened by amateur
justices of the peace. The professional common lawyers were trained at the
London Inns of Court, alternative centres of learning to the clerically dominated universities.[38]

The church courts, by contrast, were components of a Europe-wide pyramid
of justice, capped by the papal curia in Rome. Within England, cases could
come before the archbishop of Canterbury's Prerogative Court (and briefly,
Wolsey's Legatine Court), consistory courts convened by bishops in their
dioceses, or commissary courts to which they delegated authority, and at the
lowest level the courts presided over by archdeacons in their archdeaconries. In
addition, there were courts hearing cases from 'peculiar' jurisdictions, such as
parishes administered by the dean and chapter of certain cathedrals. The canon
law underpinning these courts was an amalgam of long-established compilations of decisions or canons of popes and church councils, and of rulings by
English provincial synods and Convocations.[39]

In theory, lines of demarcation between the two laws were clear. Canon law
concerned itself with matters of faith and morals: detection of heresy, regulation
of marriage, punishment of moral offences like adultery and fornication. It also
covered the internal running of the Church, and business relating to the conduct
of its personnel. Other matters of criminal or civil litigation fell within the
purview of the common law. In practice there were significant grey and shady
areas across which litigants and lawyers could wander more or less at will.

Wills and testaments were one such area. Testamentary matters (excluding
the transfer of land) were part of spiritual preparation for death, and thus
administered by the Church. But where disputed bequests revolved around
matters of property, or where debts owed to or by the deceased were at issue,
both secular and ecclesiastical courts could claim an interest. A similar conflation of categories pertained in a sphere that seemed clearly ecclesiastical – the
rights of appointment to benefices. But because advowsons were regarded as a
property right, cases relating to them were heard principally in common law
courts. There was a drift towards the common law too in cases of slander and
defamatory words. Defamation was a spiritual crime, punishable in the church
courts. But where the motivation of the plaintiff was to seek damages, or where
the accusation was one of theft (a felony) rather than fornication or adultery
(a sin), there was a standing invitation to take cases to secular courts. Conversely,
cases involving unpaid petty debts, an apparently civil matter, were increasingly

in the later fifteenth century heard in front of the courts Christian. The rationale was that the breach of faith was a spiritual offence – perjury – and payment of the debt a necessary restitution of charity.

The situation was not a free-for-all. Judges in both secular and ecclesiastical courts sometimes directed cases to the other jurisdiction, and pragmatic co-existence was often the order of the day. In a 'reading' (lecture on a legal topic) given at Gray's Inn in 1514, the common lawyer John Hales suggested the temporal and spiritual jurisdictions were like two swords, each of which should assist the other. For litigants, ambiguity about spheres of competence could represent good news, allowing them to take cases where they thought justice would be cheapest, fastest, and most likely to work in their favour.

The idea – once widespread among historians – that church courts were deeply unpopular, intrinsically intrusive, oppressive and extortionate institutions, has little to recommend it. Few, then as now, enjoyed going to court, or having to pay fees to officials and lawyers. But in their 'instance' business – that is, cases brought at the suit of an interested party – the ecclesiastical courts were often relatively cheap and efficient. 'Office' or disciplinary cases, brought by the courts on their own authority, were scarcely likely to be welcomed by the targets. But other laypeople may well have been happy to see fornicators, slanderers or notorious tithe-dodgers brought to book, and made to do public penance – clad in a sheet and bearing a lighted candle – for sins against God and their neighbours.[40]

If rivalry between practitioners of canon and common law was not ruthlessly unremitting, it was nonetheless fairly endemic, and growing rather than lessening in intensity. Common lawyers, however personally pious, were professionally and ideologically conditioned to resent the Church's legal privileges, and to assert the intrinsic superiority of common and statute law.[41] Two factors operated in their favour. Firstly, common lawyers could usually assume the crown was predisposed to support their side of the argument. Secondly, in disputing the Church's claims, they had an overarching legal and statutory principle to which they could appeal.

This was the offence of *praemunire*, codified in statutes of 1353, 1365 and 1393. When an action of praemunire was brought, the indictment ominously charged the accused with 'scheming to disinherit the King and his crown'. Praemunire – the term derives from the wording of the royal writ despatched to the sheriff, *praemunire facias* – that you forewarn (X to appear in court) – was a potent legal instrument, designed to prevent appeals from an English court to one outside the King's jurisdiction. The original purpose was to prevent unwarranted papal interference with the exercise of royal administration and justice. It was not intended to prevent appeals from English courts to Rome, deny the legitimate claims of canon law, or impede the operations of church courts in England.

Yet loose drafting in the 1393 statute, referring to people suing 'in the court of Rome or other places', allowed praemunire to be increasingly used to inhibit cases in English ecclesiastical courts, if lawyers could argue they belonged rightfully in royal ones. This particularly related to landed property, advowsons and debts, areas where the activities of ecclesiastical courts had expanded during the unsettled middle decades of the fifteenth century. Moreover, in 1462, Edward IV, newly and uneasily seated on the throne, issued a 'Charter of Liberties' to the Church, offering concessions on tithes, and guarantees to the clergy of immunity from praemunire actions and citation before secular courts. The charter, although confirmed in 1483 by Richard III, never delivered half as much as it promised. But it was a potent symbol of the flowering of ecclesiastical liberties, a plant Henry VII and his son were eager to see pruned.[42]

Common lawyers sat high in Henry VII's counsels, among them Sir James Hobart, the King's attorney general, and a member of the debt-enforcement agency known euphemistically as 'the Council Learned in the Law'. As a landowner and prominent justice of the peace in Norfolk and Suffolk, Hobart egged individuals on to praemunire actions in pursuit of their personal interests. The process was facilitated by a 1495 act allowing JPs at quarter sessions to hear information relating to offences under any statute. As attorney general, Hobart transferred numbers of these cases to King's Bench, and co-ordinated presentments (falling just short of formal praemunire charges) against the bishop of Norwich, Richard Nykke. In the face of all this, the church courts' business, at least in some regions, began to retract. Official encouragement of praemunire actions continued under Hobart's successor, John Ernley, another member of the Council Learned. As a London chronicler observed, under Henry VII, 'bishops and many other of the spiritualty' were 'vexed full uncharitably and full grievously'.[43]

Another of the lawyer-enforcers on the Council Learned was Edmund Dudley. He believed it was a royal prerogative to step in and reform matters whenever 'any manner of grudge' arose between the King's 'subjects of the spiritualty and his subjects of the temporalty, for privileges or liberties'.[44]

The guise of neutral arbiter was disingenuous, for the King was usually disposed to allow erosion of the 'liberties' of the Church, which, almost by definition, interfered with his own untrammelled exercise of authority. Through the 1490s and beyond, judicial rulings by chief justices Sir William Hussey and Sir John Fineux chipped away at rights of sanctuary. The issue came forcefully to public notice in 1516, when John Pauncefote, a Gloucestershire JP, was murdered on his way to the sessions, and one of the killers, Sir John Savage, took refuge at the Priory of St John of Jerusalem at Clerkenwell. Savage was forcibly removed from the sanctuary, but at the ensuing trial he alleged the priory's title to it through papal grant and long customary usage. Justice Fineux argued, however, that all privileges and immunities originated from the King, and laid down that no church could offer more than the customary forty days of sanctuary without a specific confirmation of the supposed privilege by a judge. Royal permission, not ancient custom or papal grant, was to be the basis for the sanctuary offered by the great ecclesiastical 'liberties'.

Coming before the royal council in November 1519, the Savage case provided another occasion for Henry VIII to expatiate on the abuses of ecclesiastical authority, and his own obligation to direct and reform it. He could not imagine the old kings and holy fathers who established the sanctuary of Westminster Abbey ever intended it 'to serve for voluntary murder and larceny done outside the sanctuary in hope of returning ... and so I will have that reformed which is encroached by abuse, and have the matter reduced to the true intent of the making thereof'.[45] It was the kind of statement Henry would make again in the future, about matters much more fundamental than the sanctuary rights of Westminster.

## Benefit of Clergy

Another privilege widely believed to have been 'encroached by abuse' was the right of clerics to avoid punishment by secular courts: so-called benefit of clergy. This was a principle hallowed by the blood of England's premier martyr-saint. In the later twelfth century, in defiance of King Henry II, Thomas Becket gave his life for the conviction that churchmen must not submit to judgement by the laity. By the later fifteenth century, as with other areas of dispute, the problem was not so much with the core principle as with its application in particular cases.

The privilege extended not just to priests, but also to clerks in so-called 'minor orders', some of whom had no intention of proceeding to ordination as a priest. Still more anomalous was the conventional mechanism for 'pleading one's clergy' upon conviction, and thus removing oneself from a secular to an ecclesiastical court for punishment. This was to demonstrate the ability to read. It might once have made sense to regard the skill as a unique and defining characteristic of a 'clerk'. But long before the turn of the sixteenth century it had come to look like a loophole through which literate laymen might leap to evade the consequences of their misdeeds. Church courts could not impose the death penalty, as clergymen were canonically banned from the shedding of blood. Offenders might have to endure lengthy periods of imprisonment, but they could expect to regain their freedom, along with, potentially, the ability to reoffend.

Such concerns prompted a tightening up. A 1489 Act of Parliament restricted full benefit of clergy to men actually in orders; others could claim it only once, and were to be branded on the thumb to prevent any second attempts. A subsequent act in 1497 removed the privilege entirely from deserters from royal armies, and those convicted of 'petty treason' (i.e.

murdering a master or employer); high treason against the crown had always been considered outside its scope. Benefit of clergy was considered again by the Parliament of 1512, when a clutch of further heinous offences was added to the list for which it could not be claimed by anyone other than bona fide clergymen: murder or other felonies committed on the open highway, in a church or other sacred place, or in a private dwelling.

This act proved astonishingly controversial. In its original drafting, it planned to restrict pleading of clergy for these offences to clerks in the three 'major orders' of sub-deacon, deacon and priest, and deny it to those in the four preliminary minor orders, reception of which did not involve laying on of hands by a bishop, or authority to perform any significant sacramental functions. Men in minor orders were always allowed to marry.

Perhaps, parliamentarians feared, career criminals were taking minor orders as an insurance policy against the penalties of the 1489 statute. But in canon law – and in the perception of rights-conscious churchmen – major or minor, clerks were clerks. The explicit redefinition was dropped from the final version of the bill, though a cloud of ambiguity hovered over exemption for 'such as be within holy orders'. Were minor orders 'holy' or not? Opposition, particularly from abbots and bishops in the Lords, likely explains why the act was to be in force only until the next Parliament, when its provisions were to be renewed or reviewed.[46]

What, from one perspective, looked like the stamping out of abuses felt from another like a trampling on the rights and traditions of the Church. In a sermon preached at Paul's Cross in 1497, at a time when Parliament was enacting a relatively minor curtailment of benefit of clergy, Bishop Alcock of Ely defiantly appropriated the words of the psalmist: 'touch not my priests'. People would say the English bishops (in Parliament) had given their consent for alterations to the law on benefit of clergy. But in Alcock's view, they could not give such consent, 'and such that did so be accursed'.

This was fighting talk, arising from a conviction that the Church of Christ was a single family, looking to the See of Rome as its mother, with liberties given by Christ not to this or that particular national Church, but to all as one. To believe Alcock – a generally level-headed educational reformer and royal administrator – martyrdom and persecution lurked just around the corner: 'it is to presume, brethren, that [if] Saint Thomas of Canterbury were now living, they which directly now do against the liberties of the Church would put him to death again'.[47]

Complaints that the liberties of the Church were under threat, and demands they be restored, were raised in the Convocation of 1504. About the same time, Bishop Nykke of Norwich penned an irate letter to Warham, his frustration with Hobart's encouragement of praemunire suits having finally boiled over. The attorney general, said Nykke, was nothing less than 'the enemy of God and his Church'. The bishop declared his intention to 'curse [excommunicate] all such promoters and maintainers of the praemunire in such cases as heretics and not-believers in Christ's Church'.[48]

Warham seems to have talked him out of this precipitate course of action. But bitterness over the treatment of the Church was palpable, and not confined to die-hard conservatives like Nykke. Christopher Urswick was a leading clerical servant of Henry VII, and a friend and patron of humanists, who once presented Erasmus with the welcome gift of a dependable horse. But as dean of St George's Chapel, Windsor, he opposed Henry VII's removal of the remains of Henry VI to Westminster Abbey, regarding it as an intolerable infringement on the liberties of his church. Urswick was a professed admirer of Becket's stance, and the owner of various texts protesting against past royal mistreatments of the Church, and implicitly criticizing present ones.[49]

There were high hopes among churchmen in 1509 that with the accession of Henry VIII the injustices suffered by the Church would abate. At the opening of the new Parliament in January 1510, Archbishop Warham's sermon urged the new King to dispense justice fairly and respect good laws made by his ancestors. Warham's mandate summoning delegates to the concurrent Convocation was less mealy mouthed. It spoke of a pressing need to defend the rights of the Church from machinations of 'malicious and wicked men'. Shortly afterwards, a bill 'for the liberties of the English Church' was introduced into the Lords; perhaps an attempt to secure confirmation for Edward IV's Charter of 1462. The bill seems to have been so heavily amended in the Commons that it was dropped by its sponsors. Determined to recover lost ground, judges in the ecclesiastical courts of Canterbury began in 1511 to order the repayment of debts by convicted parties in breach of faith cases, a practice effectively halted by the sustained pressure of praemunire actions during the previous reign.[50] The resurfacing of benefit of clergy as an issue in Parliament the following year showed there had been no real turning of the tide.

In facing these challenges, the Church did not divide between 'progressives' urging reform, and 'conservatives' defending traditional privilege. Rather, the causes of reform and church liberties were seen as intrinsically linked. Colet's excoriating sermon to Convocation in February 1512 was made at a time of 'contradiction of the laypeople'. Yet it was no part of Colet's solution that the Church should surrender any part of its jurisdictional power. His concern, rather, was for that power to be wielded more effectively and with greater moral authority.

A sermon made at the opening of the 1514 Convocation by Dr John Taylor, royal chaplain and clerk of the House of Lords, drew the same conclusion. Like Colet and other clerical reformers, Taylor denounced the idleness of monks, and the dissolute lives of secular clergy. But he drew a strong connection between reform of the Church and defence of its liberties; reform was essential so that priests might no longer be 'sold publically in fetters by the secular power, like condemned criminals'. Taylor warned his audience that 'little by little the laity were encroaching, serpent-like, upon ecclesiastical dominion', and he urged them to emulate predecessors who had stood by their rights, even with 'the parade of death before their eyes'.[51]

In February 1515, as Parliament met at Westminster, and Convocation reconvened at St Paul's, another churchman with strong reforming credentials determined to speak out. Richard Kidderminster, Benedictine abbot of Winchcombe, and latterly a nominated delegate to the Fifth Lateran Council, took to the pulpit at Paul's Cross to preach on the text Bishop Alcock interpreted in the same place nearly two decades earlier: Psalm 105, 'Touch not mine Anointed'.

Kidderminster's sermon was an uncompromising assertion of the principles behind benefit of clergy, and an attack on the act of 1512, due to come up for renewal before the new Parliament. This law was contrary to the Word of God, and those who passed it rendered themselves liable to excommunication. Addressing the ambiguity in the wording of the statute, Kidderminster declared it to be a fundamental principle that *all* clerics were in 'holy orders', and that any attempt to deny benefit of clergy to minor orders was inherently sinful. Steeling Kidderminster's resolve was the fact Rome had recently spoken.

In May 1514, during the ninth session of the Fifth Lateran Council, Leo X issued the bull *Supernae dispositionis arbitrio*. It was an ambitious reforming decree, proposing an overhaul of the lifestyle and duties of cardinals, tighter regulation of church appointments, and a crackdown on a range of abuses from blasphemy to the holding of incompatible benefices. It also emphatically reaffirmed the Church's established position that 'human and divine law give laymen no control over ecclesiastical persons'.[52]

Rome's position, which Kidderminster endorsed, was that clergymen should not even be tried, let alone sentenced, in secular courts. But the intensity of the furore provoked by his comments, which precipitated a white-hot political crisis, is explicable only in the light of preceding events in London, and the unfortunate fate of a merchant named Richard Hunne.

### Richard Hunne, Heretic

The circumstances surrounding the arrest, imprisonment and death of Hunne are as convoluted as they were controversial.[53] In February 1511, Hunne's wife gave birth to a baby boy, and most likely died after the delivery, for the child was sent to the care of a wet-nurse in the parish of St Mary Matfelon, Whitechapel. Five weeks later the boy himself died, a second personal tragedy for Hunne, but a common enough occurrence in the unforgiving conditions of the early sixteenth century. The rector of the parish, Thomas Dryfield, then demanded the cloth the child had been christened in as a mortuary, the customary payment due to the incumbent on the death of a parishioner, technically as recompense for forgotten tithes. Mortuaries – usually the best or second-best animal, or in towns, the best item of clothing – were in principle generally accepted, though they could be an unpopular tax, particularly if they were claimed cumulatively, or with threats to withhold rites of burial.

Hunne, however, took an unusual stand: a principled refusal to pay. His argument seems to have been that, not possessing property of its own, the child was not liable for the tax. He may also have made something of the fact that Dryfield was not incumbent of the parish where Hunne himself resided. Dryfield's demand for the chrisom-cloth was not unlawful, but it was unquestionably tactless. Priests did not usually insist on their rights in this matter, particularly in light of the well-established custom of burying deceased infants in their baptismal cloths as a symbol of innocence and purity.[54]

Perhaps the matter might have been quietly forgotten. But Hunne got into a dispute with another clergyman, the rector of St Michael Cornhill, over damage caused by a fire in the tenement of a friend for whom Hunne stood surety. To the clannish community of London city clergy, in light of ongoing fiscal pressures on them, and the assault on clerical immunities brewing in Parliament, Hunne looked like a dangerous troublemaker – one of those laymen who, as Christopher Urswick bemoaned in a letter to Thomas Goldstone, prior of Canterbury, sought to undermine the Church's discipline to mask their own misconduct, and whose 'detestable greed' was depriving the Church of bequests and donations.[55]

Dryfield started proceedings against Hunne in April 1512 in the Archbishop's Court of Audience. In May, Warham's chancellor, the urbane and learned Cuthbert Tunstall, found on Dryfield's behalf, but Hunne stuck to his principles and refused to hand over the christening cloth. On 27 December 1512, Hunne went to attend vespers at St Mary Matfelon. Dryfield's chaplain, Henry Marshall, refused to commence service while Hunne was in the church, saying 'thou art accursed and thou standest accursed, and therefore go thou out of the church'.

Marshall was claiming that, as an excommunicate, Hunne was barred from the sacraments and from society and fellowship of the faithful. Hunne had not yet, however, been formally excommunicated for non-compliance with the court's order, and his response was to bring a suit for defamation of character against Marshall. Pointedly, he did so not in an ecclesiastical court, but in the secular tribunal of King's Bench, on the grounds his business had been damaged by Marshall's words, and merchants with whom he usually dealt would not now trade with him. Hunne launched a second legal action in King's Bench against Dryfield, Marshall, and several officials of the church court, alleging that the initial action against him was an offence under the statute of praemunire.

This was a considerable escalation, guaranteed to raise the hackles of his opponents. It seems a disproportionate response to what was at stake in the mortuary case, unless Hunne was seeking to make legal and political points. Like the slander action, the praemunire suit was repeatedly adjourned, and never came to a conclusion, so it is now impossible to know what Hunne's stated grounds for it were. Perhaps he argued that, as matters involving property, mortuaries should not come within purview of the courts Christian. Or perhaps that the entire system of ecclesiastical justice represented a foreign jurisdiction impugning the rights of the King of England. If so, that was a radical, and perhaps desperate, claim. Thomas More, at that time Undersheriff of London, and someone who later claimed he knew the matter 'from top to toe', thought Hunne was a man possessed by 'the spirit of pride', 'set on the glory of a victory, which he hoped to have in his praemunire'. Among friends, Hunne boasted of his boldness and said he trusted to be remembered long after his death, and that in the annals of law his action should be called 'Hunne's case'.[56]

More had another explanation of events: Hunne was 'detected of heresy before the praemunire sued or thought upon'. His suit was a diversionary tactic, to slow or halt heresy investigations against him.[57] That Hunne was already marked out as a suspected heretic is by no means implausible, and would cast a different light on Marshall's heated reaction to his presence in church. In any case, on 14 October 1514 Hunne was arrested on charges of heresy by order of Richard Fitzjames, bishop of London. He was housed in the Lollards' Tower, the episcopal prison on the south side of the entrance to St Paul's Cathedral. On 2 December, Hunne was brought before Fitzjames, and charged with various offences, including speaking up for a heresy suspect, attacking tithes, denouncing priests and bishops as 'scribes and pharisees that did crucify Christ', and possessing forbidden English translations of the gospels, epistles and Book of the Apocalypse.

Two days later, Hunne was found hanging from his belt, attached to an iron staple in his cell. Judging him to have committed suicide, the Church proceeded with the case against him – death brought no exemption from charges of heresy. A sermon was preached against him at Paul's Cross on 10 December 1514, and at a trial beginning the following day, and attended by Wolsey and Bishop Smith of Lincoln, as well as Fitzjames, Hunne was pronounced guilty. On 16 December, he was formally condemned as a heretic, and on 20 December, the matter having been properly 'signified' to the secular authorities, his body was exhumed and burned.

Meanwhile, as always with suspicious deaths, a coroner's inquest was instigated, and a jury of citizens was despatched to view Hunne's body in the Lollards' Tower. The state of the corpse, and other details concerning the girdle and the stool on which Hunne supposedly stood, convinced the jurors he had been murdered. Those responsible were named: Fitzjames's chancellor, William Horsey, and two low-ranking functionaries, John Spalding, bell-ringer of St Paul's, and Charles Joseph, the bishop's former summoner. Joseph made a clumsy attempt to flee, and supplied a confession implicating the others. They were duly indicted in King's Bench and imprisoned – though everyone was acutely aware that should Horsey be convicted, he would be able to plead his clergy and escape execution.

The waters of this lake of suspicion and accusation are too murky for us ever to know what lies at its bottom. Premeditated murder on Chancellor Horsey's orders seems unlikely, not least due to the absence of plausible motive – the wheels of ecclesiastical justice were already in full motion, and steaming towards a conviction. Joseph – who had been dismissed as summoner by Horsey in October 1514 – seems an unreliable witness, though as a named co-defendant in Hunne's praemunire suit he may have entertained an animus against the merchant. It is possible Hunne was killed, accidentally or angrily, by Joseph and Spalding during a roughing-up in his cell, and that they attempted to make the death look like a suicide. But it is also conceivable that Thomas More and the church authorities were right in insisting Hunne took his own life, and no conspiracy was involved.

What is not in doubt is that Hunne's death caused a sensation, or that it was widely believed he had been slain at the behest of the clergy. Polydore Vergil, a papal official resident in London, wrote to Bishop Castellesi of Bath and Wells in March 1515 to report that 'a heretic has been put to death by the Bishop of London and created great outcry'.[58] The King ordered the royal council to undertake a thorough inquiry, and in the spring of 1515 bills were introduced in Parliament to restore to Hunne's children the property forfeited to the crown as a result of his heresy conviction, and to pursue a murder charge whatever the crown's inquiry decided on. In London there was a widespread suspicion, later to become an article of faith among Protestant writers, that Hunne was made a heretic because he had dared to sue the praemunire.[59]

The clergy did little to allay it, revealing a defensive mind-set sharpened by years of friction with common lawyers. In the midst of the furore, Bishop Nykke learned that people in Ipswich were claiming 'no bishop within his diocese shall reserve the absolution of any certain crime to himself'. Nykke's response was to write to the bailiffs, warning them that this 'savours of heresy'. Meanwhile, Bishop Fitzjames wrote in frustration to Wolsey of his certainty that 'if my chancellor be tried by any twelve men in London, they be so mali-ciously set in *favorem hereticae pravitatis*, that is, are so set upon the favour of heresy, that they will cast and condemn my clerk, though he were as innocent as Abel.' This was a serious slur upon the good name of the citizenry, and somehow the letter's contents were leaked. On 17 April 1515 the Court of Aldermen sent a deputation to have words with the bishop 'for certain perilous and heinous words as be surmised by him to be spoken of the whole body of the City touching heresy'.[60]

This was the poisoned atmosphere through which Richard Kidderminster passed to ascend the pulpit at Paul's Cross, there to assert, in all circumstances, the immunity of clerics from secular judgement, and to accuse members of the last Parliament of having committed an offence against God in passing the 1512 statute. Members of the new Parliament took exception, and petitioned the King to call a conference to review the issue. A meeting was convened at Blackfriars in February 1515, at which Kidderminster defended his position against a combative and effective spokesman for the 'temporalty'. This was Dr Henry Standish, a robust Lancashire man and popular court preacher, Warden of the London Grey Friars, and Provincial of the (Conventual) Franciscans in England. The debate touched on old fault-lines within the Church: bishops were impatient of the independence of the friars, as friars were resentful of the power, and perceived pomp and pride, of the bishops. Liberties of the Church was one hot-button issue at the Fifth Lateran Council; the autonomy of the friars was another.[61]

Standish argued that the 1512 statute was lawful and that the established custom of bringing criminous clerks before a secular judge contradicted neither divine law nor the liberties of the Church. Papal decrees that clergymen should not even appear before secular tribunals had never been formally received in England. In effect, he argued that canon law required the confirmation of royal authority.

The laymen moderating the disputation were impressed, and asked the bishops to order Kidderminster to disavow his sermon. But instead the ecclesiastical leadership was galvanized into endorsing Kidderminster's uncompromising stance: divine (i.e. canon) law was superior to all other forms, and formal 'reception' of it by a secular ruler was not required. How could the Church reform itself, or fulfil its mission to reform society, if its internal lifeblood, the canon law, was drained from it? It followed that the current practice of allowing clerics to be summoned in front of lay courts, albeit to be later punished elsewhere, was at odds with the will of God. Leading churchmen thus pushed for a major extension of the principle of benefit of clergy at the very moment when significant numbers of laymen – shocked by the Hunne affair – were more than ever convinced it should be curtailed.

Battle lines were drawn. John Taylor, clerk of Parliament and prolocutor (or chairman) of the Lower House of Convocation, recorded how 'in this Parliament and Convocation there arose the most dangerous discords between the clergy and the secular power over the liberties of the Church'.[62] Standish departed unbowed from the Blackfriars conference, and continued to make his case in sermons. The consequence was a further upping of the stakes. He was summoned before Convocation to answer articles against him, the beginning of a process for heresy.

Did Standish believe minor orders were not 'holy'? That benefit of clergy was not a matter of divine law, and that secular authorities might legitimately punish clerics if bishops proved negligent? Standish stuck to his position that the established custom of 'conventing' criminal clerics before the secular courts meant ecclesiastical ordinances to the contrary could not be binding in England. He did not believe exemption of clerics to be a positive requirement of divine law, prompting both sides to engage in some fancy footwork around what was meant by the biblical obligation to 'honour thy father'. Wisely, Standish decided to ignore the other biblical injunction about not putting your trust in princes, and appealed to Henry VIII.

The arguments were rehearsed again at a second Blackfriars conference in November 1515. Standish was not wholly isolated among the clergy. The dean of the King's chapel, Dr John Veysey, was emerging as a rising star of the 'royalist' party. He reassured Henry that summoning clerks before temporal judges for criminal causes was not against the law of God. At the conference, Veysey developed the point by analogy with priestly celibacy. Priests had once been married, but by papal decree 'received' in England and elsewhere had long since put away their wives. Yet there were Churches in the east where the decree had not been received, and priests were married still.[63] This was a slick debating point. Yet its insinuations about the uneven and historically contingent scope of papal jurisdiction, and about the federated character of wider European Christendom, perhaps lodged themselves in Henry VIII's mind.

More immediately pertinent was the response of the royal judges, as predictable as it was potent. By proceeding against Standish on the basis of a papal decree that as yet lacked royal assent, the clergy were guilty of praemunire. Convocation's formal response to the charge exuded an air of aggrieved hurt: was it fair that Members of Parliament, without fear of punishment, might criticize churchmen and church laws, while Convocation might not discuss laymen and laws of the land without risking the penalties of praemunire? There was no retraction of the claim. Standish was summoned before them because he had 'taught, affirmed and published divers matters which were thought not to stand with the laws of God and the determination of Holy Church'. Prelates had a responsibility to 'inquire of such matters and causes as appertain to the laws of God, for the redressing and reformation of all things contrary to the same'. If they failed in this, heresies would increase daily. The statement concluded by professing complete loyalty to the King, while urging him to allow Convocation to act as it had done in the days of his noble progenitors. A promise to maintain the King's laws to the best of their powers was hedged with a crucial qualification: 'as far as their order and profession shall suffer them'.[64]

It was the moment for the King to make his entrance. Leading churchmen, judges and other concerned parties were summoned before him at Baynard's Castle, a royal palace adjoining the Thames. Proceedings opened with a set-piece tableau: Wolsey knelt on the ground, and protested that none of the clergy ever intended to do anything prejudicial to the King's prerogative. For his own part, he added that 'he owed his whole advancement solely to our lord the King', and that he would 'assent to nothing that would tend to annul or derogate from his royal authority for all the world'.

This was not the abject surrender it is sometimes painted. Wolsey reiterated that conventing of clerks before secular judges 'seems contrary to the laws of God and the liberties of the Holy Church', and requested the whole matter be referred to Rome. Henry's reply that he thought that question had been answered fully by Dr Standish provoked a flurry of exchanges. Richard Fox, epitome both of a reforming bishop and of a steadfast royal servant, huffed that 'Dr Standish will not abide by his opinion at his peril'. Standish himself histrionically proclaimed, 'What should one poor friar do alone against the bishops and clergy of England?' Archbishop Warham reminded everyone how previous attempts to restrict benefit of clergy were resisted by 'divers holy fathers of the Church', some even suffering death. This was a pointed avowal – uncomfortable for kings to hear – of the literally iconic status of his predecessor Thomas Becket as a blessed martyr for the liberties of *Ecclesia Anglicana*.[65]

In all likelihood, Henry came knowing exactly what he planned to say. His words made a strong impression, as they were intended to do:

> By the ordinance and sufferance of God, we are King of England, and the Kings of England in time past have never had any superior but God alone. Wherefore know you well that we will maintain the right of our Crown and of our temporal jurisdiction, as well in this point as in all others, in as ample a wise as any of our progenitors have done before us. And as to your decrees, we are well informed that you yourselves of the Spiritualty do expressly contrary to the words of many of them, as has been well shown to you by some of our spiritual Counsel; nevertheless, you interpret your decrees at your pleasure. Wherefore, consent to your desire more than our progenitors have done in time past we will not.[66]

A final plea from Warham that Convocation might, at its own costs and charges, seek a final ruling from Rome was met with resounding royal silence.

The significance of Henry's speech, and of the 1514–15 crisis more broadly, has been much debated over the years. Was this episode the opening salvo of the English Reformation, or simply a particularly noisy moment in the ongoing sound and fury attending royal–papal relations, signifying not much more than nothing?[67]

In the wake of the 1515 conferences, most of the immediate causes of conflict were quietly defused, with shows of compromise on all sides. Horsey was quietly pardoned, and Fitzjames was able to block parliamentary moves to restore Hunne's property to his children. The praemunire suit against Convocation was dropped, as were the heresy proceedings against Standish. The 1512 act was not renewed, but in February 1516, at Wolsey's behest, Leo X reluctantly issued a bull ordering that no one was to be ordained in England for the next five years unless he took all five orders up to subdeacon simultaneously. This was an ingenious solution, but, as so often with Leo's reform initiatives, does not appear to have been implemented on the ground. A later expedient was more radical. In 1528 Wolsey secured permission from Clement VII to allow a clerk to be formally degraded from his orders by any bishop assisted by two abbots or dignitaries, a reforming exercise of the legateship that events were soon to overtake.[68]

Other than Hunne and his family, no one was very materially harmed by the events of 1514–15. Kidderminster resumed his distinguished rule of Winchcombe Abbey, and was in later years praised by the King as a man of learning and experience. Wolsey continued to soar in the King's favour. The 'royalists' reaped their rewards. Veysey was raised to the episcopate as bishop of Exeter in 1519, and in 1525 was created president of the Council in the Marches of Wales. Standish too received a bishopric, that of St Asaph in North Wales. There was an ironic sequel. Carelessly, if conventionally, Standish was consecrated by Warham before he had done the requisite homage for his temporalities and sworn to renounce any features of the papal bull of provision 'in derogation of our sovereign lord's crown and dignity'. Threatened with praemunire, Standish knelt before the royal council and begged the lords to intercede with Wolsey to secure pardon on his behalf. Wolsey undoubtedly took pleasure in this small humiliation. He probably helped ensure that after 1518 Standish never progressed further up the episcopal ladder than St Asaph, the poorest and least alluring of English and Welsh dioceses. Standish's own spleen was subsequently expended in attacks on Erasmus's New Testament, which did little to earn him the continued admiration or gratitude of the King.[69]

The following years saw continued tensions over the issue of sanctuary, but there was to be no comparable bust-up over the liberties of the Church during the period of Wolsey's legateship. Benefit of clergy and praemunire receded from the forefront of public debate. By uniting in his own person unreserved royal trust and delegated papal authority, Wolsey was able for most of the 1520s to prevent 'Church–State' conflicts from getting out of hand. Yet the unforgotten events of 1514–15 – for crown, commons and clergy alike – would cast a very long shadow.

### Whose Reform?

While the crisis was drawing to a close, Thomas More put the finishing touches to his satirical masterpiece, *Utopia*:

No official is more honoured among the Utopians than the priest, to such an extent that even if one of them commits a crime, he is not brought to court, but left to God and his own conscience. They think it wrong to lay human hands on a man, however guilty, who has been specially consecrated to God, as a holy offering, so to speak. This custom is the easier to observe because their priests are so few and so carefully selected. Besides, it rarely happens that a man chosen for his goodness and raised to high dignities solely because of his moral character will fall into corruption and vice.[70]

It is far from clear who, or what, was being satirized here. A diplomat in royal service, a common lawyer closely linked to the London merchant community, but also a supporter of the clergy's legitimate rights and an unyielding enemy of heresy, More exemplifies the contradictory impulses felt by many thoughtful and spiritual persons in early Tudor England. They longed for reformation of Church and people. But there was little clarity about who could lead that reform to fruition. The optimistic vision of a top-down overhaul of the institution by its hierarchical leaders – the head renewing the members – received little practical leadership or example from the Fifth Lateran Council, or from the distracted, politique popes in Rome. It had meanwhile become abundantly clear that the freedom of action clerical leaders felt was necessary to bring about reformation on their own terms was not to be allowed them in England. A reform agenda for the Church defined by the King's prerogative produced only Thomas Wolsey. The cardinal was a capable administrator, and, viewed in some lights, an almost plausible impression of an Erasmian idealist. But he was hardly a churchman, in More's acerbic formulation, 'chosen for his goodness and raised to high dignities solely because of his moral character'.

Henry VIII drew lessons from the crisis of 1515, and from the spat over Tournai that came sharply on its heels. Popes and bishops had their own agendas. He concluded that – as with Wolsey, who, to Henry's disappointment, never became pope – it was safest to own them absolutely, or if not, to deal with them robustly. At his coronation in 1509, Henry had sworn to 'keep and maintain the right and the liberties of Holy Church of old time granted by the righteous Christian kings of England'. But at some stage, and with his own pen, he altered the wording to make clear he meant to uphold only those rights of 'the holy Church of England not prejudicial to his jurisdiction and dignity royal'. We do not know when the changes were made; the term 'Church of England' need not imply a date after the break with Rome.[71] The basic sentiment was one Henry subscribed to from early in his reign. And even the original form of the coronation oath made clear that the Church's liberties were 'granted' by English kings; they were not God-given and inalienable.

Under both Henry VII and Henry VIII, praemunire served as a kind of thermostat control, ensuring the 'liberties' of the Church never rose above a temperature that the crown found comfortable. Thomas More, discussing with the King in 1521 the passage on the papacy in Henry's *Defence of the Seven Sacraments*, gently reminded him of 'the Statute of Praemunire, whereby a good part of the Pope's pastoral cure here was pared away'. More suggested papal authority might be 'more slenderly touched' in the book.[72] Henry did not see the objection – at that stage he perceived no inherent incompatibility between extravagant deference to the Holy See (about to reward him with a coveted title of honour) and his own 'imperial' kingship.

At various times in the first twenty-odd years of his reign, Henry VIII felt frustrated with churchmen and disappointed with popes. But the frustrations just about always resolved themselves to the King's satisfaction. The bishops were convincingly slapped down in 1515, while the Pope provided satisfaction (of a sort) over Tournai, as well as adequate recompense with grants of Wolsey's legateship and Henry's Defendership of the Faith. If, before the end of the 1520s, Henry never found his sticking-place, it was because his ecclesiastical problems never really caused him to get stuck.

The leaders of the Church in England had their own sticking-place. They would loyally serve the crown, as Convocation put it in 1515, 'as far as their order and profession shall suffer them'. In 1515 and for many years afterwards, most clergymen had little idea just how far such sufferance might have to extend.

One thing, however, was certain: it ended on this side of the line that separated orthodox faith from false and heretical belief. It was the clergy's responsibility to define and defend doctrinal orthodoxy. But as the disputes culminating in 1515 made abundantly clear, some churchmen believed that criticisms of the clergy, and attacks on their jurisdiction, were themselves potentially doctrinal matters. Anticlericalism might slip easily into heresy. The Hunne case brought to the surface acute anxieties over where, and how, the line between them was to be drawn.

In defending their status, rights and privileges, clergymen sincerely believed they were defending the faith of Christ. And by seeking out and destroying heresy and heretics, they justified the perpetuation of those rights and privileges. If other routes of reformation were blocked, this at least was a path down which the English bishops might boldly lead. As disputes over church courts crystallized at the end of the sixteenth century's first decade, the bishops prepared to demonstrate the indispensability of their jurisdiction. They launched a campaign to eradicate heresy.

# 4

## MARVELLOUS FOOLISHNESS

### Choosing to be Wrong

TRUE AND FALSE beliefs were matters only the clergy could define: 'the judging of any question concerning the supposition of heresy appertaineth only to them'. At the height of the Standish controversy, the English bishops formally set this principle down on paper, and swore they would never flinch from investigating and punishing error, 'though they themselves should suffer persecution or death for the same'.

When it came to investigating heresy, the bishops were not the people most likely to be facing persecution and death. But there is no doubting the seriousness with which heresy was taken in early Tudor England, or the determination of church leaders to see it eradicated. In February 1512, John Colet reminded the Fathers of Convocation that the realm was nowadays 'grieved of heretics, men mad with marvellous foolishness'. His provocative suggestion that the wicked lifestyle of priests itself represented a kind of heresy was calculated to concentrate minds on the problems facing the Church, and the weight of moral demand on those charged with addressing them.[1]

Heresy, like beauty, resides in the beholder's eye. It is possible to regard it as no more than a 'construct' – an artificial category created by self-proclaimed policemen, with their own reasons for identifying, or inventing, a convenient criminal enemy.[2] It was no accident that the most intense English anti-heresy campaign for a century coincided with parliamentary attempts to restrict benefit of clergy. In England, the people accused of heresy were known by the pejorative nickname of Lollard, a puzzling label which probably originally meant something like mumbler of prayers. Some historians suspect that those to whom the label was applied did not comprise any kind of 'movement' or 'sect', but were rather a haphazard assortment of the opinionated, the ignorant and the irreverent, misleadingly made to look coherent in their views by the procedures and preoccupations of persecuting authorities.[3]

But this is to tell only half the story, and to risk drawing attention away from the behaviour and beliefs of those actually accused of being heretics. These people often understood that they were going against accepted opinion; they thought they knew better than their neighbours, their curate, their bishop, even the Pope. The existence of such people is a pointer to the dynamic, and sometimes surprisingly diverse, character of later medieval religion, and to the ability of even humble parishioners to think things out for themselves.

The word heresy derives from the Greek *hairesis*, meaning choice. Orthodox churchmen were quite right when they defined heretics as people who chose their own opinions above the traditions and teachings of the Church. A heretic, Bishop John Alcock declared, was one that 'taketh the scripture of God after his will, and not after the sense of the Holy Ghost'.[4] It was not so much error in itself, but wilful pertinacity in error that made heresy so terrible. Heretics were undoubtedly worse than pagans or infidels, who never had opportunity to learn and embrace the truth. The heinous nature of the crime was brought home to parishioners through quarterly recitation in all churches of the 'great sentence', a declaration of excommunication against anyone guilty of specified offences. High on the list were heretics, who 'do willingly against the law of holy Church and the faith of Christendom, in word or deed or counsel, or in example'. The ritual pronouncement of their exclusion included the tolling of a death knell, and the extinguishing and casting to the ground of a lighted candle – accompanied by a clerical spit of scornful disdain.[5]

All the more remarkable, then, that some folk decided to risk these censures – though we should avoid the temptation, sometimes indulged by the Lollards' modern admirers, of assuming they were exceptional people, thinking thoughts their insentient Catholic neighbours were simply incapable of formulating.

Lollardy was not straightforwardly a 'cause' of the Reformation in England, or a sign that society was impatiently ready for it, in the way some Protestant historians used to imagine. Yet neither should we regard the persistent presence of heresy in officially Catholic England as a sideshow or an irrelevance. Looking at late medieval religious culture through the lens of Lollardy and anti-Lollardy repays the effort. It helps us understand how the changes that would divide and transform that culture came from within, as much as from without, and how people at all levels of society might react when those changes finally arrived.

## Heresy and Reformation of the Church

Heretics, in the early sixteenth century, were firmly linked to reformation, but not to a Protestant reformation that no one could then see coming. The 'reformation of the Church's estate', to which Colet and others were fervently committed, had heresy high on its agenda for action. By the time of the 1512 Convocation, an episcopal drive to cleanse this stain from the Church was already firmly underway. In the years 1510–14 investigations were undertaken in at least eleven English dioceses. Everyone realized something was afoot. In November 1511 Henry VIII's Latin secretary, Andrea Ammonio, wrote jokingly to Erasmus – one sophisticated European scholar trapped in rainy England to another – that the price of firewood had gone up yet again, for 'every day there are a great number of heretics to make bonfires for us'.

Ammonio was exaggerating: across England as a whole, probably fewer than a dozen people were burned at this time. A much greater number 'abjured' – that is, they formally confessed and repented of their offence and were assigned penance. A handful of these were burned in the following years for returning to their error; there were no second chances in heresy proceedings. In terms of the population as a whole, the numbers were undoubtedly small: most likely fewer than 300 persons were seriously investigated in the purge of 1510–12, and the numbers were heavily concentrated in the weald of Kent, the Chiltern Hills of Buckinghamshire, and the urban environments of Coventry and London. Nonetheless, this was the most ambitious set of prosecutions seen in England for many decades, a potent measure of episcopal concern.[6]

Heresy was virtually as old as Christianity itself, but its concentrated presence in England was a relatively recent phenomenon, traceable to the influence of a single individual, the Oxford theologian John Wyclif (d. 1384). Wyclif was never definitively condemned as a heretic in his lifetime, largely due to the political support of Edward III's son, John of Gaunt, who was attracted to Wyclif's views on the respective scope of secular and ecclesiastical power. In a world corrupted by sin, Wyclif argued, 'dominion' (i.e. temporal power derived from God) was bound to be imperfect, and churchmen should not become involved with it by maintaining wealth and estates. 'Disendowment' of the Church, on the ostensible grounds of recalling it to its true function, was a seductive idea to lay authorities in the fourteenth century, as it was to be in the sixteenth.

The growing radicalism of Wyclif's ideas alienated supporters, even as they attracted converts. Wyclif was a rigid proponent of 'realism' – the metaphysical system that posited the existence of 'universals' – underlying realities that accounted for the existence of individual things by pointing to their sharing in a common essence. In contrast, the 'nominalist' school dominant in Wyclif's Oxford denied the existence of universals other than as a system for naming things that were fundamentally unique. Why this abstruse philosophical debate mattered was that it prevented Wyclif from believing the doctrine of transubstantiation. He could not accept that a substance (bread) partaking in a universal essence could ever be completely annihilated, as, according to orthodox theology, happened during the mass. Yet, at the Last Supper, Christ could not have been lying when he told his disciples that 'this is my body'. Wyclif's eucharistic theology has been hard even for modern experts to unravel. Whether he believed Christ was really present at the mass 'virtually', 'figuratively' or 'sacramentally', or as a signification of his power and grace, one thing was certain: bread was bread.

Lay devotions in front of the consecrated host were thus superstitious and idolatrous, a critique Wyclif widened to embrace other popular practices – pilgrimage, veneration of the saints, images and prayers for the dead. The true Church was not the motley band of saints and sinners receiving instruction and sacramental grace from the priesthood, but rather an invisible congregation of those predestined to eternal life. True authority could rest only with the genuinely holy, whether ordained or not. An intense anticlericalism and anti-papalism pervaded Wyclif's writings: claims to jurisdiction and sacramental power made by the vast majority of the clergy were sinfully invalid.

All of this went well beyond a moralistic reformism that was common currency in the late medieval Church. Likewise, Wyclif's biblicism transcended the devout concern with interpretation of scripture characteristic of the late medieval schools. For Wyclif, the bible was the *only* source of truth and revelation, and nothing in faith, morals or law could be binding unless scripture expressly authorized it.

Ferocious intellectual and theological debate, conducted in Latin and within the lecture halls of the university world, was nothing new in the later fourteenth century. What transformed Wyclif from a dissenting scholar into an arch-heretic was his failure to respect the rules of the game. Courting the secular powers against the wealth and jurisdiction of the Church was disquieting enough; still more alarming was his willingness to take the key issues to the laity in the vernacular. By the early 1380s, Wyclif's disciples were preaching his doctrines to lay audiences across midland and southern England, composing tracts in English, and making willing converts. Lollard 'poor preachers' were soon equipped with a powerful weapon, a complete translation of the bible into English, produced in two versions before the end of the fourteenth century. Wyclif himself may or may not have played much of a direct role in the production of the 'Wycliffite Bible', but he inspired the team of translators. The texts themselves were fairly faithful, occasionally ponderous, translations from the Latin Vulgate. But a General Prologue publicized Wyclif's teaching on the eucharist.[7]

Wyclifism was a potent social and political force around the turn of the fifteenth century, attracting the patronage of a clutch of so-called 'Lollard knights'. The new and insecure Lancastrian dynasty saw, however, opportunities to make capital out of promoting itself as a champion of orthodox faith. An Act of Parliament in 1401 enshrined the death penalty for heresy, and in 1409 Archbishop Thomas Arundel issued a set of constitutions placing restrictions on preaching, and banning translations of the bible that did not have episcopal approval. An ill-fated rebellion against Henry IV in 1414, led by the convicted heretic Sir John Oldcastle, established an association between Lollardy and political sedition, and most of its support from the political elite ebbed away.

Lollardy was driven hard in the first decades of the fifteenth century in the places where it seems to have most firmly established itself: in Bristol, Essex, Kent and along the river valley of the Waveney, bounding Suffolk and Norfolk. But the intensity of Lollard trials slowed after the mid-1430s, and reduced to a trickle in the 1450s. There were likewise comparatively few cases in the following decade, though a significant exception was the clutch of prosecutions pursued by Bishop John Chedworth of Lincoln in 1462–4, and centred on the Buckinghamshire towns of Amersham, Great Marlow, Hughenden and High Wycombe.[8] It is unclear when Lollardy first came to the chalk hills of the Chilterns, lying to the north of the middle section of the Thames Valley as it meanders eastwards from Oxfordshire to London. But it was here the heresy put down its deepest roots.

Recorded prosecutions began to rise again towards the end of the fifteenth century. It seems unlikely that this represents a genuine resurgence of Lollardy. The lull in investigations coincided with the political turbulence of the Wars of the Roses, and came to an end with the restoration of relative stability under the Tudors. Henry VII, like Henry IV, was a usurper anxious to show that God approved of his usurpation. And the fact that so many of the new investigations took place in areas where Lollardy was present at the start of the century – Coventry, London, a Berkshire–Buckinghamshire corridor along the Thames, Kent east of the Medway – strongly suggests a continuous existence of heresy, rather than any fortuitous pattern of eradication and 'reinfestation'.[9]

Heresy-hunting around the turn of the sixteenth century was nonetheless patchy and sporadic, dependent on the vigilance of individual prelates. Concerned bishops set up commissions to investigate heresy, as James Goldwell, bishop of Norwich, did in 1494. Goldwell was a diplomat active in the service of the Yorkist kings, but after the accession of Henry VII, he withdrew from political and public engagements and concentrated on his diocese. Likewise, one of the first episcopal acts of Richard Mayhew, created bishop of Hereford in October 1504 with a lifetime of royal administrative and diplomatic service behind him, was to establish a commission to suppress heresy in the diocese. Like Fox of Winchester, these bishops may have seen attention to their dioceses as a form of penance for clerical careers overburdened by secular affairs.[10] Fox, too, was a diligent watchdog of orthodoxy, and a declared reason for his foundation of Corpus Christi College Oxford was 'the extermination of heresies and errors and the augmentation of the orthodox faith'. A godfather of humanism and Greek learning in England, the scholar William Grocyn (d. 1519) composed a treatise against Lollard eucharistic error.[11] Heresy-hunting was not the preserve of bigots inimical to reform, but a mark of diligent and conscientious churchmen.

This was the context for a co-ordinated campaign beginning in 1510, and linked to the reform agenda brought by Archbishop Warham to the Canterbury Convocation of that year. Warham conducted in parallel during 1511 a visitation of the parishes and religious houses of his diocese, and a drive to eradicate Lollardy, in the course of which fifty-three suspects were brought before him. Similar *magna abjurata* (great abjurations) were orchestrated in 1511–12 by Bishops Geoffrey Blythe in Coventry and Lichfield, Richard Fitzjames in London and William Smith in Lincoln, while other bishops stepped up their regular policing activity. Revealingly, many of the officials most heavily involved in Warham's campaign were able young scholars with theological training and humanist sympathies, rather than old-lag canon lawyers: the archbishop's chancellor, Cuthbert Tunstall, was the backbone of proceedings.[12]

Henry VIII's slapping down of the bishops in 1515, the rise of a cardinal-legate with priorities distinct from those of the archbishop, and the fizzling out of the reform euphoria created briefly by the Fifth Lateran Council, all probably contributed to a waning of episcopal enthusiasm for heresy-hunting. An earlier pattern of sporadic investigations re-established itself after 1512, though several bishops remained active and vigilant. In 1513–14 Richard Fox of Winchester brought to trial a clutch of heretics discovered in Kingston-upon-Thames and a group of villages straddling the Hampshire–Surrey border. Edmund Audley of Salisbury initiated two sets of prosecutions in 1514–19, with suspects drawn from the areas around Devizes and Bradford-on-Avon in Wiltshire. Bishop Blythe and his officials kept a close eye on Coventry, and some half-dozen of those abjuring there in 1511–12 were burned for relapse over the following decade. In London, too, the years following the Hunne case witnessed an ongoing drip of abjurations, and in 1518, two burnings: that of the wandering Lollard teacher, Thomas Man, who abjured in the Chilterns in 1511, and of John Stilman, who had sworn to orthodoxy before Bishop Audley of Salisbury in 1508.[13]

The authorities were managing to keep a lid on Lollardy, but did not succeed in scouring the pot. The early 1520s heralded the return of *magna abjurata*. In 1521, John Longland, newly appointed bishop of Lincoln, again turned to the Chilterns. He personally examined some 350 suspects, and around fifty Lollards were made to abjure. Four relapsed heretics were burned, and names unearthed in the investigation were passed to the bishops of Salisbury and Winchester. In 1527–8, Cuthbert Tunstall, now bishop of London, set in motion a major investigation centred on the Essex village of Steeple Bumpstead and the neighbouring town of Colchester.[14]

By now, the name of Luther was well known to English bishops, and there were additional reasons to be on the lookout for challenges to orthodoxy. But what was found, both here and in the Chilterns, was little different from what

had been uncovered in these places decades before. Whatever its other qualities, Lollardy was remarkably tenacious. Its persistence well into the sixteenth
century is not so much the portent of a new reformation as evidence for the
faltering of an earlier one. Lollardy's continued existence mocked the clericalist
vision of a powerful and purified Church, a channel of God's grace to obedient
laypeople, elevated by example of holy priests.

### The Inner Worlds of Lollardy

Lollardy was a proscribed activity to which no one voluntarily admitted. As a
result, we catch sight of Lollards only as they are presented through the evidence
of trials, their words and actions recorded by heresy commissioners and their
scribes. Suspects were questioned on the basis of lists of articles, often in standardized form. If they admitted holding specified errors, or confessed to
consorting with heretics or possessing forbidden English books, they could
throw themselves on the mercy of the court, and recite an abjuration prepared
by the authorities.[15]

After abjuration, the accused would be absolved, received back into the
bosom of the Church, and assigned a penance. Penances varied, but were
nearly always performances with pointedly symbolic elements. Commonly,
the penitent took part in a public procession, clad in linen shirt, and bearing
the faggot (bound bundle of sticks) that was both instrument and emblem
of the fate of the unrepentant. Abjured Lollards in Coventry and Kent in
1511–12 were ordered as part of their penance to attend and watch the burning
of a relapsed heretic. Earlier Coventry Lollards, accused of disparaging Our
Lady of the Tower, were ordered 'to carry your said faggot to this image and,
devoutly making a pilgrimage to it, offer there a candle worth a penny'. Seven
Kentish Lollards, abjuring before Warham in May 1511, were ordered to make
confession to a priest and receive the eucharist. The performance of devotional
acts, even reception of the sacraments of the Church, as a form of disciplinary
sanction suggests how permeable the line was between private devotion and
public duty in late medieval religion. Submission did not wipe the slate clean.
The bishops accepted first-time abjurations, but they were not born yesterday.
Penitents were often required to wear in perpetuity, embroidered on their outer
clothing, a badge depicting a burning faggot – a warning to others, and a
reminder of the consequence of relapse.[16]

No particular type of person was programmed to become a Lollard.
Suggestions that Lollardy was organically attached to the rural cloth industry
are too pat.[17] Yet religious nonconformity fared best where there was a little
affluence, a little leisure time, and a certain degree of distance from the sancti-
fied cycle of the farming year – very few Lollards seem to have come from the
numerically predominant agricultural labour force. The Kent heretics rounded

up by Warham in 1511–12 were mainly artisans of moderate wealth – cutlers, weavers, tailors, shoemakers, glovers. There was a similar pattern among the Coventry groups investigated by Bishop Blythe: smiths, wire-drawers, coopers and butchers were questioned, alongside workers from the city's leather and cloth industries.[18]

Nothing, however, prevented Lollard opinions from seeping up (or down) the social scale. Most London Lollards were artisans, but some were members of the prestigious livery companies who ran the city's economy. Charles Joseph, the disreputable summoner implicated in the Hunne scandal, was reported to have boasted he could 'bring my Lord of London to the doors of heretics in London, both of men and women, that be worth a thousand pound'. Lady Jane Young, widow of Sir John Young, sometime Mayor of the City, was the daughter of Joan Boughton, burned for heresy in 1494. According to a city chronicler, she 'had a great smell of an heretic after the mother'. In Amersham, the fortu-itous survival of a 1522 tax assessment to set alongside the record of Longland's investigations reveals that ten of the town's twenty richest inhabitants were Lollard suspects. The Coventry Lollards too had links to the city elite: two women abjuring there in 1511, Alice Rowley and Joan Smyth, were married to former lord mayors, and several members of the urban oligarchy were named in the course of the trials.[19]

The landed gentry had a great deal invested, financially and emotionally, in the structures of orthodox Catholicism. Overwhelmingly, they observed the conventions of traditional religion. Lollardy and gentility were not, however, mutually exclusive. Coventry Lollards in 1511 included the splendidly named Balthasar Shugborough, of the Warwickshire village of Napton, described in his abjuration as *generosus*, gentleman. The handful of known or suspected 'gentle' Lollards includes a number of wives and widows. Perhaps they had more time to think about radical ideas, and less to lose in flirting with them. But the idea that heresy per se was disproportionately attractive to women, providing them with opportunities for leadership and expression stifled by the hierarchical and patriarchal norms of late medieval Catholicism, is a fanciful one. In all of the major sweeps, women were a minority of the suspects appre-hended, and in its inner workings Lollardy could be just as patriarchal as the Catholicism against which it set its face. Women, some women, were attracted to Lollardy, not because they were women, but because they found its teachings compelling.[20]

The same holds true of another unlikely subsection of early Tudor heretics: the clergy. It is often supposed that Lollardy had little traction with priests, who derived their status from the sacramental functions Lollards tended to impugn. But, in fact, a priest or two can be found around the edges, and sometimes close to the centre, of most local networks of heresy. Two Amersham Lollards arrested in the mid-1460s claimed to have been instructed in their heresies by the rector of Chesham Bois. A Berkshire priest, Richard Molver, curate of Newbury in Berkshire, was charged in 1504 with possession of heretical books. Twenty miles to the north, the rector of Lectombe Basset in Berkshire, John Whithorn, was allowed to remain in office upon abjuring heretical articles in 1499. But there was no second chance for him after he was denounced to Bishop Audley in 1508. It emerged he had hidden English books near the high altar of his church, and sheltered two heretics who escaped from the Lollards' Tower in London. Another Lollard out of London assured Whithorn that if ever he came to the capital, he would find there 'rich heretics', with books he would want to read.[21]

In the trafficking of books between Lollard groups, clergymen, the professional literati of society, were often deeply involved. A book of English gospels, ending up in the hands of the vicar of Rickmansworth in Hertfordshire, was given to a Chilterns Lollard by Thomas Tykill, morrow mass priest of St Mary Magdalen, Milk Street, in London. A parishioner there, Joan Baker, confided to another priest, John Cawood of St Margaret's, Bridge Street, that Lady Young died 'a martyr before God'.[22]

Cawood was likely a quiet sympathizer, rather than an activist, as perhaps was James Preston, doctor of theology, and vicar of St Michael's, Coventry, from the 1480s until his death around 1507. Alice Rowley confessed that Preston borrowed a New Testament from her; she thought he favoured her and her sect. The names of several other priests emerged in the course of the Coventry investigations, and a further batch, half a dozen parish clergy and a couple of regulars, were identified as suspects during Longland's Chiltern investigations of 1518–21.[23] At Steeple Bumpstead in Essex, the Lollard John Tyball managed 'by disputing and instructing', and by sharing his collection of vernacular books, to bring the curate, Richard Fox, 'to his learning and opinions'. He then tried to convert another two local clergyman, feeling that 'if he might bring a priest once into his learning and heresies, he were sure and strong enough.'[24] Tyball was unsuccessful in this second round of persuasions, but the widespread involvement of some clergymen, over decades and in diverse regions, suggests Lollardy offered more to its adherents than unreflective anticlerical protest.

Lollardy had no priesthood of its own, and in so far as there were recognized leaders, they tended to be peripatetic laymen, like John Stilman and Thomas Mann, burnt in London in 1518. Stilman, who regarded John Wyclif as 'a saint in heaven', learned his heresy in Hampshire in the last years of the fifteenth century. He abjured in Reading in 1508, but kept silent about his books, which he later took with him to London. He was well known to the Buckinghamshire Lollards of Chesham and Amersham. Man lived and worked in Essex, Norfolk, Suffolk and London, as well as in the Lollard heartlands of the Thames Valley. He did penance before Smith of Lincoln in 1511, but kept subsequently on the move, apparently boasting that 'he and his wife had turned six or seven hundred people unto those opinions which he was abjured of'. This seems implausible, but Man was without doubt an influential figure, approaching the status of 'Lollard evangelist'.

Another of the kind was John Hacker, a frequent visitor in the late 1520s to Steeple Bumpstead, where he was known as 'Old Father Hacker'. A decade and more earlier, Hacker was teaching Lollardy in northern Hampshire, before moving, via Newbury, to Coleman Street in London. From there he ventured frequently to Burford in Oxfordshire, and to the villages of the Chilterns and the north downs of Berkshire. His teaching had a distinctly apocalyptic edge, with talk of a coming battle of priests, and of how, after a period of ascendancy, 'all the priests should be slain ... because they hold against the law of holy church'.[25]

Heretics like these kept on the move because the authorities were on their tails. Their wanderings confirm the existence of contacts and connections, maintained over decades, between different Lollard groups. But most Lollards were firmly rooted in place, their most meaningful relationships not with a nationwide corresponding club of spiritual idealists, but with people placed in day-to-day networks of family, locality and workshop. In so far as 'Lollards' had a name for themselves, they spoke about 'known men' – those whose faith was known to God, but whose understanding and discretion could be vouched for and trusted.[26]

No one was baptized into Lollardy, but parents might initiate their offspring into its mysteries at an early age. John and Agnes Grebill, of Tenterden in Kent, began to teach their sons, Christopher and John, against the sacrament of the altar when they were 'about a vii years age'. Yet, revealingly, John confessed 'he never could perceive their teachings nor give any heart thereunto till this year last past' (1510, when he was twenty), and Christopher had 'no feeling in that matter of errors till he heard John Ive teach him ... which was the space of three years past'.[27] Even at the heart of an established Lollard family, some awareness of having arrived at superior knowledge and understanding – an experience of conversion – was critical to the sense of religious belonging.

Lollardy was nourished by the natural bonds and structures of the communities where it established itself. Husbands converted wives, and vice versa. John Gest, a shoemaker from Birmingham, confessed in 1511 that he fell into heresy 'about eleven years ago, at the promptings of his wife Joan'. Hopeful conversations might be struck up and pursued with friends, neighbours and in-laws.[28]

Those in a position of social dependence – apprentices and servants, as well as children – were the easiest to draw in, though it is hard to say exactly what they were being drawn into. The modern vocabulary of religious affiliation – church, sect, denomination, cult, conventicle – is not very helpful here. With the exception of the odd code word or catchphrase, Lollardy did not develop rites or ceremonies of its own.[29] In the established centres, there were certainly meetings, either of mixed company or – more rarely – of men and women separately. Doctrines were discussed and readings were made from the scriptures or other English texts. But these were not 'services'; the numbers present were usually small, and they are not easily distinguished from the ordinary social occasions on which neighbours gathered for conversation and conviviality.

Lollardy flowed along the channels of everyday social interaction. Potentially incriminating conversations took place in alehouses and gardens, at fairs, even in churches. John Browne and William Baker of Cranbrook in Kent shared their thoughts about images and pilgrimages as they 'walked by the way', from Baker's house to a local chapel. But most of all, heresy was a domestic pursuit. Browne discussed the eucharist with Thomas and Joan Harwood at their house in Rolvenden, 'in an evening sitting by the fire in the hall'.[30]

For such occasions there was no fixed catechism or creed, and no set texts other than the bible itself, nearly always owned and consumed in the form of separate volumes of epistles and gospels. Lollards sometimes drew inspiration from copies of old Wycliffite tracts such as *The Lantern of Light* (c. 1400), but they did not produce original writings of their own. Only one heretical treatise, the pleasingly alliterative *Wyclif's Wicket*, may date from the second half of the fifteenth century.

This is often taken to indicate the fundamentally debased and decaying character of Lollard beliefs. Yet the fact that early Tudor cutlers and shoemakers did not feel inspired to attempt original theological compositions need not mean that their faith lacked vitality or even creativity. There was undoubted variation in the range and emphasis of the doctrines Lollards abjured at their trials. But to dismiss Lollardy as therefore fundamentally 'incoherent' is to set an unrealistic standard of doctrinal rectitude. There is evidence to suggest a seam of eccentric (or independent-minded) individuals in late medieval England, who held and expressed sceptical opinions about such basic Christian ideas as the incarnation or the resurrection. They sometimes ended up in the courts, and the authorities might well label such people as 'Lollards' (a straight synonym for heretic). Usually, though, they had little or no connection to established dissenting groups. In any case, at heart Lollardy was not so much about *what* you knew, as simply *that* you knew.[31] Lollards were people who had seen through the official version, and knew it was a snare and a delusion.

Certain themes nonetheless recur. Most common was a pronounced anti-sacramentalism, and an insistence the round white object the priest held above his head during the mass was not what the Church said it was – the true body of Christ. Lollards would occasionally work through the list, denying efficacy to all seven of the Church's sacraments, but it was the mass to which they most often returned. Also common was a rejection of the sacrament of penance, and the associated discipline of confession to a priest. These were the sacraments most closely tied to clerical authority and status. Virtually all Lollards, even the priests among them, seem inveterately and instinctively anticlerical. Resentment of clerical failings was scarcely uncommon in later medieval England, but Lollards rejected the theological premises on which Catholic priesthood was based. A priest, thought Richard Gilmyn of Coventry, was only a priest while saying mass, and until he returned to the altar 'he is only a layman and has no power except as a mere layman'. Agnes Grebill of Tenterden conceded that confession *could* be good and profitable, but only if 'made to a priest being the follower of Peter and being pure and clean in life'.[32]

Lollards were equally critical of practices not directly controlled by the clergy, and popular with other laypeople. Along with the eucharist, the heresies most frequently abjured in Lollard trials touched on the related topics of veneration of saints, worship of images, and pilgrimage. This seems a rough yet fair reflection of the priorities of Lollard themselves, rather than a template stamped on them by the authorities. Other areas where bishops had an obvious concern to define and defend orthodoxy – such as the existence of purgatory, or the status of the Pope – do occur in the trial record, though very much less frequently.

Lollardy's critique of orthodox popular religion was colourful and abrupt. Images of saints were 'stocks and stones'; the rood with its figure of Christ crucified was 'block Almighty'; statues of Our Lady were fuel to 'make a good fire'. John Falkys of Coventry, home to a famous image of the Virgin, swore that 'her head shall be hoary [i.e. white or grey] before I offer to her. What is it but a block?' Pilgrimages to holy places, so the Lollards of east Kent told themselves, were unprofitable for men's souls, and 'labour and money spent thereabout is but lost and done in vain.'[33]

An impression of utilitarian, rationalizing disdain for the incarnational and mysterious in religion is particularly marked in Lollard attacks on the sacrament of the altar. 'The carpenter doth make the house and not the house the carpenter.' This was a common catchphrase. Lollards liked to impress with the cogency of their sceptical reasoning. Francis Funge of Little Missenden in Buckinghamshire offered his brother a syllogistic argument he learned from Thomas Clerk of Hughenden:

> If the sacrament of the altar be very God and man, flesh and blood in form of bread, as priests say that it is, then have we many Gods, and in heaven there is but one God. And if there were a hundred houseled [given communion] in one parish, and as many in another, then there must needs be more than one God.

Clerk himself came across his brother-in-law, a priest, drying out 'singing bread' (the unleavened discs used in celebrations of the mass). He could not resist slyly suggesting 'that if every one of these were a God, then were there many Gods'.[34] There is an unattractively negative and destructive cast to such witticisms. Lollards, it seems, were the people who loved to say no.

But in their own minds, the Lollards' refusal of the norms of communal religion was not a sullen rejectionism, but a positive spiritual critique. Contempt for images and pilgrimages grew from a sense they were socially unjust, diverting resources from the poor who were the true 'image' of Christ.[35] Trial evidence also suggests that understandings of the eucharist were often more nuanced and sophisticated than a simple denial of transubstantiation. Three Maidstone Lollards, sitting around a kitchen fire in February 1510, 'communed together against the sacrament of the altar' and concluded it was bread. But they also decided it was 'done in a mind to call people together', a thoughtfully communal reflection on the social functions of eucharistic practice.

'Memorialist' understandings of the mass were favoured among the Kentish Lollards. John Bampton of Bearsted knew that what Christ gave to the disciples was not his own body, 'and so do priests in likewise give bread that cometh from God in remembrance of the bread given by Christ in his Maundy'. Local theologies of the eucharist were similarly shared by clusters of Lollards in Surrey, Essex, Coventry and elsewhere. They often concluded that while the eucharist was 'not very God', it was nonetheless a 'figure', a 'sign', a 'commemoration of Christ's passion'. Such interpretations were not directly indebted to Wyclif, who affirmed (however obscurely) some form of real presence; they may reflect the teaching of *Wyclif's Wicket*, which circulated widely among sixteenth-century groups. Eucharistic understanding was certainly not crudely unsophisticated among the Essex Lollards who taught each other to speak of the mass as *Maozim* – an obscure allusion to the strange God, 'whom his fathers knew not', mentioned in the Book of Daniel.[36]

Lollards condemned the mass, and knew the official version was a fraud. But they were virtually never accused of absenting themselves from it on Sunday. Nor did they shirk the obligation to present themselves to a priest for Lenten confession. There is a puzzling disconnect between the radicalism of Lollards' views and the conventionality of their outward behaviour. Maybe there is no great mystery. Given the consequences of being identified as a heretic, Lollards kept their heads down, and lived double lives of concealment and hypocritical pretence. Perhaps too, as a dissident and even parasitic presence, Lollardy needed the proximity of the corrupt host body to feed its righteous ire. But there is another possibility – that 'orthodoxy' and 'heresy' were not necessarily repelling magnetic fields; that Catholics and Lollards were not people with nothing to say to each other, bereft of meaningful common ground.

## Lollards and their Neighbours

How much did the neighbours know? Some Lollards took care to conceal their opinions and activities, admitting they conformed outwardly to avoid detection. Four men and four women from Reading, appearing before Bishop John Blythe of Salisbury in 1499, confessed they received the sacrament 'not for any devotion or belief that we had therein, but only for dread of the people'. A suspect appearing in 1514 before Blythe's successor, Edmund Audley, said he 'would not have come unto the church oft times, but for the rumour of the people', and in the same year a Hampshire Lollard admitted he abstained from meat on fast days 'for fear of slander and detection'. John Pykas of Colchester taught secretly against the sacrament of confession, yet 'hath yearly been confessed and houseled, but for no other cause but that people should not wonder upon him'. Some were not quite cautious enough. John and Cicely Eaton of Speen in Buckinghamshire did attend mass, but during the elevation of the host other parishioners noticed how they would 'hold down their heads, and would not look upon the sacrament'.[37]

At Christmas 1510, lively discussion of the eucharist in Edward Walker's house in Maidstone was cut short by Walker's wife: 'Sirs, it is not good that ye talk much here of these matters ... beware, for some folks will come hither anon.' Earlier, a seminar on the sacraments at the home of Robert Harrison in Canterbury ended with 'the coming into the house of a certain brother of the hospital of St John', an ecclesiastical institution located inconveniently next door. Participants in illicit discussions insisted on promises of silence and discretion. A tinker from High Wycombe spoke with Thomas Clerk about pardons, pilgrimages and the eucharist ('a holy thing, but not the body of Christ'). But he begged Clerk not to mention anything to his wife, or to her brother, a priest. Thomas Harwood of Rolvenden in Kent commanded his wife not to disclose his discussions of the eucharist with John Browne 'upon pain of her life'. Julian Yong of Coventry received books and instruction from Alice Rowley, who 'bound her under oath not to reveal her counsel and secrets'. The Grebills of Tenterden, parents and sons, made a family promise: 'none of them should discover nor betray the other of these beliefs in any wise'. Tragically, the compact was broken: both boys gave evidence against their mother, Agnes, who was burnt as a relapsed heretic in May 1511.[38]

Lollards were careful with their books. At Colnbrook in Buckinghamshire, the parish priest, Robert Freeman, was spotted reading a suspect book: 'he closed it, and carried it to his chamber'. Trial depositions mention books being hidden, and suspects admitted to concealing them. Alice Rowley of Coventry was rebuked by Thomas Banbrook for lending a book of gospels to a man they knew little about. Joan Cook, wife of a former mayor, advised Alice to burn her books.[39] Christian Clerc, wife of a Coventry hosier, urged her husband to destroy a forbidden book from which she heard him reading. John Langborowe of Kingston in Surrey was given a heretical book by John Jenyn. But when Jenyn was arrested in 1511, Langborowe burned it 'privily in the night'.

After her husband was arrested in 1514, Anne Wattys of Dogmersfield in Hampshire burned one of his books. But two others – a volume of epistles, gospels and Apocalypse, and another containing *paternoster*, *Ave*, Creed and Commandments and a treatise on baptism – she hid in a ditch. Anne's conscience perhaps rebelled at the idea of setting fire to the Word of God, but not all were so scrupulous. After the episcopal crackdown in Coventry in 1486, the fuller Matthew Markland destroyed all his gospel books. A generation later, when Roger Parker of Hughenden in Buckinghamshire reproached John Phipps for burning books including a gospel, Phipps retorted 'that he had rather burn his books, than that his books should burn him'.[40]

Given these habits of concealment, it has proved very difficult to identify individuals as Lollards on the basis of what they wrote in their wills – public documents scrutinized by the church courts.[41] In processes preceding the major abjurations, witness testimony was overwhelmingly supplied by associates and fellow suspects, not outsiders to the group. Perhaps orthodox parishioners simply did not know enough about the activities of their heterodox neighbours to incriminate them and facilitate convictions.

Yet it is hard to imagine, particularly in communities with stubbornly rooted Lollard minorities, that more conventional Christians were oblivious to the spiritual oddballs in their midst. At the 1511 episcopal visitation of Kent, the churchwardens of Tenterden reported that 'there is buried in the churchyard . . . one Agnes Roche, which was commonly known an heretic'.[42] But if she was commonly known to be a heretic, the archbishop's officers might reasonably have asked, why was she not reported earlier, and who allowed her to be buried in hallowed ground?

Some historians have suggested the existence of a parochial world of pragmatic, even benevolent, toleration of otherness, of neighbours rubbing along together until the heavy hand of external authority intruded.[43] Yet there is too much evidence that heresy was actively and widely disliked for this to be fully plausible. Suspicion was not certainty, and initiating a judicial process – requiring effort, expense and danger of retribution – was not something anyone undertook lightly. In places like Tenterden, Amersham or Colchester, where suspected Lollards were persons of wealth and local status, networks of influence worked against denunciation. After Bishop Smith's descent on Amersham in 1511, Alice, wife of the town's wealthiest inhabitant, Richard Saunders, proudly boasted that her husband had 'brought to beggary' several people who co-operated with episcopal officers. Thomas Houre was dismissed from her husband's service, and from his position as parish holy water clerk, after he told Alice 'he would lean to that way no more'. Another waverer, Thomas Rowland, was warned to 'take example' by his fate.[44]

Lollards were not always discreet and circumspect, and even where formal denunciations did not immediately ensue, their presence could cause tension and unease. This was precisely because nowhere did they comprise an insulated or self-contained 'community'. Lollards rubbed up against orthodox Catholics in countless social contexts, sometimes in the intimate bonds of marriage. William Dorset of King's Langley in Hertfordshire mocked his wife for preparing to go on pilgrimage to Our Lady of Willesden – 'Our Lady is in heaven'. John Bayly of Rolvenden in Kent scoffed that priests only wanted to make money from the pilgrimage his wife was planning. William Sweeting, a Lollard activist in Essex and London, managed the considerable feat of converting his monastic employer, the Augustinian prior of St Osyth's near Colchester. But he had less success with his spouse, who remained frustratingly wedded to lighting candles and going on pilgrimage. John Tyball was similarly able to convert a priest, but not his own wife.

The inwardness of such 'mixed marriages' eludes us. It is usually impossible to know if the wives were aware of a partner's proclivities at the time of courtship, or if conversion took place subsequent to the espousal. Both husbands and wives were occasionally assigned penance for failing to report heretical tendencies in a spouse.[45]

Other divisions can be found within families. Thanks to some 1521 testimony gathered by Bishop Longland, we can eavesdrop on discussions between two sisters, Elizabeth Copland and Isabel Morwyn of Amersham, beginning as they came from a visit to the bedside of their dying father. 'All which die,' pronounced Isabel, 'pass to hell or heaven.' 'Nay,' retorted Elizabeth, 'there is between them purgatory.' The debate resumed when Elizabeth returned from a trip, perhaps to pray for their father's soul, to a renowned crucifix known as the 'Rood of Rest'. Isabel chided her for going on pilgrimage, for saints were all in heaven. Why then, demanded Elizabeth, was pilgrimage ordained by doctors and priests? 'For gain and profit.' 'Your curate, I dare say,' Elizabeth retorted, 'never taught you so.' Isabel answered tartly that her curate never knew so much, and offered to say more if her sister would swear to keep counsel and not tell her husband. Elizabeth was in no rush to inform the authorities, but neither would she swear an oath to conceal blatant heresy.[46] Here, in an articulate and theologically informed argument between two strong-minded laywomen, we see a face of late medieval religious life usually hidden from us.

These were not the only women to engage in religious dispute. In around 1520, Mistress Alice Cottismore, widow of a Berkshire landowner, exchanged pointed words with her servant, Elizabeth Wighthill, during a visit to the house of Sir William Barentyne. Alice quietly mocked some newly gilded domestic images: 'Look, here be my Lady Barentyne's Gods!' Elizabeth was undaunted in challenging her mistress: 'They were set for remembrance of good saints.' There followed a lively exchange on the utility of religious imagery. Alice was sure that 'if I were in a house, where no images were, I could remember to pray unto Saints as well as if I did see the images'. Elizabeth insisted that 'images do provoke devotion'. Determined not to let the servant have the last word, Alice paraded her superior knowledge of the scriptures: 'ye should not worship that thing that hath ears, and cannot hear, and hath eyes and cannot see, and hath mouth, and cannot speak, and hath hands, and cannot feel' (Psalm 113, Vulgate numbering). On another occasion, Alice told the local rector that when women went to venerate saints, 'they did it to show their new gay gear'. Images were 'but carpenters' chips' and 'folks go on pilgrimage more for the green way than for devotion'.[47]

Another family argument took place at Princes Risborough, where Elizabeth Ryburn was shocked to find her brother John eating butter and eggs on the eve of the Feast of the Assumption. John mockingly told her she was 'so far in *limbo patrum* that you can never turn again', and derided her intention to go on pilgrimage, as well as her accustomed reverence to the elevated host. Another sister, Alice, heard John say the time would come when no elevation should be made. 'What service,' Alice wanted to know, 'shall we then have?' In the event, John was reported by his own father for saying that 'at sacring time he kneeled down, but he had no devotion, nor believed in the sacrament'.[48]

Lollards, then, were sometimes willing to challenge the opinions of neighbours or kinsfolk, either in hope of converting them, or simply to witness to the truth. Some clearly couldn't help themselves. Thomas Higons of Mitcheldean in Gloucestershire was 'defamed of heresy' in 1511 for repeating the old aphorism about the mass, houses and carpenters. He made the remark in a neighbour's house, 'unadvised and of my slippery tongue'.[49]

Others knew exactly what they were doing. Thomas Rave of Great Marlow went unwillingly on pilgrimage to Our Lady of Lincoln, a penance imposed on him by Bishop Smith. Even as he did so, he told pilgrims returning from the shrine of St John Shorne they were 'fools'. When he came to Lincoln, Rave 'made water in the Chapel at mass time, excusing afterward that he did it of necessity'. And, performing a further portion of his penance at Wycombe, he showed contempt for the proceedings by theatrically binding 'with a silken lace' the faggot he was obliged to carry as a symbol of defeated heresy. In London in 1520, John Southwick picked a quarrel with William Rivelay as the latter came from mass declaring he had just seen his Lord God in form of bread and wine. 'Nay, William, thou sawest not thy Lord God: thou sawest but bread, wine, and the chalice.'[50]

In the bustle and relative anonymity of the capital, Lollards had a particular tendency towards bold self-righteousness. Whenever any pauper requested Joan John for alms, 'in the worship of the Lady of Walsingham', she would snap back, 'the Lady of Walsingham help thee!' But if she did relent and decide to assist them, she would say, 'Take this in the worship of Our Lady in heaven, and let the other go.' This was mild stuff compared to the critiques of pilgrimage made by Elizabeth Sampson of Aldermanbury, who called Our Lady of Crome a 'puppet' and Our Lady of Willesden 'a burnt arse elf, and a burnt arse stock'.[51] To be 'burnt' was to suffer venereal disease; Sampson slandered revered icons in the sexual language reserved for prostitutes.

Discussion and disagreement did not always lead to immediate denunciation. Yet provocations of the sort indulged in by Sampson – who also spat at a woman attending her labour-bed for invoking the Virgin Mary – surely aroused resentment. Catholics made reverence when the consecrated host was carried through the streets to the beds of the sick and the dying, so bystanders were shocked in September 1482 to hear Thomas Wassingborne calling out, 'where goeth the costermonger?' In 1511, at Goudhurst in Kent, parishioners were sufficiently irritated by William Owyne's repeated interruptions of divine service to report him to the episcopal visitors. Owyne, they added, 'hath certain secret English books with him'.[52]

Feelings were most painfully inflamed on the rare occasions when Lollard anti-sacramentalism escalated into acts of heretical terrorism. In 1512, an image of St John was shockingly knocked down during mass in the chapel of Lincoln's Inn. Ten years later, a still greater outrage was committed in the parish of St Mary's Rickmansworth in south-west Hertfordshire. Persons unknown broke into the church, wrapped flammable cloths around the rood and rood screen, and set fire to all the images, as well as to the blessed sacrament reserved on the high altar. The resulting conflagration devastated the chancel, though an indulgence issued to raise money for rebuilding claimed that 'the blessed body of Our Lord Jesus Christ in form of bread was found upon the high altar, and nothing perished'. Rickmansworth lay close to the Lollard centres of Amersham and Chesham, and the fire was possibly started in retaliation for two Amersham Lollards burned by Bishop Longland in January 1522.[53]

Genuinely angry confrontations between heretics and orthodox Catholics were a latent possibility, particularly in places like the Essex village of Steeple Bumpstead, where Lollards were numerous enough to feel entitled and belligerent. Here, in the late 1520s, the curate Richard Fox announced, to a company assembled in the house of John Darkyn, that if he enjoyed such authority as Cardinal Wolsey he would use it to pull down all the images from the church, 'for I fear me a great many of you sin in idolatry'. One of the guests took serious exception, saying he would 'bear a faggot to burn him', and grabbed the priest's breviary, the book containing stipulated daily prayers. Unfazed, Fox remarked that in that volume was 'never a word that God ever made'. The heretic priest was asked to leave, and as he did so he asked his host if he thought he did well 'to go in pilgrimage to Our Lady of Ipswich, Walsingham, or to Canterbury?'[54]

## Heresy and Orthodoxy

Catholics and Lollards could, and did, debate furiously – but not because they had nothing in common. Rather, they shared important points of reference, and dwelled within the bounds of the same moral universe. It is not even certain we should talk emphatically about Lollards and Catholics, for Lollards *were* Catholics, to the extent that they participated in the rituals of the parish and shared its obligations and communal life. It was not always even a matter of doing the minimum they could get away with. There were cases of Lollard churchwardens and guild wardens, such as Henry Phipp of Hughenden, who implausibly allowed himself to be chosen as parish 'roodman'; that is, the person responsible for maintaining lights burning before the images on the rood loft. Other Lollards carried out the ritual and liturgical functions of parish holy water clerk, like the hapless Thomas Houre of Amersham, or the indefatigable William Sweeting, who held the post successively at Boxted and Colchester in Essex, and at Rotherhithe in Surrey.[55] There is no evidence of Lollard sympathizers among the clergy failing to perform their usual pastoral and sacramental functions. Wyclif's theology posited a 'true Church' of those predestined to salvation, but in the here-and-now many Lollards chose to live and work within the system as they found it.

Catholicism in late medieval England was universal but not uniform. Devotional preferences varied, between individuals and between regions (see Chapter 1). Whether this helps explain particular geographies of Lollard persistence, or is itself accounted for by them, is uncertain. An examination of wills in the Kentish town of Tenterden suggests 'orthodox' piety in that centre of dissent was becoming noticeably 'parsimonious' around the start of the sixteenth century, unenthusiastic about the cult of the saints, veneration of images and intercession for the souls in purgatory. But other places with a conspicuous Lollard presence display more conventional patterns of benefaction, and apparently similar shifts in priorities have been discerned in places like Beverley in East Yorkshire, where no Lollards were detected.[56]

In any case, for all their ferocious talk about pilgrimages and priests, Lollards were quite capable of aping the instincts of popular religion. When Joan Boughton was burned in 1494, supporters gathered her ashes and kept them 'for a precious relic in an earthen pot'. Wyclif himself was regarded as 'a saint in heaven'. Some Hertfordshire Lollards believed that where his bones were burnt, there 'sprang up a well or well-spring'.[57]

Not everything the Church offered was rejected. Thomas Boughton, shoemaker of Hungerford in Berkshire, confessed in 1499 that he always 'had a great mind to hear sermons and preachings of doctors and learned men of the Church'. As long as preachers 'spake the very words of the gospels and epistles such as I had heard afore in our English books', he listened to them gladly. But he rapidly became weary if they talked of tithes or offerings, or 'began to declare scripture after their doctors'. Thomas Geffrey of Uxbridge persuaded John Butler to come with him on several Sundays to London, 'to hear Doctor Colet'.

Some themes in orthodox religion evidently rang true for Lollards, including Colet's emphasis on an authentic piety unencumbered by external observances. The Londoner George Browne's rejection of the adoration of the cross in 1518 seems jarringly counter-cultural: he could see no reason for people to worship something that was 'an hurt and pain unto our Saviour Christ in the time of his passion'.[58] Yet it is unlikely Browne could have reached such a conclusion outside of the intensely Christocentric, passion-focused devotional culture of the late Middle Ages.

Lollards were book people. But not all the texts discovered in their possession were Wycliffite tracts or volumes of scripture. Quite often they were works produced for, and popular with, a mainstream orthodox readership. These included books of general religious instruction like the *Kalendar of Shepherds*, the *Prick of Conscience* and *Dives and Pauper*, as well as *Ars Moriendi* (art of dying) treatises, Books of Hours and expositions of the *paternoster*, Creed and Commandments.

Lollards no doubt often read these books against the grain of authorial intention. Alice Cottismore drew the counter-intuitive conclusion that the *Golden Legend* and an unnamed saint's *Life* 'did speak against pilgrimages'. John Edmunds of Burford was persuaded towards his memorialist position on the eucharist by reading the *Kalendar of Shepherds*, and discovering there that 'the sacrament was made in the remembrance of Christ'. In fact, the author of this hugely popular work made only the unexceptionally orthodox statement that followers of Christ 'receive the sacrament of the altar in mind of his passion'.[59] But Edmunds' misreading underlines a shared emphasis on the value of religious instruction and pious reflection in the printed vernacular.

The audacity of Wyclif's early followers in translating the bible, and then seeking to distribute it with provocative appended commentary, led to a peculiar state of affairs: the banning of all translations of scripture without explicit episcopal authorization. By contrast, vernacular translations of scripture were fairly freely available before the Reformation in France, Germany, Italy and the Low Countries. In theory at least, English book owners wishing to read the life of Christ had to make do with vernacular texts loosely based on the gospel narratives, such as Nicholas Love's hugely popular *Mirror of the Blessed Life of Jesus*.[60]

Contemporaries themselves can appear remarkably unaware of this anomaly. Thomas More asserted in 1529 that the ban was specific to Wyclif's translation, and that non-Wycliffite vernacular versions were readily to be found in English homes and churches. This was almost certainly not the case.

More probably saw Wycliffite scriptures and mistook them for non-Wycliffite ones approved by the bishop of the diocese. He believed such bibles to be orthodox because they were in the hands of orthodox people. A significant number of surviving manuscripts of the Wycliffite bible are known to have belonged to people with no plausible connections to Lollardy: a handful of religious houses, including Syon Abbey and the London and Sheen Charterhouses, several priests and seemingly orthodox laypeople, a virtually complete run of Lancastrian, Yorkist and Tudor kings. Richard III was many things, but he was certainly not a Lollard.[61]

Wycliffite bibles were even mentioned in wills, which brought them to the attention of officials of the church courts. The wealthy Suffolk clothier John Clopton, whose orthodoxy received lavish expression in the vestments, images and stained-glass windows he bestowed upon Long Melford parish church, cheerfully bequeathed 'my bible in English' to the archdeacon of Suffolk in 1504. Richard Cook, mayor of Coventry, left two English bibles in his will of 1507, one to Holy Trinity Church, Coventry, and one to the church of St Matthew's, Walsall. Cook's wife had dealings with Coventry Lollards, but there is no conclusive evidence he himself was one, and the public nature of the bequest hardly suggests a traffic in contraband goods.[62] Richard Hunne's bible was said to have been left lying around, sometimes for a month at a time, in St Margaret's Church, Bridge Street, for anyone to peruse. Witnesses reported Hunne sitting reading it openly in the doorway of his house. Hunne was at the very least a ferocious anticlerical, and the charges at his posthumous trial maintained he possessed 'books containing infinite errors'. But his bible had once belonged to a fellow parishioner, Thomas Downes, who does not look much like a Lollard. Downes asked in his will to be buried before the image of the Virgin, and left money for torches to burn before the rood, and at the elevation during mass.[63]

The fact that orthodox people used an apparently heretical and forbidden text is perhaps less surprising in view of the facts that the Wycliffite bible was a straightforward translation of the Vulgate, and that the great majority of Wycliffite bible texts circulated separately from the overtly heretical General Prologue. A large number of around 250 surviving manuscripts of Wycliffite scripture can be linked to orthodox practice. Over a third of them contain lectionaries, or more properly speaking, *capitularia*: tables enabling readers to identify the texts to be recited at mass each Sunday or feast day, and allowing them to read them in advance or even follow along during the service.[64] In all likelihood, the manuscript production of Wycliffite bibles was from an early stage geared to the needs of an orthodox clientele. The text layout, and sheer size, of many surviving manuscripts suggests they were intended for public reading in church, though how often this actually happened is unknown. What is clear is that the ambience of vernacular scripture was not overwhelmingly heretical. One Wycliffite New Testament even opens with an indulgenced prayer, offering readers 80,000 years of pardon from purgatory.[65]

There is no evidence of episcopal licensing for individuals to possess vernacular scripture. But many evidently did so, with little fear of reprimand or retribution. It seems implausible that so many manuscripts of the Wycliffite bible could have survived – far more than for any other Middle English work – if bishops had really been determined to suppress it in all circumstances.[66] Informally at least, orthodox priests and laypeople were trusted not to abuse the privilege. There was an element of class prejudice in this. The gentlefolk and urban elites, for whom engagement with vernacular scripture was one thread in a rich pattern of devotional reading and orthodox practice, were a cut above the cappers and weavers of Lollard bible circles.

But Lollards were not prosecuted for being lower middle class; or for the mere fact of possessing English books. What mattered was how they chose to interpret them. For those already believed to hold heretical opinions, the ownership of vernacular scripture might indeed clinch the case against them. In somewhat circular fashion, vernacular bibles *are* described by officials as 'books of heresy', when found in the possession of people suspected of being Lollard heretics.[67]

Lollardy matters to a study of the Reformation, though not because it suggests the terminal weakness of the Church, or the inevitability of any particular direction for future change. Lollardy was a small part of the whole, but it reminds us that the religious landscape of later medieval England was mottled and varied, and that the boundaries between orthodoxy and dissent, though at times vigilantly guarded, were also profoundly permeable. It suggests too how official definitions of tolerable and intolerable religious practice were not unquestioningly accepted, even by those who regarded themselves as conventionally Catholic and orthodox. Furthermore – an instructive straw in the wind – it reveals that the Church's institutional machinery lacked the capability to impose complete uniformity of belief and practice, even with the apparent backing of the secular authorities.

Most of all, Lollardy's existence, and persistence, reveals the capacity of ordinary men and ordinary women, orthodox and heretic alike, to think seriously and deeply about issues of conscience and belief. And it prepares us for the paradox at the very heart of the Reformation story – a story of how shared visions of faith produced deep and lasting divisions in religion.

# PART II

*Separations*

# 5

## CONVERTS

### Assertions against Heresy

IN MARCH 1518, Thomas More received a parcel of books from his friend Erasmus. It contained a treatise on rhetoric by the humanist Richard Pace, a copy of Leo X's bull proposing a crusade against the Turks, and 'the conclusions on papal pardons'. Erasmus did not say so, but the author of these conclusions, known to us as the Ninety-Five Theses, was the German friar Martin Luther, who four months earlier sent them to the archbishop of Mainz, and proposed them for wider discussion. The commotion they created in Germany at first appeared a matter of relatively little importance to people elsewhere. Some 'quarrel among friars' was how it seemed to Pope Leo, preoccupied with the more pressing matter of the crusade.[1]

In England there was little immediate sense of alarm. A leading theologian – perhaps John Stokesley – was said to have declared in a court sermon that 'Erasmus is as far outstripped by Luther in knowledge of the Scriptures as Luther is surpassed by him in style'. Erasmus was flattered. At the centre of his web of correspondence, he kept English friends abreast of developments, while presenting himself to Germans as an authority on the faraway English. In May 1519, Erasmus wrote to assure Luther that 'you have people in England who think well of what you write, and they are in high place'. The following year, Erasmus told Luther's collaborator Philip Melanchthon that Cardinal Wolsey, 'a supporter of liberal studies', could find in Luther nothing to take offence at – 'except his denial that the primacy of the supreme pontiff is part of the divine law'. No big deal, as the prince of humanists saw matters.

Erasmus also claimed credit for heading off moves to burn Luther's books. Wolsey, 'on my advice', imposed silence on anyone planning to stir up the populace. The main culprit, so Erasmus thought, was Henry Standish, an intemperate critic of his New Testament. Compared to such 'barbarians',

Luther's heart was in the right place, though Erasmus could wish his ideas 'were more courteously and moderately expressed'. Even to Thomas More, reactionary attacks on the *Novum Instrumentum* were at this stage more disturbing than the activities of Luther. In February 1520, he dismissed a rumour the Pope was about to withdraw approval from Erasmus: compared with this, 'Luther's attacks upon the Holy See would be piety itself'.[2]

Luther was a minority interest. He may have been the best-selling author in Germany, but the Oxford bookseller John Dorne sold only eleven copies of various works by him in 1520, a year in which customers bought 150 of Erasmus's works. Even so, in 1521 John Longland, newly appointed bishop of Lincoln, instructed his commissary to search Oxford bookshops for Luther's and other books 'which young indiscreet persons will desirously read and talk of'.[3]

It was at Cambridge, early in 1521, that the first overt demonstration of support for Luther took place. A French student, Pierre de Valence, defaced a display copy of the papal bull of condemnation with a quotation from Psalm 39: 'Blessed is the man whose trust is in the name of the Lord: and who hath not had regard to vanities and lying follies.' The episode brought John Fisher to Cambridge to preach against Luther, and to pronounce sentence of excommunication against the (as yet anonymous) offender.[4] It was around this time, or a little later, that, according to a famous reference in John Foxe's *Acts and Monuments*, the 'godly learned' of Cambridge began consorting together at the White Horse Tavern. This was conveniently located, on present-day King's Lane, for members of St John's, Queens' College and King's College to sneak in by a back entrance. The gatherings, whenever they began to take place, were hardly top-secret, though, for opponents soon sarcastically christened the hostelry 'Germany'.[5]

Interest in Luther's ideas was not confined to a handful of university students. Already in 1520, Polydore Vergil thought a 'large number' of Lutheran books had come into the hands of English people. In March that year, a visitor from the West Country wrote home that there was no news in London, save that 'there were heretics here, which did take Luther's opinions'. When the Pope's bull condemning Martin Luther was posted at Boxley Abbey in Kent, it was torn down by a priest named Adam Bradshawe. From his gaol cell in Maidstone, Bradshawe composed 'seditious bills against the King's Grace's most honourable council', and arranged for them to be cast into the High Street.[6]

We do not know if Bradshawe was long disaffected from traditional religion or only recently radicalized. Boxley Abbey, site of a miraculous rood, was an established target of Lollard criticism.[7] Bishops were well aware of the differences between old Lollardy and new Lutheranism. But, paradoxically, they held to the view that all heresy was fundamentally the same thing. An instinctive response was to round up the usual suspects. In parallel with his investigations at Oxford, Longland launched an investigation into the Lollards of the Chiltern Hills; a few years later, Cuthbert Tunstall, bishop of London, started to crack open the networks of Essex Lollards lurking around the northern and eastern fringes of the capital.

Still, for the first half of the 1520s, the authorities in England believed, or affected to believe, that 'Lutheran' heresy was a distant rather than domestic danger. Luther's own stance, after his initial protest at the end of 1517, became increasingly radical. In the course of public debates with able opponents in 1519, he was manoeuvred into denying the inerrancy of councils as well as popes, and into assertions of the sole authority of scripture. Rome issued a definitive condemnation in June 1520. Luther's response was to burn the papal bull at Wittenberg, and to issue a provocative manifesto on *The Babylonian Captivity of the Church*. It claimed scripture taught not seven sacraments but three (baptism, penance, eucharist); that the mass was no sacrifice; that substance of bread and wine remained on the altar alongside the body of Christ; that the Pope was not head of the Church, but rather the Antichrist. There was no going back from this. Cuthbert Tunstall, on embassy to Emperor Charles V, marvelled at such 'strange opinions': 'I pray God keep that book out of England.'[8]

The English response to Luther devolved upon the cardinal legate. Heresy was not really Wolsey's forte. As a bishop he was too preoccupied with matters of state to concern himself with hunting Lollards. Whether or not Erasmus really talked him out of burning Luther's books, Wolsey was slow to organize this symbolic ritual. He was unsure his legatine authority allowed it – perhaps the only occasion when Wolsey modestly downplayed his own jurisdictional powers. In March 1521, the Cardinal Protector at Rome, Giulio de Medici, supplied reassurances, and urged Wolsey to get a move on. Finally galvanized, Wolsey convened in London in April 1521 a conference of leading theologians. Its members included a veteran defender of the Church's rights, Abbot Kidderminster, but also several of Erasmus's Cambridge friends: Henry Bullock, Humphrey Walkenden, John Watson.[9] Whatever the hesitations of Erasmus himself, humanists were not programmed to sympathize with Luther. The country's brightest humanist stars, John Fisher and Thomas More, were soon to reveal themselves as his most implacable English opponents.

On Sunday 12 May 1521, copies of Luther's books were consigned to the flames in a splendid ceremony at the cross outside St Paul's Cathedral. Wolsey showed up – two hours late – to be greeted by the cathedral clergy, so the Venetian ambassador noted, 'as if the Pope in person had arrived', and solemnly excommunicated Luther and his followers.[10] Yet for all his customary glitz and glamour, Wolsey was not the real star. John Fisher, the austere theologian-bishop, preached for two hours against Luther and his doctrines. He defended papal primacy, and the ceremonies and traditions of the Church. But already Fisher could see, with greater clarity than others, that this was not really the

heart of the matter. Luther's challenge struck much deeper and more insidiously. At its root was a beguiling claim: 'that faith alone without works doth
justify a sinner'. If this were so, what need then for the grace of the sacraments,
for deeds of Christian charity, for ecclesiastical discipline? It was, Fisher
reflected, 'a perilous article, able to subvert all the order of the Church'.

Within three weeks, Richard Pace, dean of St Paul's and royal secretary,
translated Fisher's oration into Latin, and sent it to Leo X for him to see 'what
sort of members the Catholic Church has in this kingdom, so remote from the
rest of the world'. The Pope was predictably pleased. More significant were
efforts made by Fisher to have his sermon printed, as he delivered it, in English.
It appeared from the press of Wynkyn de Worde in the autumn of 1521, was
reprinted the following year, and again in 1527.[11] The case for traditional religion was to be presented to the people, Fisher's numerous quotations from the
Vulgate translated for the benefit of lay readers. A battle for hearts and minds
was under way.

Fisher's sermon was not Pope Leo's only literary gift from England in 1521.
Wolsey had sent the King a copy of the *Babylonian Captivity*, and on 16 April
Pace came across him reading it, and full of indignation at its impieties. Henry
had already started to write against Luther on indulgences, but with papal
encouragement he now set about a more comprehensive confutation.

As ever with Henry, the motives were mixed. Wolsey and Pace were immediately calculating the diplomatic advantages of a royal book, sent not only to
Rome, but 'into France and other nations'. It was a golden opportunity for
reviving the stalled negotiations over a papal title. And even at a moment of
danger for the faith, Henry was determined his royal rights were not to be
compromised. The King liked the look of the papal bull, but told Pace he would
have it 'well examined and diligently looked to' before permission was granted
for publication in England.[12]

Henry's *Assertio Septem Sacramentorum* (Defence of the Seven Sacraments)
– the first book ever written for the press by an English monarch – was
completed in time for Wolsey to brandish a manuscript copy at the book-
burning of May 1521. It was printed in London in July, and copies soon winged
their way to Rome. In gratitude, Leo X invested Henry with the title of *Fidei
Defensor*, defender of the faith. The King would ever after keep faith with the
title, if not with the faith itself. Henry's foray into theology was a publishing
phenomenon, with editions rapidly appearing at Rome, Strassburg and
Antwerp, along with two translations into German. It was hailed internationally as a major vindication of orthodoxy, and frequently reprinted.[13]

The success owed more to the celebrity status of the author than the intrinsic
quality of the book. Yet the *Assertio* was a robust and competent polemic,
restating scriptural and patristic proofs for all seven sacraments. Perhaps
significantly, the basis of papal primacy was not a subject Henry felt moved to

develop at length, declaring merely, 'I will not wrong the Bishop of Rome so much, as troublesomely, or carefully to dispute his right, as if it were a matter doubtful.'

Henry also postured as the astute humanist scholar, taking issue with Luther over the gender of Hebrew nouns. And he wanted readers to know he was no blind obscurantist, admitting he could see no reason in principle why the Church should not offer communion in both kinds to the laity. He waxed more passionate about the subversive implications of Luther's understanding of faith and liberty, which threatened to undermine all authority of princes and prelates. But Henry regally reined in his distemper: 'I forbear to speak of kings, lest I should seem to plead my own case.'

And it was Henry's own case, rather than, as suggested then and later, a book ghostwritten for him by Fisher, Pace or More; even, some said, by Erasmus. Nonetheless, it is likely Wolsey's 1521 conference of theologians played a part in preparing materials, and in later years Thomas More, while denying he inveigled Henry into producing the book, admitted to having been its editor, 'a sorter-out and placer of the principal matters therein contained'.[14]

Luther, in a reply published at Wittenberg in 1522, gave full vent to his stock-piles of colourful vituperation. Henry was a 'stupid and sacrilegious king', an 'ass', 'dunghill', 'lying buffoon', 'spawn of an adder', a 'mad fool with a frothy mouth and whorish face'.[15] Even friends felt he had gone too far. But the Wittenberg reformer, no respecter of earthly personages, was wholly unrepentant.

Vindication of the King's honour became an additional motive for writing in support of orthodoxy. John Fisher composed a learned *Defensio Regiae Assertionis* (Defence of the King's Argument) for European consumption. This complemented his 1522 *Sacri Sacerdotii Defensio* (Defence of the Holy Priesthood), and 1523 *Assertionis Lutheranae Confutatio* (Confutation of the Argument of Luther) – a penetrating critique of Luther's doctrines of *sola fide* (faith alone) and *sola scriptura* (the bible alone). With both the King and the learned bishop of Rochester lighting the way, England was hailed as a beacon of orthodoxy: leading German controversialists like Johan Eck, Thomas Murner, Jerome Emser and Johan Cochlaeus praised Fisher's work or wrote in Henry's defence. The Franciscan Murner came to England in the summer of 1523, hopeful for royal patronage; Eck visited in 1525.[16]

Fisher handled the serious theology, but the job of responding to Luther in kind – to which the King could not be seen to stoop – fell to Thomas More, the street-smart lawyer. Under the pseudonym 'William Ross', More published a lengthy *Responsio ad Lutherum*, which conveyed low personal invective in elevated humanist Latin – a text disconcertingly full of sewage, shit, vomit, poison, pimps, asses and pigs.[17]

Luther was an ogre, from a faraway land. Fisher, More and Henry wrote against him in Latin, to discredit him in the eyes of an elite European readership, and to burnish England's credentials for Catholic fidelity. They were joined by a host of lesser luminaries: Edward Powell, Henry Bullock, Edward Lee, William Melton and Catherine of Aragon's Spanish confessor, Alphonsus de Villasancta. When Luther's associate Johann Bugenhagen published in 1525 a hopeful *Epistola ad Anglos* (Letter to the English), on the basis of reports that 'in England too the gospel of the glory of God has been well received', More firmly slapped him down. If, by 'the gospel', Bugenhagen meant the faith of Christ and the evangelists, then it had been received everywhere in England for a thousand years. If he meant the 'new, destructive, absurd doctrines' dreamt up by Luther and spread around by himself, 'there is hardly anyone in England who welcomes that gospel of yours'.[18]

That was probably true, or almost true, at the time of writing. After Longland's sweep through the Chilterns in 1521, there is an almost complete absence of documented heresy cases before the end of 1525. Thomas Batman, hermit of St William's Chapel near Rochester, appeared before Fisher in December 1524, and admitted to Lollard-sounding critiques of shrines and images, and having praised changes taking place 'beyond the sea'. Another isolated case was that of Roger Hackman. At the church ale in North Stoke, Oxfordshire, in 1525, he tactlessly announced that 'I will never look to be saved for no good deed that ever I did, neither for any that ever I will do, without I may have my salvation by petition, as an outlaw shall have his pardon of the King.' Perhaps this was an assertion of justification by faith; perhaps a tortuous expression of the orthodox teaching that both faith and works were necessary for salvation. Either way, the authorities were becoming vigilant, and wary of theological speculations on the part of the laity.[19]

In the autumn of 1524, an official system of licensing came into operation, when Tunstall summoned London booksellers before him to warn them against the sale or importation of heretical texts. No new works were to be published or imported without prior permission from Tunstall, Wolsey, Warham or Fisher.

The bishops meant business. On 7 October 1525 Wynkyn de Worde was charged with printing without permission a text called *The Image of Love*, and, along with its translator, John Gough, was summoned before the Vicar General of London. The *Image* was a fairly innocuous work of Christocentric devotion, written by the Observant Franciscan John Ryckes as a New Year's gift for the Bridgettine nuns of Syon. Yet its strictures on finding the true image of love, 'not in painted cloths and carved images', but in scripture, sounded suspicious in these distrustful times. Thereafter, London printers towed the line, staying away from subversive or controversial publications.[20]

Through the first half of the decade, the new heresy still seemed to be what Fisher called it in his sermon of 1521, 'a thick black cloud', lowering on the distant horizon. No storm had broken in England, but that was soon to change.

## Tyndale's Testament

In the spring of 1523, a young priest called William Tyndale arrived in London from the country. After a stint at Oxford, Tyndale had returned to his native Gloucestershire to serve as a chantry priest and then as chaplain and tutor to the children of Sir John Walsh, at Little Sodbury, half a day's ride to the north-west of Bristol. His university days coincided with the publication of Erasmus's *Novum Instrumentum*. Tyndale, like other young idealists, was caught up in the excitement of the humanist spring, with its promise of a simpler, purer Christianity.

Walsh was in the habit of entertaining local clergymen to dinner: 'sundry abbots, deans, archdeacons, with other divers doctors and great beneficed men'. The table talk often turned to the ideas of Luther and Erasmus. Tyndale was not shy of challenging the opinions of his elders and betters, or of trying to win his employers to his ways of thinking. Lady Walsh wondered why she should take her lowly chaplain's opinions over those of 'a doctor which may dispend £100, and another £200, and another £300'. Tyndale was preparing his answer: a translation into English of Erasmus's *Enchiridion*. After the Walshes read it, clergymen were no longer so often invited to the house, or so welcome when they turned up.[21]

Tyndale soon set his sights on a yet more ambitious project: a translation into English, and for the press, of the New Testament itself. It is sometimes suggested that Tyndale's scriptural interests were a Lollard inheritance from his native Gloucestershire. But an interest in vernacular scripture was far from exclusive to Lollards, and the evidence for anything more than a patchy Lollard presence in the county is thin.[22] More likely, Tyndale's attraction towards scripture was initially an orthodox one, tilted in reformist directions by his discovery of Erasmus. Tyndale is recorded as debating with a learned Gloucestershire divine, badgering him with references to 'God's law' until the priest swore in exasperation that 'We were better to be without God's law than the Pope's'. Tyndale responded: 'I defy the Pope and all his laws!' and added that, 'if God spared him life, ere many years he would cause a boy that driveth the plough to know more of the Scripture' than the petulant priest did. The exchange has the pious ring of posthumous production. But if Tyndale did say it, he surely knew he was echoing the *Paraclesis* of Erasmus's *Novum Instrumentum*.[23]

The impression of these early years from the later Protestant historian John Foxe, and from Tyndale's own accounts, is of an unswerving fidelity to the cause of the Gospel, and near-martyrdom at the hands of reactionary priests. But this obscures the extent to which discussion and debate were clearly taking place *within* the social and religious settings of late medieval Catholicism. Before the Gloucestershire clergy lost patience with the Walshes' zealot of a chaplain, there were many lively arguments about the interpretation of scripture, 'reasoning and contending together'.[24]

Tyndale's next step reinforces an impression of someone eager to reform the system from within. He sought the patronage of Bishop Cuthbert Tunstall, hoping he would license his New Testament translation, in accordance with Archbishop Arundel's 1409 Constitutions. Once again, the influence of Erasmus seems key: Tyndale approached Tunstall because of praise lavished on him by the great humanist. Through an introduction from his master, Tyndale employed the offices of the controller of the royal household, Sir Henry Guildford, and prepared a translation from the Greek orator Isocrates as an example of his skill. Tyndale was not brushed off as dismissively as modern accounts usually suggest. Tunstall favoured him with a personal reply (it's unclear if they met face to face), and while the bishop explained he had no room for another chaplain in his household, he spoke warmly enough about prospects for employment within the city. There is no suggestion the bishop immediately suspected him of nefarious heresy.

For nearly a year, Tyndale sought for patronage in the capital, and his bubbling Erasmian reformism began to cool, harden and crack. At the best of times, London was a demoralizing place for an unemployed priest, let alone an argumentative idealist looking at a succession of closed doors. Tyndale came to the realization that not only was there 'no room in my lord of London's palace to translate the New Testament, but also that there was no place to do it in all England'.[25]

In the spring of 1524, Tyndale left for Hamburg, his passage paid by a wealthy member of the Drapers' Company, Humphrey Monmouth, with whom Tyndale left the manuscript of his English *Enchiridion*. Monmouth heard Tyndale preach at St Dunstan-in-the-West and, impressed, took him into his household. According to Foxe, Monmouth was already 'a scripture man', who had 'begun to smell the gospel'. But he does not look like a classic Lollard. Monmouth asked Tyndale to say masses for the souls of his parents, he possessed papal pardons acquired on a pilgrimage to Rome, and he gave financial support to various priests and religious houses of unquestioned orthodoxy. Yet it is clear that he knew and approved of what Tyndale was doing under his roof in translating the New Testament. The consciences of affluent Catholic layfolk – urban, literate and reformist, at ease with educated clergymen and impatient with ignorant ones – would be a key battleground in the struggle about to commence.[26]

Tyndale's movements in 1524 are obscure; it is possible he visited Wittenberg and met Luther. In 1525, he was in Cologne, where, assisted by a runaway Observant named William Roye, he attempted to oversee production of a printed edition of the New Testament of which he now had a complete manuscript text. Before the end of the year, news of this reached Edward Lee at Bordeaux, en route to diplomatic duties in Spain. France, Lee reported, was already 'somewhat touched with this sect'; England, he thanked God, 'is yet unblotted'. But Lee feared the arrival of Tyndale's translation. He warned Henry: 'this is the next way to fill your realm with Lutherans. For all Luther's perverse opinions be grounded upon bare words of Scripture, not well taken nor understood.' Christian faith in England 'cannot long endure if these books may come in'.[27]

In the meantime, there was a hitch. Johan Cochlaeus, a leading anti-Lutheran polemicist, was in Cologne to oversee production of a new book. He caught wind of Tyndale's plans and went to the city authorities, after hearing some printers boasting how 'all England would soon be Lutheran'. Tyndale and Roye, with copies of an incomplete text, fled up-river to Worms, a place where, Cochlaeus sneered, 'the people were in the full frenzy of Lutheranism'.[28]

The Worms edition completed in early 1526 was less elaborate than the unfinished Cologne version, which seems to have got no further than Mark's Gospel. It was physically smaller (octavo, or pocket size), and lacked the marginal notes and Prologue accompanying the earlier text, which were based closely on Luther's editorial material for the German New Testament of 1522. It was, nonetheless, a remarkable achievement: the first translation of the core texts of Christianity into English from the Greek in which they were originally written. The English of Tyndale's translation was lively and idiomatic, occasionally eccentric, but it mirrored the familiar patterns and cadences of English as it was spoken by his contemporaries.[29]

Even without marginal glosses and introductions, the Worms New Testament was a subversive document. Tyndale ended the text with an epilogue assuring readers that if they believed these 'words of health', they would be 'born anew, created afresh, and enjoy the fruits of the blood of Christ'. He supplied a primer in Luther's theology of justification, patiently explaining the distinction between Law and Gospel. The moral commandments of God (Law) were designed to elicit a sorrowful acknowledgement of sinfulness, and a recognition that it was in fact impossible to fulfil the Law's demands. But when a believer turned to the promises of the Gospel, 'so shalt thou not despair, but shall feel God as a kind and merciful father'.[30]

This was a manual for short-circuiting the Church's established mechanisms of consolation and assurance – in particular, the system of sacramental penance, with its cyclical pattern of sin, confession and absolution. Orthodox theologians did not fear there was anything in the New Testament that undermined or contradicted the sacraments and rituals of the Church, though they were all too aware scripture could be falsely translated, falsely interpreted, falsely expounded. Yet the long-standing prohibitions on translation allowed reformers to repeat a tendentious, yet nigglingly plausible claim: the clergy kept scripture from the people because they did not want them to discover its true content and meaning.[31]

The meaning of scripture, Tyndale told purchasers of his Testament, was 'plain and manifest'. There were admittedly some 'doubtful places', but these could be explicated through comparison with other passages. The conventional method of interpretation involved a four-fold approach: a passage would be scrutinized for allegorical, tropological (moral) and anagogical (prophetic) meanings, in addition to its literal ones. For Tyndale and his allies, this was simple obfuscation.[32]

But plain and manifest meanings of scripture are truth claims, not verifiable facts, and translations are invariably acts of interpretation. Some of Tyndale's linguistic choices, like those of Erasmus in Latin, were controversial, and to orthodox sensibilities, downright shocking. Tyndale's New Testament was no monument to neutral scholarship. It was a theological argument.

Several choices in particular outraged Tyndale's critics, confirming their opinion that what was being smuggled into England was not the New Testament of Christ, but a pernicious mockery of it – 'Tyndale's Testament' or 'Luther's Testament'.[33] By rendering the Greek word *charis* (*gratia* in the Vulgate), as 'favour' not 'grace', Tyndale downplayed the importance of grace-giving sacraments. Making *agape* into 'love' rather than 'charity' (*caritas*) shifted focus away from acts of charity – good works.

Other translations hit directly at structures of ecclesiastical authority. *Presbyteros*, a term of early Christian leadership, was transliterated as *presbyter* in the Vulgate, and gave rise to the English word 'priest'. Tyndale initially had it as 'senior', subsequently changed to the less foreign-sounding 'elder'. *Ekklesia* (Latin, *ecclesia*; English, church) became 'congregation'. Most crucially, the Greek verb *metanoeite* was rendered as 'repent', instead of, as the Vulgate had it, 'do penance' (*poenitentiam agite*). It signalled an interior turning to God in the heart, rather than restorative action through the sacrament of confession. In an angry and alarmist letter of February 1527, Tunstall's chaplain Robert Ridley protested to Warham's chaplain Henry Gold that 'by this translation, shall we lose all these Christian words: penance, charity, confession, grace, priest, church'. The interlocking elements of an entire framework of faith and practice were being recklessly unscrewed and discarded.[34]

That was how things appeared to Thomas More, who pursued Tyndale relentlessly over the bad faith, in every sense, of his New Testament translations. Tyndale countered with accusations of rank hypocrisy: had not More's 'darling', Erasmus, in his translation from the Greek, used 'congregatio' for 'ekklesia', as well as Latin equivalents of 'elder' and 'repent'? For More, that was beside the point. Erasmus was not advocating the abandonment of confession, or redefinitions of priesthood and the Church. Tyndale was not a heretic for translating scripture, or even for translating it incorrectly. His translation was toxic because it was made, like Luther's, with blatant heretical intent.[35]

Tyndale's New Testament was an instrument of aggression towards the Church and traditional religion. The bishops, including Tyndale's erstwhile best hope, Cuthbert Tunstall, had no hesitation in banning it. But the champions of tradition were acutely aware of the attraction exerted by the translation on people who – initially at least – thought of themselves as loyal Catholics. Tyndale, so More believed, deviously began with this 'thing that had a good visage'. Another anti-Lutheran writer took it for granted that good people were 'desirous to have the gospel in their mother tongue for the erudition and comfort of their souls'. Questioned by the authorities in May 1528, Tyndale's patron Humphrey Monmouth claimed he did not suspect anything was amiss about Tyndale until he heard Bishop Tunstall preach that the New Testament was 'naughtily translated'. Remarkably, the revised edition of Tyndale's New Testament, printed by Martin de Keyser at Antwerp in 1534, with restored notes and Lutheran prologues, also contained an appended lectionary of Old and New Testament texts to be read in church on Sundays and feast days 'after the use of Salisbury', just as many Wycliffite bibles earlier did (see p. 118). Tyndale's New Testament cheekily marketed itself as an aid to devotion for mass-going Catholics.[36]

The vernacular New Testament was a game-changer, catching the authorities on the back foot. Orthodox writers often accepted that translation was in principle meritorious, while insisting the current climate was simply not propitious for it. In 1527, and again in 1530, Henry VIII promised to allow people an English version, but only when he might 'see their manners and behaviour meet, apt and convenient to receive the same'. In the meantime, a heretical translation existed, and heretics appealed to its authority. As one Catholic author bitterly complained, they endlessly repeated 'the Word of God, the Gospel of Christ', hoping to make people believe that 'whatsoever they write or teach' was that very Word.[37]

Increasingly, religious controversies in England were an argument about the bible: who had the right to read or interpret it; which doctrines and practices did it mandate or condemn. Above all, this was a debate about authority. In the titanic literary contest between William Tyndale and Thomas More, it resolved itself into a deceptively straightforward question: which came first, the scripture or the Church?

More believed the answer to be obvious to any right-thinking person. The community established by Christ during his ministry on earth – the Catholic Church – produced a record of that ministry in the gospels, Acts of the Apostles and epistles. An authoritative understanding of those texts, guaranteed by the Holy Spirit, was preserved down the centuries in the body that created them.

Debates about meanings of scripture could safely be referred to a historic consensus of interpretation. If there were doctrines that did not seem to be scripturally grounded – for example, that Mary, the mother of Christ, remained perpetually a virgin – that was because scripture did not preserve the totality of Christ's sayings or of apostolic teachings. The end of St John's Gospel noted other things Jesus did, 'the which, if they should be written every one . . . even the world itself could not contain the books'. 'Unwritten verities' endured in the collective memory of the Church. If it were really the case that reading scripture was essential to salvation, then most Christians who ever lived were doomed to perish eternally – so unpalatable a proposition as surely to be untrue.[38]

Tyndale could hardly deny the gospels were written by Christians years after the death of Christ. For him, questions of priority were not so much chronological as existential. The 'Word' was an eternal expression of God's loving will, revealed in complete perfection in the written words of the Gospel. The Church – a congregation of believers scattered in time and space – was continually constituted by the Word, as it was received in the hearts of the faithful. More's unwritten verities were 'as true and authentic as his stories of Utopia'.[39]

It is far from certain that an episcopally approved, orthodox New Testament translation, with glosses and explanations demonstrating scripture's agreement with the customs and rituals of Catholicism, would have defused dissent, or even prevented it arising. Other parts of Europe, where translations circulated relatively freely before the Reformation, were hardly sheltered from the storm.

But the association of vernacular scripture with opposition undoubtedly proved a tactical advantage to Tyndale and his allies. The bishops' refusal to countenance an approved translation could be portrayed – with some justice – as a failure of nerve. It lent credence to claims that supporters of the status quo were opposed to lay bible-reading in principle. If corrupt translations were really the issue, then they 'have had leisure enough to put forth another well translated'. The reality was they would have done it long since, 'if ye could make your glosses agree with the text'.[40]

By defining – redefining – Christianity as a religion of the bible alone, and by refusing to concede, or even constructively discuss, the validity of practices without explicit biblical underpinning, the rebels inexorably drew their opponents onto ground of their own choosing. Another shrewd hit was William Roye's publication, in Antwerp in 1529, of an English translation of Erasmus's *Paraclesis*, with its visions of the ploughman singing 'a text of scripture at his plough-beam'. By giving all scriptural citations in the edition from the 1526 New Testament, Roye co-opted the charisma of Erasmus for the promotion of Tyndale's work.[41] The cause of the early English reformers was, as they themselves saw it, the cause of 'the gospel'. More than any other activity, production, distribution, reception and consumption of vernacular bibles provided dissidents with a missionary purpose, and a marker of measurable success.

## Abjuration

Heresy was still – officially – a problem intruding from the outside, when, at the start of 1526, and with worrying reports of Tyndale's activities arriving on his desk, Wolsey planned another public burning of Lutheran works. The King approved, showing himself – as Longland wrote effusively to Wolsey – 'as fervent in this cause of Christ's Church, and maintenance of the same, as ever a noble prince was'.[42]

It was another dazzling occasion: no fewer than thirty-six mitred abbots and bishops joined the cardinal in a packed St Paul's Cathedral. At the King's recommendation, John Fisher once again took to the pulpit. 'Great basketfuls' of confiscated books were on display, and were then carried outside for burning.

Also present, making a public abjuration of heresy, were four hapless German merchants, members of the Hanseatic community headquartered at the Steelyard on the north bank of the Thames near London Bridge. They were arrested following a raid on the premises led by Thomas More. The Germans had been reading scripture in Luther's translation, and they confessed to owning works by him and other reformers, and to eating meat on fast days. Yet they do not seem to have been importing books for wider distribution, or to have been discussing ideas very much beyond their own circle.[43] It was increasingly implausible for lapses in the nation's orthodoxy to be entirely blamed on foreigners.

Kneeling alongside the Hanseatic merchants was an English friar, Robert Barnes, prior of the Augustinian house in Cambridge. His presence was a late addition to the proceedings, and a worrying indication of the current state of things in the universities. Barnes was present at discussions at the White Horse, but that did not make him a heretic. Others participants included Stephen Gardiner, soon to be considered the model of conservative orthodoxy. Barnes, like other morally serious and intellectually curious priests, was certainly reading Luther. But the White Horse group in the early 1520s was less a cell of committed Lutherans, more a book group of reform-minded enthusiasts.[44]

A brotherhood of dissent was, however, forming in Cambridge. Thomas Bilney, fellow of Trinity Hall, underwent a profound change of heart after poring over Erasmus's Greek New Testament. His attention was caught – as Luther's was – by St Paul's passages about the justified living by faith. Bilney was in demand as a father confessor, and through this most clerical and orthodox of rites, trust in the old order was insidiously eroded. One of his penitents was Hugh Latimer, whose conventional pieties were eviscerated by Bilney's words of private counsel. It was a similar story with Barnes. Bilney – as Foxe later put it – 'converted him wholly unto Christ'.[45] It is hard to be certain what, in the early 1520s, such a phrase precisely meant. But it undoubtedly involved impatience with the current ecclesiastical leadership, indifference – if not antagonism – to much traditional piety, and a zeal for the scriptures as the key to a more authentic relationship with God.

Barnes dramatically broke cover on Christmas Eve, 1525, in a sermon at St Edward's Church, Cambridge. That Barnes did not preface his oration with the accustomed prayers for souls in purgatory was the least of it. In decidedly unfestive spirit, he argued that Christians were no more bound to serve God on holy days like Christmas than at any other times, and he queried the value of prayers made by priests who 'mumble and roar out their diriges and masses'.

The core of the sermon was an indictment of the bishops, purported successors of Christ who actually 'follow none but Judas'. Barnes excoriated their pomp, pride and 'delicious' life. There was also a digression against excommunications and ecclesiastical courts, prompted by a local churchwarden's heartless pursuit of a poor executor for a small legacy, something Barnes heard about from the distressed widow. He struck a familiar note of anticlerical grievance: no man might dare preach truly without being accused of heresy. And he implied that two Flemish Augustinians, burned three years earlier at Brussels, were true martyrs of God.[46]

Hauled before the university authorities, Barnes dragged his feet over a public recantation. The vice-chancellor informed Wolsey, and Barnes was summoned to appear at Westminster. The cardinal ordered a search of college rooms for heretical books, but a Lutheran sympathizer, the president of Queens' College, Robert Farman, put the word out, and suspect volumes were preemptively squirrelled away. Wolsey treated Barnes with surprising forbearance, and Gardiner, now in the cardinal's employ, also interceded on his behalf. Still, in the end it was turn or burn, and Barnes decided to turn.[47]

Was he at this stage a heretic? Barnes said nothing directly about justification by faith, priesthood of all believers, sole sufficiency of scripture, or other avowedly Lutheran doctrines, though he did base his sermon on a postil (sermon outline) of Luther's. Mendicant preaching was frequently hard-hitting, and famously undeferential to bishops. Gardiner believed such 'railing in a friar had been easily pardoned', had Barnes not espoused the 'anabaptist' opinion that lawsuits among Christians were forbidden. Even at a moment of growing doctrinal rebellion, jurisdictional matters remained the sorest point for some churchmen. Barnes's strictures on pluralism and clerical avarice were not wildly different from what Colet, pillar of the establishment, said to Convocation in 1512. But Colet spoke in Latin to his ecclesiastical peers; Barnes preached in English to an urban lay congregation. John Fisher, one of the commissioners appointed by Wolsey, admitted to Barnes that his insistence on a Christian's obligation to serve God with equal fervour every day of the year was something 'he would not condemn for heresy for £100'. But, Fisher added, it was 'foolish to preach this before the butchers of Cambridge'.[48]

The relative leniency with which Wolsey and Fisher treated Barnes shows they believed reconciliation to be possible. In his sermon preached at Barnes's abjuration, Fisher made a remarkable pledge. If any disciple of Luther wanted to come to him in secret, 'and break his mind at more length', he promised confidentially to hear him out: 'either he shall make me a Lutheran or else I shall induce him to be a Catholic'.[49] It was an arresting offer; not one Bishop Longland was ever tempted to make to Lollard artisans in the Chiltern villages. The authorities now recognized that heretics might be 'people like us' – students and teachers, friars and doctors. There would have to be an effort to understand what drew them to the new doctrines in order to cure them from their effects.

### Pathways to Conversion

> I have thought in times past, that the Pope, Christ's vicar, hath been Lord of all the world . . . that the Pope could have spoiled purgatory at his pleasure with a word of his mouth . . . that if I had been a friar, and in a cowl, I could not have been damned . . . that divers images of saints could have helped me, and done me much good . . . Now I abhor my superstitious foolishness.[50]

Hugh Latimer's description of a religious transformation, written in December 1531, is both revealing and enigmatic. Contemporaries believed conversions of this sort were the work of God – or of the devil. Some historians have rightly warned us that there was more to the Reformation than a succession of individual religious conversions, noting that most people didn't undergo one.[51] But without such conversions there could have been no Reformation, and attempting to untangle them draws us to the mysterious seed-beds in which change first took root. For historians have to make sense of a paradox: that a convert's radical rejection of the old and familiar could not come out of nowhere; that it must somehow be grounded in earlier attitudes and experiences.

For some, perhaps not much conversion was required. The concern of orthodox propagandists, that new Lutheranism was but old Wyclifism writ large, was a self-fulfilling prophecy. Lollards were keen to find out about the new ideas, to make contact with their proponents, and to get hold of new texts – especially the printed New Testament. A determination to prevent such contacts is the explanation for a late burst of anti-Lollard activity; in particular, Bishop Tunstall's investigations in Essex and London in early 1528, triggered by the arrest of the Lollard evangelist, John Hacker.

Hacker's testimony led to a conventicle of Lollards at Colchester, where the baker John Pykas confessed to having a copy of Tyndale's New Testament, bought in 1526 from a Lombard of London. His friend Thomas Hilles, 'a great reader amongst them', likewise had 'a book of the New Testament in English, printed'. Pykas went to Ipswich to hear Bilney preach, and considered his sermons 'most ghostly made, and best for his purposes and opinions as any that ever he heard in his life'. Yet it was not so much the message of spiritual liberation through the gratuitous grace of Christ that struck a chord with Pykas as Bilney's vigorous condemnation of pilgrimage and image worship. It was the familiar, not the strange and challenging, that Lollards first heard and responded to in 'Lutheran' teaching.[52]

Yet networks of old dissent and new reform were starting to mesh and merge in ways Tunstall and his commissaries found deeply unsettling. A regular participant in the Colchester conventicle was the London book-runner Robert Necton. Necton was a working man, not a university intellectual or affluent merchant. But neither was he some veteran Lollard artisan: he denied owning Wycliffite texts, yet he admitted keeping Tyndale's New Testament in defiance of the prohibition, and having 'read it thoroughly many times'. Necton was a Catholic who caught the bug of 'the gospel'; books – the urge to buy, sell, read and discuss them – drew him to the Lollard circles on the fringes of the capital.[53]

The other nest of Lollards disturbed in the spring of 1528 was at Steeple Bumpstead, a group closely linked to Pykas's Colchester circle. Here, the testimony is remarkable, not least for revealing convergences between old Lollardy and the people previously most immune to its blandishments: the friars. John Tyball confessed that about five years earlier he had made his confession to a Colchester Franciscan, Friar Meadow, who begged his help in escaping from 'religion'. Tyball sheltered him, shaved the distinctive tonsure from his head, and sent him – where else? – to Amersham. Tyball's curate, the irrepressible Richard Fox, meanwhile disturbed the faith of several inmates of Clare Priory, five miles east of Bumpstead across the Suffolk border. These were Augustinians – Luther's order. Friars William Gardiner, Thomas Topley and John Wyggen were acknowledged by the Bumpstead Lollards to be members of their 'sect'.[54]

It may have been through Clare that the Bumpstead Lollards secured an introduction to Robert Barnes. In the autumn of 1526, after temporary incarceration in the Fleet, Barnes was transferred to the London house of his order, so his confreres could keep an eye on him. They did not do a very good job. At Michaelmas 1526 Tyball and Thomas Hilles came to London to seek him out and 'buy a New Testament in English'.

The story is justly famous, and supplies an arresting snapshot of the coalition forming around Tyndale's vernacular bible. Tyball found the university-educated friar in his chamber, in the company of three or four others, one of them 'a merchant man reading in a book'. The two Lollards explained themselves, and boasted how their curate, Richard Fox, 'by their means was well entered into their learning'. Barnes promised to send Fox a letter of encouragement, and he sold the visitors a pair of printed New Testaments, while assuring them that in Latin the New Testament was no more than 'a cymbal tinkling and brass sounding' – itself a quotation from Tyndale's translation of I Corinthians 13:1.

The mood, however, went flat when the Bumpstead Lollards proudly brought out 'certain old books that they had' – manuscripts of the four gospels, and various epistles of Peter and Paul. Barnes was underwhelmed by these hallowed testimonies of the Wycliffite witness. These books 'the said friar did little regard, and made a twit of it . . . "A point for them! For they be not to be regarded toward the new printed Testament in English. For it is of more cleaner English." '[55]

Friar Barnes D.Th. (*Doctor Theologiae*) did not think these rustic gospellers had much to teach him. Hilles remembered his reading to them 'a chapter of Paul' – perhaps an instruction in the theology of justification that Luther found in St Paul, but which was conspicuously absent from the mental inventory of late medieval heresy. Lollardy and Lutheranism was a marriage made in heaven, but it took time for the partners to get to know each other, and there was pragmatic calculation as well as romantic attraction in the burgeoning relationship. Lollards welcomed the printed New Testament and, through their established networks, helped in its distribution. For most of them, however, it seemed a confirmation and vindication of existing preoccupations, rather than any dramatic new departure.

For their part, reformers found in Lollardy a market for their books, a sympathetic convergence of attitudes, and a reservoir of old texts in which they could selectively fish. Only later would reformers fully elaborate the idea that Lollards represented a link in the historical chain of a persecuted 'true Church', connecting believers of current times with those of the apostolic age, and providing an answer to the recurrent Catholic jeer, 'where was your Church before Luther?' Yet, from a relatively early date, the exiles edited and published antique Lollard works: some half-dozen were printed at Antwerp in 1530–2, with occasional editorial apology for their old 'barbarous' style, but also to supply evidence that 'it is no new thing, but an old practice of our prelates . . . to defame the doctrine of Christ with the name of new learning'.[56]

Some claims about Lollard contributions to the origins of the English Reformation have undoubtedly been exaggerated.[57] Lollardy's restricted geographical diffusion, its retreat from the universities, its lack of intellectual rigour, its traditions of concealment and compromise – all these amounted to a slender foundation on which to build a dynamic evangelizing movement. Heresy trials at this time suggest that many Lollards remained essentially unaffected by Luther's doctrines of grace and theology of the cross.

Others did move towards a synthesis of new and old. Thomas Harding of Amersham came to the attention of the authorities in 1506, and again in 1522, when, failing to detect other Lollards, he was forced to wear the symbol of the faggot. In 1532, dwelling at Chesham, he was spotted reading a volume of English prayers and again reported. His books now included copies of Tyndale's *Obedience of a Christian Man* and *Practice of Prelates*, as well as his New Testament. Harding confessed to holding familiar Lollard opinions about images, holy water and the eucharist, but defended his view that confession was unnecessary on the grounds that 'the faith which you have in God is sufficient for your salvation'.[58]

Lollardy was one pathway to conversion, but it was not the route taken by the majority. None of the most prominent figures of the 1520s and early 1530s – Barlow, Barnes, Coverdale, Fish, Frith, Joye, Latimer, Roye, Tyndale – had a background in Lollardy. They were all, an opponent noted, 'before fast in the Catholic faith'. The preaching of Bilney against pilgrimage and images, like aspects of Barnes's Cambridge sermon, certainly sounded Lollard. But direct influences, rather than resort to a common repertoire of anticlerical and anti-ritualist themes, are impossible to trace. The early Reformation in England had a sympathetic Lollard godmother, but its parents were orthodox and Catholic.

Catholic orthodoxy in the early sixteenth century had a pronounced humanist flavour. It would be fatuous to claim humanism directly 'caused' the Reformation. Erasmus certainly thought it was. In 1524 he responded indignantly to the accusation of some friars that he 'laid the egg and Luther hatched it'. Erasmus insisted that he had laid a hen's egg, 'and Luther has hatched a chick of a very different feather'.[59]

But Erasmian ideals undoubtedly helped foster a critical perspective on traditional piety, as well as a yearning for a simpler, more direct and authentic relationship with God. This was the starting point for Tyndale's journey of discovery, and though he subsequently became disillusioned with Erasmus, Tyndale continued in his writings to acknowledge a debt to the Dutch humanist's biblical scholarship. Erasmus's *Novum Instrumentum* had, after all, provided the base text and much of the philological groundwork for his own translation. And Tyndale carried the scars of some old scholarly battles, inviting readers of his *Answer to More* to remember how 'within this thirty years and . . . unto this day, the old barking curs, Duns's disciples and like draff called Scotists, the children of darkness, raged in every pulpit against Greek, Latin and Hebrew'.[60]

Many scholars espousing Lutheran ideas in the 1520s were on the side of Greek, Hebrew and Latin rhetoric in the university wars initiated by curricular reform and the appearance of Erasmus's New Testament. Robert Barnes studied in Louvain during Erasmus's residency, and on his return in the early 1520s began lecturing to the Cambridge Augustinians on Terence, Plautus and

Cicero. Thomas Bilney confessed, when first seeking a copy of Erasmus's New Testament, he was 'allured rather by the Latin than by the Word of God'.[61]

Purveyors of the 'new learning' knew this was their natural constituency. The strategy of the book-runner Thomas Garrett in Oxford in 1527–8 was to seek out 'all such which was given to Greek, Hebrew and the polite Latin tongue'. Pretending he was looking for instruction in the biblical languages, he brought along 'books of new things to allure them'. Thomas More knew the type well. The Lutheran-sympathizing character known as 'the Messenger' in More's *Dialogue Concerning Heresies* gave 'diligence to the Latin tongue', but rejected traditional scholastic disciplines as contaminated with a 'subtlety' inimical to faith: 'logic he reckoned but babbling . . . and as for philosophy, the most vanity of all'.[62]

Erasmus was painfully aware of the culpability foisted upon him, even in England, for luring people from the path of truth. In April 1526 he heard a (false) rumour that his *Colloquies* were banned in England, 'something which no one has attempted in Louvain or Paris' – places that were, to Erasmus, notorious centres of reactionary religion. The *Colloquies*, first published in 1518, and expanded in numerous subsequent editions, were short, witty dialogues, useful for teaching Latin and the art of speaking, but also allowing Erasmus to vent his views on various topical subjects. He protested blithely to Wolsey that there was nothing in them 'offensive or irreligious or seditious'. Yet as threats to the Church's authority grew, satirical swipes against pilgrimage, popular superstition or the religious life – Erasmus's usual range of targets –no longer seemed like the poking of harmless fun at the establishment. John Longland wrote voicing his concerns.[63]

The concerns were not misplaced. In May 1528, Tunstall summoned before him Thomas Topley, one of the Clare Augustinians under the spell of the Lollard curate Richard Fox. The priest gave Topley a copy of the *Colloquies*, drawing his attention to the dialogue 'Rash Vows', which satirized pilgrimage to Compostela and its associated indulgences. After reading it, Topley found 'my mind was almost withdrawn from devotion to saints'. His recantation warned Christians to beware of 'Erasmus's fables, for by consenting to them, they have caused me to shrink in my faith'. Tunstall too now wrote to Erasmus, expressing serious reservations about the *Colloquies*.[64]

Topley's confession reveals the combination of possible influences at work in an 'evangelical' conversion. While serving Fox's cure at Bumpstead in the latter part of 1527, Topley found in his chamber 'a certain book called *Wyclif's Wicket*'. This Lollard tract 'wounded my conscience', and caused 'great wavering' in Topley's belief in the sacrament of the altar. Yet he only 'consented' to the doctrine when he heard Fox preach upon St Anthony's Day – such public preaching was a remarkable sign of the confidence of these Essex Lollards. Still, Topley's mind remained 'much troubled' until he heard, on the fourth Sunday of Lent, the sermon of a yet more authoritative and charismatic figure: Miles Coverdale, a fellow Augustinian and Cambridge scholar. Topley and Coverdale walked the fields around Bumpstead, 'and did common together of Erasmus's works, and of confession' – a practice Coverdale condemned, since it was 'sufficient for a man to be contrite for his sins betwixt God and his conscience'. As well as winning Topley to the view that the eucharist was 'but for the remembrance of Christ's body', Coverdale's preaching persuaded him to turn against imagery of saints, since, as he pathetically confessed, 'he had no learning to defend it'.[65]

In Topley's case, the corrosive drip of Erasmian satire reacted with the sceptical materialism of Lollardy to unsettle a mind perhaps never secure in conventional monastic profession. Topley confessed to being much given to 'foolish pastimes': dancing and, worse, tennis. The decisive element was the resolution of religious doubts by a powerful authority figure. New ideas are rarely encountered as abstract propositions; more commonly, they are introduced and advocated in circles of acquaintance. This was a trump card of the emerging movement: converts trusted the ideas because they trusted the people espousing them.

Champions of orthodoxy looked on in frustration as the purveyors of heresy were reputed good and holy men. As early as 1521, John Fisher feared Martin Luther's 'pretence of virtuous life' was likely to 'overthrow the weak'. The King likewise warned the friar was trying to pass himself off with a 'visage of holiness . . . till he might enter in further credence and favour'. A work by a (temporarily) reformed heretic – William Barlow's *Dialogue describing the original ground of these Lutheran factions* – supplied an extended commentary on the theme, starting with frank recognition that many people favoured Lutheran doctrine because of 'good order . . . charitable liberality, and evangelic conversation' among its adherents. Intriguingly, something modern historians generally regard as a black mark against the new ideas, and an obstacle to their acceptance in England – the association with abroad – Barlow considered part of their allure. Germans enjoyed a reputation for 'plainness in word and deed, void of dissimulation, and for their homely familiarity without exception of persons'.[66]

Thomas More's 'Messenger' wondered how the new preachers could be entirely wrong, since they 'live so virtuously, fasting and giving their goods in alms'. From his own experience, More knew that Robert Farman, head of a Cambridge college and hawker of heretical books, grew 'in good opinion and favour' because he was a learned priest, skilled at hearing confessions, 'and among many folk well allowed in preaching'. Bilney was similarly reckoned 'a good man and a very devout'.[67]

These, of course, were false impressions. It was, defenders of the establishment insisted, simply not possible to be both a resolute heretic and a good person. Scarcely a priest coming out of Gonville College, Cambridge, so Bishop Nykke of Norwich noted sourly in May 1530, did not 'savour of the frying-pan, though he speak never so holily'. Reformers misled people about the saintliness of their lives as they deceived them about the truth of their doctrines.

This explains a vein of personal invective. Knowledge of Luther's 'open vices and boldly boasted wretchedness', the King observed, 'must needs make his doctrine suspected'. Thomas More repeatedly emphasized Luther's lewdness with a nun – that is, with his wife, the former Cistercian sister Katharina von Bora. Despite what modern commentators sometimes imply, this was a shrewd polemical thrust, not a glimpse into More's own psycho-sexual pathology.[68] There were also attempts to undermine some heretics as figures of authority by emphasizing their callow youth: More and others made sarcastic reference to 'young father Frith', while the poet John Skelton memorably characterized the troublemakers as a bunch of 'friscajoly yonkerkyns'.[69]

Yet it was hard to paint all dissidents as hypocrites and secret sybarites. Bilney was almost universally recognized as a gentle, pastorally minded physician of souls, a habitual visitor – along with Hugh Latimer – of prisoners and the sick. He followed a deeply ascetic lifestyle, eating simply and sleeping little. His Cambridge confederate George Stafford died in 1529 after contracting 'the sweat' from an ailing scholar he was seeking to dissuade from practising magic. Other members of Bilney's circle, including Thomas Arthur and Richard Smythe, were noted for charity towards the poor. One cause of Barnes's 1525 troubles was his outrage at the financial persecution of a poor parishioner.

Acts of charity to the disadvantaged, and the imposition of ascetic discipline on the self – these were not strange 'Lutheran' innovations, but traditional marks of Catholic holiness. The earliest proponents of 'the gospel' were not outsiders but insiders, exhibiting some of the best qualities of late medieval piety. Small wonder that – until they were specifically earmarked as heretics, and sometimes even after that – people listened keenly to what they had to say. More so since many of the early reformers were authority figures, members of the clergy, and – disproportionately– of the orders of friars, with their strong traditions of pastoral outreach through preaching and hearing confessions.[70]

Even at a time of high 'heresy alert', pulpits remained open to radical itinerant preachers, either because of sympathy for their views or because locals had no reason to suspect them of being heretics. In this way, in the summer of 1527, Thomas Bilney and Thomas Arthur espoused an excoriating critique of images and pilgrimage in a succession of London and East Anglian parishes: St Helen's Bishopgate, St Mary Woolchurch, St Magnus, Willesden, Newington, Kensington, Chelsea, Hadleigh, Christ Church, Ipswich.

Their qualifications were to outward appearance unimpeachable. Bilney was in 1525 granted a preaching licence (later withdrawn) by Bishop West of Ely. Arthur told the congregation at St Mary Woolchurch that he was licensed to preach by four authorities: Cardinal Wolsey, Cambridge University, the Pope and Jesus Christ, whose decree was to preach the Gospel to all. A similar concoction of delegated authority and charismatic mandate was dished up in 1527 by the book-runner priest, George Marshall. He told his congregation at Danbury in Essex that 'I am a graduate, a master of art, and a master of grammar, and I will show you the Gospel', adding that Christ and St Paul commanded no man be forbidden to preach.[71]

The orthodox feared heretics would not be recognized in their true colours; that, 'agreeing with us in the most part', they were – as Stephen Gardiner's nephew Germaine put it – 'like unto the rocks which, hid under the water, do hurt before they be spied'.[72] They were right: heretics gained an audience, and then gained recruits, because what they were saying, and how they said it, resonated in challenging ways with what thinking Catholic Christians already understood to be true.

## Justification

Yet they were also saying something radically new. 'The righteous shall live by faith'; 'A man is justified by faith without the deeds of the law'. Martin Luther found in these passages from St Paul's Letter to the Romans (1:17; 3:28) the key to unlocking the spiritual perplexity that had imprisoned him since entering the religious life. How might a sinful person become 'righteous', 'justified', acceptable in the eyes of God? His answer – after years of anguished effort to live the life of the perfect monk – was that the righteousness was not humanity's but God's; it was *imputed* to individuals, not *achieved* by them. Christ – wholly human and wholly divine – chose freely to die on the cross. And in consequence, God, of his free grace, chose to accept people as righteous, even while they remained irreparably sinful.

So confident was Luther that he had properly understood what God was saying about salvation, that in his German New Testament of 1522 he added the word 'allein' (alone) to St Paul's comments about being justified by faith.[73]

Justification by faith alone was at once a catchy slogan and a bold reinterpretation of the doctrine of salvation. But for many encountering it, it was more than an abstract theological proposition; it was a life-changing insight, seizing the emotions and shaking the affections. Looking back from the last years of his life to the moment of his theological break-through, Luther remembered how 'I felt myself straightway born afresh and to have entered through the open gates into paradise itself'. In his *Parable of the Wicked Mammon*, the first complete presentation of justification by faith to an English audience, Tyndale explained how faith, the free gift of God poured into the heart, 'renews a man and begets him afresh, alters him, changes him, and turns him altogether into a new nature'. In his *Prologue* to Paul's Letter to the Romans, Tyndale added that that this was the only way to 'quiet the conscience, and certify her that the sins are forgiven'. George Joye similarly promised that a believer would 'feel his heart eased, comforted and loosed'.[74]

For all its novelty, justification by faith made sense to people – some people – because it spoke to their lived experience, suggesting a way to resolve tensions and difficulties encumbering their spiritual lives. This was the story of Luther himself, burdened with a sense of sin, and convinced of the inadequacy of works of satisfaction to put himself right with God.

Bilney told Tunstall in 1527 that before he could 'come unto Christ', he exhausted himself in 'fastings, watching, buying of pardons, and masses' – all undertaken at the behest of 'unlearned hearers of confessions'. Reading Erasmus's New Testament, he encountered a line in Paul's First Letter to Timothy (1:15): 'Christ Jesus came into the world to save sinners; of whom I am chief.' This sentence 'through God's instruction and inward working ... did so exhilarate my heart, being before wounded with the guilt of my sins, and being almost in despair, that immediately I felt a marvellous comfort and quietness'. To Thomas More, who knew the ins and outs of Bilney's case, all this was 'superstitious fear and scrupulosity' – piety of an excessive and literal-minded kind.[75]

But if so, these were traps into which serious-minded Catholics might readily fall, as More himself knew well. His own son-in-law, William Roper, husband of his beloved Meg, turned at some point in the mid-1520s into an ardent Lutheran. More 'reasoned and argued with him', gave him 'my poor fatherly counsel', but was unable 'to call him home'. Roper's descent into heresy grew from 'a scruple of his own conscience'. Daily, he used 'immoderate fasting and many prayers', but 'thinking God therewith never to be pleased did weary himself even *usque ad taedium* [unto exhaustion]'. Driven by curiosity, Roper got hold of Tyndale's New Testament, and Luther's *Babylonian Captivity* and *Bondage of the Will*. He became convinced 'faith only did justify ... and that, if man could once believe that our Saviour Christ shed his precious blood and died on the cross for our sins, the same only belief should be sufficient for our salvation'.[76]

It is impossible to say just how frequently such intensified engagements with orthodox Catholic devotion preceded sudden disaffection from it. We should be wary of inferring from a handful of documented cases that the religion of late medieval Europe was shot through with febrile 'salvation anxiety'; that it was an over-ripe fruit on the point of falling from the tree. Yet it was a staple of the reformers' propaganda that the Church's requirements were intolerably 'burdensome' to the conscience. This was said frequently about the obligation to clerical celibacy, and the reformist critics – so often themselves celibate priests – were presumably in a position to know. Purgatory too was portrayed as a furnace of fear and dread, stoked by the clergy to make money out of masses and prayers. Yet turbulence of the spirit was easily assuaged when people recognized purgatory was simply 'feigned', an imaginary terror without warrant in scripture.[77]

Accusations of spiritual oppression often homed in on the requirement to confess sins to a priest. There was an irony here, for confession was the ideal opportunity for personalized spiritual direction, something to which the kind of people attracted to the new ideas were particularly drawn. Bilney and Farman used confession to spread their teachings, as did the Lollard priest Richard Fox. Bilney's disciple, Hugh Latimer, was even prepared to concede that 'if ever I had amendment of my sinful life, the occasion thereof came by auricular confession'.

Nonetheless, reformers frequently echoed the cynicism of the Lollards in seeing confession as a spiritually dubious exercise and an oppressive instrument of clerical surveillance. The sternest critic, Tyndale, thought 'shrift in the ear' was 'verily a work of Satan'. People were taught that without it they could not be saved, yet shame might keep them from coming to confession, or from confessing everything when they did. Those who at the end of their lives could not get a priest oft times 'die in desperation'.[78]

Liberty, mercy, freedom, release: these were the colours in which converts painted their portrait of religious enlightenment. Opponents took a predictably different view. Justification 'by faith' was licence to sin, a shameless evasion of moral responsibility. At his trial in 1528, Robert Farman was repeatedly asked how his Lutheran beliefs could be compatible with a life of virtue and restraint: surely it followed 'that folk need no more but believe, and then howsoever they live shall make no matter'? Thomas More lampooned the moral complacency caused by Luther's teaching:

> [N]either purgatory need to be feared when we go hence, nor penance need to be done while we be here, but sin and be sorry and sit and make merry, and then sin again and then repent a little, and run to the ale and wash away the sin, think once on God's promise, and then do what we list.[79]

This was more than a little unfair. But there was just enough truth in the charge to make reformers uneasy. It is not improbable that some were drawn towards heresy by its relaxation of requirements to fast, maintain vows, confess embarrassing sins, or contribute time and money to commemoration of the dead. The youthful spirit of protest and rebellion, a marked feature of the Reformation in its first phases, adds to the suspicion that not all support for change emerged from anguished crises of faith.

Nor, perhaps, did all converts get the point. John Hig, who abjured before Tunstall's vicar-general in 1528, was a passionate partisan who believed 'Martin Luther hath more learning than all the doctors in England'. He held court in alehouses, expounding the true meaning of last Sunday's gospel to anyone prepared to listen. He also maintained there was no purgatory, and that prayers and alms would do no good when he was dead. But the lesson he drew from this – 'that I would do for myself as much as I might while I was alive' – hardly sounds like a rejection of the value of good works.[80]

The relationship of faith to works was a puzzle and a challenge. St Paul seemed to assert the exclusive role of faith. But another New Testament book, the Epistle of St James, asked what use it was 'if someone says he has faith but does not have works'. It pronounced that 'faith without works is dead' (2:14, 26). Nifty footwork was required to traverse these positions, though Luther famously impugned James as an 'epistle of straw', and came close to banishing it from the canon of scripture. Among English reformers, Barnes was nearest to following this lead. But he decided that the works James referred to were those which followed rather than preceded justification – a solution that kept intact the primacy of faith, while parrying the Catholic thrust that Luther's doctrine led – literally – to no good.

The issue dominated Farman's trial in 1528. While the former president of Queens' was argued into some tight corners, he stuck doggedly to his conviction that faith necessarily implied good works, bringing them forth 'as the tree bringeth forth his leaves'. True faith 'could never be idle, as the fire must needs burn and give heat'. We can compare this with the statement of Thomas More, writing a couple of years later, that the faith of a Christian must never be 'an idle, dead, standing belief, but a belief lively, quick and stirring, and by charity and good works ever walking and going into Christ'. The sentiments here are a whisker apart, and a world away.[81]

Faith's connection to works was the subject to which Tyndale endlessly returned. He saw works, not as a cause of justification, but as its outward sign, and as reassurance to the conscience of the believer. His thinking also came to exhibit a powerful concern, not merely with how believers were declared righteous, but with how they were actually made so, through inward working of the Holy Spirit. Increasingly, Tyndale began to think of the relationship between God and humanity in terms of the Old Testament concept of covenant – a kind of sacred contract, with obligations on both sides. God's part – in Christ – was to rescue humanity from the fate to which sinful and fallen nature consigned it; humans in return undertook to strive to keep God's Commandments. This marked a shift away, in emphasis at least, from the stark polarity of 'Law' and 'Gospel' found in Luther's thought.

The concern of Tyndale and other English reformers with ethical conduct has been seen as a watering down of Luther's counter-intuitive epiphany about salvation, readmitting by the back door a role for human effort. Moral legalism – a preoccupation with the keeping of God's law – was certainly characteristic of Lollardy, and it is tempting to see the native heresy imparting some local theological flavour to the brew of English Protestantism.[82]

Yet, in taking this direction, English gospellers were not following any unique path of divergence from the main highway of the European Reformation. Among major continental reformers, Luther was unusual in his lack of concern with what followed after the Christian's justification. For him, a believer simply remained forever *simul iustus et peccator* ('at once justified, and a sinner'). Much greater interest in the moral regeneration of the justified sinner – sanctification – was to be found in the emerging 'Reformed' coalition of the Rhineland and Switzerland: in the writings of Zwingli, Oecolampadius and Bucer, all of whose works were being read by English people in the 1520s. Sanctification was also a preoccupation of Luther's close ally, Melanchthon. Here again, a golden thread leads back to humanism, and the emphasis on right conduct in the *Philosophia Christi* of Erasmus.[83]

Much about conversion remains mysterious. Why some people were immediately attracted to the new ideas, and others, from similar social milieux and subject to the same cultural influences, fervently rejected them, is a question we cannot finally answer. The 'typical' convert of the 1520s would most likely have been an educated and literate layman, perhaps a common lawyer, someone strongly drawn to the ideals of Erasmian humanism, an advocate of vernacular scripture, seriously devout, yet sharply critical of abuses within the Church, partial to an anticlerical joke. But this is a pen portrait of Thomas More.

The most we can say is that the raw materials of conversion were all, by definition, present within late medieval culture. The very notion of conversion – the transformative personal event described by Luther, Latimer, Bilney and others – was itself a long-standing ideal of devotional life, recounted in saints' *Lives* and idealized descriptions of entry into the cloister. Justification by faith alone was a novel idea. But the ideas that Christ died on the cross as a personal saviour, that salvation was dependent upon the grace of God, and that Christians should not complacently trust in their own works of righteousness: these were not inventions of the Reformation, but familiar themes from late medieval theology and sermons.

At the point of death, *Ars moriendi* texts advised that Catholics be asked, 'belief ye that ye may not be saved but by His passion and death?' 'What preacher,' Farman's interrogators demanded in 1528, 'has not told the people the parable of the poor publican ashamed of his sins, and the proud Pharisee boasting of his virtues?' Surely Farman recognized 'the Church has always taught against the putting of a proud trust in our own deeds'? His judges agreed that God freely redeemed the world without the world deserving it; that, by themselves, all the good works of mankind could not save a single soul. But they did not see how this meant there was no place for good works in human responses to God's offer of salvation.[84] It was precisely the shared premises that caused anger and mystification about the contradictory conclusions.

People like Farman were drawn to the new teaching, not despite but because of the religious concepts with which they were raised. The emotional yearnings of late medieval piety, its desire for an intensely personal relationship with Christ, for a purified heart burning with love – all this, so Farman and others came to feel, could be lived out more fully within a new framework of doctrine. But much of the language remained familiar: converts spoke in affective and sensual terms of smelling or savouring the Gospel, drawing on an existing repertoire of devotional terms and emphases. They discovered it to be 'sweet', a metaphor as ubiquitous in the texts of the heretics as in the prayer books and saints' *Lives* of the preceding decades.[85]

The most striking convergences emerged out of the Christocentric character of late medieval piety. The existing devotion to the Holy Name of Jesus was a point of connection, some early reformers instinctively retaining the devotional habit of heading their letters with the graphic icon, 'Ihus'. This point of common reference was seized upon by Thomas More to argue that if heretics were 'content that the blessed name of Jesus be had in honour and reverence', they should logically accept another form of representation – carved or painted images.[86]

References to 'the precious blood of Christ' saturate the writings of early reformers, just as they do the devotional and theological texts of the later Middle Ages. Almost identical phrases about Christians being 'redeemed and bought by the precious blood and death of Our Lord' can be found in Tyndale and in the Bridgettine John Fewterer. It was after meditating on how Christ 'shed His precious blood and died on the cross for our sins' that William Roper decided works and ceremonies were vain. His conclusion was radical, but the reflective exercise prompting it was conventionally devout and unimpeachably orthodox. It is revealing that when the London skinner John Perriman successfully persuaded an acquaintance to learn to read the New Testament, he did so by 'calling it the blood of Christ'.[87]

Resentment at the Church's jurisdictional powers, a dislike of overweening or immoral priests, exposure to the levelling wisdom of Lollardy – all these played their part in preparing people to welcome the winds of doctrinal change. But they were not the real wellsprings of the Reformation movement. It arose from deep within the devotional core of late medieval Christianity, a paradoxical tribute to the Church's success in cultivating among priests and people alike a serious concern with salvation, and in fostering a personal relationship with Christ.

## Contagion and Containment

By the later 1520s the Catholic authorities understood much about the dissent they were confronting; knowing how to contain and crush it was another matter. The contest was profoundly unequal: the forces of orthodoxy could deploy the disciplinary mechanisms of the Church and church courts, backed by the coercive power of the state. But the heretics were not without cards to play, or places to hide.

One important resource, a true birthplace of the English Reformation, was the Flemish port city of Antwerp, lying at the mouth of the River Scheldt, a hundred miles from the furthest tip of Kent. Antwerp was the 'staple', or designated port of business, of the Company of Merchant Adventurers, who enjoyed a monopoly of the export of cloth, mainstay of the late medieval English economy. Perhaps a hundred English merchants resided permanently in the city, but the transient population was much higher. Overwhelmingly, the Merchant Adventurers were Londoners, shuttling between the bustling bottlenecks of the Scheldt and Thames rivers.[88]

Antwerp was also a centre of book production, the international lustre and technical capacity of its printing houses outclassing anything to be found in London. Despite lying in imperial territory, it enjoyed proud traditions of independent-minded municipal self-governance. Religious rioting in 1525 persuaded the city authorities not to provoke trouble by harassment of the printing trade or heavy-handed policing of the foreign communities. Prohibitions on the printing of heretical works, initially at least, did not extend to vernacular bibles, and the printer Christoffel van Ruremund (who specialized in Catholic liturgical books for the English market) was able to produce in 1526, in parallel with the Worms publication, the first of several editions of Tyndale's New Testament.[89]

Tyndale himself took up residence in or near Antwerp by the spring of 1528, when his *Wicked Mammon* was published by Martin de Keyser. It was followed in short order by *The Obedience of a Christian Man*, and in 1530 by *The Practice of Prelates*, an excoriating attack on the English Catholic hierarchy. At the same time, Tyndale moved forward with his project of translating all the scriptures into English. During his continental travels he managed to learn Hebrew, and in 1530 de Keyser issued Tyndale's translation of the Pentateuch – the first five books of the Old Testament.

In the three years 1528–30, at least fifteen works by English exiles were published overseas, mainly in Antwerp. To throw the authorities off the scent, such books often claimed to have been printed 'at Marburg in the land of Hesse', by 'Hans Luft'. Luft was a real printer, based in Wittenberg and handling much of Luther's output. But the name – Luft is German for 'air'– was an appropriately breezy pseudonym for an elusive, clandestine enterprise. Tyndale was responsible for many of these titles, but other hands were at work: the common lawyer Simon Fish, the Observant friars William Roye and Jerome Barlow, the secular priests George Joye and George Constantine, the brilliant young scholar John Frith.[90] Around them gathered a coterie of sympathizers connected to the

English merchant community, relatively immune from the efforts of English authorities to seize or silence them.

The English ambassador in the Netherlands, John Hackett, worked tirelessly to prevent the publication of books, and procure the arrest of heretics. But he found himself frustrated by the cautious attitude of the Antwerp authorities. After months of wasted effort to secure the Kentish merchant Richard Harman, Hackett reflected bitterly that 'the burgomaster and the law of the town have done more diligence to save a cockatrice heretic than to please a noble prince'. Treaty arrangements between England and the Netherlands mandated the extradition of traitors. But there was no obligation – on the say-so of a bishop of London, or even a cardinal-archbishop – to return expatriates for supposed heterodoxy. As Hackett wrote plaintively to Wolsey in July 1528, 'As soon as they be past the seas, they know no more God neither King.'[91]

Heretics went out; books came back. The volume of cross-Channel commerce was sufficient to make them needles in the hay of regular trade. Books could be smuggled unbound, the small octavo leaves of the New Testament concealed between the pages of larger and innocuous publications. They could be passed off as stocks of blank paper, or hidden with bales of linen. The intended recipients in London – as Thomas More discovered from a suspect in 1531 – knew in advance the names of the shipmen, and the identifying marks on the 'fardels' (bundles) containing the contraband.

There were successes, or apparent successes, in stemming the flow. Herman Rinck, the Cologne magistrate who interrupted the printing of Tyndale's Testament in 1525, discovered at Frankfurt a cache of copies of Jerome Barlow's scurrilous verse satire, The Burial of the Mass, and bought the entire stock. A similar strategy was employed by Tunstall when, on embassy in Antwerp in the summer of 1529, he was approached by an English merchant, Augustine Packington, with an offer to purchase all copies of Tyndale's New Testament to be found in the city. As a sympathetic chronicler later told it, Packington was secretly in league with Tyndale, at that moment encumbered by piles of unexported New Testaments. Tunstall's outlay served to finance a corrected new edition: 'the bishop had the books, Packington had the thanks, and Tyndale had the money.'[92] This account of a well-planned sting operation sounds too good to be entirely true. But, even as an embroidered version of events, it illustrates the difficulties the English authorities faced, operating in an alien environment, and unsure of whom to trust.

The percentage of banned bibles successfully purchased, confiscated or burned was in any case small. One estimate is that the six editions of Tyndale's New Testament produced up to 1530 (excluding his definitive revision of 1534) may have amounted to 15,000 copies.[93] Like modern customs officials battling the trade in illegal narcotics, the authorities occasionally got lucky, arresting a runner or seizing a consignment. But they could not stop the cross-border traffic, shut down the centres of production, or easily reduce the underlying demand.

Letters found during a search of Richard Harman's Antwerp lodgings in 1528 revealed the extent of a cross-Channel fellowship. Richard Hall, a London ironmonger, requested two New Testaments from Harman, and John Sadler, draper, wrote to him in September 1526 with news from England – 'none other but that the New Testament in English should be put down and burnt'. John Andrews and Thomas Davy, countrymen of Harman from Cranbrook in Kent, also wrote concerning the New Testament, Davy telling him 'that no man may speak in England of the New Testament in English upon the pain of bearing a faggot', and urging him to bear his troubles patiently 'for the true faith of Christ'.[94]

Harman supplied bibles to Simon Fish at the Whitefriars, perhaps also to Geoffrey Lome, usher of St Anthony's School. Both men sold wholesale to Robert Necton, referred on to Fish by George Constantine, another distributor, and a collaborator of Tyndale. Necton sold New Testaments and other prohibited works in London and in the market towns of his native East Anglia – Bury St Edmunds, Norwich, Stowmarket. Lome likewise 'dispersed abroad' a variety of heretical texts. Constantine, a Shropshire man, carried books back to his county of birth. In May 1528, the curate of Atcham near Shrewsbury confessed to reading Lutheran books and discussing them with him. All were part of a distribution network that connected Antwerp to the English universities, and the countryside beyond.

Its principal depot was the church of All Hallows, Honey Lane, just north of Cheapside, where Robert Farman was rector. Farman's curate, the Oxford graduate Thomas Garrett, returned to his alma mater just before Christmas 1527, and Farman's servant John Goodale supervised the conveyance there of two 'very heavy' fardels of books. He later claimed, implausibly, that 'what was in them he knew not'.[95]

What was in them was revealed when Garrett was arrested in February 1528. His catalogue extended to over sixty titles, not just New Testaments in French and English, and numerous works by Luther, but an extensive list of past and current forbidden writers – John Wyclif and Jan Hus, as well as the German Lutherans Philip Melanchthon, Johannes Brenz, Theodore Fabricius, Urbanus Rhegius and Johannes Bugenhagen. The inventory also included authors diverging from Luther's theology: the Strassburg reformer Martin Bucer; the Frenchman François Lambert; and the Swiss theologians Johannes Oecolampadius and Huldrich Zwingli, whose views on the eucharist Luther roundly condemned. Garrett also had for sale *De Operibus Dei* [Of the Works of God] by Martin Borrhaus, a decidedly heterodox German who flirted with the radical ideas known generically as anabaptism, and who entertained apocalyptic visions of the kind fuelling the violence of the recent Peasants' War.[96]

The dissenting movement in England was not at any stage a tidily 'Lutheran' affair.

As evidence accumulated, it became clear the most active of Garrett's supporters belonged to a group located in Cardinal College – Wolsey's show-case humanist foundation – and were mainly scholars transplanted by the cardinal from Cambridge. 'We were clear without blot or suspicion till they came', the Warden of New College, John London, wrote bitterly to Longland. A dozen and more suspects were imprisoned in the Cardinal College cellar where the salt fish was stored – they included John Frith and the musician John Taverner, who had been hired to instruct the choristers. In these insalubrious surroundings, three of the prisoners died over the course of the summer – the first, largely forgotten, martyrs of the English Reformation.[97]

Only architecturally are universities cloistered communities. Longland thought that Garrett, Cardinal's senior canon, John Clerke, and another of the college group, the physician John Fryer, were 'three perilous men'. He feared 'they have infected many other parts of England'. Garrett was found to have sent over sixty books (a set of his complete reading list?) to the Benedictine prior of Reading, and Longland feared he had 'infected' other monasteries too.

Even in the usually calm and shallow waters of the English Benedictine Order, the new ideas were causing waves. One of Garrett's collaborators in the importation of books was Richard Bayfield, monk of Bury St Edmunds, who fell under the influence of Robert Barnes. Two Benedictines – one of Bury, one of Glastonbury – were in custody at Oxford, along with their books, before the end of February 1528. Another Bury monk, Edmund Rougham – who studied with Barnes at Louvain – preached at St Peter's church, Oxford, on the middle Sunday of Lent, 'the most seditious sermon that ye have [ever] heard of'. Rougham railed against Wolsey and the bishops, and with the words of Matthew's Gospel urged imprisoned preachers to face martyrdom boldly: *Nolite timere eos qui occidunt corpus* – do not fear those who kill the body (but cannot kill the soul).[98]

Yet – other than the unfortunates rotting in the Cardinal College fish cellar – there were no martyrs in 1528. In part, this was because the key players, Garrett and Farman, were willing to abjure. But it was also because the problem still appeared containable, and because to the authorities some of those impli-cated seemed almost as much victims as perpetrators. Dr London professed pity for the young men Garrett and Clerke attempted to corrupt, and Archbishop Warham, chancellor of the university, was eager to assure Wolsey that those involved were 'inexpert youth', led astray by one or two 'cankered' elders, and now 'marvellous sorry and repentant'. There were reputational concerns to think about. Warham worried that if the students were sent for public trial in London, it would bring 'obloquy and slander' to the university, and he recom-mended proceeding through a locally based commission. But his beliefs that there were varying degrees of guilt, and that the wayward should be guided back towards the true path, were undoubtedly genuine.[99]

Wolsey felt the same. He soon ordered the release of the Cardinal College detainees, and approved the lifting of excommunication for all penitent Oxford suspects. Garrett was even taken into the cardinal's employ as a scribe. The impulse to rehabilitate, rather than condemn, can be seen also in the case of the two Cambridge troublemakers, Thomas Arthur and Thomas Bilney, brought to trial in the chapter house of Westminster Abbey in November 1527 after reports surfaced of the provocative sermons preached in London and East Anglia.

The cardinal presided, assisted by no fewer than seven bishops, including Tunstall, West of Ely and Fisher of Rochester. Even before the trial, there were attempts, by Thomas More and others, privately to talk sense into the accused. Bilney, conscience-bound and conscience-stricken, was intensely reluctant to abjure. But Tunstall, handed the lead in the matter by Wolsey, took immense pains with him, repeatedly postponing sentence and striving to hand-craft an abjuration Bilney might feel able to sign.[100]

The pair did recant, at St Paul's, on 7 December 1527. And there were other, less publicly trumpeted, successes. Foxe annotated several of the names on his list of the 1528 Cardinal College detainees with such comments as 'after that, a papist', or 'afterwards fell away, and forsook the truth'. Edmund Rougham, the firebrand Benedictine of Bury, also later returned to conservative orthodoxy.[101] But the spirit of rebellion could not always be quenched by the equivalent of a serious chat in the headmaster's study. And heretics did not always stay still long enough for the authorities to talk them round.

### Exile and Return

Richard Bayfield was tried before Tunstall in 1528, but fled overseas before completing his prescribed penance. Two months later he had second thoughts, presented himself to Tunstall, and was ordered to return to his abbey. Shortly afterwards, he again took off for the continent. John Frith, released from confinement on Wolsey's orders, fled to Antwerp in the latter part of 1528. So did Robert Barnes, after an elaborate ruse involving a suicide note, and a pile of clothes on the river-bank. By 1530 he was in Wittenberg, learning at the feet of Luther. George Joye, fellow of Peterhouse, Cambridge, was spared prosecution in 1526 through the intervention of Stephen Gardiner, but at the end of 1527, he too hotfooted it to Antwerp.[102]

There was never such a thing as a hermetically sealed 'English Reformation'. The ability of suspects to flee abroad is an important reason why the nascent reform movement could not be crushed in its infancy. It was a pragmatic response to threats of persecution: Latimer remarked in a letter of 1531 that if

God had not watched over him, 'the ocean-sea, I think, should have divided my lord of London and me.'[103] But the decision for exile was also a symbolic act of commitment and defiance, one underpinned by profound biblical resonances.

The English were an island people. But in an age when maritime transportation was the principal artery of commerce and trade, this facilitated rather than inhibited contact with a wider world of change. London was the main, but not the only, point of contact. A number of thriving ports – Bristol, Southampton and Exeter on the south and west coasts; Newcastle, Hull, Boston, Lynn, Yarmouth and Ipswich on the east – had their own important trade links to the continent. Journeys from the North Sea ports in particular brought merchants and mariners into contact with developments in the Hanseatic towns of northern Germany. Six sailors from Hull served on a Dutch ship loading wheat in Bremen, and remained there for five weeks. On their return in 1528, two of the party, Robert Robinson and Henry Burnett, were charged with heresy. Robinson condemned fasting, auricular confession and the Pope; Burnett was lax in observance of fast days and loose-mouthed about what he saw in Germany: 'The people did follow Luther's works, and no masses were said there . . . the priest and all that were in the church, old and young, would sing after their mother tongue, and there was no sacring [elevation of the host].' A third member of the party, Roger Danyell, 'had the gospels in English'.

It is probable these seamen were conventionally orthodox prior to their extended stay in Germany. Burnett denied that any of them purposefully travelled 'to learn Luther's works or opinions', and they came from a part of the country without an attested Lollard tradition. They attended sermons at various places along the Friesian coast, though none of the party seems to have understood German. Perhaps an unpoliced break from fasting and confession led them to resent these tiresome obligations when they returned. Or perhaps they learned their heresy, and acquired a New Testament, from other English sailors.

An experience of witnessing the dismantling of Catholicism overseas must have been relatively common around the end of the 1520s. Lollards meeting in 1530 at the house of John Taylor in Hughenden, Buckinghamshire, were cheered by the testimony of Nicholas Field. He told them he had been 'beyond the sea in Almany [Germany], and there they used not so to fast, nor to make such holy days'.[104]

Hughenden was an old haunt of heretics. But the trails of travel and exile led from new lairs of dissent. One was the Inns of Court, where common lawyers received their training, often along with a dose of anticlericalism (see p. 82). The Inns provided a layman's equivalent to the experience of university – places where ideas were discussed, and bonds of male friendship formed.

Among the young law students succumbing to the lure of 'the gospel' was Francis Denham. In the early summer of 1528, Denham was in Paris, where he was apprehended by the English ambassadors, John Taylor and John Clerk, bishop of Bath and Wells. They were after George Constantine, at whose house Denham had been living. Denham was also acquainted with Bilney and Simon Fish, and at their suggestion translated a work by François Lambert, as well as Bugenhagen's *Epistola ad Anglos*. Denham's reading was every bit as eclectic as that of Garrett's customers in Oxford: in addition to books by Luther and Melanchthon, he had works by Savonarola, and the mystical spiritualist author Caspar Schwenckfeld.

Denham's travels took in Paris, Antwerp and the English garrison town of Calais – staple for the export of wool, as Antwerp was for cloth. There, a couple of years earlier, he 'corrupted' the Staplers' chaplain, Philip Smith, supplying him with heretical books and advice on how to read scriptures without help of old interpreters. Smith admitted selling books in Calais, and was perhaps involved in exporting them to England. As with Antwerp, the volume and regularity of English trade made Calais an ideal conduit for the importation of prohibited books. The renegade Observant William Roye dedicated his *Brefe Dialoge* (Strassburg, 1527) to 'the right noble estates and all other of the town of Calais'.[105]

Entering the Inns of Court with Denham in 1524 were others sharing his sense of disaffection from the Church. They included Simon Fish, and John Corbett, who, to the embarrassment of Bishop Clerk, formed part of his retinue on the Paris embassy. Another was an older figure, from a humble background, and already established in legal practice: Thomas Cromwell.

It was Fish who caused the biggest splash in the late 1520s. He had, as John Foxe put it, already 'begun to espy Christ from Antichrist' when, at Christmas 1526, he agreed to play the part of Cardinal Wolsey in a Gray's Inn satirical revel. Wolsey took offence. The play's producer was imprisoned, and Fish fled to Antwerp to commence his career as a book-runner. There, and most likely at Tyndale's suggestion, he translated *The Summe of the Holy Scripture*, a 1526 Dutch work representing an uneasy composite of Luther's ideas and the Swiss theology of Zwingli, Oecolampadius and Guillaume Farel.

Fish also composed a short, racy pamphlet, printed in late 1528 or early 1529. *A Supplicacyon for the Beggers* was ostensibly a petition to the King from the indigent poor against those false beggars, the mendicant orders. It was knock-about stuff. The tract highlighted the sexual voracity of the friars – 'they have made a hundred thousand idle whores in your realm' – and threw out equally implausible claims about huge sums the clergy had been siphoning off to Rome. But the *Supplicacyon*, which was rapidly translated into German and Latin, was more than a boisterous anticlerical lampoon. At its core was a revolutionary doctrinal claim: 'that there is no purgatory, but that it is a thing invented by the covetousness of the spirituality'. For those not yet ready for the raw meat of justification by faith, this was a delicate proposition to chew on, and one with momentous political and economic implications.[106]

Fish's appeal to the King signalled the growing confidence and boldness of the reformers. So did the manner of the tract's distribution in 1529. Foxe tells us it was 'strewed abroad in the streets of London', and that copies were scattered at a Candlemas Day procession at Westminster in the presence of the King. This was a step beyond the discreet exchange of texts in merchant houses and college chambers – a booming salvo in a now highly public war of propaganda.[107]

One immediate consequence was the issuing in March 1529 of a royal proc-lamation reiterating the prohibitions on unlicensed preaching, and on the writing, importation or reading of heretical books.[108] Another was that Thomas More again took up his pen, to counter the supplication of imaginary beggars with an equally fictive, and substantially longer, *Supplication of Souls*. The dead, suffering in purgatory, make a powerful social and theological case for the living to remember them in traditional and hallowed ways. But more earth-bound matters were in contention too. Fish resurrected the case of Richard Hunne – a still recent and sore memory among Londoners – suggesting that if he had not commenced his action of praemunire, 'he had been yet alive, and none heretic at all'. More denied this, as well as Fish's claim that the bishops compensated a priest, Dr John Allen, for losing a praemunire suit a decade and more earlier. Fish's strategy was 'to inflame the King's highness against the Church'. But Henry was 'a prince of excellent erudition, virtue and devotion towards the Catholic faith of Christ'. In 1529, Sir Thomas still believed, or at least hoped, this to be true.[109]

More berated Luther and Bugenhagen in the elegant Ciceronian Latin he used to defend Erasmus from his detractors. But his *Supplication of Souls* was a treatise in plain English, and it followed hot on the heels of another vernacular work, his *Dialogue Concerning Heresies*, published in the summer of 1529. As the tide of heresy continued to rise, More was a man with a special commis-sion. In March 1528, Tunstall granted him a licence to read heretical books, and to write against them in the vernacular. The authorities now accepted that simple and uneducated people (*simplicibus et idiotis hominibus*) needed help to recognize the malice of the heretics. Tunstall flattered his friend in typical humanist style as one who 'can rival Demosthenes [the most renowned of Athenian orators] in our vernacular language as well as in Latin'. But he spoke no more than the truth in describing More as 'a most eager champion of Catholic truth in all contests'.[110]

More's *Dialogue Concerning Heresies*, the first of half a dozen vernacular polemical works he produced between 1529 and 1533, stages a contest of a particular kind – a series of conversations between the author and a (fictional) character known as 'the Messenger', a bright but wilful young man fashionably drawn to the arguments of the reformers, for whom the model may have been More's son-in-law, William Roper. The Messenger is – of course – confounded. But he is given some good lines, and allowed to speak his mind in the manner Fisher had earlier envisioned. Like Fisher, Longland, Tunstall and other bishops, More saw a distinction between hard-core malevolent heretics – principally Luther and Tyndale – and basically well-meaning people who had been seduced and misled, and could, like Roper, be redirected and redeemed.

Yet optimistic hopes that heretics could peacefully be argued out of their errors were fading by the end of the decade. At the time More wrote his *Dialogue*, no heretic of the Lutheran stamp had been put to death in England. More indeed scoffed that he had never encountered any 'but he would foreswear your faith to save his life'. It was a telling contrast with the Catholic Church's glorious catalogue of martyrs down the ages. But already More saw how this might change. The concluding chapters of the *Dialogue* carry grim titles: 'concerning the burning of heretics, and that it is lawful, necessary and well done'; that 'the clergy doth no wrong in leaving heretics to secular hands'; that 'princes be bounden to punish heretics, and that fair handling helpeth little with many of them'.[111] Blood would soon spill, and with it everything would change.

## Factious Labels

Heretics and Catholics were the same sorts of people, and shared many underlying assumptions about truth and meaning. But by 1529 deep and bitter divisions over religion had emerged, and would never subsequently go away. The processes behind this were doctrinal and political, but they were also linguistic. Already in 1521 Erasmus recognized the potential of name-calling for fuelling angry theological sectarianism. In a letter to his English disciple Lord Mountjoy, he swore that neither threats nor promises would ever make him a member of any party but Christ's. 'A curse on all who rejoice in these factious labels!'[112]

The labels, at this stage, did not include the one later to define the era – 'Protestant'. The word originated from developments in Germany in 1529, when, at the Diet of Speyer, Charles V's representatives sought to rescind recent concessions to Luther's followers. Six of the princes and a number of towns issued a defiant 'protestatio'. As a result they became 'Protestants', though it was not a term they ever much used to describe themselves. In England, the word gradually entered parlance in Henry VIII's reign, but only in reference to events in Germany.[113]

The first 'Protestants' were in fact early sixteenth-century Catholics. Yet this was something their opponents were precisely concerned to deny. Luther was once, so Fisher observed in 1521, a good member of the Catholic Church. But 'he has cut himself from the Church. We came not out of them and out of his sect, but all they came out of us, and so have divided themselves from us.'[114] Heresy, a crime of the will, was at the same time a social sin, an act of with-drawal and separation. It was also, in Fisher's carefully chosen word, the delu-sion of a sect – a small band misguidedly following a charismatic but deceitful leader. More than anything else, the new heretics were called 'Lutherans' by their opponents. No one, complained Tyndale, might resist the fleshy Church of Antichrist, 'but must be called a Lutheran.'[115] It has come to sound like a neutrally descriptive label. But in the 1520s 'Lutheran', a term implying slavish adherence to a human teacher, was intended, and understood, as an insult.

Less clear is what reformers called themselves. Sarcastic references in Catholic sources suggest 'gospeller' was current among them.[116] So too was 'brethren', a scripturally evocative word echoing usage among the Lollards. A clutch of heretics uncovered at Mendlesham in Suffolk in the early 1530s confessed to meeting 'for a ghostly purpose to be done by us Christian brothers and sisters'. In London the same year the authorities received information from the mercer Thomas Keyle of arrangements 'made for the augmentation of Christian brethren of his sort', with each 'Christian brother' paying sums into a common fund. But 'Christian brethren' were a broad coalition of the like-minded, rather than a specific secret organization. Tyndale, Frith, Joye and others frequently addressed their 'brethren in Christ'.[117]

'Evangelical' (Greek, *evangelion*: good news; gospel) was another term reformers used about themselves, and one that, in attempts to avoid anachro-nism, recent historians have tended to favour. Thomas More observed in 1533 that for some years past this was the name 'by which they have been as commonly called in all the countries Catholic as by their very own name of heretic'. It was a name taken 'arrogantly to themselves'. But More observed with satisfaction how Catholics turned this good name 'to their rebuke', just as St Augustine ironically christened the heretics of his own day *Cathari*, pure ones. It was, quite literally, a matter of name and shame. Every resource of language – including constant mocking emphasis on the 'new learning' espoused by heretics – was employed to differentiate them from the body of faithful Catholic Christians.[118]

The evangelicals had their own versions of the strategy. Fisher detected a potential for violence in Luther's attitude to those 'whom he calleth so often in derision papistas, papastros, and papanos and papenses'. In 1525, More wrote against Luther on behalf of '*nos quos tu papistas vocas*' ('we, whom you call *papistas*'). The derisory term was soon anglicized as 'papist' in the writings of the overseas exiles.[119] The word was not – or not yet – used to designate a mass of ordinary, unenlightened, believers. Papists were the active agents of Antichrist: the bishops and their keenest supporters. Yet the emergent vocabulary of religious insult, against its intentions, supplied opportunities for rallying the orthodox. More wanted everyone to be aware that heretics 'call the Catholic Christian people papists', and he marvelled at the use of this 'spiteful name' against all who believed in the real presence.[120]

The language of division reflected the splintering of English Christendom, and contributed towards it. Orthodox and evangelical writers alike addressed the 'Christian reader' in what looks like a pitch for the broad middle ground. Yet in works like Tyndale's *Obedience of a Christian Man*, 'Christian' itself was becoming a term of distinctiveness: what we are, and you are not. Evangelicals inveighed against 'unchristian' bishops, and against the Pope, whom Tyndale called a 'great idol, the whore of Babylon, Antichrist of Rome'.

Unsurprisingly, much vitriol was directed against the worldly Cardinal Wolsey. But Tyndale was equally severe on the saintly Fisher of Rochester – 'abominable and shameless, yea and stark mad of pure malice'.[121] This was more than generic 'anticlericalism'. The most vocal of evangelical activists were virtually all lower-ranking clergymen. Their hostility to the authority of the bishops – none of whom, unlike in other parts of Europe, displayed any sympathy for Luther's agenda – was a personal emancipation as much as it was a theological critique.

Orthodox writers were no less fervent in castigation. The Church was one, Catholic, indivisible, united in faith and practice. By the mirror-logic of hostile stereotyping, heresy was querulous, fissiparous and fragmented. Yet stereotypes usually bear some resemblance to reality. The evangelical movement was never a tightly disciplined body with a uniform cast of mind. In particular, a decisive divide had opened between the central and north German and Scandinavian evangelicals looking to Wittenberg, and the reforming towns of the Rhineland and the Swiss Confederation.

The crux issue was the eucharist – in what sense, if any, Christ's body was really present at celebrations of the Lord's Supper. All agreed that Rome's doctrine of transubstantiation was a tortuous nonsense. But Luther held robustly to the view that Christ meant what he said when he declared over bread and wine at the Last Supper, 'This is my Body . . . This is my Blood'. His conviction jarred with the subtle textual readings of Zwingli, Oecolampadius, Bucer and others. They discerned the manner of Christ's presence to be spiritual or symbolic. In October 1529, at the Colloquy of Marburg organized by the Lutheran prince Philip of Hesse, an attempt was made to heal the rift between Luther and Zwingli. But Luther was immoveable, bluntly telling Martin Bucer, 'You have a different spirit from us.'[122]

The factious divisions of evangelicals were a favourite theme of Catholic opponents. The opinions of the heretics, Fisher preached in 1526, were repugnant not only to the Church, 'but with themselves, among themselves'. It was remarkable, observed William Barlow during his Catholic phase, that heretics 'be divided into so many sundry sects, seeing they pretend to profess the only doctrine of Christ'.[123]

English evangelicals of the 1520s cannot be neatly parcelled into 'Lutheran' and 'Zwinglian' camps. But their internal divisions were real enough. Some were matters of personality and style. Tyndale fell out badly with his erstwhile collaborator, William Roye, 'a man somewhat crafty when he cometh unto new acquaintance'. He dismissed the 'railing rhymes' Roye and Barlow produced in their satire against the mass as unworthy of a Christian.

Tyndale's quarrel with George Joye was more substantial, and showed how much easier it was for evangelicals to tear down the structures of traditional belief than to agree about what to put in their place. Purgatory was a fiction, but what was the fate of souls prior to the Second Coming and Resurrection of the Body? Concerned lest the Last Judgement be seen as a mere rubber stamp, Luther believed souls did not immediately enter heaven, but 'slept' in anticipation of ultimate bliss. Tyndale and Frith both leaned to this view, but Joye considered it a dangerous error. To make the point, he produced an unauthorized version of Tyndale's New Testament, which in some twenty places changed Tyndale's word 'resurrection' to 'the life to come', or 'the very life'. An unedifying consequence was a new preface in Tyndale's edition of 1534, lambasting Joye for dishonesty, and accusing him of causing 'no small number' of people to deny the physical resurrection of the body.[124]

Only so much dirty linen could safely be washed in public. As John Frith lay in prison in London, Tyndale advised him: 'of the presence of Christ's body in the sacrament, meddle as little as you can, that there appear no division among us'. Barnes, he warned, 'will be hot against you'. Robert Barnes was a faithful disciple of Luther on this issue. Tyndale himself was sceptical of a real physical presence; Thomas More considered, rightly, that in this he was 'a much more heretic than Luther is himself'. But, with an eye to controversies in Germany, Tyndale's instinct was for 'the presence to be an indifferent thing till the matter might be reasoned in peace'.[125]

There is little to suggest that English evangelicals collectively adhered to a 'Lutheran' view of the sacrament, till, in some tectonic shifting of theological plates, a 'Reformed' understanding superseded it. Trial evidence reveals that from the outset a radical disbelief in real physical presence was common, even among people apparently unconnected to Lollardy. The strain of thinking that opponents derisively termed 'sacramentarian' ran through works like Roye's *Brief Dialogue* and Joye's *Supper of the Lord*.

In spite of Tyndale's warning, Frith composed a tract in prison in 1532, committing himself to a spiritual and symbolic interpretation of the Lord's Supper. Following Zwingli, he used the analogy of the eucharist as a wedding ring, given to a bride (the Church) as a token of remembrance by an absent bridegroom (Christ). It was a fundamental rejection of the incarnational instincts of medieval Catholic culture, its sense of physical substances imbued with the presence of the divine. As Germaine Gardiner riposted, 'If this be idolatry, all Christian men these many hundred years have committed idolatry.'[126]

Celebration of the eucharist in fidelity to Jesus' command was the ritual core of Christianity. For Catholics, it was a moment of transcendent communication with a really present Lord. And for Christians of all kinds it was increasingly to become a crucial symbol of individual faith, and of wider group identity. Frith could agree with Tyndale that belief or disbelief in bodily presence 'is none article of our faith necessary to salvation' – a reflection of the extent to which evangelicals, in England and elsewhere, were failing to reach consensus.[127] Yet the correct interpretation of Christ's life-giving words, 'this is my body', was – quite literally – a burning issue. The campaign against heresy was about to take a decidedly more violent direction. At the very moment it did so, it was knocked out of balance by an unexpected turn of events. Heresy had found its way into the court, and was flirting with the mind of the King.

# 6

## MARTYRS AND MATRIMONY

### Anne and Catherine

IN MARCH 1522, Henry VIII, Defender of the Faith, led a band of knights in an assault on a castle. It was not very dangerous: the castle was timber and tinfoil, centrepiece of a courtly masque organized by Wolsey to impress visiting imperial ambassadors. It was 'garrisoned' by ladies of the court, each taking the identity of a romantic virtue, embroidered in gold on her headdress. One was a young gentlewoman, recently returned from France. Her name was Anne Boleyn, and the word emblazoned on her fashionable Milan bonnet was 'Perseverance'.[1]

Henry was not in love with Anne in 1522. Indeed, he was probably pursuing a dalliance with her elder sister, Mary Carey, a relationship that ended in 1525 when Mary gave birth to a son, reputedly her husband's. A previous lover, Elizabeth Blount, was the mother of an acknowledged bastard, Henry Fitzroy, born in 1519. Royal mistresses were neither shocking nor unusual presences at late medieval courts. When Anne caught Henry's eye, in 1525 or early 1526, no one expected the affair to last, or the world to change as a result. But Anne was an unusual woman, and her perseverance was the catalyst for a religious and political revolution, joining in unstable union the insurrectionary energies of evangelical reform and the imperial aspirations of the English crown.

Anne was not in any strict sense of the term a 'Lutheran'. But her imagination was enthralled by visions of Christian renewal that owed little to the clerical-humanist agenda of a Warham or Fisher. She was brought up at the French court, where she went in 1514 as part of the retinue accompanying Henry's sister Mary on her journey to wed the ageing Louis XII. Here, amidst shows of courtly dalliance – and the serial adulterizing of Louis' successor, Francis I – was a mood of moral seriousness and an impulse for reform, of which Francis's sister, Marguerite of Angoulême, was a significant patron. The moving force was Jacques Lefèvre d'Étaples, humanist, biblical scholar, friend – and occasional critic – of Erasmus. Lefèvre was scarcely the French Martin Luther. Like Erasmus, he remained within the Church, and gave priority to the cultivation of piety. But he was a sharp critic of clerical abuses, and a passionate advocate of vernacular scripture. Lefèvre's 1512 commentary on the Letters of St Paul advocated a position on justification, which, in its denigration of human effort and emphasis on the free grace of God, fell only slightly short of Luther's own.[2]

Anne came home in 1521 marked with the stamp of French 'evangelical' reformism. Her chaplain would later recall Anne 'exercising herself continually in reading the French bible and other French books of like effect', while a Protestant gentlewoman remembered her merchant father telling her that in his youth Anne commissioned him to get for her 'gospels and epistles written in parchment in French together with the Psalms'. The strength of the French connection was recognized by Anne's brother George, who personally translated as a gift for his sister two volumes of Lefèvre's biblical commentaries.[3]

It was not a shared interest in biblical commentaries that caused Henry to fall madly and doggedly in love. Anne was skilled at dancing and playing the lute, vivacious, quick-witted, unconventionally beautiful; she had the knack of drawing attention to herself. Yet biblical commentary would soon be the constant companion to their courtship.

Whether Henry's desire for an annulment of his marriage to Catherine of Aragon preceded, or proceeded from, his attraction to Anne will never be certainly known. Most likely, the growing infatuation crystallized doubts Henry already entertained about the status of his marriage. It was reported in 1532 that he discussed the question of its legality with his confessor, John Longland, 'some nine or ten years ago'.[4] By the spring of 1527, those doubts had hardened into an unshakeable conviction that Catherine was not his lawful wife. Henry wanted an annulment – a formal and legal declaration of the marriage's invalidity. Yet the word contemporaries used, divorce, captures better the legal and emotional turmoil. What Henry referred to in intimate love letters as 'Our Matter', and others euphemistically called 'the King's Great Matter', would dominate official policy-making for the next six years, and change the lives of every one of the King's subjects.

Henry married Catherine, daughter of the Spanish monarchs Ferdinand and Isabella, in the year of his accession, 1509. Doing so required formal permission from the Pope. Catherine had been married for just under five months to Henry's elder brother Arthur, prior to his premature death in April 1502. Henry and Catherine were thus related in the first degree of affinity, and the marriage required a dispensation, which Julius II duly supplied in 1503, while negotiations between England and Spain rumbled on. This was not meddlesome papal interference, but a favour to the monarchs concerned. The bull of dispensation candidly admitted that maintenance of their alliance was a compelling argument in favour of permission.

For a dozen and more years, the marriage was, as far as we can tell, a contented one. Yet, among a succession of miscarriages and stillbirths, it produced only one living child: a daughter, Mary, born in 1516. By 1525, the pregnancies had come to an end. Catherine was forty, six years her husband's senior, and the prettiness of youth was faded. The King's taking of mistresses, and perhaps also his adoption around this time of a beard, which Catherine supposedly disliked, suggests a growing physical estrangement.[5]

A male heir mattered. Violent contentions over the succession were still well within living memory, and Henry did not know the 'Wars of the Roses' were finally over. On the eve of invading France in 1513, he executed a potential Yorkist rival, Edmund de la Pole, Duke of Suffolk, a nephew of Edward IV. Edmund's exiled younger brother, Richard, went on to spend a decade and more intriguing with the French. Henry's relief was palpable – and the public celebrations lavish – when Richard was killed in the defeat of the French army at Pavia in Italy in February 1525. Richard de la Pole was the last Yorkist openly asserting a superior claim. But there were plenty of English noblemen with Yorkist blood in their veins. The later Plantagenets, unlike the Tudors, were effortlessly fecund. Dynastic anxieties were a factor in a great cause célèbre of 1521, the trial and execution for treason of Edward Stafford, Duke of Buckingham, a descendant of Edward III, who carelessly flaunted his royal ancestry.

And what of Mary? Her grandmother, Isabella of Castile, was a formidable Queen Regnant in her own right. Catherine likely saw no reason why her own daughter should not rule in due course. In 1523 she invited to England the most illustrious of Spanish humanists, Juan Luis Vives, who recommended a programme of scriptural and classical reading suitable for a future sovereign. Henry, meanwhile, hedged his bets. In 1525, a new Council was established for the governance of Wales, and Mary was despatched to Ludlow as its nominal head. Both her uncle Arthur and a great-uncle (Edward IV's son Prince Edward), served in similar capacities as part of their (abortive) preparations for kingship. But in the same year, Henry pointedly invested Henry Fitzroy with the double dukedom of Richmond and Somerset – titles with symbolic Lancastrian associations – and sent him to Yorkshire as titular head of a revived Council in the North.[6]

No illegitimate son had succeeded to the English throne since William the Bastard bloodily imposed himself in 1066. The precedents for female rule were scarcely more encouraging. Henry I's daughter, Matilda, was named successor by her father in the early twelfth century. But the arrangement was rejected by significant sections of the aristocracy, and precipitated a twenty-year civil war.

Henry VIII wanted – needed – a son born in wedlock. Catherine could not give him one; Anne, perhaps, would.

It is impossible, however, to understand what happened next if we suppose Henry was motivated solely by pragmatic calculations about the succession, or was cynically seeking nothing more than a tint of legality to daub over his desire for Anne Boleyn. The King's actions only make sense in light of his protestations of being truly, utterly convinced his marriage was unlawful, an abomination in the eyes of the Lord. Why else would God punish him by withholding the son his rank and piety had earned? Henry's 'scruple of conscience' was self-serving and self-pitying. But it was not phoney. There would be opportunities for fudge and compromise, but Henry would ultimately reject all of them, refusing to waver from his conviction that the marriage was invalid. No pope should ever have allowed it. At the heart of the matter was the authority of the bible.

### Leviticus and the Legates

The marriage restrictions of the medieval Church (see p. 71) were rooted in the taboos of the ancient Hebraic world. The Book of Leviticus, Chapter 18, laid out a series of forbidden relationships: with father, mother, sister, brother, step-mother, half-brother, grandchild, daughter-in-law, sister-in-law. Some theologians believed all the permutations to be unbreakable prohibitions under divine law. Others inferred that only directly vertical unions (parent–child–grandchild) were inimical to God's law of nature, other proscriptions being part of the ceremonial law of Moses, from which popes could legitimately dispense. Several late medieval kings and noblemen were indeed permitted to wed sisters-in-law.[7]

The scriptural texts were nonetheless eye-catching: 'Thou shalt not uncover the nakedness of thy brother's wife: it is thy brother's nakedness' (Lev. 18:16). A later verse (Lev. 20:21) added: 'And if a man shall take his brother's wife, it is an unclean thing: he hath uncovered his brother's nakedness; they shall be childless.' In these passages, Henry saw his own situation laid painfully bare. In marrying Catherine, he blatantly broke the law of God, and had paid for it in a doleful tariff of dead infants.

Others read the matter differently, noting Henry was not, in fact, childless. There was also a strong body of opinion – represented in England by John Fisher – that believed prohibitions on sleeping with a brother's wife applied only while the brother was alive. Inconveniently for Henry, another Old Testament verse (Deut. 25:5) seemingly qualified the Levitical prohibition, commanding a man to take to wife his deceased brother's widow, if there had been no child.

A further complication was the actual status of Catherine and Arthur's marriage. Catherine herself protested it had never been consummated. During negotiations between Henry VII and Ferdinand over the remarriage to Prince Henry, the Spanish and English took different views of this question, with Ferdinand and Isabella protesting vehemently to Julius II when it seemed the bull of dispensation would confirm that Catherine and Arthur had slept together. The final version stated the marriage was *forsan consummatum* ('perhaps consummated').

This mattered, because if Catherine and Arthur – a nervously inexperienced teenage couple – did not actually have sex, then Henry and Catherine were not after all related in the first degree of affinity, which coitus created. They were widely *believed* to be, so there was an impediment of 'public honesty' to overcome. The question of whether the 1503 bull adequately covered public honesty, or whether Julius II carelessly issued the wrong sort of dispensation, was something for lawyers to get their teeth into.

But Henry never showed much enthusiasm for squeezing through this loophole in the law. The King stuck rigidly to his conviction that his marriage was nullified by the unambiguous Word of God. Henry's confrontation with the Pope is often characterized as an 'act of state', devoid of meaningful spiritual content. On the contrary, it was a confrontation created by a fully primed religious conscience, and its weapon of choice was the principle of *sola scriptura*.

In May 1527, the King's conscience broke cover. Anne appeared in public with Henry for the first time, at a Greenwich reception for the French ambassador. Around the same time, Wolsey was taken aside and told of the King's 'scruple'. On 17 May, the cardinal opened a private legatine court in his house at Westminster, and summoned Henry to appear. What Wolsey did not know was that Henry was seeking an annulment with the intention of marrying Anne. For years the spider at the centre of the web of government, the cardinal was being left out of loops spun by his rivals, principally the Boleyns themselves – Anne, her father, Sir Thomas, and brother, George.

While Wolsey chewed over the prospects for finding a technical defect in the dispensation, Henry secretly sent an envoy to seek a new dispensation in Rome, allowing him to remarry if his first marriage were annulled, and to someone related to him in the first degree of affinity. An irony of this sordid entanglement was that – owing to sexual relations with her sister – Henry was 'related' to Anne as he was to Catherine, though without the direct Levitical prohibition. Henry's impatience was a tactical blunder: he revealed at an early stage how his conscientious 'scruple' was intimately linked to the prospects of Mistress Boleyn, and thus damaged its moral force.[8]

There was, as yet, little suggestion any of this might involve repudiation of papal authority. The strategy was to galvanize domestic support, and persuade the current pope, Clement VII, to pass favourable and definitive sentence, or allow Wolsey to do so. First step – in a humanistic show of concern with textual meaning and impartial search for truth – was to invite scholars to investigate the rights and wrongs. Wolsey informed Henry in July 1527 that he had 'sworn certain learned men in the law, to write their minds in that matter'. In the meantime, someone briefed the Queen. She took it, as Wolsey understatedly reported, 'displeasantly', and blamed the cardinal for her predicament.[9] Catherine had no intention of going quietly.

Ostensibly at least, the King was seeking opinions, intending nothing but 'the searching and trying out of the truth'. From the outset, those opinions would be contradictory, producing divisions at the heart of English humanism. Wolsey discussed the matter with Fisher in the summer of 1527, and found him unconvinced that the impediment was *de jure divino* (of divine law). Fisher soon set his thoughts on paper, the first of several treatises on the divorce. Deuteronomy was the key: how could God have commanded, in any circumstances, an act repugnant to his own natural law?

The answer Henry wanted came from a friend and protégé of Fisher, Robert Wakefield, fellow of St John's, and Cambridge's first official Lecturer in Hebrew. In a treatise prefaced by a letter from the King himself, Wakefield argued that because Deuteronomy did not use the explicitly sexual phraseology of Leviticus, it must refer only to unconsummated marriages, and so did not contradict the natural law prohibition. Wakefield also supplied the welcome argument that while the Latin bible referred to incestuous marriages to sisters-in-law as being without children, the Hebrew specified an absence of 'sons'. The jury remains out on the correctness of this translation. But it was a decidedly convenient application of the Erasmian technique of critiquing the Vulgate by philological comparison with the original languages, a signal of the King's commitment to truth, not custom and tradition.[10]

The fraternity of English clerical humanism presented a united front to the threat of Lutheran heresy in the early 1520s, but splintered under the pressure of the King's Great Matter. Its godfather, John Fisher, remained unwaveringly opposed, despite the daunting experience, in the Long Gallery at Westminster, of an interview with the King, flanked by the Dukes of Norfolk and Suffolk. Fisher secured Wakefield's dismissal as Hebrew lecturer at St John's, and the appointment of a replacement, Ralph Baines, who shared his loyalty to the Queen. Warham, Tunstall, Vives and Bishop Clerk of Bath and Wells were unpersuaded of the merits of Henry's case in morality or law. But other scholars were carefully positioning for royal favour. John Stokesley helped enlist Wakefield to the campaign, and Wolsey's secretaries, Edward Foxe and Stephen Gardiner, were similarly active in canvassing support.[11]

Over the course of 1527, the people whose opinion mattered were put on the spot. In October, Thomas More, light of learning and avuncular friend of the King, walked with Henry in the gallery at Hampton Court. Henry broke off their conversation to explain how his marriage was discovered to be 'not only against the positive laws of the Church and the written law of God, but also in such wise against the law of nature, that it could in no wise be dispensable by the Church'. More was aware of the arguments about the sufficiency of the dispensation. But this was his first intimation of the unbending fundamentalism of the King's intended path. Henry, the pupil instructing the master, laid a bible open before More and read out the portentous words of Leviticus. What did Sir Thomas think? The answer was a disappointment. Nevertheless, Henry accepted More's demurs 'benignly', though he commanded him to read a book 'that then was making for that matter'.[12]

More was given a pass, for now. He was not present when Henry and Wolsey assembled a group of bishops and legal experts at Hampton Court in November, to receive and revise the book setting out the King's case. Perhaps due to Wolsey's influence, the tone was more moderate than that of Wakefield's tract, and there was more attention to possible defects in the original dispensation. Like the 1521 *Assertio*, the 1527 text was a royal composition heavily edited by advisors, and designed to impress with its sweeping erudition and reflective piety. In March 1528, ambassadors presented a copy to Clement VII.[13]

If the King's case hinged on the open-mindedness of the Pope, it was in deep trouble from the start. Clement's hands were, almost literally, tied. The legatine trial of May 1527 took place under a dreadful shadow. On 6 May, unpaid and ill-disciplined imperial soldiers – many of them German Lutheran mercenaries – sacked Rome, in an orgy of unrestrained pillage, rape and murder. For the rest of the year the city was in turmoil, with the Pope holed up in the Castel Sant' Angelo as a virtual prisoner of Charles V, the son of Catherine of Aragon's sister, Joanna of Castile. For Charles, Henry's intended repudiation of his aunt was both a personal slight and an alarming lurch of policy towards France. As French and imperial armies pecked and scratched in the military cock-pit of Italy, a positive response from the papacy depended on freedom of manoeuvre purchased by French victory in the field.

In March 1528, with French arms in the ascendant, Foxe and Gardiner were despatched to Italy, to a run-down papal court-in-exile at Orvieto. Clement was a shrewd enough negotiator not to give the English exactly what they wanted: a formal papal document or 'decretal commission', allowing Wolsey to settle matters definitively in England. Instead, they received only a dispensation for Henry to marry Anne if his first marriage were dissolved, and a general commission for the case to be heard, without any guarantees it would not later be revoked to Rome. In June, Clement named a second legate-judge to sit alongside Wolsey: Lorenzo Campeggio, absentee bishop of Salisbury, and current English cardinal-protector in Rome. Arriving in late September 1528, he looked like a safe pair of hands.[14]

Frustration, however, followed in his wake. Campeggio was ill, then prevaricated about opening the trial. He wanted to explore two unlikely eventualities: reconciliation, and Catherine dissolving her marriage voluntarily by entering a nunnery. Catherine herself did her best to disrupt proceedings. In October 1528 she produced the 'Spanish Brief'. This rabbit-from-a-hat was an alternative version of Julius II's dispensation, preserved at the Spanish court, with small but significant differences. Because the terms of Wolsey and Campeggio's commission referred specifically to the previously known bull, it had the potential to scupper Henry's whole case. The King exploded in fury. Meanwhile, in Italy, the tide of French arms began to recede.[15]

Henry was also realizing that while he could flatter, bribe and browbeat churchmen and scholars, he could not so easily control what the people as a whole thought about a now open secret: that he intended to cast the Queen aside. In November 1528, the Spanish ambassador reported that as Henry and Catherine passed through a gallery from the royal residence at Bridewell to the next-door Dominican convent, 'the Queen was so warmly greeted by immense crowds of people, who publicly wished her victory over her enemies ... that the King ordered that nobody should be again admitted to the place'. A London chronicler, sympathetic to Henry, admitted frankly that 'women and other that favoured the Queen' spread the rumour Henry sent for the legate because he 'would for his own pleasure have another wife', and that anyone who spoke against the marriage 'was of the common people abhorred and reproved'.

News management was required: Henry summoned nobles, councillors, judges, mayor and aldermen to the Great Hall at Bridewell to learn 'our true meaning', which they should then 'declare to our subjects'. It was King Francis, Henry informed them, wishing to marry his son to the Princess Mary, who first sought reassurances about her legitimacy. Henry's bishops and theologians then persuaded him that he sinned mortally in his marriage. 'Think you, my lords,' he asked with shimmering pathos, 'these words touch not my body and soul; think you these doings do not daily and hourly trouble my conscience and vex my spirits?' If the matter were not settled, people could expect 'mischief and manslaughter' of the sort that in years past nearly destroyed the realm. There was nothing Henry wanted more than to be reassured his marriage was valid: the Queen was a lady 'of most gentleness, of most humility and buxomness'. All being equal, 'I would surely choose her above all other women'. Henry was a powerful and persuasive orator, but his audience was left troubled and divided: 'Every man spake as his heart served him.'[16]

The King's speech made no mention of Anne Boleyn. Yet at the start of 1529, Campeggio's letters to Rome distastefully noted how Henry 'caresses her openly and in public as if she were his wife'. Anne herself, so the Spanish ambassador observed, had begun to suspect Wolsey was sabotaging the divorce campaign, 'from fear of losing his power the moment she becomes Queen'. She had formed an alliance with the Dukes of Norfolk and Suffolk to bring about the cardinal's ruin, and Wolsey was 'no longer received at court as graciously as before'.[17]

English diplomacy adopted a Boleyn-backed strategy of intimidation. At the end of 1528, a new envoy was sent to Clement VII: Anne's bluntly spoken cousin, Francis Bryan, nicknamed 'the vicar of Hell'. He was to impress upon the Pope that, much as the King loved him, if he continued to prevaricate, it would so alienate Henry 'that he, with many other princes, his friends, with their nobles and realms, will withdraw their devotion and obedience from his Holiness and the See'.

In 1511, Henry had condemned Louis XII's defiance of Julius II as an impious laceration of the seamless robe of Christ; now he openly threatened schism. Another Boleyn policy was to present the Pope with a monster petition from all the leading men of the kingdom. Ambassador Mendoza scoffed that hardly anyone could be prevailed upon to sign it. But that would change. Smart rats were starting to leave Wolsey's leaking ship. Early in 1529, Stephen Gardiner wrote to Anne promising his unswerving devotion. 'I do trust in God,' she replied, 'you shall not repent it.'[18]

The legatine court finally got under way on 30 May 1529, with the legates summoning Henry and Catherine to appear before them at Blackfriars on 18 June. The trial was brief, and – from Henry and Wolsey's viewpoint – an unmitigated disaster. It was Catherine's finest hour. Against expectations, she appeared in person on the opening day to condemn the proceedings and appeal publicly to Rome. A few days later, both King and Queen were present.

Henry, seated in state, declared his well-rehearsed scruple of conscience. Catherine, on her knees, and in heavily accented English, addressed her husband directly: 'Twenty years I have been your true wife (or more), and by me ye have had divers children, although it hath pleased God to call them out of the world.' She swore, with God as her judge, that the marriage to Arthur was unconsummated, reminded everyone that learned men of good judgement, in England and Spain, reckoned the match lawful, lamented her lack of 'indifferent counsel', and declared an intention of acting as 'my friends in Spain will advise me'. She then rose and departed, the calls of the crier – 'Catherine Queen of England, come into the court' – ringing ineffectually in her ears.[19]

If Catherine had said her final words, her supporters had not. Her defence was conducted by Fisher, assisted by Robert Ridley and Henry Standish, two critics of Erasmus standing with one of his firmest English friends. Fisher had been the trusted spiritual advisor to Henry VIII's mother, the theological mainstay of the King's campaign against Luther, a living pledge of royal commitment to humanist piety and educational reform. Now he was openly at war with his master. In a resounding speech, he declared himself, like John the Baptist, ready to lay down his life for the sanctity of marriage. This cast Henry in the role of Herod, condemned by the Baptist for unlawfully divorcing one wife and taking another. Stephen Gardiner, in the King's name, accused Fisher of arrogance and disloyalty.[20]

The trial limped along. Witnesses supplied lurid testimony concerning consummation of the marriage to Arthur. Sir Anthony Willoughby, former household servant of the prince, recalled him emerging from his bedchamber demanding a thirst-quenching cup of ale, 'for I have been this night in the midst of Spain'. Proceedings were soon, however, tied up in technicalities. The King and Wolsey did what they could to keep the Pope in the dark. But Catherine's English supporters ensured Clement was fully aware of her formal appeal to Rome. In late June 1529, a crushing French defeat at the battle of Landriano in Lombardy increased the pressure on a stressed and vacillating pontiff.

By the middle of July Clement made the decision to revoke the case to the Roman curia. Even before this news arrived, Campeggio insisted on adjourning until the end of the summer. Again, the King was furious, and sent Norfolk and Suffolk to protest. 'By the mass,' spluttered the latter, 'now I see that the old said saw [proverb] is true, that there was never legate nor cardinal that did good in England!'[21] It was – in retrospect – a pivotal moment. If the Pope would not play by Henry's rules, then the nature of the game would have to change.

### Praemunire and Parliament

On 9 August 1529, the King sent out writs for a Parliament, the first since 1523. The French ambassador expected a demonstration of 'absolute power, in default of justice being administered by the Pope in this divorce'.[22] But it is unlikely there was as yet any thought of formally turning to Parliament to settle the Great Matter. Rather, its summoning was a continuation of the petitioning campaign begun at the end of 1528 – a measure to rally the support of the nation, and ramp up the pressure on the Pope.

After the ignominious failure of his divorce strategy, Wolsey's enemies circled. Anne poisoned the King's ear against him, but Wolsey, after years of lording it over the nobility, had critics aplenty. 'When the nobles and prelates perceived that the King's favour was from the Cardinal sore minished,' wrote Edward Hall, 'every man of the King's council began to lay to him such offences as they knew by him.' A book of thirty-four charges was presented to the King before he set off on summer progress. And prior to this, at the start of July, Lord Darcy drafted a memorandum of matters for Parliament. Among the proposals: 'that never legate nor cardinal be in England'. Eustace Chapuys, the shrewd and sophisticated Savoyard lawyer just arrived in England in September 1529 as new imperial and Spanish ambassador, heard various theories why Parliament was convening. Some believed it was to pass an act 'forbidding any more papal legates being admitted into the kingdom'.[23]

Wolsey's fall was not immediate. But his humiliation over the Blackfriars trial was compounded by a failure to maintain English interests in his greatest area of expertise: foreign policy. While Wolsey was distracted by the proceedings of the legatine court, the French and Imperialists were edging towards an understanding. The Treaty of Cambrai (5 August 1529) temporarily reconciled Henry's French ally with his imperial rival, and strengthened papal dependence on the Emperor. English interests were embarrassingly sidelined; the cardinal had to go.[24]

In autumn 1529, the talk was of parliamentary attainder, a declaration of treason demanding Wolsey's head. In the end, the King chose another path: on 9 October Wolsey was indicted in King's Bench on a charge of praemunire, specifically for obtaining from Rome the papal bulls making him a legate. On 30 October, he was found guilty, and all goods and possessions declared forfeit to the crown.[25] If anyone felt it unreasonable of Henry to prosecute a servant for exercising forms of authority the King himself laboured to obtain for him, they took care not to say so.

Wolsey prepared for a novel experience: to behave like a bishop and pastor of souls. He made plans to travel to the archdiocese of York, held since 1514, but never seen. Some of his followers – like Gardiner – had already deserted. But others remained loyal and grief-stricken. On 1 November, at Wolsey's house at Esher, his gentleman usher George Cavendish came across another of the cardinal's servants, the London lawyer Thomas Cromwell, seated by a window in the great hall, his eyes filled with tears, praying the matins of Our Lady from a Book of Hours.

Cromwell feared he was 'like to lose all that I have travailed for all the days of my life, for doing of my master true and diligent service'. He was associated with the unpopular policy of culling small monasteries to endow Oxford and Ipswich colleges. Darcy's draft indictment wanted Parliament to investigate 'whether the putting down of all the abbeys be lawful and good'. Cromwell was also bitter that Wolsey's 'idle chaplains' departed with profitable spiritual preferments, while lay servants were left with nothing.

Anticlericalism was far from the converse of piety (see pp. 64–5), though the sight of Cromwell with a traditional Catholic prayer book was one that Cavendish, recalling the scene years later, thought 'had since been a strange sight'. A man of action not contemplation, Cromwell told Cavendish he intended to head for the court 'where I will either make or mar'. Shortly after, through the patronage of Wolsey's Winchester steward, he secured election to Parliament as member for Taunton.[26]

The Parliament opened on 3 November. Wolsey's successor as Lord Chancellor opened proceedings with an eloquent oration explaining how the King, a good shepherd of his flock, summoned Parliament to make necessary laws, and to tackle 'divers new enormities' – an oblique reference to heresy. The King had also, in his wisdom, spied out a rotten 'great wether' (castrated ram), which sought to deceive him with 'fraudulent juggling'.[27]

This anti-eulogy for Wolsey was given by Thomas More. The appointment of a known opponent of the divorce to the highest office of state was, all things considered, a surprising development. The chancellorship was customarily given to a leading churchman. Archbishop Warham had held the office previously, but was unwilling to serve again. Tunstall was long considered a likely successor to Wolsey, but these were unusual times. According to Hall, the councillors tasked with discussing names all understood that the successful candidate was to be 'no man of the spirituality'. Bishops, the Pope's men in England, were to be put in their place. Another office conventionally held by a prelate, Lord Keepership of the Privy Seal, was taken from Tunstall in January 1530 and given to Anne Boleyn's father, now elevated to the earldom of Wiltshire. Suffolk was gung-ho to take the chancellorship, but Norfolk vetoed him.[28]

More was the compromise candidate, admirably qualified for the legal aspects, and a pair of clean hands untainted by association with Wolsey's regime. Henry was delighted at the nomination. It was a sign of his irrepressible confidence about prospects for the divorce that he was prepared to accept a man unwilling to play any part in bringing it about. More was reluctant, but acquiesced to a direct royal command. There was hard but necessary work ahead; a rising tide of heresy a determined chancellor might still be able to stem.

The session of Parliament sitting between November and December 1529 had business of various kinds to conduct. But it would be remembered – in the words of a 1542 chronicle – as 'a Parliament for the enormities of the clergy'. Chapuys thought its chief business was 'to legislate against all classes of the clergy', and a monastic chronicler in Suffolk characterized proceedings as a 'vehement schism between the clergy and the laypeople'.[29] Edward Hall – like Cromwell, a carpet-bagging London lawyer elected to Parliament as burgess for a West Country town – recalled that as soon as the Commons assembled, 'they began to commune of their griefs wherewith the spirituality had before time grievously oppressed them'.

The list of oppressions included excessive fines for probate of wills, as well as 'extreme exaction' in taking of mortuaries – a particularly sore point among Londoners harbouring memories of the Hunne case. There were complaints about abbots and priors keeping tanning houses, and undercutting lay merchants by dealing in cloth; about priests monopolizing tenancies of monastic farms and granges, and overcharging for agricultural products; and about pluralism and non-residence. The poor were being deprived of charity, and parishioners were starved of 'preaching, and true instruction of God's Word'.[30]

This haphazard compendium of anticlerical grievances hardly amounted to a full-frontal assault on the institution of the Church. A draft commons petition to the King did point to the anomaly of Lords Spiritual having a say in making of laws in Parliament, while 'they with the clergy in their Convocation make laws and ordinances whereby, without your royal assent, or the assent of any your lay subjects, they bind your said lay subjects'. But the actual legislative measures were relatively modest. An act against pluralism banned clergy from holding more than one benefice worth £8 a year, and insisted on residence for ten months annually. Priests were also banned from seeking papal dispensations for non-residence, a small snip at the web of ties between the English Church and Rome. Two other statutes retained the fees for probate and mortuaries, but regulated them on a sliding scale according to income.

Wolsey was the lightning rod for lay indignation. A joint committee of commons and lords produced an impressive list of forty-four charges – from usurping the jurisdiction of the bishops to exposing Henry to 'the foul and contagious disease of the great pox'. There was an anti-Wolseyan flavour to the three statutes. Excessive fees were associated with his legatine court, and his ecclesiastical career was pluralism personified. But – with Thomas Cromwell working discreetly for his old master's rehabilitation – Henry was for now disinclined to further action.[31]

Parliamentary anticlericalism, however, went beyond anti-cardinalism. Issues from 1512–15 resurfaced, as once again the spectre of heresy haunted the spaces between lay and ecclesiastical notions of legitimate authority, due process and necessary reform. In closing his list of largely fiscal grievances, Edward Hall remarked that 'these things before this time might in no wise be touched nor yet talked of by no man, except he would be made a heretic'. It was an old suspicion, voiced during the Hunne case, and now revived – at a time when 'real' heresy stalked the land, the church tribunals in active pursuit. A draft bill proposed procedural changes to protect the rights of the accused, and complained that clergy were arresting 'under the colour and name of heresy' all who 'preach, speak or reason against their detestable and shameful living'.[32]

If this was the fear, churchmen in Parliament did little to assuage it. The probate bill faced impassioned opposition, and accusations that laymen were dead-set to undermine the liberties and authority of the Church. Fisher led the counter-charge in the Lords, condemning hypocritical attempts to criticize the behaviour of priests so as 'to bring them into contempt and hatred of the laity'. He was likely thinking of Simon Fish's explosive pamphlet, recently scattered in the London streets. Laymen, Fisher stiffly reminded his audience, 'have no authority to correct' the clergy – the very point Fish bitterly emphasized. England was facing the fate of Bohemia or Germany, lands ruined by the heresies of Hus and Luther. And all this, Fisher suggested, 'ariseth from lack of faith only'.

It was a serious provocation, recalling Bishop Fitzjames's notorious remark in 1515 that any London jury would convict his official for Hunne's murder because they were 'so set upon the favour of heresy'. In the Lords, Norfolk commented ruefully that the greatest clerks were not always the wisest men. The Commons reacted with fury to the implication that 'they were infidels and no Christians, as ill as Turks or Saracens'. Speaker Thomas Audley and a delegation of MPs were sent to present a 'grievous complaint' to the King. Henry summoned Fisher, who, according to which of two sixteenth-century accounts we choose to believe, robustly 'spake his mind in defence and right of the Church', or limply explained he meant the Bohemians, not members of the Commons, acted from lack of faith. Either way, the bishop's explanation 'pleased the Commons nothing at all'.[33]

## Heresy and the Court

Henry's desire for a divorce and the evangelical yearning for sweeping reform of the Church were separate matters, connected only by coincidence in time. There was no reason why the paths should have crossed. But they did. If either demand had arisen isolated from the other, outcomes would have been different. Yet from the very start of life, the English Reformation as an 'act of state', and the English Reformation as a spiritual movement, were not remote and distant cousins; they were conjoined twins, dependent, sometimes resentfully, one upon the other.

Already, at Easter 1529, Campeggio discovered that 'certain Lutheran books, in English, of an evil sort, have been circulated in the King's court'. He tried to persuade Henry that the call in one of these books for disendowment of the Church was 'the devil dressed in angels' clothing'. Henry replied coolly that Lutherans believed churchmen sought possessions for their own advantage, lived wicked lives and 'erred in many things from divine law'. But Campeggio need not worry: he 'had been and always would remain a good Christian'.[34]

Good Christian or no, Henry's flirtations with the language of radical reform became more flagrant over the course of 1529. At a dinner at the end of November, Chapuys was subjected to a lecture about 'vain and superfluous ceremonies' in Rome, and the papacy's responsibility for numerous wars, discords and heresies. If Luther had simply castigated vices and errors of the clergy, rather than attacking the sacraments, Henry said he would have written for rather than against him. There was heresy mixed up in his books, but also 'many truths he had brought to light'. The King was set upon 'the reformation of the Church in his dominions', introducing reforms and eliminating scandal 'little by little'. When Chapuys saw him a week later, Henry claimed credit for the recent parliamentary statutes. The ambassador did not believe this concern for clerical standards was genuine or disinterested. He heard from the Queen that when she and Henry dined together on 30 November he bluntly told her that if the Pope continued to ignore well-founded theological judgements that they were not man and wife, he 'would denounce the Pope as a heretic, and marry whom he pleased'.[35]

Henry's table-talk at this time was peppered with references to a corrupt and over-funded Church needing to be recalled to its gospel mission, and to the responsibility of popes for the past and present ills of Christendom – popes who were potential heretics rather than arbiters of truth. Who had the King been talking to, or what had he been reading?

We know, in part, the answer to those questions. According to John Foxe, Simon Fish arranged for a copy of his *Supplication for the Beggars* to be sent to Anne, who, after consulting with her brother George, put it into Henry's hands. Foxe's chronology is confused, but his informant was Fish's widow, and the account looks sound in its essentials. Henry reportedly received her, and granted a petition for her husband's safe conduct. When Fish returned from Antwerp, Henry 'embraced him with loving countenance', and took him on a hunting trip. He also instructed Chancellor More to leave Fish alone.[36]

The *Supplication* might well be Campeggio's 'Lutheran book'. But the King's new opinions resembled arguments found in a still more radical text. Shortly after its publication at Antwerp in October 1528, Anne Boleyn got hold of Tyndale's *Obedience of a Christian Man*, and began marking up passages to bring to Henry's attention. In the interim, she lent the book to a lady-in-waiting, whose fiancé was caught poring over it by Richard Sampson, dean of the Chapel Royal. Anne hurried pre-emptively to the King and successfully demanded the return of the confiscated volume, which she then encouraged him to consult. Henry, seemingly, was delighted with what he found: 'This is the book for me and all kings to read!'[37]

Some refrains in *Obedience* were certainly music for royal ears. Tyndale adapted Luther's concept of temporal and spiritual 'regiments' (spheres of authority) to argue that all claims of Pope, bishops and clergy to independent power and jurisdiction were bogus and unscriptural. Structures of law, financial demands, regulation of property must rest solely in the hands of the King, for 'the King is in the room of God, and his law is God's law'. As shock waves from the German Peasants' War of 1525 continued to reverberate around Europe, Tyndale was anxious to refute allegations that the new theology was intrinsically subversive of authority. Attack, he decided, was the surest form of defence. It was the clergy who fomented rebellion and disobedience, acting as an autonomous order within the realm, and as agents for a foreign power outside it.

For centuries, Tyndale argued, popes intrigued to undermine and emasculate English rulers, resorting to violence when they could not get their way: papal lackeys murdered Richard II and Duke Humphrey of Gloucester (d. 1447), on account of their talent for spying out fake miracles. King John was no wicked tyrant, but a patriotic hero, excommunicated simply for performing 'that office which God commandeth every king to do'. The clergy always sought to doctor the historical record. But they could not erase all traces of their treachery and duplicitousness: 'read the Chronicles of England'.[38]

The fugitive Tyndale, 'captain of our English heretics' as More called him, was beginning to look like a potential royal asset. In November 1530, Wolsey lay dying at Leicester Abbey, and recalled how his final advice to the King was to 'have a diligent eye to depress this new perverse sect of the Lutherans'.[39] Yet in the same month, Cromwell's agent Stephen Vaughan departed for the continent with instructions to recruit Tyndale for the King's cause. The pair met outside Antwerp, and Vaughan conveyed the offer of a royal pardon. Tyndale, however, did not feel safe returning to England, and would not supply the guarantees about future conduct that Henry demanded. He did, though, promise to stop writing books if the King would allow only 'a bare text of the scripture [i.e. one without prologues and glosses] to be set forth among his people'.[40] Henry looked hard at this option in 1530 – the needs of the divorce made the idea of putting vernacular scripture, and the text of Leviticus 18, directly in front of the people a very tempting one. But in the end, he endorsed the clergy's opinion that the times were too unsettled.

Evangelicals nonetheless saw grounds for optimism. In the wake of the 1530 proclamation pledging a future vernacular translation, Latimer petitioned the King to remain true to his promise. The clergy withheld scripture to forestall criticism of their avarice. They were using 'means and craft' to get around the restrictions of the 1529 Parliament. And rather than lose one penny of their endowments, they would incite 'rebellion against the temporal power'.[41] These were the right notes to strike with a frustrated and anticlerical king.

Within the royal orbit, there was freedom to say the previously unsayable. In March 1531, Chapuys reported the arrest by Archbishop Warham of a priest, 'the finest and most learned preacher in England'. The cleric in question, the Cambridge scholar Edward Crome, refused to answer, on the grounds no secular lords were present at his trial, and he appealed to the King. In Henry's presence, several bishops preached against Crome, but Henry noticed one of the charges was denying the Pope to be head of the Church. This, said the King, 'ought not to be entered among the heresies, for it was quite certain and true'. Crome was let off with a token recantation. This, Chapuys believed, was at the behest of Anne Boleyn and her father, 'who are more Lutheran than Luther himself'.

Tyndale remained in the relative safety of Antwerp, and so, for the moment, did Frith, despite attempts by Cromwell and Vaughan to persuade him he would find Henry 'mercifully disposed'.[42] In November 1531, Vaughan sent Cromwell a new work by Robert Barnes, a *Supplication* to Henry, justifying his conduct since 1525, and blaming his troubles on the machinations of the clergy. Henry was less interested in the force of Barnes's arguments than in the quality of his connections. Since fleeing from England he had become intimate with Luther, Melanchthon and Bugenhagen. In the summer of 1531, a discrete approach was made for him to sound out Luther's opinion on the divorce. It was not what the King of England wanted to hear. Luther ruled that Deuteronomy had precedence over the merely Jewish ceremonial law of Leviticus, and saw no way forward for Henry other than 'the example of the patriarchs' (bigamy).

Nonetheless, Luther's letter was Barnes's passport. Thomas More wrote with clenched pen at Christmas 1531 that Friar Barnes 'is at this day come into the realm by safe conduct'. His agents kept close watch on Barnes, who took the precautions of shaving his beard and dressing like a merchant. Yet, with Cromwell's protection, he moved relatively freely, visiting evangelicals in London, and surviving a robust verbal encounter with Stephen Gardiner, who took exception to Barnes's account of the role he played in the ex-friar's troubles in 1526. With a known Lutheran swanning around the capital, graced by an interview with the King himself, official heresy policy was observably out of joint. Chapuys noted that Barnes was much in the company of a Franciscan friar, 'one of the chief writers in favour of the King'. The Franciscan was an Oxford-based Florentine, Nicholas de Burgo, and for two years he had been at the heart of a hopeful new strategy for cracking the divorce.[43]

## The Determinations of the Universities

The strategy emerged from a chance meeting in early August 1529, in the aftermath of the Blackfriars trial. In the end it did little to advance Henry's objective. But the meeting launched a career of immense significance. Stephen Gardiner and Edward Foxe were staying overnight in the Essex market town of Waltham Abbey, with a gentry family called Cressy. Another guest was a Cambridge scholar, Thomas Cranmer, a temporary refugee from the university following a seasonal outbreak of plague. Over dinner, conversation turned to the prospects for Henry's divorce – the political classes talked of little else in the summer of 1529. Cranmer thought they were going about it the wrong way. There was 'but one truth in it'. Rather than getting tangled up in legal arguments, the King should seek judgement from the experts in truth, theologians. Universities should be canvassed for their opinions. Foxe relayed the idea to Henry, who liked its blend of principle and pragmatism. Henry summoned Cranmer, and commended him to Anne Boleyn's father, who hired him as a chaplain. It was the birth of a formidable political and religious partnership.[44]

Cranmer joined an action force of royalist intellectuals, assembled in the late summer of 1529: Gardiner, Foxe, Nicholas de Burgo, Edward Lee and John Stokesley. Foxe, de Burgo and Cranmer visited More shortly after his appointment as chancellor, in a renewed effort to bring him round. But More was unmoveable, secure, so he thought, in a personal promise from the King that he need do only 'as his conscience served him'. Stokesley, Lee and Foxe had no more luck the following year with Fisher – 'self-willed and obstinate', they reported.[45]

Other theologians proved only somewhat more amenable. Foxe and Gardiner were sent to Cambridge, where, on 9 March 1530, a carefully selected panel of scholars pronounced it 'more probable' that marriage to a deceased brother's wife contravened divine law, though only if the marriage were consummated – an ambiguous rider in light of Catherine's public protestations that it had not been. Foxe and de Burgo secured a similar declaration of luke-warm support in Oxford on 8 April. But while the theologians deliberated, pro-Catherine feelings in the town ran high. De Burgo and another delegate, John Longland, were pelted with stones by a mob of angry women.[46]

Meanwhile, royal agents, copiously furnished with bribe money, solicited decisions from universities overseas. The biggest prize was Paris, with its prestigious theology faculty. In 1528, the theologians of the Sorbonne were deadlocked in an earlier debate on the King of England's marriage. But with Francis I leaning towards Henry, an unequivocally favourable determination was secured in July 1530. Other French universities – Orleans, Toulouse, Bourges, and the Paris Law Faculty – delivered similar verdicts. The Law Faculty at Angers agreed, though the theologians – perhaps out of cussedness towards a rival faculty – upheld the papal view. In Italy, the universities of Bologna, Ferrara and Padua concluded, in vague terms, that popes did not have power to dispense for marriage to a widowed sister-in-law. At the same time, English scholars were busy combing through chronicles in European university and private libraries – even, cheekily, those of the Vatican itself – for helpful historical precedent.

It hardly amounted to overwhelming international endorsement. Discounting Oxford and Cambridge, fewer than ten universities provided support, and in a surge of around fifty printed works by European canonists and theologians, many staunchly opposed the divorce.[47] Still, it was enough to freight the ship for a new course.

On 12 June 1530, Henry summoned leading nobles and office-holders to revive the policy mooted in late 1528: a giant petition of English subjects to Pope Clement, based on 'the opinion of the most famous universities and most learned men in Christendom'. The first draft, which raised the spectre of trans-ferring allegiance to a General Council, was too radical for some, and an (unnamed) 'chief favourite' threw himself on his knees to warn Henry of the dangers of popular rebellion. But the redrafted petition, despatched to Rome in July, was only slightly less provocative, warning darkly that English people would 'seek our remedy elsewhere' if the Pope, 'whom we justly call father', proved determined to make them orphans. It was endorsed by no fewer than forty-four of the secular nobility, starting with Norfolk and Suffolk, along with twenty-two heads of religious houses. Only six bishops were apparently asked to sign: Archbishops Warham and Wolsey (in one of his last public acts), Longland (the King's confessor), the aged Sherburne of Chichester, and the nonentities John Kite of Carlisle and Richard Rawlins of St David's. On a key issue of spiritual judgement, the chief pastors of the English Church were decisively sidelined.

As far as Henry was concerned, authoritative theological and moral judgement on the divorce had now been declared, and he wrote to Clement announcing 'we do separate from our cause the authority of the see apostolic'. This was not – yet – a complete withdrawal of obedience: Henry had no wish 'further to impugn your authority, unless ye do compel us'.[48]

The time had come to lay the case before the public. As popular demonstrations in favour of Catherine had shown, the King needed to persuade as well as command. The determinations of seven foreign universities were presented to Parliament in the spring of 1531 by Chancellor More, who also had the disagreeable task of denying rumours that the King pursued the divorce 'out of love for some lady, and not out of any scruple of conscience'. These *Censurae academiarum* (judgements of the academies) were published by the royal printer Thomas Berthelet, and in November appeared in Cranmer's English translation as *The Determinations of the Most Famous and Most Excellent Universities of Italy and France* – the half-hearted endorsements of Oxford and Cambridge were quietly laid aside. The determinations themselves were brief and formulaic. But an accompanying treatise, jointly authored by Stokesley, Foxe, de Burgo, Gardiner and Cranmer, examined in detail the arguments over marriage to a brother's widow, and the necessity of dissolving such marriages, whatever the Pope might say about it.[49]

### The Lion's Strength

As the *Censurae* was prepared for the press in the last months of 1530, royal positions hardened. Ambassadors in Rome were told to impress upon the Pope not only that he had no legitimate jurisdiction in this case, but that it was the custom and privilege of England that no one could be cited to submit to judgement outside the realm. In England, Suffolk and Wiltshire harangued the nuncio: they 'cared neither for Pope or Popes in this kingdom, not even if St. Peter should come to life again'. The King 'was absolute both as Emperor and Pope in his own kingdom'. Writing to Clement in December, Henry avoided the language of empire, but asserted that the laws of England did not permit his case to be heard beyond the realm, and that church councils, and the great Saints Bernard and Cyprian, believed disputes should be settled in lands where they arose.

Touchy statements that kings of England recognized no superior but God, and that privileges, laws and customs of England forbad subjects to be cited out of the realm by papal summons – these were time-honoured assertions of prerogative; often dormant, but periodically activated via the laws of provisors and praemunire (see pp. 83–4). As More would later say to Cromwell, 'If a lion knew his own strength, hard were it for any man to rule him.'[50]

But something novel was now at work. To claim that English kings enjoyed historically privileged exemption from external citation was one thing; it was another to suggest – as a universal principle – that causes must invariably be settled in whatever ecclesiastical province they originated. This was to begin to reimagine the very nature of the western Church, and the role within it of the bishop of Rome. As recently as 1526, Henry had castigated Luther as a 'perpetual enemy to the Pope', someone 'to whose highness I well know how far the estate of a king is inferior'.[51] If he knew it then, he did not know it now.

The divorce produced answers to questions Henry did not initially think to ask. The intellectuals tasked with finding persuasive arguments ranged widely and, consciously or not, they heeded Tyndale's advice – 'read the chronicles of England'. In the course of 1530–1, a wealth of evidence from history, scripture and Church Fathers was brought to bear on the marriage, and on the respective powers of king and popes. The main body of extracts was later catalogued with an inelegant title: *Collectanea satis copiosa, ex sacris scriptis et authoribus Catholicis de regia et ecclesiastica potestate* (Sufficiently large collections, from holy scripture and Catholic authors, concerning royal and ecclesiastical authority). Henry was shown the work in progress in the summer of 1530. He was thrilled with what he saw, and avidly annotated the collection with observations, headings and queries.[52]

The *Collectanea* contained a startling revelation: centralized authority in the Church under the papacy was a recent and dubious development. In the early – and therefore, according to contemporary ways of thinking, *authentic* – Church, individual provinces had autonomous jurisdiction. Moreover, historical evidence 'proved' that in each realm of Christendom supreme spiritual as well as secular authority belonged rightfully to the king. Henry's imagination was particularly caught by a letter from Pope Eleutherius to the second-century British king, Lucius I. (In fact, the letter was a thirteenth-century forgery; Lucius a mythical figure.) Lucius wrote to the Pope requesting Roman law for England, and was told he didn't need it. As a Christian king he had the scriptures, and could legislate from them for both realm and clergy. *Vicarius vero Dei estis in regno*: 'you are truly the vicar of Christ in your realm'.[53]

In the summer of 1530, Henry discovered a startling truth about himself: he was rightfully supreme head of the Church in England. If he had not hitherto exercised that role to the full, it was because he and his predecessors had carelessly allowed their powers to devolve into the hands of a usurping foreign prelate. It was nothing less than a moment of conversion, and, like other conversions, it took root because it confirmed much of what Henry already knew and felt to be true.

Why Henry did not, in the autumn of 1530, openly annul his marriage and repudiate Rome's authority is a good question. Most likely, and for all the bluster of his private and public pronouncements, he feared he would not be able to carry the political nation with him. Key advisors like Gardiner, and also Norfolk and other lords on the Council, favoured a continuation of the policy of bullying the Pope into submission. Another figure was rising in the King's favour, and admitted to the Council about this time: Thomas Cromwell. His advice was to affirm the consent of the nation by acting through Parliament.

In advance of the new session, in October 1530, Henry summoned leading clergy and lawyers to a meeting to consider whether an Act of Parliament might empower the archbishop of Canterbury to pronounce on the divorce. The experts said they did not think so, and Henry angrily postponed the Parliament till February the following year. There was more anger a couple of weeks later when the nuncio delivered Clement's negative answer to the monster petition. Using 'very threatening language', Henry pointed to a disastrous recent flooding of the Tiber as a clear sign of God's displeasure. His cause, and the larger purposes of the Almighty, were fully in alignment.

Not all subjects saw it that way. The clergy, so vigorous in their defence of 'liberties' in the past, were not prepared to roll over in front of the latest lay assaults. Fisher was uncowed by his dressing-down after his speech in Parliament against the probate bill. With two other bishops, John Clerk of Bath and Wells and Nicholas West of Ely, he attempted to appeal to Rome against the anticlerical statutes passed in 1529, perhaps in response to a minor flood of lay-instigated exchequer prosecutions generated by them. Astonishingly, the bishops invited Clement simply to annul the statutes, as infringements on ecclesiastical jurisdiction. This was a frankly implausible prospect in 1530, or at any other time. But it underlines how seriously conscientious bishops took the notion that the reform of the Church pertained to them alone.[54]

Henry's response, in September 1530, was a proclamation forbidding the importation of papal bulls prejudicial to the King's prerogative, and the three were placed under arrest. Moves to prosecute clergymen under the praemunire statute began earlier in the summer, when fourteen were indicted by the attorney general in King's Bench on charges of making compositions with Wolsey that abetted his legatine authority. In addition to Fisher, Clerk and West, five bishops were indicted: Blythe of Coventry and Lichfield, Sherburne of Chichester, Nykke of Norwich, Standish of St Asaph, and Skevington of Bangor. Standish was a strong partisan of Queen Catherine. Sherburne, Blythe and Nykke were disciplinarians, steeled in the use of church courts against heresy. Nykke in particular had a track record of opposing praemunire suits, and of voicing dark suspicions about the orthodoxy of those mounting them (see pp. 86–7) The targets were carefully singled out, but the individual cases were not pursued. Already in October Cromwell had 'another way devised': an unprecedented scheme to charge the *entire* English clergy with praemunire.[55]

In January 1531, as Parliament reconvened, Convocation assembled in parallel at Westminster Abbey.[56] Its priorities were well-established issues of clerical reform, lent urgency by the spread of Lutheran heresy. But it was to be made clear to the bishops that reformation of the Church's procedures and personnel was no longer a matter just for them.

Proceedings began with a demand from the King that the clergy compensate him for the expenses of pursuing his suit at Rome, and for securing opinions from the foreign universities – all the fault of Wolsey and other conniving bishops. The amount of the demand – £100,000 – was as outrageous as the reasoning behind it. It was accompanied by threats that the whole clergy was fallen into peril of praemunire – no longer just for collusion with Wolsey's legatine authority, but for operating a system of spiritual jurisdiction independent of royal justice. Convocation was taken aback, but not excessively intimidated. The clergy would pay, but in return wanted guarantees of immunity from prosecution, as well as clear and restricted definitions of the scope of praemunire, a modification of the statutes of 1529, and a general confirmation of the ancient rights and liberties of the Church.

It was never really about the money. Clerical assertiveness stirred Henry to greater assertiveness of his own. He now insisted the clergy acknowledge that God had committed to him the 'cure of souls' of his subjects, and recognize him as 'sole protector and supreme head' of the English Church. Through a week of urgent discussions, Henry's demands were watered down. Royal cure of souls became a vague responsibility for souls committed to clerical oversight, and the clergy agreed to recognize Henry's supreme headship 'as far as the law of Christ allows'. Fisher was instrumental in getting Convocation to adopt this cleverly subversive qualification. In early March 1531, the clergy were pardoned by parliamentary statute for breaching the acts of provisors and praemunire, and the terms of the subsidy were agreed.

The clergy felt they had won a victory, but it was a limited and tactical one. The Boleyns and their allies, eager for unilateral action, felt the wind stirring in their sails. Anne's brother George, now Lord Rochford, brought to Convocation a tract arguing that Henry's supreme authority, 'grounded on God's Word, ought in no case to be restrained by any frustrate decrees of popish laws'. Anne was said to have reacted to the demand for supremacy with 'such demonstrations of joy as if she had actually gained paradise'. Religious conservatives on the Council dutifully parroted the *Collectanea* line. In mid-January, Norfolk tried impressing Chapuys with a potted Arthurian history of Henry's 'right to empire'. The supposed clincher was an inscription copied from the seal or tomb of the great King Arthur himself – '*Britanniae, Galliae, Germaniae, Daciae Imperator*'. Chapuys had no idea who Norfolk was talking about: 'I was sorry he was not also called Emperor of Asia.'[57]

In 1531 there was little sign of the English clergy collapsing in the face of royal demands. The Convocation of the Province of York accepted a similar pardon, but with a bold proviso that the King's new title did not infringe the authority of the Holy Father. Tunstall wrote to the King explaining that temporal supremacy could in no wise extend to spiritual matters. There was protest too from the lower house of Southern Convocation. A document was sent to Rome, signed by eighteen delegates on behalf of the others. It trenchantly asserted that nothing they conceded was intended to weaken the laws and liberties of the Church, the unity of Christendom, or the authority of the Pope. The lead signatories were, predictably, charged with praemunire.[58]

The early part of 1531 brought stalemate. Henry had in all likelihood now decisively shed his remaining attachment to Rome, and assumed in his own mind his God-given destiny as supreme head of an English 'Empire'. Yet with resolution of the divorce ever the priority, policy proceeded fitfully. It was probably still something like the official line when, in January, Norfolk conceded to Chapuys that popes had jurisdiction over matters of heresy. Wolsey's death at the end of the previous year created episcopal vacancies for members of the 'think-tank' – Edward Lee went to York, and Stephen Gardiner to Winchester. York was initially offered to Henry's cousin, Reginald Pole, but he failed to give satisfactory assurances of support for the divorce. Both Lee and Gardiner were appointed in the time-honoured way: papal provision at the request of the King.[59] A final, irrevocable breach was not yet inevitable.

### Raising the Stakes

On 23 February 1530, Thomas Hitton, a Norfolk priest, was burned to death at Maidstone in Kent. Hitton was a courier for the evangelical exiles. Letters were found sewn in his coat, after he was arrested in Gravesend on suspicion of pilfering washing drying on a hedge. In the course of interrogations before Archbishop Warham he held unrepentantly to various heretical opinions, including the Zwinglian (or Lollard) view that, after consecration in the mass, there was nothing 'but only the very substance of material bread'.[60]

An undistinguished man – though a brave one – Hitton was the first evangelical to be put to death for his beliefs, giving the lie to Thomas More's taunt that heretics dared not stick to their opinions. They would scarcely admit it, but the brethren were perhaps secretly relieved. Martyrdom was uniquely potent as a gauge of truth, just as persecution was a sure indicator of the Antichrist. Soon after Hitton's death, George Joye included his name as that of a saint and martyr in the calendar prefacing his *Ortulus Anime* (Garden of the

Soul), a subversively familiar-looking vernacular version of a traditional Catholic primer.[61]

To Thomas More, Hitton was 'the devil's stinking martyr'. What particularly galled him was that to make room for this new 'Saint Thomas', Joye ejected from his calendar the name of the second-century Christian martyr St Polycarp.[62] Sixteenth-century opinion bitterly contested the claims of true and false martyrdom. All agreed with the ancient dictum of St Augustine: what created a martyr was the rightness of the cause, not the manner of the death. But the spectacle of suffering might stiffen the resolve of the victim's supporters just as much as demoralize or intimidate them. And it invariably heightened their hatred for those inflicting the punishments.

Between 23 February 1530 and 16 May 1532, when More stepped down as chancellor, at least six Englishmen – Hitton, Thomas Bilney, Richard Bayfield, John Tewkesbury, James Bainham and Thomas Benet – were burned as heretics.[63] Thomas Harding, Lollard turned quasi-Lutheran, went to the stake a fortnight later, and John Frith and his associate Andrew Hewet were burned at Smithfield the following summer. Even as the climate of relations between England and the Holy See was starting to freeze over, the temperature of persecution was – quite literally – rising.

Thomas More deserves much of the credit, or blame, for this. As chancellor, he harnessed the legal machinery of the state to the campaign against heresy, using the police powers of the Court of Star Chamber, and working closely with sympathetic bishops: Tunstall, and then Stokesley of London. The King was sidetracked and increasingly ill advised. But More, convinced of the spiritual and moral vacuity of heresy, believed the evangelicals could be defeated if bishops rose to the challenge, and dutiful laymen did their best to help. A pair of 1530 proclamations (likely drafted by More) stressed the King's detestation of 'malicious and wicked sects of heretics and Lollards', and urged state officials to 'give their whole power and diligence' to destroying them. The proclamation of June 1530, hazily promising a future vernacular bible, more concretely banned Tyndale's New and Old Testaments, his *Wicked Mammon* and *Obedience*, as well as Fish's *Sum of Scripture* and *Supplication*. It ordered the immediate arrest of anyone possessing such 'books in English tongue, printed beyond the seas'.[64]

Through 1530–1, More increasingly put the squeeze on the book-runners, receiving information from a network of informers, and arresting and interrogating suspects, some of whom were detained in his house at Chelsea.[65] Names were given up. The authorities arrested a clutch of heretics in London in the latter part of 1530, and paraded them through the streets facing backwards on horseback, cloaks heavy with tacked-on New Testaments. Chapuys worried about the lenience of the sentence and complained that 'where one spoke of them before, a hundred speak of them now'.[66]

But More's policies were securing results. He broke open a Bristol cell, headed by Richard Webbe. Rather than selling heretical books, its members were scattering them in the streets, and leaving them on doorsteps at night. 'They would of their charity,' scoffed More, 'poison men for nothing.' Webbe recanted. So – in a propaganda coup for the authorities – did William (Jerome) Barlow, who denounced his former confederates in a printed dialogue on the 'Lutheran Factions'. Evangelicals suspected it was ghostwritten by More. The greatest success was the 1531 arrest of George Constantine, who supplied both operational secrets of the book-smuggling and names of those involved – Robert Necton, the book-binder John Birt, the monk Richard Bayfield. In London, the close working partnership of two old Erasmians, More and Stokesley – one an opponent and one a supporter of the divorce – generated dozens of abjurations.[67]

Some of those tangled in the net had been caught before; there were no second chances for relapsed heretics. Richard Bayfield, former Benedictine of Bury, was tried by Stokesley and burned at the end of November 1531. John Tewkesbury was a London haberdasher who recanted before Tunstall in 1529. According to Foxe, the example of Bayfield made him 'return and constantly abide in the testimony of the truth'; More claimed Tewkesbury would have abjured all his heresies, 'and have accused Tyndale too, if it might have saved his life'. Either way, he was burned at Smithfield on 20 December.[68]

The fires of the early 1530s were beacons of evangelical resolve. Abjurations produced agonies of remorse that earlier Lollards do not seem to have felt. The lawyer James Bainham made himself conspicuous by marrying the widow of Simon Fish, and was arrested in late 1531. More and Stokesley worked hard to get him to recant, and after public penance at Paul's Cross, he was released in February 1532. But within a month, his conscience got the better of him. Bainham went to ask forgiveness of an evangelical congregation meeting secretly in a warehouse in Bow Lane. The following Sunday, he stood up in the church of the Austin Friars, 'the New Testament in his hand in English, and *The Obedience of a Christian Man* in his bosom', to make a tear-filled public confession: he had denied God, and would not 'feel such a hell again as he did feel, for all the world's good'. At a second trial, Bainham denied purgatory and transubstantiation, and was condemned to burn. The Venetian ambassador recorded a huge crowd present at his execution in April 1532, and that 'he died with the greatest fortitude'.[69]

A corrupted conscience, and the compulsion to cleanse it with an open profession of faith, were the key ingredients of a more famous martyrdom. Since his abjuration in December 1527, and his return to Cambridge in 1529, Thomas Bilney had lived under a cloud of depression and remorse. Late one evening, sometime in 1531, he announced to friends his intention to 'go up to Jerusalem' – an echo of Christ's words foretelling the passion. Norwich was

Bilney's Jerusalem. He preached there, in defiance of a prohibition, and delivered copies of Tyndale's works to Katherine Manne, an anchoress attached to the Dominican priory, whom he had 'converted to Christ'.[70]

Bilney was tried by Bishop Nykke's chancellor, Thomas Pelles, convicted as a relapsed heretic and burned at the Lollards' Pit just outside the city walls of Norwich on 19 August 1531. Everything about the case was murky and controversial. During the trial proceedings, Bilney played the same card as Edward Crome: direct appeal of his cause to the King. Pelles's dismissal of the petition created disquiet among a citizenry with experience of the heavy-handed episcopal regime of Bishop Nykke. Worried lest he should have impeded the sentence, Edward Reed, mayor and MP for the city, collected witness statements with the intention of raising the matter in the next session of Parliament. In anticipation of a parliamentary inquiry, Pelles requested Chancellor More to launch a parallel investigation through Star Chamber. It emerged that Reed was reluctant to implement Pelles's sentence: 'Master Doctor, ye know that the King hath a new title given him by the clergy, and ye were at the granting of it, of what effect it is, I know not.'[71]

The other crux of investigation was whether Bilney made a formal admission of heresy and recanted at the stake. Opinion on this was divided, but there was no doubt that before his death he was judged worthy to receive the sacrament. Within months, More was insisting that Bilney died fully reconciled to the Catholic Church – a poke in the eye for Tyndale and his tawdry tally of martyrs.[72]

Yet the perception, widespread in Norwich, that Bilney was at heart a sound Catholic, punished with unreasonable harshness, was fraught with danger for the bishops. Nykke paid a backhanded tribute to it when he heard of the preaching in Cambridge of Anne Boleyn's protégé, Nicholas Shaxton: 'Christ's Mother! I fear I have burnt Abel and let Cain go!'[73] To many, Bilney seemed another Hunne, a victim of the reactionary strategy of labelling with heresy mere honest critics of ecclesiastical abuses.

Another incident encapsulated a mood of bitterness and recrimination. A Gloucestershire gentleman, William Tracy of Toddington, died in October 1530 leaving a will that denied purgatory and asserted justification by faith. Not only did the ecclesiastical courts refuse probate, the case passed to Canterbury Convocation, which in 1531 posthumously convicted Tracy of heresy, and ordered the exhumation of his body from consecrated ground. Thomas Parker, chancellor of the diocese of Worcester, then overstepped his authority by burning the disinterred corpse, without the necessary writ for the sheriff. Encouraged by Cromwell, Tracy's son Richard went to law, and Parker was fined a swingeing £300. Meanwhile, Convocation's action served only to publicize the will, copies of which circulated in London as a reformist manifesto. Tyndale and Frith composed commentaries for an edition printed in Antwerp.

Tracy was only indirectly an evangelical martyr. But the humanist monk Robert Joseph – a friend of the vicar of Toddington – feared he 'has done more harm to the Christian religion in his death than by his pestiferous contentions before'.[74]

Only a small number of English people at the start of the 1530s were active supporters of the evangelicals. Bishop Nykke was a pessimist who feared erroneous opinions were likely to 'undo us all', but he nonetheless judged that in his diocese 'the gentlemen and the commonality be not greatly infected'; the problem lay with 'merchants, and such that hath abiding not far from the sea'. Convocation expressed satisfaction in 1532 that 'no notable personage' had yet embraced 'the abominable and erroneous opinions lately sprung in Germany'; only 'certain apostates, friars, monks, lewd priests, bankrupt merchants, vagabonds and lewd idle fellows'.[75] Large swathes of England had hardly seen a heretic. But in the parts that had, a sense was growing that the cure, in the form of episcopal zero-tolerance, might be worse than the disease. John Ashwell, Augustinian prior of Newnham in Bedfordshire, reported George Joye to Bishop Longland, but begged him to keep the denunciation secret, 'for then I shall lose the favour of many in my country'.[76]

Heresy was no longer something whispered behind closed doors. Thomas More feared it was making progress by default, through the inertia and complacency of the orthodox: 'It beginneth to grow almost in custom that among good Catholic folk they be suffered to talk unchecked.' Worse, juries at county sessions and manor courts were reluctant to present heretics. The overwhelming majority were sound in faith. But even a few birds, 'always chirking and flying from bush to bush', might seem like a great number. Similarly, busy heretics were to be found, talking and arguing, 'in every ale house, in every tavern, in every barge, and almost every boat'. Between their relentless zeal and the apathy of ordinary Catholics 'appeareth often times as great a difference as between frost and fire'.[77]

Evangelical confidence was a by-product of the King's Great Matter, which by 1530 was playing topsy-turvy with demarcations of heresy and orthodoxy. Nykke complained heretics in the diocese of Norwich were boasting that 'by Michaelmas day there shall be more that shall believe of their opinions than they that believeth the contrary'. He found his efforts against heretical books hampered by brazen claims that 'the King's Grace would that they should have the said erroneous books'. It seemed as if everyone was saying 'the King's pleasure is the New Testament in English should go forth, and men should have it and read it'.[78]

An evangelical manifesto was left in the grounds of the London palace of Bishop Tunstall, shortly before his translation to Durham: it promised 'there will come a day'. Thomas More saw it, and thought it idle boasting. Yet he also knew of unprecedented shows of evangelical strength: at one place in the diocese of London, a hundred persons assembled to attempt to rescue a known heretic from episcopal hands; elsewhere, the bishop's commissary nervously let a suspect priest go, after reports that a mob of two or three hundred was preparing to descend and burn his house. Around the same time, the Duke of Norfolk received word from Edmund Knyvet, absentee lord of the manor of Mendlesham in Suffolk, that groups of up to a hundred people had been convening there 'for a ghostly purpose'. In subversive parody of forms of local governance, they elected their own mayor, sheriff, lord and bailiff.[79]

The Christian brethren of Mendlesham were probably re-energized Lollards. A new Lollard-evangelical militancy expressed itself in 1531–2 in a wave of iconoclastic attacks along the Stour Valley and the Essex–Suffolk border. Foxe reported 'many images cast down and destroyed in many places': a roadside crucifix near Coggeshall, an image of St Christopher at Sudbury, a cross and two other images at Stoke, an image of St Petronella in the church of Great Horkesley, and another in a chapel outside Ipswich. St Petronella was a focus of local East Anglian devotion, her skull preserved as a healing relic at Bury St Edmunds. The fact she was reputedly a daughter of St Peter, first pope, perhaps increased Lollard animus against her.

The most audacious attack was directed in 1532 against the Rood of Dovercourt, a reputedly miraculous crucifix which made the eponymous village, just outside the Essex port of Harwich, a centre of regional pilgrimage. Four men travelled ten miles from Dedham by moonlight, carried the rood from the building and burned it. The Dedham iconoclasts were stirred up by the preaching of Thomas Rose, curate of nearby Hadleigh. The rood-burners gave him the coat of the 'idol', and Rose burned that too. Rose was an associate of Bilney: it seems likely the Dovercourt outrage, and perhaps other attacks too, were reprisals for Bilney's burning.[80]

Militancy was not confined to areas with a Lollard tradition. In October 1531, an Exeter schoolmaster, Thomas Benet, posted bills on the doors of the cathedral denouncing veneration of saints, and the Pope as Antichrist. Here too there was a Bilney connection: Benet was intimate with him while a fellow of Corpus Christi College, Cambridge. Sometime in 1523–4, finding himself 'very much cumbered with the concupiscence of the flesh', Benet travelled to Wittenberg, in search of Luther's counsel. The advice was predictable: choose marriage rather than ordination to sinful celibacy. Benet acquired a wife and an obscure posting in Devon, till conscience impelled him to speak out. For some, the liberation of the Gospel was a sexual liberation. In July 1532, Thomas Cranmer, on diplomatic mission in Germany, quietly married a niece of the Nuremberg Lutheran theologian, Andreas Osiander.

Benet was burned at the stake in January 1532, despite efforts by the Exeter clergy to get him to recant. Leading those efforts was a Franciscan friar, Gregory

Basset. Only a few years earlier, Basset was imprisoned for reading Luther, but he recanted and became (in Foxe's words) 'a mortal enemy to the truth all his life'.[81] Curious seekers might decide that the traditional Church had the right answers after all.

More's son-in-law, William Roper, came to that conclusion sometime before the end of the 1520s, putting his flirtations with heresy behind him. Shortly before the divorce burst onto the public stage, he commented to Sir Thomas on the happy state of the realm – a noble Catholic prince, virtuous and learned clergy, orthodoxy prevailing. More's reply was darkly prophetic:

> And yet, son Roper, I pray God, that some of us, as high as we seem to sit upon the mountains, treading heretics under our feet like ants, live not in the day that we gladly would wish to be at league and composition with them, to let them have their churches quietly to themselves, so that they would be content to let us have ours quietly to ourselves.[82]

### Submission

On 15 January 1532, the day Thomas Benet burned in Exeter, Parliament reconvened in London. The divorce remained log-jammed. Henry did not lack for advice, but much of it was contradictory. The Boleyns and their allies – Cranmer, Edward Foxe and Cromwell – wanted decisive action to settle the divorce in England, in defiance of the Pope. The Queen's supporters, represented in government by Lord Chancellor More, were doing all they could to prevent this, hoping against hope that in a time of heresy an orthodox king would return to his senses. Norfolk and other conservatives favoured an attritional policy of bullying the Pope until Henry got what he wanted.

For his part, Henry was as determined as ever to bring matters to a conclusion, and convinced of the scope of his 'imperial' rights over the Church. But something – fear, pragmatism, remembered piety? – held him back from finally and formally repudiating the Holy See.

In the meantime, the Pope was punched in his purse. At the start of the session, the government introduced a bill to abolish annates – payments made to Rome by newly beneficed senior clergy. The tone was anti-papal, with inflated claims about 'great and inestimable sums' conveyed out of the realm, and defiant assertions that religious and sacramental life would continue in the face of any interdict. Nonetheless, the act was conditional, dependent on the King's pleasure. The Pope ('our holy father') was to be compensated for administrative expenses, and no one should doubt that the King and all the English were 'as obedient, devout, Catholic and humble children of God and Holy Church as any people within any realm christened'. Henry disingenuously informed the papal nuncio that the measures 'were not taken by his consent, but were moved by the people, who hated the Pope marvellously', while Norfolk sent messages through the ambassador in Rome that 'nothing hurtful shall be done', so long as the Pope did not pronounce favourably on Catherine's appeal to Rome.[83]

In the end, 'heresy' broke the stalemate. Following More and Stokesley's intensified campaign, the Commons' sense of grievance about clerical high-handedness in heresy proceedings had grown. Norfolk was exaggerating for effect when he warned the Pope that feelings against misuse of spiritual authority were ten times what they had been in any previous Parliament. But many were clearly riled. Edward Hall recalled that as soon as the Commons began to sit, 'they sore complained of the cruelty of the Ordinaries'. Edward Reed probably brought up the case of Bilney, while London MPs were agitated about the fate of the draper Thomas Patmore, condemned to perpetual imprisonment in November 1531, despite performing public penance.[84]

The Commons' grievances were collated in a document known as 'The Supplication Against the Ordinaries', presented to the King by Speaker Audley on 18 March 1532. The Supplication drew on papers and petitions generated in the 1529 session, and Thomas Cromwell played an important role in drafting it. Was it a spontaneous expression of anticlerical frustration, a put-up job by the government, or a clever attempt by Cromwell to 'bounce' Henry into radical action? On balance, the evidence suggests Henry was not directly involved, and that though Cromwell saw an opportunity, and egged MPs on, the document was a genuine reflection of feelings in the lower house.[85]

The Supplication was a litany of miscellaneous charges about excessive fees and corrupt practices in the church courts. But the last and weightiest of the accusations complained that bishops and their officials habitually used 'such subtle interrogatories, concerning the high mysteries of our faith, as are able quickly to trap a simple, unlearned, or yet a well-witted layman without learning'.[86]

The arguments owed much to an elderly common lawyer, Christopher St German, who set out his views on the respective scope of legal systems in a Latin text of 1528: a dialogue between a doctor of canon law and a student of the laws of England. In 1530, *Doctor and Student* was extended and translated, with a further volume of *New Additions* brought out by the royal printer, Thomas Berthelet, in 1531. The running themes were a denial that ecclesiastical law was intrinsically superior to statute or common law, and an insistence the clergy be made subject to the authority of Parliament.

St German was the likely framer of a 1531 draft bill, which called for church reform and regulation across a number of fronts – abuses at pilgrimage shrines, fees for burials and masses, standards of pastoral service. The instrument of the proposed reforms was to be a 'great standing council', with authority delegated to it from Parliament. This council would also take over principal responsibility for investigation of heresy, screening cases and delivering only the truly recalcitrant for trial in the church courts.[87]

Like most common lawyers, St German was a Catholic and no Lutheran. But he was convinced that much of the blame for the spread of heresy fell on the clergy. If priests and monasteries were required by law to pray for souls without charge, 'there would be but few that would say there were no purgatory'. With the bishops unable to put their own house in order, remedies lay with 'the King in his Parliament . . . which hath not only charge on the bodies, but also on the souls of his subjects'.[88]

Henry's initial response to the ultra-royalist Supplication was studiously measured. He was at that moment annoyed with the Commons for reluctance to pass a bill reforming 'Uses' – trust arrangements allowing landowners to evade ancient feudal obligations to the King. Henry piously urged charity on all parties, and said he would hear what the clergy had to say before passing judgement. Ten days later Parliament was adjourned for its Easter recess, leaving several simmering pots about to come to the boil.[89]

On Easter Sunday, 31 March 1532, Henry and his courtiers attended mass at Greenwich, where the royal palace and Observant Priory stood conjoined in an architectural testament to Tudor patronage of reformed monasticism. William Peto, Minister Provincial of the English Observants, preached a sermon, the like of which Henry can scarcely have heard before. Peto took as his text the story of King Ahab, who, cursed with false and flattering councillors, married the heathen princess Jezebel, and allowed her to pervert him into false worship prior to his untimely death in battle. Peto warned Henry that if he followed this Old Testament pattern, 'dogs [would] lick your blood as they did his'. If this were not frank enough, after the sermon Peto told the King he was endangering his crown, for 'both great and little were murmuring at this marriage'. In no circumstances could he marry Anne, for 'it was said ye had meddled with the mother and the sister'.[90]

In riposte, Henry arranged for a royal chaplain, Richard Curwen, to preach at Greenwich the following Sunday, 'contrary to the custom of the convent'. This was too much for the warden, Henry Elstow, who openly contradicted Curwen in the King's presence. Peto, who had been treated with surprising leniency, refused to take action against Elstow, and Henry ordered both men arrested. Remarkably, his next step was to send to Rome for a commission to have members of the traditionally exempt order put on trial.[91]

These were ominous developments: Henry's actions were being publicly condemned by the most admired exemplars of English religious life. 'Murmuring' against the divorce was increasing. Chapuys reported a pro-divorce preacher in the diocese of Salisbury being violently heckled, particularly by women, and having to be rescued by the authorities. Another preacher in London, according to the Venetian ambassador, was told by a woman in his audience that the King's actions 'would be the destruction of the laws of matrimony'. A little before the recess of Parliament, a clergyman was arrested for denouncing the divorce from the pulpit of St Paul's.

Opposition in Parliament was much in evidence during the passage of the annates bill. In the Lords, all the bishops opposed it, along with the Earl of Arundel. Other lords voted in favour, but Henry had to appear in the House himself on three separate occasions. Its initial reading in the Commons was also strongly contested, and in the end involved the unusual procedure of a formal division. The Lords Spiritual also voted *en bloc* against the Citations Act, a measure limiting the ability of bishops to cite laymen to appear outside their own diocese.[92]

The epicentre of opposition remained the Convocation of Canterbury. Its members received with anger and disbelief the indictment of their stewardship contained in the Commons' Supplication. Archbishop Warham was particularly outraged by aspersions cast on his own court of audience. Maligned in the Supplication as corrupt and self-serving, the higher clergy were in fact engaged on an unprecedentedly earnest and intense programme of reform. A remarkable twenty-six new constitutions were formally ratified or proposed in 1532. They included measures to improve the quality of ordinands, provide regular preaching, tighten residence requirements, specify penances for unchaste priests, and punish simony. To show they were not deaf to lay concerns, Convocation advocated limiting fees for court officials, and – on the perennially hot-button issue of benefit of clergy – it was proposed that, in particularly scandalous cases, criminous clerks be imprisoned for a year.

This was a full-blooded revival of the policy Warham announced long ago at the Convocation of 1510, with the blessing of clerical humanists like Melton and Colet. Its watchword was reform by example, and the new statutes began by ordering every bishop, 'the pattern of the flock', to be present in his cathedral on major festivals to celebrate mass.[93] As in the past, internal reform went hand-in-hand with suppression of heresy. Convocation condemned a list of over sixty heretical books, including Frith's 1531 *Disputation of Purgatory*, a subversively clever deconstruction of the traditional doctrine, produced as a riposte to defences of it by Fisher and More. It was over purgatory that Convocation went after Hugh Latimer, now a regular court preacher and a favourite of Anne Boleyn. Like Crome and Bilney, Latimer's response was to appeal to the King. Henry allowed the case to proceed, and, after delays and evasions, Latimer made a token admission that he had erred, upon which he was again 'received into grace at the special request of the King'.[94]

The clericalist vision of reform had never aligned fully with royal priorities; now it seemed in direct conflict with them. The aged primate William Warham, so long overshadowed by Wolsey and younger colleagues like Tunstall and Fisher, sensed his moment to take a stand had come. In February 1532, he took the extraordinary step of formally registering his refusal of consent to all statutes passed in Parliament since 1529, or still to be passed, which threatened the authority of the Pope or the liberties of the Church. Warham's speeches in the Lords during passage of the annates bill were said to have made Henry so angry he swore 'were it not for his age, he would make him repent'. A trumped-up praemunire suit was prepared against the archbishop.[95]

Warham's response was to draft a defiant and brilliant defence, probably intended as a speech in the Lords, declaring the intrinsic unfairness of the case against him. Through it ran a haunting historical analogy: the refusal of his predecessor archbishop, Thomas Becket, to agree to Henry II's Constitutions of Clarendon, which aimed to abolish benefit of clergy. Becket's death at the hands of Henry II's knights was 'the example and comfort of others to speak and to do for the defence of the liberties of God's Church'. Still more bluntly, Warham reflected on the fates of earlier kings who made laws in derogation of the liberties of the Church: Henry II, abandoned by his servants to a shameful death; Edward III, dying in poverty, hated by his subjects; Richard II, starved or murdered in prison; Henry IV, stricken with leprosy – all 'punished by the hand of God'.[96]

Prophesies of disaster for the King were arising from another quarter too. Elizabeth Barton, known as the Maid or Nun of Kent, was a teenage visionary who, like Anne Wentworth a decade earlier, experienced a miraculous cure through the intervention of the Virgin Mary, and subsequently entered a convent. Her reputation for sanctity won loyal followers among the regular clergy and gentry of Kent, and brought her to the attention of the archbishop. But from the later part of 1528, her visions and prophesies began to focus on the divorce, and to hint that Henry would not remain king for six months if he repudiated Queen Catherine. Warham met her several times; Thomas Cranmer thought the nun's influence was critical in stiffening the old archbishop's sinews against the divorce.[97]

In this atmosphere Convocation, reassembled on 12 April, began to consider its response to the Supplication. It was drafted by Stephen Gardiner, newly consecrated bishop of Winchester, and a prominent cheer-leader for the divorce. But Gardiner felt as keenly as any of his episcopal colleagues the scandal of lay encroachment on the Church's domain. The statement conceded no ground to the Church's critics. It dismissed complaints against ecclesiastical jurisdiction out of hand, or regarded them as individual misdemeanours to be dealt with under existing regulations. Rather than apologize for harsh punishment of heretics, the clergy were proud of their diligence in this 'duty and office whereunto we be called'. On the fundamental issue of principle raised by the Supplication – the making of ecclesiastical canons without lay consent or royal permission – the answer was polite but firm. The clergy would listen gratefully to the King's 'mind and opinion', but he must understand that there could be no veto on a power 'grounded upon the Scripture of God and the determination of Holy Church'. The bishops could hardly have made clearer their understanding of how far 'the law of Christ' allowed Henry's supremacy to extend.[98]

In retrospect, it seems a disastrous error of judgement, a red rag to a royal bull. It is probably true that Gardiner's involvement ruled out his chances of succeeding Warham at Canterbury. Yet to concede the Supplication's demands would have meant abandoning the visions of reformation in head and members which had animated the best clerical minds for a generation and more. There was also no reason to suspect the King's hand behind the Commons' Supplication.

But the clergy's blunt assertion that their independent corporate status was prescribed by God came just when Henry's limited patience was stretched to breaking point. Opposition in the Commons to a taxation request for the improvement of coastal defences took the form of arguments that the best and cheapest form of defence was continued friendship with the Emperor. Thomas Temys, MP for Westbury in Wiltshire, had the temerity to suggest the Commons should petition the King 'to take the Queen again into his company'.

When Henry summoned Speaker Audley and a Commons delegation to an audience on 30 April, he expressed surprise and displeasure that members dared to speak openly of matters that 'touched his soul'. He also handed Convocation's statement to Audley, with words calculated to incite further anticlerical indignation: 'We think their answer will smally please you, for it seemeth to us very slender.'[99]

Henry now demanded a more satisfactory answer to the Supplication's first point about legislative competence. The bishops offered a compromise that was no compromise, retaining control over heresy and everything concerning 'the reformation and correction of sin'. In Warham's absence, clergy in Convocation's lower house seized the initiative, producing treatises on the power of ecclesiastical authority to repress heresy, and the exemption of clerics, 'by divine law', from jurisdiction of laymen. They also petitioned the upper clergy to despatch a delegation to the King for defence of their liberties. The bishops had sufficient tact to send royal favourites – Stokesley, Longland, Foxe, Dean Sampson of the Chapel Royal, and Abbots John Islip of Westminster and William Benson of Burton. But the effect of their mission was simply to harden the King's resolve.

On 10 May Convocation was presented with three royal demands: no new canons to be enacted without the King's permission, offensive ones to be annulled after assessment by a committee of clergy and laity, existing good canons to stand by royal assent. This was the moment of truth. Warham moved into crisis-management mode, transplanting Convocation from the chapter house of Westminster Abbey to the more secluded next-door chapel of St Katherine. He despatched a delegation to Rochester, to seek counsel from the

convalescing Bishop Fisher. Its gist can be imagined from a short tract, circulating at this time, which may be Fisher's composition: 'that the bishops have
immediate authority to make such laws as they shall think expedient for the
weal of men's souls'. Convocation was preparing to defend the rights of the
Church; the archbishop of Canterbury was preparing for martyrdom.[100]

Henry's counter-stroke was to unleash the anticlerical Commons. On 11
May, he again summoned Speaker Audley and a delegation of MPs. He did not
quite, like Henry II, say 'who will rid me of these turbulent priests?' But he
bewailed how the clergy seemed to be 'but half our subjects; yea, and scarce our
subjects'. Proof was in the oath bishops made to the Pope on their consecration,
'clean contrary to the oath that they make to us'. Copies of the two oaths were
produced, 'requiring you to invent some order that we be not thus deluded of
our spiritual subjects'. Audley arranged for the texts to be read in Parliament, to
great indignation. The two oaths, one qualifying the terms of the other, were
certainly anomalous, but had long co-existed as practical mechanisms of
co-operation between Church and state. Now, they were diagnosed as symptoms of a malignant growth on the heart of the English body politic.[101]

Cromwell, influenced by St German, was convinced parliamentary statute
was Henry's means to establish supremacy over the Church, and consequently
bring about the divorce. He set about drafting a bill to remove the Church's
legislative autonomy and clarify the status of 'the imperial crown of this realm'.
Chapuys thought, if it were to pass, clergymen would be reduced 'to a lower
condition than the shoemakers, who have the power of assembling and framing
their own statutes'.[102]

Parliamentary opinion was divided. A group of members, dining regularly
at the Queen's Head Tavern, sympathized strongly with the Queen. One of
them, the Warwickshire gentleman Sir George Throckmorton, son of a pious
pilgrim to Jerusalem (see p. 25), became conspicuous as a government critic.
He was a cousin of the fiery Franciscan, William Peto, who asked Throckmorton
to visit him in prison, and urged him to stick to his guns 'as I would have my
soul saved'. There was also a summons to an interview with the King himself,
Cromwell at his side. Perhaps encouraged to speak freely, Throckmorton said
to the King's face that he would be compromised by marriage to the Lady Anne
'for that it is thought ye have meddled with the mother and the sister'. 'Never
with the mother,' Henry responded, with honesty, and surprising meekness.
'Nor never with the sister neither,' Cromwell interjected angrily.

It emerged later that another eminent figure spoke privately with
Throckmorton at this time. While Cromwell's bill to muzzle the clergy was
being debated, Thomas More arranged a meeting in a little room within the
Parliament. The chancellor's words were coded, yet hardly ambiguous: 'I am
very glad to hear the good report that goeth of you, and that ye be so good a
Catholic man as ye be; and if ye do continue in the same way that ye began and

be not afraid to say your conscience, ye shall deserve great reward of God and thanks of the King's grace at length'. This hardly constitutes conclusive evidence that More was masterminding a behind-the-scenes campaign of concerted opposition. But he was willing discreetly to encourage dissent when he found it, in anticipation of the King returning to his senses.[103]

In the first days of May, More's opposition moved from the shadows into the light. Along with the bishops in the Lords, he strenuously opposed a bill proposing to remove from churchmen the power to arrest heresy suspects – the measure proposed by St German a year earlier, and one that, if passed, would represent the reversal of More's policy as chancellor over the preceding two and half years. Chapuys reported that Henry was 'exceedingly angry' with More over this, and with Bishop Gardiner.

There was no new law subordinating clergy to the King-in-Parliament in the spring of 1532. On 14 May, Henry abruptly suspended parliamentary proceedings until November, perhaps because of opposition in the Lords, perhaps because of an outbreak of plague at Westminster.[104] But there was no further compromise with Convocation. The following day, Henry sent Norfolk, Wiltshire and other councillors to enter the hallowed space of Convocation Chamber and require immediate and unreserved submission to the King's articles, and to the novel assertion that Convocation 'always hath been and must be' convened solely by royal command.

There was consternation and confusion. The lower house very likely voted to reject the demands, and in the upper, probably a mere seven bishops were present. Of these, only three – Warham, West and Veysey – subscribed unconditionally. Clerk flatly refused. Standish and Longland – crown loyalists of long standing – added qualifying clauses to the effect that good constitutions should remain unaffected; Stokesley, more bluntly, agreed to sign 'if it were not contrary to divine law, or general councils'. Only four heads of religious houses set their names to the document, on behalf of a suspiciously vague number of 'other abbots and priors'. The Submission was a document of dubious legality, and supplies no evidence that a majority of the clergy ever 'agreed' to the granting away of their rights. But it was enough. For all the talk of Magna Carta, rights, liberties and the law of the Church, the King called the clergy's bluff and exacted a public surrender.

A collapse of episcopal resistance was not inevitable, but nor was it inexplicable. Options were limited once Henry rejected all attempts at negotiation. Statutory declaration of the subordination of canon law to royal law – a still less desirable outcome – remained a real possibility. Maybe, the bishops reasoned to themselves, it was all bluster and posturing, designed to put pressure on the Pope to settle the divorce, and a crisis that would pass. Minds may have turned to the ancient maxim Warham brought to Catherine of Aragon's attention the previous year: *ira principis mors est* ('the anger of a prince is death').[105]

For the Christian, there are worse things than death. Warham was much preoccupied with the martyrdom of Becket. As the belligerent noblemen laid out Henry's demands perhaps the archbishop saw the glowering faces of Henry II's knights. If so, he looked them in the eye, and then he looked away.

The following afternoon, 16 May 1532, two old friends met in the garden of Wolsey's former palace of York Place. Thomas More placed into the King's hands a white leather pouch containing the great seal of England, tendering his resignation as chancellor on the grounds that he did not consider himself equal to the task. He intended, he said, 'to bestow the residue of my life, in mine age now to come, about the provision for my soul in the service of God, and to be your grace's beadsman and pray for you'.[106] Henry promised to be ever after a 'good and gracious lord'.[106] On both sides, the sentiments were – perhaps – genuine. But it was clear that More had fought – for the traditional relationship of crown and Church; for prioritizing heresy prosecution over the divorce – and lost badly. The same day, the Submission of the Clergy was formally subscribed before special royal commissioners, among them Thomas Cromwell. Four days later, Cromwell's ally, the Commons' Speaker, Thomas Audley, became Keeper of the Great Seal, and a few months later Lord Chancellor.

## Matters of Opinion

Change of personnel was change of direction. Erasmus, in failing health, but as active a correspondent as ever, heard More had been dismissed, and that evangelicals were jubilant. His successor immediately released many 'Lutherans' from prison – forty in number, Erasmus told one correspondent; twenty, he more cautiously informed another.[107]

A second change of personnel provided further cause for evangelical rejoicing. On 22 August 1532, death came for the archbishop. Warham passed away at his archdeacon's residence at Hackington in Kent. He was buried in the chantry chapel he prepared for himself in the north transept of Canterbury Cathedral, as near as could be to the spot where Becket had fallen.[108] Had he stuck to his guns, refused to submit and suffered the fate of his illustrious predecessor, things might just have been different. As it was, Warham's tragedy was to be remembered to posterity as a competent administrator, but not a glorious martyr.

With Gardiner in temporary disgrace, and most remaining bishops known to be at best lukewarm about the divorce, the King's prerogatives, or both, the net was cast wide. Perhaps even before Warham's demise, word reached a flabbergasted Thomas Cranmer, on embassy in Germany, that the King wanted him to be next successor to St Augustine of Canterbury. An immediate thought must have struck him: what on earth was he going to do with his wife?

The nomination was a surprise, but not a mystery. Cranmer was the Boleyns' man, and in the summer of 1532, Anne could feel her day dawning. On 1 September, Henry created her Marquess of Pembroke, a noblewoman in her own right. She was at the King's side, consort in all but name, at a state reception for Francis I at Calais in October, and danced with the French King at a masked ball. On this trip, or very shortly afterwards, Henry and Anne began sleeping together, hope or fear of papal judgement no longer a bar to dreams of conjugal happiness.

Within a week of the couple's return from France, a pamphlet was rushed out – almost certainly with official connivance – describing *The Manner of the Triumph at Calais and Boulogne*. 'My Lady Marques of Pembroke' was conspicuously listed first among the ladies dancing at the royal masque. The second to step out was her sister, Mary Carey, but description of this person simply as 'my Lady Mary' looks suspiciously like an attempt to imply Princess Mary was present, and that she consented to the precedence allotted to Anne.[109]

Modern scholarship worries whether, in the early Tudor period, we can speak of a 'public', 'public opinion' or a 'public sphere'. Yet even in a profoundly hierarchical and undemocratic age, the authorities cared deeply about what people below the level of the elite were thinking. With limited means of coercion at the government's disposal, it was vital, not merely to command, but to persuade. All political authority rests, to some degree, on consent. In periods of conflict and division, consent must be more explicitly secured. There had been 'propaganda' campaigns before: by various sides, for example, during the Wars of the Roses. The printing industry was then in its infancy, but a generation later had achieved a level of mature sophistication. The convergence of this technological flowering with the appearance of two issues – the royal divorce and the challenge to traditional orthodoxy – on which literate people at least were expected to have an opinion was a truly momentous one.

The government's 1531 experiment with vernacular translation of *The Determinations of the Universities* was followed in the autumn of 1532 by the publication, undertaken by the royal printer, of *A Glass of the Truth*. Addressed to all 'sincere lovers of the truth', it took the form of a dialogue between a canon lawyer and a divine on 'the great weighty cause of Christendom concerning the King's separation from the Queen'.

Earlier coyness about discussing matrimonial law other than in the abstract was now abandoned. Having surveyed the respective claims of Leviticus and Deuteronomy, the tract showed an extraordinary willingness to float in public intimate details of the Queen's first marriage. Some 'noblest men of this realm' knew Arthur and Catherine to have been 'fit, apt and prone to that natural act', and had sworn to hearing Arthur's lewd joke about being 'often in Spain'. A delay in granting Henry his title of Prince and heir was lest Arthur's widow might be pregnant, and inconsistencies between the bull of dispensation and the Spanish Brief suggested that Catherine had shifted her position on the fact of consummation. The *Glass* as good as called the Queen a brazen liar, saying whatever 'maketh most for her purpose'. Lawyer and doctor galloped through the doctrinal and historical findings of the *Collectanea*, and hinted that a resolution of the divorce by the archbishops in England was close, 'their unjust oath made to the Pope notwithstanding'.

Did the King himself have a hand in this anonymous treatise? Informed contemporaries believed he did, and matters of such delicacy could scarcely have been aired without Henry's explicit assent. Significantly, the tract finished on a note of entreaty rather than command, recognizing that many would condemn its arguments. Therefore, 'we most heartily pray you, gentle readers, that neither sinister affection, nor yet malicious report, do hinder the accepting of this our treatise in your hearts and judgements'. Henry was willing to place his cause squarely before the court of fair-minded public opinion. And he expected it to agree that he was right.[110]

The divorce was not the only question on which an English 'public' was being invited to form opinions. Evangelical attacks on traditional doctrine were countered with argument as well as coercion, and – since Tunstall's 1528 commission to Thomas More – in the vernacular as well as Latin. More managed – remarkably – to publish the first part of his gigantic *Confutation of Tyndale's Answer* at the start of 1532 while still serving as chancellor. But resignation freed him to devote time and energy to the literary defence of the Church.

At the end of 1532, or beginning of 1533, there appeared several editions of *A Treatise Concerning the Division between the Spiritualty and the Temporalty*. The work was anonymous, and purported to be a neutral analysis of reasons for discord between clergy and laity, with suggestions on how to repair relations. In fact, as More well knew (though he pretended not to) the author was Christopher St German, and the treatise continued his anticlerical campaign to bring the clergy firmly under control of the civil power. More rapidly composed an *Apology* – a word that in the sixteenth century meant assertion rather than retraction – combining sarcastic rebuttals of the suggestions of this 'pacifier' with renewed attacks on the evangelicals.

'It is a shorter thing, and sooner done, to write heresies than to answer them.'[111] The inequality of power between the evangelical rebels and the ecclesiastical establishment was redressed in the world of words and argument. It was easier to launch pithily destructive attacks on traditional beliefs and practices than to develop reasoned defences of rituals whose origins were frequently uncertain, and whose underlying rationales were often unspoken, social and customary. More did his frequently brilliant best. But in the preface to the *Confutation*, he confessed to reservations about the effort: 'surely the very best way were neither to read this nor theirs'.

There was a risk – of which More was acutely aware – that rebuttal would simply publicize further the heretics' views. He delayed circulating his response to Frith's unpublished treatise against the sacrament, for 'I would wish that the common people should of such heresies never hear so much as the name'. Yet hear them they did – in condemnations from the pulpit, in lists of (enticingly?) forbidden works, and indeed in More's own books. The contemporary habit of quoting at length from opponents in order to refute them meant a virtually complete text of Tyndale's *Answer* was folded into More's *Confutation*. The ex-chancellor recognized readers might choose to 'leave my words out between, and read but Tyndale alone'. But silence in the face of the heretics' onslaught was not really an option: discussion of their ideas, More lamented, 'is now almost in every lewd lad's mouth'.[112] From an early stage, and with no one intending for it to happen, the disputed tenets of both royal divorce and religious doctrine conferred on ordinary English people new opportunities to judge, discern and choose. For those with eyes to see, a subtle shift in the balance of power between rulers and ruled was starting to manifest itself.

At the close of 1532, the evangelical movement was pressed but not crushed. Its strongholds were few, and tenuously occupied, but its appeal to some devout and questing Christians was undiminished, and its fortunes had become entwined in unpredictable ways with the political and personal ambitions of the King. More than ever, an instinctively consensual and conformist culture was being forced to confront the possibility of choice, to weigh the risks of commitment, and calculate the price of division. Barely visibly, the seeds of Thomas More's hellish harvest, where adherents of rival churches might actually be forced to co-exist, were already beginning to germinate.

# 7

## SUPREMACY

### Pulpit Wars

ON THE MORNING of Sunday 16 March 1533, Hugh Latimer mounted the pulpit of St Nicholas' church in Bristol, England's third largest city. He preached again that afternoon at the Blackfriars, and the following week at St Thomas's. His words shocked and disturbed: Our Lady was a sinner; saints were not to be honoured; souls in purgatory had no need of prayers. They led to 'great strife and debate . . . among all manner of sorts of people, from the highest to the lowest'.

A year or two earlier, while Thomas More was chancellor, Latimer's temerity would have landed him in an episcopal cell. But in 1533 he visited as an honoured guest, and preached at the invitation of the mayor. Not all of the Bristol corporation sympathized with Latimer's views, but they knew he was favoured by the King and the Lady Anne. Tipped off by a local priest, Convocation ruled on 26 March that Latimer was in breach of articles he subscribed in 1532. But after the Submission of the previous year, Convocation's moral and coercive authority was dented, and Latimer was only temporarily barred from the pulpit at Easter.

Traditionalists now needed to state, and win, their case in the public arena. A trio of star preachers was summoned to Bristol: Nicholas Wilson, a seasoned inquisitor, and friend of Fisher and More; Edward Powell, long-time court preacher and prominent supporter of Queen Catherine; William Heberden, a gifted and colourful orator. They were joined by the cream of local talent: the head of the Benedictine priory of St James, the city rector John Goodrich, and the prior of the Bristol Dominicans, John Hilsey. This blitz of good Catholic preaching succeeded not in stifling but in enflaming controversy. Bristol split down the middle between Heberden's party and Latimer's. There was a crucial defection. After a personal interview, Prior Hilsey decided he had misjudged

Latimer and his cause. He and fellow conservatives 'laboured but in vain, and brought the people in greater division than they were'.[1]

Outside intervention brought the troubles to a temporary end. Evangelical sympathizers within the corporation, along with Hilsey and three other clergymen, petitioned the Council to take action against Powell and Heberden. Cromwell set up a commission of inquiry, and while it gathered evidence, Heberden was committed to the Tower, there to remain for the next five years.

Bristol's 'pulpit war', reminiscent of events in Germany around the same time, was not precisely replicated in other English towns, but it was a sign of how much had changed, and in how short a time. Ecclesiastical machinery for combating heresy was badly damaged. It did not help Heberden's cause when he announced in the pulpit 'there were twenty or thirty heretics of the inhabitants of this town of Bristol' – blanket accusations against laypeople's good faith always went down badly. And he was reported saying that anyone 'that speaks against the Pope or any point of his acts or ordinances is a heretic'. Powell too was accused of dangerously pro-papal pronouncements regarding the divorce. The most zealous defenders of traditional faith were, almost by definition, supporters of the old ecclesiastical regime, while its fiercest critics identified with the King's cause.

The stirs in Bristol drew the populace as a whole into political and religious debate. Priests and townspeople flocked to sermons, and reported to the commissioners on them in detailed terms. There is little indication that anyone felt the professionals were expostulating on high matters that did not concern them. The tone of preaching, on both sides, was harsh and recriminatory. Impelled, he said, by 'brotherly love', Latimer wrote to Heberden. But his letter was laced with the language of 'you' and 'us', seasoned with bitterness over the persecution of evangelicals, and stirred by an aggressive sense that Heberden's gang were no true Christian priests, but 'ministers of Antichrist'.[2]

In the spring and early summer of 1533, a minority of Bristolians were energized by the thrill of novel and charismatic preaching; others were outraged by a seemingly unprovoked affront to traditional pieties. The coming of reformation polarized the urban community, spurring forces of the old order to assertive resistance. Those forces were quelled, but not decisively defeated, by a brittle alliance of evangelical activists, government ministers, and municipal officials nervous of appearing to condone disloyalty. It was a local dress rehearsal for a drama soon to be played across a national stage.

### Security and Succession

On 14 March 1533, two days before Latimer started preaching in Bristol, new legislation was placed in front of the Commons. The bill was long in the making. Cromwell had been working on it since the autumn of 1532, and eight

1 A fifteenth-century carved oak sculpture of the crucified Christ, originating in Sussex and now in a private collection. It probably formed, along with statues of the Virgin Mary and St John, part of the rood grouping in a parish church. Placed above the screen that divided the chancel from the nave (the lay people's part of the church), roods drew the eye of worshippers and placed before them a powerful image of the sufferings of Jesus that had made their salvation possible.

2 The parish church of St James, in the Lincolnshire market town of Louth. The magnificent spire, placed on top of a pre-existing tower in 1501–15, was the result of energetic fundraising by parishioners and guilds, and a potent symbol of local pride and identity. In 1536, twenty-one years after a parish celebration to mark the completion of the spire, townspeople took up arms to protect their community and its traditions against the policies of Henry VIII and Cromwell.

3  A woodcut illustration of a priest elevating the host, from a French guide to the art of good living and good dying, translated into English in 1503. The elevation followed the priest at the altar's repetition of Christ's words, 'Hoc est enim corpus meum' (For this is my body), and signified that the miracle of transubstantiation had truly taken place. Onlookers worshipped their God as if he were made present among them, but later Protestants considered the action to be appalling 'idolatry'.

4  An early printing press in operation, from a French woodcut print *c.* 1520. The technology of printing with moveable type was introduced in England in the 1470s by the enterprising merchant William Caxton. Much of the output of the English presses in the ensuing decades was of Catholic devotional works of a traditional kind, but the growing availability of print was something that might have encouraged the active spiritual life of literate lay people to develop in unorthodox directions.

5 Henry VII in Star Chamber receives archbishop of Canterbury William Warham, bishop of Winchester Richard Fox, and abbot of Westminster John Islip, in a detail from an indenture linked to the King's foundation of a chantry and almshouses at Westminster. The image graphically expresses the subservient position of pre-Reformation bishops appointed by the crown, although, in fact, Warham would in time prove himself a doughty defender of the 'liberties' of the English Church.

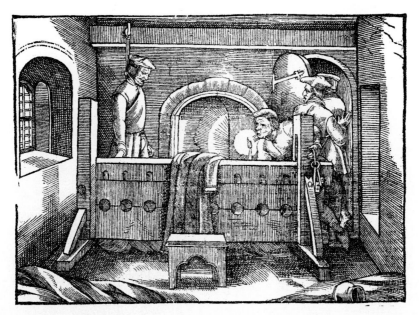

6  An imaginative depiction, from John Foxe's 1563 *Acts and Monuments*, of the death – in the bishop of London's custody in 1514 – of the London merchant Richard Hunne. Episcopal officers, including the disreputable summoner Charles Joseph, exit the cell, having rigged the death to look like a suicide. The facts of the matter remain to this day in contention, but it was widely believed in London that Hunne was accused of heresy for taking legal action against a priest, and was then done to death by culprits who could claim 'benefit of clergy'.

7  The Cambridge scholar Thomas Bilney preaching in Ipswich in 1527 and incurring the wrath of local friars, from Foxe's *Acts and Monuments*. Bilney's vehement attacks on pilgrimage and on veneration of images of saints had affinities with the teachings of the Lollards, some of whom attended his sermons. But early evangelical converts like Bilney attracted a substantial audience, in part because of their status as apparently reputable members of the Catholic establishment.

8 The fate of the London Carthusians, from a series of paintings made in the early seventeenth century by the
Italian artist Vicente Carducho for the monastery of El Paular, near Madrid. Six Carthusian monks, including
John Houghton, prior of the London Charterhouse, were executed in the early summer of 1535 for refusing
the Oath of Supremacy. The ten depicted here starved slowly to death in Newgate. The Carthusians were the
acknowledged elite of English monasticism; Henry VIII's treatment of them shocked opinion across Europe.

et singlorum Comiorum Maneriorum terrarum et tenentorum
ac Aliarum possessionum et Reddituum ac proficuorum quorumcumque
tam spualium quam temporalium omnibz et singlis monasterijs
Abbatijs Prioratibz Collegijs Hospitalibz Rectorijs vicarijs
Cantuarijs Liberis Capellis et alijs promocionibz spualibus
quibuscumque situat in et per totum Comitatum Derb spectan
et pertinen prout inferius continetur videlt

9 The title page for Derbyshire from the document known as the *Valor Ecclesiasticus*, a comprehensive survey of the income of the English Church, undertaken in 1535. The depiction of Henry in the illuminated capital letter here, surrounded by his lay councillors, is intended to underscore the King's new-found authority as Supreme Head of the Church whose wealth is being scrutinized.

10 Pontefract Castle, West Yorkshire, an eighteenth-century drawing by Thomas Pennant. The royal castle found itself at the centre of the Pilgrimage of Grace in 1536, when its custodian Thomas, Lord Darcy, surrendered the place to rebel forces and immediately assumed a key role in the leadership of the movement. The Pontefract Articles, drawn up here in December 1536, were a comprehensive indictment of Henry's policies since breaking with the Pope, whom the rebels wished to see restored as Head of the Church, 'touching *cure animarum*' (the care of souls).

11 The frontispiece to the 1539 Great Bible, printed by Richard Grafton, is a visual representation of how Henry VIII wished his Reformation to be seen: an icon of order, hierarchy and obedience. The King, seated in majesty under the protecting arms of Christ, graciously distributes the Word of God to leading lay and clerical councillors, and it is then handed down to respectable subjects by bishops and magistrates. In the lower pane, scripture is preached to common folk, who respond with grateful cries of 'Vivat Rex!' (Long live the King). Positioned opposite each other, a pulpit and a gaol represent the conjoining of powerful temporal and spiritual authority in the King's hands.

complete and four fragmentary drafts testify to its importance. It aimed to provide a secure legal basis for the final settlement of the Great Matter, prohibiting all appeals to Rome, and articulating a theory of unrestricted monarchical power.

While Cromwell was working on the theory, Henry attended to the practicalities. Before the end of 1532, Anne Boleyn was pregnant. The couple may have privately exchanged vows in November 1532, and they participated in a more formal, though still secret, marriage ceremony before a priest in January 1533.[3] Henry could finally see clearly to the exit from his marriage, and self-control was no longer a political and diplomatic imperative.

The title of the 'Act in Restraint of Appeals' underplayed its revolutionary character. It opened by declaring 'this realm of England is an empire', an entity 'governed by one supreme head and king ... unto whom a body politic, compact of all sorts and degrees of people, divided in terms, and by names of spiritualty and temporalty, be bounded'. Over all of these the King possessed 'plenary, whole and entire power'. England's Church was entirely independent of the Pope, and entirely dependent on the King.

Revolutions characteristically cloak themselves in the mantle of tradition. Innovation was couched in the language of restoration, a return to the natural order of things. Royal authority was God-given, and attested to by 'divers sundry old authentic histories and chronicles' – a summary in miniature of the arguments of the *Collectanea*.[4]

Yet ambiguities remained. If Henry's supremacy was innate and divinely ordained, why did it require an act of Parliament? The King's own view was that Parliament merely expressed the nation's assent. But Cromwell may have thought differently. The legal theorist Christopher St German, an inspiration for the parliamentary assault against the clergy in 1531–2, certainly believed that royal supremacy rested in the King-in-Parliament.[5] Like much else, how it all would work in practice remained to be seen.

The Appeals Act passed both houses of Parliament in the first week of April, though not without difficulty, even after aggressively anti-papal language found in earlier drafts had been pruned. Opposition in the Commons is sometimes said to have been motivated solely by fears of an economic embargo from Catholic states.[6] But it is likely that behind such arguments lay more fundamental concerns. Cromwell, ever watchful and alert, drew up a list of thirty-five MPs whose trustworthiness he suspected. The first name was that of George Throckmorton, the recalcitrant Warwickshire gentleman with whom the King had already exchanged private words, and who (though the government did not know it) was being egged on by Thomas More.[7]

Even while the Appeals Act seemed to write its epitaph, papal authority was invoked one last time. The required bulls for Thomas Cranmer's appointment were sought from Rome, and on 30 March he was consecrated archbishop of

Canterbury in the chapel of the Palace of Westminster. Like his predecessors, Cranmer swore an oath of loyalty to the Pope. He then swore a second oath: loyalty to the King would override anything promised in the first. He also swore to 'prosecute and reform matters wheresoever they seem to me to be for the reform of the English Church'.[8] This was a formula Warham could cheerfully have endorsed, though Cranmer meant something very different. The moral equivocations of Cranmer's appointment were an inauspicious start to a momentous career, yet such contortions of the conscience were soon to embroil the nation as a whole.

First business for the new archbishop was to end the drama of the divorce. By 2 April both houses of Convocation had agreed that marriage to a brother's widow was prohibited by divine law, and Cranmer resumed the farcical business of a trial, formally summoning Henry and Catherine to secluded Dunstable Priory in Bedfordshire. Catherine, of course, did not appear. Cranmer declared sentence against the marriage on 23 May, going through the motions of threatening Henry with excommunication if he did not comply. On 28 May, he formally pronounced the validity of Henry's marriage to Anne.[9]

It was just as well. The festivities for Queen Anne's coronation began in London the following day, climaxing in Westminster Abbey on 1 June. The pomp and pageantry were an occasion for demonstrating loyalty to the new regime; it is no accident George Throckmorton was summoned to attend as a servitor. Thomas More too was expected, and Bishops Tunstall, Gardiner and Clerk sent him £20 for a new gown. More bought the gown, but stayed provocatively at home. A more dramatic gesture was that of London town clerk William Pavier, a zealous opponent of heresy who oversaw the burning of James Bainham. In May 1533, in despair at the direction of events, Pavier hanged himself in his chamber.[10]

If the new queen knew, it is unlikely she cared. Resplendent in white and cloth of gold, Anne's moment of triumph was at hand, a vindication of the motto she adopted a few years earlier: *ainsi sera, groigne qui groigne* ('it's going to happen, grumble who will'). Crowds filled the streets for the coronation, but without demonstrations of enthusiasm or joy. Some Londoners, women in particular, did not consider Anne their rightful queen. Mrs Amadas, widow of the keeper of the royal jewels, was full of wild prophesies that, after a battle of priests, the Queen would be burned, and the King driven from his throne. Later that summer, two London women – one of them pregnant – were stripped and beaten, their ears nailed to a pillar in Cheapside, for saying 'Queen Catherine was the true queen of England'.[11]

Rumour and prophecies flourished like weeds in the summer of 1533. The most potent source – an influence on Amadas, and others too – was the young visionary nun, Elizabeth Barton.[12] She had, she said, accompanied Henry and Anne Boleyn in spirit on their visit to meet Francis I in Calais in October 1532.

As the royal party attended mass in the church of Our Lady, Henry could not see the elevated host, for Barton witnessed an angel remove it from the priest's hands, and carry it directly to her. Whatever the Pope might think, God had already excommunicated the English king.

This was heady, dangerous stuff, worse because circulating widely. The authorities later claimed that Edward Bocking and John Dering, monks of Christ Church, Canterbury, 'caused to be written sundry books, both great and small, both printed and written' containing details of Barton's revelations. Thomas More, more circumspect in dealings with the Maid than either Warham or Fisher, agreed to meet her in 1533, and afterwards wrote to warn her against discussing 'any such manner things as pertain to princes' affairs'. Around midsummer, Cranmer, perturbed by the support Barton enjoyed from 'great men of the realm' as well as 'mean men', interrogated her and sent her to Cromwell. Under intense pressure, she confessed her visions and revelations to be frauds. This was announced in a sermon preached by John Salcot at Paul's Cross in November 1533, and repeated at Canterbury in December. By then, the Nun and a half-dozen of her clerical supporters were in the Tower, and several leading figures who credited her prophesies – most prominently the Marchioness of Exeter – had written to the King begging forgiveness.

The authorities went to great lengths to discredit Barton – parading her in public, circulating details of her faked miracles and supposed sexual misbehaviour with monks. The campaign reflects anxiety about the strength of opposition, and about perceptions that Henry's actions were looked on with divine disfavour. A golden opportunity to scotch such suspicions came, and went, in September 1533. The son, whose birth would have settled the succession and vindicated the King's cause, turned out to be a daughter. Nonetheless, the King made a show of rejoicing, and pointedly arranged Princess Elizabeth's baptism for the chapel of the Observant Franciscans at Greenwich, a community becoming identified as a focus of resistance to the divorce. One of the friars later snarled that the princess was christened in hot water, 'but it was not hot enough'.[13]

As 1533 drew to a close, the Council determined on a wide-ranging plan of action to silence doubters and dissenters. Bishops were to be summoned, and challenged on whether they could prove the authority of the Pope to be greater than that of a General Council. It was assumed that they couldn't – or wouldn't – for they were to make sure all clergy preached that 'the Pope has no more jurisdiction here than any other foreign bishop'. The four orders of friars, and particularly the Observants, were to preach the same message, and nobles and London aldermen were ordered to teach it to their servants. Printed copies of the Act of Appeals were posted on every church door, along with the King's appeal against the Pope to a General Council. Meanwhile, the threat of international isolation was to be addressed by sending transcripts of Henry's appeal into other realms, 'especially Flanders', and by despatching ambassadors to conclude alliances with the King of Poland, the King of Hungary, the Landgrave of Hesse and a host of towns and principalities in Lutheran Germany. Spies were to head north into Scotland, 'to perceive their practices'.[14]

Alongside these measures, a short pamphlet appeared, comprising nine *Articles devised by the Whole Consent of the King's Most Honourable Council*. Its arguments were not new, but the tone was. The Pope was now merely 'bishop of Rome', and for denying the superiority of a General Council was said to be '*vere hereticus*, that is to say, a heretic'. For the first time, the evangelical propaganda-word 'papist' appeared in an official publication. By comparison, attention to the recent 'fair weather, with great plenty of corn and cattle', as well as 'the pureness of air, without any pestilential or contagious disease' seems banal. But it was important that people recognize how God was content 'both with our prince and his doings'.[15]

Those doings had further to run over the course of 1534. Parliament reassembled on 15 January, and processed an unprecedented plenitude of legislation. A royal proclamation had already deprived Catherine of the title of queen; an act now fixed her status as that of 'princess dowager'. The 1532 Submission of the Clergy was given explicit statutory underpinning; the act in conditional restraint of annates became absolute; and an act abolished the payment to Rome of the annual tribute of 'Peter's Pence', while transferring to the office of the archbishop of Canterbury power to issue all dispensations previously granted by the Pope.

The Dispensations Act struck an intentionally reassuring note: nobody was to suspect any intention on the part of the King or his subjects 'to decline or vary from the congregation of Christ's Church in any things concerning the very articles of the Catholic faith of Christendom'. It rather depended on what one understood by the word 'Catholic'. Once a bland synonym for orthodox, the word was fast becoming a contested trophy of sectional allegiances.

Supporters of the Pope were not true Catholics, but 'papists'. A new Heresy Act closed a potentially embarrassing loophole by declaring no one could in future be charged for condemning 'the pretended power of the bishop of Rome'. Beyond that, the act had nothing to say on which opinions were orthodox and which were not, though it aired the long-standing lay grievance that existing legislation allowed the clergy free rein to 'suspect any person'. No longer could someone be arrested solely on the basis of a bishop's suspicions. Trials must be in open court, and initiated only on basis of formal accusation, with 'two lawful witnesses at the least'. As in 1532, concerns about specific injustices fuelled the debate. The case of Thomas Phillips, imprisoned in the Tower for three years and more, was taken up by the London MP Robert Packington, and though Phillips's petition was rejected by the Lords, his plight shaped the new legislation. Heresy remained a heinous capital crime, but the chances of conviction for it were palpably receding. No suspect had been executed since John Frith and the London apprentice Andrew Huet burned together as sacramentarians at Smithfield the previous summer.[16]

Some reckonings in blood were still required. In February 1534, the government introduced into the Lords a bill of attainder, declaring Elizabeth Barton, along with the Benedictines Bocking and Dering, the Observant Franciscans Hugh Rich and Richard Risby, and the secular priests Richard Master and Henry Gold, guilty of high treason. Several others were guilty of 'misprision of treason', the offence of knowing about, yet failing to report, Barton's crimes, which incurred confiscation of goods and indefinite imprisonment. They included Catherine's chaplain Thomas Abell, as well as Bishop Fisher and Thomas More. The latter was included at Henry's personal insistence, despite Cromwell's misgivings about whether charges could be made to stick. In the event, they could not, and from concern that the measure might fail in the Lords, More's name was deleted from the amended bill passing on 21 March. Fisher was permitted to buy a pardon for £300.[17]

While Barton and her allies awaited their fate, a final, momentous bill made its way onto the statute book. The Succession Act confirmed the validity of the Boleyn marriage, and vested succession to the 'imperial crown' in the Princess Elizabeth, in default of future male heirs. Anyone slandering the marriage in print committed high treason; speaking against it was misprision of treason. Its most remarkable provision was a stipulation that all adult subjects swear a 'corporal oath' upholding the terms of the act. Cranmer, Chancellor Audley and the Dukes of Norfolk and Suffolk were appointed commissioners, and on 30 March they administered the oath to Members of Parliament.[18]

This was a novel and ambitious departure. Later medieval England was a society glued together by oaths. Solemn undertakings, invoking God and the saints as witnesses, they were sworn in courts of law, on the taking up of office, on admission to guilds and trades, or, indeed, at the contracting of marriages. Bishops had long sworn oaths of fealty to the crown, as well as to the Pope. But requiring the entire nation to be bound in conscience to a change in royal policy was something new. It was intended to be an overwhelming symbolic demonstration of the consent of the nation as well as a mechanism for identifying opponents, and forcing them into the open.

In a huge, and remarkably successful, logistical operation, commissioners administered the oath to clergy and laymen across England in the spring and early summer of 1534. It does appear to have been lay *men* who were sworn. Gardiner wrote to Cromwell in early May asking him to check with the King that they had done right in interpreting the word 'man' to apply 'only for men and not women'.[19] Not for the last time in the sixteenth century, the restricted legal and social standing of women afforded some extra space for the exercise of the conscience.

It was not, of course, only about the succession. The oath offered to laymen in 1534 avoided naming the Pope, or making precise assertions about the scope of royal supremacy – perhaps to make it more palatable to waverers. But there could be little uncertainty about the identity of the 'foreign authority or potentate' swearers were required to renounce. In any case, recognition of the Boleyn marriage involved an at least implicit rejection of Clement VII, whose definitive statement of the validity of Henry's first marriage was finally issued a week before the Succession Act passed.

If slivers of constructive obfuscation were granted to the laity, they were from the outset denied to priests: all parish clergy had to subscribe to a statement, confirmed by Convocation at the end of March, that 'the Roman bishop has no greater jurisdiction conferred to him by God in this kingdom of England than any other foreign bishop'. An oath repudiating the Pope, and affirming the royal supremacy, was demanded from newly consecrated bishops, and in all probability from existing ones as well. The friars were targeted for a similarly explicit affirmation, and by the early summer it was being required from all members of religious houses, cathedral chapters and university colleges: a clerical referendum on Henry's supreme headship in which only one possible answer was on the ballot.[20]

Henry, of course, got the result he wanted, but not without difficulty. An early stumbling block, inevitably, was the conscience of Sir Thomas More. When an oath was presented to him at Lambeth on 13 April, More declined, perhaps because the version tendered to him included assent to 'all other acts and statutes made in the present Parliament'. But it is unlikely Henry could have accepted any version of the oath More would have been prepared to swear. Sir Thomas was willing to recognize the Boleyn succession, but the validity of the Boleyn marriage was another matter entirely. Yet, ever the careful lawyer, More simply refused to say why he would not swear, despite the insistent probing of Cromwell, Cranmer and other commissioners. Such refusal was at worst misprision of treason, punishable by imprisonment but not death: on 17 April More was despatched to the Tower.[21]

Three days later, citizens of London were summoned to take the Succession Oath, and none openly demurred. Little wonder, perhaps, for on the same day Elizabeth Barton and her associates were dragged on hurdles from the Tower to Tyburn, hanged, and then beheaded. Barton's severed head was placed on London Bridge; those of the priests on the various gates of the city. It was a timely demonstration of the consequences of defying the royal will.

A handful were yet prepared to do it. No one was surprised when John Fisher refused the oath, and joined More in the Tower. But he was alone among the bishops, just as his friend Nicholas Wilson was alone among City of London clergy (and Wilson later relented). Both the Bridgettines of Syon and the London Carthusians were hesitant, yet reluctantly took the Oath of Succession, though two brethren from Mountgrace Charterhouse in Yorkshire initially refused. Greater resistance emanated from the more politically aware Observant Franciscans, whose interpretation of the mendicant life was long underpinned by papal patronage and support. In June, the governor of Calais learned that 'two carts full of friars' had been taken to the Tower. In early August, Chapuys reported that five of the seven Observant houses had been emptied for refusal to swear, and the others expected expulsion soon.[22]

Among clergy and laity nationally, there were scattered signs of resistance. The vicar of Ashlower in Gloucestershire at first declined to read the mandate summoning villagers to assemble and take the oath, saying he would rather be burned, and a couple of priests in Catherine of Aragon's orbit, Richard Barker and Richard Featherstone, flatly refused to swear. Thomas More was not quite the only layman to do likewise. Cromwell received a report in 1535 from the English hospital in Rome that a scrivener, James Holywell, had lately arrived, boasting that 'when every man were sworn to the King's Grace he said he were not nor would not'. Anthony Heron, gentleman of county Durham, may also have refused to swear in 1534, or at least he was by the following year openly maintaining that the Pope, not the King, was supreme head of the Church 'and so he will take him of his conscience during his life'. At Thanet in Kent, Gervase Shelby was arrested in June 1534 for saying 'his conscience grieved him sore to take the oath', as he believed the King 'hath broken the sacrament of matrimony'.[23]

Shelby was not alone in thinking the shabby treatment of Queen Catherine laid bare the nature of the whole exercise: 'a pitiful case to be sworn'. Indeed, the most important laypeople refusing to swear were Catherine herself and her daughter Mary – women who were emphatically not exempted from the requirement to take the oath, but who could hardly be subjected to the severities reserved for other dissidents.

Known refusers can be counted almost on fingers and toes. But the campaign was not the unalloyed triumph the raw numbers might suggest. An oath before God was the most solemn undertaking; perjury, a literally damnable offence. But medieval theologians differed over whether public oaths were by definition consensual and valid, or whether the purposes for which, and conditions under which, they were sworn might negate their binding effects. In May 1534, Chapuys was summoned before the Council to be told, in the course of a long harangue from Edward Foxe, that the King's marriage and succession were endorsed not only by Parliament but 'universally by the frank consent and voluntary oaths of all his subjects, except two women' (Catherine and Mary). Chapuys was able to retort that jurists believed coerced oaths to be illegitimate, and that many who swore 'comforted themselves by the consideration that an oath given by force and against good morals is not binding'. He added the barbed observation that oath-takers might think themselves able to violate it as honourably as the archbishop of Canterbury, 'who, the day after he had sworn fidelity and obedience to the Pope, decreed the citation against the Queen.'[24]

'An oath loosely made may loosely be broken.' That was the advice George Rowland, a Crossed or Crutched Friar of London, gave in confession in early 1536: the penitent turned out to be an evangelical, looking to entrap him. Others spoke less flippantly, but similarly regarded the oath's coercive character as inimical to its binding power. John Forest, one of the Greenwich Observants who did swear in 1534, later explained he 'denied the bishop of Rome by an oath given by his outward man, but not in the inward man'. Others used techniques of casuistry, or 'mental reservation', adding qualifications, openly or secretly, that altered the meaning of the oath. In swearing to the King's supremacy, Hugh Cooke, abbot of Reading, was supposed to have added silently, 'of the temporal Church, but not of the spiritual'.[25]

Convocation's 1531 acceptance of the royal headship 'as far as the law of Christ allows' was a helpful precedent. Prior John Houghton and the London Carthusians similarly took the Succession Oath in May 1534 'as far as it was lawful' – an equivocation they would not be allowed to repeat. The master and fellows of Balliol College, Oxford, added a proviso to their subscription in August 1534: they did not 'intend anything against divine law, nor against the rule of orthodox faith, nor against the doctrine of our mother, the holy Catholic Church'. Just how many clergy or laity took the oath in this spirit is impossible to say. John Hilsey, Latimer's erstwhile opponent, now provincial of the Dominicans and a confirmed evangelical, wrote to Cromwell in June 1534 that he had not encountered any downright refusals among the religious. But some swore 'slenderly', and with an ill will.[26]

In 1534, the government used compulsion to elicit an ostensibly free declaration of assent. It produced a legacy of evasion and suspicion with unintended but ultimately profound consequences. For into the body politic was released a germ of the notion that outward obedience and inner assent need not go together; that there were spaces for free exercise of the conscience where the tentacles of the state could not reach.

Oaths were not necessarily instruments of obedience. In June 1534, as commissioners went about their work, a serious rebellion broke out in Ireland, led by Henry's own vice-deputy, the charismatic 'Silken Thomas' Fitzgerald, Earl of Offaly, son of the Earl of Kildare. Offaly's motives were mixed, and owed much to the aristocratic jockeying for position characterizing the politics of late medieval Ireland. But Henry's breach with the papacy introduced a hitherto-lacking ideological dimension to the island's traditional unruliness. Medieval rebels usually stressed loyalty to the crown, and an intention to rescue it from the wiles of 'wicked councillors'. Offaly abandoned this nicety, repudiating fealty to Henry and placing Ireland under the direct suzerainty of the Pope. In a backhanded tribute to developments across the Irish Sea, he required followers to swear oaths of allegiance to the Pope, the Holy Roman Emperor, and himself.[27]

The story of the Reformation in Ireland is one to be told elsewhere. But by summer 1534 it was clear to Henry and his advisors that assertions of supremacy in England had stirred up a 'British problem'. In the months preceding Offaly's rebellion, Charles V grew optimistic about unrest in Ireland, and despatched an agent to help foment it. One of Offaly's leading supporters was an English-born priest, John Travers, the author of a book in support of papal supremacy.

The Franciscan Observants were international agents of trouble. The French-born Provincial of the order, Francis Faber, left England for Ireland in April 1534, promising Chapuys to 'brew up there all he could for the preserva-tion of the holy see'. As their houses closed in England, a number of Observants fled north into Scotland. English ambassadors were soon vainly pressing King James V for the extradition of 'English Observants who go about preaching there that this king is schismatic'.[28]

Charles V and Chapuys were equally upbeat about the prospects for a rising in Wales, where a power vacuum followed the fall in 1531 of the powerful Rhys ap Gruffydd, suspected of plotting rebellion. Rhys's uncle, James Gruffydd ap Hywel, fled to Scotland via Ireland in 1533, announcing himself as 'the greatest man in Wales' and declaring allegiance to Queen Catherine. James V was rather taken with him, and with his beautiful daughter. Gruffydd was briefly back in Ireland in September 1534, as rebellion continued to rage, having in the mean-time courted support in Flanders and northern Germany. Gruffydd's boast to the Lords of the Scottish Council that he and his friends could raise 10,000 men in Wales was bluster, but the English heard it, and took it very seriously.[29]

The convergence of internal treason and external invasion was Henry VIII's worst nightmare, as it had been for his father in the days of Yorkist pretenders. In conversations taking place in Isleworth, Middlesex, in May 1534, the vicar, John Hale, described his sovereign as 'the most cruellest, capital heretic, defacer, and treader under foot of Christ and of his Church . . . Whose death I beseech God may be like to the death of the most wicked John, sometime King of this realm'. This was pretty bad, but perhaps worse was Hale's prediction that the Welsh 'will join and take part with the Irish, and so invade our realm'. He added that, if they did so, 'they shall have aid and strength enough in England, for this is truth, three parts of England is against the King'.[30]

Whether or not Hale's estimation of the relative allegiances of the nation was correct, the government was in no doubt it had a serious problem, and that the best efforts of pulpit and press over the course of 1534 had failed to win round all the King's subjects. Royal propaganda indeed sometimes had the effect of galvanizing opposition. Reading the *Articles . . . of the King's Most Honourable Council* inspired the Dominican friar Thomas Charnock to compile a compendium of patristic sources in favour of papal primacy.

Meanwhile, a loyalist in Colchester warned Cromwell how the clergy there 'cannot abide to read, hear, nor see, nor yet suffer the King's subjects to read ... certain books of the King's print now of late put forth'. One Dr Thystell preached against them at the Greyfriars, likening such works to the fig tree cursed by Christ. Faced with copies of these texts, the rector of St James's, John Wayne, proved as resolute as any character portrayed by his later Hollywood name-sake: 'hence, hence, away with them: they be naught!' John Frances, sub-prior of Colchester Abbey, previously thought the King and Council merely schis-matics, but reading the *Articles* convinced him they were in fact heretics.[31]

Among both clergy and laity, much discontent focused on the marriage, and the character and deserts of the former and current queens. Frances deri-sively remarked that when Henry journeyed to Boulogne in 1532, Anne Boleyn 'followed his arse as the dog followeth his master's arse'. In July 1533, James Harrison, rector of Leigh in Lancashire, wanted to know 'who the devil made Nan Bullen, that whore, Queen?' The accusation against a Warwickshire priest, Ralph Wendon, that he called Anne Boleyn a whore and harlot, and hoped she would be burned, may have been made maliciously. But the fact his accuser expected it to be believed suggests such sentiments were widely voiced. Margaret Chanseler, of Bradfield St Clare in Suffolk, declared before witnesses in February 1534 that Anne was 'a naughty whore', a 'goggle-eyed whore', and Catherine was rightful queen. On several occasions Margaret Cowpland called Anne a strong harlot, and Henry an extortioner, knave and traitor.[32]

All this was what contemporaries called loose and idle talk – Chanseler excused her outburst by confessing to drunkenness. But this did not make such interventions harmless or politically insignificant. The mystique of the monarchy was to a considerable extent the power of the monarchy, and mocking, ribald talk punctured that mystique. Not only Anne, but Henry himself was the target of hostility, and of fantasies of violence. A Welsh priest, William ap Lli, boasted in July 1533 that if he got Henry alone on Mount Snowdon 'he would souse the King about the ears till he had his head soft enough'. Others hoped the King might break his neck falling from his horse, or believed it would be good 'if he were knocked or patted on the head'. In late 1534, or early 1535, George Taylor, of Newport Pagnell in Buckinghamshire, said he would think nothing of playing football with the King's crown, for Henry was 'a knave and liveth in adultery, and is a heretic'.[33]

Accumulations of such reports, combined with frustration over the dissi-dence of More and Fisher, and the antics of the Nun of Kent, prompted the passing of a new Treason Act in the parliamentary session of November 1534. Previous definitions required some overt action against the monarch's authority; now it became treason merely to express, in words or writing, a desire for harm to the King, Queen or heir. And it was henceforth a treasonable act simply to call the King 'heretic, schismatic, tyrant, infidel or usurper'. The virus of name-calling accompanying the outbreak of religious division in England was under no circumstances to be transmitted to the King himself.

The Treason Act troubled Members of Parliament. Visiting his brother in the Tower in early 1535, Robert Fisher, MP for Rochester, said 'there was never such a sticking at the passing of any Act in the Lower House'. Only a provision that the words must be spoken 'maliciously' helped assuage anxieties about this dramatic extension of the treason law, at a time when fears of being unjustly accused of heresy were starting to recede. Whether Henry could imagine any circumstances in which words insulting to his person were not spoken maliciously was another matter.[34]

The parliamentary session of November 1534 completed the royal takeover initiated in the stand-off with Convocation almost four years before. A second Act of Succession prescribed precise wording to be used in administration of the oath – ending an ambiguity exploited by Thomas More, who protested the oath he was offered went beyond the terms of the act. And a short Act of Supremacy definitively declared royal headship, on earth, of the Church of England, and the King's power to 'visit, repress, redress, reform, order, correct, restrain and amend' any problems or abuses within it. A practical demonstration, small but substantial, was immediately forthcoming: an act identified twenty-six locations in England as places suitable for a suffragan, or assistant, bishop, and invited prelates who wanted such a deputy in their diocese to submit two names for the King to select between.[35]

By the start of 1535, Henry's ecclesiastical authority – an expression of his imperial kingship – was total and complete, but it was not totally or completely accepted. How he would now seek to use it was a question that not only his subjects but the whole of Europe was eager to hear answered. The King's response was to delegate his authority to somebody else.

### Vicegerency, Visitation and Vengeance

In January 1535, the King's secretary Thomas Cromwell was endowed by royal commission with a new office: vicegerent (or vicar-general) in spirituals. Bishops employed vicars-general for the practical business of running their dioceses. In what must have seemed a kind of parody of this arrangement, Henry deputized another layman to exercise his untrammelled rule over the *Ecclesia Anglicana*.[36]

As vicegerent, Cromwell's powers were extensive: all bishops, including the archbishop of Canterbury, were subordinated to his authority. It was an assertion of lay control over the Church to have Warham spinning in his grave. It was not, however, the implementation of any structural master-plan; rather, a mechanism for dealing with practical and immediate problems. Cromwell's vicegerency became permanent in 1536, but his initial appointment was for the specific task of conducting a general visitation– a demonstration of the King's right to 'redress, reform, order, correct' his Church.

Something of this sort was tried in 1534, when Cranmer launched a 'metropolitical' visitation of his province of Canterbury. By precedent, the jurisdiction of diocesan bishops was suspended during such visitations. But the more independent-minded conservatives – Stokesley of London, Longland of Lincoln, Nykke of Norwich, Gardiner of Winchester – created difficulties, arguing that Cranmer's authority was uncertain under the royal supremacy. Embarrassingly, the documentation drawn up for the visitation by his officials accorded Cranmer the traditional papal style, 'Primate of All England and Legate of the Apostolic See'. For his part, Cranmer wished 'that I, and all my brethren the bishops, would leave all our styles . . . calling ourselves *apostolos Jesu Christi*'.[37] But the titles and trappings of episcopal office would stay.

Thomas Cromwell, the self-made brewer's son from Putney, and behind-the-curtain mover of so many set changes of the preceding five years, now moved into the limelight. His relationship with Cranmer was not always harmonious, but the two men liked each other, and worked closely together. It is too pat to call one the idealist and the other the pragmatist, yet Cranmer recognized Cromwell to possess skills of political management far exceeding his own. Both men were convinced and conscientious advocates of the King's royal supremacy. But both were also committed to a project-within-a-project, quietly determined to advance evangelical reform within the framework of what was once the Pope's Church in England. Their efforts would – in part – succeed, but at the cost of dividing that Church to its core, and exposing themselves to ever greater vituperation and danger.

Evangelicals were heartened by the turn events had taken by 1535. Some were now prepared to join, rather than attack, the existing religious establishment. In November 1534, with Cromwell's encouragement, Robert Barnes published a second edition of his *Supplication*, toning down his earlier critiques of episcopacy to concentrate on castigating the papacy.[38] After a decade and more of risking imprisonment, or worse, at the hands of bishops, evangelicals found themselves raised to the episcopate. Cranmer's first consecrations, in April 1534, were of two reformers he worked with over the divorce: Thomas Goodrich (Ely) and John Salcot (Bangor). The simultaneous appointment to Coventry and Lichfield of Rowland Lee, a friend of Cromwell and the cleric who reputedly married Henry and Anne, was less obviously an evangelical triumph – Cromwell's other client Stephen Vaughan thought Lee 'a papist, and idolater and a fleshy priest'. But Chapuys had no doubt Salcot was promoted 'in order to support the Lady's party'.[39]

Anne Boleyn was the link between the reformers and the good humour of the King. Contemporaries attributed key promotions to her influence: in addition to Cranmer and Goodrich, the appointment of her almoner, Nicholas

Shaxton, to Salisbury in February 1535, and of Hugh Latimer to Worcester later that year. Most likely she was instrumental in the nomination of William Barlow (reformer-turned-orthodox polemicist-turned-reformer again) to St David's in April 1535, complementing the Queen's powerbase in south-west Wales as Marquess of Pembroke. The election of John Hilsey to Rochester in August 1535, and of Edward Foxe to Hereford in August 1536 rounded off a wave of evangelical promotions.[40]

For the non-evangelical bishops, the old pathways between due deference to the crown and vigorous defence of ecclesiastical independence were now well and truly blocked off. Dilemmas of conscience were resolved for a remarkable number of conservative-minded bishops dying of natural causes in 1533–6: Nicholas West of Ely, Thomas Skevington of Bangor, Charles Booth of Hereford, Henry Standish of St Asaph, Richard Nykke of Norwich, Richard Rawlins of St David's, Robert Sherburne of Chichester. Others had to live longer with the consequences of their decisions. John Fisher's choice took him, uniquely, to the Tower; an alternative route was followed by Stephen Gardiner, who spent part of the summer of 1535 composing a fulsome defence of the royal supremacy, *De Vera Obedientia* (Of True Obedience). Chapuys was surprised and disappointed: naively, he believed Gardiner to be 'hitherto a valiant champion of apostolic authority'. Copies were soon being sent abroad to help persuade European courts of the justice of the King's cause.[41]

By the spring of 1534, Cuthbert Tunstall of Durham had reversed his former opinions and turned apologist for the King's supremacy. This was the safe and sensible course. Royal agents searched his palaces at Durham, Stockton and Bishop Auckland, on the lookout for incriminating evidence. At Auckland, in the room of Tunstall's secretary Robert Ridley, they found a copy of another Latin tract supporting the supremacy, Edward Foxe's *De Vera Differentia* – filled with critical annotations. Ridley was arrested, and likely died in prison; Tunstall decided against sharing his fate.[42]

The born-again loyalism of the conservative bishops was not down entirely to weakening of the spine. There was still reason to hope that Henry was what he professed himself to be, a dutiful Catholic king. The supremacy was to be an instrument of 'reform', but the term meant different things to different people: leading churchmen still thought of it as involving a strengthening of the clergy's guardianship over a pious and orthodox laity. Gardiner's *Obedientia* was not simply a defence of the Supremacy, but an interpretation of it: he elided the titles supreme head and *Fidei Defensor* to argue for the King's duty to protect the Church and its faith, and he defined Christian obedience as a good work, assisted by grace, but inimical to justification by faith.[43]

From the outset, the bishops were expected to be frontline agents of the break with Rome. Cromwell wrote on 3 June 1535 requiring them to preach personally in support of the King's new title, and to order all clergy to do the same. They were also to ensure the name 'papa' was physically erased from service books. Henry is often supposed to have left the Latin mass alone, but liturgical reform was in fact a hallmark of his headship. Already in the previous year Cranmer ordered that the 'collect' (special introductory prayer) for the King was to be used every day at mass, along with a new form of bidding prayers specifically referencing the royal supremacy. The Pope was to be unpicked from the prayer life of the nation, and Henry woven deep into its fabric.

Responses to Cromwell's missive are revealing: Shaxton of Salisbury sent enthusiastic congratulations; Tunstall a bare acknowledgement of receipt. Rowland Lee of Coventry and Lichfield confessed that 'hitherto I was never in pulpit', but promised to ride to his diocese from Gloucester 'with all speed' in order to give it a go. Erasmus's old foe, Edward Lee of York, protested the impracticalities in his vast and backward bishopric: 'I do not know in all my diocese twelve secular priests [that are] preachers, and few friars, and almost none of any other religion [i.e. religious order]'; still, he promised to do his best.[44]

That might not be enough: Cromwell did not trust the bishops to carry out their duties. A week after the despatch of his circular, he sent another in the King's name to sheriffs and justices of the peace, individually addressed, with flattering assurances of the 'singular trust and assured confidence which we have in you'. They were to keep watch on the bishop's activities within their shire, and if they found evidence that he, or any of his clergy, 'do omit and leave undone any part or parcel' of their orders, or executed them 'coldly and feignedly', were to report immediately. The letters illustrate the strange fusion of fanfare and paranoia surrounding implementation of the royal supremacy. Henry had complete faith in the magistrates' eagerness to carry out his orders, but if any were to 'halt, stumble or wink . . . be you assured that we like a prince of justice will so extremely correct and punish you for the same as all the world besides shall take example and beware'.[45]

The factionalized episcopate – an evangelical minority closeted uncomfortably with a conservative majority of varying degrees of fervour – was an elevated mirror of local communities across the realm. The south coast ports of Rye and Winchelsea were wracked by conflict, with claims and counterclaims about the utterances of treasonous clergy and heretical laity. Evangelicals in St Albans wrote to Cromwell and Cranmer in March 1535 to complain of 'hindrance of the pure Word of God'. The curate of St Peter's, Mr Wakefield, was Cranmer's chaplain and 'doth set [it] forth plainly'. But the curate of St Andrew's chapel, Thomas King, a man of 'small learning', warned townspeople to have nothing to do with books of Luther, Melanchthon, Tracy, Tyndale and Frith. One of his assistants said 'he trusted to see these new fashions put down', and another demanded from a young man in confession 'whether he did not believe as his fathers did before him, or believed in the new learning'.[46]

It was in London that the divisions were most visible and vocal. Through 1534 and 1535 the city pulpits resounded with competing exhortations. Preservation of 'unity and quietness' was the declared motivation in June 1534 for Cranmer to issue a mandate instructing preachers for the space of a year to steer clear of particularly controversial themes: 'purgatory, honouring of saints, that priests may have wives, that faith only justifieth, to go on pilgrimages, to forge miracles'.[47] The list is notable for its studied neutrality, and for declaring off-limits the defence of doctrines – such as purgatory and veneration of saints – lying at the heart of medieval Catholic orthodoxy.

The ordinance seems in any case to have been patchily observed. A visiting conservative preacher bemoaned at Bethlehem without Bishopsgate in August 1535 that 'these new preachers now-a-days that doth preach their iii. sermons in a day have made and brought in such divisions and seditions among us as never was seen in this realm'. The news in Rome by the autumn was of public denunciations of the mass, prayer to saints, and images.[48]

The problem was not so much a lack of regulation as one of competitive licensing regimes. 'Many preachers we have here,' Lady Lisle was informed, 'but they come not from one master.' Bishop Stokesley had authority to license preachers for his diocese, and used it to promote heresy-denouncing tradition-alists, sometimes sailing close to the wind in their opinions of royal policy. A trump card was the presence in his diocese of the pulpit at St Paul's Cross.

Cranmer could issue local and national licences, and invited Latimer to deliver the Lent sermons at court in 1534. He was also able to inveigle his own protégés, such as Hilsey, into the Paul's Cross rota. In July 1535, rather than let Hilsey attack masses for the dead, Stokesley peremptorily replaced him with the conservative Simon Mathew. 'I shall suffer for the friar to rail at the Cross at his pleasure,' Stokesley told Cromwell, but only when Stokesley himself was out of the city and would not have to listen. Cromwell enjoyed the last laugh. He waited three months, then granted Hilsey a commission to license all London preachers, including those at Paul's Cross.[49]

Evangelicals received licence, in various senses, because they were reliably and wholeheartedly anti-papal. Their books were starting to be published 'cum privilegio regali' ('with royal privilege' – a somewhat ambiguous seal of official approval). One such was the vernacular primer produced in 1534 by Cromwell's servant, William Marshall. This omitted the invocations of saints and prayers for the dead that were basic ingredients of traditional Latin primers. The Litany and *Dirige* were restored – after indignant objections – in a second edition of 1535, but Marshall's preface exuded contempt for 'mumbled, murmured and piteously puled' intercessions for departed souls, and for the 'lies and vanities' attending on traditional devotion to the saints.[50]

Another favoured author was Thomas Swynnerton, who produced two effective little tracts in 1534: *A Mustre of Schismatic Bishops of Rome* and *A Litel*

*Treatise Ageynste the Mutterynge of some Papistis in Corners.* Swynnerton's
works pedalled the official line about royal headship and papal usurpation,
while employing the evangelicals' tactic of disparaging opponents as 'papists'.
His arguments were heavily indebted to the writings of Tyndale, still a wanted
fugitive on the continent. In 1535, Swynnerton received Cranmer's licence to
preach anywhere in the country, and was soon getting up the nose of John
Longland of Lincoln. The bishop complained to Cromwell that Swynnerton's
sermons were 'not fruitful, but rather seditious', dealing with doubtful matters
not yet determined by authority. But Swynnerton offered an unanswerable
comeback: 'He sayeth that he knoweth the King's mind.'[51] That was quite a
claim. Did anyone, even Henry himself, really know the King's mind? Henry
had a clear idea of who he was – God's chosen deputy – but what his vocation
required of him was far from self-evident.

If the King was using the reformers, the reformers were also using him. By
1534–5, English evangelicalism had decisively hitched its fortunes to the
carriage of the royal supremacy. Yet its adherents did not constitute an obediently blinkered team, trotting along happily under the whip-hand of royal and
ministerial direction. There were plenty of wild horses in the pack.

Even within Cromwell's immediate circle, visions of quite startling radicalism were starting to emerge. A London grocer-turned-theologian, Clement
Armstrong, bombarded Cromwell with tracts advocating dramatic, utopian
schemes for social reform, seasoned with messianic royalism. Armstrong
wanted to sweep away institutional priesthood, yet saw the King as a sacramental figure who could personally 'minister the body of Christ in form of
bread to all men'. Robert Trueman, in a treatise drafted for Cromwell by
Thomas Derby, clerk of the royal Council, made similarly radical predictions
of the dawning of a new age, when all priesthood would disappear. The printer
Thomas Gibson, whom Latimer recommended to Cromwell as 'an honest
good man', sent the vicegerent ecstatic prophecies describing how Henry,
champion of God's Word, possessed a divine mandate to slaughter all papists
in England, and see them 'drowned in their own blood by sword'. Another,
anonymous, manuscript sent to or commissioned by Cromwell argued that
scripture required the King to instigate an international crusade against the
adherents of Antichrist, whose possessions rightfully belonged to Henry 'in
what land or country soever they be'.[52]

Cromwell was properly circumspect: none of these apocalyptic tracts was
licensed by him for publication. Anne Boleyn, too, distanced herself from the
avant-garde of the reformers. In early 1536, she refused to accept a book
dedicated to her by the Cambridge evangelical Tristram Revell. This was a
translation of a work by the French reformer François Lambert, *Farrago Rerum
Theologicarum*, which used similar language of apocalyptic warfare against the
accursed forces of Antichrist. What made it really objectionable, however, was

that it taught sacramentarianism – denial of the real presence of Christ in the eucharist. Just as Armstrong, Derby and Gibson were all Cromwell's men, Revell was no friendless outsider. He approached the Queen via the household of Archbishop Cranmer, who read the translation, before passing it to the bishop of Worcester. Latimer thought 'there were two or three extreme points in it that might not be borne', but did not completely rule out the possibility of publication.[53]

Bright sparks on the fringes of the evangelical movement threatened to consume it with the fire of their convictions. All Europe looked on aghast at events in the north German city of Münster, where, over the course of 1533–4, radicals inspired by prophecies of the world's imminent end seized control and turned society on its head. In this 'New Jerusalem', John of Leiden, a tailor's apprentice, crowned himself successor to King David, abolished infant baptism and private property, and instituted polygamy – all in preparation for the Second Coming of Christ. Evangelicals as well as Catholics breathed a sigh of relief when, in June 1535, the bishop of Münster's forces retook the city and exacted ruthless revenge.

These 'anabaptists' haunted the dreams of Europe's ruling elites. For evangelicals, there was the additional worry that their existence lent credence to Catholic claims that questioning the authority of the Church led inevitably to sedition and doctrinal anarchy. Such anxieties explain the ferocity of a March 1535 proclamation, which warned against 'strangers, born out of the King's obedience', who lately rebaptized themselves, denied the real presence in the sacrament, and taught other 'pestilent heresies'. They were to leave the country within twelve days or suffer death. In 1534, Parliament rolled back the scope of the heresy law; in his eagerness to 'defend and maintain the faith of Christ and sacraments of Holy Church', Henry now rolled it forward again: even those who recanted were subject to death if they did not depart the realm.[54]

The proclamation suggested anabaptists were, by definition, sinister foreigners – the line the bishops had taken about Lutherans a decade earlier. The authorities already knew this was not so. In or around 1532, a clutch of heretics, five Englishmen, two Flemings and a Scot, were arrested in London for possessing and distributing copies of an unspecified 'Anabaptists' Confession'. They held 'damnable opinions touching the humanity of Christ' – most likely the belief that Jesus took no flesh from the Virgin Mary and possessed a kind of celestial body. Such speculations perhaps struck a chord with surviving Lollards. In their eagerness to undermine the cult of Christ's mother some used to describe her as a 'saffron bag' – a humble container for contents of great worth.

Lines between provocative metaphor and formal 'Christological' heresy – between Lollardy, evangelicalism and radicalism – were sometimes hard to draw. In the summer of 1534, a Yorkshire priest, chaplain to the evangelical gentleman Sir Francis Bigod, scandalized conservatives with a sermon likening 'Our Lady to a pudding when the meat was out'. A year or two later, Henry Goderyck, rector of Hothfield in Kent, was teaching that Mary was not the Queen of Heaven, and could do no more for people than any other woman. She was indeed 'the Mother of Christ', but also resembled a saffron bag.[55]

The proclamation against anabaptists was no empty gesture: in May 1535 twenty-three Flemish immigrants, men and women, were arrested in London and accused of denying the humanity of Christ, the real presence and the necessity to baptize infants. After interrogation by Cranmer, they were condemned by a vicegerential commission, on which the conservative John Stokesley and the evangelical Robert Barnes sat side by side.

Ten or so recanted and were deported to the Netherlands. Another thirteen or fourteen were condemned to death. Two of them, a man and a woman, suffered together at Smithfield on 4 June. The others, in the words of the chronicler Charles Wriothesley, were 'sent to divers good towns in England, there to be burned'. John Foxe later claimed to have seen evidence that ten perished, and two were pardoned by the King. Certainly, both Henry and Cromwell made a point of personally telling Chapuys the sentences would be carried out, and a correspondent in Amiens heard by 8 June that several had been.[56]

The break with Rome brought no liberty for people to believe as they pleased. More people were burned for heresy in 1535, during Cromwell's vicegerency, and in the space of a single week, than in the preceding decade under the legateship of Wolsey and the chancellorship of More combined. They died – in part – so Henry VIII could hold his head up in front of Charles V as a pious and orthodox prince.

The summer of 1535 was a veritable season of blood. Exactly a week after the burnings at Smithfield, three Carthusians – Sebastian Newdigate, William Exmew and Humphrey Middlemore – were convicted in King's Bench of high treason for denying the King's supremacy. They spent the fortnight preceding their trial in the Marshalsea, chained to posts by necks and legs, stewing in their own excrement. It is possible Henry himself visited the prison to try to persuade them to recant. On 19 June they were dragged on hurdles to Tyburn, there to be strangled, eviscerated and dismembered.

They were not the first. Prior John Houghton and the monks of the London Charterhouse reluctantly took the Oath of Succession in 1534. But in the spring of 1535 Cromwell demanded they swear explicitly to the Supremacy. Houghton refused, along with the priors of Beauvale and Axholme, Robert Laurence and Augustine Webster, who were in London seeking a pre-emptive interview with Cromwell in the hope he might permit them to swear 'so far as the law of God might allow'. All three were executed at Tyburn on 4 May, along with the Bridgettine Richard Reynolds and the secular priest John Hale, following a trial in which Cromwell brought heavy pressure on the jury.

Arrangements were made for Thomas More, with his daughter Margaret, to watch from the window of his cell in the Tower as the monks were led out to execution: 'Dost thou not see, Meg, that these blessed fathers be now as cheerfully going to their deaths as bridegrooms to their marriage?' Conditions cannot have been very cheerful in Newgate prison, where, over the course of the next two years, a further ten dissident Carthusians starved slowly to death in chains.[57]

Carthusians were the spiritual elite of English monasticism, and, to a greater extent than other religious, members of a social elite too. Houghton was from a gentry family, Exmew the son of a former mayor of London. Newdigate had been a courtier, a gentleman of the King's Privy Chamber, who entered the order in 1531 after a profound conversion experience. The Nun of Kent could be dismissed as a deluded prophetess, surrounded by self-serving agitators. It was harder to discredit the saintly and politically quiescent contemplatives of the Charterhouse: the savagery of their punishment itself served to assert the gravity of their offence.

If Carthusian non-compliance was an embarrassment to Henry, that of the bishop of Rochester was a humiliation that could not be allowed to persist. The doughty John Fisher was tried for treason on 17 June 1535, possibly tricked in the Tower by a royal agent into explicit denial of the Supremacy.[58] In the spring of 1535, the fate of the bishop of Rochester, a theologian of European renown, was an international talking point. Pope Paul III, elected in October 1534 as successor to the dithering Clement VII, tried – ineptly – to help. On 20 May 1535, he created Fisher a cardinal. The idea was that Henry would be shamed into releasing him, and Fisher would be free to take part in the General Council Paul was hoping to convene to heal the schism with the Lutherans.

The Pope badly misjudged the reaction of the King, whom Francis I had just described to a papal ambassador as 'the most strange man in the world . . . so pertinacious and fiercely proud that it is almost impossible to bear with him'. Henry was fearful of a General Council, and incandescent with rage at so public an assertion of the English bishops' subjection to the authority of the pontiff. News of the elevation precipitated Fisher's trial, with Henry swearing 'he would give him another hat, and send the head afterwards to Rome for the Cardinal's hat'.[59] It was, presumably, acknowledgement of the bishop's age and status, rather than any literal desire to enact this threat, which resulted, on 22 June, in Fisher being beheaded rather than hanged and quartered.

Over the spring and early summer of 1535, Thomas More came under immense pressure to conform and swear the oath. He spent his months of incarceration in devotional pursuits, and in pious mental preparation for the possibility of torture and death, though his meditative writings contained sharp sideswipes at the heretics he blamed for tearing Christendom apart.

Chapuys was scarcely exaggerating when he described More and Fisher as 'persons of unequalled reputation in this kingdom'. He reported how sermons against them were ordered in London churches on Sunday 13 June in hopes of appeasing 'the murmurs of the world'. More's trial was held on 1 July, after evidence emerged of an overt denial of the Supremacy, almost certainly fabricated by the solicitor general, Richard Rich. More, once the King's friend and mentor, was likewise allowed the mercy of the axe rather than the rope and knife. He was put to death before a small crowd at the Tower early on the morning of 6 July, protesting, with his accustomed mixture of irony and conviction, that 'he died the King's good servant but God's first'.[60]

The executions of 1535 were a defining moment for English religion, an end and a beginning. The zeal and camaraderie of the evangelicals were dramatically boosted by the creation of martyrs in 1530–2; now their bitterest opponents acquired a similar badge of blood-stained honour.

Almost immediately, Henry's victims were hailed as saints and martyrs of the true faith. On the feast of St John the Baptist, two days after the beheading of Fisher, John Darlay, a perhaps traumatized member of the London Charterhouse, was visited in his cell by the ghost of a deceased brother. The apparition urged him to follow the example of Prior Houghton, a 'martyr in heaven next unto angels'. On a subsequent visit, the spirit reported 'my lord of Rochester' was there too. Reports soon spread, within England and abroad, that Fisher's head, displayed on London Bridge, was miraculously preserved from corruption. Alarmed, the authorities threw it into the Thames. But this, over the course of 1535–6, did not prevent a stream of reports of disaffected subjects praising Fisher, More and the Carthusians as 'martyrs and saints . . . for holding with our holy father the Pope'.[61]

Execution publicized the cause for which the dissidents died. Fisher announced at the block that he was 'come hither to die for the faith of Christ's holy Catholic Church'. Statements identifying the true Catholic faith with Rome seem also to have attended the execution of Reynolds and the Carthusian priors on 4 May 1535. In a letter to Reginald Pole in Italy, his former secretary Thomas Starkey, now in Cromwell's service, scoffed at the belief of the executed religious that the Pope's superiority was 'a sure truth and manifest of the law of God, and instituted by Christ as necessary to the conservation of the spiritual unity of this mystical body of Christ'. Starkey thought such obstinate and superstitious monks failed to grasp the distinction between spiritual and political unity, foolishly thinking all unity 'would run to ruin for lack of this head'.[62]

Their perception was not, however, self-evidently ridiculous, even in the sophisticated humanist circles to which Starkey himself belonged. When, at his trial, sentence was declared against him, Thomas More finally broke his famous silence. He argued the indictment was invalid because it was grounded upon an act of Parliament directly repugnant to the law of God and his Holy Church, the supreme government of which, or of any part whereof, may no temporal prince presume by any law to take upon him, as rightfully belonging to the See of Rome, a spiritual pre-eminence by the mouth of Our Saviour himself, personally present upon the earth, only to Saint Peter and his successors.[63]

More had never been an ardent papalist, and years earlier advised Henry to tone down passages in the *Assertio Septem Sacramentorum* tending too much in that direction (see p. 97). But a catastrophic confluence of heresy and schism persuaded him that papal headship was the indispensable cement of orthodoxy and unity. More drew this conclusion early, but others came to embrace the same logic. Before the early 1530s, the significance of the Pope for the religious identity of English Christians was often peripheral, implicit or unexamined, but attitudes towards the papacy were changed in positive as well as negative directions by Henry VIII's attack on it: royal policy was turning Catholics – some Catholics – into *Roman* Catholics. Henry VIII was the creator of English Roman Catholicism just as much as he was the progenitor of 'Anglicanism'.

This new religious phenomenon – dissident, oppositional Roman Catholicism – was rudderless and leaderless in the late summer of 1535. But its captain was soon to step forward. In Italy, the King's cousin, Reginald Pole, sharing the sense of European outrage at the treatment of More and Fisher, began planning to commit to paper his thoughts on the King's divorce and supremacy.

### Superstition and Sodomy

In July and August 1535, English ambassadors overseas went into overdrive to defend the executions of More and Fisher, and to justify Henry's mild and restrained treatment of detestable traitors. At home, the visitation finally got under way. One set of commissioners was tasked with financial evaluation of the income of parishes, monasteries and collegiate churches, producing a survey known as the *Valor Ecclesiasticus*. Others were specifically charged with assessing the condition of the religious houses. The King and Queen, meanwhile, avoiding the unpleasantness in the capital, set off in early June on a summer progress to the West Country.

Policy and pleasantry mixed on a holiday with a theme of reform. The royal party made a point of favouring with visits gentlemen with known evangelical sympathies: Tyndale's old patron Sir John Walsh at Little Sodbury, Latimer's friend Sir Edward Bainton at Bromham. On 23 July, Thomas Cromwell caught up with the royal progress at Winchcombe in Gloucestershire, and accompanied the itinerant court through the rest of the summer.[64]

Winchcombe Abbey was once ruled by the redoubtable Richard Kidderminster, champion of the liberties of the Church. A less imposing successor, Abbot Richard Munslow, raised no protest when Cromwell decided personally to undertake an inspection of the house. His intervention was welcomed by at least one of the monks. John Placett was an ardent evangelical convert and author of a treatise against 'the usurped power of the bishop of Rome', who found he 'cannot endure the straitness of the religion'. Placett was grateful to Cromwell for speaking to the monks 'discretely' about their vows.[65]

The sojourn at Winchcombe signalled that internal reform of the Church was on the royal agenda, and that figures besides the King were setting the pace. Barely three miles from Winchcombe lay another imposing monastery, the Cistercian abbey of Hailes, famed for its relic of a vial purporting to contain the blood of Christ. According to a generally reliable account, Anne Boleyn ordered her chaplains to go to Hailes to inspect the relic. They suspected chicanery: deception of the pilgrims with duck's blood or red wax. The Holy Blood was not confiscated or destroyed – yet. But Anne's appeals to the King resulted in its temporary removal from public display.[66]

False or forged relics were a dominant theme of the monastic visitation under way by the autumn of 1535. Injunctions carried by the commissioners ordered monks not to 'show any relics or feigned miracles for increase of lucre, but that they exhort pilgrims and strangers to give that to the poor that they thought to offer to their images or relics' – a prescription to cause Lollards to nod with vigorous approval.

It is unlikely the uncovering of 'abuses' in monasteries – a prelude to their dissolution – was the principal purpose of the visitation, at least in Henry's mind. The first three injunctions enjoined abbots and priors to faithful adherence to the Oath of Succession, to steadfast observance of statutes against the 'pretended jurisdiction' of Rome, and to consider themselves absolved from prior professions of obedience to the Pope.

The visitation, in other words, was intended for both symbolic performance and practical enforcement of the royal supremacy. And as one of the visitors observed to Cromwell, 'There can be no better way to beat the King's authority into the heads of the rude people in the North than to show them that the King intends reformation and correction of religion.'[67]

Vicegerential visitation was aimed primarily at religious houses because of anxieties about the historically rooted internationalism of the orders, and their inherited privileges and exemptions. Visitors were empowered to pore over 'foundations, charters, donations, appropriations and muniments', looking to identify and eradicate 'papistical escripts'. The concerns were more than theoretical: the behaviour over the preceding three years of the Observants of Greenwich, the Carthusians of the London Charterhouse, and various others, persuaded Henry that monks were not to be trusted.[68]

The principal visitors appointed by Thomas Cromwell – Richard Layton, Thomas Legh, John ap Rice, John Tregonwell – were not the uncultured thugs they are sometimes painted. Layton and Legh held doctorates in canon law from Cambridge, Tregonwell from Oxford. Rice was a public notary, trained, like Cromwell, at the Inns of Court. Another of the visitors, Thomas Bedyll (a graduate of New College, Oxford), was former secretary to Archbishop Warham. But all had proved their mettle in the campaign of enforcement, participating in interrogations and trials of More, Fisher and the Carthusians.

In conjunction with inspection of religious houses, they were also involved with a visitation of the universities: Layton and Tregonwell at Oxford, Legh and Rice at Cambridge. Here, too, the principal concern was with public and fulsome acknowledgement of royal supremacy from institutions that had shown disturbing signs of independent-mindedness. At the same time, the visitors were to oversee educational reforms, which doubled as political state-ments: suppression of lectures and degrees in canon law, and abandonment of scholastic commentaries in favour of enhanced concentration on the bible. As Layton boasted in a letter to Cromwell, 'we have set Duns [Scotus] in Bocardo [the town gaol] and have utterly banished him Oxford forever with all his blind glosses'. With the authority of the state behind them, humanists finally vanquished Erasmus's 'barbarians'.[69]

There was – unsurprisingly – resistance to the curricular changes, but neither at the universities nor in the monasteries did the visitors find much evidence of overt opposition to the Supremacy. At Worcester Priory in July 1535, Legh and Rice heard accusations of disloyalty against one of the brethren, though these may have been generated by ill feeling within the community. There was stronger evidence against the subprior of Lewes in Sussex, Anthony Bolney, who confessed he had preached treason and implicated his prior in concealing it. Layton also considered the monks of Battle, 'saving one or two', to be traitors as well as sodomites. The abbot was 'the veriest hayne [miser], beetle and buzzard, and the arrantest churl that I ever [did] see'. Such 'black sort of devilish monks I am sorry to know as I do: surely I think they be past amendment'.[70]

Contempt for monks and monasticism was an old tune from the humanist song sheet of the 1520s, transposed into a new key by the need to harmonize with evangelical refrains emanating from the vicegerent, the Queen, and – when the mood took him – the King himself. 'Reform' was at the outset a secondary purpose of the visitation – the injunctions and articles with which the visitors were equipped exhibited a traditional (if unusually strict) concern with matters such as enclosure, diet, alms-giving and service times. But there was a large, open-ended qualification: rules and customs of the religious life were to be observed only 'as far as they do agree with Holy Scriptures and the Word of God'.

As the visitors set about their work, despatching regular reports to Cromwell and compiling *comperta* (complaints) about what they found, two themes started to predominate. One was sexual misdemeanour, incidents of which were tabulated with statistical precision in the so-called *Compendium Compertorum* (collection of complaints) – a record of the visitation of the dioceses of York and Coventry and Lichfield, prepared for the King by Rice, Layton and Legh. In addition to twenty-eight unchaste nuns (seventeen bearing children), and 113 monks guilty of sexual relations with women, the *Compendium* identified an alarming number of confessed 'sodomites' in the northern and midland houses. But marginal annotation of the cases shows that the overwhelming majority of these (170 out of 184) were sodomites 'per voluntaria polluciones' (by voluntary pollutions) – i.e. masturbation. This sin was bracketed along with incontinence with women in a summary of the reports from Norwich, where once again it represented the most common category of offence. No episcopal visitation had ever sought to gather evidence about this.

It is unlikely the visitors simply fabricated evidence of moral turpitude, and at several houses they had nothing at all on this score to report. But there is no doubt they were actively looking to find such evidence, and that the instinct sharpened as the visitation proceeded. In January 1536, Layton reported to Cromwell that they were discovering the same 'great corruption' among religious houses in Yorkshire as in the south – nuns taking abortifacients, and monks practising *coitus interruptus*. He was about to descend on St Mary's Abbey, York, where he fully expected 'to find much evil living in the abbot and the convent'.

In a sample of forty-eight northern houses visited by Layton and Legh for which we know the size of the community, 192 of 674 monks (28 per cent) admitted to unchastity in its broadest sense. Four of these confessed to sodomy with boys, and seventy-four to fornication with women. Monastic sexual activity, it would seem, was endemic rather than epidemic. But the visitors collated the evidence in ways designed to present it in the worst possible light.[71]

The other defining theme of the visitation reports was the one Anne Boleyn brought to the King's attention near the start of the summer progress – the possession and display of bogus relics. This was a recurrent topic of the visitors' letters to Cromwell, and something of an in-joke. In August 1535, Layton sent from Bath 'a book of Our Lady's miracles, well able to match the Canterbury Tales'. He told how at Farley, a cell of Lewes, he seized 'vincula Sancti Petri' (the chains of St Peter). The monks also possessed combs of Mary Magdalen, St Dorothy and St Margaret, but were unable to tell how they came by them. At Maiden Bradley Priory in Wiltshire, Layton confiscated a collection of 'strange things': 'God's coat, Our Lady's smock, part of God's supper', as well as the stone on which Jesus was born. His sarcastic side comment was pure Erasmus: 'belike there is in Bethlehem plenty of stones and some quarry, and [they] maketh there mangers of stone'.

A similarly Erasmian tone attended Rice's report that at Bury St Edmunds were 'pieces of the holy cross enough to make a whole cross of'. 'Vanity and superstition' there also included the coals with which St Lawrence was toasted, the parings of St Edmund's nails, and 'St Thomas of Canterbury's pen-knife and his boots'.

Core institutions of the English Church were, the visitors found, riddled with 'superstition'. The *Compendium Compertorum* documented no fewer than ten pieces of the True Cross, seven portions of the Virgin's milk and numerous saints' girdles which, laywomen were encouraged to believe, assisted in the safe delivery of children. The scandal was not confined to obscure corners of the land: one of the confiscated relics of Our Lady's milk came from St Paul's Cathedral, and was found to be, the chronicler Wriothesley reported, 'but a piece of chalk'.[72]

Another relic of the Virgin's milk, preserved at the Augustinian priory at Walsingham, had been an object of Erasmus's scorn in the colloquy 'A Pilgrimage for Religion's Sake' (see pp. 29–30). Here, the visitors arrived armed with a special set of articles that relentlessly grilled the monks about forgeries and sharp practice at the shrine. The articles were in fact directly modelled on the themes and critiques of Erasmus's fictional colloquy – life imitating art.[73]

The mood music of the royal visitation was 'Erasmian', rather than overtly evangelical. But the term should not suggest for us an undogmatic stance of religious moderation; rather, it betokened an attitude of anticlerical hostility towards old-fashioned monks and friars, and of withering contempt towards the practices in popular religion they could be accused of exploiting to their own advantage.

The reasonable middle ground was nonetheless the earth on which the regime claimed to be standing. In January 1536, Cromwell despatched another royal circular to the bishops, again with the intention of regulating preaching. Bishops were to examine all licences, and remove them from persons trying to seduce the people with 'filthy and corrupt abominations of the bishop of Rome'. But there was also a warning against new notions causing 'inquietness of mind'. Cromwell added his own encouragement to suppress both papalism and 'novelties without wise and discreet qualification'. The conservative Longland of Lincoln seized the opportunity to instruct his archdeacons to send him names of all preachers in his vast diocese who 'transgressed the said order and commandment'. But he was well aware that many preachers of 'novelties' enjoyed the at least tacit support of the vicegerent.[74]

## The Fall of a Queen

On 7 January, the day Cromwell wrote to the bishops, Catherine of Aragon died at Kimbolton Castle in Huntingdonshire. She had been there under genteel house arrest since 1534, denied access to her beloved Mary as a punishment for their refusal to swear to the Supremacy. When Henry received the news he was, reported Chapuys, 'like one transported with joy'. On the following Sunday he appeared at court 'clad all over in yellow, from top to toe, except the white feather he had in his bonnet'. The greatest rebuke and challenge to the Boleyn marriage and succession was at a stroke removed. Henry paraded in his arms the Princess Elizabeth – 'the little Bastard', as Chapuys called her – proudly showing the toddler to one after another of the assembled courtiers.[75]

Chapuys believed Catherine had been poisoned, and suspected the hand of 'the Concubine'. There is no evidence for this, other than the obvious circumstance that Anne's position was strengthened by Catherine's death. But other things were thrown into flux. Chapuys feared, rightly, that greater pressure would be brought on the Princess Mary to acknowledge her father's status. He also worried that Charles V might be diplomatically outmanoeuvred, if Henry seized the opportunity for some kind of rapprochement with Rome, or at least the appearance of one. Cromwell was openly mentioning the possibility of a papal legate being allowed into England, and Chapuys thought the recent crackdown on radical preaching to be a gesture of conciliation. Others too must have wondered if Catherine's death supplied occasion to let bygones be bygones, and for Henry to reconcile himself to Rome in return for recognition of his second marriage. Such an outcome was probably never on the cards: having test-driven, at speed, his exciting new vehicle of authority, Henry was not about to return it to the shop.

Anne's triumph was short-lived. Catherine was buried on 29 January, at Peterborough Abbey, with honours due to the daughter of a queen of Spain, if not a queen of England. Her choice was for interment in a priory of the Franciscan Observants, the order to which the Spanish royal house had a particular devotion. But, as Cromwell pointed out to a servant of Chapuys, not one of their houses now remained in England. The funeral sermon was given by John Hilsey, who preached against the Pope and claimed that, at the hour of her death, Catherine acknowledged she was never Queen of England. This, almost certainly, was a lie, in the perceived service of a greater truth.[76]

On the very day of the funeral, Anne, three and a half months pregnant, miscarried a child, believed to be a boy. It was both a personal and a political disaster. Henry, inclined to feel a divine finger on all his triumphs and calamities, reportedly told her he now 'saw clearly that God did not wish to give him male children'. Their relationship had in fact been cooling for some time; Chapuys heard Henry was showing interest in 'a lady of the Court, named Mistress Semel [Jane Seymour], to whom, as many say, he has lately made great presents'.

Parliament reassembled on 4 February, for its first session since 1534, at a time of considerable uncertainty: a royal marriage in trouble, new challenges in foreign policy and continuing domestic discontent. Any hopes for a softening of the anti-papal line were soon scotched: on Sunday 6 February Cranmer preached for two hours at Paul's Cross, arguing that all scriptural passages making mention of the Antichrist referred to the Pope. To coincide with the opening of Parliament, books were published attacking images and worship of saints, as well as the doctrine of purgatory. Chapuys thought the latter 'the newest and most strange to the people', and concluded efforts were being made to undermine purgatory in order to justify the seizure of ecclesiastical endowments supporting prayer for the dead; in other words, religious houses.[77]

If partial dissolution of the religious houses was not decided upon at the start of the royal visitation, it was the conclusion to which the visitors' reports inexorably led. Even before the bill was introduced into the Lords, around 6 March, it was an open secret that smaller monasteries were to be dissolved, and Cromwell began to be besieged by landowners petitioning for grants or farms of monastic estates adjoining their own.

Such requests did not necessarily signify indifference or hostility to the religious houses, or glee at their downfall. Writing to Cromwell on 25 March, Lord De La Warr begged that Boxgrove Priory in Sussex be allowed to continue, either in its current Benedictine form, or as a college of secular priests. His ancestors were its founders and benefactors, and many lay honourably buried there. But, 'if it may not stand so with His Grace's pleasure', then De La Warr requested first refusal on rental of the lands. Small steps separated opposition to change, fatalistic acceptance of its inevitability, and opportunistic co-operation with its implementation.[78]

The government nonetheless recognized the measure required sensitive handling. The lurid findings of the *Compendium Compertorum* helped. Years later, Latimer remembered the 'enormities' of the monks being read out in Parliament, and MPs responding with cries of 'down with them'. The bill itself was carefully judged, presented as a reform measure in response to the findings of the visitation. This had revealed that 'manifest sin, vicious, carnal and abominable living is daily used and committed among the little and small abbeys'. Such sins were prevalent in houses 'under the number of twelve persons'. The figure was significant: twelve (the number of Christ's disciples) was widely seen as the viable minimum for a religious community; it echoed plans of Wolsey's, near the end of his legateship, to dissolve such supposedly dysfunctional mini-houses.

If the headlines shouted reform, and continuity with earlier humanist priorities, the small print told a different story. The actual criterion for dissolution was financial: houses were to close if their annual revenue was £200 or less. It was a calculated partial disendowment, and beyond the blunt association of size with quality (a finding in any case not really borne out by the visitation reports) there was no attempt to align standards of discipline with the fates of individual houses. Jane Messyndyne, prioress of the Cistercian nunnery of Legbourne in Lincolnshire, wrote to Cromwell to say she had heard a great number of abbeys were to be put down 'because of their misliving'. Yet she trusted in God 'ye shall hear no complaints against us, neither in our living nor hospitality keeping', and she begged that her house be allowed to stand. It was not.[79]

There was no suggestion in the Dissolution Act that the principles of monasticism itself were under attack, or that this was stage one in a larger plan of suppression. Indeed, the act went out of its way to heap praise on the 'great solemn monasteries of this realm wherein (thanks be to God) religion is right well kept and observed'. It was to such houses that monks and nuns from small monasteries not wishing to leave the religious life were to be transferred. All the abbots in the Lords voted for the measure – 'in hope', the chronicler Edward Hall sarcastically observed, 'that their great monasteries should have continued still'.

Some could see the writing on the wall. According to Hall, one member of the Lords said in debate that small abbeys 'were as thorns, but the great abbots were putrefied old oaks and they must needs follow'. Evangelicals associated religious houses with purgatory, and preaching against both intensified as the bill went through its stages. Cranmer gave a Lenten sermon arguing that money spent on masses for the dead would be better bestowed on the poor, and suggesting the King was now 'at a full point for friars and chantry priests, that they shall all away . . . saving them that can preach'. There was nothing in the act about blanket dissolution of friaries, still less of chantries. But Cranmer blithely linked their fate with that of the smaller monasteries, all the while reassuring listeners that suppression would lead to lower taxation. Latimer, meanwhile, took to the Paul's Cross pulpit on 12 March to denounce the lavish lifestyle of abbots and priors, castigating them (and bishops and other clergy too) as 'strong thieves'.[80]

Among evangelicals, expectations were high that the dissolution act was the start of real and meaningful change. But there were anxieties too. How would the cause of the Gospel be advanced if the wealth of abbeys simply disappeared into royal coffers, or the hands of courtiers and lay landowners? The question troubled no less a personage than the Queen herself. According to the biography later composed by one of her chaplains, Anne ordered Hugh Latimer to use his next sermon before the King to argue against 'utter subversion of the said houses' in favour of conversion 'to some better use'.

Either in his Paul's Cross sermon of 12 March (which Henry may have attended), or in another preached at court around this time, Latimer made an impassioned plea for the King to 'convert the abbeys and priories to places of study and good letters, and to the continual relief of the poor'. Anne urged all preachers of God's Word to press home the same message: not suppression of religious houses, but 'continual and earnest petition for the stay of the same'. Perhaps this was what the King heard from another of Anne's chaplains, Simon Haynes, in a court sermon delivered on Wednesday 8 March. An intriguing summary records Haynes saying 'that God hath brought the truth of his Word to light, and princes be the ministers of it to give commandment that it should go forward, and yet it is nothing regarded, and make of him but a Christmas king'. This sounds like a warning to Henry that if he did not live up to his responsibility for true reformation, he risked becoming a figure of ridicule.[81] To threaten a king with laughter was to pull a tiger's tail.

Boldly, recklessly, Anne now challenged Cromwell for leadership of the evangelical cause, and custodianship of the King's conscience. Chapuys heard before 1 April 1536 that 'the Concubine and Cromwell were on bad terms'. The breach between them could be read, in barely coded form, in a sermon given at court the following day by Anne's almoner, John Skip. He argued against attacks on the clergy purely for purposes of seizing their possessions, and mentioned the Old Testament story of the Persian King Ahasuerus, tricked into ordering a massacre of the Jews by his evil advisor, Haman. Tragedy was averted by the intervention of Ahasuerus's virtuous Jewish wife, Esther; Haman was hanged.

It was fairly clear who was who in this little parable. But Skip did his royal mistress few favours by invoking another Old Testament allusion: the formerly virtuous King Solomon's 'sensual and carnal aptitude in taking of many wives and concubines'. Everyone at court knew of the King's interest in Jane Seymour. Awareness was spreading too of profound disagreements surrounding the dissolution policy. Cranmer alerted Cromwell on 22 April that matters 'goeth all contrary to my expectation', and requested an urgent meeting. Did Cranmer fear that suppression would not go ahead, or that preachers and the poor would gain nothing from it?[82]

The split within the evangelical camp had foreign policy dimensions. In late summer 1535, Robert Barnes was again sent to Wittenberg to lay the groundwork for negotiations between England and the Lutheran princes of the Schmalkaldic League, a military alliance formed in 1531 to protect the German Reformation from the repressive hand of the Emperor. A formal embassy followed in October, headed by Edward Foxe. The search for allies was quickened by Paul III's drawing up of a formal bull of excommunication and deposition against Henry, and fears that its promulgation might spur the Catholic powers to military action.

The discussions at Wittenberg continued into the New Year, with theological as well as diplomatic aspects. For their part, the Schmalkaldic Leaguers hoped Henry would sign up to the Augsburg Confession, a statement of core Lutheran principles drawn up in 1530 by Melanchthon. But Henry was never one to buy his theological clothes off the peg. He welcomed advice on how 'to proceed according to the very truth of the Gospel', but not instruction. He could not, he said, 'accept at any creature's hand the observing of his and the realm's Faith'. By March 1536, a set of articles was drawn up between English ambassadors and German theologians, the prelude for a return German embassy to England.[83]

In the meantime the death of Catherine opened the possibility of rapprochement with Charles V, a safer prospect from Henry's point of view than a Lutheran alliance, and one to reduce dependence on France. Cromwell and Anne were in agreement that the change of direction made sense, and the minister – who in spite of everything enjoyed a good working relationship with Chapuys – made the running on the negotiations, which centred on Mary's restoration to the line of succession, and military support for Charles in an expected war with France. But a meeting with Chapuys on Easter Tuesday, 18 April, descended into recrimination as it became clear Henry's price was much higher: complete recognition of the Boleyn marriage, and consequently of his headship over the Church. Cromwell was left looking foolish, and dangerously exposed.

It was after this humiliation, Cromwell later informed Chapuys, that he 'planned and brought about the whole affair' (*fantasier et conspirer le dict affaire*). The fall of Anne Boleyn is a mysterious business, and Cromwell's claim to have orchestrated it cannot be taken entirely at face value.[84] His real achievement, in pushing at an open door, was to make sure it did not slam shut on his own fingers.

The one constant about Henry VIII's emotional life in the 1530s was that it was a magnet for theological and political conflict. Jane Seymour was demure and retiring (the antithesis of Anne), but she was also the tool of political conservatives – the Marquis of Exeter, the courtier Sir Nicholas Carew and others – who saw in her a means of ousting Anne and restoring the position of Mary. They coached Jane in the art of chastely piquing the King's interest. On 25 April Carew sent word to Mary 'to be of good cheer, for shortly the opposite party would put water in their wine'.[85]

Anne's already tenuous position was weakened by her own foolishly flirtatious behaviour, and an overly sexualized culture of 'dalliance' with attendants and intimates at court. One of these was a young musician, Mark Smeaton, a fantasist infatuated with the Queen. On 30 April Smeaton was arrested on Cromwell's orders, interrogated and possibly tortured. He confessed to adultery with Anne, triggering a spate of arrests of other courtiers suspected of the same offence. These included Anne's brother, George, Lord Rochford.

Smeaton, Rochford, Henry Norris (a rival of Cromwell), William Brereton and Sir Francis Weston were executed on 17 May, after indictment for the treason of sexual congress with the Queen – something not in fact a treasonable offence under the law. On the day of the executions, Cranmer declared the marriage null and void, apparently on grounds (conveniently overlooked in

1533) of Henry's prior sexual relationship with Anne's sister. Anne herself went to the block two days later, granted the dubious mercy of execution with the sword rather than the axe. All – with the exception of the pathetic Smeaton – died protesting their innocence. That Henry managed to persuade himself of the truth of the accusations is probable, though by no means certain.

It looked like an unmitigated disaster for the evangelical cause. Anne's ally Archbishop Cranmer, kept out of the loop by Cromwell, certainly feared so. When, on 2 May, he was finally briefed about what was happening, he wrote to Henry, offering consolatory words, along with a brave hope that what he heard about Anne might turn out not to be true. Yet Cranmer's principal concern was clear: 'I trust that your grace will bear no less entire favour unto the truth of the Gospel than you did before; forsomuch as your Grace's favour to the Gospel was not led by affection unto her, but by zeal unto the truth.'[86]

Carew and his allies scented victory, a future with no place in it for Cranmer or Cromwell. On the day preceding Smeaton's arrest, Chapuys detected a change in the theological weather: 'I hear from all quarters that the King has ordered the preachers to avoid new opinions touching rites and ceremonies, and preach everywhere according to the old fashion.' But there were limits to any incipient restoration. The monastic dissolution was to go ahead, and Chapuys expected no change at all 'as regards the primacy of the Pope'.[87]

Henry's fixation with recognition of his supremacy was the ledge to which Cromwell clung, and from which he was finally able to push his enemies. He managed to insinuate to Henry that Mary's obstinacy about submitting to his title was encouraged by court conservatives. Exeter was banned from meetings of the Council, along with William Fitzwilliam, Treasurer of the Household. Other supporters of Mary – Sir Francis Bryan, Sir Anthony Browne, Lady Hussey – were summarily arrested.

A second bloodbath was averted when Mary gave way. In the early summer she came under intense, unprecedented pressure. A high-level deputation, headed by the Duke of Norfolk, the Earl of Sussex and the ever-willing Bishop Rowland Lee, turned up to harangue her as an 'unnatural daughter' and 'traitress'. One of the nobles told her that 'were she his or any other man's daughter, he would beat her to death, or strike her head against the wall until he made it as soft as a boiled apple'. With Cromwell posing as her friend and protector, and even Chapuys advising submission for the sake of safety, Mary capitulated. On 22 June she signed a document acknowledging her father as supreme head of the Church, and recognizing the marriage of her parents to have been 'by God's law and man's law incestuous and unlawful'.

It was a happy ending, of sorts. For now, there were no further executions. Mary was welcomed back to court, and the embrace of her new step-mother, Queen Jane, whom Henry married on 30 May. Cromwell succeeded Anne Boleyn's father as Lord Privy Seal, and rose to the ranks of the peerage.[88] And to the immense relief of Cranmer and Anne's surviving allies, royal favour was not after all withdrawn from 'the Gospel'.

## Articles of Faith

While Mary pondered her options at the start of June 1536, a young Englishman arrived at court from Italy carrying a recently completed book. He was Michael Throckmorton, half-brother of the Sir George Throckmorton who caused Henry and Cromwell such problems in Parliament. The book was the work of his master, Reginald Pole. Its title was *Pro Ecclesiasticae Unitatis Defensione* (For the Defence of the Unity of the Church), and Pole wrote it near Padua between September 1535 and March 1536, in belated response to Henry's request for his opinion on the divorce and royal supremacy. It was a call to repentance, and a declaration of war, thinly disguised as a peace offering.

Throckmorton had instructions to tell Henry it was not too late for him; 'that God suffered His Grace to fall, to make him rise with more honour'. The moment was opportune for atonement and forgiveness, God having 'detected the iniquity of her which hath been the original cause and occasion of all these both errors and dangers'. With a General Council of the Church pending, Henry would not wish to be summoned dishonourably before its judgement. But if he returned to the unity of the Church, 'it shall be taken for one of the greatest miracles that hath been showed this many ages'.[89]

The miracle was that Henry allowed the bearer of this message to return to Italy with his head on his shoulders – Cromwell, wrong-footed for once, falsely believed he had successfully recruited him as a double agent. Throckmorton carried back to Pole a teeth-grindingly courteous reply from Henry, inviting him to return to England for further discussions, as 'their opinions differ in many points, or rather, in everything'.

That was an understatement. Pole's *De Unitate* contained vigorous debunking of the justifications for royal supremacy, and wholehearted affirmation of the identity of the true Church as the body in communion with the Pope, successor of St Peter. It combined this with virulent condemnation of Henry's actions, particularly the killing of More and Fisher, painting the King's motives as literally demonic: 'Satan promised that he would give you everything, if you would profess yourself to be supreme head of the Church.'[90]

Pole's was the most significant individual act of resistance to Henry's Reformation. It mattered because he was not only a highly regarded humanist scholar and theologian, but a high-born nobleman, with Yorkist blood in his veins. His mother Margaret, who inherited in her own right the title of Countess of Salisbury, was the only surviving child of George, Duke of Clarence, brother of Edward IV and Richard III. She was also the former governess of Princess Mary. Pole was thus a potent figurehead of opposition, spiritual and political, and his household in Italy became a magnet for disaffected English subjects. Henry would soon grow to hate him, and do more than merely wish him dead.

In the meantime, the priority was to prove Pole wrong. A committee comprising Bishops Tunstall and Stokesley, Thomas Starkey and Cromwell's client Richard Morison pored over the work. Tunstall, whom Pole particularly requested to read it, sent the first in a series of reproachful letters, denying that Henry, in taking the title supreme head, separated himself from the unity of Christendom; he sought only to preserve his realm from 'captivity of foreign powers'. Tunstall was particularly concerned to correct Pole's misapprehension that the people as a whole disapproved of the King's proceedings, or that he himself went along with them out of cowardice: since coming to understand the true history of Christianity, Tunstall never thought 'to shed one drop of my blood' for the authority of the Pope. 'The King's highness hath in this realm men as well learned in divinity as be in other countries', he sniffed, men who 'have sought in this matter even to the bottom'.[91]

Tunstall's account of a realm contentedly united under the guidance of its Christian prince glossed over the inconvenient fact that he, like other loyalist conservatives, was fighting a battle on two fronts, simultaneously defending the supremacy against papalists, while trying to prevent it serving the agenda of reforming evangelicals, including Tunstall's fellow bishops.

The divisions were openly on display in Convocation, which convened alongside a new Parliament on 8 June 1536. Once the symbol of independent clerical authority, Convocation was now to be firmly subject to secular control: Cromwell sent a lay representative, William Petre, to sit alongside Archbishop Cranmer, and himself attended on several occasions. There was no fuss or bother about an early item of business: a confirmation of the nullity of the Boleyn marriage.

Proceedings opened on 9 June with a pair of confrontational sermons from Bishop Latimer – a calculated provocation to many in his audience, and an act of revenge for treatment received at the hands of Convocation four short years earlier. Latimer castigated the English clergy as latter-day incarnations of the gospels' unjust steward (Luke 16: 1–8), men unable to give good account of their office. They had inhibited preaching and the Word of God, and advanced 'man's inventions and fantasies': fraudulent relics, gilded images, superfluous holy days – all the while extorting money and gifts from the laity in the name of 'ancient purgatory pick-purse'.

The traditionalists who still dominated Convocation's lower house responded in traditionalist fashion, drawing up and presenting to Cranmer a list of sixty-seven errors and heresies now 'commonly preached, thought and spoken', as well as of 'slanderous and erroneous books', some of which, bearing the imprint 'cum privilegio', were believed by people to have the King's approval (although, they added tactfully, 'it was not so indeed'). The document condemned people who attacked saintly intercession and saints' days, and defended pilgrimage, veneration of relics and images, and suffrages for the souls in purgatory.[92]

It was not obvious in the early summer of 1536 whether Latimer's radical reformism, or the conservatives' comprehensive rebuttal of it, came closest to expressing the official mind of the Church of England. Prominent figures extolled the unity of the realm in dealings with overseas observers, but lamented its divisions when speaking frankly at home. Thomas Starkey sent Henry a long missive in the early summer of 1536, candidly admitting 'breach of concord and unity' as the consequence of the break with Rome. There would have been virtually no opposition to repudiation of the Pope, Starkey thought, had everyone been confident 'we should have slipped thereby to no further error nor pestilent opinion'.[93] Starkey thought the dissolution of some monasteries could, and should, be justified as a measure of necessary reform. Otherwise – like Tunstall, and like Gardiner, anxiously watching developments from his diplomatic posting overseas – his preference was for some form of Catholicism without the Pope.

That was not the shape of what emerged when, in July 1536, Convocation endorsed a first formal statement of doctrine for the independent Church of England: Ten Articles, 'devised by the King's Highness's Majesty to establish Christian quietness and unity among us, and to avoid contentious opinions'.[94] Some hope. The Ten Articles were a theological camel, the proverbial horse designed by a committee. They were also, like a pantomime horse, a thing of two distinct halves. The first five articles were placed in a special category, dealing with such matters 'as are commanded expressly by God, and are necessary to our salvation'. The remainder concerned lesser issues of 'decent order and honest policy'.

The Articles had been in development for some months, and were influenced by the 'Wittenberg Articles' Barnes probably brought back from Germany in May. Already at the beginning of April a group of bishops was closeted with Cranmer 'to discuss certain articles, as well as the reformation of church ceremonies'. Chapuys' information was that they were dead set to abolish purgatory, the observance of Lent, festivals of saints, and worship of images – all with the aim of plundering St Thomas's shrine at Canterbury, and other places of pilgrimage.[95]

The Ten Articles were considerably less bold than that. The article on 'Rites and Ceremonies' defended the utility of a raft of rituals and practices of which advanced evangelicals disapproved, such as kissing the cross on Good Friday. Another, on images, allowed that 'it is meet that they should stand in the churches', though making offerings or kneeling before them was discouraged. The article on praying to saints declared 'we may pray to our blessed Lady, to St John Baptist, to all or any of the apostles, or any other saint particularly, as our devotion doth serve us; so [long] that it be done without any vain superstition'. More than one hand was at work here. A surviving draft reveals that the first part of this sentence was written by Tunstall, the qualification added by Cranmer.[96]

Saints and images belonged to the secondary matters. The five non-negotiables were the Articles of Faith (i.e. the Creed), Baptism, Penance, the Sacrament of the Altar, and Justification. But here too there was negotiation, dispute and compromise. The affirmations of the ancient creeds and of infant baptism were uncontentious, and on the eucharist there was no real prospect of the Articles not insisting that 'under the form and figure of bread and wine . . . is verily, substantially and really contained the very self-same body and blood of our Lord Jesus Christ, which was born of the Virgin Mary'.

This was an unambiguous condemnation of sacramentarianism, and could be read as a straightforward endorsement of traditional teaching on transubstantiation. But the article avoided the term itself, and its wording is remarkably close to the Wittenberg Article 'On the Supper of the Lord'.[97] A Lutheran who believed the substance of bread remained alongside the true body of Christ could probably assent. Evangelicals of all stripes would have had more difficulty, however, with the article on penance. This not only asserted its status as a sacrament – a claim from which Luther and Melanchthon had retreated – but reaffirmed the authority of the priest in confession as the instrument of divine absolution.

On the crunch question of justification, the articles were – frankly – confusing. There was some distinctly Lutheran phraseology about how the sole sufficient cause of justification was 'the only mercy and grace of the Father, promised freely unto us for his Son's sake Jesus Christ, and the merits of his blood and passion', but it was hedged about with subtle qualifications. Good works would follow from, not precede justification, but in order to attain it God nonetheless demanded from people 'inward contrition, perfect faith, and charity'. And the consequent good works were also 'necessarily required to the attaining of everlasting life'. If he still had a head, Thomas More would have been shaking it in puzzlement.

In pulpits and parishes across the land, perhaps the most controversial question was the existence of purgatory. What Latimer described in his Convocation sermon as 'this monster, purgatory' represented to reformers everything that was wrong with the old order. The doctrine mattered, as it determined how ordinary people should remember their dead kinsfolk, and whether they should themselves at the end of life allocate valuable resources to investing in suffrages. It was also, in the summer of 1536, the most politically charged of doctrinal disputes. Starkey's letter to the King warned that many would think it an uncharitable act to dissolve monasteries when one of their chief functions was to provide prayers for the dead. In another missive sent to

Henry at this time, Latimer precisely agreed. But his conclusion was much more radical: 'the founding of monasteries argued purgatory to be, so the putting of them down argueth it not to be'.[98]

The metaphysical question of whether purgatory was to be, or not to be, was scarcely settled by the Ten Articles. The last of them was headed 'Of Purgatory', but went on to declare that 'the place where [departed souls] be, the name thereof, and kind of pains there' were all 'uncertain by scripture'. Prayer and masses for the dead were laudable works of charity, which might relieve souls of some part of their pains, but how exactly this worked, 'we remit to God'. Papal indulgences, *scala coeli* masses, and other 'abuses' were roundly condemned.[99]

The inability of modern historians to agree whether the Ten Articles were a victory for orthodoxy or for reform mirrors the confusion of contemporaries. The Emperor's proctor at Rome believed 'purgatory is preached again', and even Reginald Pole thought the Ten Articles treated purgatory 'much after the old manner'. But a participant in the episcopal debates, Bishop Barlow of St David's, frustrated by reports that 'purgatory is found again', revealed in a sermon later that year that the bishops found virtually nothing in scripture to justify prayer for the dead. As an ancient custom with some sanction from Church Fathers, they judged it 'meet and expedient' to continue, but had no intention to sanction 'popish purgatory'. Robert Wymond, evangelical parishioner of Rye in Sussex, put it more succinctly: 'There is no purgatory for purgatory is pissed out.'[100]

Articles intended to resolve doubts and quieten debates thus had the effect of exacerbating the former and inflaming the latter. The bishops who drew them up were deeply divided among themselves, and within Convocation, as the returning Wittenberg negotiator Nicholas Heath reported, 'were many who assented to the meaning of these articles only with great difficulty'. Their provisional and ambiguous character is epitomized by the extraordinary circumstance that they simply ignore four of the traditional seven sacraments. In the end, it took the King's personal intervention to secure Convocation's agreement. Henry later claimed to have been forced to 'put his own pen to the book, and conceive certain articles'. How much direct input Henry actually had is unclear; conceivably, his corrections contributed to the muddiness of the article on justification. But as soon as the Articles were subscribed by Convocation on 11 July, their prescriptive status was secure. By royal order, all ordinary preaching was prohibited until the end of September, so that the Articles could be distributed across the realm.[101]

The tone and character, rather than the precise substance of the Articles were what mattered. They signalled that the crown – or the vicegerent – was ready, not merely to tolerate demands for reform, but actively to direct the process. The Articles were immediately followed by a practical ordinance with huge local impact: at royal command, Convocation passed an act for 'abrogation of certain holydays'. Henceforth, all feasts commemorating the dedication of a local church were to be held on the first Sunday in October; all feasts of the church's patron saint were to cease to be holidays at all; and all feasts of any kind falling between 1 July and 29 September (the period of harvest) were similarly redesignated as normal days of work, with the exception of feasts of the Apostles, the Virgin Mary and St George.

This was a declared measure of economic rationalization: profusion of holidays encouraged idleness and theft, and contributed to the decay of crafts and industry. There was concern too about public order – the 'excess, riot and superfluity' created by occasions of 'licentious vacation and liberty'. But the evangelical hues of Latimer's sermon were very visible. Multiplication of holy days arose from 'superstition', rather than true devotion. These were inventions of man, unlike that more appropriate day of rest, the Sabbath, ordained by God.[102]

The instrument of enforcement for this directive, and for publicizing the Ten Articles, was a set of Royal Injunctions issued to the clergy in August on Cromwell's vicegerential authority.[103] These began, predictably, with insistence on the observance of laws 'for the abolishing and extirpation of the Bishop of Rome's pretensed and usurped power'. For the next three months, all priests were to concentrate on this theme every Sunday in sermons or other addresses to parishioners, and thereafter at least twice a quarter.

Much in the Injunctions was redolent of earlier episcopal efforts at moral and educational reform: clergy were not to haunt alehouses, or spend time dicing or playing cards; they should keep hospitality and give alms to the poor; they were to encourage parents to teach their children the Ten Commandments, Creed and *paternoster* (in English). But the reformist tone of the Ten Articles was maintained, and amplified. In a direct echo of the monastic visitation injunctions, clergy were ordered 'not to set forth or extol any images, relics or miracles for any superstition or lucre'. And with respect to pilgrimages and prayer to saints, the Injunctions underlined the negative warnings of the Articles while ignoring the countervailing positives.

One aspect of the Injunctions was completely novel: incumbents of parishes were to provide, by the feast of St Peter ad Vincula (1 August) following, 'a book of the whole Bible, both in Latin, and also in English, and lay the same in the choir, for every man that will to look and read thereon'. The King, it seemed, was delivering on his promise, made in 1530, to grant his people an English bible when the time for it was right.

The order, however, was decidedly premature, and only patchily implemented by bishops. Someone, most likely Cromwell, was forcing the pace. Convocation called for an English translation in December 1534, and the following year steps were taken towards production of an official version, with the task of Englishing different books of the bible parcelled out among the bishops. Gardiner informed Cromwell in June 1535 that he had, with 'great labour', finished his translations of St Luke and St John. But the exercise ran even less smoothly than other attempts at co-operation within the divided episcopate. Stokesley, assigned the Acts of the Apostles, refused to make any effort at all, and Cranmer feared the project would be completed 'a day after doomsday'.[104]

The impetus behind vernacular scripture in fact continued to lie with the evangelical exiles. The only complete printed translation of the bible in English was that produced, probably in Antwerp, by Miles Coverdale in October 1535. Coverdale's work built on Tyndale's, though for much of the Old Testament it depended on existing Latin rather than Hebrew versions. It enjoyed no official sanction, but Coverdale clearly expected – and was likely led by Cromwell to expect – that such sanction would soon be forthcoming. The frontispiece contained the earliest version of what would become a famous motif, an enthroned Henry VIII handing out bibles to bishops and nobles. The work carried a fulsome dedicatory epistle to the King, praising Henry as a Moses, delivering his people 'from the cruel hands of our spiritual Pharaoh'.[105]

There would have been no reason to undertake the work, Coverdale wrote, had others engaged on it not suffered 'impediment'. That was to put it delicately. Tyndale was seized by imperial officials in Antwerp in the spring of 1535, lured out of the safety of the English Merchants' House by a renegade Englishman, Henry Phillips. At a time when Cromwell was offering discrete encouragement to the English exiles, Phillips was boasting to acquaintances of an episcopal commission to arrest Barnes and Joye; it is possible that the operation against Tyndale was backed by Bishop Stokesley. After sixteen months of miserable imprisonment in the castle of Vilvorde, Tyndale was convicted of heresy and burnt, most likely on 6 September 1536.[106]

Tyndale's reported words at the stake – 'Lord, open the King of England's eyes!' – suggest he died without hearing that Royal Injunctions had ordered all English subjects be given access to the bible in English. Coverdale professed to be in no doubt that Henry would discover vernacular scripture to be an instrument of 'quietness and tranquillity'. The Injunctions shared the hope, but betrayed a note of anxiety. Readers of scripture should 'in no wise stiffly or eagerly contend or strive one with another about the same', but refer matters of interpretation to those better learned than themselves.[107] It was a genuinely pious hope.

By the time the mowers laid down their scythes in the early autumn of 1536, a harvest of change had been reaped in England. Anyone expecting the break with Rome to mean little beyond a change of leadership for the *Ecclesia Anglicana* had been confounded. Evangelicals walked relatively unscathed from the debacle of the Boleyn marriage, and were filled with a cautious optimism, and a not-so-quiet determination. Commissioners were on the road across England and Wales, seeing to the closure of hundreds of religious houses.[108] Purgatory, pilgrimage, prayer to saints – venerable mainstays of popular faith – were now official objects of censure and suspicion. And the abrogation of saints' days and parish festivals cut sharply into the rhythms and patterns of local religious life.

The 'Christian quietness and unity' demanded by the Ten Articles were scarcely anywhere in evidence. Not in places like St Michael's, Wood Street, London, where twenty-two parishioners reported their curate, Sir Thomas Jennings, for speaking 'contemptuous and abused words against the Injunctions'. Some accusers were committed evangelicals, though this was a parish emerging from a bitter tithe dispute, and others may have taken occasion to settle scores. At Bishop's Stortford and at Little Hadham in Hertfordshire, the curates and sextons maintained the Feast of the Exaltation of the Cross (Holy Rood day, 14 September) 'with ringing and singing'. It caused 'much dissension' with those who 'according to the King's commandment at that day went to their bodily labour'.[109]

How many parishioners went, cheerfully or dutifully, to work on this accustomed holiday is unknown. In an effort to pre-empt anticipated difficulties, Henry wrote to the bishops on 11 August, ordering them to warn clergy not to speak of abolished festivals in any way likely to cause 'the people . . . to murmur, or to condemn the order taken therein'.[110]

'Murmur' was a significant word: inarticulate, dissatisfied rumbling in the face of legitimate commands. The crime of More and other dissidents, Simon Matthew alleged in a Paul's Cross sermon the previous summer, was to give 'pernicious occasion to the multitude to murmur and grudge at the King's laws'.[111] Murmurers could not be heard, did not deserve to be. But in October 1536, the murmuring multitude finally spoke out, loudly and clearly, and their words shook the foundations of the kingdom.

## 8

## PILGRIMAGE ENDS

### Follow the Cross

WILLIAM BREYAR WAS a criminal, branded in the hand. He was a 'sanctuary man' at Colchester, and spent the summer of 1536 wandering around the Midlands and the north, on his travels picking up a badge that identified him as a servant of the King. At the end of September, he turned up in Dent, a village in the north-western Yorkshire Dales.

Breyar arrived to find the place in uproar. A few days earlier, on 25 September, 500 men from the surrounding parishes gathered to swear solemn oaths 'to suffer no spoils nor suppressions of abbeys, parish churches, or their jewels'. A local blacksmith spotted Breyar's royal livery, and started to pick a fight. 'Thy master is a thief, for he pulleth down all our churches in the country.' But others interjected: 'It is not the King's deed but the deed of Crumwell.' They added that 'If we had him here we would crum him and crum him that he was never so crummed, and if thy master were here we would new crown him.'[1] Was Henry a tyrant to be resisted, or a liege lord to be rescued from wicked advisors? It was a dilemma the northerners never quite managed to resolve.

Henry VIII was not pulling down all churches. But he was closing monasteries, and people feared where that might lead. A hundred miles to the south-west of Dent, in the Lincolnshire village of Louth, with its magnificent church and spire (see p. 14), those fears erupted still more forcibly. On Sunday 1 October, the vicar, Thomas Kendall, urged his flock to 'go together and look well on such things as should be inquired of in the visitation'. Dozens of priests were due in Louth the next day, to be examined by Bishop Longland's chancellor. It was a time of unprecedented official inspection and intrusion: the clergy visitation was taking place alongside the roving commission for dissolution of monasteries, and another making assessments for a parliamentary subsidy.

Bold talk during the mass procession preceded Kendall's sermon. Thomas Foster, yeoman and singing-man, shouted, 'Masters, step forth and let us follow the cross this day; God knoweth whether ever we shall follow it hereafter.' After evensong, a band of parishioners, headed by 'Captain Cobbler' – the shoemaker, Nicholas Melton – took the keys from the wardens and stood overnight guard in the church. A cold welcome awaited Longland's commissary, John Frankish, when he arrived the next morning. The insurgents issued a proclamation, demanding 'new books' be handed over. English New Testaments were collected and consigned to the flames, along with a work by John Frith.[2] Nowhere in England, it seemed, was untouched by the hand-print of heresy.

The concerns of Louth were local, practical: people feared new taxes, and confiscation of their crosses and treasures. But they saw an underlying pattern: 'heretics' were subverting the commonwealth, the good ordering of society. Vicar Kendall was a local man, but he was also an Oxford-trained theologian with experience of heresy-hunting in Essex. Kendall later claimed the immediate cause of the trouble was a rumour that inhabitants of Hull had been forced to sell church jewels to buy off the royal commissioners. But beyond this, 'people grudged very sore that the King's grace should be the supreme head, and the bishop of Rome put down'. For six months, a rising was spoken of, as everyone detested new opinions concerning Our Lady and purgatory.[3]

Events after 1 October moved fast. Contagious ringing of church bells across northern Lincolnshire signalled to villagers that neighbouring parishes were 'up'. From Louth a contingent marched to interrupt officials suppressing the nearby nunnery of St Mary's, Legbourne. At Caistor, subsidy commissioners were seized and forced to draft a letter to the King. One of their captors, the gentleman John Porman, admitted 'the King to be the supreme head of the Church' – there was a spectrum of opinion on this within the rebel ranks. But there must be no more arbitrary taxation or monastic suppressions. Despite professions of loyalty to the King, the rebels had murder on their minds: Cromwell was to be handed over, along with Bishops Cranmer, Latimer, Longland, Hilsey, Goodrich and Browne of Dublin, so that all could be put to death.

The conservative Longland sits incongruously in this list of evangelical reformers, but he was the local face of hated government policies. At Horncastle on 4 October, Longland's chancellor, Dr John Raynes, was brutally done to death. A suspected royal spy, bearing the eye-catching name of Thomas Wolsey, was summarily hanged.[4]

Through the first week of October Lincolnshire's army swelled. It was as a force of at least 10,000 that the rebels entered Lincoln on 6 October, trashing Longland's episcopal palace. Priests, secular and regular, flocked to the cause: perhaps as many as 800 were directly involved in the Lincolnshire Rising.

Landed gentry – the natural custodians of order – also got involved, while the most senior local nobleman, Catherine of Aragon's former chamberlain Lord Hussey, tried to negotiate with the rebels, before fleeing the county on 7 October. For some landowners, it was a case of ride the tiger or be mauled by it, but others shared their poorer neighbours' concerns about religious changes. Gentry had their own grievances: an act passed in the spring of 1536 clamped down on 'Uses', legal trusts to prevent the King levying inheritance tax on landed estates. A petition for its repeal was the second of six articles drawn up at Lincoln on 9 October. Others demanded an end to monastic dissolution and excessive taxation, and dismissal for councillors of 'low birth and small reputation' – Cromwell and Richard Rich. Cranmer, Latimer, Hilsey, Browne, Shaxton and Barlow were named as bishops who 'subverted the faith of Christ', along with Longland as an author of 'vexation'.[5]

Henry's reaction was predictably intemperate. His reply to the articles wondered how the commoners of one shire, 'the most brute and beastly of the whole realm', presumed to lecture him on appointments to the episcopate or Council.

In the event, the Lincolnshire rebels' nerve broke. There was talk of marching south, but on 11 October, with a small but well-equipped force under the Duke of Suffolk near at hand, the rebels obeyed the Earl of Shrewsbury's order to disperse. Shortly after, Suffolk received secret royal instructions: if trouble resumed, he should 'destroy, burn, and kill man, woman and child, to the terrible example of all others'.[6]

Vengeance would have to wait. Before the Lincolnshire Rising burned itself out, sparks had ignited in half a dozen other counties, and the north was ablaze. At the centre of the flames was a hitherto obscure figure, a one-eyed Yorkshire lawyer, about thirty-six years old. Robert Aske entered Lincolnshire on 4 October, supposedly making his way to London for the new law term, and was persuaded by the rebels to take up reins of leadership. Whether Aske was already contemplating rebellion is unclear. But he was undoubtedly his own man, and not merely an agent of the northern nobles whose legal business he occasionally handled.[7] Like Thomas More, Aske was that unlikely beast, a common lawyer passionately committed to the defence of the Church. More looked on impotently as the old order was dismantled, but Aske almost succeeded in restoring it.

On 11 October, as 'chief captain' of a spate of risings breaking out across the East Riding of Yorkshire, Aske issued a proclamation, calling upon his countrymen 'to preserve the church of God from spoiling'. A couple of days later, on a hill above the small town of Market Weighton, Aske's troops met with a force commanded by William Stapleton. On parting, Aske declared that 'they were pilgrims, and had a pilgrimage gate to go'. Proclamations over the coming days repeated the idea of 'a pilgrimage of grace for the commonwealth'.

It rapidly caught on. The 'pilgrims' were loyally petitioning for favour, 'grace', just as devotees might seek the blessing of a beloved saint. But the imagery was also provocative and insubordinate, a direct riposte to attacks on pilgrimage in the recent Royal Injunctions. And when pilgrims took up arms in defence of the faith, it had a special name: crusade.[8]

The government recognized the 'Pilgrimage' for what it was: armed rebellion on an unprecedented, unmanageable scale. By late October, eight well-equipped rebel armies were on the march, together comprising some 50,000 men.[9] It was a force far larger than any the King could hope to put into the field; larger than any army deployed by the crown in the entire course of the sixteenth century. With Suffolk pacifying Lincolnshire, Thomas Howard, Duke of Norfolk, was given command of what troops were available. Outnumbered and outmanoeuvred, he had little choice but to temporize. On 26 October, Norfolk arrived at Doncaster, and proposed a truce. The rebel forces drew up in array facing him, on the far side of the River Don. Immediate danger was averted: heavy overnight rain rendered the river temporarily unfordable. To the evangelical chronicler Edward Hall it seemed 'a great miracle of God'.[10]

Over the preceding weeks, the pilgrims had achieved remarkable things. On 16 October they entered York in triumph, and posted on the door of the Minster an order for the restoration of religious houses. Meanwhile, rebel armies in North Yorkshire, and in Lancashire, Cumberland and Westmorland put the aspiration into practice. From County Durham, a force marched south under a potent symbol of everything despised by the Cromwell regime: the banner of St Cuthbert, long reputed to work miracles in battle, festooned with ancient relics. Another Cuthbert – Tunstall, bishop of Durham – fled before the banner's approach.

A second conservative prelate, Archbishop Lee, prudently left York for the King's castle at Pontefract, whose custodian, Lord Darcy, represented royal authority in south-west Yorkshire. But on 20 October, without much hesitation, Darcy surrendered Pontefract to the rebels. Both he and Lee took the oath Aske composed: to be true to 'God's faith and to holy church militant and the maintenance thereof, the preservation of the King's person and his issue, and the purifying of the nobility and to expulse all villeins' blood and evil councillors against the commonwealth'.

Virtually all participants in the Northern Risings – gentry, clergy and commons – swore some such oath. It took its cue from the Oath of Succession, turning a mechanism of government control into an instrument of subversive popular politics. Once again, questions would arise about the validity of a coerced oath: in the aftermath of the Pilgrimage, numerous gentlemen insisted they swore under duress, and in fear of their lives.[11]

Darcy's own later protestations of loyalty were not entirely disingenuous. In September 1534 he had discussed with one of Chapuys' men the prospects for a rebellion in the north. But the events of 1536 were not the expected culmination of his plans. Surprised by the scale and speed of a genuinely popular rebellion, Darcy assumed a role of leadership while working for a peaceful resolution.[12]

Peaceful resolution was far from certain. Norfolk's proposal of truce was sent along with a face-saving challenge to battle if the rebels refused to disperse, and the commanders of the Pilgrim vanguard were eager to take up the offer to fight. Among the commons, it was taken for granted the host would march on London 'to sue the King to have certain statutes revoked and the makers punished'. Only a few days before Norfolk's arrival at Doncaster, Aske himself told Lancaster Herald his intention was 'to go with his company to London on pilgrimage to the King . . . to have the faith of Christ and God's laws kept, and restitution for wrongs done to the Church'. But with an offer of negotiation on the table, Aske, Darcy and Lee argued hard for restraint, trusting in Henry and Norfolk's good faith and willingness to make concessions. Agreement was reached on 27 October. Norfolk, master dissembler, had already written to the King, asking him to 'take in good part whatever promises I shall make unto the rebels, for surely I shall observe no part thereof'.[13]

The following weeks were as taut as a drawn bowstring. The fate of the Pilgrimage, of religious reform, and of Henry's throne itself, all hung precariously in the balance. Sir Ralph Ellerker and Robert Bowes, men who joined the movement under pressure, were chosen to carry the rebels' articles to the King, while the commons in the north were left wondering how far the gentry could be trusted not to betray them. The demands, as reported by the imperial ambassador in Rome, were for restoration of the Pope's authority, recognition of Princess Mary (and her parents' marriage) as legitimate, reversal of monastic dissolution, calling of a free Parliament, without royal servants, and repeal of recent statutes.

Henry was apoplectic. In a hastily drafted reply, he was adamant he had 'done nothing that may not be defended by God's law and man's'. He would consent to neither pardon nor Parliament. There would be mercy only after ten named ringleaders were handed over for exemplary punishment. The letter was a lighted match to gunpowder. Norfolk and other councillors, serving their master more ably than he served himself, were able to prevent its despatch northward, under the pretext that the rebels were ordering fresh musters, contrary to the truce.[14]

The hope in London was for the Pilgrimage, like the Lincolnshire Rebellion, to simply collapse. But the Pilgrims' resolution held, and Darcy – a man of honour – resisted Norfolk's inducements to switch sides and betray Aske. Worse, with a third of the realm openly defiant, there were reasons to fear for the loyalty of the rest. As early as 10 October, London aldermen were commanded to confiscate all weapons larger than a meat knife from priests between the ages of sixteen and sixty. Many among the clergy, like William

Gibson of Whittington College, believed 'the Northern men rose in a good quarrel'. In Reading, priests and laymen copied out the rebel demands, and such transcripts were said to be 'universal at London'. George Throckmorton managed easily to acquire one, along with a copy of the Pilgrim Oath, and a proclamation by Aske.[15]

The reformers' enemies were emboldened; some violently so. On 13 November, a misty early morning, Robert Packington, leading mercer and evangelical, a drafter of anticlerical legislation in Parliament, was shot dead in Cheapside. There were many theories, but no one was ever arrested. Robert Barnes preached defiantly at Packington's funeral on 15 November, but such oil to the flames was the last thing the authorities wanted, and he was packed off to the Tower. Other prominent London evangelicals – John Field, John Goodale, George Marshall and possibly John Bale – were likewise imprisoned by Cromwell, for their own protection.

Later that week, Henry penned a circular to the bishops on his favoured theme of divisions inflamed by 'contrariety of preaching'. The King observed that offence taken at the railing of seditious preachers against 'honest rites, customs and ceremonial things' was the principal cause of the 'commotion and insurrection'.[16] This was a disingenuous half-truth. What was dividing the nation were official policies – the dissolution of monasteries, the banning of saints' days, the promotion of 'heretic' bishops, the royal supremacy itself. But Henry was distancing himself from the unpopular face of reform, and – perhaps – mentally preparing for the possibility of yet more dramatic reversals.

Further evidence of southerners' sympathy for the Pilgrimage came to light in subsequent years, though never its full extent. Only later did the authorities learn that, in late November 1536, a 'secret friend' came to Aske from London with news of troop movements, confirmation that Cromwell was widely hated, and assurances that 'the south parts long for our coming'.[17]

That was optimistic. Ancient antagonisms between southerners and northerners might have made a march on London seem more like invasion than liberation. But the commotion of 1536 was never simply destined to remain a regional phenomenon, or even a self-contained English one. In November, as the Pilgrims waited anxiously for the return of Ellerker and Bowes, Darcy, Aske and Sir Robert Constable decided to send an emissary to Mary of Hungary, Charles V's regent in the Netherlands. They asked for money, 2,000 hand-gunners and 2,000 horsemen. At the last minute, the messenger was recalled – a symptom of the high-level prevarication that was to be the Pilgrimage's undoing.[18]

In the end, what mattered most were the calculations of a handful of nobles. The Earls of Shrewsbury, Derby, Cumberland, Huntingdon and Rutland, as well as the Duke of Norfolk, despised Cromwell and sympathized with many of the Pilgrims' aims. For as long as the movement remained contained, natural loyalty and raw self-interest bound these men to the King. Regions where trouble might have been expected, but little was reported – south Lancashire and Cheshire, Derbyshire, Nottinghamshire – were places where the influence of one or other of these magnates was strong. The terminal indecision of Henry Percy, 6th Earl of Northumberland, gave licence for rebellion to spread across much of Yorkshire.[19]

Loyalty and trust were commodities in which the King and his councillors cynically traded. Aske believed Henry would deal fairly, and could be persuaded or pressured into making concessions. Playing for time, the King complained that the demands conveyed by Ellerker and Bowes were unhelpfully vague. So the Pilgrim leadership reconvened at Pontefract at the beginning of December to draw up a definitive statement of their programme for reform. This was no deal behind closed doors. The twenty-four articles in the Pilgrims' final manifesto were agreed in consultation with representatives of all the rebel hosts. Items drafted by an assembly of gentlemen were presented for approval to parallel meetings of commons and clergy. Inevitably, there was something for everyone. The Statute of Uses was again roundly condemned, and complaints of the north-western peasantry about oppressive landlordism were prominently aired. The priests inserted a demand to reinstate full benefit of clergy.

But the Pontefract Articles were more than a patchwork of sectional grievances, bound with a thin stitching of traditional piety. They were a largely coherent manifesto of counter-revolution, beginning with a naming of the heretics whose pernicious opinions were injurious to 'our faith': 'Luther, Wyclif, Hus, Melanchthon, Oecolampadius, Bucer, *Confessio Germaniae* [the Augsburg Confession], *Apologia Melanchthonis* [the Apology of Melanchthon], the works of Tyndale, of Barnes, of Marshall, Rastell, St German, and such other heresies of Anabaptist'.[20]

The list was a shrewd one, conveying a traditional Catholic understanding of heresy as at once infinitely varied and basically always the same. It amalgamated historical heresiarchs, leading contemporary German and English reformers, and clients and agents of Thomas Cromwell: William Marshall, who published the heretical 1534 primer; John Rastell, who first defended, and then attacked, purgatory; the arch-anticlerical Christopher St German. Marshall and St German may have been known as sponsors of a recent parliamentary bill attacking pilgrimage and relics.[21] Far from ignorantly supposing 'Anabaptist' to be a person, or failing to understand the basics of evangelical theology, the Pilgrims astutely sought to tar Cromwell's regime with the brush of radicalism. In a variant version, the sacramentarian Frith is also named.

Other articles carried the critique of heresy into the realm of practical politics, with demands for the punishment of unorthodox bishops, and of Cromwell, 'maintainer of the false sect of those heretics'. Mary was to be restored to the succession, and a Parliament held at Nottingham or York, far from the controlling hand of the court. Most provocative of all was the second article: 'to have the supreme head of the Church touching *cure animarum* to be reserved unto the see of Rome as before it was accustomed to be'. This was to tell Henry straight that he was less than he thought himself; that his hard-won spiritual enlightenment was merely a pitiful self-delusion.

The article was not as confrontational as it might have been, limiting Rome's authority to spiritual matters: *cure animarum* means 'care of souls'. Headship of the Church was an issue on which the Pilgrims were divided. This was evident from proceedings in the clerical assembly, which functioned, in effect, as a meeting of the Convocation of the Province of York. Archbishop Lee, like other bishops who crossed the line in 1534, had the instincts of a Henrician. He caused dismay when, in a sermon preached in All Saints, Pontefract, on Sunday 3 December, he denied the right of subjects to take up arms without leave of the King. Others, like Robert Sherwood, chancellor of Beverley, resolutely defended Henry's headship.

But these were a minority. In their discussions, most delegates were unabashed to use the forbidden word 'pope', and showed themselves to be either unreconstructed papalists, or else committed to the view that royal 'supremacy' was solely political. There was some support for reinstating the formula Convocation adopted in 1531, a supreme headship extending 'as far as the law of Christ allows'. But the position finally endorsed was an uncompromising one: the Pope was head of the Church 'by the laws of the Church, General Councils, interpretations of approved doctors and consent of Christian people'. Archbishop Lee balked at this, but eventually agreed to the article on the grounds that papal authority did indeed command the consent of Christian people.[22]

That consent manifested itself in the winter of 1536–7. It is often supposed that papal headship was a preoccupation of Aske and other leaders, and a matter of relatively little concern in the parishes. In fact, the opposite may be true. Commons and gentry alike, thought Aske, 'grudged chiefly at the acts of suppression of abbeys and the supremacy of the Church'. John Dakyn, rector of Kirkby Ravensworth, heard 'ignorant persons of my parish' say 'the alteration of the power of the bishop of Rome was not good and should not stand'; he experienced angry reactions in Richmond when he exhorted townsfolk to accept the King as supreme head. In many parishes, layfolk demanded that priests bid the bedes after the old fashion, and pray publicly for the Pope. Bills expressing the same sentiment appeared attached to the doors of churches. Harry Gyll, subprior of Watton in the West Riding, thought the headship of the Church was 'in every man's mouth'. People were saying of the royal supremacy that, if it 'were not laid down, it should not do well'.[23]

This was the heart of the matter. Lay protest against the break with Rome was muted in 1533–4 because it was far from clear what the change actually meant. Three years on – after monastic suppressions, royal injunctions and lashings of heretical preaching on purgatory and saints – it had begun to seem that communion with Rome might after all be the guarantor of right faith and traditional ways. Henry's propaganda sought to persuade people that the bishop of Rome was the enemy of England and the enemy of truth. But other lessons were being learned in the practical school of schism.

Henry himself received a hard lesson in humility. With Norfolk and Suffolk arguing that there was no alternative to a general pardon and the promise of a free Parliament, the King reluctantly gave way. At a meeting in the Carmelite friary in Doncaster on 6 December, Norfolk relayed these terms, and (more or less on his own authority) agreed there should be no further suppressions until a Parliament could convene to resolve the religious issues. Two days later, Aske knelt in front of the Pilgrim delegates and begged them to call him captain no longer. He tore from his tunic the emblem the Pilgrims adopted: the Five Wounds of Christ enclosing a eucharistic chalice and host. All present did likewise, and called out, 'We will all wear no badge nor sign but the badge of our sovereign lord.'[24]

It was, it seemed, a total victory. Robert Aske had become one of the most powerful men in the kingdom. There was an unexpected invitation to spend Christmas at court, where Henry, in the company of his new wife, Jane Seymour, greeted Aske with all the false bonhomie of which the King was so effortlessly capable. But the commons were restive, suspicious. Many distrusted both the King and the gentry leaders who handled the negotiations and now consulted with them no more. They were right to be sceptical. The northern Parliament remained no more than a vague promise, and nothing beyond the pardon itself was committed to the Pilgrims in writing.

The promise of the Pilgrimage withered where it first bloomed, in the East Riding of Yorkshire. John Hallam, a former captain of the commons, feared a military crackdown, and hatched a conspiracy to pre-empt it by seizing the ports of Hull and Scarborough. He made common cause with the gentleman Sir Francis Bigod – an unlikely alliance, as Bigod was a convinced evangelical. But he strongly opposed the dissolution of monasteries, places he idealistically imagined transformed into centres of reformed worship. Bigod also disliked the very concept of royal supremacy. Their rising began, ill-planned and thinly supported, on 16 January 1537, and collapsed within a few days. Nonetheless, the attempt caused a ripple of renewed insurrection across the North and West Ridings, Lancashire, Cumberland and Westmorland.[25]

The pardon was breached. Unencumbered by moral or legal constraint, Norfolk returned to restore order. He was assisted by some who had opposed him the previous year: gentlemen like Robert Bowes and Ralph Ellerker. The gentry held aloof from the new rebellions, and, hoping the December agreement could remain intact, moved to suppress them. Outside Carlisle, on

17 February, a substantial rebel army of 6,000 was crushed by a force of borderers commanded by Sir Christopher Dacre: 800 were taken prisoner, an unknown number killed. The ideal of a harmonious commonwealth unravelled into frayed strands of mistrust and recrimination.

Retribution was swift and thorough. About 150 of those involved in the new outbreaks were hanged under martial law, including around twenty clergymen. The government also moved against Lincolnshire rebels not covered by the December pardon. The principal leaders of the Pilgrimage – Aske, Darcy, Constable – were summoned to London in February and March. They went, naively expecting royal gratitude for their efforts to uphold the King's authority. All were tried and executed on shaky evidence of renewed treason, along with Lords Hussey and Lumley, Sir Thomas Percy, and a dozen other gentlemen. A couple of dozen more fled to Scotland, there to brood, plot, and enflame the King's anger.[26] There would be no Parliament at Nottingham or York.

The Pilgrimage makes nonsense of a frequently asked question: why there was 'so little opposition' to Henry's religious policies. It was a massive movement of protest, which wrested a third of the kingdom from the royal grasp, and enjoyed unknown but considerable levels of sympathy in the rest. It gave Henry, quite literally, the fright of his life. Heads were bound to roll, but if the Pilgrims had pressed their advantage, they would have been different heads.

The failure of the Pilgrimage of Grace is explicable, but it was far from inevitable. Nonetheless, that failure was a watershed moment: the champions of the old order had drawn themselves up to their full height, and had been faced down. Contemporaries drew contrasting conclusions. Some pointed to the dangers of affronting the traditionalist instincts of the populace. For others, the rebellion proved the connection of old-fashioned religion to treasonous subversion, and the necessity of pressing on boldly with reform. In a tract against the rebels, Henry's propagandist Richard Morison insisted that 'preaching of the gospel is not the cause of sedition, but rather lack of preaching of it'.[27] The contest between these contradictory counsels, among the King's advisors, and in the King's own head, produced political conditions of unprecedented volatility in the years following.

### Sugar and Mustard

'It is evident that the King of England is running openly to his ruin and that God means to punish him.' The papal nuncio in France, Rodolfo Pio, bishop of Faenza, had from the first seen the Pilgrimage of Grace as a heaven-sent opportunity to humble the heretic king of England. In February 1537, he urged the Pope to consider that 'now is perhaps the time to make use of the Cardinal of England'.[28]

Reginald Pole was raised to the Sacred College in December 1536; at the start of the following year Paul III named him legate to the Valois and Habsburg courts. The letter of appointment designated him 'an angel of peace', mandated to promote the General Council the Pope had formally announced in June, and to secure pledges of assistance against the Turks. The real plan was to send him secretly to England, to join the Pilgrims and publicly command Henry to return to obedience.

It was all too late. Pio's letter was written a day after the rebels were routed outside Carlisle. At the end of March, Paul III handed Pole a powerful piece of spiritual weaponry: a bull granting the benefits of a crusading indulgence to anyone taking up arms to return Henry VIII to the faith ('better that he and his supporters die, than for them to take others to hell').[29] But by then, Aske was on his way to London, and an appointment with the hangman.

For papalists, the Pilgrimage was an opportunity lost. Evangelicals were determined to capitalize on its defeat. Cranmer wrote on 3 April to Heinrich Bullinger, Zwingli's successor in Zürich, that the conservative bishops and clergy had been humbled and weakened. He drew a parallel with the downfall of the German peasants in 1524–5. Just as that defeat stabilized the conditions for an orderly advance of reform, 'so we hope it will be for us'. A similar message was passed to the leadership of the Lutheran Schmalkaldic League, via Cranmer's agent in Strassburg, Thomas Theobald: 'as a result of the recent uproar in England, the evangelical bishops very much have the King's ear, and ... there is good hope of furthering the cause of the gospel'. The hope on Cranmer and Cromwell's part was that stalled negotiations with the German Protestants would now recommence.[30]

In January 1537, Henry summoned a 'Great Council' of notables to advise him on responding to the rebels' demands; it seems likely they recommended looking again at the Ten Articles. The task was delegated to another body meeting towards the end of February, a clerical synod convened under Cromwell's vicegerential authority.[31] Attendees included our main source of information on proceedings, a wandering Scottish Lutheran, Alexander Alesius, apparently invited to join the discussions after running into Cromwell in the street. That no abbots or priors seemingly took part indicated how the remaining religious houses were living on borrowed time.

The King, Cromwell informed delegates, was determined 'to set a quietness in the Church', and to resolve consciences about the controversies raging throughout Christendom. The divines were to debate 'friendly and lovingly', but Henry would not countenance doctrines that could not be proved from scripture, nor 'suffer the Scripture to be wrested and defaced by any glosses, any papistical laws, or by any authority of doctors or councils'.[32]

The most contentious issue was whether the sacraments omitted from the Ten Articles – confirmation, marriage, holy orders and extreme unction – were

to be readmitted. Cranmer's view was that they 'cannot be proved to be institute of Christ, nor have any word in them to certify us of remission of sins'. He
was backed by the prelates for whose heads the rebels had called – Latimer,
Shaxton, Goodrich, Foxe – but opposed by a phalanx of conservatives not
nearly as cowed and docile as Cranmer's letter to Bullinger made out: Lee of
York (lucky to be pardoned after reluctantly throwing in his lot with the
Pilgrims), Stokesley of London, Clerk of Bath and Wells, Sampson of Chichester,
and Repps of Norwich. Gardiner was absent as ambassador in France, but
Tunstall soon added heavyweight support.

Stokesley was the most forthright, questioning the ground rules Cromwell
laid down. He refused to accept that 'nothing pertaineth unto the Christian
faith but that only that is written in the Bible', boldly asserting that unwritten
traditions transmitted from the apostles 'be of like authority with the Scripture'.
This, according to Alesius, elicited wry smiles from the evangelical bishops as
they saw him revert 'unto his old rusty sophistry'.[33]

Vigorous lobbying continued, in committee and subcommittee, through to
the summer – at Lambeth Palace, at Foxe's London residence and elsewhere.
The conservative bishops conspired on Tunstall's barge journeying back and
forth to Lambeth on the Thames. Sampson later remembered poring with
Stokesley over some texts of the Greek Fathers – a useful source of tradition
untainted by papal endorsement.[34]

In the end, there was an agreed text: *The Institution of a Christian Man*,
known, then and since, as 'The Bishops' Book'. It was the outcome of tough
negotiation, and concessions on all sides. Gardiner heard how drafts passed
between Stokesley and Foxe, each making insertions and deletions, 'and so to a
new article'. Latimer found it exhausting, and prayed 'we shall not need to have
any more such doings'. It was 'a troublous thing to agree upon a doctrine in
things of such controversy . . . every man (I trust) meaning well, and yet not all
meaning one way'.

The result pleased everybody and nobody. Gardiner later described it as 'a
common storehouse, where every man laid up in store such ware as he liked,
and could tell where to find to serve his purpose'. It was a mixture of 'sugar and
mustard'.[35] The missing sacraments were, as Archbishop Lee gleefully put it,
'found again'. But the evangelicals ensured the scriptural principle remained
paramount. They were placed in a separate section of the text, reflecting 'a
difference in dignity and necessity'. Only baptism, penance and the eucharist
were 'instituted of Christ, to be as certain instruments or remedies necessary
for our salvation'.[36]

The conservatives scored some tactical victories. In defiance of Cranmer,
the article on extreme unction affirmed an efficacy for 'remission of sins'.[37] But
such coherence as the Bishops' Book possessed tended in an evangelical direction, and there was no real dilution of the semi-Lutheranism of the Ten Articles,

whose sections on justification, purgatory and the three sacraments 'instituted of Christ' it simply reproduced. Passages on the Creed, the Commandments, Lord's Prayer and Hail Mary were extensively indebted to William Marshall's Primer of 1535, which in turn drew heavily on Luther's writings.[38]

In one crucial respect, Marshall went further than Luther himself, and the Bishops' Book, remarkably and momentously, followed him. There was, since earliest Christian times, disagreement about the numbering of the Ten Commandments, which, as preserved in Exodus and Deuteronomy, actually contain a quantity of injunctions that could be construed as between nine and fourteen. St Augustine's view – retained by Luther – was normative for the medieval western Church: the prohibition on making 'graven images', and on worshipping them, was part of the first commandment, 'Thou shalt have no other gods before me'. But Jewish tradition, followed by the Orthodox Churches of the east, always saw these as separate commandments.

Zwingli's church at Zürich, preoccupied with the dangers of 'idolatry', was responsible for reintroducing the Hebrew enumeration to the Christian west. The idea was picked up by English reformers, including Tyndale and George Joye, from whose *Ortulus Anime* the revised numbering found its way into Marshall's Primer.[39] The Bishops' Book drew back from the Zürich inference: that the second commandment prohibited all images of Christ or the saints. But the tone of its exposition was bracing, stressing the undesirability of representations of God the Father, and castigating those who 'be more ready with their substance to deck dead images gorgeously and gloriously, than with the same to help poor Christian people, the quick and lively images of God'.[40] This was the language of Latimer, and of the Lollards.

Evangelicals knew they had won a victory, albeit narrowly on points. Cranmer reacted furiously when word reached him that servants of the conservative Kentish gentleman Sir Thomas Cheyney were saying 'all things are restored by this new book to their old use'. If people were to read it carefully, Cranmer expostulated, 'they shall well perceive that purgatory, pilgrimages, praying to saints, images, holy bread, holy water, merits, works, ceremony, and such other be not restored to their late accustomed abuses, but shall evidently perceive that the word of God hath gotten the upper hand of them all'.[41]

The Word of God continued to press its advantage in the summer of 1537, as Cranmer and Cromwell strove to overcome the embarrassing anomaly of the 1536 Injunctions ordering parishes to acquire a vernacular bible, without the authorities managing to make an approved vernacular version available. In Antwerp, John Rogers completed Tyndale's translation and published it under the name of Thomas Matthew. The evangelical printer Richard Grafton financed the edition and arranged for its importation into England, sending copies to Cromwell and Cranmer with requests for a royal licence to protect his monopoly. By the second week in August, Cromwell had shown this 'Matthew

Bible' to the King and obtained authorization for it to be sold throughout the realm. On hearing the news, Cranmer told the vicegerent he had given him more pleasure 'than if you had given me a thousand pound'.[42]

Their morale high, the evangelicals pushed forward. In the week the Bishops' Book was completed, Cranmer presided at an interrogation of the vicar of Croydon, Rowland Philipps, a friend of More and Fisher, who swore the oath only reluctantly in 1534, and remained a marked man thereafter. Over two days Philipps was examined closely over comments about evangelical preaching, the relationship between faith and works, and the scope of scriptural authority.

Philipps was no ignorant country curate, to be browbeaten with episcopal learning. An intricate dance of question and response illustrates how well the two sides now understood each other. Cranmer demanded to know 'whether the apostles preached to the gentiles that which the evangelists wrote?' But Phillips tartly riposted that 'the evangelists wrote that that the apostles had preached'. It was the issue at the heart of the confrontation between Tyndale and More: which came first, the bible or the Church?

A careless reply to one question might have cost Philipps his head: 'whom he meant by the Catholic Church, when he said that the Catholic Church shall never err in things that be necessary for salvation?' His answer was a masterclass in the kind of creative obfuscation Henry's Reformation unintentionally but persistently encouraged: 'He meant the universal multitude of Christian people, as well laymen as the clergy, subjects as rulers.' Philipps did enough, for within a month William Marshall was complaining about the vicar of Croydon as one of several London clergy 'which have preached both erroneously and seditiously, and without punishment have escaped'.[43]

Although finished in July, events conspired to delay printing of the Bishops' Book and its presentation to the King: plague in London, the chronic illness of its principal compiler, Bishop Foxe, who, like his episcopal colleagues, remained unsure 'whether the book shall go forth in the King's name or that of the Bishops'. Not until the end of August 1537 was the final product ready for royal perusal.[44]

That perusal was, apparently, perfunctory. In a reply to the authors, Henry professed to be pleased with what he saw, and commanded that for three years it should be taught to the people, with parts read from the pulpit every Sunday and feast day. But he also claimed he had 'no time convenient' to look properly through the book, and being 'much otherwise occupied, we have taken, as it were, a taste'. It would not go out under the King's name.[45]

The King, of course, had much on his mind; not least, the condition of Queen Jane, seven months pregnant. But it stretches credulity that, in a matter of such importance, and involving one of his keenest interests (theology), he really only glanced lightly through the work. In fact, Henry did not entirely like what he saw, but was not ready publicly to repudiate the efforts that his bishops had gone to. It was, or should have been, a warning sign: Henry was prepared to extend the evangelicals credit, but not to underwrite their debts. It also revealed the surprising pragmatism of a king who talked much of the need to ensure unity, and to provide secure guidance to his subjects, but who in matters touching their eternal salvation was happy to refer them to a merely draft handbook.

The Bishops' Book was printed five times before the end of 1537, but already on 10 October, Cromwell's secretary Thomas Wriothesely was writing to Thomas Wyatt, English ambassador at the imperial court, to say he had not bothered to send him a copy 'because the same shall be reformed, as it had need in many points'.[46] The King himself took the task in hand, and through the remaining weeks of the year produced dozens of pages of detailed objections and emendations. He threw himself more energetically into the work after joy at the birth of the longed-for male heir, Prince Edward, on 12 October, turned into grief for the death of the baby's mother just under a fortnight later.

Henry's editorial interventions were pedantic and idiosyncratic. Most notoriously, he took it upon himself to improve the wording of both the Ten Commandments and the Lord's Prayer. He wanted the final petition of the latter to read 'and suffer us not to be led into temptation' (rather than 'lead us not into temptation'). And he amended the First Commandment ('Thou shalt have none other gods but me') to read 'Thou shalt not have nor repute any other God, or gods, but me Jesu Christ'. Cranmer took a deep breath and responded, with commendable restraint, that 'we should not alter any word in the scripture, which wholly is ministered unto us by the Ghost of God'.

There were patterns to the King's nit-pickery. One was systematic reinforcement of his authority as supreme head, and a downgrading of the spiritual powers of bishops and clergy. Where, with respect to the clergy, the book spoke of laypeople 'committed to their spiritual charge', Henry inserted a revised order of priority – 'our and their spiritual charge'. 'Holy orders' became merely 'orders'. The other tendency was an effort to weaken, even undermine, the book's emphasis on the sufficiency of faith for salvation; Henry made numerous insertions about the need for perseverance in obedience, laws, duty and 'Christian life'.[47]

Henry's revisions were written up in neat scribal copy, and by 14 January 1538 passed to Cranmer, who set aside all business to produce twenty-nine pages of detailed counter-commentary. He hoped the King would pardon his presumption, 'that I have been so scrupulous and as it were a picker of quarrels to his Grace's book, making a great matter of every light fault, or rather where no fault is at all'. The courtesy was sugar-dust on a courageous and excoriating critique. At every point, Cranmer argued against the assumption Henry inherited from late medieval Catholicism – that God's offer of saving grace was something to which the human will could productively respond with good works. For Cranmer, as for Luther, good works followed from faith. This faith was itself a gift of God – not intellectual assent, but an 'assured hope and confidence' in the boundless mercy of Christ. The emendations show Cranmer following the logic of Luther's teaching on justification further than Luther himself was prepared to go. If human free will played no part in salvation, then of his own unrestrained volition God decided the fate of every human soul: some were 'predestined' to salvation, others to damnation. 'The elect', Cranmer was convinced, would never ultimately fall away.[48]

It did little good. Henry incorporated a few suggestions, but largely stuck to his theological guns. A neat scribal copy of the Bishops' Book, so heavily emended it deserves to be called a first 'King's Book', was soon produced, but never authorized or published. The Church of England had been given a definitive statement of doctrine by its supreme temporal and spiritual head, but only Henry, and a handful of advisors, knew what it was. For the moment, as Bishop Sampson told his commissary, the King was content that 'the book lately put out . . . should be obeyed and may be taught till that His Majesty shall otherwise order'.[49]

### Things Tending to Idolatry

The King had signalled – privately – his instinctive preference for the old over the new in the great battle of ideas over salvation. But there was to be no reprieve for the institutions that epitomized the centrality of good works in late medieval Catholicism. The monasteries' part in the Pilgrimage of Grace confirmed Henry's suspicions that the religious were the least reliable of his subjects. 'All these troubles have ensued', he confided to Norfolk in February 1537, 'by the solicitation and traitorous conspiracies of the monks.'[50]

The suppression of the Pilgrimage suggested new ways forward. Several superiors, implicated to varying degrees, were executed in the spring of 1537: the heads of houses at Kirkstead and Barlings in Lincolnshire, Whalley in Lancashire, Jervaulx and Bridlington in Yorkshire. The lands and goods of traitors were forfeit to the crown, and, on the legally dubious argument that a monastery's possessions were the property of its abbot, these houses were seized and dissolved. A similar fate lay in store for Roger Pyle, Cistercian abbot of Furness in remote north-west Lancashire. He played a risky double game during the Pilgrimage, fleeing before the rebels while allowing his monks to raise tenants in their support. Henry's lieutenant, the Earl of Sussex, under orders to investigate Pyle's conduct, suggested a lifeline, and Pyle eagerly grabbed it. In a document dated 5 April 1537, the abbot declared he did 'freely and wholly surrender, give and grant unto the King's Highness' all lands, rents and properties of the house, citing 'the misorder and evil life, both unto God and our Prince, of the brethren of the said monastery' as the reason.[51]

A crucial precedent was thus established: for 'voluntary' surrender of monasteries to the crown. It was at its least voluntary in the case of the next monastery to go – the London Charterhouse, still traumatized by the execution of its prior in 1535. The monks there had sworn to the succession, but thereafter continued to resist pressure to make an unequivocal acknowledgement of the supremacy. In May 1537, as Darcy, Hussey and Aske went on trial, commissioners returned to demand it again. Ten Carthusians – three priests, a deacon and six lay brothers – refused and were carted off to Newgate, starving to death there through the stifling summer months. Twenty others, including the prior, William Trafford, reluctantly agreed to subscribe, though, according to the later account of one of their number, they did so after beseeching God to forgive the sin they were about to commit with their lips 'contrary to the law of our mind'. A month later this shattered remnant was cajoled by Cromwell's agent Thomas Bedyll into setting their seal to a surrender document, confessing that their offences merited 'the severest death', and throwing themselves on the mercy of the King.[52]

Further surrenders followed towards the end of 1537: Lewes in Sussex, Castle Acre in Norfolk, Wardon in Bedfordshire, Titchfield in Hampshire. It may have been around now that Henry made the final decision to sweep monasticism away in its entirety.[53] But if so, the intentions of the government, and the inclinations of the King, remained hard for people to read. In December, a lavish royal refoundation of the Benedictine abbey of Chertsey was completed, on the site of the dissolved priory of Austin canons at Bisham in Berkshire. The abbot and thirteen monks were to offer prayers for the King's good estate during his life, 'and for the soul of Jane his late queen'. Latimer believed the founding of monasteries to be an argument for the existence of purgatory, yet in the final, unissued, royal revision of the Bishops' Book, that word was conspicuously removed.[54]

By the beginning of 1538 the end of monasticism was widely believed to be at hand. Richard Layton wrote to Cromwell from Norfolk on 18 January to report rumours 'that the King was determined to suppress all monasteries'. Layton publicly declared that those who said so 'slandered their natural sovereign', and ordered abbots and priors 'they should not, for any such vain babbling of the people, waste, sell, grant or alienate any of their property'. In March, Cromwell despatched a circular to abbots and priors commanding such practices to stop, and assuring them the King 'does not intend in any way to trouble you or devise for the suppression of any religious house that standeth, except they shall desire it themselves'.[55]

Cromwell's denial that any such decision had been taken virtually confirms for us that it had. Maybe, in anticipating a total dissolution, the monks helped bring it on themselves: the government needed to move fast to ensure that the very considerable financial assets of the religious houses flowed undiminished into the newly established government department known as the 'Court of Augmentations'. A trickle of 'voluntary' surrenders through the early months of 1538 had by late summer become a steady flow, with commissioners travelling in circuits to bully and cajole the religious into giving up their communal life.

The dissolution of the monasteries was not only – or even primarily – an exercise in aggressive state fiscalism. It was a spectacular, public, evangelical campaign, announcing the purification of the English Church, and denigrating the values and ideals the monasteries had stood for. Deeds of surrender, their wording dictated by royal commissioners, repudiated monastic life as a farce and a fraud. The Franciscans of Bedford now realized that 'perfection of Christian living doth not consist in dumb ceremonies, wearing of a grey coat, disguising ourselves after strange fashions, ducking and becking, in girding ourselves with a girdle full of knots, and other like papistical ceremonies'. Benedictines, like those of St Andrew's, Northampton, confessed to having lived lives filled with pride, idleness and luxury. Worse, for 'damnable lucre', they seduced layfolk from the true faith of Christ, 'stirring them with all persuasions, engines and policy, to dead images and counterfeit relics'.[56]

People had been piteously deceived. That was the message the King and his advisors wanted the world to learn, as a forest of monasteries came crashing down in 1538, laying waste to a spiritual eco-system of shrines, pilgrimages and cultic images. Instances of monastic 'fraud' supplied potent justification for the King's proceedings. In February, commissioners suppressed the Cistercian monastery of Boxley (Kent), whose famous crucifix, the 'Rood of Grace', had long attracted pilgrims and offerings. They discovered, on prising it from the wall, that it had 'certain engines and old wires' in the back, allowing the eyes and lips to be moved. It is likely these mechanisms originally served some ceremonial or liturgical purpose, but the authorities seized upon this 'proof' that miracles were being faked, and pilgrims hoodwinked. The rood was paraded in the marketplace at Maidstone, then shown to King and courtiers in London. On 24 February, it was exhibited at Paul's Cross, where Bishop Hilsey denounced its 'idolatry and craft' before handing it to apprentices in the crowd for ritual dismemberment. In the same sermon, Hilsey produced another shocking revelation: the relic of Christ's Blood in the shrine at Hailes in Gloucestershire, he had it on good authority, 'was but a duck's blood'.[57]

The spring and summer of 1538 saw open season on relics and images. In March, Lord Lisle's man of business, John Husee, wrote ruefully to his master in Calais that 'pilgrimage saints go down apace'. The London chronicler Charles Wriothesley designated this as the year when 'all manner [of] images that were used for common pilgrimages both in England and Wales were taken down throughout this realm in every shire by the King's commandment', adding loyally 'that the people should use no more idolatry to them'.

London was the crucible of the campaign. Prominent crucifixes were removed from Bermondsey Abbey, and from the north door of St Paul's Cathedral. In May, iconoclasts destroyed the much venerated rood at St Margaret Pattens, believing, so they claimed, they had Cromwell's mandate for the action.[58] But efforts by zealous commissioners and evangelical bishops extended the purge into the furthest corners of the land. Sir William Basset sent Cromwell images associated with two healing wells, St Anne from Buxton, and St Modwen from Burton-on-Trent, assuring him he had confiscated the offerings and defaced the tabernacles, so that 'there should be no more idolatry and superstition there used'. In Wales, Bishop Barlow seized relics associated with the titular saint at his own cathedral of St David's, and put an end to a 'devilish delusion' at Cardigan Priory, where a miraculous candle, 'Our Lady's taper', supposedly flickered eternally. The clergy were ordered to declare to the people 'the deceitful juggling of their predecessors there'. At Worcester, Latimer removed from the cathedral the renowned image of Our Lady, 'the devil's instrument to bring many (I fear) to eternal fire'. Fire was what Latimer had in mind: he wrote to Cromwell suggesting 'our great Sibyll' be burned at Smithfield, along with 'her old sister of Walsingham, her young sister of Ipswich, with their other two sisters of Doncaster and Penrice'. In July, the two famous Virgins, of Walsingham and Ipswich, were indeed brought up to London, 'with all the jewels that hung about them', and on Cromwell's orders burned at Chelsea.[59]

For the citizens of London, these spectacles of the ritual execution of spiritually treasonous objects were interspersed with the putting to death of politically treasonous subjects. In February 1538, an Irishman and an English priest, Sir John Alane, were hanged, drawn and quartered at Tyburn, and in March the same fate befell a Plymouth gentleman, Thomas Harford, 'for seditious words of treason against the King's Majesty'.

On 22 May, the two forms of exemplary destruction came together in gruesomely spectacular fashion. A Franciscan Observant, John Forest, was burned in a suspended cage before a huge crowd at Smithfield, after a three-hour sermon by Latimer. Wood for the pyre was provided by a giant pilgrimage statute from North Wales, the image of St Derfel or Dderfel Gadarn, reputed to rescue from hell anyone who made offerings before it.

Forest reportedly made similar claims about the powers of Catholic confessors, which may have prompted the idea – on the part of Cromwell, Cranmer or Latimer – of staging this bizarre dual execution. But the principal reason Forest was burned as a heretic, rather than hanged as a traitor, was his refusal to abjure the opinion that 'the Holy Catholic Church was the Church of Rome'. Here, in its purest, most brutal form, was the logic of the royal supremacy as a religious dogma; a declaration of all-out theological war. Yet it was an experiment never to be repeated. Henry and Archbishop Cranmer shared a hatred of friars, particularly ones who hypocritically conformed (Forest took the oath with his 'outward man') while secretly proselytizing for Rome. But classifying papalists as heretics risked causing great and gratuitous offence to the Catholic powers in Europe. Ominously, just a week before Forest's execution, delegates of Charles V and Francis I began negotiations for a treaty of amity, an outcome fraught with dangers for England.[60]

In August, the truce between the Emperor and the King of France was concluded. At Nice, the two old foes swore to unite to protect Europe from the Turks, while agreeing to persuade heretics 'amicably' to return to the Church. The Pope's legate, Reginald Pole, once again saw 'the finger of God' at work, and an opportunity to remove once and for all 'that tyrant', Henry VIII.[61]

As the summer of 1538 drew to a close, traitors – political and spiritual, living and dead – loomed large in the King's imagination. Two events, seemingly unconnected, followed close upon each other with suspicious despatch. On 18 August, Cranmer wrote to Cromwell to voice his suspicion that the relic of the blood of St Thomas Becket, venerated in the cathedral at Canterbury, 'is but a feigned thing, and made of some red ochre or of such like matter'; he had ordered an investigation. On 29 August, Cromwell decided to act on information coming into his hands earlier that summer: Sir Geoffrey Pole, Reginald's younger brother, was arrested and sent to the Tower.[62]

Two exterminations proceeded in parallel: of Cardinal Pole's English family, and of the cult and memory of England's premier saint. Psychologically broken in the Tower, Geoffrey Pole began to talk. On his evidence, others were taken: Pole's elder brother, Lord Montagu, and his cousin, the Marquis of Exeter, along with their wives and children; Montagu's brother-in-law, Sir Edward Neville; Pole's mother, Margaret, Countess of Salisbury; a clutch of family chaplains and dependants. It emerged that Pole's kin had retained contact with him during his exile, and that there had been much disaffected talk among Lady Margaret's circle at Warblington Castle in Hampshire. But despite the claims of government propagandists, there was no 'Exeter Conspiracy'. Almost the worst that could be proved against the Marquis was his saying, 'I trust to see a merry world one day.'

Exeter, Montagu and Neville were beheaded on Tower Hill in December. The plebeian traitors – Montagu's servant, Hugh Holland (a bearer of letters to the cardinal), his chaplain John Collins, the chancellor of Chichester, George Croftes – were hanged and quartered at Tyburn. Geoffrey Pole was pardoned in return for his evidence, and, after two unsuccessful attempts at suicide, slunk pitifully to Rome to seek fraternal pardon for his role as the instrument of Henry VIII's vengeance.[63]

That vengeance reached down the centuries to trouble the long-dead. While Geoffrey Pole was being taken apart by his interrogators in the Tower, Cromwell was at work on a new set of Royal Injunctions. These reiterated the order from 1536 for parishes to acquire an English bible. No priest, 'privily or apertly', should discourage any man from consulting it, but rather exhort every person in his parish to read 'the very lively word of God', though the explanation of 'obscure places' was referred to 'men of higher judgement'. The purgative icon-oclasm of the preceding months now extended to the heart of parish worship. Images 'abused' with pilgrimage offerings must be taken down and destroyed ('delayed'). No lights were to burn in front of images, other than on the rood loft before the crucifix. They were also allowed at the Easter sepulchre, and before the reserved sacrament. But the banning of one of the most routine of religious acts – lighting a candle in front of the statue of a saint – signalled a profound change of devotional repertoire. Such age-old habits, along with praying on rosary beads, were 'works devised by men's fantasies', 'things tending to idolatry and superstition'.[64]

By the time the Injunctions were issued at the end of September, a further clause was added: there was to be no celebration of any kind around the feast of 'Thomas Becket, sometime Archbishop of Canterbury'. St Thomas of Canterbury was the premier domestic saint of medieval England; his shrine at Canterbury a site of European significance. But as a martyr for the liberties of the Church against royal encroachment, he embodied everything Henry VIII had grown to detest. The King himself arrived in Canterbury on 5 September, towards the end of a progress through Kent. His coming was planned to coincide with the most audacious iconoclastic spectacle of the reign to date. King and court were treated to a performance of a new play by the ex-friar John Bale, 'On the Treasons of Becket', and royal commissioners dismantled the shrine in the cathedral, removing cartloads of treasure, and burning the bones of the saint.[65]

Much that Henry sanctioned over the preceding years had scandalized opinion in Catholic Europe. But the action against Becket ramped up interna-tional indignation to new levels. In December 1538, it provoked Paul III to issue publicly the excommunication lying suspended, and in hope of Henry's amendment, since August 1535. The bull alleged that a formal trial and condemnation of Becket had taken place (improbable, but not impossible), and roundly condemned a ruler who, 'not contented with the cruel slaughter of living priests and prelates, has not been afraid to exert his savagery also upon the dead'. To Pole, writing to Charles V, it seemed that what had taken place was nothing less than an 'extraordinary and unique ungodliness'. What, he asked rhetorically, would this king not dare to do – 'Will he rewrite history?'[66]

People within England had differing perspectives of the remarkable, dizzying events of 1538. Evangelicals rejoiced: a spate of poems and treatises applauded the King's proceedings and mocked the superstitious follies swept away by them.[67] The decision to target suspect relics, forged miracles and superstitious image-worship was tactically adept. This was the soft underbelly of popular religion, equally unpalatable to the humanist reformism of the King, and the more full-blooded evangelicalism of Cromwell, Cranmer and Latimer. Conservatives could scarcely protest at the unmasking of 'abuses', and even Gardiner, returning from diplomatic service at the end of September, was able to say, perhaps through gritted teeth, that he 'misliked not' the proceedings at Canterbury. Some even deluded themselves that, shorn of 'superstition', traditional religious life might continue as before. In November 1538, Katharine Bulkeley, Benedictine abbess of Godstow in Oxfordshire, wrote solemnly to reassure Cromwell that 'there is neither pope, purgatory, image nor pilgrimage, nor praying to dead saints used amongst us'.[68]

To others, what was taking place was nothing less than sacrilege, more likely to provoke than to placate the avenging powers of heaven. A fire that broke out in the London parish of St Margaret Pattens in May 1538, taking nine lives, was thought to be a judgement on the recent destruction of the rood. In the summer, rumours spread in Salisbury that an angel had appeared to the King, commanding him to go on pilgrimage to St Michael's Mount, a message reinforced by the ghost of Jane Seymour. In the January snows of 1539, the Norfolk magistrate Roger Townsend placed in the stocks a woman from Wells for starting a rumour that Our Lady of Walsingham performed miracles after her removal to London the previous summer. He feared that, despite its destruction, 'the said image is not yet out of some of their heads'.[69]

Many Walsingham folk, robbed not only of a beloved icon but of a means of attracting wealth and trade to their little town, surely sympathized with the woman shivering in the stocks. But the young people and boys pelted her with snowballs. Here, and almost everywhere, opinion was divided, polarized – still more so than in 1533. In the garrison town of Calais, so the Welsh soldier Elis Gruffydd recalled, St Thomas of Canterbury caused 'much discussion among the people, some simple folk saying that he was a holy and saintly man, others that he was a wilful traitor to his king'. In the dedicatory epistle to the King attached to his 1538 English–Latin New Testament, Miles Coverdale bemoaned the tendency among enemies of the Gospel to break out into 'blasphemous and uncomely words'. They called loyal subjects 'heretics, new-fangled fellows, English biblers, cobblers of divinity, fellows of the new faith'.[70]

The devotees of vernacular scripture were every bit as fractious as its detractors. A Rotherham schoolmaster, William Senes, scorned the parish clerk's pious affirmation that he would believe as his father had done. 'Thy father was a liar and is in hell, and so is my father in hell also. My father never knew scripture, and now it is come forth.' At Barking in Suffolk, in autumn 1538, Hugh Buck crossed swords with the traditionalist priest John Adryan, who ordered him to believe as 'thy father and mother taught thee'. All they ever taught him, Buck riposted, was 'my *paternoster, ave* and *credo* in Latin', as well as 'idolatry'. Had they not, Adryan objected, 'bade thee love thy Lord God above all thing'? 'Nay, that was taught me since.'

Senes and Buck were men remorselessly repudiating everything that went before, including ties of ancestry and blood. It was an instinct shared by William Maldon, a young apprentice from Chelmsford in Essex, who in 1539 told his devout mother that praying in front of the crucifix was 'plain idolatry, and plainly against the commandment of God'. She was not prepared to be schooled by her own son: 'Thou thief! If thy father knew this, he would hang thee.' To Maldon, 'the glad and sweet tidings of the Gospel' heralded the dawn of a new age, just as they did for Robert Towson, instigator of a row in a Cambridge shop in April 1538. Until recently, he pronounced, there was never a good man in England – except for a few who were burned. When someone artfully asked him if the King were not a good man, Towson refused to waver: 'No, all was nought till within this six years.'[71]

In his own mind, Henry VIII's religious reforms were shaped by three core principles: unity, obedience and the refurbishment of ancient truth. Their manifest effect was to fracture unity beyond the point of obvious repair, and to stretch obedience to its very breaking point. At the same time, both opponents and supporters of the changes saw in them not stately restoration, but a transpicuous and challenging novelty. As religious houses disappeared apace from the physical and cultural landscape of the nation, the meanings of 'religion' itself were starting to alter and mutate. What had once been an inherited stake in the ritual life of the community was becoming – for some – an alternative, ideological marker of individual and group identity. In the years remaining to him, the King would redouble his efforts to compel his subjects into uniformity, while the English people increasingly worked out for themselves what, and how, to believe.

# PART III

*New Christianities*

# 9

## MUMPSIMUS AND SUMPSIMUS

### Extirpation of Diversities

IN THE SUMMER of 1538, John Harrydance, a London bricklayer, became a minor celebrity. He preached the Gospel, day and night, from his window, and from a tree in his garden – an eyewitness thought there were a thousand people at some of these sermons. Harrydance defied his critics among local clergy and laity: it was 'no marvel if the world doth persecute holy men and setters forth of light'. When the city authorities failed to silence his preaching, Cranmer hauled him in for a warning. Like the old Lollard he probably was, Harrydance recanted, and bore his faggot at Paul's Cross.[1]

John Harrydance was not the stuff of martyrs, yet this divinely inspired bricklayer was a symptom of something amiss in the commonwealth: the King's lay subjects were supposed to receive true religion – from approved texts, liturgies and preachers – not fashion it for themselves, teach it to others, or pre-empt the rulings and reasonings of royal authority. It was widely known in London that elsewhere in the realm – for example, at Hadleigh in Suffolk and Stratford in Essex – priests were saying the mass in English. Others proceeded to take wives 'without a common consent of his highness and the realm'. They did so unaware that this was a path Archbishop Cranmer had already taken, a closely guarded secret the King himself may not have known.[2]

Impatient priests and evangelical layfolk pulled ahead of the pack, yet into the late autumn of 1538, the official campaign against relics and pilgrimages continued to move forward. Hilsey preached again at Paul's Cross on 24 November, and revealed the results of an inquiry concluding that the blood of Hailes was not after all duck's blood, but 'honey clarified and coloured with saffron'.[3] But threats to true religion of a different sort were once again preying on the King's mind.

In September 1538, Henry received a letter from John Frederick, Elector of Saxony, and Philip, Landgrave of Hesse, the leading princes of the Schmalkaldic League, with whose ambassadors English delegates had engaged in weighty doctrinal discussions throughout that summer. The princes warned Henry about religious radicalism, on the march in their own lands, and enclosed a letter recently found in the possession of a captured anabaptist. Its author, Petrus Taschius, rejoiced that in England 'the truth silently but widely is propagated and powerfully increases'. The brethren there had published a book, *De incarnatione Christi* (Of the incarnation of Christ), and Taschius hoped to travel to England to further their cause.

Henry's response was swift. He ordered Cromwell to establish a commission to seek out anabaptists, 'and destroy all books of that detestable sect'. Its membership included Cranmer, and his fellow evangelicals Robert Barnes and Edward Crome, but also encompassed Stokesley and Sampson, conservative bishops whose stock was rising again, boosted by the recent return to England of Gardiner.

By the end of September, negotiations with the German Lutherans had petered to a desultory conclusion; the counsels of Cuthbert Tunstall stiffened Henry's reluctance to make concessions.[4] But the anabaptism commission brought forth grim results: a young Dutchman, Peter Franke, was burned at Colchester on 30 November, a day after his wife and another Dutchman were executed at Smithfield. A further two suspects were burned in December, grisly confirmation that breaking with Rome produced no moratorium on heresy proceedings.

Foreign anabaptists could expect little sympathy, even – or especially – from evangelicals, whose cause was compromised by wayward Christological heresies. Yet John Bale learned from eyewitnesses that Franke died nobly, standing in the midst of the fire 'without fear, sorrow, trembling, changing of countenance or dissolute moving', professing 'the Lord Jesus Christ to be his only saviour and redeemer'. The punishment of heretics was also the making of martyrs – a double-edged sword of definition. Bale claimed several onlookers were 'converted from papism unto true repentance' by Franke's heroism and conviction.[5]

Bale wrote his piece against a Catholic pamphleteer who alleged Franke was 'a limb of Lambert'. More than anything else, it was the case of John Lambert that slowed the pace of Reformation at the end of 1538, exposing splits and tensions within the evangelical cause. Lambert, alias Nicholson, was a veteran evangelical activist, imprisoned by Thomas More in the early 1530s, and later questioned by Cranmer, Latimer and Shaxton over the vehemence of his views against images. In 1538, he attended a sermon at St Peter Cornhill by the reformer John Taylor, and afterwards engaged him in argument over the eucharist. Taylor reported the affair to Robert Barnes, a true Lutheran in his devotion to the real presence. Barnes persuaded Taylor to bring the matter to Cranmer, Cranmer informed Cromwell, and Cromwell ordered Lambert's arrest. Sacramentarianism was a treacherous wind, which might bring the fragile alliance with a reformist king crashing to the ground. In 1538, the evangelical establishment closed ranks to shield themselves from it.

Lambert was prosecuted for heresy at Westminster Palace on 16 November, a trial rendered extraordinary by Henry VIII's decision to preside in person, clothed from head to foot in the white of theological purity. The conservative humanist Sir Thomas Elyot, writing the following year, extolled the 'divine influence or spark of divinity which late appeared to all them that beheld your Grace sitting in the throne of your royal estate as supreme head of the Church of England'.

Henry personally led the interrogation in robust fashion – 'tell me plainly whether thou sayest it is the body of Christ!' – and forced Lambert into an open denial. He was assisted eagerly by the leading conservative bishops, Gardiner, Tunstall and Stokesley, and less happily by Cranmer, who may have drawn comfort from the fact that Lambert's crime was denial of the real presence, rather than of transubstantiation in a more technical, scholastic sense. If the chronicler Wriothesley is to be believed, Lambert's beliefs took him far into the anabaptist camp, denying infant baptism, and asserting that Christ took no flesh of the Virgin. Only one outcome was possible: Lambert was burned at Smithfield on 22 November.[6]

On the day of Lambert's condemnation a royal proclamation was issued at Westminster. Its final section commanded the removal of all traces of 'Bishop Becket' from churches, chapels and service books. But the rest of the proclamation was visibly at odds with the drift of government policy over the preceding year. A surviving annotated draft shows that much of this was the King's personal intervention.

The proclamation attacked 'erroneous sects' of sacramentaries and anabaptists, commanding adherents to depart the realm or lose their lives. All discussion of the real presence (except by 'learned men in Holy Scripture, instructed and taught in the universities') was forbidden on pain of death. Other clauses banned importation of English books without royal licence, and placed restrictions on the import and printing of bibles. It condemned those who 'of their own sensual appetites and forward rash wills' attacked or violated laudable customs and ceremonies of the Church – use of holy bread and holy water, creeping to the cross on Good Friday and Easter Sunday, placing of lights before 'Corpus Christi' (the reserved sacrament), use of candles at the feast of the Purification of the Virgin (Candlemas), ceremonies around the churching of new mothers, and payment of offerings and tithes. Clergy were to explain to their flocks the 'true meaning' of these ceremonies, to prevent 'superstitious abuses', but the tone was different from the incessant warnings against idolatry required by the Injunctions. For good measure, clerical marriage was condemned, and priests presuming to take wives were to be dismissed and accounted laymen.[7]

Even if much of the wrangling around the Ten Articles and Bishops' Book remained behind closed committee-room doors, it was increasingly obvious that the regime spoke with multiple voices. This was reflected in a growing volume of neighbourhood disputes about the interpretation and implementation of policy. From Suffolk, Sir William Waldegrave, an enthusiastic evangelical, wrote to Cromwell complaining of difficulties in enforcing the Injunctions: local conservatives, detecting a change in the weather, were saying 'all things shall be as it hath been'.

A sense of uncertainty and opportunity was heightened by the supplementary injunctions bishops were encouraged to issue on their own authority on the back of the 1538 set. These were intended to strengthen the force of the latter, but in fact operated as interpretative glosses on them. Archbishop Lee's Injunctions for York notably lacked references to 'idolatry', or to 'abused' and 'feigned' images. Shaxton's injunctions for Salisbury, by contrast, pushed the reformers' agenda further and harder, ordering bibles to be paid for out of 'stocks given for maintaining lights before images', and that all relics should be sent to him, with appropriate documentation, so he could judge which were genuine and should be returned – it is unlikely he expected to be returning many, if any.[8]

In December, Cromwell moved to regain the initiative with a new circular to county magistrates. It reiterated in heightened terms the requirements to proclaim the Supremacy, and seek out and punish papists and rumour-mongers. In particular, magistrates were to discipline cankered priests who mumbled the Injunctions, saying they were compelled to read them, while bidding parishioners 'nevertheless to do as they did in times past'. A proclamation of February 1539 maintained the momentum, providing minimalizing explanations for the ceremonies stipulated in November: such observances were open to abuse, and valuable only as 'outward signs and tokens whereby we remember Christ'. Remarkably, the proclamation offered pardon for prior offences to repentant anabaptists and sacramentarians, lest 'great fear of punishment might turn their simplicity to obstinacy'.[9]

The pendulum swung back again with a draft proclamation in April, emphasizing the risks of unfettered bible reading. Henry's own corrections to this text insisted such reading take place 'quietly and with silence', and complained about use of the scripture to attack sacraments, or authority of magistrates, 'much contrary to his Highness' expectation'. In a now entirely predictable feature of government pronouncements, the proclamation condemned dissension, slander and railing, 'one part of them calling the other papist, the other part calling the other heretic'.[10]

Henry's vision of quietude received graphic expression in the title page to the 'Great Bible', issuing from the presses of Richard Grafton and Edward Whitchurch in April 1539. In a design perhaps created by Hans Holbein, the King sits in majesty, passing copies of 'Verbum Dei' to Cranmer and Cromwell, accompanied by bishops and lay councillors, who in turn relay it to preachers and lay elites. In the lowest plane, a preacher expounds the Word of God to a passive lay congregation, who respond (in grateful speech-ribbons) with exclamations of 'vivat rex!' It is an idyll of order and hierarchy, in which Henry plays the role of David or Solomon, shepherding God's (and his) obedient people. It was also a fantasy, a visual pageant of the kind of Reformation Henry believed he could wish and command into existence.

The April proclamation was pre-empted by the new Parliament, which got down to business in the first week of May 1539. Lord Chancellor Audley told the assembled peers that what the King desired 'above all things' was for diversities of opinions concerning religion to be 'plucked out and extirpated'. Members would find this difficult, due to time pressures, and variety of views. So the work would be shouldered by a small group, headed by Cromwell as vicegerent, and comprising the bishops of Canterbury, York, Bath and Wells, Ely, Bangor, Worcester, Durham and Carlisle. If the Lords as a whole were too divided to make meaningful progress, this committee was a microcosm of a disunited Church. Cranmer and his allies – Latimer, Goodrich, Salcot – were once again to lock horns with the traditionalists, Lee, Tunstall, Clerk and Robert Aldrich of Carlisle.[11]

First, there was the finishing of unfinished business. On 13 May Audley introduced a bill for the dissolution of monasteries. Unlike the act of 1536 this did not directly suppress religious houses, but instead provided a solid legal basis for the transfer of monks' assets to the King 'of their own free and voluntary minds'. There was no protest, even from the remaining abbots in the Lords, at what was now perceived as a fait accompli. Yet on the day the dissolution bill passed, the government rushed through another act, empowering the King to found new bishoprics, cathedrals and collegiate churches (a power he already possessed), and observing how endowments supporting the 'slothful and ungodly life' of monks might be 'turned to better use'. Its preamble spoke of support for preaching, schools, almshouses, scholarships for the universities. The intention was to promote the idea that dissolution was the prelude to a major programme of social and religious reform. In the event, all that transpired was the foundation, with monastic churches and revenues, of six new dioceses (Bristol, Chester, Gloucester, Peterborough, Oxford, Westminster) – a delayed and partial implementation of Wolsey's old plans for overhaul of the English Church.[12]

While the dissolution bill made its leisurely progress through both houses, Parliament passed another act, presented to the Lords by Cromwell on 10 May.

It was a massive bill of attainder, the largest in English history, containing the names of no fewer than fifty-three 'traitors'. Many were already dead – the leaders of the Pilgrimage, Exeter and Montagu, and their ally Sir Nicholas Carew, beheaded at the beginning of March. In the Tower, the conservative Carew experienced a change of heart, and gave thanks for the prison 'where he first savoured the life and sweetness of God's most holy Word' – a poignant symptom of the religious volatility of these years.[13]

The other targets were Pole and the little band of exiles gathered around him in Rome. The cardinal evaded the attentions of an assassin sent to the continent in 1537, but if Henry could not finish him directly, he could destroy his family. Among the attainted was Pole's mother. The proof of her treason was her needlework. Members were shown a white tunic found among the Countess's effects. On one side were depictions of the passion of Jesus, and on the other, the royal arms, in combination with pansies (symbol of the Pole family) and marigolds (representing Princess Mary), with a tree rising between them and a coat of purple hanging from its boughs, 'in tokening of the coat of Christ'.

Here was evidence that 'Pole intended to have married my Lady Mary, and betwixt them both should arise again the old doctrine'.[14] It was not as far-fetched as it sounded: Pole was a cardinal, but not yet in the major orders prohibiting marriage. As ever, the combination of a dynastic challenge and a spiritual rebuke heated Henry's anger to boiling point.

Just before Parliament assembled, Pole's former protégé Richard Morison produced two tracts – An Invective against the great and detestable voice of treason and An Exhortation to stir all Englishmen to defence of their country. The works defended the government's actions, and castigated the cardinal in bitter and personal terms: 'thou art now a Pole [pool] of little water, and that at a wonderful low ebb'. Morison was a propagandist for hire, but also a convinced evangelical. In the Invective, he portrayed England as an elect nation, and Henry as God's providential instrument, destined to banish idolatry and restore His holy Word. God moved in mysterious ways: 'of all the miracles and wonders of our time, I take the change of our Sovereign Lord's opinion in matters concerning religion to be even the greatest'.[15]

But it was becoming ever more painfully evident that Henry's opinions in matters concerning religion were not those of Morison, Cranmer or Cromwell. Already at Easter that year, Henry ostentatiously crept to the cross and served the mass. Lord Lisle's servant John Worth informed him that 'His Grace receives holy bread and holy water every Sunday, and daily uses all other laud-able ceremonies. In all London no man dare speak against them on pain of death.'

On 16 May, the Duke of Norfolk arose in the Lords to announce that the committee on religion was deadlocked, and instead the whole Parliament would be required to respond to six questions of doctrine: whether the eucharist could be the true body of the Lord without transubstantiation; whether it needed to be given to the laity under both kinds; if vows of chastity, by men and women, were to be observed by law of God; if private masses were similarly required; whether priests might take wives; and whether auricular confession was necessary, again by the law of God.[16]

Norfolk surely acted with Henry's personal authorization, and as the matter was argued out in Parliament and Convocation over the ensuing month, the King played a central role. One early casualty was the negotiations with the Schmalkaldic League. The propositions set before Parliament (on clerical celibacy, votive masses, communion in one kind) were precisely those that had stalled the talks the previous year, and at the end of May the German ambassadors finally went home empty-handed. Henry's determination to take matters more personally in hand was bolstered by reports of damaging and long-running religious disputes in the garrison town of Calais, where the conservative governor, Lord Lisle, was pitted against Cranmer's aggressively evangelical commissary, John Butler. Ominously, the King learned that 'Calais should be in some misorder by certain sacramentaries alleged to be in the same'.[17]

The Act of Six Articles passed into law at the end of June 1539. The evangelical bishops managed to retrieve a couple of spars from the wreckage. The word 'transubstantiation' disappeared from the affirmation of the real presence, and – a more substantial victory – auricular confession was declared to be 'expedient and necessary to be retained', rather than required by the law of God. Henry liked this formula, which maximized his freedom of manoeuvre as supreme head; Tunstall got a sharp rebuke when he tried to remonstrate with the King about it.[18]

In all other respects, the Six Articles were a disaster for the reformers, affirming a traditionalist line on all the propositions Norfolk placed before Parliament. They differed from the 1536 Ten Articles in having immediate statutory authority, and in prescribing extraordinarily draconian punishments. Heresy and treason became thoroughly conflated, as they no doubt were in the King's mind. Disbelief in the real presence was now a felony punishable with death by burning, and no abjuration was permitted. Public condemnation of any other article was also a capital offence; private denial meant forfeiture for a first offence, death for a second. For priests, marrying a woman became another felony punishable by death, while keeping her as a concubine meant loss of goods. The grading of punishments here made sense to Catholics, but seemed perverse to those who believed lawful matrimony an option for all Christians. A late amendment to the bill allowed married priests an additional three weeks to put their wives away without penalty. Possibly, Cromwell arranged this concession for the benefit of his friend Cranmer, whose wife and children were certainly sent to Germany around this time.[19]

The first casualties of the act were those who fought hardest against it in Convocation: Latimer of Worcester and Shaxton of Salisbury. They resigned their bishoprics, and were most likely pushed. Latimer, more relieved perhaps then Shaxton to be shot of office, even attempted to flee the country: he was intercepted at Gravesend. Cranmer's Scottish ally, Alexander Alesius, did flee abroad, on the archbishop's advice. Cranmer himself wrestled with his conscience over continued service in a Church now so clearly turning onto the wrong path.

Despite losing many tricks, Cranmer still had an ace up his sleeve. 'You were born in a happy hour . . . for, do or say what you will, the King will always well take it at your hand.' This was what Cromwell was overheard saying to him at a July dinner Henry had arranged to restore Cranmer's spirits and reconcile the quarrelling parties. The occasion was a less than total success. Norfolk combined courteous words to Cranmer with extravagant dispraise of Wolsey, and Cromwell, Wolsey's old servant, took offence. He served the cardinal willingly, he said, but would never have followed him to Rome had he been elected pope – which Norfolk, Cromwell asserted, surely would have done. At this, 'great and high words rose between them'.[20]

## A Climax of Evils

The Six Articles were a setback for evangelicals, and a shot in the arm for conservatives, but they did not signal any fundamental repudiation of the path Henry had followed since 1532. The insistence on a real, substantial presence of Christ in the eucharist was Henry's top priority, warmly welcomed by conservatives, though not intolerable to all evangelicals. The other five items were no compendium of traditional Catholicism, but an echo of specific matters in contention between English and German envoys in 1538–9.[21] Nothing was said on some of the matters proving most controversial among the King's subjects: purgatory and prayer for the dead; the status of images and ceremonies. And despite the loss of Latimer and Shaxton from the episcopal bench, there was no immediate purge or round-up of reformers.

In the weeks following the act's passing, the most emphatic official message continued to be the enormity of popish treason. On 8 July, two friars and two secular clergy were put to death in London, and on the following day two rather more distinguished prisoners, and two unnamed servants, shared their fate. Sir Adrian Fortescue was an Oxfordshire landowner whose inclusion in the 1539 attainder is mysterious, save for some family connections to the Poles. Sir Thomas Dingley, who died with him, was an eminent Knight of Malta, who had been rotting in the Tower since 1537, on account of careless words spoken about the King in Genoa, and subsequently reported back at home.[22]

Further loose ends, from the final stages of the dissolution, were ruthlessly tied up. In November 1539, three abbots of prominent Benedictine houses were tried for treason: Thomas Marshall of Colchester, Hugh Cook of Reading and Richard Whiting of Glastonbury. All were conservatives, who engaged in disaffected talk about the Supremacy. But in each case the real crime was obstructiveness in the face of seizure of their house.[23] Their executions within the locality of their abbey – in Whiting's case, hanged with two brethren on the summit of Glastonbury Tor – were designed to send a clear message: neither the King's title, nor the King's assets, were to be interfered with.

The conservative triumph, then, was far from complete, and one of its sponsors did not live to enjoy what there was of it. On 8 September 1539, John Stokesley, bishop of London, died. In later years it was reported of him that he would often reproachfully say: 'Oh, that I had holden still with my brother Fisher, and not left him when time was.' Evangelicals believed Stokesley 'to be a great papist in his heart', and in 1538 the King had fired a warning shot past him: he was briefly imperilled by praemunire charges, for admitting two brothers and a nun to Syon under papal bulls.[24]

No such fears attached to Stokesley's replacement, whose nomination seemed an overdue piece of good news for the evangelicals. Edmund Bonner was Cromwell's man, an advocate of the English bible, and an undiplomatic diplomat who in Spain acquired a reputation as a 'Lutheran'. Nor did other appointments to the episcopal bench around this time seem to be tipping it in an aggressively conservative direction. The evangelical John Salcot replaced Shaxton at Salisbury, and Salcot's successor at Bangor, John Bird, also had a reputation as a reformer. John Bell, who succeeded Latimer at Worcester was undoubtedly a conservative, but the new bishop of Rochester (Hilsey oblig-ingly died a month before his rival Stokesley) was Nicholas Heath, a protégé of Cranmer, who made a favourable impression on the German Lutherans during the negotiations of the preceding year. Anne Boleyn's former almoner John Skip was promoted to the see of Hereford, where Bonner was briefly bishop. Thomas Thirlby, elected to Westminster in 1540, was another friend of Cranmer, with non-traditional views on the sacraments. The other new dioceses were largely filled by biddable former abbots, rather than conservative warriors in the Stokesley or Gardiner mould.[25]

The changeable weather of English foreign policy served to delay further any onset of the storm evangelicals always feared was about to break. In his search for a new bride, Henry fixed his sights upon Anne, sister of Duke Wilhelm of Jülich-Cleves. Wilhelm was an Erasmian Catholic, but linked politically to the Schmalkaldic League. A German alliance was back on the table in the late summer of 1539. In the meantime, Gardiner managed to get himself expelled from the Council for criticizing the involvement in negotiations of Robert Barnes, 'a man defamed of heresy'. In September, with a marriage treaty agreed upon, the returning Saxon envoy Franz Burchard informed Melanchthon that Cranmer and Cromwell were in greater favour than ever, and that commissions to enforce the Six Articles were all suspended. 'The papistical faction (it does not confess this name, but may truly be called so) has nowise obtained its hoped-for tyranny.'[26]

Anne arrived in England on 27 December, and the King had his first sight of her at Rochester on New Year's Day. It is one of history's most famous disappointments. When Henry returned to Greenwich, Cromwell asked how he liked the Lady Anne. 'Nothing so well as she was spoken of' was the rueful reply, quickly followed by a question: 'What remedy?' Cromwell answered, 'I know none,' and said he was sorry.[27] The past callously repeats itself: an inability to provide royal marital remedy proved fatal to Cromwell's old master, Wolsey. The marriage went ahead, as it had to, on Tuesday 6 January, but Henry found himself unable to consummate, and desperate to find an exit.

On the road between Huntingdon and London, just before Christmas of 1539, two travellers discussed the news, as ordinary people often did. There was much to take note of: the arrival of the Queen, threats from Scotland, suppression of abbeys, the suspension of Gardiner and Bishop Sampson from the Council, doubts over whether Cromwell was in favour with the King, a furore in London over Cranmer's attempt to suppress preaching by a conservative ex-friar called William Watts. 'Jesus,' exclaimed one of the wayfarers, 'I had thought that schism and diversity of opinions had been pacified by the last Parliament.'[28] He did not, presumably, intend to be ironic.

Into February 1540, the reformers' morale remained buoyant. Heinrich Bullinger heard from English correspondents that 'good pastors are freely preaching the truth', and that 'the Word is powerfully preached by an individual named Barnes'.[29] Gardiner was determined to put a stop to that. His moment came when he and Nicholas Wilson were appointed Lent preachers at Paul's Cross. On Sunday 15 February, Gardiner delivered a combative sermon on the temptations of the devil. It was, he said, the accustomed trick of Satan's agents to plead with people, 'come back from fasting, come back from confession, come back from weeping for thy sins'. Nothing was necessary for salvation 'but only belief, only, only, nothing else'. Gardiner managed to make a traditionalist sermon into an attack on friars; a neat rhetorical trick. The friars had changed their coats, and now called themselves 'brethren', but they retained their wheedling ways, offering cut-price salvation through faith, in place of the pardons they once peddled.[30]

Ex-Friar Barnes was, as intended, provoked. He replied in kind from the same pulpit a fortnight later, denouncing Gardiner as a 'sower of evil herbs' in the garden of scripture. Gardiner complained to the King, who commanded the two clerics to debate in front of witnesses the question of whether 'a man could do anything good or acceptable before the grace of justification'. It was more a disciplinary process than a fair and open debate. Barnes was compelled to recant and beg Gardiner's pardon. Two other prominent evangelicals,

William Jerome and Thomas Garrett, were likewise ordered to retract. Jerome's Lenten sermon was particularly provocative. He preached that magistrates had no power 'to make that thing which of itself is indifferent to be not indifferent' – a brazen questioning of the royal supremacy's ability to prescribe rites and ceremonies.

The recantation sermons were duly preached, on 29, 30 and 31 March, but in each case retraction was patently insincere, prefaced by statements affirming justification by faith. On 3 April, the three preachers were despatched to the Tower, and on the following day Nicholas Wilson read their submissions at Paul's Cross, and warned Londoners to beware 'seditious doctrine'.[31]

Parliament reconvened on 12 April 1540, with the usual set-piece speeches. Cromwell's oration was another exhortation to the King's desired unity, and against the bitterness of spirit that produced names of heretic and papist. The problem lay in the 'rashness and licentiousness of some' and the 'inveterate superstition and stiffness of others'. The King, by contrast, 'leaned neither to the right nor to the left hand'. His only desire was to set forth to his subjects 'the pure and sincere doctrine of the Christian faith . . . without any corrupt mixtures'.

That Henry might bear any blame for the bitterly divided state of his people was not, of course, a possibility. Remedies, too, sounded depressingly familiar. There were to be new committees, one to revise the Bishops' Book, the other to consider which ceremonies should be retained, and produce guidance on their 'true use'. As before, the membership was religiously mixed, but the formidable combination of Tunstall and Gardiner was now firmly activated, and traditionalists formed majorities on both bodies.[32]

Still, Cromwell seemed to be riding high in the spring of 1540. On 18 April he was created Earl of Essex and High Chamberlain of England – a long way to come for a Putney brewer's son. Cromwell had been wary of acting to protect Barnes, but by May the new earl felt again able to move against his enemies. The defection to Rome of one of Lord Lisle's chaplains flipped the significance of the troubles in Calais: on 19 May Lisle himself was detained for treason. A week later, Cromwell secured the arrests of two leading committee members, Nicholas Wilson and Richard Sampson, on suspicion of secret correspondence with Rome. Marillac, the French ambassador, heard that Cromwell was saying 'there were still five bishops who ought to be treated thus'. Sampson's place at Paul's Cross was filled by Cranmer, who immediately began 'to put forward the contrary of what Winchester preached there in Lent'. Marillac believed Barnes was about to be released, and Latimer restored to the episcopate – 'so great is the inconstancy of the English'.[33]

The roller-coaster of court politics was soon, however, hurtling in a reverse direction. On 10 June, at a meeting of the Council, Cromwell was suddenly arrested and taken to the Tower. It was an astounding development. Most probably, Henry's unhappiness about his marriage tipped the balance of parties he was usually keen to uphold, and allowed Cromwell's enemies to seize the initiative. Gardiner gleefully welcomed Cromwell's downfall; so too did Norfolk, who despised Cromwell as an upstart. Having seen one niece become Queen of England, he now had hopes of another: since April, Henry was paying court to Catherine Howard, a delightfully, indeed suspiciously, vivacious teenager.

Within a week, an attainder was drawn up and presented to Parliament, the charges a mixture of the plausible and the preposterous. Cromwell accumulated power despite his birth being 'of as poor and low degree as few be within this realm' (true); he abused his office through many embezzlements and extortions (not true); he promoted 'damnable errors and heresies' (arguable).

There was no doubt Cromwell did advance and protect reformers, but the specific accusation was of asserting and sponsoring sacramentarianism. The most damning claim was that when Barnes and other preachers were under attack, Cromwell swore he would never abandon their teaching, saying that if the King turned from it 'I would fight in the field in mine own person, with my sword in my hand, against him and all others'.[34]

From the Tower, Cromwell wrote desperately to Henry on 12 June pleading his innocence. The principal witnesses to the alleged treasonous words were two conservatives with dubious records: Sir Richard Rich and Sir George Throckmorton. Cromwell urged Henry to remember what manner of man Rich was, and what Throckmorton 'hath ever been towards Your Grace and Your proceedings'. It is indeed unlikely that Cromwell spoke the exact words attributed to him; as Thomas More learned to his cost, Rich was an accomplished perjurer. Yet he was also Cromwell's protégé, and in 1537 Throckmorton had announced (insincerely) a conversion to the Gospel. Maybe Cromwell did speak indiscreetly in their presence. Cranmer picked up his pen on Cromwell's behalf, as he had for Anne Boleyn, professing surprise at the charges, while assuring Henry that 'if he be a traitor, I am sorry that I ever loved him'.[35]

Cromwell went to the block on 28 July; a mercy of sorts to be beheaded as a high-ranking traitor, not burned as a heretic. The office of vicegerent ended with him. At the end, Cromwell confessed his sinfulness, but said he believed in 'the holy sacrament without any grudge'. He also died, just as Fisher and More had done, affirming a commitment to 'the holy Catholic faith'.[36] The phrase meant different things to different people: the theological antagonisms of the age grappled with each other under a canopy of shared words.

With Cromwell's fall came the reckoning. On 30 July Robert Barnes, a veteran of countless political and theological battles, was burned at Smithfield, along with Garrett and Jerome. With him, the hopes for a German Lutheran alliance turned to ashes and smoke. A fortnight earlier, Cranmer annulled Henry's marriage to Anne of Cleves, on the belt-and-braces grounds of non-consummation and a supposed pre-contract with the Duke of Lorraine. Henry spent the day of Cromwell's execution celebrating his new marriage to Catherine Howard.[37]

None of this portended any rapprochement with Rome. The executions of 30 July echoed with symbolic significance. Thomas Abell, Richard Featherstone and Edward Powell were dragged on hurdles from the Tower to Smithfield alongside Barnes, Jerome and Garrett. Distinguished supporters of Catherine of Aragon, they had for years been rotting quietly in the Tower. While the evangelicals burned, the papalists were hanged and quartered in a gruesome display of judicial impartiality. European observers were shocked and appalled, and Ambassador Marillac was frankly baffled:

> [I]t is difficult to have a people entirely opposed to new errors which does not hold with the ancient authority of the Church and of the Holy See, or, on the other hand, hating the Pope, which does not share some opinions with the Germans. Yet the government will not have either the one or the other, but insists on their keeping what is commanded, which is so often altered that it is difficult to understand what it is.

To Marillac, it seemed that 'a climax of evils' had arisen in England. But in Henry's mind, his royal stance was both clear and just: the political disloyalty of the papalists was of a piece with the heretics' warped view that scripture set limits on what the Church (i.e. the King) could command to be performed or believed.[38]

With Cromwell dead, and little remaining need to appease the German Lutherans, the Six Articles were finally put into effect. Within a fortnight, as many as 500 suspects were rounded up in London. Some were charged with sacramentarianism, but, with neighbour informing against neighbour, others were arrested for transgressions that were not even offences under the act, such as criticism of images or ceremonies. The scale of the purge revealed how deeply religious divisions in London now ran, as well as the difficulties of seeking to eradicate them by judicial means. The government balked at the thought of hundreds of burnings, and on 1 August the King personally ordered a halt to the heresy quest.[39]

There was no reprieve for 'papists', another dozen of whom were hanged on 4 August. Their number included Thomas More's son-in-law, Giles Heron, as well as Thomas Empson, a former Benedictine of Westminster, whose habit was pulled from his back after he refused to seek the King's pardon. He was, wrote a later chronicler, 'the last monk that was seen in his clothing in England till Queen Mary's days'. The very last of the religious houses, Waltham Abbey in Essex, had surrendered on 23 March. For former monks, there were pensions from the Court of Augmentations, usually meagre ones. Those that could scrambled to find employment as priests in the parishes.

For the nuns, recipients of still more meagre pensions, there was no such option. Yet, cruelly and unusually, ex-nuns were still bound to chastity by the terms of the Six Articles, and thus forbidden to marry. With a unique avenue of independent existence now closed off for them, most of these women, young and old, probably went back to their families, and to undeserved historical obscurity. At Coughton in Warwickshire, Elizabeth Throckmorton, former abbess of Denny in Cambridgeshire, returned to live with her nephew, Sir George. She brought with her the wooden dole-gate of her house, through which alms were passed to the poor, as well as two or three of her nuns, possibly also family members. There, they continued to wear their Franciscan habits, and to practise discreetly a pattern of convent living in the enclosed upper rooms of the house. English monasticism fizzled, rather than flamed, out of existence at the start of the 1540s. But it possessed torches of genuine vocation, and a perhaps disproportionate number of these were carried by women.[40]

Cromwell was gone, but friends and clients endured in positions of influence around the King. In 1539, Cromwell had supervised an overhaul of the Privy Chamber, supplying reinforcements to the evangelical chief gentleman, Sir Anthony Denny. Cranmer too remained in place, apparently secure in Henry's favour. The King's trust in conservative councillors received a severe blow just after Christmas 1540, with the arrival of news that Richard Pate, English ambassador to the Emperor, had defected to Rome. Over the preceding months, Pate had been quietly insinuating to his hosts that the Six Articles and the fall of Cromwell were signs of impending reconciliation with the papacy. Paul III poured petrol on the King's rage by making the renegade Pate titular bishop of Worcester, the see traditionally held by English representatives at Rome. There was a flurried search for accomplices; Pate's uncle, the arch-loyalist Bishop Longland of Lincoln, was arrested, and his correspondence read.[41]

Evangelicals, too, trod warily. John Lassells, Cromwell's man and gentleman of the Privy Chamber, warned two fellow courtiers in September 1540 'not to be too rash or quick in maintaining the scripture'. Norfolk and Gardiner were currently in favour, but 'if we would let them alone and suffer a little time they would (I doubt not) overthrow themselves'. It sounded remarkably like the advice handed out in confession by a Kentish priest the previous summer: 'Suffer awhile, and ye shall see the Pope in as great authority as ever he was.'[42] The public cavalcade of reform created in its wake private cultures of inwardness and secrecy, of waiting for the world to change.

The early 1540s were years of minor victories, of small shifts in alignment. In October 1540, Nicholas Wilson (now rehabilitated) and Edward Crome clashed in the London pulpits over private masses and prayer for the dead: it was Crome who was made, once again, to recant. The committee on ceremonies produced, though did not publish, a cautiously conservative defence of them, the 'Rationale of Ceremonial'. On the doctrine committee, opinion drifted away from Cranmer. He was, according to his secretary Ralph Morice, abandoned by those 'he took to be his friends', by Heath, Skip, Thirlby. Not all religious journeys in these years led away from traditional Catholicism.

Another person moving back towards it, in the wake of Cromwell's downfall, was the bishop of London. In the spring of 1541, Bonner launched a renewed heresy quest under the Six Articles. This time, London juries were more circumspect: 'They ever find nothing', an exasperated Bonner complained. There was a single victim, an unfortunate case. Richard Mekyns was a teenager, an admirer of Barnes, and only possibly a sacramentarian. Understandably terrified, he wanted to recant, but the Six Articles excluded this option. His death at the stake in July 1540 laid the foundations for Bonner's reputation as a bloody persecutor.[43]

None of this amounted to any real 'reversal' of Reformation. Bloody reminders of the repercussions of Romish treason arrived with clockwork regularity. In May 1541 it was the turn of Reginald Pole's sixty-eight-year-old mother, the Countess of Salisbury. She was beheaded on Tower Green by an inexperienced youth who, according to Chapuys, 'literally hacked her head and shoulders to pieces in most pitiful manner'. The regular executioner was absent in the north, dealing with the aftermath of a scheme to seize Pontefract Castle and seek assistance from James V. The 'Wakefield Conspiracy' was a serious plot, showing Yorkshire to be neither pacified nor reconciled after the Pilgrimage. Its disclosure may have precipitated a decision to enact the attainder against Margaret Pole. When the news reached Reginald in Italy, he took it hard, but his public position was one of gratitude to God for making him the son of a martyr.[44]

Remarkably, at the very moment he was murdering the mother of a cardinal, Henry was contemplating a compromise with the Pope. In an effort to heal the schism within his German territories, Charles V invited a selection of the more malleable Lutheran and Catholic theologians to a colloquy at Regensburg in April 1541. Paul III, reluctantly, sent a delegate. Henry, unwilling to be left out, despatched Gardiner as his representative, though, typically, he paired him on the embassy with the evangelical Sir Henry Knyvett.

At a meeting in advance of the colloquy, the Emperor's chancellor, Nicholas de Granvelle, bluntly presented an offer to mediate between England and the papacy. Nonplussed, Gardiner agreed to transmit it home. When, at the start of May, the theologians reached agreement on the core issue of justification, an end to the schism seemed conceivable. The English ambassadors relayed Henry's decision that, if a similar accord were reached on the eucharist, he would allow Charles V to initiate negotiations for English reconciliation with Rome. In the event, the discussions at Regensburg collapsed over transubstantiation. Beyond the conference, intransigents on all sides rejected the formula on justification.[45] Henry's apparent willingness to consider some kind of settlement with the papacy seems surprising; most likely it points to the depth of his fears about European isolation and encirclement. For those in the know, it was a sobering reminder that nothing in life, or politics, could be taken for granted. Still, Henry was surely relieved that he would not have to eat any of his words about the usurped authority of the 'bishop of Rome'.

At home, over the course of 1541, conservative gains were offset by evangelical ones. A May proclamation, noting many places 'negligently omitted their duties' in respect of scripture, ordered copies of the Great Bible to be placed in all churches. It endorsed the Henrician ideal for bible reading – 'humbly, meekly and reverently', for private edification, for learning to observe God's Commandments, 'and to obey their sovereign lord'. There was to be no reading 'with loud and high voices in time of the celebration of the holy mass'. But the proclamation finally made a reality of a long-standing humanist-evangelical aspiration, and a requirement of the 1538 injunctions: universal access to vernacular scripture. Threatened with a 40s. fine, parishes began to comply. Prior to this, many had no bible, either because they were deliberately dragging their feet, or because of the difficulties of producing copies for all 9,000 parishes. The churchwardens of Boxford in Suffolk now laid out 6s. 5d. 'for the bible, and a chain to the bible, and the carrying of the same bible from London'.[46]

A second proclamation in July 1541 restored the feasts of Mary Magdalene, Luke and Mark, as these saints were 'many times mentioned in plain and manifest Scripture'. Yet it abrogated two feasts of the Holy Cross, as well as fasting on St Mark's day and the eve of the feast of St Lawrence. It also outlawed 'superstitious and childish observations' taking place on the feasts of St Nicholas, St Catherine, St Clement and the Holy Innocents. These were traditional occasions of festive 'misrule', which in many places involved the election of a 'Boy Bishop' to preach satirically to the adults from the parish pulpit. Even temporary and playful inversions of the social order were too much unruliness for Henry.[47]

The treatment of feasts of biblical saints, and of those promoting the cult of the rood, showed that Henry had not repudiated the didactic iconoclasm undertaken in his name in 1538. In the late summer of 1541, in the aftermath of the Wakefield Conspiracy, Henry, a king never yet seen in the north, set off on a progress to Yorkshire. At Hull, the King encountered Robert Serles, a conservative member of the cathedral chapter of Canterbury, and an arch-defender of images, who had ridden north to present a series of complaints against his archbishop. It was a ruinous misreading of the King's mood. Henry was annoyed by evidence of shrines and pilgrimage paraphernalia still standing in the north, and Serles' intervention prompted a directive to Cranmer for stricter enforcement of the 1538 injunctions.

Royal letters went out to all the bishops; Bonner issued a directive to his clergy on 14 October commanding them to enquire whether any 'superstition, hypocrisy or abuse' continued in their churches. But conservatives were learning to play within the rules. London evangelicals were soon complaining that Bonner replaced the statue of the Virgin at St Paul's with one of John the Baptist.[48]

The greatest fallen idol of 1541 fell closer to home. Before her marriage to Henry, Catherine Howard was sexually active with a succession of handsome young men; after it, she saw no reason to stop. John Lassells, the courtier who a year earlier was urging patience in the face of Howard dominance, took the bold step of presenting Cranmer with evidence of Catherine's affairs. During Henry's absence in the north, Cranmer was left in charge along with two other evangelically inclined councillors: Chancellor Audley and Jane Seymour's brother Edward, Earl of Hertford. None of them wanted to be the bearer of this extraordinarily ill news, but it could not be withheld. Just after Henry's return, on 2 November, All Souls' Day, Cranmer handed him a letter at mass. The King was at first reluctant to believe what he read, but unlike the case of Anne Boleyn, the facts here spoke for themselves.[49] Two of Catherine's lovers were tried and executed in December, and she herself was beheaded, under act of attainder, in February 1542. An asset of Howard ascendency was eliminated, and a potential avenue of influence reopened.

In January 1542, at the opening of the new Parliament that passed the attainder, Audley praised Henry as a latter-day King David, slaying the Goliath of Rome with the stone of God's Word. The fate of the Queen was in everyone's minds. But Parliament's primary task, Audley proclaimed, was, once again, 'unity of faith and concord of religion'.[50]

In truth, this was further away than ever. At the concurrent opening of Convocation, Bonner celebrated the mass and the evangelical Richard Cox preached the sermon, the mismatched pairing setting the tone for an acrimonious session. Cranmer managed to kill off a plan for revision of the Great Bible, while Gardiner and his allies scotched a scheme for a collection of official homilies. Words for prayer themselves became a battleground. In a discussion on the bible, bishops clashed over whether 'Our Lord' or 'The Lord' was the better translation of the Latin *Dominus*; traditionalists preferred the devotional intimacy of the former, evangelicals the transcendent majesty of the latter.[51]

Meanwhile, Gardiner, as chancellor of Cambridge, became embroiled in a furious row about the correct pronunciation of Greek. Following the lead of Erasmus, the evangelical scholars John Cheke and Thomas Smith wished to reconstruct the ancient pronunciation for purposes of teaching; Gardiner insisted on sticking to accustomed practice. It was, as Gardiner himself admitted, 'a trifling matter', but one that 'paves the way for more serious things'.

Authority, consensus and tradition were pitted against claims about authentic apostolic practice. To concede on this would open the door on a world of dangerous innovation.[52]

Bonner did his best to suppress innovations in the spring of 1542. He issued to his clergy a list of prohibited books, ignoring the fringe radicals to target authors closer to the hearts of evangelical bishops: Luther, Calvin, Frith, Roye, Joye, Tyndale, Barnes. On 22 March, Bonner issued a new heresy commission under the Six Articles. He also drew up a set of injunctions, which ordered preachers to follow the interpretation of 'some Catholic doctor', and pick out from the gospel or epistle of the day something to 'incense and stir the hearers to obedience of good works and prayers'. Preachers were to explain right and reverent use of the sacraments, and 'declare whereof the mass is so highly to be esteemed'.[53] The arguments among the bishops stimulated rival efforts on their part to instruct and persuade the ordinary laity – efforts which undoubtedly increased laypeople's understanding of controversial issues, and their informed ability to choose between them.

Henry's own thoughts were elsewhere in the summer and autumn of 1542. Marital disappointments were re-channelled into martial ambitions. With Francis I and Charles V once again at enmity, Henry contemplated an attack on France, while border skirmishes with Scotland escalated into full-scale war. James V's invasion ended disastrously at Solway Moss on 24 November, and a few weeks later James was dead, leaving Mary Queen of Scots as the infant heir to a fractious kingdom. James had been, for the most part, a loyal son of the papacy, and Cranmer and other evangelicals took comfort from his defeat. But within England itself, Cranmer's enemies were preparing a deadly attack of their own.

### The Advancement of True Religion

On a Sunday in Advent, 1542, Robert Serles preached at Chilham, a few miles outside Canterbury. He stayed afterwards to talk with the vicar, John Willoughby, a royal chaplain and stout traditionalist. Serles complained to his host how his charges against Cranmer were kept from the King during the ill-fated trip to Hull the previous year, and invited Willoughby to join a project of drawing up new articles of grievance. Willoughby agreed, provided the matter were 'provable'.[54]

Through the following months, Serles steadily compiled his dossier, assisted by a cathedral clergyman named William Gardiner, and a clutch of conservative Kentish magistrates. By Lent 1543, there was more than enough material in hand, and on 16 March Serles and Willoughby arrived in London to present their evidence to the King's Council, now known as the Privy Council. The following day they ran into Dr John London, a government enforcer during the dissolution of the monasteries, but a stout conservative. He was there on parallel business, to present councillors with evidence of heresy among the priests of the royal chapel of St George's, Windsor. It seems unlikely the meeting was, as they claimed, coincidental; Serles and London were old Oxford acquaintances. This 'Prebendaries' Plot' (a prebendary is a cathedral dignitary) was not from the outset woven by Stephen Gardiner, but at some stage he became aware of the various threads, and started to pull them together.[55]

By the end of April, Henry was made aware of the charges against Cranmer, and allowed the investigations to continue. The prominent evangelical Simon Heynes, dean of Exeter and canon of Windsor, was arrested, along with others linked to the chapel. Three of them – the sacramentarian priest Anthony Pearson, musician Robert Testwood, and churchwarden Henry Filmer – were burned that summer. Ripples from the investigation reached the court: ten courtiers, including a gentleman usher of the Privy Chamber, Philip Hoby, were arrested on suspicion of links to the Windsor heretics. In London, eight printers were detained for producing prohibited books, and three leading evangelicals – Thomas Becon, Robert Singleton and Robert Wisdom – publicly recanted.[56]

The principal target of all the agitation remained, however, unmolested. A famous reminiscence of Cranmer's secretary, Ralph Morice, has Henry receiving the archbishop onto his barge on the Thames, and saying to him with grim humour, 'Ah my chaplain, I have news for you, I now know who is the greatest heretic in Kent.'[57] There was to be no repeat of the spectacular fall of Cromwell – perhaps because of what Cromwell himself noticed, the King's genuine fondness for Cranmer. The archbishop, who had managed to gain personal access to Henry at a crucial moment, was himself ordered to take charge of investigations into the state of affairs in Kent.

Reports and interrogations revealed a county riven by religious conflict. Royal policy seemed almost designed to detonate tensions rather than defuse them. Robert Serles was one of six preachers attached to Canterbury Cathedral as part of its 1540 transformation from Benedictine priory into secular foundation. Henry gave directions that the appointees should be 'three of the New Learning, and three of the Old', a striking instance of his preferred policy of balancing the factions in order to control them. Yet this, as prebendary William Gardiner complained, was simply 'a mean to set us at variance'.[58]

Within Cranmer's diocese, zealous evangelical clergy, prominent among them his commissary, Christopher Nevinson, aimed at total reformation. It involved banning holy water, attacking auricular confession, and seeking complete elimination of images. The churchwardens of St George's, Canterbury, protested against the removal of their saint. They argued (correctly) that images were allowed 'where no offering was', and patriotically pointed to the status of St George as patron of England. Nevinson was unmoved: 'We have no patron but Christ.' The vicar of Adisham, John Bland, preached that it was idolatry to give honour even to the very cross on which Christ died. Encouraged by such firebrands, radical laypeople took matters into their own hands: there was a spate of iconoclastic attacks, in which images were hewed with axes, beheaded, burned. It was, in a perhaps exact sense, the revenge of the Lollards.

There was lay support too for priests of the old fashion, accused by their enemies of failing to delete the Pope's name from service books, and of keeping forbidden feasts and fasts. Large audiences gathered to hear preachers make the case for and against justification by faith, the power of the sacraments to remit sin, the merits of vernacular scripture. At times, it seemed almost as if the populace was being mobilized for religious war. On Easter Sunday 1543, William Gardiner ended his sermon with rousing cries of 'Heretics! Faggots! Fire!'

'All things among us is full of debates, dissensions and strifes.' That was the complaint in 1543 of the anonymous translator of a work by Erasmus. 'One kinsman agreeth not with another, nor one religion, as they now call it, with another.'[59] It is a revealing lament. For centuries, the word 'religion' meant an attitude of worshipful devotion towards God. Here it signified a set of ideas held by a group of people, and something now able to take aggressively plural forms.

As the investigations into heresy in Kent continued, Convocation took up a piece of crucial unfinished business. In late April 1543 it discussed the text produced by the theologians tasked with revising the Bishops' Book, in the light of Henry's comments on it, and the report of the 1540 doctrine committee. This, at last, would be a definitive King's Book.

It promised to have a sharply traditionalist edge, which Cranmer did his best to blunt. He could just about live with the disavowal that justification came by faith 'alone', for, he rationalized, faith 'hath company of other virtues'. But he balked at a denial that faith 'only' was the cause of man's salvation. Cranmer's decision to appeal directly to the King, like Tunstall's over the Six Articles, backfired badly. Henry knew what he wanted the book to say. Published in the first week of May, it began with an unambiguous statement that Christians are justified by faith, but 'neither only nor alone'. It went on to insist that every person was free to receive or refuse God's offer of grace, and to be 'a worker . . . in the attaining of his own justification'.[60]

In other regards, too, the *Necessary Doctrine and Erudition for any Christian Man*, to give it its formal title, rowed back against the current of reform. The seven sacraments were discussed without the previous two-tier ranking, and much was made of bread and wine being 'changed and turned to the very substance of the body and blood of Our Saviour Jesus Christ'. There was praise for 'laudable ceremonies', and an insistence that the second commandment did not prohibit images, but only 'godly honour' done to them. Looking upon images of Christ and the saints was a way people might be 'provoked, kindled and stirred to yield thanks to Our Lord' – 'Our Lord', rather than, as evangelicals preferred, 'the Lord': this, Gardiner later recalled, was 'the King's own device'.[61]

There was a significant exception to the traditionalist trend. The King's Book condemned in uncompromising terms 'abuses' around prayer for the dead. The impulse itself was charitable, but no one should presume to understand how, or if, masses and prayers profited an individual soul. Better to offer them for 'the universal congregation of Christian people, quick and dead'. Moreover, people must 'abstain from the name of purgatory, and no more dispute or reason thereof'. The mystery is scarcely unfathomable: more than any other Catholic doctrine, purgatory suggested the spiritual authority of the Pope. Abuses were explicitly blamed on 'supporters and maintainers of the papacy of Rome'.

Still, the article lent itself to divergent readings. A canon of Canterbury was denounced in 1543 for leaving bequests to his colleagues to say Our Lady's Psalter, 'which is thought to be against the King's Book last set forth in the article of prayer for the souls departed'. Yet early the following year, a testator in North Yorkshire requested prayers for his soul 'after the manner as it is set forth by the King's Book'. Henry himself gave mixed signals: already in 1540 he had changed the statutes of the Order of the Garter so that offerings for the souls of deceased knights might be spent on works of charity rather than masses, but at the same time he ensured prayers for the soul of Queen Jane became a duty of the new cathedral foundations. In a climate of uncertainty, growing numbers turned away from traditional habits. Across the country as a whole, requests in wills for chantries, obits and masses were running at roughly half the rate in the 1540s they had been in the 1520s.[62]

The King's Book was an ill omen for Cranmer and his allies, and worse was to follow. On 12 May, four days after it was introduced into the Lords, Parliament passed an act 'for the advancement of true religion'. It originated as a measure against erroneous books contradicting any doctrine set forth by the King since, significantly, 1540. These included Tyndale's 'crafty, false and untrue' translation of the bible. Other translations were permitted, provided annotations or preambles were blotted out. But the crucial part of the act placed tight restrictions on reading the bible in English at all. No 'artificers, apprentices, journeymen, serving men of the degrees of yeomen or under, husbandmen nor labourers' were permitted to do so. The ordinary people shown rejoicing on the title page of the Great Bible suddenly had less to cheer about.

The act also stipulated that 'no women' be allowed to read scripture, though – somewhat confusingly – this was amended later in the act to permit women of noble and gentle status to read 'to themselves alone, and not to others' – a hint of debate and revision during the act's indecorously hasty passage through Parliament. Gardiner wrote triumphantly to the vice-chancellor of Cambridge on 15 May that Henry had 'by the inspiration of the Holy Ghost, componed [settled] all matters of religion'. Others thought the inspiration was Gardiner's. But on this issue – the divisive effects of unregulated scripture – Henry needed little persuasion, especially at a time of renewed alliance with the Emperor.[63]

For many evangelicals, it was a moment of profound, shattering disillusionment. The Gospel was the source of spiritual life, the wellspring of salvation. Some wondered how a king who barred poor men and women from coming to it could retain any claim to be an instrument of God's purpose. 'They will say,' complained an angry Robert Wisdom, 'there is a book set out of most Christian doctrine for the people. To that I answer, the book of most Christian doctrine is the Holy Testament of Jesus Christ.' The most vocal critics were those who had already gone into exile, to Antwerp, Strassburg or Zürich, in the wake of the Six Articles. They included John Bale, John Hooper, the fiery physician William Turner, and a few who had taken the lonely exile road before, such as George Joye and Miles Coverdale.

'The Pope remaineth wholly still in England,' wrote the London mercer Henry Brinklow on the eve of the King's Book's publication. He did not mean, as Cromwell might have done, that the Pope's supporters still lurked in corners. Rather, it was the King's own bishops who maintained the substance of 'popedom', with their ungodly ceremonies. This claim constituted a direct challenge to Henry's right to determine the lawfulness of ceremonies and the necessity of maintaining them, even if they were not essential for salvation – the theological term here was *adiaphora*, 'things indifferent'. Some evangelicals moved from attacking *adiaphora* to questioning the Supremacy itself. Like the Catholic Pilgrims in 1536, William Turner accepted the King's right to preside over the 'politic order' of the Church. But he denied he could be its head in any spiritual sense. 'Was King Herod,' Turner asked, in a particularly tactless analogy, 'the Virgin Mary's mystical head, and spiritual head of the Apostles?'

There had always been stresses within evangelical ranks. But in the mid-1540s, the broad alliance of the Cromwellian years, confident the world was moving in the right direction, started to come apart. Among the exiles, and among a growing number of sympathizers in England, hatred of the 'popish' mass was turning towards the understanding of the eucharist current in Zürich and Strassburg, the 'sacramentarian' view for which John Lambert died. Experience of opposition and oppression encouraged a mind-set that saw the world as fundamentally divided between good and evil, with little room for ambiguity or compromise. Abroad, Bale was at work on a book, *The Image of Both Churches*. These were not the Churches of England and Rome, but rather the Church of Christ and the Church of Antichrist, whose struggle stretched back across the centuries, and would continue till the Second Coming. It was a struggle taking place within the Church of England itself, and for the moment it seemed as if Antichrist had the upper hand.[64]

For reformers prepared to stay and work pragmatically within the system, the picture was not quite so bleak. Henry's marriage in July 1543 to Catherine Parr, an attractive young widow with pious, humanist interests, seemed at least to close off a channel of potential popish influence. And the right sort of influence was at work on the young Prince Edward. His tutors, appointed in 1543–4, were John Cheke, Richard Cox and Roger Ascham. All had cautious yet distinct reformist leanings, of which the King could scarcely have been unaware. It is unlikely they indoctrinated the child, but, along with his new step-mother, they shaped his emerging world-view. When the seven-year-old carefully penned a short letter to his godfather, Archbishop Cranmer, he expressed the hope 'that you may live long, and promote the Word of God'.[65]

Promoting the Word of God was something to which Henry, in his own mind at least, remained piously committed. He fretted little about the presence at court of evangelicals because he was confident he could use and control them. Papalist treason was always more alarming to him: suspicions that conservatives were not free of all taint and trace of it accounted for his reluctance to trust them completely. In early 1544 that taint came perilously close to Gardiner himself. His nephew Germaine was one of nine arrested and charged with treason against the royal supremacy. The accusations were old stuff, relating to allegedly treasonous contacts with Pole ten years earlier in Paris. Most likely, they were resurrected as part of a retaliatory strike by Cranmer's allies: Germaine played an active role in the Prebendaries' Plot. Stephen Gardiner survived, just as Cranmer had, and perhaps by making a similar personal appeal to the King. But his cherished nephew's execution on 7 March was a bitter pill. Old scores were being settled. The victims included Thomas More's favoured parish priest, John Larke. More's son, John, was pardoned, as was his nephew, the playwright John Heywood. In July, Heywood would make a humiliating recantation at Paul's Cross for falling into such blindness as 'to think the bishop of Rome supreme head of the Universal Church'.[66]

In the spring of 1544, as the King's mind focused once more on war, and an impending campaign in France, the tide of religious reaction continued to recede. In March Parliament passed a bill drawing some of the teeth from the Six Articles. Subjects had suffered under 'secret and untrue accusations and presentments'; henceforth no one was to be arrested unless presented by a jury or by justices of the peace, and charges had to be brought punctually after the alleged offence. At the start of June, there was a small but significant victory for reform: an English Litany, composed by Cranmer, was authorized for use in parishes. The Litany, recited during special processions, was the ritual of invoking the aid of the saints in times of distress. But Cranmer's revisions pared their role back to the barest minimum, and even the hothead William Turner was pleased the King had 'begun to set out the service in English'. In contrast, traditionalists in the Kent parish of Milton marched out of church when the priest began the new English Litany, and performed for themselves the accustomed rite in Latin.[67]

Cranmer sensed possibilities for further gains. In October 1544 he informed Henry he had produced an English translation of the entire *Processionale*, the service book for ordinary processions on Sundays and feast days. This was in response to a royal command, relayed to him by William Paget, a discreet evangelical who since May had been acting as the King's principal secretary.[68] Nothing came of it, for now. But the idea of church services in the vernacular, rather than in Latin, was no longer an unthinkable one.

These baby steps failed to impress those whose evangelical energies were vigorously full-grown. On 15 December 1544, zealots cast into streets across London 'divers books of heresies . . . against the sacrament of the altar, with all other sacraments and sacramentals'. The books named Gardiner, and other bishops, 'with great rebukes'. Six days later, at Paul's Cross, the conservative Cuthbert Scott preached a despairing sermon. Laypeople now aspired to greater knowledge of scripture than the clergy. Impervious to learned argument, they might claim, 'I am one whose eyes it hath pleased God to have opened that I should see His truth.' They would also say, 'I am sure that I am one of the predestinate and elect.' Such people lacked understanding of what scripture meant by election, making it such a thing, 'as if God should appoint certain out by the head, and say, "these I will shall be saved, howsoever they do live"'. To Scott, it seemed laughable. Yet predestination, the notion that God chose certain humans for eternal life, irrespective of their merits and achievements, was no joke. In Geneva the previous year, John Calvin published a third edition of his *Institutes of the Christian Religion*, a book in which this idea was taken very seriously indeed.

'The world, the more is the pity, is full of schisms, full of diversities and contentions.' Traditionalists like William Chedsey, preaching at Paul's Cross around the same time as Scott, lamented the collapse of uniformity and consensus, and the rise of 'singularity', of people 'addicted to their own fantasies'. Blame lay with the preachers: 'Time hath been, when that those which have occupied this place have laboured and endeavoured themselves . . . to have pacified and have set at quiet the weak and feeble consciences of their audience.' Today, Chedsey bemoaned, 'He that can best dispute and reason a new matter in the pulpit, he is the best preacher.' Once, preaching was 'sweet melody'; 'now it is an unsweet noise, for the pipes jarreth'.[69]

A few sacramentarians were rounded up in the capital in January 1545, but the momentum remained with the reformers. Robert Holgate, a former monk but an evangelical sympathizer, was installed in the key archbishopric of York: the old conservative warhorse, Edward Lee, died the previous September.

Evangelicals were more than ever embedded at court, and an evangelical 'style', if not a profound moral understanding of doctrine, was becoming fashionable among sections of the nobility. One symptom of it was flagrant disregard for the requirement to abstain from meat during Lent: Norfolk's own son and heir, Henry, poet earl of Surrey, was just such a fast-breaker. Some conservatives, meanwhile, were driven to desperate, self-defeating, measures. In February 1545, a priest from Kent performed penance at Paul's Cross for 'feigning and counterfeiting a miracle'. He pricked his finger during mass, to make it seem as if the host itself was bleeding.[70]

In May, reformers chalked up another small but significant achievement: an official 'King's Primer' was authorized as the sole private prayer book for use in England. As with the Litany, victory lay in taking an old-fashioned form and subverting its traditional purposes. The calendar of saints was radically pruned, and invocations for the dead became pale shadows of their former selves. The overall tone was sombre, biblical. Cranmer composed several new prayers on the passion, which sat alongside paraphrases of scripture by the German reformer Wolfgang Capito, and meditations by the humanists Juan Luis Vives and Erasmus. One was Erasmus's prayer 'for the peace of the Church', which used a musical metaphor similar to William Chedsey's: Christendom had become a place of 'no agreement of opinions, but as it were in a misordered choir, every man singeth a contrary note'.[71]

An air of discordance pervaded the country in the summer of 1545. The war had begun promisingly. Henry himself took to the field in France in the summer of 1544, conjuring out of a now corpulent body agreeable re-enactments of his lost chivalric youth. The English secured the surrender of Boulogne, a substantial prize. But the campaign, and necessary fortifications for the captured town, were staggeringly, eye-wateringly expensive. The government resorted to an unpopular 'benevolence', and to a debasement of the coinage, which fuelled inflation and drove up prices. Not for the first time, Henry was let down by his allies. In September 1544, after Henry returned to England, Charles V made a separate peace with the French. An offensive war suddenly became a defensive one, as French fleets raided the south of England, and full-scale invasion loomed. Coastal fortifications were hastily constructed, at further ruinous expense. The Privy Council drew up an order authorizing what the Pilgrims feared in 1536: seizure of every second chalice from parish churches, and 'other silver plate as may conveniently be spared'. Fear of local reactions meant it was not implemented. The loss in July 1545 of Henry's favourite battleship, the *Mary Rose*, became almost a metaphor for sunken dreams of martial glory.[72]

A new Parliament convened in November, its urgent business the supply of money to the King. Even more than its predecessors, this Parliament was divided, factionalized. Conservatives held sway in the Upper House, where Thomas Wriothesley – another Cromwellian now distancing himself from reform – presided as Lord Chancellor. There were ardent Catholics in the Commons too, but also a tight knot of around thirty convinced evangelicals, including seven members of the King's Privy Chamber. A bill denying benefit of clergy to those 'who put forth slanderous and false accusations of treason' suggests how divisions in religion were being used to pursue private grudges and quarrels. Such divisions reached into the heart of the Parliament. Sir William Petre wrote to his fellow-secretary Paget, on royal business in Calais: 'great hurly burly about the examination of certain books, covertly thrown abroad'. Sir Peter Carew, MP for Tavistock, was found with one, and imprisoned for a time. The affair prompted the introduction into the Lords of a new bill 'for abolition of heresy, and against books containing false opinions'. But attempts at further Counter-Reformation faltered. The Lords vigorously debated the bill, before referring it to a committee under the chairmanship of Cranmer. When it was voted down in the Commons, the King was said to be 'not . . . much miscontented'.[73]

One book conservatives had in their sights was an anonymous *Lamentation of a Christian against the City of London*. It railed against auricular confession, and against the mass as 'the greatest idol under heaven'. Gardiner, abroad on a diplomatic mission to the Emperor, was sent a copy, and fretted about the author's identity. He suspected George Joye ('he writeth that word [joy] with a great letter'), but the author was in fact Henry Brinklow, one of a growing number of evangelicals to regard the Gospel, not just as a gateway to salvation for the individual, but as a cure for the ills of the 'commonwealth'. Church and clergy must be stripped of their wealth to provide for the needs of the poor. Chances were missed at the dissolution of the monasteries. But since purgatory was a fiction, and prayer for the dead but wasted breath, it was time to seize the wealth of the chantries, to 'bestow them therefore from henceforward upon the true image of Christ, which is upon the poor'.[74]

Chantries were indeed in peril; but there was little danger of the poor benefitting. Late in December an act empowered the King, if he wished, to dissolve any chantries, colleges, hospitals or guilds, and granted him the endowments of all such institutions dissolved since 1536 through underhand deals between patrons and priests. The rationale was financial necessity, rather than theological objection, though the act alleged that funds were not being used for the 'godly purposes' intended by the founders. Still, that such an extraordinary measure could be proposed and passed was an indication of how deeply the doctrine of purgatory had been eroded and discredited – by incessant evangelical preaching, and by the King's own hostile ambivalence. It was nonetheless touch-and-go in the Commons. 'The book of colleges etc. escaped narrowly and was driven over to the last hour, and yet then passed only by division of the house,' was Petre's crisp summary for Paget.[75]

Parliament concluded its business, which included the welcome grant of a subsidy to the King, on Christmas Eve. Henry himself attended the closing ceremony, and gave a speech. The King's theme was how 'charity between man and man' had become 'refrigerate'. His words were passionate, poignant, persuasive. Preachers inveighed against each other 'without charity or discretion'. People traded in opprobrious names: 'The one calleth the other heretic and anabaptist, and he calleth him again, papist, hypocrite and Pharisee.' All were 'names devised by the devil'. No one side was wholly to blame: 'Some be too stiff in their old Mumpsimus, other be too busy and curious in their new Sumpsimus.' The remedy? Bishops and clergy must mend their divisions and give example to the rest. And the whole nation must follow the lead of the King: he exhorted everyone 'to travel with him'. Henry, an emotional man, moved himself to tears as he spoke, and his audience – hardened burgesses and aristocrats – broke too into bouts of weeping.[76]

It was all, no doubt, sincerely meant. But beneath the rhetorical icing, the sentiments were hackneyed and stale. For years, royal pronouncements had vainly exhorted subjects to stop calling each other 'papist' and 'heretic'. Even 'Mumpsimus' and 'Sumpsimus' was the recycling of an old humanist joke (see p. 44). Henry's was an age that instinctively identified the best path as a middle way between extremes, Aristotle's 'Golden Mean'. Yet through a decade punctuated by brutal parallel executions, England had painfully learned that the King's 'middle way' was not a mild theological ecumenism, but an assertion of his right to discipline anything he chose to define as dissent.

Henry wanted his people to travel with him, but the destination was bafflingly uncertain. His theology was a moving target, a work in progress, a nest of contradictions. The King spoke often of 'the Word of God', but didn't trust people to read the bible faithfully; he disallowed the authority of tradition, but retained his right to prescribe venerable ceremonies on a case-by-case basis; he distrusted priests and their pretensions, but preserved the priestly prerogatives of confession and the mass. Most perplexingly of all, Henry unwired a core connection of traditional faith – that Christians could work collectively for each other's salvation, through the intercessory work of monasteries, and prayer for souls in purgatory – but he rejected the electrifying theological alternative: God's offer of justification through faith alone.[77] The one constant was an insistence on obedience and unswerving personal loyalty. For some of his subjects, this was enough. But others, in places high and low, increasingly came to see official pronouncements on religion as challenges to surmount rather than as gifts to treasure. The King could decree peace and unity in a refrigerate world, but charity's temperature had further yet to fall.

## Refrigerate Charity

In January 1546 the evangelical cause seemed poised on the brink of another significant breakthrough. Cranmer, working hand-in-glove with Paget, learned that Henry was ready to move again on the question of ceremonies, and drafted a directive for the King to sign. The order abolished the vigils of feasts of Our Lady and the Apostles, and the practice of ringing church bells on the evening of All Saints' Day (Halloween). Images would no longer be covered or 'veiled' during Lent, and the Easter custom of 'creeping to the cross' (specifically defended by proclamation in 1538) was also to cease. Such veneration of the crucifix, Cranmer ingeniously suggested, was contrary to the exposition of the Second Commandment in the King's Book.

It is a striking indication of how unwedded to tradition the King had become. But Henry remained more anxious about his position on the European stage than his domestic credentials as a reformer. Gardiner caught wind of the plan and wrote from Brussels warning it would endanger delicate negotiations with the Emperor. When Sir Anthony Denny brought the letters for Henry to sign, he found him 'now otherways resolved'.[78]

Gardiner returned to England in March, wrapped in the kudos of a fresh imperial alliance. 'It is not probable that the gospel will be purely and seriously received,' the English exile Richard Hilles wrote despairingly to Bullinger on 30 April, 'while those are alive who now hold the reins of government.' The broader international outlook was ominous: only evil 'is to be expected from those unclean birds now assembled at Trent'.[79] After years of prevarication and delay, the papacy had convened a General Council of the Church; Rome's counter-offensive was finally under way.

To evangelicals, it seemed as if agents of that counter-attack were gaining control over the English Church. The battleground of choice, for both sides, was the nature of the eucharist. This was an argument conservatives were happy to take to the public in the vernacular. Four treatises defending the real presence, and the mass as a sacrifice, appeared in 1546: one was the work of Gardiner himself, two were by the pugnacious Oxford theologian Richard Smyth, and the fourth by William Peryn, a former Dominican friar, who fled the country for Louvain in 1534, but returned in 1543 – an alarming (to evangelicals) vote of confidence in the King's Book. It was perhaps around now – though the timing is uncertain – that Cranmer finally abandoned his 'Lutheran' view of the eucharist, and came privately to agree with the sacramentarians he previously opposed.[80]

With the now ailing King firm in his belief in a real, substantial presence, the eucharist remained the reformers' political weak spot, and the spring and summer of 1546 witnessed a ruthless drive to exploit it. It started with a Lenten sermon on 11 April by Edward Crome, at which he denounced the mass as a sacrifice for the living or the dead. At what was supposed to be a recantation sermon on 9 May, he boldly restated his opinions, causing a furore in the capital. The Privy Council pulled him in, and secured royal permission to demand the names of associates, 'sundry persons of divers qualities', in the city and at the court. A wave of arrests and interrogations followed. Those implicated included the ex-bishops Latimer and Shaxton, Rowland Taylor, a clerical protégé of Cranmer, Robert Wisdom (who fled abroad), the courtiers John Lassells and Robert Huicke (a royal physician), and Anne Askew.

Askew was a young gentlewoman who came to London from rural Lincolnshire in 1544 to escape a boorish Catholic husband, and to commune with kindred spirits sharing her zeal for the Gospel. She had connections to the court, where her brother was a Cup Bearer. Anne had already been arrested and interrogated by Bonner. She was remarkably adept at refusing to state clearly her opinion: a female, evangelical version of Thomas More. The bishop – belying his reputation as a ruthless persecutor – released her after securing what barely counted as a recantation. She said she agreed with the statement prepared for her on the eucharist 'as much thereof, as the Holy Scripture doth agree to', and added that 'I, Anne Askew, do believe all manner things contained in the faith of the Catholic Church'. Askew's understanding of 'the Catholic Church' was not that of her accusers. On 24 May 1546, the Privy Council ordered her arrested again.

Crome himself recanted, plausibly if not sincerely, on 27 June. According to the imperial ambassador, this 'had a very good effect upon the common people'. A new proclamation against heretical books was issued on 8 July, offsetting the conservative failure to secure a parliamentary act to that effect the previous winter.[81]

This time, though, the enemies of the gospellers were playing for high stakes, and were not content with mere tactical point scoring. Wriothesley, more than Gardiner, was the driving force; the instrument of destruction was to be Anne Askew. She was repeatedly questioned about her connection to ladies of the court: the Countess of Hertford, Lady Denny, the Duchess of Suffolk. Implicating them in heresy was a means of bringing down their husbands. And conservatives on the Privy Council may have set their sights still higher.

John Foxe recounts a tale that seems likely to contain a kernel of truth. Queen Catherine's repeated urgings to press on with 'cleansing and purging his Church of England' began to irritate Henry, who let slip exasperated comments in the presence of Gardiner. The bishop's response was an offer to investigate the Queen's orthodoxy, and get the Council to draw up formal articles of accusation. Catherine was saved when a royal physician, the evangelical Thomas Wendy, learned what was afoot and tipped her off. She went straight to Henry, threw herself on his mercy (and his lap), and protested she only ever talked theology to distract him from bodily pains, and learn from the wisdom of his answers. Henry was mollified, and when Wriothesley arrived the following day to arrest the Queen, as she and Henry walked in the garden of Whitehall Palace, the King drove him off with stage whispers of 'arrant knave, beast and fool'.

The account is full of accurate circumstantial details, and far from intrinsically implausible. Four previous queens were toppled, for a mixture of personal and political reasons, why not a fifth? Gardiner's role may have been smaller than Foxe suggested, and the episode perhaps preceded, rather than followed, the second arrest of Askew.[82] If so, the debacle fuelled the determination of Wriothesley and his allies to break the power of the court evangelicals.

Arraigned under the Six Articles, Askew refused to retract her sacramentarian beliefs. Of those indicted with her, the city merchant Christopher White and the former bishop of Salisbury, Nicholas Shaxton, both abjured. As Askew lay condemned in the Tower, Wriothesley and Rich came and demanded names. In flagrant disregard of the law, they put her to the rack. When the Lieutenant of the Tower refused to continue with the torture, Wriothesley and Rich operated the device themselves. Geoffrey Pole had broken under much lesser pressure; Anne Askew was made of strong stuff.

Askew was burned before a large crowd at Smithfield on 16 July 1546, her body so broken she was carried to the stake in a chair. With her died an Essex tailor, John Hadlam, a former Observant friar, John Hemsley, and the courtier John Lassells. Another courtier, George Blagge, should have been there too, but was saved by the impulsive intervention of the King, who liked Blagge, and nicknamed him his 'pig'. Shaxton preached. His experiences in 1546 cauterized his reformist tendencies and reignited his earlier orthodox faith; evangelicals never forgave him.

A young scholar, John Louthe, could not keep silent: 'a vengeance of you all that doth burn Christ's member!' He slipped away as a carter tried to punch him: the crowd, a microcosm of the London population, was divided in its sympathies. Louthe later remembered that when the fire was lit some pleasant drops of rain fell, and there was a 'cracking from heaven', seeming to him like 'God's own voice'. John Bale, too, heard reports from German merchants that the sky had altered colour, and a loud thunderclap 'declared therein the high displeasure of God'. Within months, he would publish two accounts of Askew's sufferings, laying the foundations for a literature of martyrology that would do more than any other genre to steel the resolve of Christ's 'faithful members', and their contempt for 'the Pope's blind cattle'.[83]

The stakes in July 1546 were higher than almost anyone present at the burning realized. As Askew underwent her ordeal in June, a papal agent, Guron Bertano, was kicking his heels at the French court. Paul III sent him there to see if Francis I might help bring about reconciliation between England and Rome. After an Anglo-French peace was ratified on 17 July, Henry signalled he would be willing to receive Bertano, known to him from residence at the English court many years earlier. He arrived in London two weeks later, and on

3 August met with Henry. The immediate issue was English presence at the Council of Trent. Henry indicated he would be prepared to send representatives, and to 'remit his affairs' to the Council, provided it was held in a more convenient place – such as France – and was authorized by 'all the Christian Princes'. Bertano told him that there was little prospect of relocating the Council to France, but a meeting of learned men, a kind of satellite council, might take place there.[84]

Henry was engaged in the kind of tentative contact with Rome that would, and had, cost other Englishmen their heads. It seems extraordinary, and it is hard to know what exactly was going through his mind. Perhaps some kind of nominal reconciliation, linked to a universal peace, and a council at which princes called the shots, appealed briefly to his sense of grandeur.

Bertano remained in England for nearly two months, but Henry – if he ever seriously entertained it – soon rejected the Roman option. He had contemplated it once before, in 1541, when it seemed the only alternative to complete diplomatic isolation. Peace with France now liberated him from this recurrent fear. The rising men of 1546 were the military titans of the recent war, Edward Seymour, Earl of Hertford, and John Dudley, the new Lord Lisle. Seymour was a friend to the court evangelicals; Dudley's stance was more ambiguous, but he was not connected to the conservative reaction. Van der Delft, the imperial ambassador, believed the 'great prosecution of heretics and sacramentarians' ceased when Seymour and Dudley returned to the court in August.[85]

On 24 August, in a purpose-built banqueting house, festooned with tapestries, in the grounds of Hampton Court, Henry entertained the newly arrived emissary, Claude d'Annebaut, Admiral of France. Cranmer was there, supporting the ailing Henry on his arm. A few years later, he revealed to his secretary something that 'few in England would have believed'. A plan was dreamt up for Francis I, like Henry, to break 'utterly' with Rome: the two monarchs would then pressure Charles V to follow suit. At the same time, they would 'change the mass in both the realms into a communion' – a vernacular, Lutheran-style service. The King asked Cranmer to draw up proposals for sending to Francis.[86]

In the space of barely three weeks, Henry had gone from pondering submission to Rome to planning a pan-European evangelical Reformation. Mumpsimus and Sumpsimus oscillated in the King's brain. It is again hard to be sure how serious the suggestions were. The idea that Henry might abandon the mass, along with a eucharistic theology he had put dozens of people to death for denying, seems extraordinary. Perhaps it was no more than diplomatic game-playing. But that Henry should even propose it underlines just how volatile and unpredictable religious politics had become, how little constancy or coherence there was, beyond the King's enduring expectation that everyone should 'travel with him'.

Henry was in reforming mood in the late summer of 1546. A week after the meeting with d'Annebaut, he delivered his answer to ambassadors of the Schmalkaldic League, who had come to England in a desperate search for allies after Charles V renewed open war in Germany in July. Henry offered money, and more: he would personally assume leadership of the League, henceforth to be known as 'the League Christian'. He also proposed to the Landgrave of Hesse and the Duke of Saxony that they send delegates to England, to debate points of theological difference and work towards 'one opinion of religion'.[87]

While the Germans pondered their response through the autumn, the situation remained febrile, edgy. It was increasingly evident to all that the old king did not have long to live. In early November, the French ambassador, Odet de Selve, reported rumours of dissension and jockeying for position 'among the principal men of this realm'. Dudley was banished from court, after striking Gardiner during a meeting of the Council. Orders went out across the country 'to enquire secretly for such as talked treason against this king or knew of any talk or conspiracy against him'.[88]

In these fraught conditions, Gardiner committed another of his periodic, and catastrophic, errors of judgement. Henry requested an exchange of some lands between the crown and the bishopric of Winchester; Gardiner made difficulties about it, and Henry was furious. The bishop wrote abjectly on 2 December protesting he 'would not willingly offend your Majesty for no worldly thing', but the ailing King's anger was not easily assuaged. The same day, Sir Richard Southwell informed the Privy Council that he knew things about the Earl of Surrey that 'touched his fidelity to the King'. Surrey was arrested and sent to the Tower, along with his father, the Duke of Norfolk.[89]

The simultaneous disgrace of England's two most powerful religious traditionalists was coincidence not conspiracy. Southwell was himself a conservative, rather than an evangelical, and Surrey's behaviour was flagrantly self-destructive. It was said he boasted of his high blood, and cursed the 'foul churl' Cromwell; he urged his sister to become the King's mistress; he planned to massacre the Council and seize the young prince. The sole charge on which he was tried, however, was that he had quartered his arms with those of Edward the Confessor. Heraldry was a deadly serious business.

Norfolk's crime was 'misprision' (unreported knowledge) of treason. But as Paget and Sir William Paulet interrogated the duke in the Tower, they probed for evidence of papal sympathies, which might implicate Gardiner too. Did he know about letters sent from Germany in 1541, in which 'my Lord of Winchester should have said he could devise a way how the King's Majesty might save all things upright with the said Bishop of Rome'? The evangelical exiles had for years excoriated Gardiner as a 'papist'. His enemies at court now insinuated it too. There were many in London, Ambassador van der Delft noted, who 'do not conceal their wish to see the bishop of Winchester and other adherents of the ancient faith sent to the Tower to keep company with the duke of Norfolk'.[90]

The evangelical cause was on the defensive in Europe in the winter of 1546–7. The Council of Trent remained in session, and had started to promulgate a string of definitions and anathemas to give heart to the hitherto beleaguered adherents of Rome. Persecution of heretics was intensifying in France, and in Charles V's Netherlandish territories. In Germany, his armies were poised to restart campaigning, and deliver a knockout blow to the rebellious 'Protestants'.

In England, however, it seemed as if the dying Henry VIII had taken a decision to back the losing side. In the presence of Seymour, Dudley, Paget and Lord Russell, Henry told a Schmalkaldic envoy 'that if the quarrel of the duke of Saxony were nothing else against the Emperor, but for religion, he would stand to it strongly, and he would take his part'. The exiled John Hooper, writing to Bullinger from Basel in mid-December, was perhaps not in the best position to know what was going on in England. Nonetheless, he was cautiously optimistic: 'there will be a change of religion ... and the King will take up the gospel of Christ'. But Hooper had learned not to trust in the constancy of princes. This would happen only if the Emperor was defeated in Germany; should he be victorious, Henry 'will then retain his impious mass'.[91]

On 26 December, believing the end to be close, Henry summoned his councillors and told them to bring a copy of the will he had prepared before setting off for war in 1544. He ordered the names of Gardiner, and of Gardiner's ally Bishop Thirlby of Westminster, to be removed from the list of executors to serve on a regency council for his son. Another of the executors, Sir Anthony Browne, found an excuse to return to the King's bedside, and suggested that Gardiner's name must have been omitted by oversight. Henry put him straight: 'I remembered him well enough, and of good purpose have left him out ... I myself could use him, and rule him to all manner of purposes, as seemed good to me, but so shall you never do ... he is of so troublesome a nature'.[92]

This suggests something more significant than a disproportionate irritation over an exchange of episcopal lands. It was scarcely the smooth execution of an evangelical coup. Known reformers were a minority among the sixteen remaining executors, whose numbers included prominent conservatives such as Wriothesley and Tunstall.[93] But at the last Henry contemplated the most valuable of all the legacies he would leave to his son – the sublime discovery of his adult life, and the very crucible of his sense of self: his supreme headship of the Church. Who would help to keep it safe? Very likely, Henry feared the bishop of Winchester was the man to overturn his favoured policy of balance and control, and tilt the nation back towards Rome.

Henry, presumably, felt it had all been worth it. The struggles, stress, dangers and destiny of the last fifteen years represented a successful discharge of his vocation, the fulfilment of a divine plan. The irony Henry never fully discerned was that probably relatively few people other than the King himself believed, *really* believed, in the supremacy for its own sake. Conservatives welcomed the royal commitment to tradition, erratic as it was. Evangelicals desperately wanted to see Henry as the reforming instrument of providence, but experience had made many of them wary, if not cynical. As a doctrine of faith, the supremacy pointed to no truths more profound than the terms of its own formulation. Henry created it and preserved it intact, but at the cost of hundreds of lives, and of the very unity among his subjects with which the King was so consistently obsessed.

But if Henry divided his people, he also, unwittingly, helped emancipate them. With the destructive abolition of old pieties, and in the absence of coherent or compelling alternatives emanating from the crown, increasing numbers of English people were taking responsibility for their own under-standing of religious truth, helping to forge the new Christianities that would transform the face of the nation.

Surrey was beheaded on 19 January 1547. Death came for Henry nine days later. His own spiritual testament was as ambiguous as the religious course he had charted for his country. The will stipulated burial in the choir of St George's, Windsor, where an altar was to be furnished for two priests to say daily masses for him 'while the world shall endure'. There were to be four solemn annual obits, and at the funeral 1,000 marks for distribution to paupers with instruc-tions to pray for Henry's soul. All this from the monarch whose King's Book insisted that there was no certainty how, or if, individual suffrages might benefit the dead. Henry's will expressed confidence in salvation through his fulfilment of 'such good deeds and charitable works as Scripture commands'. But at the very end, he called for Cranmer, who performed for him no priestly rites or sacraments. He merely urged the King to ask for Christ's mercy, and to give some token 'that he trusted in the Lord'. Henry squeezed Cranmer's hand as hard as he could, 'and shortly after, departed'.[94]

# 10

## JOSIAH

### After Henry

IT TOOK JUST over a week for the news to spread nationwide. Thomas Butler, vicar of the small borough of Much Wenlock in Shropshire, wrote in the parish register that on 5 February 1547 'word and knowledge came thither . . . our Sovereign Lord King Henry VIII was departed out of this transitory life' – adding, 'whose soul God Almighty pardon'. The prayer was a conventional Catholic piety, but perhaps Butler did believe Henry had things for which to atone. For centuries, religious and economic life in Much Wenlock revolved around the Cluniac priory of St Milburga. In January 1540 the house was summarily dissolved. Butler's warm feeling for the dispersed community comes out in his careful recording, over many years, of the fates and fortunes of monks and servants 'sometime of the priory of St Milburga'.

Neither here, nor anywhere in England, was there open rejoicing at the death of the old king. In London, the news reportedly caused 'great lamentation and weeping', and across the country parishes rang their bells and arranged requiems on an unprecedented scale.[1] The grief was genuine, but there was also shock and disbelief, and anxious uncertainty about what followed now.

Within a couple of weeks, greater Christendom caught up with Much Wenlock. Richard Hilles, evangelical merchant, wrote from Strassburg on 25 February to pass the news to Bullinger, and to reassure him that the Earl of Hertford, the most powerful man in the new government, was 'a great enemy to the Pope of Rome'. At the same moment, Reginald Pole was writing to the Pope, pointing to a renewed opportunity to restore England to the Church, and applauding Paul III's decision to appoint new legates to France, Scotland and the Empire. Henry's death reset the clocks, instituting rival schedules of hope and ambition.

In Bologna, the news made the expatriate Welshman William Thomas the centre of attention at a dinner party in a rich merchant's house. One of his hosts wondered what on earth Thomas might find to say in Henry's favour, 'since he hath been known, and noted all over, to be the greatest tyrant that ever was in England'. The evangelical Thomas – once assured he might speak freely – found a great deal positive to say. But in the end he conceded that Henry 'did see but with one eye'. His son and heir, Thomas trusted, 'shall with no less perfection reform the true Church of Christ, not permitted by his said father to be finished, than as Solomon did the true Temple of Jerusalem, not granted to David in the time of his life'.[2]

The weight of evangelical expectation resting on the shoulders of the young king was doubtless made plain to him at his coronation on 20 February. A much-quoted address on the occasion by Archbishop Cranmer – in which he hailed the nine-year-old Edward as 'a second Josiah', the King of Judah who succeeded his father at the age of eight, and as a young adult destroyed altars and images erected to the worship of Baal – is, sadly, a clever late seventeenth-century forgery. But comparisons between Edward and Josiah were commonplace in evangelical sermons.[3]

Better documented are the revels and masks performed at the coronation, which involved the outlay of substantial sums to drapers, haberdashers and painters for 'grey kersey for friars', 'silk lace and taffeta for cardinals' hats', 'caps of crimson and black satin for priests', 'crowns and cross for the Pope'.[4] The vanquishing of popery was boisterously acted out at court, and would soon, more soberly, be attempted across the country.

That objective required firm hands on the levers of power. The sixteen-strong regency council appointed by Henry – divided between evangelicals, conservatives, pragmatists and enigmas – seemed set to oversee a continuation of the see-saw politics of Henry's last years. But even before the coronation, the balance had swung. In a move probably orchestrated by Paget, the councillors abandoned collective decision-making and elected Seymour as Lord Protector, to enjoy quasi-regal powers until the King turned eighteen. Their reward was a distribution of lands and titles Henry's will supposedly forgot to specify: William Parr became Marquis of Northampton; Wriothesley, Earl of Southampton; John Dudley, Earl of Warwick; Seymour himself, Duke of Somerset. Regency was the usual remedy for a royal minority, and a probably more sensible one than the committee government envisaged by Henry. Somerset, the new king's closest male relative, was the obvious choice for the role.

The new Duke of Somerset seemed neither a polished politician nor a single-minded gospeller. He was first and foremost a soldier, grimly determined to pursue to its conclusion the Scottish war, producing renewed conflict with France. But if fellow-councillors believed the rudder of the ship of state had passed into a safe pair of hands, willing to keep politics and religion on an even keel, they had misjudged their man. A fortnight after the coronation, Southampton was accused of abusing his office, dismissed as Lord Chancellor and removed from the Council.[5] His likely real offence was opposition to the protectorate. With Gardiner excluded, and Norfolk reprieved from execution but remaining in the Tower, conservative influence was fatally weakened.

The visage of the new regime was reflected in its choice of Lenten preachers. On Ash Wednesday, 23 February, Cranmer's protégé Nicholas Ridley preached at court, denouncing images and holy water. William Barlow, bishop of St David's, preached shortly afterwards in similar vein, to the consternation of Gardiner. He wrote to Somerset protesting it was 'a time rather to repair that [which] needeth repair, than to make any new buildings'. Still more disturbing was an outbreak of ritual iconoclasm in Portsmouth, in Gardiner's own diocese. The perpetrators pulled down an image of St John and disfigured a crucifix, piercing its side and boring out an eye. In London, too, reformers pre-empted policy. Even before the King was crowned, the curate and churchwardens of St Martin's, Ironmonger Lane, remodelled their church, taking down the images and substituting for them scriptural sentences: 'Thou shalt make no graven images, lest thou worship them.' The rood was replaced with a painting of the royal arms.

This was too much, too quickly. The Privy Council ordered the rood at least to go back up, and gave the wardens 'a grave admonition'. Henry's settlement, including the Six Articles, remained in force. On 13 April, Bonner secured a renewed commission to inquire into breaches of the Six Articles, and a handful of sacramentarians were harassed that spring in London and Norwich.[6]

Cranmer and his allies had reasons to be circumspect. One was the Holy Roman Emperor, seriously concerned at the turn of events in England, and looking out for the welfare of his cousin, the Princess Mary. It was an arithmetical rule of English foreign policy that the Emperor must not be added to the column of enemies at a time of conflict with France. On 24 April, Charles's army smashed the forces of the Lutheran Schmalkaldic League at Mühlberg, outside Leipzig. For the first time in two decades, he was in a position to enforce his will in Germany, and made plans to bring the Protestants into line.

Internal as well as external opposition was a force to be reckoned with, and a reason for proceeding with caution. Cranmer confided to his secretary Ralph Morice that 'we are now in doubt how men will take the change or alteration of abuses in the Church'. He added ruefully, with a touch of surely misplaced nostalgia, that reformation was an easier matter in the previous reign, for 'if the King's father had set forth anything for the reformation of abuses, who was he that durst gainsay it?' On 24 May, the government issued a reassuring proclamation, condemning false rumours of impending 'innovations and changes in religion'.[7]

That was a piece of misdirection and misinformation of which Cromwell might have been proud. Despite Cranmer's ruminations on Henry's bluff indefatigability, the old King was usually alert to the dangers of popular opposition, and he tacked instinctively to the centre when he perceived the need to conciliate the Emperor. In similar circumstances, and lacking the legitimacy of adult monarchical rule, the new government might be expected to do the same. In fact, it was drawing breath before embarking on a programme of daring and dizzying change.

### Visitation

The signs were there. Nine days before the proclamation, Richard Smyth, Oxford Regius Professor of Divinity, was publically humiliated. A stalwart of the conservative surge of 1546, Smyth kept up the momentum early in 1547 by publishing a treatise maintaining that the authority of apostolic tradition was equal to that of scripture. He was forced to renounce such 'unwritten verities', as well as his eucharistic beliefs, from the pulpit of Paul's Cross. Smyth's ally, the theologian William Peryn, preached in favour of images, but he too was made to recant. Peryn had once before been an exile at Louvain, and he returned there in the early summer.

He was preceded to Louvain, in April 1547, by a London rector, John Foxe – not the martyrologist, but a one-time monk of the London Charterhouse. With the assistance of two fellow former Carthusians, Thomas Munday and Thurston Hickman, Foxe planned to take with him the left arm of their martyred prior, John Houghton, which he had kept hidden in the altar of his church of St Mary Magdalene, Old Fish Street. The scheme was discovered and the relic seized. John Hooper, still in exile at Zürich, heard the story, and expressed the gruesome hope that those responsible be 'put to death in the church upon the same altar where this relic was hid' – an act of such bloodshedding would be a blessing of the building, not a desecration of it. Hickman and Munday were sentenced to death as traitors, but were pardoned early the following year – a significant indication that the new regime was reluctant to make martyrs of recalcitrant Catholics.[8] One such recalcitrant, in despair at the turn of events, made a martyr of himself. In May 1547, Richard Langryche, archdeacon of Cleveland in Yorkshire, and a closet papalist close to the exiles of Pole's circle, drowned himself by leaping into the Thames from the cloister of St Magnus the Martyr, by London Bridge.[9] Perhaps he sensed what was coming next.

There was to be a new royal visitation, picking up where Cromwell left matters in 1538. Plans for it were unveiled in May, but injunctions were not issued until July, and the visitors only set off in August. The delay was due to making ready a key instrument of reform: a Book of Homilies, which all parishes were to acquire, and from which all clergy were to read to their people, Sunday by Sunday.

There were twelve homilies in the collection, some on uncontroversial subjects, such as the wickedness of swearing and perjury. The homily 'against contention and brawling' plucked on a familiar string – uncharitable quarrelling about religion, 'upon the alebenches or other places'. It sought to shame listeners into modesty of word and demeanour. St Paul detested to hear among the Corinthians, 'I hold of Paul, I of Cephas, and I of Apollo'. What would he think if he could hear the words of contention 'which be now almost in every man's mouth': 'he is a Pharisee, he is a new-broached brother, he is a good Catholic father, he is a papist, he is a heretic'? The mystical body of Christ, once a garment without seam, was rent and torn.

It sounded like a Catholic lament, or typical Henrician hand-wringing. But there was a twist. Charity and silence were not always the appropriate responses; at times it was necessary 'to answer a fool according to his foolishness'. Christ's own example licensed righteous rebuke and godly zeal. The homily contained a revealing (and chilling) illustration from the Old Testament: Moses in his anger broke the tablets of the law 'when he saw the Israelites dancing about a [golden] calf, and caused to be killed 23,000 of his own people'. The author of this sanguinary sermon was perhaps Latimer; the opening salutation to 'good Christian people' is characteristic of his preaching style.[10]

Suffering fools was certainly no characteristic of the Homilies as a whole. The homily 'Of Good Works' culminated in a sarcastic litany of the 'false doctrine, superstition, idolatry, hypocrisy' that hindered the progress of God's Word: relics, images, shrines, monasteries, rosary beads, holy water, bells, palms, candles, fraternities, purgatory and a host of 'papistical superstitions'. Such practices were 'by Antichrist invented'.

The homily was framed as an epitaph for a vanquished world of delusions: these were things used 'of late days ... among us'. This was disingenuous; monasticism was certainly banished, but several other items on the list (the use of Palm Sunday palms, for example) were still in the required ceremonial repertoire of the Church at the time the Injunctions were issued. Underlying the mockery was a gnawing anxiety, expressed as a piece of homespun anthropology: 'Such hath been the corrupt inclination of man, ever superstitiously given to make new honouring of God [out] of his own head.'

There was a remedy. The homily on good works was paired with another, 'Of the true, lively and Christian faith'. Cranmer wrote both, along with a third, crucial, homily on salvation. The archbishop was at pains to reiterate that faith was not the alternative to good works, but their grounding and source. And he returned to the nuanced qualification made in response to the King's Book in 1543, that a true saving faith must be accompanied by other virtues, such as repentance. But there was no equivocation: 'we be justified by faith only, freely, and without works'.[11] Luther's central theological insight, the animating impulse of the evangelical movement, was – without discussion by committee, Act of Parliament, or formula agreed in Convocation – now placed at the centre of the teaching mission of the English Church.

The Homilies praised Henry for promoting God's Word, and abolishing superstition, but they directly repudiated the teaching of the King's Book on the most foundational point of disputed theology. It was the ground on which Stephen Gardiner, colossus of Henrician conservatism, chose to make his stand. Gardiner bombarded Cranmer and Somerset with letters, questioning the legality of bypassing bishops and Convocation, and emphasizing the risks of confusing laypeople, and of discrediting the clergy, by requiring priests 'to rehearse an homily made by another'. Poorly delivered preaching was worse than no preaching at all. Gardiner knew of a parish in Cambridge: 'when the vicar goeth into the pulpit . . . the multitude of the parish goeth straight out of the church home to drink'.

Along with the tactical manoeuvres and special pleading, there was a more fundamental objection to the Homilies, and to the entire scheme of reform Gardiner knew Cranmer and Somerset were preparing to unleash. It was neither sensible nor right to change Henry VIII's settlement while his son was a minor. The Council should 'deliver this realm to the King at 18 years of age, as the King his father, whose soul God assoil, left it'. It was a shrewd blow at the weakest point in the armour of the new regime. Minorities, as England's experience in the fifteenth century painfully recalled, were often times of crisis and instability: why rock the boat? Josiah was the exemplar of youthful godliness, but minds might easily turn to another Old Testament text, a poignant warning in the book of Ecclesiastes: 'woe to thee, O land, when thy king is a child'. With his lawyer's sense for a good, counter-intuitive argument, Gardiner suggested that further reforms in England would actually be pleasing to Rome, reinforcing the Pope's argument 'that where his authority is abolished, there, at every change of governors, shall be change in religion'.[12]

Gardiner's forensic brilliance could not, however, conceal a fundamental weakness in his argument. The conservatives' watchwords were tradition, obedience and authority. But through the preceding reign it was obedience to royal authority, and acceptance of the crown's right to prescribe ceremonies and traditions, which underpinned their public positions. For the royal supremacy to turn unequivocally against them was a disaster. If Catholicism without the Pope was now Catholicism without pope or king, it was hard to see where it had left to go, other than homewards to Rome. Professions of loyalty to Henry of blessed memory, to the King's Book and Six Articles, had some popular appeal. But it was a strategy without an obvious future.

For signs were starting to emerge, in his homework and Latin exercise books, that young Edward had inhaled deeply the atmosphere of evangelical humanism generated by his tutors and his step-mother, Catherine Parr. What Edward might do on reaching his majority should have filled Catholics with trepidation, not optimism.[13] The hope – unspoken, unspeakable – was that the King might fall into the hands of better guardians, able to temper his youthful enthusiasms. Somerset was not, in fact, Edward's closest blood relative. The King's half-sister, Mary, was now a resolute woman of thirty-one, and, to some, the ideal candidate for regent.

Gardiner's protests notwithstanding, the visitation got under way at the end of August. The injunctions were a version of those of 1538, with significant additions and modifications. Churches were to set up a box for offerings to the poor, an alternative repository for monies previously bestowed upon 'blind devotions'. In addition to the bible, all parishes were to purchase a copy of Erasmus's gospel *Paraphrases*, an English translation of which was begun at the end of the last reign under the supervision of Catherine Parr, to which the Princess Mary was persuaded to contribute. The final product was a less ecumenical exercise than this pedigree suggested. Its evangelical editor, Nicholas Udall, declared in the Preface that the papacy had 'infected the clear fountain of God's Word with the suds of human traditions', co-opting Erasmus as a supporter of the break with Rome.[14]

A range of devotional activities was further regulated and restricted. Recitation of the rosary was now condemned, and parish processions – an important focus of local ritual and ceremonial life – were forbidden. Thomas Foster of Louth's 1536 prediction that people would be prevented from following the cross turned out to be prescient. A new injunction based itself on the order Henry produced on his return from Hull in 1541, angered at the survival of northern superstitions. The material clutter of pilgrimage – 'shrines, covering of shrines, all tables, candlesticks, trindles or rolls of wax, pictures, paintings, and all other monuments of feigned miracles' – was to be destroyed, 'so that there remain no memory of the same'. Obliteration was to include wall-paintings and stained-glass windows, and curates must exhort parishioners 'to do the like within their several houses'.

The Injunctions did not prohibit images, though the concession of 1538 that they served as 'books of unlearned men' was dropped in favour of a grudging statement that they served no other purpose than as 'a remembrance, whereby men may be admonished of the holy lives and conversation of them that the said images do represent'. No candles were to burn in front of them – not even before the crucifix on the rood loft, where many parishes relocated their votive lights after the restrictions of 1538. The Injunctions further specified not just removal, but destruction of 'abused' images, and added censing (perfuming with incense) to the list of what constituted abuse.[15]

There was the potential for both lenient and rigorist interpretation of what the Injunctions said about images. The selection of visitors ensured the latter would prevail. Six sets of commissioners toured the country in circuits. Almost without exception, they were convinced evangelical reformers, men such as Nicholas Ridley, Richard Morison, Dean Simon Heynes of Exeter and Christopher Nevinson, a veteran of the Henrician culture wars in Cranmer's diocese of Canterbury. There were survivors – like George Constantine – of the earliest days of the evangelical movement, but also a few who burned with the zeal of recent converts. John Old, registrar to the commissioners of the midland circuit, recalled in 1556 how it had been ten or eleven years since his 'first entry into the gospel', and his emergence out of 'the damnable darkness of Antichrist's iniquity'.[16]

Armed with powers to supplement the Injunctions with ones of their own, the visitors oversaw a transformation of England's churches. In parish after parish, they ordered images removed and walls limewashed. The sometimes surprisingly large sums incurred were recorded in parish accounts: at Tilney in Norfolk the wardens paid 35 shillings 'for whiting of the church and stopping of the holes' – the niches where statues stood. The process was particularly thorough in London, where, the chronicler Charles Wriothesley neutrally recorded, 'All images in every parish church . . . were pulled down and broken by the commandment of the said visitors.'

No distinction was made between images of saints and carved figures of Christ. The great roods – visual centrepiece of every church, and material embodiment of Catholicism's incarnational theology – started to come down. At St Paul's in London, the labourers were careless: the rood fell crashing from its mounting and two of their number were killed. 'The papish priests said it was the will of God for pulling down of the said idols', Wriothesley's chronicle derisively noted. The imperial ambassador, Francis Van der Delft, noticed how destruction of roods went beyond the letter of the Injunctions, and protested to Somerset. The Lord Protector replied they would indeed have remained, were it not for 'the superstitious simplicity of the people, who constantly continued still to come and offer out of their poverty both wheat and bread' – all pocketed by avaricious priests. Somerset, his forces now heavily engaged in Scotland, blandly reassured the ambassador no further innovations were in the offing.[17]

The nationwide iconoclasm of autumn 1547 was no mere bureaucratic enforcement of regulations: it was a festival of destruction, a performance of gleeful triumph of the new ways over the old. As in 1538, there were moments of drama and revelation. Bishop Barlow preached at Paul's Cross on 27 November, taking with him into the pulpit an image of the Resurrection of Christ. This was 'made with vices', allowing a puppet Jesus to emerge from the sepulchre and bless onlookers with his hand. It was scarcely fraud of the kind John Hilsey alleged about the Rood of Boxley from the same pulpit a decade before, but that no longer mattered. Barlow preached against 'the great abomination of idolatry in images', showing as a further exhibit an image of Our Lady the clergy of St Paul's tried to hide from the visitors. After the sermon, the 'idols' were handed to the apprentice boys in the crowd and smashed to pieces.

Provincial towns staged their own spectaculars. At Shrewsbury, images of Our Lady, Mary Magdalene and St Chadd were gathered from the churches, and burned in the marketplace. A few miles to the south-east, at Thomas Butler's Much Wenlock, another bonfire was lit on 7 November: the bones of St Milburga were consumed along with four images from neighbouring parish churches. Milburga was the most indigenous of saints, an Anglo-Saxon princess and founding abbess of Wenlock's first religious house. To record the event, Butler switched from his accustomed English into Latin, a linguistic indication of distress at this violation of local pieties.[18]

Butler's pain was widely shared, but there was little that isolated traditionalists could attempt in the face of a well-orchestrated campaign with the force of law behind it. Even bishops could do little to resist or obstruct the visitors. Bonner tried, protesting he would only observe the Injunctions 'if they be not contrary to God's law and the statutes and ordinances of this Church'. He spent nearly a fortnight in the Fleet Prison before arriving at 'better consideration of my duty of obedience'. But Gardiner, the high priest of 'true obedience', had found his sticking point. He was sent to the Fleet on 25 September, and remained there for the rest of the year.[19]

Supporters of iconoclasm were a minority of the population, but more visible than its opponents, and sometimes willing to run ahead of the law. In Norwich, a band of 'curates and other idle persons' went through the city churches pulling down and taking away images. The city authorities rather impotently ordered they should 'surcease of such unlawful doings'. London, too, witnessed unofficial iconoclasm. The Privy Council at first determined on punishment for those taking down statues without authority, and for such images to be restored. But by 26 September it reached the conclusion that this 'might engender confusion among the people whether they were abused or no'.[20] A pattern was starting to emerge. The government would allow the pace to be set by pressure from below, and under guise of seeking to restrain it, edge the process decisively forwards.

## Services for the Living and Dead

Through the noise and activity of the summer and autumn, there was resounding silence – at least on the official side – about one imperative issue. The Homilies had nothing to say about the nature of the eucharist. Evangelicals were vocal, in pulpit and print, about the iniquities of the mass, but it remained the official act of worship. Moreover, the Six Articles were technically still in force, and anyone questioning the real, physical presence of Christ in the eucharist committed, in theory, a heinous, capital offence.

The remedy lay in a Parliament. It assembled, finally, on 4 November 1547, and within a week a bill entered the Lords for comprehensive abolition of all new felonies created in the reign of Henry VIII. These were, the act's preamble confidently proclaimed, less tempestuous times, not requiring such severe restraints. Heresy and treason legislation was repealed, though the new act retained some provision for treason by words only.[21] Crucially, the Six Articles were gone; respect for the mass was no longer ring-fenced by law.

At the start of December there were more words of reassurance for an anxious imperial ambassador: Somerset pointed out that the King attended mass at the opening of Parliament, and continued to have celebrations of it at court. Van der Delft was unconvinced; he had heard that mass was no longer said in the Protector's own house, in the Earl of Warwick's (Dudley's) or in Catherine Parr's. Though mass continued to be performed in the churches, common people 'are beginning to sing psalms in their own language'. Such adaptations on the ground were not unwelcome to the evangelical leadership. At the mass that opened the Parliament, Nicholas Ridley preached, and the main parts – Gloria, Creed, Sanctus, Benedictus and Agnus Dei – were all sung in English.[22]

Further ambiguous signals appeared in an Act of Parliament, passed on 10 December and reinforced by proclamation a fortnight later. The act presented itself as a measure against 'revilers of the sacrament', designed to rein in aggressive evangelical polemicists. There were threats of fines and imprisonment for people who 'marvellously abused' the eucharist with unseemly words in 'sermons, preachings, readings, lectures, communications, arguments, talks, rhymes, songs, plays, or jests'.

It was not like the defence of the sacrament undertaken by Gardiner, Peryn and Smyth in 1546. The proclamation optimistically declared scripture to contain completely clear and sufficient guidance to the nature of the eucharist. The bread was 'the communion or partaking of the body of Our Lord' – a firm statement of 'presence', which also employed the conservatives' favoured form of supplicatory address to God. But any further conjecture was arrogant and unedifying. In picking as examples of unhelpful speculation whether Christ was present 'by substance only, or else but in a figure and manner of speaking', the proclamation even-handedly rebuked sacramentarians and transubstantiationists. The high-minded tone provided useful cover for the fact that evangelicals themselves, in England as across Europe, were divided over eucharistic doctrine. The dogmatic militancy of the radicals was an embarrassment and irritation to evangelical intellectuals hoping to build a broad consensus. People who insisted on asking 'how He was there present', an exasperated Nicholas Ridley declared in a Paul's Cross sermon that November, were 'worse than dogs and hogs'.[23]

The real meat of the act was slipped in as an apparent afterthought. To be more agreeable to the first institution of the eucharist, and to the practice of the

Church for 500 years after Christ, communicants should receive under both kinds, wine as well as bread. Demands for 'the cup' were the central concern for Hussite heretics in the fifteenth century, and the clerical monopoly of communion wine was, from the 1520s onwards, a staple of evangelical attacks on traditional priesthood.

The issue, in itself, was of relatively little theological weight: few if any believed Christ was only present cumulatively in bread and wine, like a picture across interlocking pieces of a jigsaw. Yet communion in two kinds was totemic of the differences between opponents and defenders of the old order, which is why Bishops Bonner, Rugge of Norwich, Day of Chichester, Skip of Hereford and Heath of Worcester all voted against the measure in the Lords. A petition to introduce it had already come from the lower clergy in Convocation, along with calls to legalize clerical marriage. In years past, the Lower House of Convocation had been a bastion of religious conservatism. It is more likely that the royal visitors had helped to ensure the return of pliant representatives than that the clergy as a whole were swinging decisively in favour of reform.[24]

One significant measure remained to be dealt with before Parliament dispersed for its Christmas recess. A bill 'for chantries' was introduced into the Lords on 6 December, and passed on Christmas Eve. The blow had been a long time falling. Henry VIII's Chantries Act of 1545 set a precedent for dissolution, and in the meantime the doctrine of purgatory had been further undermined: in the Homilies, and in a new form of bidding prayers stipulated by the Injunctions. Prayer for the dead was refocused, away from their current condition and towards a future state of felicity: 'that they with us, and we with them at the day of judgement, may rest both body and soul, with Abraham, Isaac, and Jacob in the Kingdom of Heaven'.

The justification given for seizing the endowments of intercession, from elaborate chantries and colleges, through parish guilds and fraternities, down to anniversary observances, and simple obit lamps, was – in contrast to the Henrician act – unapologetically religious. Ignorance of the meaning of salvation through the death of Christ had been promoted by 'devising and phantasing vain opinions of purgatory and masses satisfactory, to be done for them which be departed'.

After this unequivocal statement, the act itself was long and convoluted, offering reassurances to various institutions, interests and private individuals. Corporations and craft guilds were to lose only those revenues devoted to 'superstitious' purposes; the soon-to-be-appointed chantry commissioners were granted powers to re-endow grammar schools and preaching stipends supported out of chantry funds; and where populous parishes were threatened with the loss of vital clerical manpower, they could assign revenues 'towards the sufficient finding and maintenance of one or more priests'.

The Chantries Act was emblazoned with the idealism of the evangelical reformers. It began with a promise that suppressing the blindness and ignorance of prayer for the dead would allow King and Council to convert wasted resources to 'good and godly uses': schools, universities, 'better provision for the poor and needy'.[25]

It sounded all too familiar. Promises of lavish investment in social and religious causes echoed around the last large-scale government seizure of church assets. But very little monastic wealth was returned to the localities. Financial pressures on government had in the meantime increased. To the ongoing expense of maintaining Henry VIII's meagre conquests in France, Somerset added the costs of a major offensive in Scotland. It had ambitious geo-political objectives: nothing less than the creation of an Anglo-Scots, 'British' polity through a union between King Edward and the young Mary, Queen of Scots, a marriage to which the Scots had agreed, back in 1543, but subsequently reneged.

The war began spectacularly well. On 10 September, the English were victorious at the battle of Pinkie – a slaughter of Scotsmen greater even than at Flodden in 1513. But the government in Scotland refused to capitulate, and sought aid from the French; the English campaign increasingly lost momentum and direction. Somerset's policy of consolidating English gains through establishment of numerous permanent garrisons was hugely, ruinously, expensive.[26]

Good reasons to suspect, then, that chantry revenues were destined not for preachers' stipends but for soldiers' victuals. There seems little other way to account for the extraordinary fact that on 15 December, at the fourth reading of the bill in the House of Lords, Cranmer joined with Bonner, Tunstall and other conservative bishops in voting against the measure. He was evidently sufficiently reassured to support its final passage nine days later. But, at the close of an extraordinary year of liberating, revolutionary change, it was a small but revealing portent of troubles ahead.[27]

## The Time of Schism

The second year of Edward VI was a terminus and a tipping-point. Shortly after the King's death, the churchwardens of Stanford-in-the-Vale, Berkshire, would look back and identify the early part of 1548, not 1534, as 'the time of schism, when this realm was divided from the Catholic Church'.[28]

In the depths of winter, a brisk pace was being set. On 18 January, the Council abolished ashes for Ash Wednesday, palms on Palm Sunday and – most poignantly – candles on the Feast of the Purification of the Virgin (Candlemas), then only a fortnight away. The clean-sweep of 'sacramentals' was completed shortly afterwards when Cranmer wrote to the bishops ordering them to enforce bans on holy bread, holy water and creeping to the cross on Good Friday – the measure Cranmer nearly persuaded Henry to agree to in

January 1546. It was all carried out under a cloak of restraint and moderation: a proclamation of 6 February forbad preachers or laypeople from persuading people against 'the old accustomed rites and ceremonies', or bringing in innovations of their own. But written instructions appended to episcopal copies of the proclamation made clear that the restrictions did not apply to any changes Cranmer had already ordered, or might do hereafter.[29]

A momentous order was already being prepared. Images were removed from London churches before the end of the preceding year, but in other places, reformers and conservatives argued ferociously over whether particular statues had been 'abused' in the sense intended by the Injunctions. In a Paul's Cross sermon of 18 January, Hugh Latimer fulminated against the persuasions of 'blanchers' – white-washers – who insinuated that abuse of images was a small matter, easily reformed. These people urged caution, warning that 'the people will not bear sudden alterations; an insurrection may be made'. No doubt blanchers once whispered in the ear of godly King Hezekiah. But he nonetheless 'cast out all images; he destroyed all idolatry'.

On 21 February, the Council decided Edward should be Hezekiah. Cranmer, who undoubtedly approved the order, was told to implement a complete removal of images as the only way to avoid 'strife and contention' happening in 'almost every place'. Once again, a radical leap of reform represented itself as a steady step for unity and quietness, and the emphasis was now on removal, rather than destruction. But there was a whiff of old Lollardy around the councillors' declared concern that 'the lively images of Christ should not contend for [argue over] the dead images'.

The blanket ban on church imagery was a visual and aesthetic as well as a devotional revolution. For all of the downbeat manner of its introduction, evangelicals recognized a moment of glorious triumph. John ab Ulmis, a German refugee in Oxford, wrote excitedly to Bullinger that images were 'extirpated root and branch in every part of England'. There was more: 'the mass, that darling of the papists, is shaken'.[30]

The declaration against 'irreverent speaking' about the sacrament proved a dead letter. Early Edwardian London experienced both an implosion of images, and an explosion of expository texts. It was fuelled by the removal of Henrician censorship, the patronage of evangelical presses by Somerset, Cranmer and other leading figures, and by the relocation to London of experienced continental printers, such as Steven Mierdman, a refugee from Charles V's crackdown on evangelicals in Antwerp. In the early 1540s the London presses produced around 100 editions per year; in 1547 that figure shot up to 192, and in 1548 to 268. 'What a number of books there be abroad, in every man's hand,' marvelled the evangelical writer Philip Nichols. The overwhelming majority were religious, and jostling alongside the more sombre bibles and catechisms were dozens of short, racy pamphlets attacking the Catholic clergy and the mass.

The titles of items published in 1548 speak for themselves: *The Indictment against Mother Mass*; *The Upcheering of the Popish Mass*; *A Brief Recantation of Mistress Missa*. The consecrated host was 'Round Robin', 'Jack of the box'. The authors were zealots, but not necessarily outsiders. The mock trial conducted in an *Examination of the Mass* was the brainchild of William Turner, a returning exile employed as a chaplain in Somerset's household.

For Catholics, to whom these were sacred mysteries, it all constituted an ordeal of derision and ridicule they could do little but endure. Miles Huggarde, an enterprising London hosier, composed *An Aunswer to the Ballad called the Abuse of ye Blessed Sacrament*, replying to the mockers in their own vein. Publication was suppressed, and Huggarde hauled before the Privy Council.[31]

There were serious theological critiques of the mass too – many of them in a rash of translations of the works of European divines; no fewer than thirty-seven of these appeared in 1548.[32] But it was not a time for reasoned, reflective argument, and nor did it matter that attacks on the mass were often radically incoherent, portraying it simultaneously as a ridiculous piece of empty pageantry, and a dangerous sink of Satanic infection. A growing body of evangelical believers – like the Lollards now in part subsumed into their ranks – measured themselves by their opposition to the mass. It was a backhanded tribute to the success of Catholic authorities, Roman and Henrician alike, in making eucharistic belief the touchstone of theological orthodoxy.

The wounds of a divided nation were most acutely apparent in London, but everywhere in England disunity was recognized as the new reality. In the early part of 1548, an incident took place at the free school in Bodmin, in the heart of Cornwall – undoubtedly comic, but ominously revealing of the world in which schoolchildren were growing up:

> The scholars, who used customably to divide themselves for better exploiting their pastimes, grew therethrough into two factions, the one whereof they called the old religion, the other the new. This once begun, was prosecuted among them in all exercises, and now and then handled with some eagerness and roughness . . . At last, one of the boys converted the spill of an old candlestick into a gun, charged it with powder and stone, and (through mischance or ungraciousness) therewith killed a calf. Whereupon, the owner complained, the master whipped, and the division ended.[33]

It seems highly unlikely that half the boys in Bodmin School were the sons of evangelical converts. But the selection of gang-names suggests that even children in the far corners of the land understood how the divide between reformers and conservatives was the political fact of the day. Religious allegiance, in play as in life, was becoming a matter of choice, of group solidarity, and occasionally – as the unfortunate cow discovered – of unpredictable violence.

Halfway between London and Bodmin, in the Dorset coastal town of Poole, the arrival of Thomas Hancock, a zealous evangelical curate, exacerbated tensions in an already divided community. Hancock's preaching against the mass provoked a walkout from church. 'Come from him, good people,' cried Thomas White, merchant and former mayor, 'he came from the devil and teacheth unto you devilish doctrine!' Hancock also had his supporters. They were, he later recalled, 'the first that in that part of England were called Protestants'. This nickname for German Lutherans was starting to be mockingly applied to evangelicals by their opponents; in time, they would adopt it for themselves.[34]

In London, the government believed it could control and use the pressure. But a proclamation of late 1547, condemning youths, servants and apprentices who behaved belligerently towards priests – 'reviling, tossing of them, taking violently their caps and tippets [ceremonial scarves] from them' – points to a current of religiously aggressive disorder it was difficult to turn on and off at will.[35]

On 8 March 1548 the mass, the great floating fortress of orthodoxy and tradition, moved at last on its moorings. A new 'Order for the Communion', enforced by proclamation, made an insertion into the liturgy, clarifying the arrangements for communion under both kinds. It was notable on at least two grounds. Firstly, it was in English: prayer and exhortation in the vernacular would now interrupt the flow of murmured Latin at a critical point in the celebration. Secondly, it contained a remarkable and unheralded innovation. As people prepared themselves for communion, the priest was to urge

such as shall be satisfied with a general confession [a text for this was provided], not to be offended with them that do use, to their further satisfying, the auricular and secret confession to the priest; nor those also which think needful or convenient for the quietness of their own consciences particularly to open their sins to the priest, to be offended with them that are satisfied with their humble confession to God, and the general confession to the Church.

In other words, confession to a priest – a key requirement of the Six Articles, and an obligation on all laypeople since the thirteenth century – was declared entirely optional. The implications were profound, and perhaps not entirely grasped at the time. The hold of the clergy on the consciences and compliance of laypeople was significantly weakened. Offered an opportunity to evade an onerous and often embarrassing annual duty, it is likely that a majority of laypeople, and not just convinced evangelicals, ceased confessing their sins to their curate.

The Order was not designed as a theological statement, but alert listeners heard that when Christians received the sacrament with a penitent heart, 'we spiritually eat the flesh of Christ'. If Christ was received 'spiritually', was he also there physically or 'really'?

At Easter that year, parishioners were offered opposing explanations. It was a time, complained a conservative chronicler, of 'much preaching throughout all England against the sacrament of the altar'. At St Paul's, the former friar John Cardmaker told people that 'it was but bread and wine'. In all London, only one preacher apparently stood against the innovators: William Leighton, canon of St Paul's, whose Sunday sermons caused 'much controversy and much business'. Yet in Cranmer's diocese of Canterbury several clergymen introduced the new Order with stout declarations that after consecration 'there remaineth no material bread'.

On Easter Sunday, at Womenswold, on the road between Canterbury and Dover, the vicar said two masses. The first was attended by thirty parishioners who had made Lenten confession: he administered the sacrament to them in bread only, and omitted the exhortations from the Order of Communion. There was one Church of England for the nation, but an institutionalized schism in the village of Womenswold. Some parishioners were comforted, others alarmed, by a promise in the proclamation of 8 March of further 'travail for the reformation and setting forth of such godly orders as may be most to . . . the advancement of true religion'.[36]

It is sometimes supposed that in 1547–8 the Edwardian regime was finding its feet; that changes were relatively minor, that real reformation was still to come. It did not feel like that to people in the localities, seeing ceremonies they had known their whole lives brought to an abrupt, inexplicable end. John Steynor, a merchant writing a chronicle of events in Worcester, injected notes of dismay and disbelief into his 1548 entry:

> [O]n Candlemas day was no candles hallowed nor borne. On Ash Wednesday was no ashes hallowed. 25 March was Palm Sunday, and the Annunciation of Our Lady, and then was no palms hallowed, nor cross borne, as in former times. On Good Friday was no creeping to the cross.

The litany of absences was echoed by Robert Parkyn, curate of Adwick-le-Street in Yorkshire:

> [I]n the beginning of Lent, all such suffrages as pertained to the sanctifying of ashes was omitted and left undone, and no ashes given to any persons. In the same Lent, all images, pictures, tables, crucifixes, tabernacles, was utterly abolished, and taken away forth of churches within this realm . . .[37]

Unwelcome though the orders may have been, for the most part parishes complied with them. Churchwardens' accounts from across the country in 1548 document the removal of images, the white-washing of walls and re-glazing of windows – though later discoveries of images hidden in roofs and under flooring, or buried in gardens, prove that orders to destroy them were not always obeyed.

Communities scarcely had time to react to the visitation before another set of officials was upon them. Chantry commissioners began compiling their surveys in February 1548, and were soon supervising the suppression of obits, lights and parish guilds, and arranging sales of ex-chantry lands. In most places, the commissioners were conscientious about re-endowing schools and hospitals funded from chantry income, though promises in the Chantries Act of lavish establishment for new charitable institutions proved every bit as hollow as Cranmer suspected they would be.

The dissolution was not an unmitigated disaster for education and charitable welfare, but there were losses of schools and almshouses in communities not organized enough to petition relentlessly for their retention. Most of all, there was a loss of clerical manpower. Chantry priests, like monks, were to be compensated with pensions. But with the collapse of guilds, and the outlawing of intercessory prayer, there were few remaining prospects for employment within the Church. Parishes benefiting pastorally from the contribution of chantry and fraternity priests were thrown back on the resources of their incumbent, and the odd curate or assistant. As the job market contracted, the numbers coming forward for ordination shrank: patrons would soon struggle to fill vacancies with properly qualified candidates.[38]

The local disruption experienced in 1547–8 is hard to overstate. The phrase would have meant nothing to them, but for many English people this was the moment the Middle Ages came to an end. In the little moorland parish of Morebath in Devon, the financial and devotional life of the church had long been intertwined in complex arrangements involving votive lights in front of images. These were maintained by various 'stores' – funds with their own officials, some functioning in the manner of guilds, which sustained the social and festive life of the parish. The main source of income was the sale of wool from church sheep distributed among the flocks of local farmers. The system was already under pressure in Henry's reign, but in 1547–8 it fell apart: the royal visitation forced the sale of the sheep, and, along with a cornerstone of its collective devotional life, the finances of the parish simply collapsed.

In the more substantial Devon community of Ashburton, the St Lawrence Guild doubled as the town's municipal authority, controlling the market and the local hospital. Its dissolution, with that of other intercessory institutions, left only a single priest in a parish church once served by seven. One of the commissioners' servants was set on by a mob in the market square, but the hospital's suppression went ahead.[39]

If social bonds among the living were strained by the reforms, those between the living and the dead fractured in more profound and impenetrable ways. Even through the tumult of the Henrician years, people continued to call the departed to mind in a variety of performative ways: obits, anniversaries, intercessory masses, recitation of parish bede rolls. On 1 November 1547, Thomas Hancock felt the wrath of his parishioners in Poole when he ordered his curate to ignore a request to say *Dirige* for all Christian souls: they 'as it were with one mouth [did] call me knave'.

It all came abruptly to an end in 1548. 'Superstitious' prayer for the dead was policed closely by the royal visitors, who used their supplementary injunctions to prohibit the ringing of knells at funerals, or at Halloween. After the Chantries Act, endowed prayer for the dead was effectively illegal; its virtually complete disappearance from wills after that point should occasion little surprise.

It is harder to account for the apparent indifference to monuments of the dead, which is suggested by parish accounts recording the sale of memorial brasses ripped from church floors. The churchwardens of St Andrew Holborn, London, sold a hundredweight of the stuff in 1547 for 36s., and more the following year. It was a similar story at St Thomas's, Salisbury: 36s. in 1547–8 for 'brass which was upon graves and tombs'. Long Melford, Suffolk, got rid of three hundredweight of brasses in 1548, and St Martin's, Leicester, nine hundredweight.[40] It seems an extraordinary, and extraordinarily sudden, repudiation of the cult of memory animating these communities for a hundredweight of years.

Yet, with exceptions, particularly in London, it seems less likely that communities were swept up in enthusiasm for change than that they feared more change was in the offing. Pre-emptive sales of parish assets reflected worries about imminent confiscation. Such concerns, as in 1536, were understandable. In addition to lists of church goods drawn up by the chantry commissioners, the Privy Council ordered bishops in 1547 to supply inventories of parochial plate and vestments – ostensibly to prevent embezzlement and secure assets for the use of the parish. An insensitive mishandling of the commission by William Body, archdeacon of Cornwall, provoked a 'tumultuous assembly' at Penwith in December 1547. Rather than, as he was supposed to, meet with churchwardens separately, Body summoned representatives from parishes to a single meeting, and gave them the impression that 'confiscation should have ensued to the King's majesty's behalf'. Local gentry were able to calm the situation, and Body was imprisoned for a week 'to appease the people's demonstration'.[41]

Body – a layman, and former agent of Cromwell, who in 1537 leased the archdeaconry for profit from Wolsey's bastard son, Thomas Winter – did not learn his lesson. On 5 April 1548, he was in West Cornwall, at Helston, a market town at the northern end of the Lizard Peninsula, enforcing orders for the removal of images in his usual bombastic style. Stirred up by Martin Geoffrey, a priest from nearby St Keverne, a crowd from half a dozen surrounding parishes congregated in the town. They stormed the house where Body was lodging, dragged him out and killed him. John Reseygh of Helston then made a proclamation in the market square

> that they would have all such laws as was made by the late King Henry the 8th, and none other, until the King's Majesty that now is, accomplish the age of 24 years, and that whoso would defend Body, or follow such new fashions as he did, they would punish him likewise.

This was Gardiner's position, and constituted alarming evidence of conservatives rallying around the Six Articles. Within days there were said to be 5,000 people gathered in Helston. In the event, local gentry were able to raise forces and suppress the disorder without major bloodshed. Most participants were pardoned, but leniency had limits: Geoffrey was sent to London for a traitor's death, and perhaps a dozen ringleaders were executed in Cornwall.[42]

'Unlearned and indiscreet preachers and other priests', complained a proclamation of 24 April, 'as well in confession as otherwise', incited subjects to 'insurrection and rebellion'; others were sowing false rumours of new taxes. It all sounded alarmingly reminiscent of 1536. But the government had no intention of slowing down or rolling back its policy. The immediate remedy was to ban preaching by clergymen possessing no licence from the King, the Lord Protector, or archbishop of Canterbury. Around eighty priests were formally licensed at this time, virtually all reliable evangelicals. The list included stalwarts such as Latimer and Rowland Taylor, but also firebrands like Cardmaker, Turner and 'John Knox, Scot'.[43] Parishes not blessed with visits from these luminaries had to make do with the Homilies.

A sermon of a different sort was preached at court on 29 June, St Peter's day. Stephen Gardiner had been released from prison in February, after giving grudging and qualified assent to a statement on justification. Back in his diocese, he continued to obstruct evangelical preaching, and was summoned again in front of the Council in May, and ordered to make a declaration of 'the King's Majesty's authority in his young years to be as great as if His Highness were of many more'. A couple of days before giving the sermon – of which he refused to allow the Council an advance copy – Gardiner was visited by William Cecil, Somerset's secretary. He told Gardiner that, in order to avoid trouble, he should not speak of 'doubtful matters' concerning the sacrament or the mass. Pressed to say what he meant, Cecil spelled it out: 'transubstantiation'. Condescendingly, Gardiner told the accomplished Cambridge humanist 'he wist not what transubstantiation meant'. Picking his words with lawyerly care, the bishop said he intended to speak on 'the very presence' of Christ's body and blood, 'which is the Catholic faith, and no doubtful matter, nor yet in controversy'.

Gardiner's sermon was preached before the King and a large crowd in a royal garden at Whitehall. It was a masterly exercise in crossing the line while seeming obediently to toe it. He defended the repudiation of the Pope, and the dissolution of the monasteries, though – like the old king – he believed clerical vows of chastity should be maintained. Gardiner recognized the authorities' right to remove otherwise godly things if there was evidence of abuse of them – as with images, ceremonies and chantries. He even accepted communion in two kinds, as likely to increase lay devotion to the eucharist. But Gardiner's qualified endorsement of the regime's religious policies based itself on what he knew to be a false premise: that it was committed to the defence and retention of the mass, which the bishop unapologetically termed 'a sacrifice ordained to make us the more strong in the faith and remembrance of Christ's passion'. The sermon was a subtle, but barely coded, restatement of Gardiner's view that the government was entitled to do no more than perfect the religious reformation of Henry VIII. A day after preaching it, Gardiner was sent to the Tower, to remain there, a querulous semi-martyr, for the remainder of the reign.[44]

## Common Prayer

Gardiner's assertion that the Church's eucharistic doctrine in 1548 was exactly what it was in 1546 increased the momentum for a declaration that it wasn't. For Cranmer, it was a matter of moving in step with European evangelical opinion – no easy matter, given how fractured that opinion was. But leading foreign divines were on hand to advise, as England offered itself as a haven from imperial oppression. In the wake of his military victory, Charles V imposed in June 1548 the Interim of Augsburg, restoring Catholic ceremonies and doctrines to Protestant German territories. Already in 1547, Peter Martyr Vermigli and Bernadino Ochino arrived in England: eminent Italians who five years earlier had abandoned the reformist Catholicism of Cardinal Pole's circle, with its interest in justification by faith, for full-blooded German evangelicalism. Jan Laski, a Polish exile heading the reformed Church at Emden in the Netherlands, came in October 1548; Martin Bucer of Strassburg – a prize catch – followed early the next year. Cranmer actively solicited such theological immigration. In the summer of 1548 he became enthused by a suggestion of Philip Melanchthon for an international evangelical assembly to outshine the papist proceedings at Trent: a Council of Canterbury, Westminster or Cambridge.

If such a council had convened, it would have struggled to produce a eucharistic decree acceptable to all shades of evangelical outlook. By the late summer of 1548, word was out that influential opinion in England was turning decisively against the real presence. Bartholomew Traheron, an assertively

sacramentarian MP, and a former exile in Zürich and Geneva, wrote triumphantly to Bullinger in September 1548: 'Latimer has come over to our opinion
respecting the true doctrine of the eucharist, together with the archbishop of
Canterbury and the other bishops, who heretofore seemed to be Lutherans.'[45]

New doctrine demanded a new liturgy. Drafting began with a meeting in
September 1548 at the former abbey of Chertsey. The conference produced an
accompanying commentary, apparently satisfying the conservative clergymen
taking part, such as Bishops Day, Skip and Thirlby, and Dr John Redman of
Cambridge. But when it was presented to the House of Lords in December,
traditionalists angrily noted that the sections defending adoration of the
elements, and the place of oblation (sacrifice) in the prayer of consecration
were conspicuously omitted.

Significantly, the prelude to the introduction of the new liturgy was a
debate, not in Convocation, but in the Lords: laymen participated on equal
terms with bishops, addressing the question laid in front of them by Protector
Somerset: 'whether bread be in the sacrament after the consecration or not'.
The exchanges, over four days of debate, were fractious and angry, as it became
clear to conservative bishops like Tunstall and Heath that Cranmer, his collaborator Ridley of Rochester, and their lay allies Somerset and Warwick, were
determined to take the Church in new directions. The conservative-minded
lay peers seem to have kept a low profile.

Cranmer and Ridley particularly highlighted the problem of the *manducatio impiorum* – the eating by the impious. Their insistence that unworthy
recipients of communion did not receive Christ's body in the same manner as
godly ones did was a decisive step away, not just from transubstantiation, but
from any notion of an objective real presence of Christ. It placed them firmly
on the side of 'the Reformed' – the churches of Switzerland and south-west
Germany – rather than the Lutherans, for whom the *manducatio impiorum*
was a strict test of correct eucharistic doctrine.[46]

Although the Lords' debate produced little beyond evidence of irreconcil-
able splits in the episcopate, it was immediately followed by the introduction
of legislation for a new Book of Common Prayer. An Act for 'Uniformity of
Service and Administration of the Sacraments' passed on 15 January 1549.
Bonner, Tunstall, Day, Heath, Rugge, Skip, Thirlby and Aldridge of Carlisle all
predictably voted against. So did three lay lords: the Earl of Derby, Lord Dacre
and Lord Windsor. A few weeks later, Lords Morley and Wharton joined Dacre
and Windsor in voting against the act legalizing the marriage of priests. The
statute was a belated catch-up with Convocation's decision of 1547, and a
thumb in the eye for Gardiner and other traditionalists who regarded clerical
marriage as an aberration and an abomination.[47]

The Act of Uniformity did not bill itself as a manifesto for revolutionary
change. Its declared objective was a 'uniform, quiet and godly order' throughout

the realm, through substituting a single manner of prayer and sacraments for a supposed jumble of existing liturgies: 'the Use of Sarum, of York, of Bangor, and of Lincoln'.[48] The Book of Common Prayer certainly simplified things for the clergy, compressing into one handy volume the forms of service that previously required recourse to various manuals and handbooks.

The services themselves were in some cases relatively little altered. Baptism retained a strongly sacramental character, adorned with rituals and objects that radical evangelicals found uncongenial: hallowing of water in the font, promises made by godparents, signing of the child's forehead with the cross, and wrapping it in a white chrisom cloth. Public baptism in church was the norm, but there was a form for use in people's homes, 'in time of necessity'.

The confirmation ritual followed the Sarum rite closely, as did the marriage ceremony – though the wife's traditional promise to be 'bonner and buxom in bed and at the board' was dropped: buxom, originally signifying obedient, had started to mean cheerful by the sixteenth century, and perhaps sounded indecorous. Marriage, traditionally regarded by churchmen principally as a means for producing children and avoiding fornication, was announced to be 'for the mutual society, help and comfort, that the one ought to have of the other' – an echo of the more positive appraisal of companionship in matrimony characteristic of evangelical writings like Heinrich Bullinger's *Der Christlich Eestand* (The Christian State of Matrimony, 1540), a text produced in more translated editions than any other continental evangelical work in the reigns of Henry and Edward. The rite for visitation of the sick retained a (simplified) form of unction, 'if the sick person desire to be anointed', as well as optional confession and communion at the sickbed.[49]

More fundamentally, the Prayer Book maintained a configuration of worship that was both cyclical and seasonal: a daily pattern of matins (morning prayer), mass and evensong, along with a calendar of feasts and festivals, and a menu of short prayers ('collects'), epistles and gospels appropriate to the day. In the heading provided for the eucharistic service there was an overt – perhaps even cynical – effort to signal continuity with the past: 'the Supper of the Lord, and the Holy Communion, commonly called the Mass'.

The, not Our, Lord. Cranmer, the principal author and compiler of the new liturgy, went only so far to accommodate conservative sensibilities. The new communion service was no mass of a kind English people were used to. Like the rest of the book, it was now entirely in English, the first and most fundamental fact about it noted by local chroniclers like Parkyn and Steynor.

Parkyn also noted, disbelievingly, that communion was to take place 'without any elevation'.[50] The elevation of the host was the focal, sacral moment of the medieval Latin liturgy. But it implied a change after consecration, and invited adoration – making it unacceptable to Cranmer on both counts. The great medieval prayer of consecration, or canon, explicitly identified the priest's action at the altar with the sacrifice of Christ. Cranmer's translation broke the connection. The 'oblation once offered' by Christ on the cross was not the same as the Church's offering of thanksgiving: Gardiner was answered.

Not all laypeople understood intricate points of sacramental theology. But they noticed other omissions: no kissing of the pax, no distribution of holy bread at the conclusion of mass. And, at first at least, no music – for settings of the English texts were not available to parish and cathedral choirs. There was further frugal pruning of the calendar: only the major biblical saints kept their days, and feasts of the Virgin were reduced to two, the Purification (minus candles) and the Annunciation. The Assumption was gone, along with the other great festival of summertime, Corpus Christi.

For all this, the new liturgy did not look, or feel, like the services of worship that replaced the mass in Strassburg, Zürich or Geneva. The priest still wore traditional vestments (though for communion, the cloak-like cope was recommended, rather than the poncho-like chasuble), candles were placed upon the altar, and there was a hint at least of prayer for the dead in the communion service's petition to grant mercy to 'thy servants which are departed', and – an echo of the requiem mass – in provision for 'celebration of the holy communion when there is a burial of the dead'.[51]

Potential critics were reassured that these were temporary concessions. Francisco Enzinas – known by his humanist name, Dryander – was a Spanish evangelical who fled to England from Strassburg in July 1548. In 1549 he observed that 'some puerilities have been still suffered to remain, lest the people be offended by too great an innovation'. The book spoke 'very obscurely' about the Lord's Supper. Yet it was a time to accentuate the positive. Dryander informed Bullinger on 25 March that 'the mass is abolished, and liberty of marriage allowed to the clergy; which two I consider to be the principal heads of the entire reformation'. Other, trifling matters 'may shortly be amended'.

Dryander's patron, Martin Bucer, arrived in England in April, along with the Hebrew scholar Paul Fagius. Bucer wrote home to say that the cause of religion in England was 'pretty near what could be wished'. There were faults with the new liturgy, but he had assurances 'they are only to be retained for a time, lest the people, not having yet learned Christ, should be deterred by too extensive innovations from embracing his religion'.[52] 'Moderation' was a strategy, not an intrinsic virtue.

The conciliatory face of the regime was in any case visible only from certain angles. It was not turned towards the radicals, whose numbers were feared to be growing with the influx of refugees, and whose exotic heresies alarmed and embarrassed respectable evangelical opinion. On 12 April a commission was established to seek out anabaptists: it comprised leading councillors and six bishops, Cranmer and Ridley serving alongside the conservatives Heath and Day. Several radicals were made to abjure and bear faggots at Paul's Cross in

April and May for saying a regenerate man was incapable of sin; that there was no Trinity; that baptism of infants was unprofitable. Only one refused to recant: Joan Bocher, a Kentish woman tenaciously holding to the belief that Christ's flesh was a celestial distillation, not gifted from his earthly mother. The doctrine was most likely learned from Netherlandish immigrants, though it chimed with older Lollard brags that the Virgin was a mere 'saffron bag'.

Bocher was convicted of heresy, and the authorities reflected on what to do with her. The radicalism problem remained. The zealous clerical exile John Hooper returned to England from Zürich at the start of May 1549, and joined the preaching rota at St Paul's. Soon he complained to Bullinger that anabaptists flocked to his lectures, and harangued him with wayward opinions about the incarnation and spiritual regeneration. 'Alas, not only are those heresies reviving among us which were formerly dead and buried, but new ones are springing up every day!'[53]

Zero-tolerance for the new heresies of the anabaptists was matched by antagonism towards the old errors of the Catholic bishops, who could scarcely plead ignorance as their excuse for reluctance to embrace the truth. In a sermon preached before the King at the conclusion of Parliament on 15 March, Latimer lambasted prelates who failed to enforce the Injunctions, or prevent their clergy from mangling the homilies: 'I require it in God's behalf, make them quondams [former bishops], all the pack of them!' Someone was asked how he liked the sermon: 'a seditious fellow' was the testy response. Latimer got to hear of it, and gloried in the insult. Preaching again before the King on 22 March, he noted that Christ himself was a creator of dissension. Opposition, division, 'gain-saying': all these were signs that a preacher was doing something right. 'In the popish mass-time there was no gainsaying; all things seemed to be in peace, in concord, in a quiet agreement.'[54] Disputatiousness was next to godliness.

In May 1549, the fight was taken to the heartland of disputatious conservative clericalism: the universities. New commissions were issued for royal visitations. The visitors were to a man evangelicals, and virtually all Cambridge products: Oxford, where Peter Martyr Vermigli was installed as Regius Professor of Divinity, was perceived as the more recalcitrant of the two institutions. The visitors came armed with statutes and injunctions designed to eliminate papistry, and in both universities they supervised debates on the eucharist, with the aim of demonstrating the triumph of the new thinking over the old.

In Oxford, the intention was that Richard Smyth would dispute with Vermigli, but before the visitors could arrive, Smyth decided to flee, via Scotland, back to Louvain. The defence of transubstantiation was left to a conservative B-team: William Tresham, William Chedsey and Morgan Philipps. The debate, ending on 1 June, was formally inconclusive, though in summing up, Richard Cox, Edward's tutor and, since 1547, chancellor of the university, left little doubt as to the award of laurels. He thanked 'Peter, who is worthily called Peter for the firmness of his stance ... and worthily called Martyr for the countless witnesses to the truth'. Vermigli's account of the proceedings was the one published.[55]

Two years of relentless evangelical advocacy created a wearied sense among traditionalists of being impotent, marginal, silenced. Around this time, an anonymous author penned a 'ballad of Little John Nobody'. The narrator of the verses comes across a despondent figure sitting by himself, a man needing little encouragement to condemn bitterly all 'the fashion of these new fellows'. But pressed as to what should be done, he has no answer. Each stanza ends with a poignant refrain: 'he said he was little John Nobody, that durst not speak'.[56]

One English Catholic did dare to speak. In early May, Cardinal Pole despatched emissaries to Somerset with letters that were part fatherly remonstrance, part cautious offer of reconciliation. The Protector, suggested Pole, should consider history's lessons about the dangers of a child king, and the insecurity caused by a divided episcopate. Truth and unity might return through learned debate, which Pole magnanimously offered to chair on the neutral ground of Flanders.

Somerset's reply, on 4 June, was imperiously dismissive. Pole must come home and sue for pardon, rather than write as if he were some foreign prince. All his fears were misplaced. Edward, with the advice of his faithful councillors, was ruling peerlessly. There was no dissent among the bishops, who had freely arrived at agreement, followed by debate and consent in Parliament. The outcome was 'a form and rite of service' – Somerset thoughtfully enclosed a copy of the Prayer Book along with the letter – established by statute, and set forth 'to so great a quiet as ever was in England, and as gladly received of all parts'.[57] It was an unfortunately timed boast. For even as Somerset's missive was being sealed and sent, the quiet of England was descending into raucous tumult, and thousands of little John Nobodies, in every part of the realm, rose and demanded their say.

I I

## SLAYING ANTICHRIST

### 'Item, We will have . . .'

THE NEW PRAYER Book was already in use at St Paul's and in various London parishes at the beginning of Lent 1549, but its nationwide introduction was scheduled for the end of the Easter season, the feast of Pentecost or Whitsunday, falling that year on 9 June.[1] Copies were in the meantime successfully distributed, and the new liturgy was performed in place of the Latin mass on Whitsunday even in remote rural parishes.

One of these was Sampford Courtenay, a small village in mid-Devon, on the northern fringes of Dartmoor; the elderly rector there, William Harper, did as he was required. The following day, Harper was met at the church door by a volatile crowd, demanding to know what service he planned to perform. He answered he would say the new service, as he was obliged by law to do. The protestors insisted he should not, arguing – erroneously but sincerely – that Henry VIII's will forbad innovations in religion until his son came of age. In the end, Harper 'yielded to their wills, and forthwith revested himself in his old popish attire, and said mass and all such services as in times past accustomed'.[2]

It was a small start to a national crisis, and a local cataclysm. The Devon JPs hurried to Sampford Courtenay, but lacked the resolve either to appease or intimidate the mob. A minor landowner called William Hilling remonstrated angrily with the protestors, and for his pains was set upon and hacked savagely to pieces. The rioters buried the body in the churchyard, though they aligned it north–south rather than east–west: the fate of a heretic's corpse. The domino effect seen in 1536 was once again in evidence. In the days following, contingents from numerous surrounding parishes congregated in the market town of Crediton, just north-west of Exeter, the regional capital.

A bad situation was made worse by the actions of Sir Peter Carew, a local landowner hurriedly returning from his wife's estates in Lincolnshire, either on

Somerset's orders or on his own initiative. When the rebels refused to treat with him, Carew's troops set light to barns on the outskirts of Crediton, causing panic and a retreat from the town in which several rebels were killed. Carew was a zealous evangelical, the worst choice for a negotiator with anxious traditionalists. Rebel forces regrouped at the nearby village of Clyst St Mary. Here, the trouble started a few days earlier, when another evangelical landowner, Walter Ralegh senior, berated an elderly woman on her way to church for praying on her rosary. On arrival, the woman told an already overwrought congregation that she had been warned 'except she would leave her beads, and give over holy bread and holy water, the gentlemen would burn them out of their houses and spoil them'. Class hostility rubbed salt into the wounds of religious division.

The authorities' response was hampered by strategic disagreements, between Carew and the evangelical sheriff of Devon, Peter Courtenay, on the one hand, and less confrontational local gentry on the other, allowing the rebels to encircle Exeter. By early July, trouble had spread to Cornwall, still simmering after the disturbances of the preceding year. Here, the epicentre was Bodmin, site of the pretend religious war of schoolboys, a war now starting to erupt for real. Rebels from numerous parishes, accompanied by their priests, formed camp, and elected as their leader Humphrey Arundell, one of very few local gentlemen to support the movement. Soon, the Cornishmen marched east to join the Devonians for a full-scale siege of Exeter. It commenced with a procession behind a banner of the Five Wounds, with the consecrated host carried – as on the abrogated feast of Corpus Christi just passed – in a traditional pyx.[3]

The Sampford Courtenay rebels had already sent demands to the Council in London, complaining of taxes, and the innovation (not in fact stipulated by the Prayer Book) that baptisms should take place only on Sundays. Encamped outside Exeter, the joint Devonshire-Cornish host drew up and despatched a definitive list of sixteen articles.[4] The document abandoned any conventional pretence that the rebels were modest and loyal petitioners, couching each of its demands in blunt, peremptory terms: 'Item, we will have . . .' The tone reflected a firm belief that the government lacked legitimacy for its programme of religious change; a key demand was to 'have the laws of our Sovereign Lord King Henry VIII concerning the Six Articles to be in use again'.

Other articles constituted a comprehensive repudiation of the reforms of the preceding two years. The rebels wanted holy bread, holy water, palms and ashes, and 'images to be set up again in every church'. Priests should pray by names for souls in purgatory, 'as our forefathers did'. Most of all, the rebels rejected the new liturgy: 'we will have the mass in Latin, as was before'. Communion for the laity should be in one kind, and then only at Easter; at other times the commoners were content to have the sacrament 'celebrated by the priest without any man or woman communicating with him'.

The new service was 'but like a Christmas game'. The back-and-forth dialogue of the vernacular service perhaps reminded them of the festive, semi-religious entertainments performed locally at Yuletide. The early sixteenth-century churchwardens' accounts of Ashburton contain regular payments to actors from Exeter for 'playing a Christmas game in the church'.[5] On short acquaintance, the solemnity of Cranmer's English prose clearly failed to make an impression, or to establish itself as an appropriate register for addressing the Almighty. And some rebels could not resist taking a dig at evangelical claims to have made worship accessible and relevant: 'We the Cornish men (whereof certain of us understand no English) utterly refuse this new English.'

For all their enthusiasm for the Six Articles, and their Gardiner-like stance on religious change during a minority, the rebels were not straightforwardly 'Henricians'. One article sought to tear up a central plank of King Henry's refor-mation: 'We will have the whole bible, and all books of scripture in English called in again.' There was pragmatic recognition that the availability of vernac-ular scripture weighted the scales in favour of the innovators – 'we be informed that otherwise the clergy shall not of long time confound the heretics'. Nor was it too late to reverse another of Henry VIII's proud achievements: the dissolu-tion of the monasteries. The rebels wanted to restore a measured and scaled-down monasticism, of which early sixteenth-century humanist reformers might have approved: two places in every county where 'devout persons' would pray for the King and commonwealth. That these foundations should be supported by offerings given to church-boxes was a slap in the face for reformers, who instituted the parish poor-box precisely as an alternative to 'superstitious' benefactions. Even without such offerings, the new abbeys would be generously endowed. They were to have 'the half part of the abbey lands and chantry lands, in every man's possessions, howsoever he came by them'.

This provision showed political naivety about, or perhaps proletarian disre-gard for, the concerns of the gentry, who were – in contrast to 1536 – severely under-represented in rebel counsels. Landowners paying good money for monastic or chantry lands were extremely loath, whatever their religious incli-nations, to relinquish them. An anonymous Devon gentleman, writing in late July, made his feelings plain: 'No one thing maketh me more angry with these rebels than [this] one article . . . I would, for every two strokes to be stricken for treason, strike one to keep my lands.'[6]

The articles contained one resounding silence, on the issue headlining the comparable list produced by the Pilgrims at Pontefract a dozen years before. There was no appeal for the Pope to be restored to headship of the Church. It may be this was a matter of little pressing popular concern, and the omission reflected a gut feeling that Catholicism did not have to be Roman to be orthodox. But it is equally possible the rebel leaders feared their legalistic demand for restoration of the 1546 settlement might be tactically compromised by any overt repudiation of the royal supremacy on which it was based. The rebels did, however, insist 'the Lord Cardinal Pole' be offered a free pardon, and summoned from Rome to take his place as first or second among the King's councillors. It was hard to imagine such a scenario on any basis other than reconciliation with the papacy.

Pope or no pope, the rebel demands were offensive enough. And they were infused with a rhetoric of confrontation and religious conflict that once more homed in on the eucharist – supposed symbol of Christian wholeness – as the principal point of division. The West Countrymen planned sharp remedies for anyone opposed to reserving the consecrated host above the high altar, and worshipping it there: 'We will have them die like heretics against the holy Catholic faith.'

As the situation spiralled out of control, Somerset remained under the misapprehension it was a small rebellion confined to Sampford Courtenay. He advised the local justices to make concessions, while despatching a paltry force under the command of Lord Russell. The response was inadequate because the Devon stirs were not an isolated occurrence. Disorder was breaking out across southern and midland England, and the Lord Protector was soon adrift on a sea of troubles.

The protests were the fermented product of a potent blend of religious and economic grievance. In many places, local communities were angry about enclosure – the gentry's practice of fencing or hedging areas of land to which commoners previously enjoyed access, often converting use of the land from cereals to animal pasturage. Social reformers and government advisors had for decades believed – rightly or wrongly – that the practice encouraged rural depopulation, and raised the price of commodities. As Lord Protector, Somerset professed a concern for the plight of the poor that was not wholly disingenuous. But he also worried that enclosure increased the cost and narrowed the tax-base for furtherance of the Scottish war with which Somerset was above all else obsessed. With much fanfare, enclosure commissions were sent out in 1548 to inquire into the practice, and reverse illegal instances. At the same time there was a new tax on sheep, intended to discourage anti-social conversions from arable to pasture, but – ironically – a cause of popular unhappiness in Devon and Cornwall, where most conversion took place decades earlier, and where even humble farmers (like the parishioners of Morebath) possessed good stocks of sheep.[7]

There was a troubling instance of agrarian protest in Hertfordshire in the summer of 1548, and enclosure riots broke out again – in Wiltshire, Somerset and around Bristol – in May 1549. At the start of July, a trickle of trouble became a flood, with disorders reported in virtually every county south and east of a line from the Bristol Channel to the Humber: people called it 'the commotion time.'[8]

The most serious outbreak was in Norfolk. Villagers around Wymondham, ten miles to the south-west of Norwich, threw down the hedges of the unpopular landowner John Flowerdew and found a leader when Flowerdew's local rival, Robert Kett, agreed to reverse his own enclosures and present the people's grievances to higher authority. By 12 July, as many as 20,000 were said to be camped with Kett outside Norwich, and other camps sprang up across East Anglia. In Devon, the municipal authorities managed to keep the insurgents from taking Exeter, but on 22 July Kett's followers flooded into Norwich, placing England's second city in rebellious hands.[9]

The religious complexion of the movements of 1549 mirrored the fragmented and fractious faith of the nation. In Hampshire and Sussex, conspirators planned to march in support of the West Countrymen, behind a banner of the Five Wounds. Things went further in the south Midlands. Somerset informed Russell on 12 July he had been obliged to divert reinforcements under Lord Grey of Wilton, intended to relieve the siege of Exeter, to deal with 'a stir here in Buckinghamshire and Oxfordshire, by instigation of sundry priests (keep it to yourself) for these matters of religion'. It was hardly a state secret. Rebel forces entered Oxford, and Peter Martyr was hurried off to London by his friends, leaving his wife and servants to hide themselves from the mob.[10]

There was another outbreak of religious protest in parishes along the east Yorkshire coast, near Scarborough. Archbishop Holgate's claim of 'ten or twelve thousand rebels up' may be a nervous overestimate, but it was a significant and alarming episode. The spark igniting it was the dissolution of numerous, well-integrated, local chantry foundations, and the rebels planned to join up with those in Devon. They were also reportedly inspired by prophecies 'that there should no king reign in England; the noblemen and gentlemen to be destroyed, and the realm to be ruled by four governors to be elected and appointed by the commons'.[11] Social levelling of this kind was more usually associated with radical than with conservative religion, but these were topsy-turvy days.

Where rebel demands concentrated on agrarian rather than liturgical concerns, their tone tended to be more moderate. Encouraged by the fanfare surrounding Somerset's enclosure commissions, the commons in Norfolk and elsewhere believed the government would listen seriously to their grievances and take action against local oppressors. The Lord Protector encouraged the perception, writing conciliatory letters to rebel camps in Norfolk, Suffolk, Hampshire, Hertfordshire and Essex.[12]

Somerset was prepared to treat (even if cynically) with these rebels because he did not believe them to be papists. A distinctly evangelical aura hung around the rhetoric and actions of some south-eastern bands, particularly Kett's followers in East Anglia, where justice was dispensed under an 'Oak of Reformation', and the new Prayer Book was used without protest.

Kett did not command a rustic army of evangelical converts. There were countless old-fashioned Catholics among the contingents marching to the camps behind traditional parish banners.[13] But the rhetorical language of the revolt renounced the traditionalism that could only have locked it in inflexible confrontation with the regime. Notions of 'Commonwealth' – which in 1536 evoked a vanishing Catholic world of neighbourliness and social order – now took their cue from the demands for social justice heard in the sermons of evangelical preachers, several of them frequenting Kett's encampment at Mousehold Heath. The articles drawn up by Kett during the occupation of Norwich interspersed pious evangelical aspirations with the demands for economic rights. Priests should be resident in their benefices that parishioners 'may be instructed with the laws of God'. Clergymen 'not able to preach and set forth the Word of God' should be dismissed. Leading evangelicals surely nodded in agreement at this, though they might have paused over the suggested remedy for a non-preaching parson: 'the parishioners there to choose another'. Social and spiritual hopes converged in a plea for the abolition of residual serfdom lingering on some Norfolk manorial estates: 'We pray that all bondmen be made free, for God made all free with his precious blood shedding.'[14] Consciously or not, the phrase echoed the manifestos of the rebellious German peasants of 1525. That protest too began with optimism and festivity, and ended in bloodshed and despair.

There was no social revolution in 1549; the established order gradually reasserted itself. Offers of pardon persuaded the Yorkshire rebels to disperse, and in other places local authorities proved adept at defusing tensions. In West Sussex, the rebellious commoners went home, apparently contented, after the leading regional landowner, the Earl of Arundel, listened to their grievances, and chided the gentry, at a great feast arranged in the courtyard of Arundel Castle.[15] As in 1536, the local presence of a capable magnate was an important inhibiting factor. It was no accident that the severest outbreaks occurred where Henry VIII's dynastic paranoia had lopped off potentially stabilizing hands. In 1549, both Thomas Howard, the aged Duke of Norfolk, and Edward Courtenay, the young heir to the Marquis of Exeter, were prisoners in the Tower.

In the end, however, the protest movements were not conciliated, but crushed: by government forces under loyalist noble command, and by Somerset's hired contingents of Italian and German mercenaries. Russell engaged the Devonshire forces in a sharp encounter at Fenny Bridges, east of Exeter, on 28 July, and was shortly afterwards reinforced by Lord Grey, whose troops had bloodily suppressed the risings in Buckinghamshire and Oxfordshire. On 4 August, Russell routed the rebels in a major encounter at Clyst St Mary, and broke the siege of Exeter. The remainder of the rebel forces regrouped and encamped at Sampford Courtenay. Russell marched west from the city, and on 16 August inflicted a heavy defeat on the now outnumbered Devon–Cornwall force.[16]

In the meantime, the Earl of Warwick was sent east with a well-equipped force to prise East Anglia from the grip of rebellion. The final week of August witnessed messy skirmishes in the streets of Norwich, as Warwick's troops struggled to oust Kett's tenacious followers. With his supply lines cut, Kett – like the Catholic rebels in Yorkshire – reportedly put his trust in 'feigned prophecies'. There would be a great victory at Dussindale, just outside the city. It was poorly chosen, open ground, which on 27 August enabled Warwick to unleash his cavalry to devastating effect, while the government's mercenaries made the most of their superior cohesion and firepower. There would be minor disturbances, and mopping up, in various places into the next year and beyond, but the commotion time was over.[17]

The summer of 1549 was a season of extraordinary violence and blood-letting, giving the lie to suggestions that England's reformations of religion proceeded in orderly, conformist and peaceful fashion. Contemporary esti-mates of the number of Kett's followers slaughtered at Dussindale ranged between 2,000 and 3,500.[18] The body count in the West Country was higher still. The eye-witness chronicler of events, John Hooker, did not know how many died on the government side ('they escaped not scot free'), but was told that 4,000 rebels were killed. Given the one-sided character of a series of fierce encounters, this may well be an underestimate. The campaign included at least one major atrocity. At a tense moment during the battle at Clyst St Mary, Russell ordered that the prisoners, 'which if they were newly set upon, might be a detriment and a peril unto them', should all be slaughtered. It is possible as many as 900 were 'slain like beasts'.[19]

We do not know how many perished in Lord Grey's suppression of the Oxfordshire rebellion – the young king's terse summary was of 'some slain, some taken, and some hanged'. Nor do we have numbers for those suffering under martial law across the country as a whole. The Venetian ambassador at Rome learned by letters from London in early September 'that the insurrec-tions have been entirely suppressed, but by means of the slaughter and destruc-tion of 10,000 or 11,000 natives'.[20] It seems a reasonable enough estimate. A pro-rata adjustment of numbers, relative to the recent (2013) population of England and Wales, produces a sobering figure of over 206,000 fatalities.

It was a short but bloody civil war, portrayed by many as a conflict between forces of Christ and Antichrist. A London balladeer looked into the rebels' hearts and found them 'rooted in the Pope's laws'; he hailed the Sampford Courtenay victim William Hilling as 'that martyr truly'. Philip Nichols, himself a Devonian, wrote a detailed refutation of the insurgent articles, laying the blame on 'sinister persuasions' of priests, while rebuking the lay rebels who raised tumult for no worthier cause than 'the filthy suds and dregs of stinking popery'. As in the aftermath of the Pilgrimage, government propagandists harped on the connections between popery and treason. Cranmer, in a draft treatise against the rebels, remarked snappily 'how an absolute papist varieth from a heretic or a traitor, I know not'.[21]

Definitions of popery had become decidedly elastic. The sacramental and ceremonial preferences of the rebels, not political allegiance to Rome, made them papists and traitors. Cranmer shortly afterwards denounced Gardiner as an 'English papist', one of those that 'dare not ground their faith concerning transubstantiation upon the Church of Rome'.[22]

'Papist' priests, prominent in the risings, merited exemplary and ritual punishment. In both Oxfordshire and Devon, rebel clergymen were hanged from the spires of churches – a symbolic act that came close to fulfilling Hooper's fantasy of putting idolaters to death on their own altars. Robert Welsh, a priest who played an active role in directing the siege of Exeter, was suspended and left to die in chains from the steeple of his church just outside the walls of the city. The Devon rebellion began with a priest donning old 'popish attire', and so it ended. Welsh was put to death in traditional mass vestments, with 'a holy water bucket, a sprinkler, a sacring bell, a pair of beads, and other such like popish trash hanged about him'.[23]

There was no middle ground between Christ and Antichrist. The Council issued Bonner with injunctions demanding he preach a sermon denouncing the rebels, celebrate communion in the new fashion, and affirm the King's undiminished authority in his minority. Bonner used the Prayer Book dutifully in his cathedral on 18 August, but in his Paul's Cross sermon on 1 September he said nothing about royal authority, and little about the rebellion. He did seize the opportunity to insist bread after consecration was 'the very body of Christ that was born of the Virgin Mary'. It was the catalyst for his deprivation.

Through September, a commission headed by Cranmer and Ridley interrogated the bishop of London. With his back to the wall, Bonner recovered his fighting instincts, denouncing his accusers, John Hooper and William Latimer (no relation of the former bishop), as notorious sacramentarians who 'divided themselves thereby from the unity and integrity of Christ's Catholic Church'. When Cranmer demanded what Bonner meant by talking of presence in the sacrament, Bonner nimbly turned the question around: 'What believe *you*, and how do *you* believe, my Lord?' The archbishop was not yet, clearly and unambiguously, ready to say.[24]

### 'The Perseverance of God's Word'

Somerset loomed tall in autumn 1549, while his enemies – Gardiner, Bonner, the Prayer Book rebels – lay stricken around him. But he was standing on quicksand. Resentments grew among fellow-councillors about the Protector's imperious style, and his accumulation of grand palaces. He was, they felt, doubly to blame for the terrifying tumult of the summer: by provoking conservative grievance about religious change, and by encouraging anti-landlordism with his irresponsible posturing over enclosure. Defeats to the French around Boulogne added to a gnawing discontent, crystallized by the return of the Earl of Warwick from Norfolk, and an imprudent decision by Somerset to refuse extra rewards to the victorious English and mercenary troops.

When Warwick summoned discontented councillors – Southampton (restored to the Council in early 1549), William Paulet, Richard Rich, the Marquis of Northampton – to meet with him privately, Somerset dramatically and recklessly raised the stakes. Taking Edward to Hampton Court, he issued a proclamation at the start of October, commanding all subjects to attend in arms to protect His Majesty and 'his most entirely beloved uncle the Lord Protector' against 'a most dangerous conspiracy'. Printed broadsheets appealed directly to the commons and talked of oppressions of the poor, as well as plots 'to plant again the doctrine of the devil and Antichrist of Rome'. Some four thousand commoners answered the call.

This was to court 'popularity' – the worst of political crimes in the eyes of the ruling elites; support for Somerset among his peers crumbled away. At the last, Somerset stepped back from plunging the realm into a renewed bout of internecine and class warfare, and surrendered himself to his enemies. On 13 October, the Protectorate was dissolved, and the following day Somerset was sent to the Tower.[25]

It was a classic *coup d'état*, and, almost everyone thought, a conservative one. 'We are greatly apprehensive of a change in religion,' Hooper confessed to Bullinger. From his cell in the Tower, Gardiner congratulated Warwick on saving the realm from 'tyrannous government', and anticipated his imminent release. It was a hope shared by Ambassador Van der Delft, who heard Bonner was also about to be rehabilitated, and noted the hopeful sign that Warwick had forbidden his household to eat meat on Fridays.

Writing to the Emperor on 17 October, Van der Delft remained optimistic. He acknowledged Cranmer still sat at the Council board, but thought this was merely for form's sake and unlikely to last. There were no moves yet to 'restore religion', but this was so as not to upset the people, who were 'totally infected' with heresy (the ambassador's world was London). Other councillors were all good Catholics, save for Warwick himself. But Van der Delft had good hopes of his reformation: he was 'taking up the old observances day by day'.[26]

It was all a mirage, a trick with cards. Warwick had no intention of allowing the restoration of the mass, the release of Gardiner and Norfolk, or a regency headed by the Princess Mary. Such moves would ensure his political oblivion. Conservatives, rightly, did not trust him. Yet perhaps the young King could be made to; royal favour was Warwick's best hope of long-term survival. The fate of the country, at this crucial juncture, hinged on shrewd political investment in the precocious religious enthusiasms of a twelve-year-old boy.

Warwick, working hand-in-glove with Cranmer, acted quickly to save the reformation, and to marginalize the conservatives, whose leaders, Arundel and Southampton, were already plotting against him. On 15 October, a wave of new appointments to the Privy Chamber surrounded the King with a coterie of reliable evangelicals and Warwick supporters. John ab Ulmis – briefed by Richard Cox – was sufficiently reassured to write to Bullinger a few days later, announcing 'that Antichrist . . . is again discomfited by the general sentence of all the leading men in England'. There was confirmation in a proclamation of 30 October, denying rumours the mass was to be restored, and declaring that King and Council would continue to do 'whatsoever may lend to the glory of God and the advancement of his most holy Word'.[27]

Power on the Privy Council swung further in Warwick's direction with the appointments, at the end of November, of Henry Grey, Marquis of Dorset, and Thomas Goodrich, bishop of Ely – 'the which', wrote Richard Scudamore on 5 December to his master, the evangelical courtier Philip Hoby, 'putteth all honest hearts in good comfort for the good hope that they have of the perseverance of God's Word'.[28]

On the day Scudamore wrote, almost 1,000 miles to the south-east, another journey of hope came abruptly to a halt. At the papal conclave in Rome, summoned in November to elect a successor to Paul III, Reginald Pole had the previous day come within a single vote of the required tally. Supporters were suggesting he simply be installed by acclamation; pontifical vestments were made. On 5 December, as the cardinals prepared to recommence voting, Gianpietro Carafa, archbishop of Naples, publicly accused Pole of heresy, waving a paper which detailed Pole's supposed errors concerning justification. Pole and Carafa had once been allies, sharing a humanist desire to renew the Church. But the defection of Ochino and Vermigli, and Carafa's experience as an official of the revived Roman Inquisition, had turned him into an obsessive heresy-hunter.

Pole laughed off the accusations, and his support remained high in that day's vote. But he was still short, and momentum began to slip from his campaign – not until February would the uninspiring Giovanni Maria Ciocchi del Monte emerge as a compromise candidate to take the name Julius III.[29] Whether, as pope, Pole might have done anything concrete to further reconciliation with the Protestants is a moot point. But he represented a face of Catholicism that was more conciliatory and theologically open than the one it finally adopted. The non-election of the thoughtful, reformist English cardinal was a pivotal moment for the Catholic Church, and, as events would unfold, for his native England also.

While Pole and Carafa sparred in Rome, the disgraced Somerset became the pivot of English politics. Southampton planned to destroy him, and to implicate Warwick in Somerset's treason. Warwick struck back, declaring dramatically at a council meeting on 31 December that 'he that seeketh his blood would have mine also'. With a majority now behind him, Warwick ordered Southampton and Arundel banished from court and Council. Richard Southwell and Sir Thomas Arundel – who hoped to make Mary regent – were removed about the same time. Mary herself was cautious, telling Van der Delft that the conspirators against Somerset were motivated by envy and ambition: 'no good will come of this move . . . it may be only the beginning of our misfortunes'.

Warwick was confirmed, not as Lord Protector, but more modestly as the Council's 'Lord President'. The final showdown was preceded by a proclamation on Christmas Day, ordering all old service books to be handed in to episcopal officials. Any hopes for the restoration of ceremonies in Latin 'were but a preferring of ignorance to knowledge and darkness to light'.[30] There was to be no going back.

Slowly but surely, Cranmer built up his team. The days of a deeply divided episcopate, the stop-go mechanism bedevilling the progress of reform since the mid-1530s, were coming to an end. Bonner's formal deprivation in February 1550 cleared the way for the promotion of Nicholas Ridley: at long last, the critical see of London was in safe evangelical hands. At the same time, William Rugge of Norwich, heavily in debt, and compromised over his negotiations with Kett during the rebellion, was persuaded to resign. Thomas Thirlby was transferred to Norwich, and his see of Westminster – one of the few ecclesiastical gains from the dissolution of the monasteries – was subsumed into that of London, giving Ridley a free hand in the capital.

In March, liturgical innovations prised out another conservative bishop. One glaring omission from the Prayer Book was any form of service for ordaining clergy. A new Ordinal corrected that, with input from Martin Bucer. The book was traditional to the extent it preserved a distinction between bishops and priests, and maintained the laying on of hands. But in other respects it rang a death-knell for medieval priesthood: no investiture in stole and chasuble, no reference to receiving power to offer the body of Christ. Instead, candidates obtained 'authority to preach the Word of God, and to minister the holy sacraments'. Heath of Worcester refused to accept the Ordinal, and was committed to the Fleet.[31]

'It is openly spoken,' Scudamore wrote to Hoby on 23 February, 'there shall be more quondam bishops in England shortly.' Also on the government's list was John Veysey, aged bishop of Exeter. His successor was selected, and ready on the ground – Miles Coverdale, the veteran evangelical activist, who had gone to Germany in the wake of the Six Articles and returned in 1548. Coverdale accompanied Russell's expeditionary force, preaching to the army on the eve of the Clyst St Mary massacre. He remained in the West Country in the summer of 1550, though it was another year before Veysey could finally be persuaded to step down. Tunstall of Durham was another marked man: he lost his position on the Privy Council in February 1550, and was under house arrest by the summer.[32]

Gardiner too remain caged, but not tamed, employing his enforced leisure to write defences of transubstantiation – against Peter Martyr, and against Cranmer himself. In June 1550, renewed efforts were made to secure his conformity, in which Somerset, now restored to the Council, played a leading role. He visited Gardiner in prison, and secured from him a surprisingly warm verdict on the Prayer Book: 'Touching the truth of the very presence of Christ's most precious body and blood in the sacrament, there was as much spoken in that book as might be desired.' Warwick was unconvinced of the wisdom of letting Wily Winchester loose: he insisted on a penitential acknowledgement of guilt, which the bishop was unprepared to make.[33]

Gardiner's endorsement of Cranmer's Prayer Book – part mischief-making, part tactic to win his freedom – confirmed the fears of people like Bucer, who thought the liturgy made too many concessions to the past and lent itself to popish misconstrual. There was considerable evidence at this time of conservative clergy making the new service as much as possible like the old: chanting the liturgy, ringing sacring bells, persisting with the elevation, placing candles on the altar. Cranmer issued draft visitation articles in 1549 commanding that no one 'counterfeit the popish mass'. His own words were coming back to bite him. Cranmer's official response to the western rebels condescendingly explained that what 'seemeth to you a new service . . . indeed is none other than the old: the self-same words in English which were in Latin, saving a few things taken out'.

John Bale encountered an example of a clerical counterfeiter in a church in Hampshire, an 'ape of Antichrist' who 'turned and tossed, lurked and louted [bowed], snored and smirked, gaped and gasped, kneeled and knocked, looked and licked, with both his thumbs at his ears, and other tricks more, that he made me twenty times to remember Will Somer' (Henry VIII's famous court jester). Yet it was no laughing matter if, as reported from the Welsh border counties, people 'refuse their own parish, and frequent and haunt other, where the communion is more like a mass'.[34]

A mass needed an altar, the structure topped by a stone slab at which sacrifice was performed. It was to the liturgical hardware of the churches that attention turned in the spring of 1550. Ridley, new bishop of London, set the pace. In May he commanded all altars in his diocese to be replaced with wooden 'communion tables'. Not for the first time, evangelical activists, clerical and lay, ran ahead of official policy: at least twenty London parishes removed their altars in 1549–50 prior to Ridley's order. The pattern replicates nationwide for about a fifth of the parishes for which churchwardens' accounts survive.[35] Almost nowhere can this have been a consensual, unanimously welcomed decision.

Other bishops followed suit: in November, the Privy Council noted 'altars within the more part of the churches of this our realm already upon good and godly authority taken down'. To avoid 'variance and contention', the Council ordered the remainder should be taken away – a re-run of the strategy used to sweep images from the churches in 1548. The directive flushed out another episcopal quarry: George Day of Chichester refused to implement it, was imprisoned in the Fleet, and deprived the following year.

Day was unpersuaded by Ridley's list of 'reasons why the Lord's board should be rather after the form of a table, than of an altar'. It was, argued Ridley, a question of fitness for purpose: 'The use of an altar is to make sacrifice upon it; the use of a table is to serve for men to eat upon.' Christ instituted the sacrament at a table, and if the Prayer Book mentioned altars (which it did), then it spoke 'indifferently', not meaning to specify exact forms the Lord's board should take. A key reason for making the change was educational: 'The form of a table shall move the simple from the superstitious opinions of the popish mass, unto the right use of the Lord's Supper.'[36]

Ritual and material change as a form of catechism for the uneducated made perfect sense to evangelicals. Preaching at court through Lent in 1550, John Hooper argued that 'as long as the altars remain, both the ignorant people, and the ignorant and evil-persuaded priest, will dream always of sacrifice'. On the back of his stirring sermons, King and Council offered Hooper the see of Gloucester, vacated by the death of a laid-back former monk, John Wakeman, in December 1549.[37]

### Rochets and Strangers

There was a hitch. Hooper at first declined the offer, and his Lent sermons contained clues as to why. There were things in the Ordinal 'whereat I did not a little wonder': mention of saints in the stipulated form of the Oath of Supremacy, and a requirement for bishops to be consecrated in vestments – 'rather the habit and vesture of Aaron and the gentiles, than of the ministers of Christ'.[38]

It was the start of a tense and tetchy stand-off: the bishop-elect (who was prepared to accept nomination, upon conditions) versus Cranmer and Ridley. It was also an object lesson in the vagaries of royal supremacy in the hands of a child-king. On 5 August, Cranmer received a royal dispensation to consecrate Hooper with omission of 'certain rites and ceremonies offensive to his conscience', and Hooper was confirmed in possession of the bishopric. As he prepared to swear his oath, Edward – so ab Ulmis informed Bullinger – 'chanced to notice that the saints were mentioned'. There was likely little of chance about it: Edward had been got to, his youthful godly conscience pricked. 'What wickedness is here, Hooper?' The new bishop declared his opinion about it, and the King called for a pen, scratching out the old-style petition to be helped keep the oath by 'all saints and the holy Evangelist'.

This was supreme headship with a vengeance. But Cranmer still stalled over full consecration unless Hooper was prepared to wear the stipulated garb of black chimere (an open, sleeveless gown) over full-length white rochet. Ridley worked hard to persuade councillors that Hooper's intransigence was dangerously seditious, and even Bucer and Vermigli, no fans of old-fashioned ceremony, sought to convince him he was taking a stand over the wrong issue. Hooper backed down, and was formally consecrated in March 1551 – after a short but sobering spell in the Fleet.

Hooper descended on his diocese like an avenging angel of the Lord, issuing visitation articles to smoke papists from their holes, and identifying those among his clergy – unsurprisingly, a large percentage – insufficiently familiar with scripture in English. Nicholas Heath's formal deprivation in October 1551 led to the conjoining of Worcester and Gloucester dioceses. On his first appearance in the new episcopal seat, Hooper was a perplexing creature to the chronicler John Steynor: 'Bishop Hooper came to Worcester with his wife and daughter. He had a long beard, and in all his time were no children confirmed.'[39] He was, on every count, the antithesis of a traditional Catholic bishop.

The squabble with Cranmer and Ridley over rochet and chimere was more than a storm in an episcopal teacup. It went to the heart of whether the Church could designate ceremonies as 'indifferent' (neither necessary for salvation nor prohibited by the Word of God), and require everyone to observe them. Vestments themselves – to which Cranmer was neither aesthetically nor theologically wedded – were not really the issue. It was a matter of authority, and of willingness to temper idealism with pragmatism – something Cranmer had shown in his drafting of the Prayer Book, and had learned during a long apprenticeship as the disposable conscience of an unpredictable king. It was harder to stomach for those, like Hooper, who chose to flee rather than temporize during the dark days of the 1540s, and whose natural instincts were to cleave closely to the Word of God against the mandates of popish and tyrannical bishops.

Hooper was not without supporters: his stance was vocally backed by Jan Laski, superintendent of the 'Strangers' Church'. This home from home for Protestant migrants and refugees was confirmed by royal charter in July 1550. There were two congregations: one of Dutch (or German) people worshipping at the former Austin Friars; one of French-speakers at St Anthony's chapel in Threadneedle Street. The Stranger congregations were an anomaly in a realm whose official pronouncements invariably trumpeted the virtues of 'uniformity'. The charter granted them freedom to 'exercise their own rites and ceremonies, and their own peculiar ecclesiastical discipline, notwithstanding that they do not conform with the rites and ceremonies used in our kingdom'.

For Hooper, and other evangelicals in a hurry, the Stranger Churches were a beacon and a model, pointing the sluggish English Church in the liturgical and disciplinary direction of Zürich. Ridley was suspicious of them, fearing his control over the spiritual life of his diocese might be undermined. Their independent existence was tolerated because they were considered the antidote to a greater evil threatening the body politic: the poison of anabaptist heresy. For twenty years, foreign immigration had been the channel into England of exotic heresies that horrified conservatives and evangelicals in equal measure. Such radicals, it was felt, would be easier to spot in well-ordered congregations of their own people, and less likely to infect the community at large. Edward VI wrote in his *Chronicle* that the Germans were given the Austin Friars 'for avoiding of all sects of anabaptists and suchlike'.[40]

'Anabaptism' was again at the forefront of minds in the early summer of 1550. On 2 May, after a year in Newgate, Joan Bocher was burned at the stake at Smithfield. The cream of evangelical talent exerted itself to persuade her to recant: Bishops Ridley and Goodrich, the eminent preachers Thomas Lever and Roger Hutchinson. But Joan was unshakeable in her conviction that Christ sprang only from the spiritual, not from the corporal seed of the Virgin. At her execution she harangued the appointed preacher, John Scory, as a liar.[41]

It was a moment of sombre resolution, and the loss of a kind of innocence. An ocean of blood had been spilled since Edward came to the throne, but now, for the first time, evangelicals by themselves inflicted the horrific punishment for heresy on one of their own – a woman who, a plausible later tradition maintained, had helped smuggle Tyndale's New Testament into England. Cranmer and Ridley persuaded the King of the burning's necessity, and there was little sense in the wider evangelical community of a tragic misstep. The Christian's first duty was to maintain the truth, not the liberty to be in error. Latimer dismissed Bocher as a 'foolish woman', and a versified account by the publisher Edmund Becke denounced without compunction 'the wayward Virago that would not repent / The devil's eldest daughter, which lately was brent'.[42]

The Stranger Church proved its worth as a theological drag-net when it snagged a Flemish surgeon named George van Parris, a proponent of the 'Arian' heresy denying Christ's divinity. Van Parris's excommunication from the Dutch congregation precipitated his trial before a new heresy commission in early 1551. He was burned at Smithfield on 24 April, having, like Bocher, proved immune to all persuasion. The commissions uncovered home-grown radicals too, with probable deep roots in the villages and market towns of south-east England. There were secret conventicles of anabaptists at Faversham in Kent and at Bocking in Essex – 'an assembly being of sixty persons or more'. The conventiclers here were 'freewillers': their leaders, Henry Hart and Thomas Cole, taught that 'the doctrine of predestination was meeter for devils than for Christian men'. It was also a common saying among them that 'all errors were brought in by learned men'.[43] If these were clusters of mutating Lollards, then the authorities were right to be worried about them. An inheritance of sturdy anticlericalism, and an instinctive suspicion of complex, counter-intuitive doctrines, would prove as inhospitable to the new Protestant preachers as to the popish priests they supplanted.

## Mary's Mass

For evangelicals, radical and Romanist were reflections of each other: both distorted the Word of God in the mirror of their own perverse imaginations. In a 1551 letter to John Cheke, Ridley praised a chaplain for his tirelessness in 'detecting and confuting of the anabaptists and papists in Essex'. A significant blow against 'papistry' was struck when Gardiner was brought to trial in December 1550, and in February 1551 formally deprived of his bishopric. His attempts to thwart exercise of the royal supremacy, while upholding the principle of royal supremacy, all finally came to naught. Cranmer mocked him as an oddity, an anomaly, stranded 'after the fall of the papistical doctrine, as sometimes an old post standeth when the building is overthrown'.[44]

Cranmer's ally, John Ponet, was soon installed as bishop of Winchester, though there was a more than momentary embarrassment when it transpired that Ponet had married a woman who was already the wife of a Nottingham butcher. Archbishop Robert Holgate of York fought off a lawsuit from a man claiming a pre-contract with his wife, after he married in January 1550 at the age of sixty-eight. Robert Parkyn sneered at his archbishop's 'lewd example'.[45] The legalization of clerical marriage was supposed to bring an end to scandal, but the idealism of Edwardian reformers bumped inevitably against the messy realities of human existence.

Gardiner, an old rotting post, was not the Catholic giving reformers the most cause for concern. Nor was it one of the exiles at Louvain and Paris – among them, many of the family and friends of Thomas More – sending letters of comfort to sympathizers in England and seeking to smuggle into the country Richard Smyth's books against Cranmer and Peter Martyr. The royal tutor, Roger Ascham, sneered at those who, 'to see a mass freely in Flanders, are content to forsake, like slaves, their country'.[46]

The greatest danger lay closest to home. In August 1550, a preacher at Paul's Cross railed against 'a great woman within the realm, that was a great supporter and maintainer of popery and superstition, and prayed that she might forsake her opinions'.[47] He did not name her, but everyone knew whom he meant.

In her father's reign, Princess Mary buckled and recognized the royal supremacy. In her brother's, with the mass under attack, she was determined not to repeat her apostasy. Her household, where the old service was ostentatiously performed, was a magnet for disaffected traditionalists. At first, anxious not to antagonize Charles V, Somerset and the Council informally extended her a licence to hear mass discreetly.[48] But the imperative to conciliate the Emperor was diminished after Warwick unheroically but sensibly brought to an end the ruinously expensive war with Scotland and France, returning Boulogne in a treaty of March 1550. Another, more immediate, factor was the growing exasperation of the young king that his big sister was defying him.

In April 1550, fearing her concession to hear mass was about to be with-drawn, Mary told Van der Delft she wished to flee to the Netherlands. Despite reservations, the ambassador set plans in motion. At the end of June, two impe-rial warships anchored off the coast at Maldon in Essex. In an agony of indeci-sion, and swayed by the advice of the head of her household, Robert Rochester, that she would be throwing away her right to the throne, Mary got cold feet, and the ships sailed without her. Events would prove the wisdom of Rochester's counsel.[49]

Eleven months later, in March 1551, Mary was summoned to court, to be harangued by councillors and by her brother, who 'willed her as a subject to obey' and cease hearing mass. The princess got rather the better of the encounter. When Edward said he didn't know anything about earlier threats and warnings, as he had only taken an active role in public affairs during the past year, Mary rejoined that, 'in that case, he had not drawn up the ordinances on the new religion'. She professed her willingness to die rather than give up the old religion. The King – not bereft of fraternal feeling – said 'he wished for no such sacrifice'.

Matters were left unresolved. A few days later, various gentlemen, including the courtier Sir Anthony Browne, were locked up for attending Mary's mass, but with the Emperor threatening war, Cranmer and Ridley tried to persuade a reluctant Edward that while permitting sin was itself sinful, 'to suffer and wink at it for a time might be borne'. Pressure intensified in August 1551: Mary's private mass was prohibited and her household servants were arrested and imprisoned. But the princess defiantly told visiting councillors that she would obey the King's orders in religion only when he 'shall come to such years that he may be able to judge these things himself'.[50]

Conservative opinion was not, then, entirely cowed or leaderless, five years into the reign of King Josiah. When Mary arrived in London for the March meeting, fifty knights and gentlemen rode before her, and another eighty gentleman and ladies followed after. Each ostentatiously wore at their belt 'a pair of beads'. The rosary, once a ubiquitous and unremarkable devotional object, had become a piece of daring contraband, and a material symbol of dissident confessional identity. Later that summer, as the dreadful epidemic known as 'the Sweat' swept through London, Margaret Harbotell of St Martins Ludgate harangued her evangelical curate, Nicholas Bartram, in a reversed-roles replay of the encounter that had precipitated the trouble at Clyst St Mary two years earlier. God plagued his people, she said, because Protestants 'would not suffer them to pray upon their beads'. Angrily, she shook her rosary in Bartram's face. John Hooper was no less convinced that the Sweat was 'a remarkable token of divine vengeance'. Yet his God was angered, not by the eradication of popish trappings, but by licence for some of them to remain.[51]

## The Kingdom of Christ

In the early part of 1551, the reformers took stock, recognized the strength of conservative resistance, and determined to press ahead. They did so with the encouragement of their foreign friends. In January, John Calvin wrote solemnly to Edward VI, urging him to continue 'what you have so well and happily begun', and reminded him of 'manifest abuses' remaining in the English Church. Of more practical value was the set of detailed *Censura* (criticisms) of the 1549 Prayer Book, completed by Martin Bucer a few weeks before his death on 28 February. Also published in 1551 was Bucer's *De Regno Christi* (Of the Kingdom of Christ), a manual for the creation of a truly Christian society, composed as a New Year's gift for Edward VI. It emphasized education, poor relief, the regulation of trade, industry and agriculture – all achievable through exercise of godly discipline. Bucer frankly recognized, though, that not all could be converted: in the field of the Lord, kings were empowered to cut down 'useless trees, briars and thorns'.[52]

Bucer's vision was of secular and ecclesiastical authority working seamlessly to build the Kingdom of Christ, but he was equally concerned that church property should remain in ecclesiastical hands. It was a pious hope. In March 1551, the Privy Council mandated commissions to go out to confiscate all remaining church plate, 'as the King's Majesty had need presently of a mass of money'. Just before this, orders were issued for the purging of 'superstitious books' from the royal library at Westminster. Ideological purity partnered with financial necessity: gold and silver stripped from the bindings were earmarked for Sir Anthony Aucher, the official responsible for provisioning the garrison at Calais.[53]

Leading lay evangelicals were at one neither with the preachers nor with each other. Through the spring and summer of 1551 Somerset intrigued for a restoration of his position. There were rumours the duke was plotting with the Catholic earls of Shrewsbury and Derby, to free Gardiner and reverse the religious changes. He was noticeably, even suspiciously, reticent in efforts to compel Mary to conform to the Prayer Book.

Warwick took his time, but on 16 October, a few days after his creation as Duke of Northumberland, he struck. Somerset was arrested, charged with treason and sent to the Tower. At the trial in December, Northumberland was unable to get treason charges to stick, but Somerset was convicted of felony for convoking unlawful assemblies. Northumberland's grip on government tightened on 21 December with the enforced resignation as Lord Chancellor of Richard Rich, a man suspected of involvement in Somerset's schemes. Rich drifted with the winds of self-advancement, but at heart (if he had a heart) he was a religious conservative. Only a year earlier, a reformer had dedicated a book to him, in grateful recognition of his role in suppressing 'vain ceremonies . . . that

heretofore ye have been thought to favour, uphold and maintain'. His replacement was the evangelical bishop Thomas Goodrich of Ely, the first churchman
since Wolsey to hold the office.

If Somerset did flirt with the conservatives, it was a tactical romance and
not an affair of the heart. Prior to his execution on 22 January 1552, the duke
busied himself reading the bible and composing meditations, and from the
block he urged onlookers to hold fast in the faith that, when in authority, 'I
always diligently set forth and furthered to my power'. It is impossible to guess
at the emotional hinterland of a clipped entry in his royal nephew's chronicle:
'The duke of Somerset had his head cut off upon Tower Hill between eight and
nine o'clock in the morning'.[54]

Somerset remained until the last alarmingly popular; many blamed
Northumberland for cruelly pursuing him to his death. The Lord President
exerted himself to retain the support of the reforming bishops. He encouraged,
for example, a scheme dear to Cranmer's heart: a thoroughgoing reform of
canon law, infused by the spirit of Bucer's *De Regno*. In October 1551, the
Council authorized a committee composed in equal parts of bishops, divines,
civil lawyers and common lawyers to begin working on a draft.

There was progress too with another project smiled on by the ghost of
Bucer. A revised communion service was heralded, as in 1549, by disputations
on the eucharist. In November 1551 a pair of debates took place in the London
houses of William Cecil and Richard Morison. These godly laymen, and a
third, John Cheke, joined a trio of rising clerical stars – Edmund Grindal,
Robert Horne and David Whitehead – to argue for a figurative understanding
of 'this is my body'. Their lead opponent was a learned former monk of
Evesham, John Feckenham, who was arrested by Lord Grey during the suppression of the Oxfordshire Rising. Remarkably, Feckenham's temporary release
from the Tower was extended after the debates, to allow him to travel to his
native Worcestershire, and debate there with John Hooper.

Truth would prevail, if it could be openly declared. The evangelical leadership's faith in this dictum was manifested in its sponsorship of star-quality itinerant preaching. In December 1551, Grindal was one of six preachers appointed,
with generous annual stipends of £40, as royal 'chaplains ordinary'. There were
to be two constantly in attendance upon the King, while the others were, as
Edward noted, 'always absent in preaching'. Lancashire and Wales, notoriously
dark corners of the land, were priority areas. Another name was added: that of
John Knox, currently preaching to a mixed congregation of locals and fellow
Scots exiles in Newcastle-upon-Tyne. Lincolnshire, that nursery of popish
rebellion, benefited from the folksy oratory of Hugh Latimer, who withdrew
from the court in 1550, and preached at Grimsthorpe and elsewhere as a client
of Catherine Willoughby, widowed Duchess of Suffolk, and a formidably
learned and zealous patron of evangelical religion.[55]

Parliament reassembled, after a break of almost two years, on 23 January 1552, a day after Somerset's beheading. One of the first items of business was a new Treason Act, restoring much of the scope of the Henrician legislation, in particular the penalties for calling the King 'heretic, schismatic, tyrant, infidel or usurper'. It was a symptom of the political chill following the 1549 risings, and of a fear of unrest in the counties, where 'Lords Lieutenant' loyal to Northumberland were being invested with unprecedented powers to suppress disorder. Another symptom was the return of censorship, after the carnival of print and opinion in Edward's first years. A proclamation of April 1551 banned publishing works in English, or performing plays or interludes, without written permission from six privy councillors.[56]

The crucial measure, passed in April, was a second Act of Uniformity, authorizing for worship a revised form of the Prayer Book, which Cranmer and others had been working on through the winter. As in 1549, three lay lords – Derby, Stourton, Windsor – voted against, but only two dissident bishops – Thirlby and Aldridge – now kept them company.

'A great number of people,' the act complained, 'abstain and refuse to come to their parish churches and other places where common prayer, administration of the sacraments, and preaching of the Word of God is used.' It was a charge echoed in the visitation articles of assorted bishops, and one supported by the evidence of church courts, which show marked rises in presentments for non-attendance after 1549.[57] Perhaps an age-old problem of patchy attendance was simply being policed with greater thoroughness. But bishops believed people were absenting themselves out of perversity not laziness. Ridley demanded to know 'whether there be any that privately in their private houses have their masses, contrary to the form and order of the Book of Communion?'

This was a new dimension to the religious divisions of England. For nearly a generation, argument had raged about what the worshipping community should do together in church. To some, it now seemed they should not worship together at all. The act ordered attendance at services on Sundays and holy days, 'upon pain of punishment by the censures of the Church'. The Church had always applied censures to enforce presence at worship, but statutory insistence on it was nonetheless a departure, a significant enhancement of the role of the state in regulating religious life. Revealingly, the measure was tabled in the Lords as a bill 'for the appointing of an order to come to divine service'.[58]

Divine service had taken large steps in the direction Calvin, Bullinger and Vermigli – as well as home-grown zealots like Hooper – were urging the Church to take. Cranmer's hand did not need to be forced, though; the second Prayer Book reflected his mature theology, and followed a major development in the wider evangelical movement. In the summer of 1549, Bullinger and Calvin hammered out the *Consensus Tigurinus* ('Agreement of Zürich'), first printed in March 1551. The formula combined Zwingli's insistence that the sacrament of the eucharist was a sign or seal, with Calvin's intuition of spiritual benefits for individual communicants. The eucharist was an instrument of divine grace – but only for the elect.[59] Luther, who died in February 1546, would have been horrified.

The new liturgy also reflected Cranmer's developing sense of the concessions needed to keep people on board: fewer than in 1549. The Lord's Supper was no longer, it seemed, 'commonly called the mass'. 'Altars' disappeared from the liturgy as they had from churches. The Prayer Book ordered the 'Table' to stand in the body of the church, or in the chancel (rather than in the altar's old position at the east end), and the priest to preside from a position on its long north side.

The point behind this topography of fixtures was to replace the symbolism of sacrifice with that of a minister and congregation gathered around the meal table. Distinctive ministerial garb was not abolished, but it was considerably simplified: for saying communion, the minister 'shall use neither alb, vestment, nor cope, but ... a surplice only'. Bishops 'shall have and wear a rochet' – whether Hooper liked it or not. An instruction to begin each communion service with a recital of the Ten Commandments, perhaps borrowed from the practice of the Stranger Churches, undoubtedly appealed to him more.

The theology underpinning the communion was nowhere explicitly spelled out in the Prayer Book, but there were multiple clues. Ordinary fine white bread, rather than unleavened wafers, was to be used, 'to take away the superstition which any person hath, or might have'. The words spoken by the minister on delivering communion now omitted the primordial phrase, 'the body of Christ'. Instead, people were told: 'Take and eat this, in remembrance that Christ died for thee, and feed on him in thy heart by faith, with thanksgiving.' 'Presence' was, at best, spiritual, and limited to the subjective experience of the communicant. That was certainly the implication of a homely and frugal directive: 'if any of the bread or wine remain, the curate shall have it to his own use'. The object the south-western rebels wanted to see reserved above the high altar, and devoutly worshipped there, was reduced to the status of a supper-time snack.[60]

Across a range of life-cycle rituals, the new Prayer Book emphasized the importance of faith, and sought to minimize the risk of people placing trust in ritual actions or material objects. Anointing was removed from ordination, visitation of the sick and baptism. The baptismal ceremony did away with the white chrisom robe, though in a rare concession to tradition – or perhaps as an assertion of the Trinity against anabaptist heretics – it retained making the sign of the cross on the child's forehead. There was provision for communion of the sick, but only if an impromptu congregation could be found to communicate alongside the sick person in their house, where the minister should perform the entire rite. He must not bring consecrated bread from an earlier communion in church, as permitted in 1549 – there could be no suggestion of holiness residing in an object as it was carried from place to place.

The new liturgy also addressed a recurrent concern of the earlier book's critics, by eliminating from the burial service any suggestion of prayer for the dead. 'No dirges or other devout prayers to be sung or said for such as was departed this transitory world' was Robert Parkyn's sullen summary. His chronicle contained a detailed, intelligent and caustic examination of the new liturgy, with no doubt what lay behind it: 'All this was done and brought to pass only to subdue the most blessed sacrament of Christ's body and blood.'[61]

It would be some months before Parkyn was expected to perform the new service in his parish in Yorkshire. Implementation was delayed till November 1552 while progress continued on the revision of canon law, and on another ambitious project – the production of a definitive set of articles of faith, to lay the ghost of the King's Book, and set forth the belief of the reformed English Church as emphatically as the 1530 Augsburg Confession did for German Lutherans.

Ideally, the statement would follow rather than precede an event Cranmer still hoped to see: a grand evangelical council to rival and confound the papist proceedings at Trent. In March 1552, Cranmer wrote ecumenically to Europe's three greatest anti-Roman theologians – Bullinger, Calvin and Melanchthon – inviting them to take part. Calvin warmly applauded the initiative, at a time when 'hireling dogs of the Pope are barking unceasingly'. But he excused his personal attendance on the implausible grounds of 'want of ability'. Bullinger and Melanchthon were still more evasive: the self-inflicted wounds of the European Reform were not to be bound and healed in England.[62]

Nonetheless, by the summer of 1552, there were grounds for Cranmer and other evangelical leaders to feel satisfaction: churches had been cleansed of their idolatry; papist opposition confronted and faced down. Theological opinion often held there were three signs or marks of a true Church: pure worship, correct doctrine and godly discipline. With the revision of the Prayer Book, the English Church was close to mission accomplished on the first count; the articles and new code of canon law would make it three for three. It was not to happen, and, for once, the papists could not be blamed.

### Carnal Gospelling

It was, fundamentally, a question of trust. Cranmer, Ridley and other reformers did not believe the Duke of Northumberland had the best interests of the Gospel at heart, and their suspicion gnawed at the evangelical movement from within. The problem did not come out of the blue. From the dissolution of the monasteries onwards, preachers worried that dismantling of the old order was not leading to construction of the new, and a sinister figure increasingly haunted their rhetoric: the 'carnal gospeller', who mouthed slogans of reform with the motives of material gain.[63]

Renewed orders for confiscation of church plate, and the issuing of a new commission for sale of chantry lands, brought matters to a head in April–May 1552. Cranmer's secretary Ralph Morice remembered his master offering 'to combat with the Duke of Northumberland'. The envisaged combat was (presumably) intellectual not physical, but it was a mark of Cranmer's discomfort that he found himself using the argument of religious conservatives, pleading for 'the staying of the chantries until his highness had come to lawful age'. Ridley later recalled himself and Cranmer being 'in high displeasure' with the duke for criticizing 'spoil of the church goods'.

Just before this, in March 1552, Cranmer voted in the Lords against a failed attempt by Northumberland to remove Tunstall from his diocese of Durham by act of attainder. Very likely, the archbishop had an inkling of what Northumberland was planning. It was revealed in a letter to Cecil in October, when Tunstall was finally deprived by royal commission. The scheme was to carve the great episcopal palatinate into two new dioceses, of Durham and Newcastle, on shoestring budgets, and to transfer to the crown Durham Castle, a variety of episcopal residences and lands worth £2,000 a year.[64]

Northumberland's response to such scolding was to court the bishops' critics. He backed Jan Laski against Cranmer in a squabble about who should be granted the licence to print a French translation of the Prayer Book for use in the Channel Islands. He also brought south as his chaplain John Knox, the firebrand Scot, whose preaching had impressed Northumberland on a 1551 visit to the north. In his letter to Cecil, Northumberland identified Knox as a suitable candidate for the vacant bishopric of Rochester: he would be 'a whetstone to quicken and sharpen the bishop of Canterbury, whereof he hath need'.[65]

Knox demonstrated his ability to generate sparks in a first sermon in front of King and court in late September 1552. He 'inveighed with great freedom against kneeling at the Lord's Supper'. The result was a message sent from the Privy Council to the printer Richard Grafton, ordering him to stop production and distribution of the new Prayer Book 'until certain faults therein be corrected'.[66]

The issue was a rematch of the vestments controversy of the preceding year, with Laski once again taking the side of godly rebels against the evangelical episcopal establishment. For Knox, and other purists, kneeling to receive communion implied worship of the eucharistic elements. Hooper denounced the practice of kneeling in his 1550 Lent sermons as an invitation to 'grievous and damnable idolatry' and hoped the lay authorities would insist on reception standing or seated; his preference was for the latter. For Ridley and Cranmer, it was another instance of an 'indifferent' matter. Scripture supplied no definitive instructions, and it was up to the Church to prescribe whatever was conducive to uniformity, decency and order.

Furious at being undermined and outflanked, Cranmer wrote to the Council on 7 October, emphasizing how he and 'the best learned within this realm' had already weighed the issue, and how Parliament had approved the book they produced. He trusted the councillors would not be swayed by 'glorious and unquiet spirits, which can like nothing but that is after their own fancy'. Even were the Prayer Book to be revised and reissued every year, 'yet should it not lack faults in their opinion'. Cranmer moved swiftly to a damning conclusion. The critics condemned kneeling because it was not commanded in scripture, and whatever was not commanded was unlawful. Yet this was 'the chief foundation of the error of the anabaptists . . . a subversion of all order in religion as in common policy'. It was a shrewd jab, at a moment when Cranmer was about to be named to a new heresy commission looking into the extent of anabaptism in Kent.

In the face of this tirade, and needing Cranmer's support to complete the deprivation of Bishop Tunstall, Northumberland backed down – up to a point. On 22 October the Privy Council issued on its own authority a declaration on kneeling at the communion, to be added to the Prayer Book. The last-minute character of the decision meant that early copies had the statement inserted between the leaves: a 'black rubric' not using the red ink with which liturgical instructions were conventionally printed. Kneeling would continue, though the rubric made clear that it did not imply adoration, that there was no change to the 'natural substances' of bread and wine, and that its sole purpose was to avoid 'profanation and disorder'.

The rubric added little, as theological explication, to what was already apparent from a careful reading of the Prayer Book. And in truth there was nothing in it to which Cranmer or Ridley could readily take exception. But the episode, and the manner of its resolution, illustrated the tetchiness in relations between leading figures of Church and state, and the willingness of councillors to act in religious matters on their own authority.[67]

The recriminations continued. In Lent 1553, a formidable array of preachers, at court and elsewhere, took turns to fulminate against 'covetousness' and 'ambition' in high places. They included Latimer, John Bradford, Grindal, Lever and – biting the hand until recently feeding him – Knox. Northumberland was frequently ill that winter, and so, ominously, was the King. In February, he caught a bad cold, and did not seem able to shake it off. In late April, the imperial ambassador, Van der Delft's replacement Jean Scheyve, reported that Edward was getting weaker and coughing up blood and bile: 'his doctors and physicians are perplexed and do not know what to make of it'.[68]

Edward played a reduced role at the ceremonies to mark the opening of a new Parliament on 1 March 1553. The main business, as usual, was the grant of a subsidy, for, despite sales of church goods, royal finances remained calamitous. There was also a major ecclesiastical matter: a bill to enact the proposed overhaul of canon law, now packaged in a substantial document known as the *Reformatio Legum Ecclesiasticarum* (Reform of the Ecclesiastical Laws).

The *Reformatio* was a blueprint for a meticulously reformed Church of England: the next and necessary step, after the demanding work of cleansing and destruction, towards building a new Christian society. It was not a blueprint for revolution, and aimed to reform rather than abolish the canon law system, keeping, for example, the three-fold ministry of bishops, priests and deacons. Unsurprisingly, it endorsed wholeheartedly the royal supremacy. But the document gave overtly reformed interpretations to all the remaining structures of a once-popish Church. The office of deacon was redefined, as in Calvin's Geneva, to concern itself with social welfare and support of the poor; churchwardens were to concentrate on policing morals and behaviour in the parish, rather than organizing church ales. Discipline was the recurrent theme, with detailed instructions on how preachers should supervise and regulate their flocks, and demands for strict social exclusion of excommunicates. New punishments included banishment or perpetual imprisonment for adultery and blasphemy. In line with the practice of European reformed Churches, provisions for absolute divorce in cases of adultery were introduced. There was even a canon demanding that mothers breastfeed their own children, and not avoid 'the honest and natural burdens of child-rearing'.[69]

The bill failed. Its proposals – at once utopian, compassionate and coercive – belong on the long list of might-have-beens of the English Reformation. Cranmer introduced the measure in the House of Lords, but Northumberland spoke immediately and decisively against it. This, in the imperial ambassador's account, was an act of revenge for the recent wave of sermons criticizing government policy. Yet it is also likely that Northumberland reacted against the strong strain of clericalism in the *Reformatio Legum*, and its potential for emboldening the Church to assert greater independence from the state.[70]

As discipline hit the rocks in the spring of 1553, worship and doctrine remained on a steadier course. An officially authorized primer was printed in March – a book of private prayer to complement the Book of Common Prayer, whose structure of morning and evening services it adapted for home devotional use. Virtually all traces of the traditional Catholic primers were eliminated, including the *Dirige*, and psalms and prayers of the passion. The book contained numerous prayers for sundry occasions, many of them the work of Cranmer's chaplain, Thomas Becon. Ideals of a well-ordered commonwealth, in which people knew both their place and their obligations towards others, were reflected in special petitions for landlords, merchants, lawyers, labourers, parents and children. But there was also doctrinal red meat. In a prayer 'For the glory of heaven', the reader entreated God to 'make me . . . of that number whom thou from everlasting hast predestined to be saved . . . Pluck me out of the company of the stinking goats, which shall stand on thy left side and be damned.'

'Make me' here probably meant, 'Allow me to believe that I am' – for God's mind could not be swayed or changed on the question of whom, before the beginning of time, he chose to live with him in eternity. The seeping expansion of the doctrine of predestination was a significant development of the mid-Tudor years. For believers, it gave greater depth and meaning to the perplexing divisions of England, and appreciable reassurance that being in the minority did not mean being in the wrong. The struggles, travails and contradictions experienced by the godly in this life were but echoes of another, elemental and invisible contest between the forces of light and darkness, elect and non-elect, Christ and Antichrist – the contest described in the biblical Book of Revelation and in Bale's *Image of Both Churches*, of which three editions appeared under Edward. The ultimate outcome of the contest was assured:

> The people of all manner of regions, which are predestined of God to be saved, shall walk in the clearness of the light . . . Neither shall they care for Mary nor John, roods nor relics, beads nor holy water, masses nor merits. For so shall He shine upon them, and His glory appear in them, that the clouds of Antichrist and his false prophets shall take no place.

'Antichrist is not yet slain', warned the official catechism that followed the primer in May 1553, but there was little doubt that his days were numbered.[71]

The catechism was issued jointly with a set of articles, forty-two in number, and described on their title-page as 'agreed upon by the bishops and other learned and godly men in the last Convocation'. This was misleading, a potential hostage to fortune, and added to the title page by fellow-councillors without Cranmer's knowledge. The articles were not formally discussed or adopted by Convocation, whose already weakened state as a decision-making body was eroded further in Edward's reign. Religious conservatives there would undoubtedly have put up a fight. Nor were the articles (unlike the Prayer Book) endorsed by parliamentary vote. They were drafted by Cranmer and a small circle of evangelical allies, and issued on royal authority alone. It was not the validation from a pan-European, anti-Roman General Council that Cranmer had hoped for. Such a pedigree would not in any case have conciliated conservatives. When, at the end of May, Cranmer and other bishops began to demand subscription from clergy, there were, in London at least, 'divers that denied many of the articles'.[72]

The articles themselves consolidated rather than accelerated the evangelical agenda. They avoided the recent hot-button issues of clerical vestments and kneeling at the communion, though the voice of exasperated episcopal authority was clearly audible in Article 33, maintaining that Christian customs could vary between times and places, and denouncing 'whosoever, through his private judgement, willingly and purposely doth openly break the traditions and ceremonies of the Church which be not repugnant to the Word of God'. There was predictable condemnation of papal authority, of compulsory clerical celibacy, purgatory, images, saints and transubstantiation, along with an equally emphatic rejection of a variety of anabaptist errors, such as the holding of goods in common, and the unlawfulness of oath-taking. There were declared to be but two sacraments, baptism and the eucharist, both 'effectual signs of grace', confirming and strengthening faith in Christ. Article 29, on the Lord's Supper, maintained the position of the Prayer Book (which Article 35 endorsed as 'godly, and in no point repugnant to the wholesome doctrine of the Gospel') in its denial of 'real and bodily presence', combining this with a degree of studied vagueness about what, if any, sort of presence there might actually be.

On predestination, the articles unambiguously asserted God's choice of the elect 'before the foundations of the world were laid', stressing how his 'sons by adoption' would 'walk religiously in good works' – effect following cause. There was some skirting around the full implications, however. Calvin devoted several chapters of his *Institutes of the Christian Religion* to demonstrating 'the eternal election, by which God has predestined some to salvation, and others to destruction'. By contrast, Article 17 spoke only of 'predestination to life'.

Predestination was an idea 'full of sweet, pleasant and unspeakable comfort to godly persons'. For 'curious and carnal persons', there was a danger that 'to have continually before their eyes the sentence of God's predestination' might lead to immorality or despair. The article did not say that preachers should be careful how, and how often, they treated this topic (a topic notably absent from the Homilies). But that was surely the implication, particularly since God's actual judgements 'are unknown to us'. The true, invisible Church comprised the elect only, but the rag-bag people of the visible, earthly Church still had to be managed, ordered, persuaded and cajoled into goodness.

On one point, entirely foreign to the theology of Calvin, the articles were unequivocal. 'The King of England is supreme head in earth, next under Christ, of the Church of England and Ireland.'[73] That was the legal basis for six years of exhilarating religious change, and also, to a remarkable extent, their emotional heart. Under Henry, the supremacy had often seemed no more than an instrument of convenience, and a frequently unreliable one. But evangelicals across the spectrum of temperament and opinion recognized in their young Josiah an instrument of divine providence; the mortal enemy of the Pope, and leader of the earthly struggle against Antichrist.[74] The mantle of godly royal authority enabled reformers to regard previously popish institutions as redeemed, or at least redeemable, and explains why unlikely figures, such as Hooper, were willing to serve as bishops. Even John Bale accepted promotion to the episcopate, setting off in late 1552 to serve for a few unhappy months as bishop of Ossory in the south-east of Ireland. Bale's fertile historical imagination allowed him to see King John, as well as Henry VIII, as heroic champions of Christ against Antichrist. To view Edward VI in the same light required a great deal less theological squinting.[75]

In an increasingly polarized religious world, this, ironically, was common ground between evangelicals and Catholics – some Catholics. Royal supremacy itself, it could be argued, was not the wellspring of heresy and division; a true exercise of the supremacy had been hindered and hijacked during the minority. That was the view of Gardiner, of rebels demanding the return of the Six Articles, and of others like John Proctor, a former fellow of All Souls, Oxford. At the end of 1549, just before the tightening of censorship, Proctor published an ostensibly anti-anabaptist work, sorely lamenting the 'hurly burly of Christ's religion'. He blamed irresponsible preachers and unrestrained reading of scripture for creating an England where 'every man, every woman, pretendeth to be a gospeller'. Proctor's good old days were recent ones – those of 'noble Henry, king of kings', who justly got rid of popes and superstition, but whose legacy of orthodoxy and order was now coming grievously apart.[76]

As an adult Edward would renounce the heretics and restore Henry's legacy: that was the hope, spoken or unspoken, of conservatives. A version was even shared by some Catholics who felt little nostalgia for the reign of Henry. In late 1552 or early 1553, Reginald Pole composed a letter, in the form of a preface for a new edition of his *De Unitate*, to a monarch now 'approaching adolescence'. Edward turned fifteen in October 1552, and was receiving regular instruction from William Thomas – former traveller in Italy, and now clerk of the Privy Council – on policy matters and drafting of state papers. In his letter, Pole said he had heard good reports of the King, and offered him counsel so that he would not repeat the mistakes of his father.[77]

If the letter was ever sent, there is no evidence of a reply. The young king had every intention of avoiding the mistakes of Henry VIII, though not in the way Pole meant. Edward was beyond doubt the rightful son and heir, but in 1544, on the eve of his departure to campaign in France, Henry used an Act of Parliament simply to announce the line of succession. If Edward died without lawful heirs, then the throne was to pass first to Mary and her progeny, then to Elizabeth and hers – even though both women remained, technically, bastards.

In the spring of 1553, painfully sick, and starting to despair of recovery, Edward came to a courageous and fateful decision. He would rise up to exercise his God-given supremacy, undo his father's imperious will, and rescue the realm from Antichrist.

# THE TWO QUEENS

## Devices for the Succession

Almighty and most merciful Lord . . . we most entirely appeal to Thy great mercies, graciously to restore the health and strength again of Thy servant Edward, our Sovereign Lord, that as Thou has begun by him the rooting out of error, idolatry and superstition, and the planting of true religion, true worshipping and verity, so it may please Thy merciful goodness, long to preserve him for the confirmation and establishment of the same.[1]

ON 19 JUNE 1553, this heartfelt prayer was printed for use in churches throughout the land. It petitioned for mercy, but what was needed was a miracle. After his cold in February, Edward contracted a serious illness – perhaps tuberculosis, more likely bronchial pneumonia – and through the spring he became progressively weaker. The doctors who saw him secretly on 10 June thought he had three days left, though he clung tenaciously to life for almost a month. The prayer went unheeded, but True Religion had a back-up plan.[2]

Sometime in March or April, Edward drafted a brief document headed 'My Device for the Succession'. It was a remarkable exercise of royal authority, and – since the King, a minor, could not make a valid will, or set aside an Act of Parliament – a completely illegal one. It was also an invocation of a male heir amidst a welter of women. Edward's scheme ignored his half-sisters Mary and Elizabeth, in line to succeed under the terms of the 1544 Succession Act and his father's will. He also overlooked the claims of the descendants of Henry's sister Margaret, wife of, first, James V, and then the Earl of Angus. Instead, he turned to the progeny of Margaret's younger sister, Mary.

Mary's marriage to Charles Brandon, Duke of Suffolk, produced two daughters. The elder, Frances, married Henry Grey, who inherited his father-in-law's title. They in turn had three daughters: Jane, Katherine and Mary. Edward's proposal was for the crown to pass to a future son of Frances, and failing that, to any male heir, in turn, of the three Grey sisters.

Edward's motivation was not unvarnished misogyny, or legalistic scruple over his sisters' legitimacy. The judge Sir Edward Montagu later testified to Edward telling him that he feared for 'his proceedings in religion' should Mary succeed. There was no comparable anxiety about Elizabeth. But passing over one bastard half-sister logically required the exclusion of the other. And the Greys were reliably, zealously, evangelical.

As the King's health worsened, so time ran out on the appearance of the hypothetical baby boys, and the Device was altered. The initiative was perhaps Edward's, but more likely was suggested by allies of Northumberland among the gentlemen of the Privy Chamber. The crown would now pass to 'Jane and her heirs male'. There was no logic to preferring the daughter over the mother, particularly since Jane was only sixteen. But minority rule suited Northumberland, and the decision to skip a generation was connected to the marriage, taking place on 21 May, between Jane and Northumberland's son, Guildford.

The revised Device was authenticated under letters patent on 21 June, after Northumberland bullied reluctant judges into recognizing its legality, and cajoled the rest of the Council into swearing their support. Cranmer was hesitant, but was lured on board with promises including revival of the canon-law reform, and an addition to the King's will requiring the executors 'not to suffer any piece of religion to be altered'.[3]

Edward died on the evening of 6 July. Three hours before his death, he reportedly uttered a quiet prayer (soon after printed as a broadsheet): 'Oh my Lord God, defend this realm from papistry, and maintain thy true religion.'[4]

It was the best-prepared-for royal death in more than a century. Everyone who mattered knew their part. The exception was Jane herself. On 9 July, she obeyed a summons to come to Syon, where Somerset had turned the former monastic buildings into a fine mansion house. Jane was both grief-stricken and perturbed when the councillors, having sat on news of Edward's death for three days, knelt to offer her fealty. 'The crown is not my right and pleases me not. The Lady Mary is the rightful heir!' Father, mother and husband were wheeled in to persuade her it was her religious duty to acquiesce. The following day, heralds proclaimed throughout the city Jane's right and title by letters patent of Edward VI, and that the Lady Mary was 'unlawfully begotten'.[5] There was only one flaw in the execution of the scheme; Mary herself had slipped the net.

If Jane was blissfully ignorant of Edward and Northumberland's plans, Mary was not. In late June, unnamed privy councillors began sending her updates on Edward's health, and on a plot to alter the succession. On 3 July, travelling to visit Edward at Greenwich, Mary received word he was in his final throes, and that Northumberland planned to arrest her. She rode for East Anglia, and by the time Jane was proclaimed, Mary had reached her manor house of Kenninghall, at the heart of her Norfolk estates. Here, she learned Edward was dead. According to a later tradition, the message was sent by Nicholas Throckmorton, son of Henry VIII's nemesis, Sir George Throckmorton, but himself a convert to the new faith. Not all evangelicals saw the cause of Northumberland and of the Gospel as one and the same. Hooper would soon claim how in these crucial days he rode from place to place 'to win and stay the people' for Mary.

At Kenninghall, Mary asserted her title, wrote to the councillors in London to demand obedience, and sent letters to towns and landowners across the country, asking them to muster forces. A few days later, she moved to Framlingham in Suffolk, with the nucleus of an army growing around her. England, once again, stood perched on the brink of war.[6]

It looked an unequal contest. Jane had the capital, the apparently unanimous support of the Council, the royal guard, fleet, armoury and treasury, and a considerable force of retainers already in arms. The French ambassador, Antoine de Noailles, relayed Northumberland's reassurances to Henry II, a king with a vested interest in seeing the defeat of a pro-Habsburg princess. 'They had provided so well against the Lady Mary's ever attaining the succession . . . that there is no need for you, Sire, to enter into any doubt.'[7]

The confidence proved premature. As news filtered through of forces rallying to Mary, councillors began to waver. Arundel, Pembroke, Bedford and Sir William Petre began meeting together secretly. Northumberland left London on 14 July at the head of a small army. On the eve of his departure he sternly admonished the councillors that God would not forgive them if they betrayed their 'sacred and holy oath of allegiance'.

Northumberland marched north to Cambridge, en route sacking the home of Mary's supporter John Huddlestone at Sawston Hall, where the princess had stayed during her flight. Mass books seized from the house were displayed in the pulpit by Edwin Sandys, vice-chancellor of the university, who was ordered to preach in favour of Jane.[8]

But Northumberland's support was starting to unravel. Various towns outside London declared for Jane, but others remained reticent. In some places – Coventry, Northampton, Ipswich – both queens were proclaimed by rival supporters. On 15 July, the sailors patrolling the Suffolk coast – behind Mary's lines and blocking her escape – were persuaded to change sides, and to bring ashore vital gunners and artillery. News reached London of major risings in Oxfordshire and Buckinghamshire, and there were (exaggerated) reports that Mary now had an army of 30,000 in Suffolk. It dawned on the councillors they might have backed the wrong horse; that Mary, against the odds, could actually win.

Northumberland marched for Framlingham on 18 July, but a day later fell nervously back toward Cambridge. There he learned that, meeting at Pembroke's house, a majority of the Council had proclaimed Mary rightful queen. Even Jane's father the Duke of Suffolk now publicly supported her. London's response to the proclamation of Jane on 10 July was muted. Nine days later, the celebrations were unrestrained: 'What with shouting and crying of the people, and ringing of the bells,' a chronicler noted, 'there could no one hear almost what another said.' Northumberland realized the game was up. On 20 July, he told his officers it was their duty to obey the Council. He went to the marketplace in Cambridge, threw his cap into the air and proclaimed the new sovereign. 'Queen Mary,' he told Sandys, 'was a merciful woman.'[9]

### God and the World Knoweth

London's rejoicing for the accession of Henry VIII's daughter was replicated across the nation. Mary was proclaimed at Bridgnorth in Shropshire on 22 July, the people 'casting up their caps and hats, lauding, thanking and praising God Almighty with ringing of bells and making of bonfires in every street'. There were similar scenes at Shrewsbury, and – Vicar Thomas Butler recorded with evident relish – 'also in this borough of Much Wenlock'.[10]

The summer of 1553 was the setting for a religious civil war that did not quite take place. It was not for want of trying. Jane's proclamation stressed that Mary's intention was to 'bring this noble, free realm into the tyranny and servitude of the bishop of Rome'. On the eve of departing for Framlingham, Northumberland reminded Council colleagues that they were embarked on 'God's cause, which is the preferment of his Word, and the fear of papistry's re-entrance'.

Batteries of preachers pounded at the same target. On Sunday 9 July, the eve of the coup, Ridley caused consternation by denouncing Mary and Elizabeth as bastards from the pulpit of Paul's Cross. If Mary were to become queen, 'she would bring in foreign power to reign over them, besides the subverting also of Christian religion'. In a sermon rushed to press in the course of the following week, John Bradford urged Christians to repent their sins so that 'God's Gospel should tarry with us, religion should be cherished, superstition suppressed'.[11]

Yet Northumberland – never really trusted by the gospellers, and hated by commoners for the events of 1549 – was not the man to lead a Protestant crusade. For her part, Mary stood on the rightness of her claim rather than the truth of her religion. She thus avoided driving wavering evangelicals into the arms of the opposition, though her core supporters, among the East Anglian gentry and elsewhere, were to a man firm Catholics.[12]

Mary's trump card was the endorsement of her father, which her brother's declaration for Jane simply couldn't match up to. The contest of two queens ended in the victory of one dead king over another. It was vindication of what conservatives like Gardiner had been saying for the past six years – no radical change during a minority. And no one was in any doubt that the triumph of Henry VIII's will, and of Henry VIII's daughter, meant, at the very least, the restoration of Henry VIII's religion.

To the Yorkshire priest Robert Parkyn, Mary's accession seemed nothing short of providential: 'Almighty God, which ever defendeth his true servants, ordered the matter so.' For evangelicals, at home and abroad, it was a disaster. 'Scarcely has any other thing so much distressed me as this English affair', Bullinger wrote to the Genevan reformer Theodore Beza. In faraway Zürich, no news was not good news: 'Where is our Martyr? Where is Jan Laski? Where is Hooper, bishop of Worcester? Where is Cranmer, archbishop of Canterbury?'[13]

By the time Bullinger wrote this in late August, Peter Martyr was under house arrest, waiting for the Privy Council's permission to depart from England. Laski would take ship a few weeks later. Hooper, despite his loyalty during the crisis, was on 1 September bundled off to the Fleet. Cranmer, for the moment, was at liberty, but by the middle of September was incarcerated in the Tower.

Space in the gaols was freed up by the release of the regime's friends. Bonner walked out of the Marshalsea on 5 August, and processed in honourable estate to St Paul's. 'All the people by the way bad him welcome home', wrote a friendly conservative chronicler, 'and as many of the women as might, kissed him.' Richard Cox, former chancellor of Oxford, went straight into Bonner's old cell. The following day, the aged Duke of Norfolk was released from the Tower, and the other conservative bishops – Gardiner of Winchester, Tunstall of Durham, Day of Chichester and Heath of Worcester – were set free, and restored to their former positions.[14]

The warmth of Bonner's welcome contrasted with London's reception for Northumberland. As he passed through Shoreditch on his way to the Tower 'all the people reviled him, and called him traitor and heretic'. There was similar treatment for the hapless Edwin Sandys. A woman standing in her doorway shouted at him, 'Fie on thee, thou knave . . . thou traitor, thou heretic!' But a woman on the other side of the street retorted, 'Fie on thee, neighbour! . . . Good gentleman, God be thy comfort, and give thee strength to stand in God's cause.' Londoners were as divided as ever, and women were no less willing than men to engage in rancorous public dispute.[15]

Northumberland had one more surprise up his sleeve. In the Tower on 21 August, the day before his execution, he announced a desire 'to hear mass, and receive the sacrament after the old accustomed manner'. Prominent evangelical Londoners were summoned to attend and marvel at the sudden change. Northumberland was hoping – in vain – for clemency, but his persistence in his conversion suggests it may not have been wholly cynical. From the scaffold he warned everyone to beware of 'seditious preachers and teachers of new doctrine'. Manifold plagues – 'war, famine, pestilence and death of our king, rebellion, sedition among ourselves, conspiracies' – had befallen England 'since we dissevered ourselves from the Catholic Church of Christ'.[16]

It was a devastating betrayal. The verdict of Jane, likewise a prisoner in the Tower, was scathing: 'As his life was wicked and full of dissimulation, so was his end thereafter.' Northumberland's confession was rapidly published, and widely publicized in Catholic Europe. Beza felt compelled to write a rebuttal. At the execution itself, it was reported 'there were a great number turned with his words'.[17]

The sixteenth century was a providential age; things happened for a reason. By taking away their young Josiah, evangelicals understood that God was punishing them for their sins. But was he actually judging against them? Some prominent evangelical sympathizers, such as Paget and Cecil, quickly resolved to swallow their principles, and serve the regime. Before the end of July, Elizabeth too hurried to Mary's court 'to wish the Queen joy'. Among the clergy, numerous recantations were motivated by fear. But others underwent seemingly genuine changes of heart. Distressing news reached Strassburg of countless 'fallings away' in Oxford. They included Thomas Harding, a chaplain of the Duke of Suffolk. Jane wrote harshly to Harding from her cell in the Tower, lamenting the case of a man who 'seemed sometime to be the lively member of Christ, but now the deformed imp of the devil'. In Norwich, John Barret, the city's leading evangelical preacher, rapidly and publicly conformed, and readily collaborated with the authorities. His actions undermined the morale of fellow-gospellers in a leading centre of Edwardian reform.[18]

Such reversals took place under conditions of immense psychological and political pressure. Distinctions between 'free' and 'forced' conversion are not as clear cut as we might like them to be. The portly preacher Henry Pendleton swore to his fellow-evangelical Lawrence Saunders that 'I will see the uttermost drop of this grease of mine molten away, and the last gobbet of this pampered flesh consumed to ashes, before I will forsake God and his truth'. But as soon as the pair arrived in London, Pendleton changed his tune, becoming (in John Foxe's words) 'of a faithful pastor, a false runagate, and of a true preacher, a sworn enemy of God's everlasting Testament'.

The Marian regime had many fair-weather friends. But for Pendleton and others, the direction of travel was permanently changed. Nicholas Shaxton, the former reforming bishop of Salisbury, had had his own identity crisis at the end of Henry VIII's reign. He now undertook to persuade others, employing the characteristic language of evangelical conversion against itself. 'Good brethren,

remember yourselves,' he urged the Cambridgeshire heretics Robert Pygot and
William Wolsey, 'and become new men, for I myself was in this fond opinion
that you are now in, but I am now become a new man.'[19]

The old was now the new, and the enemies of popery despaired. Mary,
reluctantly bowing to the advice of the new imperial ambassador, Simon
Renard, allowed Edward VI's funeral to take place at Westminster Abbey on 8
August using the 1552 Prayer Book. Cranmer, in his last public act as archbishop, performed the burial rites for the boy he had baptized and crowned.
The Queen, however, was at the Tower, where she ordered Gardiner to celebrate a requiem for her brother's soul. It was, contemporaries agreed, an unexpected move, which delighted traditionalists and dismayed evangelicals.[20]

Their resentment soon spilled over. There was trouble on 11 August, after a
priest said mass at the city church of St Bartholomew. It was repeated two days
later when Bonner's chaplain, Gilbert Bourne, preached at Paul's Cross on the
Edwardian sufferings of his master. Evangelicals in the crowd, angry at the
celebration of mass, shouted 'Papist!' 'You lie, for the things which he praised
and you preach were mere idolatry!' A near-riot ensued, and someone threw a
dagger which struck the pulpit. Bourne was helped to safety by John Bradford,
who urged calm and restraint. But Bradford was perhaps there in order to
orchestrate a demonstration which got out of hand, for the godly preachers
were stirring their people to acts of spiritual resistance. The Sunday before, in
a last evangelical occupancy of Paul's Cross, John Rogers preached a 'vehement'
sermon, exhorting the people 'to beware of all pestilent popery, idolatry, and
superstition'.[21]

There was a guard of 200 halberdiers when Gardiner's chaplain, Thomas
Watson, preached the following Sunday. On the day of the riot, the Council
ordered the mayor and aldermen to prevent unlicensed preaching, and to
convene a meeting of the Common Council to publicize what the Queen had
said the day before at the Tower:

> [A]lbeit her Grace's conscience is stayed in matters of religion, yet she
> meaneth graciously not to compel or constrain other men's consciences
> otherwise than God shall (as she trusteth) put in their hearts a persuasion
> of the truth that she is in, through the opening of His Word unto them by
> godly, virtuous and learned preachers . . .

This was a remarkable – and unprecedented – rejection of compulsion in religion, though its recognition of the rights of conscience was a distinctly tactical
one. Mary was aware of the strength of evangelical sentiment in the capital, and
reluctant to provoke it. There was also the consideration that, prior to parliamentary repeal of the Edwardian legislation, the Prayer Book, not the Sarum
Rite, was the legally constituted liturgy of the Church.

Mary's charm offensive was maintained in a proclamation of 18 August. It seemed pure Henry. Subjects should live together in quiet and charity, 'leaving those new-found devilish names of papist or heretic'. No books or ballads were to be printed, or plays performed, without royal licence. Yet the Queen – and this was scarcely the voice of Henry – had no mind to compel her subjects to religious conformity 'before such time as further order by common assent may be taken', even though she 'cannot now hide that religion which God and the world knoweth she hath ever professed from her infancy'.[22]

It was England's first declaration of formal religious toleration, albeit an explicitly temporary one. The proclamation implicitly declared that, whatever the law might say, the Queen was going to hear mass, and good subjects could safely do likewise. Robert Parkyn interpreted it as a proclamation 'declaring how the gracious Queen Mary did licence priests to say mass in Latin'. Even before this, Catholic lords and gentlemen were causing mass to be said in various parts of the realm, and by the beginning of September 'there was very few parish churches in Yorkshire but mass was said or sung'. On 3 September, at Much Wenlock, the vicar wrote proudly in the parish register that 'I, Thomas Butler . . . celebrated divine service and indeed mass in Latin language, in the old fashion according to the use of Sarum'. In London, around half a dozen city parishes began celebrating mass in late August, 'not by commandment, but of the people's devotion'.[23]

For a few remarkable months, the government rode the wave of a popular counter-revolution, encouraging its own subjects to break the law, and disciplining the officials who upheld it. When several priests were indicted under the Uniformity Act at the summer assizes in Kent for saying mass, James Hales, Justice of the Common Pleas, directed the grand jury that Edwardian statutes remained in force. On 6 October, Gardiner, now Lord Chancellor, refused to swear him in as a judge: 'although you had the rigour of the law on your side, yet ye might have had regard to the Queen's Highness's present doings'.[24]

Evangelicals stood precariously on the letter of the law. At Poole in Dorset, Thomas Hancock read the Queen's proclamation to his parishioners, and explained it meant merely they should 'let her alone with her religion'. Unsurprisingly, 'this satisfied not the papists', who set up an altar, and hired a French priest to say mass. Hancock's partisans pulled it down, and the Catholic faction rebuilt it in John White's house. The community was in open schism. If papists continued to attend Hancock's sermons, it was 'not for any love that they had for the Word, but to take the preacher in a trip' – that is, in hope of hearing treasonous words. For their part, Hancock's supporters warned White's man, serving at mass, that if he put his hand out of the window to ring the bell, 'a handgun should make him to smart'.

At Crowland in the Lincolnshire Fens, threats of violence came from the other side. The proclamation motivated the bailiff to urge parishioners 'to show themselves the Queen's friends' and restore the old liturgy. He ordered a reluctant curate, 'buckle yourself to mass, you knave, or by God's Blood I shall sheath my dagger in your shoulder!'[25]

The priest buckled. And so, willingly or unwillingly, did thousands of others. On 8 September, Feast of the Nativity of the Virgin, Princess Elizabeth attended mass, despite complaining of a stomach ache all the way to church. It followed a private meeting between the sisters, at which Mary made plain what was required of her sister. Elizabeth, with no powerful foreign protector, was more accommodating than, in not dissimilar circumstances, Mary herself had been. She knelt weeping before the Queen, excusing her reluctance on grounds of having 'never been taught the ancient religion'.[26] There was mass on 1 October for the Queen's coronation at Westminster Abbey, and again on 5 October for the opening of Parliament. Edwardian clergymen protested noisily but ineffectually in Convocation as Parliament swept away in a composite act all the religious legislation of Edward VI. Clerical marriage was overturned, and from 20 December the sole permissible order of divine service was that used in the last year of Henry VIII.[27]

There were pockets of resistance. The Henrician culture wars still raged at Adisham in Kent, where the iconoclast, firebrand vicar, John Bland, continued using the Prayer Book into December. His action provoked anger from conservative parishioners – 'thou art a heretic, and hast taught us nothing but heresy!' When, after Christmas, his enemies brought in another priest, Bland stood up at the chancel door to deliver an impromptu lecture on eucharistic theology, denouncing the mass as a patchwork of human inventions. He was forcibly silenced, and taken to the justices in Canterbury under escort of eighteen armed men.[28]

Another determined hold-out was Rowland Taylor, renowned preacher and rector of Hadleigh in Suffolk. Into 1554 Taylor continued to preach and use the Prayer Book as if nothing had changed. In the week before Easter, conservative parishioners finally put an altar back in the church, and brought in the rector of neighbouring Aldham to say mass. The altar had to be rebuilt, and placed under guard, after Taylor's supporters destroyed it in the night. When the mass took place, Taylor thunderously interrupted: 'Who made thee so bold to enter into this church of Christ to profane and defile it with this abominable idolatry?' Taylor, and his equally vociferous wife, were removed under guard from the church.[29]

On 3 January 1554, Bonner summoned the churchwardens of thirty London parishes, demanding why some of them 'have not the mass and service in Latin'. As late as June 1555, he received word that four Essex parishes 'do use still the English service'. But by New Year 1554, the battle for the mass was over, the old service almost everywhere restored. William Herne, rector of St Petroc in Exeter, and an evangelical convert in a region where thousands had risen for 'the mass in Latin, as was before', swore at Mary's accession he would rather be torn apart by wild horses than ever say mass again. But when the friend to whom he made the pledge encountered him in church, fully vested and ready to chant the liturgy, he could only mutter, 'It is no remedy, man; it is no remedy.'[30]

Herne's weary words might be taken as the motto of a conformist nation, over twenty and more years of unexpected change. But compliance need not mean ignorance or indifference. The abolition, revival and restoration of the Latin mass between 1547 and 1553 can be seen as a kind of protracted theological symposium, involving the participation of the entire country, and it was one in which – for a time at least – people actually had a vote. Some parishioners emerged from it strengthened and resolved in the faith of their fathers. On Christmas Eve 1553, John Come, of Linkinhorne in south-east Cornwall, came home from church in an emotional mood: he had 'seen that day that thing he saw not in four years before. For I have, thanked be God, heard mass and received holy bread and holy water.'

But Come's guests, Sampson Jackson and John Cowlyn from the neighbouring village of Stoke Climsland, saw things very differently; they wished a vengeance on the Queen and her proceedings. Cowlyn predicted that, before New Year's Day, 'outlandish men will come down upon our heads'; Plymouth was bristling with foreigners already. Jackson expected that within a year 'you shall see all houses of religion up again, with the Pope's laws'. Cowlyn believed 'we ought not to have a woman bear the sword', and Jackson added that if there was no other remedy, then 'my Lady Elizabeth ought to bear it'.[31] Their words were a compendium of the fears afflicting evangelicals – and not just evangelicals – as the dust from the succession crisis settled.

### The Clucking Hen

On 12 November 1553, James Brooks, Master of Balliol College, Oxford, and chaplain to Stephen Gardiner, took his turn in the pulpit at Paul's Cross. His sermon was a powerful lament for the sins of the schism, a time of

> change in doctrine, change in books, change in tongues, change in altars, change in placing, change in gesture, change in apparel, change in bread, change in giving, change in receiving, with many changes more, so that we had still change upon change, and like never to have left changing, till all the whole world had clean been changed.

The remedy for unending change was a return to the sure and trustworthy: the true Catholic Church, the mystical body of Christ, 'the clucking hen, under whose wings, as her chicks, the faithful are always safe'. It was a long-awaited homecoming, for the original cause of grief was 'the most unjust and ungodly divorcement' of Henry and Catherine of Aragon. Brooks's sermon was rapidly printed. But there was a curious omission: the words 'pope', 'holy father', 'bishop of Rome' appear nowhere in its pages.[32]

By Christmas 1553 Mary's government had restored the religious settlement of Henry VIII, to widespread if far from universal satisfaction. Beyond this, the waters of opinion were choppy and uncharted. Reunion with the wider Catholic Church – unless that were to mean no more than lip service to Henry VIII's fantasy federation of autonomous monarchical churches – implied some form of papal primacy. For two decades, English people had been bombarded with sermons on the iniquities of the 'bishop of Rome'; it was difficult to know how far the prescribed antipathies had penetrated, even into the minds of those instinctively drawn to the old ways.

Knotty legal and financial issues remained too: significantly, the one important Edwardian statute not repealed in 1553 was the Chantries Act. Roman canon law banned the alienation of church property; purchasers of monastic estates had reason to feel nervous. There was a further complication. Leading figures of Mary's regime, including all the restored bishops, were deeply implicated in the Henrician Schism. Gardiner was one of its leading intellectual architects. Evangelicals were keen not to let anyone forget this, rushing out an English translation of Gardiner's 1535 *De Vera Obedientia*, with a contemporary endorsement by Bonner.[33]

Rome itself watched with wonder and excitement. For three bruising decades, allegiances to the Pope had leaked away across Europe – a drainage of good news filtered only by reports of new souls won for Christ and Catholicism on the far side of the world. The victory of Mary – Queen of Heaven as well as Queen of England – seemed truly miraculous.

Reginald Pole was the man of the hour. On 5 August 1553, as soon as the outcome in England was confirmed, Julius III appointed him legate to England, with powers to reconcile penitent heretics. Aware of stumbling blocks ahead, Julius delegated to him authority to absolve for possession of ecclesiastical property – but only if people first offered to return it. Pole wrote to Mary on 13 August, hailing her as an instrument of God's mysterious providence. Just as in the *Magnificat* – the great hymn of praise recited by the Virgin in Luke's Gospel – the mighty had been cast down, the powerless exalted. Pole was ready to return and assist in whatever ways he could, but his tone was one of paternal admonition. Root of 'all the evil' was her father's departure from obedience to the Apostolic See. No good could be expected till this obedience was restored.[34]

After initial euphoria, a mood of caution returned. The view in Rome by late August was that Mary needed time – to reform her government and address the church lands question. Sending Pole too early might jeopardize his moral authority. Mary too was uncertain, and sought the advice of the imperial ambassadors. Their counsel was for delay. The property question was highly sensitive, and winning support for restored papal authority would be harder than for the mass.[35]

Gardiner's speech at the opening of Parliament in October nonetheless spoke of 'reunion', and attempts were made to secure repeal of all religious legislation going back to 1532 – restoration of papal supremacy by default. A bill declaring the validity of the marriage of Catherine of Aragon was duly passed. But, with uncertainty reigning over the status of church lands, the government encountered unexpectedly strong opposition in the Commons to any wider annulment of the Henrician statutes. The scheme was dropped. Pole, with all his legatine powers, stayed for the moment in Italy, and the English Church remained in a kind of limbo, allied to Rome, but formally independent of it.[36]

There was a still more pressing matter of policy. Catholic supporters ecstatically compared Mary to the Virgin Queen of Heaven, but no one expected her to remain permanently in a virginal state. There was an assumption the Queen must marry, both to secure an heir, and to receive the 'natural' guidance a woman expected from a husband. Gendered rules of patriarchy strained against the hierarchical rules of monarchy. Henry VIII's 1532 propaganda tract, *The Glass of the Truth* – with Mary firmly in mind – warned of the problems. A female ruler 'cannot continue long without a husband, which by God's law must then be her governor and head, and so finally shall direct this realm'. It was difficult to think of candidates 'whom the whole realm would and could be contented to have.'[37] These were prophetic, if decidedly unhelpful, words.

Mary's instinctive preference was for renewed dynastic union with the Habsburgs – the maternal stock from which she sprang. Her long-time protector Charles V was briefly considered, but the Emperor ruled himself out, and advanced instead the claims of his Spanish-born son, Philip, a widower since his wife Maria Manuela of Portugal died in 1545 giving birth to their son, Don Carlos. Some thought Reginald Pole himself a suitable candidate: he was a cardinal, but only in deacon's orders (from which the Pope could dispense), and of royal blood on his mother's side. But Pole was not interested in marriage.

There was, in fact, only one serious home-grown alternative: Edward Courtenay, Earl of Devon, newly released from imprisonment in the Tower, where he had resided since Henry VIII moved against his family in 1538. Gardiner got to know him there, and favoured his candidacy. The Spanish ambassador reported that 'the English' supported him. Did that include Cardinal Pole? Courtenay was Pole's kinsman, and the cardinal had praised the intellectual and spiritual pursuits undertaken by Courtenay in prison.

These included translating an Italian text, the *Beneficio di Christo* (Benefit of Christ Crucified), an influential and controversial work of devotion. It was a favourite of the *Spirituali*, the introspective, reform-minded Italian Catholics orbiting around Pole since the 1530s. The *Beneficio* was radically 'Augustinian' on salvation, stressing humanity's total dependence on God's grace, and in fact contained unacknowledged quotations from Calvin and other evangelical reformers. It was a pavilion for the renewal of inner spiritual life, pitched on the shared doctrinal ground which was rapidly eroding across Europe in the 1550s. And it was a prosecutor's exhibit for those, like Archbishop Carafa of Naples, who mistrusted the orthodoxy of the cool, aristocratic English cardinal.[38]

Courtenay's candidature never really got off the ground. Though some of Mary's retainers advanced his case, William Paget, the ablest politician on the Council, favoured the Spanish match from an early stage. Courtenay did not help his own cause: a prisoner from the age of twelve, he was suspected of sowing his wild oats in a belated hurry. And he was volatile and unpredictable, threatening to kill the returning exile Geoffrey Pole – Reginald's brother, and the man who, under duress, gave evidence against Courtenay's father.[39]

In any case, Mary had made up her mind. On the evening of Sunday 29 October, she sent for Ambassador Renard, and swore before the blessed sacrament to commit herself to Philip. Within days, the secret had leaked. On 16 November, Mary agreed to receive a join delegation of the Commons and the Lords, and was treated to a long disquisition, 'full of art and rhetoric and illustrated by historic examples', on the merits of marrying within the realm. Mary was irritated: 'Parliament was not accustomed to use such language to the Kings of England.'

Afterwards, Mary moaned to Renard about the duplicity of Gardiner, whom she suspected (probably rightly) of orchestrating the protest. On one day he would assure her of the people's compliance with regard to religion and urge her to press boldly on; the next he would be full of caution and woes about popular disobedience.[40] Gardiner was right that opposition to the Spanish marriage and opposition to Catholic restoration were different things. But as bishop and queen were shortly to discover, there was ominous potential for the two phenomena to combine and combust.

## Rebellion

The terms of the marriage were thrashed out in early December. Children of the match would inherit England and the Netherlands, but have no claim to Spain and its empire while Don Carlos's line continued. Philip, as joint sovereign, would receive the title of king, but retain no rights in England if Mary predeceased him. Moreover, he was not to exercise authority in his own right, grant English offices to foreigners, or take the Queen abroad without the consent of the nobles. The strikingly restrictive provisions were designed to alleviate anxieties in England. Philip considered them demeaning, and swore secretly that he did not consider himself bound by them.[41] Even without knowing that, some Englishmen decided the marriage must be stopped, and Mary removed forcibly from the throne.

The conspiracy was hatched in November, ten days after Mary rebuffed the parliamentary delegation. Four Members of Parliament, among them Sir Peter Carew and Nicholas Throckmorton, met secretly with other prominent figures, including the former clerk to the Council, William Thomas; the former lord deputy of Ireland, Sir James Croft; a former Gloucestershire MP and member of the Council in the Marches, Sir Nicholas Arnold; and the Kentish landowner and soldier Sir Thomas Wyatt. All were evangelicals.

They were soon joined by the Duke of Suffolk, who had escaped lightly – only a few days imprisonment in the Tower – for his part in the pseudo-reign of his daughter. Jane herself, with her husband Guildford, was convicted of treason on 19 November, but Mary seemingly had no intention of carrying out the sentence. In any case, Jane was not the fulcrum of the conspirators' plan. They would revert to the intention of Henry VIII, and make Elizabeth the successor to Mary – justifications for it could be found when the moment came. Elizabeth would then be married off to Courtenay, who was brought into the scheme at an early stage as a vacillating and unreliable participant. Also in the loop was the French ambassador. The Habsburg marriage was anathema to Paris, but Henry II was receiving conflicting advice, and the rebels had to formulate their plans without concrete offers of military assistance.

Elizabeth, too, was aware what was afoot, but the rumours of plots Paget and Reynard were hearing in December did not originate with her. As she left court to spend Christmas at her house at Ashridge in Hertfordshire, the princess was as discreet as ever. With scrupulous regard for appearances, she despatched a message to Mary, asking for vestments and other ornaments, so that mass could be celebrated there in appropriate style.[42]

There was no involvement of councillors, or prominent court figures. This would be a coup by outsiders. The plan was to raise co-ordinated revolts in the localities – Carew in Devon; Croft in Herefordshire; Suffolk in Leicestershire; Wyatt in Kent – and converge on the capital. The date was set for 18 March 1554, Palm Sunday.

This elaborate plan, with its multiple strands and layers of participation, failed to mesh. On 2 January Philip's emissaries arrived in London to finalize the marriage treaty. As they rode through the streets they endured a snowballing from unruly boys, while the adults, 'nothing rejoicing, held down their heads sorrowfully'. The same day, a Council summons convinced a nervous Carew that the government was onto him, and he brought forward his preparations for the rebellion in Devon, reports of which soon surfaced. Renard informed the Emperor on 18 January of suspicious activity in the French ports, and of heretics declaring house to house that 'the preachers spoke the truth when they announced that the kingdom would fall into foreign hands and the Gospel and Religion would be altered'.[43]

On 21 January, in an atmosphere of feverish rumour, Gardiner confronted his young protégé Courtenay and squeezed from him everything that he knew. The conspirators had all now left London, but Croft failed to raise Herefordshire, and Suffolk's rising in the Midlands fizzled out within a few days, even with enthusiastic backing from a caucus of evangelical activists in Coventry: 'My Lord's quarrel is God's quarrel,' declared the draper William Glover. Despite efforts to encourage rumours about the imminent arrival of hordes of rapacious Spaniards, Carew found minimal support in Devon, where his brutality in 1549 was a painful recent memory. The sheriff took action to secure Exeter against him, and on 25 January Carew boarded ship for exile in France.[44]

It was a different story in Kent. On the day Carew took flight, Wyatt raised his standard at Maidstone, while allies did the same at Rochester, Tonbridge and other places. Wyatt's propaganda kept strictly to its theme: the Spanish were coming, and would dominate the realm. The public stance was the usual one of rebels: 'We seek no harm to the Queen, but better counsel and councillors.' Only an inner core knew the plan was to depose Mary. There was also prudential silence about ideological motivation. Wyatt responded briskly to a recruit who told him 'he trusted to see the right religion restored again': 'You may not so much as mention religion, for that will withdraw from us the hearts of many.' Yet places where Wyatt's support was strong, such as Maidstone and Cranbrook, had reputations for evangelical activism.

Wyatt was more successful than the rebels of 1549 in persuading gentlemen to join his cause: some thirty are known to have done so, from around 170 landed families in the county. Fewer fought against him. Most stood aloof, suggesting the resonance of the anti-Spanish message. The sheriff, Sir Robert Southwell, had difficulty recruiting, and though he managed to rout a small rebel contingent, there was a failure to co-ordinate with other loyalist forces.

The most substantial of these was a hastily raised company of 500 London 'Whitecoats', under the command of the octogenarian Duke of Norfolk. On 28 January, Norfolk marched from London and prepared to dislodge Wyatt's followers from their position on Rochester Bridge. The battle was lost in advance, for the company officers had been suborned by French agents. At a pre-arranged signal, one of the vanguard captains made a stirring speech about 'the rule of the proud Spaniards', and the Whitecoats deserted to the rebels with cries of 'A Wyatt! A Wyatt!' Norfolk fled with a sorry remnant back to London.[45]

There was a world of difference between a rebellion in Kent and one in Yorkshire or Cornwall. Wyatt now had a force about 3,000-strong, and the capital lay, effectively undefended, only a day's march ahead of him. Anti-Spanish sentiment among the London citizens was strong. But Wyatt moved slowly, spending a whole day capturing the home of the loyalist Lord Cobham, and another responding imperiously to a government offer of negotiation.[46]

In July 1553, Mary gained the throne after fleeing from the capital; in January 1554, she kept it by ignoring advice and staying there. The Queen issued a clutch of proclamations, denouncing as bogus the rebels' professed concern for the commonwealth, and suggesting their real purpose was to kill her and place Jane on the throne. On 1 February she rode from Westminster to the Guildhall to address the citizenry. It was a bravura performance, channelling the spirit of her regal father. Mary cast herself as both mother and spouse of the nation, a woman who would consent to no marriage that would ever harm it. Wyatt stood ready to sack the city, and the marriage was 'but a Spanish cloak, to cover their pretended purpose against our religion'. The Queen finished on a rousing note: 'Good subjects, pluck up your hearts, and like true men stand fast against these rebels, both our enemies and yours, and fear them not. For I assure you, I fear them nothing at all!'[47]

Royal decisiveness trumped rebel dilatoriness. Wyatt did not arrive at Southwark until 3 February, and delayed there three days, sacking Gardiner's palace and library, while the city scrabbled to improvise its defences. With London Bridge guarded against them, the Kentishmen marched west, and on 6 February crossed the Thames at Kingston, heading back towards London along the north bank of the river. Government forces performed badly and fled; by dawn on 7 February, Ash Wednesday, Wyatt's troops were in the suburbs, past Charing Cross and approaching Ludgate, the western-most entry point in London's ancient city wall. Armed men stood back to let them pass, 'without any withstanding them'.

Prudence again dictated that Mary should flee. Instead, said a supporter, she 'placed her hope of eventual victory in God's goodness and greatness, as she had done in her most righteous bid for the throne at Framlingham'. The fate of the Queen and her religion hinged – literally – on whether a gate would remain open or shut. On his arrival, Wyatt found Ludgate closed against him, and, in the words of a contemporary chronicler, 'deceived of the aid which he hoped out of the City'. Most of his followers leaked away, and with fatalistic acceptance – 'it is no mastery now' – Wyatt allowed himself to be arrested.[48]

It was a bracing beginning to the penitential season of Lent. Mary came within a whisker of losing her recently acquired throne – not as a result of factional rivalry among her leading nobles, or of a powerful dynastic challenge, but in the blood-rush of a charismatically led popular rebellion, fuelled by a volatile blend of xenophobia and religion. What saved her was an unshakeable belief in her role as an instrument of divine providence: Mary was the Catholics' Holy Mother, no less than Edward was the Protestants' Josiah. She was saved too by an impromptu referendum among the citizenry of London, who decided on balance that loyalty to the person of the Queen outweighed their dismay at the prospect of her marriage.

There was an inevitable reckoning. In London 'one sees nothing but gibbets and hanged men', Renard wrote on 17 February. Wyatt was executed, as was the Duke of Suffolk, and about a hundred others, at various places in London and Kent. The bulk of the Kentish participants were pardoned by the Queen in choreographed shows of royal mercy, after being paraded before her with symbolic halters around their necks. There was mercy of a sort for Courtenay, who behaved loyally but unhelpfully during the attack on London, arguing over precedence of command with the Earl of Pembroke. A man, as Robert Wingfield put it, 'born . . . to spend his life in prison', he was incarcerated once again.[49]

There was merciful justice – perhaps more than she deserved – for the woman the conspirators intended to be Courtenay's consort. Letters seized from the French ambassador's courier implicated Elizabeth: Croft had told Noailles he was 'very familiar' with the princess. It was the view of Renard and Gardiner that, for the safety of the realm, Elizabeth must die. But despite some close questioning in the Tower, no really solid evidence could be found, and Wyatt performed Elizabeth a last service by swearing at his execution on 11 April that neither she nor Courtenay was privy to his plans. In May, Elizabeth was sent from the Tower to house arrest at Woodstock, Oxfordshire. Here, she let the mask slip a little, demanding an English bible and the right to recite the Litany in English, 'set forth in the King, my father's days'. But when ordered to desist, and fully conform to her sister's faith, she outwardly did so.[50]

Mary was lenient, even imprudently so, yet a full treason trial – which lacked unanimous support from the Privy Council – carried risks. In April, to the dismay and fury of the government, Nicholas Throckmorton was spectacularly acquitted of treason. It was an almost unprecedented occurrence, but Throckmorton conducted a brilliant defence, challenging the selection of jurors, and arguing it was no treason under existing law 'to talk against the coming hither of the Spaniards'. Angered by demonstrations of rejoicing at the acquittal, Mary took to her bed, and the jury was fined and imprisoned. On the day of the verdict, Wyatt's head was stolen from its place of public display – an indication that the traitor was considered, by some, to be a martyr.[51]

There was justice, but no mercy, for Jane and Guildford Dudley. The verdict against them, suspended since November, was carried out promptly on 12 February. It was from genuine solicitude for Jane's soul, rather than eagerness for a propaganda coup, that Mary despatched the gentle John Feckenham, now dean of St Paul's, to secure a last-minute recantation and conversion. But like other intrepid women of the age – Anne Askew, Joan Bocher, Mary herself – Jane's faith was one which was energized by questioning and contradiction. At the block, she asked onlookers to bear witness, 'I die a true Christian woman, and look to be saved by none other means, but only by the mercy of God in the merits of the blood of His only son, Jesus Christ.'[52] Sixteen years of age, a hapless pawn in the power plays of father and father-in-law, but a sincere, ardent believer, Jane was surely more martyr than traitor.

The rebellion had an absurd, parodic sequel. On Sunday 4 March, a battle took place in Finsbury Fields, an open space just to the north of the city. The 300 combatants were boys from city schools. They divided themselves into 'the army of the King and M. Wyatt' and that of 'the Prince of Spain and the Queen'. The fighting ended, counter-factually, with the victory of Wyatt, and a mock hanging of the Prince of Spain that nearly ended in real tragedy. These schoolboy hi-jinks, reported by both the French and Spanish ambassadors, were taken rather seriously. Mary ordered the younger lads whipped, and many of the older ones to be imprisoned in the Guildhall. It was an embarrassment to have her future husband mocked, and 'the King' – even in play – was a disquieting figure at a time when wild rumours circulated that Edward still lived. The incident undoubtedly reflects opposition to the marriage, though we cannot assume that in re-enacting the martial excitements of a few weeks earlier the boys were simply channelling the political and religious allegiances of their parents.[53]

The battle of Finsbury Fields was nonetheless a revealing episode. Like the smaller-scale boisterousness five years earlier at Bodmin, it points to an imaginative world of childhood where the natural adversaries were not aliens – Frenchmen or Scots – but neighbours of another dispensation. A generation had grown up in a world of schism. Thirteen-year-old warriors at Finsbury had been born nearly a decade after Henry VIII cast aside the authority of the Pope. They had only hazy memories of hearing Latin in church, or seeing a statue or an altar. Even older teenagers – and perhaps half the population of sixteenth-century England was under twenty – had spent their formative adolescent years in the ferment of Edwardian reform. In 1553–4, the preferred imagery of the Catholic preachers was that of the nation as a child returning to its natural parent. But for much of the population, this parent was an unfamiliar face, returning from abroad after a long absence, and someone who would have to work hard to win back affection and respect.

## Verbum Dei

On the day of the battle of Finsbury Fields, Mary sent articles to her bishops. They were a brisk memorandum of urgent tasks at hand. Processions were to be restored, along with all 'laudable and honest ceremonies which were wont to be used'. Holy days and fasts 'kept in the latter time of King Henry VIII' were reinstated. The most draconian instruction was that bishops should immediately deprive all priests who 'have married and used women as their wives', though penitent ones might after a time be admitted to another benefice. Once again, there was no mention of pope or Rome. The emphasis was on Henrician usage, and canon law from Henry's reign was to be reactivated, though there was a quiet distancing from royal headship in the stipulation that no one henceforth was to take oaths of supremacy or succession.[54]

Careful readers – and the bishops by and large were – would have noted that the Queen wrote of the 'time of King Henry VIII' without further qualification. It was conventional to refer to royal predecessors as being of 'famous', 'worthy' or 'blessed' memory. This was how Mary referred to her father in a letter to Pole of November 1553. She received in return a blistering rebuke. There was nothing blessed about the instigator of schism, the murderer of More and Fisher. Did not Christ teach that to be his disciple it was necessary to hate father and mother? If Mary could not bring herself to speak ill of her father, she should at least desist from praising him.[55]

Perhaps, for the adult Mary, it was psychologically healthy to hear this about the father who blighted the happiness of her young life. It was certainly a radical stance for a monarchical regime to espouse, sweeping aside the convenient fiction that the sins of kings were always the fault of wicked advisors. Exile and resistance, Pole's bitter inheritance, were the begetters of a new theology of politics, in which monarchs were liable to be judged, not so much by their symbolic resemblances to God, but by their fidelity in carrying out his will.

Momentum for a reconciliation with Rome was building. Pole wrote to Gardiner, sending him a copy of his book *De Summo Pontifice* (Of the Supreme Pontiff), begun during the conclave that elected Julius III, in hope that its insights would help Gardiner convey an understanding of the benefits of the papal office to the people of Winchester, and to the realm as a whole. On 12 March, Gardiner wrote back, acknowledging his own fault in agreeing to separation from the Universal Church. Pole's reply of 22 March was as barbed as it was seemingly gracious. People usually proceeded from schism into heresy, and it was a special favour of God that Gardiner had not. Though he fell into 'grave error', and was not among the 'valiant champions' who from the first defended the unity of the Church, yet God had preserved him, and through persecution and imprisonment brought him at last back to the truth.[56]

Pole was frustrated at the glacial pace of England's homeward journey, but in piling pressure on the bishop of Winchester, he was pushing at an open door. Gardiner, the arch-Henrician, had become a born-again papalist. The new vice-chancellor of Cambridge, John Young, would later remember hearing him 'sometimes in the pulpit openly, and sometime in talk at dinner among the lords of the Council', look back on Henry's reign and 'very earnestly accuse himself'. Thomas Harding testified that, in intimate talk with his chaplains, Gardiner would 'so bitterly accuse himself . . . that at the last the tears would fall from his eyes abundantly'.[57]

Gardiner's agonies of remorse were not universally echoed. There were councillors – like Rich or Southwell – who glided smoothly from Henrician to Edwardian to Marian conformism. And there were good Catholics who simply still did not see Henry's break with Rome as a catastrophic national apostasy. While Gardiner and Pole exchanged letters in March 1554, Nicholas Ridley attended a supper given by the Lieutenant of the Tower, an occasion that turned into an impromptu eucharistic debate. John Feckenham made the comment that forty years ago 'all were of one opinion' concerning the mass. That was equally true, Ridley retorted, of the Pope's supremacy. But here the Queen's secretary, Sir John Bourne, leapt in to say the cases were not the same: this was 'but a positive law'. When Ridley persisted in arguing that papal supremacy and other traditional doctrines were inextricably bound together, Bourne brushed the objection aside. 'Tush, it was not counted an article of our faith.'[58]

That was once a common enough view of the matter – perhaps the view held by Thomas More and Pole himself as humanist scholars in the carefree days before the divorce. Their minds were changed by the theological and physical violence of the Henrician schism. For others, including Gardiner, it needed the devastation of traditional Catholicism in Edward's reign to awake the realization that Catholicism without the Pope was a contradiction in terms. It was perhaps easier for Gardiner to believe that he never had any real choice in the matter than that he had made a wrong call. A few months later, he would tell a heresy suspect reproaching him for breaking his oath to Henry VIII that it was 'Herod's [a tyrant's] oath, unlawful, and therefore worthy to be broken'. Gardiner, Renard reported, was champing at the bit to bring forward in Parliament legislation 'concerning religion' – re-establishing the Pope's authority, and restoring the heresy legislation.[59]

The new Parliament convened on 2 April, as executions of conspirators continued, and feelings against the Spanish marriage remained raw. Evangelicals were conquered but not cowed. Within a few days of the opening of Parliament, a cat was found hanging from the gallows by Cheapside Cross. It was dressed in doll-size vestments, its head shaved, and a disc of paper inserted between its bound front paws, representing the host. A couple of weeks earlier, huge crowds gathered to hear mysterious oracular messages emanating from a wall in Aldersgate Street, reputedly the voice of a bird or an angel. It responded to 'God save the Lady Elizabeth' and not to 'God save Queen Mary', and gave the reply 'Idolatry', when asked the question, 'What is the mass?'[60]

In the 1530s, cut off from regular channels of place and influence, papalist Catholics turned to the alternative validations of the supernatural and miraculous. Now, the reformers did likewise. In April 1554, an ancient prophecy was supposedly discovered, foretelling an imminent apocalyptic battle, and the banishing of the Pope from England in the short-lived 'time of M'. The Aldersgate angel was exposed as a fraud: a young girl, Elizabeth Crofts, who received her instructions, along with a bird-whistle, from a cluster of evangelical plotters.[61]

In the meantime, in the tangible world of power and position, the old faith tightened its grip. In March, a slew of evangelical bishops were deprived, and on 1 April, six new Catholic ones consecrated: John White of Lincoln; Gilbert Bourne, Bath and Wells; James Brooks, Gloucester; Henry Morgan, St David's; Maurice Griffith, Rochester; George Cotes, Chester. Before the end of the year, in addition to restored bishops like Tunstall and Heath, another four were appointed: John Hopton, Norwich; Ralph Baines, Coventry; John Holyman, Bristol; Robert Warton, Hereford. Further episcopal promotions soon followed. It was, reckoned John Foxe, 'more than were made at one time since the Conquest'.[62]

Three of the old bishops – Cranmer, Latimer and Ridley – were returned to Oxford in March, and on 14 April were wheeled out for a week of public debate. It was both a rematch of the Edwardian eucharistic disputations, and an act of revenge for them, weighted as heavily against the evangelical disputants as the earlier proceedings were in their favour. The reformers held their ground, though Catholic victory was duly declared by Hugh Weston, Prolocutor of the Lower House of Convocation – a choleric clergyman who celebrated mass during Wyatt's rebellion with armour beneath his vestments. It was not, formally, a heresy trial, though to all involved it felt like a dry run.[63]

There was one thing the new bishops had in common with the evangelicals they displaced. They were, almost to a man, resident pastoral bishops, rather than absentee administrators. An immediate task, carried out with determined efficiency, was the deprivation of the married clergy. By Easter 1554, a third of London benefices were empty, either by the deprivation or resignation of the incumbent, and Essex had similar levels of enforced vacancy. About a quarter of parish clergy in Norfolk and Suffolk were deprived, though elsewhere the impact was less: around one in ten priests in Coventry, Exeter, Lincoln, Winchester and York dioceses, and barely one in twenty in the county of Lancashire.[64]

Priests married in Edward's reign for various reasons, not all of them theological. But those who did so were undoubtedly less committed to the old ways than priests remaining, whether formally or actually, celibate. Fuzzy as it is, the pattern of deprivations for marriage is as clear a snapshot of the comparative regional advances of Protestantism as we are likely to get.

A good number of penitent priests, having shed their wives, were in due course 'recycled' into new parishes, as the regulations permitted. But a hard core of evangelical sympathizers was permanently removed. Their replacements were virtually all conservatives; some were vehement ones. Wherever a zealous Catholic succeeded a fervent evangelical with a loyal parochial following, local battle lines were more than ever sharply drawn.[65]

Politics at the centre was equally fractious, though divisions did not run straightforwardly between orthodox and heretics. The Parliament of April 1554 was factionalized and ineffectual; Gardiner's initiatives were blunted by the influence of Paget, who considered them unwise at such an unsettled moment. On 1 May, the Lords voted down a heresy bill, not from sympathy with potential victims, but because councillors like Rich and Paget were convinced its real purpose was to authorize seizure of former ecclesiastical property. Plans to introduce a bill to disinherit Elizabeth had to be abandoned, and though the marriage treaty was confirmed, an attempt to extend to Philip the full protection of 'words-alone' treason law was embarrassingly defeated. The sole religious measure enacted was a rather petty one, withdrawing the pensions from married ex-religious.[66] In the early summer of 1554, the Queen remained supreme head of the Church; Pole remained in legatine limbo (Brussels); and the leading Edwardian evangelicals remained in prison, with no real legal basis for proceeding further against them.

Not everything was in suspension. After months of delay, Philip, Prince of Spain, set sail for England on 13 July, and landed at Southampton six days later, in preparation for marriage to Mary in Winchester Cathedral. London responded, upon orders of the mayor, with bonfires and bell-ringing in every parish for 'the joyful tidings of the prince's landing'. Robert Parkyn reckoned the news of the nuptials brought 'great joy and comfort to all good people in the realm', though the only event of that week Thomas Butler saw fit to record in the Much Wenlock register was that Bishop Heath stopped for an hour in the borough on his way to Bridgnorth, and was refreshed by the burgesses with wine, cakes and fruit.[67]

The entertainments were more lavish at the wedding banquet in Winchester on 25 July, where, to preserve distinctions of status, Philip was served on silver plates, and Mary on gold ones. In the proclamation of titles at the wedding, however, and in all official documents thereafter, the couple were 'Philip and Mary, by grace of God King and Queen of England, France, Naples, Jerusalem and Ireland'. It sounded, whatever the treaties said, as if precedence belonged to the husband.

It was a marriage doubtless approved of in heaven, though perhaps not made there. Mary was much taken with Philip; yet he, at twenty-seven, was more than ten years her junior, and probably shared the unkind opinion among his courtiers that the Queen, who dressed in the French fashion, was rather dowdy. The couple did not quite have a language in common: he spoke to her in Spanish; she replied in French.[68]

Nonetheless, the King's inherent Englishness was a theme of the triumphal royal entry into London on 18 August, where the 'most excellent' of several street pageants declared Philip's descent from Edward III. All the London chroniclers mention the great Cheapside Cross being newly gilded for the occasion: a special tax was levied to meet the expense. This elaborate structure, thirty-six feet high, with niches for saints, and a dove (representing the holy spirit) atop its crowning cross, was a long-standing object of civic pride. But its imagery – offensive to evangelicals even outside the walled enclosure of a church – made it a pronounced public symbol of the triumph of Catholicism. Passing through Cheapside, the royal procession paused to view the edifice, and Philip, 'perceiving the crucifix in the top thereof, very humbly put off his cap'.[69]

As the procession passed from London Bridge through Gracechurch Street, a different note was sounded. On the turrets of the water conduit were paintings of the 'nine worthies', a traditional collection of chivalric heroes, and with them, Mary, Henry VIII and Edward VI. Henry was depicted with a book in his hand, 'Verbum Dei'. It was an image of the late king familiar from the frontispiece of the Great Bible, and indeed the designer of the pageant was the producer of that bible, the evangelical printer Richard Grafton. With the possible connivance of the city authorities, a point was being made. Gardiner swiftly summoned Grafton for a dressing-down, and ordered him, before the pageants were removed, to paint out the bible and insert a pair of gloves.

Gardiner's scepticism about letting bibles loose among the people was long-standing and well known. But this was not an attempt to obliterate the past, to pretend Henry's misguided initiative never happened. Rather, it repudiated his claim to reforming virtue. Gardiner supposedly told Grafton he would have done better to place the book in Mary's hand, for it was she, not Henry, who 'reformed the Church and religion . . . according to the pure and sincere Word of God'. 'Verbum Dei' appeared again, without objection, in the final pageant, in Fleet Street by St Paul's Cathedral. Here, figures of the King and Queen were flanked by 'Justicia' and 'Veritas' – and 'Truth' carried the Word of God.[70]

The entry was a success, and Philip was not the ogre some of his new subjects had feared. On his arrival in Southampton he had told accompanying Spanish lords they must begin to live like Englishmen, and to make the point 'ordered some beer to be brought to him, and drank of it'. But, both before and after the entry, tensions between instinctively xenophobic Londoners and Philip's large entourage of Spaniards boiled over into violent altercations. Wild rumours circulated – including one that a Spanish friar was about to be appointed archbishop of Canterbury.[71]

On 19 September, the Duke of Savoy's envoy, Giovanni di Stroppiana, wrote optimistically that animus against the Spaniards 'is dying down gradually'; Renard, meanwhile, was still complaining of 'violent hatred'. But both ambassadors had good news to report: the Queen's doctors believed her to be with child. Renard was not sure it was true, but immediately leaked the news to demoralize the opposition. Stroppiana, a less cynical diplomat, hailed this latest sign of divine favour on a lady 'saved and preserved through many great dangers and raised to the throne almost by a miracle'. Miraculous too was the great work to which Mary had set her hand, 'restoration of the Catholic faith and religion'. Its daily increasing success was something Stroppiana would not have believed without seeing it with his own eyes, and this child, surely, would guarantee it.[72]

### Zeal for God's Service

Restoration of the Catholic faith took a firm step forward at the beginning of September 1554, when Bonner announced a visitation of his diocese, issuing an ambitious set of articles on which clergy and laity were to be examined. The Council was cautious and divided, and Pole still awaited permission to enter the country as the Pope's representative. 'A year has passed,' he wrote in frustration to Philip on 24 September, 'since I began to knock at the door of this royal house, and none has opened unto me.' So Bonner simply decided to move on his own, without consulting King, Queen or Council. When challenged, he was unapologetic: he acted 'out of his zeal for God's service, because in religious matters it was meet to proceed firmly and without fear'. The abdication of royal supremacy created opportunities for the revival of episcopal initiative; the visitation was 'a matter pertaining to his own post'.[73]

Bonner, the one-time loyal servant of Thomas Cromwell, fierce critic of popes and (in Foxe's assessment) 'favourer of Luther's doctrine', had become the principal architect of a new Catholicism. He wanted everyone to know that 'whatsoever opinion, good or bad, hath been conceived of him', his only intention was to do that charitable duty 'which any bishop should show to his flock'. The articles became a model for other Marian bishops, and a touchstone of what the authorities aimed to achieve.[74] Two themes predominated: restoration of liturgical life in the parishes, and the eradication of unorthodoxy. In reality, the objectives were inseparable, for the presence of the latter was an obstacle to the former, and the former, so Bonner and other bishops believed, was a sure cure for the latter.

The iconoclasm of 1547–52 left parishes emptied of nearly everything needed for the daily, weekly and seasonal performance of Catholic religion. Bonner provided an extensive shopping list of items parishes needed to have, or get quickly. Foremost was a stone high altar, with all its coverings, consecrated and dedicated, and not 'any gravestone taken from the burial . . . and put up for an altar'. Other necessary appurtenances of the mass were a chalice, cruets for the wine and water, candlesticks, a bell for ringing at the elevation, a set of vestments for the priest and surplices for the clerk, a container for incense and censer for burning it, a paxbrede, a pyx for the reserved sacrament, a curtain for veiling the altar in Lent. In addition to the missal, parishes were to have seven other liturgical books, covering a full range of services. In every church there was to be a rood and rood loft, 'as in times past hath been accustomed'. All parishes were to ensure they had the necessary cross and banners for processions. A separate cross was required for funerals, along with a bier for the dead. And, for routine and ritual blessings, there must be a chrismatory for holy oils, a stoup for holy water in church, and a vessel for carrying it about.[75] All this was the bare minimum of sacramental religion. The articles did not require the re-installation of images – devotionally desirable, but liturgically inessential.

It was a challenging list, and some churchwardens protested that the demands were simply impossible. By and large, however, the parishes of Bonner's diocese drew breath and knuckled down. After the articles were brought to the Essex port town of Harwich in early October, the accounts reveal a minor blizzard of expenditure there: 30s. for a chasuble, 6s. 8d. for a mass book, 5s. to a stranger 'for making an altar', 22d. for candle and tapers, 8d. for a sanctus bell, 6d. for a pax. The parish bought a good supply of 'holland' (plain-woven linen) to make their own albs, cloths and coverings. They were also, luckily, able to borrow a chalice from neighbouring Dovercourt, home of the miraculous rood burned by iconoclasts in 1532.[76]

In countless other places, it was a similar story of mix and mend, sometimes involving the voluntary return of items salvaged from the iconoclastic storm. At Morebath in Devon, John Williams, of neighbouring Bury, handed over an image of Mary, and part of a tableau of St George; William Morsse of Loyton gave back the figure of St John from the old rood, and various others produced books and parts of the rood loft. Vicar Christopher Trychay enthused that they all 'did like good Catholic men', though in fact Williams wanted to be paid for his trouble. Quarrels about former parochial property were sometimes acrimonious and litigious.

Across England, however, the patterns of restoration before the end of 1554 were frequently impressive. Gilbert Bourne began his episcopate at Bath and Wells in April with a visitation that found 84 per cent of parishes already had an altar, a percentage almost exactly matched in George Cotes' parallel visitation of Chester. Even if some of these altars were – as Bonner feared – recycled gravestones, the compliance rate is strikingly high, and suggests that many were hidden rather than destroyed in Edward's reign. These were conservative regions, but not necessarily untypical ones. By the end of 1554, high altars were rebuilt, and vestments and books obtained, in all 168 parishes nationwide for which Marian churchwardens' accounts survive.[77]

Parochial restoration was expensive and time-consuming, a work of years, not months, during which roods painted on cloth might have to suffice while carved ones were commissioned and saved for. Much had been sold, confiscated or destroyed, and old patterns of parish fund-raising had been disrupted and sometimes abandoned. Resuming them might be a matter of fiscal necessity, but was probably welcomed in places like Sherborne in Dorset, where the annual church ale was stopped in 1551, but raised an impressive £18 when it was restored in 1554. The evidence of the accounts suggests that many, even most, parishes were doing more refurbishment than the minimum required.

'Restoration' is a more loaded word than might at first appear. There could be no question of merely going back. Roods, altars, images and vestments were no longer what they once perhaps had been: the cultural foliage in a landscape of meaning assumed to be natural and God-given. All such objects had been profoundly, irremediably politicized – by prolonged processes of discussion, defence, denigration and destruction. Replacing them was an assertive and also a divisive act: a statement of faith in an alternative future, not an invocation of some vanished past.

It was a future some people dearly hoped not to see. In summer 1554, shortly after the rood was set up in St Paul's, a man joined a large crowd in front of it, bowed low, and addressed the image in mocking and seditious words: 'Sir, your Mastership is welcome to town. I had thought to have talked with your Mastership, but that ye be here clothed in the Queen's colours. I hope ye be but a summer's bird, in that ye be dressed in white and green.'[78]

Bonner failed to see a funny side. Those who 'played the fool in the church' were part of an extensive range of religious miscreants, clerical and lay, his articles aimed to discipline. Gone now were vague exhortations to unity and charity, with instructions not to call neighbours 'heretic' or 'papist'. Bonner knew the kind of people he was looking for, and he wanted names.

Married priests were a particular concern. There was to be a record of all who had been married, and of any still consorting with their 'concubine'. Such marriages were not just a moral lapse, but a 'schismatical' act. Without episcopal reconciliation, no married priest could celebrate mass. And nor was mass to be said by any clergyman made 'schismatically, and contrary to the old order and custom of the Catholic Church'. Priests ordained under the Edwardian Ordinal were not really priests at all. The greatest fear was of married priests, or others 'naming themselves ministers', presiding over secret assemblies or conventicles, and teaching 'doctrine or usage not allowed by the laws and laudable customs of this realm'.

It was also a worry that laypeople might attend such gatherings, or in other ways withdraw from collective Catholic worship: by failing to confess, receive the sacrament at Easter, or bring children to be confirmed. An eye was to be kept out for any who at service time 'upon feigned occasions . . . doth use to go abroad out of their own parishes into the fields', and others who 'secretly keep themselves in their houses'.

Much of the concern, however, was not about discreet withdrawal from Catholic practices, but argumentative engagement with them. Who spoke against sacraments and prayer for the dead? Or dared 'mock, jest at, threaten or beat any priest for saying mass'? Expounded scripture on their own authority? Printers or booksellers who disseminated 'slanderous books, ballads or plays' were on the list, along with anyone who, after the start of the reign, produced or sold Prayer Book or Homilies, 'having in them heretical and damnable opinions'.

Bonner's articles give the impression not so much of large-scale withdrawal of evangelicals into schism as of a variety of disruptive semi-separatisms within the parameters of the parish – heretics declining to take part in processions, or contribute towards the weekly holy loaf. They might bring their children to be baptized, but 'not suffer the priest to dip the child three times'. Worst of all, they would come to mass, but refuse to receive the pax, or find ways to express disdain for the holiest of holies: 'whether there be any at the sacring time, which do hang down their heads, hide themselves behind pillars, turn away their faces, or do depart out of the church'.[79]

The visitation met with grumbling and resistance. Renard reported in October that heretics were offended by the articles' reference to 'inquisitors', and that 'strange words' were spoken about them at the Guildhall. Assisted by his able vicar-general Nicholas Harpsfield, Bonner proceeded vigorously, 'and had sermons in every parish and place where he sat'. Londoners proved willing enough to inform on their neighbours: charges were levelled against some 450 people. Not all were convinced evangelicals, but a majority likely had some reason beyond indolence for their transgression of the rules. The commonest accusation was of failure to attend church on Sundays and holy days, though people were denounced across the range of offences Bonner expected to find. Ninety were charged with withdrawing from processions, some saying 'it was idolatry' to go on them; seventy with speaking against ceremonies; ninety with denying the real presence; forty with misbehaviour at the consecration and elevation.

Almost all of this behaviour involved giving offence to neighbours. Londoners, and people of other communities too, were increasingly together but separate. William Morris rationalized his refusal to receive communion at Easter 1554: 'He thinketh . . . it is not lawful for him to receive the communion with him or them that be of another faith.'[80]

The great majority of those brought before the courts in 1554 submitted and conformed, some performing the traditional penances in church, clad in white sheets. There was more lenient treatment for a group from St Botolph's, who confessed that 'before the Queen's reign that now is, they were maintainers and favourers of such doctrine as then was put forth, but not since'. They were admonished to go off and behave themselves like good Catholics.[81] After their Edwardian spring of freedom and ascendancy, evangelicals once again had to confront the hard question of how to comport themselves in the face of ungodly commands.

### Exiles and Nicodemites

In early 1554, John Bradford penned a treatise in the Tower. It began by posing a question very much at the forefront of his co-religionists' minds: 'whether it be lawful for a man, which knoweth the truth, to be present at the celebration of mass or no?'

Bradford's answer was, emphatically, 'no'. Those who knew it to be wrong, but conformed out of weakness and cowardice, were simply figures of contempt: 'mass-gospellers and popish protestants'. His real argument was with people who believed it was permissible to be there in body, while worshipping God secretly and inwardly. The mass had no cracks through which such freedom of the spirit might escape. It was *mare malorum* (sea of evils) – an idolatrous, insidious miasma of corruption and defilement. To hear mass, or even be in a church while it was being said there, was a sin breaking 'all God's laws generally, and every commandment particularly'. There was short shrift for the idea that attendance could be redeemed by displays of disrespect at the elevation. That was like a servant willingly accompanying thieves to his master's house, and expecting to be excused because he didn't actually steal anything himself. Nor did Bradford neglect an objection that was only indirectly theological, but presumably often posed: 'offending our brethren in not coming to mass'. Here, sadly, there was little to be done; it was a case of offence taken, not given, for the evil of the thing meant it could never be offensive to avoid and attack it. To refuse the mass was to invite retribution, but Bradford's only practical advice was for people to take up their cross and prepare to follow Christ.[82]

In evangelical circles across Europe, views were hardening, as progress of the Gospel appeared to falter, and Antichrist regrouped. Calvin condemned the dissembling of French evangelicals passing themselves off as orthodox Catholics, and gave currency to a term for the phenomenon – Nicodemism. Nicodemus was the Pharisee (John 3:1–2) who visited Jesus secretly by night, the prototype for all who lacked courage of their true convictions.

Peter Martyr Vermigli lectured on the theme in Strassburg in 1554, his words rapidly translated and published by an English disciple, with an appended sermon from Heinrich Bullinger. These were 'most unhappy days', for, 'where popery ruleth, the godly which do dwell together with the ungodly . . . are compelled to be at their masses, and most vile and filthy idolatries'. Like Bradford, the authors considered, and systematically demolished, all the reasons why anyone could think attendance acceptable, including claims of 'kindred and alliance', along with the belief that 'God will not have the government of polities or households disturbed', or wish a man's destruction.[83]

It was not only men who had the duty to resist; anti-Nicodemite rhetoric could take startlingly sexualized turns. In July 1554, John Philpot, deprived archdeacon of Winchester, wrote from prison to his sister, warning her not 'to drink of the whore's cup'. A letter from a 'godly matron', addressed to 'sisters of hers abiding in England', was published by John Knox the same year. Christ was their 'spiritual husband', so going to mass was like a bride 'giving the use of her body to another man'. In such a case, the husband was unlikely to be placated with assurances that 'you know my heart is yours'.[84]

Many of these emphatic directives against compromise and defilement came from people who had already taken themselves out of harm's way, in more senses than one. The scale of departure into exile in 1554–5 was unprecedented. The 'Strangers' were first to leave, followed by a motley assortment of preachers, university students, merchants and printers, and a smattering of gentry and nobility – perhaps a thousand persons in all.

These departures were not, in the main, daring escapes from a tightening noose. In fact, the authorities were often more than happy to see troublemakers go. Gardiner boasted to Renard in September 1553 of his 'good device for getting the Lutherans out of the country'. He would summon preachers to appear at his house, and they, fearing incarceration in the Tower, would promptly flee abroad. More considered exits required time, money and planning, with agents sometimes sent to scout the land in advance. Catherine Willoughby, Duchess of Suffolk, set off for Germany in considerable estate at the start of 1555, after her new husband, Richard Bertie, secured them a safe conduct from Gardiner. The couple left accompanied by their steward and six other servants, including a brewer, a laundress and a fool.[85]

Yet the option for exile – abandoning hearth and home for the uncertain company of strangers – was never an easy or comfortable one. For ministers, it might induce guilt about abandoning their congregation, or nagging doubts about their own motives. John Old, Edwardian visitor and vicar of Cubbington in Warwickshire, experienced the 'malicious force and rage' of his parishioners, and fled abroad before November 1554. He then discovered that 'my own conscience accuses me, for that I tarried not there still to the uttermost'.[86]

The reminiscences of a London merchant's wife, Rose Hickman, shine light on the choices she and her husband Anthony made, after 'the idolatrous mass was set up'. At the start of the reign, the Hickmans worshipped behind closed doors with other 'well-disposed Christians' – one of a number of secret conventicles meeting at various locations in the city. But after the Queen's injunctions of 4 March 1554, they decided it was no longer safe. Anthony gave financial and practical support to preachers fleeing abroad, and when this came to light he was imprisoned in the Fleet, alongside the jurors who acquitted Nicholas Throckmorton. Through the intervention of William Paulet (which Rose reckoned cost her family £200 in chests of sugar and rolls of velvet), all these prisoners were released.

Anthony took himself to Antwerp, while Rose, expecting their child, spent her confinement at a remote location in Oxfordshire. From here she smuggled a message to the imprisoned bishops – Cranmer and Ridley – asking 'whether I might suffer my child to be baptized after the popish manner'. Their reply chided Rose for not being 'gone out of England before that time'. But they conceded that baptism was the sacrament 'least corrupted' by the papists, and she might therefore use it – fear of anabaptism probably influenced this pastoral advice.

Rose's child was duly christened by a priest, but the occasion contained an unusual episode of liturgical sabotage. Part of the ritual was the placing of a pinch of salt in the child's mouth. 'But because I would avoid the popish stuff as much as I could, I did not put salt into the handkerchief that was to be delivered to the priest at the baptism, but put sugar in it instead.' As a secret protest, this seems almost pointlessly petulant, an amusing anecdote for a wealthy sugar-importer's wife to share with her godly friends. But there was a deadly seriousness to the little act of granular resistance. Rose understood, just as the Catholic bishops did, that ritual conformities shaped the inner self. Integrity and identity were bolstered by conscious acts of nonconformity, however small-scale and domestic.

Shortly afterwards, Rose joined her husband in exile in Antwerp. It meant leaving behind two 'fair houses . . . well furnished with household stuff', one in London, and one at Romford in Essex. Yet all this she accounted 'nothing in comparison to liberty of conscience for the profession of Christ'.

Antwerp was a Catholic city, but the local habit of worshipping in the cathedral meant 'it could not be easily known who came to church, and who not'.[87] Some exiles gravitated to Catholic Italy. They included the shiftless Edward Courtenay, released from confinement in early 1555, and also Sir John Cheke, who arrived at Padua in July 1554 after receiving pardon for taking part in Northumberland's coup. There, Cheke began work on a Latin treatise, *De Ecclesia*. It challenged the papal vision of the Church, but also argued for an inner realm of the spirit, able to remain pure despite outward participation in impious rites.[88]

That was the very opposite of what Bradford, Philpot and the other preachers wanted Christians to believe. But it was the path chosen by important people in England. They included Cheke's friend William Cecil, who lost formal office on Mary's accession, but breathed no outward word of religious or political disaffection. He even lodged in his own house Philip's secretary, Gonzalo Pérez, after the royal entry to London. Away from London, on land Cecil owned in the little Lincolnshire village of Barholm, the evangelical printer John Day was operating a secret press. Between October 1553 and May 1554, at least eight subversive tracts were produced there, their title pages ascribing them to 'Michael Wood of Rouen'. At the same time, Cecil was managing the estates of another scrupulous 'loyalist', the Lady Elizabeth.[89] Nicodemism was outwardly conformist, but not always politically inert.

Exiles were much more obviously political. Even Protestant authorities were sometimes reluctant to admit them, especially in Lutheran territories where the fear of offending Charles V was strong. Jan Laski's boatload of refugees from the London 'Dutch' Church was turned away successively from Denmark, Wismar, Lübeck and Hamburg, due to the exiles' refusal to adopt local Lutheran practices. They settled, in the spring of 1554, at Emden, where leadership of the congregation soon passed to John Scory, deprived bishop of Chichester.

The main correspondence networks, and the pronounced theological sympathies, of the Edwardian Church were with 'Reformed' Protestants. The natural destinations for the exiles were not the Lutheran states of northern Germany, but the Rhineland towns of Strassburg, Wesel and Frankfurt, and the Swiss cities of Zürich, Basel and Geneva. Scory was one of a handful of bishops joining the exodus – others were Barlow of Bath and Wells, Coverdale of Exeter and Ponet of Winchester. But the exile communities had no episcopate, and experimented with governance and worship. For the first time in a generation, royal supremacy was not one of their key theological co-ordinates. The structure was of linked but independent congregations, and leadership devolved to charismatic preachers, like Edmund Grindal and John Knox, or to university men like Richard Cox and Edwin Sandys.

Sandys expected a martyr's reward for his entanglements with Queen Jane, but sympathizers were able to arrange his release from the Marshalsea, and he travelled (dodging attempts to re-arrest him), via Antwerp, to Strassburg. Here he breathed a sigh of relief: 'We have lost the saving truth at home, and found it abroad: our countrymen are become our enemies, and strangers are made our friends.'[90]

Found the truth abroad, or smuggled it safe out of England? That was a point of opinion, and one triggering among the exiles a renewed outbreak of the argument about ceremonies that convulsed the later Edwardian Church.

The arena of trouble was Frankfurt, an imperial Free City of largely Lutheran complexion. It enjoyed an uneasy friendship with Charles V, after remaining loyal to him in the bout of warfare breaking out in 1552. Early in 1554, the Frankfurt Council granted permission to settle to the remnants of a small Stranger Church, a community of French weavers from Glastonbury in Somerset. As other English exiles began to arrive that summer, the Council insisted they 'should not dissent from the Frenchmen in doctrine or ceremonies' – any assertive performance of liturgies just banned in England might be seen as a provocation to Philip and Mary. In practice, the exiles found they could use the Prayer Book, but tailored it to resemble the liturgy of the French congregation, which was derived from Calvin's Geneva. New prayers and psalms were added, and the Litany and surplice discarded.[91]

This quiet local arrangement was barely in place when, on 2 August 1554, the leaders of the congregation, prominent among them William Whittingham, sent an eye-catching letter to other English exiles. It invited them to resettle in Frankfurt, where worship was 'subject to no blemish', and the Church was 'free from all dregs of superstitious ceremonies'. The implication that other refugees worshipped superstitiously was provocative, to say the least. Englishmen at Zürich and Strassburg retorted that, while minor changes were permissible, the continued use of the Prayer Book was vital: to show solidarity with persecuted brethren in England (including the book's authors, Cranmer and Ridley, awaiting trial in Oxford), and to rebut papist accusations that Protestants were constantly shifting and changing.

Positions hardened in November 1554 when John Knox – a veteran of battles over the 1552 book – was invited by the Frankfurt congregation to become their minister. He immediately allied himself with Whittingham. His co-minister, Thomas Lever, took the opposing view, as did John Bale, arriving at Frankfurt, via the Netherlands, in ignominious retreat from his episcopal ministry in Ireland. Bale was a controversialist every bit as pugnacious as Knox, and was outraged by the Scot's suggestion that the 1552 Communion Service had 'the face of the popish mass' – a serious allegation indeed. Knox and Whittingham appealed to Calvin, who wrote wearily in January 1555 urging all sides to compromise, while observing that the Prayer Book did indeed contain 'silly things'.

In March 1555, the Strassburg community decided to take matters in hand. After a conciliatory approach made by Edmund Grindal was rebuffed, a large party of exiles travelled north to Frankfurt. It was headed by the former Oxford chancellor, Richard Cox, who had escaped from house arrest to the continent in May 1554. At their first divine service, the newcomers loudly interjected Prayer Book responses omitted by the Frankfurt congregation. When challenged, they answered 'they would have the face of an English Church'. 'The Lord grant it to have the face of Christ's Church', was Knox's pious-aggressive response.

The following Sunday, Cox's supporters staged a pulpit reading of the abrogated Litany. The officiant was John Jewel, an Oxford reformer who served as notary to Cranmer and Ridley in the disputation of April 1554. Jewel's flight from Oxford was preceded by a recantation, and an attendance at mass: purists were outraged to see their pulpit occupied by a succumber to 'idolatry'. Energized, as always, by opposition, Knox gave free rein to denunciations of the Prayer Book, and of other abuses in the late Church of England – 'superstitious, impure, unclean'. But he committed a tactical error in agreeing to formal admission of the new arrivals to the Frankfurt congregation. In ongoing acrimonious debates, Cox, true to the principles of *adiaphora*, was prepared to concede that some ceremonies – even kneeling to receive communion and the surplice – might, as indifferent things, be set aside. But he drew the line at getting rid of the Litany and the great prayer of thanksgiving, the *Te Deum*. Knox's position was that only extempore prayers, or ones drawn directly from scripture, were acceptable in worship.

Knox's trump card was the standing judgement of the Frankfurt council that exiles should not deviate from the worship of the Reformed French community. The newcomers' expulsion seemed likely, but Cox's supporters delved into the box of dirty tricks. They drew the attention of the non-English-speaking councillors to Knox's *Faithful Admonition*, published the previous summer. It attacked Philip, Mary and Charles V in predictably intemperate terms: Charles was compared to the Emperor Nero. On 26 March 1555, nervous councillors expelled Knox from Frankfurt. He went to Calvin's Geneva, followed a few months later by Whittingham, his close friend Christopher Goodman, and other supporters.

Knox liked what he found there. He would later describe the city as containing within it 'the most perfect school of Christ that ever was in earth since the days of the apostles'. Its chief adornment was something the Edwardian Church signally lacked: discipline, administered in Geneva by a vigilant consistory of ministers and lay elders. 'In other places I confess Christ to be truly preached, but manners and religion so sincerely reformed, I have not yet seen.'[92]

The exiles in Geneva, unlike the leaders of the earlier Edwardian establishment, can fairly be called Calvinists. Their breathless admiration for the city's thoroughly reformed worship, and for its non-episcopal system of ecclesiastical governance, put them at odds – potentially or actually – with other evangelicals, at home and abroad. The experience of exile enabled growing numbers of English Protestants to see more clearly than ever that they were not in fact bound to the legacy of Henry VIII – limited to adapting, reforming or refining the old structures he had wrested from the control of the pope. A Church could be reconstituted from first and fundamental principles. The desire to do so, and a fear of doing so, would henceforth pull the movement of evangelical reform in ever more conflicting directions. But while new fault-lines opened up on one side of the broad religious divide, among English Catholics a twenty-year schism was drawing finally to an end, in a very different gesture of repudiation for the legacy of Henry VIII. In late 1554 the decision was at last taken: the English Church was coming home to Rome.

# 13

## TIME OF TRIAL

### Reconciliation

O N 20 NOVEMBER 1554, Reginald Pole, cardinal legate and Plantagenet prince, came ashore at Dover. It was nearly twenty-three years since he had last stood on the soil of his native land. Now he returned, on a 'greater and more praiseworthy enterprise than if one should recapture Jerusalem from the infidels'. The log-jam over church property had been broken in October 1554. Julius III agreed to enlarge Pole's powers to grant dispensations to holders of monastic estates, while Philip and Mary promised to return what property they could to the Church. A party of notables went to Brussels to escort the cardinal home: their number included William Cecil, ever outwardly loyal. Once again, law struggled to keep up with politics. Pole arrived in England still a convicted traitor. A bill reversing his attainder was quickly introduced into the Parliament convened on 12 November, and on 22 November received royal assent.[1]

Six days later, as orders went out for *Te Deum* to be sung in all parishes in thanksgiving for the Queen's presumed pregnancy, the cardinal addressed Members of Parliament summoned to the court at Westminster. It was the speech Pole had been waiting two decades to deliver, a hymn of patriotism from a man 'exiled my native country without just cause'.

England was a chosen nation, the first kingdom freely to accept the faith of Christ, as a gift from the papacy. Pole's emphasis on the 'manifold benefits that this realm hath received from the Apostolic See' was the antithesis to the antagonistic Anglo-papal history devised by William Tyndale and funnelled into the ear of Henry VIII. Pole rehearsed the disasters, 'the tumults and effusion of blood', afflicting Germany since its departure from Roman obedience, as well as the violence against the conscience raging in England since all good laws gave way to 'the lust and carnal affection of one man'.

Still, when all seemed lost and hopeless, the light of true religion burned in a few hearts. Mary, 'a virgin helpless, naked and unarmed', secured victory over tyrants and was now happily joined to 'a prince of like religion'. Pole had high hopes for Philip. Charles V was like David, who began work on the Temple of 'appeasing of controversies in religion'. His son was the Solomon who would bring it to completion. It was precisely what evangelicals said about Henry and Edward (see p. 304); Catholics and Protestants habituated the same world of biblical metaphor.

At the close of an oration of great rhetorical force, Pole begged Parliament to remove impediments standing in the way of England taking its rightful place at the heart of a united Christendom: 'I come not to destroy, but to build. I come to reconcile, not to condemn. I come not to compel, but to call again.'[2]

On 29 November, representatives of the Lords and Commons jointly prepared a petition to the crown, asking that 'this realm and dominions might be again united to the Church of Rome by the means of the Lord Cardinal Pole'. The following day, in a moving ceremony, Pole absolved the realm from the sin of schism, and reconciled England with Rome.[3] It was 30 November, the Feast of St Andrew. In a world of perfect symbolism, the event might have fallen elsewhen: St Andrew was Scotland's, not England's, patron. But in Scotland too, Protestantism was on the defensive in 1554, its English support withered since the death of Edward VI. A few months earlier, the temporizing Earl of Arran was replaced as regent by the Catholic Mary of Guise, French-born widow of James V, and mother to the young Mary Queen of Scots, now safely in France and betrothed to the Dauphin Francis. There was cause for Catholic rejoicing across Britain, yet Valois France, the dominant power in Scotland, was the sworn rival to Habsburg Spain, the dynastic partner of England.

A bill repealing no fewer than nineteen Henrician acts, and nullifying the royal supremacy, was introduced into Parliament in late December and passed on 3 January. Unusually, it contained the text of a parliamentary supplication requesting that monastic lands might remain in lay hands 'clear from all dangers of censures of the Church', as well as Pole's consequent dispensation, which was thereby given the status of statute law – an indication of the continuing nervousness around the church lands question, and a concession that Pole very grudgingly accepted. But with this question settled, the Lords who blocked the revival of medieval heresy legislation earlier in the year now cheerfully voted it through.[4]

Reconciliation with Rome was a return, but also a departure. As it transpired, the first major saint's day following passage of the legislation was 25 January, Feast of the Conversion of St Paul. It was a fitting focus for public thanksgiving, with processions and bonfires. No one could miss the symbolic point of celebrations, as Wriothesley put it, 'to give God laud and praise for the conversion of this realm to the Catholic faith'. The Grey Friars chronicler observed the 'joy of the people that were converted, likewise as St Paul was converted'.[5] There was a real flavour of evangelical fervour to the re-Romanizing of English Catholicism.

Conversion implied conscious, individual commitment, rather than just going with the flow. This was an ideal the bishops, Bonner of London once more in the lead, were eager to convert into reality. On 19 February 1555, Bonner ordered all parishioners in the forthcoming Lent to be individually absolved in confession of the sins of schism and heresy. He empowered the parochial clergy, once they themselves were reconciled, to act as his deputies for this. It was a more than merely formal exercise. Bonner anticipated that ordinary curates might not be able to 'satisfy the minds, and to appease the consciences of some of their parishioners', and so instructed his archdeacons to produce lists of the 'best learned' priests in each deanery. Those with troubled consciences could choose an expert spiritual guide to have their doubts resolved. Instructions printed that Lent for use of confessors in the diocese of York directed that, before reconciling penitents, they should examine them on their faith in the real presence, and on whether they believed 'our Holy Father the Pope . . . is and ought to be head of the universal Catholic Church'.[6]

Across England in 1555, ordinary men and women were required to identify as, and perhaps even to become, something they had never quite been before: Roman Catholics. To affirm the spiritual supremacy of the Pope in 1555 was a different matter from doing so – piously, conventionally or unthinkingly – in 1515. It was another of the regular conjunctions in the English Reformation at which official changes of policy served, not so much to confuse people, as to educate and, within limits, to empower them. As with Henry VIII's mass oath-swearing of twenty years before, the effects were equivocal. Many people (more perhaps than in 1535) were confirmed in their acknowledged allegiance to the religious and political objectives of the authorities; others internalized their doubts and said and did outwardly as they were bidden; a smaller group was encouraged and energized in conscientious opposition. A little later, Bonner would be told by Ralph Allerton, a suspect he was interrogating, that 'there are in England three religions'. The first was 'that which you hold; the second is clean contrary to the same; and the third is a neuter, being indifferent, that is to say, observing all things that are commanded outwardly, as though he were of your part, his heart being set wholly against the same'.[7] The restoration of capital punishment for heresy would soon test the categories into which people fell.

### Welcome the Cross of Christ

First to burn, at Smithfield on 4 February, was John Rogers, Tyndale's one-time collaborator on the English bible and, more recently, a prebendary of St Paul's and well-known London preacher. At an interrogation by the Privy Council in

January, Gardiner said he hoped Rogers would follow the recent example of the whole Parliament and be 'content to unite and knit yourself to the faith of the Catholic Church'. Rogers affirmed his belief in the Catholic, but 'not the Romish Church'. The Pope was not a Catholic. Tyndale and More's stark argument over the identity of the Catholic Church, diverted down some complex paths by Henry's break with Rome, was back in clear view. While the churchmen traded scriptural texts, the lay councillor Sir Richard Southwell had his own cynical take: 'Thou wilt not burn in this gear when it commeth to the purpose, I know well that.'[8]

He was wrong. Rogers went courageously to the stake amidst shows of support from the crowd. Renard reported to Philip that some of those present 'gathered the ashes and bones and wrapped them up in paper to preserve them' – the instinct to venerate relics was deep-rooted, even among those who rejected the cult of the saints. Renard was a realist. To avoid a popular backlash he advised the King against further public burnings, and thought the bishops should instead consider the merits of 'secret executions, banishment and imprisonment'. The watchword should be 'lente festinare' (make haste slowly).[9]

Another three followed within a week. The London rector Lawrence Saunders was executed at Coventry on 8 February – he had been an active evangelist in the Midlands under Edward – and on the following day two other clergymen were burned in the localities where they made an impact: Rowland Taylor at Hadleigh in Suffolk, and John Hooper in his episcopal seat of Gloucester – his death agonizingly prolonged by green wood on his pyre which at first failed to catch.[10]

All were prominent figures of the Edwardian regime – people, as Mary put it to the Council, 'as by learning would seem to deceive the simple'.[11] It was hoped, even expected, that they would 'turn', as other leading Protestants had done in the months following Mary's accession. A recantation was of greater value politically, and spiritually too, than an unrepentant death. But if the hope was for a domino effect of high-profile submissions, demoralizing the rank-and-file, it turned out to be misplaced. The eighteen months since the collapse of the evangelical regime had given its former leaders time to reflect and prepare. And in an intellectual world increasingly shaped by absolute opposi-tion of Bale's 'two churches', those of Antichrist and Christ, of idolatry and true worship, the merits of martyrdom could seem startlingly clear.

'Now is the time of trial,' Hooper wrote in one of his last letters from prison, 'to see whether we fear more God or man.' In the weeks preceding his execu-tion, Lawrence Saunders was imprisoned alongside the leading preacher and St Paul's lecturer, John Cardmaker, arrested in November 1554 while attempting to flee abroad. Cardmaker discovered he feared man more than God, and was waiting to subscribe articles of recantation, when Saunders managed to persuade him back onto the narrower path.[12] Martyrdom was a solitary vocation, but it was usually anticipated and embraced with the advice and example of others.

It was also a spectacle and a performance. The symbolism of judicial burning was of a terrible yet just punishment for the worst of imaginable crimes. The flames consumed a body that had no claim to rise in glory on the Last Day, and mimicked the hellfire that was an inexorable fate for the unrepentant heretic's soul. But the authorities could never control entirely how the meanings of the event would be perceived and understood, and the condemned thought hard about ways to make the show their own. At his burning outside Coventry, Saunders appeared 'in an old gown and a shirt, barefooted', and as he was led to the stake he 'oft times fell flat on the ground and prayed'. All Christians were called to the imitation of Christ, but execution was an opportunity to invoke comparisons with the passion in particularly intense and memorable ways. When he reached the stake, Saunders took it in his arms, kissed it and said 'welcome the cross of Christ'.[13]

Lay victims soon followed. Thomas Tomkins, a weaver, may have been first, at Smithfield on 16 March. During his interrogation, in an incident that rapidly became notorious, Bonner held Tomkins's hand over a lighted candle. It may have been the cruelty of imagined kindness, a last effort to get Tomkins to understand the implications of his refusal to recant. Prior to this, in a seemingly petty and spiteful gesture, Bonner had Tomkins' beard removed. It is a small but revealing sign of how distinctions of faith were starting to manifest in outward appearances. The evangelical preachers, to distinguish themselves from tonsured and clean-shaven popish priests, and to assert the masculinity giving them the right to marry, often sported full beards in the manner of Old Testament patriarchs. Some lay evangelicals evidently followed the fashion. Bonner sent Tomkins to the barber 'so he would look like a Catholic'.[14]

Around the same time as Tomkins, another bearded layman went to the stake, at Cardiff. Rawlins White was an illiterate fisherman, aged about sixty, who memorized scripture from the readings of his son, and who on Mary's accession placed himself at the head of an evangelizing conventicle. The background was unusual, but White's case exhibited several features characterizing the executions through that first spring and beyond. There was a vigorous and prolonged effort to induce him to recant, Bishop Kitchen of Llandaff employing both 'threatening words' and 'flattering promises' during a year of imprisonment, first in Cardiff Castle and latterly in the bishop's house at Chepstow. White's commitment to a cause he first espoused in late middle age was fervent and uncompromising. When Kitchen caused a mass to be said for his conversion, White appeared at the moment of the elevation to announce 'I bow not to this idol'. The burning was a contested, fractious event: a priest preached in favour of the real presence and the Pope, while White shouted for the crowd to give no credence to this 'false prophet'. The crowd itself was divided. White's friends grasped his hand at the stake for comfort, but others called out, 'Put fire, set to fire!'[15]

Fourteen heretics died at the stake, half of them in Essex, before Easter of 1555. They included a second bishop, Robert Ferrar of St David's, burned at Carmarthen on 30 March. On Easter Sunday itself, 14 April, a scandalous event took place in St Margaret's church by Westminster Abbey. During distribution of communion, a man came into the church and repeatedly stabbed the priest, John Cheltham, with a wood-knife. Cheltham was badly injured, and blood was splashed onto the consecrated hosts. The assailant, William Flower, was a former monk of Ely, who later admitted his actions had been wrong, and, as he claimed, unpremeditated. Yet coming into the church, 'and there seeing the people falling down before a most shameful and detestable idol', zeal for God's honour overcame him.[16]

It was a uniquely shocking case. But demonstrations of dramatic dissent during the celebration of mass, such as those made by both Taylor and White, often precipitated arrests. Heretics were punished for crimes of thought and belief, yet those who suffered were seldom, if ever, quietly minding their own business. The 'frantic' man who hanged two puddings – perhaps in mockery of the host – around the neck of one of the prebends of St Paul's going on procession on 25 March, Annunciation Day, was lucky to escape with a whipping.[17]

Flower was burned as a heretic, not hanged as a felonious assailant, on 24 April. Two days later, a properly convicted felon, John Tooley, was hanged at Charing Cross. His crime was robbing a Spaniard, yet with the connivance of evangelical fellow-inmates in the Marshalsea, his death was choreographed as a religious martyrdom. Tooley read from prayers on prepared slips of paper, including an extract from the Litany of the Edwardian Prayer Book: 'From the tyranny of the Bishop of Rome, and all his detestable enormities . . . good Lord deliver us.' Knox and Whittingham wanted to abolish the Litany, but it was a potent instrument of spiritual bonding. Three hundred in the crowd responded in unison, 'Amen, Amen, Amen.'

Linking the patriotic anti-Spanish cause with the godly anti-popish one was a conscious, and effective, strategy. A Warnyng for Englande, published at Emden in 1555, reported in lurid terms alleged Spanish atrocities in the Kingdom of Naples, soon to be visited on England – and what was almost worse, extortionate levels of taxation there. It pressed hard on a raw nerve: 'no man is so ignorant but he knoweth right well the desire of the bishops is to have the abbey lands restored'. No one, yet, had been burned for opposing this, but 'faggots be already prepared'.[18]

On 13 May, a fortnight after false rumours of the birth of a royal son prompted premature celebrations, the Venetian ambassador reported the confiscation in London of a thousand copies of a Dialogue, 'full of seditious and scandalous things . . . against their Majesties' persons'. Later that month, there was a serious outbreak of violence near the court, a crowd of 500 armed Englishmen confronting Spaniards, with five or six killed. Another incident took place on Corpus Christi Day, 13 June, with a mob assembling outside the church where the Spanish, 'including the most noble and illustrious of that nation', were attending mass, and preparing to go on procession. Only with difficulty were they persuaded to disperse. Most likely this refers to the Corpus Christi procession which Philip's Spanish Dominican chaplain, Bartolomé Carranza, organized that year in Kingston-upon-Thames, in an attempt to restart the ancient custom across the nation.[19]

In the meantime, the anti-Spanish cause had gained a surprising new recruit. The death of Julius III on 23 March was followed by the brief pontificate of Marcellus II, who died on 1 May. His successor, elected on 23 May, was the zealous inquisitor Cardinal Gianpietro Carafa. It was a blow for Reginald Pole, whose orthodoxy Carafa was known to mistrust. Also for Philip and Mary: Carafa was a patriotic Neapolitan, who might well have shared some perspectives with the *Warnyng for Englande* about the malignity of Spanish rule over his homeland. Nonetheless, the new Pope wrote swiftly to assure Philip and Mary of 'paternal goodwill', and Pole's letter of congratulation hailed their shared interest in reform of the Church.[20]

Reform and repression were two sides of a coin. On the day of the revived Corpus Christi procession, the government issued a proclamation against possession of seditious books, cataloguing a long list of forbidden authors, back to Tyndale, Frith and Barnes. It also targeted the growing literary output of the exiles: Knox's *Admonition*; Vermigli's *Treatise of the Cohabitation*; Thomas Sampson's *Letter to the Trew Professors of Christes Gospell*; John Scory's *Epistle unto all the faythfull that be in pryson*, a work already celebrating 'the most valiant, blessed and noble martyrs of our age'. Scory's tract breathes almost an air of joy and relief at the passing of an age of ascendancy and murky compromise: 'O most happy time, wherein poverty, need, pining in prison, fetters, chains, stocks, rebukes, revilings, the dens and caves of the wilderness, banishments, gallows, fires, and the cruelty of tyrants, are again restored to the Church!'[21]

Fire was restored with a generous hand through the summer months of 1555, as the Queen came to terms with the painful realization that she was not, after all, expecting a child, and Philip departed for the Netherlands.[22] Between 30 May and the end of September, fifty-one English people died at the stake, as many as were burned for heresy between the break with Rome in 1535 and the end of Henry's reign. There were a few celebrities among them – John Cardmaker on 30 May, John Bradford on 1 July, John Bland of Adisham on 12 July – and a handful were socially distinguished. Thomas Hawkes, burned in Essex on 10 June, was a gentleman, as was John Denley, dying at Uxbridge, Middlesex, on 8 August, and Robert Glover at Coventry on 19 September.

The others were humble figures – husbandmen, weavers, a sprinkling of parish clergy. There were two women, Margery Polley, burned at Dartford in Kent in July, and Elizabeth Warne, burned at Stratford le Bow in Essex in August. Where we can identify a reason for the arrest, refusals to receive the sacrament and denunciations of the mass seem to predominate. Essex's position as the main location of executions in this period was overtaken by Kent, where Richard Thornden, suffragan bishop of Dover, and another former Edwardian suffused with born-again Catholic fervour, took a leading role in prosecutions. The pattern in Canterbury, untypically at this stage, was of execution in batches: four together on 12 July, five on 23 August, and another five on 6 September.

The drive against heresy was a collective and somewhat unco-ordinated effort. Some arrests were directly instigated by the Privy Council, some by bishops, some by enthusiastic lay magistrates. Among these, there were a few zealously committed Catholics, like the cousins Edmund and Sir John Tyrell in Essex. But there were also laymen keen to attest their political loyalty by the sufferings of others. Richard, Lord Rich, prince of opportunists and time-servers, was the most active heresy-hunter in Essex. One of those he denounced was a Billericay linen draper, Thomas Watts. At his burning in Chelmsford on 10 June, Watts called out to the former Lord Chancellor, 'beware, beware, for you do against your own conscience herein, and without you repent, the Lord will revenge it'.[23]

Condemned layfolk were seldom, at their deaths, passive and silent victims. Patterns of symbolic behaviour, learned from the godly preachers, were much in evidence. Long white shirts of the kind worn by Saunders were widely favoured: light clothing facilitated a quicker death, but the garb was also designed to call to mind the white robes given to those in the Book of Revelation 'slain for the Word of God', and calling on the Lord to 'judge and avenge our blood'. Kissing or embracing the stake was another signifier of martyrdom, as was vocal prayer or singing of psalms: John Denley sang a psalm in the flames at Uxbridge on 8 August. Presiding at his execution was the lay lawyer John Story, who returned from Louvain exile on Mary's accession and served as Bonner's commissary-general. He commanded a guard to silence Denley by flinging a heavy faggot at his head. 'Truly,' he quipped, 'thou hast marred a good old song.' The burnings were legal, but also brutal and unruly events.[24]

The undoubted showcase burning of 1555 took place on 16 October, outside the city gate of Oxford, when two former bishops, Hugh Latimer and Nicholas Ridley, went together to the stake. They were finally put on trial at the end of September, before a trio of bishops: Brooks, Holyman and White. The accused maintained a defiant stand, though not without moments of unintentional comedy. Ridley, who removed his hat on entering the court, insisted on replacing it when the Pope's name was mentioned. When the commissioners demanded respectful treatment, as representatives of the cardinal legate, Ridley knelt, to show he reverenced Pole for his royal blood, but sprang up again to demonstrate his lack of esteem for Pole as the agent of a usurping power.

Latimer, predictably, interrupted White's opening oration to challenge his definition of the Catholic Church: 'Christ gave knowledge that the disciples should have persecution and trouble. How think you then, my lords, is it most like that the see of Rome, which hath been a continual persecutor, is rather the Church, or that small flock which hath been continually persecuted of it, even unto death?' Once more, we see the evangelicals' sense of rediscovered purpose, almost of relief, at knowing who they were again through the validation supplied by suffering and oppression.[25]

'Be of good comfort, Master Ridley, and play the man. We shall this day light such a candle, by God's grace, in England, as I trust shall never be put out.' Latimer's words, as the pyre was lit beneath them, have resounded down the centuries. Did he say them? They are an echo of a heavenly voice ('play the man') heard in the Roman arena by the second-century martyr St Polycarp, as recorded by the early church historian Eusebius. The words appear in the second (1570) edition of Foxe's *Acts and Monuments*, but not in the first of 1563, and without any evidence of new eye-witnesses being consulted. Whether he said them or not, Latimer undoubtedly saw himself and Ridley as links in a chain of true disciples of Christ, persecuted by the ungodly down the ages.[26]

From his prison window, Cranmer watched his friends go to their fate – a poignant echo of Thomas More's witnessing the last journey of the Carthusians, just over twenty years before. Cranmer's trial opened on 12 September, and because, unlike Ridley and Latimer, he was a bishop properly consecrated and installed under Roman rites, it was a more elaborate and formal affair. Earlier disputations covered Cranmer's favoured ground of eucharistic doctrine, but now the questioning – relentlessly pursued by Brooks, and the hard-nosed civil lawyers Thomas Martin and John Story – focused on the actions of Cranmer's own career and on the royal supremacy to which he had fatefully hitched his fortunes.

At one point, Cranmer fell headlong into a well-prepared trap. 'Was it ever so in Christ's Church?' Martin demanded – in response to Cranmer's assertion that every king was rightfully supreme head in his own dominions. 'It was so.' Then what, Martin asked, about the Emperor Nero? He was assuredly the world's mightiest ruler in the years following Christ's resurrection (and a notorious byword for tyranny and persecution). Reluctantly, Cranmer conceded that Nero, no less than Henry VIII, had been supreme head of Christ's Church on earth.

Conviction was a foregone conclusion. A succession of enemies from Cranmer's past (including Robert Serles and Richard Smyth) popped up to give evidence that the archbishop was a promoter of heretics and the author of heretical works. Cranmer himself insisted he acted 'to improve the corrupt ways of the Church' – perhaps an echo of his 1533 consecration oath to bring about changes 'wheresoever they seem to me to be for the reform of the English Church'. Paul IV's mandate for Cranmer's trial included the formal – and impractical – requirement for him to appear personally at Rome within eighty days to answer the charges against him. It served as a stay of execution, and for now, Cranmer was returned, a condemned man, to his cell.[27]

### Profitable and Necessary Doctrine

On 8 October 1555, a week before his predecessor Ridley perished in Oxford, Bishop Bonner completed his epic visitation of London, and issued clergy and laity with new injunctions. The visitation diagnosed the sickness; it was time to prescribe the remedies. The first was that all clergy with cure of souls read diligently a book 'lately made and set forth by the said Bishop of London, for the instruction and information of the people' entitled *A Profitable and Necessary Doctrine*, and expound one chapter of it to their parishioners every Sunday and Holy Day.[28]

The book was issued along with thirteen Homilies, compiled by Bonner's chaplains John Harpsfield and Henry Pendleton, and first published in July. The idea of a set of officially approved sermons, for ordinary clergy to work systematically through, was a blatant stealing of the evangelicals' clothes, and indeed two of the Homilies – on Charity and on the Misery of All Mankind – were recycled with light revisions from Cranmer's 1547 collection. The main text also had a familiar feel: it was modelled closely on an earlier *Necessary Doctrine* – the King's Book of 1543. In both title and contents, the book was a marker of stability and continuity, a nod of acknowledgement to the conservatives who, like Bonner himself, rode out the Edwardian years in stoic loyalty to the religious settlement of Henry VIII.[29]

Despite this, there was little sense of normal service being complacently resumed, after temporary intrusions of schism and heresy. Bonner's preface frankly admitted the deep and lasting damage produced by years of heretical teaching, 'sugared all over with loose liberty'. Devout religion was 'accounted and taken for superstition, and hypocrisy'. Catholic doctrines of the Church were 'with a new, envious and odious term, called and named papistry'. Bonner's aim was a fresh start, to set forth 'a very pure, sincere, and true doctrine of the faith, and religion of Christ', with errors 'weeded, purged and expelled'. In this, he praised as 'a great help' the recent proclamation banning importation of heretical books – an acknowledgement of the continuing danger posed by the writings of the exiles.

Bonner's was a compendious survey, based around the Creed, Ten Commandments, Seven Deadly Sins, Sacraments, Lord's Prayer and Hail Mary. These were Christian basics, but the intention was to accentuate the distinctiveness and exclusiveness of Catholic teaching. His exposition under-lined the key role of the Church in securing salvation, and in expounding the Second Article of the Creed ('And in Jesus Christ, his only son, Our Lord'), Bonner seized an opportunity to tackle a familiar bugbear: 'these new-fangled wits, who for a singularity, or for a glorious badge of a Protestant . . . use this peculiar fashion of speaking, "the Lord, the Lorde"'.

There was some caution in the presentation of controversial doctrines. The book devoted much attention to proofs for prayer for the dead and purgatory, for example, without ever using the name itself. Even before the accession of Edward, 'purgatory' had become a toxic term, a one-word summary of an imagined world of clerical corruption and credulous devotion. But if Bonner remained in some ways a 'Henrician', his fastidiousness on this was not shared by other Marian writers, especially returning exiles like Peryn and Smyth.[30]

'Pope' was an even more toxic linguistic legacy, and Bonner did use the term, though sparingly. But the Homilies and Necessary Doctrine can scarcely be accused of walking on doctrinal egg-shells. Of the thirteen homilies, three concerned the mass and the real presence, two were on the nature and authority of the Church, and two specifically on the supremacy. These were the calling-cards of the new Catholicism – centralizing, Roman, emotionally and doctrin-ally anchored on the mass.

Bonner followed the Necessary Doctrine in January 1556 with a catechism for children, An Honest Godlye Instruction, to be used in place of all other primers and catechisms in his diocese. The minds of the young were a key battleground, and it was regrettable that 'of late days, the youth of this realm hath been nouseled with ungodly catechisms, and pernicious evil doctrine'. Pole strongly endorsed Bonner's efforts, and in legatine visitations of 1556, repeated the order for weekly readings from the Necessary Doctrine.[31]

Yet Pole had his own, still more ambitious plans for the implanting of pure Catholic doctrine in a country recovering from schism. On 4 November 1555, a mass of the Holy Spirit, celebrated by Bonner in the Chapel Royal, marked the opening of a clerical assembly at Westminster. It was a national legatine synod, covering both provinces, rather than a meeting of Canterbury Convocation. Pole wished to tackle 'reform of the English Church' as a unified whole, and – while the process with Cranmer ran its course – he was still not installed as archbishop of Canterbury.[32]

The synod began with a grand gesture, negotiated in advance with Philip and Mary. The crown restored to the Church 'First Fruits and Tenths' – the initial year's income from a clerical benefice, and a tithe of the revenue there-after – a much-inflated replacement for papal annates, which Henry VIII had imposed as a tax on the clergy in 1534. Upon legal advice, the measure was presented for approval of the new Parliament, which convened on 21 October. There it encountered real difficulties, despite Pole's suave assurances that since pensions to the ex-religious would now be paid from this source directly by the Church, the effect on royal revenue would be neutral. Any talk of lay income being returned to the Church made parliamentarians nervous, and perhaps rightly so – Pole and Mary hoped this signal of royal renunciation would inspire individual acts of pious restoration.

The bill, in the end, passed. But another, allowing the crown to confiscate the property of exiles who refused to return to England, was on 6 December defeated in the Commons amidst dramatic scenes. Realizing a majority of those present were against the bill, the Gloucestershire MP Anthony Kingston led a party in blockading the doors, and forcing the Speaker to put the issue to a vote. Some MPs were sympathizers with the exiles' stance, but a gut instinct for the sacrosanctity of gentlemen's property was the more powerful factor.[33]

Proceedings in the synod were more sedate, albeit they began with a momentous departure. On the night of 12 November, Stephen Gardiner passed away at Whitehall in what had once been the palace of his old master, Wolsey. Conflicting accounts circulated concerning his last moments. One was that Bishop Day tried to comfort him with talk of justification by faith; another was that Gardiner was read the gospel passage on how Peter left the courtyard weeping after his denial of Christ, and commented tearfully 'Ego exivi, sed non dum flevi amare' (I have gone out, but as yet I have not wept bitterly).

As Gardiner lay dying, Pole mourned for him, and worried that 'the impious' would be emboldened. He was right. On 19 November, John Philpot wrote to a sympathizer from prison that 'I cannot but joy with you, my heartily beloved in Christ, of the fall of Sennacherib'. Why invoke this obscure Old Testament Assyrian king? Perhaps because he besieged and imprisoned the godly King Hezekiah – just as evangelicals liked to persuade themselves the limitations of Henry were imposed on him by wicked papistical councillors.[34]

Gardiner's association with Henry defined him to the end. Another old Henrician, Nicholas Heath, replaced him as Lord Chancellor, but he never wielded anything like the same influence. Gardiner's passing, and the rise of the cardinal as unrivalled ecclesiastical councillor to the crown, seemed to mark a sea change in the character of English Catholicism.

By 10 February 1556, the synod had completed its business and produced a set of decrees for 'Reformatio Angliae', the Reformation of England – a reminder that, in the sixteenth century, this word was not the exclusive property of Rome's enemies. The tone was set by the first decree: henceforth, throughout the realm, the Feast of St Andrew was to be kept as a day of solemn commemoration, with procession and a sermon, to give thanks for 'the return of this kingdom to the unity of the Church'. The relationship with Rome was a thread to be woven into the calendrical fabric of English parish life.[35]

Other decrees held a mirror up to the leaders of the Church. Prelates were to live 'soberly, chastely and piously', eschewing pomp, pride and superfluity in dress, retinue and diet: the ghost of Wolsey was to be exorcized from the Catholic episcopate. The 'great abuse' of bishops and heads of colleges failing to reside in their places of duty was to end. Absenteeism among lower clergy too was condemned, along with the pluralism giving rise to it. All clergy with cure of souls, including bishops, were required to provide sermons to the people. Pastoral office, it was noted, 'chiefly consists in the preaching of the divine word' – an assessment evangelicals could scarcely have disputed.

For decades, Catholic reformers had viewed the quality of the parish clergy as foundational to the renewal of society. Pole's decrees moved beyond ritual exhortations. Bishops were to examine ordinands with scrupulous care, and all priests presented to benefices must swear oaths they did not acquire them through simony. Most significant was the order for every diocese to establish a school, or seminary ('seed-bed'), to educate boys, especially sons of the poor, whose disposition gave 'certain hope that they will become priests'. Four such seminaries began to establish themselves over the following two years.[36] It was the beginning of a long-term solution to the haphazard training and selection of priests that for centuries was the vaguely unsatisfactory norm across the Catholic world. The Council of Trent would later take up and impose this initiative, in what is widely considered its most significant reforming measure, though the seminary system would bring with it problems of its own.

Other matters were discussed, yet did not make it into the final canons. One was vernacular scripture – in December, the New Testament was parcelled up among delegates in preparation for a new English translation. It is unclear whether the project was abandoned, or postponed for later implementation. Some supporters of the regime persisted in the old view that vernacular scripture was intrinsically divisive, practicable only when unity and obedience were universally re-established. John Standish – another Edwardian evangelical turned fervent Marian evangelist – published a treatise in 1554, *Whether it be Expedient that the Scripture should be in English*, and answered firmly, no. Other Marian churchmen included in their writings large chunks of translation from the Vulgate. Pole's initiative suggests a dawning sense that control over the meaning of vernacular scripture could no longer be ceded by default to the evangelicals; that it was time to take the fight to the enemy. To assist with the correct understanding of scripture, Pole asked Carranza to compose a new catechism.[37]

All this constituted a programme of serious-minded Catholic reform. It was a response to the rise of Protestantism, but it was not merely 'reaction', and it is wrong to see Pole as somehow stuck in or belonging to the past.[38] Much has been made of his apparently cool response to an offer of assistance, in early 1555, from Ignatius Loyola, head of the recently established Jesuit order. There were virtually no English Jesuits in 1555, and Loyola suggested Pole might send a few talented students to be trained in the Jesuit-run German College in

Rome. But Pole had his own plans for an English seminary in the city, and was keeping his powder dry.

Pole, a leading light of the early sessions of the Council of Trent, was scarcely insulated from the currents of reform jolting through the wider Catholic Church in the 1550s. He was – unlike numerous other Catholics – in no way an opponent of the Jesuits, writing a supportive letter of condolence on Ignatius's death in July 1556. And he actively supported other reformed religious movements: the Italian Cassinese Congregation, which was seeking to reinvigorate the Benedictines from within, and the Theatines – an austere order of priests (founded 1524) who dressed as secular clergy in an effort to lead by example. Carafa had been their first general, and another recruit was Thomas Goldwell, an Englishman who had shared Pole's long exile in Italy, and was consecrated bishop of St Asaph in 1555. The spirit, at least, of the Jesuits was brought to England by another returning exile, the Dominican William Peryn. In Louvain, Peryn was influenced by the mystical writer Nicholas van Ess, a priest closely linked to the early followers of Ignatius, and the author of a set of meditations much indebted to Ignatius's famous *Spiritual Exercises*. In 1557, Peryn published his own *Spirituall Exercyses*, an adaption of van Ess's work.[39]

In the summer of 1555, Peryn became prior of a restored house of Dominican friars at St Bartholomew, Smithfield. The diarist Henry Machyn thought this 'the first house that was set up again by Queen Mary's time', though in fact at Easter that year the Observant Franciscans had already returned to Greenwich, by the Queen's invitation. Some of the twenty-five brothers were 'strangers' (Spaniards), but most were indigenous former friars, led by the most venerable veterans of the English papalist cause, Henry Elstow and William Peto, exiles in the Low Countries since the early 1530s.

The appearance of monks and friars, clad in their distinctive habits, was one of the most dramatic symbols of the repudiation of Henry's, as well as Edward's, works of reformation. It was also one of the most visible pointers to the limits of restoration. There was little prospect of hundreds of dissolved religious houses springing back to life, and a line under the past was drawn by Rome itself. In a bull of June 1555, Paul IV formally dissolved all houses suppressed by Henry VIII. Any restorations would technically be new foundations. This was some further reassurance to anxious lay proprietors of ex-monastic estates, but it did not inspire in them any impulse of self-abnegating generosity. Some laypeople gave piously in their wills to refounded monasteries, but endowments for refoundation came almost entirely from the crown. Only seven religious houses were re-established nationwide between 1555 and 1558, with plans in the works for a half-dozen or so more. The most significant refoundation was that of the monastery which was never really dissolved: the royal showcase church of Westminster Abbey. On 21 November, John Feckenham, already in position as dean of Westminster, was installed as abbot, along with fourteen monks, whose numbers had grown to nearly thirty by the time of the St Andrew's Day celebrations the following year.[40]

Only around a hundred of perhaps 1,500 surviving ex-religious again took up the habit, though what monastic life lacked in quantity it made up for in quality: prestigious refoundations included the return of a resilient core of Carthusians to Sheen in November 1555, and of the Bridgettine nuns to Syon in August 1557. Others might have returned if given the chance. In Yorkshire, the former Cistercians Roland Blythe and Thomas Condall were in 1555 styling themselves 'Abbot of Rufford' and 'Abbot of Roche', in apparent expectation of restoration. After the 1538 suppression of Monk Bretton Priory, near Barnsley, a small group of monks continued living together. In Mary's reign they set about reassembling their monastic library, buying back well over a hundred volumes, in an ultimately vain hope of return to full communal life.[41]

The non-return of the monasteries, and associated non-re-establishment of a nationwide network of shrines and pilgrimage sites, along with a distinctly limited number of chantry refoundations, was a measure of the achievement, for good or ill, of the reformers under Henry and Edward. But it was also a sign of ecclesiastical priorities changing, in ways of which early sixteenth-century Catholic humanists might have approved. There was a move, supported by Peto and Peryn, to restore the house of London Conventual Franciscans. Its buildings were occupied by Christ's Hospital, a school for orphaned children, and one of five city hospitals established in Edward's reign from former monastic institutions to meet various social needs. Bonner and Gardiner disliked these showboats of unorthodox charity. When an evangelical provocatively asked of him, 'Are not all these good works, my Lord?', Gardiner scoffed that the heretics had expelled 'godly, learned and devout men', and thrust in their place 'a sort of scurvy and lousy boys'.

The scheme to restore the Grey Friars was scotched by the intervention of two Spanish mendicants: Philip's Franciscan chaplain, Alfonso de Castro, and the Dominican Juan de Villagarcía. Invited to dine in the hall at Christ's, Villagarcía was reportedly so moved by the sight of the orphans setting and serving the tables that he began to weep, declaring he 'had rather been a scullion in their kitchen than steward to the King'.[42] Common humanity, and the practical needs of a burgeoning urban population, occasionally took precedence over the scoring of confessional points.

### The Hand in the Fire

Humanity of a different sort was called for in dealing with unabashed heretics, and in 1556 Castro and Villagarcía were deeply implicated in an ongoing struggle. In February the previous year, Castro preached a remarkable court sermon, criticizing the burnings that had just started, and saying it was better for heretics to 'live and be converted'. Very likely, he spoke at the orders of Philip or Renard, at a moment of Spanish nervousness about the politically unsettling effects of the fledgling campaign. Castro was no precocious tolera- tionist, but the author of a treatise *De Iusta Haereticorum Punitione* (On the Just Punishment of Heretics), and in May 1556 he dedicated to Philip a second edition of another lengthy work justifying the death sentence for heresy.[43]

The punishment was just, of course, only for those refusing to recant. In December 1555, Villagarcía was at the forefront of efforts to secure the most spectacular recantation of all. In a succession of earnest, learned discussions with Cranmer, now being held in more comfortable conditions in Christ Church, the Spanish friar succeeded in planting doubts about the respective roles of popes and General Councils. In the New Year, encouraged by a friendly but zealously Catholic gaoler, Cranmer began attending mass. On 28 January, he put his name to a statement recognizing the authority of the Pope 'so far as God's laws and the laws and customs of this realm will permit' – an elastic formula uncannily recalling Bishop Fisher's efforts to interpret creatively the newly proclaimed royal supremacy in 1531.

Under intense psychological and emotional pressure, Cranmer made further ambiguous recantations on 15 and 16 February, but news that the date of his execution was set for 7 March precipitated a total collapse. On 26 February, he signed a comprehensive surrender, probably drafted for him by Villagarcía, affirming papal primacy, purgatory and transubstantiation.

It was a stunning reversal, and a potential propaganda triumph to place Northumberland's capitulation firmly in the shade. Yet from the start, it was oddly mishandled. A rapidly printed text of Cranmer's recantation was recalled by the Council, probably because of adverse reaction in London to the signa- tures on it of the Spanish friars Villagarcía and Pedro de Soto (who debated with Cranmer in October). Government anxiety was heightened by the discovery of a wild conspiracy, concocted by Northumberland's kinsman Henry Dudley, to raid the royal mint, support a French invasion and place Elizabeth on the throne. Cranmer's execution was postponed, and a further recantation deemed necessary.

Fatefully, Cranmer was not reprieved, as by all due processes of canon law he ought to have been. The decision to insist on the death penalty was Mary's own: Cranmer was the prime architect of twenty years of schism and heresy, as well as the dark destroyer of her parents' once-happy marriage. Mary's venge- fulness was emotionally explicable, but it was not politically astute.

Even upon learning there was no way out, Cranmer signed yet another abject recantation, and on the day of his rescheduled execution, 20 March, the authorities expected a smooth reading from the penitential script. But some- thing unclicked in the elderly archbishop's mind. In the pulpit of the University Church he unexpectedly revoked all his previous statements, and reaffirmed his writings against Gardiner on the eucharist. 'And as for the Pope, I refuse him, as Christ's enemy and Antichrist!' Bustled quickly to the place of execution, Cranmer dramatically thrust into the heart of the fire the hand with which he had signed the recantations – a gesture that erased the value of his vacillations, and underscored persecution's perverse capacity to make of victory defeat, and of defeat, victory.[44]

Some compensation for the Cranmer debacle ensued in a triumph over a lesser figure. In May 1556, Sir John Cheke, a mainstay of the exiles at Strassburg, was lured by Paget into visiting the Low Countries, and seized by Philip's agents on the road between Brussels and Antwerp. With him was the former rebel Sir Peter Carew, who betrayed Cheke in exchange for an offer of pardon. John Ponet reassured an evidently anxious Bullinger about Cheke: 'I doubt not but that he will seal his testimony to the gospel with his blood.'

Bullinger was right to be apprehensive. Cheke was worked on by an old friend and adversary, John Feckenham. They had debated eucharistic doctrine together in 1551, when Feckenham was the prisoner in the Tower, and now the favour was returned. Cheke's recantation shocked fellow Protestants: 'it is vain to place our confidence in man,' lamented Robert Horne, minister of the congregation in Frankfurt. Other prisoners were trooped in front of Cheke, to be persuaded to follow his example. The Venetian ambassador heard of 'well-nigh thirty persons, who were in prison in danger of being burned, having lately by the grace of God and through the efficacy of his language been converted'.[45]

Heresy as a whole, however, showed little sign of being demoralized into submission: 1556 was a burning-year still hotter than 1555, with eighty-five executions and a further eleven Protestants dying in prison. Of these victims, most were humble artisans, and twenty-two were women.

The suffering was not distributed evenly. There were burnings in thirteen English counties in 1556, as well as in Guernsey in the Channel Islands. But the executions were heavily concentrated in London/Middlesex, Essex, Kent and Sussex, with only a single victim each in Cambridgeshire, Derbyshire, Leicestershire, Northamptonshire and Oxfordshire (Cranmer). In the remaining twenty-six English counties there were no burnings, and none at all in Wales.[46] This was in part a topography of hatred: executions took place where bishops and lay officials were more likely to want to prosecute, and neighbours more willing to denounce. But it undoubtedly reflected the unevenness of the advance of Protestantism itself, and the thinness of support for it across much of the Midlands, north and west. In more than one sense, England was becoming increasingly divided.

Executions usually passed off without any recorded protest, though a revealing, and moving, incident took place at Laxfield in Suffolk in September 1556, at the execution of John Noyes. When the sherriff sent his men to find

hot coals to start the blaze, 'the fire in most places of the street was put out', and
the officers had to break down the door of the only house where smoke was
seen billowing from the chimney.[47] It seems implausible Laxfield's inhabitants
were making a collective evangelical protest; rather, a forlorn gesture of neigh-
bourly solidarity with a local shoemaker, burnt in his own town.

The authorities belatedly realized that killing people in their home parishes
might be unpopular: from 1556, executions increasingly shifted to selected
regional centres, and victims were consumed in batches, rather than individually: thirteen heretics, men and women, from a variety of locations were burned
together at Stratford le Bow outside London on 27 June.[48]

Sympathy for the victims was countered by assurances that they deserved to
die; that they were not martyrs but malignants. With the support of Pole, now
installed in Cranmer's place as archbishop of Canterbury, writers like James
Cancellar, chorister of the Chapel Royal, contrasted the heretics 'that lately
have been justly burned' with true martyrs 'which have suffered for the unity
of the Catholic Church' – More, Fisher and the Carthusians. Pole's conviction
that devotion to these holy men would undermine evangelical 'pseudo-martyrs'
expressed itself in encouragement to his archdeacon of Canterbury, Nicholas
Harpsfield, to compose a biography of More, and to More's nephew, William
Rastell, to produce a folio edition of his uncle's *English Works*.

The lay Catholic writer Miles Huggarde, silenced under Edward, found his
voice again in 1556 with a rollicking propaganda piece, *The Displaying of the
Protestants*. Huggarde likewise praised the Henrician martyrs, and mocked the
condemned evangelicals and their supporters. In an inversion of usual stereotypes, it was the heretics who were credulous and superstitious, rooting around
'like pigs in a sty' to collect ashes and bones, and mistaking flights of frightened
pigeons for manifestations of the Holy Spirit. Their deaths consigned them to
deserved oblivion, their only memorial to be 'enrolled in a few threehalfpenny
books which steal out of Germany'. Huggarde's insouciance fails entirely to
conceal a distinct nervousness about the exiles' propaganda, and a perceived
need to counter it.

Huggarde was a self-proclaimed expert in heresy. He even, during Lent of
1555, managed to attend a secret evangelical conventicle, meeting at a tavern in
Islington. There he listened to a sermon by the group's leader, 'Old Father
Browne'. Like Ralph Allerton, Browne believed there were three religions in
England, but his categories were rather different. There was 'my Lord
Chancellor's [Gardiner's] religion', 'Cranmer's, Latimer's and Ridley's religion',
and also 'God's religion'. The first was certainly 'nought', but the second was
'not good'.[49]

Radical Protestantism and anabaptism, bane of the Edwardian establishment, might have been expected to thrive when that enforcing hand was
removed, to be replaced by an officialdom that did not much care to distinguish

between different strains of heresy. In fact, Huggarde's experience notwithstanding, most underground congregations remained faithful to the 1552
Prayer Book and communion. In part, this was because the displaced Edwardian
preachers launched a vigorous, and remarkably successful, campaign to maintain orthodoxy within the anti-Roman ranks. From their places of imprisonment in the King's Bench and elsewhere, they sent out letters condemning the
'freewillers' who attacked predestination, and addressing individuals' doubts
about the doctrine. A number of radical conventiclers converted, bowing to the
superior learning and biblical knowledge of the clerical leaders. Where
Edwardian evangelicals were incarcerated alongside radicals, they did all they
could to silence and confound them. Included with an account of John Philpot's
prison examinations, published at Emden in 1556, was his 'Apology for Spitting
upon an Arian' – 'apology', of course, meant justification.[50]

Persecution pared, but also purified English Protestantism. In its heart, and
in its heartlands, it steeled itself to resist the onslaught of Antichrist. In May
1556, heresy commissioners in East Anglia received an alarming dossier from
a small group of beleaguered Catholic citizens in Ipswich. Some forty inhabitants had fled the town, and 'lurked in secret places'. Another twenty refused to
receive the sacrament, and a dozen (an interestingly smaller number) came to
church, but refused the pax or looked away at the elevation. There were also a
half-dozen 'priests' wives, that have access to their husbands'. Things were
worse still in the Essex town of Colchester, according to a letter from the priest
Thomas Tye, sent to Bonner in December 1556:

> The detestable sort of schismatics were never so bold since the King and
> Queen's Majesties' reigns as they are now at this present . . . They assemble
> together upon the Sabbath day in the time of divine service, sometimes in
> one house, sometime in another, and there keep their privy conventicles
> and schools of heresy . . . The ministers of the Church are hemmed at in the
> open streets, and called knaves. The blessed Sacrament of the altar is blas-
> phemed and railed upon in every alehouse and tavern. Prayer and fasting is
> not regarded. Seditious talks and news are rife, both in town and country.

All this was in spite of a spate of exemplary burnings in the town (six at once
on 28 April 1556) and a recent visit from the bishop's commissary.[51]

Colchester was very likely the most Protestant place in England. Yet
even – or especially – here, religious rivalries shaped everyday social divisions.
Protestants drank at The King's Head; Catholics at The White Hart. As Agnes
Silverside, the elderly widow of a priest, awaited execution in Colchester in
1557, Ralph Allerton wrote to remind her of 'the old law, where the people of
God were most straitly commanded that they should not mingle themselves
with the ungodly heathen'.[52]

The inspirational – or guilt-inducing – witness of the martyrs, along with the insistent finger-wagging of exiled preachers and writers, tempered the temptations of Nicodemism. Gertrude Crokehay, a London merchant's widow, was denounced as a heretic in Antwerp, on her late husband's business, and on her return was induced by Bonner's chancellor, Thomas Derbyshire, to attend evensong. She experienced 'such trouble in her conscience thereby, that she thought verily God had cast her off, and that she should be damned and never saved'. Crokehay sought the counsel of John Rough, a Scots preacher in northern England in Edward's reign, who returned from Emden in 1557 to take charge of the London underground congregation. Rough's directive to her was to confess her fault in front of the conventicle, 'and so to be received into their fellowship again'.[53]

There was no slackening in the pace of persecution in 1557. In February, Philip and Mary established a national commission to search out 'heretical opinions, Lollardies, heretical and seditious books', and before the end of the year another eighty-one burnings took place. Of these, a noticeably greater number than before were of people relapsing after earlier recantations – recantations that the authorities had sometimes gone to remarkable lengths to allow them to make. Though the commission referred to 'Lollardies' (a loose colloquialism for heresies of all kinds), this did not resemble the Lollard pattern of simply getting caught a second time. In numerous poignant cases, conscience-stricken gospellers made public declarations effectively sealing their own fate. Elizabeth Cooper, a Norwich pewterer's wife, came to St Andrew's church at service time in July 1557 to announce that 'she revoked her recantation before made in that place, and was heartily sorry that ever she did it'. A couple of months earlier, the Bristol weaver Richard Sharp came to the choir door of Temple Church during high mass, pointed to the altar and called out, 'Neighbours, bear me record that yonder idol is the greatest and most abominable that ever was, and I am sorry that ever I denied my Lord God!'[54]

Salvation lay in separation, in spurning participation with the practices of the ungodly. Rose Hickman, reluctantly, brought her child to a popish priest for baptism in 1555 (see pp. 384–5), but at Whitsun 1557, Gertrude Crockhay stood as godmother at a private baptism, using the Edwardian Prayer Book, in a midwife's house on Mincing Lane. The beleaguered Ipswich Catholics wanted the orthodoxy of midwives looked into, 'because of evil counsel at such times as the necessity of women's travail shall require a number of women assembled'. The unsupervised sociability of women was a vortex of male anxiety.

As coming into the world, so in leaving it. When, early the following year, Crockhay lay mortally ill, she was warned she would be denied Christian burial if she refused the last rites of the Church. Her reply spoke chillingly of a resolve for separation maintained through death and on into eternity: 'How happy am I, that I shall not rise with them, but against them.'[55]

Enmity was not ended by death, and nor were the dead safe from punishment. On 13 January 1557, a meeting of heads of colleges in Cambridge, convened by Vice-Chancellor Andrew Perne, determined that the former professor of Divinity, Martin Bucer, was a heretic, as was another German, the Reader in Hebrew, Paul Fagius, who died shortly after his appointment in 1549. On 6 February, the bodies of the two men were exhumed from their graves and taken to the marketplace. There, in front of a large crowd, their coffins were chained to a stake and burned, together with piles of their heretical books. In Oxford, the corpse of Catherine Dammartin, partner of Peter Martyr, was likewise disinterred. She was a priest's wife, a former nun, and a heretic buried in Christ Church near the former shrine of St Frideswide: a triple sacrilege in Catholic eyes. Her remains were reinterred in a dung-heap.

Prior to his return to England, Pole seriously considered whether the bodies of all heretics should be disinterred from churches and churchyards. A strict interpretation of canon law suggested that they should, though awareness of the outrage likely to ensue sensibly headed off this drastic course of action. Nonetheless, Spanish clergy who came over with Philip were reportedly uneasy about celebrating mass in churches 'polluted' by the presence of the heretic dead, a scruple shared by the Queen herself. Nearly forty years later, one of Mary's privy councillors, Francis Englefield, then an exile in Spain, would tell an extraordinary story. The Queen, urged on by Pole, commanded him and other courtiers secretly to exhume the body of her father, which they then burned to ashes. It would be unwise to insist it could not have happened.[56] Across the spectrum of belief, the business of existing alongside the other, in life or in death, even within the unchosen bonds of kinship, was becoming ever more freighted and fraught.

### Legacies

The exhumation of Bucer and Fagius was more than an act of petty vindictiveness: it was the symbolic face of a serious and successful campaign to reclaim the universities for Catholicism, culminating in legatine visitations of Oxford in 1556 and Cambridge in 1557. This was a particular priority of Pole, who became chancellor of Cambridge upon the death of Gardiner in 1555, and of Oxford just under a year later. New statutes, curriculum changes, including restoration of the faculties of canon law, and a thorough purge of heretical books from college libraries did much to restore official confidence in the universities' essential orthodoxy.

To a considerable extent, the universities purged themselves. A wave of exiles washed over to Germany and Switzerland, particularly from Cambridge, where, within six months of Mary's accession, only three former heads of house remained in place. The others were replaced by reliable Catholics. In a backhanded compliment to the Edwardian habit of bringing in foreign theological expertise, Carranza assisted the visitation commissioners at Oxford, where a second Spanish Dominican, Pedro de Soto, became professor of Hebrew. A third, Cranmer's nemesis Juan de Villagarcía, occupied Peter Martyr's old place as professor of Divinity. A couple of years later, Martyr himself would be told, by the returning John Jewel, that at Oxford, 'religion and all hope of good learning and talent is altogether abandoned'. 'You would scarcely believe,' Jewel told Bullinger, 'so much desolation could have been effected in so short a time.'[57]

The Catholic bishops did not know they were short of time, and neither did layfolk in the parishes. Within the churches, steady programmes of restoration and refurbishment rolled on through 1557. Only half the parishes in Bath and Wells met all the requirements about books and altars in 1554; by 1557, 86 per cent did so. In Chester, nine-tenths of parishes had a rood and necessary ornaments, and the position was still better in Lincoln diocese. In the late summer, Nicholas Harpsfield, Pole's archdeacon in Canterbury, launched a thorough visitation of the diocese. He found evidence of heresy, and some lamentable gaps in provision of statues – orders for setting up images of patron saints were issued in 1556, and in most places nationally were rapidly complied with, and often piously pre-empted. But even in Cranmer's Kent, the churches now looked and smelled Catholic again. Nearly every parish had an altar, vestments and the core set of liturgical books.[58]

Slowly and cautiously, old habits crept back. Churchwardens' accounts show that in the latter 1550s as many parishes as in the 1520s were paying for the bells to be rung at Halloween, to call for prayer for the dead. The tailors' guild of Salisbury reinstituted its obit mass in 1556, and obits and requiems started up again in Doncaster the same year. In heretic-infested Essex, the percentage of will-makers requesting masses and prayers more than doubled between 1554 and 1558, and there was a four-fold increase in East Sussex over the same period. Still, the fact that the Queen had not yet conceived an heir was a cloud on the horizon. Alan Wood, a yeoman of Snodland in Kent, established an annual obit in the parish church on his death in 1556, but took care to specify the money should go to the poor 'if the same obit by order of law be abrogated hereafter'.[59] The mutability of princes was a lesson everyone in the realm had learned.

In the absence of a direct heir, hopes and fears continued to meet in the person of Elizabeth. Philip, who had better insight than most into the likelihood of Mary's conceiving, began to think the enigmatic princess might be a better prospect than the Francophile Queen of Scots, and from a distance protected her interests. Released from confinement at Woodstock, Elizabeth, like her sister in Edward's reign, made the necessary business of travel into a public statement of confidence and expectation. In December 1556, she rode from London to her house at Hatfield 'with a great company, and her servants all in red, guarded with velvet'.[60]

In 1557, the ship of Catholic restoration was caught in the cross-winds of European politics. Early the previous year, a brief truce in the long-running Habsburg-Valois conflict broke down, and Paul IV threw the papacy's weight behind France. In September 1556, Philip – King of Spain since his father's abdication at the start of the year – sent an army to invade the Papal States. A second Sack of Rome was only narrowly averted.

Defeated by the Habsburgs in the field, the Pope flexed his spiritual muscles. On 10 April, he revoked Pole's legacy, and seemed to want to remove even the residual legatine powers adhering to the office of archbishop of Canterbury. William Peto, elderly superior of the Greenwich Observants, was implausibly made legate in Pole's place, and appointed a cardinal, though Peto tried to reject the appointment, and Mary refused to allow the courier bearing the nomination into the country.

In a further blow, Pole's friend and ally, and Philip's most obliging contact at the Roman curia, Cardinal Giovanni Morone, was arrested on 13 May and charged with Lutheran heresy. As part of the process against him, the Inquisition began to investigate Pole too. Mary flatly refused to allow him to travel to Rome. In July 1557, in tones her father might have recognized, she instructed the English ambassador there to tell the Pope any heresy trial could take place only within England.[61]

In the meantime, England was drawn directly into the Franco-Spanish conflict, initially as the result of a bizarre attempt to re-enact Wyatt's Rebellion in Yorkshire. Still more bizarrely, its leader was a nephew of Cardinal Pole, though an evangelical one: Thomas Stafford, a son of Pole's sister, Ursula. Sailing from Dieppe with a small company, on 25 April he seized Scarborough Castle, and sought (unsuccessfully) to rouse the local population against the Spanish Marriage. There was no pretence this time of rebellion as an extreme form of counsel: Mary was 'unrightful Queen', and must be deposed in favour of 'the true English blood of our own natural country' (by which Stafford seems to have meant himself). He was taken prisoner within days, and executed at Tyburn on 28 May 1557.[62]

Mary chose to believe that Henry II was directly behind the attempt. She was egged on by her husband, back in England since March to solicit military help. On 7 June, in a proclamation issued under the Queen's name alone, England declared war on France and Scotland. It began promisingly. On 10 August, English troops shared in the glory of a Spanish victory over the French at San Quentin in Picardy. But another, more deadly enemy struck closer to home. 'This summer,' wrote the chronicler Wriothesley, 'reigned in England divers strange and new sicknesses.' It was a virulent strain of influenza, the worst epidemic of the entire century, which would linger over the next two years and push mortality levels 60 per cent higher than usual. Pressures on the poor were unprecedented.[63]

Perhaps no wonder, then, if there was something of a defensive note to the sermon Cardinal Pole preached before the Queen and court on 30 November, 'Reconciliation Day', on the appropriately sombre theme of repentance. Evangelicals might glory in the contribution of the five London hospitals, but in Catholic Italy – in Rome, Venice, Florence, Bologna, Milan – there were hundreds of hospitals and religious houses, and 'in two cities only', more given to monasteries and the poor in a month, than in England in a year. Pole admitted, grudgingly, he did not expect spontaneous re-endowment of religious houses. But people who had robbed the Church, and stripped both wealth and authority from the clergy – in which England 'had gone further than any schismatical nation' – should make recompense with alms-giving.

Greed, immorality, disobedience: all were legacies of the Schism. Pole traced an inexorable logic of decline, from Henry's first assumption of his 'strange title', to the heresy and iconoclasm of recent years. Once again, More and Fisher, true martyrs who put recent false ones to shame, were his primary witnesses. Pole shared with his audience an anecdote told him by More's friend, the Italian merchant Antonio Buonvisi, now an old man. Just before the break with Rome, Buonvisi asked More what he thought of papal primacy, and he answered that he regarded it 'not a matter of so great a moment and importance, but rather as invented of men for a political order'. Having said this, More felt immediately stricken in conscience, and he asked Buonvisi to call again when he had reflected on the matter properly. Ten days later, More retracted his earlier opinion. He had come to see the primacy of the Pope as the thing 'that holdeth up all'.[64]

Rome, and a cohesive, charitable society, or schism, heresy and the collapse of all order; there was no third option. This was the theme of numerous sermons – by bishops and others at Paul's Cross, by preachers licensed by Pole for various dioceses, and by clerical officiants at the burning of unrepentant heretics. The Marian regime was as eager to proclaim its message from the pulpit as its Edwardian predecessor had been, and to emerge triumphant from an intensifying battle of ideas.[65] It was, to say the least, ironic that at the turn of 1557–8 England was embroiled in bitter conflict with a pope who considered Cardinal Pole himself to be a flagrant heretic.

The new year began badly. A surprise French attack in early January succeeded in capturing Calais, last remnant of the once-mighty English empire in France. People could hardly believe it: 'it is supposed it could not be so won without treason' was chronicler Wriothesley's pained comment.[66]

The campaign against heresy slowed down in 1558 as a result of disruption caused by the influenza epidemic, though a far from negligible forty-three people were burned over the course of the year, bringing the total for the reign to 284, with a further twenty-eight accused heretics dying in prison. Though still heavily concentrated in the south-east, the victims of 1558 were executed across eleven counties. The single burnings taking place in Exeter, and in Richmond, Yorkshire, were unusual spectacles for residents.

Almost half of those burned in 1558 were not lone dissidents, but people convicted for their membership of an illegal conventicle. John Rough's London congregation was discovered, shortly before Christmas 1557, at the Saracen's Head, Islington, under cover of watching a play. This may mean that the authorities were becoming more successful at cracking open networks, and paring away at the hard core of heretics.[67] But it may also suggest that heretics themselves were becoming more organized and determined. There is in fact little sign that the authorities thought they were close to winning the battle against heresy. A royal proclamation, issued in June 1558, was decidedly twitchy about the wave of books 'filled both with heresy, sedition and treason' continuing to be smuggled in from abroad. Any person found possessing one could immediately be executed as a rebel, 'according to the order of martial law'.[68]

Rough's congregation soon reformed itself under the leadership of Thomas Bentham, a one-time fellow of Oxford and an exile returning from Frankfurt. In a letter of 17 July 1558 to Thomas Lever, currently pastor to the exiles at Aarau near Zürich, Bentham made a surprising and revealing confession. Safe in exile in Germany, he suffered 'great grief of mind', but now – under constant threat of death – he felt 'most quiet and joyful'. A growing habit of deference to the Swiss Protestant authorities was reflected in Bentham's request for Lever to walk over to Zürich to seek advice on several thorny questions. These included whether believers could pursue lawsuits in papistical courts, and whether professors of the gospel, 'not communicating with papists', should still pay tithes to them, as well as other taxes demanded by 'evil rulers and wicked magistrates'.[69] The obligations of faith were prompting reconsideration of the most basic social and political duties.

It was certain that believers should refuse patently ungodly orders, such as to attend mass. But was it ever lawful for them to pass beyond passive disobedience into active resistance, as Wyatt and Stafford had done? Lutheran theologians had already given limited sanction for the princes of the Schmalkaldic League to oppose Charles V. They were properly constituted authorities, jointly responsible with Charles for the good order of the Empire, and could correctively step in when he failed to uphold true religion: it was hardly a charter for revolution. Calvin was almost equally guarded.[70]

Some exiles from England, faced with what they saw as a uniquely perverse and persecuting regime, went much further. In Strassburg in 1556, John Ponet published a *Short Treatise of Politike Power*, arguing that monarchs derived their sovereignty from the people, and that tyrannical rulers could legitimately be put on trial. In Geneva, in January 1558, Christopher Goodman posed the question of *How Superior Powers Ought to be Obeyed*. In terms that would have appalled Cranmer and other Henrician evangelicals, he urged readers 'to repent our former ignorance'. Obedience to God's Word meant not a stoic willingness to suffer martyrdom, but a duty 'to resist idolatry by force'. Ponet only hinted at it, but Goodman openly advocated the slaying of tyrants. Mary deserved to be 'punished with death'.

A couple of months later, Goodman's friend John Knox published a scarcely less inflammatory tract, a *First Blast of the Trumpet Against the Monstrous Regiment of Women*. Its purpose – as the title not so subtly suggested – was to argue for the unlawfulness of female rule: 'repugnant to nature, contumely [insult] to God . . . the subversion of good order'. Knox had in mind a trio of popish Marys – of England, of Scotland and of Guise – and pronounced that 'women may and ought to be deposed from authority'. If this were not enough, Knox published in July 1558 the outline for an envisioned *Second Blast*. In it he argued that monarchs should be elected, rather than succeed by inheritance; that Catholics and notorious sinners must be barred from bearing rule; that oaths of allegiance to such rulers were null; and that unfit rulers might legitimately be deposed.[71]

These were not universal, or even majority views among the exiles, let alone the more prudent evangelicals keeping their heads down at home. But in the late 1550s it was becoming more widely accepted – by Catholics as well as evangelicals – that the duty of political obedience was contingent rather than absolute, that obligations to the laws of God, or of his Church, always took precedence over merely human regulations.

Christians had always known and believed this. But for thirty years and more, the English people had been party to, and participants in, an unrelenting series of arguments, concocted in print and pulpit, and continued in homes and taverns, about what God's laws actually were. The difficulties of identifying God's laws accurately shook to the core any residual assumption that kings, Parliaments or bishops could automatically be relied on to implement them correctly.

Henry VIII's pitch to his people was simple: to trust and obey him. 'My king is not the guardian of religion,' Robert Barnes once confided to Martin Luther, 'he *is* the religion.'[72] It was a strategy not even Henry's excessive personal and regal charisma could prevent from misfiring, and one still less likely to succeed when the old King was replaced by, first, a child, and then a woman. Edward and Mary claimed to be followers, rather than embodiments, of the true religion, and they commanded their people to worship as they did. Their policies and propaganda, though diametrically opposed, had the similar effect of emboldening some in their support for official religion and confirming others in their opposition to it. A third group – perhaps the majority – were eager to obey, but had been left with an uneasy, unshakeable sense that political loyalty and religious conviction now seemed to be inherently separable things, for combining or uncoupling as circumstances demanded.

Historians have often tussled over which side was 'winning' and which 'losing' the religious struggle of Mary's reign.[73] The truth is that both sides were at once transformed and in different ways strengthened by it. On the one hand, out of the cocoon of a numerically dominant body of traditionalist lay and clerical opinion, divided and confused by the events of Henry's reign, and battered and demoralized by those of Edward's, there was emerging a more articulate, combative and committed Roman Catholicism. On the other, the networks of reformers and evangelicals, who unexpectedly gained control of the kingdom in 1547, and unexpectedly lost it in 1553, were evolving into a more determined and doctrinaire Protestant movement, and weaning themselves from dependence on the royal supremacy. The intensification of religious persecution was a crucial development. The taking of lives divided communities, but it strengthened other bonds and solidarities – among the ranks of those suffering violence, and also of those meting it out.

In January 1558 Mary informed her husband, absent from England since July the preceding year, that she believed herself to be pregnant. That she was not, and never had been, was a cruel blow of personal fortune, but it was also the decisive political fact of the reign. By April Mary once more had to admit she was mistaken, but for the moment would make no changes to a will referring to the 'heir of my body'. In the late summer, Mary developed a fever, and took to her apartments. There was no immediate cause for concern, but in late October, the Queen's health took a sharp turn for the worse. It was, perhaps, ovarian cancer.

Philip, his own claims ruled out by treaty and statute, was concerned for a smooth and stable succession, with the French left out in the cold. That meant acknowledging Elizabeth, whose trump card, like Mary's in 1553, was their father's last Act of Succession. Philip sent the Count of Feria, Renard's replacement as ambassador to England, to reason with the dying Queen. In fact, Mary herself, in a codicil to her will dated 28 October, had already added a reluctant reference to 'my next heir and successor'. Parliament reassembled on 5 November, and two days later Mary was lucid enough to receive the Speaker, and agree that a delegation be sent to Hatfield to inform Elizabeth she had been named as heir.

Mary, according to the later recollections of her lady-in-waiting, Jane Dormer, also asked for assurances that her sister was a true Catholic. Elizabeth earnestly, effortlessly provided them. Feria visited Elizabeth on 9 November, bristling with assurances of his master's goodwill towards her. He found her to be 'a very vain and clever woman', and surprisingly open with him. She joked with the envoy about Philip's attempts to wed her off to Emmanuel Philibert, Duke of Savoy, with a barbed comment about her sister losing the people's affection by marrying a foreigner. 'She puts great store by the people, and is very confident that they are all on her side.' And she made no secret of her resentment at her treatment in her sister's reign. As to religion, Feria's assessment was pessimistic: 'I am very much afraid that she will not be well disposed.' He had heard that the women around her were all heretics, and feared that the men through whom she planned to govern would prove so too. One thing was certain: her secretary would be William Cecil, 'an able and virtuous man, but a heretic'.[74]

The Queen received extreme unction on the night of 13 November. She rallied a little the next day, and died early in the morning of 17 November. Reginald Pole, in failing health since September, outlived her by twelve hours. He too, as the end approached, reconciled himself unwillingly to Elizabeth's succession, writing to her on 14 November to say that his last hope was 'to leave all persons satisfied of me, and especially your Grace, being of that honour and dignity that the providence of God hath called you unto'.[75]

God's providence was a mysterious thing. For both Catholics and Protestants, heretics and believers, it gave and it took away. One response was fatalistic acceptance. Another was to heed the signs of the times, and throw everything into arduous efforts to bring God's will to fruition. For English Protestants in 1558, hiding at home or cast into exile, the chief instrument of God's providence was now a twenty-five-year-old unmarried woman, as once it had been a nine-year-old boy. The very unlikeliness of it was part of the wonder, a sign that God still had great things in store for England.

# PART IV

Unattainable Prizes

# 14

## ALTERATION

### A Glass with a Small Neck

THE REIGN OF Elizabeth began with a declaration that nothing had changed. On the morning of Mary's death, a proclamation announcing the Queen's succession was read at Westminster, and at the Great Cross at Cheapside, and despatched to sheriffs in every county. It commanded Elizabeth's new subjects not to attempt 'breach, alteration, or change of any order or usage presently established within this our realm'.

William Cecil, who drafted the proclamation, had long been planning this moment. He was determined for nothing to go wrong, and no one to rock the boat. Cecil was confirmed as the new Queen's principal secretary at a meeting of the Privy Council at Hatfield on Sunday 20 November. Most of the old members were politely dismissed. 'A multitude', Elizabeth declared, 'doth rather make discord and confusion than good counsel.' The new Council was a smaller, more coherent group than the old, many of its members 'Edwardians', and friends and allies of Cecil. Paget's services were not required. The Lord Chancellor, Archbishop Heath, continued for a short while, but the Council then became, unprecedentedly, an entirely lay body of advisors.

While the Council met for the first time, Elizabeth's almoner, William Bill, preached at Paul's Cross on the theme of the hour: quiet and orderliness. The Catholic chronicler Henry Machyn considered it 'a godly sermon', but others were unpersuaded. The following Sunday, the bishop of Chichester, John Christopherson, managed to slip through the government net, and denounce Bill from the same pulpit: 'Believe not this new doctrine; it is not the gospel, but a new invention of new men and heretics.' Christopherson was placed under arrest: an early portent of trouble with the bishops.[1]

Once again, it took about a week for news of a royal death to percolate through to the parishes. Thomas Butler of Much Wenlock heard it on

St Catherine's Day, 25 November, direct from the sheriff of Shropshire, Richard Newport. Butler was on his way to say mass, and at the offertory came down from the altar to say, 'friends, ye shall pray for the prosperous estate of our most noble Queen Elizabeth'. He repeated the message at mass the following Sunday, 'having upon me the best cope, called St Milburga's cope'.

The old service of the mass, and the old vestments of the priests, seemed under no immediate threat. Christopher d'Assonleville, envoy of the Netherlands government, reported on 25 November that Elizabeth 'has so far continued to hear mass and vespers, as she used formerly to do'. D'Assonleville was told by a person 'in a position to know' that the Queen's intention was to settle religion where it had been in 1539, 'when the forms of the ancient religion were followed, except as regards the power of the Pope'. Someone was spinning him a line. An ambiguity about precise intentions, and a care not to alarm foreign Catholic observers, were hallmarks of the new government's public statements. Edward VI's pronouncements, as well as the first proclamation of Mary, designated the monarch 'supreme head'. Elizabeth, in her accession statement, called herself 'Defender of the faith, etc.' – an evasively tactful formula first used by her father in 1543 for securing a treaty of alliance with Charles V.[2] Charles had died, in secluded retirement in a Spanish monastery, two months before Elizabeth's accession. But his son Philip, King of Spain and former King of England, was watching developments with intense interest.

Through to the end of December, the Mantuan envoy signing himself Il Schifanoya cheerfully believed that 'matters of religion would continue in the accustomed manner'. The bishops were less sanguine. On 14 December, Mary was laid to rest in Westminster Abbey, with the full liturgical resources of Abbot Feckenham's Benedictine community. The funeral sermon was preached by the bishop of Winchester, John White. His panegyric involved pious reflections on two, apparently contradictory, passages from the Book of Ecclesiastes: 'I can commend the state of the dead above the state of the living', and 'a living dog is better than a dead lion'.

Elizabeth's affronted suspicion that these incongruous beasts were symbols for herself and Mary landed White under temporary house arrest. There was nothing ambiguous, however, about White's praise of the late Queen for asking herself, 'How can I, a woman, be Head of the Church, who by scripture am forbidden to speak in the church?' – and for recognizing she could not. Nor about his dark prognostications for the immediate future: 'I warn you, the wolves be coming out of Geneva, and other places in Germany.'[3]

They were. On the day after Mary's funeral, eleven of the leading Genevan exiles, including Knox, Goodman, Coverdale and Whittingham, wrote to their estranged brethren in Frankfurt, hoping that 'whatsoever offence hath been heretofore either taken or given, it may so cease and be forgotten'. There was a catch: unity would come when arguments ceased over 'superfluous ceremonies, or other like trifles from which God of his mercy hath delivered us'. For their part, the Frankfurters fully intended to submit themselves to 'such orders as shall be established by authority', and urged the Geneva congregation to do the same. But the visions for the future were not so very different. The Frankfurt congregation likewise hoped that true religion would not be 'burdened with unprofitable ceremonies'. If so it proved, they would 'brotherly join with you to be suitors for the reformation and abolishing of the same'.[4] The returning exiles, practical experts in doctrine and worship, had firm opinions about the forms the religious settlement should take.

Yet the exiles, trickling home over the winter of 1558–9, were not the ones running the government, or co-ordinating plans for the Parliament scheduled to meet in January. At home, Protestant voices were more cautious. Nicholas Throckmorton advised the Queen that while her authority took root, 'it shall not be meet that either the old or the new shall fully understand what you mean' – a strategy in which the Nicodemite Elizabeth needed little coaching. 'Dissimulation' was also the tactic suggested by Richard Goodrich, a leading Protestant lawyer, in a memorial submitted at Cecil's request in early December. Mindful of the fate of King John, Goodrich advised that nothing rash be attempted against the Pope, even at the coming Parliament. It would for now be enough to stop heresy prosecutions, and permit use of the Henrician Litany. Meanwhile, at her private masses, Elizabeth could, if she wished, discreetly introduce communion in two kinds, and omit the elevation.

Another memorial-writer, the former Edwardian clerk to the council, Armagil Waad, pointed to the dangers of 'alteration in religion, especially in the beginning of a prince's reign'. In a deeply divided country, too much change, too quickly, could prove disastrous:

[G]lasses with small necks, if you pour into them any liquor suddenly or violently, will not be so filled, but refuse to receive that same that you would pour into them. Howbeit, if you instil water into them by a little and little, they are soon replenished.[5]

William Cecil contemplated this advice – to soft-pedal, to compromise, to delay – and at an early stage decided boldly to ignore it. The proof is in a document, drawn up around the end of 1558, and almost certainly Cecil's work. It was titled, unambiguously, 'The Device for the Alteration of Religion', and was a manifesto for swift and decisive change, though tempered by careful weighing of threats and opportunities. It began in question and answer: 'When the alteration shall first be attempted? At the next Parliament ... for the sooner that religion is restored, God is the more glorified, and, as we trust, will be more merciful unto us, and better save and defend her Highness from all dangers.'

The dangers were many, and, in the short term at least, so the 'Device' suggested, likely to increase. The Pope might excommunicate the Queen, thus encouraging foreign powers such as France (with whom England was still at war) 'to fight against us not only as enemies but as heretics'. Scotland was the potential gateway for French invasion, while Ireland, where priests were 'addicted to Rome', would prove harder than ever to govern. In England, many would be 'very much discontented'. Opposition was expected, not just from Catholics, but from zealots objecting to any retention of old ceremonies, and scorning the alteration as 'cloaked papistry, or a mingle-mangle'.

'What remedy for these matters?' The Device's high idealism was underpinned by low Machiavellian cunning. Peace should be pursued with Scotland and France, while efforts were made to undermine the stability of both states by encouraging dissident Protestants there. Remedies for Ireland were less specific: 'some expense of money'. Domestically, it was a time to purge. In both central and local government, anyone promoted 'only or chiefly for being of the Popes' religion' must go. Leaving them in place would confirm 'wavering papists' in error, and discourage people who were 'but half inclined to that alteration'. Power at all levels must rest in the hands of men 'known to be sure in religion'. If that meant promoting justices of the peace 'meaner in substance and younger in years', then so be it.

Bishops and popish clergy should be charged with praemunire – by this means 'her Majesty's necessity of money may be somewhat relieved'. None were to be pardoned till they 'abjure the Pope of Rome, and conform themselves to the new alteration'. For the sake of order, there should be a few sharp, exemplary punishments for those that 'could be content to have religion altered, but would have it go too far'.

The chief substance of alteration must be a Book of Common Prayer to displace the mass. A text, prepared by committee, was to be cleared with the Queen and brought before Parliament. Some of the names proposed were men, like Cecil himself, who spent Mary's reign in some condition of outward conformity: Sir Thomas Smith, William Bill, William May, former dean of St Paul's, and a one-time chaplain of Anne Boleyn, Matthew Parker, like Bill, a former vice-chancellor of Cambridge. The others were former exiles of the Strassburg–Frankfurt axis: Richard Cox, Edmund Grindal, David Whitehead, James Pilkington.[6]

It is not certain the committee convened in precisely this form, but its suggested membership is an indication of how the new regime regarded itself. Everyone on the list was a convinced Protestant, nearly all with strong links to Cambridge. It was here that the evangelical faith of Cecil and others had been forged in the later years of Henry, before being brought in Edward's reign to a mature self-understanding under the influence of Cranmer and Bucer. There were no Henrician Catholics, and no 'Genevans'.

## Elevation and Coronation

Elizabeth herself gave the first clear signal of alteration, at mass on Christmas Day. The celebrant was the bishop of Carlisle, Owen Oglethorpe, and before the service started, Elizabeth sent for him, and told him to omit the elevation of the host. Oglethorpe replied, according to Feria, 'that Her Majesty was mistress of his body and life, but not of his conscience'. The version told to the Venetian ambassador was less confrontational: 'thus had he learnt the mass, and she must pardon him as he could not do otherwise'. Either way, it is hard to imagine any bishop (Fisher excepted) speaking to Henry VIII like this. But Elizabeth had her conscience too, and finally she could afford to air it in public. After the reading of the Gospel, and before the start of the consecration, the Queen rose and walked out of the chapel.

This was more than a matter of aesthetic liturgical preference. Elevation and adoration of the host was the visible face of transubstantiation; the Queen was openly declaring she did not believe in the doctrine. In Mary's reign, her action would have instigated proceedings for heresy. Within weeks, it was being reported right across Europe. On 28 December, Feast of the Holy Innocents, Elizabeth heard mass again, with a different celebrant, and this time the elevation was left out.[7]

Evangelicals responded to the accession of Elizabeth just as Catholics did to that of Mary: with jubilant performance of still forbidden forms of worship. But, unlike her sister, Elizabeth was not prepared to countenance any pre-emptive popular Reformation during a period of tense transition. A proclamation of 27 December forbad preaching by persons 'having in times past the office of ministry in the Church' – code for the returning exiles. The proclamation also prohibited celebration of forms of worship other than that 'already used and by law received' – i.e. the Latin mass – though an exception was made for the English Litany, already in use in the Chapel Royal. To permit otherwise would encourage 'unfruitful dispute in matters of religion'.

The preaching ban was bad enough. But for evangelicals who saw in the mass only idolatry and abomination, even its temporary retention was an intolerable burden. Catherine, Duchess of Suffolk, still abroad in the early part of 1559, let Cecil know exactly how unimpressed she was by reports that the Queen 'tarried but the Gospel'. When it came to the mass, 'there is no part of it good'. The underground London congregation emerged into the open in November 1558, but as a result of the December proclamation it went back to meeting in private houses as a church-within-a-church. When communion was celebrated – so Thomas Lever reported to Bullinger – 'no strangers were admitted, except such as had been kept pure from popery'. Backsliders were accepted, but only after humble acknowledgement of their offence before the entire assembly. Lever witnessed 'many returning with tears'.

Working out how to acknowledge, and to expiate, the sins of Mary's reign was to be a painful problem for the victorious but wounded Protestant community. The distinctly conditional obedience Elizabeth received from Bishop Oglethorpe was mirrored in the attitudes of some of the returning exiles. Deciding the proclamation 'was not agreeable to the command and earnest injunction of Paul, to preach the Word of God in season and out', Lever and other ministers began delivering sermons in various London churches, unlawful gatherings to which 'a numerous audience eagerly flocked'.[8]

There was both mass and sermon at Elizabeth's coronation on 15 January 1559. It was preceded, on 14 January, by a ceremonial procession into the City, with all the accustomed street pageants. At the Little Conduit in Cheapside, just as at Philip and Mary's entry of 1554, a figure of Truth stepped forward carrying a bible; this time, 'Word of Truth' rather than 'Verbum Dei'. Elizabeth ostentatiously called for the book, 'at the receipt whereof, how reverently did she with both hands take it, kiss it, and lay it upon her breast'.[9] It was a signal of good faith to Protestant subjects, and a pointed riposte to the objections Gardiner made to the presence of her father's vernacular bible in the pageant of 1554 (see p. 378).

The coronation itself, in the still monastic church of Westminster Abbey, was a messier affair. There were difficulties about who should crown the Queen. The archbishop of Canterbury was dead, and the local bishop, Bonner of London, was politically unacceptable. The government hoped the other archbishop, the emollient Nicholas Heath of York, might be willing to do it, but he declined. Responsibility devolved, once again, to the relatively junior Oglethorpe of Carlisle.

Contemporary accounts of the ceremony are confused and contradictory. Oglethorpe probably performed the coronation ritual but not the accompanying mass. Elizabeth was determined there should be no elevation, and the dean of the Chapel Royal, George Carew, an Edwardian and Marian conformist, was happy to oblige. There was a further departure from precedent, planned or accidental. Oglethorpe did not have the text of the coronation oath to administer to the Queen, and William Cecil, layman and known heretic, stepped forward to hand it to the bishop. Ambassador Feria, fearing heterodox innovations, stayed away from the coronation; he must have felt he made the right decision.[10]

### Parliamentary Problems

Ten days later, Elizabeth returned to Westminster Abbey for the state opening of Parliament. It was 25 January, Feast of the Conversion of St Paul. Three years earlier, this was the occasion for public celebrations of England's union with Rome. No one now doubted the aim of the Parliament was to bring about a divorce.

Parliamentary proceedings conventionally began with a mass of the Holy Ghost, an appropriate invocation of a hoped-for spirit of wisdom. But in 1559, the mass was said early in the morning, without elevation, and when parliamentarians convened in the Abbey, it was to hear a sermon. Elizabeth was greeted at the door by Abbot Feckenham and his robed brethren, bearing their processional candles. In what was surely a pre-meditated snub, a token of her disdain for 'superstition', the Queen called out, 'Away with those torches, for we see very well.' She had brought her own choristers, who sang that token of her discreet Marian defiance, the Litany in English, as she processed into the Abbey.

Further humiliation for the Benedictine community followed, in a sermon, preached over the course of a vehement hour and a half, by the recently returned Richard Cox. The monks deserved punishment for their impious role in the burning of poor innocents 'under pretext of heresy'. This was perhaps a jab at Feckenham, active, and effective, in campaigns to persuade heresy suspects to recant. Elizabeth herself, Cox declared, was providentially chosen to repudiate past iniquities, to destroy images, and cleanse the churches of idolatry.[11]

Parliamentary business got under way with the opening speech of Sir Nicholas Bacon, Cecil's brother-in-law. Bacon was successor to Nicholas Heath, though, with a sense of social propriety exceeding her father's, Elizabeth decided the common-born lawyer should be only Lord Keeper of the Privy Seal, rather than Lord Chancellor. Bacon announced what all knew already: that the first and chief matter before Parliament was making of laws for the 'uniting of the people of this realm into a uniform order of religion'.[12]

It was as much the throwing down of a challenge as the announcement of a legislative programme. The Lords, where twenty bishops sat, along with Abbot Feckenham, was known to be opposed to religious change. The mood of the Commons was harder to read. Some Marian exiles managed to get home in time to be elected, but their numbers were small, fewer than a dozen in an assembly of around 400. There were rock-hard Catholics too, such as the heretic-hunter John Story, chosen for a borough, Downton in Wiltshire, controlled by the redoubtable Bishop White of Winchester. Mary's last Parliament was automatically dissolved on her death in November 1558, and only about a quarter of the former MPs were returned again in January. There is little evidence the government sought systematically to 'fix' the election, yet local patrons and electors may have felt it was sensible to choose representatives who were not blatantly at odds with the new government's thinking.[13]

One item of business was firmly on the Commons' agenda, if not on the Queen's. Very early in the session, Parliament petitioned Elizabeth, as it had Mary, to marry and settle the succession. Candidates were already lining up. The brother of the King of Denmark was spoken of, though Feria deviously tried to spoil his chances by spreading the rumour among councillors he was in fact 'a very good Catholic', rather than a heretic. It was another, and genuinely good Catholic, his master Philip II, whose suit Feria advocated. The attraction of this marriage to the Spanish was evident – it would keep England in the Habsburg orbit, and out of the French one. Feria reminded Elizabeth of the ominous claims of 'the Queen Dauphine', her cousin, Mary of Scotland.

The Queen, mindful of Throckmorton's advice to keep her cards close to her chest, was not exactly saying no, though a repeat performance of the Spanish Match would have horrified MPs, and Elizabeth surely did not seriously consider it. Replying in person to the parliamentary petition, Elizabeth was guarded: she had no inclination to marry, but, if that were to change, she assured them she would do nothing 'wherewith the realm may or shall have just cause to be discontented'. That she referred to a coronation pledge to be married only to one husband, England, and held out a ring as a token of her fidelity to the kingdom, is likely a fanciful later version of the words Elizabeth actually used. The Queen was not ruling marriage out, either as a diplomatic strategy or as a matter of private inclinations. Those inclinations, about which gossip was starting to spread, leaned towards her Master of the Horse, Robert Dudley, a younger son of the late Duke of Northumberland. Here, the principal problem was not so much that Dudley was the son (and grandson) of an unpopular convicted traitor; rather that he had a wife already.[14]

Anthony Cooke – MP for Essex, former exile in Strassburg, and father of five remarkable daughters, one married to William Cecil, another to Nicholas Bacon – wrote on 12 February to Peter Martyr: 'We are now busy in Parliament about expelling the tyranny of the Pope, and restoring the royal authority, and re-establishing true religion. But we are moving far too slowly.'[15] It was to be a recurrent refrain.

A bill to restore royal supremacy was given its first reading in the Commons on 9 February, and vehemently opposed by some Catholic MPs. John Story reportedly said it was a pity Elizabeth had not been executed, as he recommended to Queen Mary. Two other bills, one for 'order of service and ministers' and one for 'the book of common prayer and ministration of the sacraments', were introduced on 15 and 16 February. The exact content of these bills is unknown, but almost certainly they were intended to restore the Edwardian Ordinal and a slightly revised version of the 1552 Prayer Book. The committee envisaged in the 'Device for the Alteration' had evidently completed its work, and the survival of a printed copy of a new prayer book, bearing signatures of privy councillors probably added in January 1559, suggests that from the outset a restoration of the 1552 liturgy, not of the more conservative 1549 one, was what the Queen and her ministers had set their minds on.[16]

In parallel with these steps, the government sponsored a lively propaganda campaign in favour of 'alteration'. The Privy Council ordered arrests of unlicensed preachers, Catholic and Protestant, in the early months of 1559, but

the traditional course of Lenten sermons at court was preached by a distinguished company of officially approved former exiles and prominent
Edwardians: Cox, Parker, Scory, Whitehead, Grindal, Sandys. Ash Wednesday
in 1559 fell on 8 February, and on the day before the introduction of the
supremacy bill, Parliament was adjourned so that all could attend Cox's sermon
in the Whitehall Palace courtyard. Il Schifanoya was there, along with, he reckoned, more than 5,000 others. But the Italian heard 'so much evil of the Pope,
of the bishops, of the prelates, of the regulars, of the Church, of the mass, and
finally of our entire faith' that he resolved to stop attending court sermons.[17]

By 21 February, the three reform measures had been rolled together into a
single bill for Supremacy and Uniformity. This passed in the Commons, but
encountered difficulties on being sent to the Lords. At its second reading on
13 March, a succession of Lords Spiritual lined up to offer impassioned arguments for papal supremacy. Their resolve was bolstered by articles drawn up
by both houses of Convocation. In addition to affirming papal supremacy,
Convocation asserted the real presence of Christ's natural body in the eucharist; transubstantiation as the means of this; and the mass as a sacrificial
offering. These were the very articles Cranmer, Latimer and Ridley were
required to respond to at the Oxford disputation of April 1554 – further
evidence that the Prayer Book just approved by the Commons was substantially
that of 1552, which the framers of the Marian debate set their sights against.

In the Lords, Cuthbert Scott, bishop of Chester, argued that faith 'is maintained and continued by no one thing so much as by unity'. Christ himself
made provision for this in the papacy, praying 'there shall be one pastor and
one sheepfold'. It was not a matter of loyalty to any individual, for, as Archbishop
Heath ruefully conceded, Paul IV had proved 'a very austere, stern father unto
us'. But forsaking communion with Rome meant forsaking all General Councils,
all ecclesiastical laws, all agreement with other princes, all unity of Christ's
Church: 'By leaping out of Peter's ship, we hazard ourselves to be overwhelmed
and drowned in the waters of schism, sects and divisions.'

Scott and Heath, like other bishops opposing the measure, were old
Henricians, one-time advocates of the royal supremacy. Their defiance of the
wishes of the crown, in support of so uncongenial a pastor as Paul IV, underlines
a profound shift in Catholic thinking, under the pressures of the Edwardian
schism, and the influence of Cardinal Pole. It now seemed quite obvious to
Heath that Henry VIII was the first 'that ever took upon him the title of
supremacy', an innovation rejected by European Protestants and Catholics alike.
If Henry was right, then Herod must have been supreme head of the Church at
Jerusalem, and Nero supreme head at Rome – most likely this was an allusion to
the confusions and concessions of the incarcerated Cranmer (see p. 397).[18]

A lay lord, and former Marian councillor, Lord Montagu, likewise spoke
fervently against the bill. He agreed with the bishops, he said, not on their

simple say-so, 'but because they teach me the ancient faith of the Fathers, delivered and received from hand to hand by continual succession of all bishops in
the Church of Christ'. Montagu, a practical man, saw concrete dangers in
severing ties with Rome: the risk of domestic instability, and the proximity of
two 'potent enemies' (Scotland and France) – concerns ironically similar to
those of Cecil's 'Device'. A couple of notable conservatives, the Earls of Arundel
and Derby, were absent from the debates, on account of (possibly feigned)
illness, but some other noblemen – the Earl of Pembroke, the Earl of Shrewsbury,
Lord Hastings – stood firmly with the bishops.[19]

Most nobles did vote for the supremacy bill, which the Lords passed on
18 March and sent back to the Commons. But over the preceding days they had
amended it out of recognition. Reform of worship was stripped out; the mass
remained, with addition, as in 1547, of provision for communion in two kinds.
Papal authority was removed, but rather than granting the title of supreme
head to the Queen, the revised bill merely said she could adopt it if she
chose to.[20]

For a flagship legislative programme, it was a crash onto the rocks without
any recent precedent – exceeding even the difficulties Mary encountered in
1554. The government scrambled to rescue what it could from the wreckage.
On 22 March a proclamation was printed, making clear that communion in two
kinds would be allowed at Easter, even though no other change to the form of
service 'can presently be established by any law'. Another casualty of the Lords'
massacring of the bill was the repeal of the Marian heresy laws. The Council had
ordered prosecutions to cease, but evangelicals remained legally exposed, and
the Commons hurriedly voted for a protective measure declaring 'no person
shall be punished for using the religion used in King Edward's last year'.[21]

Observers expected Elizabeth would come to Westminster on 24 March,
give her royal assent to the supremacy act and other legislation, and dissolve
Parliament. Instead, she conspicuously withheld assent, and instructed
Parliament to reconvene after Easter, on 3 April.

### Supremacy and Uniformity

Feria thought this was a last-minute change of plan, and perhaps it was. But
reasons had been accumulating for Elizabeth and her ministers to hold their
nerve, and not to settle for, in effect, a return to the religious settlement of
Henry VIII. In part, it was due to confirmation that there was to be peace with
France (and Scotland): the settlement formalized at the start of April 1559 as
the twin Anglo-French and Franco-Spanish Treaties of Cateau-Cambrésis.
Elizabeth was anxious not to upset the Spanish while the complex three-way
discussions were under way. But she had steeled herself to make the necessary
major concession – Calais, at least temporarily, must remain in French hands.

12  The Cluniac Priory of St Milburga, at Much Wenlock in Shropshire, was suppressed in January 1540, during the final stages of the Dissolution of the Monasteries – one of more than 800 religious houses seized by the crown, stripped of assets and left in a ruinous state. Its significance to the people of the little borough is suggested by careful records made in the parish register by the vicar Thomas Butler, documenting what became of former monks and servants of the priory.

13  The burning at Smithfield on 16 July 1546 of the gentlewoman Anne Askew, along with the courtier John Lasssells, the former Observant friar John Hemsley and the tailor John Hadlam – a social cross-section of the evangelical movement in London. Askew's courageous silence under torture thwarted a conservative plot to bring down high-ranking reformers at the court, including even the Queen, Catherine Parr. This woodcut in Foxe's *Acts and Monuments* was reused from Robert Crowley's *The confutation of .xiii. articles, wherunto N. Shaxton...subscribed* (1548). Nicholas Shaxton, formerly a prominent evangelical, abjured in 1546, and is shown here preaching at the burning. The lightning bolt emerging from the cloud represents the thunder-clap recorded by evangelical chroniclers of the event: a vindication by God of Askew's status as a true martyr.

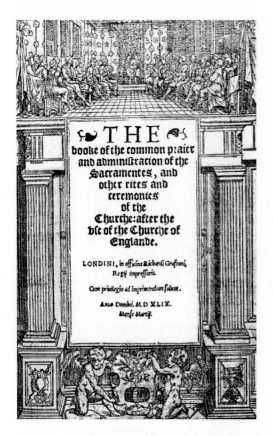

14 The Book of Common Prayer, 1549, replaced a profusion of Catholic liturgical books with a single volume containing English-language texts for church services and ceremonies. Its communion service, supplanting the Latin mass, was a shocking innovation to traditionalists and triggered a major rebellion in the south west of England. But zealous evangelicals, especially some of the foreign reformers invited to England by Thomas Cranmer, considered the Prayer Book too mired in the popish past, and pressed for its swift revision.

15 This woodcut from Foxe's *Acts and Monuments* shows Hugh Latimer delivering a sermon to a large crowd from the pulpit set up in the 'privy garden' of the Palace of Westminster. The godly young king, Edward VI, listens intently from the window of the council chamber. Preaching was the compelling vocation of Edwardian reformers, and Latimer devoted himself to it, rather than returning to the ranks of the episcopate after 1547. The ability of preachers with access to the King to influence policy was demonstrated in 1552, when criticism of the newly revised Prayer Book in a court sermon by John Knox instigated a sharp row about the meaning of kneeling to receive communion.

16 Thomas Cranmer, the deprived archbishop of Canterbury, was scheduled to read a recantation of his heretical errors on 20 March 1556 in the University Church of St Mary, Oxford, after a sermon by the Provost of Eton, Dr Henry Cole. Queen Mary's implacable determination that Cranmer should die, despite a series of abject recantations, helped produce an unexpected recovery of nerve. The image from Foxe's *Acts and Monuments* shows angry Catholic clergy pulling Cranmer from the platform after he had denounced the Pope as Antichrist. At the place of burning, Cranmer thrust into the fire his right hand, with which he had signed his earlier abjurations.

17 Cardinal Reginald Pole; a portrait *c.* 1545 by the Venetian artist Sebastiano del Piombo. A fierce critic of Henry VIII's break with Rome, Pole spent two decades in European exile, before returning to England as papal legate in 1554 to oversee reunion with Rome and replace Cranmer as archbishop of Canterbury. His reforming energies placed Mary I's England at the forefront of the emergent Counter-Reformation, but his understanding of justification led Pope Paul IV to regard him as a heretic, even as Pole was presiding over an intense prosecution of heretics in England. Full beards of the kind sported here were associated with evangelical clergy in England, yet popes and cardinals in Italy had developed the habit of wearing them. Pole himself missed becoming pope by a whisker in 1549.

18 'A Show of the Protestants' Pedigree', from a 1565 English translation by the exile Thomas Stapleton of a work by the German Catholic theologian (and convert from Protestantism) Friedrich Staphylus. The striking image of a tree of heresy, with multiple leaves and branches, was designed to put across the long-standing Catholic idea that heresy was at once infinitely fractious and a single impulse of error. Here, all the heresies of the age are traced to Luther, 'father of all the sects of Protestants', whose 'pretensed wedlock' with the ex-nun Katharina von Bora is made into the centrepiece of the design. Protestants would have found particularly offensive the idea that miscellaneous groups of radicals and anabaptists, itemized in the branch on the left, were their close theological cousins.

In nomine Domini incipit omne malum.

Fridericus Hulsius
Invent. & sculpt.

The Popes bull against the Queene.

19  Pope Pius V hands to an emissary the bull of 1570 excommunicating Elizabeth I, while forces of foreign invasion muster in the background, from George Carleton, *A Thankfull Remembrance of Gods Mercy* (London, 1630). The papal excommunication, and the Rising of the Northern Earls that immediately preceded it, intensified religious tensions in England and blurred the distinctions between spiritual and political dissidence. Henceforth, all Catholics were vulnerable to accusations of being traitors to the crown.

20 Elizabeth I sits enthroned in the House of Lords at the opening of Parliament, from a seventeenth-century edition of parliamentary proceedings. Elizabeth's relationships with successive Parliaments in her reign were frequently testy. Zealous Protestants, sometimes with the support of royal councillors, sought to use Parliament as a vehicle for advancing reform, but the Queen consistently took the line that religious matters were her prerogative, and MPs should not meddle with them.

21 A communion cup made in the 1570s or '80s for the parish of Dry Drayton in Cambridgeshire, during the incumbency of the godly rector Richard Greenham. Protestant communion services, unlike pre-Reformation Catholic ones, involved the laity receiving the sacrament 'in two kinds', wine as well as bread, and large cups were required in place of the smaller chalices used for mass. The proliferation and survival of these simple but stately objects provides material evidence of the transformation of religious culture at parish level.

R. P. Edmundus Campianus Soc: JESU. pro Fide occisus Londini in Anglia, Anno M D LXXXI Die j. Dec:   Lerch fe:

22 An engraving of the Jesuit Edmund Campion, the frontispiece to an edition of his *Decem rationes* (Ten Reasons), published in Antwerp in 1631. The mild and scholarly Campion was hailed throughout Catholic Europe as a martyr following his execution in 1581, and is here depicted with a cord around his neck and a disembowelling knife at his chest – emblems of the gruesome fate playing out in the background. Negative reactions to the death of Campion, and other missionary priests, impelled the Elizabethan regime's propagandists, including William Cecil, to embark on a literary campaign of self-justification.

Anticipating imminent news of a successful conclusion to the negotiations, Elizabeth met with Feria on the evening of Tuesday 14 March in a decidedly skittish mood. She announced, finally, that she could not marry Philip: it was because 'she was a heretic'. This was a word only ever directed towards other people, and Feria was astonished to hear Elizabeth apply it to herself. Almost as much from gallantry as diplomatic politesse, he found himself saying he 'did not consider she was heretical', though adding, pointedly, that he could not bring himself to believe she would sanction what was being discussed in Parliament. Elizabeth, however, 'kept repeating to me that she was heretical and so consequently could not marry your majesty' – an ironic compliment to Philip's supposedly immutable religious principles. Elizabeth, it seemed, was committed to breaking with Rome and to defying the 'poltroon' bishops. She assured Feria, however, that 'she would not take the title of Head of the Church'; a pledge which, it would shortly become clear, was not exactly an outright lie.[22]

The other reason for prolonging the Parliament was a government decision to tackle the poltroon bishops head on. The method was a tried and tested one, almost a cliché: a formal religious disputation. It was clearly decided upon before 20 March, when John Jewel wrote to Peter Martyr with details of the agenda and participants, including himself. Perhaps because he had just endured a gruelling fifty-seven-day journey home from Zürich, Jewel was in truculent mood, complaining that in the Lords, with no Protestant divines to expose their errors, the bishops 'reign as sole monarchs in the midst of ignorant and weak men'. He was appreciative of Elizabeth's support for 'our cause', yet complained she was 'wonderfully afraid of allowing any innovations', in part due to the influence of Feria. Things were moving, 'though somewhat more slowly than we could wish'.

Jewel was disarmingly frank about the reason for the disputation: so 'our bishops may have no ground of complaint that they are put down only by power and authority of law'. The Catholic disputants – Bishops White, Baines, Scott, Oglethorpe and Watson, along with William Chedsey, Henry Cole, Lord Montagu's chaplain Alban Langdale, and the prolocutor of an intransigent lower house of Convocation, Nicholas Harpsfield – had no chance of emerging victorious from the contest staged in Westminster Abbey on 31 March, under the presidency of Lord Keeper Bacon. Ranged against them was a phalanx of former exiles: Cox, Scory, Whitehead, Grindal, Sandys (all fresh from the Lent pulpit at Whitehall), John Aylmer, Robert Horne and Jewel, with one non-exile, Edmund Guest, a veteran of the disputations of Edwardian Cambridge. It was to be a grand public spectacle: along with privy councillors and Members of Parliament, 'a great number of all sorts of people attended'.

Three propositions were tabled: that it was against the Word of God, and the practice of the early Church, to use any language but the vernacular for public worship; that every national Church possessed authority to order its own rites and ceremonies; that the sacrificial character of the mass was unprovable by scripture. These were the fundamental issues under consideration in Parliament, but the debate soon collapsed into acrimonious procedural argument.

The bishops' requests to conduct discussion in Latin, and in writing, were turned down, and at close of debate on the first day they were denied the chance to offer rebuttal to the Protestants' statement on vernacular prayers. They expected an opportunity to do so at the start of the second day, and when Bacon insisted on moving straight to the next proposition, Bishop White refused to concede, and proceedings ended in confusion. Later that day, the Privy Council ordered White and Watson arrested. They were sent to the Tower, and their houses and papers were searched – probably for evidence the bishops were planning to excommunicate the Queen.

The government rapidly got its own version of events into print: a pamphlet which claimed that Elizabeth arranged the disputation for a free exchange of opinions intended to lead to 'some good and charitable agreement', and which explained 'the breaking up of the said conference by default and contempt of certain bishops'.[23]

New bills of supremacy and uniformity were now brought before the reconvened Parliament. The supremacy bill contained one small but significant alteration. The Queen was to be 'Supreme Governor' of the Church, rather than supreme head, and all clergy and royal office-holders were to swear an oath recognizing her as such. The change of name was a careful study in ambiguity, hinting that the monarch would not interfere with spiritual matters while not actually inhibiting her from exercising the exact same authority as her father and brother. Catholics may have found it marginally less offensive than the Henrician title, which holy martyrs died resisting, but since the act explicitly repudiated the authority of Rome, it is doubtful the formula was designed principally with their hurt feelings in mind.

It was, in fact, a necessary concession to the Queen's more fervent Protestant supporters. Some were mindful that Calvin had described Henry VIII's supreme headship as 'blasphemy'. But a vein of English Protestant unease about the title can be traced back to Tyndale, and the experience of exile and self-governance had weakened the emotional connection to it that was felt by evangelicals of Cranmer's generation. 'All scripture', Thomas Sampson stated to Peter Martyr in December 1558, nervous about the required terms of membership for the restored English Church, 'seems to assign the title of head of the Church to Christ alone.' Anthony Gilby, preparing his return from Geneva, was less circuitous: Henry VIII, 'this monstrous boar', committed treason in 'displacing Christ, our only Head'. Five months later, Jewel reassured Bullinger that the Queen was unwilling to be called 'head' because she seriously believed this honour 'cannot belong to any human being soever'. Edwin Sandys told

Parker at the end of April 1559 that it was Thomas Lever who 'wisely put such a scruple in the Queen's head'.[24]

There was another consideration: the Queen's sex. Bishop White, in his funeral sermon for Mary, openly denounced a woman's claim to be head of the Church and the smell of Knox's *First Blast of the Trumpet*, condemning female rule as inherently ungodly, hung heavily in the air. It was not a moment to give further ammunition to critics of queenship, particularly when some of its supposed champions seemed to lack the courage of their own convictions. John Aylmer, one of the Westminster disputants, and a former exile in numerous European locales, composed a riposte to Knox, published in the crucial month of April 1559. Its gist was that Elizabeth was a providential exception to the generality of women, who were 'weak in nature, feeble in body, soft in courage, unskilful in practise, not terrible to the enemy'. God, 'for some secret purpose', had simply broken his own rules. In any case, in England it was not 'so dangerous a matter to have a woman ruler as men take it to be': her power was constrained by laws, by Parliament, and by a generous buffer-zone of dependable male counsel.[25]

Yet the Queen's cautious respect for legal forms was precisely what some leading Protestants were finding intensely frustrating. On 14 April, the day the supremacy bill returned to the Lords, Jewel complained to Peter Martyr of Elizabeth's reluctance to abolish the mass 'without the sanction of law'. If she 'would but banish it from her private chapel, the whole thing might be easily got rid of'.

Protestant impatience was stretched to breaking point by Easter of 1559. At the end of March, the Privy Council ordered a search for perpetrators of 'an outrageous disorder' at Bow Church, London: 'the pulling down of images and the sacrament, and defacing the vestments and books'. In the first week of April, Henry Machyn reported, with mingled fascination and distaste, the details of a funeral at St Thomas of Acre in Cheapside: 'a great company of people'; 'neither singing nor saying till they came to the grave'; 'a collect in English'; 'the new preachers in their gowns like laymen'.

Conservative religion in London was far from cowed. On 25 April, St Mark's Day, Machyn noted various places where the people 'went with their banners abroad in their parish, singing in Latin *Kyrie Eleison* after the old fashion'. But such demonstrations of traditional piety were an invitation to violent evangelical counter-measures. At St Paul's, on Ascension Day, an apprentice seized the processional cross from its bearer, and smashed it to pieces on the ground in front of the large company of participants. He picked up and took off with him the detached figure of Christ, telling them 'he was carrying away the devil's guts'.[26]

The supremacy bill cleared both houses of Parliament by the end of April. There were some amendments at committee stage in the Lords. Most significant was a proviso that no ecclesiastical commissioners appointed by the crown could categorize as heresy anything not judged to be so by scripture, the first four General Councils, any other General Council, or any future Parliament. It was a broad remit, and what was, or was not, condemned by scripture was a perennially moot point. But conservatives were being reassured that their belief in the mass and sacraments, or even in the power of the Pope, could not easily be construed as heresy under the law.

The supremacy bill also included repeal of the Marian heresy laws, and kept the concession for communion in two kinds. That belonged more naturally in the uniformity bill, and its retention suggests that the government anticipated a hard fight over worship and ceremony: there would be a sliver of meaningful reform, even if the uniformity bill failed to pass.[27]

That almost happened. Once more, the Lords Spiritual stirred themselves to flights of impassioned oratory. At the bill's third reading, on 28 April, Bishop Scott argued that the doctrine and religion the bill proposed to abolish were ones 'which our fathers were born, brought up and lived in, and have professed here in this realm without any alteration and change by the space of ten hundred years and more'. Against this, one Act of Parliament was 'but a weak staff to lean unto'.

Contrasts between immemorial faith and flighty innovation equally coloured the arguments of Abbot Feckenham. Truth was discernible by a three-fold test: antiquity of usage, of all men, in all places; internal coherence; ability to breed quiet and obedience. The religion set forth in the Prayer Book was a triple failure. It was hitherto observed only in England, only in Edward's reign, and only for that reign's last two years. It was also 'changeable and variable'. Feckenham pointed to contrasts between the first and second Prayer Books of Edward, to broader disagreements between followers of Luther and Zwingli, and to the fact that both Cranmer and Ridley seemed at various times to be upholders of real presence. He also invited his audience to contemplate 'the sudden mutation of the subjects of this realm since the death of good Queen Mary'. Before, there had been obedience to the law, and respect for images and places of worship. Now, under the influence of 'preachers and scaffold players of this new religion, all things are changed and turned upside down, notwithstanding the Queen's Highness's most godly proclamation made to the contrary'.[28]

When votes were taken, the bill passed: twenty-one to eighteen. It might easily have been different. White and Watson were in the Tower. The now ancient Tunstall of Durham was excused from attending Parliament, and for some reason Gilbert Bourne of Bath and Wells chose not to. Much to his chagrin, no summons was sent to Pole's protégé, Thomas Goldwell of St Asaph. Feckenham, despite his eloquence in the debate, was mysteriously absent from the vote. Several conservative lay lords were in the localities on official duties, and the devoutly Catholic Thomas Percy, Earl of Northumberland, was explicitly ordered to remain in the north. It was decidedly touch-and-go. But from the government's relieved perspective, barely enough was more than sufficient.

## Alterations and Additions

For the second time in a generation, England had broken away from Rome. Yet this time around, as Feria explained it to Philip II, it was a different kind of rupture:

> [I]n the time of King Henry VIII, the whole Parliament consented without any contradiction whatever, except from the bishop of Rochester and Thomas More; whereas now, not a single ecclesiastic has agreed to what the Queen has done, and of the laymen in the lower chamber and in the upper, some opposed on the question of schism, and a great many opposed the heresies.[29]

Dissent, by definition, was not catered for in an 'Act of Uniformity'. Everyone was to attend church, on Sundays and holy days, under penalty of 12*d*. fines for each absence. Books for 'one uniform order of common services and prayers' were to be bought by all parish churches and cathedrals before the Feast of the Birth of John the Baptist (24 June), and to be in use within three weeks of purchase. The clocks had all been stopped, and reset to 1552.

Or perhaps not quite. The new Prayer Book declared itself to be the one in use at the death of Edward VI, but with certain 'alterations and additions'. One of these was the removal from the Litany of the provocative denunciation of 'the bishop of Rome, and all his detestable enormities'; another was the omission of the Black Rubric, explaining how kneeling at communion did not imply adoration. For administration of the communion itself, the words used by the minister in 1549 were coupled to those from 1552, producing a wordy, ambivalent alternative to the Catholic clarity of 'Corpus Christi':

> The body of our Lord Jesus Christ, which was given for thee, preserve thy body and soul unto everlasting life, and take and eat this, in remembrance that Christ died for thee, and feed on him in thy heart by faith with thanksgiving.

The precise eucharistic doctrine of the Church of England was, once again, destined to be a matter of informed guesswork.

It was certainly no surrender to the notion of real presence as Roman Catholics understood it. The 1552 rubric for the curate to take home and dine on leftover bread remained – a reason to think there was no permanent change in the nature of the elements. But the revised wording nonetheless stepped back from the stark memorialism of the second Edwardian Prayer Book. There was a suggestion that something 'happened' at the moment of communion, and an encouragement to reverential reception.

What the celebrant should wear while reciting these words was a critical question, addressed both in the act itself, and in a rubric of the Prayer Book. For communion and other services, 'until other order shall be therein taken by the Queen's majesty', ministers were to 'use such ornaments as were in use by the authority of Parliament in the second year of the reign of King Edward VI'.[30] That too was ambiguous: for the whole of Edward's second 'regnal year' (28 January 1548 to 27 January 1549) priests said the Latin mass in traditional Catholic vestments. But since the first Uniformity Act passed in January 1549, it seems very likely the order of the 1549 Prayer Book was intended, with cope rather than chasuble for communion.

For the returning exiles, and many Protestants who endured the crisis of Mary's reign at home, even that was bad enough. Sandys offered Parker a decidedly optimistic reading: 'Our gloss upon this text is that we shall not be forced to use them, but that others in the meantime shall not convey them away.'[31]

The 'alterations and additions' were not in themselves particularly drastic ones, and in spring 1559 Parliament largely resuscitated the still warm corpse of the Edwardian Church. This was underlined by measures restoring first fruits and tenths to the crown, and dissolving once again the fledgling Marian monasteries and chantries. Nonetheless, for those with eyes to see, a significant watershed had been reached.

For thirty years and more, reformers had striven to bring Church and society to a restored condition of apostolic purity by stages and degrees. The second Prayer Book was, reformers agreed, an improvement on the first, and – had King Edward lived to adulthood, or Queen Jane's backers succeeded – Cranmer would likely have drafted a third Prayer Book, and perhaps a fourth. The Stranger churches lighted the path to further liturgical and disciplinary reform, and its intoxicating possibilities were experienced by exiles in the free air of Frankfurt, Strassburg, Zürich and Geneva. 'Reformation' was a journey; a continual striving after elusive perfection, in the world and in oneself. The latest measures of 1559 were a staging-post, not a final destination; earnest reformers like Jewel would not long rest content with any 'leaden mediocrity'.[32] What was not yet obvious was that the new Supreme Governor simply did not see things this way. Barring some tying up of loose ends, and the necessary measures of implementation and enforcement, the Reformation, Queen Elizabeth believed, was over.

### Old Bishops, New Bishops

Enforcement of the parliamentary settlement of 1559 was at the same time a matter of discovering who was prepared to enforce it. Parliament was dissolved on 8 May, and a fortnight later, members of the Privy Council were constituted as 'ecclesiastical commissioners', to administer the Oath of Supremacy to clerics and office-holders. First in the queue were the bishops.

Their numbers were sadly depleted. In addition to Pole, several had died in the disease year of 1558 and were not replaced: James Brooks of Gloucester, John Christopherson of Chichester, William Glyn of Bangor, Maurice Griffith of Rochester, John Holyman of Bristol, John Hopton of Norwich. Feelings against the survivors were running high. John Aylmer snarled that some were gone already to taste their posthumous reward, 'and those that remain must follow, unless they wash away the spots of blood that hang upon their rochets with floods of tears of repentance'. The bishops deserved suspension, John Parkhurst told Bullinger, 'not only from office, but from a halter'.[33]

Alvaro de Quadra, the Spanish prelate replacing Feria as Philip's ambassador in May 1559, expected the oath to be put to the bishops and for all to be 'deprived at one blow'. It did not happen like that. Cecil's 'Device' envisaged the bishops being put in their place, but also remaining in their place. The tenacity of episcopal resistance in Parliament dented the expectation that they would continue to serve, but did not entirely remove it.

One deprivation, at least, was inevitable. The oath was put to Bonner first, on 29 May, and on refusal he was immediately deprived, amidst concerns for his safety at the hands of a vengeful London populace. Other likely recalcitrants were preceded against next: White, Watson, Scott, Oglethorpe, Richard Pate of Worcester and Ralph Baines of Coventry and Lichfield. Thomas Goldwell, the companion of Pole's Italian exile, fled once more to the continent before he could join these brethren in refusing the oath.[34]

All of these men (bar Bonner) were Queen Mary's appointments, new-breed bishops of the Pole era. But there were others with records of faithful episcopal and governmental service stretching back to the early 1540s: Thomas Thirlby of Ely, for example, and the former Lord Chancellor, Nicholas Heath of York, who continued to attend meetings of the Privy Council through to the start of 1559. Thirlby, unusually among Marian bishops, had been gainfully employed on ambassadorial work by the regime of Edward VI. The diplomat Sir John Mason reminded Cecil in March 1559 how Thirlby 'did great service. And so do I assuredly think he will in this time.'

Mason was proved wrong. 'I confess,' sighed Elizabeth, 'I am grieved for York and Ely.' The remark was made to a royal servant of even longer standing, Cuthbert Tunstall of Durham, who came south in July 1559 to seek audience with the Queen. She and her councillors sincerely hoped to win Tunstall round, but it was the octogenarian bishop who made the running in their encounter, telling Elizabeth that she could have all of them serving in her Council, if only she were a Catholic. Tunstall brought with him handwritten documents by Henry VIII against sacramentarian heresy, 'and begged her, at least, to respect the will of her father'.

In the end, only two of Queen Mary's bishops agreed to remain in office in 1559: the aged and undistinguished Anthony Kitchin of Llandaff, and the still less distinguished Thomas Stanley, absentee bishop of Sodor and Man, who a couple of years later was reported to be living away from his island diocese at Durham, 'at ease, and as merry as Pope Joan'.[35]

Except for these scrapings at the bottom, the episcopal barrel had to be completely refilled. Elizabeth's choice for Canterbury was Matthew Parker, a distinguished scholar, though not possessed of much high-level administrative experience. There was a filial connection. Elizabeth spoke relatively little about her mother, but Parker was Anne Boleyn's chaplain, and before her execution in 1536 she commended her infant daughter to Parker's spiritual care. Just as important was the fact that Parker, like Cecil, stayed in England through Mary's reign. It is striking that the two men Elizabeth chose to play leading roles in the making of her religious settlement were, like her, former Nicodemites. Whether Parker, like Cecil and Elizabeth, actually attended mass is tantalizingly unclear. In a letter to Nicholas Bacon, Parker referred to an injury sustained falling from his horse while fleeing from 'such as sought for me to my peril', and it was later said that Parker 'lurked secretly' at a friend's house, perhaps in the vicinity of Cambridge.[36] But no one who remained in England through all the days of 'idolatry', and who did not seek the crown of martyrdom, could easily boast of their spotlessness.

While episcopal subscriptions were being demanded in the spring and summer of 1559, Cecil drew up lists of potential or actual replacements. One identified twenty-six 'spiritual men without promotion at this present'. Around half of these were exiles, but the others were stay-at-homes, and a few had even held office in the Marian Church. For the Nicodemite Cecil, as for his mistress, a record of aversion to compromise of any sort was not in itself a powerful recommendation. In the end, exiles did supply the largest pool of qualified candidates for office, and twelve of eighteen nominations to bishoprics in the first two years of the reign went to émigrés. The earliest choices were confirmed, along with Parker, in June and July of 1559: Edmund Grindal for the key diocese of London, Richard Cox for Ely, John Jewel for Salisbury, William Barlow for Chichester and John Scory for Hereford.[37]

These were well-travelled men, but one destination was missing from their résumés: Geneva. A few successful candidates for bishoprics had links to Zürich; most belonged to the Strassburg-Frankfurt group, and to Cox's 'Prayer Book' party in the strife over ceremonies. 'Genevans' were often slower than other émigrés to return, some, like William Whittingham and Anthony Gilby, remaining to see to conclusion a major scholarly project of their exile – a new version of the complete bible in English, with extensive (and sometimes polemical) notes and commentary. A handful of talented, high-profile ministers with Genevan connections, like Thomas Lever, John Pedder and Miles Coverdale (a former bishop), were considered for highest office, but in the end passed over. Elizabeth never forgave John Knox for his *First Blast*. From the outset she associated Geneva with seditious notions of resistance.

Calvin himself wrote to Elizabeth in January 1559, enclosing a copy of a new edition of his commentary on Isaiah, dedicated to the Queen, but his gift was coldly received. Cecil was also in all likelihood less than delighted with the letter he received at the same time, urging him to use his influence with Elizabeth to advance the Gospel, while reminding him of his own silence while God's children were being slaughtered: 'if hitherto you have been timid, you may now make up for your deficiency by the ardour of your zeal'. Once the depth of Elizabeth's resentment became clear, Calvin tried to distance himself from Knox, denying knowledge of the publication of his work, but the damage was done.

By May of 1559, Knox himself was back in Scotland – Elizabeth refused permission for him to pass through England on the way. His preaching added fuel to iconoclastic rioting, which had broken out in several towns; the start of a Protestant uprising against the pro-French government of Mary of Guise. The leading Protestant nobles who banded together as 'the Lords of the Congregation' begged for English assistance, and Knox wrote to Cecil with effusive promises of 'perpetual concord betwixt these two realms'. Cecil made some efforts to effect a reconciliation, but Knox did himself few favours in a justificatory letter sent to the Queen in July. He stuck unapologetically by the arguments of the *First Blast*, instructing Elizabeth to acknowledge her complete dependence on God's special providence, while tactlessly reminding her how, in Mary's reign, 'for fear of your life, you did decline from God, and bow in idolatry'. Annotations on a copy of the letter, which may be Elizabeth's own, observed that the 'apology' was worse than the original offence; Knox's views 'put a firebrand to the state'.[38]

The Queen suspected Genevan exiles of lacking respect for royal authority; they in return suspected her and her ministers of lacking serious commitment to the cause of reform. Zealous exiles from places other than Geneva were also sometimes reluctant or cautious about accepting high office: Thomas Sampson, David Whitehead and Alexander Nowell, a critic of the Prayer Book who remained in Frankfurt, all seem to have turned down offers of bishoprics. Others, like John Parkhurst, nominated to Norwich, were slow to accept. In late 1559, Parkhurst, who evidently had a thing for hanging metaphors, boasted he had so far 'kept my neck out of that halter'.

There were few principled theological objections to episcopacy as such, though persecution had given the office of bishop a bad name in Protestant circles, despite the heroic witness of Cranmer, Ferrar, Hooper and Ridley. Jewel reassured a Zürich friend that the new bishops would be consecrated without 'superstitious and offensive ceremonies'. To remove temptations of 'royal pomp and courtly bustle', episcopal wealth was 'now diminished and reduced to a reasonable amount'. This was putting a brave face on an unpalatable parliamentary measure. The Exchange Act allowed the crown, during vacancy of a see, to trade impropriated tithes and rectories for episcopal estates. Some godly reformers detected here echoes of the cynical exploitation of the Church by the government of Northumberland. James Pilkington (later appointed to Durham) refused nomination to Winchester in 1559 on the terms being offered. After depriving the Marian bishops, Elizabeth kept sees vacant to maximize revenues. Most replacements, Parker included, were not consecrated till December 1559, or early the following year.[39] In the meantime, the business of restoring the Gospel to England had got underway without them.

### Visitation and Resistance

Preparations for a nationwide royal visitation began in May 1559, with the drawing up of lists of visitors to tour the country in six circuits, on the pattern of 1547. Lords Lieutenant and prominent county gentry were appointed to the commissions, but the actual work was undertaken by small clusters of clerical commissioners and lay lawyers. In each circuit, the lead cleric was a former exile: Robert Horne for London, Ely and Norwich; Thomas Becon for Canterbury, Rochester, Chichester and Winchester; Thomas Bentham for the midland dioceses; Jewel for the West Country; Sandys for York, and Richard Davies for Wales. And just as in 1547, the visitors interpreted their remit in the most Protestant way possible.

The visitation started in London on 19 July, as Cuthbert Tunstall – last of the Catholic bishops to hold out, and the only one to have his authority formally inhibited for the visitation – was arriving to make his doomed plea to the Queen. Tunstall was appalled by what he witnessed in the capital over the following weeks, protesting impotently to Cecil that he would not allow in Durham what 'I do plainly see to be set forth here in London, as pulling down of altars, defacing of churches by taking away of crucifixes'. The rood of St Paul's, that barometer of the religious weather, came down on 12 August, and eleven days later, there were bonfires of roods and images in St Paul's churchyard, outside St Thomas of Acre in Cheapside, and at other places in the city. Charles Wriothesley recorded conflagrations of copes, vestments, altar cloths, books, banners and 'other ornaments of the churches'. These were not ancient treasures, but expensive recent purchases: the chronicler took care to note that all this 'cost above £2000 renewing again in Queen Mary's time'. Machyn observed ruefully that the Marys, Johns and other images 'were burned with great wonder'.[40]

Nationwide, the visitation followed a regular pattern. The visitors arrived at a conveniently located church, to which churchwardens from the vicinity had been summoned. Proceedings began with a sermon, explaining and justifying what was to come, and the commission was read out, along with the articles and injunctions: it was, like previous royal visitations, a profoundly didactic public process. Churchwardens were sworn to make diligent enquiry, and to return at a future date with reports on the state of their parish. Clergy were summoned to attend at a specified time, to exhibit letters of ordination, and to subscribe to the royal supremacy, Prayer Book and Injunctions.

The subsequent work of burning and destruction was carried out most thoroughly in London, though there were conflagrations in other towns, in answer to the article inquiring whether images, 'and all other monuments of feigned and false miracles, pilgrimages, idolatry, and superstition', were 'removed, abolished and destroyed'. At Grantham in Lincolnshire, 'the rood, Mary and John, and all the other idols and pictures', along with liturgical and other Catholic books, were burned at the market cross. In Exeter, the townsfolk who venerated the images were forced to throw them into the fire. At York, Edwin Sandys preached on Jesus evicting the money-changers from the Temple, and on the duty of reformers to destroy as well as build, uproot as well as plant. The English, said Sandys, were blessed with a sovereign who, following Christ's example, had 'overthrown all polluted and defiled altars'. Entering his new episcopal seat of Worcester in the wake of the visitation, Sandys organized a burning of 'the cross and the image of Our Lady' in the cathedral churchyard. An account of the incident by the chronicler John Steynor perhaps points to the rood and an accompanying statue of Mary, but his lack of reference to the complementary 'John' might imply a new shrine image, erected in Mary's reign, a replacement for 'Our Lady of Worcester' destroyed in 1538.[41]

Most of the articles were based on ones used by Cranmer for his Canterbury visitation of 1548, though churchwardens were now asked 'whether you know any that keep in their houses undefaced any images, tables, pictures, paintings ... and especially such as have been set up in churches, chapels or oratories'. There was a determination not to allow any repetition of what had happened in Edward's reign, the smuggling away of superstitious (and costly) objects, in hope or expectation of change. In the northern circuit – the only part of the visitation for which detailed records survive – some parishioners were caught in the act of furtive removals. At St Peter's in Chester, the visitors learned that Mistress Dutton 'keepeth secretly a rood, two pictures and a mass book'; at St Mary's, Peter Fletcher 'hath certain images which he keepeth secretly'. But at Bridlington on the Yorkshire coast, the wardens could report only that 'the images be secretly kept', and at Osmotherley, on the remote western edge of the Moors, the word was 'that their images be conveyed away, but by whom they know not'. A few months later, Thomas Bentham, freshly installed bishop of Coventry and Lichfield, would complain of images 'reserved and conveyed away' across his large diocese by those 'hoping and looking for a new day'.[42]

Returning to London from his native West Country, and 'a long and trouble-some commission for the establishment of religion', John Jewel described for Peter Martyr a veritable 'wilderness of superstition sprung up in the darkness of the Marian times'. Churches were full of votive relics of saints, and cathedrals – he visited Gloucester, Bristol, Bath, Wells, Exeter and Salisbury – were 'nothing else but dens of thieves'. Nonetheless, people seemed 'sufficiently well disposed towards religion', with most of the opposition coming from priests, especially those 'who had once been on our side'.[43]

The northern visitors reported no cases of mass being said openly after midsummer 1559. As in 1553–4, the public face of worship was rapidly and comprehensively transformed. There was no space for negotiated dissent. Rather pathetically, the churchwardens of Yatton in Somerset recorded in early 1559 an outlay of 4d., 'at the visitation, for the continuance of Mary and John' – seemingly, the cost of a formal written petition to be allowed to keep their rood. Yet within a few months they found themselves shelling out the slightly larger sum of 5d. for 'taking down the rood', and another 6d. 'in expenses at taking down the images'. Churchwardens' accounts from across the country once again constitute a tableau of broad compliance with the wishes of authority: roods, images and tabernacles removed; Prayer Books, bibles and Paraphrases purchased.[44]

At St Andrew Hubbard in London, the switch-over from mass to Lord's Supper, with communion now in two kinds for the laity, was marked by the wardens paying out a substantial sum for the melting down and exchanging of 'two chalices with covers, weighing 32½ ounces, for a communion cup weighing 30½ ounces'.[45] Chalices were designed for use of the priest only; a 'communion cup' was a larger vessel, for the congregation as a whole to sip from. Here, it seems, was a literal recasting of priorities – a metallic metaphor for the swift, complete and purposeful transformation of parish liturgical and devotional life the visitors set out to oversee.

Time would have another story to tell. Twice before, in 1547 and 1553, the start of a new reign signalled a dramatic reversal of religious policy. Yet 1559 was not quite a moment of déjà vu. On both sides of a widening religious divide, local people had acquired a greater understanding of what was at stake, of what the changes meant, and of where they might lead. They were, in conse-quence, considerably less complacent and noticeably less compliant.

Lay Protestants, particularly in London, wanted not simply to follow, but to lead. An innovation, chronicled with absorbed disapprobation by Henry Machyn, was congregational singing of psalms. 'Metrification' of the psalms, so they could be sung by laypeople in unison, was a French-Genevan innovation, taken up in Edward's reign by the evangelical courtier Thomas Sternhold, whose first collection of metrical psalms, published in 1549, was expanded in multiple editions by the clergyman John Hopkins. The habit never really took off among Protestants under Edward, perhaps because of the Edwardian

Church's closeness to Bullinger's Zürich, hostile to the use in worship of music of any kind. But exile communities – in Strassburg and Frankfurt, as well as in Geneva – made psalm-singing a regular part of their liturgy, despite lack of provision for it in the Prayer Book of 1552.

Absence of prescription in the Prayer Book of 1559, or in the visitation articles, did little to discourage a burgeoning fashion. The Injunctions stated that 'modest and distinct' singing, during or after service, was permissible, but said nothing specifically about psalms. In September 1559, at St Antholin's, Budge Row, morning prayer began 'after Geneva fashion . . . men and women all do sing, and boys'. This was a 'godly' parish, where Elizabeth's accession was followed by rapid re-establishment of provision begun in Edward's reign for a 'lectureship' – a salaried minister's position dedicated solely to preaching. Londoners' psalm-singing was encouraged by a minister of French extraction, Jean Veron. There was singing to 'the tune of Geneva ways' in early 1560 at his induction to the parish of St Martin Ludgate, and at a sermon he delivered at Paul's Cross: all joined in, 'young and old'.

Singing is a powerful agent of social cohesion, binding people collectively familiar with words and melody into tighter knots of solidarity and resolution. The psalms were texts well suited to this purpose, replete with references to suffering, persecution and God's judgements on the wicked. Jewel reported in March 1560 that the habit was already spreading beyond London, and it was now possible to find 6,000 people singing together at Paul's Cross after services: 'this sadly annoys the mass priests, and the devil'.[46]

The arrival of royal visitors was sometimes a spur to direct action. At Bures, Suffolk, in September 1559, local activists were inspired to hack down the rood and other screens in the church, in the process damaging tombs belonging to the Waldegrave family, powerful local conservatives. The Waldegraves not only indicted the iconoclasts at the Bury St Edmunds sessions, they complained about them to the Privy Council; this at a time when zealots were attacking old tombs and funeral monuments in London and elsewhere, convinced – with some justification – that these were testaments in brass or stone to the ancient belief in purgatory.

The Queen responded in September 1560 with a proclamation condemning any damage to tombs as a 'barbarous disorder'. It insisted that monuments to the dead in churches were 'set up only to the memory of them to their posterity . . . and not for any religious honour' – a curious claim when countless old memorials were embellished with requests for onlookers to say prayers for the deceased's soul. Interference with the family monuments of the nobility or gentry, however, was a threat to their social power, nested as it was in lineage and inheritance. It was a line Elizabeth was not prepared to see crossed. Protestants liked to compare Elizabeth to Deborah, the (sole) female judge of biblical Israel; here was a sign she was no zealous Josiah.[47]

Most of the time, the Elizabethan authorities, including the newly appointed bishops, worried less about people going too fast, and more about them not going fast enough. Despite the zeal and energy of the visitors, implementation of the 1559 settlement was patchy and often sluggish, with churchwardens frequently proving less than fully reliable agents of enforcement. Articles and injunctions for follow-up episcopal visitations in 1560 and 1561 enquired endlessly about the retention of altars, images and Catholic service books; about priests celebrating communions for the dead; about private use of Latin primers and rosary beads.

Episcopal anxieties were not misplaced: altars were still standing in many parishes in 1561, not only in traditionalist Yorkshire, Cheshire and Staffordshire, but in Buckinghamshire, Berkshire, Hampshire, Oxfordshire and Essex. Roods came down relatively swiftly in most places, but there was a noticeable paro-chial reluctance to remove the frequently elaborate lofts on which they stood. Bishop Grindal launched a campaign to sweep rood lofts out of London churches in 1560, but there was resistance elsewhere, even after a royal order of 1561 commanded them cut down 'for avoiding of much strife and contention'.[48]

The recalcitrance of local communities was no doubt partly prudential. Elizabeth was a young, unmarried queen without heirs of her body. Parishes had recently undergone one round of expensive liturgical refurbishment, and had no desire to dig deeply into pockets again if the Protestant restoration turned out to be impermanent. It seems improbable, however, that the finan-cial investment in Catholic paraphernalia can be separated neatly or easily from investment of an emotional kind. People were often slow to comply with orders against 'idolatry' and 'superstition' precisely because they understood them all too well, and disagreed with them. And there was another crucial factor in play: the attitudes of the clergy.

Conventional wisdom holds that, barring a handful of Marian zealots, the parish priests gave very little trouble to the new regime. They had learned the habit of dutiful conformity, and few were inspired to follow the lead of the hierarchy. This was not, however, the perception of the incoming bishops. In May 1559, Grindal anticipated that not only the episcopate, but 'many other beneficed persons' would reject the changes:

> [W]e are labouring under a great dearth of godly ministers, for many who have fallen off in this persecution are now become papists in heart; and those who had been heretofore, so to speak, moderate papists, are now the most obstinate.

Grindal recognized how the Marian years had stiffened the resolve of the Catholic clergy. The perception was shared by John Jewel: 'Now that religion is everywhere changed, the mass-priests absent themselves altogether from public worship, as if it were the greatest impiety to have anything in common with the people of God.'[49]

It is hard to say exactly how many rectors and vicars conformed to the Elizabethan Settlement, and harder still to judge how they 'conformed' to it. It is certainly the case that most parochial clergy remained in post, and adapted themselves to the changes. Thomas Butler did so in Much Wenlock, as Christopher Trychay did in Morebath and Robert Parkyn in Adwick-le-Street. All three were articulate Catholic conservatives, if not ones cut from the cloth of exiles or martyrs. Their cultural cousins filled parish livings throughout the land.

Nonetheless, an often-quoted figure of only about 300 clergy deprived, or removing themselves, from ministry for reasons of conscience is certainly too low. The true figure, through to the mid-1560s, is likely to be closer to 800: this at a time when the influenza epidemic, and an acute shortage of candidates for ordination, left many parishes short of pastoral care, and the Church struggling to fill vacancies. In the diocese of Chichester, at least seventy-four parishes lost their priest due to death between November 1558 and 1561. Almost as many (sixty-one, from a total of 287 in the diocese) saw their incumbent deprived in the same period. In the diocese of Rochester, around a quarter of priests resigned or were deprived, and a fifth of the parishes in Grindal's London were similarly affected. Interestingly, the percentage was markedly lower in more 'conservative' regions, such as the Welsh dioceses. The most persuasive inference is that where attitudes and identities were forged in closer encounter with the Protestant 'other', Catholic consciences were more finely tuned.

Turnover would have been greater still had the authorities shown any real determination to weed out all the unreliables from the ranks of a now officially Protestant ministry. That would have meant a purge on a massive, unmanageable scale. Of ninety senior clergy summoned before the visitation commissioners for the northern circuit in 1559, only twenty-one appeared and subscribed, while thirty-six openly refused. Among the lower clergy, the names of 312 subscribers were recorded in 1559, probably only a third of the priests active in the province of York at the time.

Significantly, what the authorities sought was 'subscription' – a generalized acknowledgement of assent – rather than what was actually specified in the Supremacy Act, the swearing of a solemn oath on the Gospels. That might have piled more pressure on the consciences of conservative clergy than those consciences were capable of bearing. Former exiles fulminated against Nicodemites, but the Injunctions themselves drew a discreet line under the past. They admitted that there were many ministers who 'have of long time favoured fond phantasies rather than God's truth'. People, however, were not to attack or abuse them; instead, 'use them charitably and reverently for their office and ministration sake'. Even with this willingness to let bygones be bygones, the Church struggled to meet its pastoral obligations: Richard Cox of Ely reckoned in 1561 that of 152 cures in his diocese 'there are duly served but only 52'. Jewel of Salisbury reflected ruefully that 'it is no easy matter to drag the chariot without horses, especially uphill'.[50]

As bishops like Cox and Jewel came in, many of their senior clergy went out. The rate of resignation and deprivation among diocesan office-holders (chancellors, archdeacons, deans) and cathedral prebendaries was significantly higher than among ordinary parish clergy. Of such dignitaries not felled by epidemic disease in 1559–60, fewer than half were prepared to continue in office, and of those, many were regarded by their new bishops as alarmingly undependable. The result, in many places, was administrative turmoil. When Archbishop Parker sent letters to all bishops and archdeacons in 1560 and 1561, asking to be supplied with the names of cathedral clergy and of 'all and singular parsons and vicars' within their jurisdictions, along with details of residential, educational and marital status, he was not so much setting a firm hand to the ecclesiastical tiller as sending out a message in a bottle. His circulars were a confession of frank ignorance about the state of the Church's depleted resources.[51]

In circumstances of acute shortage of clergy, standards were inevitably relaxed. In London, Grindal ordained no fewer than 104 candidates to the priesthood in the year from March 1560 to March 1561. James Calfhill, himself one of this batch of quick-bake clerics, conceded a couple of years later that the shortage of good preachers was deeply regrettable, and that 'the inferior sort ... came from the shop, from the forge, from the wherry, from the loom' – though he still stoutly maintained they were better men than the Sir Johns of popish days.[52]

Church and faith were in a state of flux and confusion at the start of Elizabeth's second year. Yet the prevailing thought in the Queen's mind was that, after her own years of uncertainty and danger, matters of religion had now been brought to a satisfactory conclusion. Unusually, the 1559 Injunctions were from the outset intended, not simply as an administrative instrument for the visitation, but as a permanent set of rules for the orderly running of the Church, to be read out to parishioners four times in the year.

The Injunctions supplied the promised 'further order' for clerical attire. This was to follow the rule of the last year of Edward VI: the surplice (rather than cope or chasuble) for services, and for off-duty wear, a seemly gown and the 'square cap' that many reformers associated with the persecuting Catholic clergy. A supplementary 'Interpretation', issued by the bishops in 1560, specified 'the cope in the ministration of the Lord's Supper, and the surplice at all other ministrations'.

This was clear (if to some, unwelcome) enough. But in other respects the Injunctions worked to obfuscate rather than elucidate what expected practice should be. The scope and character of royal power over the Church were addressed, but hardly definitively settled. Elizabeth denounced false 'scruples' about the Supremacy Oath. It was simply a malicious misinterpretation that the Queen would 'challenge authority and power of ministry of divine offices in the Church'. That was, perhaps, a dependable pledge that she was not about to start ministering sacraments on her own account. But if it sounded to anyone like a more general promise to leave spiritual matters firmly in the hands of the bishops, then the added assurance that she would never push further than those 'noble kings of famous memory, King Henry VIII and King Edward VI' should have given them pause for reflection.

Other injunctions were not so much obscure as inconsistent. There was contradictory advice about sermons: one injunction said parsons and vicars should preach in their own churches at least once a month; another, that only licensed preachers could deliver sermons (others would read from the homilies), and preach at least once a quarter. Either way, in the view of many Protestants, it was not enough preaching. As to sacraments, the Prayer Book stipulated ordinary bread for the communion, but the Injunctions, 'for the more reverence to be given to these holy mysteries', were unabashed in requiring parishes to get hold of the kind of wafers 'which served for the use of the private mass', if a little thicker, and without any embossed pictures.

Another jarring mismatch was over the placement of the communion table itself. The expectation of the Prayer Book was that it would stand permanently in the chancel, oriented east–west, and only at communion time have 'a fair white linen cloth upon it'. The Injunctions directed otherwise. The table would be carried into the chancel for communion services, but at other times should be 'set in the place where the altar stood, and there commonly covered'. The 'table' of the Prayer Book was the 'holy table' in the Injunctions, where its default alignment was the north–south one suggestive of a sacrificial altar.

All of these were steps backward from the logic and momentum of Edwardian reform. So too was an injunction commanding people in church to uncover their heads and bow whenever the name of Jesus was mentioned, and another allowing processions to take place at Rogationtide for purposes of 'beating the bounds' of the parish. The Injunctions contained little of much comfort for Catholics, robbed of their mass and images, but plenty to give irritation and offence to fervent Protestants. These included a grudging concession that clerical marriage was lawful, but that due to many ministers' 'lack of discreet and sober behaviour', approval for any match must be secured from the bishop and two justices of the peace.

In this, as in virtually all else, the Injunctions were an exposition of the new order in religion to satisfy the preferences and prejudices of the Queen. Elizabeth's true religious convictions – a studied mystery in Mary's reign – were in 1559 unknown to most of her subjects and even to her bishops and leading clergymen. She had made various public, and politically expedient, gestures of commitment to the 'gospel', and she had shown herself willing enough to agree to her councillors' preference for the restoration of the 1552 Prayer Book. But the Injunctions were an early indication that Elizabeth's Protestantism was of a distinctly wilful and wayward kind. Further, deeply disconcerting, evidence of this was shortly to be forthcoming. For the moment, the Injunctions simply declared the alteration of religion to be completed; case closed. The Queen ordered her subjects henceforth 'to forbear all vain and contentious disputations in matters of religion'.[53] It was a little too late for that.

# 15

## UNSETTLED ENGLAND

### Enormities in the Queen's Closet

No sooner did the Royal Injunctions forbid contentious disputations than they broke out at the very heart of the new regime. The cause was a small object in the Queen's Chapel Royal. In the summer of 1559, while Elizabeth was on progress in Kent and Surrey, the furnishings of the chapel were reformed. Elizabeth returned to court at the end of September, and on 5 October, for the wedding of a lady-in-waiting, she ordered a silver crucifix and candles to be placed on the chapel's communion table.

It was an argument waiting to happen. Earlier that year on St George's Day, during the court procession of the Knights of the Garter, Elizabeth had noticed an omission from the usual ceremonial. 'Where', she wanted to know 'were the crosses?' The implausible explanation was that the gold and silver processional crosses had been removed to the Tower for safe keeping. Elizabeth's subsequent insistence on crucifix and candlesticks for her own chapel was a declaration that she was not to be pushed around.

The appearance of these ceremonial items caused uproar among her chaplains, but Elizabeth relented for only a few days. It was not a fuss over nothing. The place where the Queen worshipped was scarcely a 'private' one, but a shop-window of royal preferences and priorities. Ambassador de Quadra's eyes lit up at this hopeful hint of further changes: 'the crucifixes and vestments that were burnt a month ago are now set up again in the royal chapel, as they soon will be all over the kingdom'.

That, no doubt, was the fear of the bishops-elect. Jewel confessed his worry to Peter Martyr that the 'ill-omened' silver cross will 'soon be drawn into a precedent'. 'The wretched multitude', complained Thomas Sampson, 'are not only rejoicing at this, but will imitate it.' One of that multitude, the London chronicler Henry Machyn, described with evident satisfaction the uncomfortable backdrop for Protestant clergymen preaching in the Chapel Royal at the turn of 1560, 'the cross and two candles burning, and the tables standing altar-wise'.

Former exiles turned instinctively to Zürich for advice: in January 1560 Sampson wanted to know if Peter Martyr, Bullinger and Ochino agreed he should quit the ministry were the Queen to order cross and candles for all churches. The incoming bishops had been lobbying the Queen since October, when Sir Francis Knollys, among the most fervently Protestant of the lay councillors, wished Parker success in his campaign against 'enormities yet in the Queen's closet retained'. Richard Cox drafted a letter to Elizabeth explaining why he could not officiate in the Chapel Royal, 'the cross and lights being there'. A petition from a group of senior clergymen begged the Queen to consider how 'infinite millions of souls have been cast into eternal damnation by the occasion of images used in places of worship'.[1]

The bishops seemed of one mind, yet on 5 February 1560, the issue was formally debated among them at court: Jewel and Grindal versus Parker and Cox. There is no record of the disputation, and it is hard to believe Parker and Cox were sudden converts to the crucifix. Most likely, they agreed, reluctantly, to represent the royal view of the cross as an 'indifferent' item.

The stakes were high. 'Matters are come to that pass,' Jewel wrote on the eve of the debate, 'that either the crosses and tin, which we have everywhere broken in pieces, must be restored, or our bishoprics relinquished.' Edwin Sandys told Peter Martyr that Elizabeth was serious about reintroducing roods, with their figures of Mary and John, to parish churches, considering it 'not contrary to the Word of God, nay, rather for the advantage of the church'. His 'vehement' dissent, he claimed, almost cost him his bishopric.[2]

The immediate outcome was not so much compromise as stalemate. Perhaps as a result of the court debate, Elizabeth realized there was virtually no support among bishops or councillors for a restoration of parish roods, and dropped the policy. Grindal's accelerated campaign against rood lofts in London was an effort to capitalize on this while the going was good. At the beginning of March, a relieved Richard Cox wrote that 'no crucifix is nowadays to be seen in any of our churches'.[3] That was not quite true: Elizabeth stubbornly refused to give up her own cross. Rather like the Stranger Churches had been under Edward, the Chapel Royal was a pointer, hopeful or alarming, to further possibilities of change.

The row brought into the open an inconvenient truth: the Queen's priorities were not the same as those of almost her entire ecclesiastical establishment. The idea that Elizabeth was cynically uninterested in religion, or that her religious beliefs are completely impenetrable, is misplaced. There is much evidence, not least from her own writings, of a woman serious and devout in her prayerful relationship with God. But the label English reformers were starting to apply to themselves – 'Protestant' – seems at best an inexact fit.[4]

Certainly, Elizabeth was anti-papal: she was, after all, the daughter of Anne Boleyn. She was likewise impatient of 'superstition' and scholastic sacramentalism. Her endorsement of the imagery of the cross, and a leaning towards some kind of belief in real presence in the eucharist, has affinities with German Lutheranism, though the Queen's distaste for clerical marriage would scarcely have met with Luther's approval. She had a penchant for elaborate church music, and did not care to enquire too closely into the opinions of those who provided it for her. The leading court composer at the start of her reign, Thomas Tallis, was certainly a Catholic sympathizer. He would later be joined by a brilliant younger colleague whose leanings towards the old faith were even more evident: William Byrd.

There is something to be said for the suggestion that Elizabeth's faith was really that of an old-fashioned 'evangelical' of the generation bestriding her childhood. Her motto, after all, was *semper eadem*, always the same. The idea of finding solace in devout meditation on the cross of Christ was one that had been important to her last step-mother, Catherine Parr.[5] But the fervency of that first generation, and its tendency to define itself by hostility to its enemies, seems lacking in Elizabeth.

The Queen's religion was not that of her father. But it shared with his the quality of appearing idiosyncratic, uncategorizable. The difference was that while Henry's faith expressed itself in aspirations towards absolute domination, Elizabeth's was formed over two decades of finding herself at the mercy of others. She had learned the virtues of inwardness, and of knowing when, and when not, to take a principled stand. At heart, Elizabeth was a Nicodemite queen, and willing to reign as a queen of Nicodemites. She had no reason to love 'popery', but she did not see Catholics, even Roman ones, as the artful agents of Antichrist.

In so far as they already sensed this, her leading subjects found it hard to understand, and harder still to stomach. John Jewel's 'Challenge Sermon', preached before a huge crowd at Paul's Cross on 26 November 1559, and later repeated at court and again at Paul's Cross, was a defiant declaration of theological war. Jewel offered unconditional surrender to his Romanist adversaries if they could supply 'one sufficient sentence', from scripture, the Fathers or old General Councils, to prove that in its first 600 years of existence the Church maintained prayer in a foreign tongue, private or sacrificial masses, communion in one kind, transubstantiation or papal supremacy.[6]

Meanwhile, from Scotland, Christopher Goodman sent Cecil an aggrieved inventory of everything in the settlement that 'wounded the hearts of the godly'. One problem was the removal from the Litany of 'the necessary prayer against the Romish Antichrist'; another, 'which sticketh much in the hearts of many', was the failure to impose sentences of death upon the 'bloody bishops, and known murderers of God's people'.[7]

Scotland was much in Cecil's mind. By the late summer of 1559, France was sending troops in significant numbers to crush the Protestant revolt, and the Lords of the Congregation renewed their pleas for aid. Cecil was eager to oblige, from genuine sympathy with their cause, and because he had come to see Scotland as the key to English security. Henry II's death in July 1559 put his son, Francis II, on the French throne. Francis's wife was Mary Queen of Scots, now Queen of France too.

She wanted to be Queen of England. To his fury, Cecil learned from the ambassador in Paris, Nicholas Throckmorton, that Francis and Mary were using the English royal arms. He sat down to compose one of his regular 'Memorials'. It proposed a Scotland free from both French influence and 'from all idolatry', united politically with England. If Mary and Francis would not agree, the Scottish Parliament should transfer the crown to the next heir.[8] Cecil's instincts were not those of a firebrand like Knox or Goodman. But he arrived at a similarly radical conclusion to theirs: political and religious necessity could justify the removal of an anointed monarch.

In December 1559, all of Elizabeth's councillors, with the exception of the conservative Earl of Arundel, begged her to send an army to Scotland. The pleas fell on deaf ears: Cecil, in frustration, drafted a letter of resignation. At the start of the new year, Elizabeth's deep-frozen aversion to assisting rebels started slowly to thaw. In January, an English fleet blockaded the Firth of Forth, and in March, a treaty with the Lords of the Congregation provided an English army to assist in the siege of Leith, where French forces were now bottled up.

The English expeditionary force performed poorly, but growing political turmoil in France, combined with the death in June of the regent, Mary of Guise, persuaded Paris to come to terms. French and English troops both withdrew in July 1560, and a reformed settlement was rapidly endorsed by the Scots Parliament. When Mary returned to Scotland the following year, an unexpected consequence of the death of her husband, it would be to a country offering no immediate threat to the regime in England.

No military threat, at least: for Scotland was an inspiration and rebuke to disappointed English reformers. Knox and his allies rapidly drew up a 'Book of Discipline' on the Genevan model. It provided for congregational election of ministers, and moral oversight of congregations by kirk sessions staffed by elders and deacons. 'The gospel is received in Scotland', Thomas Lever wrote to Bullinger in July 1560, but here, he noted ruefully, 'no discipline is as yet established by any public authority'.[9]

Ironically, Cecil's anti-Catholic Scottish policy received political cover from the most Catholic of European monarchs. Even after it transpired Elizabeth had no intention of marrying him, Philip II used his influence at the Roman curia to dissuade popes – Paul IV, who died in August 1559; then his successor,

Pius IV – from excommunicating the Queen. The stated reason was that excommunication would make life more difficult for English Catholics; the real consideration was that it would make it easier for Mary Stewart and her Guise relatives to press their claim to the English throne.[10]

Life did get more difficult for English Catholics in the early part of 1560. On the feast of Candlemas, 2 February, worshippers attending mass at the house of the French ambassador were summarily arrested. The deposed Marian bishops hitherto enjoyed relative liberty, but in spring and early summer they were imprisoned – Bonner in the Marshalsea, well known to him from Edwardian days, others in the Fleet and the Tower.

Death had reduced their number to nine – Tunstall, last of the pre-Reformation bishops, died in November 1559; White, the funeral eulogist of Queen Mary, in January 1560. The survivors were regarded as security risks at a time of war with France. Feckenham too was sent to the Tower in May, as was Henry Cole, former dean of St Paul's, and the first writer to take up with alacrity Jewel's challenge to prove the antiquity of Catholic doctrines. The government did not know that three months earlier Cole had spoken treasonous words to the Spanish ambassador. If Philip would not stand by them in attempts to restore Catholicism, then 'they would appeal to the French, or even to the Turks, rather than put up with these heretics'.[11]

The former bishops knew the Queen was a hopeless heretic, but the Pope was not so sure. In the early part of 1560, Pius IV made preparations to reconvene the suspended Council of Trent, and optimistically thought Elizabeth might want to send English representatives. Vincenzo Parpaglia, a former client of Pole, was despatched to the Netherlands in May, in hopes of entering England as papal nuncio. Philip regarded him as alarmingly pro-French, and Ambassador de Quadra did nothing to further the mission. Nicholas Throckmorton told the secretary of the Venetian ambassador in France that Elizabeth was hedging her bets about admitting him, having decided, 'should the Council be free and universal, to send thither all her bishops and submit to it'. Elizabeth's understanding of a 'free' council probably ruled out participation on any terms acceptable to the Pope, but Cecil was annoyed with Throckmorton for encouraging Elizabeth to speculate about prospects for the Council – 'a matter of such weight being unmeet for a woman's knowledge'.

A second papal envoy, an Italian abbot, Martinengo, was appointed in January 1561, this time with Spanish blessing. There was support for his mission even within English circles of power. Elizabeth's favourite, Robert Dudley, was a free man, after his wife, Amy Robsart, broke her neck in September 1560 falling down a flight of stairs. The suspicious circumstances of her death made marriage to the Queen politically impossible – something Elizabeth soon reluctantly realized – but Dudley harboured hopes, and sought to enlist Spanish support with promises of participation at Trent. Cecil suavely

informed de Quadra in March 1561 that Elizabeth would certainly be willing
for English theologians to take part under papal chairmanship, so long as the
gathering was held in a neutral place, and judged doctrines according to the
scriptures and first four General Councils.[12]

In fact, Cecil was appalled by the prospect, and hard at work on a counter-
stroke. At the beginning of April, a commission established to search out 'mass
mongers and conjurors' claimed to have uncovered a conspiracy to bring about
the Queen's death using witchcraft, and it ordered the arrest of a clutch of
Essex Catholic gentry. They included a stalwart of July 1553, Mary's councillor
Edward Waldegrave, who died in prison in late 1561. Confiscated letters
showed the Marian bishops anticipating release from prison and freedom of
conscience for Catholics. All this – along with news of discontent in Ireland,
and of papist excitement at the discovery of the perfect image of a cross,
found in a storm-wrecked tree on a Catholic estate in Wales – was enough for
Elizabeth to endorse the Council's veto on entry for the nuncio. Cecil confided
to Throckmorton on 8 May that he meant none of them any personal harm,
but 'thought necessary to dull the papists' expectation by discovering of certain
massmongers and punishing them'. The reason for the verve of the papists?
'The Queen's lenity'.[13]

### Queen Checks Bishops

In July 1561, Elizabeth set off on an ambitious two-month progress through
Essex, Suffolk and Hertfordshire. It provided occasions, yet again, to display
differences with her leading churchmen. Already in January, the Queen had
issued a directive for better care to be taken of churches, and she was appalled
by the condition she now found many of them in, and despatched orders to her
ecclesiastical commissioners. It was reminiscent of her father during his
Yorkshire progress of 1541. But where Henry's concern had been to speed up
changes to church furnishings, Elizabeth's was to moderate them.

The Queen's order for rood lofts to be cut down (see p. 442) was a literally
halfway measure. The rood beams on which the lofts stood were to remain,
and to be decorated with 'some convenient crest' (universally understood to
mean the royal arms). There must be a 'comely partition betwixt the chancel
and the church': the old notion of a division of sacred space was retained.
Elizabeth also insisted that bells, which some Protestants saw as instruments
of popish superstition, be protected from destruction; that the role of godparents in baptism – another object of godly suspicion – be preserved; and that
communion tables be permanently embellished with 'a fair linen cloth', with a
protective covering of silk or buckram – this at a time when Bishop Parkhurst
of Norwich was ordering his clergy not to 'suffer the Lord's Table to be hanged
and decked like an altar'.[14]

None of this came near the offence the Queen unwittingly – or, more likely, wittingly – caused with an order dashed off from Ipswich in early August. It declared wives and children to be obstacles to the clergy's 'quiet and orderly profession of study and learning', and laid down that no wife, 'or other woman', was to be permitted within the precincts of cathedrals or university colleges. Elizabeth's unwillingness to grant clerical marriage a renewed statutory basis was already a sore point. 'The Queen's majesty will wink at it,' Sandys complained at the close of the 1559 Parliament, 'but not stablish it by law, which is nothing else but to bastard our children.'

In the wake of the Ipswich directive, Archbishop Parker had a meeting with the Queen and emerged from it shell-shocked. He confided to Cecil that 'I was in a horror to hear such words to come from her mild nature and Christianly learned conscience as she spake concerning God's holy order of matrimony'. Parker was aggrieved. He felt he had given everything in service of Elizabeth, procuring the hatred of papists as well as 'the foul reports of some Protestants', only to be repaid with a 'progress-hunting injunction, made upon the clergy with conference of no ecclesiastical person'. So much for the Queen's promise not to challenge authority of divine offices. The views exchanged between Queen and archbishop were bracingly frank: Elizabeth 'expressed to me a repentance that we were thus appointed in office, wishing it had been otherwise'.[15]

It was a spat, rather than a split. The story that Elizabeth once went out of her way to insult Parker's wife is probably apocryphal – 'Madam, I may not call you, and Mistress I am ashamed to call you, so I know not what to call you, but yet I do thank you.' Nonetheless, the words spoken to Parker in haste and anger – that the Queen did not, in 1559–60, get the bishops she wanted – have the ring of truth. Elizabeth's next episcopal appointment, in April 1562, was of Richard Cheyney to Gloucester. Cheyney was a Cambridge man, who had sided with Cheke and Cecil against Gardiner in the 1542 row over Greek pronunciation (see pp. 285–6). He was also a lifelong bachelor, as well as someone who had continued to hold office in the Church under Mary, and who retained a firm belief in real presence in the eucharist.[16] Like Elizabeth herself, Cheyney was more an old-style evangelical, or a Lutheran, than a Reformed Protestant. Was his appointment to Hooper's old diocese a sign of the ebbing tide of reform?

Not if the other bishops could help it. When an unknown Protestant secretly entered the Chapel Royal in August 1562, and broke to pieces the Queen's cross and candlesticks, Bishop Parkhurst could scarcely contain his glee: 'a good riddance of such a cross as that!' But a subsequent letter to Bullinger sadly reported how 'they were shortly after brought back again. . . . The lukewarmness of some persons very much retards the progress of the gospel.'[17] 'Some persons': an English bishop, writing to his foreign mentor, barely bothered to veil the criticism of his own sovereign.

Elizabeth's lukewarmness towards godly counsel depended on who was giving it. Having failed to acquire a consort's throne with Spanish help in 1561, Robert Dudley reinvented himself as a patron of advanced Protestantism, and along with other councillors pressed hard for Elizabeth to provide military assistance to beleaguered co-religionists in France. In September 1562, a treaty agreed that an English army, under the command of Robert Dudley's brother, Ambrose, Earl of Warwick, would come to the aid of the French Protestants (known as Huguenots) in Normandy; in exchange, the Huguenot leader, Louis, Prince of Condé, promised to return Calais, and handed over Newhaven (Le Havre) as a pledge of good faith.

The expedition, militarily and politically, was a flop. Newhaven was abandoned the following summer in the face of hostility from Catholics and Huguenots alike. In the meantime, the English garrison there became a laboratory of Protestant reform. Old associates of Knox – William Whittingham, William Kethe and Thomas Wood – preached to the troops, and Genevan worship displaced the Prayer Book.

In December 1562, Cecil and Robert Dudley instructed the military comptroller of Newhaven, Cuthbert Vaughan, to rein back the innovations. Vaughan bluntly replied that, so as not to offend his Huguenot hosts, Warwick would simply not comply, though he intended no criticism of usages in the Church at home.

Vaughan himself, a veteran of Wyatt's rebellion, was not himself so diplomatic: he saw 'a great difference and choice' between the experiments in France and the status quo at home. Vaughan longed to see 'full Reformation of our Church' in the coming Parliament, and removal of all 'dregs of ceremonies and superstitions'. Yet if Dudley and Cecil would not lead the charge for reform in the Parliament, 'by whom then, and when, shall we hope to be delivered?'[18]

The Parliament gathering on 11 January 1563 did not want for fiery Protestant fervour. It opened with a sermon in Westminster Abbey, preached by Alexander Nowell, dean of St Paul's. Nowell praised (with questionable sincerity) the Queen's 'clemency and mercy', but he aggressively called for sentence of death against 'obstinate' persons refusing to be reformed. A sermon that very day on the same theme at St Paul's caused de Quadra to fear that the moment of martyrdom for the Marian bishops had arrived. Nowell's sermon was overtly political, laced with demands for continued support of Scottish and French Protestants, and for the Queen to do her duty by marrying and producing an heir: 'If your parents had been of your mind, where had you been then?'

The succession was at the front of minds at the start of 1563. The previous October, Elizabeth contracted smallpox, and for a time hovered between life and death. Nowell recalled countless conversations from those anxious days: 'Alas, what trouble shall we be in, even as great or greater than France! For the succession is so uncertain, and such division for religion!' A formal petition for the Queen to marry – organized by Cecil and other councillors – soon followed from the Lords and Commons. Elizabeth eventually replied, noncommittally, that she had taken no vow not to marry, and so they should 'put out that heresy' from their minds – another instance of her playful use of a perilous term.[19]

There was nothing amusing about the thought that – like her brother and sister – Elizabeth might die only a handful of years into her reign, leaving the succession yet more uncertain than in 1553 or 1558. For Cecil and other key advisors, none of the alternatives appealed. Henry Hastings, Earl of Huntingdon, was a possibility. He was reliably Protestant, but his claim was tenuous, descending maternally (like Cardinal Pole's) from Edward IV's brother, George, Duke of Clarence. Katherine Grey (Jane's sister) had a better legal case under Henry VIII's will, but she was in disgrace for contracting an illicit marriage with Edward Seymour, son of the one-time Lord Protector, and she possessed little personally to recommend her to serious-minded councillors.

The qualifications of Mary of Scotland, in nearness of blood and experience of rule, spoke for themselves – despite Henry VIII's attempt permanently to bar the Scottish line from the succession. As an orphan and a widow (Francis II died in December 1560), Mary was now less obviously under French sway, and her stock was rising – among religious conservatives, at least. To Protestants like William Cecil, the possible advent of a second Catholic Mary was the stuff of nightmares.

In March 1563, Cecil drafted a bill for the succession, adapting constitutional arrangements already imagined by him for Scotland to a possible scenario in England. If Elizabeth were to die suddenly, then sovereign powers would pass to the Privy Council until such time as Parliament was able to choose a successor: England would become de facto a republic, and then an elective monarchy. In an era of divine right monarchy, it was an extraordinarily radical plan. Only deep religious conviction allowed Cecil to conceive it, or other councillors and Members of Parliament to entertain it. To Elizabeth, however, discussion of the succession in any form was anathema, and the bill was dropped.[20]

Parliament contented itself with tightening the Queen's security. An act 'for the Assurance of the Queen's Majesty's Royal Power' made denial of the Supremacy into a treasonable offence – a second refusal of the oath was now punishable by death. Along with schoolmasters, lawyers, candidates for degrees and ordination, MPs were added to the list of office-holders required to take the oath: Catholics, or at least open, Roman ones, were to be squeezed out of Parliament.

The bill's passage was far from smooth: a remarkable eighty-three MPs voted against it in the Commons. Robert Atkinson, member for Appleby, Westmorland, in the far north-west, presented an adroit common lawyer's case against it. Atkinson argued that support for the Pope was a religious offence, not a treasonable one. He highlighted the irony that Protestant preachers condemned the Six Articles, as well as 'the dealings in Queen Mary's days', on the grounds that religion 'must sink in by persuasion; it cannot be pressed in by violence'. A coerced oath would be self-defeating: 'Think you, that all that take it will, upon the taking of it, change their consciences? Nay, many a false shrew there is that will lay his hand to the book, when his heart shall be far off.' Far from cutting out sedition, enforced perjury would sew it into the very sinews of the state.

Atkinson concluded with a plea, not just for toleration, but for something like tolerance: 'Let us therefore, for the honour of God, leave all malice, and notwithstanding religion, let us love together. For it is no point of religion, one to hate another.' Charitable acceptance of difference was in the end inevitable: 'when we have all done, to this we must come at last'. Years of destructive warfare in Germany ended at a point where 'papist and Protestant can now quietly talk together'. Atkinson's poignant appeal fulfilled the prophecy of another Catholic common lawyer: the dark day foreseen by Thomas More, when 'we gladly would wish to be at league and composition with them, to let them have their churches quietly to themselves, so that they would be content to let us have ours quietly to ourselves' (see p. 191).

The bill was opposed in the Lords, but with the old bishops gone, the voices there lacked Atkinson's subtlety. The Earl of Northumberland saw the 'rigorous' act as an attack on the ancient aristocracy: 'when they had beheaded the clergy they would claim to do the same to the lay nobles'. Viscount Montague sounded an ominous note. Men of honour could not consent 'to receive an opinion and new religion by force and compulsion . . . And it is to be feared, rather than to die, they will seek how to defend themselves.'

Toleration of dissent, or rebellion and civil war? The government rejected this as a false choice. Defending the bill in the Commons, Cecil played the anti-Spanish card, and painted it as a measure of crucial national security at a time when Philip was threatening war over refusal to admit the papal nuncio. Yet the strength of opposition was noted. The bill was amended in the Lords, making peers themselves exempt. The Spanish ambassador again expected imminent beheading of the imprisoned bishops, but again it did not happen.

Martyrdom was a double-edged sword, wielded in a blaze of publicity whose intensity could not easily be predicted or controlled. In April, Parker, assisted by Cecil, drafted a secret memo for the (Protestant) bishops. They were empowered under the act to tender the oath to any clergyman in their jurisdiction, but where they met with refusal they were not to offer it a second time without the archbishop's explicit approval. Parker anticipated puzzlement and annoyance at this, and he did not want his brethren to think him 'a patron for the easing of such evil-hearted subjects'. There was little doubt where the pressure for 'lenity' was coming from. In a letter to Cecil, Parker admitted he was issuing the directive on his own authority so as 'not to recite the Queen's Majesty's name . . . to the discouragement of the honest Protestant'.[21]

As Cuthbert Vaughan had feared, the 1563 Parliament did little to advance reform, though an act authorizing translations of the Prayer Book and bible into Welsh was passed: an important first step towards counter-acting impressions that Protestant preaching in the principality was the imposition of an alien cultural system. There was no similar provision for Ireland. In January the previous year, the rebel Gaelic lord Shane O'Neill came to court to make a token declaration of submission to Elizabeth, his exotically clad gallowglass bodyguards exciting, according to the historian William Camden, 'as much wonderment as if they had come from China or America'. In 1563, Shane was again in rebellion, his ambitions increasingly cloaked in the mantle of Catholic resistance.[22]

The real effort of Reformation in 1563 took place not in Parliament, but in Canterbury Convocation. Its major achievement was the framing of new articles of faith, a substantial revision of the Edwardian set, reducing the number from forty-two to thirty-nine. Some explicitly anti-anabaptist articles were dropped, while some anti-Catholic ones were sharpened: in an echo of propositions placed before the Westminster disputation, worship in a language not understood by the people was declared 'repugnant to the Word of God', and national churches were noted to have authority to 'ordain, change and abolish ceremonies or rites'.

A new article announced the necessity of communion in two kinds, and transubstantiation was decreed to be a notion that 'overthroweth the nature of a sacrament'. The 'school authors' of the Edwardian articles were relabelled as 'Romish doctrine'. Catholics and Protestants, it was confirmed, recognized different bibles. The Council of Trent declared 'deutero-canonical' books such as Tobit, Ecclesiasticus and the two Books of Maccabees – found in an early Greek translation of the Old Testament but not in any Hebrew version – to be part of the canon of scripture. Article 6 denied this: the apocryphal texts were beneficial for 'example of life and instruction of manners', but could not be used as the basis of doctrine. It mattered: a key Catholic proof-text for purgatory was in the second Book of Maccabees.

On the Lord's Supper, there was a change of emphasis from 1553, though quite what it signified was a moot point. The Forty-Two Articles denounced belief in 'real and bodily presence, as they term it, of Christ's flesh and blood in the sacrament'. The 1563 formula was a more positive affirmation: 'the body of Christ is given, taken and eaten in the supper only after a heavenly and spiritual matter'.

It was still too negative for Bishop Cheyney, who seems, remarkably, to have refused to subscribe the articles. Edmund Guest of Rochester, after initial reluctance, did subscribe. In a letter to Cecil, he claimed credit for authorship of the revised article on the eucharist, and for trying to persuade Cheyney that the objectionable word 'only' was not meant to 'exclude the presence of Christ's body from the sacrament, but only the grossness and sensibleness in the receiving thereof'. Guest, like Cheyney, was a non-exile, and an alumnus of humanist, Henrician Cambridge. He did not lean as far as Cheyney towards Lutheran understandings of sacramental presence, but his eucharistic thinking encompassed the 'real' to an extent other bishops may not have realized, and would not have shared.

Elizabeth's Church now possessed a doctrinal 'Confession', but the status of the articles remained oddly provisional. There was no move to undergird them with statutory authority, though the revisions in Convocation were timely enough to make that possible: the teaching of the Church, in Elizabeth's view, was a matter for her and her clergy, not Parliament.

And in the final resort, just for her. Convocation approved thirty-nine articles, but when Elizabeth formally authorized them a few months later, there were only thirty-eight. The missing article was another on the eucharist. It stated 'the wicked, and such as be void of a lively faith, although they do carnally and visibly press with their teeth . . . yet in no wise are they partakers of Christ, but rather to their condemnation do eat and drink the sign or sacrament of so great a thing'. This negative judgement of *manducatio impiorum*, reception by the unworthy, was a long-standing English Protestant belief, upheld by Cranmer and Ridley in the Lords' debate of 1548 (see p. 323). It was also, in its unambiguous denial of any objective real presence, deeply offensive to German and Scandinavian Lutherans. Diplomatic considerations, as much as her own theological predilections, induced Elizabeth to suppress it.

There was an addition as well as a deletion. Article 20, 'Of the Authority of the Church', emerged from Convocation unchanged from 1553: 'It is not lawful for the Church to ordain anything that is contrary to God's Word written.' What Elizabeth put her name to was an article prefixing this with a declaration that 'The Church hath power to decree rites and ceremonies, and authority in controversies of faith.'[23] Here, 'the Church' really meant the Queen. Like her father, Elizabeth reserved the right to decide what counted as 'adiaphora' and to compel people to observe it.

If this was a signal to over-hasty reformers, the bishops were laying down some markers of their own. Along with the articles, Convocation authorized a second book of Homilies for reading in Church. As with its Edwardian predecessor, the twenty topics were a mixture of the moralistic ('Of Almsdeeds', 'Against Excess of Apparel') and the more directly doctrinal. 'Of the Worthy Receiving of the Sacrament' fleshed out, so to speak, the understanding of Christ's body in the eucharist. It distanced the Church from an older variety of sacramentarianism: here was 'no bare sign, no untrue figure of a thing absent'. Yet there was little comfort for quasi-Lutherans. The eucharist was 'spiritual food', 'a ghostly substance and not carnal', made real by faith. It seemed much like Calvin's 'receptionist' view.

The longest sermon in the collection was 'Against Peril of Idolatry', and probably written by John Jewel. It fulminated against ignorance and superstition, brandishing a bundle of scriptural and historical justifications for the iconoclastic work overseen by Jewel and the other visitors. The message insistently hammered home was that imagery was contrary to the second commandment, and that no images – especially images of Christ – should be erected in places of worship. Only by 'destruction and utter abolishing of all images and idols out of the church' could 'God's horrible wrath be averted' – a duty the Lord 'put in the minds of all Christian princes'. This was sailing close to the wind, for Jewel knew very well that God had put no such thought in the mind of Elizabeth.

Elizabeth mulled over the Homilies through the early summer, and when the volume was finally published at the end of July 1563, there were several changes from the presentation copy received some months earlier. A quotation from Augustine underlining the *manducatio impiorum* was gone. The Homily 'Of Common Prayer and Sacraments' was rewritten to suggest that, though only baptism and the eucharist were fully sacraments of Christ's institution, other rites such as absolution and ordination retained some sacramental character. Most significantly, the sermon on idolatry was altered to state that it was a prince's duty to remove 'all *such* images' (i.e. only abused ones) and that scripture suggested images should be banned from churches, not because they were 'filthy and dead', intrinsic sources of pollution, but only 'for fear and occasion of worshipping them, though they be of themselves things indifferent'.[24] Elizabeth did not manage to restore roods to parish churches, but she managed to say that she could, perhaps, if she wanted to. This was to rub salt into an episcopal wound, for the Queen had just thwarted another effort on the bishops' part to move things forward, not back, from the settlement of 1559.

In addition to drafting the Thirty-Nine Articles and Homilies, the 1563 Convocation produced practical proposals for further reform. These were once thought to be the schemes of radicals in the lower house, sensibly blocked by the episcopate. But painstaking analysis of various drafts proves that the bishops, including Parker, were well aware of what was being proposed, and actively supportive.

The less contentious demands were for greater clarity in the Church's teaching: a catechism written by Dean Nowell should be used in all churches and schools, and a book of doctrine set forth under royal authority. The suggestion was for this to be extracted from John Jewel's *Apologia pro Ecclesia Anglicana* (Apology for the Church of England) – an extended treatment of the anti-Catholic themes of his Challenge Sermon, appearing early in 1562. In 1564, Cecil's talented sister-in-law, Anne Bacon, produced an influential English translation, with a preface by Parker.

More provocative were calls for changes to the 1559 Prayer Book and its accompanying apparatus of worship. The petitioners – with the blessing of bishops like Sandys and Grindal – doubtless felt they were providing the same service Martin Bucer did for the Prayer Book of 1549: pointing out where liturgy remained too close to popery, and suggesting constructive improvements to bring it nearer to 'the godly purity and simplicity used in the primitive Church'. The demands included an end to the sign of the cross in baptism, and to 'superfluous' bell-ringing and 'curious' singing – organs should be banned, and music restricted to unison psalms. Inevitably, there was a request for 'the use of vestments, copes and surplices' to be 'from henceforth taken away'.

Cathedrals were to become centres of preaching, with thrice-weekly divinity lectures in English; non-preaching clergy must apply themselves to study of scripture or lose their positions. And 'discipline' – the holy grail of Protestant social reform – must be securely established: pending a thorough overhaul of canon law, there should be new laws against adulterers and fornicators, fines for failure to demonstrate basic knowledge of doctrine, public shaming for swearers and drunkards in some dedicated 'place of penitents', sharp punishments for people hearing mass or failing to take communion regularly. Not all of this appealed to lay Protestants. 'There is a great labour made by the clergy for discipline,' the poet George Ferrers wrote to his friend Thomas Challoner in January 1563, 'whereof some suppose the Bishop of Rome has gone out at one door and comes in by another.'

The most important lay Protestant was having none of it. The disciplinary reform scheme survives in a manuscript with a heading in Parker's handwriting: 'Articles drawn out by some certain [people], and were exhibited to be admitted by authority, but not so allowed'.[25] Elizabeth's stonewall reaction to the proposals of 1563 was confirmation of a mind-set: she thought the statutes, Prayer Book and injunctions of 1559 were the summit of ecclesiastical perfection and not, as most of her bishops believed, a base-camp at the foot of the mountain.

## Plague and Retribution

What God thought of it all was a matter of interpretation, though there was good reason, in the summer of 1563, to believe there was something he was not pleased about. Plague returned to England with unaccustomed vehemence, a deadly companion of the army skulking back from Newhaven. Before receding in early 1564, it took 80,000 lives, a quarter of them in London.

An official prayer was mandated to be read in churches. It enumerated blessings: 'Thou hast delivered us from all horrible and execrable idolatry, wherein we were utterly drowned, and hast brought us unto the most clear and comfortable light of Thy blessed Word'. But an ingrate people neglected God's commandments, following 'our own carnal liberty'. Small wonder God should 'show his wrath against sin, and call his people to repentance'.

The plague brought to the surface submerged anxieties about lukewarmness, neutrality and dissembling – a phenomenon, and an anxiety, that the heightened confessionalism of the mid-Tudor years helped to produce. Bishop Cox complained to Cecil in 1563 of the undermining of ministers' efforts by 'neuters, papists or carnal gospellers'. An English Protestant translation of a German Lutheran work identified a supposedly common type: 'jacks of both sides, or walkers in a mean', people who

> craftily cloak and dissemble religion, and handle themselves in all outward affairs after such sort, as if a man were familiarly linked to both parties, not altogether gone from the papists, lest he be reckoned a stubborn fellow, nor utterly divorced from the gospellers, least he be called an apostate; and by that shift to walk as it were in the middle and most safe way, to be indifferent to both sides . . .

A pervasive sense of unease, even of alarm, was exacerbated by discovery of a sect who raised the habit of dissembling to an art form, and turned Nicodemism into a theological principle. The 'Family of Love', founded by the Dutch mystic Hendrik Niclaes, established itself in parts of rural England in the 1550s, but first came to official attention through the investigations of a Surrey magistrate in 1561. Two disgruntled former Familists confessed, among other shocking revelations, that 'they hold it is lawful to do whatsoever the higher powers commandeth to be done, though it be against the commandments of God'. In Mary's reign, members of the group moved from believing attendance at mass a sin to thinking it an obligation. Their religion was so inward and pure that no outward action could defile it: 'They hold the Pope's service, and this service now used in the church, to be nought, and yet to be by them used as free in the Lord to whom nothing is unclean.'[26]

As the plague struck London, the physician William Bullein offered caustic satire, as well as medical prescriptions, in his *Dialogue Against the Fever Pestilence*. One character unashamedly confesses 'I am neither Catholic, Papist nor Protestant'; rather, 'a nulla fidian [holder of no faith], and there are many of our sect'. Two equally shady types, the scheming lawyers Avarus and Ambodexter, reflect on how the world will never be merry 'until these gospelling preachers have a sweating sickness at Smithfield'. The person to do it, 'if he were again at liberty', was 'that holy man Bishop Bonner'.

Calls for vengeance against the Marian bishops, Bonner in particular, intensified during the plague. It seemed that some kind of expiation was needed to appease God's righteous wrath. An earlier calamity ignited similar instincts. The burning of the steeple of St Paul's Cathedral, as the result of a lightning strike on 4 June 1561, was said by Catholics to be punishment for abandoning the mass and the ancient faith. In a Paul's Cross sermon, Bishop James Pilkington of Durham vigorously denied this, declaring, to the apparent rejoicing of his audience, that the Queen 'intendeth that more severity of laws shall be executed against persons disobedient, as well in causes of religion as civil'. He urged people to follow God's Word, and warned, presciently, 'of some greater plague to follow, if amendment of life in all states did not ensue'.

Just prior to the outbreak, in March 1563, a book appeared from the press of John Day, a commercial hit in spite of its intimidating length. The *Acts and Monuments of these Latter and Perilous Days* was the culmination of years of labour by John Foxe, a former member of Knox's faction at Frankfurt, and latterly a preacher in Norwich and London. It provided heart-rending accounts of the sufferings of the Marian martyrs, along with many details about their vindictive persecutors – above all, 'Bloody Bonner'.

There was thus uproar in September 1563 when the government reassigned the former bishops to comfortable house arrest with their episcopal successors, in order, it was believed, to protect them from the plague. The move was denounced in sermons at Paul's Cross and elsewhere. William Baldwin, a writer-turned-clergyman and master practitioner of anti-Catholic satire, was reported to be particularly vehement, 'wishing a gallows set up in Smithfield, and the old bishops and other papists to be hanged thereon'.[27]

In April 1564, it did seem as if Bonner's hour of reckoning had come. Bishop Horne of Winchester, in whose jurisdiction the Southwark Marshalsea prison lay, put the oath to him for the second time. Bonner refused, and was indicted in Queen's Bench to face trial for treason. It was a daring and subversive stroke, undertaken by a trio of bishops without royal knowledge or permission. The instigator was Bonner's successor, Edmund Grindal. He did not expect William Cecil to be unsympathetic, but purposely did not tell him beforehand so 'that if any misliked the matter ye might *liquido jurare* [confidently swear] ye were not privy of it'.

'Any', of course, meant Elizabeth. Grindal, girded with expert legal opinion, had Parker's written permission. The move was prompted by genuine animus against Bonner, and a determination he should face justice. But it was also an assertion of episcopal autonomy in the wake of recent checks and humiliations. Grindal envisaged the process against Bonner as the first of many: 'no more meet man to begin withal than that person'.

To step in and halt a legitimate judicial process would be legally question-able and, given the state of Protestant opinion in London, politically risky. But there is little doubt Elizabeth was privately furious. During a visit to Cambridge in August, students acted before her a comedy satirizing the imprisoned bishops. One, 'carrying a lamb in his hands as if he were eating it', was clearly supposed to represent Bonner. Elizabeth, a past mistress of the dramatic walkout, angrily left, 'using strong language'. The lights literally went out on the performance, as torch-bearers hurried to accompany the Queen.[28]

The declaration of episcopal independence went spectacularly awry. Bonner's trial in the autumn of 1564 turned into a misfire, an embarrassing rebuff to the campaign for Marian reckoning. The ex-bishop, assisted by the eminent lawyers Edmund Plowden and Christopher Wray, a Catholic and a semi-Catholic, conducted as brilliant a defence against treason as Nicholas Throckmorton did ten years earlier (see p. 372).

Bonner hinged his case on a technical defect in the indictment. The law required the oath to be tendered him by a bishop, but Horne's episcopal status, he claimed, was irregular because Archbishop Parker, who consecrated him, was himself technically deficient. The 1533 Appointment of Bishops Act stipulated the participation of four bishops, or three including an archbishop. Four (three ex-bishops and a suffragan) were eventually rounded up for Parker's consecration in December 1559, but their status depended on the Edwardian Ordinal, which had been repealed by statute in Mary's reign but not formally restored in Elizabeth's.

The validity of the episcopal orders of men their papist opponents routinely referred to as 'pseudo-bishops' was a can of worms the government wanted to stay sealed. When, in November, it seemed the judges might find merit in Bonner's arguments, the trial was permanently suspended. The new Spanish ambassador, Guzman de Silva, reported on 9 October that Cecil had ordered the bishops to treat gently 'those of the old faith', and the bishops were in consequence 'very displeased'. Archbishop Young complained to the Queen that Bonner's mistrial was a principal cause of 'inconstancy and murmuring' among Catholics in Yorkshire, encouraging a perception 'that your Majesty would have none of that sort so offending your laws punished'.

Robert Dudley, once again intriguing for Spanish support, and recently ennobled as Earl of Leicester, was happy to take credit for protecting the lives of the deprived bishops, and he assured de Silva that the Queen knew nothing beforehand about the action against Bonner. De Silva, meanwhile, impressed upon Leicester that both he and Elizabeth needed the good will of English Catholics, who 'were very numerous, much more so than those of the new religion, with whom the Queen and he were unpopular'.[29]

### Mislikers of True Religion

De Silva was surely right. Catholics, however precisely defined, were very numerous in the early 1560s. Nicholas Sander, a fellow of New College, Oxford, who fled abroad rather than take the Oath of Supremacy, wrote in 1561 a report for the protector of English interests at Rome, Cardinal Morone. He claimed that less than 1 per cent of the population was 'infected' with heresy.[30] That, undoubtedly, was an optimistic underestimate, but outside London and some other urban centres, Protestants were certainly the minority. Alarmingly, that was true even of the groups charged with responsibility for imposing the new order.

In October 1564, the Privy Council wrote to the bishops asking them to report on the reliability of justices of the peace in their dioceses. The replies placed magistrates in one of three categories: 'favourers', 'hinderers' or 'indifferent', in respect of 'true religion'. Fewer than half the JPs were reckoned to be supporters of the government's religious policies, and nearly a third positively opposed them. Catholic gentry were particularly concentrated in Hampshire, Sussex, Herefordshire and across the north. In Lancashire, only six out of twenty-five justices were thought favourable towards the settlement.

The findings underlined not only the strength of conservative feeling among the landowning elite, but also the depth of elite divisions, even within families. Edwin Sandys of Worcester placed Clement Throckmorton, one of the sons of Sir George, and sibling of Nicholas, among the 'favourers of true religion'. Their elder brother Robert was one of the 'adversaries'. Robert's son, Thomas, was put in the column for 'indifferent of religion', though Bishop Bentham of Coventry and Lichfield considered both him and his father 'no favourers'.

Bishops were shocked by what they discovered. Sandys urged the Council to consider the benefits 'if all such as mislike and condemn true religion, now by common order set forth, were put out of authority'. This was what the 'Device for the Alteration' advocated in 1558. But reality had set in: as with the parish clergy, purging every magistrate not zealously committed to reform would make England ungovernable. The Council insisted on relatively few changes to commissions for 1565.

'Misliking' true religion could mean sponsoring an alternative. Sandys complained that 'popish and perverse priests which, misliking religion, have forsaken the ministry' were 'kept in gentlemen's houses'. These skulking priests were 'had in great estimation', and 'marvellously pervert the simple'. One of their protectors was the former privy councillor and royal secretary, Sir John Bourne. During the royal visitation, Bourne removed the altar from the parish church to his house outside Worcester. Thereafter, he missed few opportunities to mock Sandys's preaching, and showed a particular animus against clerical marriage. Two ministers' wives, crossing the River Severn in a boat one day in 1563, were menaced by Bourne's son and servants: 'now you are among papists'. Bishop Scory of Hereford had similar tales to tell: office-holders in Mary's Church, 'mortal and deadly enemies to this religion', were now saying masses in the houses of suspect JPs, 'which come very seldom or not at all to church'.[31]

Catholics faced the self-same dilemma Protestants did after 1554: could they attend defective church services to fulfil the demands of the law, and the requirements of neighbourliness, or was such attendance quite literally damnable? Catholic perplexity was, if anything, greater than that of Marian Protestants: the communion service was not for them an 'idol', as the mass was for reformers. But there was at least a definitive authority to whom they could turn. In the summer of 1562, a group of leading Catholic laymen, via the Portuguese and Spanish ambassadors, petitioned the Council of Trent. They admitted that threats of imprisonment, and entreaties of friends and relatives, had induced many Catholic gentlemen 'to allow themselves to be withdrawn from their resolution' concerning presence at Protestant services; what did 'men of true piety and learning think they ought to do?'

Ambassador de Quadra, still then pursuing Philip's strategy of rapprochement with Elizabeth, added his own gloss. The 'Common Prayers' of the Church of England, he blithely declared, 'contain no false doctrine whatever, nor anything impious. It is all Scripture or prayers taken from the Catholic Church.' Attendance was not in itself evil, 'apart from the sin of dissimulation, and possible harm caused by bad example'. De Quadra was a bishop as well as a diplomat, so did not come at things from a place of theological ignorance. But the judgement of the Council Fathers, delivered in August 1562, was emphatic: 'You may not be present at such prayers of heretics, or at their sermons, without heinous offence and the indignation of God, and it is far better to suffer most bitter cruelties than to give the least sign of consent to such wicked and abominable rites.'[32]

This was a condemnation of Nicodemism as resounding as any produced by the Marian exiles. Yet there was, at first, virtually no papal effort to publicize it, even as Pius IV was quietly granting de Quadra powers to reconcile penitent heretics and schismatics – a move that provoked understandable anger on the part of the English government. Roman action against Elizabeth was still constrained by Habsburg influence. In addition to standing anxieties about France, there was a hopeful possibility that Elizabeth might marry the Archduke Charles, third son of the Emperor Ferdinand I, and a cousin of Philip of Spain.

Even Cecil thought the proposal worth considering: Charles was preferable to Leicester, and Cecil assumed (wrongly) that the Archduke would be prepared to convert to Protestantism. Negotiations did not get underway till August 1563, but in June Ferdinand reacted furiously when he heard some Englishmen at Louvain, working in concert with the imprisoned bishops, had requested the nearly concluded Council of Trent to instigate excommunication proceedings against Elizabeth. Under pressure from both Philip and Ferdinand, Pius IV dropped the idea.

Habsburg policy was to press the case for toleration, creating for English Catholics a situation analogous to that found in parts of Germany. The 1555 Peace of Augsburg, which ended the religious warfare in the Empire, embodied the famous principle, *cuius regio eius religio* (your ruler, his religion). But in some long-divided places it also confirmed arrangements for Lutherans and Catholics to worship alongside each other in uneasy co-existence. In September 1563, Ferdinand wrote to Elizabeth, thanking her for clemency towards the imprisoned bishops, and advancing a proposal from the cardinal legates at Trent: that Catholics in England be provided with at least one church in every city, to hear mass and celebrate the sacraments.

There was little chance of this being seriously entertained. Where minorities were formally tolerated in western Europe, it was usually the result of one side failing to vanquish the other in an inconclusive war. Such a war was something England, so far, had managed to avoid. Elizabeth's reply to the Emperor encapsulated a philosophy of rule where 'religion' and 'politics' were impossible to pick apart:

> To found churches for diverse rites, besides being openly repugnant to the enactments of our supreme Parliament, would be but to graft religion upon religion, to the distraction of good men's minds, the fostering of the zeal of the factious, the sorry blending [disturbing] of the functions of church and state, and the utter confounding of all things human and divine in this our now peaceful state; a thing evil in itself, of the worst example, pernicious to our people, and to those themselves, in whose interest it is craved, neither advantageous nor indeed without peril.[33]

For Elizabeth, uniformity of religious practice was, quite literally, an article of faith. This was a conventional view of things, the standard assumption of states and ecclesiastical authorities across virtually all of late medieval Europe. But forty years of rival evangelisms, state-sponsored or freelance, had placed the ideal under intolerable strain. It could be maintained in one of three ways, or by some combination of them. Nonconformists could be eliminated, by fire, sword or expulsion; they could be converted; or they could be persuaded to conform and obey, irrespective of any inner convictions about truth.

Elizabeth, who had played the game from both sides, leaned instinctively towards the third way. Sir Nicholas Bacon's son, Francis, would famously later say of her that she misliked 'to make windows into men's hearts and secret thoughts'. Yet Elizabeth reigned in a profoundly anti-Nicodemite age, and her attempts to contain religious tensions had an inescapable tendency to inflame them.

English Catholics benefited little, in the first half of the 1560s, from the muffled and mixed messages from Rome. A clearer lead came from the imprisoned bishops and senior clergy. John Feckenham wrote in 1563 a detailed account of 'considerations and causes, moving me not to be present at, nor to receive, neither use the service of the new book'. It was smuggled out of prison and circulated widely in manuscript. In 1564, Bishop Thomas Bentham complained about 'lewd priests' resorting for advice to the former bishop of Peterborough, David Pole.[34]

'Recusancy' was the legal term for refusal (Lat., *recusare*) to attend church, a statutory offence under the Act of Uniformity. It got under way without waiting for a steer from Trent or the papacy. The former Marian cathedral clergy, backbone of Pole's Catholic reformation, played a crucial role in the process.[35] The ex-dean of Durham, Thomas Robertson, was 'thought to do much hurt' in Yorkshire in 1562, while John Morren, Bonner's former chaplain and one-time canon of St Paul's, distributed a tract in the streets of Chester in 1561 warning any Catholics tempted to receive Protestant communion that in doing so 'you break your profession made in baptism, and fall into schism, separating yourselves from God and his Church'. The ex-archdeacons of Derby and Huntingdon, John Ramridge and Anthony Draycott, said recusant masses for Catholic gentlemen in East Anglia. In 1561, a batch of deprived former canons from Exeter, Worcester and other places arrived in Hereford, and placed themselves at the disposal of a band of local recusants. Bishop Scory reported with disgust the welcome they received from the citizens, with feasting and a torch-lit street procession: 'they could not much more reverently have entertained Christ himself'.

Catholic aristocrats provided shelter and protection. On completion of his visitation of Winchester in 1561, Bishop Horne told Cecil of general conformity, but also of persons 'who have purposely withdrawn themselves . . . partly under pretence that they serve noblemen'. Richard Marshall, former dean of Christ Church, Oxford, an Edwardian evangelical who under Mary became a convinced Romanist, went north after deprivation or resignation in 1559. He stayed for a time with the Earl of Cumberland, and encouraged spiritual resistance among Catholics in Yorkshire, before being arrested and persuaded by Grindal to subscribe to the Thirty-Nine Articles in December 1563 – a temporary recantation. Alban Langdale, former archdeacon of Chichester and veteran of the 1559 Westminster disputation, went to the household of Viscount Montagu, the most vocal opponent of the settlement in the House of Lords. In 1561, Langdale appeared on a list of recusants in the diocese of Chichester: 'learned, and very earnest in papistry'.[36]

The most earnest among the papists took the option favoured by zealous Protestants under Mary: flight into overseas exile, to worship as they liked, and speak and write freely against the iniquities of the regime at home. Among the first to leave was Thomas Harding, another Marian convert from evangelicalism choosing not to revert to his former opinions with the turning of the political tide. Harding went to Louvain, haven of choice for English papalists since the early 1530s. Richard Smyth, vice-chancellor of Oxford and preacher at the burning of Latimer and Ridley, attempted on Mary's death to flee to Scotland. He was arrested in the borders, and placed in Parker's custody at

Lambeth. Here, under pressure, he subscribed to the royal supremacy. Temporary submission, followed by flight, was another way in which Elizabethan exiles imitated, if not flattered, their Marian predecessors. Early in 1560, Smyth gave Parker the slip and crossed to Louvain. In 1562, he was elected vice-chancellor of Douai, a brand new university established by Philip II on the southern edge of the Spanish Netherlands.

These two university towns, of Louvain and Douai, just a little further apart from each other than Oxford was from Cambridge, attracted scholars from their English counterparts in impressive – and, to Protestants, alarming – numbers. Louvain soon had houses of study named 'Oxford' and 'Cambridge'. A contemporary Catholic estimate was of some 300 transplanted to the Low Countries in the first years of the reign. Cambridge lost its regius professors of divinity and civil law, as well as heads of several colleges, but Oxford lived up to its long-standing reputation as the more religiously conservative of the two universities: twenty-five fellows were ejected from New College alone.

By 1564, the exiles were bringing out works of religious controversy, usually published in the great printing centre of Antwerp, and initially in response to Jewel's Challenge sermon and *Apology*. It began as a trickle, and became a flood of words: five works in 1564, fifteen in 1565, twelve in 1566 – a 'havoc of books', complained Alexander Nowell. Attacks from adversaries 'beyond the sea', Parker lamented to Cecil in March 1565, were multiplying in 'books plentifully had in the court'. Jewel himself felt exhausted and beleaguered, 'always battling with these monsters'. And yet, he sighed to Bullinger, they 'must be answered'. Like Thomas More a generation earlier (see pp. 201–2), Protestants were caught up in a paradox of polemic: refuting an opponent's views inevitably involved publicizing them. Jewel's 1565 *Replie unto M. Hardinges Answeare* contained within it a complete text of Harding's attack on the Protestant Church of England.

For the most part, the exiles wrote in English, recognizing the social broadening of the battle of ideas. Simple folk, huffed Nowell, 'may much marvel at such plenty of English books'.[37] In truth, English Protestants were thrown off-balance by the ferocity and sophistication of the assault, a further tribute to the intellectual and organizational refurbishment of English Catholicism taking place in Mary's reign.

Members of the old guard – Smyth (who died in 1563) and Harding – were fully engaged. But, from the outset, leading roles devolved to members of a younger generation, writers born in the 1530s; ideological products of the Marian Church with no personal knowledge of the pre-Reformation world: Thomas Dorman, John Martiall, John Rastell, Nicholas Sander, Thomas Stapleton. Nor were the old dogs incapable of learning new tricks. Thomas Darbyshire and William Good, born in 1518 and 1527 respectively, entered the Society of Jesus in 1562–3. Jasper Heywood, son of the playwright John

Heywood, and great-nephew of Thomas More, was another early English recruit to the order.

A rising star among the exiles was a Lancashire man, William Allen, who resigned his Oxford fellowship in 1560. After a period in the Low Countries, Allen returned to Lancashire to convalesce from illness, and was horrified to find there Catholics attending church, as well as priests prepared to say both communion services and covert masses. On his own account, Allen launched an itinerant campaign for recusancy, shuttling between gentry households to persuade people 'truth was to be found nowhere else save with us Catholics'. By the spring of 1565, he was back in the Low Countries, adding to the printed chorus of condemnation against Jewel.

The exiles were mainly clergymen (though Allen was only ordained to the priesthood at Mechelen in 1565). But there was a sprinkling among them of laymen with political connections and sometimes militant convictions. Mary's privy councillor Sir Francis Englefield went abroad, under royal licence, in 1559, but judged it prudent not to return. He was already a pensioner of King Philip, and remained in his service. John Story, heretic-hunter and parliamentary troublemaker, was imprisoned in the Fleet in 1560, but in 1563, with the connivance of the Spanish ambassador, he was able to escape to Louvain. There he formally took an oath of allegiance to Philip – an unusual and provocative step revealing his conviction that faith was the higher form of patriotism.[38]

In the main, the exiles adopted a stance of scrupulous loyalty to the person of Elizabeth. Harding's 1565 *Confutation* of Jewel bore the royal arms on its title page, and was one of several works dedicated to the Queen. John Martiall invited 'indifferent' readers to note the contrast between Catholics' writings and those of the late Marian exiles: 'there is no blast blown against the monstrous regiment of women. . . . There is no libel set forth for order of succession.'

There was method in the modesty. The exiles were not strangers to English Protestantism, but astute observers of its stresses and tensions. Widening the wedge between Elizabeth and the more zealous of her clergy was a strategy that happily coincided with their long-held convictions that heresy was inherently factional and divisive. Martiall's 1564 *Treatyse of the Cross* defended the image of the crucifix with recurrent reference to the example of the Chapel Royal. Harding was well informed about an incident at a Lenten court sermon in 1564, 'your princely word commanding a preacher that opened his lewd mouth against the reverent use of the cross in your private chapel to retire from that ungodly digression'. The preacher was the dean of St Paul's, Alexander Nowell, and his temerity in raising the subject prompted a devastating royal heckle: 'To your text, Mr Dean—leave that, we have heard enough of that.' Parker took the distraught Nowell home afterwards for dinner, 'for pure pity'.[39]

Most of all, the exiles watched with vicarious delight as in 1564–5 a long-brewing storm prepared to break over the English Church. It was the question decided but not settled by the Injunctions of 1559: vestments of the clergy. In his *Fortress of the Faith*, printed at Antwerp in June 1565, Thomas Stapleton affected to marvel how anyone could acknowledge Elizabeth as Supreme Governor in spiritual causes, yet refuse to obey her in this decidedly spiritual matter. Catholics, of course, knew the value of vestments, yet 'to be apparelled priest-like' evidently seemed absurd to 'the zealous gospellers of Geneva' – people Stapleton off-handedly referred to as 'the Puritans of our country'.

This was the first documented usage of a word very likely already in circulation. Some Elizabethan commentators thought Stapleton's colleague Nicholas Sander invented the term 'Puritan', in ironic recognition of a supposedly fanatical obsession with ecclesiastical and personal purity. It was one of numerous mocking nicknames that for decades Catholics had been thinking up for their opponents; synonyms or sub-sets of 'heretic', and pay-back for the now ineradicably rooted epithet 'papist'. No one in England, at least for many years to come, would call themselves a Puritan. But the label took hold widely and quickly: Catholic oil on the internal fires of the Church of England. Anti-puritanism created Puritanism.[40] Discovering the name for a phenomenon of protest made it seem more like a movement, a party. It started to force people – most notably, the bishops themselves – to decide which side they were really on.

### Rags of Rome

Following Convocation's failure to amend the regulations on clerical vestments, some ministers decided simply to ignore them. A paper in Cecil's possession, dating from 1564/5, listed disquieting 'varieties in the service and administration used'. Communion was ministered by clergymen, 'some with surplice and cap, some with surplice alone, others with none'. There were additional irregularities. Some ministers omitted the sign of the cross in baptism; some laypeople sat, or stood, rather than knelt, to receive communion, 'some with unleavened bread, and some with leavened'. Communion tables stood variously, covered and uncovered, in naves and chancels, sometimes altarwise, sometimes not.

These were not always sins of silent omission. Among the grievances conservative parishioners in Hull, East Yorkshire, tabled in 1564 against their belligerent vicar, Melchior Smith, was that

> since the time of his being vicar there, [he] hath not used to wear a priest's cap, nor yet a surplice in the church in time of divine service, but openly in his sermons hath called priests' caps and surplices vile clouts and rags, and hath said that priests' caps are knaves' caps.

To William Turner, dean of Wells, the 'woollen horns' of the square cap were indelibly associated with the 'cruel and popish butchers which not long ago burned so many Christian martyrs'. He was said to have trained a little dog to snatch caps from the heads of visiting dignitaries.[41] Nonconformity of this sort was not confined to the provinces: it was particularly visible in London, and in the now partially decatholicized universities. Bishops like Grindal, Bentham and Parkhurst turned a strategically blind eye.

By the autumn of 1564, Elizabeth decided to put an end to it. The Spanish ambassador reported in October that 'Cecil tells these heretical bishops to look after their clergy, as the Queen is determined to reform them in their customs, and even in their dress, as the diversity that exists in everything cannot be tolerated'.

To many of the bishops, it seemed yet again an unnecessary fight over the wrong issue. 'I marvel much that this small controversy for apparel should be so heavily taken,' Pilkington groaned to Leicester. Such things might be borne with for a while, for the sake of 'Christian liberty', and 'in hope to win the weak'. Yet 'when liberty is turned to necessity, it is evil, and no longer liberty'. The unanswerable riposte was the addition Elizabeth made, without consultation of bishops, to Article 20: 'The Church hath power to decree rites and ceremonies, and authority in controversies of faith.'[42]

Parker attempted to broker a compromise, summoning to London the leaders of Oxford nonconformity, who were also the most eminent divines in the university: Laurence Humphrey, Regius Professor of Divinity, and Thomas Sampson, dean of Christ Church. Agreement – or at least a fudge – seemed possible. Humphrey and Sampson had, as usual, been soliciting Zürich for advice. They expected Bullinger to back their conscientious objection, but, much as the Swiss reformer disliked vestments, he advised that obedience to the magistrate took precedence. At a conference in December, Parker persuaded several leading churchmen, including Grindal and Horne, to sign up to the proposition that distinctions of ecclesiastical dress could be enjoined by public authority without taint of false doctrine. Humphrey and Sampson also signed, but after inscribing the words of St Paul: 'all things are lawful to me, but not all are expedient . . . not all edify'. This was – in effect – to add, as the Catholic bishops did in 1531, 'as far as the law of God allows', to reserve the judgement of their conscience. Edification – a genteel, innocuous-sounding word – was in fact anything but. For Puritans, it was the bottom line, the necessary condition for ceremonies and habits of worship. If they did not positively help towards growth in the spirit, then they positively hindered it.[43]

Elizabeth had no patience for such scruples. On 25 January 1565, she sent a letter to Parker, drafted by Cecil, instructing him to put an end to 'sufferance of sundry varieties and novelties, not only in opinions, but in external ceremonies and rites'. No one was to be admitted to ecclesiastical office without undertaking to maintain 'one manner of uniformity throughout our whole realm', and any 'superior officers' proving remiss in implementing it were to be reported, 'for we intend to have no dissension or variety grow, by suffering of persons which maintain the same to remain in office'.[44]

For the bishops, this was a moment of decision, and of fateful entanglement with some old dilemmas. Was scripture the sole storehouse of acceptable practices for Church use? Most bishops, like most Protestants, thought not. But did strictly inessential items (*adiaphora*) have to meet the test of serving wider purposes of reform – to be things that 'edified'? Or were they to be 'borne with' simply because they were desired by public authority, an authority that scripture itself enjoined Christians to obey?

It was a decision the bishops had in fact already taken, a bargain already struck, but one whose implications they now had to face up to. Grindal explained to Bullinger in 1566 that 'we who are now bishops, on our first return, and before we entered on our ministry, contended long and earnestly for the removal of those things that have occasioned the present dispute'. Having failed, 'we judged it best . . . not to desert our churches for the sake of a few ceremonies, and those not unlawful in themselves'. Mass resignations would leave the Church vulnerable to 'Lutherans and semi-papists' – Grindal had no appetite to see an episcopal bench lined by the likes of Richard Cheyney.

The bishops, then, would take a deep collective breath and enforce the Queen's wishes. On 30 January 1565, in 'obedience to her princely authority, and to avoid her heavy indignation', Parker commanded Grindal to relay Elizabeth's instructions to all bishops of the province, and to take action against offenders. In March, Grindal, along with Cox, Guest, Horne and Nicholas Bullingham of Lincoln, convened with Parker to draft a set of articles, issued early the next year as 'Advertisements [notifications] for due order in the public administration of Common Prayers' – a code of clerical discipline.

The Advertisements put preaching on a short rein. Licences issued before 1 March 1564 were suspended, with new applicants to be 'diligently examined for their conformity'. All preachers were to stress 'the reverent estimation of the holy sacraments', and urge obedience to all requirements of the Prayer Book and Injunctions. Stipulations for clerical dress were carefully, minutely, set out. At home, in private studies, clergymen might 'use their own liberty of comely apparel', but travelling in public they must at all times wear the square cap and gown prescribed by the Injunctions – a pantomime of the observance of outward uniformity insisted on by the Queen. For services, there was a (slight) relaxation of the rules. In cathedrals, and for ministration of holy communion only, the cope was to be worn. In parish churches, for public prayer and celebration of all sacraments, the required standard was now 'a comely surplice with sleeves'. The Advertisements ended, not exactly with an oath, but with a set of 'protestations' or promises for holders of ecclesiastical office to observe all the ceremonies of the Church.[45]

Elizabeth never formally assented to the Advertisements, which were issued on Parker's authority alone. Perhaps this was because the stipulation of surplice rather than cope for parish eucharists represented a retrenchment from the 1559 settlement, something the Queen was prepared to tolerate but not officially endorse. Just as probably, the Queen wanted the bishops to take responsibility for implementing a divisive and unpopular policy: it was a test of loyalty, and a form of punishment.

Enforcement began with the universities, where it proved as painful as expected. In Oxford, the resistance of Humphrey and Sampson had wide support, and while Humphrey was able to cling to office, citing legal exemptions of his college, Magdalen, Sampson was deprived of his deanery of Christ Church. Cambridge was even more recalcitrant, with something like a full-scale student rebellion stirred up by the sermons against 'popish trumpery' of George Withers and William Fulke. Cecil, chancellor of the University, stepped in to force the university authorities to impose conformity, laying down the line that was his and Parker's, but perhaps not quite Elizabeth's – that vestments 'of themselves were of none other value but to make a demonstration of obedience, and to render a testimony of unity'. The crackdown succeeded, but left a legacy of bitterness among young scholars preparing for ministry in parishes across England.

In London, showcase and nerve-centre of nonconformity, Grindal tried at the start of 1566 to broker a compromise, and managed to persuade all but a few former exiles to agree to the surplice, and a form of outdoor dress falling short of the square cap. He was still missing the point, which was full conformity to the Queen's wishes, precisely because they were the Queen's wishes. On 26 March 1566, Parker gave up waiting for royal approval of his Advertisements, and summoned the London clergy to appear before ecclesiastical commissioners at Lambeth. Grindal was now, reluctantly, on board, but privy councillors were notable by their absence. Robert Cole, rector of St Mary-le-Bow, a former opponent of the costume, modelled the gown and cap. The clergy were ordered to subscribe their willingness to wear this garb: 'be brief; make no words'. Of nearly a hundred in attendance, sixty-one agreed to subscribe, and thirty-seven refused and were immediately suspended. They included such luminaries as James Calfhill, Lady Margaret Professor of Divinity in Oxford, and the renowned authors Thomas Becon and John Foxe. Almost all the city's lecturers were among the suspended, leading the former Genevan elder Thomas Wood to complain angrily to Cecil how 'all exercises almost of interpretation of the scriptures . . . are utterly overthrown', and of 'the wonderful rejoicing also of the papists'.[46]

It was far from the end of the business. Suspended preachers refused to be silenced, and stirred up their supporters in sermons which, according to the conservative chronicler John Stow, 'vehemently' denounced the Queen,

Council and bishops. Dissidents printed two tracts, *The Voice of God* and *A Brief Discourse against the Outward Apparel*, and, in emulation of old evangelical tactics, distributed them in the streets. The prime organizer was Robert Crowley, vicar of St Giles Cripplegate, who before his ordination worked as a printer and publisher. A month after the showdown at Lambeth, Crowley blocked a funeral cortège, its accompanying clerks in surplices, from entering St Giles. The church, he said, was his: 'The Queen had given it him during his life and made him vicar thereof, wherefore he would not suffer any such superstitious rags of Rome there to enter.'

Easter 1566 saw instances of intimidation and resistance at other city churches. At St Mary Magdalen, Milk Street, the surpliced minister was unable to perform the sacrament after bread and communion cup were swiped from the holy table. Services were only possible at St Mildred, Bread Street, the Sunday after Easter, because the alderman's deputy and prominent parishioners stood guard over a stand-in minister to protect him from the suspended rector and his glowering adherents. Rival groups of parishioners came to blows at All Hallows, Thames Street, after the conforming minister was seen to smile approvingly during a sermon denouncing the vestments policy. A Scottish clergyman, who first preached against surplices and later conformed, had a rough time of it on Whit Monday in St Margaret Pattens, Rood Lane. 'A certain number of wives threw stones at him, and pulled him forth of the pulpit, rending his surplice and scratching his face' – a 'womanish brabble' was how Grindal described the incident to Cecil.

Even, or especially, in a strongly patriarchal age, female voices demanded to be heard, and to express a sometimes raucous judgement on disputed matters of religion. When, at the start of June, several leading nonconformist clergy were summoned for extended discussions with Bishop Horne of Winchester, a supportive crowd of two to three hundred women accompanied the ministers over London Bridge into Southwark, showering them with gifts, and 'animating them most earnestly to stand fast in the same their doctrine which they had taught touching surplices'. A few weeks earlier, a deputation of sixty women came to Grindal's house to petition on behalf of an arrested divinity lecturer from Crowley's parish of St Giles. Grindal delivered a patronizing message that they should 'send me half-a-dozen of their husbands, and with them I would talk'. But the bishop was on the receiving end of female wrath at the start of the following year, when he came to preach at St Margaret's, Old Fish Street, wearing the pointed square cap. The congregation, 'especially the women', hooted at him with the bull-baiting cry, 'ware horns!' One of the protestors, a Southwark tinker's wife, was forced to sit outside the church the following Saturday on two ladders 'like a cucking-stool'. But supporters gathered to tell her 'to rejoice and praise the Lord for that he had made her worthy to suffer persecution for righteousness'.[47]

How, Grindal must have been thinking, had it all come to this? Former exiles with proud records of witness against Marian oppression were being cast in the role of persecutors of the godly. 'Now my Lord of London', Parker remarked wryly to Cecil in June 1566, 'feeleth and seeth the marks and bounds of these good sprites, which, but for his tolerations etc., had been suppressed for five or six years ago.' One suspended minister, a man called Pattenson, preached sermons calling Grindal an antichrist, a heretic and a traitor. He was unashamed to repeat the charges to Grindal's face, citing the seventh chapter of Deuteronomy as condemnation of anyone who retained 'idols'. Pattenson had been ordained by Grindal, but now recognized neither his suspension, nor any authority of a 'popish licence' or obligation to remain ministering within his cure. 'My cure,' he announced solemnly, 'is wheresoever I do meet with a congregation that are willing to hear the word of God.' The Duchess of Suffolk, grande dame of the Marian exile, petitioned for Pattenson's release, but, unsurprisingly, he remained in custody.[48]

Pattenson's preoccupations with preservation from the pollution of idolatry, and with total fidelity to a literal reading of God's Word, were symptoms of a wider, and worrying, trend. The drive against nonconformity was producing a sometimes token conformity, but it was also creating more radical forms of dissent, and even withdrawal from communal worship. This was no complete novelty, for it was what some Protestant Londoners did in the reign of Mary. On 19 June 1567, a conventicle of around a hundred persons was discovered worshipping at the hall of the Plumbers' Livery Company, hired ostensibly for a wedding. The ringleaders were questioned the next day by Grindal and other ecclesiastical commissioners. The bishop put it to them that, 'in severing yourselves from the society of other Christians, you condemn not only us, but also the whole state of the Church reformed in King Edward's days, which was well reformed according to the Word of God'.

That was at least two moot points. The group's spokesman, John Smith, protested that for as long as the Word was freely preached, and sacraments ministered without 'idolatrous gear', they 'never assembled together in houses'. But when 'our preachers were displaced by your law'– a strikingly confrontational phrase – they began to look to the example of Queen Mary's days, and the congregation at Geneva, 'which used a book and order of preaching, ministering of the sacraments and discipline, most agreeable to the Word of God'.

Unfinished business from Mary's reign hung heavily over a testy encounter. Smith wanted to know if Grindal would really have him return to his parish church – the minister there 'is a very papist'. Another prisoner protested that he knew of 'one that in Queen Mary's time did persecute God's saints, and brought them forth to Bishop Bonner, and now he is minister allowed of you, and never made recantation'. It did Grindal little good to protest that a few bad apples needn't spoil the barrel, or that he himself was no fan of cope and surplice. Nor did appeals to the duty of obedience cut any ice with these perfectionists: 'It lieth not in the authority of the prince, and liberty of a Christian man,' stated Robert Hawkins, 'to use and defend that [which] appertaineth to papistry and idolatry.'

Plumbers' Hall was not some late flowering of the old sub-cultural exclusivity of Lollardy, or of the radical sectarianism of the mid-Tudor decades, for all that Stow might dismissively call such gatherings 'congregations of the anabaptists'. The separatism of late 1560s' London was an ideological creation of the Marian persecution, looking explicitly to the example of Knox's Genevan congregation. Its roots were nourished by dissident preachers within the established Church.

The fountain-head of that nourishment was the church of Holy Trinity in the Minories, a former monastic 'liberty' near the Tower of London, which retained its ecclesiastical privileges limiting episcopal control. The Duchess of Suffolk was resident in the liberty, a patroness of preachers like Pattenson and Miles Coverdale, who preached thirteen times in the church in 1567–8. Stow believed that the separatists originally 'kept their church at the Minories', before starting to hold meetings in a minister's house in Pudding Lane, a chopper's house in Thames Street, a goldsmith's dwelling near the Savoy, and many other places, including a ship moored at the dock known as St Katherine's Pool.

They 'called themselves Puritans, or Unspotted Lambs of the Lord'.[49] More likely this was what critics, such as Stow himself, called them, adopting the pejorative jargon of the overseas Catholics. Nonetheless, the movement created by the vestments crisis of 1565–7 – which we can reasonably call Puritanism – faced from the start an existential dilemma: should it work to restore a defective Church from within, or abandon it for the purity and pleasure of underground worship?

Bridges between the bishops and advocates of further godly reform were in 1566 battered, but not burned. Parliament, which reconvened in September, remained a place for harmonized action. Once again, the Lords and Commons (egged on by Cecil) petitioned the Queen to marry and produce an heir. There were moves too to introduce a bill to settle the succession – all slapped down by Elizabeth with her usual imperious indignation: 'a strange thing that the foot should direct the head in so weighty a cause'.

The question of the succession, and the cause of 'religion', were more than ever closely entwined. After deciding she could not herself marry Leicester, Elizabeth half-heartedly pushed for a match between him and the widowed Queen of Scots. But in July 1565 Mary married Henry, Lord Darnley. The marriage both strengthened and Catholicized Mary's putative place in the English succession. Darnley had his own tenable claim to the throne: he was a grandson, via her second marriage, of Henry VIII's sister, Margaret. Crucially, he was born and brought up south of the border, and though he conformed while in England, in Scotland he reverted to the Catholicism of his youth. Unstable and self-obsessed, Darnley's religious allegiances in 1565–6 fluctuated with the tide of Scottish politics. But in terms of the English succession he had an unbeatable qualification: in June 1566 Mary bore him a son.

Even before this, English exiles at Louvain were openly talking of Mary as heir to the English throne, and by October 1565 Philip II had finally come round to the conclusion 'that she is the gate by which religion must enter the realm of England'. Reformers feared that the advocates of a Stewart succession within England were often but 'dissimuled or hypocritical Protestants'. Thomas Sampson, deprived dean of Christ Church, was the probable author of a pamphlet urging Parliament to persuade the Queen to settle the succession, to avoid risks of civil war and rule by a 'stranger'. If she proved reluctant, then members should 'bestow your wisdom and power to put your country out of such peril'; in other words, act on their own authority without royal consent – once again, religious necessity was the mother of constitutional invention.[50]

The Queen forbad further discussion of the succession, but in the weeks preceding Christmas there was a push to resurrect unfinished business from the Convocation of 1563. A succession of bills was introduced into the Commons, aiming to improve education and discipline among the clergy, insisting on personal residence and condemning simony and unregulated leasing of benefices. Labelled A–F by the Clerk, the 'alphabetical bills' foundered on the rock of Elizabeth's conviction that reforms to the Church were a matter for the Supreme Governor alone. By raising them, Lord Keeper Bacon was instructed to tell MPs, 'You err in bringing her Majesty's prerogative in question.'

Bill A went furthest, in every sense. It passed through the Commons, but Elizabeth sent instructions to Lord Keeper Bacon to inhibit discussion in the Lords. The bill gave statutory authority to the Thirty-Nine Articles, and most likely proposed making subscription to them a requirement for office. Parker protested to Elizabeth that the bill was not, as she seemed to suspect, devised and introduced by the bishops. But, as in the 1563 Convocation, they were happy to bless the reforming labours of others. On Christmas Eve, Parker, along with Archbishop Thomas Young of York, Grindal, and a dozen other bishops, sent Elizabeth a letter of remonstrance enumerating the dire consequences of 'want of a plain certainty of Articles of doctrine, by law to be declared'. It was water off a duck's back. Elizabeth had nothing against the book itself, 'for it containeth the religion which she doth openly profess'. But she would not tolerate 'the manner of putting forth'.

It was another royal rebuff for a broad coalition of Protestant interests. 'The bill of religion stayed, to the comfort of the adversaries,' was Cecil's terse summary of the (non-) achievements of the 1566 Parliament. The failure increased the strain on relations between bishops and even the more moderate of the 'Puritans'. At the height of the vestments controversy, Humphrey and Sampson told Bullinger they had no wish to sow schisms, or lead a 'hostile opposition'. They disagreed with the decision, but would bear it: 'we must indeed submit to the time'. But this was 'only *for* a time, so that we may be always making progress, and never retreating'.

That was the rub: for the godly, pauses and delays were tolerable, but there could be no going back, even to the Church of Edward VI. In a dialogue by Anthony Gilby, written in 1566, a conformist character protests that, in Edwardian times, vestments were 'used of godly men'. An honest soldier puts him straight: 'That was but the first show of the light . . . we must grow to further perfection'. The question was whether the bishops possessed either the will or stamina to strive for that perfection. 'So long as the Parliament endured', Gilby reflected, 'we all had hope of amendment, and kept silence. But now that it is ended, and all hope of man is past, we must turn to God.'[51]

### The Religion Really Observed

In April 1567, Thomas Radcliffe, Earl of Sussex, prepared to travel to Vienna, to resume negotiations for a possible marriage between Elizabeth and the Archduke Charles. It was a mission of acute diplomatic sensitivity, involving a response to the Habsburg demand, which Elizabeth was reluctant to concede, for Charles to be permitted to hear mass in England.

On the eve of his departure – in a version reported to the Spanish ambassador – Sussex confessed to Elizabeth how underprepared he felt for the delicate discussions over religion: 'Although he was a native-born Englishman, and knew as well as others what was passing in the country, he was at a loss to state what *was* the religion that really was observed here'. His understanding was that the Queen and her councillors 'held by the Augsburg Confession' (i.e. practised Lutheranism), but he was also aware that Calvinism 'was being preached and being taught nearly everywhere'. Could the Council please decide upon this, so he would know what to say to his hosts?[52]

The perplexity was that of a courtier and soldier of no very fixed theological views, fretting about a mission he did not want to undertake. But the sense of uncertainty about where on the religious spectrum the Church of England really lay was one widely shared across that spectrum. In the context of Habsburg marriage negotiations, Elizabeth was anxious to show a cautious, conservative face. In summer 1565, Sussex accompanied the imperial ambassador to an elaborate choral service in the Chapel Royal. An effort to reassure him there had been no violent lurch towards heresy was reinforced by the gift of a Prayer Book, with encouragement to note the retention of old prayers, the words of administration at communion, and the rubric on vestments. Elizabeth may not have been prepared formally to endorse Parker's Advertisements at home, but she was happy to send a printed copy of them to the Spanish court, and have them received there as 'the articles of the English Church'.

A few weeks before the Austrian envoy's arrival, Bishop Guest of Rochester preached before the Queen on Christ's words, 'Hoc est corpus meum quod pro vobis tradetur' (This is my body, which is given up for you). Avoiding other issues of controversy, Guest repeatedly asserted the real presence in the sacrament. One of his listeners, it was reported, could not contain his enthusiasm, shouting out 'I do believe it, and he who doth not should be forthwith burnt!' Thomas Harding took it as a welcome sign of Elizabeth's 'good inclination towards the ancient and Catholic religion' that she had personally thanked Guest, this 'more temperate' preacher.[53]

It was precisely because Catholics might choose to interpret vestments, Prayer Book ceremonies and the Queen's cross in the Chapel Royal as signs of theological kinship that godly Protestants were more than ever convinced they must be removed. In October 1567, Elizabeth's crucifix in the Chapel Royal was vandalized for a second time. 'A certain youth' knocked it over and stamped on it during a service. Some thought him mad, but Parkhurst believed he acted 'under the influence of great zeal for God'. The image was, once again, replaced.

There were alarming reports, fuelled by the matrimonial negotiations, of people believing reconciliation with Rome to be on the cards. Cecil learned in August 1567 that Paris was full of false stories that the Queen had set the imprisoned bishops free and ordered them 'to set up mass and old religion again'. Such rumours could rise up closer to home. In May 1566, Thomas Cole, archdeacon of Essex, a fervent critic of vestments, preached at Chelmsford – not, he protested, against the order for apparel itself, but 'to hinder the disorderly talk and impudent conceit of the papists, which by reason of this order rumoured that they should have their mass again'.

Parker tried hard to persuade nonconformists that vestments could be 'a means to win the adversaries from their errors, when they see us without superstition . . . turn those things to good uses'. But his opponents were having none of it. An anonymous Puritan pamphleteer imagined the sound of 'the common voice' – the kind of opinions bishops would hear 'if you walked in the country':

> Popery is not so evil as they make it, for then they would never command these things so straitly to be observed . . . Neighbour, played we not a wise part, when we kept our mass clothes and books? For by the mass, neighbour, we shall have all again one day.

The ceremonial requirements, and the messages they emitted, were dangerous precisely because the Church at large was only patchily reformed, and in many places primed and ready for Catholic restoration. One preacher at Paul's Cross in early 1566 reckoned there were three or four thousand churches where worship continued 'according to the purification of the Jews' – that is, where clergy and laity conspired and contrived to preserve elements of the popish past.[54]

A full decade into Elizabeth's reign, few thoughtful observers truly believed 'religion' to be settled or secure. Elizabeth herself maintained it to be so, but precisely what it was she was asking the nation to value and believe seemed far from self-evident. At the local level, Protestantism continued its advance, particularly in towns. Yet its most enthusiastic proponents were often only incidentally and conditionally the agents of a state Church.

Even after years of episcopal prodding and probing, Catholic sentiment pervaded the parishes. Bishop Bullingham's visitation of Lincoln in 1566, and Archbishop Young's 1567 York visitation, revealed much evidence of altars and images, either concealed, or displayed openly in the churches. At Preston in the East Riding, the rood loft was 'full of painted pictures'. A few miles away at Swine, the episcopal visitors found 'a cross of wood standing over the north aisle, with a scutcheon [shield] having the figure of Five Wounds'. This, they may have recollected, was the badge of the 1536 Pilgrims. A dozen and more clergymen were uncovered in 1567 who 'useth the communion for the dead' – an application of new liturgical forms to old superstitious purposes. Things were even worse in North Wales, where the newly installed Bishop Nicholas Robinson of Bangor reported in October 1567 on 'images and altars standing in churches undefaced, lewd and undecent vigils and watches observed, much pilgrimage-going, many candles set up to the honour of saints, some relics yet carried about, and all the countries full of beads and knots, besides divers other monuments of wilful serving of God'. He was at least making a start: 'of which abuses, some (I thank God) are reformed'.

Slow, incomplete reformation was not limited to remote or upland regions. Numerous priests in Sussex were reported in 1569 to 'keep yet still their chalices, looking for to have mass again'. Only in 1568 did the churchwardens of Great St Mary's, Cambridge, and those of St Edmunds, Salisbury, sell off their holy water stoups, banners, vestments and processional crosses. One of these parishes lay in the intellectual home of Puritan nonconformity, the other in the episcopal seat of Bishop John Jewel.[55]

It is not quite enough to call this local recalcitrance 'conservative', if that is meant to imply only an unthinking, instinctual preference for ancestral custom. There was certainly strong attachment to traditional ways, but Catholicism was evolving in the mid-1560s, drawing strength and direction from its recent Marian reinvention. When Bishop Bentham of Coventry ordered churchwardens in 1565 to 'diligently note and mark them that wear any beads', he pinpointed an old-fashioned pious habit that was fast becoming an assertive statement of difference and dissent (see p. 344).

John Stow, London chronicler and pronounced anti-Puritan, was a nostalgic conservative whose published writings suggest a hankering for the 'merry world' of pre-Reformation times into which he was born around 1525. We don't know exactly what Stow was thinking in the mid to late 1560s, but we know what he was reading. Thirty-nine suspect books were seized from his study in a raid ordered by Bishop Grindal in February 1569. They included pre-Reformation works of devotion; late Henrician eucharistic tracts by Smyth and Gardiner; a large collection of Marian pastoral and polemical writings by Bonner, Watson, Huggarde, Brooks and others; and a half-dozen recently published controversial works by the Louvain exiles Stapleton, Dorman, Rastell and Richard Shacklock. Stow's book-list was an intellectual genealogy of English Catholicism, from its ascendancy prior to 1530, through its struggle to find and assert its voice under Henry and Edward, its confident reinvention under Mary, and its embrace of separatist resistance under Elizabeth.[56]

No doubt chastened by his experience, Stow remained, formally, in the Church of England. But Rome, finally, was moving beyond its policy of 'wait and see'. In 1566, the new pope, Pius V, an austere and orthodox Dominican, formalized the positions of Thomas Harding and Nicholas Sander as apostolic delegates for England. They had the power to absolve people from the sin of schism, and the duty to explain to them it was indeed a sin. There was, Sander insisted in a work of 1567, no truth in rumours that 'going to schismatical service is, or may be, winked at or dispensed'. Occupied with their literary war against Jewel, Harding and Sander delegated the task of going to England to publicize the ban on church-attendance to the Lancashire-born priest Laurence Vaux. Once back in the north-west, Vaux circulated letters announcing the 'definitive sentence', not just on attending communion service but against bringing infants to churches for baptism.

It was a declaration of complete spiritual separation: 'We may not communicate or associate ourselves with heretic or schismatic in divine things.' It was also a counsel of perfection for an imperfect world. Where could Catholics turn for rites of baptism and marriage, for the honourable burial of their dead?

For the gentry in particular, ceasing to worship in local churches of which they were patrons, places where their ancestors lay buried, was an act of social self-abnegation. Vaux recognized that some Catholics would find the mandate 'hard, sharp, bitter and sore'. Yet other deprived priests soon possessed 'faculties' to reconcile schismatics, and in 1567–8 the Queen directed a stream of concerned letters at the bishop of Chester and the Lancashire magistrates, ordering the arrest of seditious persons, aiming 'under colour of religion to draw sundry gentlemen and other our subjects ... from their duty of allegiance'.[57] The government was waking up to the fact that it had a real recusancy problem, its extent much greater than previous lax policing had been able to reveal.

Elizabeth's goal as Supreme Governor, in the words of a 1559 proclamation, was 'the soul health of her loving subjects, and the quieting of their consciences in the chief and principal points of Christian religion'.[58] Whatever the condition of their souls, the consciences of a great many, Protestant and Catholic, had been stirred rather than quieted by the events of the ensuing nine years. The extent of their 'loving' was also about to undergo its greatest test. On the evening of 16 May 1568, a party of weary travellers disembarked from a fishing boat at Workington in Cumberland, on the southern coast of the Solway Firth. Among them was the Queen of Scots, a refugee from her own land, and a harbinger of trouble, tragedy and treason.

# 16

## ADMONITIONS

### The Queen of Scots

'THE PERILS ARE many, great and imminent.' William Cecil's 'short memorial of the state of the realm', written at the start of 1569, made for sobering reading – purposefully so, as the intended recipient was likely Elizabeth herself. England was internally fragile and externally isolated. 'Marriage', 'children', 'alliance' headed a list of things 'the weakness of the Queen's Majesty's estate growth upon lack of'. Cecil feared renewed rebellion in Ireland, 'mixt with a Spanish practice', and saw a heavy Spanish shadow falling across Europe as a whole. Philip II's general, the Duke of Alva, seemed to have ruthlessly crushed the revolt against Spanish rule in the Netherlands. In France, the Huguenot leader, the Prince of Condé, was running out of men and money, while Spain and the Pope hurried to supply his enemies.

In November 1568, Cecil's determination to contain Spanish ambition almost turned a cold war hot. He ordered confiscation of the cargo of several Spanish ships, carrying gold to Alva, and forced by storms into English ports. The Spanish retaliated against English property in the Netherlands, and open conflict was only just averted. The apparent recklessness reflected Cecil's conviction that the Catholic powers were rampant and resurgent: the Council of Trent, he wrote in the Memorial, did much towards 'the recovery of the tyranny of Rome'. With his eye on the bigger military and diplomatic picture, Cecil took little notice of threats posed by the English exiles, though he observed the presence of Englishmen as pensioners at Philip's court, as well as the publication of 'slanderous books and histories' against the Queen.

One recent event was evidently too small a matter to be worthy of report. In September 1568, William Allen leased a house for a handful of students near the theology schools at the newly founded University of Douai. This 'English College' was a seminary, a priestly training school of the type planned by

Cardinal Pole (see p. 401), and recently mandated by Trent for dioceses across the Catholic world. Exiled English Catholicism was at the forefront of this initiative. Priests, like wine or cheese, took time to perfect. But from the outset, students were admitted to the college with more than their own spiritual formation in mind. In a letter to the president of Philip's Privy Council in the Netherlands, Allen predicted that within a few years the graduates would 'be employed in promoting the Catholic cause in England, even at peril of their lives'.

A more clear and present danger was the person Cecil never referred to by name, only as 'the Queen of Scots'. Mary's strength underlined Elizabeth's weakness. It lay in 'the universal opinion of the world for the justice of her title'; in support from 'the strongest monarchies of Christendom'; in 'secret and great numbers of discontented subjects in this realm, that gape and practise for a change by her means'.

Cecil knew the remedies. Mary must formally relinquish all claims to the English succession. The current government of Scotland, under the Earl of Moray, should be supported. A defensive alliance with the Protestant princes of Germany contracted. The secretary was a practical man. But his realism made him more, not less, an idealist for the Protestant cause. True safety lay in pushing forward: 'all means used to advance religion in this realm'.[1]

Cecil's expansive estimate of the danger posed by Mary stands in contrast to her truly disastrous personal circumstances. It is hard to imagine what else could have gone wrong with her governance of Scotland. After returning from France in 1561, Mary endured with considerable grace the incessant hectoring of John Knox, and proved pragmatic about her anomalous position as the Catholic queen of a politically Protestant nation. It was her embrace of the duty Elizabeth perversely resisted – for a female ruler to marry – that proved her undoing.

As a king and a husband, Darnley was feckless, factional and violent. But a wide swathe of opinion was nonetheless deeply shocked when, on 10 February 1567, he was found murdered, his body under a tree in the garden of his house, blown up by gunpowder, at Kirk o' Field, Edinburgh. Two months later, the chief suspect, the swaggering Earl of Bothwell, abducted and most likely raped the Queen.

Mary was (probably) innocent of complicity in Darnley's murder, but her decision – from whatever mix of motives – to agree to marry Bothwell was an error of staggering proportions. Rebel lords took possession of her child and defeated the Queen's forces in battle. She was imprisoned on a small island in Loch Leven, and on 24 July 1567 forced to abdicate the throne. Within a week, her one-year-old son was crowned as James VI.

On 2 May 1568, Mary escaped and raised an army against Moray, the Protestant regent. Eleven days later, her forces were defeated at the battle of

Langside. Rather than stay in Scotland and regroup, Mary made the fateful decision to flee to England, and throw herself on the mercy of Elizabeth.

The quality of that mercy was strained, or at least conflicted. Mary was a political rival, as well as an accused adulteress and murderess; Elizabeth refused requests to grant her an audience. She was also an anointed monarch, overthrown by rebels imbued with the Knoxian principles Elizabeth loathed with every fibre of her regal being. Elizabeth hoped Mary might be restored, under strict conditions, to her throne, but she also agreed to investigate the Scottish government's charges against her.

A 'conference' – rather than a formal trial – was convened at York in October 1568, soon afterwards moved to Westminster. Moray and the Scottish commissioners formally accused Mary of murder, and produced 'proof': a set of letters found in a casket, sent from Mary to Bothwell, and revealing her complicity in a plot to murder Darnley. Although the letters were almost certainly forged, or at least heavily doctored, the English commissioners acknowledged them as authentic.

The conference ended, in January 1569, with Elizabeth declaring nothing to be finally proven one way or the other. It was clear, however, that restoration was not an immediate option, and that English Protestant opinion was in the main firmly convinced of Mary's guilt. On decidedly hazy legal grounds, the deposed Queen of Scots remained a prisoner, and at the start of February was moved from Bolton Castle in North Yorkshire to the secure custodianship of the Earl of Shrewsbury at Tutbury Castle in Staffordshire – far from the escape routes of the coast, and further from the Catholic heartlands of the north.[2]

### Counter-Reformation in the North

That may have been Cecil's doing. High on his January 1569 to-do list was 'to inquire and regard the state of the country northward, where her person is, and to keep suspected persons in some awe from harkening to practices, and the common people from riots and mutinies which are the cloaks and preparatives of rebellion'. They were prescient words, if not quite prescient enough.

Like other good Protestants, Cecil lay awake at night worrying about the slow progress of reform in the north. Archbishop Thomas Young of York was among the more pragmatic and accommodating of Elizabeth's bishops. His death in June 1568 produced an opportunity for a firmer anti-Catholic hand at the tiller. Parker and Cecil favoured Grindal for the post, but Elizabeth, predictably, refused to make a decision, and the key diocese remained vacant.

The new, hawkish, Spanish ambassador, Guerau de Spes, was also looking to the north, hopefully rather than fearfully. In May 1569 he reported to Philip that nearly all Wales and the north were Catholic, and strongly attached to the Queen of Scots. In July he added that 'a rising in the north is feared', and that heretic ministers from there were arriving in London, driven out by their congregations. But Spanish hopes did not rest on the grievances of Yorkshire farmfolk; great men were in play. The Duke of Norfolk (grandson of the 3rd duke, who died in 1554) and the Earl of Arundel had assured the ambassador of their good will towards the King of Spain. Norfolk, wrote de Spes, adhered to the 'Augustinian' (Lutheran) Creed, but Arundel was confident he could convert him. The Earl of Northumberland was likewise pledged to support moves to restore the Catholic faith. And, at second-hand, a message from the imprisoned Mary: 'Tell the ambassador that, if his master will help me, I shall be queen of England in three months, and mass shall be said all over the country.'[3]

It was a tangled web of threads, drawing into a pattern by the late summer of 1569. One solution to the Mary problem was – fourth time presumably lucky – for her to wed again, though the marriage to Bothwell, a fugitive and prisoner in Denmark, was not formally annulled. The proposal originated with the wily Scots politician William Maitland of Lethington, who put it to Norfolk at the York Conference. Safely married to a Protestant husband, Mary would cease to be a magnet of discontent, and Elizabeth could recognize her as heir, removing uncertainty over the English succession.

Norfolk, son of the executed Earl of Surrey, and England's premier duke, though scarcely its leading statesman, was transfixed by the idea. Other leading Protestants saw merit in the scheme, including Nicholas Throckmorton and Leicester, for whom it promised a welcome reduction in the influence of William Cecil. Conservative nobles like Arundel and Pembroke were drawn to it for the same reason. Thomas Percy, Earl of Northumberland, was another number in a matrix of whispered discussions, connecting Tutbury to Rome and Madrid, via Ambassador de Spes, John Leslie, exiled bishop of Ross and Mary's chief advisor, and Roberto Ridolfi, an energetic Florentine banker based in London. Ridolfi held an appointment as *nunzio segreto* (secret envoy) of the Pope. Northumberland was initially unenthusiastic about the marriage, later confessing he advised Mary that many of her supporters were wary of Norfolk's Protestantism, and that 'if she looked to recover her estate, it must be by advancing the Catholic religion.'[4]

There were only two problems with the plan: Elizabeth would never agree to it, and she was bound to find out. The Queen already knew what was afoot before Leicester confessed all to her on 6 September, a day after Bonner died in the Marshalsea, and was buried secretly at midnight on Grindal's orders. The laying of one shade of the Marian past coincided with the rising spectre of another. Like Princess Mary in 1553, Norfolk ignored a summons to the court, and retreated to his estate at Kenninghall in East Anglia. But he lacked the nerve to raise a rebellion there, and at the start of October decided to go back to London and excuse himself to the Queen.

Norfolk was plotting a wedding, not a war, but he was privy to bold talk, and by the end of the summer had been drawn into the audacious plans of the northern Catholics. On the eve of his return to London he sent a message to the Earls of Northumberland and Westmorland, pleading that 'they should not rise, for if they did, it would cost him his head'. Norfolk had a close connection to Charles Neville, Earl of Westmorland, husband of his sister, Jane. In a separate message he begged Westmorland not to take to arms, whatever Northumberland decided. But Jane was made of sterner stuff than her brother: 'What a simple man the duke is, to begin a matter and not go through with it.'

Bereft of political support in the south, the northern earls – who *were* plotting a rebellion – quickly rethought their plans. Westmorland was an instinctive waverer, but his uncles Christopher and Cuthbert Neville were resolute warriors. Northumberland too was egged on by hawks in his retinue: Thomas Markenfield, a returnee from continental exile, and Richard Norton, a grizzled veteran of the rebellion of 1536. Most hawkish of all was the Countess of Westmorland. When it seemed – due to the suspicions of the government, and the growing preparedness of the president of the Council in the North, the Earl of Sussex – that action might be indefinitely postponed, she remonstrated with the procrastinating earls, lamenting 'they and their country were shamed for ever, and that they must seek holes to creep into'.[5]

A summons to present themselves at court finally bounced the earls into action. On 9 November 1569, church bells began ringing at Topcliffe in North Yorkshire, chief residence of the Earl of Northumberland. The Neville tenantry had for days been trooping to the Earl of Westmorland's castle at Brancepeth in County Durham, and Northumberland hastened to meet him there. He too was kept on his mettle by his (pregnant) wife, reported to Cecil as 'the stouter of the two'. She 'doth hasten him, and encourage him to persevere, and rides up and down with their army'.

Anne Percy was a sister of William Somerset, Catholic earl of Worcester. The rebels spread rumours he was raising Wales on their behalf, though in fact Worcester remained conspicuously loyal. As in 1536, there were fears of a more general conflagration. Bishop Sandys of Worcester wrote to Cecil about 'counterfeited countenances and hollow hearts'. Cecil himself issued an order for the arrest in Oxford and Cambridge of 'all young men being the sons or kinsfolk of any of the rebels in the north, or of any suspected persons for religion'.[6] But the insurgency remained confined to the north, and to those parts of the north – County Durham and the North Riding of Yorkshire – where the earls and their lieutenants exercised immediate sway.

For all that, things were serious enough. Writing to the Queen from York on 26 November, Sir Ralph Sadler estimated the rebels' strength to be about 6,000 foot and 1,000 horse, all well armed. It was at least as large an army as that fielded by the western rebels in 1549, and larger than that with which

Wyatt nearly toppled Queen Mary in 1554. As usual, government forces on the ground were badly outnumbered. The Earl of Sussex was happier mustering horse and harness than discussing theology at the Austrian court, but even when reinforced by Sadler and Lord Hunsdon he commanded at York only a fraction of the rebel numbers. Tutbury was a hundred miles away, but the government was taking no chances: on 22 November orders were issued to move the Queen of Scots further south to Coventry.[7]

On the eve of the rising, as the earls and their confederates debated their options at Topcliffe, the question arose of what they were actually rebelling for. To Norton and Markenfield, it seemed obvious: 'for religion'. But Westmorland demurred: 'No; those that seem to take that quarrel in other countries are accounted as rebels, and therefore I will never blot my house which hath been this long preserved without staining.' It was of a piece with Mary's emphasis on legitimacy during her campaign in 1553, and with Wyatt's determination to 'not so much as mention religion' (see p. 370). Once the rising was under way, a manifesto drawn up in the name of the two earls (and, to their acute embarrassment, in the names of Norfolk, Arundel and Pembroke) protested loyalty to the Queen, emphasized the need to clarify the succession and spoke in conventional terms about 'subversion of the commonwealth' by sinister councillors.[8] The rebellion is often seen as a last gasp of the old feudal nobility, angered at their exclusion from the corridors of power. It was sustained, certainly, by traditional faith, but this too was the Indian summer of a passing world.

This interpretation is understandable, but in significant respects wrong. The Rising of the Northern Earls was the last in the great sequence of 'Tudor Rebellions' – conservative attempts to restore the upset balance of the commonwealth. But it was also, even more than Wyatt's Rebellion, something new: an attempt at regime-change motivated by religion as a political ideology. It supplies compelling evidence of a mutation in English Catholicism, under way in the 1550s and accelerated in the 1560s, as traditional Christianity – or some strands of it – allowed itself to be reinvented as sectarian Roman Catholicism. It was also the closest that England came in the sixteenth century to a French-style war of religion.

The manifesto sent to the Earl of Derby, and forwarded by him to the court, spoke in deliberately ambiguous terms of the rebel leadership as 'favourers of God's Word'. But other proclamations issued by the earls, with the aim of drumming up recruits in the north, highlighted a duty to set forth God's 'true and Catholic religion', and to resist the 'new-found religion and heresy' imposed on the realm by traitors.

Northumberland was himself, in a sense, a recent convert. In 1567, he was formally reconciled to Rome by a priest named Copley, one of those exercising a wandering ministry after refusal to submit to the settlement of 1559. Earlier in 1569, Northumberland took counsel with Nicholas Morton, sent from Rome by Pius V to gauge the situation of English Catholics, and authorized to grant powers of reconciliation to other priests. The rebel leadership scrupled over whether they might legitimately take up arms against Elizabeth before she was 'lawfully excommunicated by the head of the Church'. Morton told anyone who would listen that Elizabeth was already excommunicated, by virtue of her refusal to admit the papal nuncio. On 8 November, the very eve of their revolt, the earls wrote to Rome for guidance. But Northumberland was already radicalized by reading the works of the Louvain exiles. Harding, Sander, Stapleton and others illuminated for him 'the unity which ever hath been, throughout Christendom, among those called papists; the disagreement and great dissension continually growing, and that ever hath been, among the Protestants'.[9]

The leadership of the 1569 rising was unitedly 'Roman', in a way that that of 1536 was not (see p. 251). More surprisingly, this seems to have been true to a remarkable extent of the rank-and-file. These were not in the main Percy or Neville tenants activated by ancestral loyalty, but volunteers, emboldened by the earls' leadership to express their uncompromising rejection of the state religion – though the loyalist gentleman Sir George Bowes claimed sourly that many were bribed or coerced into taking part.

That was not the case at Sedgefield, a village ten miles south of Durham. Here, as locals later testified, 'the parish met together, and consulted to set in the altar stone'. They knew precisely where it was: buried in 'Gibson's garth' (a yard or garden). A crowd – some said thirty, others eighty – dragged the altar to the church with ropes, and re-erected it with lime and mortar. Processional restoration was followed by iconoclastic destruction. The parish's Protestant books – bible, homilies and psalters – were collected and taken to the town gate. There, before a 'great multitude', they were torn to shreds and thrown onto a fire. 'Lo,' cried the husbandman Roland Hixson, 'where the Homilies flee to the devil!' Mass was said in Sedgefield church for the first time in over a decade, accompanied by a combative sermon from the priest, Richard Hartborn. Witnesses recalled him saying that 'the doctrine of England was naught, and that this realm was cut off from all other nations'; 'they were all out of the way, and worse than a horse that hath been in the mire'. Parishioners knelt, and Hartborn reconciled them from the sin of schism.

The events at Sedgefield were far from unique: Prayer Books and bibles were destroyed in at least eighty-five Yorkshire and County Durham churches. The most dramatic episodes were in Durham itself, after the entry of the earls on 14 November. The full splendour of the Latin liturgy returned to Durham Cathedral, one of the great churches of northern Europe. Later protestations by the cathedral's minor canons, lay clerks and choristers, that they took part in these triumphal rituals unwillingly, have a decidedly unconvincing air. Sermons about schism, and formal submission to Rome, were the core of the

proceedings. The priest William Holmes 'willed all that was disposed to be
reconciled to kneel down; whereupon he pronounced a *forma absolutionis* in
Latin, in the name of Christ and Bishop Pius'. It was St Andrew's Day, 30
November, anniversary of the Marian reunion with Rome. It is doubtful that
many, if any, in the cathedral remained standing. Holmes also invited priests to
his lodging, for individual reconciliation.[10]

There was real revivalist fervour behind this local outbreak of the Counter-
Reformation, heightened by the fact that, in James Pilkington (who sensibly
fled south), Durham had endured the rule of one of England's most zealously
Protestant bishops. The regime at the cathedral, where the 'Genevan' William
Whittingham served as dean, was positively puritanical. Whittingham's French
Huguenot wife used holy water stoups for salting beef in her kitchen, and was
suspected of having burned the banner of St Cuthbert – the miracle-working
relic, carried by the Pilgrims in 1536. Deprived of this totem, the rebels marched
behind another familiar symbol of Catholic rebellion, the Five Wounds of
Christ. It was also reported that 'all their force, both of horse and foot' wore red
crosses on their clothes. The cross of St George was the conventional symbol of
English soldiery in the field, but the hostility of Protestants to the religious
iconography of the cross lent it new potency as a partisan emblem. Another
witness declared that the wearing of a great crucifix around the neck was 'the
ensign of the order of these rebels'.[11]

For some, it was all too much. John Browne, priest of Witton Gilbert, a
chapelry just north-west of Durham, stepped emotionally into the pulpit to ask
mercy from God and his parishioners: 'I have these eleven years taught you the
wrong way.' He renounced his office, insisting that 'wheresoever you meet me,
in town or field, take me as a stranger, and none of your curate'. Browne's
Nicodemism was a millstone around the conscience, not a lightly worn outward
conformity. He was not the only clergyman at this time publically to beg his
people's forgiveness for leading them astray.[12]

The Catholic carnival of 1569 burned bright and brief. Hoped-for support
in Lancashire and Cheshire was not forthcoming, and the earls fatefully turned
back north in the last week of November, rather than press on to capture a
thinly garrisoned York. While a large royal army gathered in the south, a
handful of competent loyalist commanders – Sadler, Hunsdon, Sir John Forster,
Sir Thomas Gargrave – helped shore up resistance, and prevent disorder from
spreading, all the while seeking to convince a suspicious Elizabeth that Sussex
had not deliberately allowed things to get out of hand. By mid-December, with
the Queen's army finally approaching the River Tees, the earls' nerve gave out.
They disbanded their foot soldiers, and fled with the fast-moving cavalry. Just
after Christmas, they crossed the border into Scotland to seek shelter with
Marian sympathizers.

It was not quite all over. A potential supporter in the far north-west, Leonard
Dacre, was in London through the autumn contesting a lawsuit for control of

the family estates. Ironically, his adversary was Norfolk, widowed step-father to the daughters of his brother, the fourth Lord Dacre. Leonard returned to the family seat at Naworth in Cumberland at the end of the year, but was soon under suspicion of raising troops to assist the rebels, rather than, as he claimed, to resist them. The assassination of the Earl of Moray by a Marian supporter on 23 January 1570 made a second rebellion, with Scottish support, seem a real possibility, and the government ordered Dacre's arrest.

On 20 February, Dacre's borderers pre-emptively offered battle to Lord Hunsdon on heathland near the River Gelt, a few miles east of Carlisle. It was a bloody and decisive encounter: Hunsdon's horsemen charged Dacre's infantry, and killed three or four hundred and captured a further two or three hundred. The single day's death toll surpassed the four-year tally of Marian martyrs – another reminder that the 'peaceful' character of the English Reformation should never be blithely asserted.

Dacre himself escaped to Scotland, and within a year was in Antwerp, collecting a meagre pension from Philip II. Westmorland also fled from Scotland to the Spanish Netherlands, as did Markenfield and Norton. Northumberland's courageous countess likewise made it to the Low Countries, but the earl was not so fortunate. On crossing into Scotland in December 1569, he was betrayed by border reivers and handed over to Moray. The Scots held him as a bargaining chip, and in June 1572 sold him to the English government.[13]

## Aftermath

After the rising, the reckoning. With most of the leaders beyond her reach, Elizabeth's vengeance fell on the ordinary rebels. Martial law was declared in the north, and the Privy Council authorized use of torture to discover the full extent of local treason. Sussex and his officers drew up lists of rebels, and fixed a number, generally between 20 and 40 per cent, of those to die in each district. The arbitrariness was almost the point, in a retaliation more brutal than that following any previous sixteenth-century rebellion. Sussex's provost marshal, Sir George Bowes, travelled through the towns of Durham and North Yorkshire, with authority to hang more or fewer as he judged best. Writing to his cousin on 23 January, Bowes reckoned he had now executed 'six hundred and odd', adding that 'the people are in marvellous fear, so that I trust there shall never such thing happen in these parts again'.[14]

Not in these parts, not in any parts. Despite its limited extent, and inept execution, the rebellion was widely seen, not as a little local difficulty, but as an existential threat to the survival of the Queen and the Protestant religion. A prayer of thanksgiving, ordered to be read in all churches, praised the Almighty's ability 'to vanquish infinite multitudes of thine enemies'. In 1570, a new 'Homily against Disobedience and Wilful Rebellion', of gruelling length, was added to the collection rebellious parishioners had burned copies of the previous year. Grindal's translation to the smouldering see of York was hastily approved.

The rebellion inspired a rash of printed ballads and pamphlets, unofficial and semi-official. 'Between Doncaster and Penrith [i.e. the whole region, from the River Trent northwards] / Be many popish hearts / Would their heads were in carts'. The quotation is from a mock funeral liturgy for Edmund Bonner. For many Protestants, the cruelties of the popish past underlined the dangers in the present; the rising was a wake-up call about the risks of leniency, of the sort Bonner had consistently received.

Most prolific of the pamphleteers was Thomas Norton, a godly lawyer who in 1561 produced the first English translation of Calvin's *Institutes*. He was also the parliamentary agent, the 'man of business', for William Cecil. In one of half a dozen tracts written in 1569–70, Norton painted the papist, 'one that believeth all the Pope's doctrine to be true', as by definition an enemy and traitor. Moreover, 'no clemency, gentleness, benefits or loving dealing can win a papist, while he continues a papist, to love her Majesty'. Norton's defence of the Queen barely masked a critique of her policy towards Catholics, a view shared by Bishop Horne of Winchester, who complained to Cecil in January 1570 of the 'troubles and charges overmuch forbearing of the papists hath wrought'.[15]

That policy was changing even as the events of the rising played out. Cecil's memorandum looked to have 'the lawyers of the realm reformed'. In the autumn there was a purge of the Inns of Court, suspected to be nests of popery, as once they were of rebellious evangelicalism. In parallel, in November 1569, the government mounted a concerted nationwide drive to make justices of the peace take the Oath of Supremacy and subscribe to the Act of Uniformity and Book of Common Prayer. 'Mislikers' remaining in post through the 1560s – such as Nicholas Throckmorton's brother, Robert, in Warwickshire – were now removed from the county commissions.

In Berkshire, Edmund Plowden, the Catholic lawyer who defended Bonner in 1564, found he could not subscribe, though with legal fastidiousness, he requested time to read carefully through every line of the act and Prayer Book. The exercise turned Plowden into a recusant, since he attended church regularly through the 1560s. A Herefordshire JP, John Scudamore, declared his willingness to be loyal and obedient in everything 'saving matters of religion, or any manner thing touching the same . . . I do not refuse of obstinacy, but for conscience's sake'.

The authorities were not prepared to accept any formal distinction between spiritual and temporal obedience: it made mockery of the principles on which the royal supremacy was founded. But another form of mockery – of which Robert Atkinson warned in the Parliament of 1563 – was the taking of an oath while dissimulating one's inward dissent. Many Catholic sympathizers did just that, among them Nicholas and Robert's brother, John Throckmorton, a significant regional office-holder as vice-president of the Council in Wales.

Atkinson himself, faced with expulsion from the Inner Temple, claimed evasively that he attended church whenever he was in the country; he was nonetheless disbarred. Bishop Horne observed how southern papists 'stamp and stare at the rebels, and cry out at their lewd enterprise'. Yet he considered such protestations hypocritical; their real grievance with the northerners was 'that they dealt the matter so foolishly it could take no better effect'.[16]

## Regnans and Ridolfi

Suspicions that Catholics – all Catholics – were potential traitors were in the spring of 1570 powerfully confirmed by Rome itself. For years, exiles had been pressing the papacy to excommunicate Elizabeth. Nicholas Morton returned to Rome in the summer of 1569 with assurances of support in England for such a move, and news arriving after Christmas of the long-awaited rebellion convinced Pius V the time had come to act.

The process in Rome was not entirely arbitrary. Elizabeth was subject, in absentia, to a formal trial, whose proceedings opened on 5 February. The charges were of compelling her subjects to take a wicked oath; of depriving duly consecrated bishops and installing heretics in their place; of imprisoning people for hearing mass; of encouraging 'Calvinistic' sermons; and of ordaining heretical celebration of the Lord's Supper. Twelve expert witnesses – all English and Welsh clerical exiles – testified to the truth of the charges. They included Thomas Goldwell, bishop of St Asaph and latterly delegate at Trent, an incarnation of Catholic resistance since the days of Henry VIII.

On 25 February 1570 Pius V promulgated the bull known from its opening words as *Regnans in Excelsis* (Ruling in the highest). The phrase referred to God, rather than the Pope, but the document exuded a high self-estimation of papal authority. Elizabeth, 'pretended Queen of England', was declared to be a heretic, cut off from the unity of the body of Christ, and 'deprived of the right which she pretends to the foresaid kingdom'. All English people were absolved from 'all manner of duty, fidelity and obedience'. Indeed, they were positively instructed 'that they shall not once dare to obey her or any her directions'.[17]

The Pope, occupant of the oldest throne in Europe, thus revealed himself as much a political radical as any Knox or Goodman. He deposed a queen from her throne, and as good as authorized her subjects to rise in rebellion against her. An irritated Philip II was not consulted in advance, and thought 'his Holiness allowed himself to be carried away by his zeal'. Philip also believed, rightly, that in current circumstances the measure was impractical and would simply drive Elizabeth and her ministers 'the more to oppress and persecute the few good Catholics still remaining in England'. The Emperor Maximilian went as far as to ask the Pope to withdraw the excommunication. But even though news of the earls' defeat, along with the unwillingness of Catholic powers to help enforce it, made the bull a virtual dead letter, Pius had written what he had written.

To be canonically valid, a bull needed to be 'published'. Its promulgation in England was an occasion of high drama, akin to a formal declaration of war. Copies of the bull were smuggled into London, largely through the efforts of the ubiquitous Roberto Ridolfi, already questioned, and temporarily imprisoned, on suspicion of advancing money to the northern rebels. Early in the morning of 25 May 1570 the bull appeared nailed to the door of the bishop of London's palace, near St Paul's Cathedral. A wave of searches and arrests produced the name of John Felton, a wealthy layman resident in Surrey. Felton freely confessed to the deed, but was tortured to get him to admit to contacts with the Spanish ambassador. Felton was hanged and quartered in St Paul's churchyard, near the scene of the crime, on 8 August. The hangman's name, providentially, was Bull.[18]

Felton's execution for treason, for publicizing an authoritative papal teaching, marked the start of a new and dangerous phase of religious conflict. Since Henry VIII's days, no Catholic had been put to death in England solely for refusal to recognize the royal supremacy. There was, in both Edward's reign and the first decade of Elizabeth's, a pragmatic willingness to distinguish between the religious errors of Catholics and words and actions constituting a capital offence under the law. After *Regnans in Excelsis* that distinction became thoroughly muddied – in the eyes of the government, and in the minds of Catholics themselves.

A second treason trial confirmed the gloves were off. In August 1570, William Cecil, working at second and third hand with a team of agents in the Netherlands, arranged the kidnapping of John Story, now working for the Spanish authorities as a searcher of ships, for contraband and heretical literature. At his trial, Story claimed to have forsaken his country 'for conscience's sake', and further, that he was no longer the Queen's subject but 'the subject of the most Catholic and mighty prince, King Philip'. Story hoped this would confer immunity; for his judges, it merely measured the depth of his treason.

Story's real offence – now Bonner was dead – was to be the remembered face of the Marian persecution. His hanging and quartering at Tyburn on 1 June 1571 was a settling of old scores, and a delayed acknowledgement of long-ignored Protestant cries for vengeance. The publication in 1570 of a second, much expanded, edition of Foxe's *Acts and Monuments* helped keep that resentful memory alive. In November that year, Cecil and a selection of godly privy councillors wrote to Parker instructing, ambitiously, that all parish churches acquire a copy of this huge work, it being 'very profitable to bring her Majesty's subjects to good opinion, understanding and dear liking of the present government ... by true rehearsal and conference of times past'. Story's fate was also a warning to other exiles – no longer just scholarly priests, but military men like Westmorland, Norton and Markenfield – that no one was beyond the government's reach.[19]

While Story's case trundled to its gruesome conclusion, the government became aware of another threat to the security of the Queen, and the Protestant religion. Once again, Roberto Ridolfi, papal agent and money-man, was the prime mover. He hatched a scheme for the overthrow and, if it proved necessary, assassination of Elizabeth, and the enthronement of Mary, after a second Catholic rebellion precipitated by the arrival of 8,000 Spanish troops under the Duke of Alva. Ridolfi persuaded Norfolk to agree to lead the revolt, and to profess a Catholicism for which he probably felt little personal enthusiasm. Norfolk had been treated with quite remarkable leniency by Elizabeth, released from the Tower into comfortable London house arrest in August 1570. But he remained obsessed with marriage to Mary – for reasons of honour and ambition, rather than any romantic attraction. Mary herself, through the bishop of Ross, signalled her assent.

Ridolfi left for the continent in March 1571, to drum up support from a highly sceptical Alva, a persuadable Philip II and an enthusiastic Pius V. The cheerfully indiscreet Ridolfi revealed details of the scheme to numerous others, including his own sovereign, Cosimo de Medici, Grand Duke of Tuscany, who felt honour-bound to send Elizabeth a warning. In fact, Cecil – since February 1571 ennobled as Lord Burghley – already knew what was afoot. Two weeks after Ridolfi's departure, one of Mary's servants was arrested at Dover and found in possession of ciphered letters from Ridolfi to Norfolk and his former brother-in-law, Lord Lumley. In August, two of Norfolk's secretaries were caught trying to convey £600 in gold from the French ambassador to supporters of Mary in Scotland. This time, letters were deciphered proving Norfolk's involvement, and he returned to the Tower to await trial for treason.[20]

The Ridolfi Plot was an implausible intrigue. Yet even without following so close upon the Northern Rising and the papal excommunication, it would have produced alarm in government circles, and, to Burghley, proof that the dark prognostications of his 1569 memorandum were fully justified. The Spanish were evidently willing to contemplate an 'Enterprise of England', and the Queen of Scots was the black widow spider, at the centre of a web of dangers, ensnaring enemies abroad and traitors at home.

As a new Parliament assembled at the start of April 1571, English Protestantism seemed refocused, reinvigorated, replenished. Episcopal appointments, in the wake of Grindal's transfer to York, displayed a firmly evangelical face – no more mavericks of the Richard Cheyney school. Edwin Sandys replaced Grindal at London, and Nicholas Bullingham, a stout former exile, replaced Sandys at Worcester. Energetic Protestant reformers, Thomas

Cooper and Richard Curteys, were installed in early 1571 in the key dioceses of Lincoln and Chichester. Richard Barnes, appointed to Carlisle in August 1570, proved a reliable royal agent in the post-rebellion clear-up.[21]

Catholicism, 'popery', had revealed its true face: it was not just a parody of Christian faith, but a principle of violence and subversion, infiltrating the realm from outside, and infecting the weak-willed within. The time had come for Protestants of all stripes to close ranks, overcome their differences and concentrate on defeating this existential threat. Or so one might have thought.

### The Scrupulosity of Princes

On 25 February 1570, Queen Elizabeth attended a court Lenten sermon, the like of which she can scarcely have heard before. The preacher, Edward Dering, launched a fierce assault on the failings of the English Church. These were first and foremost problems of the ministry, beset by ignorance, pleasure-seeking, pluralism and non-residence. Far too many ministers were 'dumb dogs', unable to preach and edify their congregations: 'Have we not made us priests like the people of the country?'

Like people like priest. Dering's diatribe bore remarkable resemblances to the sermons of late medieval Catholic reformers (see pp. 42–3). Clericalism – an elevated sense of the status of ecclesiastical ministry, expressing itself through ferocious denunciation of that ministry's unworthy practitioners – was as much a Protestant as a Catholic trait.

This was tough but standard fare. What made Dering's sermon dynamite was that he called the bluff of the royal supremacy, laying responsibility, and blame, squarely on Elizabeth herself. 'And yet you in the meanwhile that all these whoredoms are committed; you, at whose hands God will require it; you sit still and are careless, and let men do as they list.' In a sermon replete with examples of the unenviable fates of unworthy biblical rulers, Dering threatened the Queen with divine judgement: 'Let these things alone, and God is a righteous God; He will one day call you to your reckoning.'[22] It was the very same day that Pius V, with a radically different understanding of God's unhappiness with Elizabeth, issued his bull of deposition.

To say Elizabeth was displeased would be an understatement, even if Dering, speaking directly to the Queen in recognized 'prophetic' mode, did not do anything overtly or legally treasonous. Born in around 1540, Dering was too young to have been part of the Marian exile; he was one of a new generation of Protestant clergymen whose faith was formed in the fractious 1560s. Yet his sermon had nothing to say about surplices, caps, kneeling at communion, or other staple Puritan grievances. There was a sense that more fundamental matters needed to be looked to, if popery was to be rooted out, and true religion secured.

In the spring of 1570, Thomas Cartwright, newly appointed Lady Margaret Professor of Divinity in Cambridge, delivered a series of lectures on the Acts of the Apostles. Cartwright was a veteran of the controversies over vestments, and withdrew for a time to serve as chaplain to Archbishop Adam Loftus of Armagh. In Ireland, the exposed front line of the struggle against popery, Puritans were usually welcomed by the bishops as brothers-in-arms, not shunned as disagreeable troublemakers.

Yet the office of bishop itself was under scrutiny as Cartwright – to the delight of younger scholars in his audiences – expounded the first two chapters of Acts, and argued that the organizational model of the early Church was prescriptive for Christianity in all subsequent ages. The Church of England, with its government by deans, archdeacons, bishops and archbishops, straight off the peg of medieval popery, stood rebuked by scripture. The primitive Church knew only of pastors and deacons. It had no elaborate hierarchies, but an equality of status among ministers. And it was evident from scripture that those ministers should be called to serve faithfully in one congregation, not pitched here and there by officials and patrons. Cartwright gave theological underpinning to the anti-episcopal prejudices inherited from Mary's reign, and heightened by the vestments controversy. The word was not yet in use, but one day there would be a name for this: presbyterianism.

As Cambridge divided into pro- and anti-Cartwright factions, the establishment moved to assert its dominance. A new set of statutes, designed to place control of the university in the hands of conformist heads of houses, was drawn up by Andrew Perne, Master of Peterhouse, an arch-Nicodemite, holding the post since 1554, and by a rising academic star, John Whitgift, Master of Trinity. One of the statutes forbad public attacks on the established order of religion, and in December 1570, Whitgift, in his role as first vice-chancellor elected under the new constitution, deprived Cartwright of his professorship. Cartwright withdrew to Geneva, and to a teaching position in its Academy, working there alongside Calvin's successor, Theodore Beza, a robust theologian who believed episcopacy to be a worthless, man-made institution, and monarchical authority to be rooted in the consent of the people.[23]

Most educated English Protestants were by the early 1570s 'Calvinists' – in the sense that they accepted the doctrine of predestination. But to be a 'Genevan' meant something else: a political critic of the structure and governance of the English Church. Whether that criticism was loyal and constructive, or an instinct of insidious subversion, was very much a moot point.

For Members of Parliament meeting in April 1571, the issue was not so much whether to counter the threat from Rome, but whether the best way to counter it was to resume the neglected task of reforming the structures and practices of the Church of England. Elizabeth, wary and weary of being (literally) preached at, conveyed a message via Lord Keeper Bacon at the opening of the session: the Commons 'should do well to meddle with no matters of state, but such as be propounded unto them'.

There were no difficulties about the passing of an act making it treason to call the sovereign 'heretic, schismatic, tyrant, infidel or an usurper' (as it had been under Henry), or another allowing for confiscation of the property of religious exiles. A third made it high treason to introduce papal bulls into England, and misprision of treason to conceal them. This act also threatened with penalties of praemunire anyone importing objects 'called by the name of an Agnus Dei [a wax disc, with imprinted religious picture], or any crosses, pictures, beads or such like', blessed by the Pope or anyone on his behalf – a further indication of how material objects of devotion were becoming politicized as tokens of nonconformist identity.

It was a different matter, however, with a more stringent measure for controlling the Catholic population at home. This bill proposed increasing the fine for non-attendance at church at least once a quarter to £12, and instituting a fine of 100 marks (£66) for failure to receive communion at least once in the year. With the enthusiastic backing of the bishops (and the likely tacit support of Burghley in the Lords), the bill passed both houses. Elizabeth vetoed it.[24]

This was, in its way, a defining moment. As the papal bull made clear, Catholics thought, or were supposed to think, that the Protestant eucharist was heretical; participating in it, a literally damnable matter. 'Communion', as the name implied, was a social act, signifying full membership of a community. The bill was intended to force religious conservatives to become de facto practising Protestants, or to identify themselves as outsiders, and face crippling financial penalties. It was designed to scotch Nicodemism, or to drive it so far in upon itself that it lost its moral compass.

It was not Elizabeth's way – perhaps because she feared provoking resentful Catholics into a second round of rebellion; perhaps because of that instinctive reluctance to make windows into hearts that grew from her own life experience of concealment and compliance. Either way, the veto was an emphatic confirmation of an existing arrangement, whereby church attendance was a statutory duty, but participation in the sacraments was left to the feeble discipline of the church courts. The arrangement lent itself to the whispered suspicion that attendance at public worship could be a purely civil duty, divorced from the actual cultivation of a spiritual life. And it represented the implicit offer of a bargain between Elizabeth and her Catholic subjects: obey me, conform outwardly, and I will leave your souls alone. It was an offer the Protestant clergy, most of them, did not want Elizabeth to make, and one the Catholic clergy, most of them, did not want their people to accept.

In other respects, the Parliament of 1571 witnessed an agitated accumulation of alternate agendas. Elizabeth's standing insistence that religious matters belonged to her sole prerogative was cheerfully ignored in an assembly many of whose members regarded the state of the Church as a standing item of business. 'Puritan' reformers enjoyed the tacit encouragement of leading councillors like Knollys and Leicester. The bishops had by no means given up on hopes of further substantial reform. But possibilities for collaboration with the godly laity were frayed by the disciplinary campaigns of the late 1560s, and by an understandable swelling of episcopal dignity on the part of men whose role and status were starting to be questioned.

Lay reformers in the Commons seized for themselves an abandoned episcopal project: the Church of England's missing discipline. On 6 April, William Strickland, MP for Scarborough, revealed that Thomas Norton possessed a newly printed copy of Cranmer's rejected plan for reform of the canon law, the *Reformatio Legum*. He called on Norton to bring it forth for consideration. The printing was organized by John Foxe, and the choreographed episode was intended to precipitate a wider reform of doctrine and worship – the two other marks of a true Church. Foxe's preface to the reissued *Reformatio* criticized the Prayer Book, which Strickland's speech damned with faint praise as merely 'drawn very near to the sincerity of the truth'. Use of the sign of the cross, and permission for women, in necessity, to baptize were things 'more superstitious . . . than in such high matters be tolerable'.

The *Reformatio Legum* was unacceptable to Elizabeth for much the same reason Northumberland disliked it: it strengthened the independent authority of the clergy. Nonetheless, a committee was established to confer about it with the bishops. In the meantime, Strickland continued to spearhead proposals for reform, calling for reintroduction of the 'alphabet' measures from 1566, and introducing his own bill for wholesale revision of the Prayer Book. This proposed the abolition of private baptism, 'needless' confirmation of children, vestments, kneeling at communion, and exchange of rings at the wedding service – a practice godly reformers viewed, with great seriousness, as a form of marital idolatry.

All this was too much even for sympathizers among the councillors. Knollys argued in the Commons that heresies in the Prayer Book were certainly to be reformed, 'but if they are but matters of ceremony, then it behoveth to refer the same to her Majesty'. Almost apologetically, he urged his fellow parliamentarians towards a weary acceptance of the limits of the possible:

> [W]hat cause there might be to make her Majesty not to run and join with those who seem to be earnest, we are not to search. Whether it be for that, orderly and in time, she hopeth to bring them all with her, or what secret cause or other scrupulosity there may be in princes, it is not for all sorts to know.

Strickland was too earnest for his own good, and during Parliament's Easter recess, the Council – probably on the Queen's orders – excluded him, and sent him to the Tower. Parliament had as keen a sense of its prerogatives as the Queen did of hers, and a rash of angry speeches about encroachment on the liberties of the House brought about Strickland's release on 21 April. The Prayer Book bill died a quiet death, as attention turned to another piece of unfinished business: the Articles of Religion.[25]

In Convocation, the bishops overcame the reservations of Edmund Guest and restored the missing Article 29, with its stricture on the *manducatio impiorum* (see p. 458). Elizabeth, unwilling to face a fight on two fronts – against bishops in Convocation and radical MPs in Parliament – agreed to the reinsertion, and to the principle of statutory underpinning for the now Thirty-Nine Articles. This, too, proved a less than straightforward matter.

Two bills concerning the articles were introduced by reformers into the Commons. One required clergymen to subscribe them; the other confirmed the articles, but only a selection of the core 'doctrinal' ones, omitting those unpalatable to Puritan consciences, such as articles concerning the Homilies and consecration of bishops. It was a blatant attempt to redefine the Church of England's priorities through selective editing, and while it passed the Commons, Elizabeth halted its progress in the Lords.

The Subscription Act did pass and receive royal assent. Henceforth, all new clergymen would have to subscribe the Articles, as would existing ministers ordained in any form other than that 'set forth by Parliament in the time of . . . Edward VI, or now used' – a symptom of continuing mistrust of the large number of Marian priests still ministering in the parishes.

Strickland and his allies scored one notable rear-guard success. The requirement was for clergymen to subscribe only those Articles of Religion 'which . . . concern the confession of the true Christian faith, and the doctrine of the sacraments' – whichever those were. In practice, bishops required new ordinands to subscribe *in toto*. Still, it was hardly a masterclass in smooth co-operation between Church and state. The Church of England had an agreed final text of its 'confession of faith', but Parliament stopped short of confirming the articles as normative or mandatory for the nation's spiritual health. Instead, it required clergymen, some clergymen, to express assent to them – some of them. For good measure, even as she signed the bill, Elizabeth sent a message through Lord Keeper Bacon that it was really a matter for Convocation and bishops. Parliament should never have discussed it in the first place: those who 'so audaciously and arrogantly have dealt in such matters may not look to receive further favour'.[26]

Elizabeth was even-handedly noncommittal in her dealings with Convocation. In response to the parliamentary committee on the *Reformatio Legum*, the bishops undertook to draw up new canons. These upheld the disciplinary requirements around vestments, and clerical subscription to (all of) the articles, but the prevailing tone was evangelical. 'Preacher' was the term used to designate parish clergymen, and schoolteachers were ordered to use Dean Nowell's very Protestant catechism, which Thomas Norton had just translated into English. Elizabeth received the canons in June, and allowed them to be printed, but they went forth in the bishops' names, not the Queen's.[27]

Beyond Westminster, beyond the court, not everyone was simply waiting to decode confused instructions from the centre; reformation was following its own courses. In the forefront were county and market towns. On 5 June 1571, the day after Archbishop Parker sent the canons to the Queen, another set of orders was drawn up by the mayor and justices of Northampton, with 'consent of the bishop of Peterborough', Edmund Scambler. The document closely regulated times and patterns of services in the town's churches, all to take place without any 'singing and playing of organs'. Services should finish punctually to allow attendance at a weekly sermon in All Saints, 'chief church' of the town, where 'the communion table standeth in the body of the church', the orders adding, 'according to the book'. Since Prayer Book and Injunctions contradicted each other (see p. 445), selective obedience was a technique of local empowerment. It was also a cause of contention: in East Anglia, Bishop Parkhurst encountered 'earnest disputations' in many places about wafers or common bread for the communion, 'the one alleging the book, the other her Majesty's Injunctions'.

In Northampton, on Thursdays, there was a weekly lecture, after which the mayor and his brethren, along with the preacher, minister and justices, would correct cases of 'notorious blasphemy, whoredom, drunkenness, railing against religion', reported by 'certain sworn men appointed for that service in each parish'. This body was not called a consistory, but the allure of Genevan-style discipline for the town governors of Northampton was quite evident. It was also reflected in an order for the town's youth to be instructed every Sunday 'in a portion of Calvin's catechism'.

Another injunction described a recent innovation. Every Saturday morning, from nine until eleven, there was 'an exercise of the ministers, both of town and country, about the interpretation of scriptures'. In front of an audience of laypeople, ministers would take turns to preach on a given text, and then withdraw 'into a privy place there to confer among themselves, as well touching doctrine as good life'.

The inspiration for this came not from Geneva, but from Zürich. Zwingli instituted these clerical workshops, where two or three proficient ministers would deliver sermons, and others take notes on how it should be done. The occasion was known as the *prophezei*, 'prophesying'. Returning exiles imported the practice, and it was positively encouraged by several bishops: prophesyings began in Grindal's London in the 1560s, and were starting to spring up elsewhere in the early 1570s, often at local initiative. By bringing people into the town, prophesyings were good for local business, but, most importantly, they were oases of preaching, in what many bishops still saw as a parched and desert land.[28]

Elizabeth herself gave only one order for the augmentation of preaching in the later part of 1571: a sermon of thanksgiving at Paul's Cross, along with special prayers in churches, for the great victory on 7 October of the Spanish and papal fleet over the Ottoman Turks at Lepanto in the eastern Mediterranean. Whatever their differences, Catholics and Protestants shared in the common faith of Christendom against its external enemies, and church bells across London rang in celebration.

Not everyone saw it that way. One owner of a copy of an earlier prayer, issued to give thanks for the lifting of the Ottoman siege of Malta in 1565, replaced all references to 'Turk' and 'Turks' with 'pope' and 'papists'. Thomas Cartwright, back in Cambridge from Geneva in the spring of 1572, suggested it would actually be safer for Protestants to copy their 'indifferent ceremonies' from Islam than from popery. The internationalist sympathies of Puritans were focused not on the beleaguered Catholics and Orthodox of Europe's eastern frontier, but on the persecuted Protestants of France and the Netherlands. Their heroes were the Dutch 'Sea Beggars', godly privateers whom Elizabeth banned from English ports in the spring of 1572, but who reignited the rebellion in the Netherlands that April with their daring seizure of the port of Brill. The Sea Beggars' motto was 'rather Turkish than popish', and they provocatively wore as a badge on their clothes the Islamic crescent moon.[29] No English Protestant went that far. But many knew who their real enemies were, and how close they lay at hand.

### An Axe or an Act?

Almost the last thing Elizabeth I wanted was a new Parliament, less than a year after the dissolution of the last. But the revelations of the Ridolfi Plot spurred the Privy Council into taking a firm line and insisting. One issue was in almost everyone's minds: what to do about the Queen of Scots?

On 13 May 1572, less than a week after Parliament assembled, the Council presented the case against Mary to a committee of both Houses. She stood accused of laying claim to the English throne, of seeking a marriage with Norfolk to advance that claim, of instigating rebellion in the north, and of plotting an invasion of the realm.

Solutions, it seemed to most MPs, were staring them in the face: either Mary should be formally excluded from the succession by statute, or she should be tried for treason as if she were an English subject. Paul Wentworth, Puritan sympathizer and member for the Cornish borough of Liskeard, bluntly asked that 'it may be put to the question of the House, whether we should call for an axe or an act'.

A taste for the axe was not limited to a bloodthirsty radical fringe. It was the preferred option for Burghley, for most of the Privy Council and for nearly all the bishops. By 19 May, a bill was prepared containing a petition for the Queen of Scots to be attainted. The language of Commons speeches was fiery, intemperate. Mary, said Nicholas St Leger, MP for Maidstone, was 'the monstrous and huge dragon, and mass of the earth'. Thomas Norton revisited the themes of his tracts against the northern rebels. It was said mercy was good in a prince, but 'mercy without her Majesty's safety, causeth misery'.

More was at stake than Elizabeth's personal well-being, and some MPs were not shy of saying it. 'Since the Queen in respect of her own safety is not to be induced therein,' argued Robert Newdigate, 'let us petition she will do it in respect of our safety. I have heard she delighteth to be called our mother.' Newdigate was being archly ironic. Others, like Thomas Dannet, were bluntly forthright. Elizabeth's reluctance to settle the succession was nothing less than a refusal 'to put us in safety after her death'. If she would not take necessary steps to prolong her subjects' safety by preserving her own life, 'true and faithful subjects, despairing of safety by her means, shall be forced to seek protection elsewhere'.

The inescapable conclusion from such language was that loyalty to Elizabeth was not absolute, but conditional on a willingness to defend the Protestant Church and succession. Remarkably – or perhaps, not so remarkably – the theme was developed most powerfully in a paper presented by the bishops, men with more cause than most to lament the Queen's religious fecklessness. It drew on every resource of scripture to justify the harshest treatment for 'the late Queen of Scots', someone who 'wrought by all means she can to seduce the people of God in this realm from true religion'. A wicked, criminal ruler was justly deposed.

But the bishops went further. The first Book of Kings recorded how King Saul spared the life of Agag, a defeated Amalekite king who persecuted the Jews. In consequence, 'God took from the same Saul his good spirit and transferred the Kingdom of Israel from him and his heirs'. It was, the bishops doubtless felt, a warning rather than a threat. But there was no doubt 'her Majesty must needs offend in conscience before God if she do not punish her [Mary] according to the measure of her offence'. The bishops also gave a surprisingly different spin to a text usually used to argue for absolute political obedience. St Paul's Letter to the Romans 13:1, declared: 'Let every soul be subject unto the higher powers, for there is no power but of God. The powers that be are ordained of God.' The bishops read Paul to be saying that 'the magistrate is the minister of God, and the revenger of wrath towards him that hath done evil'. If magistrates neglected this duty, 'God threateneth heavy punishment'.

'Magistrate' was a telling word – not an anointed sacral monarchy, but an office in the commonwealth, with prescribed responsibilities – and one which hinted at possibilities of dismissal. The bishops' moralizing essay was part of a co-ordinated front of censorious advice, an attempt to jostle Elizabeth down a road she did not wish to travel. Burghley arranged for a young clergyman, Tobie Matthew, to preach in front of her. He expostulated on Elizabeth's duty to execute Mary; all, even queens, 'must live within the lists of one's own vocation'.[30]

Elizabeth I was not frightened of Burghley, or of bishops, however many blood-curdling Old Testament stories they had at their elbows. The Queen instructed Parliament to abandon ideas of an attainder, and proceed instead with a bill for exclusion. That bill passed both Houses, but when the moment for royal assent came, Elizabeth held back, saying 'she is not yet fully resolved'. She did, however, make one significant concession, agreeing to the execution of the Duke of Norfolk, who had been tried and convicted in January for his role in the Ridolfi affair. The duke, asserting his Protestant faith, was beheaded at the Tower on 2 June.[31]

The wider cause of reform fared no better in the 1572 Parliament than in that of the preceding year, though reformers adopted a (seemingly) more moderate tack. Two MPs, Tristram Pistor and Robert Snagge, brought forward a bill, not to abolish the Prayer Book, but to make strict observance of the 1559 Act of Uniformity apply 'only to such as shall say any papistical service'. Good Protestants – with consent of their bishop – would be free to omit ceremonies that were only included 'in respect of the great weakness of the people'. In addition, individual bishops could license petitioning clergymen to use the forms of service employed by the French and Dutch Stranger Churches.

It was a prescription for liturgical free-for-all, making nonsense of any concept of uniformity. Yet it expressed an optimistic conviction that the times were right for evolutionary, rather than revolutionary, change:

> Through this long continuance of preaching the Gospel under Your Highness's authority . . . many congregations within Your Highness's realm are grown to desire of attaining to some further form than in that book is prescribed. . . . A great number of learned pastors and zealous ministers . . . have omitted the precise rule and strait observation of the form prescribed . . . [while] a number of malicious adversaries of the truth do cover their malice under pretence of conformity and obedience . . .

The disobedient, in other words, were the most loyal and reliable. This perplexingly paradoxical logic was not entirely dismissed by leading figures of the government. Knollys helped to revise the bill, stripping out its most contentious aspect (permission to use Stranger Church liturgies), and assigning permission to alter Prayer Book usages to the bishops as a whole. In that form, many of them would have welcomed the bill. But bishops had learned, as MPs perhaps still had not, that Elizabeth would countenance no tinkering with the

1559 Prayer Book. Elizabeth read the drafts, and criticized them rather more courteously than was her wont. But she said she could consider no bills of religion that did not enjoy prior episcopal approval.[32]

Even while these collaborative plans were struggling to stay afloat in the Commons, the ship of reformation entered new, dangerously confrontational waters. Around the end of June 1572, an anonymous pamphlet was published in London. *An Admonition to the Parliament* was the work of two young clergymen, John Field and Thomas Wilcox, and it raised the piratical flag of ecclesiastical mutiny.

## Ambitious Spirits

The *Admonition* was a cocktail of finely distilled theological critique and home-brewed satirical mockery. Wilcox specialized in the former, Field, the latter. The Prayer Book, readers learned, was a work 'culled and picked out of that popish dunghill, the mass book', a 'reading service' containing no 'edification'. Its formal solemnity of alternating lines of text and response meant merely that congregations 'toss the psalms in most places like tennis balls'.

'Popish abuses yet remaining in the English Church' included private communion and baptism (and use of the sign of the cross), holy days dedicated to saints, kneeling at communion, wafer bread, vestments. The ceremony of 'churching' women – readmitting them to worship after a period of separation following childbirth – 'smelleth of Jewish purification'. Superstitious rituals marred the rites of confirmation, marriage and burial. Any special role for ministers at funerals was simply a means 'whereby prayer for the dead is maintained'. Indeed, a fundamental misunderstanding of clerical ministry accounted for many of the Church's failings: 'by the Word of God, it is an office of preaching, they make it an office of reading'.

Who were 'they'? The most inflammatory feature of the *Admonition* was its repudiation of any recognition of the bishops as fellow, albeit tardy, sojourners on the road to righteousness. They were not part of the solution, but the very root of the problem. Embittered by the experience of subscription and suspension, and energized by the theological insights of Cartwright, Field and Wilcox mapped out a presbyterian future for the Church, placing it in the hands 'of lawful pastors, of watchful seniors and elders, and careful deacons'. 'Archbishop' and 'bishop' were names and roles 'drawn out of the Pope's shop'. Governance of the Church by them was naught but an 'Antichristian tyranny'.[33]

For all its scurrility and ribald humour, the *Admonition* was not to be laughed off. By the end of August 1572, the work had run into its third edition, and in November 1572 *A Second Admonition to Parliament* added flesh to the bones, with more detailed exposition of what a 'well reformed Church' would look like: locally elected pastors reporting to regional 'conferences' of

ministers; above them, synods provincial. This was not just blue-sky theo-
rizing: Field had for some time been meeting in regular conference with other
London ministers, and was in correspondence with like-minded clergymen in
various English counties. An embryonic presbyterian organization was growing
within the womb of the English Church.

The *Second Admonition* defined the conference – what Beza and other
continental Calvinists would have called a *classis* – as 'the meeting of some
certain ministers, and other brethren' at a significant town, or in a deanery, to
discuss policy and exercise discipline. They were occasions when ministers
would 'confer and exercise themselves in prophesying, or in interpreting the
scriptures'. The passing use of the word 'prophesying' was a fateful conflation.
Subversive models of alternative church government might easily now be associated with the forms of in-service training smiled on by many of the bishops
themselves.

The author of the *Second Admonition* was widely supposed to have been
Cartwright, though a likelier candidate is Christopher Goodman, back from a
spell in Ireland to a ministry in his native Chester, but still *persona non grata* on
account of his earlier embrace of Knoxian resistance theory. Cartwright,
however, was soon in the thick of things. John Whitgift, rapidly emerging as
the leading voice of clerical 'conformity', completed an *Answer* to the
*Admonition* in October 1572, shortly after depriving Cartwright of his
Cambridge fellowship. Cartwright issued a *Reply* in April 1573, from the same
secret press that produced the *Second Admonition*. Whitgift's *Against the Reply*
provoked Cartwright's *Second Reply* and a subsequent *Rest of the Second Reply*.

The 'Admonition Controversy' was one of the great print-debates of the
century, comparable to More's titanic duel with Tyndale, or Jewel's Challenge to
the Louvainists. Cartwright and Whitgift were barely in disagreement with each
other on issues of soteriology – the theology of salvation. Both recognized that
good works played no instrumental role, and that God predestined to eternal
life those he freely chose. Nor was there a total divergence on ecclesiology – the
theology of the Church. They agreed there was both an invisible and a visible
Church. Cartwright's instinct, however, was to mould the latter to fit the shape
of the former. It should be possible to identify the elect, through their unswerving
obedience to the commandments of God, and to place them in leadership roles.
Conversely, the recognizably unworthy and ungodly – very probably the
damned, and so not even part of the true, invisible Church – should be excluded
from sacraments and full membership of the visible Church.

Whitgift's contrary instinct was for a kind of agnostic separation of the
invisible and visible Churches. It was not possible to know who was saved and
who was damned; the visible Church unavoidably contained within its ranks
both good and evil people. This meant it was essential for the Church to
exercise discipline and impose universal obedience to its rules, including

observance of its ceremonies. Moreover, that discipline should be 'according to the kind and form of government used in the commonwealth'. It was the Queen's God-given right as Supreme Governor to prescribe rules for the governance of the Church, just as she did in temporal matters for the state, regardless of whether individual rituals were judged able to 'edify'. This was music to royal ears. Whitgift's was the antithesis of a political theology stressing at every turn the obligation on the 'magistrate' to conform herself to the commands of God in scripture, as interpreted for her by, of course, the clergy.[34]

In the meantime, Field and Wilcox were identified as the *Admonition*'s authors and imprisoned in Newgate. In June 1573, a royal proclamation condemned the work, and its sequel, and demanded surrender of all copies. The godly were far from uniformly supportive of the presbyterian agitation. Thomas Sampson and Robert Crowley, veteran leaders of the vestments protest, distanced themselves from these younger firebrands. Thomas Norton, the most resolutely 'political' of lay Puritans, thought the *Admonition* 'fond' (i.e. foolish): it 'hath hindered much good and done much hurt, and in nothing more than in increasing the papists' triumph against our Church'. Catholics liked nothing better than an intra-Protestant feud.

Nonetheless, the bishops felt abandoned and beleaguered. Parker complained to Burghley in November 1572 that, 'among such as profess themselves Protestants', the agitators were being praised 'and we judged to be extreme persecutors'. There was clearly considerable lay support for the stance of the Puritan preachers. Early the next year, Parker warned darkly that, if action were not taken, 'I fear ye shall feel Müntzer's Commonwealth attempted shortly' – half a century on, the horrors of the German Peasants' War continued to haunt the imaginations of all 'respectable' Protestants.

In April 1573, Bishop Scambler of Peterborough lamented that 'those whom men do call Puritans' were out of control in various towns in Rutland and Northamptonshire, preaching without licence and administering sacraments in ways 'contrary to the form prescribed by the public order of the realm'. In August, Sandys of London wrote to Bullinger in alarmist tones about 'new orators', men 'seeking the complete overthrow and rooting up of our whole ecclesiastical polity'. Among their outlandish opinions was that 'the civil magistrate has no authority in ecclesiastical matters' – a view Sandys could reliably expect the clerical leader of Zürich, where institutions of Church and state were closely integrated, to find disturbingly abhorrent.

Closer to home, sympathy was in short supply. Councillors and courtiers scarcely rushed to take the bishops' side. Sandys reflected bitterly that 'ambitious spirits', undermining religion 'under the colour of Reformation', were 'favoured by some of great calling'. He had received 'sundry letters from noblemen' interceding for Field and Wilcox. Prior to release in the summer of 1573, they were transferred to more comfortable conditions, probably due to the influence of Leicester and Warwick. Like his father, the Duke of Northumberland, Leicester enjoyed posing as the patron of radical preachers who were able to keep the bishops on their toes. Goodman was a protégé, and told Leicester he was sorry that 'for my sake your Lordship should grow in suspicion to be a maintainer of such as go about the undermining of the estate'; Parker suspected the earl of plotting against him with 'certain precisians'.

Without backing from powerful laymen, the bishops – who had limited access to the Queen, and few powerful disciplinary tools of their own – remained relatively weak. In the summer of 1573, Sandys was reduced to begging Burghley and Leicester for help in regaining control of preaching in the capital, where supporters of Cartwright shamelessly expounded his ideas at Paul's Cross, and where, despite the June proclamation, there was 'not one book brought in'.[35]

Privy Council support for a crackdown was eventually forthcoming, probably thanks to the direct intervention of the Queen. On 14 October 1573, in the vicinity of Temple Bar, a radically Puritan – and probably unhinged – law student named Peter Birchet stabbed and seriously wounded the renowned sea captain Sir John Hawkins. It was an unfortunate case of mistaken identity. Hawkins's fine clothing led Birchet to confuse him with Christopher Hatton, gentleman of the Privy Chamber and captain of the Yeomen of the Guard. Hatton had recently swept into public awareness as a new royal favourite. Some suspected him of secret papist sympathies, and many of the godly blamed him for the failure of reforming and anti-Marian measures in the Parliament of 1572.

Six days after the attack, a royal proclamation demanded stricter enforcement of the Act of Uniformity, and imprisonment for anyone preaching or writing against the Prayer Book. Somewhat spitefully, the Queen ascribed blame for the disorder to 'the negligence of the bishops'. In November, the Privy Council established special commissions to investigate Puritan nonconformity, and to enforce subscription to articles upholding liturgical and ceremonial rules. A warrant was issued for Cartwright's arrest: he went into hiding, and escaped before the end of the year to the Calvinist university town of Heidelberg. There he oversaw the printing of polemics against Whitgift, as well as *A Brief Discourse of the Troubles begun at Frankfurt* (1574) – a compilation of documents put together by Field and Thomas Wood, designed to show that the Puritan cause of the 1570s had a venerable ancestry in the principled actions of Marian exile.

London witnessed a renewed drive to impose use of the surplice: leading Puritans were rounded up and imprisoned. Robert Johnson, preacher at St Clement Danes, was incarcerated in the Westminster Gatehouse, spending his time there composing witty diatribes against Sandys and the dean of Westminster, Gabriel Goodman, whom he considered no better than a papist. Johnson died, a martyr to insanitary conditions, before April 1574. He was not the first. There were, claimed Thomas Wood in February, 'three lately dead by the bishops' imprisonment'. Yet, as in any persecution, there were apostates as well as martyrs, and some – like Edward Dering – who failed to take the bold stand the irreconcilables hoped they would.

Beyond the capital, waves of episcopally enforced subscription and suspension crashed along the Puritan shorelines of Northamptonshire, Warwickshire, Leicestershire and East Anglia. Wood grieved to Dean Whittingham of Durham that 'the poor famished sheep of Christ are daily spoiled of their godly and learned shepherds', driven out, in some bishoprics, 'twelve at a clap'. In fact, enforcement of conformity was decidedly patchy. In Norwich, Parkhurst was as reluctant to become a persecutor of Puritans as he had been to become a bishop in the first place. He implemented some temporary suspensions, but those affected were still allowed to take part in the prophesyings.[36]

The furore surrounding the *Admonition*, and the failed parliamentary reform efforts of 1571–2, revealed English Protestantism to be deeply, perhaps fatally, fractured. The emerging fault lines lay not just between a mainstream drive for continuing reformation within the Church and the eccentric conservatism of its Supreme Governor, but between those committed to principles of hierarchy and order and those who felt licensed by their insight into the mind of God to build a godly society from the bottom up.

It was, nonetheless, a crisis that never quite became a conflagration. The deranged Birchet aside, and despite the vehemence of their language, Puritans were not minded to resort to actual violence in pursuit of their goals. Their political patrons were willing to offer protection, and happy to see bishops discomfited and embarrassed, but they would not write the Puritans a blank cheque, or endorse plans to overthrow the established ecclesiastical order.

There was also an abiding sense that, however bitter it became, this was still a family quarrel. Beyond the hearth, beyond the home, dangerous forces stirred. The third printing of the *Admonition* in 1572 coincided with dreadful news from France. On St Bartholomew's Day (24 August), during an uneasy peace in the religious wars, Catholics in Paris, believing they had the blessing of the King, turned on their Huguenot neighbours and killed at least 2,000 of them in three days of savage slaughter. Thousands more died in copy-cat attacks in the provinces over the following weeks. The English ambassador, Francis Walsingham, would never forget, or forgive, what he witnessed in the French capital.

Was this the fate English Protestants narrowly escaped through exposure of Ridolfi's Plot and Alva's invasion plan? Parker reported to Burghley in September 1572 that the 'imps' (priests) of the English papists were 'rejoicing much at this unnatural and unprincely cruelty and murder'. Some 'looked for such slaughter at home'. Robert Beale, Clerk of the Privy Council, and a secretary to Walsingham in Paris at the time of the massacre, drew up an analysis for

Burghley. It concluded that there was a 'detestable conspiracy' of the papacy, Spanish and French to divide the world between them, and that no trust could be placed in any Catholic in England 'who thinketh in conscience, under the damnation of his soul, to owe a more obedience to a higher power'. Special prayers – quite different in tone from those appointed after Lepanto – were ordered to be read in church. The words of Psalm 22 expressed deep feelings of anxiety and persecution: 'the wicked conspireth against us, and our enemies are daily in hand to swallow us up'.

The Privy Council ordered improvement of coastal defences, and for the navy to be put to sea. It also asked for names and statuses of papists throughout the realm. To compile such a register, thought Parker, 'were an infinite matter', the number of papists was growing so fast.[37] Yet Burghley received that year an annotated list of 'noblemen, gentlemen, yeomen and chief franklins' within Hampshire. Of the 246 names, ninety-seven were marked 'p' and a further forty-seven 'pp': 'papists' and 'earnest papists'. In a world of politicized faith, the unknowable reaches of the heart were redacted into formulaic abbreviation.

The episcopal authorities were far from complacent: in early 1573, for example, Bishop Bentham of Coventry hauled before him the curate Richard Cook for 'too much familiarity and bearing with them in Stone (Staffordshire) which are judged to be papists'. But after the immediate shock of St Bartholomew subsided there was a sense that the domestic papist problem was containable. Parker even blamed the apparent flare-up of Catholic militancy in late 1572 on the fact that 'they be exasperated by the disordered preachings and writings of some Puritans'. Bishop Horne of Winchester reported patriotically to Bullinger at the start of 1573 that England, 'having secured tranquillity at home and peace abroad, is sailing as it were with full sails and a prosperous breeze'. The Church, admittedly, was dangerously agitated, but this was not so much due to papists, 'who are daily restrained by severe laws', as to 'false brethren, who seem to be sliding into anabaptism'.[38]

The severe laws were invoked in June 1573, when a priest, Thomas Woodhouse, was hanged, drawn and quartered at Tyburn after unwisely sending Burghley a letter defending the papal deposition, and forcibly defending his views in a subsequent interview with the Lord Treasurer. At least one cleric was executed under martial law in the north in 1569, but Woodhouse was the first priest formally to suffer under an Elizabethan statute.

He was also a human hinge between Catholicisms past and pending. Ordained under Mary, Woodhouse had been in the Fleet for religious disaffection since 1561. Yet in the year of his execution he wrote to Paris requesting admission to the Society of Jesus, and he died a Jesuit.

Jesuits were not – yet – a prime target of English Protestant hatred and fear. In fact, four years on from the Northern Rising and papal bull, the government felt able to show some magnanimity to its Catholic opponents. In 1574, the

Privy Council ordered Abbot Feckenham and the former bishop of Lincoln, Thomas Watson, to be released from the Marshalsea, and Henry Cole, and the brothers John and Nicholas Harpsfield to be removed from the Fleet, on receipt of promises not to agitate publicly against the established religion.

Even as this small band of aged clergymen laid down the sword and shield of religious struggle, another group of younger ones prepared to pick them up. In 1573, the first graduates of Allen's Douai seminary were ordained to the priest-hood, and in 1574 four of them – Lewis Barlow, Henry Shaw, Martin Nelson and Thomas Metham – crossed secretly to England. Another seven followed in 1575. A new phase in the story of English Catholicism was under way.

The Council's relatively compassionate attitude to the surviving pillars of the Marian regime contrasted with the outlook of some Puritans, for whom to forgive was to forget, and to forget was not an option. On 29 September 1574, Robert Crowley preached at the Guildhall, at the election of a new Lord Mayor. His text was Psalm 139 ('Do I not hate them, O Lord, that hate thee?'), and his theme was the purity of Christian hatred. More than any other miscreant, Crowley admonished, a papist 'must be so hated, that he be not chosen to supply any place in any public ministration'. At the start of the preceding year, John Browning, a Cambridge colleague of Cartwright, caused uproar when he preached in Great St Mary's that no Protestant who attended an idolatrous mass could ever be forgiven for it; he even implied that death was the appro-priate penalty for such apostasy. Among the outputs of Cartwright's Heidelberg press was a satirical attack on Matthew Parker, claiming that while the faithful were giving their lives, Parker passed his time in 'pleasant rest and leisure'. Only after Mary was safely dead did he creep 'out of his lurking hole into the open sight of the world'.[39]

Parker may not have been burned, but he was certainly bruised by a decade and more of holding the line, at first Elizabeth's, but increasingly his own, against those who – as he observed with bitter irony to the Lord Treasurer in April 1575 – saw both himself and Burghley as 'great papists':

> Does your Lordship think I care either for cap, tippet, surplice, or wafer-bread, or any such? But [only] for the laws so established I esteem them, and not more for exercise of contempt against law and authority, which I see will be the end of it, nor for any other respect.

Dictating his letter from the sickbed that was soon to be his deathbed, Parker declared he had done his duty, and hoped Burghley would continue to do his, helping 'her Majesty's good government in princely constancy'.

He did not feel like the beneficiary of much constancy himself; in a final indignity, the Queen had just unexpectedly levied a charge on Parker for mounting a visitation of Winchester diocese. 'Her majesty told me that I had supreme government ecclesiastical; but what is it to govern cumbered with such subtlety?' With remarkable frankness, the ailing archbishop confessed to Burghley he did not really understand what the royal supremacy was. Certainly, the Queen's powers were more than the papists would grant her, yet, 'whatsoever the ecclesiastical prerogative is, I fear it is not so great as your pen hath given it in the Injunctions'.

In signing off, Parker's mind turned to prophecies, and to an 'old verse' that kept springing into his head. *Femina morte cadet, postquam terram mala tangent*: A woman falls dead, and afterwards evils touch the land. However infuriating Parker – and Burghley – might find Elizabeth, her continued survival was all that was standing between them and the collapse of everything they held dear. It was not intended to be a comforting thought.

Parker died at Lambeth on 17 May 1575, doubtless wishing he had spent more time on his beloved antiquarian research – designed to show the Church of ancient Britain as resolutely non-Roman and proudly proto-Protestant – and less time dealing with ingrate Puritans.[40] He left a modern Church formally intact, but wracked by mistrust and recrimination: between Puritans and bishops; between bishops and nobles; between almost everyone and a frustratingly impassive queen. His successor would need to possess in abundance the vision, direction and charisma that the weary and disillusioned Parker so patently lacked. As it turned out, all those things would still not be enough.

### Grindal

On Friday 22 July 1575, the fires of Smithfield, doused since June 1558, were set alight once more. Two foreigners burned to death, after being convicted of heresy by an ecclesiastical commission headed by Bishop Sandys of London. John Foxe, John Field and other Puritans were there to see and hear them perish in agony, since no small bags of gunpowder (sometimes hung around the neck to hasten the end of heretics) were placed on their bodies.

Hendrik Terwoort and Jan Pietersz were members of a group of twenty-seven Flemish anabaptists, found worshipping at a house in Whitechapel on Easter Sunday – just a few of several thousand foreigners, economic and religious refugees, living in London and its suburbs. The discovery was an embarrassment to the Dutch Stranger Church, to which resident aliens were supposed to belong, and whose ministers (acting as interpreters) were active in efforts to get the prisoners to recant. Five did so, at Paul's Cross on 15 May. The others would not, declaring in a petition to the Queen that they could not agree Christ took his flesh from the Virgin, 'seeing we do not find the word "substance" expressed in the scripture'. Infant baptism was intolerable, as 'we dare use no religious rites or ceremonies without a command from God'.

Most of the convicted anabaptists were deported, but two were held back for exemplary punishment. The Privy Council authorized the commission to pass the death sentence, and Elizabeth herself signed the warrant. It was, in part, a gesture towards a slight thaw in relations with Spain, tested to the limit over preceding years by English moral support for the Dutch rebels, and by the depredations in the Spanish Caribbean of pirate captains like John Hawkins and Francis Drake. In March 1575, Alva's replacement as governor in the Netherlands, Luis de Requesens, agreed to expel from Spanish territory English participants in the rebellion of 1569. At the same time, the seizure of English ships by Dutch rebels had harmed their relations with the English government. It was an opportune moment for Elizabeth to show Philip she was no sympathizer with the most damnable views of some of his rebellious subjects.

After the conviction, the Stranger Churches and their English friends campaigned for clemency, or even for hanging rather than burning. To consign people to the flames, Foxe wrote in an impassioned direct appeal to Elizabeth, 'is more after the Roman example, than a Christian custom'. Yet an important principle was, as it were, at stake. Among the doctrinal statements members of the Stranger Churches were required to subscribe in the summer of 1575, in order to prove their antipathy to anabaptism, was that Christian magistrates might legitimately impose the death penalty on obstinate heretics.[41]

The executions of Pietersz and Terwoort posed to English Puritans a profoundly painful question: did their sympathies lie with Christians seeking to apply to all aspects of life a literalist test of scriptural purity, or with church and state authorities willing to administer the unpalatable remedies of Pole and Bonner?

For all their dislike of judicial burning, even the bishops' sternest critics in the fledgling presbyterian movement were genuinely horrified by the errors of the anabaptists. Their perverse and wilful *misreading* of scripture put them on a par with papists. Periodic eruptions of Christological heresy were a reminder to all 'magisterial' Protestants of their shared doctrinal ground, and of the need to defend it against both ravaging romanists and subversive sectarians.

What was needed was a strong archiepiscopal voice, to heal the hurts, and harness Puritan energies for the common good of the Church. Even as Parker lay dying, Burghley knew whose voice that should be. On 15 May 1575, he wrote to Francis Walsingham that 'the meetest man to succeed should be the Archbishop of York . . . both for knowledge of government and good proof of the same in the north'. Walsingham was another friend of the godly, a determined Protestant who in 1573 joined the Privy Council and succeeded Burghley in the role of principal secretary.[42]

Edmund Grindal had certainly done his best in a region he described on arrival in 1570 as resembling 'another church, rather than a member of the rest'. He prided himself on importing preachers into the archdiocese, and, working with an energetic dean, Matthew Hutton, on making York Minster into a beacon of Protestant sermonizing in a notoriously conservative city. Visitations in 1571 and 1575 revealed how deeply planted Catholic practices and attitudes remained across much of the north. But Grindal worked hard at rooting them out. He collaborated closely with the Earl of Huntingdon, godly president of the Council of the North, and made good use of the powerful York Ecclesiastical Commission – rather than the moribund ordinary machinery of the church courts – to identify, fine and punish recusants.

Papists, not Puritans, were the principal problem, and Grindal was able to assure Parker at the height of the crackdown in December 1573 that in the diocese of York the Prayer Book was 'universally observed', though elsewhere in the province there were, he admitted, 'some novelties'. Grindal showed in London that he could enforce the line against dissidents when he needed to, but to supporters in 1575 he represented change, not continuity, with the entrenched and confrontational policies of Parker.

Parker himself mapped out a continuation of the disciplinary drive in his final letter to Burghley. For the pivotal see of Norwich (vacant since the death of Parkhurst in February 1575), he recommended three notoriously anti-Puritan candidates: John Whitgift, Dean Gabriel Goodman of Westminster and John Piers, Master of Balliol, Oxford. Men of this stamp were preferable to 'my Lord of Leicester's chaplains'. He did not say who his own replacement should be.

Elizabeth might have preferred Richard Cox of Ely, a man battling Puritanism since before its name was discovered. But in 1568 Cox committed a major faux pas, remarrying with unseemly haste after the death of his first wife. Whitgift was as yet only a dean. Henry VIII had fast-forwarded a lowly archdeacon to the see of Canterbury in 1533, but Elizabeth's sense of decency and decorum was always stricter than her father's. The bishop of Rochester, Edmund Freke, was transferred to Norwich, and though Elizabeth delayed the appointment until the end of the year, the archbishop of York was accepted for Canterbury.

Grindal was sound but not a stickler, an enthusiastic evangelical sharing much of the mind-set of sensible, moderate Puritans. Leading councillors breathed a sigh of relief at his appointment, hoping for reorientation of the Church towards reform rather than repression, and a renewed focus on combatting Catholicism. Sir Walter Mildmay, Chancellor of the Exchequer, and by instinct a moderate Puritan, wrote to assure Grindal that 'it is greatly hoped for by the godly and well-affected of this realm that your lordship will prove a profitable instrument in that calling'. Grindal himself confessed to 'many conflicts with myself about that matter'. He would, however, accept the appointment, 'lest in resisting the same I might with Jonah offend God'.[43] Multiple disasters befell Jonah, after he defied the Lord's commandment to go and preach in Nineveh. Yet Grindal's obedience to God would not save him from his own ordeal in the belly of the whale.

Grindal arrived in London just in time for the new session of Parliament, opening on 8 February 1576. Mildmay expressed hopes this would be an occasion for 'consultation . . . with some of your brethren how some part of those Romish dregs remaining [in the Church], offensive to the godly, may be removed'. A reforming coalition of councillors, bishops, and pious MPs was, it seemed, back in business.

This time there was to be no provocative Prayer Book bill; rather, a seemly petition. The call was made by Tristram Pistor, veteran of the parliamentary manoeuvres of 1572, and responded to in the establishment of a committee, well staffed with privy councillors. Their petition carefully avoided matters of liturgy and ceremony, calling instead for imposition of 'true discipline'. Not discipline in the presbyterian sense, but crackdowns on non-residence and pluralism, and on procedural abuses by the church courts, along with greater encouragement for preaching.

Elizabeth's reply was gracious, claiming (disingenuously?) these were all issues she was already thinking about, and intent on redressing. Once more she insisted, however, that such matters should be addressed, not by Parliament, but by clerics in Convocation. A new set of canons was duly produced there, with earnest but unexceptionable directions for closer scrutiny of ordination candidates, and catechizing of parish youth. Unlike the canons of 1571, these did receive official royal sanction, though also some royal corrections. The canon that veered closest to the concerns of militant Puritans, requiring that private baptisms be performed only by a 'lawful minister', was omitted from the printed version. Mildmay would later describe the 1576 canons as 'little or nothing to the purpose'.

Elizabeth saw off the sole attempt to pass an act on religious matters. This was a revival of the 1571 proposal to make reception of communion a statutory requirement, and to increase fines for non-attendance at church. The bishops introduced the bill into the Lords, and Grindal, along with Burghley and Leicester, sat on the committee to which the bill was referred after its second reading. The committee tried to mollify the Queen by dropping the communion clause, but the bill made no further progress.[44]

Parliamentary routes to further reformation remained, as it seemed, blocked. But godly hopes in Grindal were not yet snuffed out. In June 1576, he persuaded the Privy Council to agree to a major overhaul of his archiepiscopal Court of Faculties. This was the body that, since the days of Henry VIII, had taken over the issuing of dispensations from the rulings of canon law that once pertained to the Roman curia. Puritans detested it: Field and Wilcox named the Court of Faculties 'the filthy quagmire and poisoned plash of all the abominations that do infect the whole realm'. Henceforth, some more notorious abuses – such as licences for clergymen to hold three benefices in plurality – were no longer permitted.

Another gesture of episcopal reconciliation with the reformers concerned the bible. The Geneva Bible of 1560 (see p. 436) was the translation preferred by godly preachers, and by devout householders for domestic use. No edition of it was printed in England while Parker was alive. Indeed, he sponsored an alternative: an official replacement for the folio Great Bible of 1539, produced as a collective episcopal effort. The work was finally ready in October 1568, and in presenting this 'Bishops' Bible' to the Queen, Parker pointedly noted how some churches were using for worship 'translations which have not been laboured in your realm'. English-made was best, and a guiding principle of the Bishops' Bible was to avoid definitive determination on controversial questions, and the 'bitter notes' allegedly characteristic of the Geneva version. The canons of 1571 ordered churchwardens to acquire a copy for their parish, 'if it may conveniently be'.

The Bishops' Bible possessed all the consistency and flair of a translation produced by a committee lacking a firm editorial hand. Grindal dutifully contributed, but was not a devotee of the project. In 1576, however, an edition of the Geneva Bible, the first of many, was produced in London by the Queen's printer, Christopher Barker. It was a symptom of a new spring of evangelical reform.[45]

The Geneva Bible's preface urged owners to study it regularly, at least twice a day. Yet, for many Protestant clergy, simply reading the scripture was never quite enough. The 'Word' was not synonymous with printed words on the page. In order to awake within an individual a necessary awareness of saving faith, words of scripture had to be brought alive; they had to be preached. To its most ardent proponents, the Protestant Reformation was nothing if it was not a perpetual pageant of preaching. The Church's most fundamental problem was a shortage of competent preachers; printed Homilies were, at best, an inadequate stop-gap solution. That, of course, was not how Elizabeth saw things.

## Prophesyings

The Queen seemingly became aware of prophesyings in 1574, when a message was passed to Sandys, via Parker, that 'the exercises in your diocese called prophesyings should stay [cease]'. Sandys protested vigorously; like most bishops, he saw prophesyings as a valued resource for disseminating Protestant teaching in a still inadequately protestantized land. Parker sent a similar message to Parkhurst of Norwich, who requested further instructions after being assured by the councillors Knollys, Mildmay and Sir Thomas Smith that the order was intended to apply only to 'schismatical and seditious' meetings.

Under pressure from Parker, Parkhurst issued an order on 7 June 1574 to suppress all the 'exercises' in his diocese. He was afterwards informed by Freke of Rochester that no such order had been issued in his diocese, or in London, and that he and Sandys had simply tried to ensure 'no matter of controversy' was raised in the exercises. Shortly after Parkhurst ordered his chancellor to act, a leading Norfolk gentleman, Sir Christopher Heydon, secured letters signed by Sandys and two privy councillors for the restitution of prophesyings in the county. Then, on summer progress in 1575, Elizabeth learned about prophesyings at Welwyn in Hertfordshire, and ordered Bishop Cooper of Lincoln to suppress them. He did so, banning some, but not all, of the other exercises in the southern counties of his vast diocese.[46]

It was, then, a decidedly messy pattern: of orders issued, evaded and countermanded, of bishops quietly thwarting the Queen's wishes with the covert encouragement of privy councillors. It came to an end in the summer of 1576. Grindal was not temperamentally cut out to play this kind of game, and Elizabeth's hostility to the prophesyings became more insistent after she was informed of 'disorders' in the Midlands, especially in the Warwickshire town of Southam. In June, Leicester, Burghley and Walsingham all wrote to Grindal, informing (and warning) him of the Queen's displeasure.

With Elizabeth in imperious mood, the limits of noble patronage for Puritans were cruelly exposed. In August, Thomas Wood wrote reproachfully to Leicester: 'It is commonly reported among the godly ... that your lordship hath been the chief instrument, or rather the only, of the overthrow of a most godly exercise at Southam.' Leicester indignantly denied the charge, and enumerated his prodigious efforts over many years for the furtherance of preaching and godly reform. But he wanted Wood to understand that he was not someone 'fantastically persuaded in religion'. He feared 'the over busy dealing of some hath done so much hurt in striving to make better that which is by permission good enough already'. When the chips were down, Leicester was a man of the establishment, not the opposition.[47]

Which was Grindal? On 12 June 1576 the archbishop was summoned to Elizabeth's presence, and told to suppress prophesyings throughout the province of Canterbury. Grindal requested time to consider, and to consult with his bishops. Their letters to him were almost universally supportive of the prophesyings as 'profitable' and 'necessary'. Even Cheyney of Gloucester said he approved, 'so they meddle not with matters in controversy'. The other 'conservative' on the episcopal bench, Edmund Guest, now bishop of Salisbury, was also in favour, though he was unhappy about the designation: prophecy was a gift to the Church of the Apostles, no longer present in the current age.

The exotic name was certainly a problem, perhaps conjuring in the Queen's mind visions of ecstatic utterance and wild-eyed oratory. Grindal admitted as much, and was content with the staid description, 'an exercise of the ministers'.

But, whether they were called prophesyings or exercises, these were occasions without sanction in the Injunctions of 1559, or in any subsequent canons – that was the taproot of Elizabeth's objection. It made the prophesyings vulnerable to denunciation, from conservative laity in the localities, or from more powerful figures in the orbit of the Queen. Bishop Cooper suspected the trouble started with 'one or two of some countenance and easy access unto the prince, that have small liking to that, or any other thing whereby religion may be further published'. The name of nemesis whispered in court circles was that of Christopher Hatton.

Suspicion of prophesyings was an anti-Puritan trait, but it was more than paranoia and prejudice. In many places, exercises may indeed have been almost painfully respectable, yet the moving spirits of the prophesying movement were sometimes fiery ones. Eusebius Paget, moderator of the Southam exercise, was a deprived Northamptonshire minister who likened bishops to Pharisees, cardinals and abbots. Among Grindal's episcopal correspondents, Scory of Hereford and Cox of Ely, survivors from Edwardian days, were frankly hostile. Scory suppressed prophesyings in his diocese because he feared an occurrence of what he heard was happening elsewhere: promotion of Cartwright's presbyterian ideas 'under colour of such exercise'.[48]

On 18 November, Elizabeth again summoned Grindal, ruled out further consultation, and ordered him to suppress prophesyings without additional delay. It was probably on this occasion that Elizabeth flatly told Grindal she 'thought that three or four preachers may suffice for a shire'. It was an assessment of the Church's needs leaving the evangelical archbishop almost literally speechless. But in any case it was a curt and abrupt interview, he 'not being permitted to explain in person how it seemed to him'.

Yet explain he did, in a 6,000-word missive composed just under three weeks later. It was perhaps the most extraordinary letter ever sent by a bishop to an English monarch; it sealed Grindal's fate, and set the Church of England on a new course.

What the Queen received was a candid lecture on the basics of Christian faith: 'Public and continual preaching of God's Word is the ordinary means and instrument of the salvation of mankind.' Reading Homilies was all very well, 'but is nothing comparable to the office of preaching'. There followed an impassioned defence of the prophesyings: dignified and orderly occasions, where 'the gravest and best learned pastors are appointed of the bishop to moderate', laymen were not permitted to speak, and 'no controversy of this present time and state shall be moved'. Prophesyings made ministers 'apter to teach their flocks'; drew them from idleness and gaming; elevated them in 'the opinion of laymen' – 'nothing, by experience, beateth down popery more'.

And then Grindal said it: 'I cannot with safe conscience, and without the offence of God, give my assent to the suppressing of the said exercises.' Perhaps he should have stopped there, but the archbishop's pen was liberated by the convictions of his courage. Just as Warham once likened himself to Becket, Grindal compared himself to Ambrose, fourth-century bishop of Milan, who defied the eastern and western emperors, Theodosius and Valentinian, over their toleration of Arian heresy and claims to control over Christian basilicas. Ambrose brought Theodosius to heel, by his innate moral authority, and by use of excommunication against him – it was, in the circumstances of the 1570s, an extraordinarily tactless historical analogy.

Parker said he did not know the bounds of royal supremacy; Grindal was sure that he did. Disputed matters of secular law were not simply decided by the Queen, but referred to the judges; likewise, 'matters of doctrine or discipline of the Church' pertained to the bishops. Grindal respectfully suggested that 'when you deal in matters of faith and religion . . . you would not use to pronounce too resolutely and peremptorily . . . as ye may do in civil and extern matters'. In God's causes, 'the will of God, and not the will of any earthly creature, is to take place'.

The letter ended with sombre admonition: 'remember, Madam, that you are a mortal creature'. If Elizabeth did not follow God's will – interpreted for her by her bishops – there would be an inevitable reckoning:

> Ye have done many things well, but except ye persevere to the end, ye cannot be blessed. For if ye turn away from God, then God will turn his merciful countenance from you. And what remaineth then to be looked for, but only a terrible expectation of God's judgments, and a heaping up of wrath against the day of wrath.[49]

For Grindal himself, the day of wrath was temporarily postponed, as privy councillors, including Burghley and Leicester, busied themselves, first of all to delay Elizabeth from seeing the archbishop's letter, and then to broker some kind of compromise. Grindal was warned to stay away from court, but for five months he continued to function as archbishop of Canterbury.

During those five months, the temperature in the higher reaches of the Church perceptibly changed. Sandys's translation to York as Grindal's successor created a vacancy in the key diocese of London. His successor, appointed in March 1577, was John Aylmer. A stalwart of the Marian exile, Aylmer blotted his episcopal prospects with his ham-fisted defence of female monarchy (see p. 431). But in the intervening years he slowly climbed the ladder of ecclesiastical promotion, and in the 1570s emerged as an outspoken critic of the prophesyings and a clerical protégé of Christopher Hatton.

John Whitgift, another pronounced anti-Puritan, and firm ally of Hatton, was enthroned as bishop of Worcester in May 1577. The crackdown hoped for by the dying, embittered Parker was seemingly under way. John Piers became bishop of Rochester in 1576, and transferred to Salisbury the following year. Pier's replacement at Rochester, John Young, probably also owed his appointment to Hatton, the suspected crypto-papist. Aylmer approvingly described Young as a man 'fit to bridle innovators'.

The first generation of Elizabethan bishops, largely united in background and attitude, sworn servants to ideals beyond obedience to monarchical command, was passing away: Parkhurst's death in 1575 was followed by that of Pilkington in 1576; Bentham would die in 1579 and Horne in 1580. Grindal's words of warning to the Queen in December 1576 belonged in a tradition of prophetic guidance and reproach, which the bishops collectively invoked over the fate of Mary in 1572. It expressed a profoundly Protestant sense of stewardship, of holders of roles and offices – including the crown – being ultimately accountable to God and the Christian commonwealth. It was an outlook Burghley, for all his affectionate loyalty to Elizabeth, wholeheartedly shared.

It was not the outlook of Whitgift or Aylmer. These were bulldog bishops of a new breed, and, in a strict sense of the term, 'Elizabethans'. Nor was it the outlook of Christopher Hatton. In a pair of intimate letters, written to Hatton in the early part of 1578, Aylmer revealed his 'mark to aim at': correction of 'offenders on both sides which swerve from the right path of obedience ... both the papist and the Puritan'. He went on, in only semi-ironic mode: 'I study with my eyes on my book, and my mind is in the court. I preach without spirit. I trust not of God, but of my sovereign, which is God's lieutenant, and so another God unto me.'[50] It was almost a parodic inversion of Grindal's letter of royal remonstrance.

Grindal himself was summoned before the Privy Council on 27 May 1577, and, after refusing to retract his position, formally suspended from exercise of office. A few weeks earlier, on 7 May, Elizabeth demonstrated her own understanding of the royal supremacy, writing personally to all the bishops commanding them to suppress the 'schismatical' prophesyings, and to ensure preaching was restricted to duly licensed persons, lest she was forced 'to make some example in reforming of you according to your deserts'.

The next step was deprivation; Elizabeth seemed intent on it. The only modern precedent, Cranmer's removal by Mary I, was not a happy one; it was an eventuality leading councillors were desperate to avoid. Burghley saw 'peril' in the prospect of proceedings that 'cannot but irritate our merciful God'. Knollys wrote in January 1578 that, if Grindal were deprived, 'then up starts the pride and practice of the papists'. A combination of Grindal's own ill health, and of intercessions from councillors – even from the decidedly non-vindictive Hatton – kept the moment of reckoning at bay. The archbishop of Canterbury remained in limbo, while practical church leadership devolved on Aylmer of London.

Zealous Protestants in government could feel the ship of state veering alarmingly off course. Yet there was still something they could do to right the direction. The official logic of the crackdown on prophesyings and Puritans was that their offences mirrored the disobedience of papists. Renewed attention to the Catholic threat might, then, concentrate the mind of the Queen, and mitigate the severity of the anti-Grindal reaction, without the need openly to oppose it.

In June 1577, Abbot Feckenham and other Catholics freed on parole were returned to confinement, accused of meeting with 'evil disposed' persons whom they further 'perverted in religion'. In October, with Star Chamber proceedings hanging over Grindal's head, Francis Walsingham worked with Aylmer to instruct the bishops to undertake at high speed a survey of recusancy in their dioceses. On 12 November, at the meeting during which Hatton was sworn to its membership, the Privy Council, with Burghley, Leicester, Bacon and Walsingham in attendance, ordered the immediate implementation of a death sentence on a priest, the first since 1573. Cuthbert Mayne was an alumnus of Allen's Douai seminary, arrested in Cornwall in the summer, and found in possession of a papal bull. The bull pertained to an expired papal jubilee, and was not brought from Rome, but purchased from a bookseller in Douai, apparently as a kind of souvenir. But it was enough to make Mayne technically a traitor under the statute of 1571. His head was displayed on a spike at Launceston, and his quartered body parts at Bodmin, Torquay, Barnstaple and Wadesbridge – a literal posting of the popish threat across the market towns of Devon and Cornwall.

In February 1578, shortly after Burghley received news, from the newly appointed royal secretary, Sir Thomas Wilson, that Elizabeth was 'much offended by the archbishop, and disliketh our darings for dealing with him', another two Catholics went to the scaffold at Tyburn. The priest John Nelson and the layman Thomas Sherwood were arrested in London for attending Catholic services, and convicted of treason after describing the Queen as a heretic and schismatic – words their interrogators worked hard to get them to use. The Privy Council ordered Sherwood put to the rack when it seemed he 'fain would retract his words in respect he affirmed her Majesty to be a heretic and usurper'.

The middle way of the Elizabethan Church, like Henry VIII's middle way before it, was not an easy-going forbearance, but a course defined by coercion and violence. In front of the Privy Council, Grindal was hectoringly told by an unnamed councillor that the prophesyings, and his refusal to suppress them, were a source of 'great divisions and sects'; a cause 'that religion, which of its own nature should be uniform, would against his nature have proved milliform; yea, in continuance, nulliform'.[51]

An official campaign against milliformity intensified at the beginning of Elizabeth's third decade on the throne. Some deviations – quiet, unobtrusive, preferably kept secret in the silent utterances of the heart – might be allowed to pass unexamined. But public or assertive performances of nonconformity contradicted the firmly held belief of both Queen and councillors that secure political authority required a dutiful uniformity in religious practice and allegiance. This belief was not, in its own terms, wrong. Yet a rigid determination to enforce that uniformity now promised only further effusions of blood. Rather than restoring the true 'nature' of religion, it risked simply proving how far its meanings had changed.

# 17

## WARS OF RELIGION

### A Shot Across the Bows

THE QUEEN WAS seated in her royal barge, on the Thames, between Greenwich and Deptford, 17 July 1579, a pleasant summer's evening, when her reign almost came to an abrupt and bloody end. A bullet passed within six feet of her, striking one of the rowers through both arms. On the vessel, consternation erupted, yet – according to contemporary printed accounts – Elizabeth herself took charge, calmly seeing to the welfare of her wounded boatman.

It was not, in fact, an assassination attempt. A young servant, Thomas Appletree, had a new gun, and to test it rowed out in a little boat with a couple of friends, firing random shots across the water. Stupidity was no defence at law, and Appletree was sentenced to death. At the gallows, Sir Christopher Hatton declared all the reasons he deserved to die, before unexpectedly producing a royal reprieve: the cue for much popular rejoicing at the Queen's merciful nature.

Hatton's speech underlined a fact privy councillors wanted people to remember; something they themselves could rarely banish from mind: the precariousness of peace and Protestantism. Had the bullet slain the Queen, 'our religion, and true faith in Jesus Christ, which we enjoy with unspeakable comfort of free conscience, might hereby have suffered confusion, and persecution of blood'. At the chance pace of a rower's stroke, twenty years of happy government could easily have been 'turned to bloody wars'.

Appletree himself was a pious, if thoughtless, youth. On the eve of his expected execution, he composed a lengthy prayer calling for God's blessing on the Queen, and for 'the establishing of a perfect government of thy Church, according to the rule of thy blessed Word' and 'the rooting out of all superstition and relics of Antichrist'.[1]

Yet if godly Protestants like Appletree had been privy to the barge-talk that summer's evening, they might well have thought it more likely to comfort Antichrist than confound him. Sitting beside the Queen was a charming French ambassador, Jean de Simier. He was in England to discuss the prospects for a marriage between Elizabeth and his master – Francis, Duke of Anjou, youngest son of Henry II and Catherine de Medici, heir presumptive to his brother, Henry III, and, of course, a Roman Catholic.

It was not the first time Elizabeth contemplated a papist consort. She weighed the credentials of the Austrian Archduke Charles in the mid-1560s (see p. 478), and briefly considered Francis's elder brother Henry – before his accession to the French throne – in 1570–1. The substitute merits of Francis, then Duke of Alençon, were thereafter periodically mooted by the French, but without much enthusiasm on the English side.

In 1579, the courtship came dramatically to life. Francis was no longer a teenager, but a personable young man of twenty-four. He visited in person in August, and Elizabeth professed herself enchanted with her 'frog'. An heir was not literally inconceivable, though Elizabeth had turned forty-five in September 1578. The attractions of the match were more political than personal. The revolt in the Netherlands had spread to the Catholic provinces of the south, and Anjou, with an established reputation as a protector of French Huguenots, was raising troops to aid the insurgents. Elizabeth had already (in 1575) turned down an offer from the Dutch rebels to recognize her as their sovereign, and was resisting calls from Leicester and other councillors to intervene directly. Marriage to Anjou would increase diplomatic pressure on Philip II, and ideally lead to a peaceful resolution in the Netherlands, or at least a military one where French ambitions were being safely directed from London.[2]

The Privy Council was divided. Sussex was in favour of the match; Burghley, at best, sceptical; Leicester and Walsingham were strongly against. Proponents cheerfully predicted that Anjou would see the light and convert to Protestantism, but however strongly Elizabeth appeared to reject it, the reality was that marriage must mean toleration: minimally of Anjou and his entourage to hear mass in England; maximally of English Catholics generally.

That prospect galvanized Protestant opposition in the spring and summer of 1579. Preachers of the Lent sermons at court spoke 'very violently against this marriage'. The Spanish ambassador supposed – not implausibly – that since the preachers escaped without punishment they must have the support of high-ranking figures. Elizabeth's willingness to tolerate criticism had limits, however, and London preachers, many of whom were 'covertly' guiding their texts towards criticism of the marriage, were ordered at the start of April to steer well clear.[3]

The most forceful critique of the marriage crossed a line. In August 1579, a London lawyer, John Stubbs, perhaps being fed information by Leicester or Walsingham, published *The discoverie of a gaping gulf whereunto England is like to be swallowed*. A royal marriage to a papist could be nothing but a heinous sin, calling down the vengeful judgement of God. The work bristled with belligerent religious nationalism, comparing England to the Kingdom of Israel, and naming France 'a principal prop of the tottering house of Antichrist'. The union would inevitably lead to the erection of an 'idolatrous altar' in London, 'our Jerusalem'. And alongside its tub-thumping anti-popery, Stubbs's tract advanced a novel constitutional claim: the Queen must contract no marriage 'before she parley in Parliament with all her subjects'.

Stubbs's pugnacious Puritanism, in toxic combination with disdain for the royal prerogative, explains the fury of Elizabeth's response. An unusually long proclamation, issued on 27 September, defended the Queen's record as a champion of Protestantism. It denounced Stubbs as a 'seditious libeller', and demanded the destruction of copies of his tract 'seditiously dispersed into sundry corners of the realm'. Aylmer summoned London ministers to his palace and exhorted them to condemn Stubbs. Even Grindal was brought temporarily out of suspended animation. His friends on the Privy Council (Burghley, Knollys, Walsingham, Wilson) wrote in early October, in half-hope of rehabilitation, ordering him to convene prominent preachers and warn them against Stubbs's iniquity.

Stubbs's punishment, inflicted on 3 November, was suitably Old Testament. Elizabeth wanted him to hang, but a jury refused to convict for felony and he was retried under a Marian statute for inciting sedition. Prior to imprisonment, the public hangman struck off with a cleaver the right hand that wrote the *Gaping Gulf*. A similar punishment was inflicted on William Page – no lowly acolyte, but an MP and secretary to a leading councillor, the Earl of Bedford. Page's crime was to have sent fifty copies to his friend, Sir Richard Grenville, for circulation in the West Country. The tract's printer, Hugh Singleton, was spared on account of his advanced years. At that very moment, Singleton's presses were producing the poet Edmund Spenser's *Shepherd's Calendar*, a work packed with coded attacks on the Anjou match. Spenser had recently become secretary to Leicester, who may or may not have been Stubbs's secret patron.[4] It is difficult here to pin down the policy priorities of any unified Elizabethan 'regime'.

Among Protestants, Stubbs's mutilation went down badly. The crowd at his punishment was ominously and unusually silent. In Norwich, magistrates even debated whether to publicize the September proclamation, as they were required to do. Elizabeth was angered by the opposition, both in the country and on the Privy Council, openly voiced at a meeting in October 1579. Her instinct was to push ahead. It is to this juncture that we can ascribe reports, originating with the French ambassador, of Elizabeth considering a major change to the composition of the Council, dismissing Walsingham, the most dogged opponent of the match, and recruiting four heavyweight Catholics, including Viscount Montagu, and Henry Percy, brother and successor to the rebel Earl of Northumberland.

Protestants were right to be anxious. The marginalization of papists from political life, even to the point of extinction, was not, after all, an unalterable fact. Among Catholics, hopes for change were cautiously stirring. The most enthusiastic written endorsement of the marriage was a manuscript treatise by Henry Howard, younger brother of the executed Duke of Norfolk. Howard conformed outwardly, but was widely regarded as a secret papist. He had close links to Catholic supporters of Mary Queen of Scots.

Between them, Stubbs, the preachers, and the self-justificatory royal proc-lamation, all helped to ensure that the implications of the Anjou marriage were not a lofty preserve of policy-makers, but something discussed avidly by common folk in markets and alehouses. In these heady days, complete reversal of the Reformation did not seem implausible. In rural Warwickshire, one of the curates of the vicar of Wooton, 'upon rumour of a change in religion ... did shave his beard', the symbol of a Protestant minister (see p. 393). 'What if the world change, as it did in King Henry VIII's time and in Queen Mary's time?' was the saucy response of a parishioner of Thornton-in-Craven, Yorkshire, presented for recusancy in 1580.

In the end, Elizabeth drew back from a policy bound to fracture any func-tioning concord on her Council, and to provoke resistance, vocal and perhaps violent, from the country at large. Characteristically, she did not admit to retreat, instructing her councillors to draw up terms for a marriage treaty. This recognized, reluctantly, the claims of Anjou and his servants to 'exercise of their religion', but the form of the wedding was left unresolved, and Elizabeth reserved her right to repudiate the treaty if she found she could not obtain her people's consent. In January 1580, Elizabeth regretfully informed Anjou that her subjects' objections had not been overcome, and asked him to rethink his insistence on freedom to hear mass. The negotiations continued, but the court-ship's moment had passed.[5]

English Catholics' hopes of toleration, of readmission to the social and political life of the nation, took a blow – to the immense relief of bishops and councillors, whose alertness to a growing domestic danger had been heightened by the 1577 recusancy survey. 'The papists,' Aylmer remarked to Walsingham, 'marvellously increase both in numbers and in obstinate with-drawal of themselves from the church.'[6] That obstinacy was about to receive a major infusion of awkwardness, as the international Counter-Reformation turned its gaze to the prospects of England.

## Jesuits

On 1 May 1579, Pope Gregory XIII issued a bull of foundation for a new institute in Rome. It decreed the formal conversion of the old English hospice (see p. 70) into an English College, to instruct young men of a nation that 'once flourished with great wealth and concern for the Catholic Faith, but is now devastated by the dreadful taint of heresy'.

For some years, a process of transformation had been under way, seeing the hospice become a centre for clerical exiles, rather than itinerant pilgrims. From 1577, there was an influx of students from William Allen's seminary at Douai, which, in March 1578, to escape political turmoil in the Netherlands, transferred itself to Rheims in northern France.

The mind-set of Allen's students put them at odds with the existing regime in the hospice. They were imbued with an ethos of mission and conversion, while the current rector, Morris Clynnog, saw his task as the education and useful employment of expatriate priests, who would return to England only after a formal restoration of Catholicism there. The quarrel was overlaid with ethnic tensions, the English new arrivals accusing Clynnog of favouring fellow Welshmen among the students.

It was all rather mystifying to Pope Gregory, who had no idea the Welsh and English were separate species. Bombarded with memorials and petitions, he removed Clynnog in March 1579 and asked the General of the Society of Jesus, Everard Mercurian, a judicious Luxembourger, to take over control. An Italian Jesuit, Alfonso Agazzari, was installed as rector, and a change of direction was signalled in the declaration of the bull of foundation that henceforth graduates would 'return to England to enlighten others who had fallen away'. All students would now take an oath, affirming their willingness to travel to England whenever their superiors commanded them – a local adaptation of the famous 'fourth vow' of the Jesuits, to offer 'special obedience' to the Pope in respect of missions.[7]

The coup in Rome was the capstone of a rising edifice of Catholic activism, with William Allen as its master-builder. Allen met with other English Catholic exiles at the start of 1576, and discussed with them the prospects for a joint papal-Spanish invasion. Philip was sympathetic, but military commitments in the Netherlands, and the continuing Ottoman threat in the Mediterranean, limited his offers of support to moral ones.

By 1578, that was starting to change. Philip helped to fund a scheme for the invasion of Ireland. It was the brainchild of Thomas Stukley, a colourful English exile and professional soldier, in Habsburg service, off and on, since the mid-1550s. Stukley set off from Civita Vecchia, the port of Rome, in February 1578. Docking en route at Lisbon, he was persuaded by the devout and charismatic King Sebastian I to join an expedition against the Moors in Morocco. Sebastian promised Stukley that, having dealt with the infidels, the crusade would then proceed to Ireland to confound the heretics. Both men, and an entire Portuguese army, perished in the sand at the battle of Alcazar on 4 August 1578.

The death of the childless King Sebastian provoked a Portuguese succession crisis. His heir was his uncle Henry, archbishop and cardinal; also childless. Henry's death in 1580 prompted Philip to assert his own dynastic claim. It was enforced with a successful invasion: a demonstration, not lost on the English government, of what the King of Spain could do when he put his mind to it.

Meanwhile, the Irish enterprise entered a second phase under a new leader: James Fitzmaurice Fitzgerald, a veteran rebel and exile, in possession of a papal brief promising a plenary indulgence to all Irish people who supported his insurgency. With a force of 700 Italian and Spanish troops, Fitzmaurice landed at Smerwick in south-west Ireland on 17 July 1579, unfurled a papal banner, and issued a proclamation calling on Irish lords to join him in overthrowing the heretic 'she-tyrant', Elizabeth. The papal bull of excommunication was perhaps not such a damp squib after all.

By Fitzmaurice's side was the proclamation's author, the English priest Nicholas Sander, who planned to raise an Irish army for the invasion of England. Sander was the most radical of Catholic resistance theorists. His 1571 work *De visibili monarchia ecclesiae* (Of the Visible Monarchy of the Church) praised John Felton as a martyr, and portrayed popes as world-bestriding sovereigns, whom other rulers were obligated to obey.[8] This was a different brand of Catholicism from the one Elizabeth was (literally) flirting with in 1579, but to Englishmen like John Stubbs, the distinction was largely meaning-less. Whatever aspect it chose to present, the face of Antichrist was the visage of sedition.

In the autumn of 1579, William Allen finalized his plans. There was to be a spiritual invasion of England, to parallel the military invasion of Ireland, and perhaps prepare for its progression across the intervening North Sea. Allen's chosen instrument was the Society of Jesus, which, despite growing numbers of English recruits, had so far held largely aloof from the English mission. The still undecided fate of the Anjou negotiations strengthened the case for a show of Catholic strength, and, despite his reservations, General Mercurian agreed to the undertaking. He did, however, prepare instructions for the participants insisting on the purely religious nature of their assignment. Ambiguities about motive – and perhaps the sheer impossibility of separating spiritual aims from political ones – would from the outset dog the missionaries' steps.

Allen knew the men he wanted. One was Robert Persons, a robust and resourceful Somerset man, of yeoman stock. In the late 1560s, Persons began an academic career at Oxford, still far from fully purged of Catholic sympa-thizers. Increasingly, he was drawn into their orbit, before decamping to the continent in 1574 and the following year joining the Society of Jesus. The other man was widely considered one of the most brilliant scholars of his generation, and, like Persons, was a convert to Catholicism from a Protestant, or at least conformist, background.

Edmund Campion was the son of a London bookseller, raised in a world of words and print. He prospered in Oxford as a fellow of St John's, but, even before his ordination in 1569 as a Church of England deacon, was increasingly troubled at having taken the Oath of Supremacy. After a spell of semi-retirement in Ireland (a refuge for crypto-papists, as well as Puritans), Campion finally declared himself. He fled to Douai in 1571, and entered the Society of Jesus as a novice in Rome in 1573. At the time he received Allen's summons, Campion, an exemplar of Jesuit scholarly internationalism, was teaching rhetoric and philosophy in Prague.

On 14 April 1580, Pope Gregory received Campion and Persons in audience in Rome. They sent him in advance nineteen questions, relating to 'consolation and instruction of Catholics who are perplexed'. Several involved the day-to-day dilemmas of living among heretics. Was it ever acceptable to forego fast days and eat meat? (Yes, in cases of necessity, and without heretical intent.) Could a Catholic, outside of service times, pray in a church controlled by heretics? Again, yes, so long as scandal was avoided.

More thorny questions involved attendance at churches while services were taking place. What if someone, taking no part in 'their heretical supper', simply read Catholic prayers quietly? Or made plain their disapproval by sitting with a hat on? The Jesuits also posed the specific instance – perhaps prompted by a real case – of a Catholic noblewoman of the Queen's household, dutifully accompanying her mistress into the 'secret chamber from which Elizabeth hears the divine service of heretics'.

Gregory's answers were less rigidly anti-Nicodemite than one might have expected. The noblewoman should seek to avoid such dangerous occasions, but if that proved impossible, she must take care 'to show that she does not consent in any way to heresy'. Laypeople in general should follow the same course.

This note of pastoral flexibility, recognizing the difficult situation of Catholics, extended to the main meat of the questions: the status of *Regnans in Excelsis*. Gregory formally reissued the bull; there was no doubt that Elizabeth, a tyrant, remained excommunicated. Nonetheless, the Pope explained, it was legitimate to call her queen and obey her in civil matters. Catholics could even take civil oaths of loyalty to her, adding an evasive 'etc.' to the Queen's regnal title.

In short, English Catholics were not obliged by the bull to take up arms against Elizabeth: they were off the hook on which Pius V had snagged them. Or not quite. 'Things being as they are', there was no expectation of hopeless sacrifice. But if 'everything has been so arranged that hope of victory is certain', then it was incumbent on people to help overthrow Elizabeth. In response to the most sensitive question of all, the Pope affirmed that 'it is not lawful for a private person to kill any tyrant'. But if such an action were guaranteed to deliver control of the government, then killing Elizabeth would be lawful. As things stood, however, 'it is much better not ever to talk at all about that matter'.[9]

Rome was ruling nothing out. English Catholics were allowed to be 'loyal', but their licence for loyalty could at any time be revoked – or should be revoked by themselves – if political or military circumstances changed. It was a slippery and perilous mandate for the Jesuits (still, it seems, unaware of what was happening in Ireland) to carry with them into a hostile land. It positively invited the hypothetical 'bloody question' that Burghley would soon start putting to arrested priests: if a foreign power invaded to implement the 1570 bull, whose side would you be on?

Campion and Persons, and a third Jesuit, the lay brother Ralph Emerson, crossed secretly and separately to England in June 1580, though their coming was well heralded and expected. The expedition from Rome to the Channel was something of a triumphal procession; among those accompanying the priests was the aged Bishop Thomas Goldwell, in disappointed hope he would be allowed to return with them. The journey included a moment of audacious theatre, when the party turned up in Geneva and demanded an impromptu disputation with Beza. Force of argument, the Jesuits believed, would carry all before it.

They arrived in a country rendered defensively fearful by the bloody course of the rebellion in Ireland, and by an earthquake that in April shook the capital and south-east, and seemed to many a portent of God's judgement and displeasure. In London, the Lord Mayor recommended banning plays within the liberties; in Coventry, the traditional cycle of Corpus Christi mystery plays, revised but not abolished over preceding decades, was finally brought to an end. Troops were mustered that summer in every English county. In July, a proclamation warned people against spreading or heeding rumours that 'the Pope, the King of Spain, and some other princes are accorded to make a great army to invade this realm', while simultaneously reassuring them that if such a thing were to happen, the nation was fully prepared.[10]

Once in England, the Jesuits made contact with priests in the capital, and in the second week of July convened a meeting with lay and clerical leaders. At the 'Synod of Southwark' disagreement emerged over strategies for survival. Given the intense pressure from the authorities, some nobles and gentlemen hoped for concessions to attend heretical services, but on this Campion and Persons proved more Catholic than the Pope, insisting on strict recusancy as the only acceptable way.

Shortly afterwards, on a press secretly set up in East Ham, just outside London, Persons inaugurated his career as a brilliant polemicist and produced *A Brief Discourse Concerning Certain Reasons why Catholics Refuse to go to*

*Church*. It is a work underlining just how far the meaning of 'religion' had changed over several decades of creative conflict. It was in the nature of a religion, Persons contended, to require some 'sign or mark' of its members' allegiance and identity. For Catholics in England, absence from church was that 'sign distinctive'. Non-absentees were not Catholics but 'schismatics'. Mischievously, Persons observed that 'the hotter sort of Protestants, called the Puritans . . . do utterly condemn the service which now the Protestants have, and thereupon do refrain from it as much as Catholics'. That was only partly true, but divisions among the heretics rarely went unremarked by the Catholic exiles. Persons in fact claimed that England now contained four religions, 'distinct both in name, spirit, and doctrine: that is to say, the Catholics, the Protestants, the Puritans, and the householders of Love'.[11]

Persons's uncompromising anti-Nicodemism offered only the same cold comfort that Protestants had received from their leaders under Mary: God would reward suffering in due time. But Catholic priests, unlike Protestant preachers, were accustomed to think in terms of 'casuistry' – the application, and sometimes adjustment, of general principles to fit particular cases.

Persons launched into print in response to a manuscript circulating among Catholic landowners imprisoned for recusancy, the work of Lord Montagu's chaplain, Alban Langdale. It did not defend church-going as a general principle, but it argued that 'God doth more regard the will and intention of the doer than the deed'. There were, for example, many parishes in England 'where neither the curate nor parishioners are open professors of Protestantism nor known Protestants but dissembling Catholics': in such places attendance hardly connoted Protestant commitment. Langdale denied a mere 'corporate presence' was the crux of distinction between heretics and believers: 'If I pray not with them, if I sit when they kneel, if I refuse their communion etc, be not these *signa distinctiva?*'

Whatever these new Jesuits said, there were various ways to be a faithful Catholic. In time of persecution, it was possible to accept the Queen's proposal – never openly stated, but implicit in the scope of her legislation – that church-going was primarily a matter of civil obedience rather than spiritual conviction.

For anxious Protestants (and for later tidy-minded historians), this was bad news. However many, or few, names appeared on lists of convicted recusants, it was impossible to know how many 'real' Catholics were actually out there. In the Warwickshire village of Rowington, in the cool shade of Anjou's courtship, the Catholic gentleman William Skinner was hopeful of an imminent declaration of religious toleration; that 'every man should live as he like'. He taunted the Protestant parish clerk: when such a decree was made, 'how many thinkest thou . . . would come to church? Not passing ten of our parish, I warrant thee.'[12]

After the synod, Persons and Campion separated, and traversed a network of Catholic houses in the Thames Valley, the Midlands, the West Country and the north: saying mass, hearing confessions, reconciling 'schismatics' and preaching sermons – sometimes to large audiences. Before leaving London, the Jesuits agreed that each should draft a statement of intentions, underlining Mercurian's insistence on the mission's purely spiritual character, for use if they were arrested. The statements were supposed to remain sealed, but Campion's 'Letter to the Council' was copied and widely circulated among supporters. By January 1581, it had twice been printed for refutation by outraged Protestant critics: the Puritan Meredith Hanmer christened it 'Campion's Brag'.

The Letter was a kind of riposte to Jewel's Challenge sermon of two decades before. Campion declared himself eager to debate with councillors and divines, certain that 'none of the Protestants, nor all the Protestants living . . . can maintain their doctrine in disputation'. Nor did he do much to allay Protestant fears about the Society of Jesus:

> As touching our Society, be it known unto you that we have a league [with] all the Jesuits in the world, whose succession and multitude must overreach the practice of England, cheerfully to carry the cross which God shall lay upon us and never to despair [of] your recovery while we have a man left to enjoy your Tyburn, or to be racked with your torments, or to be consumed with your prisons. The expense is reckoned, the enterprise is begun. It is of God; it cannot be withstood.[13]

Parliament reconvened in early 1581, in the midst of a moral panic about Jesuits. Ireland was spiralling further out of control. Fitzmaurice had been killed, but the Earl of Desmond and Viscount Baltinglass now carried the banner of Catholic rebellion across the southern provinces of Munster and Leinster. Wales too was causing concern, amidst fears it might serve as the point of entry for an invasion from Ireland. The start of 1581 witnessed the appearance of a Welsh Elizabeth Barton (see pp. 206–7). Elizabeth Orton was a teenager from Flintshire, whose ecstatic visions of purgatory involved denunciations of the established Church and exhortations to strict recusancy. Local Catholics circulated manuscript accounts of her utterances, which were reportedly sent to Ireland, and even to France and Rome.

In his speech before Parliament of 25 January, Sir Walter Mildmay, Chancellor of the Exchequer, denounced the Jesuits: 'a rabble of vagrant friars newly sprung up and coming through the world to trouble the Church of God'. The news, as Mildmay reported it, was not all bad: Fitzmaurice's death was a token of God's providential care, as was the fate of Spaniards recently 'pulled out by the ears' by 'a noble captain', the deputy of Ireland, Lord Grey of Wilton.

It was an upbeat way to describe an atrocity. In November 1580, a second, newly arrived, papal contingent, besieged in a fort outside the town of Smerwick in County Kerry, surrendered to Grey under a white flag, and handed over its weapons and standards. After excoriating the Pope who sent them – a 'detest-able shaveling' – Grey ordered the systematic slaughter of the defenders: perhaps 600 in total, including accompanying priests and a leavening of women and children. In Ireland, militant Protestantism waged a brutal religious war, without mercy or regret. The English government sanctioned it, out of indiffer-ence to native Irish lives, and in hopes of cauterizing there the infection of seditious rebellion.[14]

## The Execution of Justice

Within England itself, the law might still suffice. In Parliament, Mildmay spoke for the Privy Council as a whole in claiming Catholic disobedience was encour-aged by 'mildness of the laws hitherto'. Parliament passed new legislation making it a treasonable offence to convert anyone to Catholicism with intent to withdraw them from royal obedience. Attendance requirements under the Act of Uniformity were now to be enforced with crippling fines of £20 per month.

It was a persuasive inducement to conform, if not convert. People indicted for recusancy would be discharged if they agreed to 'submit and conform' themselves before their bishop. Once again, however, it was not the act the bishops really wanted. They backed a bill originating in the Lords to give the ecclesiastical Court of High Commission rights to levy heavy fines on non-communicants. The Commons put forward a still harsher bill, with death penalties and indefinite imprisonments. The bill that passed, limiting itself to physical attendance at church, bore the characteristic royal fingerprints.[15]

Meanwhile, Campion, Persons and Emerson remained at large, in defiance of a proclamation calling for the arrest of persons trained overseas, 'whereof some of them carry the name of Jesuits, under the colour of a holy name to deceive and abuse the simpler sort'.

It was not the 'simpler sort' the authorities needed to worry about. Whether in Bolivia or Berkshire, Jesuits habitually targeted the elites, aiming to convert society through a downward osmosis of spiritual influence. On 27 June 1581, the Jesuits pulled off an extraordinary propaganda coup at the heart of the Protestant intellectual establishment. Oxford students congregating in the University Church of St Mary found copies of a Latin treatise strewn on the benches. It was a work by Campion: *Rationes decem* (Ten Reasons) in defence of the Catholic religion, freshly printed in 400 copies on Persons's secret press, now relocated from East Ham to the manor house at Stonor Park in south Oxfordshire.

Campion's 'Reasons' combatted the reformers' claims across a broad series of fronts. Protestants' scripturalism involved ignoring inconvenient texts (like the Epistle of James); their assertions of antiquity were contradicted by a host of early councils and Fathers. And any suggestion that Catholicism was a novel or alien creed was confounded by witness of simple observation. Habits of law,

rituals of monarchy and nobility, customs of ordinary people, forms of archi-
tecture, fashions of dress – all were shaped by a faith 'embedded in the very
roots of our culture'. With scrupulous courtesy, Campion appealed directly to
Elizabeth, inviting her to take her rightful place in a line of distinguished kings
and emperors: 'One heaven cannot hold both Calvin and the princes I have
named.'[16]

The challenge could not be allowed to go unanswered, and barely three
weeks later Campion was called to account. On 17 July 1581, along with two
other priests and a handful of laymen, he was arrested at Lyford Grange in
Berkshire, after being reported by an informer.

The blaze of publicity accompanying the Jesuit mission intensified in the
months after Campion's arrest. 'There is tremendous talk here of Jesuits,'
Persons wrote to Agazzari in August, 'and more fables perhaps are told about
them than were told of old about monsters.' Campion was granted in the Tower
the disputation he asked for, against a tag-team of prominent Protestant
divines, all determined to refute the Jesuit's theological claims, and to unmask
him as a seditious traitor rather than the simple pastor he claimed to be.

The disputation, spread over four sessions in August and September, was
not intended to be fair. Campion had no access to books, and received no noti-
fication of topics. He was nonetheless acknowledged, even by his enemies, to
have acquitted himself remarkably well. There were risks for the government in
allowing Campion even a stage-managed platform for his views. But there were
risks too in seeming to run scared of the free debate for which the Jesuit had
called.

From the pulpit, and in print, government supporters waged a clamorous
anti-Campion campaign, to win over 'public opinion'. As the Jesuit went to trial
in November 1581, the professors of divinity in Oxford and Cambridge,
Laurence Humphrey and William Whitaker, produced learned Latin confuta-
tions of his *Rationes decem*. Both were anti-vestiarian Puritans, a type little to
Aylmer's taste. But at this moment of crisis, Elizabeth's Church needed the
intellectual firepower of godly Protestantism, and the bishop of London asked
for their help. Some yet more radical figures, among them John Field, took
time out from their quarrel with the bishops to denounce the Jesuits in print.

Puritans, including Cartwright, also rallied round to condemn a sensa-
tional Catholic publication of 1582: a translation of the New Testament into
English, undertaken at Rheims under the direction of Gregory Martin. It was a
rendition from the Vulgate rather than the original Greek, and in places
cautiously and even curiously Latinate in its translations. Still, with its polemical preface and notes, it was a further sign of the eagerness of Catholic exiles
to engage wholeheartedly in a battle of ideas – and, in its belated endorsement
of vernacular scripture, an indication of their willingness to take the fight to
the enemy.

Alongside the learned denunciations of Campion were a rash of racy, vernacular pamphlets, blackening him by association with popish superstition and subversion. Their leading producer was a slippery character, Anthony Munday, pamphleteer and actor, who gave evidence against Campion at his trial. Munday had lived in 1579 as a seminarian in the English College, and recounted his experiences there in a scandalous exposé, *The English Roman Life* (1582). After dinner, he reported, students would habitually sit with Jesuits around the fire, 'and in all their talk, they strive who shall speak worst of her Majesty, of some of her Council, of some bishop'.

Spies, reporting to either Walsingham or Burghley, proliferated among the penniless overseas exiles, though it may well be that Munday initially went to Rome as a curious Catholic, rather than a patriotic Protestant. Even in his lurid anti-papal polemics, there were some who thought he protested too much, and in a world demanding outward professions of certainty, not everyone was sure how true allegiance was to be known.[17]

There were ways to make windows into men's hearts. Any impression of Campion being crushed by sheer force of truth was illusory. In parallel with the Tower debates, he was subjected to bouts of rigorous interrogation, and periodic applications of excruciating torture. Campion never denied his faith, or confessed to treasonous intents, but he gave up names of Catholics who sheltered him, leading to a wave of arrests: perhaps as many as 500 landowners were interrogated on whether they 'entertained' Campion in their houses.

The increasing use of judicial torture was an innovation of the Elizabethan regime. It was illegal under the common law, and took place under authority of Privy Council warrants, granting the torturers immunity from prosecution. Thomas Norton, nicknamed 'rack master' by Persons, oversaw its use in the Tower. Both at the disputation, and his trial, Campion publicized the fact he had been tortured, creating billows of outrage in England and overseas. Soon after, Norton wrote to Walsingham to justify the practice. He insisted – a seemingly circular argument – that 'none was put to the rack that was not first by manifest matter known to the Council to be guilty of treason . . . there was no innocent tormented'. It was important for Norton, in the era of the Spanish Inquisition, to assert, and presumably believe, that 'no man was tormented for matter of religion, nor asked what he believed of any point of religion, but only to understand of particular practices for setting up their religion, by treason or force against the Queen'.[18]

The resort to torture reflected, then, not only the regime's profound insecurity, but some important claims about the limits of 'religion' itself. These were soon enshrined in print. At the end of 1583, Norton's apology for torture was printed, along with a short tract called *The Execution of Justice in England*. Its anonymous author was none other than Burghley, and its publication was an admission that the authorities had a serious problem.

Campion was executed at Tyburn on 1 December 1581, along with two other missionary priests, Alexander Bryant and Ralph Sherwin. Seven more priests were executed before May 1582, and another four by the close of the year. A further three priests and a layman were hanged in 1583. All were convicted as traitors, but Catholics insisted they died 'for religion' – a perception lent credence as much by Campion's pious demeanour and courtesy to opponents as by his unfailing insistence on the spiritual nature of his mission. On the scaffold, Campion was urged by the attending minister to pray with him and make conventional gestures of penitence. This he politely refused to do, telling the preacher, 'You and I, we are not of one religion.'

Campion's status as a saintly martyr was soon being broadcast throughout Europe. Persons, having escaped to France in the summer of 1581, published in 1582 *De persecutione Anglicana libellus* (Book of the Persecution in England), rapidly reprinted in numerous editions, and translated into English, Italian, German, French and Spanish. The same year, William Allen produced *A Brief History of the Glorious Martyrdom of Twelve Reverend Priests*, intended to show 'how by colour of contrived treason and conspiracy (the cause indeed being religion) the enemies of the Christian faith have shed their innocent blood'.

Persecution and martyrdom were words Protestants had become accustomed to owning; they disliked having them thrown in their face. A royal proclamation of April 1582 complained of numerous 'letters, libels, pamphlets and books', falsely insinuating Campion and others 'were without just cause condemned'. Henceforth, all Jesuits and seminary priests were *ipso facto* to be considered traitors.

Capital punishment as such was not the crux of Catholic criticism. John Hamerton, of Hellifield in North Yorkshire, was in June 1582 accused of treason, after saying Campion, like Felton and Story, was unjustly put to death for religion; they died like apostles and martyrs. Hamerton was anything but squeamish: he nostalgically recalled how 'he was Bonner's man, and helped to set fire to the faggots to the most that were burned in Smithfield'. Indeed, 'he yet rejoices to think how they fried in the flame, and what service he had done God in furthering their death'.[19] Martyrs were not those who died for a cause. Martyrs were those who died for the truth.

On 2 August 1581, an Englishman was burned at the stake in Rome. Richard Atkins was a zealot, and possibly a lunatic, who travelled to Italy intending 'to charge the Pope publicly with his sins'. He was arrested and sentenced to death after knocking the chalice from the priest's hands at a mass in St Peter's. Robert Persons reported the affair in the form of a printed letter 'sent by an English gentleman from beyond the seas, to his friend in London'. The timing was significant, even instructive. Atkins perished only two days after the seminary priest Everard Hanse was put to death at Tyburn, and Persons claimed that as he finished writing news reached him of 'the betraying and apprehension of Master Campion'.

The contrast between these paragons and the deranged Atkins was palpable; Persons signed off by suggesting to his friend that 'if you communicate the case to Master Fox, perhaps he can make something of it'. It was a sarcastic jibe, yet in the 1583 edition of *Acts and Monuments*, Foxe did include a 'true report of the horrible and merciless martyrdom of one Richard Atkins, an Englishman, with extreme torments', largely lifted from a chapter of the ubiquitous Anthony Munday's *English Roman Life*.[20] More than ever, truth claims were tied up with the sufferings of acknowledged brethren, inflicted on them by unjust persecutors. A great deal was at stake in deciphering the deaths of growing numbers of Jesuits and seminary priests.

Burghley's counter-attack, in the *Execution of Justice*, was itself partly a matter of numbers. Even by their own reckoning, papists could recite no more than sixty names of 'martyrs' from the past twenty-five years. They chose to forget the times of Queen Mary, when, in little more than five years, almost 400 died from 'imprisonment, torments, famine and fire'. What the recent sufferers lacked in quantity, they also wanted for in quality. The denizens of the seminaries ('seedmen of sedition') were a rabble of social malcontents, disappointed scholars, bankrupt merchants. None was prosecuted for holding 'contrary opinions in religion', but only for treason and incitement to rebellion. They were convicted, not under strange or novel statutes, 'but by the ancient temporal laws of the realm' – technically true in the case of Campion, indicted under a statute of 1352.

The logic of Burghley's propaganda propelled him towards definitions of 'religion' that few Protestant, let alone Catholic, clergy would readily have recognized. It seemed to be a matter of internally held doctrinal propositions, divorced from speech or action in the world. In a hastily produced rebuttal, William Allen flatly rejected the premise: 'as though, forsooth, there were no question pertaining to faith and religion but touching our inward belief'. It was indeed a religious matter 'to demand and press us by torture where, in whose houses, what days and times we say or hear mass; how many we have reconciled; what we have heard in confession; who resorteth to our preachings'.[21]

It is reasonable, if not particularly helpful, to observe that both men had a point. They were struggling to make sense of a newly emerging world, one in which inherited conceptions about the indivisibility of truth came up against pragmatic recognition that religious minorities might have to be accommodated, rather than simply wished out of existence. Nonetheless, neither the exiled opposition, nor in truth the government, was prepared to acknowledge a purely secular sphere of 'politics', or a sealed private one of 'faith'. Both were playing for total victory, in a game where the stakes were very high. Caught in the middle were the Catholic laity, trying to reconcile their duties as loyal subjects with what was needed to save their souls.

In February 1583, Burghley interviewed Lord Vaux of Harrowden, a prominent Northamptonshire landowner, imprisoned for recusancy and for sustaining the fugitive Campion. The minister was surprisingly sympathetic to Vaux's plight, and helped him draft a statement of submission to Elizabeth, acknowledging his fault and begging to be remitted his recusancy fine. Vaux's capitulation was not total, however. He professed a willingness to listen to arguments or instruction, but asked 'to be forborne to be compelled to come to the church, not for that I should so do in contempt of her Majesty or of her laws, but that my conscience only . . . did stay me'.

There was no right of conscience in Elizabethan England, and no relaxation of the recusancy laws for Vaux. Like his brother-in-law, Sir Thomas Tresham (who also sheltered Campion), and his cousin, Thomas Throckmorton of Coughton (another brother-in-law of Tresham), Vaux continued to face indictments and fines for failure to attend church.[22] All protested their loyalty to the Queen, but could a papist ever be a good subject?

### Country Divinity

Plenty of people were convinced the answer was no. One of the many publications spawned by the Campion affair was *A dialogue between a Papist and a Protestant* (1582), which replayed in fictional form the kind of theological disputation conducted in the Tower. Its author was George Gifford, vicar of the Essex parish of Maldon, and a preacher of determinedly godly inclinations.

Gifford's 'papist' objects to the label: 'Wherefore should ye call me papist? I am obedient to the laws, and do not refuse to go to the church'. To his Protestant antagonist, this is a distinction without a difference: 'there are papists which will not come at the church, and there are papists which can keep their conscience to themselves'. The test of loyalty proposed by the Queen's legislation was, in the view of zealous reformers like Gifford, entirely inadequate. The long discussion between the men ends, not, as we might expect, with the papist's submission and conversion, but with the Protestant recognizing its impossibility: 'I leave you to the Lord; no hope I see to win you.'[23]

Yet Puritan ministers like Gifford, with years of pastoral parish experience, knew that the world was not in fact neatly divided between hopeless papists and dependable Protestants. In 1581, Gifford had published another dialogue: *A Brief Discourse of Certain Points of the Religion, which is [found] among the Common Sort of Christians, which may be termed the Country Divinity*. Its characters are a minister, 'Zelotes', and a middle-aged rural parishioner, 'Atheos'.

Atheos means 'without God', but this well-meaning householder is no atheist in any sense we might today recognize. He is a diligent church-goer, who tries to follow the Ten Commandments and do well by his neighbours, and who protests that 'I love God above all, and put my whole trust in him'.

Atheos rejects indignantly any imputation to him of popery: 'What tell you me of the Pope? I care not for him; I would both he and his dung were buried in the dunghill.'

Nonetheless, Atheos's religion, his 'country divinity', does not count as Christianity by Zelotes's (or Gifford's) standards. He shows too little respect for preaching, and far too much for the faith of his forefathers: 'What, should we seek for to be wiser or better than they?' Most fundamentally, Atheos fails to grasp the key theological insight of the reformers – justification by faith alone – and believes people will be judged by the good they do in the world. 'If a man be sorry, and ask God forgiveness, is he not even as well as they which are the more precise? The mercy of God must save all.'

Calvinist clergy knew that was not going to happen. From before the beginning of the world, God selected some people for eternal life, consigned others to eternal perdition. It was a certainty that the latter significantly outnumbered the former. For anyone with eyes to see, predestination was the unmistakable teaching of scripture. But it was more than an abstract proposition. It demanded a searching within oneself for signs of the saving faith that gave the Christian optimistic hope, 'assurance', of membership among the elect.

It was to this intent that another Essex Puritan minister, Richard Rogers, kept a diary in the 1580s, scrupulously recording both 'torment' and 'sound peace', as he analysed daily thoughts and motives. True faith meant moving beyond externals, beyond even the externals of right belief, to confront the unconquered wilfulness within. The *Country Divinity* contains a revealing exchange. Atheos is asked what he thinks of images, and dutifully replies that he never put any trust in them, or thought they could do him any good. Zelotes corrects him: 'I do not speak of that outward giving of God's worship, but of another, which is inward in the mind.'[24] Idols were not merely material or ritual residues of the Catholic past, but any temptation of the will inserting itself between the believer and the true, unstinted worship of God.

Godly clergy in the 1580s worried that the parishes were full of Atheoses, people who failed to grasp there was more to being a Protestant than not being a papist. It was little good, thought Edward Dering, to 'use thy liberty, say thou art a Protestant, renounce the Pope, except thou love righteousness'. We live in scandalous times, preached John Udall, a young lecturer at Kingston-upon-Thames, when someone can 'put on the name of a Protestant' and be 'taken of others to be of a true and sound religion, yea though his life and conversation do swear the contrary'. In his own version of a Giffordesque dialogue, Udall has 'Demetrius', a usurer, comically declare: 'Yea, by St Mary, I am a Protestant, for I love to eat flesh on the Friday.'

Twenty-five years after the accession of Elizabeth, it seemed to men like Gifford, Dering and Udall that the real task of reformation had barely begun. Formidable obstacles stood in its way, not least the attitudes of Atheos and his

ilk, who considered godly preachers 'busy controllers', and moaned that 'nowadays, there is nothing among many of ye but damnation, damnation'.

It was not a purely rural problem. 'What kicking and pricking hath here
been against the preachers?' complained the anonymous author of a 1582
memorial about conditions in Southampton. They lacked adequate financial
support, and found themselves 'belied and railed upon behind their backs,
upon credit of wicked and slanderous libels'. Examples of such self-pitying jeremiads can easily be multiplied.[25]

In many places outside London, preachers, or clergy of any kind with the
education and motivation to bring about change, were still in short supply. In
the midlands diocese of Coventry and Lichfield – not untypically of the country
as a whole – a mere 14 per cent of beneficed clergy were graduates in 1584,
though things were better in the hinterlands of the universities: 50 per cent in
the diocese of Oxford in 1580.

Non-graduates, in the 1580s as in the 1510s, could be conscientious and
popular pastors, just as they could be troublemakers and ne'er-do-wells. The
gradual spread and acceptance of clerical marriage most likely reduced, though
it certainly did not remove, scope for sexual misbehaviour and for parishioners
to complain about it. At the start of the 1580s, the proportion of clerical will-
makers who can be shown to be, or to have been, married varied between 40
per cent in the northern province and 71 per cent in Essex. Will-makers were
by definition the elder generation of clergy, so actual percentages may already
have been higher. Catholics, and other parishioners when they felt provoked,
might still derisively call the minister's lawful wife 'priest's whore', but the
number of such cases was relatively low. The realities of parish life, and the tiresome duty of paying tithes, produced levels of 'anticlericalism' in Elizabethan
England that may have been lower than before the Reformation only because
there were now fewer clergy around.

If anything, moralists like Gifford worried not so much about anticlericalism as about clergymen proving too popular with their parishioners, sitting
with them in the alehouse rather than reproving them from the pulpit. Atheos's
own minister was not Zelotes but a certain 'Sir Robert'. The traditional form of
address (see p. 41) was still common in rural communities – at Bridlington in
East Yorkshire, in 1584, there is a record of a parishioner receiving a similarly
named curate at his home, 'Sir Robert, you are welcome!'

Atheos's Sir Robert is 'a very good fellow: he will not stick when . . . honest
men meet together to spend his groat at the alehouse'. Sir Robert is not some
dissolute rake, but a charitable reconciler, 'for if there be any that do not agree,
he will seek for to make them friends', getting them to play together at cards or
bowls. Yet clerical 'Sirs', almost by definition, were not preachers. They could
not awake in people a faith-filled awareness of Christ's redeeming grace; they
could not save souls.

The concern was shared by powerfully placed friends of the godly. In the aftermath of the prophesyings debacle, Sir Walter Mildmay wrote an excoriating letter to Bishop Scambler of Peterborough about matters in Northampton, 'left destitute of a sufficient preacher'. It was a scandalous case for 'a town so great, so notorious and so peopled'. Mildmay lectured the bishop on his duty to ensure provision: 'Your whole diocese is your charge; it is your parish and your flock.' The responsibility could not be left to 'a scraping chancellor or a covetous commissary'. Mildmay's general experience of the diocese was that 'the chiefest places want preachers; that the ministers be for the most part unfitted and unmeet for so holy and so divine a vocation'.

It was with such deficiencies in mind that in January 1584 Mildmay founded a new Cambridge college, Emmanuel. The scriptural, Hebrew name ('God with us') stood out among the rows of colleges named for saints or monarchs. Emmanuel had a remit to train preachers, and a curriculum restricted to theology, Latin and Greek. From the outset, it had the reputation of a Puritan foundation, a godly retort to the priest-factories of Rheims and Rome.[26] At least two missions to convert the nation were under way in the early 1580s: the Jesuit and seminarist crusade co-ordinated by Allen and Persons, and the godly drive to transform a tangled growth of country divinity into a harvest of productive faith.

Preachers like Gifford or Rogers were inclined to regard any people who did not share their vision of godly reformation as not really Protestants at all. But it would be a mistake simply to take their word for it. Another meticulous diarist of the 1580s was Richard Stonley, an official of the London Exchequer, who witnessed Campion and his companions drawn on hurdles to Tyburn in December 1581. Stonley was sharply censorious of Puritan deviations from prescribed norms, noting occasions in church where clergymen officiated 'contrary to the order of the Book of Common Prayer', and commenting approvingly when his minister 'began service with the surplice on his back'. Yet Stonley hardly looks like an old-fashioned religious 'conservative'. He was an aficionado of sermons at Paul's Cross, presided over family prayers at home, and sometimes spent whole Sundays reading the Geneva Bible. He was also strongly anti-papist. A diary entry recording the execution of the priest Everard Hanse is accompanied by a quotation from Psalm 139: 'I hate them with an unfeigned hatred, as they were mine utter enemies.'[27]

Protestant Reformation, moving into Elizabeth's third decade, was starting to lay down roots in the parishes, even if not in the exact forms the most zealous godly clergy would have liked. The process is not always easy for us to discern – very few laypeople were, like Stonley, keepers of diaries, and quiet conformity with the rules represents a type of behaviour by definition less likely to generate written documentation than any sort of assertive challenge to them. Nonetheless, the gradual normalization of a broadly Protestant culture in the localities can be inferred from parish inventories showing an absence of old Catholic items and an accumulation of bibles, psalters, homilies, paraphrases and injunctions, along with copies of Jewel's *Apology* and (to a lesser extent) Foxe's *Acts and Monuments*.

It is evident too in mundane records of expenditure in parish accounts, including the wine (often in copious quantities) required for celebrations of the Protestant communion at Christmas, Easter, Whitsun and other occasional times of the year. Though they might now be stripped of many of their ancient furnishings, a real concern for the fabric and upkeep of parish churches survived through, or revived after, the tumult of the mid-Tudor decades. There were a few cases of shocking neglect, but in the main churches were well cared for, through the efforts of parishioners, and also – though a bugbear of Puritans – of the lay impropriators of tithes who were the institutional successors of the monks in 'appropriated' parishes (see p. 47). In episcopal visitations of the late 1570s and 1580s, fewer than 15 per cent of parishes in Yorkshire and Nottinghamshire were reporting their chancel to be in a condition of dilapidation.[28]

Even in an age of confessional conflict and growing doctrinal awareness, the practice of faith remained to a considerable extent habitual. Medieval Christians were shaped by the mass; Elizabethan ones by the liturgies of the Prayer Book they heard recited week upon week on Sundays, and at regular ritual observances of birth, marriage and death. Godly clergy were sometimes suspicious of popular attachment to the official worship of the Church. 'They do make the Book of Common Prayer a cloak for their papistry,' the minister of Flixton in Suffolk, Thomas Deynes, said of his parishioners at the end of the 1580s. But Puritan condemnation of the Prayer Book as a compendium of 'popish abuses' did not cause everyone to forget, and should not cause us to forget, that its author was Thomas Cranmer, the flower of Protestant martyrdom, or that its language resonated with the core theological insights of the Reformation. Laypeople were never required to own copies of the Prayer Book, but some did, and bequeathed them fondly in their wills. It was one of a number of texts shaping the religious culture of the nation by the sheer magnitude of its physical presence: over fifty editions were published in the first three decades of Elizabeth's reign.

Other formative texts were Protestant catechisms and books of religious instruction. Well over one hundred such works in English were published between 1559 and 1586, many in multiple editions. The bible itself was an ever more ubiquitous object, in homes as well as in churches: fifty-three editions of the complete bible, and forty-one of the New Testament appeared in 1560–89. Still more prevalent were copies of the Psalms: eighty-one editions of Sternhold and Hopkins' version were printed in the same period.

Growing rates of literacy, and the increasing output of the press, helped ensure that by the 1580s the cultural imprint of Protestantism was becoming ever more widely and deeply felt, even by those experiencing within themselves no particular effusion of evangelical zeal. William Shakespeare, born in 1564, and receiving his grammar school education in Stratford in the 1570s, was very likely raised in a Catholic household, and as an adult and an author he never exhibited much enthusiasm for Protestantism of the 'godly' variety. But his dramatic works are permeated with allusions to the Prayer Book and Homilies, and to the bible, in both Bishops' and Geneva versions.[29]

As more and more people born and raised in 'days of popery' died of old age, along with parish clergymen who had served their apprenticeship in the Henrician or Marian Church, it seemed that the passage of time, along with changes of perception and perspective achieved by a kind of cultural inhalation, was taking care of England's gradual transformation into a properly Protestant nation. The types of people variously referred to by historians as 'parish anglicans' or 'Prayer Book Protestants', as exponents of 'unspectacular orthodoxy' or of 'commonplace piety', were conformists in the sense that they practised their religion in accordance with the dictates of the law, civil and ecclesiastical.[30] It would be unwise to assume they were typically 'mere conformists', failing to engage meaningfully with any part of the spectrum of spiritual possibilities cast through the prism of the Elizabethan Settlement.

Quietly conformist Protestants were very likely in the majority in most places by the start of the 1580s.[31] But to some true believers, their predominance scarcely represented a triumph of the Gospel at all. It seemed to promise only the mechanistic observance of a kind of 'cold statute Protestantism', in a Church but half-reformed. The life-giving soar of the spirit, the zeal to transform society out of an overwhelming love of Christ, and an equally all-encompassing hatred of sin, were tragically absent. As Zelotes parted company with Atheos on the road outside Chelmsford, some of his brothers in spirit paused and took breath before stepping up their efforts to save the Church of England from its own mediocrity; others prepared to shake its dust from their feet, and to follow another path entirely.

## Without Tarrying for Any

In June 1583, a new proclamation condemned 'sundry seditious, schismatical, and erroneous books and libels', sent into England from beyond the seas, as well as their authors, 'fled out of the realm as seditious persons'.

The guilty parties named were not exiled papists, but a pair of puritanical Protestants, who had abandoned the Church of England and established their own congregation at Middelburg in Zealand, a town liberated from the Spanish a few years earlier and already a centre for English Puritan printing. Robert Browne and Robert Harrison became friends at Cambridge, where Browne dissuaded Harrison from taking orders in a Church tainted by the unscriptural abomination of episcopacy. The parishes of the Church of England were all in spiritual bondage, and 'whoever would take charge of them, must also come into bondage with them'. Far better to begin creating God's kingdom with 'the worthiest, were they never so few'.

The two men started holding conventicles in Cambridge, and in 1580 transferred operations to Norwich, where they organized a petition to Elizabeth, bearing the signatures of 175 supporters, and claiming the support of 'infinite more'. It called for removal of 'the government of Antichrist', and institution of 'that holy eldership, the very sinew of Christ's Church, which is so plainly described and so weightily authorised in God's Word'.

These were not anabaptists, espousing strange Christological heresies, but radical Puritans, reshaping the Church from the bottom up. In East Anglia they formed their own congregation, 'in one covenant and fellowship together', with the intention of making its members fully 'obedient to Christ'. Sustained harassment from Bishop Freke prompted the move to Middelburg in the summer of 1582. There Browne rapidly published several tracts, including *A Treatise of Reformation without Tarrying for any, and of the Wickedness of those Preachers which will not Reform themselves and their Charge, because they will tarry till the Magistrate Command or Compel them.*

The 'wicked' preachers included those still hoping to alter the governance of the Church from within, even presbyterians such as Thomas Cartwright and Walter Travers. As chaplains to the English Merchant Adventurers, they found themselves uncomfortable neighbours of Browne and Harrison in Middelburg, after the Company moved its operations there from Antwerp in October 1582.

Middelburg's separatist congregation soon separated from itself. Towards the end of 1583, having quarrelled with Harrison, Browne departed for Scotland, hoping in vain to find there the perfectly ordered Church he endlessly sought. Harrison tried, and failed, to bring about a merger with Cartwright's merchant flock, and a depleted Middelburg congregation limped on for a few years more.[32] In England, separatism faced more harrowing trials.

Browne's disciples were particularly concentrated in Bury St Edmunds, a Suffolk market town that also contained a strong bloc of Puritans, in bitter dispute with Bishop Freke. In 1582 some Brownists arranged to have a quotation from the Book of Revelation (2:19) painted around the royal arms in the parish church: 'I know thy works and thy love, and service, and faith'.

It seemed innocuous enough. But one of the preachers brought from Cambridge to assist Freke against the Puritans realized something. The succeeding verse in Revelation went on to say, 'Notwithstanding, I have a few things against thee, that thou sufferest the woman Jezebel, which calleth herself a Prophetess, to teach and to deceive my servants, to make them commit fornication, and to eat meats sacrificed unto idols.' It was a coded but venomous attack against Elizabeth, and the antichristian remnants such as vestments ('meat sacrificed to idols') still corrupting her Church.

The astute scriptural detective was Richard Bancroft, a chaplain of Christopher Hatton, and a deadly anti-Puritan, who wasted no time before trying to tar nonconformist Puritans with the same brush used to highlight the rejectionism of the Brownists: several Puritan ministers were imprisoned in Bury gaol. It went harder on proven separatists. At the Bury Assizes, the tailor Elias Thacker and the shoemaker John Copping were tried and convicted for distributing the writings of Browne and Harrison. Thacker was hanged on 4 July 1583; Copping the following day. On both occasions, piles of forbidden books burned by the gallows.

It was another turning point. The authorities had on previous occasions executed anabaptist heretics, but this was the first official killing to target christologically orthodox fellow Protestants. The charge, of course, was sedition. But, as with the seminarist priests, distinctions between dying for treason and dying for religion lay squarely in the eye of the beholder. A third separatist, William Dennis, was hanged nearby about the same time, at Thetford in Norfolk. Presiding at the Bury Assizes was Chief Justice Sir Christopher Wray, a legal chameleon who defended Bonner in 1565, and in 1581 prosecuted Campion. Wray wrote to Burghley to warn him 'there be many of Copping and Elias' opinions'.[33]

On 8 May 1582, while the Bury 'stirs' were still simmering, remarkable events took place eight miles away, in the parish of Cockfield. Its rector was the Puritan minister John Knewstub, renowned for Paul's Cross sermons against the Family of Love. No fewer than sixty ministers, 'appointed out of Essex, Cambridgeshire and Norfolk', attended a meeting there. The purpose was 'to confer of the Common Book; what might be tolerated, and what necessarily to be refused'. It must have been difficult to conceal, or explain, the presence of so many clergymen in a small Suffolk village. Nonetheless, as the Suffolk minister Oliver Pig wrote a week later to John Field, 'our meeting was appointed to be kept very secretly, and to be made known to none'.

The ministers met again at the end of September, at Wethersfield in Essex, where the diarist Richard Rogers was lecturer. They heard a sermon from Edmund Chapman, a deprived prebendary of Norwich, and lecturer at Dedham, a parish on the Essex–Suffolk border. It was the talk of the village alehouse. 'What make all these knaves here today?' demanded a local farmer, a veritable Atheos. 'What, will they make a god of Rogers?'

Chapman was the host when the ministers assembled again at Dedham in October, and agreed to convene there regularly, the Monday after the first Sunday in every month. It was, in effect, a *classis*, a regional conference of ministers of the kind advocated by Wilcox, Field and Cartwright – a presbyterian sapling rooting itself in the undergrowth of the episcopal Church of England.

The ministers meeting at Dedham did not see themselves as revolutionaries; rather as colleagues offering mutual advice and support on 'further reformation' in their respective parishes. Like the participants in earlier prophesyings, they heard and critiqued sermons. Sometimes, the meeting was devoted to a fast: Puritans despised the prescribed fast days of the popish Church, but saw spiritual benefit in event-specific days of prayer and abstinence from food. They debated theological questions – such as how strictly the Sabbath should be observed – and discussed practical pastoral problems.

A recurrent issue was access to the sacraments, and whether parishioners falling short of the highest standards should be barred from receiving communion or from bringing their children to baptism. Puritan parish clergymen wrestled in their own minds with the question of whether their ministry was to the great mass of good and bad, or solely to a subset of the spiritually worthy.[34]

In August 1583, an ominous note entered the record: 'it was said our meetings were known and threatened'; the ministers determined to seek legal advice on 'how we may meet by law'. In October, they agreed 'it were good the Archbishop should be written unto, to be favourable to our Church and to discipline'.

The 'Archbishop' was not Edmund Grindal. In July 1583, his health worn down by years of unremitting royal disfavour, suspended but never dismissed, Grindal died at his palace at Croydon. His successor, nominated by the Queen on 14 August, was widely anticipated. John Whitgift, bishop of Worcester, was enthroned on 23 October. He was indeed favourable to discipline, but not the sort of discipline the Dedham petitioners had in mind.

On 17 November 1583 – the twenty-fifth anniversary of Elizabeth's accession – Whitgift preached at Paul's Cross, laying out his priorities for government. The theme was obedience to magistrates and higher powers, foremost among them the Queen, 'nursing-mother' of the Church. Obedience was under threat from three sorts of people: papists, anabaptists, 'and our wayward and conceited persons' – men who coloured their doings with titles of 'faith' and 'perfection'. These, it seemed, were to be the chief object of archiepiscopal attention. Robert Beale, Clerk of the Privy Council, and an industrious friend of the godly, told Whitgift the sermon 'dismayed both myself and sundry others, who supposed your lordship would have run another course than it appeareth you have taken in hand'.

The course, however, was set, its sails billowing with something no archbishop of Canterbury had enjoyed for a very long time: the unconditional support of the Queen. Articles, approved by Elizabeth, were circulated to the dioceses on 29 October. They contained disciplinary and reform measures unexceptionable to most Protestants: a crackdown on recusants, closer examination of ordination candidates. The twist was in a final clause demanding all clergymen subscribe to three articles. The first, affirming the royal supremacy, and the third, declaring all Thirty-Nine Articles 'agreeable to the Word of God' were relatively uncontentious. The second required ministers to agree that the Book of Common Prayer 'containeth nothing in it contrary to the Word of God', and to promise to 'use the form of the said book prescribed, in public prayer and administration of the sacraments'.

This was a net with a narrow mesh. The demand was bound to meet opposition, not just from hard-core Puritans and presbyterian activists among the salaried lecturers, but from a broader spectrum of godly beneficed clergy. Whitgift knew what he was doing. In a letter to Walsingham, he declared: 'I have taken upon me the defence of the religion and rites of the Church of England, to appease the sects and schisms therein, to reduce all the ministers thereof to uniformity and due obedience. Herein, I intend to be constant, and not to waver with every wind.'[35]

He encountered a hurricane of opposition. County by county, ministers in their dozens refused to subscribe, or offered subscription in only limited and conditional fashion, especially in the Puritan heartlands of Essex, Norfolk and Suffolk. Somewhere between three and four hundred ministers declined subscription in the form Whitgift demanded: George Gifford and Richard Rogers were among those suspended.

Whitgift's campaign had the inadvertent effect of encouraging dissident clergymen to correspond and organize, especially after the widely divergent reasons for refusal offered by early non-subscribers threatened to provide the archbishop with a propaganda coup. Field drew up a list of errors in the Prayer Book, and the Dedham Conference was at the heart of efforts to co-ordinate resistance, sending and receiving letters with suggested rationales for declining to subscribe.

How far could resistance go? Dedham itself was divided: Chapman and other moderates were for exploring terms for some acceptable form of subscription. But William Tey, rector of Peldon, declared that 'the bishop's authority is antichristian; ergo, not to be obeyed'. Ministers should preach, even when ordered not to by lay magistrates. The membrane between tarrying and not tarrying, dissenting and seceding, was here stretched very thin.

It was not just ministers who were unhappy. In May 1584, Whitgift had an awkward meeting with a delegation of twenty-five angry Kentish gentlemen, and the Privy Council was swamped with petitions from town corporations and landowners. In June, pressure from the Council forced Whitgift into a partial climb-down. He agreed to demand full subscription to only the first and third articles, along with a promise to use the Prayer Book 'and none other'. Catholics were notorious casuists, but Puritans too understood how to find unstated meanings in a verbal declaration. They would use the Prayer Book, but not the whole of the Prayer Book. On that basis, all but a handful (the hold-outs included John Field) were prepared to subscribe.

Whitgift, however, was not done. He turned to the power of High Commission to pursue the most intransigent opponents, drawing up a set of twenty-four interrogatories explicitly aimed at Puritans. They demanded to know whether 'you deem and judge the said whole Book to be a godly and virtuous Book', whether 'you have at the time of communion ... worn only your ordinary apparel', and whether 'you have used private conferences and assemblies'. Suspects were required to answer upon an oath known as *ex officio mero*, unknown to the traditions of common law. The oath, previously used only against recusants, required defendants to swear they would answer truthfully any questions put to them, without knowing in advance what the questions were going to be. It took away any right of silence, potentially requiring people to incriminate themselves.

Use of the procedure against Essex dissidents such as Gifford provoked fresh waves of complaint to the Privy Council. In July, Burghley told the archbishop he thought his new articles to be 'formed in a Romish style ... so full of branches and circumstances, as I think the inquisitors of Spain use not so many questions to comprehend and trap their preys'. On 20 September, a majority of councillors wrote to Whitgift and Aylmer complaining about the treatment of the Essex ministers. The signatories did not include Hatton, whom Whitgift had thanked earlier that summer for his support in the face of 'some unkind speeches ... only for doing my duty'. The councillors included with their letter a survey of ministers in Essex, compiled by the Puritans themselves, and designed to demonstrate that the conformist clergy approved of by Whitgift were typically idle, immoral, non-resident or unsound in doctrine – a veritable flock of 'Sir Roberts'. Those reluctant to subscribe were demonstrably more learned and reliable.[36]

Leading laymen professed bafflement that the archbishop of Canterbury was troubling good Protestants at a time of unprecedented Roman threats. Knollys appealed fruitlessly to Whitgift in June 1584 to allow non-subscribing ministers to preach, and afterwards wrote in frustration to Burghley:

> [I]t grieves my heart to see the course of popish treason to be neglected, and to see the zealous preachers of the Gospel, sound in doctrine, who are the most diligent barkers against the popish wolf to save the fold and flock of Christ, to be persecuted and put to silence, as though there were no enemies to her Majesty and to the state but they ...

As far as Knollys was concerned, 'absolute authority of bishops ... hath no foundation in the Word of God'. It threatened the Queen's safety that direction of policy 'should be taken from all councillors of her Majesty's estate, and ... given over to the rule of bishops'. The Pope's adherents 'laugh in their sleeve, and hope for a day'.

Burghley refrained from such anti-episcopal jibes, but asked Whitgift to comment on reports that papists in Cheshire and elsewhere rejoiced at the disciplinary campaign against Puritans. The archbishop affected not to see it: 'They are urged to subscribe against the usurped power of the bishop of Rome – how can that please the papist? They subscribe that in our Book of Common Prayer there is nothing contrary to the Word of God – this cannot please the papists, which wholly condemn it.'

Nonetheless, Catholics tracked Protestant divisions with considerable interest. In the summer of 1584, an anonymous tract, *The Copy of a letter written by a Master of Arts*, was printed at Rouen. Universally known as *Leicester's Commonwealth*, it took the form of courteous dialogue between a Protestant gentleman, a Protestant scholar and a Catholic lawyer. Their conversation was constructed to convey an insistent message: that the real threat to the realm was the Earl of Leicester – portrayed as scheming and debauched – along with his Puritan 'faction'. Each speaker recognized that subjects naturally wished for 'a prince and state of their own religion', but that was not the world as it was. In England, refusing the religion of the state was made into treason. Yet, the lawyer explained, this 'treason' was different from 'some actual attempt or treaty against the life of the state or prince'. Catholics might be 'traitors' in either category, but the same was true of 'hot Puritans ... whose differences from the state, especially in matters of government, is very well known'.

The safest way forward was surely a toleration, to 'content all divisions, factions and parties among us, for their continuance in peace, be they papists, Puritans, Familians, or of whatsoever nice difference'. The tone was scrupulously loyal, prescribing remedies in Elizabeth's best interests. If, as seems likely, Robert Persons was instrumental in the tract's production, this was disingenuous as well as tendentious: he was up to his elbows in schemes for the Queen's overthrow. But Puritan disobedience, and the patronage extended to it by nobles like Leicester, allowed papists to claim that they were just as good, if not better, subjects of the Queen.[37]

## Bonds and Associations

The councillors, most of them, did not believe that; in the summer of 1584 the Queen's safety was very much at the forefront of their minds. On 10 July, William of Orange, leader of the Dutch Revolt and a key English ally, was shot dead with a pistol by a Catholic assassin, a deed lauded by Philip of Spain.

Councillors did not need to ask themselves, 'Could it happen here?' In October the previous year, a Warwickshire squire, John Somerville, had been arrested for plotting the very prototype of the deed. He 'meant to shoot her [Elizabeth] through with his dag [pistol] and hoped to see her head to be set upon a pole for that she was a serpent and a traitor'. Somerville – deluded, if not deranged – did not get far with his plan. His habit of announcing his intentions in front of company in alehouses meant he was arrested before getting out of Oxfordshire. Yet the government took his case extremely seriously. Prior to Somerville's hanging himself in custody, he was personally interrogated by Elizabeth's security chief and spy-master, Francis Walsingham.

Walsingham was on the cusp of neutralizing a more serious threat, details of which emerged with the arrest of Francis Throckmorton in November 1583. In truth, Throckmorton was a bit-player in the plot bearing his name, though he provides an intriguing study in trends within English Catholicism. His father was the royal office-holder, and 'church papist', Sir John Throckmorton, but Francis and his brother Thomas were red-bloodedly Roman, radicalized during time spent in the Low Countries in the late 1570s. The phenomenon was familiar to contemporaries. 'You have at this day,' a preacher warned at Paul's Cross in 1578, 'many young gentlemen . . . that are more obstinate and stubborn papists than their fathers.'

Than fathers, but perhaps not mothers. Sir John's wife Margaret was a more constant papist than her spouse, a common pattern in Catholic families, and a by-product of recusancy legislation able to fine husbands but not wives, who in theory possessed no property of their own. 'Such have a common saying,' Protestants scoffed, 'the unbelieving husband shall be saved by the believing wife.'

Francis Throckmorton also exemplified the genetic intimacy of popery and Protestantism. His uncle was the former royal councillor Sir Nicholas Throckmorton, and a Warwickshire cousin was a fiery Puritan activist, Job Throckmorton. Nicholas's son, Arthur, was to be found socializing with all branches of the family during hunting trips to the Midlands. His diary entry for November 1579 reads: 'I wrote to my cousin Job Throckmorton; I wrote to my cousin Francis Throckmorton.' Such family ties, stretched but not broken across religious divides, were by no means unusual. But as details of the treason emerged, bonds of kinship were erased: references in Arthur's diary to 'my cousin Francis Throckmorton' become simply 'Francis Throckmorton.'

Francis was the courier, carrying letters between English exiles, the French and Spanish ambassadors, and Mary Queen of Scots. The serious players were William Allen, who helped hatch the scheme at a meeting in Paris in June 1583, and Henry, Duke of Guise, Mary's cousin and leader of the militant wing of French Catholicism. The plan was for a Spanish–Italian force to invade via Lancashire, triggering a Catholic rebellion in the north. A second French army under Guise would land in Sussex, where it was hoped the influence of the Catholic magnates Henry, Earl of Northumberland, and Philip, Earl of Arundel, would generate local support.

This was a more plausible business than the Ridolfi Plot of a decade earlier, yet it proved fatal for only a few of those involved. Throckmorton was executed at Tyburn in July 1584. Northumberland took his own life in the Tower in 1585, while the government decided whether to bring treason charges. The more peripherally involved Arundel, a son of the late Duke of Norfolk, had been converted to Catholicism by Campion's bravura performances in the Tower. He was sent there himself in 1585, and never left. The Spanish ambassador, Bernadino de Mendoza, was ignominiously expelled in January 1584.[38]

The main effect of the Throckmorton Plot was to reignite the campaign to 'do something' about the Queen of Scots. The something on this occasion was a dramatic political gesture, with far-reaching constitutional implications.

At the Privy Council meeting on 12 October 1584, Burghley and Walsingham presented their colleagues with 'the instrument of an Association for the preservation of the Queen's Majesty's royal person'. It was a document binding signatories to resist to the full extent of their power 'any act, counsel or consent to anything that shall tend to the harm of her Majesty's royal person'. If, God forbid, the Queen should be assassinated, then they swore 'never to accept, avow or favour any such pretended successors, by whom or for whom any such detestable act shall be committed'. In fact, the bondsmen promised to pursue such persons 'to the death, with our joint and particular forces, and to take the uttermost revenge of them'.

This was religious politics in the red and raw. The Lord Treasurer, the Queen's Secretary, and other leading officers of state made a public declaration that if anyone took Elizabeth's life to advance the claims of Mary Stewart, then – without trial or legal nicety – they would kill Mary, whether she knew of the plan or not. The first Elizabeth heard about it was when she was presented with a copy at Hampton Court, freighted with the signatures of her leading nobles. It was not her way of doing politics, but, not for the first time, Burghley had seized the initiative.

The Bond was affirmed by all the great and the good: in a ruthlessly cynical move, Mary herself was prevailed upon to sign – a pledge of her loyalty, and a kind of pre-emptive suicide note. But its utility as both a practical and propaganda instrument depended upon wide diffusion. A day after Privy Council signatures were collected on 19 October, Walsingham claimed that 'divers good and well affected subjects' had somehow 'got knowledge' of the document and were eager to sign it. In fact, he and Burghley were actively soliciting the signatures of JPs and gentlemen, county by county. 'The more public the matter is made,' Walsingham reflected, 'the better it is like to work.'

The intention was not quite to replicate what Henry VIII had aimed at in 1534, an oath sworn by all adult males. But in various places, humbler folk earnestly asked to be allowed to take part, and sometimes did so in great numbers. Justices in Yorkshire informed the Earl of Huntingdon they had taken signatures from 'such of the meaner sort of gentlemen and of the principal freeholders and clothiers about them as sued to be accepted into the society'. By late November, Huntingdon reckoned he had at least 7,500 signatories.

Joining the association was a solemn ritual, a blood oath. It was sworn upon copies of the gospels, and the oath itself threatened retribution against backsliders, to be pursued by the rest 'as perjured persons and as public enemies to God'. The Earl of Derby reported to Leicester on solemn proceedings in the parish church of Wigan: the gentry of Lancashire, in batches of six, reverently took their oath before the bishop of Chester, 'upon their knees, bareheaded'. In this most 'backward' of counties, Catholics were surely among their number. The Bond, sensibly, spoke only of protection of the Queen from unnamed enemies, and said nothing explicitly about religion.[39] But no one who seriously weighed the matter could be in any doubt this was an endeavour to protect the Protestant succession and prevent a Catholic one; an exercise in which ideological politics trumped monarchical rank, and the settled rules of inheritance.

Discovery of Catholic conspiracy, as in 1572, led to the summoning of Parliament: an Act for the Security of the Queen, for which the Association laid the foundations, was the Council's chief priority. But the ecclesiastical wrangles of the preceding year were far from played out. At the opening ceremony on 23 November 1584, Whitgift preached on how contempt for good laws by 'many orators' was threatening all order. In an arresting image, he foresaw the unjust being 'swept away like the spider in his cobweb'. The opening speech of the Lord Chancellor, Thomas Bromley, carried the now customary warning from Elizabeth against 'the cause of religion to be spoken among them': an injunction that not only many MPs, but also leading members of the Queen's government fully intended to ignore.

The archbishop's opponents lobbied tirelessly. Just before Parliament opened, the Dedham conference decided that from every county 'some of the best credit and most forward for the gospel should go up to London, to solicit the cause of the Church'. MPs from Essex, Warwickshire and Lincolnshire presented petitions, bearing signatures of 'gentlemen of the greatest worship in the same shires', and complaining against restrictions on preachers. In December, at the request of the Earl of Leicester, there was a conference at Lambeth. In Leicester's presence, and that of Burghley and Walsingham, Whitgift and Sandys debated with Travers and the Lincolnshire minister Thomas Sparke over disputed passages in the Prayer Book. The inconclusive disputation was a victory for the Puritans if only because the archbishop had been forced to contend with them on equal terms. Rumours they had been vanquished were countered by a pamphlet (probably the work of Field), whose title – *The Unlawful Practices of Prelates* – deliberately evoked Tyndale's famous polemic against Wolsey. The bishops, said Edward Lewkenor, MP for George Gifford's Maldon, a client of Leicester, 'were rather deformers than reformers'.

Some godly clergy now sought sweeping solutions. Their surrogate in Parliament was the physician Dr Peter Turner, son of the preacher William Turner. On 14 December, he presented the Commons with 'a bill and book'. The book was the liturgy of Calvin's Geneva, as used by Knox's Marian congregation. The bill imposed its use, along with an explicitly presbyterian structure for the Church, henceforth to be governed by pastors and elders, with consistories in each congregation, and synods of ministers and laymen in every county.

This was too radical even for friends of further reform: Francis Knollys and others spoke against the measure, and it was not put to a vote. But Knollys and Mildmay backed a Commons measure in the form of a petition to the Lords against 'disorders' in episcopal government. It lambasted the gamut of Whitgift's policies: subscription, the *ex officio* oath, vexing of honest ministers 'for omitting small portions, or some ceremony prescribed in the Prayer Book'. At the same time, and without using the word, the petition demanded restoration of prophesyings ('some common exercises and conferences'), and suggested dramatic dilutions of episcopal authority: bishops should only be able to ordain with assistance from six other ministers, and only for specified vacant benefices, where candidates had already proved an ability to preach. These were the presbyterian tenets of equality of orders, and congregational calling of ministers, in scarcely veiled form. Whitgift's sniffy response was that the proposals undermined the rights of patrons, and 'savoureth of popular elections'.

The archbishop need not have worried. At the beginning of March 1585, the Speaker returned from a meeting with Elizabeth, charged to admonish the House for ignoring her directive about religion, and to remind them that the Queen 'knows, and thinks you know, that she is Supreme Governor of this Church'. If abuses existed, she would take them in hand, but it was

> her resolute pleasure [that] she will receive no motion of alteration or change of any law whereby the religion or Church of England stands established at this day. . . . For as she found it at her first coming in, and so hath maintained it these twenty-seven years, she meant in like state, by God's grace, to continue it and leave it behind her.

It was Elizabeth's clearest statement to date of what still seemed barely comprehensible to wide swathes of pious opinion, clerical and lay: the Church of England was flawless as it was. Even after hearing it, the Commons proceeded to discuss, and pass, a bill proposing harsh sanctions against unworthy ministers. In the Lords, where the bill disappeared, it was 'greatly inveighed against' by Whitgift. Leicester, a diarist recorded, seemed 'much to mislike the bishops' order of dealing'.[40]

The parliamentary session closed at the end of March, without a single bill for religion being passed, just as Elizabeth intended. The sorry state of affairs provoked one Puritan, the former Genevan exile William Fuller, to send the Queen that summer an extraordinary 'book' of impassioned remonstrance. Fuller had once been Elizabeth's servant, when she lived in the household of Catherine Parr – a connection granting him access to the court, and in his own mind at least, a licence to speak freely: he had already offered criticisms at a personal audience in 1580.

In 1585, Fuller wrote fired by a sense of impending crisis and disaster, 'in this last and worst age of the world'. He declared frustrated disappointment with a sovereign who as a child enjoyed glowing reports 'for religion and all virtue and good learning'. God placed her on the throne, not only 'to maintain his Church and kingdom, but also to put down that monstrous and deceitful Antichrist' – even though she was already proved unworthy in her sister's reign, 'by reason of your yielding to that idolatry'.

Elizabeth's offence was compounded by her agreeing 'to be crowned and anointed at a most monstrous and idolatrous mass', and afterwards by preserving in her chapel 'that foul idol, the cross'. Worse, she permitted, without condign punishment, 'divers Antichristians of this kingdom to have and adore secretly . . . that abominable idol and false god of bread', all the while making peace with 'Antichristian neighbours'. Steps to advance God's kingdom were 'so little as it is most lamentable to consider'. Satan's kingdom was currently poised for bloody assault upon England, 'and then to all the true churches of God in Europe'. These dangers were directly attributable to 'your Majesty's proceedings, which were neither hot nor cold'. The jeer was a common Puritan take on the Elizabethan 'middle way': an allusion to the Book of Revelation, where God threatens to spit out of his mouth the Church of Laodicea, for being 'lukewarm'.

All this, perhaps, was more than enough. But Fuller felt emboldened to comment on the Queen's personal habits. God's Commandments forbad swearing, and yet 'your gracious Majesty in your anger hath used to swear, sometimes by that abominable idol, the Mass, and often and grievously by God, and by Christ, and by many parts of His glorified body, and by Saints, Faith, Troth, and other forbidden things'. Elizabeth was a Catholic when it came to profanity – a trait she shared with many of her nominally Protestant subjects.

Fuller learned the fate of his book from a contact at court. The Queen read it, the morning after receipt. Burghley came into the chamber, and she told him about it. The book was lying on a chair, and 'as he went out he took it with him'. Elizabeth later asked a lady-in-waiting to get it back for her, but she dared not bother the Lord Treasurer.[41]

Burghley had more important things on his mind than the grievances of an old and uppity Puritan. He had seen to it that the 1585 Parliament did pass an Act for the Queen's Safety, a legal colouring for the vigilantism of the Bond of Association. A special commission of privy councillors and nobles would sit in

judgement on anyone caught conspiring against the Queen; intended beneficiaries would be barred from claims to the throne; and private subjects were
empowered to 'pursue to death' the conspirators, and anyone knowing about or
agreeing to their plans. No potential pretender was identified; she did not need
to be.

Accompanying the measure was a severe Act against Jesuits and Seminarists,
which mimicked Burghley's *Execution of Justice* in arguing that such creatures
came to England solely to withdraw subjects from their obedience, and to 'stir
up and move sedition, rebellion and open hostility'. Henceforth, any priest
entering the country after ordination abroad was *ipso facto* guilty of treason;
any layperson assisting or sheltering him, a felon.

As the bill passed through the Commons, various proposed amendments
plumbed the depths of anti-Catholic sentiment: any exiles not returning by a
specified date should be proclaimed traitors; penalties should apply to foreign
as well as native-born priests. Most draconian was a suggestion 'that whosoever should teach the Romish religion should be as a traitor'. This threatened to
conflate entirely the categories of treason and heresy, and to undermine fatally
the government's strategy for driving a wedge between 'good' and 'bad'
Catholics. MPs were persuaded by the counter-argument the measure would
help papists, allowing them to claim that 'seeing we could not convince their
doctrine by doctrine, we sought to quench it by making it treason'.

Only one MP spoke against the act in principle. In December 1584, William
Parry, member for Queenborough in Kent, warned there was 'nothing therein
but blood . . . nothing but despair and terror to us all'. His intervention caused
uproar, and demands he be committed to the Tower: Parry was forced to apologize, kneeling at the bar of the House.

Before the bill reached the statute book, Parry was dead: hanged and quartered in Westminster Palace Yard on 2 March 1585, the only elected serving
member of any Elizabethan Parliament to be tried and executed for treason.
Parry was an extreme example of a recognizable type: the double agent who
lost a sure grasp of which side he was really on. On the run from debt, Parry
spent the early 1580s associating with Catholic exiles overseas, and sending
self-aggrandizing reports on them to Burghley and Walsingham. At the same
time, he was formally reconciled to the Catholic Church, and after boasting of
a desire to kill 'the greatest subject in England' (Leicester), it was put to him by
Thomas Morgan, a wandering agent of Mary Stewart, that Elizabeth herself
would make the better target.

Back in England at the end of 1583, Parry was able to secure an audience
with Elizabeth, attempting, bizarrely, to persuade her of the reality of a plot
against her. Reading Allen's *Modest Defence* reawakened in Parry a desire to
undertake the deed himself. He recruited a co-conspirator, Edmund Neville,
whose arrest in February 1585 precipitated Parry's own. At their 1583 interview,

Elizabeth told Parry that 'never a Catholic should be troubled for religion or supremacy, so long as they lived like good subjects', a crisp summary of her philosophy of governance. But commenting on Parry's ignominious end, the Puritan pamphleteer Philip Stubbes declared 'that all papists are traitors in their hearts, howsoever otherwise they bear the world in hand'.[42]

## War

William Fuller's vision, of the forces of Antichrist massing for an attack on England, was not the apocalyptic fantasy of a solitary zealot. It was the long-held conviction of councillors like Burghley, Leicester and Walsingham that the prospects of the Protestant religion in England, and the victories of the Catholic powers abroad, were entwined threads of a single fate.

In October 1584, in the wake of the assassination of William of Orange, the Privy Council had convened to discuss the situation of the Dutch rebels, and to address Burghley's imperative question: 'If her Majesty shall not take them into her defence, then what shall she do or provide for her own surety against the King of Spain's malice and forces, which he shall offer against this realm, when he hath subdued Holland and Zealand?'

The case for action was strengthened at the end of the year, when Philip signed the Treaty of Joinville with the Guises and the militant Catholic League, formed in France to resist the unpalatably 'politique' Henry III. The catalyst was the death of Elizabeth's suitor, the Duke of Anjou, and Henry's recognition as his heir of the Huguenot Henry of Navarre. As Burghley had been predicting since the 1560s, the forces of Spanish and French Catholicism were converging, on a sworn mission to destroy Protestantism in both France and the Netherlands.

Elizabeth took time to be persuaded, but by August 1585 she was ready to sign the Treaty of Nonsuch, which pledged to the States General of the Netherlands an annual subsidy, and the despatch of an army of 6,400 foot and 1,000 horse. Command of the expedition was assigned to the Earl of Leicester, an appointment welcomed by godly Protestants who admired his opposition to Whitgift, and saw in the war in the Netherlands a straight contest of Christ with Antichrist. Without fanfare or formal declaration, England was at war with Spain. Overt hostilities commenced in September, with the sailing of a fleet under Francis Drake, to intercept treasure fleets and harass Spanish colonies in the West Indies.

Early in the new year, Drake attacked and plundered the settlements of Santo Domingo in Hispaniola, and Cartagena on the Colombian coast. After the English left, letters home to the King contained aggrieved accounts of how the 'Lutherans' treated the cities as 'an enemy of their religion', burning churches, monasteries, nunneries and hospitals. The dean and chapter of Santo

Domingo reported their cathedral becoming an empty shell, 'for its altars, reta-bles [altarpieces], crucifixes, images, choir, screens, organs, bells, and all other objects usual in such churches, they broke up, overthrew, burned and destroyed'.[43] Sailors who were still unborn at the time of the orderly iconoclasm in English parish churches could indulge in an orgy of destruction, confident they were doing God's work. William Fuller must have regretted he was not there to see it.

Closer to home, war made the bloody question about papist responses to foreign invasion less than ever a hypothetical one. On 25 April 1586, two priests, Robert Anderton and William Marsden, were put to death on the Isle of Wight, where stormy weather had forced their ship into land. Two weeks later, a royal proclamation offered an extended justification for their execution. After initial arrest, the priests persuaded the Winchester Assize judges that 'they would at all times adventure their lives in defence of her Majesty and her realms against the Pope or any foreign power', and their lives were spared. But further questioning in London produced more dubious responses. Anderton said he could not truthfully answer as to what he would do in case of a papally sanctioned invasion, as 'in the meantime he may possibly become a Protestant' – the kind of insolently equivocal response that drove interrogators to distraction.

Campion's martyrdom cast a long shadow: the government was acutely anxious to demonstrate it acted justly, and that priests were executed solely for treasonous intents – even though the recent act against Jesuits and seminarists declared the very fact of their priesthood to be sufficient evidence of treason. Another execution under that act, driven through by zealous local authorities, caused widespread unease. In March 1586, a York butcher's wife, Margaret Clitherow, was indicted for sheltering missionary priests, and then pressed to death with weights after she refused to plead. The possibility she was pregnant – which Clitherow refused to confirm or deny – left a particularly bad odour.[44]

If disquiet attended the execution, on questionable legal grounds, of a mere butcher's wife, what might be the reaction, at home and abroad, to the unjust slaying of a queen? In 1585, Mary had been transferred to the custody of Sir Amyas Paulet, a close ally of Walsingham and a grimly determined supporter of the international Calvinist cause. Mary considered him 'one of the most zealous and pitiless men I have ever known'. The Queen of Scots' letters, and even her private apartments, were regularly searched for evidence of involve-ment in conspiracy, but nothing sufficient was found.

In July 1586, Walsingham got the evidence he needed. Earlier that summer, another Catholic plot crystallized. Its central figure was the Derbyshire gentleman Anthony Babington, egged on by the priest John Ballard, who was in touch with Mendoza, now Spanish ambassador in Paris, and able to elicit promises of Guise and Spanish forces. Babington recruited to the cause a handful of young Catholic radicals, who swore to assassinate Elizabeth as a prelude to foreign invasion. One of the conspirators, Gilbert Gifford, was, like Anthony Munday, a shiftless wanderer, expelled from the English College in Rome in 1580 in murky circumstances. In 1586, he was already secretly in the pay of Walsingham.

Crucially, Gifford was employed to carry letters to and from Mary at Chartley in Staffordshire, and suggested to her a scheme (in fact, devised by Walsingham) whereby messages were placed in sealed packets inside the beer barrels brought in and out by a 'trustworthy' brewer. Mary's entire correspondence could now be removed, deciphered and replaced by Walsingham's agents. The government did not cook up the Babington Plot, but allowed it to simmer near to boiling point.

Babington informed Mary that 'the dispatch of the usurper' was to be undertaken by 'six noble gentlemen, all my private friends', and the letter she wrote in reply on 17 July was fatally incriminating:

> The affair being thus prepared, and forces in readiness both without and within the realm, then shall it be time to set the six gentlemen to work taking order; upon the accomplishing of their design, I may be suddenly transported out of this place, and that all your forces in the same time be on the field to meet me in tarrying for the arrival of the foreign aid . . .

Mary had explicitly given her consent to foreign invasion and to the assassination of her cousin; she had signed her own death warrant.

The conspirators were dealt with first. Babington and his confederates were put on trial in mid-September, charged with seeking to murder the Queen, stir up sedition and 'subvert the true Christian religion'. He and six others were executed on 20 September. They experienced the full horror of the penalties for treason: cut down while still alive, castrated and disembowelled. Another seven conspirators followed the next day, though these were allowed to hang until dead. The contemporary historian William Camden said this was because Elizabeth 'detested the former cruelty'. In fact, she told Burghley, she wanted the deaths of her would-be murderers to serve 'for more terror'; adverse reactions from the crowd may have prompted the (relatively) greater leniency.[45]

There was no question of such indignities in death for an anointed queen, but Protestant councillors were this time determined that Mary must die. The commission envisaged under the Act for the Queen's Safety convened at Fotheringhay Castle in Northamptonshire on 12 October, and finished its proceedings three days later. Elizabeth demanded a delay in pronouncing sentence, and the guilty verdict was read out in the Star Chamber at Westminster on 25 October.

In the meantime, Parliament was recalled. The sole purpose was to lobby for the death of Mary – advice that Elizabeth, who stayed away from the opening ceremony, did not want to hear. In the first week, privy councillors queued up to recount Mary's crimes and call for her blood, without distinction of more or less godliness among them. Christopher Hatton named Mary 'the hope of all idolatry', and concluded, *Ne periat Israel, periat Absalom*: 'if Israel is not to perish, Absalom must perish'. This was a reference to the rebellious son of King David (2 Samuel: 17–18), slain by his commander, Joab. David mourned for Absalom, as everyone knew Elizabeth would mourn for her cousin. Loyal subjects would harden their hearts on her behalf.

Amidst a torrent of bitter and impassioned speeches, that of Job Throckmorton, MP for Warwick, stood out. Mary was the inversion of all female propriety, 'the daughter of sedition, the mother of rebellion, the nurse of impiety, the handmaid of iniquity, the sister of unshamefastness'. Throckmorton catalogued crimes of Catholics from the time of the 'horrible slaughter' in Paris, and named the guilty men: 'an Allen, a Campion, a Bristow, a Sander, a Gifford, and I know not who'. He forbore to mention, though it cannot have been far from his mind, that his own cousin bestowed the family name on a popish conspiracy to murder Elizabeth.

To Puritans like Throckmorton, the death of Mary involved more than the personal safety of the Queen. His speech ended on a controversial constitutional note. 'Under the warrant of God's law, what may not this House do?' If anyone said Parliament was 'not able to cut off ten such serpents' heads as this, not able to reform religion, and establish succession: it is treason'.

Lords and Commons, in a joint petition sent to Elizabeth on 12 November, demanded death for the former Queen of Scots. At its core was the argument that Mary was seeking to 'supplant the gospel'. This evil threatened to overtake not England and Scotland alone, but 'all parts beyond the seas where the gospel of God is maintained . . . if defection should happen in these two most valiant kingdoms'. The fate of the entire European Reformation, the Queen must understand, now rested upon her resolve.

Nonetheless, Elizabeth prevaricated, replying that the petition pointed towards 'a course contrary to her own disposition and nature'. The Queen's hesitation was not simply tenderness or squeamishness. The proposal was for Elizabeth to put to death, for political and religious reasons, a kinswoman and fellow monarch: she balked at the implications.[46]

On 4 December 1586, Elizabeth agreed to public proclamation of the sentence against Mary, but she still refused to sign the death warrant. Indeed, she hoped to evade responsibility entirely, and rely on the Bond of Association. A letter was sent to Sir Amyas Paulet, suggesting he should simply do away with Mary as he was sworn to do. Mary's gaoler indignantly refused: 'God forbid that I should make so foul a shipwreck of conscience'.

Elizabeth signed the warrant on 1 February 1587, amidst rumours (fostered by Burghley himself) of a Spanish landing in Wales. Even then, she did not think she was committing herself to immediate action, but, with steely unanimity of purpose, the Privy Council hastily despatched the warrant to Fotheringhay before the Queen could change her mind.

Mary was beheaded, on a scaffold in the great hall of Fotheringhay Castle, on 8 February. She was denied the ministrations of a priest, but scrupulously acted the part of Catholic martyr, approaching the block with Agnus Dei around her neck, crucifix in her hand, rosary at her belt. The undergarments to which she was stripped proved to be crimson – the liturgical colour for commemoration of martyrs. Mary declined an invitation from the dean of Peterborough to renounce 'the vanity of her religion'.

Elizabeth received the news the following day, and in her fury even considered imprisoning Burghley and Walsingham. In the end, William Davison, the hapless secretary to whom the warrant was entrusted, took the blame. He went to the Tower, and stayed there for the best part of two years.[47]

Reactions in Catholic Europe were, if anything, more stunned and aggrieved than at news of the executions of More and Fisher, half a century before. In Paris, pictures of the royal martyrdom were set up in the churchyard of St Severin, alongside tableaux depicting the hanging and quartering of Jesuits in England. The English ambassador, Sir Edward Stafford, complained to Walsingham that 5,000 people a day were coming to see the display, and that 'English knave priests . . . point with a rod and show everything, affirm it to be true and aggravate it'.

The pictures were the work of the English priest Richard Verstegan, and published that year in his *Theatrum crudelitatum haereticorum nostri temporis* (Theatre of Cruelty of the Heretics of Our Times) – a work of Catholic martyrology designed to out-Foxe Foxe, and to bring European opinion up to crusading temperature. In Rome, Sixtus V elevated William Allen to the status of cardinal, making him the unquestioned leader of all English Catholics, a national governor-in-waiting. In Madrid, Philip II accelerated preparations for the Enterprise of England, while Allen and Persons pored over genealogies to justify the King of Spain's dynastic claim (through the House of Lancaster) to the English throne. Mary, before the end, had named Philip as her successor.[48]

In England, the immediate emotion in many quarters was one of relief; not crisis impending, but crisis resolved. No longer was a formidable Catholic claimant rattling at the door of Protestant dynastic hopes. In a Commons speech on 27 February, Job Throckmorton praised the 'very worthy act that was lately done at Fotheringhay'. But he lampooned any tendency towards satisfied complacency: 'What, shall we thereupon set up all our sails and sing peace upon Israel?'

Even while the storm clouds were gathering over Fotheringhay, Puritans stepped up their efforts to purge the Church of its impurities. They now had an instrument with which to accomplish it, a *Book of Discipline*, drafted either by Cartwright or Travers over the course of 1585–6, and sent to all the regional conferences: a copy was received before April 1587 at Dedham, where it elicited mixed views. The *Book* contained a detailed outline of 'the synodical discipline', a presbyterian structure of church government based on the model of Scotland and other European Churches. Public worship was to be conducted from the Genevan Prayer Book.

Privy councillors employed the 1586 Parliament as an echo chamber for their advice on Mary Queen of Scots. But the godly, as ever, saw Parliament as the highest court of ecclesiastical policy, a place to debate and settle momentous issues. They revived the orchestrated petitioning campaign of 1584: supplications for unfettered preaching and reform of the ministry now purported to come from thousands of ordinary Christians rather than gentlemen and justices of the peace. There were further county-based 'surveys of the ministry'. Warwickshire's was probably compiled by Job Throckmorton, and offered considerable evidence of clerical dead wood mouldering in the midland parishes: numerous incumbents who once were 'popish priests', and several suspected, very revealingly, of 'the vice of good fellowship'.

Throckmorton was part of a clique of Puritan MPs determined to bring presbyterian reform to fruition. Others included Anthony Cope, Edward Lewkenor and Peter Wentworth. Cope reintroduced a new 'bill and book' to the Commons. The bill's lengthy preamble contained a potted history of the Reformation to date, praising Henry, Edward and Elizabeth for making a good start, but noting the 'imperfections, corruptions and repugnancies with the Word of God, yet continued in the order and discipline of this Church'. Throckmorton, already in trouble for urging the Queen to accept an offer of sovereignty from the States General of the Netherlands, spoke passionately in the bill's favour. He also attacked the propensity to caricature proponents of 'bettering and reformation':

> To bewail the distresses of God's children, it is Puritanism. To find fault with corruptions of our Church, it is Puritanism. To reprove a man for swearing, it is Puritanism. To banish an adulterer out of the house, it is Puritanism. To make humble suit to her Majesty and the High Court of Parliament for a learned ministry, it is Puritanism.

Throckmorton resented the lazy application of a demeaning label. But he had spotted something that was indeed stirring in the upper reaches of the Elizabethan establishment. The disciplinary crackdown on godly nonconformity was starting to evolve and mutate into a full-blooded ideology of anti-Puritanism.

It was short shrift for the bill and book, and a death-knell for Puritan attempts to use Parliament to change the face of the English Church. On 27 February, amidst scenes of confusion, the Speaker tried to prevent the bill being read in the Commons, and on the following day a message arrived from the Queen ordering members to desist. Attempts to evade the prohibition put Cope, Wentworth and three other members in the Tower, charged with holding extra-parliamentary conferences. They were soon joined there by Throckmorton, whose unflattering references to 'the young imp of Scotland' (James VI) offended Elizabeth and broke the unwritten rule against any discussion of the succession.[49]

On 4 March, a mixed trio of government spokesmen took turns to justify rejection of the bill and book: Sir Thomas Egerton, solicitor general, as voice of the establishment; Chancellor of the Exchequer Mildmay, the sorrowful face of moderate Puritanism; and Whitgift's ally Christopher Hatton, shortly to be appointed Lord Chancellor. Hatton's speech was the most interesting, not least because it was probably written for him by his chaplain, Richard Bancroft, nemesis of the Bury separatists.

Hatton's defence of the ecclesiastical status quo was a smooth concoction of the principled and pragmatic. The reformation begun in King Edward's time was, he said, brought by Elizabeth 'to such perfection, as the profession of this reformed religion in England hath ever since been the chief key and stay thereof in all the reformed churches of Christendom'. By altering forms of service people had now used over decades, thinking them good and godly, 'you shall drive them by thousands either to become atheists or papists'.

Yet the real weight of Hatton's punch lay in his suggestion that presbyterians, and by extension godly Puritan internationalists, were intrinsically subversive individuals, inevitable opponents of royal supremacy. Who did not know of the 'outrageous assertions' in books of 'your chief presbytery men'? Here, Hatton made mention of works on resistance theory by three leading Calvinist intellectuals – the Genevan leader Theodore Beza, the Scotsman, George Buchanan and the Huguenot, Philippe de Mornay. The implication was that these luminaries were embarrassing liabilities, rather than allies to feel proud of.

Monarchical jurisdiction was excised from the system being proposed: appeals passed only from presbytery (or *classis*) to provincial and then national synods – just as in the past all disputed ecclesiastical cases went ultimately to Rome. And Hatton inferred that Elizabeth herself might be subject to a presbytery's censure or excommunication (a point on which the bill and book had understandably not touched). 'I pray you, wherein differ these men in cause from the papists? The Pope denieth the supremacy of princes; so do in effect these.'

It was a significant shift of emphasis. For decades, Protestant writers located truth's centre of gravity through reference to the counter-balancing errors of papists and anabaptists. This revised theological triangulation, measuring equidistance from papalist Catholicism and Calvinist presbyterianism, was something different, marking the advent of a new, more dogmatic style of Protestant conformity.

A straw in the wind was the outcome of a pulpit battle of 1586. The location was Temple Church in London, the spiritual home of lawyers from the nearby Inns of Court. The Master, appointed in 1585 on the recommendation of Aylmer, was an Oxford scholar, Richard Hooker. The benchers (senior members of the Inns) thereupon hired Cartwright's ally Walter Travers as lecturer. Hooker politely declined Travers's invitation to submit his own appointment to congregational approval.

Over several months, Travers's afternoon lectures jostled against Hooker's morning sermons. His principal objection to Hooker's teaching was the latter's claim that the medieval Church had maimed, rather than completely over-thrown, the doctrine of justification by faith. It followed that pre-Reformation Catholics, and presumably also contemporary ones, could be saved. Such sympathetic words about papists, Travers indignantly complained, had not been heard in the realm since the days of Queen Mary. Whitgift himself had reservations about aspects of Hooker's theology, but in March 1586 it was Travers whom he banned from preaching. A month earlier, Whitgift joined the Privy Council, its first episcopal member since Heath.[50]

The status of bishops themselves was another sign of changing times. Episcopal governance of the Church was an obvious continuation of medieval Catholic practice, and was generally defended, even by conservative Protestants like Whitgift, on utilitarian rather than doctrinal grounds. In 1587, however, the dean of Salisbury, John Bridges, published a weighty (1,400-page!) *Defence of the Government Established in the Church of England*. This attack on the Puritans suggested that episcopacy, rather than presbyterianism, was to be found in the pages of the New Testament. The office of bishop was of direct apostolic institution, and episcopacy was *iure divino* – rooted in, if not neces-sarily required by, divine law. If this was so, it implied a more distant relation-ship with European Churches (Zürich, Geneva) that Puritans typically saw as the 'best reformed', but which conspicuously rejected this divinely ordained instrument of governance.[51]

Episcopal authority received a boost with the defection of one of its fiercest critics. After leaving Middelburg for Scotland, and wandering around for a while in Europe, Robert Browne returned to England. He was soon arrested, and in October 1585 subscribed a document recognizing the authority of Archbishop Whitgift, and the Church of England as a true Church of God. Former brethren bewailed the betrayal, while others were suspicious of its sincerity. The Puritan layman Stephen Bredwell attacked Browne in a tract alleging that he 'still seduceth, and carrieth away from the ordinary assemblies as many as he can'.

'Brownism' survived the surrender of its eponymous leader. On 8 October 1587, more than twenty separatists, men and women, were arrested at a conventicle in the London parish of St Andrew-by-the-Wardrobe. One of them, Margaret Maynard, confessed she had not been to church in ten years, and 'sayeth that there is no Church in England'. A leading light of the group was John Greenwood, formerly a curate in Norfolk, who 'disgraded myself through God's mercy by repentance'. A close associate was Henry Barrow, son of a Norfolk gentleman, who was himself arrested on going to visit the prisoners in the Clink.

Barrow wrote a detailed account of his appearances before Whitgift and High Commission, for whom he refused to swear the *ex officio* oath. A first meeting with the archbishop set the tone for discussion. Whitgift demanded to know, 'Of what occupation are you?' Barrow: 'A Christian.' Whitgift: 'So are we all.' Barrow: 'I deny that.'

Barrow and Greenwood produced from prison a steady stream of letters, tracts and petitions, smuggled out by sympathizers and printed overseas. The separatists refused to recognize any spiritual kinship with people outside their group, but they participated willingly enough in a common enterprise of Reformation Christians: the attempt to engage, shape and change opinion through the long-distance medium of print.[52]

## Armada and Marprelate

In December 1587, the Earl of Leicester returned ingloriously from the Netherlands, having fallen out with his Dutch allies and achieved little of military consequence. At the Inner Temple in London, there was talk of the war, and much sympathy for 'her Highness' poor afflicted neighbours in Flanders'. But two of the butlers there, Thomas Martin and Edward Mellers, reportedly rejoiced at news of English setbacks. Martin 'useth publicly in all his public speeches to extol the King of Spain . . . terming him a wise and valiant prince'.

Late in the previous year, in the Devon parish of Morchard Episcopi, the gentleman John Easton drank the health of King Philip at a neighbour's house, while asking each man present 'what part he would take if there were any war or stir?' Easton himself boasted his willingness to be 'the foremost horseman'. He seemed to mean in the Queen's army, not the King of Spain's, but his companions were not so sure, and reported him to the magistrate.[53]

The loyalties of English Catholics were more than ever under scrutiny as Philip finalized his preparations for an Armada against England. In the Netherlands, they had already proved fickle. Early in 1587, Sir William Stanley, commander of a regiment in Leicester's army, defected to the Duke of Parma and handed to the Spanish the strategically important town of Deventer. William Allen published a justification of Stanley's treason, as the actions of an informed Catholic conscience in the circumstances of an unjust war. In 1588, in his *Admonition to the Nobility and People of England*, Cardinal Allen dropped all pretence and called openly on Catholics to overthrow Elizabeth – no longer the unwitting victim of evil counsel, but a heretical and sacrilegious tyrant, 'an incestuous bastard, begotten and born in sin of an infamous courtesan'. Elizabeth herself had shamefully 'abused her body', with the Earl of Leicester 'and divers others'. Copies of the tract, printed but not published, sat ready to be shipped to England, once Spanish forces had established their bridgehead, propaganda fuel for the expected Catholic rebellion.

It is hard to say whether such a rebellion would have taken place. There is no evidence of preparation for it, and much evidence of lay Catholics loudly protesting their willingness to take up arms for the Queen. But there is equally no doubting the genuine fears among Protestants. At the height of the scare, Richard Rogers confided to his diary, 'We are now in peril of goods, liberty, life by our enemies the Spaniards, and at home papists in multitudes ready to come on us unawares.' Catholic houses were searched for weapons in the summer of 1588, and Lords Lieutenant ordered by the Privy Council to commit to prison 'the most obstinate and noted' recusants in their counties.[54]

The great Armada sailed from Lisbon in May 1588: 130 ships, aiming to collect a Spanish army in the Netherlands and reclaim England for the faith. The Armada's progress was delayed by unseasonable weather, but in late July and early August it met the English fleet in the Channel in a succession of sharp engagements. A combination of superior naval tactics and luck secured victory for the English, while Dutch allies kept Parma's troops bottled up in the Flemish ports. Powerful south-westerly winds bustled the Spanish out of the Channel in the second week of August, and refused thereafter to let up. Through September, the defeated Armada limped counter-clockwise around the British coast: only half the departing vessels returned to Spanish ports.

A military and patriotic triumph was portrayed, inevitably, as a religious one too. Sermons of thanksgiving began at Paul's Cross as soon as the fact of victory became clear. Dean Nowell preached on 20 August, and at the sermon on 8 September eleven banners from Spanish ships were on display; one, bearing an image of the Virgin with Christ in her arms, was waved triumphantly over the pulpit. A day of national celebration was decreed for 19 November, an occasion for bonfires and bells in provincial town and rural parish alike. Elizabeth herself attended a thanksgiving service at St Paul's on 24 November.

Pamphleteers hailed the evidence of a protective divine providence, and a narrow escape from spiritual as well as foreign tyranny. The Suffolk minister Thomas Rogers's hastily published *Historical Dialogue touching Antichrist and Popery* cautioned that Catholics, no matter how loudly they protested their

loyalty, were not to be trusted, 'papists being the solicitors, papists the prosecu-
tors of this war, papists the soldiers'.

That was pretty much an official line. A prayer of thanksgiving, appointed
to be read in churches, declared how the Spaniards came with the intention
'wholly to suppress thy Holy Word, and blessed Gospel of thy dear son, Our
Saviour, Jesus Christ, which they, being drowned in idolatries and superstitions, do hate most deadly'. Privy councillors did their part to reinforce the
message: a published letter purporting to be from an English Jesuit to the
former ambassador Mendoza, and confessing how the Armada's defeat 'by no
reason could proceed of man, or of any earthly power, but only of God', was in
fact the work of Burghley.

In February 1589, in the opening speech of a new Parliament, Lord
Chancellor Hatton recited a litany of historical papal perfidy, from supposed
plots against King John, via Clement VII and Paul III's 'fury against her
Majesty's father', to the 'raging bull' of Pius V, the inspiration for the traitors
Story, Harding, Felton, Sander, Campion, Somerville, Throckmorton and
Babington – not to mention 'that shameless atheist and bloody Cardinal, Allen'.
It was he who made it 'a point of the Romish religion' for all priests and
Catholics to solicit the aid of the Pope and the Spaniard. Constant vigilance
was required against 'those vile wretches, those bloody priests and false trai-
tors, here in our bosoms, but beyond the seas especially'.[55]

Priests in England paid a high price for the government's fear of domestic
rebellion, and for the spiritual militarism of Cardinal Allen. The sailing of the
Armada launched a wave of arrests and, from July 1588 onwards, a spate of
killings: twenty-one priests and ten laypeople were put to death in the second
half of the year, fourteen executions taking place in just three days, 28–30
August, when the military outcome was already clear. One of the victims was
female. Margaret Ward, a gentlewoman's attendant, smuggled into prison a
rope, which enabled the priest William Watson to escape from Bridewell. Ward
was flogged prior to her trial, and in her cell was hung cruelly from her wrists.
She refused to beg for Elizabeth's pardon, saying she was sure the Queen, if she
had the compassion of a woman, would have done the same thing.

Ward featured in a broadside ballad, one of thirty or so published in connection with the defeat of the Armada. Sold to be sung 'to the tune of Greensleeves',
it rattled rhythmically through the fourteen false traitors slain in late August,
saying of Ward: 'This wicked woman / void of grace, / would not repent in any
case, / But desp'rately even at that place, / she died as a foe to England.'[56]

Texts such as this suggest a growing identification of Protestantism and
patriotism, which, with official encouragement, the Armada crisis did much to
cement. In November 1588, the churchwardens of St Peter's church, St Albans,
dutifully paid bellmen 'to ring for our good success against the Spaniards', after
a court apparitor delivered a note requiring them to do it. Like countless other

parishes, St Peter's spent a few shillings every year to ring the church bells on 17 November, to commemorate the accession of Elizabeth. But only from 1590 onwards did the wardens typically pay the ringers 'on coronation day'. Prior to that, the transaction was frequently recorded as taking place on St Hugh's Day, the designation of 17 November under the old Catholic calendar. It was a small but significant gesture of forgetting and remembering. Across the country, the late 1580s also witnessed the final instances of episcopal complaints about ringing of parish bells taking place a couple of weeks earlier – on the abolished Catholic feast day of All Souls.[57] Amidst the diffusion of a widespread popular anti-popery, Protestant England was finding its cultural bearings.

It was not, however, the kind of Protestant England the most resolute Protestants wanted. The Armada year was a year of unprecedented Puritan activism, which took the campaign for further reformation out of Parliament, out of the clerical conferences, and into the fractious forum of popular opinion. John Field, the acknowledged leader of the presbyterian movement, died in March 1588. September saw the death of the Puritans' most powerful political protector, the Earl of Leicester (Mildmay died in the spring of the following year, and Walsingham early the year after). These departures brought both fragmentation and increased radicalization in Puritan patterns of behaviour, and produced an unforgiving official response.

The trail is laid out with printers' ink. In April 1588, under instructions from Whitgift, officials of the Stationers' Company, the body regulating the book trade, raided the London premises of Robert Waldegrave, and confiscated his press. Waldegrave was a veteran printer of Puritan books; he had produced works by Field and John Udall, as well as editions of Calvin and Knox. His current offence was to start printing a fiercely anti-episcopal assessment of *The State of the Church of England*, formerly ascribed by historians to Udall, but quite probably the work of Job Throckmorton.

Waldegrave re-equipped, and moved his operations underground. Through Udall he had been introduced to the minister John Penry, already in trouble with High Commission for aggressive lobbying of Parliament about deplorably superstitious conditions in his native Wales. In May or June 1588 Waldegrave and Penry set up a secret press in East Moseley, Surrey, in the house of Elizabeth Crane, the widow of a prominent Puritan gentleman. That summer, as naval battles raged in the Channel, Waldegrave anonymously printed presbyterian works by Penry and Udall. In October, he produced, in around a thousand copies, a short work called *An Epistle to the Terrible Priests of the Convocation House*. Within weeks, a determined hunt for its author was under way.

That author identified himself as 'Martin Marprelate'. Martin was a nod to Luther, iconic father of the Reformation; Marprelate summed up an attitude towards the senior clergy who were its supposed guardians. Martin's real identity remains uncertain, though stylistic similarities to his known works make

Job Throckmorton the likeliest candidate for principal authorship of the *Epistle*, and of six subsequent tracts appearing from Waldegrave's press up to September 1589, as it moved across country from one safe-house to another to avoid detection. Others – Penry, Udall, Elizabeth Crane's second husband, George Carleton – may have chipped in. 'Marprelate' was always a project and a team, rather than any single individual.

The aim of the project was to step down from the high ground of scriptural and theological argument, and to pulverize the bishops with the base weapons of sarcasm, satire and cutting comedy. There were hints of this strategy in earlier Puritan works by Field, Gilby and others. But Marprelate took it much further, pitching directly for a populist, plebeian readership, and representing himself as the voice of an irrepressible Everyman: if he was to be hanged, 'there will be twenty Martins spring in my place'. Despite relatively small print-runs, the pamphlets passed widely from hand to hand, spread by pedlars and small shopkeepers. A principal distributor was the cobbler Humphrey Newman, nicknamed 'Brown-bread'. The participation of such people in discussions of church governance seemed to herald a dissolution of all social order. The dean of Exeter, Matthew Sutcliffe, caricatured presbyterian discipline as a world where people like himself must submit themselves to the judgement of 'Hick, Hob and Clim of Clough; yea, and Margaret and Joan too'. 'As they shoot at bishops now,' warned the Earl of Hertford, 'so they will do at the nobility also, if they be suffered.'[58]

Yet Martin was popular because he was funny, with knowing winks towards more learned readers, as well as belly laughs for the multitude. The original target was John Bridges's ponderous *Defence of the Government* ('a very portable book: a horse may carry it if he be not too weak'), which had unwisely challenged Puritans to make public, if they could, any allegations of misconduct against bishops. Martin cheerfully obliged, itemizing the financial misdeeds, habitual swearing and alleged addiction to bowling of Aylmer ('Dumb John of London'), and mocking the rest of the bishops, individually and collectively, as a pack of 'petty popes and petty antichrists'.

The approach was not entirely novel: it evoked how some evangelicals of an earlier generation spoke about Wolsey or Gardiner. And it amounted to a declaration by at least a section of English Puritans that they had cut all ties with the ecclesiastical establishment, regarding themselves now as travellers on a different road to Reformation, not the faster lane of a common one. In tone, and in some aspects of substance, it had more in common with the separatism of Barrow than the godliness of Grindal.

Retaliation was slow but inexorable. Whitgift remarked to Burghley in August 1589 that while, for his own part, 'I make small account of their malice', stern punishment was needed – in respect of the archbishop's 'calling and profession', and of the scandal caused among people 'apt to believe anything'.

Disciplinary proceedings, he suggested, should be instigated by Burghley, rather than the bishops, so everyone might know 'we are not cast off as abjects of the world', or for 'doing of our duties in suppressing sects and wicked opinions'.

Whitgift wrote after agents of the Earl of Derby had tracked Waldegrave's press to a house just outside Manchester. Three printers taken in the raid were sent to London, the Privy Council instructing interrogators that 'if they cannot bring them to confess the truth, then to put them all to the torture'. A final tract, *The Protestation of Martin Marprelate*, was defiantly printed in September on a hastily reassembled press, the type-setting perhaps done by Penry and Throckmorton themselves. Waldegrave and Penry fled to Scotland, but most of the other Marprelaters were eventually taken and questioned. Throckmorton, protected to some extent by his gentleman status, brazenly denied involvement – 'I am not Martin; I knew not Martin.' He was released following an inconclusive trial.

The affair provided an excuse for Whitgift and High Commission to go after the presbyterian ministers. In the midland counties of Northamptonshire and Warwickshire, studies were searched and documents seized: the archbishop learned a great deal about the clandestine activities of ministerial conferences over the preceding few years. Nine leading preachers were put on trial, first in High Commission and then in Star Chamber. They included Thomas Cartwright, despite his disavowals of sympathy for Marprelate. Burghley did what he could to protect Cartwright, but in the face of the Queen's expressed displeasure, that was little enough. The ministers were stripped of their offices and orders, and banned from holding positions in the Church.[59]

That was as far as Puritan martyrdoms went, though Penry was to be tried and hanged for sedition in May 1593, after returning from Scotland and joining a separatist congregation in London (Barrow and Greenwood suffered the same fate a few weeks earlier). There was no need for a holocaust of presbyterians in 1589–90: their organization had been hollowed out and broken.

More importantly, presbyterianism was discredited, or at least substantial efforts were made to discredit it. At the heart of the campaign was Hatton's chaplain, Richard Bancroft. On 9 February 1589, just after the opening of Parliament and three days before the issuing of a proclamation against the Marprelate Tracts, Bancroft preached a ferocious anti-Puritan sermon at Paul's Cross. Robert Beale was shocked at its vehemence. It seemed to him that Bancroft believed 'all such persons as have desired a perfect reformation of sundry abuses remaining in this Church' were 'in a yoke with papists, anabaptists and rebels'. The gist of Bancroft's indictment was that Puritans were not troublesome spirits working within the Church, but sinister schismatics assailing it from without. For good measure, he affirmed the apostolic origins of episcopacy, bringing that controversial opinion to a wider audience than Bridges's weighty tome had managed to reach.

It was Bancroft, too, who suggested to Whitgift the tactic of having Marprelate and his fellows 'answered after their own vein'. Archiepiscopal patronage lay behind a burst of activity from a knot of London writers – Robert Greene, John Lyly, Thomas Nashe – who in 1589 produced a rash of popular pamphlets, mocking Puritans as seditious holy hypocrites.

Not everyone thought this a good idea. Francis Bacon, son of the former Lord Keeper, and a young man just entering on government service, wrote in about 1590 a memorandum 'touching the controversies of the Church of England'. He considered it time for an end to 'this immodest and deformed manner of writing lately entertained, whereby matters of religion are handled in the style of the stage'. In fact, they were literally being handled on the stage, in a brace of anti-Puritan plays helping to establish comic templates soon to be developed by Shakespeare and Ben Jonson. The Privy Council shared Bacon's anxiety, and in November 1589 wrote to Whitgift instructing him to establish procedures for the vetting of comedies and tragedies. Actors must not 'handle in their plays certain matters of divinity and state, unfit to be suffered'.[60] It was the recurrent, self-deluded fallacy of Tudor government authorities to believe that opinions and prejudices, once conjured into being by controversy and conflict, could be simply ordered back into oblivion. The Marprelate affair gave voice to a vein of undeferential popular Puritanism, and at the same time licensed the open expression of a belligerent popular anti-Puritanism; neither would thereafter go quietly away, and a half century later, they would go to war with each other.

### Strange Contrariety of Humours

The late 1580s did not herald the end of endeavours to reform the worship, habits and thoughts of the people of England. But more than one grandiose project of Reformation peaked and ebbed in the period around 1587–9. Never again would such an opportunity present itself to restore England to the fraternity of Catholic nations, its traditional faith remade and renewed, under the tutelage of Jesuits and other educated priests, and inspired by the universalism of a resurgent Rome. In the coming years, doubts within the Catholic community about the wisdom of the strategies pursued by Robert Persons and Cardinal Allen would be ever more vocally expressed, and internal divisions would widen – about organization, the necessity of recusancy, and relations with the English state.

Simultaneously, the years around 1590 produced a climacteric of disappointment for the decades-long campaign to encourage the Protestant Church of England to become the best version of itself. The increasingly evident failure of bishops to make the case for continuing reformation pushed Puritanism into becoming a political movement – a movement that first broke against the crown's determination not to allow Parliament to be used as a forum for the reform of religion, and then suffered the consequences of choosing to work and organize beyond it. Puritanism's cultural potential as a force for the transformation of English society was barely yet tapped. As a political force it would eventually return with a variety of vengeances. But for the moment, at least, it was cowed, defeated and divided.

Yet the generals of the ascendant disciplinarian and conformist forces that seemingly triumphed over Puritanism in 1589–90 should have realized the shakiness of the ground on which they stood. Despite the – never entirely dependable – backing of the crown, the programme of Whitgift and his allies rested on a narrow base of support, distrusted and disliked by many of the lay elites, on the Council and in the counties. It commanded the loyalty, theological and otherwise, of only an uncertain percentage of the English clergy. Decades' worth of discussion, division and debate made its vision of a total religious uniformity – of a collective obedience to the rules, precisely because they were the rules – no more than a fantasy and a delusion.

These were not the only proposals mooted at this time as to how English Christians should live in relation to each other. In the early weeks of 1587, an important and much anticipated book appeared in the shops of London booksellers. It was a revised edition of the *Chronicles* of Raphael Holinshed. In fact the work of a team of authors, 'Holinshed' was an exhaustive compilation of histories of England, Scotland and Ireland, brought up to date with accounts of the events of recent years.

One of those noteworthy events was the 1571 battle of Lepanto, where a coalition of papal and Venetian naval forces routed the Turkish fleet, and halted, for a while at least, the Ottoman advance in the Mediterranean – an event marked at the time in London with prayers of thanksgiving and festive bonfires (see p. 502). The account of the battle in 'Holinshed' finishes with a remarkable postscript:

> [S]uch is the malice of the time, that the Christians have more pleasure to draw their weapons one against another, than against that common enemy of us all, who regardeth neither Protestant nor Catholic . . . It were therefore to be wished . . . that Princes would permit their subjects to live in liberty of conscience concerning matters of faith, and that subjects again would be ready in dutiful wise to obey their Princes in matters of civil government, so that, compounding their controversies among themselves, with tolerable conditions, they might employ their forces against the common enemy, to the benefit of the whole Christian world, which, the more is the pity, they have so long exercised one against another . . .

It was the writer's considered opinion that 'matters in variance about religion' should be settled by the word rather than by the sword, 'an instrument full unfit for that purpose'.

Almost certainly, the author of this arresting passage was the antiquarian John Stow. Earlier in the reign, Stow showed distinct leanings towards Catholicism (see p. 481), and perhaps he still felt their pull. He had become, however, a conforming member of the Church of England, rather than a conscientious dissident from it. In various published writings, Stow waxed nostalgic for the culture of the pre-Reformation past, a time of spiritual fellowship and social harmony. But here he recognized that such days were irrevocably gone, and that plurality of religion was an established social fact. There was level-headed pragmatism, as well as lofty idealism, in his suggestion that loyalty to the state be recast as a civil matter, to allow religion to be argued over without violence or coercion, in a social and private sphere.

An idealist, but also a realist, Stow recognized his propositions were 'rather to be wished than hoped for, by any apparent likelihood, considering the strange contrariety of humours now reigning among men'. Perhaps he would not have been overly surprised, had he learned later that year of the approach Elizabeth was secretly making to the Ottoman Sultan Murad III, asking for military aid against Philip of Spain and the 'idolatrous princes' supporting him.

Not only did Stow's proposal not get off the ground, it was roundly criticized in the very text promoting it. The general editor of the second edition of *Holinshed's Chronicles* was Abraham Fleming, a fervent Protestant, shortly to be ordained as a minister. His account of the deaths of the Babington conspirators ('venomous vipers . . . their tigers' hearts burned in the fire') was so vehement that the Privy Council demanded it be toned down prior to publication. Stow's plea for English people to be allowed to pursue their religion in peace prompted Fleming to add in the margin a sharp corrective note: 'good counsel, if that faith be the faith of Christ and his true Church'.[61]

Fleming's editorial intervention begged the elemental questions with which the whole spectacle described in this book began and ended: what actually was the true Church, and what did the faith of Christ really look like? To virtually all the people making use of the word, 'Reformation' suggested a lineal process of betterment and change – of agent acting progressively upon object to produce one perfected, or at least improved, bastion of faith. The experience of the English Reformation, for those who lived through it, could scarcely have been less like that. Its meanings and directions were at every stage bitterly disputed. England's sixteenth-century wars of religion were usually metaphorical, but sometimes shockingly bloody. They were literary as well as theological, cultural as much as political, pitting papist against Protestant, Protestant against Puritan, in a profoundly perplexing contest, where the assertions of one party often confirmed the opposing convictions of the other, and where even catastrophic defeats could be chalked up as glorious martyrs' victories.

The Reformation changed what it meant to be a Christian in England, affecting not just what people believed but how they believed it. At the same time it planted new, volatile and hazardous conditions deep into the furrows of English social, community and political life. John Stow's proposal for coming to terms with pluralism by putting aside coercion, and for offering liberty of conscience in return for lawful obedience in matters of 'civil government', in the end offered the only viable solution for learning to live with the challenge of these permanently changed circumstances. Yet centuries would have to pass before everyone finally admitted that he had been right.

# POSTSCRIPT

WILLIAM SALESBURY, ELIZABETHAN translator of the Prayer Book and New Testament into Welsh, looked back over a childhood spent in Denbighshire and Lancashire, from his adulthood in the middle years of the sixteenth century, not with nostalgia, but with a mixture of revulsion and relief:

> And as I was thus tangled, and abominably deceived, and trained and brought up in tender age in the Pope's holy like religion, before Christ's second birth here in England, even so were the Jews before his first birth in Judea wondrously deceived, and shamefully seduced.

Salesbury's is an important testimony, one of several bequeathed to us by Protestant converts from this period. He interpreted the passage of his own life as a journey from enslavement into liberty, from delusion to enlightenment, from a sham ('holy like') faith to one that was reliable and authentic: 'Christ's true religion here among us'.[1]

Much of the scholarship produced by previous generations of Reformation historians would probably have been disposed to take Salesbury's assessment as not just true 'for him', but as true, period, and might not have balked unduly at his arresting characterization of the English Reformation as 'Christ's second birth' in the country.[2] Even today, some intelligent people, both religious-minded and secular, remain strongly persuaded that at the Reformation a bad form of Christianity was replaced by a good or at least a better one. Others incline to thinking that the opposite may well be true, or at least that a popular form of Christianity was displaced by a less popular one, an assessment which had a good deal more respectable scholarly weight behind it by the end of the twentieth century than it did twenty or thirty years earlier.[3]

Most historians working today take the understandable view that it is not their business to pronounce on whether the aims and achievements of the Reformation were inherently virtuous, though that has not stopped them from offering a variety of responses to the seemingly perennial question of whether the Reformation should be judged a success or a failure. The teasing out of answers to this conundrum often involves attention to various long-term continuities in English religious culture, and sometimes leads to the paradoxical conclusion that the Reformation succeeded as an agent of social transformation precisely because of how little it actually managed to change, and how slowly it managed to change it.[4]

The approach taken in this book, however, represents a deliberate revisiting of themes that caught the attention of earlier Reformation historians: conflict, conversion and the ecstatic or agonizing experience of change. Arguably, it doesn't always pay as much attention as it should to the unremarkable and sometimes almost unmeasurable modulations of alteration and sameness in the rhythms of everyday life.

There certainly were important stabilities and continuities – most obviously, in the fact that the majority of people continued to worship, week on week, in the same church building as their parents and grandparents. The quirky conservatism of Elizabeth I helped to ensure that links to the past of various kinds remained in place there, and many ordinary parishioners undoubtedly valued them. At the very end of the sixteenth century, Elizabeth's idiosyncratic version of Protestantism received powerful intellectual validation. Richard Hooker's *Laws of Ecclesiastical Polity* argued for a positive spiritual value in ceremonies and rituals, and for an unbroken line of succession from the medieval Church to the latter day Church of England. Here, indeed, were the origins of what would later be called 'Anglicanism'.

Anglicanism typically prizes continuity. Yet the Reformation in England, I am convinced, was nothing if not a volcanic eruption of change, whose seismic impact remains fundamental to an informed understanding of almost all the country's subsequent social and political developments.

The unresolved issues of a splintered world of faith persisted far beyond the death of Elizabeth I in 1603, and the accession to the English throne of Mary Queen of Scots' Protestant son, James I. Puritanism, politically quiescent in the 1590s, resuscitated its demands for an onward march of official Reformation, to receive at the Hampton Court Conference a famous put-down from a monarch who thought he understood the implications for royal authority of any prior commitment to the perceived teachings of scripture: 'no bishop, no king'.

A recurring strain of Roman Catholic radicalism asserted itself in the attempt to blow up both bishops and king in the Gunpowder Plot of 1605. English Catholics, increasingly divided among themselves, mostly disapproved of such extreme measures. As the most obviously defeated party in the fall-out from the Reformation, Catholics, the erstwhile repressors of all dissent, were often the most enthusiastic advocates of toleration. The hand of government repression fell less heavily under James I, and his successor Charles I, than it did under Elizabeth (both monarchs had Catholic consorts), but an increasingly deep-rooted English hostility to popery, cultural and xenophobic as much as it was theological, made formal toleration a practical impossibility.

Fears that Charles I, and his bench of anti-Calvinist, *iure divino* bishops, were seeking to lead England back towards subjection to Rome were a major factor in the breakdown of political trust that culminated in the outbreak of war between Charles and Parliament in August 1642. It is too simplistic to say without qualification that the British Civil Wars were wars of religion, but many of the participants undoubtedly believed they were fighting in God's cause, and addressing themselves to the unfinished business of the sixteenth century.

On the eve of the conflagration, John Milton, poet and religious visionary, published a pamphlet entitled *Of Reformation touching Church-Discipline in England, and the Causes that hitherto have Hindered it*. Milton looked back over the events of the sixteenth century with an unforgiving eye. Cranmer, Latimer and Ridley, the episcopal martyrs of Mary's reign, were nothing but 'halting and time-serving prelates', men who suffered themselves 'to countenance with their prostituted gravities every politic fetch [stratagem] that was then on foot, as oft as the potent statists pleased to employ them'.[5]

Milton's Puritanism embodied in a distilled form the anti-episcopal, anti-monarchical instincts of radical Elizabethan presbyterianism. And parliamentary victory over the King in the Civil War permitted at long last the implementation of a sweeping Puritan agenda for reform of the rituals and structures of the Protestant Church of England. Yet this too was a pyrrhic victory, as both the ideal and reality of Puritan-style uniformity collapsed in the 1650s, in quarrels between presbyterians, who wanted to maintain the structure of a national Church, and Congregationalists and Independents, for whom the autonomy of local communities of believers came first. At the same time, the willingness of ordinary people, whatever their level of formal education, to assert the rights of religious conscience and interpret scripture according to their own lights, was dramatically affirmed in a carnivalesque procession of new sects: Baptists, Quakers, Ranters, Seekers, Diggers, Muggletonians, Fifth Monarchists and others. The Catholic polemicists of the 1520s and '30s would have been dismayed, but not surprised, to see all their dire predictions about the fissiparous character of heresy confirmed.

The alternative, conformist face of English Protestantism reasserted itself with the Restoration of the monarchy in 1660, but uniformity was a long lost cause. Puritans finally departed from a Church of England that can now properly be called 'Anglican', to populate a variety of Dissenting, Nonconformist Protestant Churches (as some had already done in the American colonies). Formal toleration for Dissenters would follow in 1689, after a short interlude during which King James II showed himself no more adept than his great-grandmother, Mary Queen of Scots, at playing the part of Catholic ruler in a politically Protestant nation.

James's overthrow in 1688 was an emphatic vindication of the contested Reformation principle that the rights of true religion trumped the claims of dynastic inheritance, and of monarchs claiming to rule by divine mandate; it also showed the nation was not ready, yet, to allow religion to become a purely private business, rather than a matter of policy and state.

That happened, slowly. Penal laws, excluding Catholics from public life, began to be lifted in the 1770s; Catholics were allowed to vote for, and sit as, Members of Parliament in 1829, and (along with other nonconformists) to take up Oxford and Cambridge fellowships in 1871. In 1974, the law was changed to clarify that Roman Catholics were once again permitted to hold Wolsey and More's office of Lord Chancellor, and in 2013 changed again to allow a (hypothetical) Catholic to marry the heir to the throne. The position of British monarch remains, however, the preserve of a Protestant; its holder still Supreme Governor of the Church of England.

In the United Kingdom, the unravelling of the Reformation legacy has been a leisurely but inexorable process. Other than in isolated pockets, sectarian hatreds are in mainland Britain a thing of the past, and ecumenical relations between the Churches have become warmer as the commitment to Christianity of the nation as a whole has emphatically cooled and waned. For much of the population today, if they have heard of it at all, the Reformation probably evokes feelings similar to how Prime Minister Neville Chamberlain regarded the 1938 crisis in Czechoslovakia: 'a quarrel in a faraway country, between people of whom we know nothing'.

Yet the Reformation, whether we choose to recognize it or not, is a foundational fact of modern England and Britain, as also, at a remove, of America and other places around the globe where British people have settled over the centuries. The inheritance represents much more than a nostalgic lost legacy of medieval works of art, and a surviving one of monastic ruins, now places of secular pilgrimage, scattered like beads across the rural landscape of England and Wales. Nor, conversely, should it be seen solely as a tradition of towering works of Protestant literature – Milton, Bunyan, the English bible itself – or of the attainments of great thinkers, like Isaac Newton, who stood squarely, if heretically, in the Reformation, anti-Catholic lineage.

The real significance of the English Reformation, I would suggest, lies not in the achievement, but in the struggle itself. Though never anything like an exercise in proto-democracy, the Reformation was nonetheless, from first to

last, a vocal, vibrant national conversation, about issues of uttermost importance, and one from which few voices were ever entirely excluded.

Victories were regularly declared, but never completely secured. Within
Christianity itself, the possibility of alternatives has over the centuries encouraged believers of all sorts to become more thoughtful about the theory and
practice of their faith, and to preserve and value the traditions that best maintain it, while quietly discarding others. It has also allowed for possibilities
of choice and change, including, but not requiring, the complete rejection of
Christian belief. England is now a fairly secular place, but the challenge of
living successfully with difference, religious and otherwise, remains a very real
one as we approach the third decade of the twenty-first century.

To modern people who are familiar with it, believers and non-believers
alike, the era of the Reformation may not seem like much of a recommendation
for the religion of Jesus, the messenger of peace and forgiveness. A streak of
violence in thought, word and action; a rigid intolerance of dissent; an unap-
pealing zealotry in belief and practice: these can all too easily come across as
the dominant notes and accents of the age.

Forays into the past in search of people sharing the modern (very modern)
western values of tolerance and inclusivity are usually doomed to end in disappointment or delusion. Efforts to identify, and to reward or castigate, historical
heroes and villains are always likely to reveal more about our contemporary
beliefs and preoccupations than about those of the society being ransacked for
moral edification. Yet the people of the sixteenth century were no less complex,
or conflicted, than we are in the twenty-first. Even at times of the most deaf-
ening discord and division, the quiet Christian impulse to control and conquer
hatred might make itself heard.

At his trial in 1535, after sentence was pronounced against him, Thomas
More was asked by his judges if he had anything further he wanted to say.
More's mind turned to scripture, to the Acts of the Apostles, and he reflected
on how Paul, then a Pharisee, had approved the stoning to death of the disciple
Stephen, 'and yet be they now both twain holy saints'. In the same way, More
hoped that he, and the judges who condemned him, 'may yet hereafter in
heaven all merrily meet together, to our everlasting salvation'.

Three years earlier, the lawyer James Bainham burned at the stake at
Smithfield, after being convicted as a heretic through the efforts of Lord
Chancellor More. As the fire took hold, Bainham uttered 'God forgive thee' to
the man setting it, and added 'the Lord forgive Sir Thomas More'. Jesus himself,
from the cross, prayed that his Father would forgive his persecutors, as 'they
know not what they do'. In their determination to follow the pattern of Christ,
several of the martyrs of Mary's reign made the prayer their own. Elizabeth
Folkes, a Colchester maidservant, barely twenty years old, fell to her knees after
her condemnation in 1557: 'Lord, if it be thy will, forgive them that this have

done against me.' One of her judges, the archdeacon of Middlesex, William Chedsey, wept as the sentence against her was read, 'that the tears trickled down his cheeks'.

In London in July 1580, on the eve of his departure on the mission that would lead within a year to arrest, and then to torture and death, Edmund Campion signed off his 'Letter to the Council' with a declaration of how he intended to react if all his offers and arguments were ignored, and his entreaties responded to with rejection and 'rigour':[6]

I have no more to say but to recommend your case and mine to Almighty God, the searcher of hearts. Who, send us of his grace, and set us at accord before the Day of Payment, to the end at the last we may be friends in Heaven, where all injuries shall be forgotten.

# ACKNOWLEDGEMENTS

Behind this book stands a small army of believers. Fortunately for me, many of them are also heretics, whose robust independence of thought has redounded to my immense advantage. Four remarkably loyal friends, all of them brilliant historians of the Reformation, read the entire text in manuscript, and saved me from numerous traps of my own making: Eric Carlson, Alec Ryrie, Jonathan Willis and Alex Walsham. It goes without saying that they bear no responsibility for errors or infelicities I have managed to retain. Tom Freeman offered me the benefit of his very considerable expertise on Lollards. The friendship and encouragement of Eamon Duffy has also been invaluable.

I have been worrying about the English Reformation for quite a long time now. As an undergraduate in the 1980s, I was enthused by the insurgent lectures of Chris Haigh, and I have continued to find his ground-breaking work a source of challenge and stimulation. As a doctoral student, I could have wished for no finer supervisor than Susan Brigden; she remains for me the platonic ideal of a scholar and mentor. I'm a firm believer that you only really learn something by teaching it, and I owe a lot to successive generations of Warwick undergraduate students who have cheerfully taken classes with me on 'Religion and Religious Change in England, 1470–1558' and 'The Elizabethan Reformation'. There is a still more direct debt to the lively band of PhD students I was supervising during the writing of this book: Stephen Bates, Laura Branch, Alice Byrne, Pat Cox, Edward Geall, Todd Marquis, Katie Nelson, Anastasia Stylianou and Anne Thompson. At Warwick, I have also been extremely fortunate in the quality of moral and practical support from three outstanding heads of department – Margot Finn, Maria Luddy and Dan Branch – and from some exceptional administrators, in particular, Jayne Brown and Robert Horton. Among many interested and supportive academic colleagues, I hope it will not be invidious to pick out Bernard Capp, whose unfailingly compassionate interest in my scholarly travails has, over many years, meant a very great deal.

A number of the ideas in this book were first tried out on conference and lecture audiences in a variety of far-flung locations, and I am grateful to an international roll-call of hugely hospitable academic hosts: John Craig in Vancouver, Sasha Handley in Manchester, Per Ingesman in Aarhus, James Kelly in Durham, Liz Tingle in Plymouth, Lynn Tribble in Dunedin, Susan Wabuda in New York and Dorothea Wendebourg in Berlin. Welcome financial support for the research and writing of this book has come from the Leverhulme Trust, and from the Social Sciences and Humanities Research Council of Canada – though still more welcome has been the companionship and intellectual stimulation provided over several years by fellow researchers on the SSHRC-funded project 'Early Modern Conversions': among others, Patsy Badir, Torrance Kirby, Steven Mullaney, Ben Schmidt, Helen Smith, John Sutton, Mark Vessey, Bronwen Wilson, Stephen Wittek and Paul Yachnin. Heartfelt thanks are due also, for information, favours or simple reassurance, to Stephen Alford, Felicity Heal, Gerard Kilroy, Suzie Lipscomb, John Morgan, Richard Rex, Susan Royal, Bill Sheils, Fred Smith and Lucy Wooding. It seems appropriate for a historian to thank the dead as well as the living, though it is a cause of real sadness that several exceptional historians of the Reformation, at whose hands I received much kindness and encouragement, passed away during the time of writing: Margaret Aston, John Bossy, Patrick Collinson, Cliff Davies, Eric Ives, David Loades, Tom Mayer and Jenny Wormald.

This book would never have come to fruition without the persistent belief in it of my editor at Yale, Heather McCallum. I am very grateful to her, and to Rachael Lonsdale and Melissa Bond for further guidance and support. I must also thank Yale's five anonymous readers (two of the proposal, and three of the first draft of the finished typescript) who between them encouraged me to sharpen up my act.

The most long-standing bills are usually the most unpayable. My mother, Elma Marshall, died in 2013 as I was starting in earnest to write chapter drafts. Her faith in me was unwavering, and her memory has helped keep me anchored to the truly important things. My father, George Marshall, has equally been a supporter and a believer for as long as I can remember. At home, the sometimes sombre and solitary task of writing has been considerably lightened by the intermittent presence of bright and delightful young people: my daughters, Bella, Maria and Kit Marshall, and Dani Reynolds. Finally, an old debt re-acknowledged. Ali Marshall was the dedicatee of my first book, nearly a quarter of a century ago. Without her unfailing love and friendship, I could never have got from there to here.

*PM*
*Leamington Spa*
*Michaelmas, 2016*

# NOTES

## Abbreviations

*Place of publication is London, unless otherwise specified.*

| | |
|---|---|
| *APC* | *Acts of the Privy Council*, ed. John Roche Dasent (46 vols, 1890–1964) |
| Bernard | George Bernard, *The King's Reformation* (New Haven, 2005) |
| BL | British Library |
| Brigden | Susan Brigden, *London and the Reformation* (Oxford, 1989) |
| Burnet | Gilbert Burnet, *The History of the Reformation of the Church of England*, ed. N. Pocock (7 vols, Oxford, 1865) |
| CCED | Clergy of the Church of England database, online at http://theclergydatabase.org.uk/ |
| *CGF* | J. G. Nichols, ed., *Chronicle of the Grey Friars of London* (1853) |
| *CJ* | Commons' Journals |
| *CQJ* | J. G. Nichols, ed., *The Chronicle of Queen Jane* (1850) |
| Cranmer | Thomas Cranmer, *Miscellaneous Writings*, ed. J. E. Cox (Cambridge, 1846) |
| *CRP* | Thomas Mayer, ed., *Correspondence of Reginald Pole* (4 vols, Aldershot, 2002–8) |
| *CSP* | Calendars of State Papers |
| *CWE* | *Collected Works of Erasmus* (Toronto, 1974–) |
| Dickens | A. G. Dickens, *The English Reformation* (2nd edn, 1989) |
| Duffy | Eamon Duffy, *The Stripping of the Altars: Traditional Religion in England, 1400–1580* (New Haven, 1992) |
| *EHR* | *English Historical Review* |
| Folger | Folger Shakespeare Library, Washington DC |
| Foxe | John Foxe, *Acts and Monuments*, various editions (using 'modern' page references given in the online edition, www.johnfoxe.org) |
| Gee | Henry Gee and William J. Hardy, eds, *Documents Illustrative of English Church History* (1896) |
| Haigh | Christopher Haigh, *English Reformations: Religion, Politics, and Society under the Tudors* (Oxford, 1993) |
| Hall | Edward Hall, *The Union of the two noble and illustre fameilies of Lancastre [and] Yorke* (1548) |
| Hartley | T. E. Hartley, ed., *Proceedings in the Parliaments of Elizabeth I* (3 vols, Leicester, 1981–95) |
| Haugaard | William Haugaard, *Elizabeth I and the English Reformation* (Cambridge, 1968) |

| | |
|---|---|
| *HJ* | *Historical Journal* |
| HMC | Historical Manuscripts Commission |
| *JEH* | *Journal of Ecclesiastical History* |
| *Liturgies* | Joseph Ketley, ed., *The Two Liturgies . . . in the Reign of King Edward VI* (Cambridge, 1844) |
| *LJ* | Lords' Journal |
| Lloyd | C. Lloyd, ed., *Formularies of Faith put forth by Authority during the Reign of Henry VIII* (Oxford, 1856) |
| *LP* | J. S. Brewer, J. Gairdner and R. H. Brodie, eds, *Letters and Papers, Foreign and Domestic, of the Reign of Henry VIII* (21 vols in 33 parts, 1862–1910) |
| *LSG* | James A Muller, ed., *The Letters of Stephen Gardiner* (Cambridge, 1933) |
| MacCulloch | Diarmaid MacCulloch, *Thomas Cranmer: A Life* (New Haven, 1996) |
| Machyn | J. G. Nichols, ed., *The Diary of Henry Machyn* (1847) |
| Marshall | Peter Marshall, *Religious Identities in Henry VIII's England* (Aldershot, 2006) |
| Mears | Natalie Mears et al., eds, *National Prayers: Special Worship since the Reformation, Volume I* (Woodbridge, 2013) |
| *Narratives* | J. G. Nichols, ed., *Narratives of the Days of the Reformation* (1859) |
| *ODNB* | *Oxford Dictionary of National Biography*, online edition |
| *OL* | Hastings Robinson, ed., *Original Letters relative to the English Reformation* (2 vols, Cambridge 1846–7) |
| Parker | John Bruce, ed., *Correspondence of Matthew Parker* (Cambridge, 1853) |
| Roper | William Roper, 'The Life of Sir Thomas More', in Richard S. Sylvester and Davis P. Harding, eds, *Two Early Tudor Lives* (New Haven, 1962) |
| RSTC | Revised Short Title Catalogue |
| *SCJ* | *Sixteenth Century Journal* |
| SP | National Archives, State Papers |
| STAC | National Archives, records of Star Chamber |
| Strype | John Strype, *Ecclesiastical Memorials* (3 vols, Oxford, 1822) |
| Strype, *Annals* | John Strype, *Annals of the Reformation* (4 vols, Oxford, 1824) |
| *TRHS* | *Transactions of the Royal Historical Society* |
| *TRP* | P. L. Hughes and J. F. Larkin, eds, *Tudor Royal Proclamations* (3 vols, New Haven, 1964–9), |
| *VAI* | W. H. Frere and W. P. M. Kennedy, eds, *Visitation Articles and Injunctions of the Period of the Reformation* (3 vols, 1910) |
| 'Wenlock' | 'The Register of Sir Thomas Botelar, Vicar of Much Wenlock', *Transactions of the Shropshire Archaeological and Natural History Society*, 6 (1883) |
| Wilkins | David Wilkins, ed., *Concilia Magna Britanniae et Hiberniae* (4 vols, 1737) |
| Wriothesley | Charles Wriothesley, *A Chronicle of England*, ed. W. D. Hamilton (2 vols, 1875–77) |
| *ZL* | Hastings Robinson, ed., *The Zurich Letters* (2nd edn, Cambridge, 1846) |

## Preface

1. Edwin Sandys, *Sermons*, ed. John Ayre (Cambridge, 1841), 49.
2. For discussion of this concept, see Ute Lotz-Heumann, 'Confessionalization', in David Whitford, ed., *Reformation and Early Modern Europe: A Guide to Research* (Kirksville, MO, 2008), 136–57.
3. Folger, L.d.980.

## 1 The Imitation of Christ

1. David Starkey, *Henry: Virtuous Prince* (2008), 11–13; William Tyndale, *Doctrinal Treatises*, ed. H. Walter (Cambridge, 1848), 277.
2. R. W. Scribner, *Popular Culture and Popular Movements in Reformation Germany* (1987), 5–8, 39–41, 259–62.

3. Berndt Hamm, *The Reformation of Faith in the Context of Late Medieval Theology and Piety*, ed. Robert J. Bast (Leiden, 2004), 136–42; Steven Ozment, *The Reformation in the Cities* (New Haven, 1975), 22–8, 49–56; Peter Marshall, *The Catholic Priesthood and the English Reformation* (Oxford, 1994), 9–13; SP 1/102, 67r.

4. C. A. Sneyd, ed., *A Relation, or Rather a True Account of the Island of England* (1847), 23; Marshall, *Priesthood*, 43; Duffy, 100–2.

5. John Bossy, 'The Mass as a Social Institution, 1200–1700', *Past and Present*, 100 (1983), 29–61; Mervyn James, 'Ritual, Drama and the Social Body in the Late Medieval English Town', *Past and Present*, 98 (1983), 3–29; Miri Rubin, *Corpus Christi: The Eucharist in Late Medieval Culture* (Cambridge, 1991), 243–71; W. H. Hale, ed., *A Series of Precedents and Proceedings in Criminal Causes* (1847), 53–4; Duffy, 94, 126–7.

6. Duffy, 127; A. H. Thompson, ed., *Visitations in the Diocese of Lincoln, 1517–1531* (3 vols, Lincoln, 1940–7), 6.

7. Peter Marshall, *Reformation England* (2nd edn, 2012), 3–4; Penry Williams, *The Later Tudors* (Oxford, 1995), 177; David Harris Sacks, 'London's Dominion', in Lena Cowen Orlin, ed., *Material London, ca. 1600* (Philadelphia, 2000), 22–3.

8. For what follows, see especially Ronald Hutton, *The Rise and Fall of Merry England: The Ritual Year 1400–1700* (Oxford, 1994), 5–48; Duffy, 11–52.

9. For this concept, see Willem Frijhoff, *Embodied Belief: Ten Essays on Religious Culture in Dutch History* (Hilversum, 2002).

10. Robert S. Bayley, *Notitiae Ludae, or Notices of Louth* (1834), 146–7.

11. Katherine French, 'Parochial Fund-Raising in Late Medieval Somerset', in French, Gary G. Gibbs and Beat A. Kümin, eds, *The Parish in English Life 1400–1600* (Manchester, 1997), 115–32; Beat Kümin, *The Shaping of a Community: The Rise and Reformation of the English Parish, c. 1400–1560* (Aldershot, 1996), 103–25; G. W. Bernard, *The Late Medieval English Church* (New Haven, 2012), 101–3; Paul Whitefield White, *Drama and Religion in English Provincial Society, 1485–1660* (Cambridge, 2008), 9–26.

12. David Dymond and Clive Paine, eds, *Five Centuries of an English Parish Church: 'The State of Melford Church'*, Suffolk (Cambridge, 2012), 67–71; K. Wood-Legh, ed., *Kentish Visitations of Archbishop William Warham and his Deputies, 1511–1512* (Maidstone, 1984), 224; Marshall, *Priesthood*, 200.

13. Peter Marshall, *Beliefs and the Dead in Reformation England* (Oxford, 2002), 23–4.

14. Charles Henderson and E. Jervoise, *Old Devon Bridges* (Exeter, 1938), 92; Duffy, 288–9. The definitive study is R. N. Swanson, *Indulgences in Late Medieval England* (Cambridge, 2007).

15. Marshall, *Beliefs*, 22–32; Brigden, 33.

16. Robert Swanson, *Church and Society in Late Medieval England* (Oxford, 1989), 280–4; Duffy, 141–54; David Crouch, *Piety, Fraternity, and Power: Religious Gilds in Late Medieval Yorkshire* (York, 2000), 217–18; Caroline Barron, 'The Parish Fraternities of Medieval London', in Barron and Christopher Harper-Bill, eds, *The Church in Pre-Reformation Society* (Woodbridge, 1985), 13–37.

17. Clive Burgess, 'A Service for the Dead: the Form and Function of the Anniversary in Late Medieval Bristol', *Transactions of the Bristol and Gloucestershire Archaeological Society*, 105 (1987), 183–211.

18. Marshall, *Beliefs*, 14–15, 19–20, 24–5; *The Interpretacyon and Sygnyfycacyon of the Masse* (1532), C1v; Robert Whiting, *Local Responses to the English Reformation* (Basingstoke, 1998), 71–2; *Dives and Pauper* (1534), 266v–268r.

19. Duffy, 8; A. N. Galpern, 'The Legacy of Late Medieval Religion in Sixteenth-Century Champagne', in C. Trinkaus and H. O. Oberman, eds, *The Pursuit of Holiness in Late Medieval and Renaissance Religion* (Leiden, 1974), 149.

20. F. W. Weaver, ed., *Somerset Medieval Wills 1501–30* (1903), 72. See, e.g., J. Weaver and A. Beardwood, eds, *Some Oxfordshire Wills Proved in the Prerogative Court of Canterbury, 1393–1510* (Oxford, 1958), 96; J. Raine, ed., *Testamenta Eboracensia . . . Vol. V* (Durham, 1884), 33.

21. *Here begynneth a Lytel Boke that speketh of Purgatorye* (?1531), A1r.

22. Marshall, *Beliefs*, 41–6; Brigden, 389n.

23. G. Marc'hadour, 'Introduction', in Thomas More, *The Supplication of Souls*, ed. F. Manley et al. (New Haven, 1990), lxx; N. F. Blake, 'Caxton, William (1415x24–1492)', *ODNB*; 'Worde, Wynkyn de (*d.* 1534/5)', *ODNB*.

24. Duffy, 68–87, 209–32.

25. Jo Ann Hoeppner Moran, *The Growth of English Schooling, 1340–1548* (Princeton, 1985), 18–20; Sneyd, *Relation*, 23; Richard Rex, *Henry VIII and the English Reformation* (2nd edn, Basingstoke, 2006), 88–91.

26. BL, Harley MS 651, 194v–196v; Thomas More, *A Dialogue Concerning Heresies*, ed. T. M. C. Lawler et al. (New Haven, 1981), 95–6; Diarmaid MacCulloch, *Suffolk and the Tudors* (Oxford, 1986), 143–6; Richard Rex, 'Wentworth, Jane [the Maid of Ipswich] (*c.*1503–1572?)', *ODNB*. There is uncertainty about the girl's Christian name: it is given as Anne in a Protestant source of the 1550s.

27. Henry Ellis, ed., *The pylgrymage of Sir Richard Guylforde to the Holy Land, AD 1506* (1851), 23; Warwickshire Record Office, CR1998/Box 73/2. For suggestions of disengagement from the parish church, see Colin Richmond, 'Religion and the Fifteenth-Century English Gentleman', in R. B. Dobson, ed., *The Church, Politics and Patronage in the Fifteenth Century* (Gloucester, 1984), 193–203.

28. J. T. Fowler, ed., *Rites of Durham* (Durham, 1902), 94–6; Diana Webb, *Pilgrimage in Medieval England* (2000), 72–7; Eamon Duffy, 'The Dynamics of Pilgrimage in Late Medieval England', in Colin Morris and Peter Roberts, eds, *Pilgrimage: The English Experience from Becket to Bunyan* (Cambridge, 2002), 164–77.

29. Christine Peters, *Patterns of Piety: Women, Gender and Religion in Late Medieval and Reformation England* (Cambridge, 2003), 97–102; Ronald Finucane, *Miracles and Pilgrims* (London, 1977), Part II; Duffy, 178–81; Wendy R. Larson, 'Maternal Patronage of the Cult of St Margaret', in Mary C. Erler and Maryanne Kowaleski, eds, *Gendering the Master Narrative* (New York, 2003), 94–104.

30. Peter Heath, 'Urban Piety in the Later Middle Ages', in R. B. Dobson, ed., *The Church, Politics and Patronage in the Fifteenth Century* (Gloucester, 1984), 214; Richard Pfaff, *New Liturgical Feasts in Later Medieval England* (Oxford 1970); Duffy, 44–6, 260–1; Robert Lutton, *Lollardy and Orthodox Religion in Pre-Reformation England* (London, 2006), 69–70; William Smith, *The Use of Hereford: The Sources of a Medieval English Diocesan Rite* (Aldershot, 2015), 689–92; Eamon Duffy, 'Religious Belief', in Rosemary Horrox and W. Mark Ormrod, eds, *A Social History of England 1200–1500* (Cambridge, 2006), 338–9.

31. Peters, *Patterns*, 62–5; Hugh Latimer, *Sermons and Remains*, ed. G. E. Corrie (Cambridge, 1845), 364; Webb, *Pilgrimage*, 97–9; Richard Suggett, 'Church-Building in Late Medieval Wales', in R. A. Griffiths and P. R. Schofield, eds, *Wales and the Welsh in the Middle Ages* (Cardiff, 2011), 186.

32. Norman P. Tanner, *The Church in Late Medieval Norwich, 1370–1532* (Toronto, 1984), 99; Vanessa Harding, *The Dead and the Living in Paris and London, 1500–1670* (Cambridge, 2002), 225–6; Lutton, *Lollardy*, 69–80; Peter Marshall, 'Catholic Puritanism in Pre-Reformation England', *British Catholic History*, 32 (2015), 431–50.

33. Maximilian von Habsburg, *Catholic and Protestant Translations of the Imitatio Christi, 1425–1650* (Farnham, 2011), 89–94, 278–9; Michael K. Jones and Malcolm G. Underwood, *The King's Mother: Lady Margaret Beaufort* (Cambridge, 1992), 184–5.

34. D. F. S. Thomson and H. C. Porter, eds, *Erasmus and Cambridge* (Toronto, 1963), 148.

35. Thomson and Porter, *Erasmus*, 148–9; *The Poems of Desiderius Erasmus*, ed. C. Reedijk (Leiden, 1956), 303; *The Colloquies of Erasmus*, ed. C. R. Thompson (Chicago and London, 1965), 285–310.

36. *John Colet's Commentary on First Corinthians*, ed. and tr. Bernard O'Kelly and Catherine A. L. Jarrott (New York, 1985), 165.

37. Thomson and Porter, *Erasmus*, 18.

38. Richard Rex, 'The New Learning', *JEH*, 44 (1993), 26–44.

39. *CWE*, II, 122.

40. Erasmus, *Praise of Folly*, ed. A. Levi, tr. B. Radice (Harmondsworth, 1971), 126–30, 152–75.

41. Thomas More, *Utopia*, ed. George M. Logan and Robert M. Adams (Cambridge, 1989), 66, 101, 86.

42. Thomas More, *In Defense of Humanism*, ed. D. Kinney (New Haven, 1986), 285–9.

43. See, e.g., Susan Boynton and Diane J. Reilly, eds, *The Practice of the Bible in the Middle Ages: Production, Reception and Performance in Western Christianity* (New York, 2011).

44. James D. Tracy, *Erasmus of the Low Countries* (Berkeley and Los Angeles, 1996), 61–2.

45. *CWE*, II, 213; Maria Dowling, *Humanism in the Age of Henry VIII* (Beckenham, 1986), 20–1.

46. John C. Olin, ed., *Christian Humanism and the Reformation: Selected Writings of Erasmus* (3rd edn, New York, 1987), 97–108.

47. Erika Rummel, *Erasmus* (2004), 74–9; R. J. Schoeck, *Erasmus of Europe: The Prince of the Humanists* (Edinburgh, 1993), 187–8; Tracy, *Erasmus*, 108–9.

48. *CWE*, VI, 948.

49. Richard Marius, *Thomas More* (1984), 145–51; *CWE*, IV, 115–16; J. B. Trapp, *Erasmus, Colet and More: The Early Tudor Humanists and their Books* (1991), 73–4.

50. *CWE*, IV, 44–5.

51. S. Thompson, 'Fitzjames, Richard (*d.* 1522)', *ODNB*; Peter Iver Kaufman, *The 'Polytyque Churche': Religion and Early Tudor Political Culture, 1485–1516* (Macon, GA, 1986), 66–8.

52. Tracy, *Erasmus*, 120; John A. F. Thomson, *The Early Tudor Church and Society* (1993), 48.

53. Margaret Harvey, 'Reaction to Revival: Robert Ridley's Critique of Erasmus', in Kate Cooper and Jeremy Gregory, eds, *Revival and Resurgence in Christian History* (Woodbridge, 2008), 77– 86 (quotation at 85).

54. Thomson and Porter, *Erasmus*, 182, 187, 190, 194; Tracy, *Erasmus*, 121; *CWE*, VI, 316–17.

55. More, *Humanism*, 130–49; Craig W. D'Alton, 'The Trojan War of 1518: Melodrama, Politics, and the Rise of Humanism', *SCJ*, 28 (1997), 727–38.

56. See J. I. Catto and Ralph Evans, eds, *The History of the University of Oxford. Volume II: Late Medieval Oxford* (Oxford, 1992); D. R. Leader, *A History of the University of Cambridge. Volume 1: The University to 1546* (Cambridge, 1988).

57. Malcolm Underwood, 'John Fisher and the Promotion of Learning', in Brendan Bradshaw and Eamon Duffy, eds, *Humanism, Reform and the Reformation* (Cambridge, 1989), 25–46; David Knowles, *The Religious Orders in England: III The Tudor Age* (Cambridge, 1959), 161–2, 470.

58. John Venn, *Biographical History of Gonville and Caius College* (Cambridge, 1897), 21–2; Leader, *Cambridge*, 279, 287.

59. J. R. Lander, *Government and Community: England, 1450–1509* (Cambridge, MA, 1980), 123; *Statutes of the Colleges of Oxford . . . Corpus Christi College* (Oxford, 1853), 50–1.

60. D'Alton, 'War', 733–4.

61. Dowling, *Humanism*, 26; Jonathan Woolfson, 'Croke, Richard (1489–1558)', *ODNB*; *CWE*, V, 225.

62. Richard Rex, 'Melton, William (*d.* 1528)', *ODNB*; James K. McConica, *English Humanists and Reformation Politics* (Oxford, 1965), 90–2; Underwood, 'Fisher', 25, 30; Leader, *Cambridge*, 289, 313–14; 252; J. E. B. Mayor, ed., *Early Statutes of the College of St John* (Cambridge, 1859); Peter Gwyn, *The King's Cardinal* (1990), 343–4; Hugh Aveling and W. A. Pantin, eds, *The Letter Book of Robert Joseph* (Oxford, 1967), xxxiv.

## 2 Lights of the World

1. STAC.2, 2/267; *The Orcharde of Syon* (1519), B6v, T6v; John Fisher, *The English Works*, ed. J. E. Mayor (1876), 179; Craig W. D'Alton, 'The Suppression of Heresy in Early Henrician England', University of Melbourne PhD Thesis (1999), 26–7.

2. John Gleason, *John Colet* (Berkeley, CA, 1989), 181–4, dates the sermon to 1510, a revision accepted by Haigh, 9–10, but convincingly rebutted by D'Alton, 'Suppression', 50.

3. J. H. Lupton, *Life of John Colet* (1887), 293–304; Christopher Harper-Bill, 'Dean Colet's Convocation Sermon and the Pre-Reformation Church in England', in Peter Marshall, ed., *The Impact of the English Reformation 1500–1640* (1997), 17–37; Robert Swanson, *Church and Society in Late Medieval England* (Oxford, 1989), 27–82; John A. F. Thomson, *The Early Tudor Church and Society* (1993), 139–87; Felicity Heal, *Reformation in Britain and Ireland* (Oxford, 2003), 59–80; G. W. Bernard, *The Late Medieval English Church* (New Haven, 2012), 68–86.

4. Brigden, 58; Peter Heath, *English Parish Clergy on the Eve of the Reformation* (1969), 81–2.

5. Lucy Wooding, *Rethinking Catholicism in Reformation England* (Oxford, 2000), 36; Marshall, 157–65.

6. Peter Marshall, *The Catholic Priesthood and the English Reformation* (Oxford, 1994), 99, 176; Christopher Harper-Bill, *The Pre-Reformation Church in England 1400–1530* (1989), 50–1; Bernard, *Church*, 69; K. Wood-Legh, ed., *Kentish Visitations of Archbishop William Warham and his Deputies, 1511–1512* (Maidstone, 1984), 47; Heath, *Clergy*, 56.

7. Stephen Lander, 'Church Courts and the Reformation in the Diocese of Chichester, 1500–58', in Rosemary O'Day and Felicity Heal, eds, *Continuity and Change: Personnel and Administration of the Church in England 1500–1642* (Leicester, 1976), 223–4.

8. Susan Brigden, 'Tithe Controversy in Reformation London', *JEH*, 32 (1981), 285–301; Haigh, 45–6; Bernard, *Church*, 154–5; Marshall, *Priesthood*, 231.

9. Helen Parish, *Clerical Celibacy in the West, c. 1100–1700* (Farnham, 2010); P. S. and H. M. Allen, eds, *Letters of Richard Fox* (Oxford, 1929), 151; Marshall, *Priesthood*, 144–5; Heal, *Reformation*, 76–9.

10. J. R. Lander, *Government and Community: England, 1450–1509* (Cambridge, MA, 1980), 120; Maria Dowling, *Fisher of Men: A Life of John Fisher* (Basingstoke, 1999), 50–1; Peter Gwyn, *The King's Cardinal* (1990), 312–13.

11. Tim Cooper, *The Last Generation of English Catholic Clergy* (Woodbridge, 1999), 77–91; Peter Marshall, *The Face of the Pastoral Ministry in the East Riding, 1525–1595* (York, 1995), 19–20; Michael Zell, 'Economic Problems of the Parochial Clergy in the Sixteenth Century', in Rosemary O'Day and Felicity Heal, eds, *Princes and Paupers in the English Church 1500–1800* (Leicester, 1981), 25–9; John Pound, 'Clerical Poverty in Early Sixteenth-Century England', *JEH*, 37 (1986), 389–96.

12. Andrew A. Chibi, *Henry VIII's Bishops* (Cambridge, 2003), 26–9; D. G. Newcombe, 'Stanley, James (c.1465–1515)', *ODNB*; Jonathan Hughes, 'Audley, Edmund (c.1439–1524)', *ODNB*.

13. Peter Marshall, 'The Dispersal of Monastic Patronage in East Yorkshire, 1520–90', in Beat Kümin, ed., *Reformations Old and New* (Aldershot, 1996), 124–34; James E. Oxley, *The Reformation in Essex to the Death of Mary* (Manchester, 1965), 263.

14. Heath, *Clergy*, 33; Margaret Bowker, *The Henrician Reformation: The Diocese of Lincoln under John Longland 1521–1547* (Cambridge, 1981), 44, 79–80; J. J. Scarisbrick, 'Warham, William (1450?–1532)', *ODNB* (who doubts the archdeacon of Canterbury was Warham's son); MacCulloch, 108–9 (who suspects he was); Dowling, *Fisher*, 61–2.

15. Steven Gunn, 'Edmund Dudley and the Church', *JEH*, 51 (2000), 521–4.

16. J. J. Scarisbrick, *The Reformation and the English People* (Oxford, 1984), 166–7; Marshall, *Priesthood*, 196–9; Diarmaid MacCulloch, *Suffolk and the Tudors* (Oxford, 1986), 175.

17. Heath, *Clergy*, 93–103; Marshall, *Priesthood*, 88–9; Heal, *Reformation*, 62–4; Susan Wabuda, *Preaching during the English Reformation* (Cambridge, 2003), 107–22; Robert Whiting, *The Blind Devotion of the People: Popular Religion and the English Reformation* (Cambridge, 1989), 239–40; Barrie Dobson, 'English Monastic Cathedrals in the Fifteenth Century', *TRHS*, 6th ser. 1 (1991), 151–72.

18. William Langland, *Piers the Ploughman*, ed. J. F. Goodridge (Harmondsworth, 1959), 120–1; William Lyndwood, *Provinciale*, ed. J. V. Bullard and H. C. Bell (1929), 20–1, 26; Marshall, *Priesthood*, 90–1; Wabuda, *Preaching*, 33; Whiting, *Devotion*, 237–8.

19. Dowling, *Fisher*, 87; James Raine, ed., *The Fabric Rolls of York Minster* (Durham, 1858), 258; *The Book of Margery Kempe*, ed. Lynn Staley (Kalamazoo, MI, 1996), 52, 58, 61.

20. John Alcock, *[Sermon on Luke VIII]* (Westminster, ?1497), B4v; Brigden, 72; Hall, 60r–v.

21. J. Raine et al., eds, *Testamenta Eboracensia: a Selection of Wills from the Registry at York (1300–1551), Vol. V* (Durham, 1884), 61; Brigden, 72–3; Wabuda, *Preaching*, 21, 47–52, 64, 166–7, 177; Whiting, *Devotion*, 237–8.

22. Dowling, *Fisher*, 72–89; Wabuda, *Preaching*, 68–72; *The imytacyon and folowynge the blessed lyfe of our moste mercyfull Sauyour cryste*, tr. William Atkinson (1517), B6v; *Diues [and] paup[er]* (1493), P6v–7r.

23. A. G. Ferrers Howell, *S. Bernardino of Siena* (1913), 218–19; Richard Whitford, *A Werke for Housholders* (1530), D4r–v.

24. James G. Clark, 'The Religious Orders in Pre-Reformation England', in Clark, ed., *The Religious Orders in Pre-Reformation England* (Woodbridge, 2002), 6–7.

25. David Knowles and R. Neville Hadcock, *Medieval Religious Houses, England and Wales* (Harlow, 1971).

26. Penn Szittya, *The Antifraternal Tradition in Medieval Literature* (Princeton, 1986); G. Geltner, *The Making of Medieval Antifraternalism: Polemic, Violence, Deviance, and Remembrance* (Oxford, 2012).

27. Philip Hughes, *The Reformation in England* (3 vols, 1950–4), I, 57–8; David Knowles, *The Religious Orders in England III: The Tudor Age* (Cambridge, 1959), 62, 74–5; Thomson, *Church*, 198–206; Benjamin Thompson, 'Monasteries, Society and Reform in Late Medieval England', in Clark, *Orders*, 184–9; John Alcock, *An exhortacyon made to Relygyous systers in the tyme of theyr consecracyon* (Westminster, 1497), 5v–6r.

28. Clark, 'Orders', 16–24; Joan Greatrex, 'After Knowles: Recent Perspectives in Monastic History', in Clark, *Orders*, 35–47; David N. Bell, 'Monastic libraries: 1400–1557', in Lotte Hellinga and J. B. Trapp, eds, *The Cambridge History of the Book in Britain, Volume 3, 1400–1557* (Cambridge, 1999), 229–54; Roger Bowers, 'The Almonry Schools of the English Monasteries, c. 1265–1540', in Benjamin Thompson, ed., *Monasteries and Society in Medieval Britain* (Stamford, 1999), 176–222; Knowles, *Orders*, 21–7; Bernard, *Church*, 179.

29. *LP*, IV (2), 4692; Thomas Starkey, *A Dialogue between Pole and Lupset*, ed. T. F. Mayer (1989), 99, 103–4, 133–4; Bowker, *Reformation*, 17–28.

30. Alcock, *Exhortacyon*, A2v; Barry Collett, ed., *Female Monastic Life in Early Tudor England* (Burlington, VT, 2002); Dowling, *Fisher*, 56–7; Cecilia A. Hatt, ed., *English Works of John Fisher, Bishop of Rochester* (Oxford, 2002), 350–400.

31. Gwyn, *Wolsey*, 464–70, 477–9; Knowles, *Orders*, 162; Martin Heale, *Monasticism in Late Medieval England, c. 1300–1535* (Manchester, 2009), 43.

32. Gwyn, *Wolsey*, 270–4; *LP*, IV, 414; Heale, *Monasticism*, 127, 135–6; John Longland, *Ioannis Longlondi Dei gratia Lincolnien[sis] Episcopi, tres conciones* (1527), C1r–v.

33. Gwyn, *Wolsey*, 270–1; Thomson, *Church*, 206–7; James G. Clark, *The Benedictines in the Middle Ages* (Woodbridge, 2011), 308–9; Knowles, *Orders*, 35–51.

34. Gwyn, *Wolsey*, 265–6, 272–3, 316–23, 329–30, 471–2.

35. Keith Brown, 'Wolsey and Ecclesiastical Order: The Case of the Franciscan Observants', in S. J. Gunn and P. G. Lindley, eds, *Cardinal Wolsey: Church, State and Art* (Cambridge, 1991), 219–38.

36. Bert Roest, 'Observant Reform in Religious Orders', in Miri Rubin and Walter Simons, eds, *Christianity in Western Europe c. 1100–c. 1500* (Cambridge, 2009), 446–57; Henry A. Jeffries, *The Irish Church and the Tudor Reformations* (Dublin, 2010), 36.

37. J. H. Elliott, *Imperial Spain, 1469–1716* (Harmondsworth, 1970), 104; Jeremy Catto, 'Franciscan Learning in England, 1450–1540'; Michael Robson, 'The Grey Friars in York, c. 1450–1530', in Clark, *Orders*, 97–104, 109–19; Nelson H. Minnich, 'Prophecy and the Fifth Lateran Council (1512–1517)', in Marjorie Reeves, ed., *Prophetic Rome in the High Renaissance Period* (Oxford, 1992), 63–87.

38. Clark, *Benedictines*, 310–11.

39. Swanson, *Church*, 274; Norman P. Tanner, *The Church in Late Medieval Norwich, 1370–1532* (Toronto, 1984), 64–6; R. N. Swanson, *Religion and Devotion in Europe, c. 1215–c.1515* (Cambridge, 1995), 113–15; Duffy, chs 6–7; Mary C. Erler, *Women, Reading and Piety in Late Medieval England* (Cambridge, 2002).

40. Thomas Betson, *Here begynneth a ryght profytable treatyse* (Westminster, 1500), A2r; *Here begyn[n]eth the medled lyfe compyled by mayster Water [sic] Hylton* (1530);

C. Annette Grisé, 'The Mixed Life and Lay Piety in Mystical Texts Printed in Pre-Reformation England', *Journal of the Early Book Society*, 8 (2005), 97–124; Alexandra da Costa, *Reforming Printing: Syon Abbey's Defence of Orthodoxy 1525-1534* (Oxford, 2012), 52–79, 143–63.

41. Whitford, *Werke*, A2v–B1v; J. T. Rhodes, 'Syon Abbey and its Religious Publications in the Sixteenth Century', *JEH*, 44 (1993), 11–25; Alexandra da Costa, 'John Fewterer's Myrrour or Glasse of Christes Passion and Ulrich Pinder's Speculum Passionis', *Notes and Queries*, 56 (2009), 27–9; da Costa, *Printing*, 41–2.

42. Brigden, 73–4; Roper, 198; Knowles, *Orders*, 222–8; A. G. Dickens, ed., *Clifford Letters of the Sixteenth Century* (Durham, 1962), 62–3.

43. Michael Sargent, 'The Transmission by the English Carthusians of some Late Medieval Spiritual Writings', *JEH*, 27 (1976), 225–40; Thomas More, *In Defense of Humanism*, ed. Daniel Kinney (New Haven, 1986), 271; *The Pomander of prayer* (1530), A1r-v; Emily Richards, 'Writing and Silence: Transitions between the Contemplative and the Active Life', in Robert Lutton and Elisabeth Salter, eds, *Pieties in Transition* (Aldershot, 2007), 163–79; James McConica, *English Humanists and Reformation Politics* (Oxford, 1965), 38; Glyn Coppack, '"Make straight in the desert a highway for our God": Carthusians and Community in Late Medieval England', in Janet Burton and Karen Stöber, eds, *Monasteries and Society in the British Isles in the Later Middle Ages* (Woodbridge, 2008), 169–73.

44. R. B. Dobson, *Durham Priory 1400-1450* (Cambridge, 1973), 125–31; Nancy Bradley Warren, *Spiritual Economies: Female Monasticism in Later Medieval England* (Philadelphia, 2001), 66; Knowles, *Orders*, 260–4; Barbara Harvey, *Living and Dying in England 1100-1540: The Monastic Experience* (Oxford, 1993), 149–53.

45. Knowles, *Orders*, 266–7; Allison Fizzard, 'Retirement Arrangements and the Laity at Religious Houses in Pre-Reformation Devon', *Florilegium*, 22 (2005), 63; Marilyn Oliva, *The Convent and Community in Late Medieval England* (Woodbridge, 1998), 127; Harvey, *Living*, 179–209.

46. A. G. Dickens, *Late Monasticism and the Reformation* (1994), 50, 51–2, 53, 54–5, 57, 68; Neil S. Rushton, 'Monastic Charitable Provision in Tudor England', *Continuity and Change*, 16 (2001), 9–44.

47. Bernard, *Church*, 166–7; Claire Cross, 'The Origins and University Connections of Yorkshire Religious, c. 1480–1540', in Peter Biller and Barrie Dobson, eds, *The Medieval Church: Universities, Heresy and the Religious Life* (Woodbridge, 1999), 271–91; Knowles, *Orders*, 64; Oliva, *Convent*, 52–61; Bernard, *Church*, 166–7; Paul Lee, *Nunneries, Learning, and Spirituality in Late Medieval English Society* (Woodbridge, 2001), 57–67.

48. SP 1/35, 48r; 1/34, 240r-v.

49. Robert Whiting, 'Local Responses to the Henrician Reformation', in Diarmaid MacCulloch, ed., *The Reign of Henry VIII* (Basingstoke, 1995), 206; Bernard, *Church*, 178; Bowker, *Reformation*, 48; David Palliser, *The Reformation in York, 1534-1553* (York, 1971), 2; Andrew D. Brown, *Popular Piety in Medieval England* (Oxford, 1995), 29, 44, 35; Vanessa Harding, 'Burial Choice and Burial Location in Later Medieval London', in Steven Basset, ed., *Death in Towns* (1992), 122–4; Tanner, *Norwich*, 108, 189.

50. Thomson, *Church*, 222–3; Warwickshire Record Office, CR 1998/Box 52; Robert N. Swanson, 'Mendicants and Confraternity in Late Medieval England', in Clark, *Orders*, 121–41.

51. Whiting, *Devotion*, 119; Janet E. Burton, *Monastic and Religious Orders in Britain, 1000-1300* (Cambridge, 1994), 243–5; James G. Clark, 'Religion and Politics in English Monastic Towns', *Cultural and Social History*, 6 (2009), 277–96; Robert S. Gottfried, *Bury St Edmunds and the Urban Crisis, 1290-1539* (Princeton, 1982), 215–36; Jeanette Martin, 'Leadership and Priorities in Reading during the Reformation', in Patrick Collinson and John Craig, eds, *The Reformation in English Towns 1500-1640* (Basingstoke, 1998), 115–16.

52. Dickens, *Monasticism*, 155; Sean Field, 'Devotion, Discontent, and the Henrician Reformation: The Evidence of the Robin Hood Stories', *Journal of British Studies*, 41 (2002), 6–22; A. J. Pollard, *Imagining Robin Hood* (Abingdon, 2004), 111–33.

53. Peter Happé, 'Heywood, John (*b.* 1496/7, *d.* in or after 1578)', *ODNB*; RSTC 3545, 3546, 3547, 3547a; A. Barclay, *The Ship of Fools*, ed. T. H. Jamieson (2 vols, 1874), II, 61.

54. John Skelton, *The Complete English Poems*, ed. John Scattergood (1983), 268–9; Brigden, 76–7; John Heywood, *A dialogue conteinyng the nomber in effect of all the prouerbes in the englishe tongue* (1546), C4r; Thomas More, *A Dialogue Concerning Heresies*, ed. T. M. C. Lawler et al. (New Haven, 1981), 296–7.

55. Brigden, 76–8; John Scattergood, 'Skelton, John (*c.*1460–1529)', *ODNB*; Nicholas Orme, 'Barclay, Alexander (*c.*1484–1552)', *ODNB*; Sebastian Brandt, *The shyppe of fooles*, tr. Henry Watson (1509), A2v.

### 3 Head and Members

1. George Cavendish, *The Life and Death of Cardinal Wolsey*, ed. R. S. Sylvester and D. P. Harding (New Haven, 1962), 17; J. H. Lupton, *Life of John Colet* (1887), 193–8.

2. John Alcock, *[Sermon on Luke VIII]* (Westminster, ?1497), C6r.

3. Phillip H. Stump, *The Reforms of the Council of Constance (1414–1418)* (Leiden, 1994).

4. A theme largely absent, e.g., from Duffy, and from J. J. Scarisbrick, *The Reformation and the English People* (Oxford, 1984).

5. *LP*, I, 1048, 1083 (5), 1170; William E. Wilkie, *The Cardinal Protectors of England* (Cambridge, 1974), 45; Nelson E. Minnch, 'Erasmus and the Fifth Lateran Council', in Jan Sperna Weiland and Willem T. Frijhoff, eds, *Erasmus of Rotterdam: The Man and the Scholar* (Leiden, 1988), 46–60.

6. Diarmaid MacCulloch, *Reformation: Europe's House Divided 1490–1700* (2003), 88.

7. D S. Chambers, *Popes, Cardinals and War* (2006), 110–33.

8. Cathy Curtis, 'Richard Pace on Pedagogy, Counsel and Satire', University of Cambridge PhD thesis (1996); Aysha Pollnitz, *Princely Education in Early Modern Britain* (Cambridge, 2015), 70–1 (reasserting the case for Erasmus's authorship); *CWE*, VIII, 242.

9. T. F. Simmons, ed., *The Lay Folks Mass Book* (1879), 74–5; *Diues [and] paup[er]* (1493), n3v; *The Ordynarye of crystyanyte or of crysten men* (1502), H7r; Duffy, 58, 65, 159, 238–9.

10. R. N. Swanson, *Indulgences in Late Medieval England* (Cambridge, 2007); Pamela Neville-Sington, 'Press, Politics and Religion', in Lotte Hellinga and J. B. Trapp, eds, *The Cambridge History of the Book in Britain, Volume 3, 1400–1557* (Cambridge, 1999), 584.

11. George B. Parks, *The English Traveler to Italy: Volume 1, The Middle Ages (to 1525)* (Rome, 1954), 337–82; John A. F. Thomson, ' "The Well of Grace": Englishmen and Rome in the Fifteenth Century', in R. B. Dobson, ed., *The Church, Politics and Patronage in the Fifteenth Century* (Gloucester, 1984), 107; Judith F. Champ, *The English Pilgrimage to Rome* (Leominster, 2000), 52.

12. Michael Mullett, *Martin Luther* (2004), 46–7; *A sermon of Cuthbert Bysshop of Duresme* (1539), B8v–C1r.

13. For the following, see Thomson, ' "Well" ', 99–114; Thomson, *The Early Tudor Church and Society* (1993), 32–9, 234–7; Felicity Heal, *Reformation in Britain and Ireland* (Oxford, 2003), 24–7; Peter D. Clarke, 'Petitioning the Pope: English Supplicants and Rome in the Fifteenth Century', in Linda Clark, ed., *The Fifteenth Century* (Woodbridge, 2012), 41–60; Clarke, 'Canterbury as the New Rome: Dispensations and Henry VIII's Reformation', *JEH*, 64 (2013), 20–44.

14. Charles Donahue, *Law, Marriage and Society in the Later Middle Ages* (Cambridge, 2007), 28–30.

15. Thomson, *Church*, 235.

16. S. B. Chrimes, *Henry VII* (1972), 66, 241, 78–9, 330–1; C. S. L. Davies, 'Bishop John Morton, the Holy See, and the Accession of Henry VII', *EHR*, 102 (1987), 2–30; Wilkie, *Protectors*, 12–13; James Gairdner, ed., *Letters and Papers Illustrative of the Reigns of Richard III and Henry VII* (2 vols, 1861–3), I, 94–5.

17. *Our holy fadre the Pope Innocent the. viij. To the p[er]petuall memory of this here after* (1486); Chrimes, *Henry*, 331.

18. J. Wickham Legg, 'The Gift of the Papal Cap and Sword to Henry VII', *Archaeological Journal*, 57 (1900), 183–203; R. L. Storey, *The Reign of Henry VII* (1968), 184–5; Thomas S. Freeman, '"*Ut Verus Christi Sequester*": John Blacman and the Cult of Henry VI', in Linda Clark, ed., *Of Mice and Men: Image, Belief and Regulation in Late Medieval England* (Woodbridge, 2005), 127–42; Peter I. Kaufman, 'Henry VII and Sanctuary', *Church History*, 53 (1984), 465–76.

19. Champ, *Pilgrimage*, 57–8; Davies, 'Morton', 18–19; *CSP, Venetian*, I, no. 577; Wilkie, *Protectors*, 17–27, 28–31; Brian Newns, 'The Hospice of St Thomas and the English Crown 1474–1538', *Venerabile*, 21 (1962), 161; Parks, *Traveler*, 364.

20. Kenneth Pickthorn, *Early Tudor Government: Henry VII* (Cambridge, 1934), 178; Storey, *Henry*, 82–5.

21. D. S. Chambers, 'Bainbridge, Christopher (1462/3–1514)', *ODNB*; Kenneth M. Setton, *The Papacy and the Levant (1204–1571): Volume 3* (Philadelphia, 1984), 124; Richard J. Schoeck, 'The Fifth Lateran Council', in G. F. Lytle, ed., *Reform and Authority in the Medieval and Reformation Church* (Washington, 1981), 107; J. J. Scarisbrick, *Henry VIII* (1968), 26–9; Lucy Wooding, *Henry VIII* (2nd edn, Abingdon, 2015), 74.

22. *LP*, I, 842; Scarisbrick, *Henry*, 33–4.

23. *LP*, II, 967, 1418, 1456, 1928.

24. SP 1/14, 255r–258r. Long-term political and constitutional importance is emphasized by Thomas F. Mayer, 'Tournai and Tyranny: Imperial Kingship and Critical Humanism', *HJ*, 34 (1991), 257–77, and 'On the Road to 1534: The Occupation of Tournai and Henry VIII's Theory of Sovereignty', in Dale Hoak, ed., *Tudor Political Culture* (Cambridge, 1995), 11–30. More sceptical views: C. S. L. Davies, 'Tournai and the English Crown, 1513–1519', *HJ*, 41 (1998), 1–26; G. W. Bernard, *The Late Medieval English Church* (New Haven, 2012), 41–3.

25. Wilkie, *Protectors*, 89–96; Peter Gwyn, *The King's Cardinal* (1990), 85–6, 95–6.

26. Roper, 235; Thomas Malory, *Le Morte D'Arthur*, ed. Janet Cowen (2 vols, Harmondsworth, 1969), I, 167–71; Anthony Goodman, 'Henry VII and Christian Renewal', in Keith Robins, ed., *Religion and Humanism* (Oxford, 1981), 125; Jon Whitman, 'National Icon: The Winchester Round Table and the Revelation of Authority', *Arthuriana*, 18 (2008), 33–65.

27. Christopher Harper-Bill, *The Pre-Reformation Church in England 1400–1530* (1989), 13–14; Bernard, *Church*, 22–3.

28. Robert Swanson, *Church and Society in Late Medieval England* (Oxford, 1989), 116–18; Steven Gunn, 'Edmund Dudley and the Church', *JEH*, 51 (2000), 515–18; G. R. Elton, ed., *The Tudor Constitution* (Cambridge, 1960), 62–3; Celsus Maffeus, *Celsi Veronensis dissuasoria* (1505); Thomson, *Church*, 31; J. J. Scarisbrick, 'Clerical Taxation in England, 1485–1547', *JEH*, 11 (1960), 41–54.

29. John A. F. Thomson, *Popes and Princes 1417–1517* (1980), 152–3; Thomson, *Church*, 29–30; Swanson, *Church*, 80–2; Kenneth Carleton, *Bishops and Reform in the English Church, 1520–1559* (Woodbridge, 2001), 7–9.

30. Rosemary O'Day, *The Longman Companion to the Tudor Age* (1995), 107–8.

31. Thomson, *Church*, 46–60; Haigh, 9–11; Stephen Thompson, 'The Bishop in his Diocese', in Brendan Bradshaw and Eamon Duffy, eds, *Humanism, Reform and the Reformation: The Career of Bishop John Fisher* (Cambridge, 1989), 250; Stephen Thompson, 'The Pastoral Work of the English and Welsh Bishops, 1500–1558', University of Oxford, D. Phil thesis (1984), 9–19.

32. M. M. Condon, 'Ruling Elites in the Reign of Henry VII', in Charles Ross, ed., *Patronage, Pedigree and Power in Later Medieval England* (Gloucester, 1979), 111; Margaret Bowker, 'Smith, William (d. 1514)', *ODNB*; Roper, 200; P. S. and H. M. Allen, eds, *Letters of Richard Fox, 1486–1527* (Oxford, 1929), 82–3; Dowling, *Fisher*, 54.

33. On this, and for the following, see Gwyn, *Cardinal*, 265–353; S. J. Gunn and P. G. Lindley, 'Introduction', in Gunn and Lindley, eds, *Cardinal Wolsey: Church, State and Art* (Cambridge, 1991), 1–53; Richard Rex, 'Cardinal Wolsey', *Catholic Historical Review*, 78 (1992), 607–14; Sybil M. Jack, 'Wolsey, Thomas (1470/71–1530)', *ODNB*.

34. *LP*, III, 600.

35. Thomson, *Popes*, 74–5.

36. Erika Rummel, *Jiménez de Cisneros: on the Threshold of Spain's Golden Age* (Tempe, AZ, 1999).

37. Gwyn, *Cardinal*, 49–50.

38. Eric Ives, *The Common Lawyers of Pre-Reformation England* (Cambridge, 1983).

39. R. M. Helmholz, *Roman Canon Law in Reformation England* (Cambridge, 1990); Ralph Houlbrooke, *Church Courts and the People during the English Reformation 1520–1570* (Oxford, 1979), 7–54.

40. Swanson, *Church*, 140–90; Thomson, *Church*, 74–90; Harper-Bill, *Pre-Reformation*, 55–63; John H. Baker, *The Oxford History of the Laws of England: Vol. VI, 1483–1558* (Oxford, 2003), 237, 242–3; Margaret Bowker, 'Some Archdeacons' Court Books and the Common's Supplication Against the Ordinaries', in D. A. Bullough and R. L. Storey, eds, *The Study of Medieval Records* (Oxford, 1971), 282–316; Richard Wunderli, *London Church Courts and Society on the Eve of the Reformation* (Cambridge, MA, 1981).

41. John Guy, 'Thomas Cromwell and the Intellectual Origins of the Henrician Revolution', in Alistair Fox and John Guy, eds, *Reassessing the Henrician Age* (Oxford, 1986), 165.

42. Swanson, *Church*, 184–5; P. R. Cavill, ' "The Enemy of God and His Church": James Hobart, Praemunire, and the Clergy of Norwich Diocese', *Journal of Legal History*, 32 (2011), 127–50; Wilkins, III, 583–5.

43. R. L. Storey, *Diocesan Administration in Fifteenth-Century England* (2nd edn, York, 1972), 29–32; Ralph Houlbrooke, 'The Decline of Ecclesiastical Jurisdiction under the Tudors', in Rosemary O'Day and Felicity Heal, eds, *Continuity and Change: Personnel and Administration of the Church in England 1500–1642* (Leicester, 1976), 240–1; Gunn, 'Dudley', 514–15; Cavill, ' "Enemy" ', 148.

44. Edmund Dudley, *The Tree of Commonwealth*, ed. D. M. Brodie (Cambridge, 1948), 41.

45. E. W. Ives, 'Crime, Sanctuary and Royal Authority under Henry VIII: the Exemplary Sufferings of the Savage Family', in M. S. Arnold et al., eds, *On the Laws and Customs of England* (Chapel Hill, NC, 1981), 296–320; Gregory O'Malley, *The Knights Hospitaller of the English Langue 1460–1565* (Oxford, 2005), 174–5 (noting that by 1520, the priory's privilege of sanctuary had effectively been lost); Bradin Cormack, *A Power to Do Justice: Jurisdiction, English Literature, and the Rise of Common Law, 1509–1625* (Chicago, 2007), 76–8; Bernard, *Church*, 37–9.

46. Swanson, *Church*, 149–53; Bernard, *Church*, 34–5; P. R. Cavill, 'A Perspective on the Church–State Confrontation of 1515: The Passage of 4 Henry VIII, c. 2', *JEH*, 63 (2012), 655–70.

47. Alcock, *[Sermon on Luke VIII]*, C4r–v, C6r.

48. Gwyn, *Cardinal*, 45; Cavill, ' "Enemy" ', 129–32

49. Gunn, 'Dudley', 515–16; J. B. Trapp, 'Urswick, Christopher (1448?–1522)', *ODNB*; J. B. Trapp, *Erasmus, Colet and More: The Early Tudor Humanists and their Books* (1991), 13–29.

50. J. P. Cooper, 'Henry VII's Last Years Reconsidered', *HJ*, 2 (1959), 124–5; Wilkins, III, 651; Houlbrooke, 'Decline', 240–1.

51. Lupton, *Colet*, 298; Gwyn, *Cardinal*, 46; P. R. N. Carter, 'Taylor, John (*d.* 1534)', *ODNB*; Richard J. Schoeck, 'Common Law and Canon Law in the Writings of Thomas More: The Affair of Richard Hunne', in Stephan Kuttner, ed., *Proceedings of the Third International Congress of Medieval Canon Law* (Vatican City, 1971), 239.

52. Arthur Ogle, *The Tragedy of the Lollards' Tower* (Oxford, 1949), 140–3; J. Duncan M. Derrett, 'The Affairs of Richard Hunne and Friar Standish', in Thomas More, *The Apology*, ed. J. B. Trapp (New Haven, 1979), 225–7; John C. Olin, ed., *The Catholic Reformation: Savonarola to Ignatius Loyola* (2nd edn, New York, 1992), 56–64 (quotation at 64).

53. The following paragraphs draw on the discussions of the case by Derrett, 'Hunne'; S. F. C. Milsom, 'Richard Hunne's Praemunire', *EHR*, 76 (1961), 80–2; John Fines, 'The Post-Mortem Condemnation for Heresy of Richard Hunne', *EHR*, 78 (1963), 523–31; Schoeck, 'Law', 237–54; Richard Wunderli, 'Pre-Reformation London Summoners and the Murder of Richard Hunne', *JEH*, 33 (1982), 218–24; Brigden, 98–103; Gwyn, *Cardinal*, 34–41; Haigh, 76–80; Bernard, *Church*, 1–16.

54. Peter Heath, *English Parish Clergy on the Eve of the Reformation* (1969), 153–6; Peter Marshall, *The Catholic Priesthood and the English Reformation* (Oxford, 1994), 186–7; Margaret Harvey, 'Some Comments on Northern Mortuary Customs in the Later Middle Ages, *JEH*, 59 (2008), 272–80; Will Coster, 'Tokens of Innocence: Infant Baptism, Death and Burial in Early Modern England', in Bruce Gordon and Peter Marshall, eds, *The Place of the Dead: Death and Remembrance in Late Medieval and Early Modern Europe* (Cambridge, 2000), 272–3.
55. Peter Iver Kaufman, 'Polydore Vergil and the Strange Disappearance of Christopher Urswick', *SCJ*, 17 (1986), 79–80.
56. More, *Apology*, 126; Thomas More, *A Dialogue Concerning Heresies*, ed. T. M. C. Lawler et al. (New Haven, 1981), 318, 326–7.
57. Thomas More, *Letter to Bugenhagen. Supplication of Souls. Letter against Frith*, ed. Frank Manley et al. (New Haven, 1990), 132–3.
58. *LP*, II, 215.
59. Gwyn, *Cardinal*, 39–40; E. Jeffries Davis, 'The Authorities for the Case of Richard Hunne', *EHR*, 30 (1915), 483–4; More, *Dialogue*, 318.
60. Davis, 'Hunne', 477–8.
61. Andrew A. Chibi, 'Standish, Henry (c.1475–1535)', *ODNB*. For what follows, Derrett, 'Hunne', 227–37; Gwyn, *Cardinal*, 47–50; *LP*, II, 1313; Gwyn, *Wolsey*, 47.
62. Schoeck, 'Law', 241.
63. *LP*, II, 1313.
64. SP 1/12, 16r–19r.
65. Ogle, *Tower*, 151–2.
66. Ogle, *Tower*, 153.
67. Compare Dickens, 13, with Scarisbrick, *Reformation*, 47 and Haigh, 82–3.
68. G. R. Elton, *Reform and Reformation: England 1509–1558* (1977), 56; LP, *II*, 1532; Henry Maynard Smith, *Pre-Reformation England* (1938), 66–7; Heath, *Clergy*, 124–5.
69. Peter Cunich, 'Kidderminster, Richard (c.1461–1533/4)', *ODNB*; Nicholas Orme, 'Veysey, John (c.1464–1554)', *ODNB*; Andrew A. Chibi, 'Standish, Henry (c.1475–1535)', *ODNB*.
70. Thomas More, *Utopia*, ed. George M. Logan and Robert M. Adams (Cambridge, 1989), 102.
71. BL, Cotton MS Tiberius E VIII, 89. For a variety of views on the dating of the revisions, see Walter Ullman, 'This Realm of England is an Empire', *JEH*, 30 (1979), 179; Haigh, 82; Pamela Tudor-Craig, 'Henry VIII and King David', in Daniel Williams, ed., *Early Tudor England* (Woodbridge, 1989), 187–9; Mayer, 'Tournai', 257n. On balance, a time in the late 1520s or 1530s seems most likely.
72. Roper, 235.

## 4 Marvellous Foolishness

1. SP 1/12, 17v–18r; J. H. Lupton, *Life of John Colet* (1887), 298.
2. See particularly R. I. Moore, *The Formation of a Persecuting Society* (2nd edn, Oxford, 2007); *The War on Heresy: The Battle for Faith and Power in Medieval Europe* (2012).
3. R. N. Swanson, *Catholic England* (Manchester, 1993), 35–8; G. W. Bernard, *The Late Medieval English Church* (New Haven, 2012), 216–31.
4. John Alcock, *[Sermon on Luke VIII]* (Westminster, ?1497, STC 285), C1v. This was a formula produced in the twelfth century by the ecclesiastical jurist Gratian: Andrew E. Larson, *The School of Heretics: Academic Condemnation at the University of Oxford, 1277–1409* (Leiden, 2011), 5–6.
5. John Mirk, *Instructions for Parish Priests*, ed. E. Peacock (1868), 22–4.
6. CWE, II, 189; John A. F. Thomson, *The Later Lollards 1414–1520* (Oxford, 1965), 237–8.
7. Richard Rex, *The Lollards* (Basingstoke, 2002), xii, 75–6; Mary Dove, *The First English Bible* (Cambridge, 2007).
8. Thomson, *Lollards*, 20–30, 68–72, 117–38, 173–90; Norman Tanner, ed., *Heresy Trials in the Diocese of Norwich, 1428–1431* (1977).

9. The term is Anne Hudson's: *The Premature Reformation* (Oxford, 1988), 121.

10. Thomson, *Lollards*, 47–8, 134; Rosemary C. E. Hayes, 'Goldwell, James (d. 1499)', *ODNB*; D. G. Newcombe, 'Mayhew, Richard (1439/40–1516)', *ODNB*.

11. Stephen Thompson, 'The Pastoral Work of the English and Welsh Bishops, 1500–1558', University of Oxford, D.Phil thesis (1984), 125; Margaret Aston, *Lollards and Reformers* (1984), 257.

12. Norman Tanner, ed., *Kent Heresy Proceedings 1511–12* (Stroud, 1997), ix–xii; Craig D'Alton, 'Heresy Hunting and Clerical Reform: William Warham, John Colet, and the Lollards of Kent, 1511–1512', in Ian Hunter, John C. Laursen and Cary J. Nederman, eds, *Heresy in Transition: Transforming Ideas of Heresy in Medieval and Early Modern Europe* (Aldershot, 2005), 103–14; D'Alton, 'The Suppression of Heresy in Early Henrician England', University of Melbourne PhD Thesis (1999), 25–47. The term 'abjuratio magna' was coined by the first major historian of Lollardy, John Foxe: Foxe (1583), 842.

13. J. Patrick Hornbeck, '*Wycklyffes Wycket* and Eucharistic Theology: Cases from Sixteenth-Century Winchester', in Mishtooni Bose and Hornbeck, eds, *Wycliffite Controversies* (Turnhout, 2011), 279–94; Thomson, *Lollards*, 49–51, 170–1; D'Alton, 'Suppression', 90–1; Brigden, 86–106.

14. Thompson, 'Bishops', 126; Thomson, *Lollards*, 90–4; John F. Davis, *Heresy and Reformation in the South East of England 1520–1559* (1983), 57–65; Bernard, *Church*, 211–15.

15. For procedures in heresy trials, see Thomson, *Lollards*, 220–36; Ian Forrest, *The Detection of Heresy in Late Medieval England* (Oxford, 2005), 197–206.

16. Norman Tanner, 'Penances Imposed on Kentish Lollards by Archbishop Warham 1511–12', in Margaret Aston and Colin Richmond, eds, *Lollardy and the Gentry in the Later Middle Ages* (Stroud, 1997), 229–49; Shannon McSheffrey and Norman Tanner, eds and tr, *Lollards of Coventry, 1486–1522* (2003), 7–11, 79, 85–6, 94, 242.

17. J. F. Davis, 'Lollard Survival and the Textile Industry in the South-East of England', in G. J. Cuming, ed., *Studies in Church History* (Leiden, 1966), 191–201.

18. Tanner, *Kent*, xviii; McSheffrey and Tanner, *Coventry*, 25.

19. Brigden, 96–8; Foxe (1583), 184; Andrew Hope, 'Lollardy: the Stone the Builders Rejected', in Peter Lake and Maria Dowling, eds, *Protestantism and the National Church in Sixteenth-Century England* (1987), 2–6; Derek Plumb, 'The Social and Economic Status of the Later Lollards', in Margaret Spufford, ed., *The World of Rural Dissenters 1520–1725* (Cambridge, 1995), 103–31, 132; McSheffrey and Tanner, *Coventry*, 27–31.

20. McSheffrey and Tanner, *Coventry*, 144–5; Andrew Hope, 'The Lady and the Bailiff: Lollardy among the Gentry in Yorkist and Tudor England', in Aston and Richmond, *Gentry*, 250–277; Shannon McSheffrey, *Gender and Heresy: Women and Men in Lollard Communities, 1420–1530* (Philadelphia, 1995), *passim*, against the drift of Margaret Aston, *Lollards*, 49–70, and Claire Cross, ' "Great Reasoners in Scripture": the Activities of Women Lollards, 1380–1530', in D. Baker, ed., *Medieval Women* (Oxford, 1978), 359–80.

21. Hudson, *Premature*, 467, 478; Margaret Aston and Colin Richmond, 'Introduction', in *Gentry*, 14; Thomson, *Lollards*, 82, 85–6. 'Rich' seems a more accurate translation of 'locupletes' than Thomson's 'trusty'. Cf. Brigden, 97. Other cases of Lollard clergy: McSheffrey, *Gender*, 146; Thomson, *Lollards*, 49; Norman P. Tanner, *The Church in Late Medieval Norwich, 1370–1532* (Toronto, 1984), 163.

22. Foxe (1583), 853; Brigden, 94; Hope, 'Lady', 250–1.

23. McSheffrey and Tanner, *Coventry*, 29, 41, 77, 104, 109 127, 139, 160; Hudson, *Premature*, 113; Foxe (1583), 854, 857.

24. Strype, I (2), 52–3.

25. Derek Plumb, 'A Gathered Church? Lollards and their Society', in Spufford, ed., *Dissenters*, 154–6; Hudson, *Premature*, 464–6; Brigden, 104–6; Foxe (1583), 839–40, 854.

26. Anne Hudson, *Lollards and their Books* (1985), 165–80.

27. Tanner, *Kent*, 19–21.

28. McSheffrey and Tanner, *Coventry*, 154. R. G. Davies, 'Lollardy and Locality', *TRHS*, 6th ser., 1 (1991), 191–212 is the best discussion of the social dynamics of Lollardy in its local settings.

29. For such 'secret sayings', Foxe (1583), 843; McSheffrey and Tanner, *Coventry*, 127.
30. Tanner, *Kent*, xviii–xix, 45–6.
31. A variation on R. G. Davies's celebrated conclusion that 'if Wyclifism was *what* you knew, Lollardy was *who* you knew': 'Locality', 212.
32. McSheffrey and Tanner, *Coventry*, 73; Tanner, *Kent*, 19.
33. Foxe (1583), 801, 827, 831, 854, 858, 861; Margaret Aston, 'Lollards and the Cross', in Fiona Somerset, Jill C. Havens and Derrick G. Pitard, eds, *Lollards and Their Influence in Late Medieval England* (Woodbridge, 2003), 113; McSheffrey and Tanner, *Coventry*, 66, 71; Tanner, *Kent*, 65, 67.
34. Thomson, *Lollards*, 112; Tanner, *Kent*, 65; Hudson, *Premature*, 285; Foxe (1583), 853–4.
35. Margaret Aston, *England's Iconoclasts* (Oxford, 1988), 124–32; Tanner, *Kent*, 53; Foxe (1583), 799, 843; McSheffrey and Tanner, *Coventry*, 66, 72, 96, 104, 151, 160, 199, 235.
36. Tanner, *Kent*, 52–3, 54; Hudson, *Premature*, 281–90; McSheffrey and Tanner, *Coventry*, 21; Hornbeck, '*Wycket*'; J. Patrick Hornbeck, *What is a Lollard? Dissent and Belief in Late Medieval England* (Oxford, 2010), 90–103 (to which I am indebted for the phrase 'local theologies'); Hope, 'Lady', 260.
37. Thomson, *Lollards*, 80; Hudson, *Premature*, 148, 149–50, 468; BL, Harley MS 421, 17v–18r; Foxe (1583), 1009.
38. Tanner, *Kent*, 6, 20, 47, 55; Foxe (1583), 854; McSheffrey and Tanner, *Coventry*, 218.
39. Foxe (1583), 854; McSheffrey and Tanner, *Coventry*, 160. The editors argue (29) that this implies Cook was hostile to Lollardy, but it might as easily suggest she was a cautious sympathizer. For hiding of books, ibid., 208, 218, 245, 248, 260, 263–4, 267, 270, 274.
40. McSheffrey and Tanner, *Coventry*, 189, 153; Hornbeck, '*Wycket*', 284, 286; Foxe (1583), 857.
41. J. A. F. Thomson, 'Knightly Piety and the Margins of Lollardy', in Aston and Richmond, *Gentry*, 95–111; Plumb, 'Status', 121–6; Bernard, *Church*, 217–18.
42. K. Wood-Legh, ed., *Kentish Visitations of Archbishop William Warham and his Deputies, 1511–1512* (Maidstone, 1984), 207.
43. Plumb, 'Church?', 132–3; McSheffrey, *Gender*, 73. Robert Lutton, *Lollardy and Orthodox Religion in Pre-Reformation England* (London, 2006), 170–1, 194–5 postulates in addition a degree of active sympathy among the orthodox with Lollard calls for reform.
44. Foxe (1583), 852–3; Hope, 'Lollardy', 4.
45. Foxe (1583), 839, 842, 859; McSheffrey, *Gender*, 94–5; Hope, 'Lady', 250–77; Strype, I (2), 55–6.
46. Foxe (1583), 850.
47. Foxe (1583), 859, 1008. For some of the complexities of the case, and a possible liaison between Cottismore and the priest, see McSheffrey, *Gender*, 114–16.
48. Foxe (1583), 1008–9.
49. Robert L. Williams, 'Aspects of Heresy and Reformation in England 1515–1540', University of Cambridge, PhD thesis (1976), 10.
50. Foxe (1583), 838, 853.
51. Foxe (1583), 799, 827.
52. Foxe (1583), 838; W. H. Hale, ed., *A Series of Precedents and Proceedings in Criminal Causes* (1847), 8–9; Wood-Legh, *Visitations*, 283.
53. Aston, *Iconoclasts*, 142; Margaret Aston, *Faith and Fire: Popular and Unpopular Religion, 1350–1600* (1993), 231–260.
54. BL, Harley MS 421, 28r–v.
55. Hudson, *Premature*, 480; Plumb, 'Status', 124–5; Davies, 'Locality', 206; Hope, 'Lady', 255, 264; Foxe (1583), 842.
56. Robert Lutton, 'Heresy and Heterodoxy in Late Medieval Kent', in Sheila Sweetinburgh, ed., *Later Medieval Kent 1220–1540* (Woodbridge, 2010), 178–9; Lutton, *Lollardy*, esp. 140–95; David Lamburn, *The Laity and the Church: Religious Developments in Beverley in the First Half of the Sixteenth Century* (York, 2000), 11–16.
57. Hudson, *Premature*, 172; Aston, *Lollards*, 263.
58. McSheffrey, *Gender*, 70; Foxe (1583), 827, 851.

59. Aston, *Lollards*, 208–12; Shannon McSheffrey, 'Heresy, Orthodoxy and Vernacular Religion, 1480–1525', *Past and Present*, 186 (2005), 64–7. On the *Kalendar of Shepherds*, see Duffy, 50–1, 365–6. A forthcoming Cambridge doctoral thesis by Morgan Ring argues for some ambivalence towards the status of imagery and pilgrimage in the *Golden Legend*.

60. Sabrina Corbellini, 'Instructing the Soul, Feeding the Spirit and Awakening the Passion: Holy Writ and Lay Readers in Medieval Europe', in Bruce Gordon and Matthew MacLean, eds, *Shaping the Bible in the Reformation* (Leiden, 2010), 15–40; Andrew Gow, 'Challenging the Protestant Paradigm: Bible Reading in Lay and Urban Contexts of the Later Middle Ages', in T. J. Hefferman and T. E. Burman, eds, *Scripture and Pluralism* (Leiden, 2005), 161–91; James Simpson, *Reform and Cultural Revolution* (Oxford, 2002), 434–40.

61. Thomas More, *A Dialogue Concerning Heresies*, ed. T. M. C. Lawler et al. (New Haven and London, 1981), 314–16; F. A. Gasquet, *The Old English Bible and Other Essays* (1897), 121–34; Rex, *Lollards*, 76; Dove, *Bible*, 38–40, 44–55.

62. Gail McMurray Gibson, *The Theater of Devotion: East Anglian Drama and Society in the Late Middle Ages* (Chicago, 1989), 28–30; Aston and Richmond, 'Introduction', in *Gentry*, 19. After his death, Cook was rumoured to have been a member of the 'sect', yet he was in office during, and apparently co-operated with, the episcopal crackdown of 1486: McSheffrey and Tanner, *Coventry*, 189, 315.

63. Greg Walker, *Persuasive Fictions* (Aldershot, 1996), 133; Brigden, 102, 107.

64. Lectionaries contain full texts of the readings, while *capitularia* are reference aids giving the opening and closing words of the lesson: Matti Peikola, 'The Sanctorale, Thomas of Woodstock's English Bible, and the Orthodox Appropriation of Wycliffite Tables of Lessons', in Bose and Hornbeck, *Controversies*, 163–4.

65. Dove, *Bible*, 61–7; Hudson, *Premature*, 198–9; Christopher de Hamel, *The Book: A History of the Bible* (2001), 166–7.

66. Hamel, *Book*, 187, noting such suppression was eminently possible: some mainstream Lollard texts do not survive in a single copy.

67. McSheffrey and Tanner, *Coventry*, 31–2; McSheffrey, 'Heresy', 61–2.

## 5 Converts

1. *CWE*, V, 327; Richard Rex, 'The Friars in the English Reformation', in Peter Marshall and Alec Ryrie, eds, *The Beginnings of English Protestantism* (Cambridge, 2002), 38.

2. *CWE*, VIII, 261, VI, 392, VII, 283, 313; *LP*, III, 640.

3. F. Madan, ed., 'The Daily Ledger of John Dorne, 1520', in *Collectanea*, Oxford Historical Society (1885), 71–178; Margaret Bowker, *The Henrician Reformation: The Diocese of Lincoln under John Longland, 1521–1547* (Cambridge, 1981), 58–9.

4. Richard Rex, 'The Early Impact of Reformation Theology at Cambridge University', *Reformation and Renaissance Review*, 2 (1999), 41–2; Maria Dowling, *Fisher of Men: A Life of John Fisher* (Basingstoke, 1999), 109–10.

5. Foxe (1583), 1216.

6. *The Anglica Historia of Polydore Vergil*, ed. Denys Hay, Camden Soc., 54 (1950), 277; *Manuscripts of Shrewsbury and Coventry Corporations [etc]: Fourth report, Appendix: Part X* (1899), 48; SP 1/22, 207r.

7. Diana Webb, *Pilgrimage in Medieval England* (2000), 243.

8. Maria Dowling, *Humanism in the Age of Henry VIII* (Beckenham, 1986), 41.

9. *LP*, III, 1210, 1234; Richard Rex, 'The English Campaign against Luther in the 1520s', *Transactions of the Royal Historical Society*, 5th ser. 39 (1989), 87–8.

10. Strype, I (2), 20–5.

11. Cecilia A. Hatt, ed., *English Works of John Fisher, Bishop of Rochester* (Oxford, 2002), 52–3, 85; RSTC 10894, 10894.5, 10895.

12. Henry Ellis, ed., *Original Letters* (4 vols, 1827), I, 286–8.

13. Erwin Doernberg, *Henry VIII and Luther* (1961), 17–19; David Bagchi, *Luther's Earliest Opponents* (Minneapolis, 1991), 123–8; Rex, 'Campaign', 98–9; Gergely Juhász,

'Henry VIII, Assertio Septem Sacramentorum' (Cat. Entry 18), in *Tyndale's Testament*, ed. Paul Arblaster et al. (Turnhout, 2002), 73–4.

14. Henry VIII, *Assertio Septem Sacramentorum*, ed. and tr. Louis O'Donovan (New York, 1908), 202–4, 216, 234–6, 312–14; Roper, 234–5; Rex, 'Campaign', 87; J. J. Scarisbrick, *Henry VIII* (1968), 112–13.
15. Martin Luther, *Contra Henricum Regem Angliae* (Wittenberg, 1522), extracts collated and translated in John Milner, *Letters to a Prebendary* (1801), 288.
16. *LP*, III, 3270; Rex, 'Campaign', 100–1.
17. Thomas More, *Responsio ad Lutherum*, ed. John H. Headley (New Haven, 1969), 11, 198–9.
18. Rex, 'Campaign', 89, 97; Thomas More, *Letter to Bugenhagen, Supplication of Souls, Letter Against Frith*, ed. Frank Manley et al. (New Haven, 1990), 399, 15, 17.
19. Dowling, *Fisher*, 65; Foxe (1583), 1008; Fisher, *Works*, 77.
20. John Ryckes, *The ymage of loue* (1525), E1v. See E. Ruth Harvey, 'The Image of Love', in Thomas More, *A Dialogue Concerning Heresies*, ed. T. M. C. Lawler et al. (New Haven and London, 1981), 729–59.
21. Foxe (1583), 1099.
22. Compare Donald D. Smeeton, *Lollard Themes in the Reformation Theology of William Tyndale* (Kirksville, MO, 1986) with Richard Rex, 'New Light on Tyndale and Lollardy', *Reformation*, 8 (2003), 143–71.
23. Foxe (1583), 1100.
24. Foxe (1583), 1099.
25. *Tyndale's Old Testament*, ed. D. Daniell (New Haven, 1992), 4–5.
26. Strype, I (2), 363–8; Foxe (1583), 1020–1.
27. BL, Cotton MS Vespasian C III, 211v–212r.
28. Elizabeth Vandiver et al., eds, *Luther's Lives* (Manchester, 2002), 181–2.
29. David Daniel, *The Bible in English* (New Haven, 2003), 133–9; Allan K. Jenkins and Patrick Preston, *Biblical Scholarship and the Church* (Aldershot, 2007), chs 4–5.
30. [*The New Testament*] (Worms, 1526), facsimile edition (Bristol, 1862), Tt1v–Tt2r.
31. [William Barlow], *A proper dyaloge, betwene a gentillman and a husbandman* (Antwerp, 1530), A7v; William Tyndale, *The Obedience of a Christen man* (Antwerp, 1528), 63v; Tyndale, 'To the Reader', in [*The Pentateuch*] (Antwerp, 1530); William Roye, *A Brefe Dialoge bitwene a Christen Father and his stobborne Sonne*, ed. Douglas H. Parker and Bruce Krajewski (Toronto, 1999), 99.
32. Tyndale, *Obedience*, 129v.
33. More, *Dialogue*, 285.
34. A. W. Pollard, ed., *Records of the English Bible* (1911), 124.
35. More, *Dialogue*, 284–90, 512–16; *The Confutation of Tyndale's Answer*, ed. L. A. Schuster et al. (New Haven, 1973), 143–5; *Supplication*, 161.
36. More, *Dialogue*, 368; William Barlow, *A dyaloge describing the originall grou[n]d of these Lutheran faccyons* (1531), X3r; Strype, I (2), 366; *Tyndale's New Testament*, ed. David Daniell (New Haven, 1995), 391–428.
37. Richard Rex, *The Theology of John Fisher* (Cambridge, 1991), 158–61; More, *Dialogue*, 337–8; Henry VIII, *A copy of the letters* (1527); Wilkins, III, 727–37; *TRP*, I, 196; Barlow, *Dyaloge*, A3v.
38. More, *Responsio*, 89; *Confutation*, 225–7, 254–9, 800, 805–12; *The Apology*, ed. J. B. Trapp (New Haven, 1979), 13.
39. William Tyndale, *An Answer to Sir Thomas More's Dialogue*, ed. Henry Walter (Cambridge, 1850), 24–30; Tyndale, *Expositions and Notes*, ed. Henry Walter (Cambridge, 1849), 100.
40. *A compendious olde treatyse* (Antwerp, 1530), A1v; Tyndale, *Answer*, 168.
41. *An exhortation to the diligent studye of scripture, made by Erasmus Roterodamus*, tr. William Roye (Antwerp, 1529).
42. *LP*, IV, 995, misdated to 1525.
43. *LP*, IV, 1962. Foxe (1583), 1217, suggests five 'Steelyard men' abjured, but records of examination survive for only four. Fisher, *Works*, 145–74.

44. James P. Lusardi, 'The Career of Robert Barnes', in More, *Confutation*, 1369-70; *LSG*, 166.
45. Foxe (1583), 1216; P. R. N. Carter, 'Bilney, Thomas (*c*.1495-1531)', *ODNB*.
46. Robert Barnes, *A supplicatyon* (Antwerp, 1531), 23r-35v; *A supplicacion* (1534), F1r-H1r.
47. Lusardi, 'Career', 1371-1382.
48. *LSG*, 166; Barnes, *Supplicacion* (1534), F1r-v. Fisher may have been suggesting that, as purveyors of meat, butchers had a vested interest in abolishing distinctions between feast days and fast days.
49. Fisher, *Works*, 147.
50. Hugh Latimer, *Sermons and Remains*, ed. G. E. Corrie (Cambridge, 1845), 332-3.
51. Ethan Shagan, *Popular Politics and the English Reformation* (Cambridge, 2003), 6-7.
52. BL, Harley MS 421, 11r-v, 17r-18r.
53. Strype, I (2), 63-5.
54. Strype, I (2), 55, 56, 60-2.
55. Strype, I (2), 54-5; BL, Harley MS 421, 35r. Hilles's testimony suggested the encounter took place around Whitsuntide 1527 rather than Michaelmas 1526.
56. Margaret Aston, *Lollards and Reformers* (1984), 220-9.
57. See, e.g., John F. Davis, *Heresy and Reformation in the South East of England 1520-1559* (1983), chs 4-5; Dickens, ch. 3.
58. Anne Hudson, *The Premature Reformation* (Oxford, 1988), 505-7.
59. More, *Apology*, 9; *CWE*, X, 464.
60. Jenkins and Preston, *Scholarship*, 83; Tyndale, *Answer*, 75.
61. Lusardi, 'Career', 1369; E. G. Rupp, *Studies in the Making of the English Protestant Tradition* (Cambridge, 1947), 17.
62. SP 1/47, 16v; More, *Dialogue*, 33.
63. *CWE*, XII, 165-71, 189-90.
64. Foxe (1583), 1070-1; Erasmus, *Colloquies*, 4-7; P. S. Allen, ed., *Opus Epistolarum Des. Erasmi Roterodami* (12 vols, Oxford, 1906-58), VIII, no. 2226.
65. Foxe (1583), 1071.
66. Fisher, *Works*, 92-5; Henry VIII, *Letters*, 6v-7v; Barlow, *Dyaloge*, B4v, C1v.
67. More, *Dialogue*, 257, 379, 418, 421.
68. BL, Cotton MS Cleopatra E V, 389v; Henry VIII, *Letters*, A7v; More, *Dialogue*, 165, 304, 346, 349, 360, 366, 368, 375-6, 378, 426, 434; *Confutation*, 41-2, 48-9, 181, 191, 204, 207, 209, 228, 262, 306, 443, 493-4, 496, 600, 638, 690, 726, 766, 808, 925-7, 932, 940.
69. More, *Confutation*, 35; *Apology*, 124-5; Germaine Gardiner, *A letter of a yonge gentylman* (1534), 3v, 5r; John Skelton, *The Complete Poems*, ed. John Scattergood (Harmondsworth, 1983), 374.
70. Rex, 'Impact', 55; P. R. N. Carter, 'Bilney, Thomas (*c*.1495-1531)', *ODNB*; D. R. Leader, *A History of the University of Cambridge. Volume 1* (Cambridge, 1988), 150; Rex, 'Friars'.
71. J. F. Davis, 'The Trials of Thomas Bilney and the English Reformation', *HJ*, 24 (1981), 775-90; Davis, *Heresy and Reformation in the South East of England 1520-1559* (London, 1983), 47-8; Brigden, 111.
72. Gardiner, *Letter*, 41r.
73. Martin Luther, *On Translating: An Open Letter (1530), Luther's Works*, 55 vols (St Louis, 1960), XXXV, 187-9, 195.
74. E. G. Rupp and B. Drewery, eds, *Martin Luther* (1970), 5-6; William Tyndale, *Parable of the Wicked Mammon* (Antwerp, 1528), 7v; *Testament*, ed. Daniell, 224; George Joye, *The Letters whyche Iohan Ashwell Priour of Newnham Abbey besydes Bedforde sente* (Strassburg, 1531), A6v-7r.
75. Foxe (1583), 1029; More, *Dialogue*, 255.
76. Nicholas Harpsfield, *The Life and Death of Sir Thomas More*, ed. E. V. Hitchcock and R. W. Chambers (1932), 83-9.
77. Helen Parish, *Clerical Marriage and the English Reformation* (Aldershot, 2000), esp. ch. 5; Peter Marshall, *Beliefs and the Dead in Reformation England* (Oxford, 2002), 47-64.
78. SP 1/104, 202r; Roye, *Dialoge*, 150; Tyndale, *Obedience*, 83r, 96v.
79. More, *Dialogue*, 389; *Confutation*, 90-1. See also Brigden, 119.

80. SP 1/47, 75r-v.

81. Mark U. Edwards, *Printing, Propaganda and Martin Luther* (Minneapolis, 1994), 113-14; Carl Trueman, *Luther's Legacy: Salvation and English Reformers 1525-1556* (Oxford, 1994), 169-71; More, *Dialogue*, 382, 393; Thomas More, *The Answer to a Poisoned Book*, ed. S. M. Foley and C. H. Miller (New Haven, 1985), 39.

82. Trueman, *Legacy*, 84-120. For the claim that Tyndale 'renounced his discipleship to Luther', William A. Clebsch, *England's Earliest Protestants, 1520-1535* (New Haven, 1964), 154-74 (quote at 155). For Lollard influence, Diarmaid MacCulloch, 'England', in Andrew Pettegree, ed., *The Early Reformation in Europe* (Cambridge, 1992), 172-3.

83. Alister E. McGrath, 'Sanctification', in Hans J. Hillerbrand, ed., *The Oxford Encyclopedia of the Reformation* (4 vols, Oxford, 1996), III, 480-2.

84. Marshall, 24-6; Brigden, 22; More, *Dialogue*, 380, 391.

85. Susan Wabuda, *Preaching During the English Reformation* (Cambridge, 2003), 84-5; Marshall, 30-2.

86. More, *Dialogue*, 139; Wabuda, *Preaching*, 168-75; Robert Lutton, '"Love this Name that is IHC": Vernacular Prayers, Hymns and Lyrics to the Holy Name of Jesus in Pre-Reformation England', in Elisabeth Salter and Helen Wicker, eds, *Vernacularity in England and Wales c. 1300-1550* (Turnhout, 2011), 119-45.

87. John Fewterer, *The Myrrour or glasse of christes passion* (1534), 30r; William Tyndale, *A path way i[n]to the holy scripture* (1536), D1r. See Ralph Werrell, *The Blood of Christ in the Theology of William Tyndale* (Cambridge, 2015); Caroline Walker Bynum, *Wonderful Blood: Theology and Practice in Later Medieval Northern Germany and Beyond* (Philadelphia, 2007). Harpsfield, *More*, 85-6; Foxe (1583), 1067.

88. Donald J. Harreld, *High Germans in The Low Countries: German Merchants and Commerce in Golden Age Antwerp* (Leiden, 2004), 51-2; John D. Fudge, *Commerce and Print in the Early Reformation* (Leiden, 2007), 16-17.

89. Paul Arblaster, 'Totius Mundi Emporium: Antwerp as a Centre for Vernacular Bible Translations, 1523-1545', in Jan L. de Long and Marc Van Vaeck, eds, *The Low Countries as a Crossroads of Religious Belief* (Leiden, 2004), 9-31; Wim François, 'The Antwerp Printers Christoffel and Hans (I) van Ruremund', *Archiv für Reformationsgeschichte*, 101 (2010), 7-28.

90. Anthea Hume, 'English Protestant Books Printed Abroad, 1525-1535: An Annotated Bibliography', in More, *Confutation*, 1065-80.

91. Fudge, *Commerce*, 164-7; Elizabeth F. Rogers, ed., *The Letters of Sir John Hackett 1526-1534* (Morgantown, 1971), 156, 201.

92. More, *Confutation*, 20; Andrew Hope, 'On the Smuggling of Prohibited Books from Antwerp to England in the 1520s and 1530s', in Arblaster, *Testament*, 35-7; Hall, 185r-v.

93. Brooke Foss Westcott, *A General View of the History of the English Bible* (3rd edn, New York, 1916), 37.

94. Hackett, *Letters*, 173.

95. SP 1/47, 99r-100v; Brigden, 114-16; A. G. Dickens, *Late Monasticism and the Reformation* (1994), 119.

96. SP 1/47, 11r.

97. SP 147, 16v; Foxe (1583), 1056.

98. SP 1/47, 10v, 65r, 149v; Andrew Hope, 'Bayfield, Richard (d. 1531)', *ODNB*; Foxe (1583), 1045.

99. SP 1/47, 16v; *LP*, III (1), 1193 (assigned to 1521, but contents and context of Warham's letter clearly place it in 1528).

100. Rupp, *Tradition*, 21-2; Dickens, 100; Craig W. D'Alton, 'The Suppression of Lutheran Heretics in England, 1526-1529', *JEH*, 54 (2003), 252; Davis, 'Bilney', 775-90; Greg Walker, *Persuasive Fictions* (Aldershot, 1996), 143-65; D'Alton, 'Suppression', 241-6.

101. Foxe (1583), 1056; (1563), 711.

102. Foxe (1583), 1045-6, 1056; Carl R. Trueman, 'Barnes, Robert (c.1495-1540)', *ODNB*; H. L. Parish, 'Joye, George (1490x95-1553)', *ODNB*.

103. Latimer, *Remains*, 334.

104. Maryanne Kowaleski, 'Port Towns: England and Wales 1300–1540', in David M. Palliser, ed., *The Cambridge Urban History of Britain Volume 1: 600–1540* (Cambridge, 2000), 467–94; Fudge, *Commerce,* 115–20; A. G. Dickens, *Lollards and Protestants in the Diocese of York* (Cambridge, 1959), 24–7; Foxe (1583), 1009.

105. *LP,* IV (2), 4396, 4407, 5097; Fudge, *Commerce,* 197–202; Brigden, 116–17.

106. Foxe (1583), 1037–8; Rodney M. Fisher, 'Simon Fishe, Cardinal Wolsey and John Roo's Play at Gray's Inn, Christmas 1526', *Archiv für Reformationsgeschichte,* 69 (1978), 293–8. The *Supplycacyon* is reproduced in More, *Bugenhagen,* 412–22.

107. Foxe (1583), 1038, 1041. Confusion surrounds the dating of this episode. Several authorities assert – on no clear basis – that it coincided with opening of Parliament (3 November 1529). David Starkey points out the King's itinerary has him at Greenwich at Candlemas: *Six Wives: The Queens of Henry VIII* (2003), 449. Yet Starkey's redating to 1532 is implausible. Foxe states that Wolsey warned Henry about it, placing the episode in the first half of 1529. Either Foxe was confused about the day, or, more likely, about the presence of the King.

108. *TRP,* I, 181–5.

109. More, *Bugenhagen,* 111–69, quotations at 128, 132, 162.

110. More, *Correspondence,* 386–8.

111. More, *Dialogue,* 201, 405–6, 410, 415.

112. *CWE,* VIII, 259–61.

113. Peter Marshall, 'The Naming of Protestant England', *Past and Present,* 214 (2012), 87–128.

114. Fisher, *Works,* 164

115. Tyndale, *Answer,* 107.

116. Henry VIII, *Letters,* E6r; More, *Apology,* 5; Gardiner, *Letter,* 37v. Revealingly, since the author was himself an abjured heretic, the phrase 'new gospeller' occurs repeatedly in Barlow's *Dyaloge*: C2v, M2v, N1r, O1r, Y1r.

117. SP 1/65, 91v; SP 1/237, 95r; More, *Apology,* 5, 7, 14, 17, 156–7, 313; *Confutation,* 14, 18, 333; Gardiner, *Letter,* 20v; Rupp, *Tradition,* 6–9.

118. Thomas More, *The Debellacyon of Salem and Bizance* (1533), 29r–30v; R. Rex, 'The New Learning', *JEH,* 44 (1993), 26–44.

119. Fisher, *Works,* 95; More, *Responsio,* 224; Jerome Barlow and William Roye, *Rede me and be nott wrothe* (Strassburg, 1528), B8v; John Frith, *The revelation of Antichrist* (Antwerp, 1529), 54r–v; Roye, *Dialogue,* 150; Tyndale, *Expositions,* 242; *Answer,* 190; [*Pentateuch*], note on Deut. 1:43–4 (modern numbering); [George Joye?], *The Souper of the Lorde,* in More, *Poisoned,* 309.

120. More, *Poisoned,* 147; *Confutation,* 962.

121. Barlow, *Dialogue,* C2v; John Gwynneth, *The co[n]futacyon of the fyrst parte of Frythes boke* (St Albans, 1536), Prologue; [Joye], *Souper,* 325, 326, 327, 335; Tyndale, *Answer,* 21, 32, 36, 63, 107; *Obedience,* 42r, 65r, 159r.

122. Willem Nijenhuis, *Ecclesia Reformata* (Leiden, 1994), 42.

123. Fisher, *Works,* 150; Barlow, *Dyaloge,* G1v–4v

124. William Tyndale, *Doctrinal Treatises,* ed. H. Walter (Cambridge, 1848), 37–4; Marshall, *Beliefs,* 223–4; *Testament,* ed. Daniell, 13–16.

125. More, *Confutation,* 301; Foxe (1583), 1105.

126. Stephen M. Foley and Clarence H. Miller, 'The Shape of the Eucharistic Controversy', in More, *Poisoned,* xvii–lxi; John Frith, *A Christen Sentence,* in More, *Bugenhagen,* 425–33; Gardiner, *Letter,* 26v.

127. Frith, *Sentence,* 428.

### 6 Martyrs and Matrimony

1. *LP,* II, p. 1559; Hall, 81v–82r; David Starkey, *Six Wives: The Queens of Henry VIII* (2003), 264–6.

2. Jonathan A. Reid, *King's Sister – Queen of Dissent: Marguerite of Navarre (1492–1549)* (2 vols, Leiden, 2009); Philip Hughes, *Lefèvre: Pioneer of Ecclesiastical Renewal in France* (Grand Rapids, MI, 1984).

3. William Latymer, 'A Chronicle of Anne Boleyn', ed. Maria Dowling, *Camden Miscellany XXX* (1990), 63; Maria Dowling and Joy Shakespeare, eds, 'Religion and Politics in Mid Tudor England through the Eyes of an English Protestant Woman: The Recollections of Rose Hickman', *Bulletin of the Institute of Historical Research*, 55 (1982), 97.

4. *LP*, V, 1114.

5. Lucy Wooding, *Henry VIII* (2nd edn, Abingdon, 2015), 136.

6. Judith M. Richards, *Mary Tudor* (2008), 45–8; Beverley A. Murphy, 'Fitzroy, Henry, duke of Richmond and Somerset (1519–1536)', *ODNB*.

7. Henry Ansgar Kelly, *The Matrimonial Trials of Henry VIII* (Stanford, 1976), 5–17; J. J. Scarisbrick, *Henry VIII* (1968), 177–8.

8. Starkey, *Wives*, 284–94; Wooding, *Henry VIII*, 132–3; Eric Carlson, *Marriage and the English Reformation* (Oxford, 1994), 68–9; Peter Gwyn, *The King's Cardinal* (1990), 501–2.

9. SP 1/42, 158r–161v.

10. SP 1/42, 158v; Jonathan Woolfson, 'Wakefield, Robert (*d.* 1537/8)', *ODNB*; Cathy Curtis, 'Pace, Richard (1483?–1536)', *ODNB*; Kelly, *Trials*, 35–6; Virginia Murphy, 'The Literature and Propaganda of Henry VIII's First Divorce', in Diarmaid MacCulloch, ed., *The Reign of Henry VIII* (Basingstoke, 1995), 138–42; Richard Rex, *The Theology of John Fisher* (Cambridge, 1991), 165–9. David S. Katz, in *The Jews in the History of England, 1485–1850* (Oxford, 1994), 21–2, suggests the term *aririm* refers generally to barrenness.

11. Rex, *Fisher*, 165, 168; Wooding, *Henry VIII*, 149–50; Murphy, 'Literature', 142–3.

12. *LP*, VII, 289; Strype, I (2), 196–7.

13. Murphy, 'Literature', 144–5.

14. Nicholas Pocock, ed., *Records of the Reformation* (2 vols, 1870), I, 88–9: Starkey, *Wives*, 321–9; Scarisbrick, *Henry*, 206–9.

15. Scarisbrick, *Henry*, 212–19; Starkey, *Wives*, 338–9.

16. *CSP, Spain*, III (2), no. 586; Hall, 180r–v.

17. J. S. Brewer, *The Reign of Henry VIII* (2 vols, 1884), II, 486; *CSP, Spain*, III (2), no. 621.

18. *LP*, IV, 4977; *CSP, Spain*, III (2), no. 600; Eric Ives, *The Life and Death of Anne Boleyn* (Oxford, 2004), 114–15.

19. George Cavendish, *The Life and Death of Cardinal Wolsey*, ed. R. S. Sylvester and D. P. Harding (New Haven, 1962), 80–8.

20. Scarisbrick, *Henry*, 225.

21. *LP*, IV, 5774, 5778; Scarisbrick, *Henry*, 225–7; Stanford E. Lehmberg, *The Reformation Parliament 1529–1536* (Cambridge, 1970), 2; Hall, 83r.

22. *LP*, IV, 5862.

23. Hall, 183r; John Guy, *The Public Career of Sir Thomas More* (New Haven, 1980), 206; *CSP, Spain*, IV (1), no. 601.

24. Stella Fletcher, *Cardinal Wolsey* (2009), 153–5.

25. *LP*, IV, 6035; Lehmberg, *Reformation*, 4–5.

26. Cavendish, 'Wolsey', 107–13; SP 1/55, 198r; Guy, *Career*, 206.

27. Hall, 187r.

28. Hall, 184v; Charles Sturge, *Cuthbert Tunstall* (1938), 177; Guy, *Career*, 32–3.

29. *The chronicle of Fabyan* (1542), 487.

30. Hall, 188r.

31. Lehmberg, *Reformation*, 81–6, 91–4, 101–4.

32. Hall, 188r; Lehmberg, *Reformation*, 84.

33. Maria Dowling, *Fisher of Men: A Life of John Fisher, 1469–1535* (Basingstoke, 1999), 139–40; Hall, 188v–189r.

34. *LP*, IV, 5416.

35. *CSP, Spain*, IV (1), no. 224. Chapuys writes the date as 28 Oct., misleading some historians, but context makes clear 28 Nov. was meant.

36. Foxe (1583), 1038; Thomas S. Freeman, 'Research, Rumour and Propaganda: Anne Boleyn in Foxe's "Book of Martyrs"', *HJ*, 38 (1995), 802–3, 805–10.

37. *Narratives*, 52–7; S. W. Singer, ed., *The Life of Cardinal Wolsey by George Cavendish* (London, 1827), 438–41.

38. William Tyndale, *The Obedie[n]ce of a Christen Man* (Antwerp, 1528), quotes at 79r, 157r, 157v.
39. Thomas More, *The Answer to a Poisoned Book*, ed. S. M. Foley and C. H. Miller (New Haven, 1985), 9; Cavendish, 'Wolsey', 183–4.
40. Brad C. Pardue, *Printing, Power, and Piety* (Leiden, 2012), 123–37 (quotation at 133).
41. Foxe (1583), 1176.
42. *LP*, V, 148, 246, 248; *CSP, Spain*, IV (2), no. 664.
43. *LP*, V, 532, 533; William A. Clebsch, *England's Earliest Protestants, 1520–1535* (New Haven, 1964), 51–4; Thomas More, *The Confutation of Tyndale's Answer*, ed. L. A. Schuster et al. (New Haven, 1973), 9, 885; Foxe (1583), 1218; James P. Lusardi, 'The Career of Robert Barnes', in More, *Confutation*, 1390–5; *LP*, V, 593.
44. *Narratives*, 240–2; MacCulloch, 44–7. The idea of defending the King's cause in foreign universities was mooted by Wakefield in 1527: Bernard, 15.
45. *LP*, VII, 289; *CSP, Spain*, IV (1), no. 547.
46. Murphy, 'Literature', 152–3; Guy Bedouelle, 'The Consultations of the Universities', in David C. Steinmetz, ed., *The Bible in the Sixteenth Century* (Durham, NC, 1990), 25–6; Kelly, *Trials*, 175–6; Virginia Murphy, 'Burgo, Nicholas de (*fl.* 1517–1537)', *ODNB*.
47. Bedouelle, 'Consultations', 26–9; J. Christopher Warner, *Henry VIII's Divorce: Literature and the Politics of the Printing Press* (Woodbridge, 1998), 22.
48. *CSP, Spain*, IV (1), no. 354; *LP*, IV, 6513; Ives, *Boleyn*, 135; Burnet, IV, 169–73.
49. *LP*, IV, 6738; V, 171; Edward Surtz and Virginia Murphy, eds, *The Divorce Tracts of Henry VIII* (Angers, 1988), i–xxxiii; Murphy, 'Literature', 155–7.
50. SP 1/58, 108r–112v; *CSP, Spain*, IV (1), no. 445; *LP*, IV, 6759; Roper, 228.
51. Richard Rex, 'The Religion of Henry VIII', *HJ*, 57 (2014), 29.
52. BL, Cotton MS Cleopatra E VI, 16r–135r.
53. Graham D. Nicholson, 'The Nature and Function of Historical Argument in the Henrician Reformation', University of Cambridge PhD (1977), 182–3.
54. R. N. Swanson, 'Problems of the Priesthood in Pre-Reformation England', *EHR*, 417 (1990), 864.
55. *CSP, Milan*, 831; *CSP, Venice*, IV, 629, 634; Guy, *Career*, 136–8; G. R. Elton, *Reform and Reformation: England, 1509–1558* (1977), 139–40; *LP*, IV, 6699.
56. The following draws selectively on J. J. Scarisbrick, 'The Pardon of the Clergy, 1531', *Cambridge Historical Journal*, 12 (1956), 22–39; Scarisbrick, *Henry*, 273–80; Lehmberg, *Reformation*, 109–16; Elton, *Reform*, 139–45; Guy, *Career*, 136–8, 147–51; Guy, 'Henry VIII and the Praemunire Manoeuvres of 1530–31', *EHR*, 97 (1982), 481–503; G. W. Bernard, 'The Pardon of the Clergy Reconsidered', *JEH*, 37 (1986), 258–87.
57. Lehmberg, *Reformation*, 114; *CSP, Spain*, IV (2), no. 635; *LP*, V, 45.
58. Scarisbrick, *Henry*, 276–8.
59. *LP*, V, 45; *CSP, Spain*, IV (2), no. 641; Scarisbrick, *Henry*, 281; Guy, *Career*, 178–9.
60. More, *Confutation*, 13–17; Foxe (1583), 2159–60.
61. [George Joye], *Ortulus anime* (Antwerp, 1530), A3v.
62. More, *Confutation*, 13, 17.
63. In the Calendar prefixed to the 1563 and 1583 editions of *Acts and Monuments*, Foxe listed a further four persons supposedly martyred in 1531. Of these, Valentine Freez and his wife must have been executed in or after 1540, when they appear in the York records: A. G. Dickens, *Lollards and Protestants in the Diocese of York* (Cambridge, 1959), 32–3. An 'old man of Buckinghamshire', burned for eating pork in Lent (Foxe (1563), 546), disappeared from the text (though not the Calendar) after 1563, probably because Foxe could not verify the story. Of 'Davy Foster, martyr', noted tersely in the Calendar for 11 March, nothing further is known.
64. Thomas More, *The Apology*, ed. J. B. Trapp (New Haven, 1979), 162; *TRP*, I, 181–6 (misdated to 1529), 193–7.
65. Though recycled in modern history books (and novels), allegations (publicized by Foxe) that More supervised the torture of suspects were refuted by him in systematic detail (*Apology*, 116–20), and are probably largely groundless.

66. James Davis, 'The Christian Brethren and the Dissemination of Heretical Books', in R. N. Swanson, ed., *The Church and the Book* (Woodbridge, 2004), 194–5; *LP*, IV, 6738.
67. More, *Confutation*, 813; Louis A. Schuster, 'Thomas More's Polemical Career, 1523–1533', in More *Confutation*, 1250–1; Brigden, 197–8.
68. Andrew Hope, 'Bayfield, Richard (*d.* 1531)', *ODNB*; More, *Confutation*, 21; Foxe (1583), 1048–50.
69. Foxe (1583), 1051–4; *CSP*, Venice, IV, no. 765.
70. Foxe (1583), 1032; Mary C. Erler, *Women, Reading and Piety in Late Medieval England* (Cambridge, 2002), 100–2.
71. SP 1/68, 76v.
72. More, *Confutation*, 22–6.
73. Foxe (1583), 1035.
74. Lehmberg, *Reformation*, 117; John Craig and Caroline Litzenberger, 'Wills as Religious Propaganda: the Testament of William Tracy', *JEH*, 44 (1993), 424–5; Hugh Aveling and W. A. Pantin, eds, *The Letter Book of Robert Joseph* (Oxford, 1967), 101.
75. BL, Cotton MS Cleopatra E V, 389v; Gee, 162.
76. George Joye, *The letters which Iohan Ashwel . . . sente secretely to the Bishope of Lyncolne* (Antwerp, 1531), A3r.
77. More, *Poisoned*, 4–5; *Apology*, 135, 158–60.
78. BL, Cotton MS Cleopatra E V, 389r.
79. More, *Apology*, 156–8; SP 1/65, 191r–192r.
80. Foxe (1583), 1054–5; Walter F. Schirmer, *John Lydgate*, tr. Ann E. Keep (1961), 157–8; Margaret Aston, *Faith and Fire: Popular and Unpopular Religion, 1350–1600* (1993), 263–6.
81. BL, Harley MS 419, 125r–v; Foxe (1583), 1061–4; Thomas S. Freeman, 'Dusgate, Thomas (*d.* 1532)', *ODNB*; MacCulloch, 71–2.
82. Roper, 216.
83. Lehmberg, *Reformation*, 135–8; *LP*, V, 832; *CSP*, Spain, IV (2), no. 926; Gee, 178–95.
84. SP 1/69, 121r; Hall, 202r; Brigden, 205–6.
85. For government sponsorship, G. R. Elton, 'The Commons' Supplication of 1532', *EHR*, 66 (1951), 507–34; for Cromwell's directing role, Guy, *Career*, 186–99, Haigh, 111–14; for spontaneity (and confusion), J. P. Cooper, 'The Supplication against the Ordinaries Reconsidered', *EHR*, 72 (1957), 616–41; M. J. Kelly, 'The Submission of the Clergy', *TRHS*, 5th ser., 15 (1965), 97–119; Bernard, 58–66.
86. Gee, 145–53.
87. SP 6/7, 16r–20r.
88. T. F. T. Pluncket and J. L. Barton, eds, *St German's Doctor and Student* (1974), 327–8.
89. Hall, 202v.
90. *LP*, V, 941; Nicholas Harpsfield, *A Treatise on the Pretended Divorce*, ed. Nicholas Pocock (1878), 202–33; John Stow, *Annales* (1615), 561; Guy, *Career*, 210.
91. *LP*, V, 941, 989; Lehmberg, *Reformation*, 146n.
92. *CSP*, Spain, IV (2), nos 922, 926; *CSP*, Venice, IV, 761; *LP*, V, 879, 898.
93. Gerald Bray, ed., *The Anglican Canons, 1529–1947* (Woodbridge, 1998), 2–67.
94. *LP*, V, 860; Jonathan M. Gray, *Oaths and the English Reformation* (Cambridge, 2013), 185–8.
95. Wilkins, III, 746; *CSP*, Venice, IV, 754; Lehmberg, *Reformation*, 144.
96. SP 1/70, 209r–215v.
97. Marshall, 126–7; MacCulloch, 103; Bernard, 175.
98. Gee, 154–76.
99. Hall, 203r, 205r; *LP*, V, 989.
100. Kelly, 'Submission', 112–13; SP 6/2, 22r–39v; 6/1, 36r–40v.
101. Hall, 205r–v.
102. Guy, *Career*, 197–8; *CSP*, Spain, IV (2), no. 951.
103. Guy, *Career*, 207–8, 210–11. For More as political plotter, see G. R. Elton, 'Sir Thomas More and the opposition to Henry VIII', *Bulletin of the Institute of Historical Research*, 41 (1968), 19–34.

104. *CSP, Spain*, IV (2), no. 951; *LP*, V, 1013; Hall, 203v.

105. Kelly, 'Submission', 115-17; Lehmberg, *Reformation*, 151-2; Wilkins, III, 749; *LP*, V, 287.

106. Elizabeth F. Rogers, ed., *St Thomas More: Selected Letters* (New Haven, 1961), 202.

107. *Opus epistolarum Des. Erasmi Roterodami*, ed. P. S. Allen and H. M. Allen (12 vols, Oxford, 1906-58), X, 116, 135, 180.

108. J. J. Scarisbrick, 'Warham, William (1450?-1532)', *ODNB*. ·

109. MacCulloch, 75-7, 82-3; Ives, *Boleyn*, 156-61.

110. *A glasse of the truthe* (1532), quotations at B2r, D4v, D8v, E5r, E5v, E7v, F2r-v.

111. More, *Apology*, 8.

112. More, *Confutation*, 6, 7, 37; *Apology*, 11, 123.

## 7 Supremacy

1. Thomas Wright, ed., *Three Chapters of Letters relating to the Suppression of Monasteries* (1843), 8-9, 12.

2. Hugh Latimer, *Sermons and Remains*, ed. G. E. Corrie (Cambridge, 1845), 317-21.

3. MacCulloch, 637-8.

4. Gee, 187-9.

5. John Guy, *Tudor England* (Oxford, 1988), 133-4.

6. Stanford E. Lehmberg, *The Reformation Parliament 1529-1536* (Cambridge, 1970), 174-5; Bernard, 211.

7. *LP*, IX, 1077 (misdated to 1535).

8. MacCulloch, 88-9.

9. Lehmberg, *Reformation*, 177-9; MacCulloch, 83-4.

10. *LP*, VI, 562 (i); Roper, 229-30; Brigden, 217.

11. *CSP, Spain*, IV (1), no. 547; Eric Ives, *The Life and Death of Anne Boleyn* (Oxford, 2004), 177-8; *LP*, VI, 923-4; C. L. Kingsford, ed., *Two London Chronicles from the Collection of John Stow* (1910), 8.

12. For what follows, see Diane Watt, 'Barton, Elizabeth (c.1506-1534)', *ODNB*; Ethan Shagan, *Popular Politics and the English Reformation* (Cambridge, 2003), 61-85; Cranmer, 272-4; L. E. Whatmore, ed., 'The Sermon against the Holy Maid of Kent and her Adherents', *EHR*, 58 (1943), 463-75.

13. SP 1/185, 21r; MacCulloch, 98.

14. *LP*, VI, 1487-8.

15. *Articles deuisid by the holle consent of the kynges moste honourable counsayle* (1533), 1r-10v.

16. *TRP*, I, 209-11; Lehmberg, *Reformation*, 190-9; Gee, 225; J. A. Guy, 'The Law of Heresy', in Thomas More, *The Debellation of Salem and Bizance*, ed. J. Guy, R. Keen, C. H. Miller and R. McGugan (New Haven, 1987), lxii-lxvii; Brigden, 218-19.

17. Lehmberg, *Reformation*, 194-6.

18. Jonathan M. Gray, *Oaths and the English Reformation* (Cambridge, 2013), 57-8.

19. *LSG*, 57.

20. Gray, *Oaths*, 58-77.

21. G. R. Elton, *Policy and Police* (Cambridge, 1972), 222-4; Peter Marshall, 'The Last Years', in George Logan, ed., *The Cambridge Companion to Thomas More* (Cambridge, 2011), 121-3.

22. Kenneth Carleton, 'Wilson, Nicholas (d. 1548)', *ODNB*; David Knowles, *The Religious Orders in England III: The Tudor Age* (Cambridge, 1959), 209-11, 215-16, 229-30; SP 3/7, 166r; *LP*, VII, 1057.

23. Elton, *Policy*, 120-1; Gray, *Oaths*, 118; SP 1/92, 171v; 1/97, 58r; 1/76, 200r.

24. *LP*, VII, 690.

25. SP 1/102, 73v; 1/132, 155; *LP*, XIII (2), 613.

26. Knowles, *Religious*, 229-31; L. E. Whatmore, *The Carthusians under King Henry VIII* (Salzburg, 1983), 27; Thomas Rymer, *Foedera* (20 vols, London, 1704-35), XIV, 498; SP 1/84, 239.

27. Felicity Heal, *Reformation in Britain and Ireland* (Oxford, 2003), 130–1; Henry A. Jefferies, *The Irish Church and the Tudor Reformations* (Dublin, 2010), 71–3.
28. R. Dudley Edwards, 'Venerable John Travers and the Rebellion of Silken Thomas', *Studies: An Irish Quarterly Review*, 23 (1934), 687–99; Colm O'Clabaigh, *The Franciscans in Ireland, 1400–1534* (Dublin, 2002), 78; *LP*, VIII, 48.
29. Peter Marshall, '"The Greatest Man in Wales": James ap Gruffydd ap Hywel and the International Opposition to Henry VIII', *SCJ*, 39 (2008), 681–704.
30. *LP*, VIII, 609.
31. *LP*, VII, 259, 406, 140.
32. Elton, *Policy*, 208n, 347; *LP*, VI, 1492; VIII, 196; VII, 1609.
33. *LP*, VI, 790 (i); XIII (2), 307; IX, 74; VIII, 278. For other cases of people stating or implying Henry was a heretic, Shagan, *Politics*, 32–6.
34. Gee, 247–52; *LP*, VIII, 856; Lehmberg, *Reformation*, 203–6.
35. Gee, 243–7, 253–6.
36. The following paragraphs draw on F. Donald Logan, 'Thomas Cromwell and the Vicegerency in Spirituals: a Revisitation', *EHR*, 103 (1988), 658–67; MacCulloch, 125–35; Malcolm B. Yarnell, *Royal Priesthood in the English Reformation* (Oxford, 2013), 151–4.
37. Cranmer, 304–5.
38. Douglas H. Parker, *A Critical Edition of Robert Barnes's A Supplication Vnto the Most Gracyous Prince Kynge Henry the. VIIJ. 1534* (Toronto, 2008), 16–20.
39. Philip Hughes, *The Reformation in England* (3 vols, 1950–54), I, 266n; *LP*, VI, 1460.
40. Ives, *Boleyn*, 261–2; Andrew A. Chibi, *Henry VIII's Bishops* (Cambridge, 2003), Appendix.
41. *LP*, IX, 965; Tracey Sowerby, '"All our books do be sent into other countries and translated": Henrician Polemic in its International Context', *EHR*, 121 (2006), 1271–99.
42. Richard Rex, 'Ridley, Robert (*d.* 1536?)', *ODNB*.
43. C. D. C. Armstrong, 'Gardiner, Stephen (*c.*1495x8–1555)', *ODNB*; Richard Rex, 'The Crisis of Obedience: God's Word and Henry's Reformation', *HJ*, 39 (1996), 885–7.
44. Elton, *Policy*, 231–5; Aude de Mézerac-Zanetti, 'Reforming the Liturgy under Henry VIII: The Instructions of John Clerk, Bishop of Bath and Wells', *JEH*, 64 (2013), 96–111; SP 1/93, 29; Henry Ellis, ed., *Original Letters Illustrative of English History* (3rd ser.,4 vols, 1846), II, 338–9.
45. Folger, L.b.339 (a copy sent to the JPs of Surrey); *TRP*, I, 230.
46. Elton, *Policy*, 85–9; *LP*, VIII, 406–7.
47. Cranmer, 460–1.
48. *LP*, IX, 1059, 681.
49. Brigden, 258; *LP*, VIII, 1054; BL, Add. MS 48022, 87r–88r.
50. Duffy, 82–3.
51. Rex, 'Crisis', 879–80; Brad C. Pardue, *Printing, Power, and Piety: Appeals to the Public during the Early Years of the English Reformation* (Leiden, 2012), 175–7; SP 1/103, 331v.
52. Ethan Shagan, 'Clement Armstrong and the Godly Commonwealth', in Peter Marshall and Alec Ryrie, eds, *The Beginnings of English Protestantism* (Cambridge, 2002), 60–83; Karl Gunther and Ethan Shagan, 'Protestant Radicalism and Political Thought in the Reign of Henry VIII', *Past and Present*, 194 (2007), 35–74; Yarnell, *Royal*, 163–4; I. Gadd, 'Gibson, Thomas (*d.* 1562)', *ODNB*; Karl Gunther, *Reformation Unbound: Protestant Visions of Reform in England, 1525–1590* (Cambridge, 2014), 87–9.
53. *LP*, X, 371; Gunther, *Reformation*, 74–5; Ives, *Boleyn*, 326; MacCulloch, 147.
54. *TRP*, I, 227–8; R. W. Heinze, *The Proclamations of the Tudor Kings* (Cambridge, 1976), 135.
55. SP 1/237, 284r; A. G. Dickens, *Lollards and Protestants in the Diocese of York* (Oxford, 1959), 75; Strype, I (1), 442; BL, Cotton MS Cleopatra E V, 397r–v.
56. *LP*, VIII, 771, 826, 846; Wriothesley, I, 28; Foxe (1583), 1073.
57. Wriothesley, I, 28; Knowles, *Religious*, 229–36; Roper, 242.
58. Whatmore, *Carthusians*, 4, 101–10, 140–2; Nicholas Harpsfield, *The Life and Death of Sir Thomas Moore*, ed. E. V. Hitchcock (1932), 232–40.

59. *LP*, VIII, 742, 876; Maria Dowling, *Fisher of Men: A Life of John Fisher, 1469-1535* (Basingstoke, 1999), 159-67.

60. *LP*, VIII, 876; Marshall, 'Last', 123-33.

61. Wright, *Letters*, 34-5; *LP*, IX, 46, 873; XI, 486; Elton, *Policy*, 157, 355-6.

62. Hughes, *Reformation*, I, 280; Whatmore, *Carthusians*, 73-4, 83; Strype, I (1), 304-6; *LP*, VIII, 801.

63. Roper, 248.

64. Dowling, *Fisher*, 170-3; David Starkey and Susan Wabuda, 'Acton Court and the Progress of 1535', in *Henry VIII: A European Court in England* (1991), 118.

65. *LP*, IX, 321-2.

66. Maria Dowling, ed., 'William Latymer's Cronickille of Anne Bulleyne', *Camden Miscellany XXX* (1990), 60-1.

67. *LP*, VIII, 955.

68. Joyce Youings, *The Dissolution of the Monasteries* (1971), 151-2; G. W. Bernard, 'The Dissolution of the Monasteries', *History*, 96 (2001), 390-409.

69. Knowles, *Religious*, 270-3; F. D. Logan, 'The First Royal Visitation of the English Universities, 1535', *EHR*, 106 (1991), 861-88 (though noting that Aristotelian logic continued to be taught).

70. Bernard, 247; SP 1/98, 22r.

71. Bernard, 258-64; Knowles, *Religious*, 289; Wright, *Letters*, 97: A. N. Shaw, 'The *Compendium Compertorum* and the Making of the Suppression Act of 1536', University of Warwick PhD thesis (2003), chs 3-4. Shaw demonstrates (335-6) that the decision to record cases of masturbation was taken at a meeting of Cromwell with the principal visitors at Winchester in September 1535, after the visitation was under way.

72. SP 1/95, 38r-v; Wright, *Letters*, 58-9, 85; SP 1/102, 85r-104r; Wriothesley, I, 31.

73. Marshall, 136-7.

74. Elton, *Policy*, 244-5; Duffy, 387-9; Margaret Bowker, *The Henrician Reformation: The Diocese of Lincoln under John Longland 1521-1547* (Cambridge, 1981), 144-5.

75. *LP*, X, 59, 141. Though for scepticism about Chapuys' report, see Suzannah Lipscomb, *1536: The Year that Changed Henry VIII* (Oxford, 2009), 52-3.

76. *LP*, X, 284.

77. *LP*, X, 282, 283, 351.

78. Hughes, *Reformation*, I, 387; Wright, *Letters*, 119.

79. Hugh Latimer, *Sermons*, ed. G. E. Corrie (Cambridge, 1844), 123; Youings, *Dissolution*, 155-6; Wright, *Letters*, 116-17.

80. Lehmberg, *Reformation*, 226; Wright, *Letters*, 38; MacCulloch, 151-2.

81. Latymer, 'Cronickille', 57-8 (noting that Anne slapped down petitioners who believed her a supporter of monasticism per se); Wright, *Letters*, 37. My account of the fall of Anne largely follows the interpretation of Ives, *Boleyn*, 306-37, though Ives makes no mention of the Haynes sermon.

82. MacCulloch, 155-6.

83. Rory McEntegart, *Henry VIII, The League of Schmalkalden, and the English Reformation* (2002), 29-58 (quote at 47); *LP*, IX, 1016.

84. Ives, *Boleyn*, 312-16; *CSP, Spain*, V (2), no. 61. For a different reading, stressing Anne's own culpability, see George Bernard, *Anne Boleyn: Fatal Attractions* (New Haven and London, 2010), 135-92.

85. *LP*, X, 752.

86. Cranmer, 323-4.

87. *LP*, X, 752.

88. Ives, *Boleyn*, 360-2; *CSP, Spain*, V, pt 2, no. 70; *LP*, X, 1137.

89. Burnet, VI, 172-6.

90. *LP*, X, 1093; Marshall, 242; Reginald Pole, *Defense of the Unity of the Church*, tr. Joseph Dwyer (Westminster, MD, 1965), 283.

91. Burnet, VI, 177-84.

92. MacCulloch, 160; Latimer, *Sermons*, 33-57; Duffy, 391-2.

93. Thomas Starkey, *Life and Letters*, ed. S. J. Herrtage (1878), lii-liii.

94. Lloyd, xi-xxxii, 1-20.

95. Alan Kreider, *English Chantries: The Road to Dissolution* (Cambridge, MA, 1979), 246–7; *CSP, Spain*, V (1), no. 43. MacCulloch, 165, argues the Wittenberg Articles only arrived in England with Foxe in July.
96. MacCulloch, 162–3.
97. Reproduced in Gerald Bray, ed., *Documents of the English Reformation* (Cambridge, 1994), 137.
98. Latimer, *Sermons*, 50; Starkey, *Life*, lv; BL, Cotton MS Cleopatra E V, 140r–142r.
99. Lloyd, 16–17.
100. *LP*, X, 1043; XI, 376; SP 1/101, 184r–185r; SP 1/113, 90r. For the Articles as fundamentally orthodox, Richard Rex, *Henry VIII and the English Reformation* (2nd edn, Basingstoke, 2006), 117–19; as quasi-Lutheran, Haigh, 128–30; Dickens, 200.
101. Kreider, *Chantries*, 121–2; *LP*, XI, 1110; MacCulloch, 165.
102. Wilkins, III, 823–4.
103. *VAI*, II, 1–11.
104. Bernard, 524; Rex, *Henry VIII*, 98–9; *LSG*, 66.
105. *Biblia the Bible, that is, the holy Scripture of the Olde and New Testament* (1535), ✠2r–4v. RSTC gives place of publication as Cologne, but a persuasive case for Antwerp is made by David Daniell, *The Bible in English* (New Haven, 2003), 179–80.
106. J. F. Mozley, *William Tyndale* (1937), 299–304. The traditional dating of Tyndale's execution to 6 October is corrected by Paul Arblaster, 'An Error of Dates?', *Tyndale Society Journal*, 25 (2003), 50–1.
107. *VAI*, II, 9.
108. In the event, only 243 of over 400 houses assessed at £200 were closed in 1536. The others were exempted, either in return for payments, or because room could not be found in larger monasteries for all inmates wishing to stay in the religious life: Peter Marshall, *Reformation England 1480–1642* (2nd edn, 2012), 46.
109. SP 1/113, 93r; Brigden, 279; SP 1/106, 228r.
110. Wilkins, III, 824.
111. Simon Matthew, *A sermon made in the cathedrall churche of Saynt Paule* (1535), C7v.

## 8 Pilgrimage Ends

1. *LP*, XI, 563, 564; 841.
2. *LP*, XII (1), 380; XI, 828, 854.
3. A. B. Emden, *A Biographical Register of the University of Oxford, 1501–40* (Oxford, 1974), 327–8; SP 1/110, 142r–v; *LP*, XII (1), 70.
4. Geoffrey Moorhouse, *The Pilgrimage of Grace* (2002), 52–3, 56–7; *LP*, XI, 853.
5. Anthony Fletcher and Diarmaid MacCulloch, *Tudor Rebellions* (6th edn, 2016), 27–8; SP 1/108, 45r–v; *LP*, XI, 780.
6. S. J. Gunn, *Charles Brandon, Duke of Suffolk c. 1484–1545* (Oxford, 1988), 144–6; *LP*, XI, 780.
7. For Aske as an instrument of the Percies, see G. R. Elton, 'Politics and the Pilgrimage of Grace', in B. Malament, ed., *After the Reformation* (New Haven, 1980), 25–56.
8. Michael Bush, *The Pilgrims' Complaint* (Farnham, 2009), 253; *LP*, XI, 828 (xii), 786; Michael Bush, 'The Pilgrimage of Grace and the Pilgrim Tradition of Holy War', in Colin Morris and Peter Roberts, eds, *Pilgrimage: The English Experience* (Cambridge, 2002), 178–98.
9. Bush, 'Pilgrimage', 187.
10. Hall, 230v.
11. Fletcher and MacCulloch, *Rebellions*, 32–3; Jonathan Gray, *Oaths and the English Reformation* (Cambridge, 2013), 143–69.
12. *CSP, Spain*, V (1), no. 257; R. W. Hoyle, 'Darcy, Thomas, Baron Darcy of Darcy (*b.* in or before 1467, *d.* 1537)', *ODNB*; Hoyle, *The Pilgrimage of Grace and the Politics of the 1530s* (Oxford, 2001), which arguably overstates the case for Darcy's loyalism.
13. *LP*, XII (1), 393, 946, 1175; XI, 826; Fletcher and MacCulloch, *Rebellions*, 34.
14. *LP*, XI, 1204, 957, 995.

15. Michael Bush, *The Pilgrimage of Grace* (Manchester, 1996), 399; Brigden, 251–2; SP 1/113, 60r–65r.
16. Marshall, 60–9; Duffy, 399–400.
17. G. R. Elton, *Policy and Police* (Cambridge, 1972), 63–4, 119, 138, 149–50, 157–9, 296, 350, 362–3; *LP*, XI, 1128.
18. *LP*, XII (1), 1080.
19. G. W. Bernard, 'Talbot, George (1468–1538)', *ODNB*.
20. Hoyle, *Pilgrimage*, 342–55, 460–3 (who is less inclined to see coherence in the articles).
21. Bush, *Complaint*, 103–4.
22. Ethan Shagan, *Popular Politics and the English Reformation* (2003), 101–6; Bush, *Complaint*, 46–53.
23. Mary Bateson, ed., 'The Pilgrimage of Grace and Aske's Examination', *EHR*, 5 (1908), 559; SP 1/117, 205v; Bush, *Complaint*, 53–61.
24. Moorhouse, *Pilgrimage*, 232–9.
25. The fullest study of the 'post-pardon revolts' is Michael Bush and David Bownes, *The Defeat of the Pilgrimage of Grace* (Hull, 1999).
26. Moorhouse, *Pilgrimage*, 309–46; Bush and Bownes, *Defeat*, 363–7, 413–14.
27. Richard Morison, *A Remedy for Sedition* (1536), E3r.
28. *LP*, XI, 848, 1194; XII, 463.
29. *CRP*, I, 120–1, 133, 149; *CSP, Spain*, V (2), nos 128, 134.
30. Emil Egli and Rudolf Schoch, eds, *Johannes Kesslers Sabbata, mit kleineren Schriften und Briefen* (St Gallen, 1902), 464; Rory McEntegart, *Henry VIII, The League of Schmalkalden, and the English Reformation* (2002), 82.
31. P. J. Holmes, 'The Last Tudor Great Councils', *HJ*, 33 (1990), 10–13.
32. Alexander Alesius, *Of the Auctorite of the Word of God agaynst the Bisshop of London* (?Leipzig, ?1537), sigs A5v–6v.
33. Alesius, *Auctorite*, sigs A8r, B6r–7r.
34. MacCulloch, 189–91; Strype, I (2), 381–2.
35. Hugh Latimer, *Sermons and Remains*, ed. G. E. Corrie (Cambridge, 1845), 380; *LSG*, 351.
36. *LP*, XII (1), 789; Lloyd, 128–9.
37. Lloyd, 125.
38. E. G. Rupp, *Studies in the Making of the English Protestant Tradition* (Cambridge, 1947), 140–7; Haigh, 132–3.
39. Margaret Aston, *England's Iconoclasts* (Oxford, 1988), 371–80, 413–25.
40. Lloyd, 134–8.
41. Cranmer, 351; MacCulloch, 199n.
42. *LP*, XII (2), App. 35; Cranmer, 344–6.
43. Cranmer, 338–40; SP 1/106, 22v.
44. Rupp, *Studies*, 139; *LP*, XII (2), 330.
45. Cranmer, 469–70.
46. G. F. Nott, ed., *The Works of Henry Howard, Earl of Surrey, and of Sir Thomas Wyatt the Elder* (2 vols, 1815–16), II, 423.
47. Cranmer, 83–114.
48. MacCulloch, 208–12.
49. Alan Kreider, *English Chantries: The Road to Dissolution* (Cambridge, MA, 1979), 133–4.
50. J. W. Clay, ed., *Yorkshire Monastic Suppression Papers* (Worksop, 1912), 34.
51. Bernard, 433–9; Hoyle, *Pilgrimage*, 239–40.
52. Thomas Wright, ed., *Three Chapters of Letters relating to the Suppression of Monasteries* (1843), 162–3; Gray, *Oaths*, 132; *LP*, XII (1), 1232–3; XII (2), 64.
53. As suggested by Bernard, 447–8, noting that pensions were now for the first time paid to all inmates of the dissolved houses.
54. P. H. Ditchfield and William Page, eds, *A History of the County of Berkshire: Volume 2* (1907), 82–5; Kreider, *Chantries*, 134–6.
55. *LP*, XIII (1), 102, 573.
56. G. W. O. Woodward, *The Dissolution of the Monasteries* (1966), 119; SP 1/192, 143r–v.

57. Marshall, 138–9.
58. Muriel St Clare Byrne, ed., *The Lisle Letters* (6 vols, Chicago, 1981), V, 1129; Wriothesley, I, 77, 84; Brigden, 290.
59. Wright, *Letters*, 143, 183–7; Latimer, *Remains*, 395; Wriothesley, I, 83.
60. Wriothesley, I, 77; Marshall, 199–226.
61. Susan Brigden, 'Henry VIII and the Crusade against England', in Thomas Betteridge and Suzannah Lipscomb, eds, *Henry VIII and the Court* (Farnham, 2013), 221; *CRP*, I, 196.
62. Cranmer, 378; *CSP, Spanish*, VI (1), no. 7.
63. Wriothesley, I, 92; Desmond Seward, *The Last White Rose* (2010), 273–9.
64. *VAI*, II, 34–43.
65. Peter Roberts, 'Politics, Drama and the Cult of Thomas Becket in the Sixteenth Century', in Morris and Roberts, *Pilgrimage*, 199–237.
66. *LP*, XIII (2), 1087; Arthur James Mason, *What became of the Bones of St Thomas?* (Cambridge, 1920), 132–4.
67. Marshall, 142–3.
68. *LP*, XIII (2), 442, 911.
69. Wriothesley, I, 81; *LP*, XIII (2), 596, 62; Henry Ellis, ed., *Original Letters Illustrative of English History* (3rd ser., 4 vols, 1846), III, 162–3. Duffy, 403, ascribes the letter to 1538, but 1539 is a better fit.
70. Roberts, 'Becket', 199; *The Newe Testamente both Latine and Englyshe* (Southwark, 1538), +2r–3r.
71. SP 1/123, 202v; *LP*, XIII (2), 571; *Narratives*, 350; *LP*, XIII (1), 975.

## 9 Mumpsimus and Sumpsimus

1. Brigden, 273–4.
2. Wriothesley, I, 83; *TRP*, I, 274.
3. Wriothesley, I, 90.
4. *LP*, XIII (2), 264–5, 427, 498; Rory McEntegart, *Henry VIII, The League of Schmalkalden, and the English Reformation* (2002), 116–30.
5. Wriothesley, I, 90; *CGF*, 42; John Bale, *A mysterye of inyquyte* (Antwerp, 1545), 54v.
6. Foxe (1583), 1125–45; Tom Betteridge, 'Lambert, John (*d.* 1538)', *ODNB*; MacCulloch, 232–4; Wriothesley, I, 89.
7. *TRP*, I, 270–6; G. R. Elton, *Policy and Police* (Cambridge, 1972), 255–8.
8. *LP*, XIII (2), 1179; Duffy, 412–15.
9. Burnet, VI, 223–7; *TRP*, I, 278–80.
10. *TRP*, I, 284–6.
11. *LJ*, I, 105.
12. Stanford Lehmberg, *The Later Parliaments of Henry VIII* (Cambridge, 1977), 61–4, 66–7.
13. Marshall, 32, 238.
14. *LP*, XIV (1), 980.
15. Tracey Sowerby, *Renaissance and Reform in Tudor England* (Oxford, 2010), 90–106 (quotes at 98, 102).
16. *LP*, XIV (1), 967; *LJ*, I, 109.
17. MacCulloch, 243–8; Muriel St Clare Byrne, ed., *The Lisle Letters* (6 vols, Chicago, 1981), V, 462–3.
18. Bernard, 504–5.
19. Gee, 303–19; *LJ*, I, 122; MacCulloch, 249.
20. *LP*, XIV (1), 1219, 1227–8; MacCulloch, 251–2; Foxe (1583), 1213.
21. McEntegart, *Schmalkalden*, 158–63.
22. Wriothesley, I, 101; Richard Rex, 'Fortescue, Sir Adrian (*c.*1481–1539)', *ODNB*; G. J. O'Malley, 'Dingley, Sir Thomas (1506x8–1539)', *ODNB*.
23. Bernard, 467–74.
24. R. Bayne, ed., *The Life of Fisher* (1921), 108; Wriothesley, I, 81, 105.
25. Alec Ryrie, *The Gospel and Henry VIII* (Cambridge, 2003), 214–17.
26. *LP*, XIV (2), 750, 423.

27. Burnet, IV, 424–5.
28. *LP*, XIV (2), 750.
29. *OL*, II, 614, 627.
30. *LSG*, 168–70.
31. *LP*, XV, 306, 312, 334; Foxe (1583), 1221–3; Brigden, 309–12; Wriothesley, I, 114.
32. Lehmberg, *Parliaments*, 90–2.
33. *LP*, XV, 495, 539, 697, 736–7.
34. Burnet, I (2), 292–301.
35. Peter Marshall, 'Crisis of Allegiance: George Throckmorton and Henry Tudor', in Peter Marshall and Geoffrey Scott, eds, *Catholic Gentry in English Society* (Aldershot, 2009), 49–50, 57–8; MacCulloch, 270.
36. Bodleian Library, Fol. Δ 624, 462.
37. MacCulloch, 272–4.
38. *LP*, XV, 953, 954. See Ethan H. Shagan, *The Rule of Moderation* (Cambridge, 2011), 85–98.
39. Brigden, 320–2; Ryrie, *Gospel*, 40–1.
40. Wriothesely, I, 121; Raphael Holinshed, *Chronicles* (1587), vol. VI, 95; Marshall, 'Crisis', 52–6. For other documented cases of nuns trying to maintain communal religious life, see Peter Cunich, 'The Ex-Religious in Post-Dissolution Society', in James G. Clark, ed., *The Religious Orders in Pre-Reformation England* (Woodbridge, 2002), 235–7.
41. Ryrie, *Gospel*, 202; Susan Brigden, *Thomas Wyatt* (2012), 519, 530–1.
42. Alec Ryrie, 'Lassells, John (d. 1546)', *ODNB*; *LP*, XIV (1), 1074.
43. MacCulloch, 277; Brigden, 330–5.
44. *CSP, Spanish*, VI (1), no. 166; A. G. Dickens, *Reformation Studies* (1982), 1–20; Thomas F. Mayer, *Reginald Pole* (Cambridge, 2000), 112–13.
45. Glyn Redworth, *In Defence of the Church Catholic: The Life of Stephen Gardiner* (Oxford, 1990), 130–55.
46. *TRP*, I, 296–8; Ronald Hutton, 'The Local Impact of the Tudor Reformations', in Christopher Haigh, ed., *The English Reformation Revised* (Cambridge, 1987), 118; Peter Northeast, ed., *Boxford Churchwardens' Accounts 1530–1561* (Woodbridge, 1982), 37.
47. *TRP*, I, 301–2.
48. Duffy, 431; Cranmer, 490; Foxe (1583), 1317; Brigden, 338.
49. Lacey Baldwin Smith, *A Tudor Tragedy* (1961), 160–6.
50. *LJ*, I, 164–5.
51. MacCulloch, 289–94.
52. Ryrie, *Gospel*, 183–7.
53. Brigden, 339; *VAI*, II, 88–9.
54. *LP*, XVIII, 546 (pp. 324–5).
55. The best reconstruction of these complex events is MacCulloch, 297–322.
56. Ryrie, *Gospel*, 48–9; Brigden, 345–51.
57. *Narratives*, 252. MacCulloch, 315, dates the episode to early September 1543.
58. MacCulloch, 264–5, 285. For the following, see Duffy, 434–42; Shagan, *Politics*, 197–227.
59. *Here folowith a scorneful image* (1543), C4r–v.
60. *LSG*, 336–7; Lloyd, 223, 365.
61. Lloyd, 263, 299, 310; *LSG*, 259.
62. Peter Marshall, *Beliefs and the Dead in Reformation England* (Oxford, 2002), 77–81; Duffy, 443; Richard Rex, 'The Religion of Henry VIII', *HJ*, 57 (2014), 24–5.
63. Lehmberg, *Parliaments*, 186–8; *LSG*, 122.
64. Ryrie, *Gospel*, 62–4, 107, 252–3, 266–70; Karl Gunther, *Reformation Unbound: Protestant Visions of Reform in England, 1525–1590* (Cambridge, 2014), 54–60.
65. Cranmer, 413; Ryrie, *Gospel*, 198.
66. *LP*, XIX (1), 444 (6), 853; Brigden, 353–4.
67. *LJ*, i, 253; Lehmberg, *Parliaments*, 198; Mears, 15–23; Cranmer, 494–5; Ryrie, *Gospel*, 52; *LP*, XX (1), 1118.
68. MacCulloch, 330–1.
69. *CGF*, 48; *Two notable sermones lately preached at Pauls Crosse* (1545), H7r, C2v–3v.

70. Brigden, 343–4, 358–9; Wriothesley, I, 152.
71. Duffy, 444–7.
72. Lehmberg, *Parliaments*, 200–1; *LP*, XX (1), 16.
73. Lehmberg, *Parliaments*, 214–15, 222–3, 225; *LP*, XX (2), 995.
74. *LSG*, 159–63; Henry Brinklow, *The lamentacyon of a Christen*, ed. J. M. Cowper (1874), 89–90, 98; Ryrie, *Gospel*, 145–56.
75. Alan Kreider, *English Chantries: The Road to Dissolution* (Cambridge, MA, 1979), 165–85; *LP*, XX (2), 1030.
76. SP 1/212, 110v–111r; Hall, 261r–262r
77. For an intriguing attempt to make sense of Henry's personal theology, see Alec Ryrie, 'Divine Kingship and Royal Theology in Henry VIII's Reformation', *Reformation*, 7 (2002), 49–77.
78. Cranmer, 414–15; Foxe (1583), 1268–9.
79. *OL*, II, 253–4.
80. Stephen Gardiner, *A detection of the deuils sophistrie* (1546); Richard Smyth, *The assertion and defence of the sacramente of the aulter* (1546); Smyth, *A defence of the blessed masse, and the sacrifice therof* (1546); William Peryn, *Thre godlye and notable sermons, of the sacrament of the aulter* (1546); Marshall, 245; MacCulloch, 354–5.
81. Susan Wabuda, 'Crome, Edward (d. 1562)', *ODNB*; Elaine Beilin, ed., *The Examinations of Anne Askew* (Oxford, 1996), xvii–xviii, 58–64; *CSP, Spanish*, VIII, no. 291; *TRP*, I, 373–6.
82. This is persuasively argued by Thomas S. Freeman, 'One Survived: The Account of Katherine Parr in Foxe's "Book of Martyrs"', in Thomas Betteridge and Suzannah Lipscomb, eds, *Henry VIII and the Court* (Farnham, 2013), 235–52; Foxe (1570), 1461–4.
83. Brigden, 373–7; *Narratives*, 41–4; Beilin, *Examinations*, 127–34, 154–5.
84. *LP*, XXI (2), 'Preface', vii–x.
85. MacCulloch, 356–7; *LP*, XXI (2), 605.
86. Wriothesely, I, 173; Foxe (1583), 1269.
87. *LP*, XXI (1), 1526; McEntegart, *Schmalkalden*, 212–13.
88. *LP*, XXI (2), 347, 381.
89. *LSG*, 246–9; Stanford Lehmberg, 'Southwell, Sir Richard (1502/3–1564)', *ODNB*.
90. *LP*, XXI (2), 554, 555; *CSP, Spanish*, VIII, no. 370.
91. Foxe (1583), 1315; *OL*, I, 41
92. Foxe (1583), 1315. Foxe got the report from Ralph Morice, who overheard Denny speaking of it to Cranmer. Another account in Foxe (1563), 871, has Paget and other councillors unsuccessfully urging the reinstatement of Gardiner.
93. Suzannah Lipscomb, *The King is Dead: The Last Will and Testament of Henry VIII* (2015), 82–90; Lucy Wooding, *Henry VIII* (2nd edn, Abingdon, 2015), 292–3;
94. Lipscomb, *Will*, 171–201; Foxe (1583), 1314;

## 10 Josiah

1. 'Wenlock', 98–110; W. K. Jordan, ed., *The Chronicle and Political Papers of King Edward VI* (Ithaca, NY, 1966), 4; John Cooper, *Propaganda and the Tudor State* (Oxford, 2003), 18–19.
2. *CRP*, II, nos 514–16; *OL*, I 257–8; William Thomas, *The Pilgrim*, ed. J. A. Froude (1861), 8, 80.
3. Cranmer, 126–7. For the forgery, Diarmaid MacCulloch, *All Things Made New: Writings on the Reformation* (2016), 321–58; for genuine comparisons, Stephen Alford, *Kingship and Politics in the Reign of Edward VI* (Cambridge, 2002), 50–3.
4. Folger, L.b.8.
5. *Calendar of Patent Rolls, Edward VI* (6 vols, 1924–9), I, 97; SP 10/1, 28r–v; Jennifer Loach, *Edward VI* (New Haven, 1999), 24–7.
6. *LSG*, 255–67, 273–5, 288; *APC*, II, 25–7; John Foxe, *Acts and Monuments*, ed. S. R. Cattley and G. Townsend (8 vols, 1837–41), V, App. XX; MacCulloch, 371; Muriel C. McLendon, 'Religious Toleration and the Reformation: Norwich Magistrates in the Sixteenth Century', in Nicholas Tyacke, ed., *England's Long Reformation 1500–1800* (1998), 95–6.

7. Foxe (1583), 1269; *TRP*, I, 387.

8. J. Andreas Löwe, *Richard Smyth and the Language of Orthodoxy* (Leiden, 2003), 34–8; L. E. C. Wooding, 'Peryn, William (*d.* 1558)', *ODNB*; Brigden, 427; Wriothesley, I, 184–5; John Hooper, *An Answer unto my lord of wynchesters booke* (Zürich, 1547), Q2v, not naming the church, but surely referring to the same episode.

9. *LP*, XI, 1350; Charles Kingsford, ed., *Two London Chronicles* (1910), 44 – not, as suggested by various authorities, the steeple of St Magnus.

10. R. B. Bond, ed., *Certain Sermons or Homilies (1547)* (Toronto, 1987), 190, 199–200. Cf. *Sermons*, ed. G. E. Corrie (Cambridge, 1844), 496, 521.

11. Bond, *Sermons*, 79–113, quotations at 82, 110, 112.

12. *LSG*, 278, 291 (quotations), 294, 308, 314–15, 330, 355–6, 362, 367, 371. In early 1549, the MP John Story was imprisoned for citing this text in the Commons: Julian Lock, 'Story, John (1503/4?–1571)', *ODNB*.

13. Diarmaid MacCulloch, *Tudor Church Militant: Edward VI and the Protestant Reformation* (1999), 20–30.

14. James McConica, *English Humanists and Reformation Politics* (Oxford, 1965), 231–2, 240–6; *The first tome or volume of the Paraphrase of Erasmus vpon the Newe Testamente* (1548), 3r.

15. *VAI*, II, 114–30; Duffy, 450–3.

16. John Strype, *Memorials of Thomas Cranmer* (3 vols, Oxford, 1848–53), II, 13–14; John Old, *A Confession of the Most Auncient and True Christen Catholike Olde Belefe* (Emden, 1556), E7r, A2v.

17. Duffy, 453–4, 480–1; *CGF*, 54–5; Wriothesley, II, 1; *CSP, Spain*, IX, 218–19.

18. Wriothesley, II, 1; W. A. Leighton, ed., 'Early Chronicles of Shrewsbury, 1372–1606', *Transactions of the Shropshire Archaeological and Natural History Society*, 3 (1880), 258; Donald Attwater, *The Penguin Dictionary of Saints* (1965), 246; 'Wenlock', 106.

19. *CGF*, 54; *APC*, II, 126–7; *LSG*, 378–400.

20. *APC*, II, 518; McClendon, 'Toleration', 96.

21. G. R. Elton, *Reform and Revolution* (1977), 342.

22. *CSP, Spain*, IX, 219–22; Wriothesley, I, 187.

23. Gee, 322–8; *TRP*, I, 410–12; Foxe (1563), 911.

24. *LJ*, I, 306; MacCulloch, 377.

25. *VAI*, II, 130; Gee, 328–57 (quotes at pp. 328–9, 339).

26. M. L. Bush, *The Government Policy of Protector Somerset* (1975), 13–19, 32–7.

27. *LJ*, I, 308, 313.

28. W. Haines, ed., 'Stanford Churchwardens' Accounts (1552–1602)', *Antiquary*, 17 (1888), 70.

29. *VAI*, II, 184–5; *TRP*, I, 416–17.

30. *APC*, II, 140–1; Hugh Latimer, *Sermons and Remains*, ed. G. E. Corrie (Cambridge, 1845), 76; Cranmer, 510; *OL*, II, 377.

31. Andrew Pettegree, 'Printing and the Reformation: The English Exception', in Peter Marshall and Alec Ryrie, eds, *The Beginnings of English Protestantism* (Cambridge, 2002), 171–2; Philip Nichols, *Here begyneth a godly new story* (1548), A3v; Whitney R. Jones, *William Turner* (1988), 19, 143–50; Brigden, 436–41; C. Bradshaw, 'Huggarde, Miles (*fl.* 1533–1557)', *ODNB*.

32. Alec Ryrie, *The Age of Reformation* (2009), 151–2.

33. Alec Ryrie, 'Counting Sheep, Counting Shepherds: The Problem of Allegiance in the English Reformation', in Marshall and Ryrie, *Beginnings*, 109.

34. *Narratives*, 77–8.

35. *TRP*, I, 407.

36. *Liturgies*, 3–8; *CGF*, 54–5; Brigden, 436; C. E. Woodruff, ed., 'Extracts from Original Documents illustrating the Progress of the Reformation in Kent', *Archaeologia Cantiana*, 31 (1915), 96–7; *TRP*, I, 417–18.

37. Diarmaid MacCulloch and Pat Hughes, eds, 'A Bailiff's List and Chronicle from Worcester', *Antiquaries Journal*, 74 (1995), 245–6; A. G. Dickens, *Reformation Studies* (1982), 295.

38. Ronald Hutton, 'The Local Impact of the Tudor Reformations', in Christopher Haigh, ed., *The English Reformation Revised* (Cambridge, 1987), 121–4; Duffy, 490–1; J. J. Scarisbrick, *The Reformation and the English People* (Oxford, 1984), 112–21; Peter Marshall, *The Catholic Priesthood and the English Reformation* (Oxford, 1994), 229–30.
39. Eamon Duffy, *The Voices of Morebath* (New Haven, 2001), 24–32, 119–23.
40. *Narratives*, 78; W. K. Jordan, *Edward VI: The Young King* (1968), 165; Duffy, *Morebath*, 120; Peter Marshall, *Beliefs and the Dead in Reformation England* (Oxford, 2002), 103–5.
41. William Page, ed., *The inventories of church goods for the counties of York, Durham, and Northumberland* (Durham, 1896), x–xi; *APC*, II, 534–5.
42. Frances Rose-Troup, *The Western Rebellion of 1549* (1913), 70–92; Cooper, *Propaganda*, 58–60.
43. *TRP*, I, 421–3; R. W. Dixon, *History of the Church of England* (3rd edn, 6 vols, 1895–1902), II, 485–6.
44. Foxe (1576), 1326–7, 1706–9; C. D. C. Armstrong, 'Gardiner, Stephen (*c.*1495x8–1555)', *ODNB*; Glyn Redworth, *In Defence of the Church Catholic: The Life of Stephen Gardiner* (Oxford, 1990), 275–81 (over-inclined to take Gardiner's 'support' for the regime's policies at face value).
45. Anne Overell, *Italian Reform and English Reformations, c. 1535–c.1585* (Aldershot, 2008), chs 2–5; MacCulloch, 394–6; *OL*, I, 322.
46. Francis A. Gasquet and Edmund Bishop, *Edward VI and the Book of Common Prayer* (3rd edn, 1891), 397–43. Cf. MacCulloch, 404–7.
47. *CJ*, I, 5; *LJ*, I, 330, 343.
48. Gee, 358–9.
49. Brian Cummings, ed., *The Book of Common Prayer* (Oxford, 2011), 46–57, 58–63, 64–71, 72–81; Carrie Euler, *Couriers of the Gospel: England and Zurich, 1531–1558* (Zürich, 2006), 237–55.
50. MacCulloch and Hughes, 'Bailiff's', 246; Dickens, *Studies*, 298–9.
51. Cummings, *Prayer*, 30, 89. Helpful discussions: ibid., xxv–xxxi; MacCulloch, 410–21; Duffy, 464–6.
52. *OL*, I, 348–51; II, 535–6.
53. Burnet, II, 203–4; Andrew Hope, 'Bocher, Joan (*d.* 1550)', *ODNB*; *OL*, I, 65–6.
54. Hugh Latimer, *Sermons*, ed. G. E. Corrie (Cambridge, 1844), 121–2, 129–30, 134.
55. *VAI*, II, 197–212; Peter Martyr Vermigli, *The Oxford Treatise and Disputation on the Eucharist*, ed. and tr. Joseph C. McLelland (Kirksville, MO, 2000), xvii–xxx; Overell, *Reform*, 106–9 (108 for 'B team').
56. Strype, *Cranmer*, III, 636–8. The action of the poem takes place in December, but its implication that the Prayer Book is a recent innovation, and an absence of reference to the summer tumults, may place composition in spring 1549.
57. Thomas F. Mayer, *Reginald Pole* (Cambridge, 2000), 169–70; SP 10/7, 74r–79r (quote at 76v).

## 11 Slaying Antichrist

1. Wriothesley, II, 9.
2. John Hooker, *The Description of the Citie of Excester*, ed. W. J. Harte et al. (3 vols, Exeter, 1919), II, 57.
3. Barret L. Beer, *Rebellion and Riot* (Kent, OH, 1982), 51–9; Hooker, *Excester*, II, 62–3; Anthony Fletcher and Diarmaid MacCulloch, *Tudor Rebellions* (6th edn, 2016), 54–7. A convincing case for the Cornish outbreak following, rather than preceding, Sampford Courtney is made by Mark Stoyle, ' "Fullye Bente to Fighte Oute the Matter": Reconsidering Cornwall's Role in the Western Rebellion of 1549', *EHR*, 129 (2014), 560–5.
4. Nicholas Pocock, ed., *Troubles Connected with the Prayer Book of 1549* (1884), 16; Fletcher and MacCulloch, *Rebellions*, 153–5.
5. Alison Hanham, ed., *Churchwardens' Accounts of Ashburton, 1479–1580* (Torquay, 1970), xi, 95, 100.
6. Frances Rose-Troup, *The Western Rebellion of 1549* (1913), 491–2.

7. Joyce Youings, 'The South-Western Rebellion of 1549', *Southern History*, 1 (1979), 105–7.

8. Amanda C. Jones, '"Commotion Time": The English Risings of 1549', University of Warwick PhD (2003), Map 1.1, and *passim*.

9. Andy Wood, *The 1549 Rebellions and the Making of Early Modern England* (Cambridge, 2007), 59–66.

10. Jones, 'Commotion', 112–22; Pocock, *Troubles*, 26; Katherine Halliday, 'New Light on the "Commotion Time" of 1549: The Oxfordshire Rising', *Historical Research*, 82 (2009), 657.

11. A. G. Dickens, *Reformation Studies* (1982), 28–38.

12. Ethan Shagan, 'Protector Somerset and the 1549 Rebellions: New Sources and New Perspectives', *EHR*, 114 (1999), 34–63.

13. Eamon Duffy, *The Voices of Morebath* (New Haven, 2001), 130–1.

14. Kett's articles: Fletcher and MacCulloch, *Rebellions*, 158–60.

15. Dickens, *Studies*, 37; Beer, *Rebellion*, 153–4.

16. Beer, *Rebellion*, 78–81.

17. Nicholas Sotherton, *The Commoyson in Norfolk 1549*, ed. Susan Yaxley (Stibbard, 1987), 41; Fletcher and MacCulloch, *Rebellions*, 73–4.

18. Frederic Russell, *Kett's Rebellion in Norfolk* (1859), 147; W. K. Jordan, ed., *The Chronicle and Political Papers of King Edward VI* (Ithaca, NY, 1966), 16. For England's 'largely peaceful Reformation', Christopher Haigh, ed., *The English Reformation Revised* (Cambridge, 1987), 5, 17.

19. Hooker, *Excester*, II, 88, 96; John Hayward, *The Life and Raigne of King Edward the Sixth*, ed. Barret L. Beer (Kent, OH, 1993), 82.

20. Edward, *Chronicle*, 13; *CSP, Venice*, V, no. 579.

21. [*Ballad on the defeat of the Devon and Cornwall rebels*] (1549); Pocock, *Troubles*, 141, 190; Cranmer, 165.

22. Thomas Cranmer, *Writings and Disputations*, ed. J. E. Cox (Cambridge, 1844), 302.

23. Stoyle, 'Rebellion', 570; Halliday, 'Light', 669–70; Hooker, *Excester*, II, 94.

24. Foxe (1583), 1328, 1337–8; Susan Brigden, ed., 'The Letters of Richard Scudamore', *Camden Miscellany XXX* (1990), 87; Brigden, 447–52.

25. MacCulloch, 443–5; Brigden, 497–9; *TRP*, I, 483; Barrett L. Beer, 'Seymour, Edward, duke of Somerset (*c*.1500–1552)', *ODNB*.

26. *OL*, I, 69; *LSG*, 440–1; *CSP, Spain*, IX, 458–9, 462.

27. *APC*, II, 344–5; *OL*, II, 395; *TRP*, I, 484.

28. Brigden, 'Scudamore', 96; *CSP, Spain*, IX, 489.

29. Thomas Mayer, *Cardinal Pole in European Context* (Aldershot, 2000), ch. 4.

30. David Loades, *John Dudley, Duke of Northumberland* (Oxford, 1996), 144–5; Edward, *Chronicle*, 19. There is debate around the timing of this episode, which Loades ascribes to 11 or 12 December. But Scudamore dates the confrontation to 'immediately after my writing of my last letters': Brigden, 'Scudamore', 107. *CSP, Spain*, X, 445; *TRP*, I, 485.

31. MacCulloch, 454–7; Peter Marshall, *The Catholic Priesthood and the English Reformation* (Oxford, 1994), 140; *APC*, II, 405.

32. Brigden, 'Scudamore', 122; Rose-Troup, *Rebellion*, 267; *OL*, II, 483; MacCulloch, 458–9.

33. 'Gardiner', *ODNB*; Foxe (1563), 843–4; Glyn Redworth, *In Defence of the Church Catholic: The Life of Stephen Gardiner* (Oxford, 1990), 286–7.

34. *OL*, II, 547; *VAI*, II, 191–3, 241–2, 292; Foxe (1583), 1330; John Bale, *An expostulation or complaint against the blasphemies of a frantic papist of Hampshire* (1551), C1v–2r.

35. Kenneth Fincham and Nicholas Tyacke, *Altars Restored: The Changing Face of English Religious Worship, 1547–c.1700* (Oxford, 2007), 15–18.

36. *APC*, III, 167–73, 176–8; Nicholas Ridley, *Works*, ed. Henry Christmas (Cambridge, 1843), 321–3.

37. John Hooper, *Early Writings*, ed. Samuel Carr (Cambridge, 1843), 488; *OL*, I, 87.

38. Hooper, *Early*, 479.

39. Foxe (1583), 1528; *Liturgies*, 169; Diarmaid MacCulloch, 'Peter Martyr and Thomas Cranmer', in Emidio Campi, ed., *Peter Martyr Vermigli* (Geneva, 2002), 190–1; *VAI*, II, 267–309; Diarmaid MacCulloch and Pat Hughes, eds, 'A Bailiff's List and Chronicle from Worcester', *Antiquaries Journal*, 74 (1995), 247.

40. Andrew Pettegree, *Foreign Protestant Communities in Sixteenth-Century London* (Oxford, 1986), 22–45 (quote at 35); Edward, *Chronicle*, 37.

41. Edward, *Chronicle*, 28; *CGF*, 66; W. K. Jordan, *Edward VI: The Threshold of Power* (1970), 328–9.

42. Andrew Hope, 'Bocher, Joan (*d.* 1550)', *ODNB*; Latimer, *Remains*, 114; Edmund Becke, *A brefe confutacion* (1550).

43. Andrew Pettegree, 'Parris, George van (*d.* 1551)', *ODNB*; Edward, *Chronicle*, 58; Champlin Burrage, *The Early English Dissenters* (2 vols, Cambridge, 1912), II, 1–6.

44. Ridley, *Works*, 331; Cranmer, *Disputations*, 196.

45. D. G. Newcombe, 'Ponet, John (*c.*1514–1556)', *ODNB*; H. L. Parish, 'Holgate, Robert (1481/2–1555)', *ODNB*; Dickens, *Studies*, 298.

46. *APC*, II, 232; Brigden, 453–5.

47. *CGF*, 67

48. *CSP, Spain*, IX, 444.

49. John Edwards, *Mary I* (New Haven, 2011), 71–4.

50. *CSP, Spain*, X, 258–60; Edward, *Chronicle*, 55–6; *CGF*, 69; SP 10/13, 73v.

51. Machyn, 4–5; F. W. Fincham, 'Notes from the Ecclesiastical Court Records at Somerset House', *TRHS*, 4th ser., 4 (1921), 117; *OL*, I, 94.

52. *OL*, II, 707–11; N. Scott Amos, 'Bucer, Martin (1491–1551)', *ODNB*; William Pauck, ed., *Melanchthon and Bucer* (1969), 174 ff, quote at 180.

53. *APC*, III, 228, 224; Edward, *Chronicle*, 53.

54. Brigden, 510–17; MacCulloch, 496–7; Jordan, *Threshold*, 54–6, 92–101; William Salesbury, *The Baterie of the Popes Botereulx* (1550), A2r; Foxe (1576), 1345; Edward, *Chronicle*, 107.

55. *APC*, III, 382; John Strype, *Life of Sir John Cheke* (Oxford, 1821), 70–86; C. S. Knighton, 'Feckenham, John (*c.*1510–1584)', *ODNB*; Patrick Collinson, *Archbishop Grindal* (1979), 60; Jane Dawson, *John Knox* (New Haven, 2015), 62–3; Susan Wabuda, 'Latimer, Hugh (*c.*1485–1555)', *ODNB*.

56. G. R. Elton, ed., *The Tudor Constitution* (2nd edn, Cambridge, 1982), 68; Penry Williams, *The Later Tudors* (Oxford, 1995), 154–5; *TRP*, I, 517.

57. *LJ*, I, 421; Gee, 369; *VAI*, II, 234, 247–8, 263, 291; Ralph Houlbrooke, *Church Courts and the People during the English Reformation* (Oxford, 1979), 243–4.

58. *VAI*, II, 238; *LJ*, I, 394.

59. Paul Sanders, 'Consensus Tigurinus', in Hans Hillebrand, ed., *The Oxford Encyclopedia of the Reformation* (4 vols, Oxford, 1996), I, 414–15.

60. *Liturgies*, 217, 265–6, 279, 282–3. For the Stranger connection, MacCulloch, 505–6.

61. Duffy, 472–5; Dickens, *Studies*, 304–5.

62. Cranmer, 430–4; *OL*, II, 711–13; MacCulloch, 518.

63. Catharine Davies, *A Religion of the Word: The Defence of the Reformation in the Reign of Edward VI* (Manchester, 2002), 204–9.

64. Edward, *Chronicle*, 119; 121–2; *Narratives*, 247; Ridley, *Works*, 59; *LJ*, I, 417–18; SP 10/15, 79r–v.

65. Diarmaid MacCulloch, 'The Importance of Jan Laksi in the English Reformation', in Christoph Strohm, ed., *Johannes a Lasco* (Tübingen, 2000), 335–6; Dawson, *Knox*, 63; SP 10/15, 79r.

66. *OL*, II, 591; *APC*, IV, 131.

67. Hooper, *Early*, 536; Peter Lorimer, *John Knox and the Church of England* (1875), 103–5; MacCulloch, 525–9.

68. MacCulloch, 532; Jennifer Loach, *Edward VI* (New Haven, 1999), 159; *CSP, Spain*, XI, 535.

69. Gerald Bray, ed., *Tudor Church Reform: The Henrician Canons of 1535 and the Reformatio Legum Ecclesiasticarum* (Woodbridge, 2000), 171–213, 225, 349–51, 341–3, 469–71, 267, 225, 267–73, 257, 519.

70. *CSP, Spain*, XI, 33; MacCulloch, 532–5.

71. Text of Primer in *Liturgies*, 357–484 (quote at 475), 520; Duffy, 537–8; Seymour Baker House, 'Becon, Thomas (1512/13–1567)', *ODNB*; John Bale, *Select Works*, ed. Henry Christmas (Cambridge, 1849), 612.

72. MacCulloch, 535–7; *CGF*, 77–8.

73. *Liturgies*, 535, 533, 536, 534, 530; John Calvin, *Institutes*, tr. Henry Beveridge (2 vols in 1, Grand Rapids, MI, 1989), II, 202–58.

74. Stephen Alford, *Kingship and Politics in the Reign of Edward VI* (Cambridge, 2002), 100–115; Ryan Reeves, *English Evangelicals and Tudor Obedience* (Leiden, 2014), 98–9.

75. *The Vocacyon of Johan Bale to the Bishoprick of Ossorie in Ireland* (1553); Leslie Fairfield, *John Bale* (West Lafayette, IN, 1976), chs 3–4.

76. John Proctor, *The Fal of the late Arrian* (1549), D3r, A8v, B3r. See Alec Ryrie, 'Paths Not Taken in the British Reformations', *HJ*, 52 (2009), 7–10.

77. J. G. Nichols, ed., *Literary Remains of King Edward VI* (2 vols, 1857), I, clxii–clxv; *CRP*, II, no. 601.

## 12  The Two Queens

1. Mears, 41–2.

2. For what follows, see Eric Ives, *Lady Jane Grey: A Tudor Mystery* (Chichester, 2009), 137–68; Dale Hoak, 'The Succession Crisis of 1553 and Mary's Rise to Power', in Elizabeth Evenden and Vivienne Westbrook, eds, *Catholic Renewal and Protestant Resistance in Marian England* (Farnham, 2015), 17–42. For the medical possibilities, Jennifer Loach, *Edward VI* (New Haven, 1999), 159–62.

3. MacCulloch, 538–41.

4. *The prayer of kynge Edwarde the syxte* (1553).

5. Ives, *Jane*, 189; Machyn, 35; Wriothesley, II, 86.

6. Robert Wingfield, 'Vita Mariae Angliae Reginae', ed. and tr. Diarmaid MacCulloch, *Camden Miscellany XXVIII* (1984), 251; Richard Garrnett, ed., *The accession of Queen Mary: being the contemporary narrative of a Spanish merchant resident in London* (1892), 89; C. V. Malfatti, ed., *The accession, coronation and marriage of Mary Tudor as related in four manuscripts of the Escorial* (Barcelona, 1956), 7; J. G. Nichols, ed., *The Legend of Sir Nicholas Throckmorton* (1874), 29; Ives, *Jane*, 227–8, 235–6.

7. Hoak, 'Crisis', 36; Linda Porter, *Mary Tudor* (2007), 192.

8. Hoak, 'Crisis', 39; *CQJ*, 6; Foxe (1583), 2110.

9. Jennifer Loach, *Parliament and Crown in the Reign of Mary Tudor* (Oxford, 1986), 1–5; Ives, *Jane*, 210–24, 241–4; *CQJ*, 11–12; Foxe (1583), 2111.

10. 'Wenlock', 108.

11. Loach, *Parliament*, 7; *CGF*, 78; Foxe (1583), 1432; John Bradford, *A sermon of repentaunce* (1553), A3r-v.

12. Anna Whitelock and Diarmaid MacCulloch, 'Princess Mary's Household and the Succession Crisis, 1553', *HJ*, 50 (2007), 265–87.

13. A. G. Dickens, *Reformation Studies* (1982), 307; *OL*, II, 741.

14. Andrew Pettegree, *Foreign Protestant Communities in Sixteenth-Century London* (Oxford, 1986), 114; Mark Taplin, 'Vermigli, Pietro Martire [Peter Martyr] (1499–1562)'; D. G. Newcombe, 'Hooper, John (1495x1500–1555)', *ODNB*; Machyn, 39; *CGF*, 82–4.

15. *CGF*, 81; Foxe (1583), 2111.

16. *CQJ*, 18–19; *The saying of Iohn late Duke of Northumberlande vppon the scaffolde* (1553).

17. *CQJ*, 25; Brigden, 531; Eamon Duffy, *Fires of Faith* (New Haven, 2009), 88, 219n.

18. Wingfield, 'Vita', 271; *OL*, I, 373; Foxe (1583), 1444; Ralph Houlbrooke, 'The Clergy, the Church Courts and the Marian Restoration in Norwich', in Eamon Duffy and David Loades, eds, *The Church of Mary Tudor* (Aldershot, 2006), 124–46.

19. Foxe (1583), 1523, 1740.

20. John Edwards, *Mary I* (New Haven, 2011), 117–19; Wingfield, 'Vita', 272; *Accession of Queen Mary*, 101.

21. Brigden, 528–9; Wingfield, 'Vita', 272–3; Wriothesley, II, 97–8; *Accession of Queen Mary*, 104–5; Foxe (1583), 1433, 1508.

22. *CGF*, 83; *APC*, IV, 317; *TRP*, II, 5–8.

23. Dickens, *Studies*, 308–9; 'Wenlock', 109; Wriothesley, II, 101.

24. Foxe (1583), 1556–7.

25. *Narratives*, 80–3; Foxe (1583), 2124.
26. *CSP*, *Spain*, XI, 220.
27. Machyn, 45–6; *OL*, I, 373; Gee, 377–80; Brigden, 533.
28. Foxe (1583), 1689–90.
29. Foxe (1583), 1543.
30. *CQJ*, 34; *APC*, V, 150; Eamon Duffy, *The Voices of Morebath* (New Haven, 2001), 153.
31. SP 11/2, 2r.
32. James Brooks, *A sermon very notable, fruictefull, and godlie* (1553), C4v, D6v.
33. *De vera obedientia An oration made in Latine, by the right Reuere[n]de father in God Stepha[n] bishop of Wi[n]chestre* ('Rome' [Wesel?], 1553).
34. *CRP*, II, 129–33; *CSP*, *Venice*, V, no. 766.
35. *CRP*, II, 169–70; *CSP*, *Spain*, XI, 214–21.
36. *CSP*, *Venice*, V, no. 813; Edwards, *Mary*, 141–2; Glyn Redworth, *In Defence of the Church Catholic: The Life of Stephen Gardiner* (Oxford, 1990), 300–6.
37. *A glasse of the truthe* (London, 1532), A3r–v.
38. Edwards, *Mary*, 147–9; *CRP*, II, 209–10; *CSP*, *Spain*, XI, 263. See M. A. Overell, 'Edwardian Court Humanism and *Il Beneficio di Cristo*, 1547–1553', in Jonathan Woolfson, ed., *Reassessing Tudor Humanism* (Basingstoke, 2002), 151–73.
39. Ian W. Archer, 'Courtenay, Edward, first earl of Devon (1526–1556)', *ODNB*.
40. *CSP*, *Spain*, XI, 328–9, 363–5; *CQJ*, 32.
41. Edwards, *Mary*, 156–8.
42. Edwards, *Mary*, 160–1; Patrick Collinson, 'Elizabeth I (1533–1603)', *ODNB*.
43. *CQJ*, 34; *CSP*, *Spain*, XII, 31.
44. David Loades, *Two Tudor Conspiracies* (2nd edn, Bangor, 1992), 25–49 (quote at 31).
45. Loades, *Conspiracies*, 59–60; Michael Zell, 'Landholding and the Land Market', in Zell, ed., *Early Modern Kent* (Woodbridge, 2000), 49; *CQJ*, 38–9.
46. Anthony Fletcher and Diarmaid MacCulloch, *Tudor Rebellions* (6th edn, 2016), 94.
47. Machyn, 53; *TRP*, II, 26–9; Foxe (1583), 1442–3.
48. Fletcher and MacCulloch, *Rebellions*, 94–5; Wingfield, 'Vita', 283; *CQJ*, 49–52.
49. *CSP*, *Spain*, XII, 106; Loades, *Conspiracies*, 123; Machyn, 56–7; Judith Richards, *Mary Tudor* (2008), 152; Archer, 'Courtenay'.
50. John Guy, *The Children of Henry VIII* (Oxford, 2013), 154–61; Collinson, 'Elizabeth'; *CQJ*, 73–4.
51. Stanford Lehmberg, 'Throckmorton, Sir Nicholas (1515/16–1571)', *ODNB*; Brigden, 551–2.
52. *CQJ*, 57; Foxe (1583), 1443–6.
53. *CSP*, *Spain*, XII, 146; *CQJ*, 67; A. G. Dickens, *Late Monasticism and the Reformation* (1994), 177–90.
54. *VAI*, II, 322–9.
55. Eamon Duffy, 'Hampton Court, Henry VIII and Cardinal Pole', in Thomas Betteridge and Suzannah Lipscomb, *Henry VIII and the Court* (Farnham, 2013), 210.
56. *LSG*, 496–501, Duffy, *Fires*, 41–2.
57. R. Bayne, ed., *The Life of Fisher* (1921), 107–10.
58. Foxe (1583), 1450–2.
59. Foxe (1583), 1544; *CSP*, *Spain*, XII, 216.
60. Wriothesley, II, 114; Machyn, 59; *CSP*, *Spain*, XII, 154–5.
61. Brigden, 548–9.
62. Machyn, 58; *ODNB*, by name; Foxe (1583), 1491.
63. MacCulloch, 562–7; C. S. Knighton, 'Weston, Hugh (c.1510–1558)', *ODNB*.
64. Brigden 575–6; Helen Parish, *Clerical Marriage and the English Reformation* (Aldershot, 2000), 186–91.
65. Thomas S. Freeman, 'Burning Zeal: Mary Tudor and the Marian Persecution', in Susan Doran and Thomas S. Freeman, eds, *Mary Tudor: Old and New Perspectives* (Basingstoke, 2011), 181–3.
66. Loach, *Parliament*, 91–104.
67. Wriothesley, II, 118; *CGF*, 91; Dickens, *Studies*, 311; 'Wenlock', 109–10.
68. Richards, *Mary*, 158–61; Edwards, *Mary*, 186–92.

69. *CGF*, 91; Machyn, 65; Wriothesley, II, 122; *CQJ*, 145–51 (quote at 149); C. L. Kingsford, ed., 'Two London Chronicles', *Camden Miscellany XII* (1910), 36; William Andrews, *Old Church Lore* (Hull, 1891), 142.

70. *CQJ*, 78–9, 150–1; Foxe (1576), 1427; Edwards, *Mary*, 198–9.

71. *CQJ*, 81–2, 139n; Brigden, 56–7.

72. *CSP, Spain*, XIII, nos 60–1.

73. *CSP, Spain*, XIII, nos 63, 76; *VAI*, II, 330–59.

74. Foxe (1583), 1112, *VAI*, II, 331; Duffy, 543–4.

75. *VAI*, II, 342–7.

76. Duffy, 546; J. E. Oxley, *The Reformation in Essex* (Manchester, 1965), 188.

77. Duffy, *Morebath*, 162–3; Haigh, 211–12, 129; Ronald Hutton, *The Rise and Fall of Merry England* (Oxford, 1994), 96.

78. Foxe (1583), 1496–7.

79. *VAI*, II, 331–4, 337, 343, 348–54.

80. *CSP, Spain*, XIII, 64, 68 (see *VAI*, II, 358); Wriothesley, II, 122; Meriel Jagger, 'Bonner's Episcopal Visitation of London, 1554', *Bulletin of the Institute of Historical Research*, 45 (1972), 306–11; Brigden, 562–9 (quote at 566).

81. Brigden, 572; W. H. Hale, ed., *A Series of Precedents and Proceedings in Criminal Causes* (1847), 144.

82. John Bradford, *Writings . . . Letters, Treatises, Remains*, ed. A. Townsend (Cambridge, 1853), 300–2, 314, 320, 327, 340, 343, 351.

83. Carlos N. M. Eire, 'Calvin's Attack on Nicodemism and Religious Compromise', *Archiv für Reformationsgeschichte*, 76 (1985), 120–45; Peter Martyr Vermigli, *A treatise of the cohabitacyon of the faithfull with the vnfaithfull* (Strassburg, 1555), 17r, 68r, 75v, 82r–v.

84. Foxe (1583), 1859; John Knox, *A Percel of the. vi. Psalme expounded* (1554), E1v–2r.

85. *CSP, Spain*, XI, 217; Foxe (1583), 2102–3.

86. C. Bradshaw, 'Old, John (*d.* 1557)', *ODNB*; Jonathan Wright, 'Marian Exiles and the Legitimacy of Flight from Persecution', *JEH*, 52 (2001), 222–3.

87. Maria Dowling and Joy Shakespeare, eds, 'Religion and Politics in Mid Tudor England through the Eyes of an English Protestant Woman: The Recollections of Rose Hickman', *Bulletin of the Institute of Historical Research*, 55 (1982), 98–101.

88. Alan Bryson, 'Cheke, Sir John (1514–1557)', *ODNB*; John F. McDiarmid, ' "To Content God Quietlie": The Troubles of Sir John Cheke under Queen Mary', in Evenden and Westbrook, *Renewal*, 197–9.

89. Stephen Alford, *Burghley: William Cecil at the Court of Elizabeth I* (New Haven, 2008), 65–70; Andrew Pettegree, 'Day, John (1521/2–1584)', *ODNB*.

90. Philip Benedict, *Christ's Churches Purely Reformed* (New Haven, 2002), 75; Andrew Pettegree, *Marian Protestantism* (Aldershot, 1996), 13–14; Edwin Sandys, *Sermons*, ed. John Ayre (Cambridge, 1841), ix–xvi, 296.

91. My account of the 'Troubles at Frankfurt' draws on Jane Dawson, *John Knox* (New Haven, 2015), 90–106; Dickens, 344–7; Karl Gunther, *Reformation Unbound: Protestant Visions of Reform in England, 1525–1590* (Cambridge, 2014), 170–81; Ryan Reeves, *English Evangelicals and Tudor Obedience* (Leiden, 2014), 140–5.

92. John Knox, *Works*, ed. David Laing (6 vols, Edinburgh, 1846–64), IV, 240.

## 13  Time of Trial

1. *CRP*, II, 350–61 (quote at 353); Stephen Alford, *Burghley: William Cecil at the Court of Elizabeth I* (New Haven, 2008), 70; Jennifer Loach, *Parliament and Crown in the Reign of Mary Tudor* (Oxford, 1986), 105–6.

2. Wriothesley, II, 76–7; *CQJ*, 153–9.

3. *CJ*, I, 38.

4. Gee, 384, 385–415; Loach, *Parliament*, 107–15.

5. Wriothesley, II, 126; *CGF*, 94.

6. Foxe (1583), 1555; Eamon Duffy, *Fires of Faith* (New Haven, 2009), 15–17.

7. Foxe (1583), 2038.

8. Foxe (1583), 1508–10.

9. *CSP, Spain*, XIII, 138.
10. Tom Betteridge, 'Saunders, Lawrence (*d.* 1555)', *ODNB*; Eric Josef Carlson, 'Taylor, Rowland (*d.* 1555)', *ODNB*; D. G. Newcombe, 'Hooper, John (1495x1500–1555)', *ODNB*.
11. John Edwards, *Mary I* (New Haven, 2011), 258.
12. Foxe (1576), 1464; Thomas S. Freeman, 'Cardmaker, John (*c.*1496–1555)', *ODNB*.
13. Foxe (1583), 1522.
14. Foxe (1583), 1557–8.
15. Foxe (1583), 1580–3 (shown as bearded in the accompanying woodcut).
16. 'Appendix: The Marian Martyrs', in Susan Doran and Thomas S. Freeman, eds, *Mary Tudor: Old and New Perspectives* (Basingstoke, 2011), 229–30; Machyn, 84–5; Foxe (1583), 1597–1601.
17. *CGF*, 95. Machyn, 109 dates the incident to 15 May.
18. Wriothesley, II, 128; Foxe (1583), 1607–8; *Liturgies*, 233; *A Warnynge for Englande* (Emden, 1555), A1r–8r;
19. Edwards, *Mary*, 267; *CSP, Venice*, VI, nos 80, 97, 150; John Edwards, 'Corpus Christi at Kingston upon Thames', in Edwards and Ronald Truman, eds, *Reforming Catholicism in the England of Mary Tudor* (Aldershot, 2005), 139–51 (not mentioning the disturbance).
20. *CRP*, IV, 105, 107.
21. *TRP*, II, 57–60; John Scory, *An Epistle* (Emden, 1555), A3r, A4r.
22. Edwards, *Mary*, 268.
23. Thomas S. Freeman, 'Burning Zeal: Mary Tudor and the Marian Persecution', in Susan Doran and Thomas S. Freeman, eds, *Mary Tudor: Old and New Perspectives* (Basingstoke, 2011), 185–7; 'Marian Martyrs', 231–7; Michael Zell, 'Thornden, Richard (*c.*1490–1558)', *ODNB*.
24. Foxe (1583), 1710; Duffy, *Fires*, 123.
25. *CRP*, III, 169; David Loades, *The Oxford Martyrs* (2nd edn, Bangor, 1992), 203–12.
26. John King, 'Fiction and Fact in Foxe's *Book of Martyrs*', in David Loades, ed., *John Foxe and the English Reformation* (Aldershot, 1997), 23–4.
27. MacCulloch, 573–9.
28. *VAI*, II, 360–1.
29. Duffy, 534–6.
30. Edmund Bonner, *A profitable and necessarye doctrine with certayne homelyes adioyned* (1555), A2r–4r, D2v; William Wizeman, *The Theology and Spirituality of Mary Tudor's Church* (Aldershot, 2006), 25–6, 245–8.
31. Duffy, *Fires*, 66–7; *VAI*, II, 401.
32. *CRP*, III, 183, 191, 193–4
33. Loach, *Parliament*, 135–43.
34. James Muller, *Stephen Gardiner and the Tudor Reaction* (1926), 291–3; *CRP*, III, 194; 2 Kings: 18–19.
35. Gerald Bray, ed., *The Anglican Canons, 1529–1947* (Woodbridge, 1998), 69, 75–7, 137.
36. Bray, *Canons*, 95–103, 107, 113–15, 123, 127–9; Duffy, *Fires*, 197.
37. Thomas F. Mayer, *Reginald Pole* (Cambridge, 2000), 242; Wizeman, *Theology*, 62–4. Carranza's catechism would later supply the basis for the Catechism of the Council of Trent: Duffy, *Fires*, 206.
38. As, for example, Dickens, 309–15.
39. *CRP*, III, 24; Duffy, *Fires*, 30–3; John Edwards, *Archbishop Pole* (Farnham, 2014), 192, 196–200; Mary C. Erler, *Reading and Writing during the Dissolution* (Cambridge, 2013), 108–10.
40. Machyn, 171–2; Wriothesely, II, 128, 136; Mayer, *Pole*, 288; Edwards, *Pole*, 189–95; *CSP, Venice*, VI, no. 743.
41. Claire Cross, 'Monasteries and Society in Sixteenth-Century Yorkshire', in Janet E. Burton and Karen Stöber, eds, *Monasteries and Society in the British Isles in the Later Middle Ages* (Woodbridge, 2008), 236; Cross, 'A Yorkshire Religious House and its Hinterland', in Simon Ditchfield, ed., *Christianity and Community in the West* (Aldershot, 2001), 83.
42. Brigden, 477–8; *Narratives*, 182–3; William Lemprière, ed., *John Howes' MS., 1582* (1904), 66.
43. Foxe (1583), 1553; Duffy, *Fires*, 113–14.

44. MacCulloch, 584–605; David Loades, *Two Tudor Conspiracies* (2nd edn, Bangor, 1992), 213–33
45. McDiarmid, 'Cheke', 205–17; *OL*, I, 117–18, 133; *CSP, Venice*, VI, no. 690.
46. 'Marian Martyrs', 239–50.
47. Foxe (1583), 2046.
48. Duffy, *Fires*, 129–30; 'Marian Martyrs', 245–6.
49. Duffy, *Fires*, 171–87 (quotes at 175, 177); Miles Huggarde, *The Displaying of the Protestantes* (1556), 124v.
50. Brigden, 601; Thomas Freeman, 'Dissenters from a Dissenting Church', in Peter Marshall and Alec Ryrie, eds, *The Beginnings of English Protestantism* (Cambridge, 2002), 129–56; *The examinacion of the constaunt martir of Christ, Iohan Philpot* (Emden, 1556), Part 2, A1r.
51. Foxe (1583), 2113–14, 2030; 'Marian Martyrs', 242–3.
52. Mark Byford, 'The Birth of a Protestant Town', in Patrick Collinson and John Craig, eds, *The Reformation in English Towns* (Basingstoke, 1998), 30–1.
53. Foxe (1583), 2168.
54. Foxe (1583), 2029, 2076; Duffy, *Fires*, 142–6.
55. Foxe (1583), 2114, 2168; Brigden, 601–2.
56. *CRP*, II, 339; Edwards, *Pole*, 136, 187–8; Foxe (1583), 1992; Eamon Duffy, 'Hampton Court, Henry VIII and Cardinal Pole', in Thomas Betteridge and Suzannah Lipscomb, *Henry VIII and the Court* (Farnham, 2013), 198.
57. Andrew Hegarty, 'Carranza and the English Universities', in Edwards and Truman, *Reforming*, 156–60; Claire Cross, 'The English Universities, 1553–58', in Eamon Duffy and David Loades, eds, *The Church of Mary Tudor* (Aldershot, 2006), 63–70.
58. Ronald Hutton, *The Rise and Fall of Merry England* (Oxford, 1994), 96; Haigh, 211–12; Duffy, 555–64.
59. Peter Marshall, *Beliefs and the Dead in Reformation England* (Oxford, 2002), 116–17.
60. Machyn, 120.
61. Edwards, *Pole*, 208–11.
62. Michael Hicks, 'Stafford, Thomas (c.1533–1557)', *ODNB*.
63. Wriothesley, II, 139; Steve Rappaport, *Worlds Within Worlds: Structures of Life in Sixteenth-Century London* (Cambridge, 1989), 71.
64. Strype, III (2), 482–510 (quotes at 484, 485, 488, 492).
65. Duffy, *Fires*, 17–21.
66. Wriothesley, II, 140.
67. The argument of Duffy, *Fires*, 7, 168–70. 'Marian Martyrs', 260–5; Richard L. Greaves, 'Rough, John (c.1508–1557)', *ODNB*.
68. *TRP*, II, 90–1.
69. Strype, III (2), 133–5.
70. Peter Marshall, *The Reformation: A Very Short Introduction* (Oxford, 2009), 72.
71. Ryan Reeves, *English Evangelicals and Tudor Obedience* (Leiden, 2014), 150–7; Jane Dawson, *John Knox* (New Haven, 2015), 140–6.
72. Scott Hendrix, *Martin Luther: Visionary Reformer* (New Haven, 2015), 248.
73. Duffy, *Fires*, is the most optimistic assessment, anticipated by Haigh, 227–34. Forthright scepticism about the potential of Marian restoration in Dickens, 289–315, finds more nuanced expression in Andrew Pettegree, *Marian Protestantism* (Aldershot, 1996) and David Loades, *The Religious Culture of Marian England* (2010).
74. Edwards, *Mary*, 326–8; Henry Clifford, *The Life of Jane Dormer*, ed. J. Stevenson (1887), 90; David Loades, *Mary Tudor* (2006), 199–201.
75. Edwards, *Mary*, 332; Strype, *Annals*, I (1), 72.

## 14 Alteration

1. *TRP*, II, 99–100; Winthrop S. Hudson, *The Cambridge Connection and the Elizabethan Settlement of 1559* (Durham, NC, 1980), 9–12, 25; Machyn, 178; *ZL*, 4–5.
2. 'Wenlock', 112; H. N. Birt, *The Elizabethan Religious Settlement* (1907), 4; *TRP*, I, 99; Marshall, 117.

3. *CSP, Venice*, VII, no. 2; Strype, III (2), 536–50.

4. Karl Gunther, *Reformation Unbound: Protestant Visions of Reform in England, 1525–1590* (Cambridge, 2014), 180–1.

5. J. E. Neale, ed., 'Sir Nicholas Throckmorton's Advice to Queen Elizabeth on Her Accession to the Throne', *EHR*, 65 (1950), 91–2; SP 12/1, 156r–158r; 12/1, 150v.

6. Strype, *Annals*, I (2), 392–8.

7. *CSP, Simancas*, I, no. 6; *CSP, Venice*, VII, no. 1; C. G. Bayne, 'The Coronation of Queen Elizabeth I', *EHR*, 22 (1907), 662–3. Feria reported the 28 December mass as 'said by another bishop': this seems likely to be a misidentification of George Carew, dean of the Chapel Royal.

8. *TRP*, II, 102–3; *CSP, Foreign*, I, no. 379; *ZL*, 57–8.

9. Germanine Warkentin, ed., *The Queen's Majesty's Passage and Related Documents* (Toronto, 2004), 98.

10. Bayne, 'Coronation', 650–73; William P. Haugaard, 'The Coronation of Elizabeth I', *JEH*, 19 (1968), 161–70; Stephen Alford, *Burghley: William Cecil at the Court of Elizabeth I* (New Haven, 2008), 96.

11. *CSP, Venice*, VII, no. 15.

12. Hartley, I, 34.

13. Norman L. Jones, *Faith by Statute* (1982), 62–72; P. W. Hasler, ed., *The House of Commons 1558–1603* (3 vols, 1981), I, 67–9.

14. *CSP, Simancas*, I, nos 4, 6; Susan Doran, *Monarchy and Matrimony: The Courtships of Elizabeth I* (1996), 1–2.

15. *ZL*, 19.

16. Jones, *Faith*, 89–94; Cyndia S. Clegg, 'The 1559 Books of Common Prayer and the Elizabethan Reformation', *JEH*, 67 (2016), 94–121.

17. *APC*, VII, 36, 47–8, 52, 59, 62, 64, 65, 67; Machyn, 189–90; *CSP, Venice*, VII, no. 23.

18. Wilkins, IV, 179–80; Jones, *Faith*, 96–7; Strype, *Annals*, I (2), 400, 401, 409–10.

19. Hartley, I, 9–10; *CSP, Venice*, VII, no. 45.

20. *CSP, Venice*, VII, no. 45; *CSP, Simancas*, I, no. 18; *LJ*, I, 564–5.

21. *TRP*, II, 109–11; *CJ*, I, 58.

22. *CSP, Simancas*, I, no. 18.

23. *ZL*, 22–3; Haugaard, 96–104; Jones, *Faith*, 123–9; *The Declaracyon of the procedynge of a Conference begon at Westminster* (RSTC suggests a publication date of 1560, but 1559 is more likely).

24. Jones, *Faith*, 130–1; *ZL*, 2, 41–2; John Knox, *Works*, ed. David Laing (6 vols, Edinburgh, 1846–64), IV, 564; Parker, 66.

25. John Aylmer, *An harborowe for faithfull and trewe subiectes* (London, 1559), B3r, H3r–v.

26. *ZL*, 29; *APC*, VII, 77; Machyn, 193, 196; *CSP, Venice*, VII, no. 71.

27. Jones, *Faith*, 130, 142–4.

28. Hartley, I, 19–20; 27–31.

29. Jones, *Faith*, 77–80, 150–1.

30. Gee, 458–67; Brian Cummings, ed., *The Book of Common Prayer* (Oxford, 2011), xxxiii–xxxiv, 102, 137, 140.

31. Parker, 65.

32. *ZL*, 33.

33. *ODNB*, by name; Aylmer, *Harborowe*, D3v–4r; *ZL*, 38.

34. *CSP, Simancas*, I, no. 32; *ZL*, 40; *CSP, Venice*, VII, no. 81; Haugaard, 37–8.

35. *APC*, VII, 38; *CSP, Foreign*, I, no. 422; 'Dr Nicholas Sander's Report to Cardinal Moroni', in J. Pollen, ed., *Catholic Record Society Miscellanea I* (1905), 35–6; *CSP, Simancas*, I, no. 54; Parker, 222.

36. David J. Crankshaw and Alexandra Gillespie, 'Parker, Matthew (1504–1575)', *ODNB*; Parker, 59.

37. SP 12/4, 131r; Brett Usher, *William Cecil and Episcopacy, 1559–1577* (Aldershot, 2003), 7–23; Andrew Pettegree, *Marian Protestantism* (Aldershot, 1996), 112; Haugaard, 43.

38. Haugaard, 47–50; David Daniell, *The Bible in English* (New Haven, 2003), 294; *Letters of John Calvin*, ed. Jules Bonnet (4 vols, Philadelphia, 1858), IV, 16; Knox, *Works*, VI, 31, 40–4, 47–50; Jane Dawson, *John Knox* (New Haven, 2015), 172–3.

39. Patrick Collinson, *The Elizabethan Puritan Movement* (1967), 46–7; *ZL*, 63–5, 71; David Marcombe, 'Pilkington, James (1520–1576)', *ODNB*; Norman Jones, *The Birth of the Elizabethan Age* (Oxford, 1993), 31.

40. Haugaard, 136–7; *TRP*, II, 117; *SP*, 12/6, 49r; Wriothesley, II, 146; Machyn, 207.

41. C. J. Kitching, ed., *The Royal Visitation of 1559* (Gateshead, 1975), xx–xxi; *VAI*, III, 2; Margaret Aston, *Broken Idols of the English Reformation* (Cambridge, 2016), 123; Ronald Hutton, *The Rise and Fall of Merry England* (Oxford, 1994), 105; Edwin Sandys, *Sermons*, ed. John Ayre (Cambridge, 1852), 235–55 (quote at 250); Diarmaid MacCulloch and Pat Hughes, eds, 'A Bailiff's List and Chronicle from Worcester', *Antiquaries Journal*, 74 (1995), 249.

42. Kitching, *Visitation*, 69, 85; *VAI*, III, 6; Aston, *Idols*, 236–8.

43. *ZL*, 54, 60.

44. Edmund Hobhouse, ed., *Church-wardens' accounts of Croscombe, Pilton, Yatton, Tintinhull, Morebath, and St. Michael's, Bath* (1890), 170–1; Jones, *Birth*, 29.

45. Clive Burgess, ed., *The Church Records of St Andrew Hubbard, Eastcheap c.1450–c.1570* (1999), 183.

46. Jonathan Willis, *Church Music and Protestantism in Post-Reformation England* (Farnham, 2010), 54–8; *VAI*, III, 23; Collinson, *Movement*, 50; Machyn, 212, 228; *ZL*, 90.

47. Peter Marshall, *Beliefs and the Dead in Reformation England* (Oxford, 2002), 169–71.

48. Duffy, 571; Ronald Hutton, 'The Local Impact of the Tudor Reformations', in Christopher Haigh, ed., *The English Reformation Revised* (Cambridge, 1987), 134–6; *VAI*, III, 108.

49. *ZL*, 45, 54.

50. Peter Marshall and John Morgan, 'Clerical Conformity and the Elizabethan Settlement Revisited', *HJ*, 59 (2016), 1–22; *ZL*, 6.

51. Eamon Duffy, *Fires of Faith* (New Haven, 2009), 197; Parker, 27–7, 153–4.

52. Birt, *Settlement*, 439; James Calfhill, *An Answer to John Martiall's Treatise of the Cross*, ed. Richard Gibbings (Cambridge, 1846), 52.

53. *VAI*, III, 9–10, 14, 18–19, 20, 23, 25–8, 61; Cummings, *Prayer*, 124.

## 15  Unsettled England

1. Haugaard, 185–7; Margaret Aston, *Broken Idols of the English Reformation* (Cambridge, 2016), 748–50; Machyn, 226–9; *ZL*, 79; Parker, 93, 97.

2. *ZL*, 86, 98.

3. *ZL*, 89.

4. The best discussions of this thorny issue are Patrick Collinson, *Elizabethan Essays* (1994), 87–118; Susan Doran, 'Elizabeth I's Religion: Clues from her Letters', *JEH*, 52 (2001).

5. Diarmaid MacCulloch, *Tudor Church Militant* (1999), 187–9.

6. Machyn, 218; Norman Jones, *The Birth of the Elizabethan Age* (Oxford, 1993), 69–70.

7. *CSP, Foreign*, II, no. 145.

8. Stephen Alford, *Burghley: William Cecil at the Court of Elizabeth I* (New Haven, 2008), 104–8.

9. Alec Ryrie, *The Origins of the Scottish Reformation* (Manchester, 2006), 161–3, 189–90; Alford, *Burghley*, 109–11; *ZL*, 108–9.

10. Norman L. Jones, *Faith by Statute* (1982), 53–4.

11. Haugaard, 310–11; T. F. Mayer, 'Cole, Henry (1504/5–1579/80)', *ODNB*; C. S. Knighton, 'Feckenham, John (c.1510–1584)', *ODNB*; *CSP, Simancas*, I, nos 85–6,

12. *CSP, Venice*, VII, no. 178; C. J. Bayne, *Anglo-Roman Relations, 1558–1565* (Oxford, 1913), 69–70; Susan Doran, *Monarchy and Matrimony: The Courtships of Elizabeth I* (1996), 42–50; *CSP, Simancas*, I, no. 125.

13. Jones, *Birth*, 36–8; Bayne, *Relations*, 99–102; *CSP, Foreign*, IV, no. 187.

14. Elizabeth Goldring et al., eds, *John Nichols's The Progresses and Public Processions of Queen Elizabeth I* (5 vols, Oxford, 2014), I, 184–5; *VAI*, III, 98, 108–10.

15. Parker, 66, 146, 156–60.

16. Brett Usher, 'Queen Elizabeth and Mrs Bishop', in Susan Doran and Thomas S. Freeman, eds, *The Myth of Elizabeth* (Basingstoke, 2003), 207–8; Jane Reedy Ladley, 'Cheyney, Richard (*d.* 1579)', *ODNB*.
17. *ZL*, 161, 173.
18. Wallace MacCaffrey, *The Shaping of the Elizabethan Regime* (1969), 92–7; C. P. Croly, 'Vaughan, Cuthbert (*c.*1519–1563)', *ODNB*; *CSP, Foreign*, V, 1299.
19. Alexander Nowell, *A Catechism*, ed. George E. Corrie (Cambridge, 1853), 223–9; *CSP, Simancas*, I, no. 208; Hartley, I, 58–62, 115.
20. MacCaffrey, *Shaping*, 108–9; Alford, *Burghley*, 123–5.
21. Jones, *Faith*, 172–6; Strype, *Annals*, I (1), 444–5, 446–55; *CSP, Simancas*, I, nos 210, 213; Parker, 173–5.
22. Haugaard, 126; Christopher Maginn, 'O'Neill, Shane (*c.*1530–1567)', *ODNB*.
23. Haugaard, 248–53; Peter Marshall, *Beliefs and the Dead in Reformation England* (Oxford, 2002), 54; SP 12/41, 135r; Gerald Bray, ed., *Documents of the English Reformation* (Cambridge, 1993), 296–7, 303.
24. Ashley Null, 'Official Tudor Homilies', in Peter McCullough et al., eds, *The Oxford Handbook of the Early Modern Sermon* (Oxford, 2011), 359–60; Margaret Aston, *England's Iconoclasts* (Oxford, 1988), 320–4; John Griffiths, ed., *Certain Sermons or Homilies* (Oxford, 1850), 168, 239, 398–9.
25. Haugaard, 60–2, 166–82; David Crankshaw, 'Preparations for the Canterbury Provincial Convocation of 1562–63: A Question of Attribution', in Susan Wabuda and Caroline Litzenberger, eds, *Belief and Practice in Reformation England* (Aldershot, 1998), 60–93; *CSP, Foreign*, VI, no. 136; David J. Crankshaw and Alexandra Gillespie, 'Parker, Matthew (1504–1575)', *ODNB*.
26. Mears, 56–68; BL, Lansdowne MSS, Vol. 6, 202r; Johan Wigand, *De neutralibus et mediis, grossly Inglished, Jacke of both sydes* (1562), B1r, B3r; Folger, L.b.98.
27. William Bullein, *A dialogue both pleasant and piety-full, against the fever pestilence* (1564), B4r–v, C5v; *The true report of the burnyng of the steple and church of Poules* (1561), A7r–8v; Thomas S. Freeman, 'Foxe, John (1516/17–1587)', *ODNB*; John N. King, 'Baldwin, William (*d.* in or before 1563)', *ODNB*; 'Historical Memoranda in the Handwriting of John Stow', in James Gairdner, ed., *Three Fifteenth Century Chronicles* (1880), 126.
28. SP 12/34, 1r; *CSP, Simancas*, I, no. 263.
29. Geoffrey de C. Parmiter, 'Bishop Bonner and the Oath', *Recusant History*, 11 (1972), 215–36; SP 15/12, 173r; *CSP, Simancas*, I, nos 270, 272, 274, 277.
30. Dr Nicholas Sander's Report to Cardinal Moroni', in J. Pollen, ed., *Catholic Record Society Miscellanea I* (1905), 45.
31. Alan Dures, *English Catholicism 1558–1642* (Harlow, 1983), 6; Jones, *Birth*, 74–5; Mary Bateson, ed., 'A Collection of Original Letters from the Bishops to the Privy Council, 1564', in *Camden Miscellany IX* (1895), 2, 3, 7–8, 19, 46, 77–8; Strype, *Annals*, I (2), 15–22.
32. Ginerva Crosignani et al., eds, *Recusancy and Conformity in Early Modern England* (Toronto, 2010), 3, 7, 19.
33. Doran, *Matrimony*, 73–4; Haugaard, 304–6, 315, 324; *CSP, Vatican*, I, no. 278.
34. Francis Bacon, *Works, vol. I* (1838), 387; Crosignani, *Recusancy*, 30–57; Bateson, 'Letters', 40.
35. Frederick Smith, 'The Origins of Recusancy in Elizabethan England Reconsidered', *HJ*, forthcoming.
36. Haigh, 254–5; SP 12/19, 45r; 12/17, 47r; Smith, 'Recusancy'; Christopher Haigh, 'Marshall, Richard (*b.* 1517, *d.* in or after 1575)', *ODNB*; Jonathan Wright, 'Langdale, Alban (*fl.* 1532–1580)', *ODNB*.
37. J. Andreas Löwe, *Richard Smyth and the Language of Orthodoxy* (Leiden, 2003), 57–75; Gary W. Jenkins, *John Jewel and the English National Church* (Aldershot, 2006), 117–23; Nicholas Sander, *Rise and Growth of the Anglican Schism*, ed. David Lewis (1877), 261; J. H. Pollen, *The English Catholics in the Reign of Queen Elizabeth* (1920), 109; Parker, 233; Karl Gunther, *Reformation Unbound: Protestant Visions of Reform in England, 1525–1590* (Cambridge, 2014), 192–3.

38. Paul Arblaster, 'Darbyshire, Thomas (1518–1604)', *ODNB*; Thomas M. McCoog, 'Good, William (1527–1586)', *ODNB*; Dennis Flynn, 'Heywood, Jasper (1535–1598)', *ODNB*; Eamon Duffy, 'Allen, William (1532–1594)', *ODNB*; A. J. Loomie, 'Englefield, Sir Francis (1522–1596)', *ODNB*; Julian Lock, 'Story, John (1503/4?–1571)', *ODNB*.

39. Christopher Highley, *Catholics Writing the Nation in Early Modern Britain and Ireland* (Oxford, 2008), 29; Lucy Wooding, *Rethinking Catholicism in Reformation England* (Oxford, 2000), 195–6; Thomas Harding, *A confutation of a booke intituled An apologie of the Church of England* (Antwerp, 1565), *2v; Stanford Lehmberg, 'Nowell, Alexander (c.1516/17–1602)', *ODNB*; Parker, 235.

40. Thomas Stapleton, *A fortresse of the faith* (Antwerp, 1565), 134v; Patrick Collinson, 'Antipuritanism', in John Coffey and Paul C. H. Lim, eds, *The Cambridge Companion to Puritanism* (Cambridge, 2008), 19–22.

41. John Strype, *The Life and Acts of Matthew Parker* (3 vols, Oxford, 1821), I, 302; J. S. Purvis, ed., *Tudor Parish Documents of the Diocese of York* (Cambridge, 1948), 212; Patrick Collinson, *Richard Bancroft and Elizabethan Anti-Puritanism* (Cambridge, 2013), 15.

42. *CSP, Simancas*, I, no. 270; James Pilkington, *Works*, ed. J. Scholefield (Cambridge, 1842), 658–62.

43. Ryan Reeves, *English Evangelicals and Tudor Obedience* (Leiden, 2014), 184; Patrick Collinson, *The Elizabethan Puritan Movement* (1967), 68–9; John S. Coolidge, *The Pauline Renaissance in England* (Oxford, 1970), 27–41.

44. Parker, 223–7.

45. *ZL*, 243–4; Parker, 227–30; *VAI*, III, 172–3, 175, 178–80.

46. C. M. Dent, *Protestant Reformers in Elizabethan Oxford* (Oxford, 1983), 34–9; Strype, *Annals*, I (2), 155; Jones, *Birth*, 57–9; Parker, 279–70; Collinson, *Movement*, 72–6; Patrick Collinson, ed., *Letters of Thomas Wood, Puritan* (1960), xi, 1.

47. Stow, 'Memoranda', 135–40; Edmund Grindal, *Remains*, ed. John Williamson (Cambridge, 1843), 288–9. For another instance of 'ware horns', Shakespeare, *Troilus and Cressida*, V, vii, 12.

48. Parker, 284; SP 12/44, 53r–53Ar.

49. Patrick Collinson, *Archbishop Grindal* (1979), 177–9; Grindal, *Remains*, 201–4; A. P. House, 'The City of London and the Problem of the Liberties, c.1540–c.1640', Oxford D.Phil. Thesis (2006), 83–4; Stow, 'Memoranda', 143–4.

50. Hartley, I, 147; Pollen, *Catholics*, 112; *CSP, Vatican*, I, no. 348; MacCaffrey, *Shaping*, 144; Mortimer Levene, *The Early Elizabethan Succession Question* (Stanford, 1966), 168–70.

51. Hartley, I, 171; Jones, *Birth*, 64; Parker, 290–4; *ZL*, 236–7; Anthony Gilby, *A Pleasaunt Dialogue* (Middelburg, 1581), A7v, G8r.

52. *CSP, Simancas*, I, no. 418.

53. Doran, *Matrimony*, 76, 234; *CSP, Simancas*, I, no. 295; Harding, *Confutation*, *2v.

54. Aston, *Iconoclasts*, 313–14; SP 70/93, 22r; *Historical Manuscripts Commission: Report on the Pepys Manuscripts* (1911), 90; *An answere for the tyme* (Rouen, 1566), H6v; Gunther, *Unbound*, 119, 212.

55. Purvis, *Documents*, 15–34 (quotes at 32, 34); Marshall, *Beliefs*, 126; SP 12/44, 62r; H. N. Birt, *The Elizabethan Religious Settlement* (1907), 429; Duffy, 572–4, 585.

56. *VAI*, III, 168; John Strype, *Life and Acts of . . . Edmund Grindal* (Oxford, 1821), 516–19.

57. Crosignani, *Recusancy*, xix, 60–3, 70; John J. LaRocca, 'Vaux, Laurence (1519–1585)', *ODNB*; Alexandra Walsham, *Church Papists* (Woodbridge, 1993), 23; SP 12/46, 45r, 69r–v.

58. *TRP*, II, 133.

### 16 Admonitions

1. Samuel Haynes, ed., *A Collection of State Papers* (1740), 579–88; T. F. Knox, ed., *The First and Second Diaries of the English College, Douay* (1878), xxviii–xxix; Stephen Alford, *The Early Elizabethan Polity* (Cambridge, 1998), 182–9. Alford dates the Memorial to July/August due to its mention of 'the new rebellion in Ireland': revolt broke out there in July. But this appears on a list of *envisaged* threats and dangers. References to Mary being in the north, to military action 'this spring', and an absence of references to the death of Condé (in March 1569) make January the likelier date.

2. The best among countless biographies is John Guy, *'My Heart is My Own': The Life of Mary Queen of Scots* (2004).

3. Haynes, *Papers*, 587; Brett Usher, *William Cecil and Episcopacy, 1559–1577* (Aldershot, 2003), 105–6; *CSP, Simancas*, II, nos 70, 95, 99, 119.

4. Anthony Fletcher and Diarmaid MacCulloch, *Tudor Rebellions* (6th edn, 2016), 101–2; *CSPD, Elizabeth Addenda 1566–1579*, 403.

5. K. J. Kesselring, *The Northern Rebellion of 1569* (2007), 46–56; Kenneth Carleton, 'Bonner, Edmund (d. 1569)', *ODNB*; R. R. Reid, 'The Rebellion of the Earls, 1569', *TRHS*, 20 (1906), 191, 196.

6. Cuthbert Sharp, ed., *Memorials of the Rebellion of 1569* (1840), 77; W. R. B. Robinson, 'Somerset, William, third earl of Worcester (1526/7–1589)', *ODNB*; H. N. Birt, *The Elizabethan Religious Settlement* (1907), 358, 529.

7. Sharp, *Memorials*, xvi, 71.

8. Reid, 'Rebellion', 192; Haynes, *Papers*, 564–5.

9. Sharp, *Memorials*, 42–3n, 204, 212–13; Kesselring, *Rebellion*, 58–9. A Robert Copley was deprived as rector of Walton-on-the-Hill, Surrey, in 1562: CCED, person ID 106441.

10. Sharp, *Memorials*, 43–5; James Raine, ed., *Depositions and other Ecclesiastical Proceedings from the Courts of Durham* (1845), 143–4, 162, 184–93; Kesselring, *Rebellion*, 69–70.

11. Geoffrey Moorhouse, *The Last Office* (2008), 243–4; Kesselring, *Rebellion*, 67.

12. Raine, *Depositions*, 174–5, 180.

13. Fletcher and MacCulloch, *Rebellions*, 104–7; Henry Summerson, 'Dacre, Leonard (d. 1573)', *ODNB*; Roger N. McDermott, 'Neville, Charles, sixth earl of Westmorland (1542/3–1601)', *ODNB*; Julian Lock, 'Percy, Thomas, seventh earl of Northumberland (1528–1572)', *ODNB*; Sharp, *Memorials*, 219–20.

14. Kesselring, *Rebellion*, 122–5; Sharp, *Memorials*, 163.

15. Mears, 127–8; Usher, *Episcopacy*, 106; 'Lemeke Avale', *A commemoration or dirige of bastarde Edmonde Boner* (1569), C3r; Thomas Norton, *A warning agaynst the dangerous practises of papistes* (1569), B1r–v; Birt, *Settlement*, 332.

16. Haynes, *Papers*, 588; SP 12/48, 179r; Norman Jones, *The Birth of the Elizabethan Age* (Oxford, 1993), 84–6; Birt, *Settlement*, 419, 518–19

17. J. H. Pollen, *The English Catholics in the Reign of Queen Elizabeth* (1920), 142–9; Robert S. Miola, ed., *Early Modern Catholicism: An Anthology of Primary Sources* (Oxford, 2007), 486–8.

18. Birt, *Settlement*, 499–500; Pollen, *Catholics*, 155; Julian Lock, 'Felton, John (d. 1570)', *ODNB*.

19. R. Pollitt, 'The Abduction of Dr John Story', *Sixteenth Century Journal*, 14 (1983), 131–56; *A Declaration of the Lyfe and Death of Iohn Story* (1571), B3v–4v; Elizabeth Evenden and Thomas S. Freeman, 'Print, Profit and Propaganda: The Elizabethan Privy Council and the 1570 Edition of Foxe's "Book of Martyrs"', *EHR*, 119 (2004), 1288–1307.

20. Michael A. R. Graves, 'Howard, Thomas, fourth duke of Norfolk (1538–1572)', *ODNB*; L. E. Hunt, 'Ridolfi, Roberto di (1531–1612)', *ODNB*.

21. Usher, *Episcopacy*, 115–17.

22. Edward Dering, *A sermon preached before the Quenes Maiestie* (?1570), E4r, F1r–v.

23. Patrick Collinson, *The Elizabethan Puritan Movement* (1967), 109–10, 112–13; William Joseph Sheils, 'Whitgift, John (1530/31?–1604)', *ODNB*.

24. Hartley, I, 199, 201–5; *Statutes of the Realm* (11 vols, 1810–28), IV, 526–34; Wallace T. MacCaffrey, *Queen Elizabeth and the Making of Policy* (Princeton, 1981), 125–6.

25. Hartley, I, 200–1, 220; Gerald Bray, ed., *Tudor Church Reform: The Henrician Canons of 1535 and the Reformatio Legum Ecclesiasticarum* (Woodbridge, 2000), lxxvi–xcix; T. Freeman, 'Thomas Norton, John Foxe and the Parliament of 1571', *Parliamentary History*, 16 (1997), 131–47; MacCaffrey, *Policy*, 60.

26. Haugaard, 254–5; Gee, 478; MacCaffrey, *Policy*, 59–61.

27. Gerald Bray, ed., *The Anglican Canons, 1529–1947* (Woodbridge, 1998), xlviii–xlix, 197–9, 201.

28. Claire Cross, *The Royal Supremacy in the Elizabethan Church* (1969), 213–15; Ralph Houlbrooke, ed., *The Letter Book of John Parkhurst* (Norwich, 1974), 243; Patrick Collinson, ed., 'The Prophesyings and the Downfall of Archbishop Edmund Grindal,

1576–1583', in Melanie Barber et al, eds, *From the Reformation to the Permissive Society* (Woodbridge, 2010), 4–5.

29. Peter Marshall, ' "Rather with Papists than with Turks": The Battle of Lepanto and the Contours of Elizabethan Christendom', *Reformation*, 17 (2012), 135–59.

30. Hartley, I, 270–2, 274–82, 298, 325, 376; Patrick Collinson, *Elizabethan Essays* (1994), 46–7; Rosamund Oates, 'Puritans and the "Monarchical Republic"', *EHR*, 127 (2012), 819.

31. Hartley, I, 302–10, 332–3, 418; Graves, 'Norfolk'.

32. Hartley, I, 330, 359, 369–70; MacCaffrey, *Policy*, 62–3; W. H. Frere and C. E. Douglas, eds, *Puritan Manifestoes* (1907), 149–51.

33. Frere and Douglas, *Manifestoes*, 8–37; Collinson, *Movement*, 118–20.

34. Collinson, *Movement*, 133–40; Frere and Douglas, *Manifestoes*, 96–8, 107–8; Sheils, 'Whitgift'.

35. *TRP*, II, 375–6; Collinson, *Movement*, 12, 146–9; Thomas Wright, ed., *Queen Elizabeth and her Times* (2 vols, 1838), I, 475–6; *ZL*, 439–40; Parker, 410, 426, 434; Patrick Collinson, ed., *Letters of Thomas Wood, Puritan* (1960), xxx–xxxi; John Strype, *Life and Acts of John Whitgift* (3 vols, Oxford, 1822), III, 32–5.

36. Collinson, *Movement*, 150–4; Wallace T. MacCaffrey, 'Hatton, Sir Christopher (*c.*1540–1591)', *ODNB*; *TRP*, II, 379–81; Collinson, *Wood*, xvi, 7–8.

37. Stephen Alford, *The Watchers* (2012), 52, 129–30; Mears, 134; Parker, 398–9.

38. Birt, *Settlement*, 420; Folger, L.a.651; CCED Record ID: 99389; *ZL*, 414.

39. Sharp, *Memorials*, 188; Thomas M. McCoog, 'Woodhouse, Thomas (*d.* 1573)', *ODNB*; *APC*, VIII, 218, 264, 269, 284; Patrick McGrath, *Papists and Puritans under Elizabeth I* (1967), 111; Robert Crowley, *A sermon made in the chappel at the Gylde Halle* (1575), F2v; Robert Harkins, 'Elizabethan Puritanism and the Politics of Memory in Post-Marian England', *HJ*, 57 (2014), 904–5, 908–9.

40. Parker, 477–9; David J. Crankshaw and Alexandra Gillespie, 'Parker, Matthew (1504–1575)', *ODNB*.

41. Alastair Duke, 'Martyrs with a Difference: Dutch Anabaptist Victims of Elizabethan Persecution', *Nederlands Archief voor Kerkgeschiedenis*, 80 (2000), 263–81.

42. SP 12/103, 111r.

43. Patrick Collinson, *Archbishop Grindal* (1979), 190, 199, 215, 221–2; William Nicholson, ed., *The Remains of Edmund Grindal* (Cambridge), 347, 357; Parker, 477–8; Felicity Heal, 'Cox, Richard (*c.*1500–1581)', *ODNB*; Collinson, 'Prophesyings', 3 (noting Grindal's correspondent was 'almost certainly' Mildmay).

44. Collinson, *Movement*, 161–4; Hartley, I, 445–7; Bray, *Canons*, 211–15; Collinson, *Grindal*, 225.

45. Collinson, *Grindal*, 228–32; Frere and Douglas, *Manifestoes*, 32; Parker, 336, 338; Bray, *Canons*, 193.

46. MacCaffrey, *Policy*, 84–5; Parker, 457–60; Houlbrooke, *Parkhurst*, 46–7, 242–6.

47. Collinson, *Grindal*, 233; 'Wood', 10, 12–16.

48. Susan Doran, *Elizabeth I and Her Circle* (Oxford, 2015), 152; Collinson, 'Prophesyings', 13–16, 40; Richard L. Greaves, 'Pagit, Eusebius (1546/7–1617)', *ODNB*.

49. Collinson, 'Prophesyings', 40, 19–25.

50. Collinson, 'Prophesyings', 8; *Movement*, 201; Strype, *Annals*, IV, 317; Harris Nicolas, *Memoirs of the Life and Times of Sir Christopher Hatton* (1847), 56, 58–9.

51. Collinson, *Grindal*, 248–9, 263; Patrick Collinson, 'Grindal, Edmund (1516x20–1583)', *ODNB*; C. S. Knighton, 'Feckenham, John (*c.*1510–1584)', *ODNB*; *APC*, X, 83–5, 111; Peter Lake, 'A Tale of Two Episcopal Surveys', *TRHS*, 18 (2008), 129–63; Edmund Grindal, *Remains*, ed. John Williamson (Cambridge, 1843), 471.

## 17  Wars of Religion

1. William Elderton, *A newe ballade, declaryng the daungerous shootynge of the gunne at the courte* (1579); John Stow, *The chronicles of England* (1580), 1200–1; *A briefe discourse of the most haynous and traytorlike fact of Thomas Appeltree* (1579).

2. Susan Doran, *Monarchy and Matrimony: The Courtships of Elizabeth I* (1996), 130–48.

3. *CSP, Simancas*, II, no. 31; Edmund Lodge, ed., *Illustrations of British History* (3 vols, 1838), II, 150.

4. Doran, *Matrimony*, 160–7; Peter Lake, *Bad Queen Bess: Libels, Secret Histories, and the Politics of Publicity* (Oxford, 2016), 99–103; *TRP*, II, 445–9; John Strype, *Life and Acts of Edmund Grindal* (2 vols, Oxford, 1821), II, 584–6; Patrick Collinson, *This England* (Manchester, 2011), 77–8.

5. Lake, *Bess*, 103–8; Albert Peel, ed., *The Seconde Parte of a Register* (2 vols, Cambridge, 1915), II, 166; J. C. H. Aveling, *Catholic Recusants of the West Riding* (Leeds, 1963), 211; Doran, *Matrimony*, 172–6.

6. Patrick McGrath, *Papists and Puritans under Elizabeth I* (1967), 116.

7. Michael E. Williams, *The Venerable English College, Rome* (2nd edn, Leominster, 2008), 7–8, 273–4; Thomas M. McCoog, *The Society of Jesus in Ireland, Scotland and England, 1541–1588* (Leiden, 1996), 106–8.

8. Peter Holmes, 'Stucley, Thomas (*c.*1520–1578)', *ODNB*; T. F. Mayer, 'Sander, Nicholas (*c.*1530–1581)', *ODNB*; McCoog, *Society*, 116–17; Gerard Kilroy, *Edmund Campion: A Scholarly Life* (Farnham, 2015), 127–8. On the longer-term impact and significance of the bull, see Aislinn Muller, 'Queen Elizabeth's Excommunication and its Afterlife, c. 1570–1603', Cambridge PhD thesis (2016).

9. Victor Houliston, 'Persons [Parsons], Robert (1546–1610)', *ODNB*; Michael A. R. Graves, 'Campion, Edmund [St Edmund Campion] (1540–1581)', *ODNB*; Ginerva Crosignani et al., eds, *Recusancy and Conformity in Early Modern England* (Toronto, 2010), 94–100.

10. Kilroy, *Campion*, 145–6, 150–9; Alexandra Walsham, *Providence in Early Modern England* (Oxford, 1999), 130–5; *TRP*, II, 469–71.

11. McGrath, *Papists*, 167–70; Robert Parsons, *A Brief Discours Contayning Certayne Reasons* (Douai, i.e. East Ham, 1580), ‡3r, 15v–16r, 39v–40r.

12. Crosignani, *Recusancy*, 117–29; SP 12/167, 60r.

13. Kilroy, *Campion*, 190; Meredith Hanmer, *The great bragge and challenge of M. Champion* (1581), 20r, 24v.

14. Hartley, I, 502–5; Alexandra Walsham, 'The Holy Maid of Wales: Visions, Imposture and Catholicism in Elizabethan Britain', *EHR* (forthcoming); John Cooper, *The Queen's Agent* (2011), 248–50.

15. *Statutes of the Realm* (11 vols, 1810–28), IV, 657–8; Wallace T. MacCaffrey, *Queen Elizabeth and the Making of Policy* (Princeton, 1981), 131–2.

16. *TRP*, II, 483; Kilroy, *Campion*, 203–5.

17. Leo Hicks, ed., *Letters and Memorials of Father Robert Persons* (1942), 83; Peter Lake with Michael Questier, *The Antichrist's Lewd Hat* (New Haven, 2002), 255–62; Peter Milward, *Religious Controversies of the Elizabethan Age* (Lincoln, NB, 1977), 46–64; Anthony Munday, *The English Romayne Life*, ed. G. B. Harrison (Edinburgh, 1966), 39; Peter Marshall, 'Religious Ideology', in Paulina Kewes et al., eds, *The Oxford Handbook of Holinshed's Chronicles* (Oxford, 2013), 423.

18. Kilroy, *Campion*, 243–55; SP 12/152, 124r.

19. Stephen Alford, *Burghley* (New Haven, 2009), 248; Henry Ellis, ed., *Holinshed's Chronicles* (6 vols, 1807–8), IV, 459; Stefania Tutino, *Law and Conscience* (Aldershot, 2007), 35; William Allen, *A Briefe Historie* (Rheims, 1582), A2v–3r; *TRP*, II, 488–91; SP 15/27/1,141r.

20. Robert Persons, *The copie of a double letter* (Rheims, 1581), 5, 7, 10–11, 21, 23; Foxe (1583), 2174–5; Munday, *Life*, 100–5.

21. Robert M. Kingdon, ed., *The Execution of Justice in England* (Ithaca, NY, 1965), 5, 8, 9–10, 20, 40, 70.

22. Alford, *Burghley*, 245–6; Jesse Childs, *God's Traitors* (2014), 99–101; Peter Marshall, *Faith and Identity in a Warwickshire Family* (Stratford-upon-Avon, 2010) 21–2.

23. Antoinina Bevan Zlatar, *Reformation Fictions* (Oxford, 2011), 115–23.

24. George Gifford, *A briefe discourse* (1581), 4r–5r, 7r, 12r–v, 13v, 22r, 68r; Zlatar, *Fictions*, 178–85; M. M. Knappen, ed., *Two Elizabethan Puritan Diaries* (Chicago, 1933), 53–102 (quote at 55).

25. Peter Marshall, 'The Naming of Protestant England', *Past and Present*, 214 (2012), 103–5; Gifford, *Discourse*, 2v, 34r; SP 12/156, 70v; Haigh, 279–84.

26. Rosemary O'Day, *The English Clergy* (Leicester, 1979), 132; Patrick Collinson, *The Religion of Protestants* (Oxford, 1982), 94; Anne Thomson, 'Clergy Wives in Elizabethan England', University of Warwick PhD (2016), 26–31, 247–61; Gifford, *Discourse*, 1v–2r, 5v; Borthwick Institute, York, CP G 2169; Folger, X.c.28; L. L. Ford, 'Mildmay, Sir Walter (1520/21–1589)', *ODNB*.

27. Folger, V.a.459, 5r, 10v, 11v, 19r, 21r, 30r, 33v, 73r.

28. John Craig, 'Erasmus or Calvin? The Politics of Book Purchase in the Early Modern English Parish', in Polly Ha and Patrick Collinson, eds, *The Reception of Continental Reformation in Britain* (Oxford, 2010), 39–62; Craig, *Reformation, Politics and Polemics* (Aldershot, 2001), 50–63; Lucy Kaufman, 'Ecclesiastical Improvements, Lay Impropriations, and the Building of a Post-Reformation Church in England, 1560–1600', *HJ*, 58 (2015), 1–23.

29. Craig, *Reformation*, 32; Judith Maltby, *Prayer Book and People in Elizabethan and Early Stuart England* (Cambridge, 1998), 24–8; Ian Green, *The Christian's ABC* (Oxford, 1996), 'Finding List', 580–750; Green, *Print and Protestantism in Early Modern England* (Oxford, 2000), 50, 248, 513; Patrick Collinson, *Elizabethan Essays* (1994), 251–2.

30. Christopher Haigh, 'The Church of England, the Catholics, and the People', in Peter Marshall, ed., *The Impact of the English Reformation 1500–1640* (1997), 253–4; Maltby, *Prayer Book*, 11; Martin Ingram, *Church Courts, Sex and Marriage in England, 1570–1640* (Cambridge, 1987), 123; Christopher Marsh, *Popular Religion in Sixteenth-Century England: Holding their Peace* (Basingstoke, 1998), 26.

31. This can be inferred from will preambles, avoiding for the most part both traditional Catholic invocations and high-Calvinist declarations of assurance: Caroline Litzenberger, 'Local Responses to Religious Change: Evidence from Gloucestershire Wills', in Eric Carlson, ed., *Religion and the English People 1500–1640* (Kirksville, MO, 1998), 245–70.

32. *TRP*, II, 501–2; Michael E. Moody, 'Browne, Robert (1550?–1633)', *ODNB*; Ronald Bayne, 'Harrison, Robert (d. c.1585)', rev. Michael E. Moody, *ODNB*; Albert Peel, ed., *The Writings of Robert Harrison and Robert Browne* (1953), 404; Peel, ed., *The Seconde Parte of a Register* (2 vols, Cambridge, 1915), I, 157–61; Peel and Leland H. Carlson, eds, *Cartwrightiana* (1951), 48.

33. Craig, *Reformation*, 103–7; Patrick Collinson, *Richard Bancroft and Elizabethan Anti-Puritanism* (Cambridge, 2013), 32–6.

34. Patrick Collinson et al., eds, *Conferences and Combination Lectures in the Elizabethan Church* (Woodbridge, 2003), xlix–l, lxxxii–xc; Collinson, *The Elizabethan Puritan Movement* (1967), 220.

35. Collinson, *Conferences*, 9; Collinson, *Movement*, 244–7; William Joseph Sheils, 'Whitgift, John (1530/31?–1604)', *ODNB*; Whitgift, *Works*, ed. J. Ayre (3 vols, Cambridge, 1851–3), III, 586–96; MacCaffrey, *Policy*, 107.

36. Collinson, *Movement*, 249–72; Collinson, *Conferences*, xcii; John Strype, *Life and Acts of John Whitgift* (3 vols, Oxford, 1822), III, 81–7; Harris Nicolas, *Memoirs of the Life and Times of Sir Christopher Hatton* (1847), 380.

37. SP 12/171, 41r; HMC, *Bath*, II, 26; Lake, *Bess*, 116–32.

38. Stephen Alford, *The Watchers* (2012), 134–5, 152–66, 174–8; J. O. W. Haweis, *Sketches of the Reformation and Elizabethan Age* (1844), 195; Marshall, *Faith*, 17–19; A. L. Rowse, *Ralegh and the Throckmortons* (1962), 213.

39. BL, Add. MS 48027, 248r–249r; David Cressy, 'Binding the Nation: The Bonds of 1584 and 1696', in DeLloyd Guth and John W. McKenna, eds, *Tudor Rule and Revolution* (Cambridge, 1982), 217–25; SP 12/175, 6r.

40. Hartley, II, 20–1, 29, 45–50, 53, 54–5, 185–6; Collinson, *Movement*, 268–9, 279–88; Strype, *Whitgift*, III, 118–24.

41. Peel, *Register*, II, 49–64; Natalie Mears, 'Fuller, William (d. 1586?)', *ODNB*.

42. *Statutes*, IV, 704–8; Hartley, II, 77, 154–5; Lake, *Bess*, 178–83.

43. HMC, *Salisbury*, III, 67; MacCaffrey, *Policy*, 348–9; Irene A. Wright, ed. and tr., *Further English Voyages to Spanish America, 1583–1594: Documents from the Archives of the Indies* (1951), 27–8, 40, 51.

44. Richard Challoner, *Memoirs of Missionary Priests* (2 vols in 1, Philadelphia, 1839), I, 114–15; *TRP*, II, 518–21; Peter Lake and Michael Questier, *The Trials of Margaret Clitherow* (2011), 83–108.

45. John Guy, *'My Heart is My Own': The Life of Mary Queen of Scots* (2004), 456–8, 483; *A Complete Collection of State Trials* (2nd edn, 6 vols, 1730), I, 121; Penry Williams, 'Babington, Anthony (1561–1586)', *ODNB*; Alford, *Watchers*, 210–35.

46. Guy, *Mary*, 488–94; Hartley, II, 214–18, 228–32, 244–7, 372.

47. John Guy, *The Tudors* (Oxford, 2013), 100; Alford, *Burghley*, 286–92; Elizabeth Goldring et al., eds, *John Nichols's The Progresses and Public Processions of Queen Elizabeth I* (5 vols, Oxford, 2014), III, 360–1.

48. *CSP, Foreign, Elizabeth*, XXI (1), 316; Anne Dillon, *The Construction of Martyrdom in the English Catholic Community, 1535–1603* (Aldershot, 2002), 165–7, 243–76; McCoog, *Society*, 239–40.

49. Hartley, II, 285, 310–19; Collinson, *Conferences*, xcvii–xcviii; Peel, *Register*, II, 162, 165, 166, 167, 169, 170, 173, 212–13; Collinson, *Movement*, 303–11.

50. Hartley, II, 333–54; Lee W. Gibbs, 'Life of Hooker', in Torrance Kirby, ed., *A Companion to Richard Hooker* (Leiden, 2008), 11–13; Anthony Milton, *Catholic and Reformed* (Cambridge, 1995), 286; *APC*, XIV, 5.

51. Peter Lake, *Anglicans and Puritans?* (1988), 90–6; M. R. Sommerville, 'Richard Hooker and his Contemporaries on Episcopacy: An Elizabethan Consensus', *JEH* (1984), 177–87.

52. Moody, 'Browne'; Moody, 'Greenwood, John (*c*.1560–1593)', *ODNB*; Stephen Bredwell, *The rasing of the foundations of Brownisme* (1588), 126; SP 12/204, 17r; Leland H. Carlson, ed., *The Writings of Henry Barrow, 1587–1590* (1962), 67.

53. MacCaffrey, *Policy*, 386–7; SP 12/203, 97r; 12/198, 76r–77r.

54. Alford, *Watchers*, 250–1; Eamon Duffy, 'Allen, William (1532–1594)', *ODNB*; Lake, *Bess*, 302–11; Knappen, *Diaries*, 80; Marshall, *Faith*, 27; Childs, *Traitors*, 159.

55. Strype, *Annals*, III (2), 26–8; Thomas Rogers, *An historical dialogue* (1589), 85; Mears, 182–8; Alford, *Burghley*, 308; Hartley, II, 414–26.

56. McGrath, *Papists*, 202–3; Edwin H. Burton and J. H. Pollen, eds, *Lives of the English Martyrs* (1914), 432–7; John J. McAleer, 'Ballads on the Spanish Armada', *Texas Studies in Literature and Language*, 4 (1963), 602–12; *A Warning to all False Traitors* (1588).

57. Anthony Palmer, ed., *Tudor Churchwardens' Accounts* (Cambridge, 1985), 114, 116, 130, 136, 139, 142, 149, 152, 155; Peter Marshall, *Beliefs and the Dead in Reformation England* (Oxford, 2002), 128–32.

58. A. J. Mann, 'Waldegrave, Robert (*c*.1554–1603/4)', *ODNB*; Collinson, *Bancroft*, 60–9; Matthew Sutcliffe, *A treatise of ecclesiasticall discipline* (1590), A3r; Brian Cummings, 'Martin Marprelate and the Popular Voice', in Kate Cooper and Jeremy Gregory, eds, *Elite and Popular Religion* (Woodbridge, 2006), 225–39.

59. Joseph L. Black, ed., *The Martin Marprelate Tracts* (Cambridge, 2008), 9, 32–3, 37; Collinson, *Bancroft*, 60–2; Strype, *Whitgift*, I, 602; *APC*, XVIII, 62; Collinson, *Movement*, 403–31.

60. Mary Morrissey, *Politics and the Paul's Cross Sermons, 1558–1642* (Oxford, 2011), 208–13; Collinson, *Bancroft*, 77–82

61. Holinshed, IV, 263–4; James McDermott, *England and the Spanish Armada* (New Haven, 2005), 170; Cyndia Susan Clegg, 'Fleming, Abraham (*c*.1552–1607)', *ODNB*.

### Postscript

1. William Salesbury, *The Baterie of the Popes Botereulx* (1550), A4r, F2r; R. Brinley Jones, 'Salesbury, William (*b*. before 1520, *d. c*.1580)', *ODNB*.

2. The standard mid- to late twentieth-century account, A. G. Dickens's *The English Reformation* (1964), was a meticulously scholarly study, regarding itself as non-sectarian, but still able to conclude (340) that the achievement of the English Reformation was 'to cast aside misleading unessentials and accretions', and bring Christians 'nearer in love to the real person of the Founder'.

3. Haigh and Duffy are the leading exemplars of this 'revisionist' school, sometimes – not entirely accurately – termed 'Catholic revisionism'. It is important to note, however, that Duffy's magnificent *Stripping of the Altars* was not intended as a comprehensive history of the Reformation, but as an account of the heyday and demise of 'traditional religion'.
4. For summary and assessment of a rich 'post-revisionist' literature on the social history of the Reformation, see my '(Re)defining the English Reformation', *Journal of British Studies*, 48 (2009), 564–86, and *Reformation England 1480–1642* (2nd edn, 2012), especially ch. 6.
5. John Milton, *Of Reformation* (1641), 9–10.
6. Roper, 250; Foxe (1583), 1079, 2032; BL, Harley MS 422, 133r.

# INDEX

benefit of clergy (1489, 1497, 1512) 85–6; *de heretico comburendo* (1401) 101; conditional restraint of annates (1532) 191–2, 194; Citations Act (1532) 194; Appeals Act (1533) 205, 207; appointment of bishops (1533) 463; Dispensations Act (1534) 208; Heresy Act (1534) 208–9; Succession Act (1534) 209; Treason Act (1534) 214–15; dissolving monasteries (1536) 231–3; restricting Uses (1536) 246; dissolving monasteries (1539) 273–4; restricting bible reading (1543) 289–90; ameliorating Six Articles (1544) 291; Succession Act (1544) 355, 356; Chantries Act (1545) 294, 366; against 'revilers of the sacrament' (1547) 312; Chantries Act (1547) 313–14, 319; Act of Uniformity (1549) 323–4; legalizing clerical marriage (1549) 323; Treason Act (1552) 347; Act of Uniformity (1552) 347; declaring validity of Aragon marriage (1553) 367; repealing religious legislation (1554) 390; restoring first fruits and tenths (1555) 399; Act of Supremacy (1559) 430–2; Act of Uniformity (1559) 430–2, 433; restoring first fruits and tenths to crown (1559) 434; Act of Exchange (1559) 438; 'for the Assurance of the Queen's Majesty's Royal Power' (1563) 455; treasonous words (1571) 498; confiscating exiles' property (1571) 498; against importation of papal bulls (1571) 498; Subscription Act (1571) 500; increasing recusancy fines (1581) 533; Act for the Queen's Safety (1585) 554–5; against Jesuits and Seminarists (1585) 555
Steelyard, Hanseatic headquarters 135
Steeple Bumpstead, Essex 103, 106, 115, 138–9, 142
Sternhold, Thomas 440
Stewart, Henry, Lord Darnley 476–7, 484
Stewart, James, Earl of Moray 484, 485, 491
Steynor, John 318, 341, 439
Stilman, John 103, 106
Stoke, Suffolk 190
Stokesley, John, bishop of London 123, 168, 179–80, 181, 187, 196, 198, 216, 219, 222, 237, 242, 255, 270, 277
Stone, Staffordshire 510
Stonley, Richard 541
Story, John 397, 425, 426, 469, 494, 536, 566
Stourton, Charles, Lord 347
Stow, John, chronicler 473–4, 481, 572–3
Stowmarket, Suffolk 152
Stranger Churches 341–2, 348, 384, 386, 434, 504, 512–13

Stratford, Essex 269
Stratford-upon-Avon 18
Strickland, William 499–500
Stroppiana, Giovanni di, Savoyard ambassador 378–9
Stubbes, Philip 556
Stubbs, John 525, 528
Stukley, Thomas 527–8
Sudbury, Suffolk 190
Surrender of the Clergy (1532) 196–7, 208
Sutcliffe, Matthew, dean of Exeter 568
Sweeting, William 113, 116
Swine, Yorkshire 480
Swit, John 72
Swynnerton, Thomas 219–20
Syon Abbey, Middlesex 52, 59–60, 62, 118, 128, 210, 403

Talbot, Francis, fifth Earl of Shrewsbury, 345, 428
Talbot, George, fourth Earl of Shrewsbury 246, 249,
Talbot, George, sixth Earl of Shrewsbury 485
Tallis, Thomas 449
Taschius, Petrus 270
Taverner, John 153
Tavistock Abbey, Devon, 1527 protest against 63
Taylor, George 214
Taylor, Dr John 87–8, 92, 156
Taylor, John, Lollard 155
Taylor, John, reformer 271
Taylor, Rowland 297, 321, 364, 392
Temys, Thomas, 196
Ten Articles (1536) 238–40, 254
Tenterden, Kent 107, 112, 116
tertiaries, monastic 59
Terwood, Hendrik 512–13
Testwood, Robert 287
Tewkesbury, John 186, 187
Tey, William 547
Thacker, Elias 545
Thanet, Kent 211
Theobald, Thomas 254
Thetford, Norfolk 545; Priory 61
Theydon-Garnon, Essex 11
Thirlby, Thomas, bishop of Ely 277, 283, 301, 323, 338, 347, 435
Thirty-Nine Articles (1563) 457–8, 477, 500, 546
Thomas, William 304, 355, 369
Thornden, Richard, bishop of Dover 396
Thornton-in-Craven, Yorkshire 526
Throckmorton, Arthur 550
Throckmorton, Clement 464